Lecture Notes in Computer Science 12264

More information about this series at http://www.springer.com/series/7412

Anne L. Martel · Purang Abolmaesumi ·
Danail Stoyanov · Diana Mateus ·
Maria A. Zuluaga · S. Kevin Zhou ·
Daniel Racoceanu · Leo Joskowicz (Eds.)

Medical Image Computing and Computer Assisted Intervention – MICCAI 2020

23rd International Conference
Lima, Peru, October 4–8, 2020
Proceedings, Part IV

 Springer

Editors
Anne L. Martel (iD)
University of Toronto
Toronto, ON, Canada

Purang Abolmaesumi (iD)
The University of British Columbia
Vancouver, BC, Canada

Danail Stoyanov (iD)
University College London
London, UK

Diana Mateus (iD)
École Centrale de Nantes
Nantes, France

Maria A. Zuluaga (iD)
EURECOM
Biot, France

S. Kevin Zhou (iD)
Chinese Academy of Sciences
Beijing, China

Daniel Racoceanu (iD)
Sorbonne University
Paris, France

Leo Joskowicz (iD)
The Hebrew University of Jerusalem
Jerusalem, Israel

ISSN 0302-9743   ISSN 1611-3349 (electronic)
Lecture Notes in Computer Science
ISBN 978-3-030-59718-4   ISBN 978-3-030-59719-1 (eBook)
https://doi.org/10.1007/978-3-030-59719-1

LNCS Sublibrary: SL6 – Image Processing, Computer Vision, Pattern Recognition, and Graphics

This Springer imprint is published by the registered company Springer Nature Switzerland AG
The registered company address is: Gewerbestrasse 11, 6330 Cham, Switzerland

Preface

The 23rd International Conference on Medical Image Computing and Computer-Assisted Intervention (MICCAI 2020) was held this year under the most unusual circumstances, due to the COVID-19 pandemic disrupting our lives in ways that were unimaginable at the start of the new decade. MICCAI 2020 was scheduled to be held in Lima, Peru, and would have been the first MICCAI meeting in Latin America. However, with the pandemic, the conference and its program had to be redesigned to deal with realities of the "new normal", where virtual presence rather than physical interactions among attendees, was necessary to comply with global transmission control measures. The conference was held through a virtual conference management platform, consisting of the main scientific program in addition to featuring 25 workshops, 8 tutorials, and 24 challenges during October 4–8, 2020. In order to keep a part of the original spirit of MICCAI 2020, SIPAIM 2020 was held as an adjacent LatAm conference dedicated to medical information management and imaging, held during October 3–4, 2020.

The proceedings of MICCAI 2020 showcase papers contributed by the authors to the main conference, which are organized in seven volumes of *Lecture Notes in Computer Science* (LNCS) books. These papers were selected after a thorough double-blind peer-review process. We followed the example set by past MICCAI meetings, using Microsoft's Conference Managing Toolkit (CMT) for paper submission and peer reviews, with support from the Toronto Paper Matching System (TPMS) to partially automate paper assignment to area chairs and reviewers.

The conference submission deadline had to be extended by two weeks to account for the disruption COVID-19 caused on the worldwide scientific community. From 2,953 original intentions to submit, 1,876 full submissions were received, which were reduced to 1,809 submissions following an initial quality check by the program chairs. Of those, 61% were self-declared by authors as Medical Image Computing (MIC), 6% as Computer Assisted Intervention (CAI), and 32% as both MIC and CAI. Following a broad call to the community for self-nomination of volunteers and a thorough review by the program chairs, considering criteria such as balance across research areas, geographical distribution, and gender, the MICCAI 2020 Program Committee comprised 82 area chairs, with 46% from North America, 28% from Europe, 19% from Asia/Pacific/Middle East, 4% from Latin America, and 1% from Australia. We invested significant effort in recruiting more women to the Program Committee, following the conference's emphasis on equity, inclusion, and diversity. This resulted in 26% female area chairs. Each area chair was assigned about 23 manuscripts, with suggested potential reviewers using TPMS scoring and self-declared research areas, while domain conflicts were automatically considered by CMT. Following a final revision and prioritization of reviewers by area chairs in terms of their expertise related to each paper, over 1,426 invited reviewers were asked to bid for the papers for which they had been suggested. Final reviewer allocations via CMT took account of reviewer bidding, prioritization of area chairs, and TPMS scores, leading to allocating about 4 papers per reviewer. Following an initial double-blind review phase by reviewers, area chairs provided a meta-review summarizing key points of reviews and a recommendation for each paper. The program chairs then evaluated the reviews and their scores, along with the recommendation from the area chairs, to directly accept 241 papers (13%) and reject 828 papers (46%); the remainder of the papers were sent for rebuttal by the authors. During the rebuttal phase, two additional area chairs were assigned to each paper using the CMT and TPMS scores while accounting for domain conflicts. The three area chairs then independently scored each paper to accept or reject, based on the reviews, rebuttal, and manuscript, resulting in clear paper decisions using majority voting. This process resulted in the acceptance of a further 301 papers for an overall acceptance rate of 30%. A virtual Program Committee meeting was held on July 10, 2020, to confirm the final results and collect feedback of the peer-review process.

For the MICCAI 2020 proceedings, 542 accepted papers have been organized into seven volumes as follows:

- Part I, LNCS Volume 12261: Machine Learning Methodologies
- Part II, LNCS Volume 12262: Image Reconstruction and Machine Learning
- Part III, LNCS Volume 12263: Computer Aided Intervention, Ultrasound and Image Registration
- Part IV, LNCS Volume 12264: Segmentation and Shape Analysis
- Part V, LNCS Volume 12265: Biological, Optical and Microscopic Image Analysis
- Part VI, LNCS Volume 12266: Clinical Applications
- Part VII, LNCS Volume 12267: Neurological Imaging and PET

For the main conference, the traditional emphasis on poster presentations was maintained; each author uploaded a brief pre-recorded presentation and a graphical abstract onto a web platform and was allocated a personal virtual live session in which they talked directly to the attendees. It was also possible to post questions online allowing asynchronous conversations – essential to overcome the challenges of a global conference spanning many time zones. The traditional oral sessions, which typically included a small proportion of the papers, were replaced with 90 "mini" sessions where all of the authors were clustered into groups of 5 to 7 related papers; a live virtual session allowed the authors and attendees to discuss the papers in a panel format.

We would like to sincerely thank everyone who contributed to the success of MICCAI 2020 and the quality of its proceedings under the most unusual circumstances of a global pandemic. First and foremost, we thank all authors for submitting and presenting their high-quality work that made MICCAI 2020 a greatly enjoyable and successful scientific meeting. We are also especially grateful to all members of the Program Committee and reviewers for their dedicated effort and insightful feedback throughout the entire paper selection process. We would like to particularly thank the MICCAI society for support, insightful comments, and continuous engagement with organizing the conference. Special thanks go to Kitty Wong, who oversaw the entire process of paper submission, reviews, and preparation of conference proceedings. Without her, we would have not functioned effectively. Given the "new normal", none of the workshops, tutorials, and challenges would have been feasible without the true leadership of the satellite events organizing team led by Mauricio Reyes: Erik Meijering (workshops), Carlos Alberola-López (tutorials), and Lena Maier-Hein (challenges). Behind the scenes, MICCAI secretarial personnel, Janette Wallace and Johanne Langford, kept a close eye on logistics and budgets, while Mehmet Eldegez and his team at Dekon Congress and Tourism led the professional conference organization, working tightly with the virtual platform team. We also thank our sponsors for financial support and engagement with conference attendees through the virtual platform. Special thanks goes to Veronika Cheplygina for continuous engagement with various social media platforms before and throughout the conference to publicize the conference. We would also like to express our gratitude to Shelley Wallace for helping us in Marketing MICCAI 2020, especially during the last phase of the virtual conference organization.

The selection process for Young Investigator Awards was managed by a team of senior MICCAI investigators, led by Julia Schnabel. In addition, MICCAI 2020 offered free registration to the top 50 ranked papers at the conference whose primary authors were students. Priority was given to low-income regions and Latin American students. Further support was provided by the National Institutes of Health (support granted for MICCAI 2020) and the National Science Foundation (support granted to MICCAI 2019 and continued for MICCAI 2020) which sponsored another 52 awards for USA-based students to attend the conference. We would like to thank Marius Linguraru and Antonion Porras, for their leadership in regards to the NIH sponsorship for 2020, and Dinggang Shen and Tianming Liu, MICCAI 2019 general chairs, for keeping an active bridge and engagement with MICCAI 2020.

Marius Linguraru and Antonion Porras were also leading the young investigators early career development program, including a very active mentorship which we do hope, will significantly catalize young and briliant careers of future leaders of our scientific community. In link with SIPAIM (thanks to Jorge Brieva, Marius Linguraru, and Natasha Lepore for their support), we also initiated a Startup Village initiative, which, we hope, will be able to bring in promising private initiatives in the areas of MICCAI. As a part of SIPAIM 2020, we note also the presence of a workshop for Peruvian clinicians. We would like to thank Benjaming Castañeda and Renato Gandolfi for this initiative.

MICCAI 2020 invested significant efforts to tightly engage the industry stakeholders in our field throughout its planning and organization. These efforts were led by Parvin Mousavi, and ensured that all sponsoring industry partners could connect with the conference attendees through the conference's virtual platform before and during the meeting. We would like to thank the sponsorship team and the contributions of Gustavo Carneiro, Benjamín Castañeda, Ignacio Larrabide, Marius Linguraru, Yanwu Xu, and Kevin Zhou.

We look forward to seeing you at MICCAI 2021.

October 2020

Anne L. Martel
Purang Abolmaesumi
Danail Stoyanov
Diana Mateus
Maria A. Zuluaga
S. Kevin Zhou
Daniel Racoceanu
Leo Joskowicz

Organization

General Chairs

Daniel Racoceanu   Sorbonne Université, Brain Institute, France
Leo Joskowicz   The Hebrew University of Jerusalem, Israel

Program Committee Chairs

Anne L. Martel   University of Toronto, Canada
Purang Abolmaesumi   The University of British Columbia, Canada
Danail Stoyanov   University College London, UK
Diana Mateus   Ecole Centrale de Nantes, LS2N, France
Maria A. Zuluaga   Eurecom, France
S. Kevin Zhou   Chinese Academy of Sciences, China

Keynote Speaker Chair

Rene Vidal   The John Hopkins University, USA

Satellite Events Chair

Mauricio Reyes   University of Bern, Switzerland

Workshop Team

Erik Meijering (Chair)   The University of New South Wales, Australia
Li Cheng   University of Alberta, Canada
Pamela Guevara   University of Concepción, Chile
Bennett Landman   Vanderbilt University, USA
Tammy Riklin Raviv   Ben-Gurion University of the Negev, Israel
Virginie Uhlmann   EMBL, European Bioinformatics Institute, UK

Tutorial Team

Carlos Alberola-López (Chair)   Universidad de Valladolid, Spain

Clarisa Sánchez   Radboud University Medical Center, The Netherlands
Demian Wassermann   Inria Saclay Île-de-France, France

Challenges Team

Lena Maier-Hein (Chair)	German Cancer Research Center, Germany
Annette Kopp-Schneider	German Cancer Research Center, Germany
Michal Kozubek	Masaryk University, Czech Republic
Annika Reinke	German Cancer Research Center, Germany

Sponsorship Team

Parvin Mousavi (Chair)	Queen's University, Canada
Marius Linguraru	Children's National Institute, USA
Gustavo Carneiro	The University of Adelaide, Australia
Yanwu Xu	Baidu Inc., China
Ignacio Larrabide	National Scientific and Technical Research Council, Argentina
S. Kevin Zhou	Chinese Academy of Sciences, China
Benjamín Castañeda	Pontifical Catholic University of Peru, Peru

Local and Regional Chairs

Benjamín Castañeda	Pontifical Catholic University of Peru, Peru
Natasha Lepore	University of Southern California, USA

Social Media Chair

Veronika Cheplygina	Eindhoven University of Technology, The Netherlands

Young Investigators Early Career Development Program Chairs

Marius Linguraru	Children's National Institute, USA
Antonio Porras	Children's National Institute, USA

Student Board Liaison Chair

Gabriel Jimenez	Pontifical Catholic University of Peru, Peru

Submission Platform Manager

Kitty Wong	The MICCAI Society, Canada

Conference Management

DEKON Group
Pathable Inc.

Program Committee

Ehsan Adeli	Stanford University, USA
Shadi Albarqouni	ETH Zurich, Switzerland
Pablo Arbelaez	Universidad de los Andes, Colombia
Ulas Bagci	University of Central Florida, USA
Adrien Bartoli	Université Clermont Auvergne, France
Hrvoje Bogunovic	Medical University of Vienna, Austria
Weidong Cai	The University of Sydney, Australia
Chao Chen	Stony Brook University, USA
Elvis Chen	Robarts Research Institute, Canada
Stanley Durrleman	Inria, France
Boris Escalante-Ramírez	National Autonomous University of Mexico, Mexico
Pascal Fallavollita	University of Ottawa, Canada
Enzo Ferrante	CONICET, Universidad Nacional del Litoral, Argentina
Stamatia Giannarou	Imperial College London, UK
Orcun Goksel	ETH Zurich, Switzerland
Alberto Gomez	King's College London, UK
Miguel Angel González Ballester	Universitat Pompeu Fabra, Spain
Ilker Hacihaliloglu	Rutgers University, USA
Yi Hong	University of Georgia, USA
Yipeng Hu	University College London, UK
Heng Huang	University of Pittsburgh and JD Finance America Corporation, USA
Juan Eugenio Iglesias	University College London, UK
Madhura Ingalhalikar	Symbiosis Center for Medical Image Analysis, India
Pierre Jannin	Université de Rennes, France
Samuel Kadoury	Ecole Polytechnique de Montreal, Canada
Bernhard Kainz	Imperial College London, UK
Marta Kersten-Oertel	Concordia University, Canada
Andrew King	King's College London, UK
Ignacio Larrabide	CONICET, Argentina
Gang Li	University of North Carolina at Chapel Hill, USA
Jianming Liang	Arizona State University, USA
Hongen Liao	Tsinghua University, China
Rui Liao	Siemens Healthineers, USA
Feng Lin	Nanyang Technological University, China
Mingxia Liu	University of North Carolina at Chapel Hill, USA
Jiebo Luo	University of Rochester, USA
Xiongbiao Luo	Xiamen University, China
Andreas Maier	FAU Erlangen-Nuremberg, Germany
Stephen McKenna	University of Dundee, UK
Bjoern Menze	Technische Universität München, Germany
Mehdi Moradi	IBM Research, USA

Mentorship Program (Mentors)

Ehsan Adeli   Stanford University, USA
Stephen Aylward   Kitware, USA
Hrvoje Bogunovic   Medical University of Vienna, Austria
Li Cheng   University of Alberta, Canada
Marleen de Bruijne   University of Copenhagen, Denmark
Caroline Essert   University of Strasbourg, France
Gabor Fichtinger   Queen's University, Canada
Stamatia Giannarou   Imperial College London, UK
Juan Eugenio Iglesias Gonzalez   University College London, UK
Bernhard Kainz   Imperial College London, UK
Shuo Li   Western University, Canada
Jianming Liang   Arizona State University, USA
Rui Liao   Siemens Healthineers, USA
Feng Lin   Nanyang Technological University, China
Marius George Linguraru   Children's National Hospital, George Washington University, USA
Tianming Liu   University of Georgia, USA
Xiongbiao Luo   Xiamen University, China
Dong Ni   Shenzhen University, China
Wiro Niessen   Erasmus MC - University Medical Center Rotterdam, The Netherlands
Terry Peters   Western University, Canada
Antonio R. Porras   University of Colorado, USA
Daniel Racoceanu   Sorbonne University, France
Islem Rekik   Istanbul Technical University, Turkey
Nicola Rieke   NVIDIA, USA
Julia Schnabel   King's College London, UK
Ruby Shamir   Novocure, Switzerland
Stefanie Speidel   National Center for Tumor Diseases Dresden, Germany
Martin Styner   University of North Carolina at Chapel Hill, USA
Xiaoying Tang   Southern University of Science and Technology, China
Pallavi Tiwari   Case Western Reserve University, USA
Jocelyne Troccaz   CNRS, Grenoble Alpes University, France
Pierre Jannin   INSERM, Université de Rennes, France
Archana Venkataraman   Johns Hopkins University, USA
Linwei Wang   Rochester Institute of Technology, USA
Guorong Wu   University of North Carolina at Chapel Hill, USA
Li Xiao   Chinese Academy of Science, China
Ziyue Xu   NVIDIA, USA
Bochuan Zheng   China West Normal University, China
Guoyan Zheng   Shanghai Jiao Tong University, China
S. Kevin Zhou   Chinese Academy of Sciences, China
Maria A. Zuluaga   EURECOM, France

Additional Reviewers

Alaa Eldin Abdelaal
Ahmed Abdulkadir
Clement Abi Nader
Mazdak Abulnaga
Ganesh Adluru
Iman Aganj
Priya Aggarwal
Sahar Ahmad
Seyed-Ahmad Ahmadi
Euijoon Ahn
Alireza Akhondi-asl
Mohamed Akrout
Dawood Al Chanti
Ibraheem Al-Dhamari
Navid Alemi Koohbanani
Hanan Alghamdi
Hassan Alhajj
Hazrat Ali
Sharib Ali
Omar Al-Kadi
Maximilian Allan
Felix Ambellan
Mina Amiri
Sameer Antani
Luigi Antelmi
Michela Antonelli
Jacob Antunes
Saeed Anwar
Fernando Arambula
Ignacio Arganda-Carreras
Mohammad Ali Armin
John Ashburner
Md Ashikuzzaman
Shahab Aslani
Mehdi Astaraki
Angélica Atehortúa
Gowtham Atluri
Kamran Avanaki
Angelica Aviles-Rivero
Suyash Awate
Dogu Baran Aydogan
Qinle Ba
Morteza Babaie

Hyeon-Min Bae
Woong Bae
Wenjia Bai
Ujjwal Baid
Spyridon Bakas
Yaël Balbastre
Marcin Balicki
Fabian Balsiger
Abhirup Banerjee
Sreya Banerjee
Sophia Bano
Shunxing Bao
Adrian Barbu
Cher Bass
John S. H. Baxter
Amirhossein Bayat
Sharareh Bayat
Neslihan Bayramoglu
Bahareh Behboodi
Delaram Behnami
Mikhail Belyaev
Oualid Benkarim
Aicha BenTaieb
Camilo Bermudez
Giulia Bertò
Hadrien Bertrand
Julián Betancur
Michael Beyeler
Parmeet Bhatia
Chetan Bhole
Suvrat Bhooshan
Chitresh Bhushan
Lei Bi
Cheng Bian
Gui-Bin Bian
Sangeeta Biswas
Stefano B. Blumberg
Janusz Bobulski
Sebastian Bodenstedt
Ester Bonmati
Bhushan Borotikar
Jiri Borovec
Ilaria Boscolo Galazzo

Alexandre Bousse
Nicolas Boutry
Behzad Bozorgtabar
Nadia Brancati
Christopher Bridge
Esther Bron
Rupert Brooks
Qirong Bu
Tim-Oliver Buchholz
Duc Toan Bui
Qasim Bukhari
Ninon Burgos
Nikolay Burlutskiy
Russell Butler
Michał Byra
Hongmin Cai
Yunliang Cai
Sema Candemir
Bing Cao
Qing Cao
Shilei Cao
Tian Cao
Weiguo Cao
Yankun Cao
Aaron Carass
Heike Carolus
Adrià Casamitjana
Suheyla Cetin Karayumak
Ahmad Chaddad
Krishna Chaitanya
Jayasree Chakraborty
Tapabrata Chakraborty
Sylvie Chambon
Ming-Ching Chang
Violeta Chang
Simon Chatelin
Sudhanya Chatterjee
Christos Chatzichristos
Rizwan Chaudhry
Antong Chen
Cameron Po-Hsuan Chen
Chang Chen
Chao Chen
Chen Chen
Cheng Chen
Dongdong Chen

Fang Chen
Geng Chen
Hao Chen
Jianan Chen
Jianxu Chen
Jia-Wei Chen
Jie Chen
Junxiang Chen
Li Chen
Liang Chen
Pingjun Chen
Qiang Chen
Shuai Chen
Tianhua Chen
Tingting Chen
Xi Chen
Xiaoran Chen
Xin Chen
Yuanyuan Chen
Yuhua Chen
Yukun Chen
Zhineng Chen
Zhixiang Chen
Erkang Cheng
Jun Cheng
Li Cheng
Xuelian Cheng
Yuan Cheng
Veronika Cheplygina
Hyungjoo Cho
Jaegul Choo
Aritra Chowdhury
Stergios Christodoulidis
Ai Wern Chung
Pietro Antonio Cicalese
Özgün Çiçek
Robert Cierniak
Matthew Clarkson
Dana Cobzas
Jaume Coll-Font
Alessia Colonna
Marc Combalia
Olivier Commowick
Sonia Contreras Ortiz
Pierre-Henri Conze
Timothy Cootes

Luca Corinzia
Teresa Correia
Pierrick Coupé
Jeffrey Craley
Arun C. S. Kumar
Hui Cui
Jianan Cui
Zhiming Cui
Kathleen Curran
Haixing Dai
Xiaoliang Dai
Ker Dai Fei Elmer
Adrian Dalca
Abhijit Das
Neda Davoudi
Laura Daza
Sandro De Zanet
Charles Delahunt
Herve Delingette
Beatrice Demiray
Yang Deng
Hrishikesh Deshpande
Christian Desrosiers
Neel Dey
Xinghao Ding
Zhipeng Ding
Konstantin Dmitriev
Jose Dolz
Ines Domingues
Juan Pedro Dominguez-Morales
Hao Dong
Mengjin Dong
Nanqing Dong
Qinglin Dong
Suyu Dong
Sven Dorkenwald
Qi Dou
P. K. Douglas
Simon Drouin
Karen Drukker
Niharika D'Souza
Lei Du
Shaoyi Du
Xuefeng Du
Dingna Duan
Nicolas Duchateau

James Duncan
Jared Dunnmon
Luc Duong
Nicha Dvornek
Dmitry V. Dylov
Oleh Dzyubachyk
Mehran Ebrahimi
Philip Edwards
Alexander Effland
Jan Egger
Alma Eguizabal
Gudmundur Einarsson
Ahmed Elazab
Mohammed S. M. Elbaz
Shireen Elhabian
Ahmed Eltanboly
Sandy Engelhardt
Ertunc Erdil
Marius Erdt
Floris Ernst
Mohammad Eslami
Nazila Esmaeili
Marco Esposito
Oscar Esteban
Jingfan Fan
Xin Fan
Yonghui Fan
Chaowei Fang
Xi Fang
Mohsen Farzi
Johannes Fauser
Andrey Fedorov
Hamid Fehri
Lina Felsner
Jun Feng
Ruibin Feng
Xinyang Feng
Yifan Feng
Yuan Feng
Henrique Fernandes
Ricardo Ferrari
Jean Feydy
Lucas Fidon
Lukas Fischer
Antonio Foncubierta-Rodríguez
Germain Forestier

Reza Forghani
Nils Daniel Forkert
Jean-Rassaire Fouefack
Tatiana Fountoukidou
Aina Frau-Pascual
Moti Freiman
Sarah Frisken
Huazhu Fu
Xueyang Fu
Wolfgang Fuhl
Isabel Funke
Philipp Fürnstahl
Pedro Furtado
Ryo Furukawa
Elies Fuster-Garcia
Youssef Gahi
Jin Kyu Gahm
Laurent Gajny
Rohan Gala
Harshala Gammulle
Yu Gan
Cong Gao
Dongxu Gao
Fei Gao
Feng Gao
Linlin Gao
Mingchen Gao
Siyuan Gao
Xin Gao
Xinpei Gao
Yixin Gao
Yue Gao
Zhifan Gao
Sara Garbarino
Alfonso Gastelum-Strozzi
Romane Gauriau
Srishti Gautam
Bao Ge
Rongjun Ge
Zongyuan Ge
Sairam Geethanath
Yasmeen George
Samuel Gerber
Guido Gerig
Nils Gessert
Olivier Gevaert

Muhammad Usman Ghani
Sandesh Ghimire
Sayan Ghosal
Gabriel Girard
Ben Glocker
Evgin Goceri
Michael Goetz
Arnold Gomez
Kuang Gong
Mingming Gong
Yuanhao Gong
German Gonzalez
Sharath Gopal
Karthik Gopinath
Pietro Gori
Maged Goubran
Sobhan Goudarzi
Baran Gözcü
Benedikt Graf
Mark Graham
Bertrand Granado
Alejandro Granados
Robert Grupp
Christina Gsaxner
Lin Gu
Shi Gu
Yun Gu
Ricardo Guerrero
Houssem-Eddine Gueziri
Dazhou Guo
Hengtao Guo
Jixiang Guo
Pengfei Guo
Yanrong Guo
Yi Guo
Yong Guo
Yulan Guo
Yuyu Guo
Krati Gupta
Vikash Gupta
Praveen Gurunath Bharathi
Prashnna Gyawali
Stathis Hadjidemetriou
Omid Haji Maghsoudi
Justin Haldar
Mohammad Hamghalam

Bing Han
Hu Han
Liang Han
Xiaoguang Han
Xu Han
Zhi Han
Zhongyi Han
Jonny Hancox
Christian Hansen
Xiaoke Hao
Rabia Haq
Michael Hardisty
Stefan Harrer
Adam Harrison
S. M. Kamrul Hasan
Hoda Sadat Hashemi
Nobuhiko Hata
Andreas Hauptmann
Mohammad Havaei
Huiguang He
Junjun He
Kelei He
Tiancheng He
Xuming He
Yuting He
Mattias Heinrich
Stefan Heldmann
Nicholas Heller
Alessa Hering
Monica Hernandez
Estefania Hernandez-Martin
Carlos Hernandez-Matas
Javier Herrera-Vega
Kilian Hett
Tsung-Ying Ho
Nico Hoffmann
Matthew Holden
Song Hong
Sungmin Hong
Yoonmi Hong
Corné Hoogendoorn
Antal Horváth
Belayat Hossain
Le Hou
Ai-Ling Hsu
Po-Ya Hsu

Tai-Chiu Hsung
Pengwei Hu
Shunbo Hu
Xiaoling Hu
Xiaowei Hu
Yan Hu
Zhenhong Hu
Jia-Hong Huang
Junzhou Huang
Kevin Huang
Qiaoying Huang
Weilin Huang
Xiaolei Huang
Yawen Huang
Yongxiang Huang
Yue Huang
Yufang Huang
Zhi Huang
Arnaud Huaulmé
Henkjan Huisman
Xing Huo
Yuankai Huo
Sarfaraz Hussein
Jana Hutter
Khoi Huynh
Seong Jae Hwang
Emmanuel Iarussi
Ilknur Icke
Kay Igwe
Alfredo Illanes
Abdullah-Al-Zubaer Imran
Ismail Irmakci
Samra Irshad
Benjamin Irving
Mobarakol Islam
Mohammad Shafkat Islam
Vamsi Ithapu
Koichi Ito
Hayato Itoh
Oleksandra Ivashchenko
Yuji Iwahori
Shruti Jadon
Mohammad Jafari
Mostafa Jahanifar
Andras Jakab
Amir Jamaludin

Won-Dong Jang
Vincent Jaouen
Uditha Jarayathne
Ronnachai Jaroensri
Golara Javadi
Rohit Jena
Todd Jensen
Won-Ki Jeong
Zexuan Ji
Haozhe Jia
Jue Jiang
Tingting Jiang
Weixiong Jiang
Xi Jiang
Xiang Jiang
Jianbo Jiao
Zhicheng Jiao
Amelia Jiménez-Sánchez
Dakai Jin
Taisong Jin
Yueming Jin
Ze Jin
Bin Jing
Yaqub Jonmohamadi
Anand Joshi
Shantanu Joshi
Christoph Jud
Florian Jug
Yohan Jun
Alain Jungo
Abdolrahim Kadkhodamohammadi
Ali Kafaei Zad Tehrani
Dagmar Kainmueller
Siva Teja Kakileti
John Kalafut
Konstantinos Kamnitsas
Michael C. Kampffmeyer
Qingbo Kang
Neerav Karani
Davood Karimi
Satyananda Kashyap
Alexander Katzmann
Prabhjot Kaur
Anees Kazi
Erwan Kerrien
Hoel Kervadec

Ashkan Khakzar
Fahmi Khalifa
Nadieh Khalili
Siavash Khallaghi
Farzad Khalvati
Hassan Khan
Bishesh Khanal
Pulkit Khandelwal
Maksym Kholiavchenko
Meenakshi Khosla
Naji Khosravan
Seyed Mostafa Kia
Ron Kikinis
Daeseung Kim
Geena Kim
Hak Gu Kim
Heejong Kim
Hosung Kim
Hyo-Eun Kim
Jinman Kim
Jinyoung Kim
Mansu Kim
Minjeong Kim
Seong Tae Kim
Won Hwa Kim
Young-Ho Kim
Atilla Kiraly
Yoshiro Kitamura
Takayuki Kitasaka
Sabrina Kletz
Tobias Klinder
Kranthi Kolli
Satoshi Kondo
Bin Kong
Jun Kong
Tomasz Konopczynski
Ender Konukoglu
Bongjin Koo
Kivanc Kose
Anna Kreshuk
AnithaPriya Krishnan
Pavitra Krishnaswamy
Frithjof Kruggel
Alexander Krull
Elizabeth Krupinski
Hulin Kuang

Serife Kucur
David Kügler
Arjan Kuijper
Jan Kukacka
Nilima Kulkarni
Abhay Kumar
Ashnil Kumar
Kuldeep Kumar
Neeraj Kumar
Nitin Kumar
Manuela Kunz
Holger Kunze
Tahsin Kurc
Thomas Kurmann
Yoshihiro Kuroda
Jin Tae Kwak
Yongchan Kwon
Aymen Laadhari
Dmitrii Lachinov
Alexander Ladikos
Alain Lalande
Rodney Lalonde
Tryphon Lambrou
Hengrong Lan
Catherine Laporte
Carole Lartizien
Bianca Lassen-Schmidt
Andras Lasso
Ngan Le
Leo Lebrat
Changhwan Lee
Eung-Joo Lee
Hyekyoung Lee
Jong-Hwan Lee
Jungbeom Lee
Matthew Lee
Sangmin Lee
Soochahn Lee
Stefan Leger
Étienne Léger
Baiying Lei
Andreas Leibetseder
Rogers Jeffrey Leo John
Juan Leon
Wee Kheng Leow
Annan Li

Bo Li
Chongyi Li
Haohan Li
Hongming Li
Hongwei Li
Huiqi Li
Jian Li
Jianning Li
Jiayun Li
Junhua Li
Lincan Li
Mengzhang Li
Ming Li
Qing Li
Quanzheng Li
Shulong Li
Shuyu Li
Weikai Li
Wenyuan Li
Xiang Li
Xiaomeng Li
Xiaoxiao Li
Xin Li
Xiuli Li
Yang Li (Beihang University)
Yang Li (Northeast Electric Power
    University)
Yi Li
Yuexiang Li
Zeju Li
Zhang Li
Zhen Li
Zhiyuan Li
Zhjin Li
Zhongyu Li
Chunfeng Lian
Gongbo Liang
Libin Liang
Shanshan Liang
Yudong Liang
Haofu Liao
Ruizhi Liao
Gilbert Lim
Baihan Lin
Hongxiang Lin
Huei-Yung Lin

Jianyu Lin
C. Lindner
Geert Litjens
Bin Liu
Chang Liu
Dongnan Liu
Feng Liu
Hangfan Liu
Jianfei Liu
Jin Liu
Jingya Liu
Jingyu Liu
Kai Liu
Kefei Liu
Lihao Liu
Luyan Liu
Mengting Liu
Na Liu
Peng Liu
Ping Liu
Quande Liu
Qun Liu
Shengfeng Liu
Shuangjun Liu
Sidong Liu
Siqi Liu
Siyuan Liu
Tianrui Liu
Xianglong Liu
Xinyang Liu
Yan Liu
Yuan Liu
Yuhang Liu
Andrea Loddo
Herve Lombaert
Marco Lorenzi
Jian Lou
Nicolas Loy Rodas
Allen Lu
Donghuan Lu
Huanxiang Lu
Jiwen Lu
Le Lu
Weijia Lu
Xiankai Lu
Yao Lu

Yongyi Lu
Yueh-Hsun Lu
Christian Lucas
Oeslle Lucena
Imanol Luengo
Ronald Lui
Gongning Luo
Jie Luo
Ma Luo
Marcel Luthi
Khoa Luu
Bin Lv
Jinglei Lv
Ilwoo Lyu
Qing Lyu
Sharath M. S.
Andy J. Ma
Chunwei Ma
Da Ma
Hua Ma
Jingting Ma
Kai Ma
Lei Ma
Wenao Ma
Yuexin Ma
Amirreza Mahbod
Sara Mahdavi
Mohammed Mahmoud
Gabriel Maicas
Klaus H. Maier-Hein
Sokratis Makrogiannis
Bilal Malik
Anand Malpani
Ilja Manakov
Matteo Mancini
Efthymios Maneas
Tommaso Mansi
Brett Marinelli
Razvan Marinescu
Pablo Márquez Neila
Carsten Marr
Yassine Marrakchi
Fabio Martinez
Antonio Martinez-Torteya
Andre Mastmeyer
Dimitrios Mavroeidis

Jamie McClelland
Verónica Medina Bañuelos
Raghav Mehta
Sachin Mehta
Liye Mei
Raphael Meier
Qier Meng
Qingjie Meng
Yu Meng
Martin Menten
Odyssée Merveille
Pablo Mesejo
Liang Mi
Shun Miao
Stijn Michielse
Mikhail Milchenko
Hyun-Seok Min
Zhe Min
Tadashi Miyamoto
Aryan Mobiny
Irina Mocanu
Sara Moccia
Omid Mohareri
Hassan Mohy-ud-Din
Muthu Rama Krishnan Mookiah
Rodrigo Moreno
Lia Morra
Agata Mosinska
Saman Motamed
Mohammad Hamed Mozaffari
Anirban Mukhopadhyay
Henning Müller
Balamurali Murugesan
Cosmas Mwikirize
Andriy Myronenko
Saad Nadeem
Ahmed Naglah
Vivek Natarajan
Vishwesh Nath
Rodrigo Nava
Fernando Navarro
Lydia Neary-Zajiczek
Peter Neher
Dominik Neumann
Gia Ngo
Hannes Nickisch

Dong Nie
Jingxin Nie
Weizhi Nie
Aditya Nigam
Xia Ning
Zhenyuan Ning
Sijie Niu
Tianye Niu
Alexey Novikov
Jorge Novo
Chinedu Nwoye
Mohammad Obeid
Masahiro Oda
Thomas O'Donnell
Benjamin Odry
Steffen Oeltze-Jafra
Ayşe Oktay
Hugo Oliveira
Marcelo Oliveira
Sara Oliveira
Arnau Oliver
Sahin Olut
Jimena Olveres
John Onofrey
Eliza Orasanu
Felipe Orihuela-Espina
José Orlando
Marcos Ortega
Sarah Ostadabbas
Yoshito Otake
Sebastian Otalora
Cheng Ouyang
Jiahong Ouyang
Cristina Oyarzun Laura
Michal Ozery-Flato
Krittin Pachtrachai
Johannes Paetzold
Jin Pan
Yongsheng Pan
Prashant Pandey
Joao Papa
Giorgos Papanastasiou
Constantin Pape
Nripesh Parajuli
Hyunjin Park
Sanghyun Park

Seyoun Park
Angshuman Paul
Christian Payer
Chengtao Peng
Jialin Peng
Liying Peng
Tingying Peng
Yifan Peng
Tobias Penzkofer
Antonio Pepe
Oscar Perdomo
Jose-Antonio Pérez-Carrasco
Fernando Pérez-García
Jorge Perez-Gonzalez
Skand Peri
Loic Peter
Jorg Peters
Jens Petersen
Caroline Petitjean
Micha Pfeiffer
Dzung Pham
Renzo Phellan
Ashish Phophalia
Mark Pickering
Kilian Pohl
Iulia Popescu
Karteek Popuri
Tiziano Portenier
Alison Pouch
Arash Pourtaherian
Prateek Prasanna
Alexander Preuhs
Raphael Prevost
Juan Prieto
Viswanath P. S.
Sergi Pujades
Kumaradevan Punithakumar
Elodie Puybareau
Haikun Qi
Huan Qi
Xin Qi
Buyue Qian
Zhen Qian
Yan Qiang
Yuchuan Qiao
Zhi Qiao

Chen Qin
Wenjian Qin
Yanguo Qin
Wu Qiu
Hui Qu
Kha Gia Quach
Prashanth R.
Pradeep Reddy Raamana
Jagath Rajapakse
Kashif Rajpoot
Jhonata Ramos
Andrik Rampun
Parnesh Raniga
Nagulan Ratnarajah
Richard Rau
Mehul Raval
Keerthi Sravan Ravi
Daniele Ravì
Harish RaviPrakash
Rohith Reddy
Markus Rempfler
Xuhua Ren
Yinhao Ren
Yudan Ren
Anne-Marie Rickmann
Brandalyn Riedel
Leticia Rittner
Robert Robinson
Jessica Rodgers
Robert Rohling
Lukasz Roszkowiak
Karsten Roth
José Rouco
Su Ruan
Daniel Rueckert
Mirabela Rusu
Erica Rutter
Jaime S. Cardoso
Mohammad Sabokrou
Monjoy Saha
Pramit Saha
Dushyant Sahoo
Pranjal Sahu
Wojciech Samek
Juan A. Sánchez-Margallo
Robin Sandkuehler

Rodrigo Santa Cruz
Gianmarco Santini
Anil Kumar Sao
Mhd Hasan Sarhan
Duygu Sarikaya
Imari Sato
Olivier Saut
Mattia Savardi
Ramasamy Savitha
Fabien Scalzo
Nico Scherf
Alexander Schlaefer
Philipp Schleer
Leopold Schmetterer
Julia Schnabel
Klaus Schoeffmann
Peter Schueffler
Andreas Schuh
Thomas Schultz
Michael Schwier
Michael Sdika
Suman Sedai
Raghavendra Selvan
Sourya Sengupta
Youngho Seo
Lama Seoud
Ana Sequeira
Saeed Seyyedi
Giorgos Sfikas
Sobhan Shafiei
Reuben Shamir
Shayan Shams
Hongming Shan
Yeqin Shao
Harshita Sharma
Gregory Sharp
Mohamed Shehata
Haocheng Shen
Mali Shen
Yiqiu Shen
Zhengyang Shen
Luyao Shi
Xiaoshuang Shi
Yemin Shi
Yonghong Shi
Saurabh Shigwan

Hoo-Chang Shin
Suprosanna Shit
Yucheng Shu
Nadya Shusharina
Alberto Signoroni
Carlos A. Silva
Wilson Silva
Praveer Singh
Ramandeep Singh
Rohit Singla
Sumedha Singla
Ayushi Sinha
Rajath Soans
Hessam Sokooti
Jaemin Son
Ming Song
Tianyu Song
Yang Song
Youyi Song
Aristeidis Sotiras
Arcot Sowmya
Rachel Sparks
Bella Specktor
William Speier
Ziga Spiclin
Dominik Spinczyk
Chetan Srinidhi
Vinkle Srivastav
Lawrence Staib
Peter Steinbach
Darko Stern
Joshua Stough
Justin Strait
Robin Strand
Martin Styner
Hai Su
Pan Su
Yun-Hsuan Su
Vaishnavi Subramanian
Gérard Subsol
Carole Sudre
Yao Sui
Avan Suinesiaputra
Jeremias Sulam
Shipra Suman
Jian Sun

Liang Sun
Tao Sun
Kyung Sung
Chiranjib Sur
Yannick Suter
Raphael Sznitman
Solale Tabarestani
Fatemeh Taheri Dezaki
Roger Tam
José Tamez-Peña
Chaowei Tan
Jiaxing Tan
Hao Tang
Sheng Tang
Thomas Tang
Xiongfeng Tang
Zhenyu Tang
Mickael Tardy
Eu Wern Teh
Antonio Tejero-de-Pablos
Paul Thienphrapa
Stephen Thompson
Felix Thomsen
Jiang Tian
Yun Tian
Aleksei Tiulpin
Hamid Tizhoosh
Matthew Toews
Oguzhan Topsakal
Jordina Torrents
Sylvie Treuillet
Jocelyne Troccaz
Emanuele Trucco
Vinh Truong Hoang
Chialing Tsai
Andru Putra Twinanda
Norimichi Ukita
Eranga Ukwatta
Mathias Unberath
Tamas Ungi
Martin Urschler
Verena Uslar
Fatmatulzehra Uslu
Régis Vaillant
Jeya Maria Jose Valanarasu
Marta Vallejo

Fons van der Sommen
Gijs van Tulder
Kimberlin van Wijnen
Yogatheesan Varatharajah
Marta Varela
Thomas Varsavsky
Francisco Vasconcelos
S. Swaroop Vedula
Sanketh Vedula
Harini Veeraraghavan
Gonzalo Vegas Sanchez-Ferrero
Anant Vemuri
Gopalkrishna Veni
Ruchika Verma
Ujjwal Verma
Pedro Vieira
Juan Pedro Vigueras Guillen
Pierre-Frederic Villard
Athanasios Vlontzos
Wolf-Dieter Vogl
Ingmar Voigt
Eugene Vorontsov
Bo Wang
Cheng Wang
Chengjia Wang
Chunliang Wang
Dadong Wang
Guotai Wang
Haifeng Wang
Hongkai Wang
Hongyu Wang
Hua Wang
Huan Wang
Jun Wang
Kuanquan Wang
Kun Wang
Lei Wang
Li Wang
Liansheng Wang
Manning Wang
Ruixuan Wang
Shanshan Wang
Shujun Wang
Shuo Wang
Tianchen Wang
Tongxin Wang

Wenzhe Wang
Xi Wang
Xiangxue Wang
Yalin Wang
Yan Wang (Sichuan University)
Yan Wang (Johns Hopkins University)
Yaping Wang
Yi Wang
Yirui Wang
Yuanjun Wang
Yun Wang
Zeyi Wang
Zhangyang Wang
Simon Warfield
Jonathan Weber
Jürgen Weese
Donglai Wei
Dongming Wei
Zhen Wei
Martin Weigert
Michael Wels
Junhao Wen
Matthias Wilms
Stefan Winzeck
Adam Wittek
Marek Wodzinski
Jelmer Wolterink
Ken C. L. Wong
Jonghye Woo
Chongruo Wu
Dijia Wu
Ji Wu
Jian Wu (Tsinghua University)
Jian Wu (Zhejiang University)
Jie Ying Wu
Junyan Wu
Minjie Wu
Pengxiang Wu
Xi Wu
Xia Wu
Xiyin Wu
Ye Wu
Yicheng Wu
Yifan Wu
Zhengwang Wu
Tobias Wuerfl

Pengcheng Xi
James Xia
Siyu Xia
Yingda Xia
Yong Xia
Lei Xiang
Deqiang Xiao
Li Xiao (Tulane University)
Li Xiao (Chinese Academy of Science)
Yuting Xiao
Hongtao Xie
Jianyang Xie
Lingxi Xie
Long Xie
Xueqian Xie
Yiting Xie
Yuan Xie
Yutong Xie
Fangxu Xing
Fuyong Xing
Tao Xiong
Chenchu Xu
Hongming Xu
Jiaofeng Xu
Kele Xu
Lisheng Xu
Min Xu
Rui Xu
Xiaowei Xu
Yanwu Xu
Yongchao Xu
Zhenghua Xu
Cheng Xue
Jie Xue
Wufeng Xue
Yuan Xue
Faridah Yahya
Chenggang Yan
Ke Yan
Weizheng Yan
Yu Yan
Yuguang Yan
Zhennan Yan
Changchun Yang
Chao-Han Huck Yang
Dong Yang

Fan Yang (IIAI)
Fan Yang (Temple University)
Feng Yang
Ge Yang
Guang Yang
Heran Yang
Hongxu Yang
Huijuan Yang
Jiancheng Yang
Jie Yang
Junlin Yang
Lin Yang
Xiao Yang
Xiaohui Yang
Xin Yang
Yan Yang
Yujiu Yang
Dongren Yao
Jianhua Yao
Jiawen Yao
Li Yao
Chuyang Ye
Huihui Ye
Menglong Ye
Xujiong Ye
Andy W. K. Yeung
Jingru Yi
Jirong Yi
Xin Yi
Yi Yin
Shihui Ying
Youngjin Yoo
Chenyu You
Sahar Yousefi
Hanchao Yu
Jinhua Yu
Kai Yu
Lequan Yu
Qi Yu
Yang Yu
Zhen Yu
Pengyu Yuan
Yixuan Yuan
Paul Yushkevich
Ghada Zamzmi
Dong Zeng

Guodong Zeng
Oliver Zettinig
Zhiwei Zhai
Kun Zhan
Baochang Zhang
Chaoyi Zhang
Daoqiang Zhang
Dongqing Zhang
Fan Zhang (Yale University)
Fan Zhang (Harvard Medical School)
Guangming Zhang
Han Zhang
Hang Zhang
Haopeng Zhang
Heye Zhang
Huahong Zhang
Jianpeng Zhang
Jinao Zhang
Jingqing Zhang
Jinwei Zhang
Jiong Zhang
Jun Zhang
Le Zhang
Lei Zhang
Lichi Zhang
Lin Zhang
Ling Zhang
Lu Zhang
Miaomiao Zhang
Ning Zhang
Pengfei Zhang
Pengyue Zhang
Qiang Zhang
Rongzhao Zhang
Ru-Yuan Zhang
Shanzhuo Zhang
Shu Zhang
Tong Zhang
Wei Zhang
Weiwei Zhang
Wenlu Zhang
Xiaoyun Zhang
Xin Zhang
Ya Zhang
Yanbo Zhang
Yanfu Zhang

Contents – Part IV

Shape Models and Landmark Detection

Segmentation

Deep Volumetric Universal Lesion Detection Using Light-Weight Pseudo 3D Convolution and Surface Point Regression

Jinzheng Cai[1]([✉]), Ke Yan[1], Chi-Tung Cheng[2], Jing Xiao[3], Chien-Hung Liao[2], Le Lu[1], and Adam P. Harrison[1]

[1] PAII Inc., Bethesda, MD, USA
caijinzheng883@paii-labs.com
[2] Chang Gung Memorial Hospital, Linkou, Taiwan, ROC
[3] Ping An Technology, Shenzhen, China

Abstract. Identifying, measuring and reporting lesions accurately and comprehensively from patient CT scans are important yet time-consuming procedures for physicians. Computer-aided lesion/significant-findings detection techniques are at the core of medical imaging, which remain very challenging due to the tremendously large variability of lesion appearance, location and size distributions in 3D imaging. In this work, we propose a novel deep anchor-free one-stage volumetric lesion detector (VLD) framework that incorporates (1) pseudo 3D convolution operators to recycle the architectural configurations and pre-trained weights from the off-the-shelf 2D networks, especially ones with large capacities to cope with data variance, and (2) a new surface point regression method to effectively regress the 3D lesion spatial extents by pinpointing their representative key points on lesion surfaces. Experimental validations are first conducted on the public large-scale NIH DeepLesion dataset where our proposed method delivers new state-of-the-art quantitative performance. We also test VLD on our in-house dataset for liver tumor detection. VLD generalizes well in both large-scale and small-sized tumor datasets in CT imaging.

Keywords: Volumetric universal lesion detection · Light-weight pseudo 3D convolution · Surface point regression

1 Introduction

Automated lesion detection is an important yet challenging task in medical image analysis, as exploited by [8,16,19,22,23,27,29] on the public NIH DeepLesion dataset. Its aims include improving physician's reading efficiency and increasing the sensitivity for localizing/reporting small but vital tumors, which are more

Electronic supplementary material The online version of this chapter (https://doi.org/10.1007/978-3-030-59719-1_1) contains supplementary material, which is available to authorized users.

© Springer Nature Switzerland AG 2020
A. L. Martel et al. (Eds.): MICCAI 2020, LNCS 12264, pp. 3–13, 2020.
https://doi.org/10.1007/978-3-030-59719-1_1

prone to be missed, e.g. human-reader sensitivity is reported at 48–57% with small-sized hepatocellular carcinoma (HCC) liver lesions [1]. Automated lesion detection remains difficult due to the tremendously large appearance variability, unpredictable locations, and frequent small-sized lesions of interest [12,22]. In particular, two key aspects requiring further research are (1) the best means to effectively process the 3D volumetric data (since small and critical tumors require 3D imaging context to be differentiated) and (2) to more accurately regress the tumor's 3D bounding box. This work makes significant contributions towards both aims.

Computed tomography (CT) scans are volumetric, so incorporating 3D context is the key in recognizing lesions. As a direct solution, 3D convolutional neural networks (CNNs) have achieved good performance for lung nodule detection [5,6]. However, due to GPU memory constraints, shallower networks and smaller input dimensions are used [5,6], which may limit the performance for more complicated detection problems. For instance, universal lesion detection (ULD) [16,17,21,29], which aims to detect many lesions types with diverse appearances from the whole body, demands wider and deeper networks to extract more comprehensive image features. To resolve this issue, 2.5D networks have been designed [2,16,17,20,21,29] that use deep 2D CNNs with ImageNet pre-trained weights and fuse image features of multiple consecutive axial slices. Nevertheless, these methods do not fully exploit 3D information since their 3D related operations operate sparsely at only selected network layers via convolutional-layer inner products. 2.5D models are also inefficient because they process CT volumes in a slice-by-slice manner. Partially inspired by [3,14,24], we propose applying pseudo 3D convolution (P3DC) backbones to efficiently process 3D images. This allows our volumetric lesion detector (VLD) framework to fully exploit 3D context while re-purposing off-the-shelf deep 2D network structures and inheriting their large capacities to cope with lesion variances.

Good lesion detection performance also relies on accurate bounding box regression. But, some lesions, e.g. liver lesions, frequently present vague boundaries that are hard to distinguish from background. Most existing anchor-based [15] and anchor-free [18,28] algorithms rely on features extracted from the proposal *center* to predict the lesion's extent. This is sub-optimal since lesion *boundary* features should intuitively be crucial for this task. To this end, we adopt and enhance the RepPoint algorithm [25], which generates a point set to estimate bounding boxes, with each point fixating on a representative part. Such a point set can drive more finely-tuned bounding box regression than traditional strategies, which is crucial for accurately localizing small lesions. Different from RepPoint, we propose surface point regression (SPR), which uses a novel triplet-base appearance regularization to force regressed points to move towards lesion boundaries. This allows for an even more accurate regression.

In this work, we advance both volumetric detection and bounding box regression using deep volumetric P3DCs and effective SPR, respectively. We demonstrate that our P3DC backbone can outperform state-of-the-art 2.5D and 3D detectors on the public large-scale NIH DeepLesion dataset [22], e.g. we increase the strongest baseline's sensitivity of detecting small lesions from 22.4% to 30.3% at 1 false positive (FP) per CT volume. When incorporating SPR, our VLD

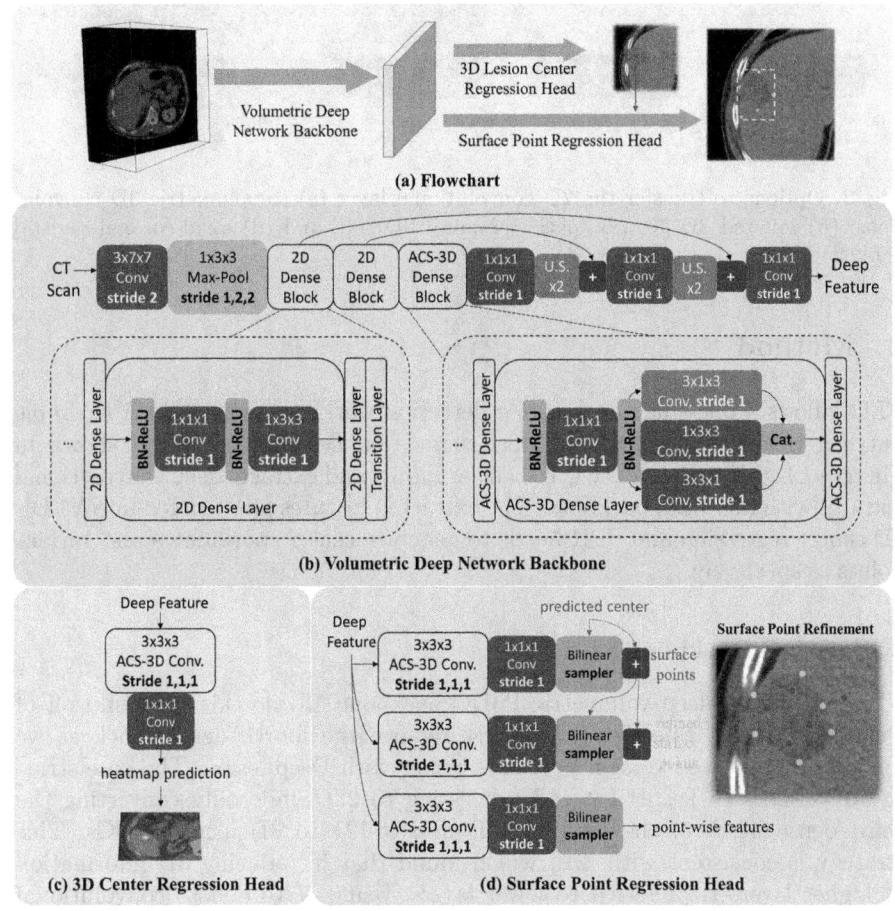

Fig. 1. Overview of VLD. We show (a) the complete workflow; (b) the detailed pseudo 3D convolution (P3DC) backbone; (c) 3D lesion center regression head; and (d) surface point regression (SPR) head for bounding box generation.

outperforms the best baseline [2] by >4% sensitivity for all operating points on free-response receiver operating characteristic (FROC). We also evaluate VLD on an extremely challenging dataset (574 patient studies) of HCC liver lesions collected from archives in Chang Cung Memorial Hospital. Many patients suffer from cirrhosis, which make HCC detection extremely difficult. P3DC alone accounts for 63.6% sensitivity at 1 FP per CT volume. Adding SPR boosts this sensitivity to 69.2%. Importantly, for both the DeepLesion and in-house HCC dataset, our complete VLD framework provides the largest performance gains for small lesions, which are the easiest to miss by human readers and thus should be the focus for any detection system.

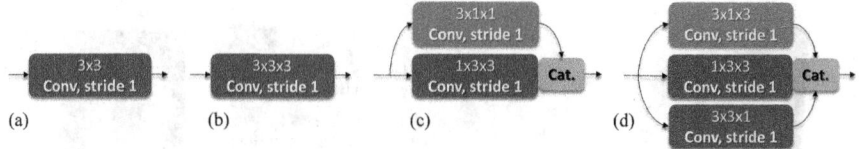

Fig. 2. Options to transfer the 2D convolutional layer (a) to volumetric 3D convolutions: (b) inflated 3D [3], (c) spatio-temporal 3D [14], and (d) axial-coronal-sagittal 3D [24].

2   Method

VLD follows a one-stage anchor-free detection workflow [2,28], which is simple but has yielded state-of-the-art performance on DeepLesion [2]. As shown in Fig. 1, VLD takes volumetric CT scans as inputs and extracts deep convolutional features with its P3DC backbone. The extracted features are then fed into VLD's 3D center regression and SPR heads to generate center coordinates and surface points, respectively.

2.1   P3DC Backbone

VLD relies on a deep volumetric P3DC backbone. To do this, we build off of DenseNet-121 [7]. Specifically, we first remove the fourth dense block as we found this truncated version performs better with DeepLesion. The core strategy of VLD is to keep front-end processing to 2D, while only converting the third dense block of the truncated DenseNet-121 to 3D using P3DCs. This strategy is consistent with [21], which found that introducing 3D information at higher layers is preferred to lower layers. Using N to denote convolutional kernel sizes throughout, for the first two dense blocks the weight parameters, (c_o, c_i, N, N), are reshaped to $(c_o, c_i, 1, N, N)$ to process volumetric data slice-by-slice. When processing dynamic CTs with multiple contrast phases, e.g., our in-house dataset, we stack the multi-phase input and inflate the weight of the first convolutional kernel along its second dimension [3].

To implement 3D processing, we convert the third dense block and task-specific heads and investigate several different options for P3DCs, which include inflated 3D (I3D) [3], spatio-temporal 3D (ST-3D) [14], and axial-coronal-sagittal 3D (ACS-3D) [24]. These options are depicted in Fig. 2. I3D [3] simply duplicates 2D kernels along the axial (3D) direction and downscales weight values by the number of duplications. Thus, I3D produces true 3D kernels. ST-3D [14] first reshapes (c_o, c_i, N, N) kernels into $(c_o, c_i, 1, N, N)$ to act as "spatial" kernels and introduces an extra $(c_o, c_i, N, 1, 1)$ kernel as the "temporal" kernel. The resulting features from both are fused using channel-wise concatenation. There are alternative ST-3D configurations; however, the parallel structure of Fig. 2(c) was shown to be best in a liver segmentation study [27]. ACS-3D [24] splits the kernel (c_o, c_i, N, N) into axial (c_{oa}, c_i, N, N), coronal (c_{oc}, c_i, N, N), and sagittal

(c_{os}, c_i, N, N) kernels, where $c_o = c_{oa} + c_{os} + c_{oc}$. Thereafter, it reshapes the view-specific kernels correspondingly into $(c_{oa}, c_i, 1, N, N)$, $(c_{oc}, c_i, N, 1, N)$, and $(c_{os}, c_i, N, N, 1)$. Like ST-3D, ACS-3D fuses the resulting features using channel-wise concatenation. Compared to the extra temporal-kernels introduced by ST-3D, ACS-3D requires no extra model parameters, keeping the converted model light-weight. In our implementation, we empirically set the ratio of $c_{oa} : c_{oc} : c_{os}$ to $8 : 1 : 1$ as the axial plane usually holds the highest resolution.

VLD has two task-specific network heads, one to locate the lesion centers and one to regress surface points. Before inputting the deep volumetric features into the heads, we use an feature pyramid network (FPN) [10] with three $(c_o, c_i, 1, 1, 1)$ convolutional layers to fuse outputs of the dense blocks, which helps VLD to be robust to lesions with different sizes. Focusing first on the center regression head, it takes the output of the FPN (i.e. "deep feature" in Fig. 1) and processes it with an ACS-3D convolutional layer followed by a $(1, c_i, 1, 1, 1)$ convolutional layer. Both layers are randomly initialized. Like CenterNet [28], the output is a 3D heat map, $\hat{Y}$, that predicts lesion centers. Ground-truth heat map, Y, is generated as a Gaussian heat map with the radius in each dimension set to half of the target lesion's width, height, and depth. We use focal loss [2,11,28] to train the center regression head:

$$\mathcal{L}_{ctr} = \frac{-1}{m} \sum_{xyz} \begin{cases} (1 - \hat{Y}_{xyz})^\alpha \log(\hat{Y}_{xyz}) & \text{if } Y_{xyz} = 1 \\ (1 - Y_{xyz})^\beta (\hat{Y}_{xyz})^\alpha \log(1 - \hat{Y}_{xyz}) & \text{otherwise} \end{cases}, \quad (1)$$

where m is the number of lesions in the CT and $\alpha = 2$ and $\beta = 4$ are focal-loss hyper-parameters [28]. The ground-truth heat map is <1 everywhere except at the lesion center voxel. Like recent work [2], when possible we also exploit hard negatives by generating negative-valued heatmaps in Y, which will magnify their loss contributions more than 0-valued regions. See Cai et al. [2] for more details.

2.2   Surface Point Regression

The P3DC backbone and center regression head are effective at locating lesions. But, once the lesion is located its extent must also be determined. To do this, we directly regress a 3D point set (actually offsets from the center point), using backbone features located at the center point:

$$\mathcal{P} = \{(x_k, y_k, z_k)\}_{k=1}^n, \quad (2)$$

where n is the total number of points. This requires a $1 \times 1 \times 1$ convolution with $3n$ outputs. Empirically, we find $n = 16$ delivers the best results. Because $\mathcal{P}$ is computed from center-point features, it may suffer from inaccuracies. Thus, we also compute offsets to refine $\mathcal{P}$:

$$\mathcal{P}_r = \{(x_k + \Delta x_k, y_k + \Delta y_k, z_k + \Delta z_k)\}_{k=1}^n, \quad (3)$$

where $\{(\Delta x_k, \Delta y_k, \Delta z_k)\}$ are the predicted offsets of the refined surface points. To do this, for each location in $\mathcal{P}$, we bilinearly interpolate corresponding backbone features and regress location-specific offsets. This only requires a $1 \times 1 \times 1$

convolution with 3 outputs. To actually supervise the $\mathcal{P}$ and $\mathcal{P}_r$ regression, we compute their minimum and maximum coordinates and ensure they match with the ground-truth bounding box. More formally, if we denote the ground-truth box using its top-right-front and bottom-left-rear corners $\{(x_{trf}, y_{trf}, z_{trf}),$ $(x_{blr}, y_{blr}, z_{blr})\}$, the regression of $\mathcal{P}$ and $\mathcal{P}_r$ can be trained using the following loss:

$$\mathcal{L}_{pts} = \sum_{i \in (x,y,z)} |i_{blr} - \min_{1 \le k \le n}(i_k)| + |i_{trf} - \max_{1 \le k \le n}(i_k)|$$
$$+ |i_{blr} - \min_{1 \le k \le n}(i_k + \Delta i_k)| + |i_{trf} - \max_{1 \le k \le n}(i_k + \Delta i_k)|. \quad (4)$$

One important limitation of (4) is that ellipsoid lesions do not fit perfectly in cuboid boxes. As a result, regressed points may still satisfy (4) if they lay outside the lesion, but still inside the box. Such points may be more prone to produce inaccurate offsets, i.e. (3), during inference. To address this, we propose an appearance-based similarity constraint to encourage points to only fixate on lesion surfaces so that the point set can represent fine-grained lesion geometry correctly. The idea is to force surface-point appearance to be more similar to regions inside the lesion than to those outside it. This constraint is achieved by adding a triplet-loss with the lesion center as the positive anchor (inside) and box corners as negative anchors (outside). Specifically, we compute *point-wise* features from the center and eight corners of the bounding box with bilinear sampling and denote them as a^p and $\{a_j^n\}_{j=1}^8$, respectively. We also extract point-wise features from P_r: $\{a_k\}_{k=1}^n$. The triplet-loss is then formulated as

$$\mathcal{L}_{tri} = \frac{1}{m} \sum_{k=1}^n \sum_{j=1}^8 \max(0, \|a^p - a_k\|_2 - \|a^p - a_j^n\|_2 + 1). \quad (5)$$

With the supervision of $\mathcal{L}_{pts}$ and $\mathcal{L}_{tri}$, we expect surface points will either move toward lesion surfaces or to the center. This constitutes our surface point regression (SPR). The extracted point-wise features are designed to be semantic in nature (healthy versus lesion tissue). Thus, complex lesion appearances, e.g., cavitations, should be mapped to a similar semantic space. We optimize the SPR together with the center regression head by minimizing a joint loss function:

$$\mathcal{L} = \mathcal{L}_{ctr} + 0.1(\mathcal{L}_{pts} + \mathcal{L}_{tri}). \quad (6)$$

2.3   Implementation Details

We implement our system in Pytorch [13] on four NVIDIA Quadro RTX 6000 GPUs. The P3DC backbone weights were initialized with the pre-trained Lesion Harvester weights [2], which were trained using the official DeepLesion data split so there is no data leakage. We also tried ImageNet-pretrained weights and random initialization, but performance was not as good. All other layers were randomly initialized. The FPN's output, i.e., "deep feature" in Fig. 1, has 512 channels. In the task-specific heads, each ACS-3D layer consists of an ACS-3D convolutional layer with a kernel size of 3 and $c_{ao} + c_{co} + c_{so} = 256$. The output channels of the lesion center heat map, $\mathcal{P}$, $\mathcal{P}_r$, and point-wise features are 1, 48 (16 points), 3, and 128, respectively. We adopt the Adam [9] optimizer and set a base learning rate to 0.0001, which was reduced by a factor of 10 after the validation loss reached its minimum value.

3   Experimental Results

Datasets. We evaluate our approach on two datasets. **DeepLesion** [23] is a large-scale benchmark for ULD that comprises 32,735 retrospectively clinically annotated lesions from 10,594 CT scans of 4,427 unique patients. Many works report performance on DeepLesion, but most are either 2D [16,17,29] or 2.5D [20, 21]. We use the 3D annotations and hard-negatives from [2] to both train and evaluate DeepLesion. The volumetric test set of DeepLesion [2] includes 272 fully-annotated sub-volumes and more accurately reflects the 3D lesion detection performance. **HCC Liver Dataset:** We also evaluate on our in-house dataset of 574 dynamic CT studies of patients with HCC liver lesions. HCC is one of the most fatal cancers and detection at early stages is crucial. However, HCC often co-occurs with liver fibrosis, challenging lesion discovery. Human sensitivities have been reported to be 48–57% for small-sized lesions [1]. We randomly split the dataset patient-wise into 384, 92, and 98 studies for training, validation, and testing, respectively.

Evaluation and Comparison Methods. A detected bounding-box is regarded as correct when the 3D-IoU between the detected box and a ground-truth box exceeds 0.3. The FROC is used for evaluation. We first evaluate different P3DC backbones: ST-3D, I3D, and ACS-3D. We also test a shallow fully-3D UNet [4] backbone within the CenterNet [28] framework and also against the 2.5D Lesion Harvester [2], which reports the highest performance to date for the DeepLesion dataset. These two competitors directly regress a lesion's size using features sampled from the predicted lesion center and can also naturally learn from hard-negatives [2]. In addition, we also report results using CenterNet (2D) [28], Faster R-CNN (2.5D) [15], and MULAN (2.5D) [21], drawn from Cai et al.'s experiments [2]. This represents a comprehensive comparison across many different detector variants. To measure the impact of our proposed SPR, we also implement VLD with deep representative points (DRP) [26] that foregoes the appearance-based triplet loss. Finally, we evaluate our proposed VLD framework: P3DC + SPR.

Results. In Table 1, we compare our proposed approach against alternative approaches. Using FROC analysis, the average sensitivities on DeepLesion are: CenterNet-2D 27.9%; CenterNet-3D 18.7%; Faster R-CNN 25.4%; MULAN 27.9%; Lesion Harvester 31.9%, and our strongest P3DC variant 36.4%. As can been seen, P3DC significantly outperforms the previous SOTA Lesion Harvester

Table 1. Sensitivities (%) at various FPs per CT volume.

Method	Backbone	FPs per volume								Avg.
		0.25	0.50	0.75	1.00	1.25	1.50	1.75	2.00	
DeepLesion volumetric test set										
CenterNet-3D	3D UNet	9.6	14.1	16.7	18.9	20.3	22.2	23.5	24.9	18.7
Faster R-CNN [15]	2.5D DenseNet-121	9.0	14.8	19.8	25.6	29.3	32.8	35.5	36.7	25.4
CenterNet [28]	2D DenseNet-121	15.0	19.8	24.3	28.5	31.2	33.3	35.0	36.6	27.9
MULAN [21]	2.5D DenseNet-121	14.5	20.8	25.6	31.0	34.4	38.1	40.3	42.8	30.9
Lesion Harvester [2]	2.5D DenseNet-121	15.8	24.6	28.4	32.7	35.5	37.5	39.8	41.0	31.9
P3DC	I3D	**22.3**	27.7	32.7	36.5	38.3	39.5	41.4	43.0	35.1
P3DC	ST-3D	18.8	26.7	30.5	32.7	35.5	37.3	39.1	41.2	32.7
P3DC	ACS-3D	19.8	27.5	32.2	35.5	38.9	41.1	41.8	43.1	34.9
P3DC	ACS-3D+DRP	20.4	26.3	31.0	34.4	37.4	40.0	41.3	42.1	34.1
P3DC	ACS-3D+SPR	20.1	**29.1**	**34.4**	**37.1**	**40.3**	**42.1**	**43.6**	**45.1**	**36.4**
HCC Liver test set										
P3DC	ACS-3D	50.5	57.0	61.7	63.6	67.3	71.0	71.0	71.0	64.1
P3DC	ACS-3D+DRP	**57.9**	**65.4**	68.2	**69.2**	70.1	71.0	72.9	73.8	68.5
P3DC	ACS-3D+SPR	55.1	64.5	**69.2**	**69.2**	**72.0**	**76.6**	**77.6**	**77.6**	**70.2**

and MULAN methods by 4.5% and 8.5%, respectively, which validates the effectiveness of P3DC over its 2.5D counterparts. We choose ACS-3D over I3D for it produces comparable performance to I3D, meanwhile it keeps VLD light-weight.

From Table 1, we also observe that adding the original DRP method actually underperforms the baseline P3DC. This in fact motivated our development of SPR. The DRP method lacks explicit constraints on point locations, making it challenging to automatically learn effective point-wise feature from CT images. In contrast, SPR introduces surface constraints to force the regressed points to distribute onto lesion surfaces. Tests on our in-house dataset also confirms that our proposed SPR can improve sensitivities on HCC liver lesion detection.

While these results demonstrate the value of our P3DC backbone and SPR bounding-box regression, even more convincing conclusions can be drawn when analyzing performance based on lesion size. In DeepLesion, we use 2 cm and 5 cm as cut-off sizes. However, our HCC liver dataset has hardly any lesions smaller than 2 cm, so we only stratify based on a 5 cm cut-off. As Table 2 indicates, compared to Lesion Harvester, our P3DC backbone can yield improvements of 7% sensitivity for small-size lesions in DeepLesion. These are the most critical lesions to detect, since these are the easiest for human observers to miss. Adding the SPR boosts small-size performance even further, indicating that SPR's aggregation of boundary features can produce improved fine-grained bounding boxes. Moving to the HCC dataset, our SPR can produce boosts in sensitivity of over 4% compared to direct CenterNet-style regression, further validating our SPR regression strategy. These are clinically significant performance improvements. Visual examples can be found in Fig. 3, and our supplementary material, depicting the process of SPR's more refined regression of bounding box extents.

Table 2. Size-stratified sensitivities (%) at FP = 1 per CT volume.[†]: P3DC+DRP produces FPs with high confidences, thus at FP = 1, it has lower sensitivity than P3DC+SPR on HCC Liver.

	DeepLesion				HCC liver		
Lesion size (cm)	<2	2–5	>5	All	<=5	>5	All
Distribution (%)	62%	29%	9%	100%	65%	35%	100%
UNet 3D	16.5	38.8	30.8	18.9			
Lesion Harvester [2]	22.4	**67.1**	**75.6**	32.7			
P3DC (ACS-3D)	29.9	62.4	57.7	35.5	61.4	86.5	63.6
P3DC (ACS-3D) + DRP	28.7	64.7	60.3	34.4	58.6[†]	**94.6**	69.2
P3DC (ACS-3D) + SPR	**30.3**	63.9	62.8	**37.1**	**65.7**	**94.6**	**69.2**

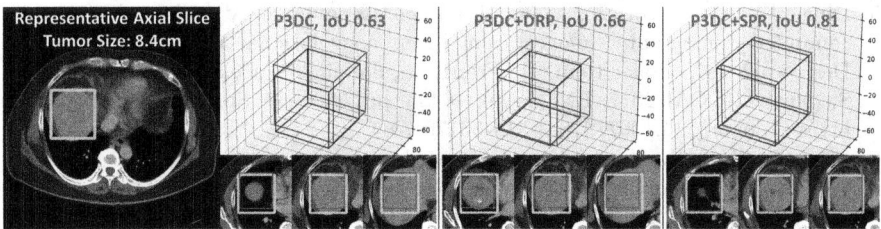

Fig. 3. Visualization of different methods. We show an instance of liver tumor overlaid with its ground-truth box in the 1st column. In the 2nd, 3rd, and 4th columns, we show the detection results from P3DC with general box regression, P3DC+DRP, and P3DC+SPR, respectively. For each example, we display the result in 3D and show three representative axial slices. We render the ground-truth box in **Green**, the detection results in **Blue**, and the regressed surface points, when applicable, in **Red**. Best viewed in color. (Color figure online)

4   Conclusion

In this work, we tackle challenges of lesion detection in CT scans by proposing a very deep volumetric lesion detection model VLD. It processes CT scans directly in 3D so as to fully incorporate 3D context for better performance. It has very deep backbones with large capacities so that it can handle lesions with large appearance variability. Its surface point regression head can effectively estimate the 3D lesion spatial extents. It also generalize well with small-scaled medical datasets as it is light-weight and can be initialized with pre-trained 2D networks. Compared with 2D, 2.5D, and fully 3D variants, our method is superior in accuracy, model size, and speed (see our supplementary material). The proposed VLD achieved new SOTA performance on the large-scale NIH DeepLesion dataset. It has also validated its generalization capability on our in-house HCC liver dataset.

References

1. Addley, H., et al.: Accuracy of hepatocellular carcinoma detection on multidetector CT in a transplant liver population with explant liver correlation. Clin. Radiol. **66**, 349–356 (2011)
2. Cai, J., et al.: Lesion harvester: iteratively mining unlabeled lesions and hard-negative examples at scale. CoRR abs/2001.07776 (2020)
3. Carreira, J., Zisserman, A.: Quo vadis, action recognition? A new model and the kinetics dataset. In: CVPR 2017, pp. 4724–4733. IEEE (2017)
4. Çiçek, Ö., Abdulkadir, A., Lienkamp, S.S., Brox, T., Ronneberger, O.: 3D U-Net: learning dense volumetric segmentation from sparse annotation. In: Ourselin, S., Joskowicz, L., Sabuncu, M.R., Unal, G., Wells, W. (eds.) MICCAI 2016. LNCS, vol. 9901, pp. 424–432. Springer, Cham (2016). https://doi.org/10.1007/978-3-319-46723-8_49
5. Ding, J., Li, A., Hu, Z., Wang, L.: Accurate pulmonary nodule detection in computed tomography images using deep convolutional neural networks. In: Descoteaux, M., Maier-Hein, L., Franz, A., Jannin, P., Collins, D.L., Duchesne, S. (eds.) MICCAI 2017. LNCS, vol. 10435, pp. 559–567. Springer, Cham (2017). https://doi.org/10.1007/978-3-319-66179-7_64
6. Dou, Q., Chen, H., Yu, L., Qin, J., Heng, P.: Multilevel contextual 3-D CNNs for false positive reduction in pulmonary nodule detection. IEEE Trans. Biomed. Eng. **64**(7), 1558–1567 (2017)
7. Huang, G., Liu, Z., van der Maaten, L., Weinberger, K.Q.: Densely connected convolutional networks. In: CVPR 2017, pp. 2261–2269. IEEE (2017)
8. Jiang, C., Wang, S., Xu, H., Liang, X.: Elixirnet: relation-aware network architecture adaptation for medical lesion detection. In: AAAI 2020, pp. 11093–11100. AAAI Press (2020)
9. Kingma, D.P., Ba, J.: Adam: a method for stochastic optimization. In: Bengio, Y., LeCun, Y. (eds.) ICLR 2015 (2015)
10. Lin, T., Dollár, P., Girshick, R.B., He, K., Hariharan, B., Belongie, S.J.: Feature pyramid networks for object detection. In: CVPR 2017, pp. 936–944. IEEE (2017)
11. Lin, T., Goyal, P., Girshick, R.B., He, K., Dollár, P.: Focal loss for dense object detection. In: ICCV 2017, pp. 2999–3007. IEEE (2017)
12. Litjens, G., et al.: A survey on deep learning in medical image analysis. Med. Image Anal. **42**, 60–88 (2017)
13. Paszke, A., et al.: Pytorch: an imperative style, high-performance deep learning library. In: NeurIPS, pp. 8024–8035 (2019)
14. Qiu, Z., Yao, T., Mei, T.: Learning spatio-temporal representation with pseudo-3D residual networks. In: ICCV 2017, pp. 5534–5542. IEEE (2017)
15. Ren, S., He, K., Girshick, R., Sun, J.: Faster R-CNN: towards real-time object detection with region proposal networks. In: NIPS 2015, pp. 91–99 (2015)
16. Shao, Q., Gong, L., Ma, K., Liu, H., Zheng, Y.: Attentive CT lesion detection using deep pyramid inference with multi-scale booster. In: Shen, D., et al. (eds.) MICCAI 2019. LNCS, vol. 11769, pp. 301–309. Springer, Cham (2019). https://doi.org/10.1007/978-3-030-32226-7_34
17. Tang, Y., Yan, K., Tang, Y., Liu, J., Xiao, J., Summers, R.M.: Uldor: a universal lesion detector for CT scans with pseudo masks and hard negative example mining. In: ISBI 2019, pp. 833–836. IEEE (2019)
18. Tian, Z., Shen, C., Chen, H., He, T.: FCOS: fully convolutional one-stage object detection. In: ICCV 2019, pp. 9626–9635. IEEE (2019)

19. Wang, X., Cai, Z., Gao, D., Vasconcelos, N.: Towards universal object detection by domain attention. In: CVPR 2019, pp. 7289–7298. IEEE (2019)

20. Yan, K., Bagheri, M., Summers, R.M.: 3D context enhanced region-based convolutional neural network for end-to-end lesion detection. In: Frangi, A.F., Schnabel, J.A., Davatzikos, C., Alberola-López, C., Fichtinger, G. (eds.) MICCAI 2018. LNCS, vol. 11070, pp. 511–519. Springer, Cham (2018). https://doi.org/10.1007/978-3-030-00928-1_58

21. Yan, K., et al.: MULAN: multitask universal lesion analysis network for joint lesion detection, tagging, and segmentation. In: Shen, D., et al. (eds.) MICCAI 2019. LNCS, vol. 11769, pp. 194–202. Springer, Cham (2019). https://doi.org/10.1007/978-3-030-32226-7_22

22. Yan, K., Wang, X., Lu, L., Summers, R.M.: Deeplesion: automated mining of large-scale lesion annotations and universal lesion detection with deep learning. J. Med. Imaging 5(3), 036501 (2018)

23. Yan, K., et al.: Deep lesion graphs in the wild: Relationship learning and organization of significant radiology image findings in a diverse large-scale lesion database. In: CVPR 2018, pp. 9261–9270. IEEE (2018)

24. Yang, J., Huang, X., Ni, B., Xu, J., Yang, C., Xu, G.: Reinventing 2D convolutions for 3D medical images. CoRR abs/1911.10477 (2019)

25. Yang, Z., Liu, S., Hu, H., Wang, L., Lin, S.: Reppoints: point set representation for object detection. In: ICCV 2019, pp. 9656–9665. IEEE (2019)

26. Yang, Z., et al.: Dense reppoints: representing visual objects with dense point sets. CoRR abs/1912.11473 (2019)

27. Zhang, J., Xie, Y., Zhang, P., Chen, H., Xia, Y., Shen, C.: Light-weight hybrid convolutional network for liver tumor segmentation. In: Kraus, S. (ed.) IJCAI 2019, pp. 4271–4277. ijcai.org (2019)

28. Zhou, X., Wang, D., Krähenbühl, P.: Objects as points. CoRR abs/1904.07850 (2019)

29. Zlocha, M., Dou, Q., Glocker, B.: Improving RetinaNet for CT lesion detection with dense masks from weak RECIST labels. In: Shen, D., et al. (eds.) MICCAI 2019. LNCS, vol. 11769, pp. 402–410. Springer, Cham (2019). https://doi.org/10.1007/978-3-030-32226-7_45

DeScarGAN: Disease-Specific Anomaly Detection with Weak Supervision

Julia Wolleb[✉], Robin Sandkühler, and Philippe C. Cattin

Department of Biomedical Engineering, University of Basel, Allschwil, Switzerland
`julia.wolleb@unibas.ch`

Abstract. Anomaly detection and localization in medical images is a challenging task, especially when the anomaly exhibits a change of existing structures, e.g., brain atrophy or changes in the pleural space due to pleural effusions. In this work, we present a weakly supervised and detail-preserving method that is able to detect structural changes of existing anatomical structures. In contrast to standard anomaly detection methods, our method extracts information about the disease characteristics from two groups: a group of patients affected by the same disease and a healthy control group. Together with identity-preserving mechanisms, this enables our method to extract highly disease-specific characteristics for a more detailed detection of structural changes. We designed a specific synthetic data set to evaluate and compare our method against state-of-the-art anomaly detection methods. Finally, we show the performance of our method on chest X-ray images. Our method called DeScarGAN outperforms other anomaly detection methods on the synthetic data set and by visual inspection on the chest X-ray image data set.

Keywords: Anomaly detection · Weak supervision · Disease-specific

1 Introduction

For medical applications, it is of great interest to find an automated way to show visual manifestations of a disease. In the past, artificial neural networks have shown a great performance in the task of image segmentation. As the manual generation of pixel-wise annotations is time consuming and requires expert knowledge, the training data is limited in number or even unavailable. Furthermore, the manually generated labels are affected by human bias. Using only image-level class labels for training of the networks overcomes those issues. In this paper, we propose a new disease-specific and weakly supervised method for anomaly detection and localization. The task we aim to solve is to highlight the pathological changes in an image of a diseased subject, as well as the classification into diseased and healthy subjects. This can improve diagnosis, lead

Electronic supplementary material The online version of this chapter (https://doi.org/10.1007/978-3-030-59719-1_2) contains supplementary material, which is available to authorized users.

A. L. Martel et al. (Eds.): MICCAI 2020, LNCS 12264, pp. 14–24, 2020.
https://doi.org/10.1007/978-3-030-59719-1_2

the attention to relevant parts of the anatomy and provide a starting point for further studies.

Classical anomaly detection algorithms are trained only on healthy subjects and detect abnormal parts of images as outliers. Variational Autoencoders (VAEs) can be used to detect lesions in the brain [4,25]. Beside VAEs, Generative Adversarial Networks (GANs) [8] are used for anomaly detection in medical images [7]. VAGAN [3] proposes the generation of an additive map to make an image of a diseased subject appear healthy. PathoGAN [2] provides a weakly supervised segmentation algorithm for brain tumors based on image-to-image translation. StarGAN [5] follows a similar idea as CycleGAN [24] and simplifies the architecture to only one generator and one discriminator. This idea can be used for anomaly detection by taking the difference between original and translated images. Fixed-Point GAN (FP-GAN) [20] improves StarGAN by preserving features that should not be changed during translation, outperforming f-Anogan [18] and others [1] in brain lesion detection. The problem of combining GANs with a classification network is tackled by semi-supervised GANs [15,17]. Class activation maps [19,23] visualize the features of the input image that lead to the classification score, but limitations in the resolution lead to blurry maps. Another approach is the generation of saliency maps [13,21] by computing the gradient of the classification score with regard to the input image.

We are interested in cases where the anomaly occurs in the form of deformations of existing structures, e.g., atrophy, rather than in lesions. Both VAGAN and FP-GAN are designed to only generate an additive map rather than a complete new image. We claim that this restriction to additive maps may hinder the methods from showing deformations. What is more, VAGAN is not designed to perform classification and assumes that the class label for each input image is provided in advance. VAEs are only trained on the healthy control group and may not be able to point out the characteristics of a specific disease, due to natural variations in the data. Our method for detection of structural changes in anatomical regions, further called DeScarGAN, is designed to address these issues.

Our method performs image-to-image translation between a set of healthy and a set of diseased subjects in order to find the visual manifestations that make the distributions of the two datasets differ from each other. We introduce a novel disease-specific architecture with skip connections, a splitting of the networks into weight-sharing subnetworks and an identity loss as identity-preserving mechanisms. This ensures that the difference between the generated healthy and the real input image is accurate enough to highlight the regions of interest, resulting in more detailed maps of the characteristics of the disease than previous methods.

We point out that compared to classical anomaly detection, we train only on one specific disease and extract information about its characteristics. With this approach, changes of already existing structures can be detected in a detailed manner, which is different from the presence or absence of lesions.

We evaluate our method on a synthetic dataset designed for this task. Furthermore, we apply it on the Chexpert dataset [12] of X-ray images of lungs in order to detect pleural effusions. Our method outperforms state-of-the-art anomaly detection algorithms in showing deformations of already existing structures. Furthermore, it provides better classification results than standard classification algorithms. With the addition of visually highlighting the regions of interest, the attention is led to the relevant parts of the image, making a step towards *interpretable machine learning*. The code is publicly available at https://github.com/JuliaWolleb/DeScarGAN.

2   Method

Let $\mathcal{F} = \{x \mid x : \mathbb{R}^2 \to \mathbb{R}\}$ be a set of medical images from the same imaging modality showing the same anatomical structures, with $\mathcal{P} \subset \mathcal{F}$ the set of images of patients affected by a specific disease and $\mathcal{H} \subset \mathcal{F}$ the set of images of a healthy control group. The aim of our method is, given a new image of unknown class, to detect regions in the image that show the same characteristics as the images in $\mathcal{P}$ and to assign a class label.

Let p be the class of the images in $\mathcal{P}$ and h the class of the images in $\mathcal{H}$, with $c, \bar{c} \in \{h, p\}$ and $c \neq \bar{c}$. The main idea is to translate a real image r_c of either class c to an artificial image $a_{\bar{c}}$ of class $\bar{c}$. The pathological region is then defined as the difference $d := a_h - r_c$ between the artificial healthy image a_h and the real input image r_c of class c. Thus we perform image-to-image translation between the unpaired sets $\mathcal{P}$ and $\mathcal{H}$. A diagram showing the workflow of our method is given in Fig. 1. Given any image r_c, the generator both generates an artificial image a_c of the same class c and an artificial image $a_{\bar{c}}$ of class $\bar{c}$. To ensure that r_c and a_h only differ in the pathological region, we add the identity loss $\mathcal{L}_{id}$ and the reconstruction loss $\mathcal{L}_{rec}$ for cycle consistency.

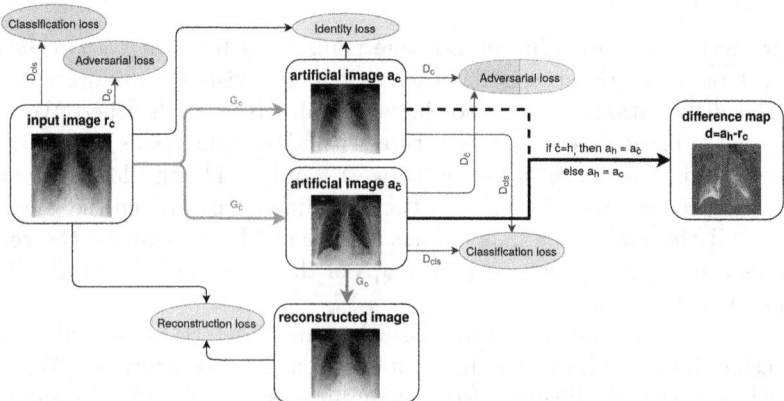

Fig. 1. Workflow of our method. The components of the loss functions for the discriminator are shown in green, the ones for the generator in orange. (Color figure online)

The generator consists of two branches, its architecture is shown in Fig. 2. We refer to the generator $G_p : \mathcal{F} \to \mathcal{P}$ for generating images of class p and generator $G_h : \mathcal{F} \to \mathcal{H}$ for generating images of class h.

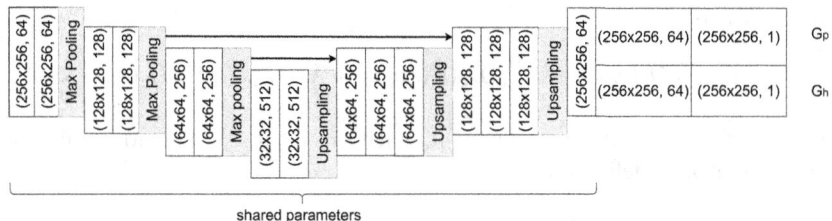

Fig. 2. The architecture of the generator network. Every box stands for a convolutional layer with the stated output size (image width $\times$ image height, feature channels) and kernelsize 3, followed by a batch normalization layer and a ReLU activation function.

The skip connections of the generator ensure that the artificial image maintains the detailed structures of the input image. This is a way to alter only the necessary features, thus making the difference map d more accurate. The skip connection in the uppermost layer turned out to be too restrictive to perform the translation to another class. By omitting this skip connection, we enable the generator to perform structural changes.

The discriminator network has the task to both classify images into healthy and diseased subjects and to distinguish between real and artificial images. Therefore, it consists of three subnets that share parameters, as shown in Fig. 3. $D_p : \mathcal{P} \to \mathbb{R}$ distinguishes between real and artificial images of class p, $D_h : \mathcal{H} \to \mathbb{R}$ does the same for class h and $D_{cls} : \mathcal{F} \to \mathbb{R}$ is the network for classification, following the structure of a VGG net [22]. The branching of the generator and discriminator gives a higher range of flexibility compared to StarGAN, which turned out to be beneficial for image-to-image translation.

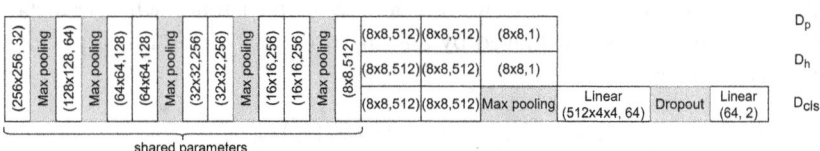

Fig. 3. The architecture of the discriminator with three subnets D_p, D_h and D_{cls} that share parameters. Every box stands for a convolutional layer with kernelsize 3 and with the stated output size, followed by a ReLU activation function.

With the notation from above, D_c can be D_p or D_h interchangeably, and $D_{\bar{c}}$ denotes the discriminator for the contrary class. The same applies for the generator G.

2.1   Loss Functions

Adversarial Loss. The generator aims to generate images that the discriminator cannot distinguish from real images. Following the idea of Wasserstein GANs [9], we add a gradient penalty loss and define the adversarial loss for the discriminator as

$$\mathcal{L}_{adv,d} = -\mathbb{E}_{r_c,c}[(D_c(r_c))] + \mathbb{E}_{r_c,\bar{c}}[D_{\bar{c}}(G_{\bar{c}}(r_c))] + \lambda_{gp}\mathbb{E}_{\hat{x},c}[(\parallel \nabla_{\hat{x}} D_c(\hat{x}_c) \parallel_2 -1)^2], \tag{1}$$

where $\hat{x}_c$ is given by $\hat{x}_c = tr_c + (1 - t)a_c$ with $t \sim U([0, 1])$. The adversarial loss for the generator is defined as

$$\mathcal{L}_{adv,g} = -\mathbb{E}_{r_c,\bar{c}}[D_{\bar{c}}(G_{\bar{c}}(r_c))]. \tag{2}$$

Identity Loss. Considering an input image r_c, we aim for identity between r_c and $G_c(r_c)$. Therefore, the identity loss for the generator is defined as

$$\mathcal{L}_{id} = \mathbb{E}_{r_c,c}[\parallel r_c - G_c(r_c) \parallel_2]. \tag{3}$$

Classification Loss. The classification subnet D_{cls} of the discriminator has to correctly classify r_c to belong to class c. The objective function for the discriminator is described as

$$\mathcal{L}_{cls,d} = \mathbb{E}_{r_c,c}[-\log D_{cls}^c(r_c)], \tag{4}$$

where the term $D_{cls}^c(r_c)$ describes the computed probability score that r_c belongs to class c. The generator aims for classification of an artificial image $a_{\bar{c}} = G_{\bar{c}}(r_c)$ to belong to class $\bar{c}$. Therefore, the classification loss for the generator is defined as

$$\mathcal{L}_{cls,g} = \mathbb{E}_{r_c,\bar{c}}[-\log D_{cls}^{\bar{c}}(G_{\bar{c}}(r_c))]. \tag{5}$$

Reconstruction Loss. When an input image r_c of class c is translated into an image $a_{\bar{c}} = G_{\bar{c}}(r_c)$ of class $\bar{c}$, we aim for cycle consistency when translating $a_{\bar{c}}$ back to class c. This is achieved by adding a reconstruction loss term for the generator, given by

$$\mathcal{L}_{rec} = \mathbb{E}_{r_c,c}[\parallel r_c - G_c(G_{\bar{c}}(r_c)) \parallel_2]. \tag{6}$$

Total Loss Objective. The overall loss function for the generator is defined as

$$\mathcal{L}_g = \lambda_{adv,g}\mathcal{L}_{adv,g} + \lambda_{rec}\mathcal{L}_{rec} + \lambda_{id}\mathcal{L}_{id} + \lambda_{cls,g}\mathcal{L}_{cls,g}, \tag{7}$$

and for the discriminator as

$$\mathcal{L}_d = \lambda_{adv,d}\mathcal{L}_{adv,d} + \lambda_{cls,d}\mathcal{L}_{cls,d}. \tag{8}$$

3 Synthetic Dataset

The purpose of weakly supervised algorithms is to overcome the need for pixel-wise labels and the human bias within these labels. In order not to be affected by this human bias, we designed a synthetic data set for the evaluation of our method. Two ellipses e_1 and e_2 are present in the image, one larger than the other and both with variable contour thickness, origin and orientation. The background is structured in concentric waves with two variable origins and variable wave length; this provides a higher level of complexity. Images of the healthy group $\mathcal{H}$ keep this structure. If the image is deformed such that the smaller ellipse e_1 shrinks to an even smaller ellipse, the background is also deformed. Images with this characteristics belong to the diseased group $\mathcal{P}$. Implementation details are provided in the supplementary material.

In Fig. 4, exemplary images of the two sets $\mathcal{H}$ and $\mathcal{P}$ are shown. The pixel-wise ground truth (GT) is known by definition. We generate a training set of 2000 images of each class, and a validation and a test set with 200 images of each class.

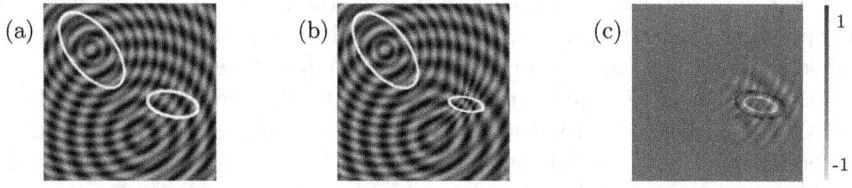

Fig. 4. Images (a) and (b) show exemplary images of the sets $\mathcal{H}$ and $\mathcal{P}$ respectively. Image (c) corresponds to the ground truth given by the difference (a)–(b).

4 Results and Discussion

We compare our method against StarGAN, FP-GAN, the VAE proposed in [4] and VAGAN. To train our model, we use the Adam optimizer [14] with $\beta_1 = 0.5$, $\beta_2 = 0.999$, and a learning rate of 10^{-4}. For every update of the parameters of the generator, we update the discriminator 5 times. We manually choose the hyperparameters $\lambda_{adv,d} = 20$, $\lambda_{gp} = 10$, $\lambda_{id} = \lambda_{rec} = 50$, $\lambda_{adv,g} = \lambda_{cls,g} = 1$, and $\lambda_{cls,d} = 5$. The number of trained parameters is 8528262 for the generator and 18170180 for the discriminator.

4.1 Synthetic Dataset

As a measure for the pixel-wise error for the anomaly detection task, we choose the Dice score, AUROC_{pix} [10] for pixel-wise classification, the Mean Square Error (MSE) and the Structural Similarity Index (SSIM) between d and GT, and finally the MSE between an input image $r_h \in \mathcal{H}$ and the corresponding artificial image a_h. For the calculation of the Dice score and the $AUROC_{pix}$, we perform a thresholding based on the average Otsu [16] threshold value on the GT images. The results are shown in Table 1. All methods classify the images almost perfectly on the test set, so we omit those results. VAGAN is not designed to take an image $r_h \in \mathcal{H}$ as input, but we still report the result for completeness.

Table 1. Results on the synthetic dataset.

	Dice	$AUROC_{pix}$	$MSE(d, GT)$ (var)	SSIM	$MSE(r_h, a_h)$ (var)
StarGAN	0.710	0.962	0.0229 (0.128)	0.888	0.0025 (0.002)
FP-GAN	0.766	0.975	0.0160 (0.004)	0.917	0.0027 (0.003)
VAGAN	0.442	0.954	0.1321 (0.132)	0.869	0.0036 (0.002)
VAE	0.288	0.809	0.0734 (0.071)	0.668	0.0316 (0.031)
DeScarGAN	**0.853**	**0.988**	**0.0086 (0.002)**	**0.954**	**0.0018 (0.001)**

In Fig. 5, exemplary real images $r_p \in \mathcal{P}$ of the synthetic dataset with the corresponding artificial images $a_h \in \mathcal{H}$ of the different methods are shown. Our method provides the most accurate difference map d. The results of FP-GAN are good as well, but the method fails to generate a proper unshrunken ellipse e_1. VAE and VAGAN fail to generate an accurate image of class h, resulting in a difference map not close to the ground truth. For visualization, we omit the StarGAN method since it is outperformed by its extension FP-GAN.

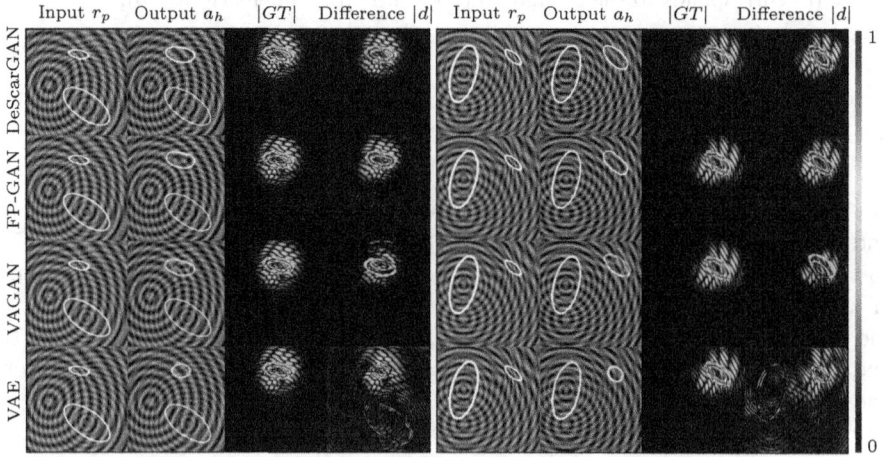

Fig. 5. Visualization of the results of our DeScarGAN, FP-GAN, VAGAN and VAE for two samples of the synthetic dataset.

4.2   Chexpert Dataset

For the Chexpert dataset introduced in [12], we used a training set of 14179 images of healthy subjects and 16776 images of subjects that suffer from pleural effusions. The test and validation set each consist of 200 images for each class.

Table 2. Classification results and MSE(r_h, a_h) on the Chexpert dataset.

	Accuracy$_{cls}$	Kappa score	AUROC$_{image}$	MSE(r_h, a_h) (var)
StarGAN	0.853	0.705	0.923	0.0534 (0.095)
FP-GAN	0.875	0.750	0.939	0.0060 (0.007)
VAGAN	×	×	×	0.0638 (0.065)
VAE	×	×	×	0.0231 (0.030)
Densenet169	0.893	0.785	0.951	×
D_{cls}	0.890	0.780	0.949	×
DeScarGAN	**0.898**	**0.795**	**0.953**	**0.0035 (0.003)**

For classification, we compare DeScarGAN against the classification results of StarGAN, FP-GAN, Densenet169 [11] and the classifier D_{cls} without the GAN mechanism. The result for the image-level classification is measured in classification accuracy, the Cohen's kappa score [6] and the AUROC score. Further, we

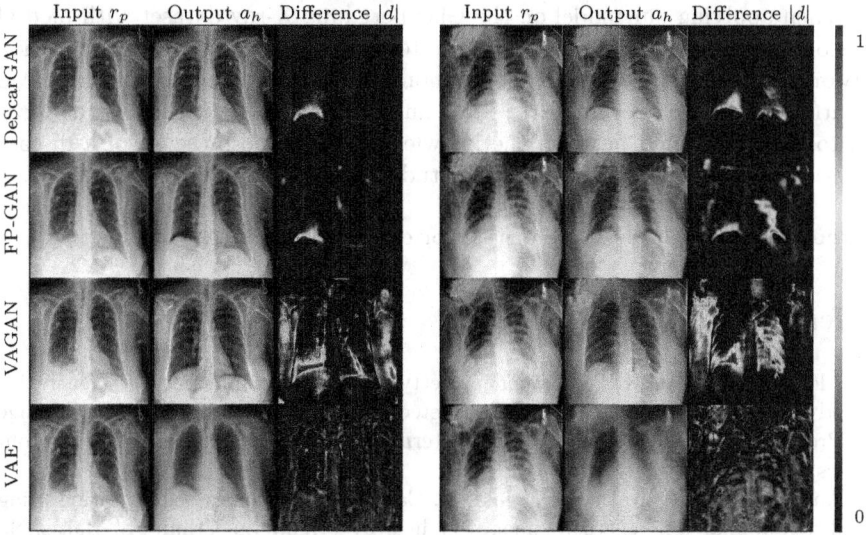

Fig. 6. Comparison of our DeScarGAN against FP-GAN, VAGAN and VAE for two samples of the Chexpert dataset.

measure the MSE between real images $r_h \in \mathcal{H}$ and artificial images $a_h \in \mathcal{H}$. The scores are summarized in Table 2.

DeScarGAN achieves better classification results than the pure classification networks D_{cls} and Densenet169, indicating that the GAN mechanism supports the classification network. The results of the different methods are visualized in Fig. 6. We observe that the VAE fails to detect pleural effusions. Although FP-GAN detects similar regions as our method, the generated maps appear blurry and mark regions outside the thorax. The additive map of VAGAN also outlines parts of the arms and upper chest as abnormal. Our method generates the most detailed difference map, not highlighting any regions outside the pleural space.

5   Conclusion

We proposed DeScarGAN, a method to generate disease-specific, detailed maps that show pathological changes of existing anatomical structures. The novelty of our method is the introduction of a new architecture with skip connections, a splitting of the networks into weight-sharing subnetworks and an identity loss as identity-preserving mechanisms. This setup enables the detection of deformations of existing anatomical structures, e.g., atrophy or changes in the pleural space due to pleural effusions.

When comparing our DeScarGAN against state-of-the-art anomaly detection algorithms, we outperform FP-GAN, VAE, StarGAN and VAGAN on a synthetic dataset. Although FP-GAN provides good results by generating additive maps, DeScarGAN generates a complete new image and provides more precise maps that reliably outline the regions of pathological changes.

When applying our model on the Chexpert lung X-ray dataset with pleural effusions, our classification scores are better than state-of-the-art classification networks. The generated maps detect anomalies in a detailed manner and lead the attention to the relevant parts of the anatomy. This approach has the potential to bridge the gap between the knowledge about the presence of a disease and setting the focus of a longitudinal study observing the region of interest.

Acknowledgement. This work was supported by Novartis FreeNovation.

References

1. Alex, V., Safwan, K.P.M., Chennamsetty, S.S., Krishnamurthi, G.: Generative adversarial networks for brain lesion detection. In: Medical Imaging 2017: Image Processing, vol. 10133, pp. 113–121. International Society for Optics and Photonics, SPIE (2017)
2. Andermatt, S., Horváth, A., Pezold, S., Cattin, P.: Pathology segmentation using distributional differences to images of healthy origin. In: Crimi, A., Bakas, S., Kuijf, H., Keyvan, F., Reyes, M., van Walsum, T. (eds.) BrainLes 2018. LNCS, vol. 11383, pp. 228–238. Springer, Cham (2019). https://doi.org/10.1007/978-3-030-11723-8_23

3. Baumgartner, C.F., Koch, L.M., Can Tezcan, K., Xi Ang, J., Konukoglu, E.: Visual feature attribution using wasserstein GANs. In: Proceedings of the IEEE Conference on Computer Vision and Pattern Recognition, pp. 8309–8319 (2018)
4. Chen, X., Konukoglu, E.: Unsupervised detection of lesions in brain MRI using constrained adversarial auto-encoders. arXiv preprint arXiv:1806.04972 (2018)
5. Choi, Y., Choi, M., Kim, M., Ha, J.W., Kim, S., Choo, J.: Stargan: unified generative adversarial networks for multi-domain image-to-image translation. In: Proceedings of the IEEE Conference on Computer Vision and Pattern Recognition, pp. 8789–8797 (2018)
6. Cohen, J.: A coefficient of agreement for nominal scales. Educ. Psychol. Measur. **20**(1), 37–46 (1960)
7. Di Mattia, F., Galeone, P., De Simoni, M., Ghelfi, E.: A survey on GANs for anomaly detection. arXiv preprint arXiv:1906.11632 (2019)
8. Goodfellow, I., et al.: Generative adversarial nets. In: Advances in Neural Information Processing Systems, vol. 27, pp. 2672–2680 (2014)
9. Gulrajani, I., Ahmed, F., Arjovsky, M., Dumoulin, V., Courville, A.C.: Improved training of wasserstein GANs. In: Advances in Neural Information Processing Systems, vol. 30, pp. 5767–5777 (2017)
10. Hanley, J.A., McNeil, B.J.: The meaning and use of the area under a receiver operating characteristic (ROC) curve. Radiology **143**(1), 29–36 (1982)
11. Huang, G., Liu, Z., Van Der Maaten, L., Weinberger, K.Q.: Densely connected convolutional networks. In: 2017 IEEE Conference on Computer Vision and Pattern Recognition, pp. 2261–2269 (2017)
12. Irvin, J., et al.: Chexpert: a large chest radiograph dataset with uncertainty labels and expert comparison. In: Proceedings of the AAAI Conference on Artificial Intelligence, pp. 590–597 (2019)
13. Karargyros, A., Syeda-Mahmood, T.: Saliency U-net: a regional saliency map-driven hybrid deep learning network for anomaly segmentation. In: Medical Imaging 2018: Computer-Aided Diagnosis, vol. 10575, pp. 413–418. International Society for Optics and Photonics, SPIE (2018)
14. Kingma, D.P., Ba, J.: Adam: a method for stochastic optimization. arXiv preprint arXiv:1412.6980 (2014)
15. Odena, A.: Semi-supervised learning with generative adversarial networks. arXiv preprint arXiv:1606.01583 (2016)
16. Otsu, N.: A threshold selection method from gray-level histograms. IEEE Trans. Syst. Man Cybern. **9**(1), 62–66 (1979)
17. Salimans, T., Goodfellow, I., Zaremba, W., Cheung, V., Radford, A., Chen, X.: Improved techniques for training GANs. In: Proceedings of the 30th International Conference on Neural Information Processing Systems, pp. 2234–2242 (2016)
18. Schlegl, T., Seeböck, P., Waldstein, S.M., Langs, G., Schmidt-Erfurth, U.: f-AnoGAN: fast unsupervised anomaly detection with generative adversarial networks. Med. Image Anal. **54**, 30–44 (2019)
19. Selvaraju, R.R., Cogswell, M., Das, A., Vedantam, R., Parikh, D., Batra, D.: Grad-cam: visual explanations from deep networks via gradient-based localization. In: 2017 IEEE International Conference on Computer Vision, pp. 618–626 (2017)
20. Siddiquee, M.M.R., et al.: Learning fixed points in generative adversarial networks: from image-to-image translation to disease detection and localization. In: Proceedings of the IEEE International Conference on Computer Vision, pp. 191–200 (2019)
21. Simonyan, K., Vedaldi, A., Zisserman, A.: Deep inside convolutional networks: visualising image classification models and saliency maps. arXiv preprint arXiv:1312.6034 (2013)

22. Simonyan, K., Zisserman, A.: Very deep convolutional networks for large-scale image recognition. In: International Conference on Learning Representations (2015)
23. Zhou, B., Khosla, A., Lapedriza, A., Oliva, A., Torralba, A.: Learning deep features for discriminative localization. In: 2016 IEEE Conference on Computer Vision and Pattern Recognition, pp. 2921–2929 (2016)
24. Zhu, J.Y., Park, T., Isola, P., Efros, A.A.: Unpaired image-to-image translation using cycle-consistent adversarial networks. In: 2017 IEEE International Conference on Computer Vision, pp. 2242–2251 (2017)
25. Zimmerer, D., Isensee, F., Petersen, J., Kohl, S., Maier-Hein, K.: Unsupervised anomaly localization using variational auto-encoders. In: Medical Image Computing and Computer Assisted Intervention, pp. 289–297 (2019)

KISEG: A Three-Stage Segmentation Framework for Multi-level Acceleration of Chest CT Scans from COVID-19 Patients

Xiaohong Liu[1], Kai Wang[2], Ke Wang[1], Ting Chen[1], Kang Zhang[3], and Guangyu Wang[1(✉)]

[1] Department of Computer Science and Technology & BNRist, Tsinghua University, Beijing, China
wangguangyu@tsinghua.edu.cn
[2] University of California, San Diego, CA, USA
[3] Faculty of Medicine, Macau University of Science and Technology, Macau, China

Abstract. During the ongoing COVID-19 outbreak, it is critical to perform an accurate diagnosis of COVID-19 pneumonia by computed tomography (CT). Although chest lesion segmentation plays a pivotal role in computer-aided diagnosis (CAD), accuracy is hindered by the lack of a publicly available CT dataset with manual annotation. In addition, for clinical deployment, how to balance the accuracy versus efficiency for the semantic segmentation model remains challenging. To address these issues, we construct the first CT dataset of COVID-19 pneumonia with pixel-wise lesion annotations. We propose a three-stage framework, called KISEG (Key and Intermediate frame of Segmentation), to enhance performance on serial CT image segmentation with multi-level acceleration. We first take a policy to divide frames of serial CT into two groups, key frames and intermediate frames. Then KISEG employs a main model (accurate but cumbersome) for key frame segmentation. And third, an auxiliary model was employed for intermediate frame segmentation with incorporating the information of key frames during the fusion module. Moreover, we propose a Gaussian Kernel Dropout for data augmentation. Experiments on our dataset demonstrate that our proposed KISEG achieves comparable accuracy with state-of-the-art methods and fewer GFLOPs, speeding up from 2.88× to 9.16×. This dataset has been made public for further research of COVID-19 for AI community, released on http://ncov-ai.big.ac.cn/download.

Keywords: Chest CT · COVID-19 dataset · Semantic segmentation · Multi-level acceleration

1 Introduction

The world is experiencing an outbreak of coronavirus disease (COVID-19) and many infected patients develop pneumonia. Computed tomography (CT) tests

© Springer Nature Switzerland AG 2020
A. L. Martel et al. (Eds.): MICCAI 2020, LNCS 12264, pp. 25–34, 2020.
https://doi.org/10.1007/978-3-030-59719-1_3

are widely used for chest diseases detection including pneumonia, and the accurate segmentation of lung lesions in CT slices benefits diagnosis and severity analysis. For example, ground-glass opacity and consolidation on chest CT images are important features to differentiate COVID-19 pneumonia from other forms of pneumonia [1]. However, there is a lack of publicly available images of manually segmented COVID-19 pneumonia CT lesions. In addition, as a CT scan consists of a series of images, how to efficiently trade off between the accuracy and speed of segmentation during clinical applications remains challenging. Thus, we proposed the speed-up segmentation framework to lessen a radiologist's overall workload and allow them to respond effectively in emergency situation.

Many recent studies have focused on image segmentation for different medical imaging modalities, including brain tumor segmentation in magnetic resonance imaging (MRI) [2], X-ray, and cerebral CT [3]. As for medical image semantic segmentation, Convolutional Neural Networks (CNNs) have recently achieved significant success. Long et al. proposed fully convolutional networks (FCN) that up-sample the output activation maps from which the pixel-wise output can be calculated [4]. Ronneberger et al. [5] proposed a U-Net architecture for biomedical image segmentation, which follows an encoder-decoder structure and consists of a contracting path to capture context and a symmetric expanding path at different scales that enables precise localization. The fusion of features extracted at different scales yields significant improvements on the performance.

To obtain high accuracy in medical image segmentation, one typically trains very cumbersome models which could be an ensemble of separately trained models or a single very large model and can't meet the efficiency requirements of real-world deployment. Attempts have been made to alleviate this issue by designing different network architectures. For example, ENet [6] is a deep neural network architecture with several bottleneck blocks, designed for real-time semantic segmentation. DFANet [7] is an efficient CNN architecture for semantic segmentation which aggregates discriminative features through sub-network and sub-stage cascades. MobileNets [8] are a class of small, low latency models based on a streamlined architecture which are proposed for mobile and embedded vision applications. Another approach for model acceleration is shrinking, or compressing pre-trained networks to obtain small networks. As for model compression, pruning [9] has been proposed to induce sparsity in a deep neural network's various connection matrices. Another popular approach is distillation [10] which transfers the knowledge from an ensemble of models to a small model for deployment.

Here, we introduce a novel framework for multi-level of semantic segmentation acceleration, named **Key Intermediate Frame Seg**mentation (KISEG). The design of our framework is inspired by the H264 codec [11] for video compression. H264 introduces *IPB-frames*, which employs intra-frame compression, while B-frames and P-frames only store differential information to key frames and can be decoded with key frames as a reference. As for our segmentation framework, we first take a policy to divide frames of serial CT scan into two groups, key frames and intermediate frames. Then we use an accurate "main model" for key frames segmentation and the rest of intermediate frames are consumed by a fast "auxiliary model" with the key frames information as reference.

Our contributions are as follows. First, we construct a large-scale chest CT dataset for the study of COVID-19 which consists of 21,471 CT images from 150 CT scans. Of these, we manually annotated 750 CT images with four defined classes at the pixel-level: background, lung field (except lesion field), ground-glass opacity, and consolidation. To the best of our knowledge, this is the first annotated CT dataset of COVID-19. Second, we propose a novel three-stage framework, KISEG, for multi-level accelerating semantic segmentation of image series. This framework provides trade-off between efficiency and accuracy for clinical applications. Third, we propose a Gaussian Kernel Dropout (GKD) layer to improve the generalization of models. Experimental results demonstrate that our proposed methods achieve a 2.88× speedup almost without harming accuracy and an up to 9.16× speedup with a very slight loss of accuracy.

2 Dataset Construction

We construct a chest CT dataset of COVID-19 patients which consists of 21,471 CT images from 150 CT scans[1]. COVID-19 diagnosis is confirmed by a real-time reverse-transcriptase polymerase-chain-reaction (rt-PCR) assay. The CT resolution is 1.0 mm. COVID-19 pneumonia has typical lesions of ground-glass opacity and consolidation which are quite different from other pneumonia.

We select five CT images from each CT scan on average and have radiologists manually annotate a total of 750 CT images. The lung CT segmentation is annotated by five radiologists who had at least 10 years of experience. Each image is labelled on each pixel with 4 classes of segmentation regions: background (BG), lung field (LF), ground-glass opacity (GGO), and consolidation (CL). Next, 20% of images are randomly checked and verified by a second tier of three senior independent radiologists, each with over 20 years of clinical experience.

3 Methods

3.1 The Overall Framework

KISEG is a three-stage framework for accelerating semantic segmentation of high correlated image series of CT, which uses a KI-frame (Key and Intermediate frame) strategy to achieve balance between accuracy and efficiency, as shown in Fig. 1(a). Given an image series of $X = [x_1, x_2, \cdots, x_L]$, the framework $\mathbb{M}$ outputs the segmentation results $Y = \mathbb{M}(X)$, where $Y = [y_1, y_2, \cdots, y_L]$, L is the length of the image series, $x_i \in \mathbb{R}^{D \times W \times H}$ is an image with D channels, and $y_i \in \{1, 2, \cdots, C\}^{W \times H}$ is a mask with C-classes at the pixel-level. The three stages are as follows. In the first stage, KISEG uses a key frame selection policy π to determine which frames are key frames (K-frames): $\pi(X) = \{k_{m1}, k_{m2}, \cdots, k_M\}$,

---

[1] The dataset is released on http://ncov-ai.big.ac.cn/download.

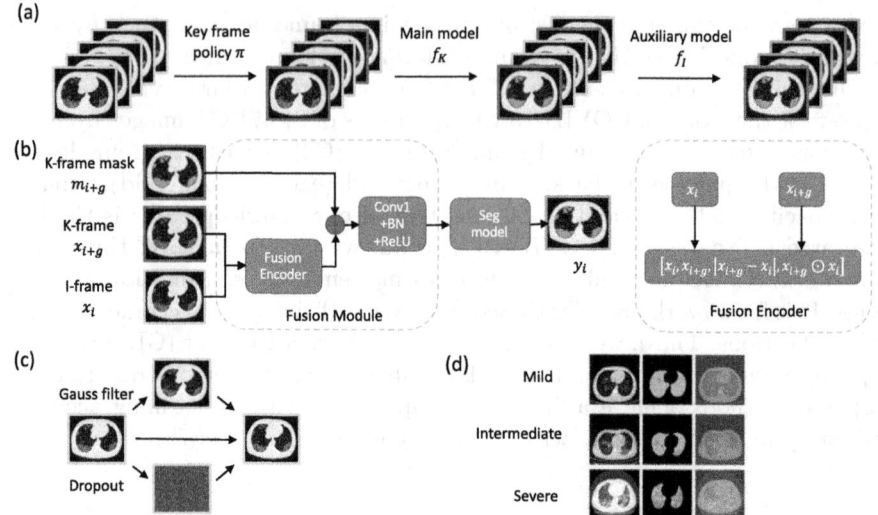

Fig. 1. (a) The workflow and components of KISEG. (b) Fusion module. (c) The process of Gaussian Kernel Dropout. (d) CT samples of COVID-19 patients, and the three rows represent different severity levels: mild, intermediate and severe.

where k_m is an index of K-frame and M is the number of K-frames. And the rest are intermediate frames (I-frames). In the second stage, a main model f_K segments each K-frame x_k to obtain segmented mask y_i and a probability tensor m_i, where $m_i \in \mathbb{R}^{C \times W \times H}$ will be used as a prior distribution (prior) for I-frame segmentation. And in the third stage, each I-frame, its nearest K-frame, and the corresponding K-frame prior are combined and go through a fusion model to generate a tensor. Then an auxiliary model f_I performs on this tensor to obtain a segmented mask of the I-frame.

3.2 Auxiliary Model for Fast Segmentation

The framework contains two segmentation models, a main model f_K and an auxiliary model f_I, for K-frames and I-frames, respectively. We choose f_K from high-performance segmentation models whereas f_K may cost a large (but acceptable) number of GFlops. Meanwhile f_I requires fewer GFlops to accelerate segmentation. We suppose that neighbouring frames are highly correlated, so models can easily achieve accurate segmentation by focusing features capturing the difference between frames, even using small models. Thus, we propose a fusion module for fusing information from the I-frame and the K-frame information before sending the input to f_I. Concretely, the current frame x_i, the nearest K-frame x_{i+g} with the interval g and the corresponding mask prior m_{i+g} are fused by a fusion module to form the input of f_I, as shown in Fig. 1(b). First, two frames x_i and x_{i+g} go through a fusion encoder layer *FuseEnc* to obtain a cross-input. Following the SentInfer architecture [12], *FuseEnc* extracts the fusing information of x_i and x_{i+g} by three operations: (i) concatenation of the two input (x_i, x_{i+g}), (2) element-wise product $x_i \odot x_{i+g}$, and (3) absolute element-wise difference $|x_i - x_{i+g}|$. That is

$$[x_i, x_{i+g}, |x_i - x_{i+g}|, x_i \odot x_{i+g}] = FuseEnc(x_i, x_{i+g}). \tag{1}$$

Then *Conv1* with 3 output channels is applied. It is a 3×3 convolutional kernel with stride 1, and padding 1, following a Batch Normalization layer and an ReLU layer: $y_i = f_I(Conv1(FuseEnc(x_i, x_{i+g}) \oplus m_{i+g}))$.

3.3   Key Frame Selection

By a key frame selection strategy, we can down-sample the CT frames processed by the main model f_K, thus accelerating the process of segmentation for the whole image series. The key-frame selection policy π is required to select fewer but more informative key frames. Given an image series X with $L = |X|$ frames and $M = |\pi(X)|$ selected K-frames, the average computation cost per frame can be approximated by $c_K M/L + c_I(1 - M/L)$, where c_K and c_I are computation costs of the models f_K and f_I, respectively. For simplicity, we denote the down-sampling ratio $r = M/L$, and the average computation cost can be rewritten as $c_K r + c_I(1 - r)$. We apply a uniform sampling policy as π. The π takes the first frame of a given image series as K-frame, then takes other K-frames by fixed intervals g. With such a policy, assuming that the maximum intervals between K-frames and I-frames is g, then r will be approximately $1/(2g+1)$. An example is the series of $IKIIIIKIIIIK \cdots$, which implies $g = 2$ and $r = 1/5$. We expect c_I to be much smaller than c_K such that we gain around $(1/r-1)$ times speed-up. Thus, with different g, we promise to generate multi-level accelerating models.

3.4   Data Augmentation and Loss Function

There are two constraints when training KISEG: (1) f_I trends to reach a local optimum if f_I learns to segment only utilizing the I-frame while ignoring information from K-frame. This is because the I-frame provides direct information for segmentation during the fusion module, and can overshadow the information from K-frame. (2) There exists a problem of class imbalance, where most areas are easy background that contribute less useful learning for segmentation of regions of our interest. Thus causing inefficient training.

We propose a Gaussian Kernel Dropout (GKD) layer as data augmentation to overcome the first constraint. The GKD layer blurs the current frame to encourage the model to learn with the K-frame. Rather than replacing the chosen pixel with zero like Dropout [13], the GKD layer sets pixels with Gaussian filtered values. Formally, given an image x, the GKD layer generates a zero-one mask $x_{01} = Dropout(x)$ with probability p using Dropout. Meanwhile the GKD layer uses a Gaussian kernel (μ, Σ) of size $s \times s$ to filter x, obtaining a Gaussian blurred frame $x_g = Gauss(x, \mu, \Sigma, s \times s)$. Then, the GKD combines both to generate the output $x_o = GKD(x)$, where the element at position (i, j) is:

$$x_o(i, j) = \begin{cases} x(i, j) & \text{if } x_{01}(i, j) = 0, \\ x_g(i, j) & \text{otherwise.} \end{cases} \tag{2}$$

In addition, class imbalance is encountered in many image segmentation problems. In the study, we introduce the focal loss (FL) [14] as loss function to up-weights region of interests. Based on cross entropy loss, FL adds a modulating factor $\alpha_t(1 - p_t)^\gamma$ to increase the importance of correcting misclassified examples, that is $FL(p_t, y = t) = -\alpha_t(1 - p_t)^\gamma \log(p_t)$, where t is the true class, p_t is the predicted probability of class t, and two introduced hyperparameters α_t and γ are a class balanced factor and focusing factor, respectively. We apply the GKD layer for I-frames during the training process, and do not apply it during inference. We apply FL for image segmentation at the pixel-level.

4   Experiments and Results

4.1   Experiments

We conduct three experiments to evaluate KISEG: speed and accuracy comparisons, training strategy study, and ablation study. To measure the effectiveness of our framework, we choose U-Net as the K-frame segmentation model f_K and ENet as the I-frame segmentation model f_I. In training strategy study, we choose two strategies with fixed intervals and ranged intervals in the training set for f_I. The ablation study is conducted to investigate the effectiveness of FL and GKD.

Data. We divide the 150 CT scans (750 annotated slice images) into training, validation and testing sets equally (50:50:50). The 7,500 unlabelled images (neighbors of the annotated images) are used in the training process of f_I, in which these images are used as K-frames segmented by f_K to provide mask priors.

Evaluation Metrics. We use the Intersection over Union (IoU) to measure the percent overlap between the predicted mask P and the ground truth mask G. Let P_c and G_c represent the set of pixels labelled as class $c \in C$ in the predicted mask and the ground truth mask, respectively. The definition of IoU_c and $mIoU$ are as follows: $IoU_c = \frac{P_c \cap G_c}{P_c \cup G_c}$ and $mIoU = \frac{1}{|C|} \sum_{c \in C}^{C} IoU_c$. We reported the metrics for f_I with different testing K-frame intervals in the last two experiments to gain insight of the effect of K-frames, since intuitively near K-frames will be more helpful than far K-frames.

Table 1. Comparison among state-of-the-art models, baseline models and KISEGs with different intervals

Methods	GFlops	Speedup	mIoU(%)	BG(%)	LF(%)	GGO(%)	CL(%)
ENet	4.01	58.46×	74.72	99.67	93.67	51.54	53.99
UNet	234.42	1.0×	78.89	99.73	94.90	58.75	62.18
KISEG(1)	81.28	2.88×	78.75	99.72	94.49	56.74	64.03
KISEG(2)	50.65	4.63×	78.13	99.71	94.28	55.29	63.24
KISEG(3)	37.52	6.25×	77.59	99.70	94.13	54.19	62.23
KISEG(4)	30.23	7.75×	77.13	99.69	94.00	53.34	61.49
KISEG(5)	25.59	9.16×	76.74	99.69	93.88	52.62	60.76

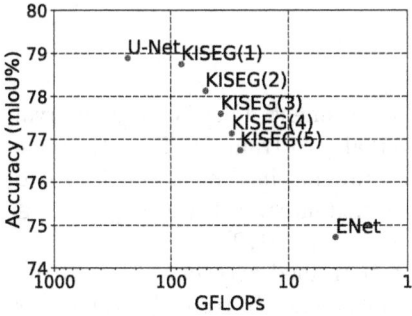

Fig. 2. Comparison of GFLOPs and mIoUs performance between different methods.

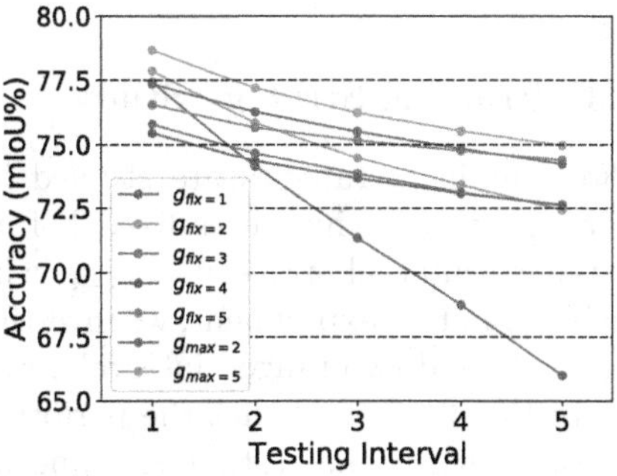

Fig. 3. Comparison of mIoUs with different training and testing K-frame intervals.

Implementation. All CT images are resized to 512×512 in advance. Thus the masks for the prior have shape $4 \times 512 \times 512$ for $C = 4$. The network is implemented in *PyTorch* [15] and an Adam optimizer [16] with learning rate of 0.01 and batch size of 4. The total number of training epochs is set to 50. All experiments were conducted on an NVIDIA 1080Ti GPU. The parameters in GKD used in f_I are $\Sigma = diag(10, 10)$, $\mu = [0, 0]^T$, and the kernel size is 5×5. The dropout rate is 0.1, and the focal loss is adopted with $\gamma = 2.0$.

4.2 Speed and Accuracy Comparisons

The results in Table 1 show that U-Net achieves the best mIoU of 78.89%, and ENet has the least computing consumption of 4.01 GFlops during inference, but with an mIoU of only 74.72%. From KISEG(1) to KISEG(5), KISEG obtains a series of segmentation models that achieve different trade-offs in speed and performance from 2.88× speedup and 78.75% mIoU to 9.16× speedup and 76.74% mIoU. The accuracy (mIoU) and speed (GFLOPs) of the models are shown in Fig. 2. We observe that KISEGs can generate multi-level of accuracy and efficiency,

Table 2. Ablation study on focal loss and Gaussian Kernel Dropout.

Settings	1	2	3	4	5
$p = 0.0$	77.39	75.96	75.04	74.34	73.68
$p = 0.1$	77.30	75.99	75.07	74.30	73.75
$p = 0.0$ (FL)	75.12	73.79	72.89	72.20	71.64
$p = 0.1$ (FL)	**78.68**	**77.20**	**76.23**	**75.53**	**74.97**
$p = 0.3$ (FL)	77.00	75.64	74.67	73.94	73.21

and promise to be more flexible segmentation acceleration models for clinical application which fill in the gap between U-Net and ENet.

4.3 Training Strategy Study

Two training strategies are studied in this experiment. One is fixed interval strategy $g_{fix=i}$, which uses fixed K-frame interval i to train f_I. The other one is ranged interval strategy $g_{max=i}$, which uses ranging intervals from 1 to i to train f_I. In this experiment, we investigate five fixed interval strategies $g_{fix=i}, i \in [1, \cdots, 5]$ and two ranged interval strategies $g_{max=i}, i \in [1, 2]$.

In Fig. 3, we find that the performance of f_I trained with $g_{fix=1}$ drastically degrades when the testing K-frame interval increases. f_I trained with larger fixed intervals, such as $g_{fix=2}$ and $g_{fix=3}$, can gain performance improvements on large testing intervals, but get hurt on small testing intervals. The best result is obtained by training with $g_{max=5}$, performing well on all of testing intervals. This experimental result suggests using ranged intervals to train f_I is a good choice to improve its generalization.

4.4 Ablation Study

The ablation study on focal loss and GKD is conducted on KISEG using $g_{max=5}$. Results are shown in Table 2. Without focal loss and GKD, f_I obtains 77.39% and 73.68% with K-frame intervals of 1 and 5, respectively. We can see that with both the focal loss and the GKD ($p = 0.1$) applied in the training process, f_I achieves the best performance and obtains an improvement of 1.29% and 1.29% with K-frame intervals of 1 and 5, respectively. But a high dropout rate ($p = 0.3$) leads to performance degradation. This result suggests focal loss and GKD are effective to improve segmentation with ranging K-frame intervals.

5 Conclusion

In this study, we construct the first CT dataset of COVID-19 pneumonia with pixel-wise lesion annotations. We propose a three-stage framework for chest CT segmentation, called KISEG. We also propose a Gaussian Kernel Dropout layer for better generalization when training models within KISEG. Experimental results demonstrate that our proposed KISEG and GKD are effective by achieving superior speed while maintaining comparable accuracy.

Acknowledgements. We thank Dr. Julian McAuley for helping the revision of the manuscript. This work is supported by the National Key R&D Program of China (2019YFB1404804), the National Natural Science Foundation of China (grants 61906105, 61872218, 61721003 and 61673241), Tsinghua-Fuzhou Institute of Digital Technology, Beijing National Research Center for Information Science and Technology (BNRist), and Tsinghua University-Peking Union Medical College Hospital Initiative Scientific Research Program. The funders had no roles in study design, data collection and analysis, the decision to publish, and preparation of the manuscript.

References

1. Zhang, K., Liu, X., Shen, J., et al.: Clinically applicable AI system for accurate diagnosis, quantitative measurements, and prognosis of COVID-19 pneumonia using computed tomography. Cell **181**(6), 1423–1433 (2020). e11 in Cell

2. Chen, C., Liu, X., Ding, M., Zheng, J., Li, J.: 3D dilated multi-fiber network for real-time brain tumor segmentation in MRI. In: Shen, D., et al. (eds.) MICCAI 2019. LNCS, vol. 11766, pp. 184–192. Springer, Cham (2019). https://doi.org/10.1007/978-3-030-32248-9_21

3. Manvel, A., Vladimir, K., Alexander, T., Dmitry, U.: Radiologist-level stroke classification on non-contrast CT scans with deep U-Net. In: Shen, D., et al. (eds.) MICCAI 2019. LNCS, vol. 11766, pp. 820–828. Springer, Cham (2019). https://doi.org/10.1007/978-3-030-32248-9_91

4. Long, J., Shelhamer, E., Darrell, T.: Fully convolutional networks for semantic segmentation. In: CVPR (2015)

5. Ronneberger, O., Fischer, P., Brox, T.: U-Net: convolutional networks for biomedical image segmentation. In: Navab, N., Hornegger, J., Wells, W.M., Frangi, A.F. (eds.) MICCAI 2015. LNCS, vol. 9351, pp. 234–241. Springer, Cham (2015). https://doi.org/10.1007/978-3-319-24574-4_28

6. Paszke, A., Chaurasia, A., Kim, S., Culurciello, E.: Enet: a deep neural network architecture for real-time semantic segmentation. arXiv:1606.02147 (2016)

7. Li, H., Xiong, P., Fan, H., Sun, J.: Dfanet: deep feature aggregation for real-time semantic segmentation. In: CVPR (2019)

8. Howard, A.G., Zhu, M., Chen, B., et al.: Mobilenets: efficient convolutional neural networks for mobile vision applications. arXiv:1704.04861 (2017)

9. Zhu, M., Gupta, S.: To prune, or not to prune: exploring the efficacy of pruning for model compression. In: ICLR (Workshop) (2018)

10. Hinton, G., Vinyals, O., Dean, J.: Distilling the knowledge in a neural network. arXiv:1503.02531 (2015)

11. Wiegand, T., Sullivan, G.J., Bjontegaard, G., Luthra, A.: Overview of the H. 264/AVC video coding standard. IEEE Trans. Circ. Syst. Video Technol. **13**(7), 560–576 (2003)

12. Conneau, A., Kiela, D., Schwenk, H., Barrault, L., Bordes, A.: Supervised learning of universal sentence representations from natural language inference data. In: EMNLP (2017)

13. Srivastava, N., Hinton, G., Krizhevsky, A., Sutskever, I., Salakhutdinov, R.: Dropout: a simple way to prevent neural networks from overfitting. J. Mach. Learn. Res. **15**(1), 1929–1958 (2014)
14. Lin, T.-Y., Goyal, P., Girshick, R., He, K., Dollár, P.: Focal loss for dense object detection. In: ICCV (2017)
15. Paszke, A., Gross, S., Massa, F., et al.: Pytorch: an imperative style, high-performance deep learning library. In: NIPS (2019)
16. Kingma, D.P., Ba, J.: Adam: a method for stochastic optimization. In: ICLR (Poster) (2015)

CircleNet: Anchor-Free Glomerulus Detection with Circle Representation

Haichun Yang[1], Ruining Deng[2], Yuzhe Lu[2], Zheyu Zhu[2], Ye Chen[2], Joseph T. Roland[1], Le Lu[3], Bennett A. Landman[2], Agnes B. Fogo[1], and Yuankai Huo[2(✉)]

[1] Vanderbilt University Medical Center, Nashville, TN 37215, USA
[2] Vanderbilt University, Nashville, TN 37215, USA
yuankai.huo@vanderbilt.edu
[3] PAII Inc., Bethesda, MD 20817, USA

Abstract. Object detection networks are powerful in computer vision, but not necessarily optimized for biomedical object detection. In this work, we propose CircleNet, a simple anchor-free detection method with circle representation for detection of the ball-shaped glomerulus. Different from the traditional bounding box based detection method, the bounding circle (1) reduces the degrees of freedom of detection representation, (2) is naturally rotation invariant, (3) and optimized for ball-shaped objects. The key innovation to enable this representation is the anchor-free framework with the circle detection head. We evaluate CircleNet in the context of detection of glomerulus. CircleNet increases average precision of the glomerulus detection from 0.598 to 0.647. Another key advantage is that CircleNet achieves better rotation consistency compared with bounding box representations.

Keywords: Detection · CircleNet · Anchor-free · Pathology

1 Introduction

Detection of Glomeruli is a fundamental task for efficient diagnosis and quantitative evaluations in renal pathology. Recently, deep learning techniques have played important roles in renal pathology to reduce the clinical working load of pathologists and enable the large-scale population based research [1,2,4,6,10]. Many traditional feature-based image processing methods have been proposed for detection of glomeruli. Such methods strongly rely on "hand-crafted" features from feature engineering, such as edge detection [18], Histogram of Gradients (HOG) [8,9,11], median filter [13], shape features [19], Gabor filtering [5], and Hessian based Difference of Gaussians (HDoG) [25].

In recent years, deep convolutional neural network (CNN) based methods have shown superior performance on detection of glomeruli with "data-driven" features. Temerinac-Ott *et al.* [23] proposed a glomerulus detection method by comparing the CNN performance on different stains. Gallego *et al.* [3] conducted glomerulus detection by integrating detection and classification, while other researchers [1,2,4,6,10] combined detection and segmentation. With the rapid development of detection technologies in computer vision, the anchor-based detection methods (e.g. Faster-RCNN [22])

© Springer Nature Switzerland AG 2020
A. L. Martel et al. (Eds.): MICCAI 2020, LNCS 12264, pp. 35–44, 2020.
https://doi.org/10.1007/978-3-030-59719-1_4

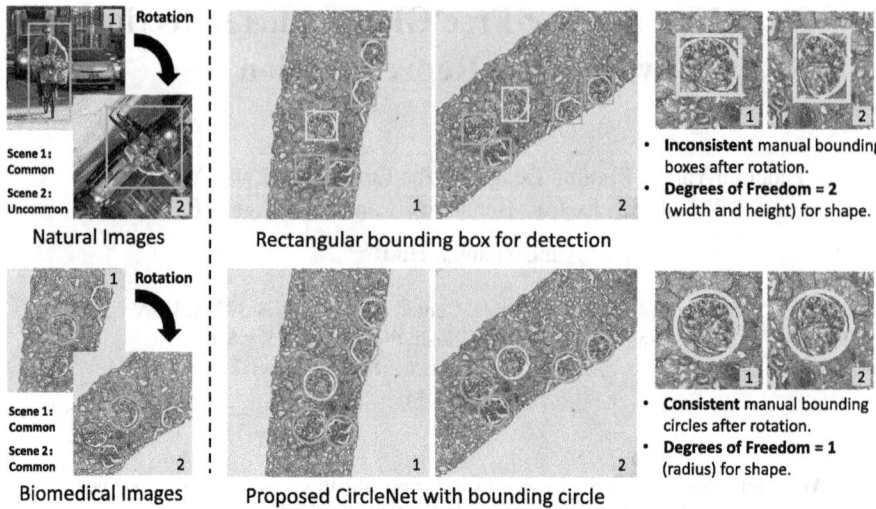

Fig. 1. Comparison of rectangular bounding box and CircleNet. The left panel shows that the samples of glomeruli can be acquired and presented with any angles of rotation (both scenes are "common" for radiologist). The right panel shows that the rectangular bounding box is not optimized for the ball-shaped glomerulus. Using the proposed CircleNet, a more consistent representation with less degrees of freedom is able to be achieved.

have become the *de facto* standard glomerulus detection approach due to their superior performance. Kawazoe *et al.* [12] and Lo *et al.* [17] proposed the Faster-RCNN based method, which achieved the state-of-the-art performance on glomerulus detection. However, anchor-based methods typically yields higher model complexity and lower flexibility [12,22] since anchors are preset on the images and refined several times as detection results. Therefore, recent academic attention has been shifted toward anchor-free detection methods (means without preset anchors) with simpler network design, less hyper parameters, and even with superior performance [14,26,27].

However, the "computer vision" oriented detection approaches are not necessarily optimized for biomedical objects, such as the detection of glomeruli, shown in Fig. 1. In this paper, we propose a circle representation based anchor-free detection method, called CircleNet, for robust detection of glomeruli. Briefly, the "bounding circle" is introduced as the detection representation for the ball-shaped structure of the glomerulus. After detecting the center location of the glomerulus, the degrees of freedom (DoF) = 1 (radius) are required to fit the bounding circle, while the DoF = 2 (height and width) are needed for bounding box. Briefly, the contributions of this study are in three areas:

- **Optimized Biomedical Object Detection:** To the best of our knowledge, the proposed CircleNet is the first anchor-free approach for detection of glomeruli with optimized circle representation.
- **Circle Representation:** We propose a simple circle representation for ball-shaped biomedical object detection with smaller DoF of fitting and superior detection

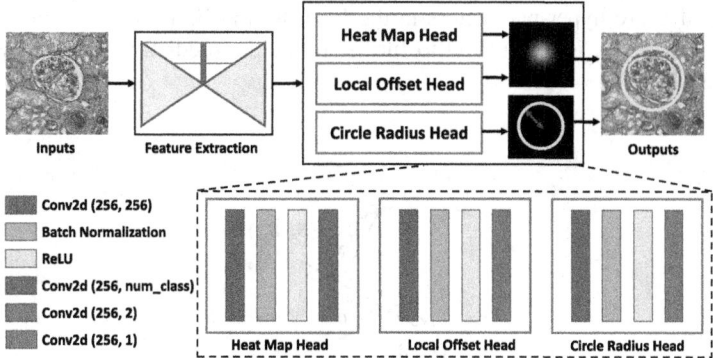

Fig. 2. The network structure of proposed CircleNet. The role of the center point localization network is to achieve feature maps for the resulting head networks. Then three network heads are used to achieve the central location and the radius of a bounding circle.

performance. We also introduce the circle intersection over union (cIOU) and validate the effectiveness of both circle representation and cIOU

- **Rotation Consistency:** The proposed CircleNet achieved better rotation consistency for detection of glomeruli.

2 Methods

2.1 Anchor Free Backbone

In Fig. 2, the center point localization (CPL) network is developed based on the anchor-free CenterNet implementation [26], as it possesses an ideal combination of high performance and simplicity. Throughout, we follow the definition of the terms from Zhou *et al.* [26]. The input image I is defined as $I \in R^{W \times H \times 3}$ with height H and width W. The output of the CPL network is the center localization of each object, which is formed as a heatmap $\hat{Y} \in [0,1]^{\frac{W}{R} \times \frac{H}{R} \times C}$. C indicates the number of candidate classes, while R is the downsampling factor of the prediction. The heatmap $\hat{Y}$ is expected to be equal to 1 at lesion centers, while 0 otherwise. Following standard practice [14,26], the ground truth of the target center point is modeled as a 2D Gaussian kernel:

$$Y_{xyc} = \exp\left(-\frac{(x - \tilde{p}_x)^2 + (y - \tilde{p}_y)^2}{2\sigma_p^2}\right) \tag{1}$$

where the $\tilde{p}_x$ and $\tilde{p}_y$ are the downsampled target center points and σ_p is the kernel standard deviation. The predicted heatmap is optimized by pixel regression loss L_k with focal loss [15]:

$$L_k = \frac{-1}{N} \sum_{xyc} \begin{cases} (1 - \hat{Y}_{xyc})^\alpha \log(\hat{Y}_{xyc}) & \text{if } Y_{xyc} = 1 \\ (1 - Y_{xyc})^\beta (\hat{Y}_{xyc})^\alpha & \\ \quad \log(1 - \hat{Y}_{xyc}) & \text{otherwise} \end{cases} \tag{2}$$

where α and β are hyper-parameters in the focal loss [15]. Then, the ℓ_1-norm offset prediction loss L_{off}, is formulated to further refine the prediction location, which is identical as [26].

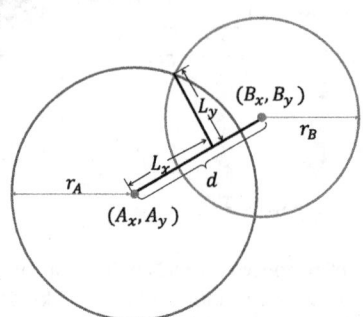

Fig. 3. The parameters that are used to calculate the circle IOU (cIOU).

2.2   From Center Point to Bounding Circle

Once the peaks of the all heatmaps are obtained, the top n peaks are proposed whose value is greater or equal to its 8-connected neighbors. The set of n detected center points is defined as $\hat{\mathcal{P}} = \{(\hat{x}_i, \hat{y}_i)\}_{i=1}^n$. Each key point location is formed by an integer coordinate (x_i, y_i) from $\hat{Y}_{x_i y_i c}$ and L_k. Meanwhile, the offset $(\delta\hat{x}_i, \delta\hat{y}_i)$ is obtained from L_{off}. Then, the bounding circle is formed as a circle with center point $\hat{p}$ and radius $\hat{r}$ as:

$$\hat{p} = (\hat{x}_i + \delta\hat{x}_i, \ \hat{y}_i + \delta\hat{y}_i). \quad \hat{r} = \hat{R}_{\hat{x}_i, \hat{y}_i}. \tag{3}$$

where $\hat{R} \in \mathcal{R}^{\frac{W}{R} \times \frac{H}{R} \times 1}$ is the radius prediction for each pixel location, optimized by

$$L_{radius} = \frac{1}{N} \sum_{k=1}^{N} \left| \hat{R}_{p_k} - r_k \right|. \tag{4}$$

where r_k is the true radius for each circle object k. Finally, The overall objective is

$$L_{det} = L_k + \lambda_{radius} L_{radius} + \lambda_{off} L_{off}. \tag{5}$$

We set $\lambda_{radius} = 0.1$ and $\lambda_{off} = 1$ referring from [26].

2.3   Circle IOU

In canonical object detection, intersection over union (IOU) is the most popular evaluation metric to measure the similarity between two bounding boxes. The IOU is defined as the ratio between area of intersection and area of union. For CircleNet, as the objects are presented as circles, we introduce the cIOU as:

$$\text{cIOU} = \frac{\text{Area}(A \cap B)}{\text{Area}(A \cup B)} \tag{6}$$

where A and B represent the two circles respectively as Fig. 3. The center coordinates of A and B are defined as (A_x, A_y) and (B_x, B_y), which are calculated by:

$$A_x = \hat{x}_i + \delta\hat{x}_i, A_y = \hat{y}_i + \delta\hat{y}_i \tag{7}$$

$$B_x = \hat{x}_j + \delta\hat{x}_j, B_y = \hat{y}_j + \delta\hat{y}_j \tag{8}$$

Then, the distance between the center coordinates d is defined as:

$$d = \sqrt{(B_x - A_x)^2 + (B_y - A_y)^2} \tag{9}$$

$$L_x = \frac{r_A^2 - r_B^2 + d^2}{2d}, L_y = \sqrt{r_A^2 - L_x^2} \tag{10}$$

Finally, the cIOU can be calculated from

$$\text{Area}(A \cap B) = r_A^2 \sin^{-1}\left(\frac{L_y}{r_A}\right) + r_B^2 \sin^{-1}\left(\frac{L_y}{r_B}\right) - L_y\left(L_x + \sqrt{r_A^2 - r_B^2 + L_x^2}\right) \tag{11}$$

$$\text{Area}(A \cup B) = \pi r_A^2 + \pi r_B^2 - \text{Area}(A \cap B) \tag{12}$$

3 Data and Implementation Details

Whole scan images from renal biopsies were utilized for analysis. Kidney tissue was routinely processed, paraffin embedded, and $3\,\mu m$ thickness sections cut and stained with hematoxylin and eosin (HE), periodic acid–Schiff (PAS) or Jones. Samples were deidentified, and studies were approved by the Institutional Review Board (IRB). 704 glomeruli from 42 biopsy samples were used as training data, 98 glomeruli from 7 biopsy samples were used as validation data, while 147 glomeruli from 7 biopsy samples were used as testing data. For all training and testing data, the original high-resolution whole scan images ($0.25\,\mu m$ per pixel) is downsampled to lower resolution ($4\,\mu m$ per pixel), considering the size of a glumerulus [21] and its ratio within a patch. Then, we randomly sampled image patches (each patch contained at least one glomerulus with 512×512 pixels) as experimental images for detection networks. Eventually, we formed a cohort with 7040 training, 980 validation, and 1470 testing images.

The Faster-RCNN [22], CornerNet [14], ExtremeNet [27], CenterNet [26] were employed as the baseline methods due to their superior performance in object detection. For different detection methods, ResNet-50 [7], stacked Hourglass-104 [20] network and deep layer aggregation (DLA) network [24] were employed as backbone networks, respectively. The implementations of detection and backbone networks followed the authors' official PyTorch implementations. All the models used in this study were initialized by the COCO pretrained model [16]. The same workstation with NVIDIA 1080Ti GPU was used to perform all experiments in this study.

Table 1. The detection performance.

Methods	Backbone	AP	$AP_{(50)}$	$Ap_{(75)}$	$Ap_{(S)}$	$Ap_{(M)}$
Faster-RCNN [22]	ResNet-50	0.584	0.866	0.730	0.478	0.648
Faster-RCNN [22]	ResNet-101	0.568	0.867	0.694	0.460	0.633
CornerNet [14]	Hourglass-104	0.595	0.818	0.732	0.524	**0.695**
ExtremeNet [27]	Hourglass-104	0.597	0.864	0.749	0.493	0.658
CenterNet-HG [26]	Hourglass-104	0.574	0.853	0.708	0.442	0.649
CenterNet-DLA [26]	DLA	0.598	0.902	0.735	0.513	0.648
CircleNet-HG (Ours)	Hourglass-104	0.615	0.853	0.750	0.586	0.656
CircleNet-DLA (Ours)	DLA	**0.647**	**0.907**	**0.787**	**0.597**	0.685

4   Results

4.1   Detection Performance

The standard detection metrics were used to evaluate different methods, including average precision (AP), AP_{50} (IOU threshold at 0.5), AP_{75} (IOU threshold at 0.75), AP_S (small scale with area <1000), AP_M (median scale with area >1000). In the experiment, state-of-the-art anchor-based (Faster-RCNN) and anchor-free detection methods (CornerNet, ExtremeNet, CenterNet) were employed as benchmarks. From Table 1, the proposed method outperformed the benchmarks with a remarkable margin, except for AP_M. However, the performance of the proposed method still achieved the second best performance for AP_M.

4.2   Circle Representation and cIOU

We further evaluated if the better detection results of circle representation sacrificed the effectiveness for detection representation. To do that, we manually annotated 50 glomerulus from the testing data to achieve segmentation masks. Then, we calculated the ratio between the mask area and bounding box/circle area, called mask detection ratio (MDT), for each glomerulus. From the right panel of Fig. 4, both box and circle representations have the comparable mean MDT, which shows that the bounding circle does not sacrifice the effectiveness for detection representation.

For bounding box and bounding circle, the IOU and cIOU were used as the overlap metrics for evaluating the detection performance (e.g., AP_{50} and AP_{75}) between manual annotations and predictions. Herein, we compared the performance of bounding box and bounding circle as similarity metrics for detection of glomeruli. To test this, we added random displacements with random directions on all testing glomeruli to simulate different detection results. Then, we calculated the IOU and cIOU, respectively. Figure 5 presents the results of mean IOU and mean cIOU on all testing glomeruli, with the displacements varying from 0 to 100 pixels. The results show that the cIOU behaves nearly the same as a IOU, which shows that the cIOU is a validated overlap metrics for detection of glomeruli.

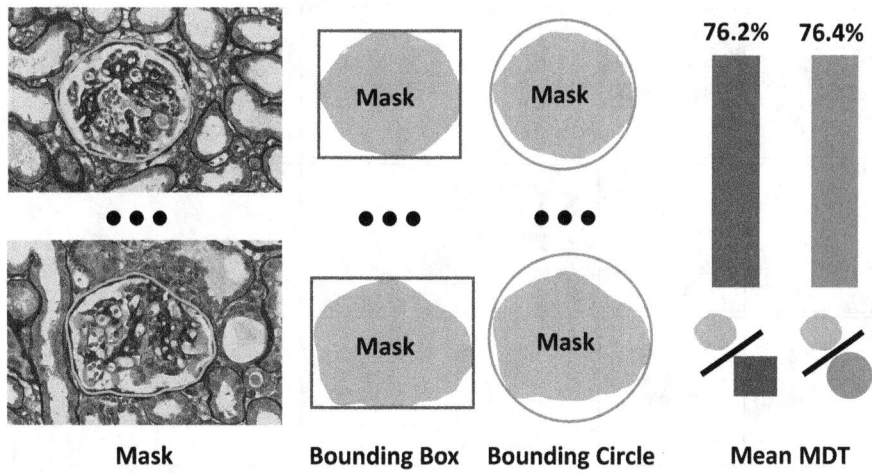

Fig. 4. The ratio between the mask area and bounding box/circle area, called mask detection ratio (MDT). The masks and representations were manually traced (left and middle panel) on 50 randomly selected glomerulus from the testing cohort. As the result, the mean MDT was close across rectangular box representations and circle representations

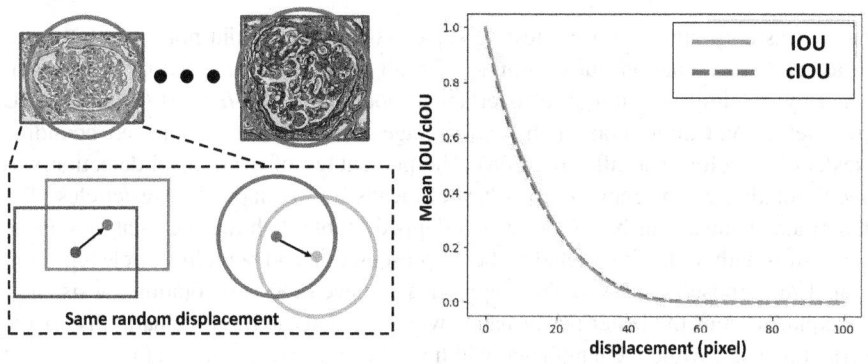

Fig. 5. The effectiveness of IOU and cIOU metrics. For every testing glomerulus, we shifted the bounding box/circle with certain displacement in a random direction (left panel). Then, the IOU and cIOU values between the original and shifted bounding boxes/circles were calculated for different displacement (right panel).

4.3 Rotation Consistency

Another potential benefit for circle representation is better rotation consistency than rectangular boxes. As shown in Fig. 6, we evaluated the consistency of bounding box/circle detection by rotating the original testing images. To avoid the impact from intensity interpolation, we rotated the original image 90° rather than an arbitrary degree. By doing this, detected bounding box/circle on rotated images were conveniently able to be converted to the original space. To fairly compare the rotation consistency, the

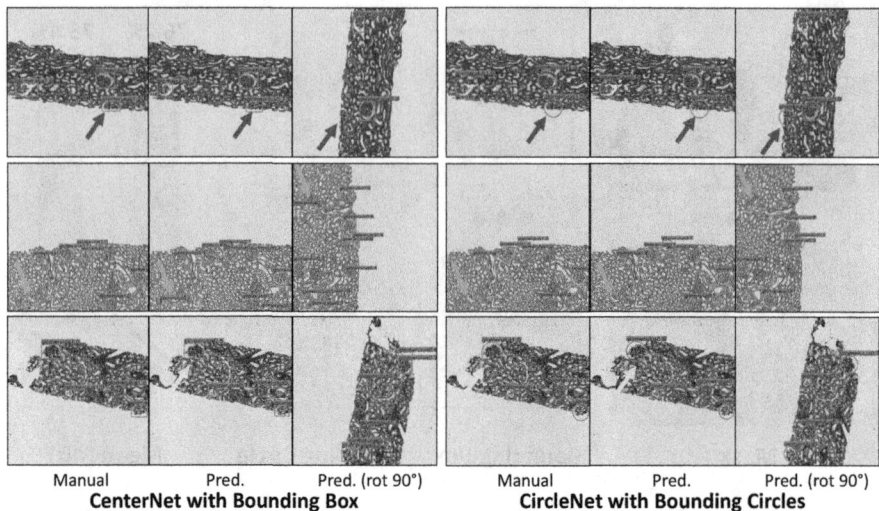

Fig. 6. The qualitative results of detection and rotation consistency. Each row indicates a different example patches. The arrows indicate the inconsistent detection results in different cases.

rotation was only applied during testing stage. Therefore, we did not apply any rotation as data augmentation during training for all methods. The consistency was calculated by dividing the number of overlapped bounding boxes/circles (IOU or cIOU > 0.5 before and after rotation) by the average number of total detected bounding boxes/circles (before and after rotation). The percentage of overlapped detection was named "rotation consistency" ratio, where 0 means no overlapped boxes/circles after rotation and 1 means all boxes/circles overlapped. Table 2 shows the rotation consistency results with traditional bounding box representation and bounding circle representation. The proposed CircleNet-DLA approach achieved the best rotation consistency. One explanation of the better performance would be that the radii are naturally spatial invariant metrics, while the length and width metrics are sensitive to rotation.

Table 2. Rotation consistency results of bounding box and bounding circle.

Representation	Methods	Backbone	Rotation consistency
Bounding Box	CenterNet-HG [26]	Hourglass-104	0.833
Bounding Box	CenterNet-DLA [26]	DLA	0.851
Bounding Circle	CircleNet-HG (Ours)	Hourglass-104	0.875
Bounding Circle	CircleNet-DLA (Ours)	DLA	**0.886**

5 Conclusion

In this paper, we introduce CircleNet, an anchor-free method for detection of glomeruli. The proposed detection method is optimized for ball-shaped biomedical objects, with the superior detection performance and better rotation consistency. The new circle representation as well as the cIOU evaluation metric were comprehensively evaluated in this study. The results show that the circle representation does not sacrifice the effectiveness with less DoF compared with traditional representation for detection of glomeruli. The method is optimized for quasi-disk shape detection, so it might not be optimal for other types of objects, such as stick-like objects.

Acknowledgements. This work was supported by NIH NIDDK DK56942(ABF), NSF CAREER 1452485 (Landman).

References

1. Bueno, G., Fernandez-Carrobles, M.M., Gonzalez-Lopez, L., Deniz, O.: Glomerulosclerosis identification in whole slide images using semantic segmentation. Comput. Methods Programs Biomed. **184**, 105273 (2020)
2. Gadermayr, M., Dombrowski, A.K., Klinkhammer, B.M., Boor, P., Merhof, D.: CNN cascades for segmenting whole slide images of the kidney. arXiv preprint arXiv:1708.00251 (2017)
3. Gallego, J., et al.: Glomerulus classification and detection based on convolutional neural networks. J. Imaging **4**(1), 20 (2018)
4. Ginley, B., et al.: Computational segmentation and classification of diabetic glomerulosclerosis. J. Am. Soc. Nephrol. **30**(10), 1953–1967 (2019)
5. Ginley, B., Tomaszewski, J.E., Yacoub, R., Chen, F., Sarder, P.: Unsupervised labeling of glomerular boundaries using Gabor filters and statistical testing in renal histology. J. Med. Imaging **4**(2), 021102 (2017)
6. Govind, D., Ginley, B., Lutnick, B., Tomaszewski, J.E., Sarder, P.: Glomerular detection and segmentation from multimodal microscopy images using a Butterworth band-pass filter. In: Medical Imaging 2018: Digital Pathology, vol. 10581, p. 1058114. International Society for Optics and Photonics (2018)
7. He, K., Zhang, X., Ren, S., Sun, J.: Deep residual learning for image recognition. In: Proceedings of the IEEE Conference on Computer Vision and Pattern Recognition, pp. 770–778 (2016)
8. Kakimoto, T., et al.: Automated image analysis of a glomerular injury marker desmin in spontaneously diabetic torii rats treated with losartan. J. Endocrinol. **222**(1), 43 (2014)
9. Kakimoto, T., et al.: Quantitative analysis of markers of podocyte injury in the rat puromycin aminonucleoside nephropathy model. Exp. Toxicol. Pathol. **67**(2), 171–177 (2015)
10. Kannan, S., et al.: Segmentation of glomeruli within trichrome images using deep learning. Kidney Int. Rep. **4**(7), 955–962 (2019)
11. Kato, T., et al.: Segmental hog: new descriptor for glomerulus detection in kidney microscopy image. BMC Bioinform. **16**(1), 316 (2015)
12. Kawazoe, Y., et al.: Faster R-CNN-based glomerular detection in multistained human whole slide images. J. Imaging **4**(7), 91 (2018)
13. Kotyk, T., et al.: Measurement of glomerulus diameter and bowman's space width of renal albino rats. Comput. Methods Programs Biomed. **126**, 143–153 (2016)

14. Law, H., Deng, J.: Cornernet: detecting objects as paired keypoints. In: Proceedings of the European Conference on Computer Vision (ECCV), pp. 734–750 (2018)
15. Lin, T.Y., Goyal, P., Girshick, R., He, K., Dollár, P.: Focal loss for dense object detection. In: Proceedings of the IEEE International Conference on Computer Vision, pp. 2980–2988 (2017)
16. Lin, T.-Y., et al.: Microsoft COCO: common objects in context. In: Fleet, D., Pajdla, T., Schiele, B., Tuytelaars, T. (eds.) ECCV 2014. LNCS, vol. 8693, pp. 740–755. Springer, Cham (2014). https://doi.org/10.1007/978-3-319-10602-1_48
17. Lo, Y.-C., et al.: Glomerulus detection on light microscopic images of renal pathology with the faster R-CNN. In: Cheng, L., Leung, A.C.S., Ozawa, S. (eds.) ICONIP 2018. LNCS, vol. 11307, pp. 369–377. Springer, Cham (2018). https://doi.org/10.1007/978-3-030-04239-4_33
18. Ma, J., Zhang, J., Hu, J.: Glomerulus extraction by using genetic algorithm for edge patching. In: 2009 IEEE Congress on Evolutionary Computation, pp. 2474–2479. IEEE (2009)
19. Marée, R., Dallongeville, S., Olivo-Marin, J.C., Meas-Yedid, V.: An approach for detection of glomeruli in multisite digital pathology. In: 2016 IEEE 13th International Symposium on Biomedical Imaging (ISBI), pp. 1033–1036. IEEE (2016)
20. Newell, A., Yang, K., Deng, J.: Stacked hourglass networks for human pose estimation. In: Leibe, B., Matas, J., Sebe, N., Welling, M. (eds.) ECCV 2016. LNCS, vol. 9912, pp. 483–499. Springer, Cham (2016). https://doi.org/10.1007/978-3-319-46484-8_29
21. Puelles, V.G., Hoy, W.E., Hughson, M.D., Diouf, B., Douglas-Denton, R.N., Bertram, J.F.: Glomerular number and size variability and risk for kidney disease. Curr. Opin. Nephrol. Hypertens. 20(1), 7–15 (2011)
22. Ren, S., He, K., Girshick, R., Sun, J.: Faster R-CNN: towards real-time object detection with region proposal networks. In: Advances in Neural Information Processing Systems, pp. 91–99 (2015)
23. Temerinac-Ott, M., et al.: Detection of glomeruli in renal pathology by mutual comparison of multiple staining modalities. In: Proceedings of the 10th International Symposium on Image and Signal Processing and Analysis, pp. 19–24. IEEE (2017)
24. Yu, F., Wang, D., Shelhamer, E., Darrell, T.: Deep layer aggregation. In: Proceedings of the IEEE Conference on Computer Vision and Pattern Recognition, pp. 2403–2412 (2018)
25. Zhang, M., Wu, T., Bennett, K.M.: A novel hessian based algorithm for rat kidney glomerulus detection in 3D MRI. In: Medical Imaging 2015: Image Processing, vol. 9413, p. 94132N. International Society for Optics and Photonics (2015)
26. Zhou, X., Wang, D., Krähenbühl, P.: Objects as points. arXiv preprint arXiv:1904.07850 (2019)
27. Zhou, X., Zhuo, J., Krahenbuhl, P.: Bottom-up object detection by grouping extreme and center points. In: Proceedings of the IEEE Conference on Computer Vision and Pattern Recognition, pp. 850–859 (2019)

Weakly Supervised One-Stage Vision and Language Disease Detection Using Large Scale Pneumonia and Pneumothorax Studies

Leo K. Tam[1(✉)], Xiaosong Wang[1], Evrim Turkbey[2], Kevin Lu[1], Yuhong Wen[1], and Daguang Xu[1]

[1] NVIDIA, 2788 San Tomas Expy, Santa Clara, CA 95051, USA
lk.tam1@gmail.com
[2] National Institute of Health Clinical Center,
10 Center Dr., Bethesda, MD 20814, USA

Abstract. Detecting clinically relevant objects in medical images is a challenge despite large datasets due to the lack of detailed labels. To address the label issue, we utilize the scene-level labels with a detection architecture that incorporates natural language information. We present a challenging new set of radiologist paired bounding box and natural language annotations on the publicly available MIMIC-CXR dataset especially focussed on pneumonia and pneumothorax. Along with the dataset, we present a joint vision language weakly supervised transformer layer-selected one-stage dual head detection architecture (LITERATI) alongside strong baseline comparisons with class activation mapping (CAM), gradient CAM, and relevant implementations on the NIH ChestXray-14 and MIMIC-CXR dataset. Borrowing from advances in vision language architectures, the LITERATI method demonstrates joint image and referring expression (objects localized in the image using natural language) input for detection that scales in a purely weakly supervised fashion. The architectural modifications address three obstacles – implementing a supervised vision and language detection method in a weakly supervised fashion, incorporating clinical referring expression natural language information, and generating high fidelity detections with map probabilities. Nevertheless, the challenging clinical nature of the radiologist annotations including subtle references, multi-instance specifications, and relatively verbose underlying medical reports, ensures the vision language detection task at scale remains stimulating for future investigation.

Keywords: Deep learning · Weak supervision · Natural language processing · Vision language · Chest x-ray · Electronic health record

1 Introduction

Recently, the release of large scale datasets concerning chest x-rays has enabled methods that scale with such datasets [7,18,25]. Whereas image classification

© Springer Nature Switzerland AG 2020
A. L. Martel et al. (Eds.): MICCAI 2020, LNCS 12264, pp. 45–55, 2020.
https://doi.org/10.1007/978-3-030-59719-1_5

implementations may reach adequate performance using scene-level labels, significantly more effort is required for annotation of bounding boxes around numerous visual features of interest. Yet there is detailed information present in released clinical reports that could inform natural language (NL) methods. The proposed method brings together advances in object detection [5], language [3], and their usage together [26, 28].

Typically object detection algorithms are either multi-stage with a region proposal stage or single stage with proposed regions scored to a certain object class when proposed [4, 20]. The single stage detectors have the benefit of fast inference time at often nearly the same performance in accuracy [20, 21]. The object detection networks benefit from using the same classification network architecture as their image classification cousins, where the visual features carry significance and shared modularity of networks holds. The modularity of network architectures is further realized with recent vision language architectures.

Vision language networks seek to encode the symbolic and information dense content in NL with visual features to solve applications such as visual question and answering, high fidelity image captioning, and other multi-modal tasks, some of which have seen application in medical imaging [16, 26, 27, 31]. Recent advances in NLP incorporate the transformer unit architecture, a computational building block that allows the attention of every word to learn an attentional weighting with regards to every other word in a sequence, given standard NLP tasks such as cloze, next sentence prediction, etc. [24]. Furthermore, deep transformer networks of a dozen or more layers trained for the language modeling task (next word prediction) were found to be adaptable to a variety of tasks, in part due to their ability to learn the components of a traditional NLP processing pipeline [23]. The combination of NLP for the vision task of object detection centers around the issue of visual grounding, namely given a referring phrase, how the phrase places an object in the image. The computational generation of referring phrases in a natural fashion is a nontrivial problem centered on photographs of cluttered scenes, where prevailing methods are based on probabilistically mapped potentials for attribute categories [10]. Related detection methods on cluttered scenes emphasize a single stage and end-to-end training [8, 10].

In particular, our method builds on a supervised single stage visual grounding method that incorporates fixed transformer embeddings [29]. The original one-stage methods fuses the referring expression in the form of a transformer embedding to augment the spatial features in the YOLOv3 detector. Our method alters to a weakly supervised implementation, taking care to ensure adequate training signal can be propagated to the object detection backbone through the technique adapted for directly allowing training signal through a fixed global average pooling layer [12]. The fast and memory efficient backbone of the DarkNet-53 architecture combines with fixed bidirectionally encoded features [3] to visually ground radiologist-annotated phrases. The fixed transformer embeddings are allowed increased flexibility through a learned selection layer as corroborated by the concurrent work [14], though here our explicit reasoning is to boost the NL information (verified by ablation study) of a more sophisticated phrasing then encountered in the generic visual grounding setting. To narrow our focus for object detection, we consider two datasets – the ChestXray-14 dataset [25], which was released with 984 bounding box annotations spread across 8 labels, and the MIMIC-CXR dataset [7], for which we collected over 400 board-certified radiologist bounding box annotations. Our weakly supervised transformer layer-selected one-stage dual head detection architecture (LITERATI) forms a strong baseline on a challenging set of annotations with scant information provided by the disease label.

2 Methods

The architecture of our method is presented in Fig. 1 with salient improvements numbered. The inputs of the model are anteroposterior view chest x-ray images and a referring expression parsed from the associated clinical report for the study. The output of the model is a probability map for each disease class (pneumonia and pneumothorax) as well as a classification for the image to generate the scene level loss. Intersection over union (IOU) is calculated for the input and ground truth annotation as $\frac{A \cap B}{A \cup B}$ where A is the input and B is the ground truth annotation.

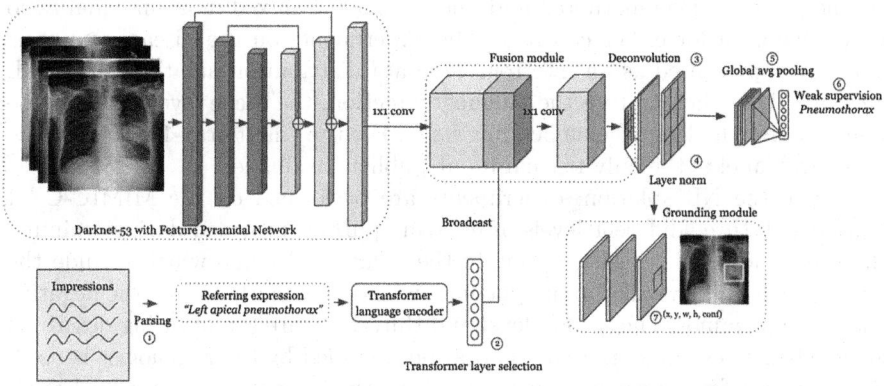

Fig. 1. The LITERATI network architecture is a vision language one-stage detector adapted from the supervised method of [28] for the weakly supervised case of medical imaging visually grounded object detection. The changes are highlighted by numbers and described in Sect. 2.2.

2.1 Preprocessing

The MIMIC-CXR dataset second stage release [7] included a reference label file built on the CheXpert labeler [6], which we used for our filtering and data selection. The CheXpert labels are used to isolate pneumonia and pneumothorax images and the corresponding chest x-ray reports retrieved by subject and study number. The images are converted from the full resolution (typically 2544×3056) to 416×416 to match the preferred one-stage resolution. For the ChestXray-14 dataset, the 1024×1024 PNG files are converted in PNG format.

For the MIMIC-CXR dataset, the radiologist reports are parsed to search for referring expressions, i.e. an object of interest is identified and located in the image [10]. The referring expression is created using tools adapted from [10]. Namely, the tooling uses the Stanford CoreNLP [15] parser and the NLTK tokenizer [13] to separate sentences into the R1–R7 attributes and reformed where there is an object in the image as either subject or direct object. Specifically, the referring phrase consists of the R7 attributes (generics), R1 attributes (entry-level name), R5 attributes (relative location), and finally R6 attributes (relative object) [10]. Sample referring phrases in the reports are "confluent opacity at bases", "left apical pneumothorax", and "multifocal bilateral airspace consolidation". As occasionally, the referring phrase does not capture the disease focus, the reports are additionally processed to excerpt phrases with "pneumonia" and "pneumothorax" to create a disease emphasis dataset split. For example, a phrase that does not qualify as a canonical referring expression but is present for the disease is, "vague right mid lung opacity, which is of uncertain etiology, although could represent an early pneumonia" which is a positive mention, standing in contrast to, "no complications, no pneumothorax" as a negative mention. To include the presence of normal and negative example images, data negative for pneumothorax and pneumonia was mixed in at an equal ratio to positive data for either category. The experiments on the disease emphasis phrases are presented as an interrogative data distribution ablation of the NL function. To further capture the language function, the scene level label can be submitted for the language embedding itself. For the ChestXray-14 dataset, the scene level label is the only textual input publicly available.

During the NL ablation, experiments are performed on the MIMIC-CXR dataset with three different levels of referring phrases provided during training. The tersest level of phrasing is simply the scene level label, which include the cases pneumonia, pneumothorax, pneumonia and pneumothorax, or the negative phrase 'no pneumo'. The second level and third level are the phrasing described previously. At test time, the full annotation provided by the radiologist is used.

Once the referring expressions are in place, the ingredients are set for board-certified radiologist clinical annotations. We pair the images and highlight relevant phrases in the clinical report by building functionality on the publicly available MS COCO annotator [2]. The radiologist is given free rein to select phrases that are clinically relevant in the report to highlight. The radiologist has annotated 455 clinically relevant phrases with bounding boxes on the MIMIC-CXR dataset, which we release at https://github.com/leotam/MIMIC-CXR-annotations. As of writing, the annotations constitute the largest disease focussed bounding box labels with referring expressions publicly released, and we hope is a valuable contribution to the clinical visual grounding milieu.

2.2   Network Architecture

There are six modifications to [28] noted in Fig. 1 beyond the parsing discussed. To adapt the network from supervised to weakly supervised, the classification layer must be not be trained to reduce partitioning of the data information. To achieve that purpose, a global average pooling layer [12] was combined with a cross-entropy loss on the scene labels, Fig. 1 (5, 6), to replace the convolution-batch norm-convolution (CBC) layer that generates the bounding box anchors in the original implementation. To replace the CBC layer, a deconvolution layer norm layer was prepended to the pooling layer Fig. 1 (3), which additionally allowed grounding on an image scale probability map Fig. 1 (7), instead of the anchor shifts typically dictated by the YOLOv3 implementation [21].

For the NL implementation, the ability of transformer architectures to implement aspects of the NLP pipeline [23] suggests a trained layer may be successful in increasing the expressivity of the language information for the task. Normally, a fully connected layer is appended to a transformer model to fine-tune for a given task for various classification tasks [19]. The architecture includes a convolutional 1D layer in the language mapping module Fig. 1 (2) that allows access to all the transformer layers instead of the linear layers on the averaged last four transformer layers output in the original implementation [28]. Such a modification echos the custom attention on layers mechanism from a concurrent study on the automatic labeler work [14].

For the bounding box generation, we move to the threshold detection method similar to [25], which differs from the threshold detection method in [28]. The current generation method uses the tractable probability map output after the deconvolution-layer norm stage close to the weak supervision signal to select regions of high confidence given a neighborhood size. Specifically, a maximal filter is applied to the map probabilities as follows:

$$M = \left\{ \frac{e^{c_i}}{\sum_i e^{c_i}} \mid c_i \in C \right\} \tag{1}$$

$$S = \{m \mid \max(m \in M) \,\forall\, m \mid \|m - x_0\| < d\} \tag{2}$$

$$x_0 \equiv \frac{\sum_{}^{N}(x - x_0)}{N} = d \mid x \in S. \tag{3}$$

First the M map probabilities are generated from the convolutional outputs C via softmax, followed by maximal filtering (with the threshold d as a hyperparameter set by tree-structured parzen estimator [1], as are all hyperparameters across methods) to generate the regions S, and then x_0 center of masses collected as bounding box centers. The original method [21] used the confidence scores to assign a probability to a superimposed anchor grid. As the LITERATI output is at parity resolution with the image, the deconvolution and maximal filtering obviates the anchor grid and offset prediction mechanism.

2.3   Training

The implementation in PyTorch [17] allows for straight-forward data parallelism via the nn.DataParallel class, which we found was key to performance in a timely fashion. The LITERATI network was trained for 100 epochs (as per the original implementation) on a NVIDIA DGX-2 (16×32 GB V100) with 16-way data parallelism using a batch size of 416 for approximately 12 h. The dataset for the weakly supervised case was split in an 80/10/10 ratio for training, test, and validation respectively, or 44627, 5577, and 5777 images respectively. The test set was checked infrequently for divergence from the validation set. The epoch with the best validation performance was selected for the visual grounding task and was observed to always perform better than the overfitted last epoch. For the supervised implementation of the original, there were not enough annotations and instead the default parameters from [28] were used.

3   Results and Discussion

In Table 1, experiments are compared across the ChestXray-14 dataset. The methods show the gradient CAM implementation derived from [9,22] outperforms the traditional CAM implementation [30], likely due to the higher resolution localization map. Meanwhile the LITERATI with scene label method improves on the grad CAM method most significantly at IOU = 0.2, though lagging at IOU = 0.4 and higher. Above both methods is the jointly trained supervised and unsupervised method from [11]. The LITERATI method and the one-stage method were designed for visual grounding, but the performance for detection on the supervised one-stage method with minimal modification is not strong at the dataset size here, 215 ChestXray-14 annotations for specifically pneumonia and pneumothorax as that is the supervision available.

Table 1. ChestXray-14 detection accuracy

IOU	0.1	0.2	0.3	0.4	0.5
CAM [30] WS	0.505	0.290	0.150	0.075	0.030
Multi-stage S + WS [11]	**0.615**	**0.505**	**0.415**	**0.275**	**0.180**
Gradient CAM WS	0.565	0.298	0.175	**0.097**	**0.049**
LITERATI SWS	**0.593**	**0.417**	**0.204**	0.088	0.046
One-stage S	0.115	0.083	0.073	0.021	0.003

Supervised (S), weakly supervised (WS), and scene-level NLP (SWS) methods

While we include two relevant prior art baselines without language input, the present visual grounding task is more specifically contained by the referring expression label and at times further removed from the scene level label due to an annotation's clinical importance determined by the radiologist. The data in

Table 2. MIMIC-CXR detection accuracy

IOU	0.1	0.2	0.3	0.4	0.5
Gradient CAM WS	0.316	0.104	0.049	0.005	0.001
LITERATI NWS	0.349	0.125	0.060	0.024	0.007
One-stage S	0.209	0.125	0.125	0.125	0.031

Supervised (S), weakly supervised (WS), and NLP (NWS) methods

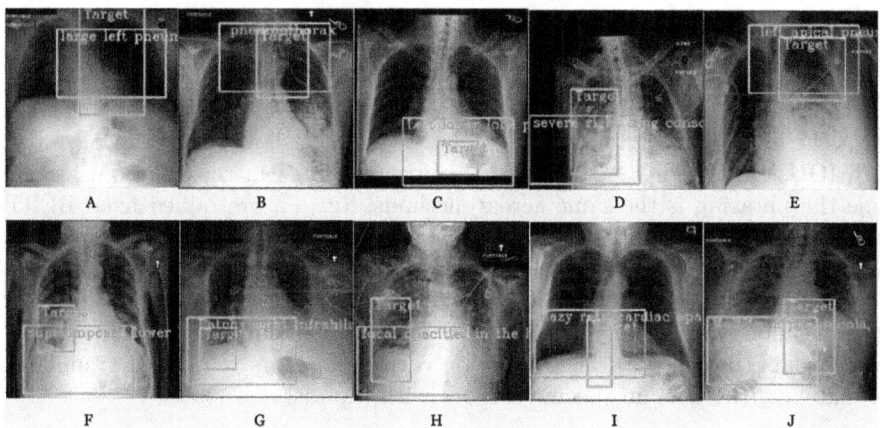

Fig. 2. Qualitative detection results using the LITERATI method. The referring expressions (A–J) are "large left pneumothorax", "pneumothorax", "left lower lobe pneumonia", "severe right lung consolidation", "left apical pneumothorax", "superimposed lower lobe pneumonia", "patchy right infrahilar opacity", "focal opacities in the lateral right mid lung and medial right lower lung", "hazy retrocardial opacity", and "multifocal pneumonia". In the top row (A–E), mainly disease focussed referring phrases are localized. In the bottom row (F–J), examples of difficult annotations where the referenced location may be vague or spatially ambiguous are presented.

Table 2 shows detection accuracy on the visual grounding task. The LITERATI method improves on the supervised method at IOU = 0.1 and on gradient CAM at all IOUs. We present qualitative results in Fig. 2 that cover a range of annotations from disease focussed ("large left pneumonia") to more subtle features ("patchy right infrahilar opacity"). Of interest are the multi-instance annotations (e.g. "multifocal pneumonia" or "bibasilar consolidations") which would typically fall out of scope for referring expressions, but were included at the radiologist's discretion in approximately 46 of the annotations. Considering the case of "bibasilar consolidations", the ground truth annotation indicates two symmetrical boxes on each lung lobe. Such annotations are especially challenging for the one-stage method as it does not consider the multi-instance problem.

The ablation study on different levels of NL information is given in Table 3. Note, the table retains the same architecture and training procedure from the

Table 3. Ablation with differing NL information supplied during training

IOU	0.1	0.2	0.3	0.4	0.5
Scene label	0.337	0.123	0.048	0.012	0.000
Referring expression	**0.349**	**0.125**	0.051	0.014	0.002
Referring disease emphasis	**0.349**	**0.125**	**0.060**	**0.024**	**0.007**

Weakly supervised experiments with varying language input, i.e. scene label ("pneumonia"), referring expression ("patchy right infrahilar opacity"), or referring expression with scene label disease ("large left pneumonia").

LITERATI description in Sect. 2.2. The improvements using detail ranging from the scene level label to a full disease related sentence show performance gain at high IOUs. Although the training NL phrasing differs in the ablation, at test time the phrasing is the same across methods. Since a pretrained fixed BERT encoder is used, the ablation probes the adaptability from the NL portion of the architecture to the task. Since the pretrained encoder is trained on a large generic corpora, it likely retains the NLP pipeline (named entity recognition, coreference disambiguation, etc.) necessary for the visual grounding task. In limited experiments (not shown), fine-tuning on corpora appears to depend granularly on matching the domain specific corpora with the task.

4   Conclusion

We present a weakly supervised vision language method and associated clinical referring expressions dataset on pneumonia and pneumothorax chest x-ray images at scale. The clinical reports generate expressions that isolate discriminative objects inside the images. As parsing into referring expressions is accurate and mostly independently of vocabulary (i.e. it's tractable to identify a direct object without knowing exactly the meaning of the object) [10], the referring phrases represent a valuable source of information during the learning process.

Though not necessarily motivated by learning processes in nature, algorithms including NL bend towards explainable mechanisms, i.e. the localized image and language pairs form clear concepts. The explainable nature of visually grounded referring expressions in a clinical setting, while cogent here, merits further investigation on the lines of workflow performance. For pure NLP tasks, training on a data distribution closely matching the testing distribution has encountered success. An appropriately matching referring expressions dataset may draw from an ontology [25,27] or from didactic literature.

The study suggests that vision language approaches may be valuable for accessing information within clinical reports.

References

1. Bergstra, J., Bardenet, R., Bengio, Y., Kégl, B.: Algorithms for hyper-parameter optimization. In: Shawe-Taylor, J., Zemel, R.S., Bartlett, P.L., Pereira, F.C.N., Weinberger, K.Q. (eds.) Advances in Neural Information Processing Systems 24: 25th Annual Conference on Neural Information Processing Systems 2011. Proceedings of a meeting held 12–14 December 2011, Granada, Spain, pp. 2546–2554 (2011). http://papers.nips.cc/paper/4443-algorithms-for-hyper-parameter-optimization
2. Brooks, J.: Coco annotator (2019). https://github.com/jsbroks/coco-annotator/
3. Devlin, J., Chang, M., Lee, K., Toutanova, K.: BERT: pre-training of deep bidirectional transformers for language understanding. CoRR abs/1810.04805 (2018). http://arxiv.org/abs/1810.04805
4. Girshick, R.B.: Fast R-CNN. In: 2015 IEEE International Conference on Computer Vision, ICCV 2015, Santiago, Chile, 7–13 December 2015, pp. 1440–1448. IEEE Computer Society (2015). https://doi.org/10.1109/ICCV.2015.169
5. Huang, J., et al.: Speed/accuracy trade-offs for modern convolutional object detectors. CoRR abs/1611.10012 (2016). http://arxiv.org/abs/1611.10012
6. Irvin, J., et al.: Chexpert: a large chest radiograph dataset with uncertainty labels and expert comparison. CoRR abs/1901.07031 (2019). http://arxiv.org/abs/1901.07031
7. Johnson, A.E.W., et al.: MIMIC-CXR: a large publicly available database of labeled chest radiographs. CoRR abs/1901.07042 (2019). http://arxiv.org/abs/1901.07042
8. Johnson, J., Karpathy, A., Fei-Fei, L.: Densecap: fully convolutional localization networks for dense captioning. In: Proceedings of the IEEE Conference on Computer Vision and Pattern Recognition (CVPR), June 2016
9. Kao, H.: Gradcam on chexnet, March 2020. https://github.com/thtang/CheXNet-with-localization
10. Kazemzadeh, S., Ordonez, V., Matten, M., Berg, T.L.: Referitgame: referring to objects in photographs of natural scenes. In: Moschitti, A., Pang, B., Daelemans, W. (eds.) Proceedings of the 2014 Conference on Empirical Methods in Natural Language Processing, EMNLP 2014, Doha, Qatar, 25–29 October 2014, A meeting of SIGDAT, a Special Interest Group of the ACL, pp. 787–798. ACL (2014). https://doi.org/10.3115/v1/d14-1086
11. Li, Z., et al.: Thoracic disease identification and localization with limited supervision. CoRR abs/1711.06373 (2017). http://arxiv.org/abs/1711.06373
12. Lin, M., Chen, Q., Yan, S.: Network in network. In: Bengio, Y., LeCun, Y. (eds.) 2nd International Conference on Learning Representations, ICLR 2014, Banff, AB, Canada, 14–16 April 2014, Conference Track Proceedings (2014). http://arxiv.org/abs/1312.4400
13. Loper, E., Bird, S.: NLTK: the natural language toolkit. CoRR cs.CL/0205028 (2002). https://arxiv.org/abs/cs/0205028
14. Lyubinets, V., Boiko, T., Nicholas, D.: Automated labeling of bugs and tickets using attention-based mechanisms in recurrent neural networks. CoRR abs/1807.02892 (2018). http://arxiv.org/abs/1807.02892

15. Manning, C.D., Surdeanu, M., Bauer, J., Finkel, J.R., Bethard, S., McClosky, D.: The stanford corenlp natural language processing toolkit. In: Proceedings of the 52nd Annual Meeting of the Association for Computational Linguistics, ACL 2014, Baltimore, MD, USA, 22–27 June 2014, System Demonstrations, pp. 55–60. The Association for Computer Linguistics (2014). https://doi.org/10.3115/v1/p14-5010

16. Moradi, M., Madani, A., Gur, Y., Guo, Y., Syeda-Mahmood, T.: Bimodal network architectures for automatic generation of image annotation from text. In: Frangi, A.F., Schnabel, J.A., Davatzikos, C., Alberola-López, C., Fichtinger, G. (eds.) MICCAI 2018. LNCS, vol. 11070, pp. 449–456. Springer, Cham (2018). https://doi.org/10.1007/978-3-030-00928-1_51

17. Paszke, A., et al.: Pytorch: an imperative style, high-performance deep learning library. CoRR abs/1912.01703 (2019). http://arxiv.org/abs/1912.01703

18. Rajpurkar, P., et al.: Chexnet: radiologist-level pneumonia detection on chest x-rays with deep learning. CoRR abs/1711.05225 (2017). http://arxiv.org/abs/1711.05225

19. Rajpurkar, P., Jia, R., Liang, P.: Know what you don't know: unanswerable questions for squad. CoRR abs/1806.03822 (2018). http://arxiv.org/abs/1806.03822

20. Redmon, J., Divvala, S.K., Girshick, R.B., Farhadi, A.: You only look once: Unified, real-time object detection. CoRR abs/1506.02640 (2015). http://arxiv.org/abs/1506.02640

21. Redmon, J., Farhadi, A.: Yolov3: an incremental improvement. CoRR abs/1804.02767 (2018). http://arxiv.org/abs/1804.02767

22. Selvaraju, R.R., Das, A., Vedantam, R., Cogswell, M., Parikh, D., Batra, D.: Gradcam: why did you say that? Visual explanations from deep networks via gradient-based localization. CoRR abs/1610.02391 (2016). http://arxiv.org/abs/1610.02391

23. Tenney, I., Das, D., Pavlick, E.: BERT rediscovers the classical NLP pipeline. CoRR abs/1905.05950 (2019). http://arxiv.org/abs/1905.05950

24. Vaswani, A., et al.: Attention is all you need. CoRR abs/1706.03762 (2017). http://arxiv.org/abs/1706.03762

25. Wang, X., Peng, Y., Lu, L., Lu, Z., Bagheri, M., Summers, R.M.: Chestx-ray8: hospital-scale chest x-ray database and benchmarks on weakly-supervised classification and localization of common thorax diseases. CoRR abs/1705.02315 (2017). http://arxiv.org/abs/1705.02315

26. Wang, X., Peng, Y., Lu, L., Lu, Z., Summers, R.M.: Tienet: text-image embedding network for common thorax disease classification and reporting in chest x-rays. CoRR abs/1801.04334 (2018). http://arxiv.org/abs/1801.04334

27. Yan, K., Wang, X., Lu, L., Summers, R.M.: Deeplesion: automated deep mining, categorization and detection of significant radiology image findings using large-scale clinical lesion annotations. CoRR abs/1710.01766 (2017). http://arxiv.org/abs/1710.01766

28. Yang, Z., Gong, B., Wang, L., Huang, W., Yu, D., Luo, J.: A fast and accurate one-stage approach to visual grounding. In: 2019 IEEE/CVF International Conference on Computer Vision, ICCV 2019, Seoul, Korea (South), 27 October–2 November 2019, pp. 4682–4692. IEEE (2019). https://doi.org/10.1109/ICCV.2019.00478

29. Yang, Z., Gong, B., Wang, L., Huang, W., Yu, D., Luo, J.: A fast and accurate one-stage approach to visual grounding. CoRR abs/1908.06354 (2019). http://arxiv.org/abs/1908.06354

30. Zhou, B., Khosla, A., Lapedriza, À., Oliva, A., Torralba, A.: Learning deep features for discriminative localization. CoRR abs/1512.04150 (2015). http://arxiv.org/abs/1512.04150
31. Zhu, W., Vang, Y.S., Huang, Y., Xie, X.: DeepEM: deep 3D ConvNets with EM for weakly supervised pulmonary nodule detection. In: Frangi, A.F., Schnabel, J.A., Davatzikos, C., Alberola-López, C., Fichtinger, G. (eds.) MICCAI 2018. LNCS, vol. 11071, pp. 812–820. Springer, Cham (2018). https://doi.org/10.1007/978-3-030-00934-2_90

Diagnostic Assessment of Deep Learning Algorithms for Detection and Segmentation of Lesion in Mammographic Images

Thomas Boot[1($\boxtimes$)] and Humayun Irshad[1,2]

[1] BostonMeditech Inc, Concord, MA 01742, USA
tboot@bostonmeditech.com
[2] Synthesis AI, San Francisco, CA 94108, USA

Abstract. Computer-aided detection or diagnosing support methods aims to improve breast cancer screening programs by helping radiologists to evaluate digital mammography (DM) exams. This system relates to the use of deep learning for automated detection and segmentation of soft tissue lesions at the early stage. This paper presents a novel deep learning approach, based on a two stage object detector combining an enhanced Faster R-CNN with the Libra R-CNN structure for the Object Detection segment. A segmentation network is placed on top of previous structure in order to provide accurate extraction and localization of masses various features, i.e: margin, shape. The segmentation head is based on a Recurrent Residual Convolutional Neural Network and can lead to an additional feature classification for specific instance properties. A database of digital mammograms was collected from one vendor, Hologic, of which 1,200 images contained masses. The performance for our automated detection system was assessed with the sensitivity of the model which reached a micro average recall: 0.892, micro average precision: 0.734, micro average F1 score: 0.805. Macro average recall: 0.896, macro average precision: 0.819, macro average F1 score: 0.843. The segmentation performance for the same test set was evaluated to a mean IOU of 0.859.

Keywords: Mammography · Computer aided diagnosis · Mass detection · Mass segmentation

1 Introduction

Breast cancer is the most common non-skin related malignancy among women in the US. The average risk of a woman in the United States to develop breast cancer in her lifetime is around 13%, approximately a chance of 1 in 8 women to develop breast cancer [2]. Every year, new cases of breast cancer are detected and early screening of those new cases is primordial for the patient's health

© Springer Nature Switzerland AG 2020
A. L. Martel et al. (Eds.): MICCAI 2020, LNCS 12264, pp. 56–65, 2020.
https://doi.org/10.1007/978-3-030-59719-1_6

and survival against the disease. According to [4], breast cancer death rates declined by 40% from 1989 to 2016 among women. This progress is attributed to improvements in breast screening early detection programs, where mammograms are the best tools at our disposal, nonetheless this technique is not flawless, it has its own limitations.

Breast Cancer screening programs with mammography is the standard and efficient screening has proven to reduce breast cancer related mortality among women by 38–48% according to [19]. During a mammography screening examination, X-ray images are taken from 2 angles for each breast. Each paired view (i.e., medio-lateral oblique and cranio-caudal) are highly relational and complementary when it comes to mass identification within those views. Each scan is evaluated by a radiologist, a human reader. This process is lengthy, tiring and time consuming. Several studies have shown that a significant number of cases diagnosed as being wrongly marked negative were already visible on previous mammograms [6,12]. Additionally, the effectiveness of early screening is highly correlated with the radiologist's ability to detect abnormalities; experience and artifacts play a role in the interpretation of mammograms. Regardless of these pitfalls, the shortage of radiologists specialized in breast imaging suggests that there needs to be a different solution in order to reduce the false negative screens and improve the reliability of the exams.

Computer-aided detection (CAD) systems are developed to help radiologists to overcome the pitfalls and limitations. These systems usually provide specific tools to explore and mark suspicious areas, which should be reviewed by radiologists. Recent developments in machine learning and perceptive field, especially deep neural networks, have greatly improved the performance of such algorithms and outperformed as compared to previous methods [17]. Convolutional neural networks (CNN) have reached, or even surpassed human performance in various image classification and object detection tasks [3]. Needless to say, that the next generation of CNN have tremendous potential to significantly improve the breast cancer screening programs sensitivity.

Many contributions are being made developing deep learning based CAD systems. Some studies showed that they used patch based approaches to select the candidate regions and classify into benign and malignant [14,25]. This method does not fully utilize the mammography information available and makes the training process time consuming. In our work, we studied the use of recently proposed object detection frameworks that allows to train an end-to-end model that classifies soft tissue, while fully utilizing and enforcing the information flow from low level features into high level features. Our CAD system performs detection and classification step in one phase, the second stage is devoted to segmentation and mass properties classification (margin, shape, mass density).

2   Literature Review

Object detection is one of the booming perceptive fields which detect and classify different objects in an image. R-CNN [10] is the first method that uses selective search to provide regions proposals, which are fed into CNN and later classified using support vector machine. Fast R-CNN method [9] extends the R-CNN by building a faster object detection algorithm. Faster R-CNN [22] tries to tackle the major bottleneck of R-CNN and Fast R-CNN by replacing the selective search with Region Proposal Network (RPN) that learns the attention mechanisms of the model. The RPN generates objectness scores for each anchor and refine the bounding box coordinates to the exact location of the object. Mask R-CNN [11] extends Faster R-CNN by adding a mask head in parallel to the object classification and regression heads. Mask R-CNN introduced an improved version of ROI Pooling called ROI Align, which is a quantization free layer that preserves the spatial locations by using the computed value of each of the sampling points using bilinear interpolation from nearby grid points.

Current CAD systems for Mammography mainly rely on extracting mass-centered image patches automatically and apply a CNN method for automated mass detection in full-field digital mammograms (FFDM). Some papers deal with mass segmentation from whole mammograms as in [26], while others spend focus on mass detection using more recent object detectors, [13] or a combination of deep learning and machine learning algorithms, [8]. While all papers claim to reach state-of-the art results on public datasets, the application of those methods on more recent mammograms does not show any significant improvement compared to our own implemented method. A limitation of previous papers in mammography is the generalization of those methods regarding specific problems, with that in mind, we diminish the user interaction in preparing the training scheme and come up with a more recent state-of-the art combination of models to adapt our models to current more advanced imaging technologies.

Previously proposed methods for object detection do not tackle various imbalance problems that weaken CAD systems into maximizing their sensitivity and accuracy. We handle this problem by enhancing a common object detection framework for the task of breast cancer detection, where imbalance problems can lead to clinical insufficiency of the CAD systems.

3   Materials and Methods

3.1   Data Sets

The objective of the proposed system is to detect any kind of lesions, from benign to malignant. We used two data sets, one is publicly available INbreast [1] and another is an in-house data set. All the images are biopsy-proven cancer or benign lesions. The in-house data set incorporated 1,200 biopsy-proven lesions acquired from a Hologic scanner, with pixel-level ground truth annotations from experienced breast radiologists. The average number of lesions present per breast lies around ~1.1−~1.5 per image. The INbreast data set contains 115 FFDMs with pixel-level annotations. 113 cases containing proven masses were used for this study. In both data sets, the height and width of bounding boxes which enclose lesions in our data set are shown in the Fig. 1. Mean height is around 315 pixels in training, 374 pixels in validation. Mean width is 320 and 367 pixels

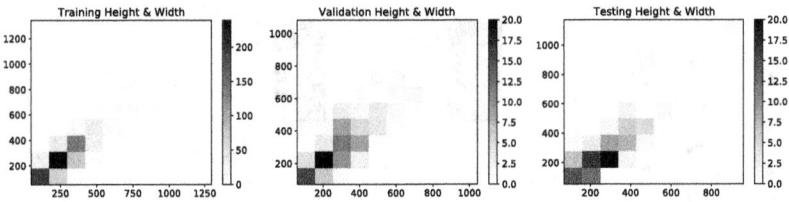

Fig. 1. Mass size distribution of the dataset

for training and validation. The number of benign and malignant masses in our inhouse dataset is 252 and 1003, for INbreast, it is 38 and 75.

3.2   Image Preprocessing

Preprocessing includes two steps. The first step is converting the 16-bit DICOM file into a 8-bit PNG file by rescaling to the integer range of [0–255]. This step allows us to reduce the computational cost without losing too much information. The second step includes the breast cropping using independent trained Mask R-CNN to remove pectoral and other tissue regions.

Transfer learning has been successful through every kind of application in computer vision and medical imaging applications. Due to the scarcity of medical data, it is preferable to use pretrained network features on natural images such as ImageNet or COCO [7,16,24], in order to take advantage of the computational and performance gain for specific related tasks. To make our domain specific task compatible with those pretrained networks, we simply duplicate the grey channel over a RGB image format in order to fully utilize the shallow and mid-deep features of the network.

3.3   Deep Learning Frameworks

The proposed system consists of two models in sequence which includes extended Faster-RCNN to propose region proposals and a modified U-Net with an edge focus loss head to calculate edge information.

Mass Detector Framework. We enhanced the Faster RCNN model by providing a deeper and more incentive approach to train networks and preserve the information while training. We proposed an end-to-end model that englobes the feature pyramid network (FPN) [15], path aggregation network (PANet) [18], and Libra R-CNN [21] for object balanced learning as shown in Fig. 2. This framework helps to tackle four common problems in object detection tasks: class imbalance, scale imbalance, spatial imbalance and objective imbalance. It handles the class imbalance problem by adopting a hard sampling method with IoU -based sampling [21] to handle the "foreground-background" imbalance. The objects in both data sets are imbalance and have various scales. To tackle object

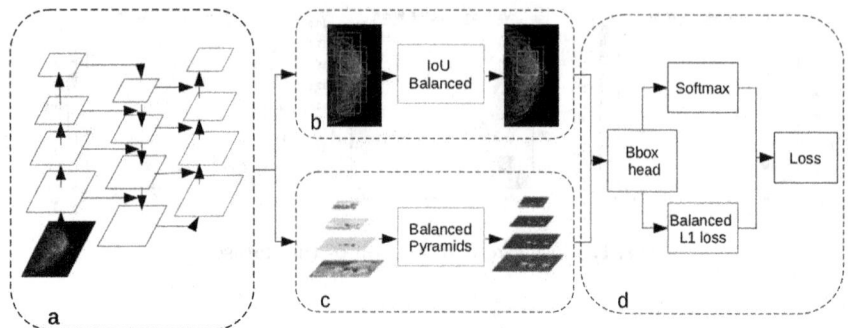

Fig. 2. Illustration of Mass Detector framework. (a) FPN Backbone mounted on ResNeXt-101-32x4d and PANet bottom-up path augmentation, (b) IoU balancing sampling, (c) balanced feature pyramid, (d) Balanced L1-loss

level imbalance and scale problems, we modified the FPN implementation and extended it with a combined PANet. In addition, we employed Libra R-CNN structure to improve the feature level imbalance with the bottom-up path augmentation [18] and the balanced feature pyramid method [21].

The spatial imbalance relates to the spatial properties of the bounding boxes which can be divided into three sub-types of spatial imbalance: 1) imbalance in regression loss that is related to the contribution of individual objects to the regression task, 2) IoU distribution loss that is related to the biases in the distribution of IoUs, 3) object location imbalance is about the location distribution of object instances in an image and therefore the design of anchors and the sampled subset to train the detection network.

The objective imbalance refers to the multi-task loss function to minimize (i.e classification and regression task). Both could be incompatible in terms of range and therefore a balanced objective strategy can be developed to find a solution in acceptable terms. The most common strategy is to use task weighting which balances the loss terms by an additional hyper-parameter as the weighting factor. The hyper-parameter is set using a validation set.

The backbone of mass detector is ResNeXt-101 with 32x4d [27], on top of which we have a PA-FPN neck that extracts and strengthens low level features in higher semantic layers in order to increase localization information. The Libra R-CNN module helps us to equally select positive and negative samples as hard negative samples are hard to consider during training due to extreme sample imbalance. In parallel, the multi-layer features are deeply integrated in order to obtain semantic balanced features. This approach aggregates features from low-level to high-level at the same time and is complementary with the PA-FPN structure. On top of that, a balanced L1 loss, derived from conventional smooth L1 loss, is used to promote crucial regression gradients, i.e. gradients from accurate samples (in-liners), to re-balanced samples in order to achieve a more balanced training for classification and localization. The detector framework optimized multi-task loss composed of the classification loss L_{cls}, which is based on balanced cross entropy loss, and the bounding box loss L_{bbox}, which is based on balanced L1 loss, where w_1 and w_2 are factors to balance the different losses.

$$L_{detect} = w_1 L_{cls} + w_2 L_{bbox} \tag{1}$$

The detector framework is trained with SGD optimizer using gradual warmup strategy for the first epochs until 0.001, and reducing the learning rate every 20 epochs by a factor of 10. All loss factors are set to 1.

Mass Segmentor Framework. As opposed to traditional two-stage object detector frameworks, we decided not to integrate the mask prediction head on an end-to-end training framework, as it reduced its sensitivity and precision. Adding an additional loss to minimize makes our general task more complicated and more sensitive to outliers, this is a typical case of objective imbalance, where one of the loss functions is dominating during training. We performed experiments in order to accurately battle the objective imbalance as we are adding a term (mask loss) to the linear multi-task loss function of the object detector framework. Based on detection results, we compute the deviation in bounding box prediction compared to the ground truth and add this deviation factor into a custom augmentation technique for our segmentation task as shown in Fig. 3. In addition, we also add a random uncertainty translation during training to make our segmentor robust against detection uncertainties.

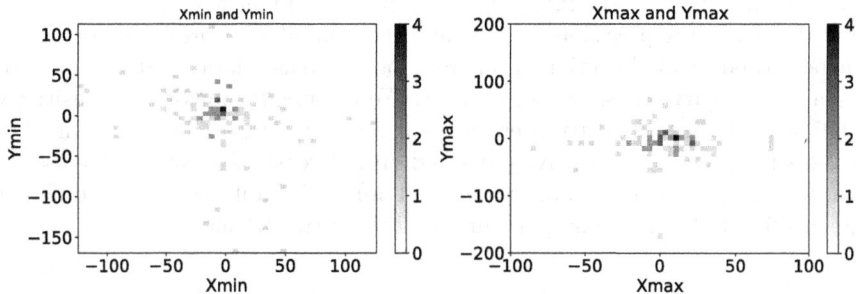

Fig. 3. Deviation of the bounding box coordinates compared to ground truth

In mass segmentor framework, We implemented a Recurrent Residual U-Net based on [5], which allows to speed up convergence and improve segmentation results compared to [23]. By applying convolution of Sobel kernels on both ground truth and predicted mask, [28] we can compute the difference between both edge maps using the mean square error between the target y and the prediction $\hat{y}$:

$$L^2(y, \hat{y}) = M_2(abs(y - \hat{y}))^2 \tag{2}$$

The L^2 distance defined in (2) can be added linearly to the soft dice loss of the R2UNet as in (3):

$$L_{seg} = w_3 L_{dice} + w_4 L_{edge} \tag{3}$$

4 Results

4.1 Evaluation Metrics

For mass detection task, we used standard metrics like sensitivity, precision and F1-score, and the free receiver operating characteristic (FROC) analysis. The FROC curve shows sensitivity (fraction of correctly localized lesions) as a function of the number of false positive marks on an image. To compute the FROC curve, for each threshold T, the average true-positive rate (TPR) per image versus the average number of false positives per image. A lesion is being correctly predicted if there is a candidate that lies within 1 cm of the center of the mass. The performance of the mass segmentation framework was evaluated with IoU metrics.

4.2 Detection and Segmentation Results

Table 1 compares our method with other state-of-the art object detection methods on the in-house data set. All values displayed are macro averages. First, we can notice the increase by 9% in sensitivity while introducing Libra R-CNN combined with the FPN into our training scheme, followed by a +8% increase in precision and an overall increase of +7% in the overall F1-score. Eventually, adding the specificity of the PAN net architecture, we manage to increase the sensitivity by +2%, the precision by +2% and the general F1-score by almost +3%. The performance of detection framework on INbreast data is also computed with a FROC curve as shown in Table 1. We obtained a maximum sensitivity of 0.95 with 0.3 false positives per image at a detection confidence threshold of 0.6. This is the highest sensitivity reached on INBreast. The qualitative assessment of segmentation framework is depicted in Fig. 4. Table 2 compares different segmentation IOUs depending on current state-of-the art models.

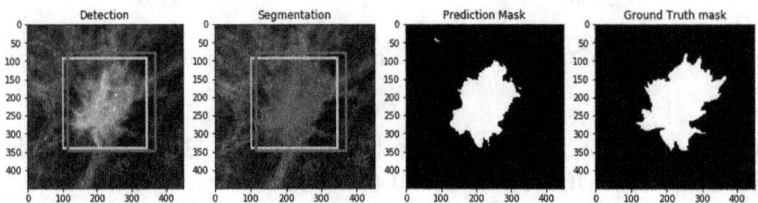

Fig. 4. Lesion detection and segmentation with proposed framework. Red bounding box is the prediction while Green bounding box is the ground truth. (Color figure online)

Table 1. Comparison between different approaches on test data sets.

Model	Backbone	Neck			Metrics		
		FPN	LibraRCNN	PANet	Recall	Precision	F1-Score
in-house							
Faster R-CNN	Resnet-101	✓			0.74	0.676	0.698
Faster R-CNN	ResNeXt101-32x4d	✓			0.784	0.719	0.741
HRNet w40	HRNet				0.787	0.703	0.729
Cascade R-CNN	ResNeXt101-32x4d	✓	✓		0.829	0.778	0.795
Faster R-CNN	ResNeXt101-32x4d	✓	✓		0.879	0.793	0.818
Faster R-CNN	ResNeXt101-32x4d	✓	✓	✓	**0.896**	**0.819**	**0.843**
INBreast							
Faster R-CNN	ResNeXt101-32x4d	✓	✓	✓	**0.956**	**0.758**	**0.846**

Table 2. Model segmentation metrics on in-house test data set.

Method	Unet	R2UNet	Att-UNet [20]	R2UNet + Edge Loss [28]
IoU	0.801	0.852	0.848	**0.859**

5   Discussion

In this paper, we proposed a novel system that combines an enhanced Faster R-CNN and a Recurrent Residual U-Net for the lesion detection in mammography. Our main contribution relies on trying to tackle the four main object detection imbalance problems, by combining an end-to-end CAD system deployed as we speak in hospitals. Further our paper discusses several approaches on how to increase sensitivity and accuracy in breast cancer detection by handling several key imbalance factors that can limit the networks capacity for object detection.

The lesion detection framework showed promising results in terms of detection sensitivity for benign and malignant lesions. A preprocessing strategy is added to enhance the breast search area to finally improve the overall accuracy. Our experimental results demonstrated that on INbreast data set, the maximum sensitivity was reached at 0.95 for 0.3 false positives per image. We explored that most false positives contain lesions which are too small to provide any conclusion. On the other hand, we extended our experiment to a more recent data set, that contained more samples. Indeed we can see that the results are comparable, the maximum sensitivity is 0.896 at confidence score above 0.6, while maintaining a high F1-score of 0.843.

Our detection framework reaches some limitations when it encounters benign, transparent masses that are under sampled in our data set. More specifically, fat-containing masses have shown difficulties to be detected by our framework. Further, most non-detected masses are present in heavily dense breasts, where the texture of the tissue tends to misclassify regions when provided to RPN. Regarding our Segmentation framework, our method tends to under segment when the edges are not clearly defined, as shown in Fig. 4. When the mass texture is similar to surrounding tissues, the segmentor tends to over segment. This effect is limited by the accurate instance detection within the breast, and additional data augmentation scheme provided to counter this undesired effect of over segmenting unnecessary breast tissue. Under segmentation tends to be significant on ill-defined and obscured masses, as every patch is mean centered, edge pixels with similar tissue intensity as neighborhood pixels might be lost. This would impact the following stages of mass properties classification such as the soft tissue margin.

In order to fully extend our research into how those individual imbalance problems successfully contribute to breast cancer detection, we hope to extend our database to a level where significant improvements could provide useful information for breast screening. In the meantime, we investigate further the prospect of integrating a mass property branch to further analyze individual lesions that would simplify and accelerate the breast screening.

References

1. Moreira, I.C. et al.: INbreast: toward a full-field digital mammographic database. In: Academic Radiology 19.2, pp. 236–248 (2012). https://doi.org/10.1016/j.acra.2011.09.014. http://www.sciencedirect.com/science/article/pii/S1076633211 00451X. ISSN: 1076-6332
2. (2010).   www.cancer.org/cancer/breast-cancer/about/how-common-is-breast-cancer.html
3. Bejnordi, B.E., et al.: Diagnostic assessment of deep learning algorithms for detection of lymph node metastases in women with breast cancer. JAMA Neurol. **318**(22), 2199–2210 (2017). https://doi.org/10.1001/jama.2017.14585
4. (2019). www.cancer.org/latest-news/facts-and-figures-2019.html
5. Alom, M.Z., Yakopcic, C., Hasan, M., Taha, T.M., Asari, V.K.: Recurrent residual u-net for medical image segmentation. J. Med. Imaging **6**(1), 014006 (2019). https://doi.org/10.1117/1.jmi.6.1.014006. https://europepmc.org/articles/PMC6435980
6. Birdwell, R.L., Ikeda, D.M., O'Shaughnessy, K.F., Sickles, E.A.: Mammographic characteristics of 115 missed cancers later detected with screening mammography and the potential utility of computer-aided detection. Radiology **219**(1), 192–202 (2001). https://doi.org/10.1148/radiology.219.1.r01ap16192. pMID: 11274556
7. Deng, J., Dong, W., Socher, R., Li, L., Li, K., Fei-Fei, L.: Imagenet: a large-scale hierarchical image database, pp. 248–255 (2009)
8. Dhungel, N., Carneiro, G., Bradley, A.P.: Automated mass detection in mammograms using cascaded deep learning and random forests, pp. 1–8 (2015)
9. Girshick, R.: Fast R-CNN (2015)
10. Girshick, R., Donahue, J., Darrell, T., Malik, J.: Rich feature hierarchies for accurate object detection and semantic segmentation (2013)
11. He, K., Gkioxari, G., Dollár, P., Girshick, R.: Mask R-CNN (2017)
12. Hoff, S.R., Abrahamsen, A.L., Samset, J.H., Vigeland, E., Klepp, O., Hofvind, S.: Breast cancer: missed interval and screening-detected cancer at full-field digital mammography and screen-film mammography–results from a retrospective review. Radiology **264**(2), 378–386 (2012). https://doi.org/10.1148/radiol.12112074. pMID: 22700555

13. Jung, H., et al.: Detection of masses in mammograms using a one-stage object detector based on a deep convolutional neural network. PLoS ONE **13** (2018). https://doi.org/10.1371/journal.pone.0203355
14. Kooi, T., Litjens, G., Van Ginneken, B., et al.: Large scale deep learning for computer aided detection of mammographic lesions. Med. Image Anal. **35**, 303–312 (2017). https://doi.org/10.1016/j.media.2016.07.007
15. Lin, T.Y., Dollár, P., Girshick, R., He, K., Hariharan, B., Belongie, S.: Feature pyramid networks for object detection (2016)
16. Lin, T.Y., et al.: Microsoft coco: common objects in context (2014)
17. Litjens, G., et al.: A survey on deep learning in medical image analysis. Med. Image Anal. **42**, 60–88 (2017). https://doi.org/10.1016/j.media.2017.07.005
18. Liu, S., Qi, L., Qin, H., Shi, J., Jia, J.: Path aggregation network for instance segmentation (2018)
19. Moss, S.M., Nyström, L., Jonsson, H., et al.: The impact of mammographic screening on breast cancer mortality in Europe: a review of trend studies. J. Med. Screen. **19**(Suppl. 1), 26–32 (2012). https://doi.org/10.1258/jms.2012.012079
20. Oktay, O., et al.: Attention u-net: learning where to look for the pancreas (2018)
21. Pang, J., Chen, K., Shi, J., Feng, H., Ouyang, W., Lin, D.: Libra R-CNN: towards balanced learning for object detection (2019)
22. Ren, S., He, K., Girshick, R., Sun, J.: Faster R-CNN: towards real-time object detection with region proposal networks (2015)
23. Ronneberger, O., Fischer, P., Brox, T.: U-net: convolutional networks for biomedical image segmentation (2015)
24. Russakovsky, O., et al.: ImageNet large scale visual recognition challenge. Int. J. Comput. Vision **115**(3), 211–252 (2015). https://doi.org/10.1007/s11263-015-0816-y
25. Shen, L., Margolies, L.R., Rothstein, J.H., Fluder, E., McBride, R., Sieh, W.: Deep learning to improve breast cancer detection on screening mammography. Sci. Rep. **9**(1) (2019). https://doi.org/10.1038/s41598-019-48995-4
26. Sun, H., Li, C., Liu, B., Zheng, H., Feng, D.D., Wang, S.: Aunet: attention-guided dense-upsampling networks for breast mass segmentation in whole mammograms (2018)
27. Xie, S., Girshick, R., Dollár, P., Tu, Z., He, K.: Aggregated residual transformations for deep neural networks (2016)
28. Zimmermann, R.S., Siems, J.N.: Faster training of mask R-CNN by focusing on instance boundaries. Comput. Vis. Image Underst. **188**, 102795 (2019). https://doi.org/10.1016/j.cviu.2019.102795

Efficient and Phase-Aware Video Super-Resolution for Cardiac MRI

Jhih-Yuan Lin[(✉)], Yu-Cheng Chang, and Winston H. Hsu

National Taiwan University, Taipei, Taiwan
peter850706@gmail.com

Abstract. Cardiac Magnetic Resonance Imaging (CMR) is widely used since it can illustrate the structure and function of the heart in a non-invasive and painless way. However, it is time-consuming and high-cost to acquire high-quality scans due to the hardware limitation. To this end, we propose a novel end-to-end trainable network to solve CMR video super-resolution problem without the hardware upgrade and the scanning protocol modifications. We incorporate the cardiac knowledge into our model to assist in utilizing the temporal information. Specifically, we formulate the cardiac knowledge as the periodic function, which is tailored to meet the cyclic characteristic of CMR. Besides, the proposed residual of residual learning scheme facilitates the network to learn the LR-HR mapping in a progressive refinement fashion. This mechanism enables the network to have the adaptive capability by adjusting refinement iterations depending on the difficulty of the task. Extensive experimental results on large-scale datasets demonstrate the superiority of the proposed method compared with numerous state-of-the-art methods.

Keywords: Cardiac MRI · Video super-resolution

1 Introduction

Magnetic Resonance Imaging (MRI) has been widely used to examine almost any part of the body since it can depict the structure inside the human non-invasively and produce high contrast images. Notably, cardiac MRI (CMR) assessing cardiac structure and function plays a key role in evidence-based diagnostic and therapeutic pathways in cardiovascular disease [13], including the assessment of myocardial ischemia, cardiomyopathies, myocarditis, congenital heart disease [14]. However, obtaining high-resolution CMR is time-consuming and high-cost as it is sensitive to the changes in the cardiac cycle length and respiratory position [23], which is rarely clinically applicable.

To address this issue, the single image super-resolution (SISR) technique, which aims at reconstructing a high-resolution (HR) image from low-resolution (LR) one, holds a great promise that does not need to change the hardware or

---

J.-Y. Lin and Y.-C. Chang—Equal contribution.

© Springer Nature Switzerland AG 2020
A. L. Martel et al. (Eds.): MICCAI 2020, LNCS 12264, pp. 66–76, 2020.
https://doi.org/10.1007/978-3-030-59719-1_7

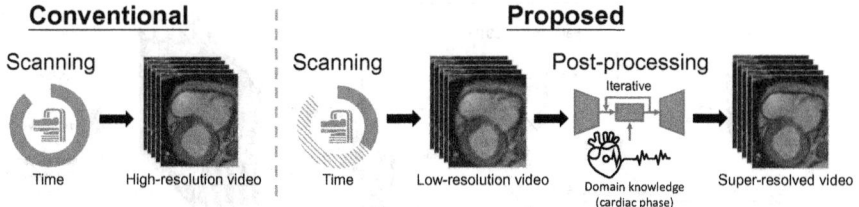

Fig. 1. We present efficient post-processing to facilitate the acquisition of high-quality cardiac MRI (CMR) that is conventionally time-consuming, high-cost, and sensitive to the changes in the cardiac cycle length and respiratory position [23]. Specifically, we utilize the domain knowledge and iteratively enhance low-resolution CMR by a neural network, which can reduce the scan time and cost without changing the hardware or scanning protocol.

scanning protocol. Most of the MRI SISR approaches [3, 21, 24] are based on the deep learning-based methods [5, 16], which learn the LR-HR mapping with extensive LR-HR paired data. On the other hand, several previous studies [11, 31] adapt the self-similarity based SISR algorithm [8], which does not need external HR data for training. However, straightforwardly employing the aforementioned methods is not appropriate for CMR video reconstruction since the relationship among the consecutive frames in CMR video is not well considered. Therefore, we adopt the video super-resolution (VSR) technique, which can properly leverage the temporal information and has been applied in numerous works [7, 10, 22, 27, 30], to perform CMR video reconstruction.

In this work, we propose an end-to-end trainable network to address CMR VSR problem. To well consider the temporal information, we choose ConvL-STM [28], which has been proven effective [6, 9], as our backbone. Moreover, we introduce the domain knowledge (*i.e.*, cardiac phase), which has shown to be important for the measurement of the stroke volume [15] and disease diagnosis [29], to provide the direct guidance about the temporal relationship in a cardiac cycle. Combined with the proposed *phase fusion module*, the model can better utilize the temporal information. Last but not the least, we devise the *residual of residual learning* inspired by the iterative error feedback mechanism [2, 19] to guide the model iteratively recover the lost details. Different from other purely feed-forward approaches [10, 18, 22, 27, 30], our iterative learning strategy can make the model easier in representing the LR-HR mapping with fewer parameters.

We evaluate our model and multiple state-of-the-art baselines on two synthetic datasets established by mimicking the acquisition of MRI [4, 31] from two publicly datasets [1, 26]. It is worth noting that one of them is totally for external evaluation. To properly assess the model performance, we introduce the cardiac metrics based on PSNR and SSIM. The experimental results turn out that the proposed network can stand out from existing methods even on the large-scale external dataset, which indicates our model has the generalization ability. To

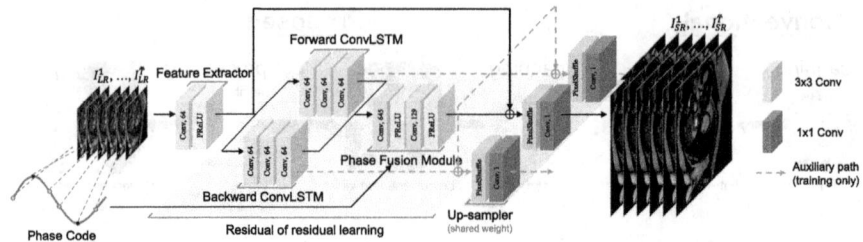

Fig. 2. Model overview. The bidirectional ConvLSTM [28] utilizes the temporal information from forward and backward directions. The *phase fusion module* exploits the informative phase code to leverage the bidirectional features. With the *residual of residual learning*, the network recovers the results in a coarse-to-fine fashion. Auxiliary paths are adopted for stabilizing the training procedure.

our best knowledge, this work is the pioneer to address the CMR VSR problem and provide a benchmark to facilitate the development in this domain.

2   Proposed Approach

Let $I_{LR}^t \in \mathbb{R}^{H \times W}$ denote the t-th LR frame obtained by down-sampling the original HR frame $I_{HR}^t \in \mathbb{R}^{rH \times rW}$ with the scale factor r. Given a sequence of LR frames denoted as $\{I_{LR}^t\}$, the proposed end-to-end trainable model aims to estimate the corresponding high-quality results $\{I_{SR}^t\}$ that approximate the ground truth frames $\{I_{HR}^t\}$. Besides, $\oplus$ refers to the element-wise addition.

2.1   Overall Architecture

Our proposed network is illustrated in Fig. 2. It consists of a feature extractor, a bidirectional ConvLSTM [28], a phase fusion module, and an up-sampler. The feature extractor (FE) first exploits the frame I_{LR}^t to obtain the low-frequency feature L^t. Subsequently, the bidirectional ConvLSTM [28] comprising a forward ConvLSTM ($ConvLSTM_F$) and a backward ConvLSTM ($ConvLSTM_B$) makes use of the low-frequency feature L^t to generate the high-frequency features H_F^t, H_B^t. With the help of its memory mechanism, the bidirectional ConvLSTM can fully utilize the temporal relationship among consecutive frames in both directions. In addition, we can update the memory cells in the bidirectional ConvLSTM in advance instead of starting with the empty states due to the cyclic characteristic of the cardiac videos. This can be done by feeding n consequent updated frames before and after the input sequence $\{I_{LR}^t\}$ to the network.

Furthermore, to completely integrate the bidirectional features, the designed phase fusion module (PF) applies the cardiac knowledge of the $2N + 1$ successive frames from $t - N$ to $t + N$ in the form of the phase code $P^{[t-N:t+N]}$, which can be formulated as $H_P^t = PF(H_F^{[t-N:t+N]}, H_B^{[t-N:t+N]}, P^{[t-N:t+N]})$, where H_P^t represents the fused high-frequency feature. After that, the fused

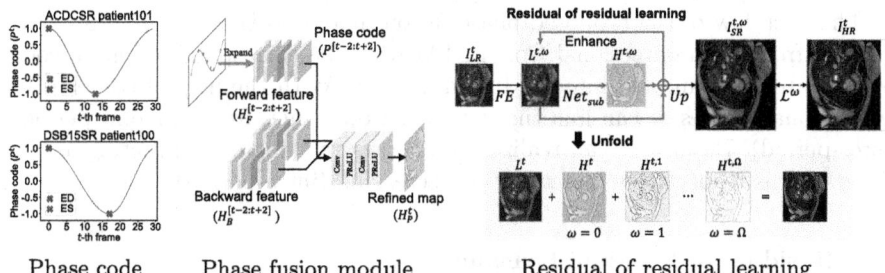

Phase code   Phase fusion module   Residual of residual learning

Fig. 3. Proposed components. (a) *Phase code* formulated as the periodic function contains domain knowledge (*i.e.*, cardiac phase). (b) *Phase fusion module* can realize the phase of the current sequence with the cardiac knowledge to thoroughly integrate the bidirectional features. (c) *Residual of residual learning* aims at directing the model to reconstruct the results in a coarse-to-fine manner.

high-frequency feature H_P^t combined with the low-frequency feature L^t through the global skip connection is up-scaled by the up-sampler (Up) into the super-resolved image $I_{SR}^t = Up(H_P^t \oplus L^t)$. We further define the sub-network (Net_{sub}) as the combination of $ConvLSTM_F, ConvLSTM_B$ and PF. The purpose of Net_{sub} is to recover the high-frequency residual $H_P^t = Net_{sub}(L^t)$. Besides, we employ the deep supervision technique [17] to provide the additional gradient signal and stabilize the training process by adding two auxiliary paths, namely $I_{SR,F}^t = Up(H_F^t \oplus L^t)$ and $I_{SR,B}^t = Up(H_B^t \oplus L^t)$. Finally, we propose the residual of residual learning that progressively restores the residual that has yet to be recovered in each refinement stage ω. To simplify the notation, ω is omitted when it equals to 0, *e.g.*, L_F^t means the low-frequency feature of the t-th frame at the 0-th stage $L_F^{t,0}$.

2.2   Phase Fusion Module

The cardiac cycle is a cyclic sequence of events when the heart beats, which consists of systole and diastole process. Identification of the end-systole (ES) and the end-diastole (ED) in a cardiac cycle has been proved critical in several applications, such as the measurement of the ejection fraction and stroke volume [15], and disease diagnosis [29]. Hence, we embed the physical meaning of the input frames into our model with the informative phase code generated by projecting the cardiac cycle to the periodic Cosine function as depicted in Fig. 3a. Specifically, we map the process of the systole and the diastole to the half-period cosine separately:

$$P^t = \begin{cases} Cos(\pi \times \frac{t-ED}{ES-ED}), & \text{if } ED < t \leq ES \\ Cos(\pi \times (1 + \frac{(t-ES)\%T}{T-(ES-ED)})), & \text{otherwise} \end{cases} \tag{1}$$

where % denotes modulo operation and T is the frame number in a cardiac cycle.

The overview of the proposed phase fusion module is shown in Fig. 3b. The features from the bidirectional ConvLSTM with the corresponding phase code are concatenated and fed into the fusion module. With the help of consecutive $2N + 1$ phase codes, it can link the same-position frames from different periods (inter-period). Besides, it can realize the heart is relaxing or contracting as the phase code is respectively increasing or decreasing (intra-period).

2.3   Residual of Residual Learning

In the computer vision field, the iterative error-correcting mechanism plays an essential role in several topics, such as reinforcement learning [19], scene reconstruction [20], and human pose estimation [2]. Inspired by this mechanism, we propose the residual of residual learning composing the reconstruction process into multiple stages, as shown in Fig. 3c. At each stage, the sub-network (Net_{sub}) in our model estimates the high-frequency residual based on the current low-frequency feature, and then the input low-frequency feature is updated for the next refinement stage. Let $L^{t,0}$ be the initial feature from the feature extractor (FE) and $L^{t,\omega}$ denote the updated feature at the iteration ω, the residual of residual learning for Ω stages can be described as the recursive format:

$$L^{t,\omega} = \begin{cases} FE(I_{LR}^t), & \text{when } \omega = 0 \\ L^{t,\omega-1} \oplus Net_{sub}(L^{t,\omega-1}), & \text{if } 0 < \omega \leq \Omega \end{cases} \tag{2}$$

Then, the network generates the super-resolution result $I_{SR}^{t,\omega}$ based on the current reconstructed feature $L^{t,\omega}$, which can be written as:

$$I_{SR}^{t,\omega} = Up(L^{t,\omega} \oplus Net_{sub}(L^{t,\omega})) \tag{3}$$

The model progressively restores the residual that has yet to be recovered in each refinement stage, which is so-called the residual of residual learning. Compared to other one-step approaches [10,18,22,27,30], the proposed mechanism tries to break down the ill-posed problem into several easier sub-problems in the manner of divide-and-conquer. Most notably, it can dynamically adjust the iteration number depending on the problem difficulty without any additional parameters.

2.4   Loss Function

In this section, we elaborate on the mathematical formulation of our cost function. At each refinement stage ω, the super-resolved frames $\{I_{SR}^{t,\omega}\}$ are supervised by the ground-truth HR video $\{I_{HR}^t\}$, which can be formulated as $\mathcal{L}^\omega = \frac{1}{\tilde{T}} \sum_{t=1}^{\tilde{T}} \parallel I_{SR}^{t,\omega} - I_{HR}^t \parallel_1$, where $\tilde{T}$ indicates the length of the video sequence fed into the network. We choose the L1 loss as the cost function since the previous works have demonstrated that the L1 loss provides better convergence compared to the widely used L2 loss [18,32]. Besides, we apply the deep

Table 1. Quantitative results. The red and blue indicate the best and the second-best performance, respectively. We adopt CardiacPSNR/CardiacSSIM to fairly assess the reconstruction quality of the heart region. It is worth noting that the large-scale DSB15SR dataset is entirely for external evaluation.

Dataset	Scale	SISR			VSR				Model (Ours)
		Bicubic	EDSR[18]	DUF[10]	EDVR[27]	RBPN[7]	TOFlow[30]	FRVSR[22]	
ACDCSR	×2	33.0927 / 0.9362	37.3022 / 0.9681	37.4008 / 0.9688	- / -	37.5017 / 0.9694	36.6510 / 0.9641	- / -	37.5003 / 0.9696
	×3	29.0724 / 0.8472	32.8177 / 0.9201	32.7942 / 0.9203	- / -	32.9099 / 0.9225	32.4535 / 0.9136	- / -	32.9342 / 0.9231
	×4	26.9961 / 0.7611	30.2536 / 0.8631	30.2420 / 0.8621	30.2817 / 0.8655	30.3294 / 0.8653	30.0087 / 0.8538	30.1693 / 0.8592	30.4060 / 0.8668
DSB15SR	×2	34.1661 / 0.9597	40.1723 / 0.9815	40.3548 / 0.9822	- / -	40.3792 / 0.9824	39.5042 / 0.9794	- / -	40.4635 / 0.9821
	×3	29.1175 / 0.8854	33.9893 / 0.9424	33.9736 / 0.9428	- / -	34.1320 / 0.9445	33.6656 / 0.9386	- / -	34.2169 / 0.9451
	×4	26.5157 / 0.8065	30.6354 / 0.8907	30.7411 / 0.8918	30.8564 / 0.8949	30.7985 / 0.8933	30.3153 / 0.8836	30.5800 / 0.8889	30.9104 / 0.8956

supervision technique as described in Sect. 2.1 by adding two auxiliary losses $\mathcal{L}_F^\omega = \frac{1}{T}\sum_{t=1}^{\tilde{T}} \parallel I_{SR,F}^{t,\omega} - I_{HR}^t \parallel_1$ and $\mathcal{L}_B^\omega = \frac{1}{T}\sum_{t=1}^{\tilde{T}} \parallel I_{SR,B}^{t,\omega} - I_{HR}^t \parallel_1$. Hence, the total loss function can be summarized as $\mathcal{L} = \sum_{\omega=0}^{\Omega}(\mathcal{L}^\omega + \mathcal{L}_F^\omega + \mathcal{L}_B^\omega)$, where Ω denoted as the total number of refinement stages.

3 Experiment

3.1 Experimental Settings

Data Preparation. To our best knowledge, there is no publicly available CMR dataset for the VSR problem. Hence, we create two datasets named ACDCSR and DSB15SR based on the public MRI datasets. One is the Automated Cardiac Diagnosis Challenge dataset [1], which contains four dimension MRI scans of a total of 150 patients. The other is the large-scale Second Annual Data Science Bowl Challenge dataset [26] composed of 2D cine MRI videos that contain 30 images across the cardiac cycle per sequence. We use its testing dataset comprising 440 patients as the external assessment to verify the robustness and generalization of the algorithms. To more accurately mimic the acquisition of LR MRI scans [4,31], we project the HR MRI videos to the frequency domain by Fourier transform and filter the high-frequency information. After that, we apply the inverse Fourier transform to project the videos back to the spatial domain and further downsample by bicubic interpolation with the scale factor 2, 3, and 4.

Evaluation Metrics. PSNR and SSIM criteria have been widely used in previous studies to evaluate the SR algorithms. However, the considerable disparity of the proportion of the cardiac region to the background region in MRI images makes the results heavily biased towards the insignificant background region. Therefore, we introduce CardiacPSNR and CardiacSSIM to assess the performance more impartially and objectively. Specifically, we employ a heart ROI detection method similar to [25] to crop the cardiac region and calculate PSNR and SSIM in this region. This can reduce the influence of the background region and more accurately reflect the reconstruction quality of the heart region.

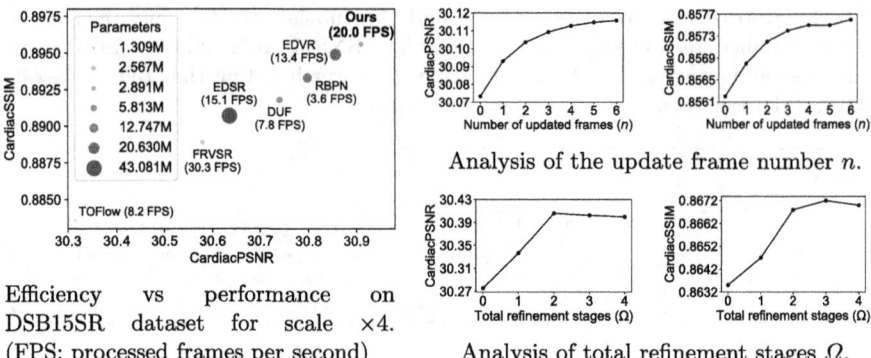

Efficiency vs performance on DSB15SR dataset for scale ×4. (FPS: processed frames per second)

Analysis of the update frame number n.

Analysis of total refinement stages Ω.

Fig. 4. Experimental analysis. (a) Our network outperforms other baselines with fewer parameters and higher FPS. (b) The performance is progressively enhanced as n increases, which indicates that the prior sequence can provide useful information. (c) The performance can be improved with Ω increasing.

Training Details. For training, we randomly crop the LR clips of $\tilde{T} = 7$ consecutive frames of size 32×32 with the corresponding HR clips. We experimentally choose $n = 6$ and $\Omega = 2$ as detailed in Sect. 3.3, while $N = 2$ in the phase fusion module. We use the Adam optimizer [12] with learning rate 10^{-4} and set the batch size to 16. For other baselines, we basically follow their original settings except the necessary modifications to train them from the scratch.

3.2   Experimental Results

To confirm the superiority of the proposed approach, we compare our network with multiple state-of-the-art methods, namely EDSR [18], DUF [10], EDVR [27], RBPN [7], TOFlow [30], and FRVSR [22]. We present the quantitative and qualitative results in Table 1 and Fig. 5 respectively. Our approach outperforms almost all the existing methods by a huge margin in all scales in terms of CardiacPSNR and CardiacSSIM. In addition, our method can yield

Table 2. Ablation study. *Memory*: the memory cells in the ConvLSTM [28] are activated; *Updated memory*: the memory cells are updated by feeding n consecutive frames; *Bidirection*: bidirectional ConvLSTM is adopted; *Phase fusion module* and *Residual of residual learning*: the proposed components are adopted.

Memory	Updated memory ($n = 6$)	Bidirection	Phase fusion module	Residual of residual learning ($\Omega = 2$)	CardiacPSNR/CardiacSSIM
					29.7580 / 0.8458
✓					30.0733 / 0.8562
✓	✓				30.1790 / 0.8596
✓	✓	✓			30.2380 / 0.8623
✓	✓	✓	✓		30.2754 / 0.8635
✓	✓	✓	✓	✓	**30.4060 / 0.8668**

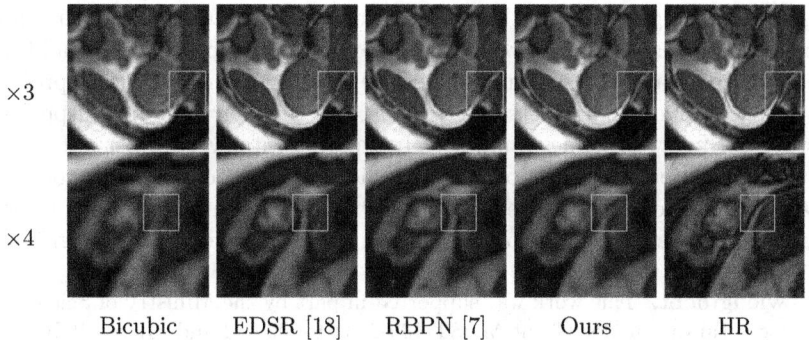

$\times 3$

$\times 4$

Bicubic   EDSR [18]   RBPN [7]   Ours   HR

Fig. 5. Qualitative results. Zoom in to see better visualization.

more clear and photo-realistic SR results which subjectively closer to the ground truths. Moreover, the results on the external DSB15SR dataset are sufficiently convincing to validate the generalization of the proposed approach. On the other hand, the comparison with regard to the model parameters, FPS, and the image quality in the cardiac region plotted in Fig. 4a demonstrates that our method strikes the best balance between efficiency and reconstruction performance.

3.3 Ablation Study

We adopt the unidirectional ConvLSTM as the simplest baseline. As shown in the Table 2, the temporal information is important since the model performance is worse when the memory cells in ConvLSTM are disabled. As the cardiac MRI video is cyclic, we can refresh the memory by feeding n successive frames. Accordingly, we analyze the relation between n and model performance. The result in Fig. 4b turns out that the network significantly improves as the updated frame number increases. Moreover, the forward and backward information is shown to be useful and complementary for recovering the lost details.

In Sect. 2.2, we exploit the knowledge of the cardiac phase to better fuse the bidirectional information. The result in Table 2 reveals that the phase fusion module can leverage the bidirectional temporal features more effectively. Besides, we explore the influence of the total number of refinement stages Ω in the residual of residual learning. It can be observed from Fig. 4c that the reconstruction performance is improved as the total refinement stages continue to increase. The possible reason for the saturation or degradation of the overall performance when Ω equals to 3 or 4 is overfitting (violate the Occam's razor).

4   Conclusion

In this work, we define the cyclic cardiac MRI video super-resolution problem which has not yet been completely solved to our best knowledge. To tackle this issue, we bring the cardiac knowledge into our network and employ the residual of residual learning to train in the progressive refinement manner, which enables the model to generate sharper results with fewer model parameters. In addition, we build large-scale datasets and introduce cardiac metrics for this problem. Through extensive experiments, we demonstrate that our network outperforms the state-of-the-art baselines qualitatively and quantitatively. Most notably, we carry out the external evaluation, which indicates our model exhibits good generalization behavior. We believe our approach can be seamlessly applied to other modalities such as computed tomography angiography and echocardiography.

Acknowledgment. This work was supported in part by the Ministry of Science and Technology, Taiwan, under Grant MOST 109-2634-F-002-032 and Microsoft Research Asia. We are grateful to the NVIDIA grants and the DGX-1 AI Supercomputer and the National Center for High-performance Computing. We thank Dr. Chih-Kuo Lee, National Taiwan University Hospital, for the early discussions.

References

1. Bernard, O., et al.: Deep learning techniques for automatic MRI cardiac multi-structures segmentation and diagnosis: is the problem solved? IEEE Trans. Med. Imaging **37**(11), 2514–2525 (2018)
2. Carreira, J., Agrawal, P., Fragkiadaki, K., Malik, J.: Human pose estimation with iterative error feedback. In: Proceedings of the IEEE Conference on Computer Vision and Pattern Recognition, pp. 4733–4742 (2016)
3. Chen, Y., Shi, F., Christodoulou, A.G., Xie, Y., Zhou, Z., Li, D.: Efficient and accurate MRI super-resolution using a generative adversarial network and 3D multi-level densely connected network. In: Frangi, A.F., Schnabel, J.A., Davatzikos, C., Alberola-López, C., Fichtinger, G. (eds.) MICCAI 2018. LNCS, vol. 11070, pp. 91–99. Springer, Cham (2018). https://doi.org/10.1007/978-3-030-00928-1_11
4. Chen, Y., Xie, Y., Zhou, Z., Shi, F., Christodoulou, A.G., Li, D.: Brain MRI super resolution using 3D deep densely connected neural networks. In: 2018 IEEE 15th International Symposium on Biomedical Imaging (ISBI 2018), pp. 739–742. IEEE (2018)
5. Dong, C., Loy, C.C., He, K., Tang, X.: Image super-resolution using deep convolutional networks. IEEE Trans. Pattern Anal. Mach. Intell. **38**(2), 295–307 (2015)
6. Finn, C., Goodfellow, I., Levine, S.: Unsupervised learning for physical interaction through video prediction. In: Advances in Neural Information Processing Systems, pp. 64–72 (2016)
7. Haris, M., Shakhnarovich, G., Ukita, N.: Recurrent back-projection network for video super-resolution. arXiv preprint arXiv:1903.10128 (2019)
8. Huang, J.B., Singh, A., Ahuja, N.: Single image super-resolution from transformed self-exemplars. In: Proceedings of the IEEE Conference on Computer Vision and Pattern Recognition, pp. 5197–5206 (2015)
9. Huang, Y., Wang, W., Wang, L.: Bidirectional recurrent convolutional networks for multi-frame super-resolution. In: Advances in Neural Information Processing Systems, pp. 235–243 (2015)
10. Jo, Y., Wug Oh, S., Kang, J., Joo Kim, S.: Deep video super-resolution network using dynamic upsampling filters without explicit motion compensation. In: Proceedings of the IEEE Conference on Computer Vision and Pattern Recognition, pp. 3224–3232 (2018)

11. Jog, A., Carass, A., Prince, J.L.: Self super-resolution for magnetic resonance images. In: Ourselin, S., Joskowicz, L., Sabuncu, M.R., Unal, G., Wells, W. (eds.) MICCAI 2016. LNCS, vol. 9902, pp. 553–560. Springer, Cham (2016). https://doi.org/10.1007/978-3-319-46726-9_64

12. Kingma, D.P., Ba, J.: Adam: a method for stochastic optimization. arXiv preprint arXiv:1412.6980 (2014)

13. von Knobelsdorff-Brenkenhoff, F., Pilz, G., Schulz-Menger, J.: Representation of cardiovascular magnetic resonance in the AHA/ACC guidelines. J. Cardiovasc. Magn. Reson. **19**(1), 70 (2017). https://doi.org/10.1186/s12968-017-0385-z

14. von Knobelsdorff-Brenkenhoff, F., Schulz-Menger, J.: Role of cardiovascular magnetic resonance in the guidelines of the European society of cardiology. J. Cardiovasc. Magn. Reson. **18**(1), 6 (2015). https://doi.org/10.1186/s12968-016-0225-6

15. Lalande, A., et al.: Left ventricular ejection fraction calculation from automatically selected and processed diastolic and systolic frames in short-axis cine-mri. J. Cardiovasc. Magn. Reson. **6**(4), 817–827 (2004)

16. Ledig, C., et al.: Photo-realistic single image super-resolution using a generative adversarial network. In: Proceedings of the IEEE Conference on Computer Vision and Pattern Recognition, pp. 4681–4690 (2017)

17. Lee, C.Y., Xie, S., Gallagher, P., Zhang, Z., Tu, Z.: Deeply-supervised nets. In: Artificial Intelligence and Statistics, pp. 562–570 (2015)

18. Lim, B., Son, S., Kim, H., Nah, S., Mu Lee, K.: Enhanced deep residual networks for single image super-resolution. In: Proceedings of the IEEE Conference on Computer Vision and Pattern Recognition Workshops, pp. 136–144 (2017)

19. Mnih, V., et al.: Playing atari with deep reinforcement learning. arXiv preprint arXiv:1312.5602 (2013)

20. Montemerlo, M., Thrun, S., Koller, D., Wegbreit, B., et al.: FastSLAM: a factored solution to the simultaneous localization and mapping problem. In: AAAI/IAAI, pp. 593–598 (2002)

21. Pham, C.H., Ducournau, A., Fablet, R., Rousseau, F.: Brain MRI super-resolution using deep 3D convolutional networks. In: 2017 IEEE 14th International Symposium on Biomedical Imaging (ISBI 2017), pp. 197–200. IEEE (2017)

22. Sajjadi, M.S., Vemulapalli, R., Brown, M.: Frame-recurrent video super-resolution. In: Proceedings of the IEEE Conference on Computer Vision and Pattern Recognition, pp. 6626–6634 (2018)

23. Salerno, M., et al.: Recent advances in cardiovascular magnetic resonance: techniques and applications. Circ.: Cardiovasc. Imaging **10**(6), e003951 (2017)

24. Shi, J., Liu, Q., Wang, C., Zhang, Q., Ying, S., Xu, H.: Super-resolution reconstruction of MR image with a novel residual learning network algorithm. Phys. Med. Biol. **63**(8), 085011 (2018)

25. Tautz, L., Friman, O., Hennemuth, A., Seeger, A., Peitgen, H.O.: Automatic detection of a heart ROI in perfusion MRI images. In: Handels, H., Ehrhardt, J., Deserno, T., Meinzer, H.P., Tolxdorff, T. (eds.) Bildverarbeitung für die Medizin 2011, pp. 259–263. Springer, Heidelberg (2011). https://doi.org/10.1007/978-3-642-19335-4_54

26. National Heart, Lung, and Blood Institute: Data science bowl cardiac challenge data (2015)

27. Wang, X., Chan, K.C., Yu, K., Dong, C., Change Loy, C.: EDVR: video restoration with enhanced deformable convolutional networks. In: Proceedings of the IEEE Conference on Computer Vision and Pattern Recognition Workshops (2019)

28. Xingjian, S., Chen, Z., Wang, H., Yeung, D.Y., Wong, W.K., Woo, W.C.: Convolutional LSTM network: a machine learning approach for precipitation nowcasting. In: Advances in Neural Information Processing Systems, pp. 802–810 (2015)

29. Xu, H.Y., et al.: Volume-time curve of cardiac magnetic resonance assessed left ventricular dysfunction in coronary artery disease patients with type 2 diabetes mellitus. BMC Cardiovasc. Disord. **17**(1), 145 (2017). https://doi.org/10.1186/s12872-017-0583-5

30. Xue, T., Chen, B., Wu, J., Wei, D., Freeman, W.T.: Video enhancement with task-oriented flow. Int. J. Comput. Vision **127**(8), 1106–1125 (2019)

31. Zhao, C., Carass, A., Dewey, B.E., Prince, J.L.: Self super-resolution for magnetic resonance images using deep networks. In: 2018 IEEE 15th International Symposium on Biomedical Imaging (ISBI 2018), pp. 365–368. IEEE (2018)

32. Zhao, H., Gallo, O., Frosio, I., Kautz, J.: Loss functions for neural networks for image processing. arXiv preprint arXiv:1511.08861 (2015)

ImageCHD: A 3D Computed Tomography Image Dataset for Classification of Congenital Heart Disease

Xiaowei Xu[1], Tianchen Wang[2], Jian Zhuang[1], Haiyun Yuan[1], Meiping Huang[1], Jianzheng Cen[1], Qianjun Jia[1], Yuhao Dong[1], and Yiyu Shi[2(✉)]

[1] Guangdong Provincial People's Hospital, Guangzhou, China
`xiao.wei.xu@foxmail.com`, `zhuangjian5413@tom.com`, `huangmeiping@126.com`
[2] University of Notre Dame, Notre Dame, USA
`{twang9,yshi4}@nd.edu`

Abstract. Congenital heart disease (CHD) is the most common type of birth defects, which occurs 1 in every 110 births in the United States. CHD usually comes with severe variations in heart structure and great artery connections that can be classified into many types. Thus highly specialized domain knowledge and time-consuming human process is needed to analyze the associated medical images. On the other hand, due to the complexity of CHD and the lack of dataset, little has been explored on the automatic diagnosis (classification) of CHDs. In this paper, we present ImageCHD, the first medical image dataset for CHD classification. ImageCHD contains 110 3D Computed Tomography (CT) images covering most types of CHD, which is of decent size compared with existing medical imaging datasets. Classification of CHDs requires the identification of large structural changes without any local tissue changes, with limited data. It is an example of a larger class of problems that are quite difficult for current machine-learning based vision methods to solve. To demonstrate this, we further present a baseline framework for automatic classification of CHD, based on a state-of-the-art CHD segmentation method. Experimental results show that the baseline framework can only achieve a classification accuracy of 82.0% under selective prediction scheme with 88.4% coverage, leaving big room for further improvement. We hope that ImageCHD can stimulate further research and lead to innovative and generic solutions that would have an impact in multiple domains. Our dataset is released to the public [1].

Keywords: Dataset · Congenital heart disease · Automatic diagnosis · Computed tomography

1 Introduction

Congenital heart disease (CHD) is the problem with the heart structure that is present at birth, which is the most common type of birth defects [3]. In recent

© Springer Nature Switzerland AG 2020
A. L. Martel et al. (Eds.): MICCAI 2020, LNCS 12264, pp. 77–87, 2020.
https://doi.org/10.1007/978-3-030-59719-1_8

years, noninvasive imaging techniques such as computed tomography (CT) have prevailed in comprehensive diagnosis, intervention decision-making, and regular follow-up for CHD. However, analysis (e.g., segmentation or classification) of these medical images are usually performed manually by experienced cardiovascular radiologists, which is time-consuming and requires highly specialized domain knowledge.

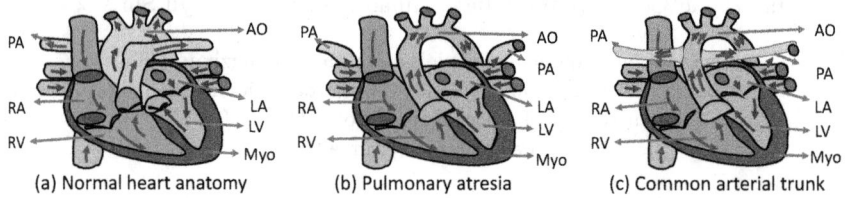

(a) Normal heart anatomy   (b) Pulmonary atresia   (c) Common arterial trunk

Fig. 1. Examples of large heart structure and great artery connection variations in CHD (LV-left ventricle, RV-right ventricle, LA-left atrium, RA-right atrium, Myo-myocardium, AO-aorta and PA-pulmonary artery). Best viewed in color. (Color figure online)

On the other hand, automatic segmentation and classification of medical images in CHD is rather challenging. Patients with CHD typically suffer from severe variation in heart structures and connections between different parts of the anatomy. Two examples are shown in Fig. 1: the disappearance of the main trunk of pulmonary artery (PA) in (b) (c) introduces much difficulty in the correct segmentation of PA and AO. In addition, CHD does not necessarily cause local tissue changes, as in lesions. As such, hearts with CHD have similar local statistics as normal hearts but with global structural changes. Automatic algorithms to detect the disorders need to be able to capture such changes, which require excellent usage of the contextual information. CHD classification is further complicated by the fact that a patient's CT image may exhibit more than one type of CHD, and the number of types is more than 20 [3].

Various works exist in segmentation and classification of heart with *normal anatomy, e.g.,* [4–6,8,9,13,17,20,22–25, ?], most of which are based on deep neural networks (DNNs) [15, ?]. Recently, researchers started to explore heart segmentation in CHD. The works [7,14,18,19,21] adopt DNNs for blood pool and myocardium segmentation only. The only automatic whole heart and great artery segmentation method in CHD [16] in the literature uses a deep learning and shape similarity analysis based method. A 3D CT dataset for CHD segmentation is also released there. In addition to segmentation, there are also some works about classification of adult heart diseases [2] but not CHD. The automatic classification of CHD still remains a missing piece in the literature due to the complexity of CHD and the lack of dataset.

In this paper, we present ImageCHD, the first medical image dataset for CHD classification. ImageCHD contains 110 3D Computed Tomography (CT) images which covers 16 types of CHD. CT images are labelled by a team of four experienced cardiovascular radiologists with 7-substructure segmentation and CHD type classification. The dataset is of decent size compared with other medical imaging datasets [17,21]. We also present a baseline method for automatic CHD classification based on the state-of-the-art CHD segmentation framework [16], which is the first automatic CHD classification method in the literature. Results show that the baseline framework can achieve a classification accuracy of 82.0% under selective prediction scheme with 88.4% coverage, and there is still big room for further improvement.

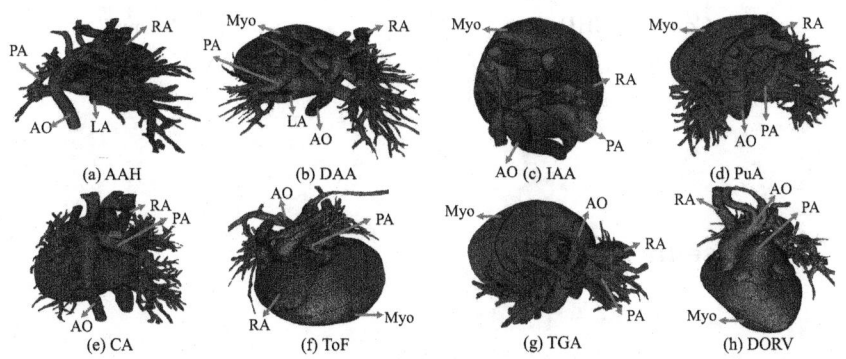

Fig. 2. Examples of CT images in the ImageCHD dataset with its types of CHD.

2   The ImageCHD Dataset

The ImageCHD dataset consists of 3D CT images captured by a Siemens biograph 64 machine from 110 patients, with age 1 month and 40 years (mostly 1 month and 2 years). The size of the images is $512 \times 512 \times (129\text{--}357)$, and the typical voxel size is $0.25 \times 0.25 \times 0.5\,\mathrm{mm}^3$. The dataset covers 16 types of CHD, which include eight common types (atrial septal defect (ASD), atrioventricular septal defect (AVSD), patent ductus arteriosus (PDA), pulmonary atresia (PuA), ventricular septal defect (VSD), co-arctation (CA), tetrology of fallot (TOF), and transposition of great arteries (TGA)) plus eight less common ones (pulmonary artery sling (PAS), double outlet right ventricle (DORV), common arterial trunk (CAT), double aortic arch (DAA), anomalous pulmonary venous drainage (APVC), aortic arch hypoplasia (AAH), interrupted aortic arch (IAA), double superior vena cava (DSVC)). The number of images associated with each is summarized in Table 1. Several examples of images in the dataset are shown in Fig. 2. Due to the structure complexities, the labeling including segmentation and classification is performed by a team of four cardiovascular radiologists who have extensive experience with CHD. The segmentation label of each image is fulfilled by only one radiologist, and its diagnosis is performed by four. The time to label each image is around 1–1.5 h on average. The segmentation include seven substructures: LV, RV, LA, RA, Myo, AO and PA.

Table 1. The types of CHD in the ImageCHD dataset (containing 110 3D CT images) and the associated number of images. Note that some images may correspond to more than one type of CHD.

Common CHD								
ASD	AVSD	VSD	TOF	PDA	TGA	CA	PuA	
26	18	44	12	14	7	6	16	
Less Common CHD								Normal
PAS	DORV	CAT	DAA	APVC	AAH	IAA	DSVC	
3	8	4	5	6	3	3	8	6

3   The Baseline Method

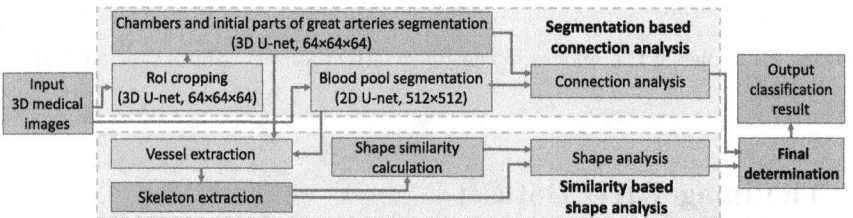

Fig. 3. Overview of the baseline method for CHD classification.

Overview: Due to the lack of baseline method for CHD classification, along with the dataset we establish one as shown in Fig. 3, which modifies and extends the whole heart and great artery segmentation method in CHD [16]. It includes two subtasks: segmentation based connection analysis and similarity based shape analysis. Accordingly, the parts and connections most critical to the classification are extracted.

Segmentation Based Connection Analysis: Segmentation is performed with multiple U-Nets [11]. There are two steps in segmentation: blood pool segmentation, and chambers and initial parts of great arteries segmentation. The former is fulfilled by a high-resolution (input size 512×512) 2D U-net, while the latter is performed with a 3D low-resolution (input size $64 \times 64 \times 64$) 3D U-net. A Region of Interest (RoI) cropping is also included with a 3D U-net before the 3D segmentation. With the segmentation results, connection analysis can be

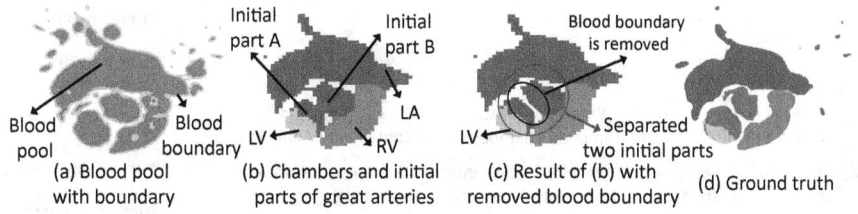

Fig. 4. Connection analysis between LV/RV and great arteries (AO and PA).

processed, which mainly extracts the connection features between great arteries (AO and PA) and LV/RV, and between LV/LA and RV/RA. With the segmentation results, two connection analyses between chambers, AO and PA are then performed by the connection analysis module. The first one analyzes the connections between LV/RV and great arteries. We remove high resolution boundary from low resolution substructures as shown in Fig. 4(a)–(c). Compared with the ground truth in Fig. 4(d), Fig. 4(c) shows that the two initial parts are correctly separated (but not in (b) where they will be treated as connected). The second one has a similar process as the first one.

Similarity Based Shape Analysis: The flow of this subtask is shown in Fig. 5. With the segmentation results, vessel extraction removes the blood pool corresponding to chambers, and vessel refinement removes any remaining small islands in the image, and smooths it with erosion. Then, the skeleton of the vessels are extracted, sampled, normalized, and fed to the shape similarity calculation module to obtain its similarity with all the templates in a pre-defined library. Similarity module is performed using earth mover's distance (EMD) which is a widely used similarity metric for distributions [12]. Two factors need to be modeled: the *weight* of each bin in the distribution, and the *distance* between bins. We model each sampled point in the sampled skeleton as a bin, the Euclidean distance between the points as the distance between bins, and the volume of blood pool around the sampled point as the weight of its corresponding bin. Particularly, the weight is defined as r^3 where r is the radius of the inscribed sphere in the blood pool centered at the sampled point. The template library is manually created in advance and contains six categories of templates corresponding to five types of CHDs and the normal anatomy as shown in Fig. 5, covering all the possible shapes of great arteries in our dataset. Each category contains multiple templates. Finally, the shape analysis module takes the skeleton and its similarities to obtain two kinds of features. The type of the template with the highest similarity is extracted as the first kind. The second kind includes two skeleton features: whether a circle exists in the skeleton, and how the r of the sample points varies. These two features are desired because if there is a circle in the skeleton, the test image is with high possibility to be classified as DAA; If a sampled point with a small r is connected to two sampled points with a much larger r, narrow vessel happens, which is a possible indication of CA and PuA.

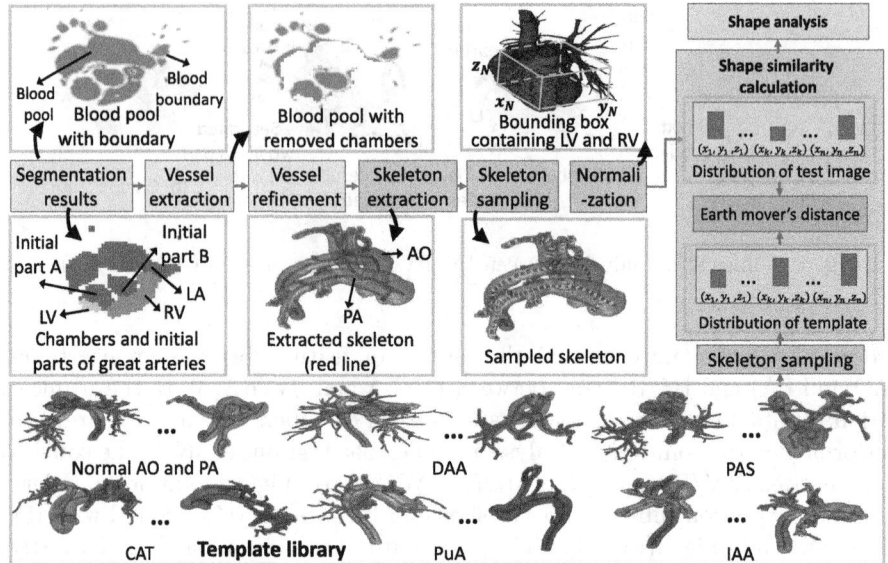

Fig. 5. Similarity based shape analysis of great arteries. Best viewed in color. (Color figure online)

Final Determination: With the extracted connection and shape features, the classification can be finally determined using a rule-based automatic approach. Specifically, ASD and VSD have unexpected connection between LA and RA, and LV and RV, respectively. AVSD is a combination of ASD and VSD, and the three can be classified according to the connection features between LA/LV and RA/RV. DORV has two initial parts of great arteries, both of which are connected to RV. TOF has connected LV and RV, as well as connected LV, RV and the initial part of AO. CHD with specific shapes including CAT, DAA, PuA, PAS and IAA as shown in Fig. 5 can be classified by their shape features. PDA and CA are determined by analyzing the shapes and skeletons such as the variety of r along the skeleton. DSVC can be easily classified by analyzing the skeleton of RV, and APVC is determined by the number of islands that the LA has. Note that if the connection and shape features do not fit any of the above rules, the classifier outputs *uncertain* indicating that the test image cannot be handled and manual classification is needed.

4   Experiment

Experiment Setup: All the experiments run on a Nvidia GTX 1080Ti GPU with 11 GB memory. We implement the 3D U-net using PyTorch based on [8]. For 2D U-net, most configurations remain the same with those of the 3D U-net except that it adopts 5 levels and the number of filters in the initial level is 16. Both Dice loss and cross entropy loss are used, and the training epochs are 2 and 480 for 2D U-net and 3D U-net, respectively. Data augmentation and normalization are also adopted with the same configuration as in [8] for 3D U-net. For both networks and all the analyses, three-fold cross validation is performed (about 37 images for testing, and 73 images for training). We split the dataset such that all types of CHD are present in each subset. The classification considers a total of 17 classes, including 16 types of CHD and the normal anatomy. The templates in the template library are randomly selected from the annotated training set.

In the evaluation, we use selective prediction scheme [10] and report a case as uncertain if at least one chamber is missing (which does not correspond to any type in our dataset) in the segmentation results, or in the similarity calculation the minimum EMD is larger than 0.01. For these cases, manual classification by radiologists is needed. To further evaluate how the baseline method performs against human experts, we also extract manual CT classification from the electronic health records (the manual results can still be wrong).

Results and Analysis: The CHD classification result is shown in Table 2. Each entry (X, Y) in the table corresponds to the number of cases with ground truth class suggested by its row header and predicted class by its column header, where X, and Y are the results from the baseline, and those from radiologists respectively. Again, an image can contribute to multiple cases if it contains more than one types of CHD. From the table we can see that for the baseline method, due to segmentation error or feature extraction failure, 22 cases are classified as uncertain, yielding a 88.4% coverage; Out of the remaining 167 cases, 137 are correct. Thus, for the baseline the overall classification accuracy is 72.5% for full prediction, and 82.0% for selective prediction. For the modified baseline, the overall classification accuracy is 39.2% for full prediction and 50.3% for selective prediction. On the other hand, the manual classification from experienced radiologist can achieve an overall accuracy of 90.5%. It is interesting to note that out of the 17 classes, the baseline method achieves higher accuracy in one (PuA) and breaks even in four (VSD, CAT, DAA, and AAH) compared with manual classification. In addition, Out of the 110 cases, the five radiologists only unanimously agreed on 78 cases, which further reflects the difficulty of the problem and the value of an automated tool.

The mean and standard deviation of Dice score of our baseline method for six substructures of chambers and initial parts of great vessels segmentation, and blood pool segmentation are shown in Table 3. We can notice that blood pool has the highest score, and initial parts of great vessels has the lowest, and the overall segmentation performance is moderate. Though the segmentation performance of initial parts is low, its related types of CHDs (e.g., ToF, TGA) still achieve high classification accuracy which is due to the fact that only the critical segmentation determines the types of CHDs. Comparing the performance of segmentation and classification, we can also notice that accurate segmentation usually helps classification, but not necessarily.

Classification Success: Six types of CHD including TGA, CAT, DAA, AAH, PAS and PuA achieve relatively high accuracy, which is due to their clear and stable features that distinguish them from normal anatomy. Such features can be

Table 2. Number of cases (X, Y) with ground truth class and predicted class suggested by the row and column headers respectively, where X, and Y correspond to automatic classification by the baseline, and manual classification, respectively. Green numbers along the diagonal suggest correct cases. (U-Uncertain, 1-ASD, 2-AVSD, 3-VSD, 4-TOF, 5-PDA, 6-TGA, 7-CA, 8-IAA, 9-PAS, 10-DORV, 11-CAT, 12-DAA, 13-APVC, 14-AAH, 15-PuA, 16-DSVC, N-Normal)

Type	U	1	2	3	4	5	6	7	8	9	10	11	12	13	14	15	16	N
1	6,0	18,24																2,2
2	3,0	1,3	9,14	5,1														
3	1,0	1,2		42,42														
4	1,0			4,2	7,10													
5						7,14												7,0
6	1,0						6,7											
7	1,0						4,6								1,0			
8									2,3									1,0
9	1,0									2,3								
10	1,0		3,1	1,1							3,6							
11												4,4						
12													5,5					
13	1,0													3,6				2,0
14	1,0														2,2			0,1
15	2,0			0,2		0,1						0,1				14,10		
16	1,0															5,7		2,1
N	2,0																	4,6

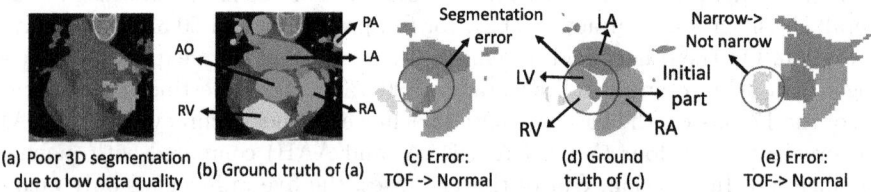

(a) Poor 3D segmentation due to low data quality · (b) Ground truth of (a) · (c) Error: TOF -> Normal · (d) Ground truth of (c) · (e) Error: TOF-> Normal

Fig. 6. Examples of classification failure: uncertain classification in (a–b), and wrong classification of TOF in (c) and (e). Best viewed in color. (Color figure online)

easily captured by either connection or shape features extracted by the baseline method. For example, CAT has a main trunk that AO and PA are both connected to; DAA has a circular vessel which is composed of two aortic arches; PAS has a PA with very different shape; PuA has a very thin PA without main trunk; AAH has a long period of narrow vessels in the arch; and TGA has a reversed connection to LV and RV.

Classification Failure: Test images are classified as uncertain due to segmentation error. Figure 6 shows some examples of such error. The test image in Fig. 6(a) has very low contrast, and its blood pool and boundary are not clear compared with other areas, resulting in segmentation error: compared with the

Table 3. Mean and standard deviation of Dice score of our baseline method (in %) for six substructures of chambers and initial parts of great vessels segmentation, and blood pool segmentation.

LV	RV	LA	RA	Initial parts of great vessels	Blood pool	Average
77.7 ± 16.2	74.6 ± 13.8	77.9 ± 11.2	81.5 ± 11.5	66.5 ± 15.1	86.5 ± 10.5	75.6 ± 10.2

ground truth in Fig. 6(b), only RA and part of the initial parts of great arteries are segmented. As for the cases where a CHD type is predicted but wrong, we will use TOF as examples, and leave the comprehensive discussion for all classes in the supplementary material. Segmentation error around the initial parts of great arteries is the main reason of the classification failure of TOF as shown in Fig. 6. Compared with the ground truth in Fig. 6(d), the 3D segmentation in Fig. 6(c) labels part of LV as RV, resulting in the initial part only connected to RV rather than RV and LV. As one of the main features of TOF is that one initial part is connected to both RV and LV, missing such feature leads to misclassification of TOF as VSD. Another main feature of TOF is the narrow vessels in the initial part and its connected RV part, which can also lead to wrong classification if not detected correctly as shown in Fig. 6(e). A precise threshold to decide whether the vessels are narrow or not is still missing even in clinical studies.

Discussion: We can notice that segmentation accuracy is important for successful classification of CHD. Higher segmentation accuracy can lead to better connection and shape feature extraction. In addition, so far we have only considered the connection features in the blood pool and the shapes of the vessels. More structural features associated with classification should be considered to improve the performance, which due to the lack of local tissue changes, need innovations from the deep learning community and deeper collaboration between computer scientists and radiologists.

5   Conclusion

We introduce to the community the ImageCHD dataset [1] in hopes of encouraging new research into unique, difficult and meaningful datasets. We also present a baseline method for comparison on this new dataset, based on a state-of-the-art whole-heart and great artery segmentation method for CHD images. Experimental results show that under selective prediction scheme the baseline method can achieve a classification accuracy of 82.0%, leaving big room for improvement. We hope that the dataset and the baseline method can encourage new research that be used to better address not only the CHD classification but also a wider class of problems that have large global structural change but little local texture/feature change.

References

1. https://github.com/XiaoweiXu/ImageCHD-A-3D-Computed-Tomography-Image-Dataset-for-Classification-of-Congenital-Heart-Disease
2. Bernard, O., et al.: Deep learning techniques for automatic MRI cardiac multi-structures segmentation and diagnosis: is the problem solved? IEEE Trans. Med. Imaging **37**(11), 2514–2525 (2018)
3. Bhat, V., BeLaVaL, V., Gadabanahalli, K., Raj, V., Shah, S.: Illustrated imaging essay on congenital heart diseases: multimodality approach Part I: clinical perspective, anatomy and imaging techniques. J. Clin. Diagn. Res. JCDR **10**(5), TE01 (2016)
4. Dou, Q., et al.: PnP-AdaNet: plug-and-play adversarial domain adaptation network at unpaired cross-modality cardiac segmentation. IEEE Access **7**, 99065–99076 (2019)
5. Habijan, M., Leventić, H., Galić, I., Babin, D.: Whole heart segmentation from CT images using 3D U-net architecture. In: 2019 International Conference on Systems, Signals and Image Processing (IWSSIP), pp. 121–126. IEEE (2019)
6. Liu, T., Tian, Y., Zhao, S., Huang, X., Wang, Q.: Automatic whole heart segmentation using a two-stage U-net framework and an adaptive threshold window. IEEE Access **7**, 83628–83636 (2019)
7. Pace, D.F., et al.: Iterative segmentation from limited training data: applications to congenital heart disease. In: Stoyanov, D., et al. (eds.) DLMIA/ML-CDS -2018. LNCS, vol. 11045, pp. 334–342. Springer, Cham (2018). https://doi.org/10.1007/978-3-030-00889-5_38
8. Payer, C., Štern, D., Bischof, H., Urschler, M.: Multi-label whole heart segmentation using CNNs and anatomical label configurations. In: Pop, M., et al. (eds.) STACOM 2017. LNCS, vol. 10663, pp. 190–198. Springer, Cham (2018). https://doi.org/10.1007/978-3-319-75541-0_20
9. Piccini, D., Littmann, A., Nielles-Vallespin, S., Zenge, M.O.: Respiratory self-navigation for whole-heart bright-blood coronary MRI: methods for robust isolation and automatic segmentation of the blood pool. Magn. Reson. Med. **68**(2), 571–579 (2012)
10. Pidan, D., El-Yaniv, R.: Selective prediction of financial trends with hidden Markov models. In: Advances in Neural Information Processing Systems, pp. 855–863 (2011)
11. Ronneberger, O., Fischer, P., Brox, T.: U-Net: convolutional networks for biomedical image segmentation. In: Navab, N., Hornegger, J., Wells, W.M., Frangi, A.F. (eds.) MICCAI 2015. LNCS, vol. 9351, pp. 234–241. Springer, Cham (2015). https://doi.org/10.1007/978-3-319-24574-4_28
12. Rubner, Y., Tomasi, C., Guibas, L.J.: The earth mover's distance as a metric for image retrieval. Int. J. Comput. Vision **40**(2), 99–121 (2000)
13. Wang, C., MacGillivray, T., Macnaught, G., Yang, G., Newby, D.: A two-stage 3D Unet framework for multi-class segmentation on full resolution image. arXiv preprint arXiv:1804.04341 (2018)
14. Wolterink, J.M., Leiner, T., Viergever, M.A., Išgum, I.: Dilated convolutional neural networks for cardiovascular MR segmentation in congenital heart disease. In: Zuluaga, M.A., Bhatia, K., Kainz, B., Moghari, M.H., Pace, D.F. (eds.) RAMBO/HVSMR-2016. LNCS, vol. 10129, pp. 95–102. Springer, Cham (2017). https://doi.org/10.1007/978-3-319-52280-7_9

15. Xu, X., et al.: Quantization of fully convolutional networks for accurate biomedical image segmentation. In: Proceedings of the IEEE Conference on Computer Vision and Pattern Recognition, pp. 8300–8308 (2018)

16. Xu, X., et al.: Whole heart and great vessel segmentation in congenital heart disease using deep neural networks and graph matching. In: Shen, D., et al. (eds.) MICCAI 2019. LNCS, vol. 11765, pp. 477–485. Springer, Cham (2019). https://doi.org/10.1007/978-3-030-32245-8_53

17. Xu, Z., Wu, Z., Feng, J.: CFUN: combining faster R-CNN and U-net network for efficient whole heart segmentation. arXiv preprint arXiv:1812.04914 (2018)

18. Yang, X., Bian, C., Yu, L., Ni, D., Heng, P.-A.: Class-balanced deep neural network for automatic ventricular structure segmentation. In: Pop, M., et al. (eds.) STACOM 2017. LNCS, vol. 10663, pp. 152–160. Springer, Cham (2018). https://doi.org/10.1007/978-3-319-75541-0_16

19. Yang, X., Bian, C., Yu, L., Ni, D., Heng, P.-A.: Hybrid loss guided convolutional networks for whole heart parsing. In: Pop, M., et al. (eds.) STACOM 2017. LNCS, vol. 10663, pp. 215–223. Springer, Cham (2018). https://doi.org/10.1007/978-3-319-75541-0_23

20. Ye, C., Wang, W., Zhang, S., Wang, K.: Multi-depth fusion network for whole-heart CT image segmentation. IEEE Access **7**, 23421–23429 (2019)

21. Yu, L., Yang, X., Qin, J., Heng, P.-A.: 3D FractalNet: dense volumetric segmentation for cardiovascular MRI volumes. In: Zuluaga, M.A., Bhatia, K., Kainz, B., Moghari, M.H., Pace, D.F. (eds.) RAMBO/HVSMR-2016. LNCS, vol. 10129, pp. 103–110. Springer, Cham (2017). https://doi.org/10.1007/978-3-319-52280-7_10

22. Zhang, R., Chung, A.C.S.: A fine-grain error map prediction and segmentation quality assessment framework for whole-heart segmentation. In: Shen, D., et al. (eds.) MICCAI 2019. LNCS, vol. 11765, pp. 550–558. Springer, Cham (2019). https://doi.org/10.1007/978-3-030-32245-8_61

23. Zheng, H., et al.: HFA-Net: 3D cardiovascular image segmentation with asymmetrical pooling and content-aware fusion. In: Shen, D., et al. (eds.) MICCAI 2019. LNCS, vol. 11765, pp. 759–767. Springer, Cham (2019). https://doi.org/10.1007/978-3-030-32245-8_84

24. Zhou, Z., et al.: Cross-modal attention-guided convolutional network for multi-modal cardiac segmentation. In: Suk, H.-I., Liu, M., Yan, P., Lian, C. (eds.) MLMI 2019. LNCS, vol. 11861, pp. 601–610. Springer, Cham (2019). https://doi.org/10.1007/978-3-030-32692-0_69

25. Zhuang, X., Shen, J.: Multi-scale patch and multi-modality atlases for whole heart segmentation of MRI. Med. Image Anal. **31**, 77–87 (2016)

Deep Generative Model-Based Quality Control for Cardiac MRI Segmentation

Shuo Wang[1(✉)], Giacomo Tarroni[2], Chen Qin[2,3], Yuanhan Mo[1],
Chengliang Dai[1], Chen Chen[2], Ben Glocker[2], Yike Guo[1], Daniel Rueckert[2],
and Wenjia Bai[1,4]

[1] Data Science Institute, Imperial College London, London, UK
shuo.wang@imperial.ac.uk
[2] BioMedIA Group, Department of Computing,
Imperial College London, London, UK
[3] Institute for Digital Communications, University of Edinburgh, Edinburgh, UK
[4] Department of Brain Sciences, Imperial College London, London, UK

Abstract. In recent years, convolutional neural networks have demonstrated promising performance in a variety of medical image segmentation tasks. However, when a trained segmentation model is deployed into the real clinical world, the model may not perform optimally. A major challenge is the potential poor-quality segmentations generated due to degraded image quality or domain shift issues. There is a timely need to develop an automated quality control method that can detect poor segmentations and feedback to clinicians. Here we propose a novel deep generative model-based framework for quality control of cardiac MRI segmentation. It first learns a manifold of good-quality image-segmentation pairs using a generative model. The quality of a given test segmentation is then assessed by evaluating the difference from its projection onto the good-quality manifold. In particular, the projection is refined through iterative search in the latent space. The proposed method achieves high prediction accuracy on two publicly available cardiac MRI datasets. Moreover, it shows better generalisation ability than traditional regression-based methods. Our approach provides a real-time and model-agnostic quality control for cardiac MRI segmentation, which has the potential to be integrated into clinical image analysis workflows.

Keywords: Cardiac segmentation · Quality control · Generative model

1 Introduction

Cardiovascular diseases (CVDs) are the leading cause of death globally, taking more than 18 million lives every year [1]. Cardiac magnetic resonance imaging

Electronic supplementary material The online version of this chapter (https://doi.org/10.1007/978-3-030-59719-1_9) contains supplementary material, which is available to authorized users.

© Springer Nature Switzerland AG 2020
A. L. Martel et al. (Eds.): MICCAI 2020, LNCS 12264, pp. 88–97, 2020.
https://doi.org/10.1007/978-3-030-59719-1_9

(MRI) has been widely used in clinical practice for evaluating cardiac structure and function. To derive quantitative measures from cardiac MRI, accurate segmentation is of great importance. Over the past few years, various architectures of convolutional neural networks (CNNs) have been developed to deliver state-of-the-art performance in the task of automated cardiac MRI segmentation [2–5]. Although satisfactory performance has been achieved on specific datasets, care must be taken when deploying these models into clinical practice. In fact, it is inevitable for automated segmentation algorithms (not limited to CNN-based) to generate a number of poor-quality segmentations in real-world scenarios, due to differences in scanner models and acquisition protocols as well as potential poor image quality and motion artifacts. Therefore, reliable quality control (QC) of cardiac MRI segmentation on a per-case basis is highly desired and of great importance for successful translation into clinical practice.

Related Work: Numerous efforts have been devoted into quality control of medical images [6–8] and segmentations [9,10]. In this work, we focus on the latter, i.e. segmentation quality control. Existing literature can be broadly classified into two categories:

Learning-Based Quality Control: These methods consider quality control as a regression or classification task where a quality metric is predicted from extracted features. Kohlberger et al. proposed 42 hand-crafted features based on intensity and appearance and achieved an accuracy of 85% in detecting segmentation failure [11]. Robinson et al. developed a CNN-based method for real-time regression of the Dice similarity metric from image-segmentation pairs [12]. Hann et al. integrated quality control into the segmentation network by regressing the Dice metric [13]. Most of these methods require poor-quality segmentations as negative samples to train the regression or classification model. This makes quality control specific to the segmentation model and the type of poor-quality segmentations used for training. Liu et al. used a variational auto-encoder (VAE) for learning the shape features of segmentation in an unsupervised manner and proposed to use the evidence lower bound (ELBO) as a predictor [14]. This model-agnostic structure provides valuable insights and an elegant theoretical framework for quality control.

Registration-Based Quality Control: These methods perform image registration between the test image with a set of pre-selected template images with known segmentations. Then the quality metric can be evaluated by referring to the warped segmentations of these template images. Following this direction, the concept of reverse classification accuracy (RCA) was proposed to predict segmentation quality [15] and achieved good performance on a large-scale cardiac MRI dataset [9]. These methods can be computationally expensive due to the cost of multiple image registrations, which could potentially be reduced by using GPU acceleration and learning-based registration tools [16].

Contributions: There are three major contributions of this work. Firstly, we propose a generic deep generative model-based framework which learns the manifold of good-quality segmentations for quality control on a per-case basis. Secondly, we implement the framework with a VAE and propose an iterative search strategy in the latent space. Finally, we compare the performance of our method with regression-based methods on two different datasets, demonstrating both the accuracy and generalisation ability of the method.

2   Methodology

2.1   Problem Formulation

Let F denote an arbitrary type of segmentation model to be deployed. Given a test image I, the segmentation model provides a predicted segmentation $\hat{S} = F(I)$. The ground-truth quality of $\hat{S}$ is defined as $q(S_{gt}, \hat{S})$ where S_{gt} is the ground-truth segmentation and q is a chosen quality metric (e.g. Dice metric). The aim of quality control is to develop a model Q so that $Q(\hat{S}; I) \approx q(S_{gt}, \hat{S})$.

2.2   Deep Generative Model-Based Quality Control

Quality control would be trivial if the ground-truth segmentation S_{gt} was available. Intuitively, the proposed framework aims to find a good-quality segmentation S_{sur} as a surrogate for ground truth so that $q(S_{sur}, \hat{S}) \approx q(S_{gt}, \hat{S})$. This is realised through iterative search on the manifold of good-quality segmentations (Fig. 1).

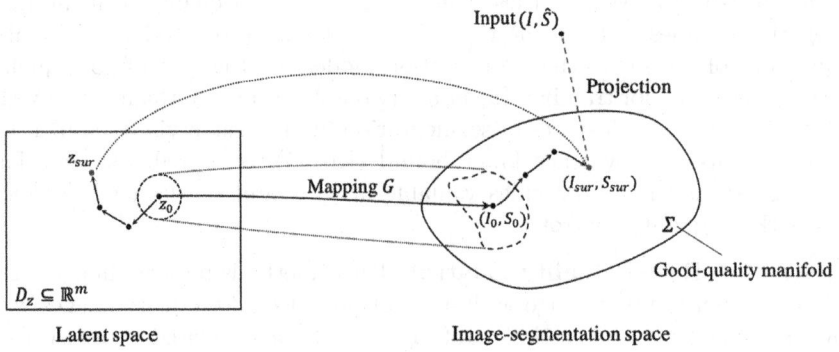

Fig. 1. Overview of the deep generative model-based quality control framework. The generative model G is trained to learn a mapping $G(z)$ from the low-dimensional latent space D_z to the good-quality manifold Σ. The input image-segmentation pair $(I, \hat{S})$ is projected to (S_{sur}, I_{sur}) on the manifold through iterative search, which is in turn used as surrogate ground truth for quality prediction. z_0 is the initial guess in the latent space and it converges to z_{sur}.

Good-Quality Manifold: The core component of this framework is a deep generative model G which learns how to generate good-quality image-segmentation pairs. Formally, let $X = (I, S) \in D_I \times D_S$ represent an image-segmentation pair, where D_I and D_S are the domains of images and possible segmentations. The key assumption of this framework is that good-quality pairs (I, S_{gt}) are distributed on a manifold $\Sigma \subset D_I \times D_S$, named as *good-quality manifold*. The generator G learns to construct a low-dimensional latent space $D_z \subseteq \mathbb{R}^m$ and a mapping to the good-quality manifold:

$$G(z) : D_z \ni z \mapsto X = G(z) \in D_I \times D_S \tag{1}$$

where z denotes the latent variable with dimension m. The mapping $G(z)$ is usually intractable but can be approximated using generative models such as generative adversarial networks (GANs) or VAEs.

Iterative Search in the Latent Space: To incorporate the generator into the quality control framework, we develop an iterative search scheme in the latent space to find a surrogate segmentation for a given image-segmentation pair as input. This surrogate segmentation is used for quality prediction. Finding the closest surrogate segmentation (i.e. projection) on the good-quality manifold is formulated as an optimisation problem,

$$z_{sur} = \underset{z \in D_z}{\operatorname{argmin}} \ \mathcal{L}(G(z), (I, \hat{S})) \tag{2}$$

which minimises the distance metric $\mathcal{L}$ between the reconstructed $G(z)$ and the input image-segmentation pair $(I, \hat{S})$. This problem can be solved using the gradient descent method as explained in Algorithm 1.

Algorithm 1. Iterative search of surrogate segmentation for quality prediction

---

Require: A trained generator $G : D_z \ni z \mapsto G(z) = (I, S) \in \Sigma$
Input: Image-segmentation pair $(I, \hat{S})$
Output: Quality prediction $Q(\hat{S}; I)$
 1: **Initialization** $z = z_0 \in D_z$
 2: **while** L not converge **do**
 3:     $L = \mathcal{L}(G(z), (I, \hat{S}))$
 4:     $grad = \nabla_z L$ # calculate gradient through back-propagation
 5:     $z = z - \alpha \cdot grad$ # gradient descent with learning rate α
 6: **end while**
 7: $S_{sur} = G(z_{sur})$
 8: $Q(\hat{S}; I) = q(S_{sur}, \hat{S})$ # perform quality control q (e.g. Dice)

2.3   Generative Model Using VAE

The proposed framework can be implemented with different generative models as long as a good-quality segmentation generator with smooth latent space is

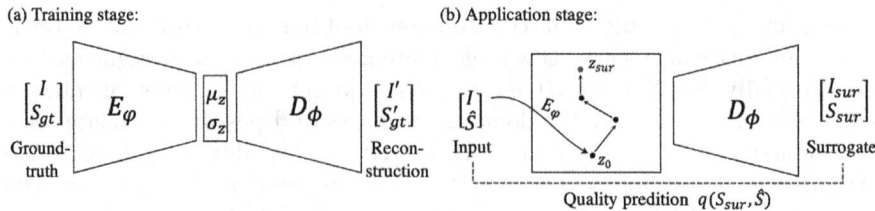

Fig. 2. Framework implementation using the variational autoencoder (VAE). In the training stage, the ground-truth image-segmentation pairs are used. In the application stage, the VAE decoder is used as the generator for iterative search of the surrogate segmentation on the good-quality manifold. Initial guess z_0 is from the encoder.

available. In this paper, we employ the VAE (Fig. 2) which includes an encoder E_φ and a decoder D_ϕ, where φ and ϕ denote the model parameters [17]. The image-segmentation pair (I, S) is encoded by E_φ to follow a Gaussian distribution $\mathcal{N}(\mu_z, \sigma_z^2)$ in the latent space, where μ_z and σ_z^2 denote the mean and variance respectively. A probabilistic reconstruction of the image-segmentation pair (I', S') is generated from the decoder D_ϕ.

At the training stage, the ground-truth image-segmentation pairs are used to train the VAE. The loss function includes a reconstruction loss and a KL divergence term for regularisation [18]:

$$\mathcal{L}_{VAE} = \mathcal{L}_{recon} + \beta \cdot D_{KL}(\mathcal{N}(\mu_z, \sigma_z^2) \| \mathcal{N}(0, \mathbf{I})) \tag{3}$$

$$\mathcal{L}_{recon} = BCE(S_{GT}, S'_{GT}) + MSE(I, I') \tag{4}$$

where β is the hyperparameter that balances between reconstruction loss and regularisation. The reconstruction loss is evaluated using the binary cross entropy (BCE) for segmentation and the mean square error (MSE) for image, respectively. The effects of the weight β and the latent space dimension m will be evaluated in the ablation study.

At the application stage, the VAE decoder D_ϕ is used as the generator, reconstructing image-segmentation pairs from the latent space. The initial guess z_0 in the latent space is obtained from the encoder E_φ. Following Algorithm 1, the surrogate segmentation S_{sur} can be found via iterative search (Fig. 2b). Finally, the quality metric is evaluated by $q(S_{sur}, \hat{S})$, e.g. Dice metric.

3   Experiments

3.1   Datasets

UK Biobank Dataset: Short-axis SSFP cardiac cine MRI of 1,500 subjects at the end-diastolic (ED) frame were obtained from UK Biobank and split into three subsets for training (800 cases), validation (200 cases) and test (500 cases). The in-plane resolution is 1.8×1.8 mm with slice thickness 8 mm and slice gap of 2 mm. A short-axis image stack typically consists of 10 to 12 image slices.

Ground-truth good segmentations were generated from a publicly available fully-convolutional network (FCN) that has demonstrated a high performance [2], with manual quality control by an experienced cardiologist.

ACDC Dataset: 100 subjects were obtained from ACDC dataset [4] and resampled to the same spatial resolution as UK Biobank data. This includes one normal group (NOR) and four pathological groups with cardiac abnormalities: dilated cardiomyopathy (DCM); hypertrophic cardiomyopathy (HCM); myocardial infarction with altered left ventricular ejection fraction (MINF); and abnormal right ventricle (RV). The ground-truth segmentations at the ED frame were provided by the ACDC challenge organisers.

3.2 Experimental Design

In this study, we evaluate the performance of our proposed method and compare with two regression-based methods for quality control of cardiac MRI segmentation. Specifically, we focus on the left ventricular myocardium, which is a challenging cardiac structure to segment and of high clinical relevance.

VAE Implementation and Training: The VAE encoder is composed of four convolutional layers (each was followed by *ReLU* activation), and one fully connected layer. The decoder has a similar structure with reversed order and the last layer is followed by *Sigmoid* function. The latent space dimension m was set to 8 and the hyperparameter β was set to 0.01 from ablation study results. The architecture is shown in Supplementary Fig. S1. The model was implemented in PyTorch and trained using the Adam optimiser with learning rate 0.0001 and batch size 16. It was trained for 100 epochs and an early stopping criterion was used based on the validation set performance. To improve the computational efficiency, the VAE was trained on a region of interest (ROI) centered around the myocardium with the window size of 96×96 pixel, which was heuristically determined to include the whole cardiac structure. The cropped image intensity was normalised to the $[0, 1]$ range and stacked with the binary segmentation.

Baseline Methods: Two regression-based methods were used as baselines: a) a support vector regression (SVR) model with 42 hand-crafted features about shape and appearance [11] and b) a CNN regression network (ResNet-18 backbone) with the image-segmentation pair as input [12]. Both baseline methods use the Dice metric as the regression target.

Experiment 1: UK Biobank. Besides the ground-truth segmentations, we generated poor-quality segmentations by attacking the segmentation model. White noise with different variance level was added to the original images, resulting in a dataset of poor-quality segmentations with uniform Dice distribution. The quality prediction was performed on the test set of the attacked segmentations.

Experiment 2: ACDC. We deployed a UK Biobank trained segmentation model on ACDC dataset without fine-tuning. This reflects a real-world clinical setting, where segmentation failures would occur due to domain shift issues.

Ablation Study: We adjusted the dimensionality of the latent space m and the hyperparameter β and performed a sensitivity analysis on the UK Biobank validation dataset. The result is reported in the Supplementary Table S1.

4   Results and Discussion

Quality control performance is assessed in terms of Dice metric prediction accuracy. Pearson correlation coefficient r and mean absolute error (MAE) between predicted Dice and real Dice are calculated. Table 1 compares the quantitative performance of the methods and Fig. 3 visualises the predictions. On UK Biobank dataset, the hand-crafted feature method performed the worst. The proposed method achieved a similar performance ($r = 0.96$, MAE $= 0.07$) as the CNN regression method ($r = 0.97$, MAE $= 0.06$). However, on ACDC dataset, the proposed method ($r = 0.97$, MAE $= 0.03$) outperformed the CNN regression method ($r = 0.97$, MAE $= 0.17$) with a smaller MAE. As shown in Fig. 3, on ACDC dataset, the prediction of the proposed method aligns well with the identity line, whereas the CNN regression method clearly deviates from the line, even though the r coefficient is still high.

Table 1. Quality control performance of three models on two cardiac datasets. The Pearson correlation coefficient r and the mean absolute error (MAE) between predicted and true Dice metrics are reported. MAE is reported as mean (standard deviation). For ACDC dataset, the performance on five subgroups [4] are aslo reported.

Dataset	Hand-crafted features [11]		CNN regression [12]		Proposed model	
	r	MAE	r	MAE	r	MAE
UK Biobank	0.909	0.100(0.100)	**0.973**	**0.061(0.049)**	0.958	0.067(0.052)
ACDC	0.728	0.182(0.130)	0.968	0.165(0.044)	**0.969**	**0.033(0.028)**
DCM	0.802	0.353(0.123)	0.956	0.186(0.034)	**0.964**	**0.036(0.020)**
HCM	0.838	0.131(0.075)	0.836	0.155(0.027)	**0.896**	**0.023(0.015)**
MINF	0.815	0.184(0.123)	0.969	0.156(0.051)	**0.976**	**0.033(0.029)**
NOR	0.775	0.114(0.065)	**0.985**	0.158(0.040)	**0.985**	**0.026(0.017)**
RV	0.877	0.129(0.073)	**0.974**	0.169(0.053)	0.960	**0.045(0.042)**

A possible explanation for this is that the proposed generative method works by learning the good-quality manifold and proposing the surrogate ground truth for quality assessment. Thus it is agnostic to the types of poor-quality segmentations. The training of hand-crafted features and CNN-based regression methods require poor-quality segmentations and may be overfitted to the UK Biobank data. When they are deployed onto ACDC dataset, there is a shift not only for

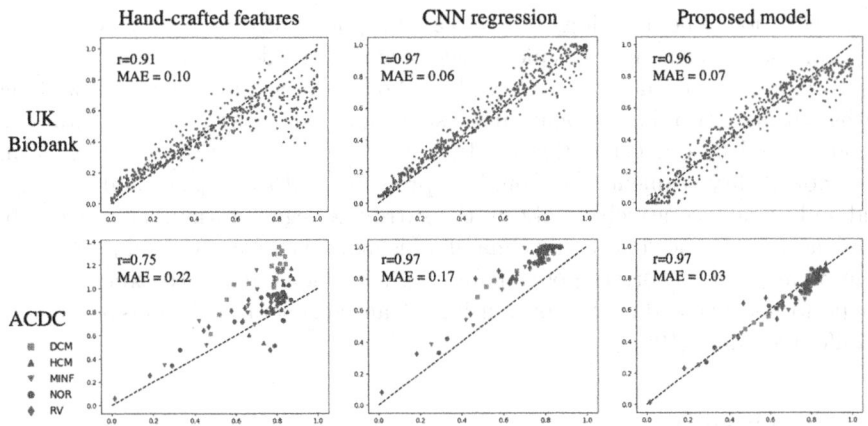

Fig. 3. Comparison of the performance of different quality control methods. The x-axis is the real Dice of each subject and the y-axis is the predicted Dice by each method. The dashed line is the $y = x$, plotted for reference. Top row: UK Biobank data ($n = 500$). Bottom row: ACDC data ($n = 100$), with five subgroups plotted in different colors.

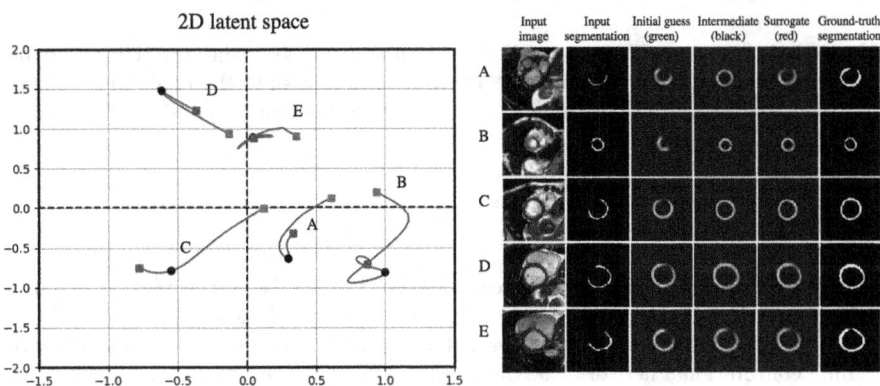

Fig. 4. Visualisation of searching path in a two-dimensional latent space. Left: searching paths for five exemplar samples (green point: initial guess from the VAE encoder; black point: intermediate state during iterative search; red point: convergence point for surrogate segmentation). Right: the input image and segmentation, reconstructed segmentations along the searching path and the ground-truth segmentation. (Color figure online)

image appearance (e.g. difference 1.5T and 3.0T MRI scanner) but also for types of segmentation failures. In addition, the ACDC dataset consists of more pathological cases, whereas the UK Biobank comes from a general healthy population. Due to the domain shift, the performance of regression-based methods degraded. In contrast, the proposed method maintained a high prediction accuracy against domain shift. This indicates the advantage of a generative model-based framework for generalisation. It also can be potentially used as a system to monitor the performance of deployed segmentation models over time.

To gain insights into our proposed method, we visualised several searching paths within a two-dimensional latent space and corresponding segmentations reconstructed by our generative model (Fig. 4). Following the searching path, the poor-quality segmentation could be projected onto the good-quality manifold and refined iteratively to obtain the surrogate segmentation. The surrogate segmentation on the good-quality manifold is more plausible and can potentially be used as *prior* to correct poor-quality segmentations. It is also expected that the performance could be improved using advanced generative models and better manifold learning [19].

5   Conclusion

Here we propose a generative-model based framework for cardiac image segmentation quality control. It is model-agnostic, in the sense that it does not depend on specific segmentation models or types of segmentation failures. It can be potentially extended for quality control for different anatomical structures.

Acknowledgements. This research has been conducted using the UK Biobank Resource under Application Number 18545: the authors wish to thank all UK Biobank participants and staff. The authors also acknowledge funding by EPSRC Programme (EP/P001009/1).

References

1. WHO: Scale up prevention of heart attack and stroke. https://www.who.int/cardiovascular_diseases/world-heart-day/en/. Accessed 16 Mar 2020
2. Bai, W., et al.: Automated cardiovascular magnetic resonance image analysis with fully convolutional networks. J. Cardiovasc. Magn. Reson. **20**(1), 65 (2018)
3. Tao, Q., et al.: Deep learning-based method for fully automatic quantification of left ventricle function from cine MR images: a multivendor, multicenter study. Radiology **290**(1), 81–88 (2019)
4. Bernard, O., et al.: Deep learning techniques for automatic MRI cardiac multi-structures segmentation and diagnosis: is the problem solved? IEEE Trans. Med. Imaging **37**(11), 2514–2525 (2018)
5. Zheng, Q., Delingette, H., Duchateau, N., Ayache, N.: 3-D consistent and robust segmentation of cardiac images by deep learning with spatial propagation. IEEE Trans. Med. Imaging **37**(9), 2137–2148 (2018)
6. Tarroni, G., et al.: Learning-based quality control for cardiac MR images. IEEE Trans. Med. Imaging **38**(5), 1127–1138 (2018)
7. Carapella, V., et al.: Towards the semantic enrichment of free-text annotation of image quality assessment for UK biobank cardiac cine MRI scans. In: Carneiro, G., et al. (eds.) LABELS/DLMIA-2016. LNCS, vol. 10008, pp. 238–248. Springer, Cham (2016). https://doi.org/10.1007/978-3-319-46976-8_25

8. Zhang, L., et al.: Automated quality assessment of cardiac MR images using convolutional neural networks. In: Tsaftaris, S.A., Gooya, A., Frangi, A.F., Prince, J.L. (eds.) SASHIMI 2016. LNCS, vol. 9968, pp. 138–145. Springer, Cham (2016). https://doi.org/10.1007/978-3-319-46630-9_14

9. Robinson, R., et al.: Automated quality control in image segmentation: application to the UK biobank cardiovascular magnetic resonance imaging study. J. Cardiovasc. Magn. Reson. **21**(1), 18 (2019)

10. Albà, X., Lekadir, K., Pereanez, M., Medrano-Gracia, P., Young, A.A., Frangi, A.F.: Automatic initialization and quality control of large-scale cardiac MRI segmentations. Med. Image Anal. **43**, 129–141 (2018)

11. Kohlberger, T., Singh, V., Alvino, C., Bahlmann, C., Grady, L.: Evaluating segmentation error without ground truth. In: Ayache, N., Delingette, H., Golland, P., Mori, K. (eds.) MICCAI 2012. LNCS, vol. 7510, pp. 528–536. Springer, Heidelberg (2012). https://doi.org/10.1007/978-3-642-33415-3_65

12. Robinson, R., et al.: Real-time prediction of segmentation quality. In: Frangi, A.F., Schnabel, J.A., Davatzikos, C., Alberola-López, C., Fichtinger, G. (eds.) MICCAI 2018. LNCS, vol. 11073, pp. 578–585. Springer, Cham (2018). https://doi.org/10.1007/978-3-030-00937-3_66

13. Hann, E., et al.: Quality control-driven image segmentation towards reliable automatic image analysis in large-scale cardiovascular magnetic resonance aortic cine imaging. In: Shen, D., et al. (eds.) MICCAI 2019. LNCS, vol. 11765, pp. 750–758. Springer, Cham (2019). https://doi.org/10.1007/978-3-030-32245-8_83

14. Liu, F., Xia, Y., Yang, D., Yuille, A.L., Xu, D.: An alarm system for segmentation algorithm based on shape model. In: Proceedings of the IEEE International Conference on Computer Vision, pp. 10652–10661 (2019)

15. Valindria, V.V., et al.: Reverse classification accuracy: predicting segmentation performance in the absence of ground truth. IEEE Trans. Med. Imaging **36**(8), 1597–1606 (2017)

16. Haskins, G., Kruger, U., Yan, P.: Deep learning in medical image registration: a survey. Mach. Vis. Appl. **31**(1), 1–18 (2020)

17. Kingma, D.P., Welling, M.: Auto-encoding variational bayes. In: International Conference on Learning Representations (2014)

18. Higgins, I., et al.: beta-VAE: learning basic visual concepts with a constrained variational framework. In: International Conference on Learning Representations (2017)

19. Bojanowski, P., Joulin, A., Lopez-Paz, D., Szlam, A.: Optimizing the latent space of generative networks. In: International Conference on Machine Learning (2018)

DeU-Net: Deformable U-Net for 3D Cardiac MRI Video Segmentation

Shunjie Dong[1], Jinlong Zhao[1], Maojun Zhang[1], Zhengxue Shi[1], Jianing Deng[1], Yiyu Shi[2], Mei Tian[1], and Cheng Zhuo[1(✉)]

[1] Zhejiang University, Hangzhou, China
{sj_dong,zhaojl,zhmj,sjwo,dengjn,meitian,czhuo}@zju.edu.cn
[2] University of Notre Dame, Notre Dame, USA
yshi4@nd.edu

Abstract. Automatic segmentation of cardiac magnetic resonance imaging (MRI) facilitates efficient and accurate volume measurement in clinical applications. However, due to anisotropic resolution and ambiguous border (e.g., right ventricular endocardium), existing methods suffer from the degradation of accuracy and robustness in 3D cardiac MRI video segmentation. In this paper, we propose a novel *Deformable U-Net* (DeU-Net) to fully exploit spatio-temporal information from 3D cardiac MRI video, including a Temporal Deformable Aggregation Module (TDAM) and a Deformable Global Position Attention (DGPA) network. First, the TDAM takes a cardiac MRI video clip as input with temporal information extracted by an offset prediction network. Then we fuse extracted temporal information via a temporal aggregation deformable convolution to produce fused feature maps. Furthermore, to aggregate meaningful features, we devise the DGPA network by employing deformable attention U-Net, which can encode a wider range of multi-dimensional contextual information into global and local features. Experimental results show that our DeU-Net achieves the state-of-the-art performance on commonly used evaluation metrics, especially for cardiac marginal information (ASSD and HD).

1 Introduction

Magnetic Resonance Imaging (MRI) is widely used by cardiologists as the golden modality for cardiac assessment [10]. The segmentation of kinetic MR images along the short axis is complicated but essential to precise morphological and pathological analysis, diagnosis, and surgical planning. In particular, one has to delineate left ventricular endocardium (LV), myocardium (MYO), and right ventricular endocardium (RV) to calculate the volume of the cavities in cardiac MRI video, including end-diastolic (ED) and end-systolic (ES) phases [7].

Electronic supplementary material The online version of this chapter (https://doi.org/10.1007/978-3-030-59719-1_10) contains supplementary material, which is available to authorized users.

A. L. Martel et al. (Eds.): MICCAI 2020, LNCS 12264, pp. 98–107, 2020.
https://doi.org/10.1007/978-3-030-59719-1_10

Recent studies [4,6,8,11,14,15] proposed deep learning based approaches to learn robust contextual and semantic features, achieving the state-of-the-art segmentation performance. However, automatic and accurate 3D cardiac MRI video segmentation still remains very challenging due to significant variations in the subjects, ambiguous borders, inhomogeneous intensity and artifacts, especially for RV. There are two key issues that needs to be resolved: (1) In cardiac MRI video, the RV segmentation performance is influenced by complicated shape and inhomogeneous intensity, especially the partial volume effect close to the free wall. (2) Subtle structures (e.g., MYO) have ambiguous borders and different orientations in different anatomical planes of MRI video, causing segmentation inaccuracy. Thus, it is highly desired to have precise and robust cardiac MRI video segmentation.

In this paper, we propose a new *Deformable U-Net* (DeU-Net) to address the aforementioned issues by fully exploiting the spatio-temporal information from 3D cardiac MRI video and aggregating temporal information to boost segmentation performance. The DeU-Net consists of two parts: Temporal Deformable Aggregation Module (TDAM) and a Deformable Global Position Attention (DGPA) network. To address the partial volume effect of RV in [14,15], the TDAM utilizes the spatio-temporal information of the MRI video clip to produce fused feature maps by a temporal aggregation deformable convolution. To handle the issue of subtle structures in [6], the U-Net based DGPA network jointly encodes a wider range of multi-dimensional contextual information into global and local features, guaranteeing clear and continuous borders of every segmentation map. We then quantitatively and qualitatively evaluate the proposed method on ACDC MICCAI 2017 Challenge dataset [1] with additional labeling done by experience radiologists [11]. The experimental results show that our proposal achieves the state-of-the-art performance on commonly used metrics, especially for cardiac marginal information (ASSD and HD).

2   Method

The architecture of DeU-Net is plotted in Fig. 1, including a Temporal Deformable Aggregation Module (TDAM) and a Deformable Global Position Attention (DGPA) network. The proposed TDAM consists of two phases: a temporal deformable convolution and an offset prediction network based on U-Net to predict deformable offsets. The fused features (target frame) produced by temporal deformable convolution are fed into DGPA for the final segmentation results. The DGPA network which also employs U-Net as backbone introduces deformable convolution for encoders and utilizes the deformable attention block to augment the spatial sampling locations.

2.1   Temporal Deformable Aggregation Module

Many existing methods design very complicated neural networks to achieve performance gain. However, most approaches ignore the spatio-temporal information of 3D MRI video, and treat each frame as a separate object, thereby causing

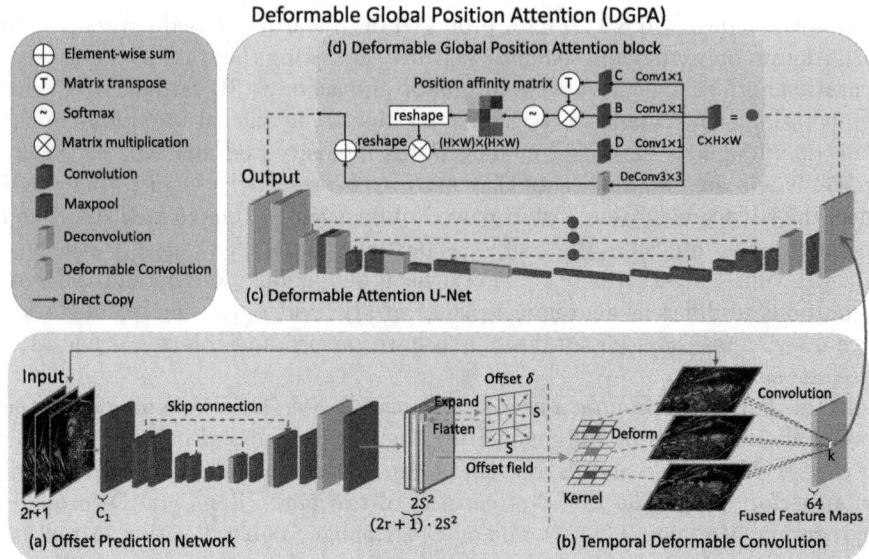

Fig. 1. The architecture of DeU-Net for 3D cardiac MRI video segmentation. Given a video clip ($2r + 1$ concatenated frames) as input, an offset prediction network is designed for deformable offset. Temporal deformable aggregation convolution exploits the offset field to fuse temporal information. The fused feature maps are used by a deformable attention U-Net to enhance segmentation performance. Herein, temporal radius $r = 1$ and deformable kernel size $S = 3$.

performance degradation in ASSD and HD. Moreover, in the process of data sampling, various semantic details of the video clips may get lost due to fast variation of cardiac borders with time and regular convolution, inevitably distorting video local details and pixel-wise connections between the frames. Thus, we propose a Temporal Deformable Aggregation Module (TDAM) to adaptively extract temporal information (motion field) for image interpretation. The proposed TDAM takes a target frame along with its neighboring reference frames as inputs to jointly predict an offset field, that is, the motion field. Then, the enhanced contextual information can be fused into the target frame by a temporal aggregation deformable convolution.

We denote the dimension of an input 3D MRI video as $[x, y, z, t]$, where $x - y$ plane is the short-axis plane, z is the short axis, and t is the temporal dimension. Considering the large inter-slice gap in MRI cardiac images along z axis, we select images within the dimension $[x, y, t]$ where stronger correlation may exist. Specially, we define $C_{t_0} \in \mathbb{R}^{H \times W}$ as the target frame in a 3D MRI video at time t_0, where H and W are the height and width of the input feature map. In order to leverage temporal information, we take the preceding and succeeding r frames as the reference to improve the quality of the target frame C_{t_0}. For a 3D cardiac MRI video clip $\{C_{t_0-r}, \cdots, C_{t_0}, \cdots, C_{t_0+r}\}$, the conventional temporal fusion

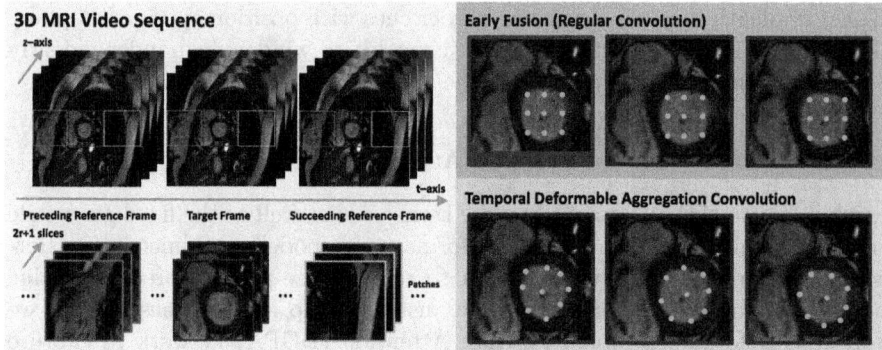

Fig. 2. Comparison between the fixed receptive field in Early Fusion [5] and the adaptive receptive field in TDAM. Each canonical clip is extracted using the samples from the same position in the $x - y$ plane. The yellow points denote the sampling positions of 3×3 convolution window centered at green points. The temporal change of cardiac borders are highlighted, corresponding to the relevant context in the 3D MRI video. The patches are the images collected at different timestamps with the same position.

scheme (i.e., Early Fusion [5]) can be formulated as a multichannel convolution directly applied on the target frames as:

$$\mathcal{F}(\mathbf{k}) = \sum_{t=t_0-r}^{t_0+r} \sum_{s=1}^{S^2} K_{t,s} \cdot C_t(\mathbf{k} + \mathbf{k}_s), \tag{1}$$

where $\mathcal{F}(\cdot)$ represents the quality-enhanced feature map. S is the size of convolution kernel and $K_t \in \mathbb{R}^{S^2}$ denotes the kernel for t-th channel. $\mathbf{k}$ represents an arbitrary spatial position and $\mathbf{k}_s$ indicates the regular sampling offsets. However, noisy content can be easily introduced due to cardiac temporal change in video. Inspired by Multi-Frame Quality Enhancement [13] for Video Quality Enhancement (VQE), we design TDAM to augment the regular sampling offset with extra learnable offset $\delta_{(t,\mathbf{k})} \in \mathbb{R}^{2S^2}$ for the potential spatio-temporal correlations:

$$\mathbf{k}_s \leftarrow \mathbf{k}_s + \delta_{(t,\mathbf{k}),s}. \tag{2}$$

Note that the deformable offset $\delta_{(t,\mathbf{k})}$ is designed for each convolution window centered at a spatio-temporal position $(t, \mathbf{k})$, as shown in Fig. 1. We propose to take the whole clip into consideration and jointly predict all the deformable offsets with a U-Net based network [8]. Maxpool and deconvolutional layers are used for downsampling and upsampling, respectively. Convolutional layer with stride 1, zero paddings are designed to retain the feature size. With such a scheme, the spatial deformations with temporal dynamics in 3D MRI video clips can be simultaneously modeled.

Compared with the existing VQE approaches which achieve explicit motion compensation before fusion to alleviate the negative effects of temporal motion,

TDAM implicitly focuses on cardiac border cues with position-specific sampling. As shown in Fig. 2, adjacent deformable convolution windows can independently sample the contents, achieving higher flexibility and performance boost.

2.2 Deformable Global Position Attention

Regular convolution is restricted by the kernel size as well as the fixed geometric structures, which results in limited performance in modeling geometric transformations. In practice, it is very difficult to reduce false-positive predictions due to unclear borders between the cardiac instances. To address these issues, we propose a Deformable Global Position Attention (DGPA) network to capture a sufficiently large receptive field and semantic global contextual information, including Deformable Attention U-Net and DGPA block. Compared with the existing attention method [9], we introduce deformable convolution on the learning of attention in U-Net. DGPA augments the spatial sampling locations in the modules with additional offsets, which is designed to model complex geometric transformations. Thus, long-range contextual information can be collected, which helps obtain more discriminative cardiac border for pixel-level prediction.

As shown in Fig. 1, the fused local features $I \in \mathbb{R}^{N \times H \times W}$ are regarded as input to the DGPA block, where N represents the number of input channels, H and W indicate the height and width of the input features, respectively. We first feed the input features I with a 3×3 deformable convolution layer to capture cardiac geometric information. The formulation is as below:

$$O = I \otimes \mathcal{K}_{l,\delta'}, \tag{3}$$

where $O \in \mathbb{R}^{N \times H \times W}$ the feature map, $\mathcal{K}$ is deformable convolution kernel, l is the kernel size and δ' is the deformable offset. The input feature map is reshaped to three new feature maps $B, C, D \in \mathbb{R}^{N \times M}$, where M denotes the number of pixels ($M = H \times W$). In order to exploit the high-level features of cardiac borders, a dot-product is conducted between B and the transpose of C. Then the result is applied into a softmax layer to calculate the attention map $P \in \mathbb{R}^{N \times N}$:

$$p_{ji} = \frac{\exp(B_i \cdot C_j^T)}{\sum_{i=1}^{N} \exp(B_i \cdot C_j^T)}, \tag{4}$$

where p_{ji} represents the ith pixel's impact on the jth pixel. The more similar feature representations of the two pixels indicate a stronger correlation between them. Then we perform a matrix multiplication between the transpose of P and D to reshape the result to $\mathbb{R}^{N \times H \times W}$. Finally, an element-wise sum operation is applied with the feature map O from deformable block to obtain the output features $\mathcal{Z} \in \mathbb{R}^{N \times H \times W}$ as below:

$$\mathcal{Z}_j = \alpha \sum_{i=1}^{N} (p_{ji} \cdot D_i) + O_j, \tag{5}$$

where α is the scale parameter belonging to the position affinity matrix. Each element in $\mathcal{Z}$ is a weighted sum of the features globally and selectively aggregates input features I. Long-range dependencies of the feature map are calculated to improve intra-class compact and semantic consistency.

3 Experiments and Results

3.1 Setup

Evaluation Datasets. We evaluate our proposal and competitive approaches on the publicly available data of ACDC MICCAI 2017 Challenge [1] with additional labeling done by experience radiologists [11]. The dataset has right ventricle, myocardium, and left ventricle segmentation frames from MRI videos with labels provided by experienced radiologists. The collected images following the common clinical SSFP cine-MRI sequence have similar properties as 3D cardiac MRI videos. The MRI sequence, as a series of short-axis slices of end diastolic and end systolic instant, starts from the mitral valves down to the apex of the left ventricle. We resize the exams into 256×256 images, and no additional pre-processing was conducted. The dataset has 150 exams from different patients with 100 for training and 50 for testing.

Implementation Details. The proposed method is implemented based on PyTorch library with reference to MMDetection toolbox [3] for deformable convolution, using a NVIDIA GTX 1080Ti GPU. For the training set, standard data augmentation (i.e., mirror, axial flip or rotation) is further used to exploit training samples better. We use Adam optimizer to update the network parameters. The initial learning rate is set to 2×10^{-4} and a weight decay of 1×10^{-4}. We use a batch size of at least 12. The number of reference frames r from Eq. 1 is set as 1. The training is stopped if the Dice score does not increase by 20 epochs. In our experiments, we perform 5-fold cross-validation.

Comparison Methods. We compare the proposed DeU-Net with several state-of-the-art approaches for 3D Cardiac MRI Video segmentation: (1) kU-Net [2] combined convolutional and recurrent neural networks to exploit the intra-slice and inter-slice contexts, respectively. (2) GridNet [15] incorporated a shape prior whose registration on the input image is learned by the model, learning both high-level and low-level features. (3) Attention U-Net [6] proposed a novel self-attention gating module to learn irrelevant regions in an input image for dense label predictions. For a fair comparison, all these methods are modified and fully trained for 3D cardiac MRI video segmentation.

3.2 Results

For quantitative evaluation, Table 1 details the comparison among U-Net, Grid-Net, Attention U-Net, kU-Net, and the proposed DeU-Net on average symmetric

Table 1. Average scores of the 3D cardiac MRI video different metrics and approaches.

Method	ASSD LV		ASSD MYO		ASSD RV		ASSD
	ED	ES	ED	ES	ED	ES	Average
U-Net	0.34 ± .09	0.51 ± .08	0.36 ± .07	0.41 ± .05	0.81 ± .06	1.65 ± .07	0.78 ± .06
kU-Net	0.20 ± .12	0.32 ± .07	0.34 ± .03	0.41 ± .07	0.62 ± .08	0.58 ± .06	0.51 ± .11
GridNet	0.16 ± .10	0.25 ± .09	0.24 ± .07	0.26 ± .09	0.27 ± .11	0.49 ± .08	0.38 ± .08
Attention U-Net	0.17 ± .13	0.32 ± .11	0.24 ± .09	0.27 ± .09	0.26 ± .08	0.56 ± .13	0.39 ± .12
ToFlow U-Net	0.12 ± .07	0.28 ± .04	0.21 ± .05	0.15 ± .04	0.30 ± .06	0.57 ± .08	0.27 ± .10
DeU-Net(t)	0.07 ± .08	0.23 ± .09	0.19 ± .02	0.18 ± .06	0.22 ± .04	0.51 ± .09	0.24 ± .08
DeU-Net(d)	0.10 ± .04	0.18 ± .06	0.17 ± .03	0.20 ± .03	0.19 ± .05	0.49 ± .02	0.22 ± .05
DeU-Net	**0.04 ± .01**	**0.12 ± .04**	**0.12 ± .02**	**0.12 ± .00**	**0.13 ± .03**	**0.41 ± .03**	**0.19 ± .04**
Method	HD LV		HD MYO		HD RV		HD
	ED	ES	ED	ES	ED	ES	Average
U-Net	6.17 ± .88	8.29 ± .62	15.26 ± .98	17.92 ± .23	20.51 ± .54	21.21 ± .88	19.89 ± .73
kU-Net	4.59 ± .32	5.40 ± .55	7.11 ± .79	6.45 ± .64	11.92 ± .52	14.83 ± .42	14.38 ± .70
GridNet	5.96 ± .42	6.57 ± .41	8.68 ± .45	8.99 ± .84	13.48 ± .53	16.66 ± .83	15.06 ± .25
Attention U-Net	4.39 ± .76	5.27 ± .74	7.02 ± .88	7.35 ± .90	12.65 ± .58	10.99 ± .41	13.95 ± .21
ToFlow U-Net	3.21 ± .47	4.32 ± .63	6.20 ± .91	6.02 ± .69	10.39 ± .81	13.00 ± .24	11.19 ± .43
DeU-Net(t)	4.08 ± .32	4.59 ± .09	5.91 ± .33	5.31 ± .70	11.58 ± .12	12.23 ± .13	9.28 ± .14
DeU-Net(d)	2.76 ± .36	4.27 ± .55	4.77 ± .40	4.22 ± .43	12.13 ± .23	11.97 ± .09	7.69 ± .24
DeU-Net	**2.48 ± .27**	**3.25 ± .30**	**4.56 ± .29**	**4.20 ± .14**	**9.88 ± .17**	**9.02 ± .11**	**6.80 ± .17**
Method	Dice LV		Dice MYO		Dice RV		Dice
	ED	ES	ED	ES	ED	ES	Average
U-Net	0.96 ± .00	0.90 ± .01	0.78 ± .01	0.76 ± .02	0.88 ± .02	0.80 ± .02	0.81 ± .03
kU-Net	0.96 ± .00	0.90 ± .00	0.88 ± .02	0.89 ± .03	0.91 ± .03	0.82 ± .03	0.83 ± .01
GridNet	0.96 ± .01	0.91 ± .01	0.88 ± .03	0.90 ± .03	0.90 ± .01	0.82 ± .03	0.85 ± .02
Attention U-Net	0.96 ± .01	0.91 ± .02	0.88 ± .02	0.90 ± .01	0.91 ± .01	0.83 ± .02	0.84 ± .03
ToFlow U-Net	0.96 ± .00	0.91 ± .01	**0.90 ± .01**	0.90 ± .01	0.92 ± .01	0.84 ± .02	0.87 ± .02
DeU-Net(t)	0.96 ± .00	0.91 ± .00	0.89 ± .00	0.90 ± .01	0.92 ± .01	0.83 ± .01	0.86 ± .03
DeU-Net(d)	0.96 ± .01	0.91 ± .01	0.88 ± .01	**0.91 ± .01**	0.92 ± .00	0.84 ± .00	0.88 ± .02
DeU-Net	**0.97 ± .00**	**0.92 ± .00**	0.90 ± .00	0.91 ± .01	**0.93 ± .00**	**0.86 ± ± .01**	**0.90 ± .01**

surface distance (ASSD), Hausdorff distance (HD), and Dice score. In addition
to the scores at ED and ES phases, we evaluate the average score of the entire
3D cardiac MRI video for all the three metrics (with more detailed statistics
reported in the supplementary material due to the space limit). We can observe
that DeU-Net significantly outperforms all the prior networks on most metrics.
It is worth noting that our proposal substantially improves segmentation performance on RV, where the ventricle has complicated shape and intensity inhomogeneities. Note that, the proposed method achieves the best results on ASSD
that is lower than GridNet by an average of 0.19 mm. Compared to existing
methods, HD is lower for our approach by an average of 7.15 mm, and the Dice
score is better by an average of 5%. This is a strong indication that DeU-Net
exploits spatio-temporal information and reduces the negative effect of cardiac
border ambiguity.

To separate the contributions of TDAM and DGPA, we also evaluate the
performance of three variants of DeU-Net: (1) DeU-Net(t), the variant without
TDAM. (2) DeU-Net(d), the variant without DGPA. (3) ToFlow U-Net, the variant replacing TDAM by Task-oriented Flow (ToFlow) [12]. For the differences

| Ground Truth | GridNet | Attention U-Net | ToFlow U-Net | DeU-Net |

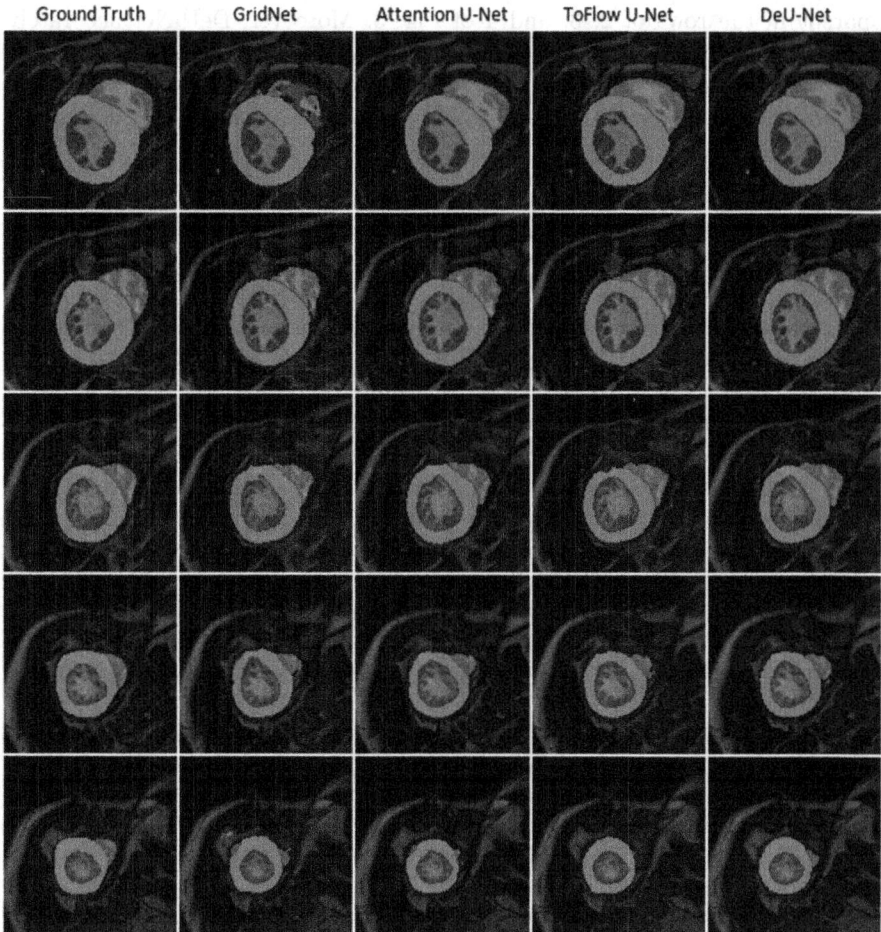

Fig. 3. Visualization of the segmentation results by different methods on the testing data. RV, MYO, and LV are labeled in red, green and blue, respectively. (Color figure online)

among RV, MYO and LV, Table 1 shows that DeU-Net(d) works better than ToFlow U-Net and DeU-Net(t) on both HD and ASSD, indicating that TDAM can fully explore temporal correspondences across multiple frames, especially close to the borders. Moreover, DeU-Net also performs better over all the three variants, validating the necessity of having both TDAM and DGPA in the flow.

Finally, Fig. 3 illustrates a visual comparison of the ground truth, GridNet, Attention U-Net, ToFlow U-Net and DeU-Net in a 3D cardiac MRI video clip. It can be seen that GridNet and Attention U-Net successfully produce accurate results on most slices of each 3D volume, but the shape of the target region is not as accurate as ToFlow U-Net and DeU-Net. Such observations are especially apparent in the rows of 2, 3, and 4 of Fig. 3. Moreover, DeU-Net accurately extracts the borders of the target regions on most of the slices, as shown in the last row of Fig. 3. Note that, the segmentation performance of RV, labeled as blue, is significantly lower than that of MYO and LV due to the irregular shape and the ambiguous borders.

4   Discussions and Conclusions

In this paper, we propose a *Deformable U-Net* (DeU-Net) to fully exploit spatio-temporal information from 3D cardiac MRI video, including a Temporal Deformable Aggregation Module (TDAM) and a Deformable Global Position Attention (DGPA) network. Based on the temporal correlation across multiple frames, TDAM aggregates temporal information with learnable sampling offsets, and capture sufficient semantic context. To obtain the discriminative and compact features in subtle structures, the DGPA network encodes a wider range of multi-dimensional fused contextual information into global and local features. Experimental results show that our proposal achieves the state-of-the-art performance on commonly used metrics, especially for cardiac marginal information (ASSD and HD). In the future, it would be of interest to apply our proposal to other datasets (such as myocardial contrast echocardiography). Our segmentation method will facilitate the translation of neural networks to clinical practice.

Acknowledgement. This work was supported in part by National Key Research and Development Program of China [No. 2018YFE0126300], Key Area Research and Development Program of Guangdong Province [No. 2018B030338001], and Information Technology Center, Zhejiang University.

References

1. Bernard, O., et al.: Deep learning techniques for automatic MRI cardiac multi-structures segmentation and diagnosis: is the problem solved? IEEE Trans. Med. Imaging **37**(11), 2514–2525 (2018)
2. Chen, J., Yang, L., Zhang, Y., Alber, M., Chen, D.Z.: Combining fully convolutional and recurrent neural networks for 3D biomedical image segmentation. In: Advances in Neural Information Processing Systems, pp. 3036–3044 (2016)
3. Chen, K., et al.: MMDetection: open MMLab detection toolbox and benchmark. arXiv preprint arXiv:1906.07155 (2019)
4. Deng, J., Wang, L., Pu, S., Zhuo, C.: Spatio-temporal deformable convolution for compressed video quality enhancement. In: Proceedings of the AAAI Conference on Artificial Intelligence, pp. 10696–10703 (2020)
5. Karpathy, A., Toderici, G., Shetty, S., Leung, T., Sukthankar, R., Fei-Fei, L.: Large-scale video classification with convolutional neural networks. In: Proceedings of the IEEE Conference on Computer Vision and Pattern Recognition, pp. 1725–1732 (2014)
6. Oktay, O., et al.: Attention U-net: learning where to look for the pancreas. arXiv preprint arXiv:1804.03999 (2018)

7. Peng, P., Lekadir, K., Gooya, A., Shao, L., Petersen, S.E., Frangi, A.F.: A review of heart chamber segmentation for structural and functional analysis using cardiac magnetic resonance imaging. Magn. Reson. Mater. Phys. Biol. Med. **29**(2), 155–195 (2016). https://doi.org/10.1007/s10334-015-0521-4

8. Ronneberger, O., Fischer, P., Brox, T.: U-Net: convolutional networks for biomedical image segmentation. In: Navab, N., Hornegger, J., Wells, W.M., Frangi, A.F. (eds.) MICCAI 2015. LNCS, vol. 9351, pp. 234–241. Springer, Cham (2015). https://doi.org/10.1007/978-3-319-24574-4_28

9. Vaswani, A., et al.: Attention is all you need (2017)

10. Vick III, G.W.: The gold standard for noninvasive imaging in coronary heart disease: magnetic resonance imaging. Curr. Opin. Cardiol. **24**(6), 567–579 (2009)

11. Wang, T., et al.: MSU-net: multiscale statistical U-net for real-time 3D cardiac MRI video segmentation. In: Shen, D., et al. (eds.) MICCAI 2019. LNCS, vol. 11765, pp. 614–622. Springer, Cham (2019). https://doi.org/10.1007/978-3-030-32245-8_68

12. Xue, T., Chen, B., Wu, J., Wei, D., Freeman, W.T.: Video enhancement with task-oriented flow. Int. J. Comput. Vision **127**(8), 1106–1125 (2019)

13. Yang, R., Xu, M., Wang, Z., Li, T.: Multi-frame quality enhancement for compressed video. In: Proceedings of the IEEE Conference on Computer Vision and Pattern Recognition, pp. 6664–6673 (2018)

14. Zheng, H., et al.: HFA-Net: 3D cardiovascular image segmentation with asymmetrical pooling and content-aware fusion. In: Shen, D., et al. (eds.) MICCAI 2019. LNCS, vol. 11765, pp. 759–767. Springer, Cham (2019). https://doi.org/10.1007/978-3-030-32245-8_84

15. Zotti, C., Luo, Z., Humbert, O., Lalande, A., Jodoin, P.-M.: GridNet with automatic shape prior registration for automatic MRI cardiac segmentation. In: Pop, M., et al. (eds.) STACOM 2017. LNCS, vol. 10663, pp. 73–81. Springer, Cham (2018). https://doi.org/10.1007/978-3-319-75541-0_8

Learning Directional Feature Maps for Cardiac MRI Segmentation

Feng Cheng[1], Cheng Chen[1], Yukang Wang[1], Heshui Shi[2,3], Yukun Cao[2,3], Dandan Tu[4], Changzheng Zhang[4], and Yongchao Xu[1(✉)]

[1] School of Electronic Information and Communications,
Huazhong University of Science and Technology, Wuhan, China
yongchaoxu@hust.edu.cn
[2] Department of Radiology, Union Hospital, Tongji Medical College, Huazhong University of Science and Technology, Wuhan, China
[3] Hubei Province Key Laboratory of Molecular Imaging, Wuhan, China
[4] HUST-HW Joint Innovation Lab, Wuhan, China

Abstract. Cardiac MRI segmentation plays a crucial role in clinical diagnosis for evaluating personalized cardiac performance parameters. Due to the indistinct boundaries and heterogeneous intensity distributions in the cardiac MRI, most existing methods still suffer from two aspects of challenges: inter-class indistinction and intra-class inconsistency. To tackle these two problems, we propose a novel method to exploit the directional feature maps, which can simultaneously strengthen the differences between classes and the similarities within classes. Specifically, we perform cardiac segmentation and learn a direction field pointing away from the nearest cardiac tissue boundary to each pixel via a direction field (DF) module. Based on the learned direction field, we then propose a feature rectification and fusion (FRF) module to improve the original segmentation features, and obtain the final segmentation. The proposed modules are simple yet effective and can be flexibly added to any existing segmentation network without excessively increasing time and space complexity. We evaluate the proposed method on the 2017 MICCAI Automated Cardiac Diagnosis Challenge (ACDC) dataset and a large-scale self-collected dataset, showing good segmentation performance and robust generalization ability of the proposed method. The code is publicly available at https://github.com/c-feng/ DirectionalFeature.

Keywords: Cardiac segmentation · Deep learning · Direction field

1 Introduction

Cardiac cine Magnetic Resonance Imaging (MRI) segmentation is of great importance in disease diagnosis and surgical planning. Given the segmentation results,

---

F. Cheng and C. Chen—Equal contributions.

A. L. Martel et al. (Eds.): MICCAI 2020, LNCS 12264, pp. 108–117, 2020.
https://doi.org/10.1007/978-3-030-59719-1_11

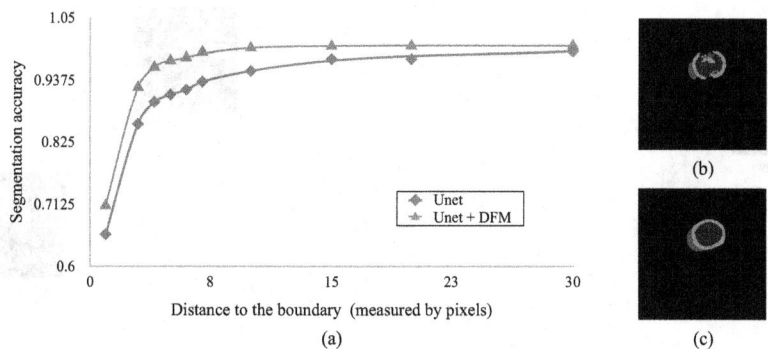

Fig. 1. (a) is the comparison of segmentation accuracy between U-Net and the proposed method at different distances from pixel to boundary; (b) and (c) are the segmentation visualizations of U-Net and the proposed method, respectively. Compared with the original U-Net, the proposed method effectively mitigate the problems of inter-class indistinction and intra-class inconsistency.

doctors can obtain the cardiac diagnostic indices such as myocardial mass and thickness, ejection fraction and ventricle volumes more efficiently. Indeed, manual segmentation is the gold standard approach. However, it is not only time-consuming but also suffers from the inter-observer variations. Hence, the automatic cardiac cine MRI segmentation is desirable in the clinic.

In the past decade, deep convolutional neural networks (CNNs) based methods have achieved great successes in both natural and medical image segmentation. U-Net [11] is one of the most successful and influential method in medical image segmentation. Recent works typically leverage the U-shape networks and can be roughly divided into 2D and 3D methods. 2D methods take a single 2D slice as input while 3D methods utilize the entire volume. nnU-Net [5] adopts the model fusion strategy of 2D U-Net and 3D U-Net, which achieves the current state-of-the-art performance in cardiac segmentation. However, the applicability is somewhat limited since it requires a high cost of memory and computation.

The MRI artifacts such as intensity inhomogeneity and fuzziness may make it indistinguishable between pixels near the boundary, leading to the problem of inter-class indistinction. As depicted in Fig. 1(a), we observe that the cardiac MRI segmentation accuracy drops dramatically for those pixels close to the boundary. Meanwhile, due to the lack of restriction on the spatial relationship between pixels, the segmentation model may produce some anatomical implausible errors (see Fig. 1(b) for an example). In this paper, we propose a novel method to improve the segmentation feature maps with directional information, which can significantly improve the inter-class indistinction as well as cope with the intra-class inconsistency. Extensive experiments demonstrate that the proposed method achieves good performance and is robust under cross-dataset validation.

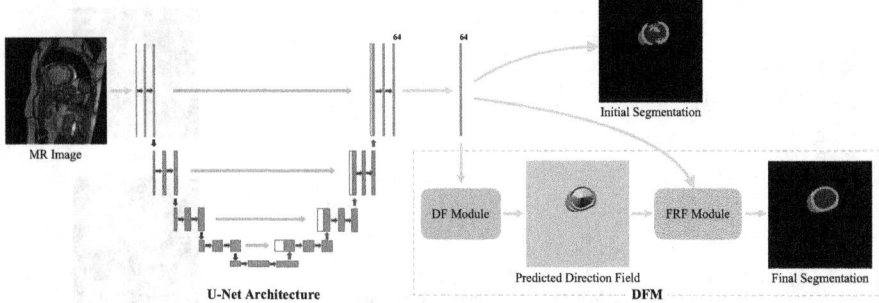

Fig. 2. Pipeline of the proposed method. Given an image, the network predicts an initial segmentation map from U-Net and a direction field (DF) (visualized by its direction information), based on which we reconstruct and fuse the original segmentation features via a feature rectification and fusion (FRF) module to produce the final segmentation.

Recent approaches in semantic segmentation have been devoted to handling the inter-class indistinction and the intra-class inconsistency. Ke *et al.* [6] define the concept of adaptive affinity fields (AAF) to capture and match the semantic relations between neighboring pixels in the label space. Cheng *et al.* [2] explore the boundary and segmentation mask information to improve the inter-class indistinction problem for instance segmentation. Shusil *et al.* [3] propose a multi-task learning framework to perform segmentation along with a pixel-wise distance map regression. This regularization method takes the distance from the pixel to the boundary as auxiliary information to handle the problem of inter-class indistinction. Nathan *et al.* [9] propose an adversarial variational auto-encoder to assure anatomically plausible, whose latent space encodes a smooth manifold on which lies a large spectrum of valid cardiac shapes, thereby indirectly solving the intra-class inconsistency problem.

Directional information has been recently explored in different vision tasks. For instance, TextField [14] and DeepFlux [12] learn similar direction fields on text areas and skeleton context for scene text detection and skeleton extraction, respectively. They directly construct text instances or recover skeletons from the direction field. However, medical images are inherently different from natural images. Such segmentation results obtained directly from the direction field are not accurate for the MRI segmentation task. In this paper, we propose to improve the original segmentation features guided by the directional information for better cardiac MRI segmentation.

2   Method

Inter-class indistinction and intra-class inconsistency are commonly found in both natural and medical image segmentation. Meanwhile, segmentation models usually learn individual representations and thus lack of restrictions on the relationship between pixels. We propose a simple yet effective method to exploit the directional relationship between pixels, which can simultaneously strengthen the differences between classes and the similarities within classes. The pipeline of the proposed method, termed as DFM, is depicted in Fig. 2. We adopt U-Net [11] as our base segmentation framework. Given an input image, the network produces the initial segmentation map. Meanwhile, we apply a direction field (DF) module to learn the direction field with the shared features from U-Net. A feature rectification feature (FRF) module is then proposed to combine the initial segmentation feature with the learned direction field to generate the final improved segmentation result.

2.1   DF Module to Learn a Direction Field

We first detail the notation of the direction field. As shown in Fig. 3(a, b), for each foreground pixel p, we find its nearest pixel b lying on the cardiac tissue boundary and then normalize the direction vector $\overrightarrow{bp}$ pointing from b to p by the distance between b and p. We set the background pixels to $(0,0)$. Formally, the direction field DF for each pixel p in the image domain Ω is given by:

$$DF(p) = \begin{cases} \frac{\overrightarrow{bp}}{|\overrightarrow{bp}|} & p \in foreground, \\ (0,0) & otherwise. \end{cases} \tag{1}$$

We propose a simple yet effective DF module to learn the above direction field, which is depicted in Fig. 3. This module is made up of a 1×1 convolution, whose input is the 64-channel feature extracted by U-Net and output is the two-channel direction field. It is noteworthy that we can obtain the ground truth of the direction field from the annotation easily by distance transform algorithm.

2.2   FRF Module for Feature Rectification and Fusion

The direction field predicted by the DF module reveals the directional relationship between pixels and provides a unique direction vector that points from the boundary to the central area for each pixel. Guided by these direction vectors, we propose a Feature Rectification and Fusion (FRF) module to utilize the characteristics of the central area to rectify the errors in the initial segmentation feature maps step by step. As illustrated in Fig. 4, the N-steps improved feature maps $F^N \in \mathbb{R}^{C \times H \times W}$ are obtained with the initial feature maps $F^0 \in \mathbb{R}^{C \times H \times W}$ and the predicted direction field $DF \in \mathbb{R}^{2 \times H \times W}$ step by step. Concretely, the improved feature of the pixel p is updated iteratively by the feature of the position that $DF(p)$ points to, which is calculated by the bilinear interpolation. In other words, $F(p)$ is rectified by the features of the central area gradually. The whole procedure is formalized as below:

$$\forall p \in \Omega, F^k(p) = F^{(k-1)}(p_x + DF(p)_x, p_y + DF(p)_y), \tag{2}$$

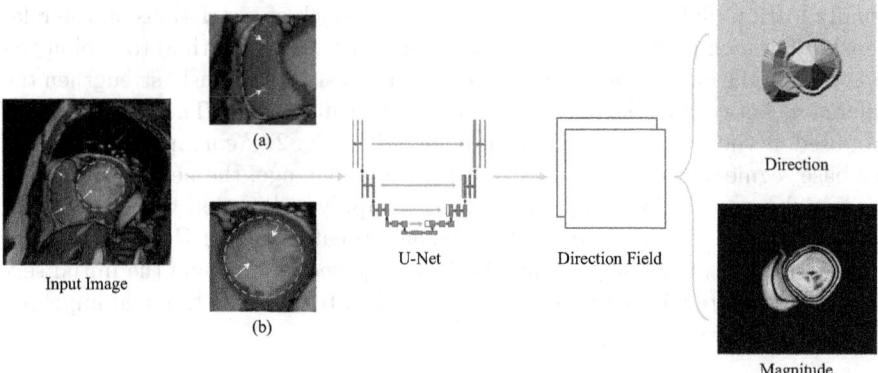

Fig. 3. Illustration of the DF module. Given an image, the network predicts a novel direction field in terms of an image of two-dimensional vectors. (a) and (b) show the vector from the nearest boundary pixel to the current pixel. We calculate and visualize the direction and magnitude information of the direction field on the right side.

where $1 \leq k \leq N$ denotes the current step, N is the total steps (set to 5 if not stated otherwise), and p_x (*resp.* p_y) represents the x (*resp.* y) coordinate of the pixel p.

After performing the above rectification process, we concatenate F^N with F^0, and then apply the final classifier on the concatenated feature maps to predict the final cardiac segmentation.

2.3   Training Objective

The proposed method involves loss function on the initial segmentation L_{CE}^i, final segmentation L_{CE}^f, and direction field L_{DF}. We adopt the general cross-entropy L_{CE} as the segmentation loss to encourage class-seperate feature, which is commonly used in semantic segmentation. Formally, L_{CE} is given by $L_{CE} = -\sum_i y_i log(\hat{y}_i)$, where y_i and $\hat{y}_i$ denote the ground truth and the prediction, respectively. For the loss to supervise the direction field learning, we choose the L_2-norm distance and angle distance as the training objective:

$$L_{DF} = \sum_{p \in \Omega} w(p)(||DF(p) - \hat{DF}(p)||_2 + \alpha \times ||cos^{-1}\langle DF(p), \hat{DF}(p)\rangle||^2) \quad (3)$$

where $\hat{DF}$ and DF denote the predicted direction field and the corresponding ground truth, respectively, α is a hyperparameter to balance the L_2-norm distance and angle distance, and is to 1 in all experiments, and $w(p)$ represents the weight on pixel p, which is calculated by:

$$w(p) = \begin{cases} \frac{\sum_{i=1}^{N_{cls}} |C_i|}{N_{cls} \cdot |C_i|} & p \in C_i, \\ 1 & otherwise, \end{cases} \quad (4)$$

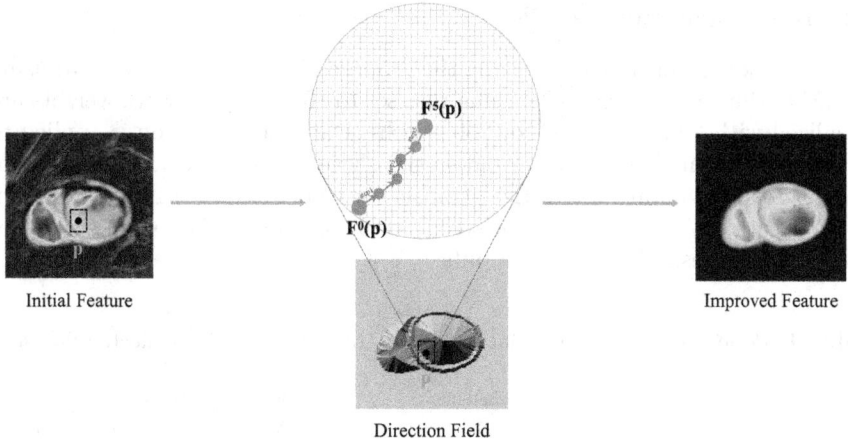

Fig. 4. Schematic illustration of the FRF module. We use the learned direction field to guide the feature rectification. The feature for pixels close to the boundary is rectified with the feature (having the same semantic category) far from the boundary.

where $|C_i|$ denotes the total number of pixels with label i and N_{cls} is the number of classes. The overall loss L combines L_{CE} and L_{DF} with a balance factor $\lambda = 1$:

$$L = L^i_{CE} + L^f_{CE} + \lambda L_{DF} \tag{5}$$

3 Experiments

3.1 Datasets and Evaluation Metrics

Automatic Cardiac Diagnosis Challenge (ACDC) Dataset contains cine-MR images of 150 patients, split into 100 train images and 50 test images. These patients are divided into 5 evenly distributed subgroups: normal, myocardial infarction, dilated cardiomyopathy, hypertrophic cardiomyopathy and abnormal right ventricle, available as a part of the STACOM 2017 ACDC challenge. The annotations for the 50 test images are hold by the challenge organizer. We also further divide the 100 training images into 80% training and 20% validation with five non-overlapping folds to perform extensive experiments.

Self-collected Dataset consists of more than 100k 2D images that we collected from 531 patient cases. All the data was labeled by a team of medical experts. The patients are also divided into the same 5 subgroups as ACDC. A series of short axis slices cover LV from the base to the apex, with a thickness of 6 mm and a flip angle of 80°. The magnitude field strength of images is 1.5 T and the spatial resolution is 1.328 mm^2/pixel. We also split all the patients into 80% training and 20% test.

Evaluation Metrics: We adopt the widely used 3D Dice coefficient and Hausdorff distance to benchmark the proposed method.

3.2   Implementation Details

The network is trained by minimizing the proposed loss function in Eq. (5) using ADAM optimizer [8] with the learning rate set to 10^{-3}. The network weights are initialized with [4] and trained for 200 epochs. Data augmentation is applied to prevent over-fitting including: 1) random translation with the maximum absolute fraction for horizontal and vertical translations both set to 0.125; 2) random rotation with the random angle between $-180°$ and $180°$. The batch size is set to 32 with the resized 256×256 inputs.

Table 1. Performance on ACDC dataset (train/val split) and Self-collected dataset.

	Methods	Dice coefficient				Hausdorff distance (mm)			
		LV	RV	MYO	Mean	LV	RV	MYO	Mean
ACDC dataset	U-Net	0.931	0.856	0.872	0.886	24.609	30.006	14.416	23.009
	Ours	**0.949**	**0.888**	**0.911**	**0.916**	**3.761**	**6.037**	**10.282**	**6.693**
Self-collected dataset	U-Net	0.948	0.854	0.906	0.903	2.823	3.691	2.951	3.155
	Ours	**0.949**	**0.859**	**0.909**	**0.906**	**2.814**	**3.409**	**2.683**	**2.957**

Table 2. Results on the ACDC leaderboard (sorted by Mean Hausdorff Distance).

Rank	User	Mean DICE	Mean HD (mm)
1	Fabian Isensee [5]	0.927	7.8
2	Clement Zotti [15]	0.9138	9.51
3	**Ours**	**0.911**	**9.92**
4	Nathan Painchaud [9]	0.911	9.93
5	Christian Baumgartner [1]	0.9046	10.4
6	Jelmer Wolterink [13]	0.908	10.7
7	Mahendra Khened [7]	0.9136	11.23
8	Shubham Jain [10]	0.8915	12.07

3.3   In-Dataset Results

We first evaluate the proposed method on the ACDC dataset (train/val split described in Sect. 3.1) and the self-collected dataset. Table 1 presents the performance of the proposed DFM on two datasets. LV, RV and MYO represent the left ventricle, right ventricle and myocardium, respectively. Our approach consistently improves the baseline (U-Net), demonstrating its effectiveness. To further make comparison with the current state-of-the-arts methods, we submit the results to the ACDC leadboard. As shown in Table 2, compared with

Table 3. Comparisons with different methods aiming to alleviate the inter-class indistinction and intra-class inconsistency on ACDC dataset (train/val split).

Methods	Dice coefficient				Hausdorff distance (mm)			
	LV	MYO	RV	Mean	LV	MYO	RV	Mean
U-Net	0.931	0.856	0.872	0.886	24.609	30.006	14.416	23.009
AAF [6]	0.928	0.853	0.891	0.891	13.306	14.255	13.969	13.844
DMR [3]	0.937	0.880	0.892	0.903	7.520	9.870	12.385	9.925
U-Net+DFM	**0.949**	**0.888**	**0.911**	**0.916**	**3.761**	**6.037**	**10.282**	**6.693**

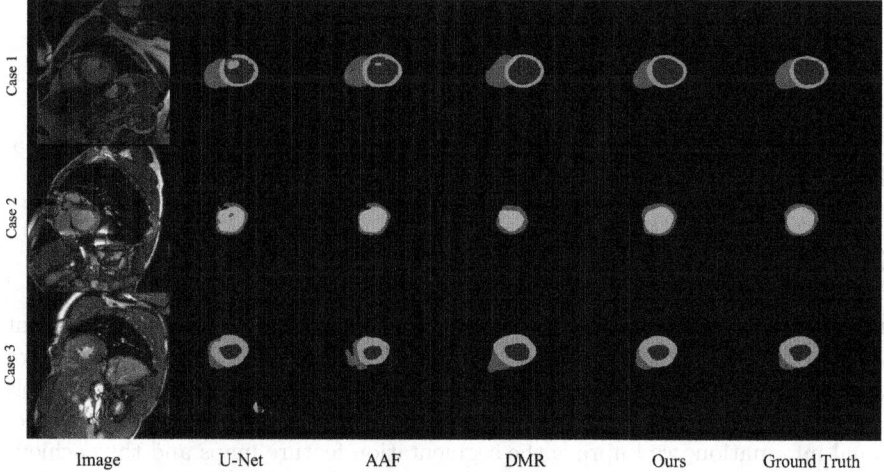

Fig. 5. Qualitative comparison on ACDC dataset. The proposed DFM achieves more accurate results along with better smoothness and continuity in shape.

those methods that rely on well-designed networks (*e.g.* 3D network in [5] and Grid-like CNN in [15]) or multi-model fusion, the proposed DFM achieves competitive performance with only two simple yet effective modules added to the baseline U-Net. We also compare our approach with other methods dedicated to alleviate the inter-class indistinction and intra-class inconsistency. As depicted in Table 3, the proposed DFM significantly outperforms these methods. Some qualitative comparisons are given in Fig. 5.

3.4 Cross Dataset Evaluation and Ablation Study

To analyze the generalization ability of the proposed DFM, we performed a cross-dataset segmentation evaluation. Results listed in Table 4 show that the proposed DFM can consistently improve the cross-dataset performance compared with the original U-Net, validating its generalization ability and robustness. We also conduct ablation study on ACDC dataset to explore how the number of steps N

Table 4. Cross-dataset evaluation compared with the original U-Net.

Methods	ACDC to self-collected dataset		Self-collected dataset to ACDC	
	Mean dice	Mean HD (mm)	Mean dice	Mean HD (mm)
U-Net	0.832	25.553	0.803	4.896
U-Net+DFM	**0.841**	**17.870**	**0.820**	**4.453**

Table 5. Ablation study on the number of steps N on ACDC dataset.

Number of steps	0	1	3	5	7
Mean dice	0.910	0.913	0.914	**0.916**	0.910
Mean HD (mm)	10.498	17.846	9.026	**6.693**	13.880

involved in the FRF module influences the performance. As shown in Table 5, the setting of $N = 5$ gives the best performance.

4   Conclusion

In this paper, we explore the importance of directional information and present a simple yet effective method for cardiac MRI segmentation. We propose to learn a direction field, which characterizes the directional relationship between pixels and implicitly restricts the shape of the segmentation result. Guided by the directional information, we improve the segmentation feature maps and thus achieve better segmentation accuracy. Experimental results demonstrate the effectiveness and the robust generalization ability of the proposed method.

Acknowledgement. This work was supported in part by the Major Project for New Generation of AI under Grant no. 2018AAA0100400, NSFC 61703171, and NSF of Hubei Province of China under Grant 2018CFB199. Dr. Yongchao Xu was supported by the Young Elite Scientists Sponsorship Program by CAST.

References

1. Baumgartner, C.F., Koch, L.M., Pollefeys, M., Konukoglu, E.: An exploration of 2D and 3D deep learning techniques for cardiac MR image segmentation. In: Pop, M., et al. (eds.) STACOM 2017. Lecture Notes in Computer Science, vol. 10663, pp. 111–119. Springer, Cham (2017). https://doi.org/10.1007/978-3-319-75541-0_12
2. Cheng, T., Wang, X., Huang, L., Liu, W.: Boundary-preserving mask R-CNN. In: Proceedings of European Conference on Computer Vision (2020)
3. Dangi, S., Linte, C.A., Yaniv, Z.: A distance map regularized CNN for cardiac cine MR image segmentation. Med. Phys. **46**(12), 5637–5651 (2019)
4. He, K., Zhang, X., Ren, S., Sun, J.: Delving deep into rectifiers: surpassing human-level performance on ImageNet classification. In: Proceedings of IEEE International Conference on Computer Vision and Pattern Recognition, pp. 1026–1034 (2015)

5. Isensee, F., Petersen, J., Kohl, S.A., Jäger, P.F., Maier-Hein, K.H.: NNU-net: breaking the spell on successful medical image segmentation. arXiv preprint arXiv:1904.08128 (2019)
6. Ke, T.W., Hwang, J.J., Liu, Z., Yu, S.X.: Adaptive affinity fields for semantic segmentation. In: Proceedings of European Conference on Computer Vision, pp. 587–602 (2018)
7. Khened, M., Kollerathu, V.A., Krishnamurthi, G.: Fully convolutional multi-scale residual DenseNets for cardiac segmentation and automated cardiac diagnosis using ensemble of classifiers. Med. Image Anal. **51**, 21–45 (2019)
8. Kingma, D.P., Ba, J.: Adam: a method for stochastic optimization. arXiv preprint arXiv:1412.6980 (2014)
9. Painchaud, N., Skandarani, Y., Judge, T., Bernard, O., Lalande, A., Jodoin, P.M.: Cardiac MRI segmentation with strong anatomical guarantees. In: Shen, D., et al. (eds.) MICCAI 2019. LNCS, vol. 11765, pp. 632–640. Springer, Cham (2019). https://doi.org/10.1007/978-3-030-32245-8_70
10. Patravali, J., Jain, S., Chilamkurthy, S.: 2D-3D fully convolutional neural networks for cardiac MR segmentation. In: Pop, M., et al. (eds.) STACOM 2017. LNCS, vol. 10663, pp. 130–139. Springer, Cham (2018). https://doi.org/10.1007/978-3-319-75541-0_14
11. Ronneberger, O., Fischer, P., Brox, T.: U-net: convolutional networks for biomedical image segmentation. In: Navab, N., Hornegger, J., Wells, W., Frangi, A. (eds.) MICCAI 2015. LNCS, vol. 9351, pp. 234–241. Springer, Cham (2015). https://doi.org/10.1007/978-3-319-24574-4_28
12. Wang, Y., Xu, Y., Tsogkas, S., Bai, X., Dickinson, S., Siddiqi, K.: DeepFlux for skeletons in the wild. In: Proceedings of IEEE International Conference on Computer Vision and Pattern Recognition, pp. 5287–5296 (2019)
13. Wolterink, J.M., Leiner, T., Viergever, M.A., Išgum, I.: Automatic segmentation and disease classification using cardiac cine MR images. In: Pop, M., et al. (eds.) STACOM 2017. LNCS, vol. 10663, pp. 101–110. Springer, Cham (2017). https://doi.org/10.1007/978-3-319-75541-0_11
14. Xu, Y., Wang, Y., Zhou, W., Wang, Y., Yang, Z., Bai, X.: TextField: learning a deep direction field for irregular scene text detection. IEEE Trans. Image Process. **28**(11), 5566–5579 (2019)
15. Zotti, C., Luo, Z., Lalande, A., Jodoin, P.M.: Convolutional neural network with shape prior applied to cardiac MRI segmentation. IEEE J. Biomed. Health Inf. **23**(3), 1119–1128 (2018)

Joint Left Atrial Segmentation and Scar Quantification Based on a DNN with Spatial Encoding and Shape Attention

Lei Li[1,2,3], Xin Weng[2], Julia A. Schnabel[3], and Xiahai Zhuang[2(✉)]

[1] School of Biomedical Engineering, Shanghai Jiao Tong University, Shanghai, China
[2] School of Data Science, Fudan University, Shanghai, China
zxh@fudan.edu.cn
[3] School of Biomedical Engineering and Imaging Sciences, King's College London, London, UK

Abstract. We propose an end-to-end deep neural network (DNN) which can simultaneously segment the left atrial (LA) cavity and quantify LA scars. The framework incorporates the continuous spatial information of the target by introducing a spatially encoded (SE) loss based on the distance transform map. Compared to conventional binary label based loss, the proposed SE loss can reduce noisy patches in the resulting segmentation, which is commonly seen for deep learning-based methods. To fully utilize the inherent spatial relationship between LA and LA scars, we further propose a shape attention (SA) mechanism through an explicit surface projection to build an end-to-end-trainable model. Specifically, the SA scheme is embedded into a two-task network to perform the joint LA segmentation and scar quantification. Moreover, the proposed method can alleviate the severe class-imbalance problem when detecting small and discrete targets like scars. We evaluated the proposed framework on 60 LGE MRI data from the MICCAI2018 LA challenge. For LA segmentation, the proposed method reduced the mean Hausdorff distance from 36.4 mm to 20.0 mm compared to the 3D basic U-Net using the binary cross-entropy loss. For scar quantification, the method was compared with the results or algorithms reported in the literature and demonstrated better performance.

Keywords: Atrial scar segmentation · Spatial encoding · Shape attention

1 Introduction

Atrial fibrillation (AF) is the most common cardiac arrhythmia which increases the risk of stroke, heart failure and death [2]. Radiofrequency ablation is a promising procedure for treating AF, where patient selection and outcome prediction of such therapy can be improved through left atrial (LA) scar localization and quantification. Atrial scars are located on the LA wall, thus it

© Springer Nature Switzerland AG 2020
A. L. Martel et al. (Eds.): MICCAI 2020, LNCS 12264, pp. 118–127, 2020.
https://doi.org/10.1007/978-3-030-59719-1_12

normally requires LA/LA wall segmentation to exclude confounding enhanced tissues from other substructures of the heart. Late gadolinium enhanced magnetic resonance imaging (LGE MRI) has been an important tool for scar visualization and quantification. Manual delineations of LGE MRI can be subjective and labor-intensive. However, automating this segmentation remains challenging, mainly due to the various LA shapes, thin LA wall, poor image quality and enhanced noise from surrounding tissues.

Limited studies have been reported in the literature to develop automatic LA segmentation and scar quantification algorithms. For LA segmentation, Xiong et al. proposed a dual fully convolutional neural network (CNN) [11]. In an LA segmentation challenge [14], Chen et al. presented a two-task network for atrial segmentation and post/pre classification to incorporate the prior information of the patient category [1]. Nunez et al. achieved LA segmentation by combining multi-atlas segmentation and shape modeling of LA [9]. Recently, Yu et al. designed an uncertainty-aware semi-supervised framework for LA segmentation [12]. For scar quantification, most of the current works adopted threshold-based methods that relied on manual LA wall segmentation [6]. Some other conventional algorithms, such as Gaussian mixture model (GMM) [4], also required an accurate initialization of LA or LA wall. However, automatic LA wall segmentation is complex and challenging due to its inherent thin thickness (1–2mm) [5]. Recent studies show that the thickness can be ignored, as clinical studies mainly focus on the location and extent of scars [7,10]. For example, Li et al. proposed a graph-cuts framework for scar quantification on the LA surface mesh, where the weights of the graph were learned via a multi-scale CNN [7]. However, they did not achieve an end-to-end training, i.e., the multi-scale CNN and graph-cuts were separated into two sub-tasks.

Recently, deep learning (DL)-based methods have achieved promising performance for cardiac image segmentation. However, most DL-based segmentation methods are trained with a loss only considering a label mask in a discrete space. Due to the lack of spatial information, predictions commonly tend to be blurry in boundary, and it leads to noisy segmentation with large outliers. To solve this problem, several strategies have been employed, such as graph-cuts/CRF regularization [3,7], and deformation combining shape priors [13].

In this work, we present an end-to-end multi-task learning network for joint LA segmentation and scar quantification. The proposed method incorporates spatial information in the pipeline to eliminate outliers for LA segmentation, with additional benefits for scar quantification. This is achieved by introducing a spatially encoded loss based on the distance transform map, without any modifications of the network. To utilize the spatial relationship between LA and scars, we adopt the LA boundary as an attention mask on the scar map, namely surface projection, to achieve shape attention. Therefore, an end-to-end learning framework is created for simultaneous LA segmentation, scar projection and quantification via the multi-task learning (MTL) network embedding the spatial encoding (SE) and boundary shape attention (SA), namely MTL-SESA network.

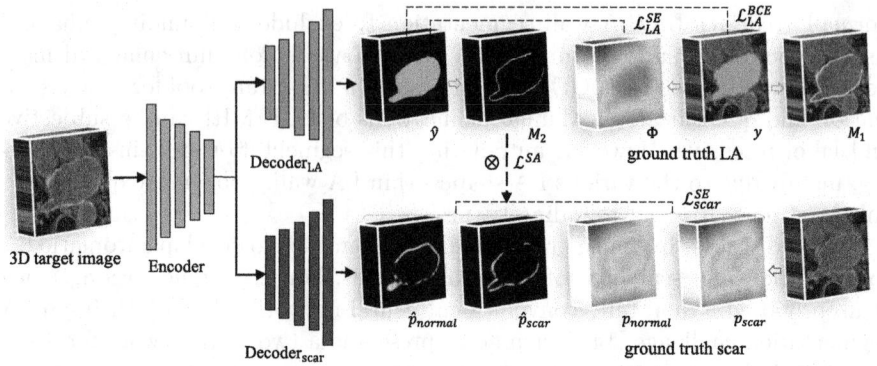

Fig. 1. The proposed MTL-SESA network for joint LA segmentation and scar quantification. Note that the skip connections between the encoder and two decoders are omitted here.

2   Method

Figure 1 provides an overview of the proposed framework. The proposed network is a modified U-Net consisting of two decoders for LA segmentation and scar quantification, respectively. In Sect. 2.1, a SE loss based on the distance transform map is introduced as a regularization term for LA segmentation. For scar segmentation, a SE loss based on the distance probability map is employed, followed by a spatial projection (see Sect. 2.2). Section 2.3 presents the specific SA scheme embedded in the MTL network for the predictions of LA and LA scars in an end-to-end style.

2.1   Spatially Encoded Constraint for LA Segmentation

A SE loss based on the signed distance transform map (DTM) is employed as a regularization term to represent a spatial vicinity to the target label. Given a target label, the signed DTM for each pixel x_i can be defined as:

$$\phi(x_i) = \begin{cases} -d^\beta & x_i \in \Omega_{in} \\ 0 & x_i \in S \\ d^\beta & x_i \in \Omega_{out} \end{cases} \quad (1)$$

where Ω_{in} and Ω_{out} respectively indicate the region inside and outside the target label, S denotes the surface boundary, d represents the distance from pixel x_i to the nearest point on S, and β is a hyperparameter. The binary cross-entropy (BCE) loss and the additional SE loss for LA segmentation can be defined as:

$$\mathcal{L}_{LA}^{BCE} = \sum_{i=1}^{N} y_i \cdot log(\hat{y}(x_i; \theta)) + (1 - y_i) \cdot log(1 - \hat{y}(x_i; \theta)) \quad (2)$$

$$\mathcal{L}_{LA}^{SE} = \sum_{i=1}^{N} (\hat{y}(x_i; \theta) - 0.5) \cdot \phi(x_i) \tag{3}$$

where $\hat{y}$ and y ($y \in \{0, 1\}$) are the prediction of LA and its ground truth, respectively, and $\cdot$ denotes element-wise product.

2.2 Spatially Encoded Constraint with an Explicit Projection for Scar Quantification

For scar quantification, we encode the spatial information by adopting the distance probability map of normal wall and scar region as the ground truth instead of binary scar label. This is because the scar region can be very small and discrete, thus its detection presents significant challenges to current DL-based methods due to the class-imbalance problem. In contrast to traditional DL-based algorithms optimizing in a discrete space, the distance probability map considers the continuous spatial information of scars. Specifically, we separately obtain the DTM of the scar and normal wall from a manual scar label, and convert both into probability maps $p(x_i) = [p_{normal}, p_{scar}]$. Here $p = e^{-d'}$ and d' is the nearest distance to the boundary of normal wall or scar for pixel x_i. Then, the SE loss for scar quantification can be defined as:

$$\mathcal{L}_{scar}^{SE} = \sum_{i=1}^{N} \|\hat{p}(x_i; \theta) - p(x_i)\|_2^2, \tag{4}$$

where $\hat{p}$ ($\hat{p} = [\hat{p}_{normal}, \hat{p}_{scar}]$) is the predicted distance probability map of both normal wall and scar region. Note that the situation of $\hat{p}_{normal} + \hat{p}_{scar} > 1$ sometimes exists. One can compare these two probabilities to extract scars instead of employing a fixed threshold.

To ignore the wall thickness which varies from different positions and patients [5], the extracted scars are explicitly projected onto the LA surface. Therefore, the volume-based scar segmentation is converted into a surface-based scar quantification through the spatially explicit projection. However, the pixel-based classification in the surface-based quantification task only includes very limited information, i.e., the intensity value of one pixel. In contrast to extracting multi-scale patches along the LA surface [7], we employ the SE loss to learn the spatial features near the LA surface. Similar to [7], the SE loss can also be beneficial to improving the robustness of the framework against the LA segmentation errors.

2.3 Multi-task Learning with an End-to-End Trainable Shape Attention

To employ the spatial relationship between LA and atrial scars, we design an MTL network including two decoders, i.e., one for LA and the other for scar segmentation. As Fig. 1 shows, the Decoder$_{LA}$ is supervised by $\mathcal{L}_{LA}^{BCE}$ and $\mathcal{L}_{LA}^{SE}$, and the Decoder$_{scar}$ is supervised by $\mathcal{L}_{scar}^{SE}$. To explicitly learn the relationship between the two tasks, we extract the LA boundary from the predicted LA as an attention mask for the training of Decoder$_{scar}$, namely explicit projection mentioned in Sect. 2.2. An SA loss is introduced to enforce the attention of Decoder$_{scar}$ on the LA boundary:

$$\mathcal{L}^{SA} = \sum_{i=1}^{N} (M \cdot (\nabla \hat{p}(x_i; \theta) - \nabla p(x_i)))^2 \tag{5}$$

where $\nabla \hat{p} = \hat{p}_{normal} - \hat{p}_{scar}$, $\nabla p = p_{normal} - p_{scar}$, and M is the boundary attention mask, which can be generated from the gold standard segmentation of LA (M_1) as well as the predicted LA (M_2). Hence, the total loss of the framework is defined by combining all the losses mentioned above:

$$\mathcal{L} = \mathcal{L}_{LA}^{BCE} + \lambda_{LA} \mathcal{L}_{LA}^{SE} + \lambda_{scar} \mathcal{L}_{scar}^{SE} + \lambda_{M_1} \mathcal{L}_{scar M_1}^{SA} + \lambda_{M_2} \mathcal{L}_{scar M_2}^{SA} \tag{6}$$

where λ_{LA}, λ_{scar}, λ_{M_1} and λ_{M_2} are balancing parameters.

3   Experiments

3.1   Materials

Data Acquisition and Pre-processing. The data is from the MICCAI2018 LA challenge [14]. The 100 LGE MRI training data, with manual segmentation of LA, consists of 60 post-ablation and 40 pre-ablation data. In this work, we chose the 60 post-ablation data for manual segmentation of the LA scars and employed them for experiments. The LGE MRIs were acquired with a resolution of $0.625 \times 0.625 \times 0.625$ mm and reconstructed to $1 \times 1 \times 1$ mm. All images were cropped into a unified size of $208 \times 208 \times 80$ centering at the heart region and were normalized using Z-score. We split the images into two sets, i.e., one with 40 images for training and the other with 20 for the test.

Gold Standard and Evaluation. The challenge provides LA manual segmentation for the training data, and scars of the 60 post-ablation data were manually delineated by a well-trained expert. These manual segmentations were considered as the gold standard. For LA segmentation evaluation, Dice volume overlap, average surface distance (ASD) and Hausdorff distance (HD) were applied. For scar quantification evaluation, the manual and (semi-) automatic segmentation results were first projected onto the manually segmented LA surface. Then, the *Accuracy* measurement of the two areas in the projected surface, Dice of scars (Dice$_{scar}$) and generalized Dice score (GDice) were used as indicators of the accuracy of scar quantification.

Implementation. The framework was implemented in PyTorch, running on a computer with 1.90 GHz Intel(R) Xeon(R) E5-2620 CPU and an NVIDIA

TITAN X GPU. We used the SGD optimizer to update the network parameters (weight decay = 0.0001, momentum = 0.9). The initial learning rate was set to 0.001 and divided by 10 every 4000 iterations. The balancing parameters in Sect. 2.3, were set as follows, $\lambda_{LA} = 0.01$, $\lambda_{scar} = 10$, $\lambda_{M_1} = 0.01$ and $\lambda_{M_2} = 0.001$, where λ_{LA} and λ_{M_2} was multiplied by 1.1 every 200 iterations as it achieved more robust results compared to the fixed values. The inference of the networks required about 8 s to process one test image.

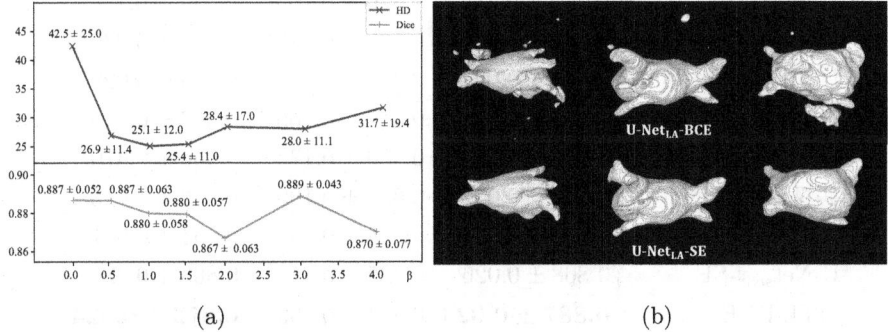

(a)   (b)

Fig. 2. Quantitative and qualitative evaluation results of the proposed SE loss for LA segmentation: (a) Dice and HD of the LA segmentation results after combining the SE loss, i.e., U-Net$_{LA}$-SE with different β for DTM; (b) 3D visualization of the LA segmentation results of three typical cases by U-Net$_{LA}$-BCE and U-Net$_{LA}$-SE.

Table 1. Summary of the quantitative evaluation results of LA segmentation. Here, U-Net$_{LA}$ uses the original U-Net architecture for LA segmentation; MTL means that the methods are based on the architecture in Fig. 1 with two decoders; BCE, SE, SA and SESA refer to the different loss functions. The proposed method is denoted as MTL-SESA.

Method	Dice	ASD (mm)	HD (mm)
U-Net$_{LA}$-BCE	0.889 ± 0.035	2.12 ± 0.80	36.4 ± 23.6
U-Net$_{LA}$-SE	0.880 ± 0.058	2.36 ± 1.49	25.1 ± 11.9
MTL-BCE	0.890 ± 0.042	2.11 ± 1.01	28.5 ± 14.0
MTL-SE	0.909 ± 0.033	1.69 ± 0.69	22.4 ± 9.80
MTL-SESA	$\mathbf{0.913 \pm 0.032}$	$\mathbf{1.60 \pm 0.72}$	$\mathbf{20.0 \pm 9.59}$

Table 2. Summary of the quantitative evaluation results of scar quantification. Here, LA_M denotes that scar quantification is based on the manually segmented LA, while LA_{U-Net} indicates that it is based on the U-Net$_{LA}$-BCE segmentation; U-Net$_{scar}$ is the scar segmentation directly based on the U-Net architecture with different loss functions; The inter-observer variation (Inter-Ob) is calculated from randomly selected twelve subjects.

Method	Accuracy	Dice$_{scar}$	GDice
LA_M+Otsu [10]	0.750 ± 0.219	0.420 ± 0.106	0.750 ± 0.188
LA_M+MGMM [8]	0.717 ± 0.250	0.499 ± 0.148	0.725 ± 0.239
LA_M+LearnGC [7]	0.868 ± 0.024	0.481 ± 0.151	0.856 ± 0.029
LA_{U-Net}+Otsu	0.604 ± 0.339	0.359 ± 0.106	0.567 ± 0.359
LA_{U-Net}+MGMM	0.579 ± 0.334	0.430 ± 0.174	0.556 ± 0.370
U-Net$_{scar}$-BCE	0.866 ± 0.032	0.357 ± 0.199	0.843 ± 0.043
U-Net$_{scar}$-Dice	0.881 ± 0.030	0.374 ± 0.156	0.854 ± 0.041
U-Net$_{scar}$-SE	0.868 ± 0.026	0.485 ± 0.129	0.863 ± 0.026
MTL-BCE	$\mathbf{0.887 \pm 0.023}$	0.484 ± 0.099	$\mathbf{0.872 \pm 0.024}$
MTL-SE	0.882 ± 0.026	0.518 ± 0.110	0.871 ± 0.024
MTL-SESA	0.867 ± 0.032	$\mathbf{0.543 \pm 0.097}$	0.868 ± 0.028
Inter-Ob	0.891 ± 0.017	0.580 ± 0.110	0.888 ± 0.022

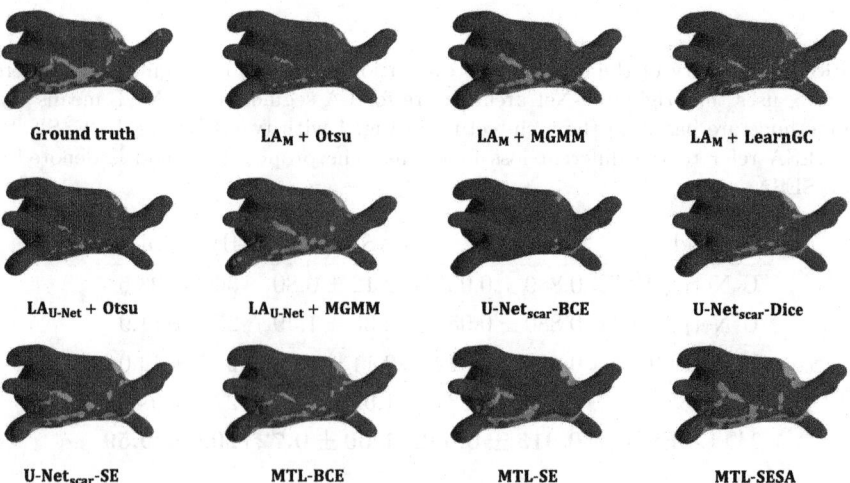

Fig. 3. 3D visualization of the LA scar localization by the eleven methods. The scarring areas are labeled in orange on the LA surface, which is constructed from LA_M labeled in blue. (Color figure online)

3.2   Result

Parameter Study. To explore the effectiveness of the SE loss, we compared the results of the proposed scheme for LA segmentation using different values of β for DTM in Eq. (1). Figure 2 (a) provides the results in terms of Dice and HD, and Fig. 2 (b) visualizes three examples for illustrating the difference of the results using or without using the SE loss. One can see that with the SE loss, U-Net$_{LA}$-SE evidently reduced clutter and disconnected parts in the segmentation compared to U-Net$_{LA}$-BCE, and significantly improved the HD of the resulting segmentation ($p < 0.001$), though the Dice score may not be very different. Also, U-Net$_{LA}$-SE showed stable performance with different values of β except for too extreme values. In the following experiments, β was set to 1.

Ablation Study. Table 1 and Table 2 present the quantitative results of different methods for LA segmentation and scar quantification, respectively. For LA segmentation, combining the proposed SE loss performed better than only using the BCE loss. For scar quantification, the SE loss also showed promising performance compared to the conventional losses in terms of Dice$_{scar}$. LA segmentation and scar quantification both benefited from the proposed MTL scheme comparing to achieving the two tasks separately. The results were further improved after introducing the newly-designed SE and SA loss in terms of Dice$_{scar}$ ($p \leq 0.001$), but with a slightly worse *Accuracy* ($p \leq 0.001$) and *G*Dice ($p > 0.1$) due to slight over-segmentation. Figure 3 visualizes an example for illustrating the segmentation and quantification results of scars from the mentioned methods in Table 2. Compared to U-Net$_{scar}$-BCE and U-Net$_{scar}$-Dice, MTL-BCE improved the performance, thanks to the MTL network architecture. When the proposed SE and SA loss were included, some small and discrete scars were also detected, and an End-To-end scar quantification and projection was achieved.

Comparisons with Literature. Table 2 and Fig. 3 also present the scar quantification results from some state-of-the-art algorithms, i.e., Otsu [10], multi-component GMM (MGMM) [8], LearnGC [7] and U-Net$_{scar}$ with different loss functions. The three (semi-) automatic methods generally obtained acceptable results, but relied on an accurate initialization of LA. LearnGC had a similar result compared to MGMM in Dice$_{scar}$ based on LA$_M$, but its *Accuracy* and *G*Dice were higher. The proposed method performed much better than all the automatic methods in terms of Dice$_{scar}$ with statistical significance ($p \leq 0.001$). In Fig. 3, one can see that Otsu and U-Net$_{scar}$ tended to under-segment the scars. Though including Dice loss could alleviate the class-imbalance problem, it is evident that the SE loss could be more effective, which is consistent with the quantitative results in Table 2. MGMM and LearnGC both detected most of the scars, but LearnGC has the potential advantage of small scar detection. The proposed method could also detect small scars and obtained a smoother segmentation result.

4   Conclusion

In this work, we have proposed an end-to-end learning framework for simultaneous LA segmentation and scar quantification by combining the SE and SA loss. The proposed algorithm has been applied to 60 image volumes acquired from AF patients and obtained comparable results to inter-observer variations. The results have demonstrated the effectiveness of the proposed SE and SA loss, and showed the superiority of segmentation performance over the conventional schemes. Particularly, the proposed SE loss substantially reduced the outliers, which frequently occurs in the prediction of DL-based methods. Our technique can be easily extended to other segmentation tasks, especially for discrete and small targets such as lesions. A limitation of this work is that the gold standard was constructed from the manual delineation of only one expert. Besides, the target included in this study is only post-ablation AF patients. In future work, we will combine multiple experts to construct the gold standard, and consider both pre- and post-ablation data.

Acknowledgement. This work was supported by the National Natural Science Foundation of China (61971142), and L. Li was partially supported by the CSC Scholarship.

References

1. Chen, C., Bai, W., Rueckert, D.: Multi-task learning for left atrial segmentation on GE-MRI. In: Pop, M., et al. (eds.) STACOM 2018. LNCS, vol. 11395, pp. 292–301. Springer, Cham (2018). https://doi.org/10.1007/978-3-030-12029-0_32
2. Chugh, S.S., et al.: Worldwide epidemiology of atrial fibrillation: a global burden of disease 2010 study. Circulation **129**(8), 837–847 (2014)
3. Kamnitsas, K., et al.: Efficient multi-scale 3D CNN with fully connected CRF for accurate brain lesion segmentation. Med. Image Anal. **36**, 61–78 (2017)
4. Karim, R., et al.: A method to standardize quantification of left atrial scar from delayed-enhancement MR images. IEEE J. Transl. Eng. Health Med. **2**, 1–15 (2014)
5. Karim, R., et al.: Algorithms for left atrial wall segmentation and thickness-evaluation on an open-source CT and MRI image database. Med. Image Anal. **50**, 36–53 (2018)
6. Karim, R., et al.: Evaluation of current algorithms for segmentation of scar tissue from late gadolinium enhancement cardiovascular magnetic resonance of the left atrium: an open-access grand challenge. J. Cardiovasc. Magn. Reson. **15**(1), 105 (2013)
7. Li, L., et al.: Atrial scar quantification via multi-scale CNN in the graph-cuts framework. Med. Image Anal. **60**, 101595 (2020)
8. Liu, J., et al.: Myocardium segmentation from DE MRI using multicomponent Gaussian mixture model and coupled level set. IEEE Trans. Biomed. Eng. **64**(11), 2650–2661 (2017)
9. Nuñez-Garcia, M., et al.: Left atrial segmentation combining multi-atlas whole heart labeling and shape-based atlas selection. In: Pop, M., et al. (eds.) STACOM 2018. LNCS, vol. 11395, pp. 302–310. Springer, Cham (2019). https://doi.org/10.1007/978-3-030-12029-0_33

10. Ravanelli, D., et al.: A novel skeleton based quantification and 3-D volumetric visualization of left atrium fibrosis using late gadolinium enhancement magnetic resonance imaging. IEEE Trans. Med. Imaging **33**(2), 566–576 (2013)
11. Xiong, Z., Fedorov, V.V., Fu, X., Cheng, E., Macleod, R., Zhao, J.: Fully automatic left atrium segmentation from late gadolinium enhanced magnetic resonance imaging using a dual fully convolutional neural network. IEEE Trans. Med. Imaging **38**(2), 515–524 (2018)
12. Yu, L., Wang, S., Li, X., Fu, C.W., Heng, P.A.: Uncertainty-aware self-ensembling model for semi-supervised 3D left atrium segmentation. In: Shen, D., et al. (eds.) MICCAI 2019. LNCS, vol. 11765, pp. 605–613. Springer, Cham (2019). https://doi.org/10.1007/978-3-030-32245-8_67
13. Zeng, Q., et al.: Liver segmentation in magnetic resonance imaging via mean shape fitting with fully convolutional neural networks. In: Shen, D., et al. (eds.) MICCAI 2019. LNCS, vol. 11765. Springer, Cham (2019). https://doi.org/10.1007/978-3-030-32245-8_28
14. Zhao, J., Xiong, Z.: 2018 atrial segmentation challenge (2018). http://atriaseg2018.cardiacatlas.org/

XCAT-GAN for Synthesizing 3D Consistent Labeled Cardiac MR Images on Anatomically Variable XCAT Phantoms

Sina Amirrajab[1]([✉]), Samaneh Abbasi-Sureshjani[1], Yasmina Al Khalil[1], Cristian Lorenz[2], Jürgen Weese[2], Josien Pluim[1], and Marcel Breeuwer[1,3]

[1] Eindhoven University of Technology, Eindhoven, The Netherlands
{s.amirrajab,s.abbasi,y.al.khalil,j.pluim,m.breeuwer}@tue.nl
[2] Philips Research Laboratories, Hamburg, Germany
{cristian.lorenz,juergen.weese}@philips.com
[3] Philips Healthcare, MR R&D - Clinical Science, Best, The Netherlands

Abstract. Generative adversarial networks (GANs) have provided promising data enrichment solutions by synthesizing high-fidelity images. However, generating large sets of labeled images with new anatomical variations remains unexplored. We propose a novel method for synthesizing cardiac magnetic resonance (CMR) images on a population of virtual subjects with a large anatomical variation, introduced using the 4D eXtended Cardiac and Torso (XCAT) computerized human phantom. We investigate two conditional image synthesis approaches grounded on a semantically-consistent mask-guided image generation technique: 4-class and 8-class XCAT-GANs. The 4-class technique relies on only the annotations of the heart; while the 8-class technique employs a predicted multi-tissue label map of the heart-surrounding organs and provides better guidance for our conditional image synthesis. For both techniques, we train our conditional XCAT-GAN with real images paired with corresponding labels and subsequently at the inference time, we substitute the labels with the XCAT derived ones. Therefore, the trained network accurately transfers the tissue-specific textures to the new label maps. By creating 33 virtual subjects of synthetic CMR images at the end-diastolic and end-systolic phases, we evaluate the usefulness of such data in the downstream cardiac cavity segmentation task under different augmentation strategies. Results demonstrate that even with only 20% of real images (40 volumes) seen during training, segmentation performance is retained with the addition of synthetic CMR images. Moreover, the improvement in utilizing synthetic images for augmenting the real data is evident through the reduction of Hausdorff distance up to 28% and an increase in the Dice score up to 5%, indicating a higher similarity to the ground truth in all dimensions.

S. Amirrajab, S. Abbasi-Sureshjani, Y. Al Khalil—Contributed equally.

Electronic supplementary material The online version of this chapter (https://doi.org/10.1007/978-3-030-59719-1_13) contains supplementary material, which is available to authorized users.

© Springer Nature Switzerland AG 2020
A. L. Martel et al. (Eds.): MICCAI 2020, LNCS 12264, pp. 128–137, 2020.
https://doi.org/10.1007/978-3-030-59719-1_13

Keywords: Conditional image synthesis · Cardiac Magnetic
Resonance imaging · XCAT anatomical phantom

1 Introduction

The medical image analysis community is suffering from limited annotated data, constrained sharing policies, and imbalanced samples, which directly lead to limitations in the adoption of novel and reliable deep learning methods. This is particularly reflected in clinical practice, where deep learning models lack robustness and generalizability to the diverse patient population, as well as variations in imaging protocols, acquisition parameters and manufacturing specifications of imaging devices [25]. The image synthesis techniques by Generative Adversarial Networks (GANs) [9] have gained lots of attention as a potential approach to address these problems by augmenting and balancing the data in various domains [13, 26]. For instance, leveraging the synthetic data obtained by domain translation techniques led to significant performance improvements in the application of cardiac cavity segmentation [5–7]. However, in most domain translation approaches, the variations in the synthetic images are constrained by the source domain i.e., either the input label maps or the images in the source domain have limited anatomical variations. Thus, generating new anatomically-plausible instances is not possible.

1.1 Related Work

Separating the style (often called domain-specific features) from the shape (often called domain-invariant features) has enabled various domain translation techniques [10, 16, 22], which can synthesize high-resolution photo-realistic images with detailed textures from semantic label maps using conditional GANs. A recent work by [17] showed the effectiveness of translating the simulated to realistic images for the task of liver segmentation in laparoscopic images using a conditional unpaired image-to-image translation approach [10]. The works by [7, 15] used the same technique to combine the styles from domains with few or no labels with the contents of another domains with more labels and use them in adapting the segmentation networks. Even though such techniques provide flexibility by using unpaired sets, paired image-to-image translation techniques [16, 22] provide more control over image generation. They enable generating semantically consistent labeled synthetic images, which are more useful for medical image analysis (such as the work by [21]). However, the only possible variation in synthetic data can be created by learning different styles (often via Variational Auto-Encoders (VAE) [14]) and then mixing them with the existing shape information provided by the annotated label maps with limited anatomical variations. Although it is possible to model and create new shape deformations statistically [8] or via VAEs [12], such models are not necessarily anatomically plausible and structurally accurate.

1.2 Contributions

In this paper, we address the above-mentioned challenges by proposing a novel framework for synthesizing a diverse labeled database of 3D consistent Cardiac

Magnetic Resonance (CMR) images on anatomically-plausible XCAT derived labels. The new framework, called XCAT-GAN, is tailored to transfer the modality-specific MR image characteristics to new anatomical representations to generate a new realistic-looking synthetic CMR image database in two ways: 4-class and 8-class image synthesis. We rely on the eXtended CArdiac Torso (XCAT) [20] phantoms as the source of the computerized human phantoms to generate 33 virtual subjects with various anatomical features. Our synthetic database comprises heterogeneous images of virtual subjects that are variable in terms of anatomical representation and diverse in terms of image appearance. Manual annotation is not required since the anatomical model used for image generation serves as the ground truth label map for synthetic images. Real annotated datasets are needed for training the network, but the existing annotations are limited to a few classes of the heart. For improving the guidance in image generation, multi-tissue label maps of surrounding regions of the heart are obtained by leveraging a segmentation network trained on a set of simulated images [2]. Using these new label maps leads to a substantial improvement in the consistency of the synthesis particularly of the organs for which the annotations are not available. Finally, we demonstrate that the synthetic data can be used not only for augmenting the datasets but also for replacing the real images since they provide accurate and realistic shapes and appearances. Compared to our concurrent image synthesis approach in [1], we achieve anatomical consistency in the third dimension by incorporating more labels for the organs visible in the background. Furthermore, we validate the utility of the synthetic images for a clinical task quantitatively, which has not been explored previously.

2   Methodology

We demonstrate a novel image synthesis approach with two different settings; for the first one we only use available ground truth labels for the heart (4-class), and in the second one we increase the number of labels (8-class) when training the XCAT-GAN. A general overview of the networks is illustrated in Fig. 1.

Three neural networks are used for image generation and evaluation. Network 1 is a modified U-Net [19] that predicts multi-tissue segmentation maps for a set of real images. This component is only used for the 8-class image synthesis to provide more guidance for our XCAT-GAN. Network 2 is a conditional GAN architecture [16], trained on paired real images and label maps (either 4 or 8-class maps). After the training is done, it synthesizes images on the XCAT labels as the new anatomical representations. In the 4-class image synthesis additional images are used to add variations in the style of generated images at the inference time. The new synthetic images with their corresponding cardiac labels are evaluated in different experiment settings by network 3 that is an adapted version of the 2D U-Net architecture [11]. All three networks are trained separately so that the output of the first network is used as the input of the second network in the training time and the output of the second network is used as the data augmentation for the third network. In the following sections, we explain the

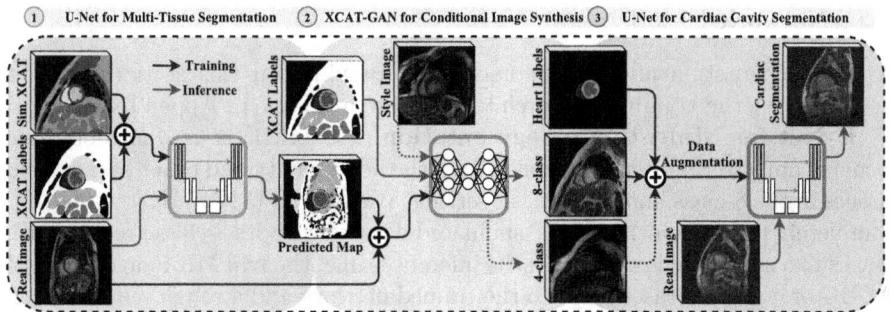

Fig. 1. An overview of the three networks used in our proposed approaches. The first U-Net is trained completely on the simulated CMR data with 8-class ground truth labels. The paired images and label maps (4 or 8 classes) are used to train the second network for conditional image synthesis. At the inference, the XCAT derived labels are used for synthesizing 3D CMR images. New styles are also transferred to the synthetic images in the 4-class XCAT-GAN. The synthetic data with its ground truth labels are evaluated by the third network in a supervised cardiac cavity segmentation task.

data used at each stage and elaborate on the particular strategies for training and inference times.

2.1 Material

We utilize four real CMR image datasets and one simulated CMR image dataset in our proposed framework. The simulated dataset contains 66 simulated CMR image volumes that are generated with MRXCAT analytical approach [23] on variable XCAT phantoms [2] with anatomical variabilities such as heart size, location and orientation with respect to other organs. One sample of a simulated XCAT image and its corresponding label map is shown at the top left of Fig. 1. The Automated Cardiac Diagnosis Challenge (ACDC) dataset [4] is the main real dataset used for training the XCAT-GAN. The Sunnybrook Cardiac Data (SCD) [18] and York Cardiac MRI (York) [3] datasets are only used for adding style variations in the 4-class image synthesis at the inference time and are not seen during the training. Moreover, 156 internal clinical CMR (cCMR) volumes are used for our quantitative evaluation step[1]. All datasets are pre-processed by sub-sampling them to 1.3×1.3 mm in-plane resolution and taking a central crop of the images with 256×256 pixels. All intensity values are normalized to the range $[-1, 1]$. Data is augmented during the training by random scaling, rotations, elastic deformation, and mirroring. Further details about each dataset are available in Appendix A, Table 1.

---

[1] All data used in this study were obtained with the required approvals and patient consent.

2.2   Network Details

A brief explanation about each network is provided in this section. Further details about the training and architectures are available in Appendix B.

U-Net for Multi-tissue Segmentation (network 1) is used for obtaining a coarse multi-tissue segmentation map of the heart cavity and other background tissues in the 8-class image synthesis setting. We adopt a U-Net architecture [19], completely trained on the XCAT simulated dataset with its 8-class ground truth masks in a supervised manner. In the inference time, the real MR image from the ACDC or cCMR dataset is fed to the trained network and a rough segmentation map is created. The heart labels are replaced with the manual annotations before feeding them to the next network, along with their corresponding real images.

XCAT-GAN for Conditional Image Synthesis [16] is a mask-guided image generation technique that employs spatially-adaptive denormalization layers resulting in semantically-consistent image synthesis. During the training, the network takes the (predicted) label maps of the ACDC dataset with their corresponding real images and learns their underlying modality-specific features for each class. Since the guidance in the 4-class synthesis case is limited to three heart classes and the background contains various organs, we provide more guidance to the network by using a style encoder in a VAE setting [16] without instance normalization layers that often lead to the removal of semantic information. This helps in learning and transferring new styles and structures in the background. At the inference time, the label maps are replaced with the XCAT labels. Also, additional style images are used as the input of the style encoder.

U-Net for Cardiac Cavity Segmentation (network 3) is employed for segmentation of heart cavities in real cardiac data with the addition of labelled synthetic XCAT images in different augmentation settings. This network is a modified 2D U-Net, designed and optimized following the recommendations of the nnU-Net framework [11], as explained in Appendix B.

2.3   Experiments and Results

Image Synthesis: For synthesizing the images, we utilize 66 XCAT volumes including both end-diastolic (ED) and end-systolic (ES) phases (33 subjects). For the 4-class case, we utilize 22 random volumes generated with three different styles from the York, SCD, and ACDC dataset, respectively; while for the 8-class case, we use 66 volumes synthesized only with the ACDC style. Throughout the whole experiments, we keep the number of 4-class and 8-class synthetic images the same (66 volumes) to have a fair comparison in our segmentation task.

Figure 2 depicts sample synthetic images generated by 4-class (with the ACDC style) and 8-class XCAT-GANs. Moreover, a sample 4-class synthetic image with the SCD style is depicted in Fig. 1, between networks 2 and 3. As seen in Fig. 2(a), in the background region, both the texture and the anatomical content including the surrounding organs and structures to the heart such as the

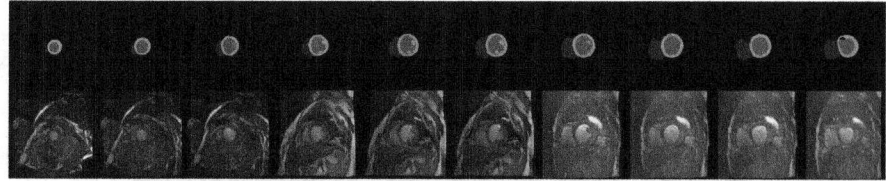

(a) The synthetic image for a 4-class label map

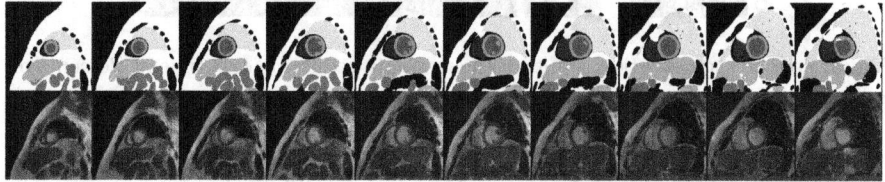

(b) The synthetic image for an 8-class label map

Fig. 2. Sample images generated by (a) 4 and (b) 8-class XCAT-GAN with their corresponding XCAT labels for 10 short axis slices from the apex to the base of the heart.

fat layer of the outer layer of the body, lung and abdominal organs are generated well by the network. Although the synthetic texture for heart classes seems to be consistent and robust for different slices across the heart long axes view, the synthetic content for the background class changes. Considering the complexity of the anatomical content and style for the background class, this inconsistency comes as no surprise. To alleviate this, the 8-class XCAT-GAN is proposed.

The 8-class XCAT-GAN uses the predictions by network 1. A sample of a full predicted map is depicted in Fig. 1, between the first and second networks. As seen in Fig. 2(b), as a result of utilizing more labels for training the XCAT-GAN, more local characteristic for each visible structure in the image are learned. Subsequently at the inference time, when we feed XCAT labels with eight classes, the synthetic images are consistent in the third direction. Two 3D visualizations of the synthetic images for the ED and ES phases are available at https://github.com/sinaamirrajab/XCAT-GAN.

Cardiac Cavity Segmentation: To quantitatively evaluate the usefulness of the synthetic cardiac images, we combine them with real images to train a network for cardiac cavity segmentation task. As a baseline, we first train our network on the existing ACDC and cCMR images for three classes: left ventricular myocardium (MYO), left ventricle blood pool (LV) and right ventricle blood pool (RV). In the first set of experiments, we evaluate the effect of adding synthetic images to the real MR data during training (*Augmentation*). Other experiments focus on gradually reducing real MR data in the training set, while the number of synthetic images is kept constant (*Real Data Reduction*). The aim is to evaluate whether the synthetic data are realistic enough to replace real MR data. We use the same data for inference in all experiments, namely the subsets of both

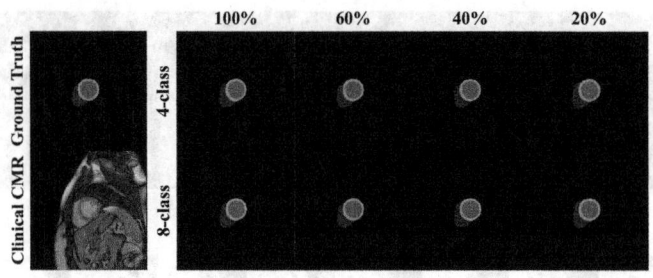

Fig. 3. Sample segmentation results of the real data reduction experiment. Percentages indicate the ratio of used real data relative to the baseline experiment (200 volumes).

cCMR and ACDC datasets. Reference Dice scores (DSC) achieved on the ACDC dataset are 0.968, 0.946 and 0.902 for the ED phase and 0.931, 0.889 and 0.919 for the ES phase on LV, RV, and MYO classes, respectively [4]. A configuration summary of all experiments and results can be found in Table 1.

The *augmentation* experiments show that utilizing the synthetic data improves the segmentation performance of the network trained on cCMR and ACDC images in terms of the mean DSC and Hausdorff distance (HD) for most cases. Moreover, utilizing 8-class synthetic data improves the HD significantly across all experiments.

The *real data reduction* experiments indicate that segmentation performance is retained in cases when synthetic XCAT data is added to fewer real data in the training set compared to the baseline model (trained with 200 cCMR and ACDC images). Since the number of total volumes used for training is decreased in each

Table 1. Segmentation results for augmentation and real data reduction experiments.

Exp.	Training set				Clinical MR test set (n = 50)						ACDC test set (n = 50)					
	Real set		Synthetic set		LV		MYO		RV		LV		MYO		RV	
	Name	# Vol.	Name	# Vol.	DSC	HD	DSC	HD	DSC	HD	DSC	HD	DSC	HD	DSC	HD
Augmentation	cCMR	100	–	–	0.91	10.11	0.84	13.74	0.88	11.73	0.86	**12.57**	0.80	14.61	0.87	22.73
	cCMR	100	4-class	66	0.93	10.73	0.86	13.98	0.89	9.94	0.90	14.25	0.90	15.54	0.86	16.72
	cCMR	100	8-class	66	**0.94**	**9.84**	**0.86**	**8.06**	**0.89**	**8.08**	**0.91**	12.98	**0.91**	**13.40**	**0.87**	**11.87**
	ACDC	100	–	–	0.88	**20.46**	0.81	31.26	0.82	26.28	0.94	11.21	0.90	12.94	0.92	14.14
	ACDC	100	4-class	66	0.88	33.50	0.81	41.39	0.84	20.59	0.95	11.81	0.91	12.25	**0.94**	11.87
	ACDC	100	8-class	66	**0.89**	21.84	**0.82**	**25.71**	**0.84**	**18.89**	**0.96**	**9.73**	**0.92**	**11.91**	0.93	**10.67**
Real data reduction	cCMR+ACDC	200	–	–	0.93	**9.84**	0.85	13.79	0.89	10.63	0.95	8.71	0.90	11.33	0.91	12.86
	cCMR+ACDC	200	4-class	66	0.93	12.15	0.85	15.27	0.89	12.93	0.95	9.51	0.91	15.99	0.92	16.63
	cCMR+ACDC	200	8-class	66	0.93	9.89	**0.86**	**13.22**	0.89	**9.43**	0.95	**7.99**	**0.92**	**9.07**	**0.92**	**10.32**
	cCMR+ACDC	120	–	–	0.90	12.11	0.83	15.73	0.86	14.39	0.94	9.14	0.89	15.08	0.88	16.35
	cCMR+ACDC	120	4-class	66	0.92	10.64	0.85	14.27	0.87	12.20	0.95	10.12	0.90	12.77	0.92	12.21
	cCMR+ACDC	120	8-class	66	**0.92**	**9.98**	0.85	13.27	**0.89**	**10.11**	0.95	**8.89**	**0.91**	**11.31**	**0.93**	**12.08**
	cCMR+ACDC	80	–	–	0.87	17.22	0.82	**18.01**	0.86	15.76	0.92	16.51	0.87	17.22	0.87	18.11
	cCMR+ACDC	80	4-class	66	0.92	21.34	0.85	24.77	0.88	18.77	0.93	16.75	0.89	19.57	0.89	19.15
	cCMR+ACDC	80	8-class	66	**0.92**	**14.67**	0.85	18.82	**0.88**	**11.72**	**0.94**	**11.30**	**0.91**	**12.79**	**0.90**	**14.76**
	cCMR+ACDC	40	–	–	0.85	21.13	0.79	22.69	0.83	18.91	0.89	19.74	0.85	19.11	0.85	20.05
	cCMR+ACDC	40	4-class	66	0.90	26.29	0.82	38.73	0.85	24.42	0.92	22.79	0.89	27.13	0.88	28.33
	cCMR+ACDC	40	8-class	66	**0.91**	**16.28**	**0.84**	**19.04**	**0.87**	**13.75**	**0.94**	**15.49**	**0.90**	**15.76**	**0.90**	**17.38**

experiment, we expect the performance to decrease accordingly. However, we do not observe a significant drop in performance as we introduce new shape priors through the addition of synthetic images. This holds even in cases when only 20% of the baseline MR real images are used in the training set. Some sample segmentation results on the cCMR dataset for this experiment are also depicted in Fig. 3, which shows the segmentation maps remain accurate when replacing the real data with synthetic ones.

3   Discussion and Conclusion

In this paper, we propose a novel framework for generating a database of synthetic 3D consistent labeled CMR images for medical data augmentation. Our XCAT-GAN combines the anatomically accurate XCAT labels with the learned modality-specific image characteristics to synthesize plausible images. In the 4-class image synthesis setting, XCAT-GAN can learn both the texture of the heart and the underlying content information for the background. Furthermore, by incorporating more labels for the surrounding regions of the heart in the 8-class synthesis, we achieve more consistency and robustness in synthesising 3D image volumes, despite the fact that we used 2D networks for all of our experiments.

We evaluate the usefulness of this synthetic database in data augmentation for the supervised cardiac cavity segmentation task. For both 4-class and 8-class synthesis, it is demonstrated that the segmentation performance is retained even when the network is trained on fewer real data i.e., a significant number of real MR images (up to 80%) can be replaced by synthetic images during training, which is a promising step towards addressing the lack of available medical data. While the DSC is slightly improved in the 8-class augmentation compared to 4-class, the false positives of the background tissues are significantly reduced due to 3D consistency achieved by providing more labels in the process of synthesis. This is also demonstrated by obtaining a smaller HD. However, such results could also be the effect of training and evaluation with a 2D segmentation network only. Thus, future work includes utilizing the 8-class images in a 3D segmentation setting. Nevertheless, images synthesized with the method proposed in this paper can supplement or be utilized instead of real data.

Our rough segmentation maps by the first network are not perfect due to the gap between the simulated images (used for training) and real images (used for testing). This leads to false conditioning in the XCAT-GAN in some regions. It is possible to improve the quality of the segmentation maps, by improving the segmentation network or using the domain adaptation techniques such as [24]. The other option is to use other labeled real sets with labels covering all regions rather than only the heart classes (if available). Moreover, the style or modality-specific feature mentioned in this paper is learned from the real data with cine MR contrast. Since all the datasets we used have very similar styles, the main advantage of the VAE setup for the 4-class image synthesis is to introduce more control over the surrounding regions. Rather than memorizing and generating the same background, it learns to transfer some structures from the style image as well, which is why the 4-class and 8-class synthetic images lead to comparable results in our experiments. Transferring the style of other MR modalities such as T1-weighted and late gadolinium enhancement conditioned on each anatomical label class is considered as a future direction. Finally, it is worth mentioning that it is possible to extend the image synthesis to 4D by using the parameterized motion model of the XCAT heart and generating 3D+t CMR images.

Acknowledgments. This research is a part of the openGTN project, supported by the European Union in the Marie Curie Innovative Training Networks (ITN) fellowship program under project No. 764465.

References

1. Abbasi-Sureshjani, S., Amirrajab, S., Lorenz, C., Weese, J., Pluim, J., Breeuwer, M.: 4D semantic cardiac magnetic resonance image synthesis on XCAT anatomical model. In: Medical Imaging with Deep Learning (2020)
2. Amirrajab, S., Al Khalil, Y., Lorenz, C., Weese, J., Breeuwer, M.: Towards generating realistic and hetrogeneous cardiac magnetic resonance simulated image database for deep learning based image segmentation algorithms. Proceedings of the 12th Annual Meeting ISMRM Benelux Chapter 2020, P-077 (2020)
3. Andreopoulos, A., Tsotsos, J.K.: Efficient and generalizable statistical models of shape and appearance for analysis of cardiac MRI. Med. Image Anal. **12**(3), 335–357 (2008)
4. Bernard, O., Lalande, A., Zotti, C., Cervenansky, F., et al.: Deep learning techniques for automatic MRI cardiac multi-structures segmentation and diagnosis: is the problem solved? IEEE Trans. Med. Imaging **37**(11), 2514–2525 (2018)
5. Chaitanya, K., Karani, N., Baumgartner, C.F., Becker, A., Donati, O., Konukoglu, E.: Semi-supervised and task-driven data augmentation. In: Chung, A.C.S., Gee, J.C., Yushkevich, P.A., Bao, S. (eds.) IPMI 2019. LNCS, vol. 11492, pp. 29–41. Springer, Cham (2019). https://doi.org/10.1007/978-3-030-20351-1_3
6. Chartsias, A., Joyce, T., Dharmakumar, R., Tsaftaris, S.A.: Adversarial image synthesis for unpaired multi-modal cardiac data. In: Tsaftaris, S.A., Gooya, A., Frangi, A.F., Prince, J.L. (eds.) SASHIMI 2017. LNCS, vol. 10557, pp. 3–13. Springer, Cham (2017). https://doi.org/10.1007/978-3-319-68127-6_1
7. Chen, C., et al.: Unsupervised multi-modal style transfer for cardiac MR segmentation. arXiv e-prints arXiv:1908.07344 (Aug 2019)
8. Corral Acero, J., et al.: SMOD - data augmentation based on statistical models of deformation to enhance segmentation in 2D cine cardiac MRI. In: Coudière, Y., Ozenne, V., Vigmond, E., Zemzemi, N. (eds.) FIMH 2019. LNCS, vol. 11504, pp. 361–369. Springer, Cham (2019). https://doi.org/10.1007/978-3-030-21949-9_39
9. Goodfellow, I., Pouget-Abadie, J., Mirza, M., Xu, B., et al.: Generative adversarial nets. In: Ghahramani, Z., Welling, M., Cortes, C., Lawrence, N.D., Weinberger, K.Q. (eds.) Advances in Neural Information Processing Systems, vol. 27, pp. 2672–2680. Curran Associates Inc., New York (2014)
10. Huang, X., Liu, M.-Y., Belongie, S., Kautz, J.: Multimodal unsupervised image-to-image translation. In: Ferrari, V., Hebert, M., Sminchisescu, C., Weiss, Y. (eds.) ECCV 2018. LNCS, vol. 11207, pp. 179–196. Springer, Cham (2018). https://doi.org/10.1007/978-3-030-01219-9_11

11. Isensee, F., Petersen, J., Kohl, S.A.A., Jäger, P.F., Maier-Hein, K.: nnU-Net: breaking the spell on successful medical image segmentation. ArXiv abs/1904.08128 (2019)
12. Joyce, T., Kozerke, S.: 3D medical image synthesis by factorised representation and deformable model learning. In: Burgos, N., Gooya, A., Svoboda, D. (eds.) SASHIMI 2019. LNCS, vol. 11827, pp. 110–119. Springer, Cham (2019). https://doi.org/10.1007/978-3-030-32778-1_12
13. Kazeminia, S., et al.: Gans for medical image analysis (2018)
14. Kingma, D.P., Welling, M.: Auto-encoding variational Bayes. arXiv e-prints arXiv:1312.6114, December 2013
15. Ma, C., Ji, Z., Gao, M.: Neural style transfer improves 3D cardiovascular MR image segmentation on inconsistent data. In: Shen, D., et al. (eds.) MICCAI 2019. LNCS, vol. 11765, pp. 128–136. Springer, Cham (2019). https://doi.org/10.1007/978-3-030-32245-8_15
16. Park, T., Liu, M.Y., Wang, T.C., Zhu, J.Y.: Semantic image synthesis with spatially-adaptive normalization. In: 2019 IEEE/CVF Conference on Computer Vision and Pattern Recognition (CVPR), Los Alamitos, CA, USA, pp. 2332–2341. IEEE Computer Society, June 2019
17. Pfeiffer, M., et al.: Generating large labeled data sets for laparoscopic image processing tasks using unpaired image-to-image translation. In: Shen, D., et al. (eds.) MICCAI 2019. LNCS, vol. 11768, pp. 119–127. Springer, Cham (2019). https://doi.org/10.1007/978-3-030-32254-0_14
18. Radau, P., Lu, Y., Connelly, K., Paul, G., Dick, A., Wright, G.: Evaluation framework for algorithms segmenting short axis cardiac MRI, July 2009
19. Ronneberger, O., Fischer, P., Brox, T.: U-Net: convolutional networks for biomedical image segmentation. In: Navab, N., Hornegger, J., Wells, W.M., Frangi, A.F. (eds.) MICCAI 2015. LNCS, vol. 9351, pp. 234–241. Springer, Cham (2015). https://doi.org/10.1007/978-3-319-24574-4_28
20. Segars, W., Sturgeon, G., Mendonca, S., Grimes, J., Tsui, B.M.: 4D XCAT phantom for multimodality imaging research. Med. Phys. **37**(9), 4902–4915 (2010)
21. Tang, Y.B., Oh, S., Tang, Y.X., Xiao, J., Summers, R.M.: CT-realistic data augmentation using generative adversarial network for robust lymph node segmentation. In: Mori, K., Hahn, H.K. (eds.) Medical Imaging 2019: Computer-Aided Diagnosis, vol. 10950, pp. 976–981. International Society for Optics and Photonics, SPIE (2019)
22. Wang, T.C., Liu, M.Y., Zhu, J.Y., Tao, A., Kautz, J., Catanzaro, B.: High-resolution image synthesis and semantic manipulation with conditional GANs. In: 2018 IEEE/CVF Conference on Computer Vision and Pattern Recognition, pp. 8798–8807, June 2018
23. Wissmann, L., Santelli, C., Segars, W.P., Kozerke, S.: MRXCAT: realistic numerical phantoms for cardiovascular magnetic resonance. J. Cardiovasc. Magn. Reson. **16**(1), 63 (2014)
24. Wu, Z., Wang, X., Gonzalez, J.E., Goldstein, T., Davis, L.S.: ACE: adapting to changing environments for semantic segmentation. CoRR abs/1904.06268 (2019)
25. Yasaka, K., Abe, O.: Deep learning and artificial intelligence in radiology: current applications and future directions. PLOS Med. **15**(11), 1–4 (2018)
26. Yi, X., Walia, E., Babyn, P.: Generative adversarial network in medical imaging: a review. Med. Image Anal. **58**, 101552 (2019)

TexNet: Texture Loss Based Network for Gastric Antrum Segmentation in Ultrasound

Guohao Dong[1], Yaoxian Zou[1], Jiaming Jiao[1], Yuxi Liu[1], Shuo Liu[1], Tianzhu Liang[1],
Chaoyue Liu[1], Zhijie Chen[1], Lei Zhu[1], Dong Ni[2], and Muqing Lin[1(✉)]

[1] Shenzhen Mindray Bio-Medical Electronics, Co., Ltd., Shenzhen, China
linmuqing@mindray.com
[2] National-Regional Key Technology Engineering Laboratory for Medical Ultrasound, School
of Biomedical Engineering, Health Science Center, Shenzhen University, Shenzhen, China

Abstract. Gastric Antrum (GA) cross-sectional area measurement using ultrasound imaging is an important point-of-care (POC) application in intense care unit (ICU) and anesthesia. GA in ultrasound images often show substantial differences in both shape and texture among subjects, leading to a challenging task of automated segmentation. To the best of our knowledge, no work has been published for this task. Meanwhile, dice similarity coefficient (DSC) based loss function has been widely used by CNN-based segmentation methods. Simply calculating mask overlap, DSC is often biased towards shape and lack of generalization ability for cases with diversified and complicated texture patterns. In this paper, we present a robust segmentation method (TexNet) by introducing a new loss function based on multiscale information of local boundary texture. The new texture loss provides a complementary measure of texture-wise accuracy in contour area which can reduce overfitting issues caused by using DSC loss alone. Experiments have been performed on 8487 images from 121 patients. Results show that TexNet outperforms state of the art methods with higher accuracy and better consistency. Besides GA, the proposed method could potentially be an ideal solution to segment other organs with large variation in both shape and texture among subjects.

Keywords: Gastric antrum · Ultrasound · Point-of-care · Segmentation · Texture loss · Channel attention

1 Introduction

Gastric content volume (GCV) is the key factor to assess the risk of regurgitation and aspiration before anesthesia. As an important point-of-care (POC) application in intense care unit (ICU), gastric emptying time (GET) and gastric motility index (GMI) are calculated for early diagnosis and management of gastrointestinal motility dysfunction [1]. The above parameters are usually acquired by measuring the area of gastric antrum (GA) at different time points using ultrasound. In current manner, clinicians mainly use traditional two-diameter method (TDM) or manual tracing to estimate the area of GA [2] which often lead to low efficiency and inevitable intra-operator error. Therefore,

© Springer Nature Switzerland AG 2020
A. L. Martel et al. (Eds.): MICCAI 2020, LNCS 12264, pp. 138–145, 2020.
https://doi.org/10.1007/978-3-030-59719-1_14

developing automated methods to segment the area of GA in ultrasound can provide important values in improving current clinical workflow.

In the field of ultrasound image segmentation, many deep learning methods have been proposed for organs with various shapes, such as placenta [3], prostate [4] and follicle [5]. Current published works mainly solve cases with large variation of shape while texture patterns among subjects are usually similar or at least not significantly different. Meanwhile, dice similarity coefficient (DSC) has been widely used as loss function for those segmentation networks. In general, DSC loss is shape-oriented and competent for cases with different shapes but similar texture patterns.

Due to individual differences of acoustic properties and status of empty or full stomach, ultrasound images of GA sometimes are completely dissimilar not just in shape but also in texture pattern and image quality (Fig. 1). For such diversified and sophisticated cases, DSC loss tends to arise overfitting problems (Fig. 1 e–h). This is mainly because the training process is solely driven by maximizing mask overlap between groundtruth and prediction without any specific metrics to assess textural differences.

To overcome this challenge, we introduce a new loss function based on local boundary texture (texture loss) and further propose a robust segmentation network (TexNet). Other than DSC loss which is biased towards shape, texture loss can provide complementary measure of texture-wise accuracy by quantifying the image similarity between groundtruth and prediction in contour area. To further assess texture-wise accuracy at multiscale, the new loss function is integrated into a structure of deep supervision. DSC loss and texture loss are combined to achieve both shape-wise and texture-wise assessment at training stage which can alleviate the issue of overfitting. To the best of our knowledge, TexNet is the first deep learning method for automated segmentation of GA in ultrasound images. Extensively validated on a large clinical dataset, the results show the benefits of TexNet over state of the art methods.

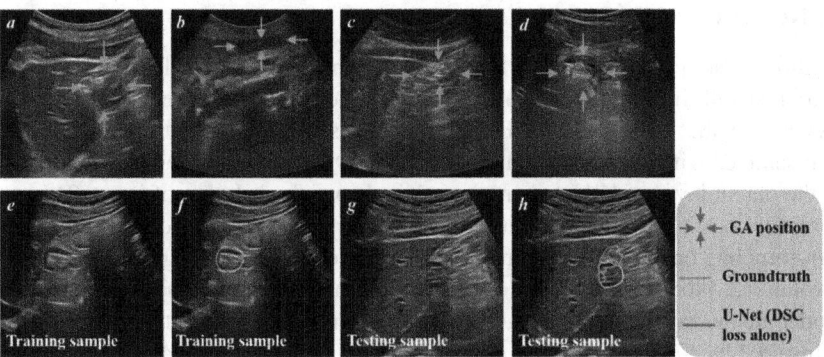

Fig. 1. Typical ultrasound images of GA. (a)–(d): GA with various shapes and texture patterns. (e): GA from training set. (f): Prediction of (e) using U-Net with DSC loss. (g): GA similar to (e) from testing set. (h): Prediction of (g) using U-Net with DSC loss.

2 Methods

Figure 2 illustrates the framework of TexNet and its loss function consists of both DSC loss and texture loss. Following the manner of deep supervision, the hybrid loss function is calculated in each spatial resolution and further combined to attain multiscale assessment of accuracy at training stage.

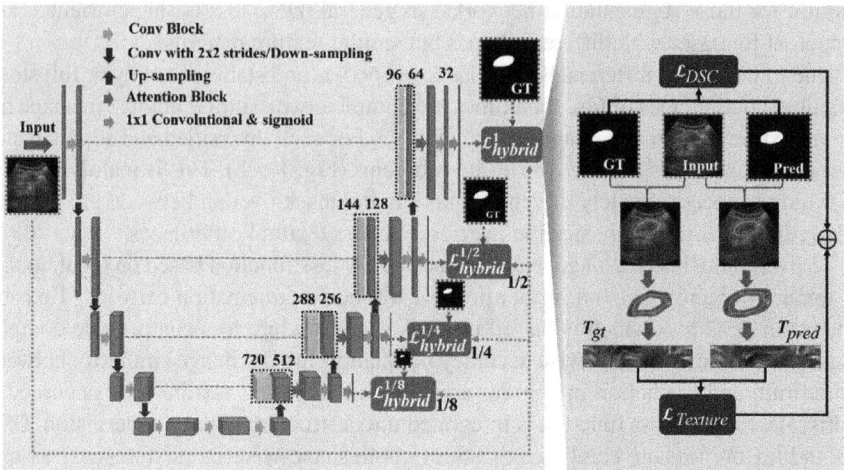

Fig. 2. The illustration of the proposed pipeline for GA segmentation. The diagram of the encoder part is simplified only for the purpose of demonstration. Major backbone structures (such as MobileNet, EfficientNet, etc.) can all be adopted in the proposed framework.

2.1 Network Architecture

Attention U-Net [6] is adopted as basic model with a backbone of EfficientNet-B2 [7] pre-trained with ImageNet while any other end-to-end networks are also applicable. It is noteworthy that for the original EfficientNet, the spatial resolution of input is directly down-sampled with a stride of 2 in the first layer. On the other hand, both the first layer and the output layer of U-Net share the original spatial resolution of input. Therefore, in order to match the spatial resolution between encoder and decoder, we remove the down-sampling operation in the first layer of EfficientNet by setting the corresponding convolutional block with a stride of 1. Besides, the channel numbers of encoder and decoder are the same as the original EfficientNet and U-Net, respectively.

Inspired by SE block [8], we design a modified version to adapt the structure of U-Net and further improve the localization of GA with attention guidance. The attention blocks are inserted to all the modules of skip connection (concatenate) accordingly. Figure 3 presents the schematics of the modified SE block. Compared to the original SE block which only uses features from encoder as input, the modified version takes additional input from decoder. Specifically, decoder features from higher layer which have lower spatial resolution but more semantic information are resized to match encoder features by up-sampling and 1×1 convolution. Following the manner of attention

U-Net [6], encoder features are reweighted by channel-wise attention vector and further concatenated with decoder features.

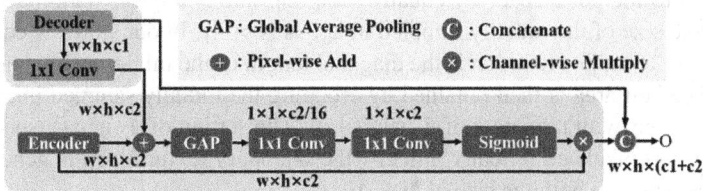

Fig. 3. Schematics of the proposed attention block which takes inputs from both encoder and decoder. The module with blue background is the same as the original SE block [8].

2.2 Texture Loss

For medical image segmentation, common loss functions (DSC, Hausdorff distance, cross entropy, etc.) only evaluate shape-wise accuracy which is usually sufficient for cases with similar texture patterns among subjects. However, for dataset with limited subjects and large variation in both shape and texture (such as GA), models based on the shape-wise loss functions often suffer from overfitting issues. Therefore, a complementary measure which assesses texture-wise accuracy could potentially be the key to improve the generalization ability of current models.

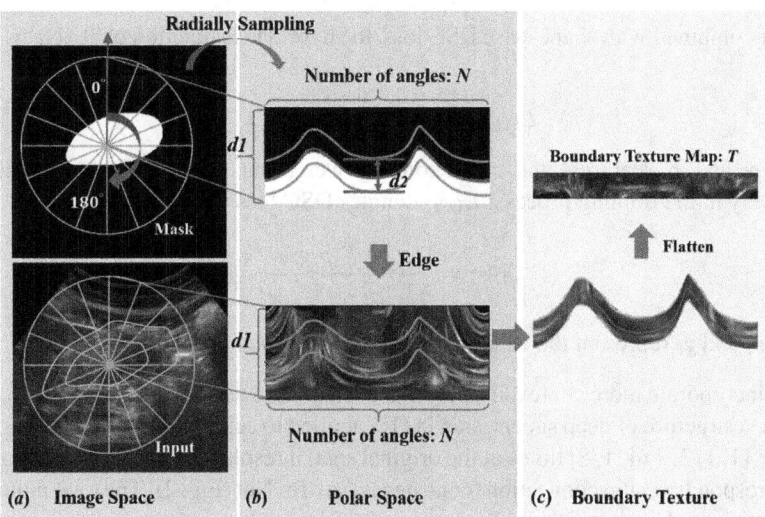

Fig. 4. Illustration of generating boundary texture map.

Generation of Boundary Texture Map. In order to achieve better sensitivity of segmentation, texture loss is calculated only within a belt area of mask contour (Fig. 4). Specifically, the input image and its corresponding mask (groundtruth or prediction) are first mapped to the polar space by equally sampling into N angles. With the sampling radius d_1, the size of the radially sampled image is $N \times d_1$. In our study, N equals 360 while d_1 is set to half of L which is the diagonal length of the minimized bounding box of mask. The belt area is then obtained by cropping the radially sampled image along the mask contour with thickness of d_2 (Fig. 4 b). The setting of d_2 is task-specific and we set d_2 to 40 pixels empirically. Finally, the boundary texture map is generated by warping the belt area with the size of $N \times d_2$.

Multi-scale Texture Loss Function. It is clear that the boundary texture maps of prediction T_{pred} and groundtruth T_{gt} tend to be the same if automated segmentation is accurate. Therefore, texture loss is calculated as the image similarity between T_{pred} and T_{gt}. Specifically, structural similarity (SSIM) index [10] which has been widely applied in medical image analysis is adopted to quantify the image similarity. Given reference image x and prediction image y, SSIM index is calculated by:

$$\text{SSIM}(x, y) = \frac{2\mu_x\mu_y + C_1}{\mu_x^2 + \mu_y^2 + C_1} \cdot \frac{2\delta_x\delta_y + C_2}{\delta_x^2 + \delta_y^2 + C_2} \cdot \frac{2\delta_{xy} + C_3}{\delta_x\delta_y + C_3} \tag{1}$$

where μ_x/μ_y and δ_x/δ_y are the mean and the variance of x and y, respectively; δ_{xy} is the covariance of x and y; constants C_1, C_2 and C_3 are used to stabilize the dividing operation. To adapt the process of minimization, texture loss is defined by:

$$\mathcal{L}_{\text{texture}} = 1.0 - \text{SSIM}\left(T_{gt}, T_{pred}\right) \tag{2}$$

Further combined with shape-wise DSC loss, the hybrid loss function of TexNet is given by:

$$\mathcal{L}_{hybrid} = \alpha\mathcal{L}_{\text{texture}} + \beta\mathcal{L}_{\text{DSC}} \tag{3}$$

where α and β represent the corresponding weighting factors which are changed adaptively in the training process; $\mathcal{L}_{\text{DSC}}$ denotes DSC loss which is defined by:

$$\mathcal{L}_{\text{DSC}} = \frac{2\sum_i^N p_i g_i}{\sum_i^N p_i^2 + \sum_i^N g_i^2} \tag{4}$$

where p_i and g_i represent the value of predicted and groundtruth at location i.

To incorporate more context information of shape and texture in different spatial resolution, a structure of deep supervision [11] is applied to achieve multiscale assessment. For $i = [1, 1/2, 1/4, 1/8]$ times of the original spatial resolution, $\mathcal{L}_{hybrid}^i$ is calculated in the corresponding skip connection (concatenate) of TexNet (Fig. 2). The total multiscale loss function is hence defined by:

$$\mathcal{L}_{\text{total}} = \sum_{i=1}^4 \left(w[i] \cdot \mathcal{L}_{hybrid}^i\right) \tag{5}$$

where $w[i] = [0.6, 0.2, 0.1, 0.1]$ is the multiscale weighting factor which is set by empirical.

3 Experiments

Materials. Experiments were carried on a representative and challenging dataset of 2D GA ultrasound images. Approved by local IRB, all the images were anonymized and scanned by experts. The dataset consisted of 141 videos from 121 patients (96 for training, 25 for testing) with age ranges from 17 to 92 years old. There were totally 6336 images and 2151 images in the training set and the testing set, respectively. All the images were resized and cropped into the resolution of 448×448 while all the labels are annotated by three senior experts.

Implementation Details. Our proposed network was implemented using Keras with the backend of TensorFlow. Both training and testing were performed on two 16G NVidia V100 GPUs. The strategy of data augmentation includes flipping, cropping, rotation, and translation. For the configuration of training, Adam optimizer is adopted (batch size $= 8$, momentum $= 0.9$). The initial learning rate is 1×10^{-3} and it decreases by a factor of 0.95 after every epoch. In the first 10 epochs, the weighting factors of the hybrid loss function are set as $\alpha = 0$ and $\beta = 1$, which implies only DSC loss is used for initial training. Then in the following epochs, α increases by 0.1 (until $\alpha = 1$) and β decreases by 0.1 (until $\beta = 0$) iteratively, which means texture loss gradually dominates the hybrid loss function after initial training. In our study, the training process converges after 60 epochs.

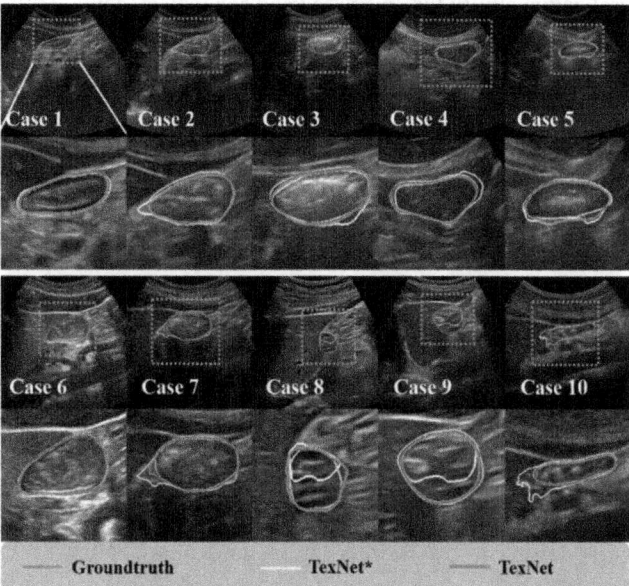

Fig. 5. Segmentation results of TexNet using DSC loss alone (TexNet*) and hybrid loss (TexNet).

Qualitative and Quantitative Analysis. To qualitatively show the improvement in overfitting issues, we present several difficult cases of TexNet using DSC loss alone (TexNet*) and the hybrid loss function (DSC loss + texture loss) in Fig. 5. The quantitative comparisons can be further found in Table 1. Clearly, TexNet using both DSC loss and texture loss outperforms with higher accuracy and better consistency, indicating texture-wise accuracy is an important and useful measure for cases with large variation in shape and texture pattern among subjects.

For quantitative validation, two metrics were used to evaluate the accuracy of automated segmentation: DSC and Hausdorff distance (HD, in pixel). Several state of the art methods were implemented for comparison, including U-Net [9], DeepLabV3+ [12], ResUNet [4], CR-UNet [5] and U-Net + LSTM [13]. For U-Net + LSTM, time-sequence based inputs (3 successive frames) were used as we assume higher accuracy could be achieved with additional temporal information.

The segmentation results are summarized in Table 1. Overall, the proposed TexNet (DSC loss + texture loss) outperforms all the other methods with the highest DSC of 0.9284 and the lowest HD of 9.54. The improvement of DSC and HD is within 5% and 5 pixels, respectively. On the other hand, we further select two difficult groups from the cases with relatively poor DSC and HD (below 30th percentile), respectively. For the performance on these difficult groups, TexNet shows significant improvement both in DSC (5% to 10%) and HD (5 pixels to 13 pixels) which demonstrates the robustness of TexNet. It is notable that even without any temporal information, our method still outperforms U-Net + LSTM both in DSC and HD, indicating the proposed texture loss has ideal generalization ability for diversified and sophisticated images.

Table 1. Performance comparison of GA segmentation

Method	Loss function	DSC	DSC lowest 30%	HD	HD highest 30%
ResUNet [4]	DSC loss	0.8927	0.7476	12.50	31.23
DeepLabV3 + [12]		0.9061	0.7938	11.97	23.55
UNet + LSTM [13]		0.9106	0.8011	11.23	24.50
CR-UNet [5]		0.9078	0.7965	11.93	24.54
UNet [9]		0.8838	0.7364	14.50	32.15
TexNet*		0.9128	0.8138	10.69	22.99
TexNet	**DSC loss + texture loss**	**0.9284**	**0.8553**	**9.54**	**19.52**

4   Conclusion

In this paper, we propose a robust segmentation method for GA in ultrasound images by introducing a novel texture loss. TexNet achieves the highest DSC and the lowest HD among state of the art methods. Based on the encouraging results, we believe that besides the traditional shape-wise metrics, texture-wise accuracy could also play an important role in image segmentation, especially for objects like GA which has substantial differences in both shape and texture pattern among subjects. For future works, TexNet will be further tested on more clinical tasks to better validate the advantages demonstrated in this paper.

Acknowledgments. This work was supported by the National Key R&D Program of China [2019YFC0118300].

References

1. Cubillos, J., et al.: Bedside ultrasound assessment of gastric content: an observational study. Can. J. Aneth. **59**(4), 416–423 (2012)
2. Kruisselbrink, R., et al.: Intra- and interrater reliability of ultrasound assessment of gastric volume. Anesthesiology **121**(1), 46–51 (2014)
3. Qi, H., et al.: UPI-Net: Semantic Contour Detection in Placental Ultrasound. In: ICCV (2019)
4. Anas, E.M.A., et al.: A deep learning approach for real time prostate segmentation in freehand ultrasound guided biopsy. Med. Image Anal. **48**, 107–116 (2018)
5. Li, H., et al.: CR-Unet: a composite network for ovary and follicle segmentation in ultrasound images. IEEE J. Biomed. Health Inf. (early access)
6. Oktay, O., et al.: Attention u-net: learning where to look for the pancreas. In: Medical Imaging with Deep Learning (MIDL) (2018)
7. Tan, M., Le, Q.V.: EfficientNet: rethinking model scaling for convolutional neural network. In: ICML (2019)
8. Hu, J., Shen, L., Sun, G.: Squeece-and-excitation networks. In: CVPR (2018)
9. Ronneberger, O., Fischer, P., Brox, T.: U-Net: convolutional networks for biomedical image segmentation. In: Navab, N., Hornegger, J., Wells, W.M., Frangi, A.F. (eds.) MICCAI 2015. LNCS, vol. 9351, pp. 234–241. Springer, Cham (2015). https://doi.org/10.1007/978-3-319-24574-4_28
10. Wang, Z., Bovik, A.C., Sheikh, H.R., Simoncelli, E.P.: Image quality assessment: from error visibility to structural similarity. IEEE Trans. Image Process. **13**(4), 600–612 (2004)
11. Yang, X., et al.: Towards Automatic Semantic Segmentation in Volumetric Ultrasound. In: Descoteaux, M., Maier-Hein, L., Franz, A., Jannin, P., Collins, D.Louis, Duchesne, S. (eds.) MICCAI 2017. LNCS, vol. 10433, pp. 711–719. Springer, Cham (2017). https://doi.org/10.1007/978-3-319-66182-7_81
12. Chen, L.-C., Zhu, Y., Papandreou, G., Schroff, F., Adam, H.: Encoder-decoder with atrous separable convolution for semantic image segmentation. In: Ferrari, V., Hebert, M., Sminchisescu, C., Weiss, Y. (eds.) ECCV 2018. LNCS, vol. 11211, pp. 833–851. Springer, Cham (2018). https://doi.org/10.1007/978-3-030-01234-2_49
13. Chen, J., Yang, L., Zhang, Y., Alber, M., Chen, D.Z.: Combining fully convolutional and recurrent neural networks for 3D biomedical image segmentation. In: NIPS (2016)

Multi-organ Segmentation via Co-training Weight-Averaged Models from Few-Organ Datasets

Rui Huang[1], Yuanjie Zheng[2(✉)], Zhiqiang Hu[1], Shaoting Zhang[1],
and Hongsheng Li[3,4(✉)]

[1] SenseTime Research, Hong Kong, China
`huangrui@sensetime.com`
[2] School of Information Science and Engineering, Shandong Normal University,
Jinan, China
`zhengyuanjie@gmail.com`
[3] CUHK-SenseTime Joint Laboratory, The Chinese University of Hong Kong,
Hong Kong, China
`hsli@ee.cuhk.edu.hk`
[4] Centre for Perceptual and Interactive Intelligence (CPII), Hong Kong, China

Abstract. Multi-organ segmentation requires to segment multiple organs of interest from each image. However, it is generally quite difficult to collect full annotations of all the organs on the same images, as some medical centers might only annotate a portion of the organs due to their own clinical practice. In most scenarios, one might obtain annotations of a single or a few organs from one training set, and obtain annotations of the other organs from another set of training images. Existing approaches mostly train and deploy a single model for each subset of organs, which are memory intensive and also time inefficient. In this paper, we propose to co-train weight-averaged models for learning a unified multi-organ segmentation network from few-organ datasets. Specifically, we collaboratively train two networks and let the coupled networks teach each other on un-annotated organs. To alleviate the noisy teaching supervisions between the networks, the weighted-averaged models are adopted to produce more reliable soft labels. In addition, a novel region mask is utilized to selectively apply the consistent constraint on the un-annotated organ regions that require collaborative teaching, which further boosts the performance. Extensive experiments on three publicly available single-organ datasets LiTS [1], KiTS [8], Pancreas [12] and manually-constructed single-organ datasets from MOBA [7] show that our method can better utilize the few-organ datasets and achieves superior performance with less inference computational cost.

Keywords: Multi-organ segmentation · Co-training · Few-organ datasets

© Springer Nature Switzerland AG 2020
A. L. Martel et al. (Eds.): MICCAI 2020, LNCS 12264, pp. 146–155, 2020.
https://doi.org/10.1007/978-3-030-59719-1_15

1   Introduction

In medical image segmentation, obtaining multi-organ annotations on the same set of images is labor-intensive and time-consuming, where only experienced radiologists are qualified for the annotation job. On the other hand, different medical centers or research institutes might have annotated a subset of organs for their own clinical and research purposes. For instance, there are publicly available single-organ datasets, such as LiTS [1], KiTS [8] and Pancreas [12], each of which only provides a single organ's annotations, as shown in Fig. 1. However, existing methods cannot effectively train a multi-organ segmentation network based on those single-organ datasets with different images.

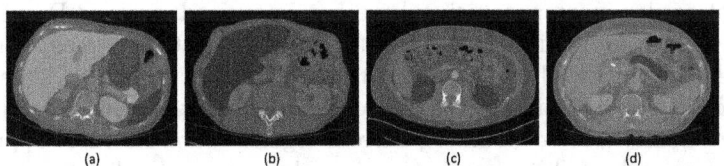

Fig. 1. (a) Multi-organ segmentation is required to achieve more comprehensive computer-aided analysis. (b) LiTS dataset [1] contains only liver annotations. (c) KiTS [8] dataset contains only kidney annotations. (d) Pancreas [12] dataset contains only pancreas annotations.

This work focuses on learning multi-organ segmentation from few-organ datasets for abdominal computed tomography (CT) scans. An intuitive solution is to segment each organ by a separate model using a training dataset. However, this solution is computationally expensive and the spatial relationships between different organs cannot be well exploited. Furthermore, some researches adopt self-training [10], which generates pseudo labels for un-annotated organs in each dataset using a trained single-organ segmentation model, and constructs a pseudo multi-organ dataset. The multi-organ segmentation model can be learned from the pseudo multi-organ dataset. Obviously, the pseudo labels might contain much noise due to the generalization inability of each single-organ segmentation model, as well as the domain gap between different datasets. The inaccurate pseudo labels would harm the training process and limit the performance of self-training.

To tackle the challenge, we propose to co-train a pair of weight-averaged models for unified multi-organ segmentation from few-organ datasets. Specifically, to provide supervisions for un-annotated organs, we adopt the temporally weight-averaged model to generate soft pseudo labels on un-annotated organs. In order to constrain error amplification, two models' weight-averaged versions are used to provide supervisions for training each other on the un-annotated organs via consistency constraints, in a collaborative manner. A novel region mask is proposed to adaptively constrain the network to mostly utilize the soft pseudo labels on the regions of un-annotated organs. Note that our proposed framework with two networks is only adopted during training stage and only one network is used for inference without additional computational or memory overhead.

The contributions of our works are threefold: (1) We propose to co-train collaborative weight-averaged models for achieving unified multi-organ segmentation from few-organ datasets. (2) The co-training strategy, weight-averaged model and the region mask are developed for more reliable consistency training. (3) The experiment results show that our framework better utilizes the few-organ datasets and achieves superior performance with less computational cost.

2   Related Work

Recently, CNNs have made tremendous progress for semantic segmentation. Plenty of predominant approaches have been proposed, such as DeepLab [4], PSPNet [16] for natural images and UNet [11], VoxResNet [2] for medical images. Due to the difficulty of obtaining multi-organ datasets, many approaches are dedicated to the segmentation of one particular organ. Chen et al. [3] proposed a two-stage framework for accurate pancreas segmentation. As these approaches are designed under fully-supervised setting, they cannot be directly applied to train a multi-organ segmentation model from few-organ datasets.

Konstantin et al. [5] firstly present a conditional CNN framework for multi-class segmentation and demonstrate the possibility of producing multi-class segmentations using a single model trained on single-class datasets. However, the inference time of their method is proportion to the number of organs, which is inefficient. Zhou et al. [17] incorporated domain-specific knowledge for multi-organ segmentation using partially annotated datasets. But their training objective is difficult to optimized and it needs some specific optimization methods.

Teacher-student model is a widely used technique in semi-supervised learning (SSL) and model distillation. The key idea is to transfer knowledge from a teacher to a student network via consistency training. Deep mutual learning [15] proposed to train two networks collaboratively with the supervision from each other. Mean-teacher model [13] averaged model weights over different training iterations to produce supervisions for unlabeled data. Ge et al. [6] proposed a framework called Mutual Mean Teaching for pseudo label refinery in person re-ID. Note that these methods are designed under fully-supervised or semi-supervised settings. In this work, we exploit the integration of co-training strategy and weight-averaged models for unifying multi-organ segmentation from few-organ datasets.

3   Method

Single-organ datasets are special cases of few-organ datasets. Without loss of generality, we discuss how to train multi-organ segmentation networks from single-organ datasets in this section. The method can be easily extended to handle few-organ datasets. Formally, given K single-organ datasets $\{\mathbb{D}_1, \cdots, \mathbb{D}_K\}$, where $\mathbb{D}_k = \{(x_i^k, y_i^k)|i = 1, \cdots, N_k, k = 1, \cdots, K\}$, let x_i^k and y_i^k denote the i-th training sample in the k-th single-organ dataset and its associated binary segmentation mask for organ k out of all K organs. Our goal is to train a unified network that can output segmentation maps for all K organs simultaneously.

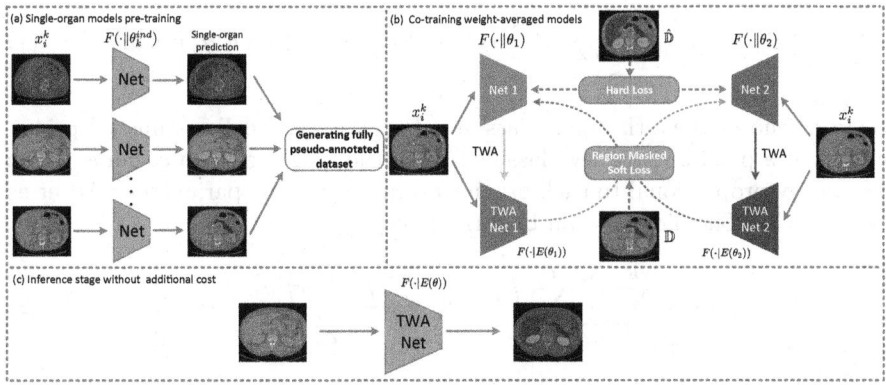

Fig. 2. (a) The pipeline of generating fully pseudo-annotated dataset. (b) The overall framework of our method. (c) In inference phase, only one network is used without requiring additional computational cost.

Pre-training Single-Organ and Multi-organ Models. We choose DeepLab [4] with dilated Resnet-50 [14] and IBN modules [9] as our segmentation backbone for its strong capability on different semantic segmentation tasks. Note that other segmentation networks could also be adopted in our proposed framework. We first pre-train K segmentation models on the K single-organ datasets, respectively. Each model is responsible for segmentation of one individual organ, denoted as $F(\cdot \| \theta_k^{ind})$, where θ_k^{ind} denotes network parameters of the k-th single-organ network. With the pre-trained models, for each single-organ dataset $\mathbb{D}_k$, we can generate pseudo labels for those un-annotated organs to create a fully-annotated dataset with pseudo labels $\hat{\mathbb{D}}_k$, where the label of organ k is manually annotated and the others are hard pseudo labels(see Fig. 2(a)). We can then construct a joint fully pseudo-annotated dataset $\hat{\mathbb{D}} = \{\hat{\mathbb{D}}_1, \cdots, \hat{\mathbb{D}}_K\}$.

Based on pseudo segmentation masks, we can pre-train a multi-organ segmentation model $\hat{F}$ on $\hat{\mathbb{D}}$. Obviously, the quality of pseudo labels is vital to the final performance. It is inevitable that some pseudo label maps might be inaccurate due to the generalization inability of each single-organ segmentation model. The noisy pseudo labels would therefore harm the final segmentation accuracy.

Co-training Weight-Averaged Models for Pseudo Label Regularization. Our framework is illustrated in Fig. 2(b). We train a pair of collaborative networks, $F(\cdot \| \theta_1)$ and $F(\cdot \| \theta_2)$, with the same structure as our pre-trained multi-organ network $\hat{F}$ but with randomly initialized parameters. The training utilizes both the fully pseudo-annotated dataset $\hat{\mathbb{D}}$ with hard pseudo labels and the original dataset $\mathbb{D} = \{\mathbb{D}_1, \cdots, \mathbb{D}_K\}$ with online generated soft pseudo labels. Both the networks are trained with the weighted focal loss and dice loss using hard labels in the fully pseudo-annotated dataset $\hat{\mathbb{D}}$, for handling the high variability of organ size in abdomen. The weighted focal loss is defined as

$$\mathcal{L}_{\text{focal}}(\theta) = -\sum_{k=1}^{K}\sum_{i=1}^{N_k}\sum_{c=1}^{C}\alpha_c\left(1 - F(x_i^k|\theta)_c\right)^{\gamma}\log\left(F(x_i^k|\theta)_c\right), \tag{1}$$

where c denotes the c-th organ class and $F(x_i^k|\theta)_c$ is model's estimated probability that a pixel is correctly classified. α_c is the weight of each organ c, which is inversely proportional to each organ's average size. The parameter γ is set as 2 empirically. The dice loss can be formulated as

$$\mathcal{L}_{\text{dice}}(\theta) = \sum_{k=1}^{K}\sum_{i=1}^{N_k}\sum_{c=1}^{C}\left(1 - 2\frac{\sum \hat{y}_i^{k,c}F(x_i^k|\theta)_c + \epsilon}{\sum \hat{y}_i^{k,c} + \sum F(x_i^k|\theta)_c + \epsilon}\right), \tag{2}$$

where $\hat{y}_i^k$ and $F(x_i^k|\theta)_c$ represent the hard labels and model's predictions for organ c, respectively. ϵ is a small value to ensure numerical stability. Note that the above losses are applied to both networks' parameters, θ_1 and θ_2.

Since the hard pseudo labels are quite noisy, to properly regularize the learning process, we also adopt the online generated soft pseudo labels for un-annotated organs when training the networks on the original data $\mathbb{D}$. For training network 1, $F(\cdot\|\theta_1^{(t)})$, at iteration t with image $x_i^k \in \mathbb{D}_k$, the ground-truth labels for organ k are used while other organs' predicted soft labels are generated from the network 2, $F(\cdot\|\mathbb{E}_t(\theta_2))$, with temporally averaged parameters $\mathbb{E}_t(\theta_2)$:

$$\mathbb{E}_t(\theta_2) = \alpha\mathbb{E}(\theta_2^{(t-1)}) + (1-\alpha)\theta_2^{(t)}, \tag{3}$$

where $\alpha \in [0,1]$ controls how fast the parameters are temporally averaged. Similarly, network 2's parameters $\theta_2^{(t)}$ are trained by temporally weight-averaged model of network 1 $F(\cdot\|\mathbb{E}_t(\theta_1))$'s predictions. Intuitively, the temporally weight-averaged version is a temporal ensemble of a network over its past iterations, which can generate more robust online soft pseudo labels for the un-annotated organs than the network at a specific iteration. In addition, we adopt one network's temporal average to supervise the other network. This strategy can avoid each network using its own previous iterations' predictions as supervisions, which might amplify its segmentation errors from previous iterations.

For each image x_i^k, pixels belong to organ-k are with ground-truth annotations. We would avoid adopting the soft pseudo labels for training networks on regions of ground-truth organs. We morphologically dilate the hard pseudo labels for each un-annotated organ to generate a region mask $\mathcal{T}(y_i^k)$:

$$\mathcal{T}(y_i^k) = \begin{cases} 1, & \text{regions without annotations or background,} \\ 0, & \text{regions with organ-k ground-truth annotations.} \end{cases}$$

Therefore, the segmentation loss with soft pseudo labels are formulated as:

$$\mathcal{L}_{\text{soft}}(\theta_1^{(t)}|\theta_2^{(t)}) = -\sum_{k=1}^{K}\sum_{i=1}^{N_k}(\mathcal{T}(y_i^k) \cdot F(x_i^k|\mathbb{E}_t(\theta_2) \cdot \log F(x_i^k|\theta_1^{(t)})), \tag{4}$$

$$\mathcal{L}_{\text{soft}}(\theta_2^{(t)}|\theta_1^{(t)}) = -\sum_{k=1}^{K}\sum_{i=1}^{N_k}(\mathcal{T}(y_i^k) \cdot F(x_i^k|\mathbb{E}_t(\theta_1) \cdot \log F(x_i^k|\theta_2^{(t)})). \tag{5}$$

The key difference between our method and mean teacher [13] is that we use the temporally weight-averaged version of one network to supervise another network. Such a collaborative training manner can further decouple the networks' predictions. In addition, the region masks are important to enforce the soft label supervisions are only applied to un-annotated regions.

Overall Segmentation Loss. Our framework is trained with the supervision of the hard loss and the soft loss. The overall loss function optimizes the two networks simultaneously, which is formulated as:

$$\begin{aligned}\mathcal{L}(\theta_1, \theta_2) =&\lambda_{\text{focal}}(\mathcal{L}_{\text{focal}}(\theta_1) + \mathcal{L}_{\text{focal}}(\theta_2)) + \lambda_{\text{dice}}(\mathcal{L}_{\text{dice}}(\theta_1) + \mathcal{L}_{\text{dice}}(\theta_2))\\ &+ \lambda_{\text{rampup}}\lambda_{\text{soft}}(\mathcal{L}_{\text{soft}}(\theta_1|\theta_2) + \mathcal{L}_{\text{soft}}(\theta_2|\theta_1)),\end{aligned} \tag{6}$$

where $\lambda_{\text{focal}}, \lambda_{\text{dice}}$ and λ_{soft} are loss weights. Since the predictions at early training stages might not be accurate, we apply a ramp-up strategy to gradually increase λ_{rampup}, which makes the training process more stable.

4   Experiments

The proposed framework was evaluated on three publicly available single-organ datasets, LiTS [1], KiTS [8], Pancreas [12] and a manually-constructed single-organ dataset MOBA [7]. LiTS consists of 131 training and 70 test CT scans with liver annotations, provided by several clinical sites. KiTS consists of 210 training and 90 test CT scans with kidney annotations, collected from 300 patients who underwent partial or radical nephrectomy. Pancreas consists of 281 training and 139 test CT scans with pancreas annotations, provided by Memorial Sloan Kettering Cancer Center. Since the annotation is only available for the training set, we use their training sets in our experiments. MOBA is a multi-organ dataset with 90 CT scans drawn from two clinical sites. The authors of [7] provided segmentation masks of eight organs, including spleen, left kidney, gallbladder, esophagus, liver, stomach, pancreas and duodenum. Specifically, the multi-organ segmentation masks are binarized and stored separately, i.e., we have manually constructed eight single-organ datasets. All datasets are divided into training and test sets with a 4:1 ratio. We use the Dice-Score-Coefficient (DSC) and Hausdorff Distance (HD) as the evaluation metric: $\text{DSC}(\mathcal{P}, \mathcal{G}) = \frac{2\times|\mathcal{P}\cap\mathcal{G}|}{|\mathcal{P}|+|\mathcal{G}|}$, where $\mathcal{P}$ is the binary prediction and $\mathcal{G}$ is the ground truth. HD measures the largest distance from points in $\mathcal{P}$ to its nearest neighbour in $\mathcal{G}$ and the distances of two directions are averaged to get the final metric: $\text{HD}(\mathcal{P}, \mathcal{G}) = (d_H(\mathcal{P}, \mathcal{G}) + d_H(\mathcal{G}, \mathcal{P}))/2$.

For preprocessing, all the CT scans are re-sampled to $1 \times 1 \times 3$ mm. The CT intensity values are re-scaled to $[0, 1]$ using a window of $[-125, 275]$ HU for better contrast. We then center crop a 352×352 patch as the network input.

4.1   Implementation Details

All models were trained for 10 epochs using synchronized SGD on 8 NVIDIA 1080 Ti GPUs with a minibatch of 24 (3 images per GPU). The initial learning rate is 0.05 and a *cosine* learning rate policy is employed. Weight decay of 0.0005 and momentum of 0.9 are used during training. The hyper-parameters $\lambda_{focal}, \lambda_{dice}$ and λ_{soft} are set to 1.0, 0.1 and 0.1, respectively. The smoothing coefficient α is set as 0.999. During inference, only one of the two weight-averaged models with better validation performance is used as the final model.

Table 1. Ablation studies of our proposed methods on the LiTS-KiTS-Pancreas dataset. CT: co-training strategy. WA: weight-averaged model. RM: region mask.

Method	Liver	Kidney	Pancreas	Avg DSC
Individual	95.90	**95.30**	77.05	89.41
Self-training	95.94	94.02	78.54	89.50
CT	95.89	94.42	78.15	89.49
WA	95.90	94.49	78.52	89.63
CT+WA	95.93	94.31	79.12	89.78
CT+WA+RM	**95.96**	95.01	79.25	90.07
Ours (CT+WA+RM+IBN)	95.90	94.98	**79.78**	**90.22**

Table 2. DSC(%) and execution time of conditionCNN [5] and our method.

Method	conditionCNN [5]	Ours
Liver	**95.93**	95.90
Kidney	**95.33**	94.98
Pancreas	77.90	**79.78**
Avg DSC	89.72	**90.22**
Time (s)	12.9	**4.28**

Table 3. DSC (%) and HD (mm) comparison on MOBA dataset.

Organ	DSC (%)					HD (mm)		
	Individual	Combine	Self-training	Ours	ConditionCNN [5]	Individual	Self-training	Ours
Spleen	**96.00**	95.28	95.69	94.95	80.77	**16.81**	32.54	23.15
Kidney(L)	94.51	94.35	94.60	**95.03**	81.51	29.20	26.29	**22.33**
Gallbladder	78.59	79.55	**80.43**	79.65	66.15	54.22	**31.58**	34.35
Esophagus	66.07	62.90	71.87	**72.25**	55.03	26.85	26.58	**24.47**
Liver	**96.61**	96.12	96.23	96.18	94.47	**31.99**	45.89	43.07
Stomach	**91.35**	87.65	90.08	89.68	82.56	57.64	43.71	**42.93**
Pancreas	78.04	73.69	78.10	**79.35**	60.55	28.61	31.04	**29.68**
Duodenum	58.16	54.53	57.72	**61.63**	47.60	41.28	38.43	**35.08**
Avg	82.41	82.02	83.09	**83.60**	62.37	35.82	34.51	**31.88**

4.2   Experiments on LiTS-KiTS-Pancreas Dataset

For the single-organ datasets, LiTS, KiTS and Pancreas, we first train three single-organ models separately for each organ, denoted as "individual" in Table 1. It achieves 95.90%, 95.30%, 77.05% DSC for liver, kidney, pancreas, respectively, and an average DSC of 89.41%.

Ablation Study. In this section, we evaluate each component's effect in our framework. The ablation results are shown in Table 1. We can observe that when training a multi-organ segmentation model directly with hard pseudo labels (denoted as "self-training"), the performance is slightly better than single-organ models (89.41% to 89.50%), which means that even the noisy pseudo labels can improve the segmentation of un-annotated organs. Meanwhile, by applying the co-training scheme, weight-averaged model, region mask and IBN module, our proposed framework achieves a remarkable improvement of 0.81% in terms of average DSC (89.41% to 90.22%) without any additional computational cost for inference. Especially, we observe a significant performance gain of 2.73% for the segmentation of the pancrea, which is more challenging because of its smaller sizes and irregular shapes. Note that when only applying the co-training scheme, the performance is just comparable with self-training, which demonstrates that using the weight-averaged model for supervising the other model can produce more reliable soft labels. The weight-averaged model, region mask and IBN module bring performance gains of 0.29%, 0.29%, and 0.15%, respectively.

Comparison with State-of-the-Art. We compare our method with state-of-the-art conditionCNN [5], which targets at the same task as our work. Since their full dataset is not publicly available and their code is not open-sourced, we re-implement their method using the above mentioned datasets and our baseline model, and tune the hyper-parameters to achieve their best performance for a fair comparison. The results are shown in Table 2. We can see that our method outperforms conditionCNN by a considerate margin (0.5%). In addition, the inference time of conditionCNN is proportion to the number of organs, which makes it inefficient when handling a large number of organs. Some qualitative results are shown in Fig. 3. Our method shows more superior results with less computational cost, compared with existing methods.

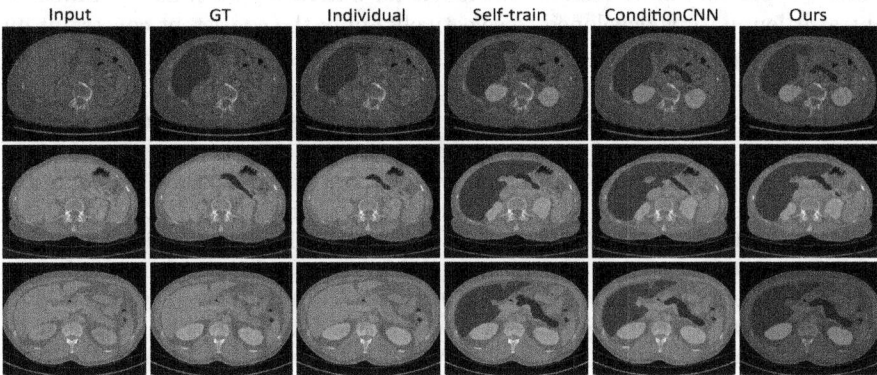

Fig. 3. Qualitative comparison of different methods. Top to bottom: a LiTS dataset image with liver annotation, a Pancreas dataset image with pancreas annotation, and a KiTS dataset image with kidney annotation.

4.3   Experiments on MOBA Dataset

To validate the generalization ability of our method, we also conduct experiments on MOBA dataset, which is more challenging with eight target organs. Since MOBA has multi-organ annotations, we can train a multi-organ segmentation model directly for comparison. The results are shown in Table 3. Our method obtains a significant performance gain of 1.19% compared with the baseline "individual" model (82.41% to 83.60%). Similarly, a large improvement can be observed for those organs with smaller size and irregular shape, such as esophagus (66.07% to 72.25%) and duodenum (58.16% to 61.63%), which demonstrate the effectiveness and robustness of our framework. Interestingly, our method even outperforms the fully-supervised results (denoted as "combine"). We speculate that it might result from the MOBA has more organs to segment and there is severe class imbalance among organs, and our framework can alleviate the imbalance problem by the proposed online-generated soft pseudo labels. We further calculate Hausdorff Distance in Table 3. Our method shows much better HD than baseline "individual" and self-training strategy, bring gains of 3.94 and 2.63 respectively.

Additionally, conditionCNN [5] fails to achieve high performance on MOBA. The accuracy drops dramatically, especially for those organs with smaller sizes and irregular shapes. We suspect it's because conditionCNN cannot handle too many organs with high variation by simply incorporating the conditional information into a CNN.

5   Conclusion

We propose to co-train weight-averaged models for achieving unified multi-organ segmentation from few-organ datasets. Two networks are collaboratively trained to supervise each other via consistency training. The weight-averaged models are utilized to produce more reliable soft labels for mitigating label noise. Additionally, a region mask is developed to selectively apply the consistent constraint on the regions requiring collaborative teaching. Experiments on four public datasets show that our framework can better utilize the few-organ data and achieves superior performance on multiple public datasets with less computational cost.

Acknowledgements. This work is supported in part by the General Research Fund through the Research Grants Council of Hong Kong under Grants CUHK14208417, CUHK14239816, CUHK14207319, in part by the Hong Kong Innovation and Technology Support Programme (No. ITS/312/18FX), in part by the National Natural Science Foundation of China (No. 81871508; No. 61773246), in part by the Taishan Scholar Program of Shandong Province of China (No. TSHW201502038), in part by the Major Program of Shandong Province Natural Science Foundation (ZR2019ZD04, No. ZR2018ZB0419).

References

1. Bilic, P., et al.: The liver tumor segmentation benchmark (LITS). arXiv preprint arXiv:1901.04056 (2019)

2. Chen, H., Dou, Q., Yu, L., Qin, J., Heng, P.A.: VoxresNet: deep voxelwise residual networks for brain segmentation from 3D MR images. NeuroImage **170**, 446–455 (2018)
3. Chen, H., Wang, X., Huang, Y., Wu, X., Yu, Y., Wang, L.: Harnessing 2D networks and 3D features for automated pancreas segmentation from volumetric CT images. In: Shen, D., et al. (eds.) MICCAI 2019. LNCS, vol. 11769, pp. 339–347. Springer, Cham (2019). https://doi.org/10.1007/978-3-030-32226-7_38
4. Chen, L.C., Zhu, Y., Papandreou, G., Schroff, F., Adam, H.: Encoder-decoder with atrous separable convolution for semantic image segmentation. In: Proceedings of the European Conference on Computer Vision (ECCV), pp. 801–818 (2018)
5. Dmitriev, K., Kaufman, A.E.: Learning multi-class segmentations from single-class datasets. In: Proceedings of the IEEE Conference on Computer Vision and Pattern Recognition, pp. 9501–9511 (2019)
6. Ge, Y., Chen, D., Li, H.: Mutual mean-teaching: pseudo label refinery for unsupervised domain adaptation on person re-identification. arXiv preprint arXiv:2001.01526 (2020)
7. Gibson, E., et al.: Automatic multi-organ segmentation on abdominal CT with dense V-networks. IEEE Trans. Med. Imaging **37**(8), 1822–1834 (2018)
8. Heller, N., et al.: The kits19 challenge data: 300 kidney tumor cases with clinical context, CT semantic segmentations, and surgical outcomes. arXiv preprint arXiv:1904.00445 (2019)
9. Pan, X., Luo, P., Shi, J., Tang, X.: Two at once: enhancing learning and generalization capacities via IBN-net. In: Proceedings of the European Conference on Computer Vision (ECCV), pp. 464–479 (2018)
10. Papandreou, G., Chen, L.C., Murphy, K.P., Yuille, A.L.: Weakly-and semi-supervised learning of a deep convolutional network for semantic image segmentation. In: Proceedings of the IEEE International Conference on Computer Vision, pp. 1742–1750 (2015)
11. Ronneberger, O., Fischer, P., Brox, T.: U-Net: convolutional networks for biomedical image segmentation. In: Navab, N., Hornegger, J., Wells, W.M., Frangi, A.F. (eds.) MICCAI 2015. LNCS, vol. 9351, pp. 234–241. Springer, Cham (2015). https://doi.org/10.1007/978-3-319-24574-4_28
12. Simpson, A.L., et al.: A large annotated medical image dataset for the development and evaluation of segmentation algorithms. arXiv preprint arXiv:1902.09063 (2019)
13. Tarvainen, A., Valpola, H.: Mean teachers are better role models: weight-averaged consistency targets improve semi-supervised deep learning results. In: Advances in Neural Information Processing Systems, pp. 1195–1204 (2017)
14. Zhang, H., et al.: Context encoding for semantic segmentation. In: Proceedings of the IEEE Conference on Computer Vision and Pattern Recognition, pp. 7151–7160 (2018)
15. Zhang, Y., Xiang, T., Hospedales, T.M., Lu, H.: Deep mutual learning. In: Proceedings of the IEEE Conference on Computer Vision and Pattern Recognition, pp. 4320–4328 (2018)
16. Zhao, H., Shi, J., Qi, X., Wang, X., Jia, J.: Pyramid scene parsing network. In: Proceedings of the IEEE Conference on Computer Vision and Pattern Recognition, pp. 2881–2890 (2017)
17. Zhou, Y., et al.: Prior-aware neural network for partially-supervised multi-organ segmentation. In: Proceedings of the IEEE International Conference on Computer Vision, pp. 10672–10681 (2019)

Suggestive Annotation of Brain Tumour Images with Gradient-Guided Sampling

Chengliang Dai[1]([✉]), Shuo Wang[1], Yuanhan Mo[1], Kaichen Zhou[4],
Elsa Angelini[2], Yike Guo[1], and Wenjia Bai[1,3]

[1] Data Science Institute, Imperial College London, London, UK
c.dai@imperial.ac.uk
[2] ITMAT Data Science Group, Imperial College London, London, UK
[3] Department of Brain Sciences, Imperial College London, London, UK
[4] Department of Computer Science, University of Oxford, Oxford, UK

Abstract. Machine learning has been widely adopted for medical image analysis in recent years given its promising performance in image segmentation and classification tasks. As a data-driven science, the success of machine learning, in particular supervised learning, largely depends on the availability of manually annotated datasets. For medical imaging applications, such annotated datasets are not easy to acquire. It takes a substantial amount of time and resource to curate an annotated medical image set. In this paper, we propose an efficient annotation framework for brain tumour images that is able to suggest informative sample images for human experts to annotate. Our experiments show that training a segmentation model with only 19% suggestively annotated patient scans from BraTS 2019 dataset can achieve a comparable performance to training a model on the full dataset for whole tumour segmentation task. It demonstrates a promising way to save manual annotation cost and improve data efficiency in medical imaging applications.

Keywords: Suggestive annotation · Brain tumour segmentation · MR

1 Introduction

Machine learning techniques have been widely used in medical imaging applications, achieving performance comparable to or even surpassing human-level performance in a variety of tasks [1]. The prevalence of machine learning techniques comes with some evident challenges and one of them is the requirement for large amount of annotated data for training. In medical imaging applications, the availability of imaging data itself is usually not the real challenge since thousands of people are examined by MRI, CT or X-ray scanners everyday, generating large quantities of medical images. The real challenge comes from the scarcity of human expert annotations for these images. Annotating medical images can

Electronic supplementary material The online version of this chapter (https://doi.org/10.1007/978-3-030-59719-1_16) contains supplementary material, which is available to authorized users.

be expensive in terms of both time and expertise. For instance, annotating the brain tumour image of one patient may take several hours even for a skilled image analyst [2].

Many efforts have been devoted to addressing the challenge of the lack of annotated data. One perspective is to maximise the use of existing data annotations. For instance, transfer learning [3] and domain adaptation [4] were proposed to utilise features learnt from annotations in an existing domain for applications in a target domain where annotations are limited. Semi-supervised and weakly-supervised learning [5] is another example, which leverages unlabelled or weakly-labelled data, together with labelled data, to achieve a better performance than using labelled data alone.

Another perspective to address the challenge is to optimise the annotation process, which is in line with what we have explored in this paper. As has been observed in [6,7], different data samples contribute to the training of a machine learning model to different extents. Selecting more *informative* samples for manual annotation and for model training can therefore potentially reduce the annotation cost and improve efficiency. To improve the efficiency of annotation, active learning [8] was proposed for querying annotations for the most informative samples only. The informativeness of an unannotated data sample is normally defined by two equally important metrics: uncertainty, the confidence of the model in predicting the correct label; and representativeness, which describes how much characteristics of a data sample can represent the dataset it belongs to. To select the most informative biomedical images for annotation, multiple fully convolutional networks (FCNs) were used in [9] to measure the uncertainty of data and the cosine similarity was used to find representative samples among all candidates. In [10], a coreset-based method, which used a small set of data points to approximate all of the data points, were combined with uncertainty sampling for selecting brain lesion images that were both uncertain and representative. [11] proposed a dual-criteria method, which utilised local sensitive hashing and prediction confidence ranking to select informative samples. These methods have shown effectiveness in selecting samples that contribute more to model training.

In this work, we propose a gradient-guided sampling method that utilises the gradient from the training loss to guide the selection of informative samples from a data manifold learnt by a variational autoencoder (VAE) [12]. There are two major contributions of this work: (1) Medical images are suggested for annotation using the loss gradient projected onto the data manifold. Although the loss gradient was explored in the context of adversarial attack and learning [13], its role in suggestive annotation has not been investigated in depth. (2) To further reduce annotation cost, we takes the data redundancy in 3D volume into account, investigating and comparing patient-wise vs. image-wise suggestions. The proposed method was evaluated on a challenging annotation task, brain tumour annotation, and it achieved a promising performance.

2   Methods

2.1   Overview

The framework of gradient-guided suggestive annotation is illustrated in Fig. 1, consisting of three steps: (1) A VAE is trained with an unannotated dataset to learn a data manifold in the latent space. (2) An image segmentation model (base model), where we use a 2D UNet [14] as an example, is trained in an active learning manner. To initialise the model, the first batch of training data is randomly selected from the unannotated dataset and suggested for annotation. After training for several epochs, the gradient of the training loss is backpropogated to the image space. (3) Gradient-integrated image is further projected to the latent space using the VAE encoder. New unannotated samples are selected in the latent space based on the gradient and suggested for the next round of annotation. The model is then trained on images using annotations from both step (2) and (3).

Step (2) and (3) can be done iteratively to suggest more batches of samples. In this work, we perform it for just one iteration as the research focus here is on investigating of whether such sampling method works and how well it works compared to other methods, such as random suggestion or oracle method.

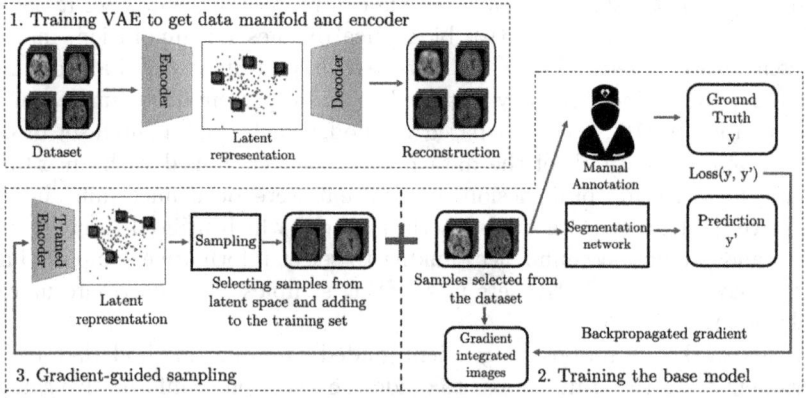

Fig. 1. An overview of the suggestive annotation method. The framework consists of three steps: (1) Training a VAE for learning the data manifold. (2) Training the segmentation model and backpropagating the loss gradient to image space. (3) Sampling on the learnt manifold guided by the gradient.

2.2   Learning the Data Manifold

Representativeness is important for selecting informative samples. Learning a data manifold that can reflect the structure of a given dataset is the prerequisite for the proposed framework. The VAE is used here for learning the data manifold given its good potential shown in many other works [15]. Let us denote an unannotated medical images dataset by $X = \{x_1, x_2, ..., x_n\}$. A VAE is trained on X with the loss function formulated as

$$\mathcal{L}_{vae}(\theta, \phi; x_i) = MSE(f_\theta(g_\phi(x_i)), x_i) + D_{KL}(q_\phi(z|x_i)\|p_\theta(z)), \qquad (1)$$

where $g_\phi(\cdot)$ and $f_\theta(\cdot)$ denote the encoder and decoder, which typically consist of a number of convolutional layers [12]. MSE denotes the mean square error function and D_{KL} denotes the KL-divergence, which regularises the optimisation problem by minimising the distance between the latent variable distribution and a Gaussian distribution [12]. Once trained, the VAE can be used to obtain the latent representations $Z = \{z_1, z_2, ..., z_n\}$ given X. It will be used for sampling purpose in the later stage.

2.3   Training the Base Model

We train the base segmentation model which can provide the gradient for sample suggestion. As revealed in [16,17], less *informative* samples are more important at the early stage of model training, while *harder* samples are more important at the later stage. Therefore, we first randomly select a subset $S = \{x_1, x_2, ..., x_m\}$ of m samples, which are used to initialise the model training and explore the hard samples in the manifold.

An annotated dataset $\mathcal{D} = \{(x_1, y_1), (x_2, y_2), ..., (x_m, y_m)\}$ is thus constructed, where y denotes the annotation by the expert. A base model is trained on $\mathcal{D}$ with the Dice loss function defined by,

$$\mathcal{L}_{Dice}(y_i, \hat{y}_i) = -\frac{2\sum \hat{y}_i y_i}{\sum \hat{y}_i + \sum y_i}, (x_i, y_i) \in \mathcal{D}. \qquad (2)$$

where $\hat{y}_i$ denotes the output of the base model given x_i, which is a probability map of segmentation and y_i denotes the ground truth annotation from the expert.

After the base model is trained, for each of the m samples $x_i \in S$, its gradient of loss is backpropagated to the image space according to,

$$x'_i = x_i + \alpha \frac{\partial L_{Dice}}{\partial x_i}, \qquad (3)$$

where the gradient informs the direction to harder samples and α denotes the step length along the gradient.

2.4   Gradient-Guided Sampling

Here, we describe gradient-guided sampling, which selects informative samples on the learnt data manifold and strikes a balance between exploring uncertain samples and representative samples. Using the VAE encoder $g_\phi(\cdot)$, the hard sample x'_i can be projected to the latent space by,

$$z'_i = g_\phi(x'_i). \qquad (4)$$

Theoretically, images can be synthesised from z_i' via the VAE decoder $f_\theta(\cdot)$ and suggested to the expert for annotation. However, the synthetic image may not be of high quality, which would prevent the expert from producing reliable annotation. To mitigate this issue, we propose to sample in the real image space, searching for existing real images that are most similar to the synthesised image in the latent space. In this way, the expert would be able to annotate on high-quality real images.

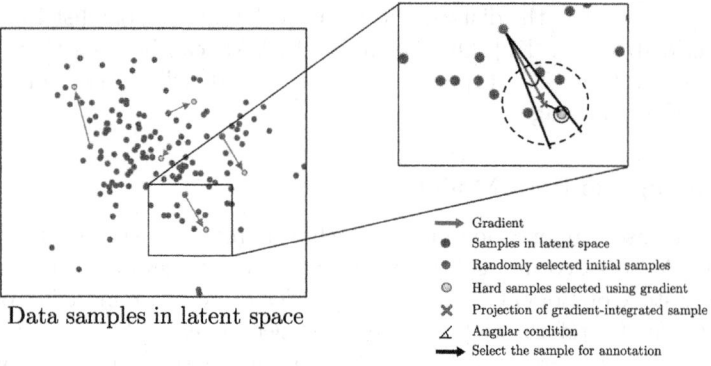

Fig. 2. Sampling process in the latent space. The zoomed view shows an example of a new sample suggested by the proposed gradient-guided sampling method. (Color figure online)

Figure 2 illustrates the sampling process in the latent space. The red dots are the latent representation of S that are randomly selected initially. After training the base model with these samples, for any x_i from S, the loss gradient is backpropagated and integrated to x_i (Eq. 3), then projected to z_i' in the latent space (Eq. 4 and red cross in Fig. 2). One of two criteria we use to find an existing real image is to find a $z_j \in Z$ (yellow dot) that has the shortest Euclidean distance to z_i'. However, we have found that using the Euclidean distance alone sometimes may fail to find an existing image that is similar to the synthesised image. To mitigate this issue, we introduce an angular condition to limit the search angle (black angle in Fig. 2). The angular condition is similar to the cosine distance widely used in machine learning, which in our case was used to constrain the search in the VAE manifold with respect to similar cases. The result of an ablation study is given in Supplementary Table S1.

By using the gradient-guided sampling method, one or more samples can be found given each z_i'. To simplify the process, we only select one sample $z_j \in Z$ for each z_i' in our work, which corresponds to image $x_j \in X$. In this way, we select m informative samples and suggest them to the expert for manual annotation. A new training dataset with m more samples $\mathcal{D}' = \{(x_1, y_1), (x_2, y_2), ..., (x_{2m}, y_{2m})\}$ can be constructed, which consists of initial samples and new samples suggested by the proposed method. The new training set can be used for further training the base network.

3 Experiments

3.1 Dataset

To demonstrate the proposed sampling method in this paper, we used a brain tumour dataset from the 2019 BraTS Challenge [18–22]. The dataset contains T1, T1 gadolinium (Gd)-enhancing, T2 and T2-FLAIR brain MRI volumes for 335 patients diagnosed with high grade gliomas (HGG) or low grade gliomas (LGG), acquired with different clinical protocols from multiple institutions. Two main contributors of the dataset are Center for Biomedical Image Computing and Analytics (CBICA) for 129 patients and The Cancer Imaging Archive (TCIA) for 167 patients. The dataset was pre-processed with skull-striping, interpolation to a uniform isotropic resolution of $1\,mm^3$ and registered to SRI24 space [23] with a dimension of $240 \times 240 \times 155$. We further processed the provided image volume with zero padding and z-score intensity normalisation. The first and last few image slices of the volume were discarded which were normally blank, resulting in a volume of dimension of $256 \times 256 \times 150$ after pre-processing. The annotations of the dataset have four labels: background, Gd-enhancing tumour, the peritumoral edema and the necrotic and non-enhancing tumour core. The latter three labels were combined to form the whole tumour label, which was an important structure for evaluating segmentation accuracy [18]. The dataset was split into 260/75 for training and test.

3.2 Experimental Design

The VAE with the encoder and decoder built by residual blocks [24] was used for learning the data manifold. It was trained for 50 epochs on the images with the Adam optimizer, the loss given by Eq. 1 and a learning rate of 1e−4. The VAE were trained with empirically selected z dimension numbers of 5. The UNet, as the base model for segmentation, was trained with Adam optimizer using Dice as the loss function and a learning rate of 1e-3. We used a 2D network for segmentation due to the computational constraint, as it is challenging to feed a whole 3D volume to 3D VAE network and segmentation network on a standard GPU that we use (Titan X, 12 GB RAM).

To further reduce annotation cost, we investigate two methods of suggestive annotation: image-wise suggestion and patient-wise suggestion. Ideally image-wise suggestion is preferred because it can select several representative image slices for each patient and the expert does not need to annotate all the slices for the same patient, which may contain high data redundancy. Patient-wise suggestion, on the other hand, would require similar slices from the same patient to be annotated. In reality, however, it may be difficult for the expert to annotate the brain tumour on just a few slices from each patient without assessing other slices in the context due to the reason that the vessel may look similar to a tumour on MR images [18]. Here we test the two suggestion strategies under an empirical assumption that if one image slice is suggested for annotation by image-wise suggestion method, two adjacent slices would also be given to the expert for reference.

Patient-Wise Suggestion: Assuming that we use 20 patients' volumes to test our method, we first randomly select 10 patients (equivalent to 150×10 slices) for initial model training of 30 epochs. Then we apply the proposed method to select 10 more volumes from the rest of dataset for suggestive annotation. The model is then trained on the new set of 20 patients for 30 more epochs. To sample the patient in latent space, the latent representations of 150 image slices for each patient was calculated and averaged to form a patient-wise representation.

Image-Wise Suggestion: To compare with the case of using 20 patients' volumes, 1000 (150 * 20/3) image slices in total will be used, of which 500 slices will be randomly selected initially to train the model for 30 epochs, then 500 more will be selected by the proposed method. The step size α is set to $1e-4$ for both image- and patient-wise suggestion.

The baseline method is random suggestion, which randomly selects the same number of patients or images for training the segmentation model. An oracle method was also evaluated, which assumes that the annotations are already available for all the data and we select the posteriori 'best' (in our case, the most challenging samples in terms of Dice score) samples according to the goal of optimizing the segmentation model. The oracle method serves as an upper-bound for suggestive annotation. Each experiment was repeated 10 times for evaluating the averaged performance.

We evaluate the performance of our method in two scenarios, *training from scratch* and *transfer learning*. For training from scratch, we sample from the full BraTS dataset. For transfer learning, we use the CBICA dataset to pre-train the UNet for segmentation and then sample from the TCIA dataset for fine-tuning the network with the proposed method. This is common in medical imaging applications, where we have trained a network using data from one site and then need to deploy it to data from another site. In this scenario, TCIA dataset was split into 130/37 for training and test. The data manifold was learnt from TCIA training set only to avoid a data manifold that has bias towards the pre-training (CBICA) dataset.

3.3   Results

Figure 3 compares the performance of the proposed method to the baseline random suggestion method and the oracle method, in terms of the Dice score for segmentation. It shows that when training from scratch (Fig. 3 (A)), the proposed method outperforms the random suggestion under all circumstances. In addition, it yields similar or sometimes better performance compared to the oracle method. Training with 50 out of the full 260 volumes in BraTS dataset (19%) or 2,500 out of 39,000 image slices (7%) suggested by the proposed method achieved comparable performance to training on full dataset (a Dice score of 0.853 on full dataset is observed). For the transfer learning scenario (Fig. 3 (B)), the proposed method also consistently outperformed random suggestion and achieved comparable performance as the oracle method. Some examples of images suggested by proposed method for annotation are given in Fig. 4. More detailed result can be found in Supplementary Table S2.

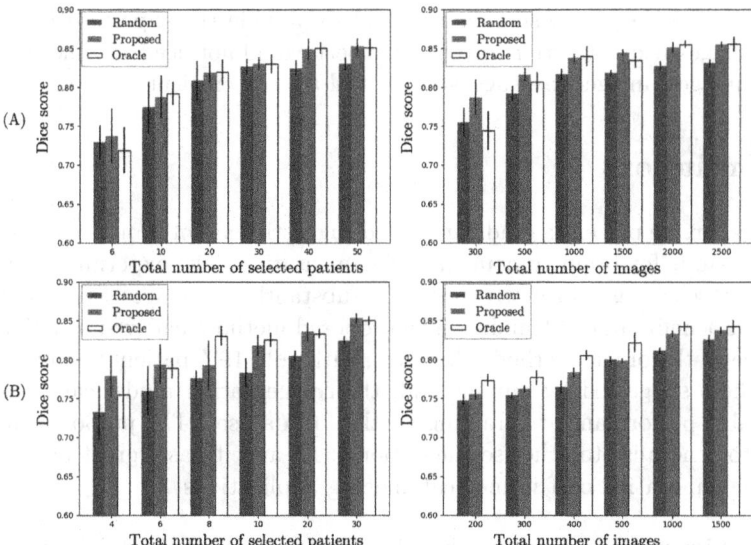

Fig. 3. Comparison of the proposed suggestive annotation method with the baseline random suggestion method and the oracle method. Row (A): training from scratch; Row (B): transfer learning from CBICA to TCIA. Left column: patient-wise suggestion; right column: image-wise suggestion. For the total number of n patients or images, $n/2$ are randomly selected for initial model training and $n/2$ are selected using one of the methods: random, proposed or oracle.

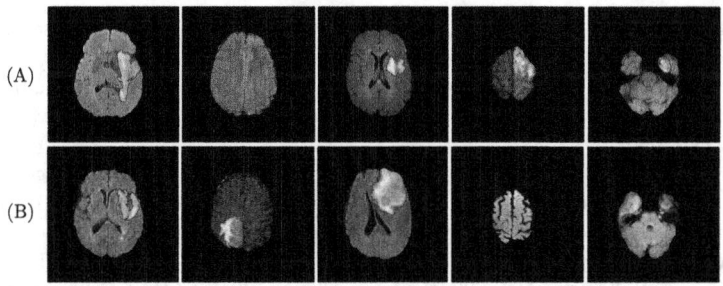

Fig. 4. Interpretation of the proposed method. Row (A): initial samples (red contour: whole tumour), which provide the gradient for search; Row (B): samples suggested by proposed method, which appear quite different from the initial samples. (Color figure online)

When we compare patient-wise suggestion to image-wise suggestion, the latter is better in annotation efficiency since much less images slices are suggested for annotation. In Fig. 3 (A), 2,500 images are suggested for annotation, which can achieve a similar performance as annotating 50 volumes (7,500 images).

Even though some image slices are needed to provide the expert with the context in image-wise suggestion, given the expert would not need to annotate these context images, image-wise suggestion is still a more efficient method.

4   Conclusions

In this paper, we present a gradient-guided suggestive annotation framework and demonstrate it for brain tumour image segmentation. The experimental results show that selecting informative samples substantially reduces the annotation costs and benefits model training. The proposed method achieved a similar performance as the oracle method. Moreover, with only 19% patient volumes or 7% image slices suggested by our method, the segmentation model can achieve a comparable performance to training on the full dataset. The proposed method is easy to generalise to other segmentation tasks and it has a great potential to lower the annotation cost in medical imaging applications.

Acknowledgements. This research is independent research funded by the NIHR Imperial Biomedical Research Centre (BRC). The views expressed in this publication are those of the author(s) and not necessarily those of the NHS, NIHR or Department of Health. We gratefully acknowledge the support of NVIDIA Corporation with the donation of the GPU used for this research.

References

1. Liang, H., et al.: Evaluation and accurate diagnoses of pediatric diseases using artificial intelligence. Nat. Med. **25**(3), 433–438 (2019)
2. Fiez, J.A., Damasio, H., Grabowski, T.J.: Lesion segmentation and manual warping to a reference brain: intra-and interobserver reliability. Hum. Brain Mapp. **9**(4), 192–211 (2000)
3. Tajbakhsh, N., et al.: Convolutional neural networks for medical image analysis: full training or fine tuning? IEEE Trans. Med. Imaging **35**(5), 1299–1312 (2016)
4. Kamnitsas, K., et al.: Unsupervised domain adaptation in brain lesion segmentation with adversarial networks. In: Niethammer, M., et al. (eds.) IPMI 2017. LNCS, vol. 10265, pp. 597–609. Springer, Cham (2017). https://doi.org/10.1007/978-3-319-59050-9_47
5. Cheplygina, V., de Bruijne, M., Pluim, J.P.: Not-so-supervised: a survey of semi-supervised, multi-instance, and transfer learning in medical image analysis. Med. Image Anal. **54**, 280–296 (2019)
6. Katharopoulos, A., Fleuret, F.: Not all samples are created equal: deep learning with importance sampling. In: International Conference on Machine Learning, pp. 2525–2534 (2018)
7. Fan, Y., Tian, F., Qin, T., Bian, J., Liu, T.Y.: Learning what data to learn. arXiv preprint arXiv:1702.08635 (2017)
8. Settles, B.: Active learning literature survey. Technical report, University of Wisconsin-Madison Department of Computer Sciences (2009)

9. Yang, L., Zhang, Y., Chen, J., Zhang, S., Chen, D.Z.: Suggestive annotation: a deep active learning framework for biomedical image segmentation. In: Descoteaux, M., Maier-Hein, L., Franz, A., Jannin, P., Collins, D.L., Duchesne, S. (eds.) MICCAI 2017. LNCS, vol. 10435, pp. 399–407. Springer, Cham (2017). https://doi.org/10.1007/978-3-319-66179-7_46

10. Sharma, D., Shanis, Z., Reddy, C.K., Gerber, S., Enquobahrie, A.: Active learning technique for multimodal brain tumor segmentation using limited labeled images. In: Wang, Q., et al. (eds.) DART/MIL3ID 2019. LNCS, vol. 11795, pp. 148–156. Springer, Cham (2019). https://doi.org/10.1007/978-3-030-33391-1_17

11. Shi, X., Dou, Q., Xue, C., Qin, J., Chen, H., Heng, P.-A.: An active learning approach for reducing annotation cost in skin lesion analysis. In: Suk, H.-I., Liu, M., Yan, P., Lian, C. (eds.) MLMI 2019. LNCS, vol. 11861, pp. 628–636. Springer, Cham (2019). https://doi.org/10.1007/978-3-030-32692-0_72

12. Kingma, D.P., Welling, M.: Auto-encoding variational Bayes. In: International Conference on Learning Representations (2014)

13. Kurakin, A., Goodfellow, I., Bengio, S.: Adversarial machine learning at scale. In: International Conference on Learning Representations (2017)

14. Ronneberger, O., Fischer, P., Brox, T.: U-Net: convolutional networks for biomedical image segmentation. In: Navab, N., Hornegger, J., Wells, W.M., Frangi, A.F. (eds.) MICCAI 2015. LNCS, vol. 9351, pp. 234–241. Springer, Cham (2015). https://doi.org/10.1007/978-3-319-24574-4_28

15. Liu, M.Y., Breuel, T., Kautz, J.: Unsupervised image-to-image translation networks. In: Advances in Neural Information Processing Systems, pp. 700–708 (2017)

16. Kumar, M.P., Packer, B., Koller, D.: Self-paced learning for latent variable models. In: Advances in Neural Information Processing Systems, pp. 1189–1197 (2010)

17. Bengio, Y., Louradour, J., Collobert, R., Weston, J.: Curriculum learning. In: Proceedings of the 26th Annual International Conference on Machine Learning, pp. 41–48 (2009)

18. Bakas, S., Reyes, M., Jakab, A., Bauer, S., Rempfler, M., et al.: Identifying the best machine learning algorithms for brain tumor segmentation, progression assessment, and overall survival prediction in the BraTS challenge. arXiv:1811.02629 (2018)

19. Bakas, S., et al.: Segmentation labels and radiomic features for the pre-operative scans of the TCGA-LGG collection. The Cancer Imaging Archive 286 (2017)

20. Bakas, S., et al.: Segmentation labels and radiomic features for the pre-operative scans of the TCGA-GBM collection. the cancer imaging archive (2017) (2017)

21. Bakas, S., et al.: Advancing the cancer genome atlas glioma MRI collections with expert segmentation labels and radiomic features. Sci. Data 4, 170117 (2017)

22. Menze, B.H., et al.: The multimodal brain tumor image segmentation benchmark (BRATS). IEEE Trans. Med. Imaging 34(10), 1993–2024 (2014)

23. Rohlfing, T., Zahr, N.M., Sullivan, E.V., Pfefferbaum, A.: The SRI24 multichannel atlas of normal adult human brain structure. Hum. Brain Mapp. 31(5), 798–819 (2010)

24. Szegedy, C., Ioffe, S., Vanhoucke, V., Alemi, A.A.: Inception-v4, inception-ResNet and the impact of residual connections on learning. In: Thirty-first AAAI Conference on Artificial Intelligence (2017)

Pay More Attention to Discontinuity for Medical Image Segmentation

Jiajia Chu[1], Yajie Chen[1], Wei Zhou[1], Heshui Shi[2,3], Yukun Cao[2,3],
Dandan Tu[4], Richu Jin[4], and Yongchao Xu[1(✉)]

[1] School of Electronic Information and Communications,
Huazhong University of Science and Technology, Wuhan, China
yongchaoxu@hust.edu.cn
[2] Department of Radiology, Union Hospital, Tongji Medical College, Huazhong
University of Science and Technology, Wuhan, China
[3] Hubei Province Key Laboratory of Molecular Imaging, Wuhan, China
[4] HUST-HW Joint Innovation Lab, Wuhan, China

Abstract. Medical image segmentation is one of the most important
tasks for computer aided diagnosis in medical image analysis. Thanks to
deep learning, great progress has been made recently. Yet, most existing
segmentation methods still struggle at discontinuity positions (including
region boundary and discontinuity within regions), especially when generalized to unseen datasets. In particular, discontinuity within regions
and being close to the real region contours may cause wrong boundary
delineation. In this paper, different from existing methods that focus only
on alleviating the discontinuity issue on region boundary, we propose to
pay more attention to all discontinuity including the discontinuity within
regions. Specifically, we leverage a simple edge detector to locate all the
discontinuity and apply additional supervision on these areas. Extensive
experiments on cardiac, prostate, and liver segmentation tasks demonstrate that such a simple approach effectively mitigates the inaccurate
segmentation due to discontinuity and achieves noticeable improvements
over some state-of-the-art methods.

Keywords: Discontinuity · Medical image segmentation · Edge
detection

1 Introduction

Medical image segmentation which extracts anatomy information is one of the
most important tasks in medical image analysis. In recent years, great progress
has been made thanks to the development of deep learning. Yet, it is still challenging to accurately delineate the region boundary between regions of interest,
which is important in clinical usage.

Different from semantic segmentation of natural images that mainly focus on
incorporating contextual information, state-of-the-art methods in medical image

© Springer Nature Switzerland AG 2020
A. L. Martel et al. (Eds.): MICCAI 2020, LNCS 12264, pp. 166–175, 2020.
https://doi.org/10.1007/978-3-030-59719-1_17

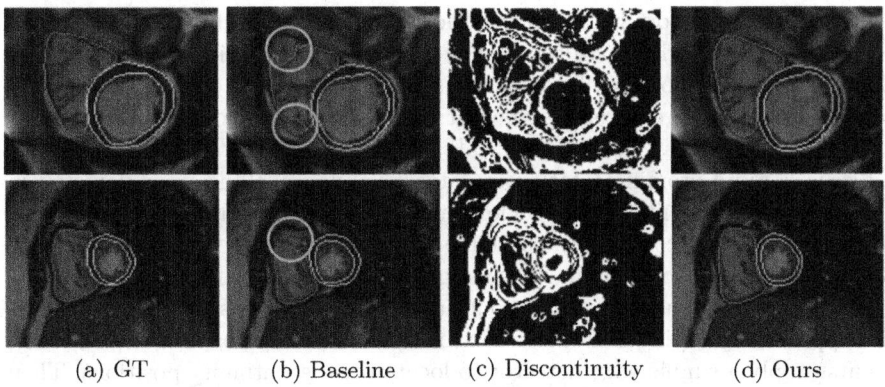

(a) GT   (b) Baseline   (c) Discontinuity   (d) Ours

Fig. 1. Some segmentation examples. Top row: in-dataset validation. Bottom row: cross-dataset validation. By paying more attention to all discontinuity positions in (c) obtained with a simple edge detector, we can avoid the confusing delineation (see the yellow ellipses in (b)) caused by discontinuity within regions and being close to the region boundary, and thus achieve accurate segmentation in (d). (Color figure online)

segmentation put much effort in either improving the network design, incorporating the anatomical prior information, or developing dedicated loss functions, to improve the segmentation accuracy. They can be roughly categorized into these three classes.

For the methods that rely on novel network design, the U-net [1] is one of the most popular convolutional network architecture used in medical image segmentation. Some following methods [2–4] aim to improve the architecture of U-net and achieve boosted performance. Isensee *et al.* [5] proposed nnU-net (no-new-Net) [5] which can automatically design simple U-net and has achieved important improvement over the original U-net [1].

Medical images usually have some anatomical prior structure, based on which some methods [6,7] attempt to integrate such prior information to improve the segmentation accuracy. For example, Yue *et al.* [6] take into account the spatial information by predicting the spatial positions for each slice and regularizes the segmentation result into a desired realistic shape. In [7], the authors leverage an adversarial variational autoencoder to automatically correct the anatomically inaccurate shapes.

Some other methods focus on developing novel loss functions for medical image segmentation. Popular examples are Dice loss [2] and focal loss [8] which can mitigate the class imbalance problem faced by many medical image segmentation tasks. They result in improved accuracy but do not explicitly extract precise boundaries, which is crucial in clinical usage. In [9], Kervadec *et al.* proposed boundary loss that explicitly forces the boundary of segmentation result to align with the ground-truth region boundary. Chen *et al.* [10] developed a novel loss based on active contour models that also achieves accurate boundaries.

Despite much effort in improving the segmentation accuracy, it is still difficult to accurately delineate the region boundary. In practice, it is reasonable that a quasi-flat region may have similar segmentation output, and discontinuity positions may cause different segmentation outputs. Therefore, the discontinuity within regions may cause implausible boundary delineation. This discontinuity issue is more prominent for cross-dataset validation. Indeed, as depicted in Fig. 1, the discontinuity within regions and being close to the region boundary (see yellow ellipses) confuses the baseline model falsely regard such discontinuity positions as the region boundary, leading to inaccurate segmentation results.

In this paper, to address the discontinuity issue, we propose a simple yet effective approach by paying more attention to all discontinuity positions. Specifically, we first apply a simple edge detector to locate the discontinuity positions. Then in addition to the normal loss (*e.g.*, Dice loss [2]) on the whole image, we add an extra loss (*e.g.*, Dice loss [2]) on the discontinuity areas. Such a simple approach effectively alleviates the discontinuity issue and yields accurate boundary delineation (see for example Fig. 1). Extensive experiments on three medical image segmentation tasks (*i.e.*, cardiac, prostate, and liver segmentation) demonstrate the usefulness of the proposed approach.

The main contributions of this paper are three-folds: 1) In addition to region boundary which may pose problems for accurate medical image segmentation, to the best of our knowledge, we reveal for the first time that the discontinuity within regions can also cause inaccurate boundary delineation in medical image segmentation. 2) We propose a simple yet effective approach to alleviate such issue by simply paying more attention to the discontinuity obtained with a simple edge detector. 3) Without bells and whistles, the proposed method consistently achieves noticeable improvements over some related state-of-the-art methods on three medical image segmentation tasks.

2   Method

2.1   Motivation

Current mainstream medical segmentation methods are based on deep convolutional neural networks. They have achieved impressive performance in many segmentation tasks. Yet, the performance usually drops a lot when generalized to unseen datasets, which is the case in clinical usage. It is also crucial to accurately delineate the region boundaries, which usually correspond to some discontinuity positions. Indeed, we observe that quasi-flat regions usually have the same segmentation output, and areas around discontinuity positions are more likely to have different segmentation output. The discontinuity within regions and especially for those near the region contour can somehow confuse the segmentation model to make wrong boundary decision. Based on this finding, we propose to simply pay more attention to all discontinuity positions which may trigger inaccurate segmentation. The overall pipeline is depicted in Fig. 2. Hopefully, this will alleviate the problem of predicting some discontinuity positions within regions as the region boundary.

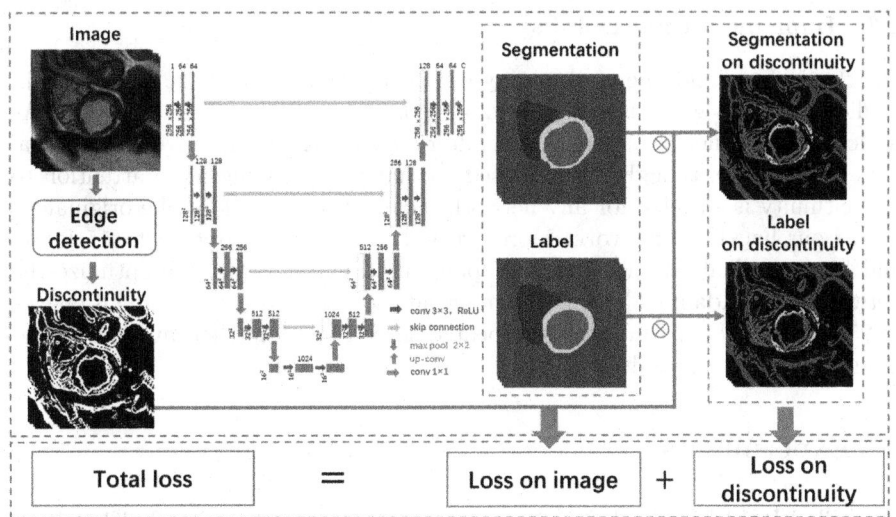

Fig. 2. Pipeline of the proposed method. We build the proposed approach on U-net baseline [1] by adding an additional loss on the discontinuity positions obtained by a simple edge detector.

2.2   Paying More Attention to Discontinuity

Most existing medical image segmentation methods apply cross-entropy loss or Dice loss [2] on the image domain Ω. Specifically, The Dice loss [2] L_d is less sensitive to class imbalance issue. It is given by:

$$L_d(\Omega) = 1 - \frac{1}{K} \sum_{c=1}^{K} \left(\frac{2 \sum_{x \in \Omega} p_c(x) \times g_c(x)}{\sum_{x \in \Omega} p_c(x) + \sum_{x \in \Omega} g_c(x)} \right) \tag{1}$$

where $p_c(x)$ and $g_c(x)$ represent the probability of the pixel x belonging to the class c in prediction and ground truth, respectively.

In practice, we observe that discontinuity positions near the region boundary can be easily misclassified, resulting in boundary misalignment between segmentation result and ground truth segmentation. To mitigate such effect, we propose to pay more attention to all discontinuity positions. This is achieved by adding extra supervision on the discontinuity areas. Specifically, we first extract the discontinuity by applying a simple edge detector (*e.g..*, Scharr Filter [11]) on the image. We regard the top 25% edge responses in the image as the candidate discontinuity positions $\mathbb{D}$. Then we apply an additional Dice loss on the discontinuity areas $\mathbb{D}$. Therefore, the total loss is given by:

$$L = L_d(\Omega) + \lambda \times L_d(\mathbb{D}) \tag{2}$$

where λ is a hyper-parameter which is set to 1 in all experiments.

2.3 Implementation Details

For the segmentation network, many different architectures have been used in medical image segmentation. The most popular and classic is U-net [1]. As noticed in nnU-net [5], many U-net alternatives slightly improve the original U-net. Therefore, though the proposed mechanism of paying more attention to discontinuity is suitable for any network architecture, we adopt the original U-net as our backbone network. More precisely, we employ U-net with 15 layers and batch normalization without dropout in all experiments. We optimize the network using Adam [12] with a learning rate set to 0.001, and resize all images to 256×256. All experiments are repeated three times and their average is considered as the final result.

3 Experiments

To demonstrate the effectiveness of the proposed method, we conduct experiments on three medical image segmentation tasks: cardiac, liver, and prostate segmentation.

3.1 Dataset and Evaluation Metrics

Cardiac500 Dataset: The Cardiac500 Dataset was collected by ourselves from a large hospital. It contains 531 patients divided into 5 subgroups: normal subjects, myocardial infarction, dilated cardiomyopathy, hypertrophic cardiomyopathy, and abnormal right ventricle. Each patient was collected at 25 time points, constructing a large-scale 4D cardiac dataset. Each case has 8–12 slices, and the whole dataset contains more than 100K 2D cardiac images. The right ventricles (RV), left ventricles (LV), and myocardium (Myo) are annotated by the cardiac physician. We divide the dataset into training set and test set according to the proportion of 8:2 in terms of patient level, resulting in 2645 test cases. All images are resized to 256×256. We train the network for 10 epochs on the training set and report results on the test set.

ACDC Dataset: The ACDC dataset [13] was acquired from two MRI scanners (1.5T and 3.0T) and used in the STACOM 2017 ACDC challenge[1]. It comprises 150 patients divided into the same 5 subgroups and annotated with the same three classes as the self-collected Cardiac500 dataset. The MRI data with associated annotations for 100 patients is publicly released, and the MRI data for the other 50 patients is released with their annotations hold by the challenge organizer. We leverage the MRI data for the 100 released patients with annotations for cross-dataset validation.

Liver Segmentation: The Liver dataset (T2-SPIR) is provided by the Combined Healthy Abdominal Organ Segmentation (CHAOS) Challenge in which

---

[1] https://www.creatis.insa-lyon.fr/Challenge/acdc/index.html.

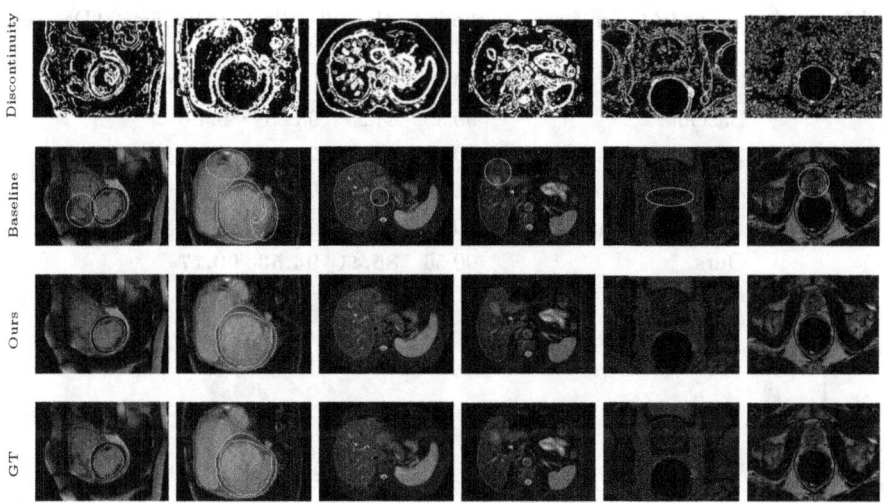

Fig. 3. Some qualitative illustrations. The discontinuity within regions and being close to the region boundary may be falsely regarded as the region boundary for the baseline method. By paying more attention to all discontinuity pixels (see the first row) obtained with a simple edge detector, the proposed method can alleviate such issue.

all images are acquired by a 1.5T Philips MRI and of size 256×256. CHAOS dataset contains 20 fully annotated subjects and 20 without annotation. We split the 20 fully annotated subjects into 15 for training and 5 for testing.

Prostate Segmentation: The Prostate dataset contains 40 patients from the PROSTATE-DIAGNOSIS collection [14] scanned with a 1.5T Philips Achieva MRI scanner. It is split into 30 patients for training, 5 for testing, and 5 for the competition (not used in our experiments). The labels are provided by Cancer Imaging Archive (TCIA) site [15]. The image size is 400×400 or 432×432. This dataset has two labeled categories, peripheral zone (PZ) and central gland (CG). Following [16], we consider both PZ and CG as the prostate region, and use 28 subjects with correct annotations to train the network and test on 5 test subjects.

Evaluation Protocol: We follow the common evaluation protocol relying on the 3D Dice coefficient.

3.2 Results

We compare the proposed method with the popular baseline U-net [1] with Dice loss, alternative (termed Boundary-enhanced loss) that applies larger loss weight on ground-truth region boundary, and two state-of-the-art methods that present novel loss functions: boundary loss [9] and active contour loss [10], on cardiac, liver, and prostate segmentation.

Table 1. Dice scores (%) of different methods on the self-collected Cardiac500 Dataset.

Methods	RV	Myo	LV	Average
Baseline	90.39	84.24	93.83	89.49
Boundary loss [9]	90.47	85.08	93.91	89.82
Active contour loss [10]	**90.68**	84.72	94.43	89.94
Boundary-enhanced loss	90.65	84.93	94.33	89.97
Ours	90.56	**85.41**	**94.53**	**90.17**

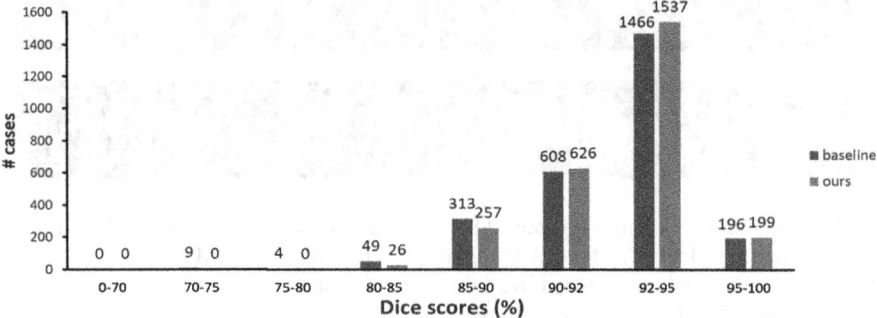

Fig. 4. Distribution of dice scores for 2645 cardiac cases in the self-collected Cardiac500 dataset. Compared with the baseline method, the proposed approach have more cases with Dice scores larger than 90%, and no cases (VS 13 cases for the baseline method) with Dice scores smaller than 80%.

Cardiac Segmentation. We first conduct experiments on the large-scale self-collected Cardiac500 dataset. Some segmentation results are illustrated in Fig. 3 (left two columns). Qualitatively, the proposed approach mitigates the false boundary delineation on discontinuity within regions suffered by the baseline method, and thus achieves accurate segmentation results. The quantitative comparison with other methods is depicted in Table 1. Compared with the baseline method and the alternative by enhancing loss weights on ground-truth region boundary, paying more attention to discontinuity brings 0.68% and 0.2% Dice improvements. Since the self-collected Cardiac500 is a very large-scale dataset, such improvement over the baseline method is still noticeable. The proposed method also consistently improves boundary loss [9] and active contour loss [10] by 0.35% and 0.23% in terms of Dice score, respectively.

To further demonstrate the effectiveness of the proposed method, we also analyze the distribution of Dice scores for the proposed method and the baseline method. As shown in Fig. 4, the proposed method has 92 more images achieving Dice scores larger than 90% compared with the baseline, and there is no images (VS 13 images for the baseline method) with Dice scores below 80%. This demonstrates the robustness of the proposed method in clinical usage.

Table 2. Cross-dataset validation in terms of Dice scores (%) for different methods trained on the self-collected Cardiac500 Dataset and tested on ACDC Dataset.

Methods	RV	Myo	LV	Average
Baseline	63.84	74.14	81.14	73.04
Boundary loss [9]	66.34	79.69	85.14	77.06
Active contour loss [10]	64.96	79.20	84.95	76.37
Boundary-enhanced loss	65.19	78.49	83.95	75.88
Ours	**68.52**	**80.03**	**85.88**	**78.14**

Table 3. Dice scores (%) of different methods on liver and prostate segmentation.

Methods	Liver	Prostate
Baseline	92.70	89.48
Boundary loss [9]	92.76	90.00
Active contour loss [10]	93.10	89.59
Boundary-enhanced loss	92.78	89.99
Ours	**93.79**	**90.28**

We then evaluate the proposed method and the competing methods under cross-dataset validation to further demonstrate the robustness of the proposed approach. As shown in Table 2, for the model trained on the large-scale self-collected Cardiac500 dataset, the proposed method outperforms all other methods when testing on the ACDC dataset [13]. Specifically, the proposed method achieves a Dice score of 78.14%, improving the baseline method and the alternative that enhances the loss weights on ground-truth region boundary by 5.1% and 2.26%, respectively. Compared with the boundary loss [9] and the active contour loss [10], the proposed method yields a Dice improvement of 1.08% and 1.77%, respectively.

Liver Segmentation. To further evaluate the effectiveness of the proposed method, next, we conduct experiments on liver segmentation. Some qualitative illustrations are shown in Fig. 3 (two columns in the middle). The same observation as on the cardiac segmentation also holds on liver segmentation. The quantitative comparison is depicted in Table 3. Similar to the result on cardiac segmentation, the proposed method outperforms all other methods in terms of Dice score. Precisely, the proposed method gives 1.09% and 1.01% Dice improvement over the baseline method and the alternative one, respectively. Compared with boundary loss [9] and active contour loss [10], the proposed method brings 1.03% and 0.69% Dice improvement, respectively.

Prostate Segmentation. We then conduct experiments on prostate (including peripheral zone (PZ) and central gland (CG)) segmentation. We show some qualitative results in the right two columns of Fig. 3. The proposed method aligns the ground-truth boundary better. The quantitative comparison is given in Table 3. The proposed method also consistently outperforms all other methods.

4   Conclusion

In this paper, we first reveal that the discontinuity within regions especially those near the region boundary may confuse the segmentation model in deducing accurate region boundary. Based on this observation, we propose a simple yet effective approach to alleviate such effects. Specifically, we propose to simply pay more attention to all discontinuity positions obtained by an edge detector. This is achieved by applying an additional loss on the discontinuity areas to supervise the network training. Despite its simplicity, we consistently achieve noticeable improvements over some state-of-the-art methods on three medical image segmentation tasks. The proposed method makes the segmentation more robust without requiring extra runtime. It is noteworthy that the proposed method is only beneficial for segmenting regions with discontinuity inside, and does not bring performance when the discontinuity within regions is not severe.

Acknowledgement. This work was supported in part by the Major Project for New Generation of AI under Grant no. 2018AAA0100400, NSFC 61703171, and NSF of Hubei Province of China under Grant 2018CFB199. Dr. Yongchao Xu was supported by the Young Elite Scientists Sponsorship Program by CAST.

References

1. Ronneberger, O., Fischer, P., Brox, T.: U-Net: convolutional networks for biomedical image segmentation. In: Navab, N., Hornegger, J., Wells, W.M., Frangi, A.F. (eds.) MICCAI 2015. LNCS, vol. 9351, pp. 234–241. Springer, Cham (2015). https://doi.org/10.1007/978-3-319-24574-4_28
2. Milletari, F., Navab, N., Ahmadi, S.-A.: V-net: Fully convolutional neural networks for volumetric medical image segmentation. In: Proceedings of International Conference on 3D Vision, pp. 565–571 (2016)
3. Jegou, S., Drozdzal, M., Vazquez, D., Romero, A., Bengio, Y.: The one hundred layers tiramisu: fully convolutional DenseNets for semantic segmentation. In: Proceedings of IEEE International Conference on Computer Vision and Pattern Recognition, pp. 1175–1183 (2017)
4. Oktay, O., et al.: Attention u-net: Learning where to look for the pancreas. In: Proceedings of International Conference on Medical Imaging with Deep Learning (2018)
5. Isensee, F., et al.: NNU-Net: self-adapting framework for u-net-based medical image segmentation. arXiv preprint arXiv:1809.10486 (2018)
6. Yue, Q., Luo, X., Ye, Q., Xu, L., Zhuang, X.: Cardiac segmentation from LGE MRI using deep neural network incorporating shape and spatial priors. In: Shen, D., et al. (eds.) MICCAI 2019. Lecture Notes in Computer Science, vol. 11765, pp. 559–567. Springer, Cham (2019). https://doi.org/10.1007/978-3-030-32245-8_62

7. Painchaud, N., Skandarani, Y., Judge, T., Bernard, O., Lalande, A., Jodoin, P.-M.: Cardiac MRI segmentation with strong anatomical guarantees. In: Shen, D., et al. (eds.) MICCAI 2019. LNCS, vol. 11765, pp. 632–640. Springer, Cham (2019). https://doi.org/10.1007/978-3-030-32245-8_70

8. Lin, T.-Y., Goyal, P., Girshick, R., He, K., Dollàr, P.: Focal loss for dense object detection. IEEE Trans. Pattern Anal. Mach. Intell. **42**(2), 318–327 (2018)

9. Kervadec, H., Bouchtiba, J., Desrosiers, C., Granger, E., Dolz, J., Ayed, I.B.: Boundary loss for highly unbalanced segmentation. In: Proceedings of International Conference on Medical Imaging with Deep Learning, pp. 285–296 (2019)

10. Chen, X., Williams, B.M., Vallabhaneni, S.R., Czanner, G., Williams, R., Zheng, Y.: Learning active contour models for medical image segmentation. In: Proceedings of IEEE International Conference on Computer Vision and Pattern Recognition, pp. 11632–11640 (2019)

11. Jähne, B., Scharr, H., Körkel, S.: Principles of filter design. In: Handbook of Computer Vision and Applications, vol. 2, pp. 125–151 (1999)

12. Kingma, D.P., Ba, J.: Adam: a method for stochastic optimization. arXiv preprint arXiv:1412.6980 (2014)

13. Bernard, O., et al.: Deep learning techniques for automatic MRI cardiac multi-structures segmentation and diagnosis: is the problem solved? IEEE Trans. Med. Imaging **37**(11), 2514–2525 (2018)

14. Bloch, B.N., Jain, A., Jaffe, C.C.: Data from prostate-diagnosis. The Cancer Imaging Archive, 9 (2015). 10.7937K

15. Bloch, N., et al.: NCI-ISBI: challenge: automated segmentation of prostate structures. The Cancer Imaging Archive 370, 2015 (2013)

16. Liu, Q., Dou, Q., Yu, L., Heng, P.A.: MS-net: multi-site network for improving prostate segmentation with heterogeneous MRI data. IEEE Trans. Med. Imaging (2020)

Learning 3D Features with 2D CNNs via Surface Projection for CT Volume Segmentation

Youyi Song[1]([✉]), Zhen Yu[2], Teng Zhou[3], Jeremy Yuen-Chun Teoh[4],
Baiying Lei[5], Kup-Sze Choi[1], and Jing Qin[1]

[1] Center for Smart Health, School of Nursing, The Hong Kong Polytechnic
University, Hong Kong, China
youyisong.song@connect.polyu.hk
[2] Central Clinical School, Monash University, Melbourne, Australia
[3] Department of Compute Science, Shantou University, Shantou, China
[4] Department of Surgery, The Chinese University of Hong Kong, Hong Kong, China
[5] School of Biomedical Engineering, Shenzhen University, Shenzhen, China

Abstract. 3D features are desired in nature for segmenting CT volumes. It is, however, computationally expensive to employ a 3D convolutional neural network (CNN) to learn 3D features. Existing methods hence learn 3D features by still relying on 2D CNNs while attempting to consider more 2D slices, but up until now it is difficulty for them to consider the whole volumetric data, resulting in information loss and performance degradation. In this paper, we propose a simple and effective technique that allows a 2D CNN to learn 3D features for segmenting CT volumes. Our key insight is that all boundary voxels of a 3D object form a surface that can be represented by using a 2D matrix, and therefore they can be perfectly recognized by a 2D CNN in theory. We hence learn 3D features for recognizing these boundary voxels by learning the projection distance between a set of prescribed spherical surfaces and the object's surface, which can be readily performed by a 2D CNN. By doing so, we can consider the whole volumetric data when spherical surfaces are sampled sufficiently dense, without any information loss. We assessed the proposed method on a publicly available dataset. The experimental evidence shows that the proposed method is effective, outperforming existing methods.

Keywords: Learning 3D features by 2D CNNs · Surface projection · CT image segmentation.

1 Introduction

Computed tomography (CT) images are frequently used in clinical practice, with a wide range of applications, e.g. diseases diagnosis, therapeutic assistance, radiotherapy planning, surgery simulation, and injury prediction, to mention a

© Springer Nature Switzerland AG 2020
A. L. Martel et al. (Eds.): MICCAI 2020, LNCS 12264, pp. 176–186, 2020.
https://doi.org/10.1007/978-3-030-59719-1_18

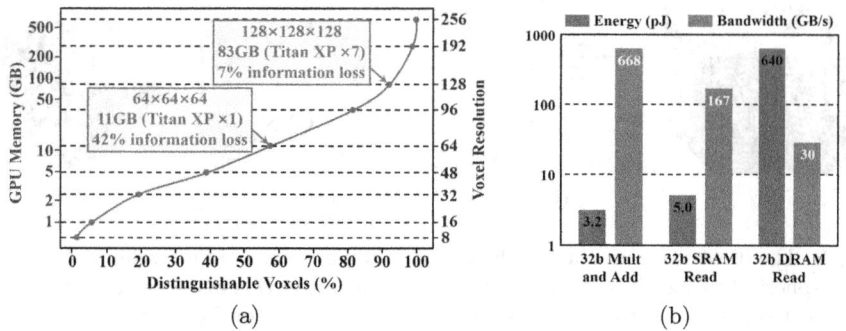

Fig. 1. 3D CNNs are expensive to use; (a) GPU memory consumption is large (here 3D U-Net with batch size of 16 is used), and (b) memory operations are expensive (off-chip DRAM access consumes far more energy than arithmetic operations: multiplication and addition, while the bandwidth is far less).

few [1]. In order to automatically interpret or analyze these images, often it is a prerequisite to segment the object or organ of interest in them, for quantitatively extracting information as required by the application at hand.

For segmenting CT images, 3D features are desired in nature in the machine learning context. However, it is computationally expensive to employ a 3D convolutional neural network (CNN) to learn 3D features [2–4]. As shown in Fig. 1 (a), GPU memory consumption of 3D CNNs grow cubically with voxel's resolution, making 3D CNNs memory-prohibitive to process high-resolution data. But with a low resolution there is information loss, making many voxels distinguishable, which may greatly degrades segmentation performance. Furthermore, 3D CNNs also consume large memory footprint, making memory operation is far more expensive than arithmetic operation for extracting features, as shown in Fig. 1(b).

In the literature, there is a direction that learns 3D features by using 2D CNNs while trying to consider more 2D slices. Existing methods can be classified into three main streams: (1) **2D slice distillation** [5–8], (2) **2.5D** [9–12], and (3) **2D multiple views** [13–15]. Methods in the first stream distill 3D features from 2D features learned by 2D CNNs from 2D slices by mainly employing a conditional random field [16,17] or recurrent neural network [19,20]. 2.5D-based methods learn 3D features by feeding several neighboring 2D slices into a 2D CNN. Methods is the third stream model 3D features from 2D features learned by 2D CNNs from different views (often three views: axial, coronal, and sagittal). While they consider more information than plain 2D CNNs, they cannot consider the whole volumetric data up until now, which leads to information loss.

In this paper, we propose a simple and effective technique that learns 3D features by 2D CNNs, for segmenting CT images. Our key idea is that all boundary voxels of a 3D object form a 2D surface that can be represented by using a 2D matrix, and hence they can be perfectly recognized by a 2D CNN in theory. We concrete this idea by employing a 2D CNN to predict the projection

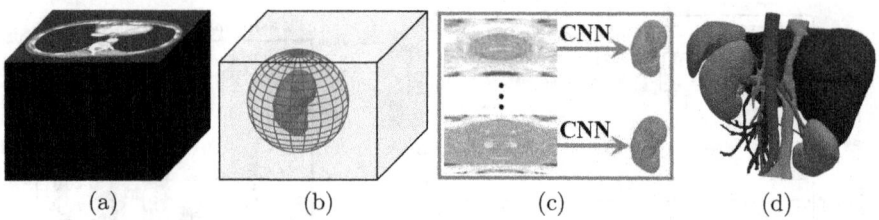

Fig. 2. The illustrative pipeline of the introduced method: (a) input volume, (b) sampling spherical surface (the red mesh), (c) predicting projection distance, and (d) fusing constructed 3D results to produce segmentation result. (Color figure online)

distance between a set of prescribed spherical surfaces and the object's surface, and then fusing the predicted projection distance to identify boundary voxels for the segmentation. We can consider the whole volumetric data by sampling spherical surfaces sufficiently dense, without any information loss. The introduced method is assessed on a publicly available CT dataset. The experimental evidence shows that the introduced method is effective to learn 3D features, working better than existing methods.

2   Methodology

Figure 2 shows the pipeline of the introduced method. For a given CT volume (Fig. 2 (a)), we first sample spherical surfaces (the red mesh in Fig. 2 (b)); to do so, the object is coarsely segmented. Next, we (1) organize the sampled surface into a 2D plane, (2) employ a 2D U-Net [21] to predict the projection distance (defined later), and (3) identify boundary voxels based on the predicted projection distance (Fig. 2 (c)). Finally, we fuse all surfaces' results to produce the segmentation result (Fig. 2 (d)). Technical details are presented below.

2.1   Spherical Surfaces Sampling

We begin by presenting how to sample spherical surfaces. For sampling a spherical surface $\mathbf{S}_n$, we have to determine the origin of coordinates and the radius, denoted by $\mathbf{p}_n$ and r_n, respectively. For determining $\mathbf{p}_n$, we first employ a 2D U-Net to segment the objects of interest (implementation details are given in Sect. 3.3). We then place $\mathbf{p}_n$ at the centerline of the segmented objects, with a distance interval as d. Here we just need a coarse segmentation; the effect of its accuracy to the final segmentation accuracy is analyzed in Sect. 3.4, in which we also analyzed how to set the value of r_n and d such that the sampled surfaces are sufficiently dense.

For the moment, we just focus on how to sample $\mathbf{S}_n$ and organize it into a 2D plane, given $\mathbf{p}_n$ and r_n. To do so, we choose the angular coordinate system; two indexes of $\mathbf{S}_n$ are $\theta \in [0, 360)$ and $\varphi \in [0, 180)$, and $\mathbf{S}_n$ is organized as

$$\mathbf{S}_n(\theta, \varphi) = \mathbf{V}(\mathbf{p}_n + r_n\mathbf{d}(\theta, \varphi)), \tag{1}$$

where $\mathbf{V}(x, y, z)$ represents the intensity value of the voxel at the position (x, y, z) in the given CT volume, and $\mathbf{d}$ represents the 3D unit vector in the Cartesian coordinate system; $\mathbf{d} = (\cos\theta\cos\varphi, \cos\theta\sin\varphi, \sin\theta)$.

2.2 Surface's Projection Distance Predicting

We now go into how to use a 2D CNN (U-Net here) to learn 3D features, by employing the 2D CNN to learn the projection distance between sampled spherical surfaces and the object's surface. We start by presenting how to predict the projection distance. The projection distance is defined as the distance of the voxel in $\mathbf{S}_n$ to the object's surface, along the line from the voxel to the object's center. It has a positive value when the voxel is outside the object's surface, and a negative value otherwise. We train a 2D U-Net to predict the projection distance by solving for the following problem

$$\operatorname*{argmin}_{\omega} \frac{1}{M} \sum_{n=1}^{M} \| f(\mathbf{S}_n; \omega) - \mathbf{G}_n \|_2^2, \tag{2}$$

where ω denotes the parameters of the 2D U-Net f, M denotes the number of training examples, and $\mathbf{G}_n$ denotes the ground truth of $\mathbf{S}_n$, storing the distance information. The operation $\|A - B\|_2^2$ counts the average square Euclidean distance of pixels between two images A and B. Here note that for the purpose of validating our idea, we just use the simplest and most straightforward loss function; for the practical usage, more advanced loss function is suggested.

Optimization details of above problem (Eq. 2) are presented in Sect. 3.3. We now proceed with how to identify boundary voxels based on the predicted distance of $\mathbf{S}_n$. For each voxel indexed by (θ, φ) in $\mathbf{S}_n$, if its predicted projection distance is ℓ, then the voxel at position $\mathbf{p}_n + (r_n - \ell)\mathbf{d}(\theta, \varphi)$ in the input CT data is regarded as a boundary voxel. Below we present an intuitive explanation of why 3D features can be learned by the introduced way. 3D features are learned from mainly the intensity and geometrical information. If we learn it by a plain 2D CNN, then geometrical information among 2D slices is disregarded. By the introduced way, geometrical information is provided by the ground truth while the sampled surfaces provide the intensity information, and so both geometrical and intensity information are preserved. In addition, the mapping of intensity to geometrical information can be well memorized by the properly trained 2D CNN, as revealed by the recent studies [22–24], so it is guaranteed that the geometrical information can be well utilized.

2.3   Surfaces' Projection Distance Fusing

For exploiting comprehensive geometric and intensity information, we sampled not only one surface for the object. We here present how to fuse these complementary information from different surfaces. Specifically, suppose that we sampled N surfaces for the object, and there are K voxels in the input CT volume. Let $\mathbf{D} \in \mathbb{B}^{K \times N}$ be the joint segmentation result matrix; $\mathbf{D}(k, n) = 1$ meaning that the voxel k is segmented as a foreground voxel according to $\mathbf{S}_n$. For estimating the unknown truth segmentation $\mathbf{G} \in \mathbb{B}^K$, we first estimate all surfaces segmentation accuracy, denoted by $\mathbf{A}_n = (\delta_n, \xi_n)$ (of $\mathbf{S}_n$), where δ_n and ξ_n stand for the true positive rate and true negative rate, the fraction of object voxels and non-object voxels to be segmented correctly. We then use the estimated $\mathcal{A} = [\mathbf{A}_1, \mathbf{A}_2, \cdots, \mathbf{A}_N])$ and $\mathbf{D}$ to estimate $\mathbf{G}$. The fusing procedure can be mathematically expressed as

$$\mathcal{A}^* = \operatorname*{argmax}_{\mathcal{A}} p(\mathbf{D}, \mathbf{G}|\mathcal{A}) \text{ and } \mathbf{G}^* = \operatorname*{argmax}_{\mathbf{G}} p(\mathbf{G}|\mathbf{D}, \mathcal{A}^*), \qquad (3)$$

where $p(\mathbf{D}, \mathbf{G}|\mathcal{A})$ denotes the mass probability function of the complete data $(\mathbf{D}, \mathbf{G})$.

Below we present how we solve for Eq. 3 in an iterative manner. We initialize $\mathcal{A}$ by computing $\{\delta_n, \xi_n\}_{n=1}^N$ in the training set. We then update the estimation of $\mathbf{G}$ (at t-th iteration) by

$$\mathbf{G}^t(k) = p\big(\mathbf{G}(k) = 1 \big| \mathcal{A}^t, \sum_{n=1}^N \mathbf{D}(k, n)\big) = \frac{\mathbf{F}^t(k)}{\mathbf{F}^t(k) + \mathbf{B}^t(k)}, \qquad (4)$$

where

$$\mathbf{F}^t(k) = p\big(\mathbf{G}(k) = 1\big) \prod_{n}^{\mathbf{D}(k,n)=1} \delta_n^t \prod_{n}^{\mathbf{D}(k,n)=0} (1 - \delta_n^t),$$

$$\mathbf{B}^t(k) = p\big(\mathbf{G}(k) = 0\big) \prod_{n}^{\mathbf{D}(k,n)=0} \xi_n^t \prod_{n}^{\mathbf{D}(k,n)=1} (1 - \xi_n^t). \qquad (5)$$

The prior probability $p(\mathbf{G}(k) = 1)$ is set to the fraction of voxels at the position k to be the object in the training set. Next, we update $\mathcal{A}$ as

$$\delta_n^{t+1} = \sum_{k}^{\mathbf{D}(k,n)=1} \mathbf{G}^t(k) \bigg/ \sum_{k} \mathbf{G}^t(k),$$

$$\xi_n^{t+1} = \sum_{k}^{\mathbf{D}(k,n)=0} \big(1 - \mathbf{G}^t(k)\big) \bigg/ \sum_{k} \big(1 - \mathbf{G}^t(k)\big). \qquad (6)$$

The updating finally is terminated when $\mathbf{G}$ and $\mathcal{A}$ reached a stable value.

3   Experimental Evaluation

3.1   Dataset

We assessed the proposed method on a publicly available CT dataset [27][1]. It contains 90 CT volumes, 43 from [28–30] and 47 from [31,32], and has 8 organs labeled: (1) liver, (2) spleen, (3) left kidney, (4) stomach, (5) pancreas, (6) gallbladder, (7) esophagus, and (8) duodenum. Each volume's resolution at three directions are varying hugely, from 0.6 to 0.9 mm (in-plane) and from 0.5 to 5.0 mm (inter-slice spacing).

3.2   Evaluation Metric

We employed two metrics: DSC (Dice similarity coefficient) and ASD (average surface distance), to evaluate the segmentation accuracy. DSC measures the match of the segmentation result and ground truth by normalizing voxels' number in their intersection over the average of voxels' number in them. ASD measures the average distances of boundary voxels of the segmentation result to boundary voxels of the ground truth. DSC takes its value in the range of $[0, 1]$ while ASD of $[0, \infty]$, and a better segmentation algorithm has a larger value of DSC while a smaller value of ASD.

3.3   Implementation Details

CT volumes are first aligned by linear interpolation to let them have the same spacing resolution. Next, the U-Net for the coarse segmentation has the same architecture as [21], and is trained by the Dice loss function. As for the U-Net (for predicting the projection distance), it's architecture is automatically searched by employing [33] instead of manually designing. These two U-Nets are optimized by Adam [34], with the initial learning rate as 0.0003, and terminated to optimize when the loss function cannot be decreased in the validation set. In addition, for sampling spherical surfaces sufficiently dense, we set d, the distance interval to place $\mathbf{p}_n$, to 3, and r_n is from 5 to $1.5r$ with the interval of 5, where r is the radius of the minimum ball that covers the object segmented by the first U-Net; the effect of d, r_n, and the segmentation accuracy of the first U-Net on the final segmentation accuracy is analyzed later (Sect. 3.4).

3.4   Experimental Results

Segmentation Accuracy Improvement: We first look at how much extent the segmentation accuracy can be improved by the proposed method. We hence compare it to four existing methods: (1) 2D-CRF, (2) 2D-RNN, (3) 2.5D, and (4) 2D-MV. 2D-CRF [6] and 2D-RNN [7] belong to 2D slice distillation-based methods, modeling 3D features on the learned 2D features by employing CRF

---

[1] Available on https://zenodo.org/record/1169361#.XSFOm-gzYuU.

Table 1. Segmentation accuracy comparison with existing methods; DSC (%) and ASD (mm).

	Raw		Coarse	
	DSC	ASD	DSC	ASD
2D-CRF [6]	84.2 ± 6.5	1.69 ± 1.37	85.1 ± 6.3	1.65 ± 1.35
2D-RNN [7]	84.8 ± 6.3	1.65 ± 1.33	85.4 ± 6.2	1.61 ± 1.32
2.5D [11]	84.7 ± 6.4	1.68 ± 1.32	85.2 ± 6.1	1.62 ± 1.34
2D-MV [13]	84.5 ± 6.3	1.64 ± 1.41	85.0 ± 6.2	1.60 ± 1.37
Ours	—	—	**87.5 ± 5.6**	**1.57 ± 1.24**

Table 2. Ablation study results.

	DSC	ASD
Voting	86.2 ± 6.0	1.60 ± 1.30
Pro-S	84.1 ± 6.8	1.69 ± 1.37
Sur-B	86.3 ± 6.0	1.63 ± 1.31
Sur-S	86.9 ± 5.8	1.58 ± 1.29
Ours	**87.5 ± 5.6**	**1.57 ± 1.24**

and RNN, respectively. 2.5D [11] learns 3D features by feeding several neighboring 2D slices to the 2D CNN; here we feed 6 slices by which 2.5D network produces the most accurate segmentation result. 2D-MV learns 3D features from different views [13]; here we used three views: axial, coronal, and sagittal. We use the same architecture of U-Nets, and train them in the same learning setting (Dice loss and Adam with the same initial learning rate: 0.0003). For a fair comparison, we also tested them on the coarse segmentation results which we used to sample spherical surfaces. The results were acquired based on a 5-fold cross-validation, and are presented in Table 1 where 'Raw' and 'Coarse' stand for the method takes the input as the raw image and the coarse segmentation result, respectively. From Table 1, we can see that the introduced method yields the best segmentation accuracy, demonstrating its effectiveness (Table 4).

Superior Accuracy to 3D CNNs: We here compare the introduced method to 3D CNNs. For a fair comparison, we place them in the same GPU memory consumption. Specifically, we allocated 40%, 60%, 80%, and 100% of GPU memory to search 3D and 2D U-Nets by employing [33]. 3D U-Nets are trained with two manners: patch- and low resolution-based, meaning that the 3D U-Net takes respectively the 3D patch and the low-resolution counterpart as the input. We used Dice loss and Adam with the same initial learning rate (0.0003) to train them. The results were acquired based on a 5-fold cross-validation, and are presented in Table 2 where '-P-R', '-P-C', 'R-R', and 'R-C' stand for 3D patch-based training from raw images, 3D patch-based training from coarse segmentation results, low resolution-based training from raw images, and low resolution-based training from coarse segmentation results, respectively. We can see from Table 2 that the introduced method works better than 3D U-Nets under the same amount of GPU memory consumption.

Coarse Segmentation Sensitivity: The introduced method sample spherical surfaces from the coarse segmentation results, so we here evaluate how the coarse segmentation results to affect the final segmentation results. To do so, we allocated 40%, 60%, 80%, and 100% of GPU memory to search U-Net's architecture for the coarse segmentation, and trained them using the same learning setting. The results were acquired based on a 5-fold cross-validation, and are presented in Table 3. We can see from Table 3 that the final segmentation accuracy just varies slightly, meaning that the introduced method is not sensitive to the coarse segmentation results.

Table 3. Segmentation accuracy comparison with 3D CNNs, under the same amount of GPU memory consumption (from 40% to 100%).

	40%		60%		80%		100%	
	DSC	ASD	DSC	ASD	DSC	ASD	DSC	ASD
3D-P-R	78.4 ± 7.4	1.81 ± 1.52	82.6 ± 6.9	1.74 ± 1.43	84.3 ± 6.5	1.67 ± 1.39	85.1 ± 6.3	1.65 ± 1.35
3D-P-C	79.7 ± 7.1	1.77 ± 1.47	83.1 ± 6.7	1.72 ± 1.40	85.7 ± 6.1	1.64 ± 1.32	86.2 ± 6.0	1.62 ± 1.31
3D-R-R	76.9 ± 7.6	1.84 ± 1.54	81.9 ± 7.1	1.76 ± 1.47	83.2 ± 6.8	1.72 ± 1.41	84.4 ± 6.5	1.68 ± 1.39
3D-R-C	78.1 ± 7.4	1.79 ± 1.50	82.7 ± 6.8	1.73 ± 1.42	84.4 ± 6.6	1.68 ± 1.37	85.3 ± 6.1	1.63 ± 1.34
Ours	$\mathbf{86.4 \pm 5.9}$	$\mathbf{1.62 \pm 1.29}$	$\mathbf{87.1 \pm 5.7}$	$\mathbf{1.59 \pm 1.27}$	$\mathbf{87.4 \pm 5.6}$	$\mathbf{1.57 \pm 1.26}$	$\mathbf{87.5 \pm 5.6}$	$\mathbf{1.57 \pm 1.24}$

Table 4. Segmentation accuracy comparison under different coarse segmentation results produced by 4 different U-Net's architectures.

40%		60%		80%		100%	
DSC	ASD	DSC	ASD	DSC	ASD	DSC	ASD
87.2 ± 5.7	1.60 ± 1.26	87.4 ± 5.6	1.58 ± 1.25	87.5 ± 5.5	1.58 ± 1.24	87.5 ± 5.6	1.57 ± 1.24

Parameters Sensitivity: The introduced method has two parameters: (1) the distance interval, d, to place $\mathbf{p}_n$, and (2) the radius interval, I_r, to sample surfaces. Their values are significant, deciding how much extent of the CT data the 2D CNN can exploit to learn 3D features. We hence look at their effect on the segmentation accuracy here. To do so, we set different values to them, both from 1 to 10. The results are presented in Fig. 3; based on a 5-fold cross-validation. We can see from Fig. 3 that when d and I_r are set to 3 and 5, respectively, the introduced method yields the most accurate segmentation results.

Ablation Study: We go into why we concrete our idea as the introduced one. We first look at why we employ the introduced fusing procedure. It can be simply done by the majority voting, but experimental evidence shows it works worse; the results are presented in Table 2 (denoted by 'Voting'). We then look at why we have to predict the projection distance, rather than predicting voxels in the sampled surfaces to be object or non-object. We denote this way by 'Pro-S'; it is in spirit similar to [18]. From Table 2, we can see that Pro-S works worse, probably because it uses geometrical information not as effective as ours. We now look at why the surface is spherical. We experimented two different surfaces, denoted by 'Sur-B' and 'Sur-S' in Table 2, standing for the surface to be a box and the mean shape (estimated from the training dataset), respectively. From Table 2, we can see that they do not work better than the introduced method. In addition, they are more difficult to implement; it is complicated to organize data on them into 2D planes.

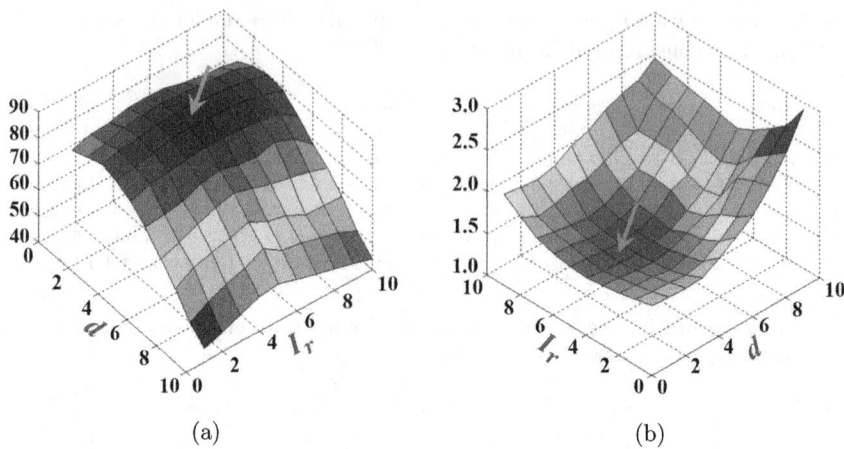

Fig. 3. Parameters' sensitivity to segmentation accuracy; (a) *DSC* and (b) *ASD*.

4 Conclusion

In this paper, we introduced a simple and effective technique to learn 3D features with 2D CNNs for segmenting CT images via surface projection. It is of great impractical importance, because directly employing a 3D CNN to learn 3D features is computationally expensive. Our idea is to predict the projection distance of voxels on a set of prescribed spherical surfaces to the object's surface, which can be readily implemented by existing 2D CNNs. By doing so, a 2D CNN can exploit both intensity and geometrical information to progressively form representative 3D features. The experimental evidence from a publicly available dataset shows that the introduced method is effective, working better than existing methods.

Acknowledgement. The work described in this paper is supported by a grant from the Hong Kong Research Grants Council (Project No. PolyU 152035/17E), a grant from the Natural Foundation of China (Grant No. 61902232), a grant from the Li Ka Shing Foundation Cross-Disciplinary Research (Grant no. 2020LKSFG05D), a grant from the Innovative Technology Fund (Grant No. MRP/015/18), and a grant from the General Research Fund (Grant No. PolyU 152006/19E).

References

1. Cerrolaza, J., Picazo, M., Humbert, L., et al.: Computational anatomy for multi-organ analysis in medical imaging: a review. Med. Image Anal. **56**, 44–67 (2019)
2. Roth, H., Shen, Ch., Oda, H., et al.: Deep learning and its application to medical image segmentation. Med. Imaging Technol. **36**(2), 63–71 (2018)
3. Roth, H.R., et al.: A multi-scale pyramid of 3D fully convolutional networks for abdominal multi-organ segmentation. In: Frangi, A.F., Schnabel, J.A., Davatzikos, C., Alberola-López, C., Fichtinger, G. (eds.) MICCAI 2018. LNCS, vol. 11073, pp. 417–425. Springer, Cham (2018). https://doi.org/10.1007/978-3-030-00937-3_48

4. Kakeya, H., Okada, T., Oshiro, Y.: 3D U-JAPA-Net: mixture of convolutional networks for abdominal multi-organ CT segmentation. In: Frangi, A.F., Schnabel, J.A., Davatzikos, C., Alberola-López, C., Fichtinger, G. (eds.) MICCAI 2018. LNCS, vol. 11073, pp. 426–433. Springer, Cham (2018). https://doi.org/10.1007/978-3-030-00937-3_49

5. Chen, J., Yang, L., Zhang, Y., et al.: Combining fully convolutional and recurrent neural networks for 3D biomedical image segmentation. In: Advances in Neural Information Processing Systems, pp. 3036–3044 (2016)

6. Christ, P., et al.: Automatic liver and lesion segmentation in CT using cascaded fully convolutional neural networks and 3D conditional random fields. In: Ourselin, S., Joskowicz, L., Sabuncu, M.R., Unal, G., Wells, W. (eds.) MICCAI 2016. LNCS, vol. 9901, pp. 415–423. Springer, Cham (2016). https://doi.org/10.1007/978-3-319-46723-8_48

7. Cai, J., Lu, L., Xie, Y., et al.: Improving deep pancreas segmentation in CT and MRI images via recurrent neural contextual learning and direct loss function. arXiv preprint arXiv:1707.04912 (2017)

8. Novikov, A., Major, D., Wimmer, M., et al.: Deep sequential segmentation of organs in volumetric medical scans. IEEE Trans. Med. Imaging **38**(5), 1207–1215 (2018)

9. Li, X., Chen, H., Qi, X., et al.: H-DenseUNet: hybrid densely connected UNet for liver and tumor segmentation from CT volumes. IEEE Trans. Med. Imaging **37**(12), 2663–2674 (2018)

10. Xia, Y., Xie, L., Liu, F., Zhu, Z., Fishman, E.K., Yuille, A.L.: Bridging the gap between 2D and 3D organ segmentation with volumetric fusion net. In: Frangi, A.F., Schnabel, J.A., Davatzikos, C., Alberola-López, C., Fichtinger, G. (eds.) MICCAI 2018. LNCS, vol. 11073, pp. 445–453. Springer, Cham (2018). https://doi.org/10.1007/978-3-030-00937-3_51

11. Yu, Q., Xia, Y., Xie, L., et al.: Thickened 2D networks for 3D medical image segmentation. arXiv preprint arXiv:1904.01150 (2019)

12. Ambellan, F., Tack, A., Ehlke, M., et al.: Automated segmentation of knee bone and cartilage combining statistical shape knowledge and convolutional neural networks: data from the osteoarthritis initiative. Med. Image Anal. **52**, 109–118 (2019)

13. Wang, Y., Zhou, Y., Shen, W., et al.: Abdominal multi-organ segmentation with organ-attention networks and statistical fusion. Med. Image Anal. **55**, 88–102 (2019)

14. Wang, Z., Wang, G.: Triplanar convolutional neural network for automatic liver and tumor image segmentation. International Journal of Performability Engineering **14**(12), 3151–3158 (2019)

15. Li, Y., et al.: Volumetric medical image segmentation: a 3D deep coarse-to-fine framework and its adversarial examples. In: Lu, L., Wang, X., Carneiro, G., Yang, L. (eds.) Deep Learning and Convolutional Neural Networks for Medical Imaging and Clinical Informatics. ACVPR, pp. 69–91. Springer, Cham (2019). https://doi.org/10.1007/978-3-030-13969-8_4

16. Quattoni, A., Collins, M. and Darrell, T.: Conditional random fields for object recognition. In: Advances in Neural Information Processing Systems, pp. 1097–1104 (2005)

17. Zheng, S., Jayasumana, S., Romera-Paredes B., et al.: Conditional random fields as recurrent neural networks. In: IEEE International Conference on Computer Vision, pp. 1529–1537 (2015)

18. Tianwei, N., Lingxi, X., Huangjie, Zh, et al.: Elastic boundary projection for 3D medical image segmentation. In: IEEE International Conference on Computer Vision, pp. 2109–2118 (2019)
19. Lipton, Z., Berkowitz, J. and Elkan, C.: A critical review of recurrent neural networks for sequence learning. arXiv preprint arXiv:1506.00019 (2015)
20. Mandic, D. and Chambers, J.: Recurrent neural networks for prediction: learning algorithms, architectures and stability. (2001)
21. Ronneberger, O., Fischer, P., Brox, T.: U-Net: convolutional networks for biomedical image segmentation. In: Navab, N., Hornegger, J., Wells, W.M., Frangi, A.F. (eds.) MICCAI 2015. LNCS, vol. 9351, pp. 234–241. Springer, Cham (2015). https://doi.org/10.1007/978-3-319-24574-4_28
22. Zhang, C., Bengio, S., Hardt, M., et al.: Understanding deep learning requires rethinking generalization. In: International Conference on Learning Representations, pp. 1–15 (2017)
23. Arpit, D., Jastrzebski, S., Ballas, N., et al.: A closer look at memorization in deep networks. In: International Conference on Machine Learning, pp. 233–242 (2017)
24. Ma, X., Wang, Y., Houle, M., et al.: Dimensionality-driven learning with noisy labels. In: International Conference on Machine Learning, pp. 3361–3370 (2018)
25. Warfield, S., Zou, K., Wells, W.: Simultaneous truth and performance level estimation (STAPLE): an algorithm for the validation of image segmentation. IEEE Trans. Med. Imaging **23**(7), 903–921 (2004)
26. Soler, L., Hostettler, A., Agnus, V., et al.: 3D image reconstruction for comparison of algorithm database: a patient specific anatomical and medical image database. Technical report IRCAD, Strasbourg, France (2010)
27. Gibson, E., Giganti, F., Hu, Y., et al.: Automatic multi-organ segmentation on abdominal CT with dense v-networks. IEEE Trans. Med. Imaging **37**(8), 1822–1834 (2018)
28. Clark, K., Vendt, B., Smith, K., et al.: The cancer imaging archive (TCIA): maintaining and operating a public information repository. J. Digit. Imaging **26**(6), 1045–1057 (2013)
29. Roth, H.R., et al.: DeepOrgan: multi-level deep convolutional networks for automated pancreas segmentation. In: Navab, N., Hornegger, J., Wells, W.M., Frangi, A.F. (eds.) MICCAI 2015. LNCS, vol. 9349, pp. 556–564. Springer, Cham (2015). https://doi.org/10.1007/978-3-319-24553-9_68
30. Roth, H., Farag, A., Turkbey, E., et al.: Data from pancreas-CT. The cancer imaging archive. (2015)
31. Landman, B., Xu, Z., Eugenio, I., et al.: MICCAI multi-atlas labeling beyond the cranial vault-workshop and challenge (2015)
32. Xu, Z., Lee, C., Heinrich, M., et al.: Evaluation of six registration methods for the human abdomen on clinically acquired CT. IEEE Trans. Biomed. Eng. **63**(8), 1563–1572 (2016)
33. Isensee, F., Petersen, J., Klein, A., et al.: NNU-Net: self-adapting framework for u-net-based medical image segmentation. arXiv preprint arXiv:1809.10486 (2018)
34. Kingma, D., Ba, J.: Adam: a method for stochastic optimization. arXiv preprint arXiv:1412.6980 (2014)
35. Çiçek, Ö., Abdulkadir, A., Lienkamp, S.S., Brox, T., Ronneberger, O.: 3D U-Net: learning dense volumetric segmentation from sparse annotation. In: Ourselin, S., Joskowicz, L., Sabuncu, M.R., Unal, G., Wells, W. (eds.) MICCAI 2016. LNCS, vol. 9901, pp. 424–432. Springer, Cham (2016). https://doi.org/10.1007/978-3-319-46723-8_49

Deep Class-Specific Affinity-Guided Convolutional Network for Multimodal Unpaired Image Segmentation

Jingkun Chen[1], Wenqi Li[2], Hongwei Li[3], and Jianguo Zhang[1(✉)]

[1] Department of Computer Science and Engineering, Southern University of Science and Technology, Shenzhen, China
zhangjg@sustech.edu.cn
[2] NVIDIA, Santa Clara, USA
[3] Technical University of Munich, Munich, Germany

Abstract. Multi-modal medical image segmentation plays an essential role in clinical diagnosis. It remains challenging as the input modalities are often not well-aligned spatially. Existing learning-based methods mainly consider sharing trainable layers across modalities and minimizing visual feature discrepancies. While the problem is often formulated as joint supervised feature learning, multiple-scale features and class-specific representation have not yet been explored. In this paper, we propose an affinity-guided fully convolutional network for multimodal image segmentation. To learn effective representations, we design class-specific affinity matrices to encode the knowledge of hierarchical feature reasoning, together with the shared convolutional layers to ensure the cross-modality generalization. Our affinity matrix does not depend on spatial alignments of the visual features and thus allows us to train with unpaired, multimodal inputs. We extensively evaluated our method on two public multimodal benchmark datasets and outperform state-of-the-art methods.

Keywords: Segmentation · Class-specific affinity · Feature transfer

1 Introduction

Medical image segmentation is a key step in clinical diagnosis and treatment. Fully convolutional networks [1–3] have been established as powerful tools for the segmentation tasks. Benefiting from the learning capability of these models, researchers start to address more challenging and critical problems such as learning from multiple imaging modalities. This is an essential task because different modalities provide complementary information and joint analysis can provide valuable insights in clinical practice.

Multi-modal learning is inherently challenging for two reasons: 1) supervised feature learning is often *modality-dependent*; features learned from a single modality can not easily be combined with those from other modalities; 2) joint

© Springer Nature Switzerland AG 2020
A. L. Martel et al. (Eds.): MICCAI 2020, LNCS 12264, pp. 187–196, 2020.
https://doi.org/10.1007/978-3-030-59719-1_19

learning often requires images from different modalities being *spatially* well-aligned and paired; obtaining such training data is itself a costly task and often infeasible. Figure 1 shows sample slices from cardiac scans in different modalities. It can be observed that although they all reveal parts of the heart anatomy, their visual appearances vary. Segmentation networks are often sensitive to such discrepancies, which has become a major obstacle for model generalization across modalities.

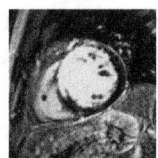 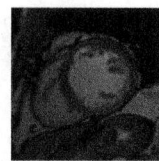 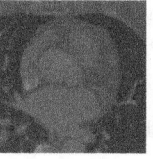 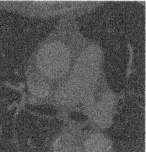

Fig. 1. Left to right: slices of MR (left two) and CT (right two) cardiac scans.

Spatial misalignment is another issue. Existing image registration methods are often infeasible, as the spatial correspondences among modalities can be highly complex and finding a good similarity measurement is non-trivial.

To mitigate these issues, joint learning with unpaired data is emerging as a promising direction [7,9,10]. MultiResUNet [4] has been proposed to improve upon U-Net in multimodal medical image analysis. In brain image segmentation, Nie et al. [5] trained networks independently for single modalities and then fused the high-layer outputs for final segmentation. Yang et al. [8] used disentangled representations to achieve CT and MR adaptation. Existing methods didn't take into account class-specific information, even though the features obtained by supervised training are highly correlated with the tasks (Fig. 2).

Our assumption is that, with the same network architecture, the underlying anatomical features should be extracted in a similar manner across modalities. At the same time, each network instance should have modality-specific modules to tolerate the imaging domain gaps. With this assumption, to facilitate effective joint feature learning, we adopt an FCN for all modalities, where the convolutional kernels are shared, while the modality-specific batch feature normalizations remain local to each modality. More importantly, we extract class-specific affinity measurements at multiple feature scales, and minimize an affinity loss during training. Different from cross-modal feature consistency loss, our design ensures that the networks extract modality independent features in a similar hierarchical manner. Intuitively, this could be interpreted as "high-order" feature extraction consistency compared with the feature map consistency loss. We show that this is a more appropriate joint model regularizer that effectively guides the anatomical feature extractions.

In summary, our main contributions are: 1) we propose a novel unpaired multimodal segmentation framework, which explicitly extracts the *modality-agnostic* knowledge; 2) we introduce a joint learning strategy and a *class-specific* affinity matrix to guide the training, which is capable of distilling between-layer

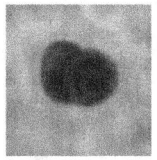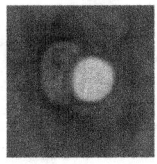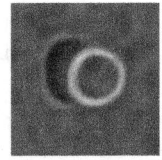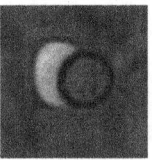

Fig. 2. Visualization of feature maps of one cardiac slice in four classes. Left to right: the background, RV, myo and LV. The higher brightness part indicates the region for the corresponding class; it could be observed that class-specific feature representation is brighter than the other parts, which is highly correlated with the ground truth mask in this class.

relationships at multiple scales; 3) we extensively evaluated our method on two public multimodal benchmark datasets, and the proposed method outperforms the state-of-the-art multimodal segmentation approaches.

2   Methodology

This section details the proposed joint training for segmentation tasks.

2.1   Multimodal Learning

We adopt an FCN as the backbone of our framework. Without any loss of generality, we present our framework in the case of training with two imaging modalities. The overall architecture is illustrated in Fig. 3. The training of the system operates on random unpaired samples from both modalities, the same set of convolutional layers of the network are updated, while the batch normalization layers are initialized and updated individually for each modality.

2.2   Modality-Specific Batch Normalization

Using two independent sets of parameters for joint training leads to large models and thus tends to overfit. Karani et al. [11] showed that using a domain-specific batch normalization is effective in addressing domain gaps issue while keeping the model compact. Here we employ the same technique for modality-specific feature extraction. Specifically, the batch normalization layer matches the first and the second moment of the distributions of feature x:

$$x^* = \gamma \frac{x - E(x)}{\sqrt{Var(x) + \epsilon}} + \beta \tag{1}$$

where γ, β are trainable parameters and are modality-dependent in our design. ϵ is a very small positive number to avoid dividing by zero.

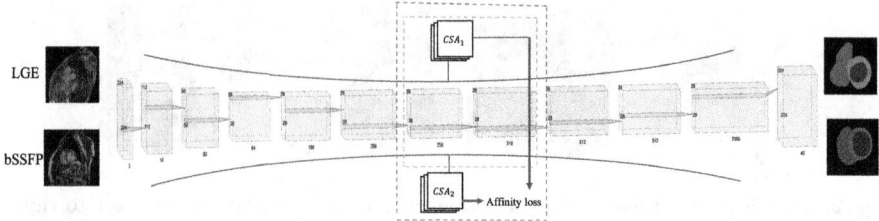

Fig. 3. Architecture of the proposed class-specific affinity guided learning for multi-modal segmentation (CSA denotes class-specific affinity). The overall structure of the proposed method contains two streams of FCNs with shared layers. For the detail of the CSA module, please see Fig. 5.

2.3 Class-Specific Affinity

It has been shown that feature maps in a network could reflect the saliency of the class of interest in a multi-class setting [6] in a recent study by Levine et al. Such a saliency map could give a robust interpretation of the reasoning process of model predictions. Motivated by this study, in the multi-modal segmentation network, since all the modalities share the same tasks (e.g., multi-class heart region segmentation), we hypothesized that the reasoning process of model-specific channels should be similar and its feature map should reflect class-specific saliency (i.e., interpretation of the class of interest). As shown in Fig. 2, ideally, the region of interest in a learned feature map should be salient and aligned well with its class-label. Therefore, for a learned feature map $F(l)$ of layer l and a given class c, we introduce the *class-specific* feature map $F^c(l)$ defined as

$$F^c(l) = F(l) \odot M^c \tag{2}$$

where M^c denotes the ground truth mask of size (h, w) for class c (reshape to the size of feature map if necessary), and $\odot$ represents Hadamard product.

Suppose that $F_m^c(l)$ and $F_n^c(k)$ are the m-th and n-th class-specific feature maps from layer l and k respectively, we measure their relationships using an *affinity* defined by their cosine similarity, i.e.,

$$a_{m,n}^c = \frac{1}{S_c} * cos(F_m^c(l), F_n^c(k)) \tag{3}$$

Where S_c is the size of the region of interest in M^c. Such a normalization is to ensure that the affinity is invariant to the size of the saliency region. Suppose that layer l and layer k have M and N number of class-specific feature maps, we construct the between-layer affinity matrix $A_{m,n}^c$, where the entry at (m, n) is $a_{m,n}^c$. The size of A^c is M by N. Since the affinity is computed based class-specific on feature map, we term this as the *class-specific affinity* (CSA) matrix.

Figure 4 shows our design of a class-specific affinity (CSA) layer. Our CSA could be computed for each of the modality, based on which we build the CSA module. It is worth noting that our design is based on a class-specific feature

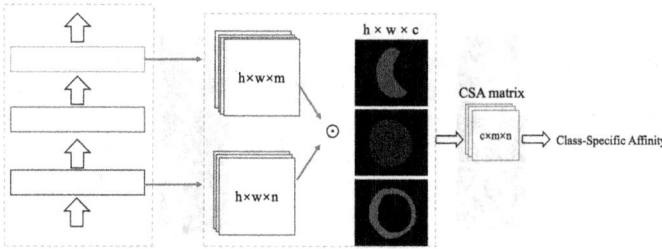

Fig. 4. The proposed class-specific affinity guided learning layer. The dotted box on the left shows three convolutional layers for feature extraction. The dotted box in the middle shows the affinity computation by incorporating feature maps at multiple scales as well as the multi-class ground truth segmentation map.

map, and independent to the choice of modalities; therefore, our network does not require inputs spatial alignment.

2.4   CSA Module

Suppose that we have two modalities using the same network architecture for joint learning. We compute $A^{c,1}$ for modality-1 (e.g., CT) and $A^{c,2}$ modality-2 (e.g. MR) across layer l and k. The knowledge encoded by CSA for a specific class c could be transferred by enforcing the consistency of CSA between the two modalities using an L2 norm. We then aggregate all of the consistencies for all of the classes to formulate a consistency loss function as below:

$$L_{CSA} = \frac{1}{C} \sum_c^C \left\| \frac{1}{P} \sum_{i=1}^P (A_i^{c,1} - A_i^{c,2}) \right\|_2^2 \tag{4}$$

where C is the number of classes. P is the total number of entries in A^c, i.e., MN. Normalizing by P is to ensure that the consistency is invariant to the number of feature channels.

When minimizing the CSA loss, the affinity consistency between the two modalities could be maximized thus ensuring joint learning. For the segmentation loss, we use a Dice coefficient loss L_{dice} to ensure good segmentation at region level, and a L_{ce} cross-entropy loss for pixel-level segmentation. Taking all of the three losses together, the final loss of our multi-modal learning framework for two modalities 1 and 2 is defined as:

$$L = \alpha(L_{dice}^1 + L_{dice}^2) + \beta(L_{ce}^1 + L_{ce}^2) + \lambda L_{CSA} \tag{5}$$

Where L_{CSA} is the CSA transfer loss, α, β, λ are the system parameters to weight the loss components.

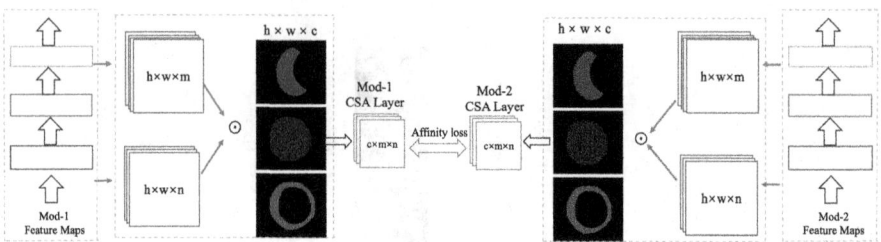

Fig. 5. The CSA guided multi-modal knowledge sharing. The CSA Layer computes affinity from "Mod-1" and "Mod-2" respectively (according to Sect. 2.3). The affinity loss between two modalities is computed according to Sect. 2.4.

3   Experiments

Datasets. We evaluated our multimodal learning method on two public datasets: MS-CMRSeg 2019 [13,14] and MM-WHS [15]. MS-CMRSeg 2019 contains 45 patients who had previously suffered from cardiomyopathy. Each patient has images in three cardiac MR modalities (LGE, T2, and bSSFP) with the three segmentation classes: left ventricles, myocardium, and right ventricles. We use LGE and bSSFP in our experiments. For each slice, we crop the image and get region of interests with a fixed bounding box (224 × 224), enclosing all the annotated regions. we randomly divided the dataset into 80% for training and 20% for testing according to the patients. MM-WHS contains the MR and CT images whole heart from the upper abdomen to the aortic arch. The segmentation task includes four structures: left ventricular myocardium (LVM), left atrium (LAC), left ventricle (LVC), and ascending aorta (AA). We crop each slice with a region with a 256 × 256-pixel bounding box in the coronal plane and randomly divided the dataset into training (80%) and test sets (20%). For preprocessing, we use *z-score* normalization [12] to calibrate the intensity of each 2D slice from all modalities in both datasets.

Implementation. Our architecture consists of nine convolutional operation groups, one deconvolutional group and one softmax layer. Each group contains two to four shared convolutional layers and domain-specific batch normalization layers. We implemented the proposed method with Python-based on Tensorflow 1.14.0 library using Nvidia Quadro RTX GPU (24G). We optimize our network with Adam optimizer with a batch size of 8. The learning rate is initialized to 1×10^{-4} and decayed by 5% per 1000 iterations. Besides, we incorporated dropout layers (drop rate of 0.75) into the network to validate the performance. In the training stage, we used three loss functions. Empirically, α, β and λ are set to 1, 1 and 0.5 respectively. Our assumption is that the higher layer features are too closely related to the ground truth mask, so the affinity features of the migration process are not obvious, so we choose the feature maps from the intermediate layer. We believe that the information between remote feature maps is difficult to express completely with affinity feature maps, so we used the feature maps from the layers relatively close to each other in our experiment.

Comparison and Analysis. We designed the following five experimental settings (single training of separate modalities (Single), Unpaired Multi-modal Segmentation via Knowledge Distillation (UMMKD) [10], Joint training of two modalities in shared BN model (Joint), Modality-specific batch normalization only (MSBN), Affinity-guided learning (Affinity), and CSA guided learning (ours)). For all settings, the network architecture and datasets are fixed so that different methods can be compared fairly. In terms of quantitative performance measurements, we adopt the volume Dice score and surface Hausdorff distance as listed in Table 1, 2 and 3.

Table 1. Average Dice score (%) and Surface Hausdorff distance (mm) on LGE and bSSFP, the highest performance in each class is highlighted.

Method	LGE_Dice			bSSFP_Dice			LGE_Dist.			bSSFP_Dist.		
	LV	myo	RV	LV	myo	RV	LV	myo	RV	LV	myo	RV
Single [3]	90.17	80.31	86.51	92.89	85.11	88.76	6.63	3.61	25.10	47.80	2.45	11.58
UMMKD [10]	90.41	80.48	86.99	93.38	85.69	89.91	5.00	3.46	8.66	3.00	2.24	5.39
Joint	90.22	80.91	86.61	92.74	85.19	89.12	4.00	6.08	5.12	3.16	2.45	5.00
MSBN	90.23	80.81	86.08	93.46	85.57	89.91	5.75	3.61	5.48	3.00	2.24	5.10
Affinity	90.65	81.18	87.27	93.54	85.93	89.93	5.00	3.16	9.72	3.00	2.24	5.10
Ours	**91.89**	**83.39**	**87.66**	93.48	85.72	**90.64**	4.12	**3.00**	**5.00**	**3.00**	**2.24**	**4.12**

1) Results on MS-CMRSeg 2019: Table 1 lists the results of three classes cardiac segmentation. As can be observed, compared with individual training and the other multi-modal learning, our methods showed a significant performance gain. The overall *average* Dice score of three classes on two modalities increased to 87.65% and 89.95% which is much higher than single training of separate modalities (85.66% and 88.92%) and UMMKD (85.96% and 89.66%), and the *average* Hausdorff distance of three classes on LGE modality of UMMKD decreased from 5.71 mm to 4.04 mm. This indicates that class-based cross-modal knowledge transfer is effective. We have conducted the Wilcoxon signed-rank test for the improvements of our method over UMMKD on the results based on the patient-level predictions (the p-value is 0.010 for LGE, and 0.048 for bSSFPP), indicating that improvements are statistically significant. It is observed that the affinity guided learning also achieved the better result on the two modalities, especially on the bSSFP modality, but it is still lower than the CSA module, as the CSA module learned to share the class-based semantic knowledge.
2) Results on MM-WHS: The proposed method was also used to segment six classes cardiac MRI and CT, and achieves promising segmentation performance on this relatively large dataset (Table 2 and 3), with an *average* Dice

score of 79.27% for LVM, 87.46% for LAC, and 81.42% for AA on CT modality; 88.89% for LVM, 92.53% for LVC, and 96.07% for AA. Hausdorff distance of our method on the two modalities is also lower in most of the classes. The differences when comparing with the models trained in MS-CMRSeg 2019 were the number of samples for training and the weight of the CSA loss increased to 0.5. Overall, it can be seen that the proposed methods (ours) outperforms both the single modality model and the multi-modal method, which confirms their effectiveness. We tested the CSA learning between the more distant layers and the closer layers, and we found that the performance within the closer layers is better. The CSA knowledge between the closer layers can be better learned and also easier to be migrated.

Table 2. Average Dice score (%) on MRI and CT.

Method	CT				MRI			
	LVM	LAC	LVC	AA	LVM	LAC	LVC	AA
Single [3]	78.17	85.84	93.07	81.08	87.56	90.29	91.66	94.26
UMMKD [10]	78.73	83.47	93.29	81.41	87.89	91.68	91.88	95.32
Joint	77.92	83.96	93.51	80.08	84.03	88.41	90.92	94.67
MSBN	78.82	86.07	94.40	80.57	87.57	92.30	91.88	96.02
Affinity	78.63	87.13	94.35	79.49	85.31	91.06	91.84	92.24
Ours	**79.27**	**87.46**	94.22	**81.42**	**88.89**	91.18	**92.53**	**96.07**

Table 3. Surface Hausdorff distance (mm) on CT and MRI.

Method	CT				MRI			
	LVM	LAC	LVC	AA	LVM	LAC	LVC	AA
Single [3]	5.00	10.63	5.00	13.38	8.50	15.03	4.47	6.00
UMMKD [10]	5.83	14.40	6.01	13.97	10.05	8.94	4.47	3.61
Joint	5.39	14.32	4.24	13.30	6.40	40.17	9.84	4.47
MSBN	5.00	10.63	4.24	13.93	4.12	9.06	4.47	3.00
Affinity	6.00	10.63	4.89	15.13	10.05	12.08	5.00	67.09
Ours	5.39	**10.30**	**4.24**	15.80	**4.12**	9.49	**4.12**	**2.83**

Visualization. Figure 6 shows the predicted masks from the five methods. It could be seen that our methods improve the performance of only using single-modal method and the other multi-modal method, especially for the LGE modality. These observations are consistent with those shown in the Table 1, 2 and 3.

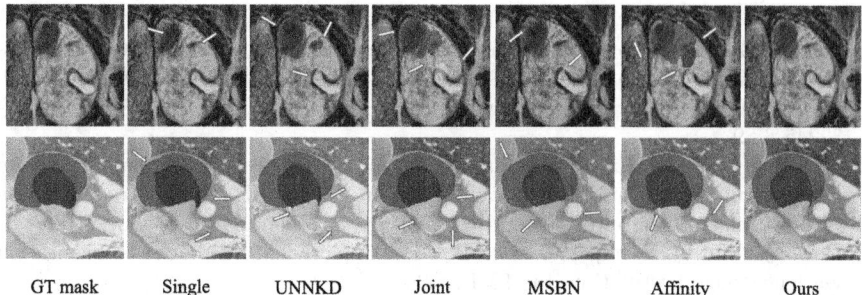

| GT mask | Single | UNNKD | Joint | MSBN | Affinity | Ours |

Fig. 6. Segmentation maps on CT (top) and MRI (bottom). Left to right: Ground Truth mask, Single, UMMKD, Joint, MSBN, Affinity and CSA.

4   Conclusion

We propose a new framework for unpaired multi-modal segmentation, and introduce class-specific affinity measurements to regularize the jointly model training. We have derived the formulations and experimented with spatially 2D feature maps. As future work, the same concepts could be extended to spatially 3D cases. The results based on the proposed class-specific affinity loss are encouraging. Further quantitative analysis of the feature maps and investigating model interpretability is also an interesting future direction.

References

1. Ronneberger, O., Fischer, P., Brox, T.: U-Net: convolutional networks for biomedical image segmentation. In: Navab, N., Hornegger, J., Wells, W.M., Frangi, A.F. (eds.) MICCAI 2015. LNCS, vol. 9351, pp. 234–241. Springer, Cham (2015). https://doi.org/10.1007/978-3-319-24574-4_28
2. Badrinarayanan, V., Kendall, A., Cipolla, R.: SegNet: a deep convolutional encoder-decoder architecture for image segmentation. IEEE Trans. Pattern Anal. Mach. Intell. **39**(12), 2481–2495 (2017)
3. Long, J., Shelhamer, E., Darrell, T.: Fully convolutional networks for semantic segmentation. In: CVPR, pp. 3431–3440 (2015)
4. Ibtehaz, N., Rahman, M.S.: MultiResUNet: rethinking the U-Net architecture for multimodal biomedical image segmentation. Neural Netw. **121**, 74–87 (2020)
5. Nie, D., Wang, L., Gao, Y., Shen, D.: Fully convolutional networks for multi-modality isointense infant brain image segmentation. In: ISBI, pp. 1342–1345, April 2016
6. Levine, A., Singla, S., Feizi, S.: Certifiably robust interpretation in deep learning. arXiv preprint arXiv:1905.12105 (2019)
7. Wolterink, J.M., Dinkla, A.M., Savenije, M.H.F., Seevinck, P.R., van den Berg, C.A.T., Išgum, I.: Deep MR to CT synthesis using unpaired data. In: Tsaftaris, S.A., Gooya, A., Frangi, A.F., Prince, J.L. (eds.) SASHIMI 2017. LNCS, vol. 10557, pp. 14–23. Springer, Cham (2017). https://doi.org/10.1007/978-3-319-68127-6_2

8. Yang, J., Dvornek, N.C., Zhang, F., Chapiro, J., Lin, M.D., Duncan, J.S.: Unsupervised domain adaptation via disentangled representations: application to cross-modality liver segmentation. In: Shen, D., et al. (eds.) MICCAI 2019. LNCS, vol. 11765, pp. 255–263. Springer, Cham (2019). https://doi.org/10.1007/978-3-030-32245-8_29

9. Valindria, V.V., et al.: Multi-modal learning from unpaired images: application to multi-organ segmentation in CT and MRI. In 2018 IEEE Winter Conference on Applications of Computer Vision (WACV), pp. 547–556. IEEE, March 2018

10. Dou, Q., Liu, Q., Heng, P.A., Glocker, B.: Unpaired Multi-modal Segmentation via Knowledge Distillation. In: TMI (2020)

11. Karani, N., Chaitanya, K., Baumgartner, C., Konukoglu, E.: A lifelong learning approach to brain MR segmentation across scanners and protocols. In: Frangi, A.F., Schnabel, J.A., Davatzikos, C., Alberola-López, C., Fichtinger, G. (eds.) MICCAI 2018. LNCS, vol. 11070, pp. 476–484. Springer, Cham (2018). https://doi.org/10.1007/978-3-030-00928-1_54

12. Chen, J., Li, H., Zhang, J., Menze, B.: Adversarial convolutional networks with weak domain-transfer for multi-sequence cardiac MR images segmentation. In: Pop, M., et al. (eds.) STACOM 2019. LNCS, vol. 12009, pp. 317–325. Springer, Cham (2020). https://doi.org/10.1007/978-3-030-39074-7_34

13. Zhuang, X.: Multivariate mixture model for cardiac segmentation from multi-sequence MRI. In: Ourselin, S., Joskowicz, L., Sabuncu, M.R., Unal, G., Wells, W. (eds.) MICCAI 2016. LNCS, vol. 9901, pp. 581–588. Springer, Cham (2016). https://doi.org/10.1007/978-3-319-46723-8_67

14. Zhuang, X., et al.: Cardiac segmentation on late gadolinium enhancement MRI: a benchmark study from multi-sequence cardiac MR segmentation challenge. arXiv preprint arXiv:2006.12434 (2020)

15. Zhuang, X., et al.: Evaluation of algorithms for multi-modality whole heart segmentation: an open-access grand challenge. Med. Image Anal. **58**, 101537 (2019)

Memory-Efficient Automatic Kidney and Tumor Segmentation Based on Non-local Context Guided 3D U-Net

Zhuoying Li[1], Junquan Pan[1], Huisi Wu[1(✉)], Zhenkun Wen[1], and Jing Qin[2]

[1] College of Computer Science and Software Engineering, Shenzhen University,
Shenzhen, China
hswu@szu.edu.cn
[2] Centre for Smart Health, School of Nursing, The Hong Kong Polytechnic
University, Hong Kong, China

Abstract. Automatic kidney and tumor segmentation from CT volumes is essential for clinical diagnosis and surgery planning. However, it is still a very challenging problem as kidney and tumor usually exhibit various scales, irregular shapes and blurred contours. In this paper, we propose a memory efficient automatic kidney and tumor segmentation algorithm based on non-local context guided 3D U-Net. Different from the traditional 3D U-Net, we implement a lightweight 3D U-Net with depthwise separable convolution (DSC), which can not only avoid over fitting but also improve the generalization ability. By encoding long range pixelwise dependencies in features and recalibrating the weight of channels, we also develop a non-local context guided mechanism to capture global context and fully utilize the long range dependencies during the feature selection. Thanks to the non-local context guidance (NCG), we can successfully complement high-level semantic information with the spatial information simply based on a skip connection between encoder and decoder in the 3D U-Net, and finally realize a more accurate 3D kidney and tumor segmentation network. Our proposed method was validated and evaluated with KiTS dataset, including various 3D kidney and tumor patient cases. Convincing visual and statistical results verified effectiveness of our method. Comparisons with state-of-the-art methods were also conducted to demonstrate its advantages in terms of both efficiency and accuracy.

Keywords: Kidney and tumor segmentation · U-Net · Memory-efficient network · Non-local context guided network

1 Introduction

Kidney and tumor segmentation from 3D CT volumes is a requisite step for kidney disease diagnosis and surgery planning. Without high accuracy and efficient segmentation tools, radiologists can only manually and roughly draw the kidney

A. L. Martel et al. (Eds.): MICCAI 2020, LNCS 12264, pp. 197–206, 2020.
https://doi.org/10.1007/978-3-030-59719-1_20

and tumor contours slice by slice. Obviously, segmentation by hand is not only a very tedious and time-consuming process but also an error-prone job for radiologists. Thus, automatic kidney and tumor segmentation from 3D CT volumes become an essential problem that is needed to be solved in clinical practice.

As the kidney and tumor may appear with various scales, irregular shapes and blurred contours, automatic kidney and tumor segmentation from 3D CT volumes remains a very challenging problem. Traditional kidney and tumor segmentation methods [1,12] usually heavily rely on specific image or volume features (such as edge or level-set) which still cannot achieve high enough accuracy for real clinical applications.

Recently, deep learning techniques have exhibited promising performance in medical image segmentation. Among current CNN-based methods, U-Net [15] and 3D U-Net [6] architecture were widely used in medical image segmentation tasks, such as prostate segmentation [17], brain segmentation [2,4,14] and pancreas segmentation [13]. It is, however, difficult to directly harness U-Net in kidney and tumor segmentation. We observed that, after extending U-Net from 2D to 3D, the parameters and required memory resources may dramatically increase, which hinders it from being used in clinical practice. Too many parameters not only makes the training difficult to converge but also easily leads to overfitting when the training data are limited. More important, traditional 3D U-Nets usually ignore the global context or long range dependency in the feature selection process, which may also degrade the segmentation performance.

In this paper, we propose a novel automatic approach to segmenting kidney and tumor from 3D CT volumes based on a memory efficient and non-local context guided 3D U-Net. Unlike the traditional 3D U-Net, we employ a depthwise separable convolution (DSC) [10] to implement a lightweight 3D U-Net. Based on our memory efficient setting, we can also avoid overfitting and improve the generalization ability. To capture global context and fully utilize the long range dependencies during the feature selection, we further propose a non-local context guided mechanism to encode long range pixel-wise dependencies in features and recalibrate the weight of channels. Based on the non-local context guidance (NCG) [16], we can complement high-level semantic information with the spatial information simply based on a skip connection between encoder and decoder in the 3D U-Net, and finally obtain a more accurate 3D kidney and tumor segmentation network. Our proposed method was validated and evaluated with famous KiTS dataset. Comparisons with state-of-the-art methods were also conducted to demonstrate the advantages of our method.

2   Method

The framework of our memory-efficient and non-local context guided U-Net is shown in Fig. 1. To reduce memory cost of the vanilla U-Net in kidney and tumor segmentation, we first employ depthwise separable convolution (DSC) to implement a relatively lightweight and memory-efficient network. We further develop a new mechanism to leverage non-local context to enhance the segmentation accuracy.

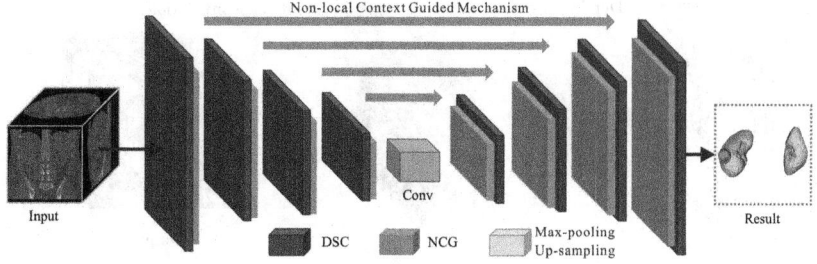

Fig. 1. Framework of our memory-efficient and non-local context guided U-Net.

2.1 Depthwise Separable Convolution

Unlike natural image segmentation which may have massive and ubiquitous collected labels, we can only perform the kidney and tumor segmentation under small datasets with limited labels. To handle natural image segmentation, traditional segmentation networks usually sacrifice computing and memory cost to improve the accuracy. As a result, most of them are too complex and require too many computing resources to be used in real clinical applications. To avoid overfitting and improve the generalization ability, we have to design a lightweight and more memory efficient network for kidney and tumor segmentation. In our implementation, we employ depthwise separable convolution [5,10] to reduce the parameters of the vanilla 3D U-Net, which can still maintain the accuracy of kidney and tumor segmentation under a memory efficient implementation. The Fig. 2 shows the process of depthwise separable convolution.

Assume that features $\mathbf{F} = H \times W \times S \times M$ and $\mathbf{G} = H \times W \times S \times N$ are the input and output of the convolution, where H, W, S, M, N denote the height, width, slice, the number of the input and output channels, respectively, if the convolution kernel K has the kernel size $T \times T \times T$, a vanilla convolutional layer operation can be formulated as,

$$\mathbf{G}_{h,w,s,n} = \sum_{i,j,k,m} \mathbf{K}_{i,j,k,m,n} \cdot \mathbf{F}_{h+i-1,w+j-1,s+k-1,m} \tag{1}$$

where the i, j, k denote the position of the pixel. The memory cost of the vanilla convolution layer depends on the values of M, N, T, H, W and S. Instead, depthwise separable convolution (DSC) splits the convolution layer into two parts, which are depthwise convolution and pointwise convolution, respectively. Depthwise convolution only employs a single filter to convolute each input channel, where the operation can be formulated as,

$$\hat{\mathbf{G}}_{h,w,s,m} = \sum_{i,j,k,m} \hat{\mathbf{K}}_{i,j,k,m} \cdot \mathbf{F}_{h+i-1,w+j-1,s+k-1,m}. \tag{2}$$

As depthwise convolution focuses on a single channel for each kernel, it may lack the channel-wise correlation. We can further use pointwise convolution to

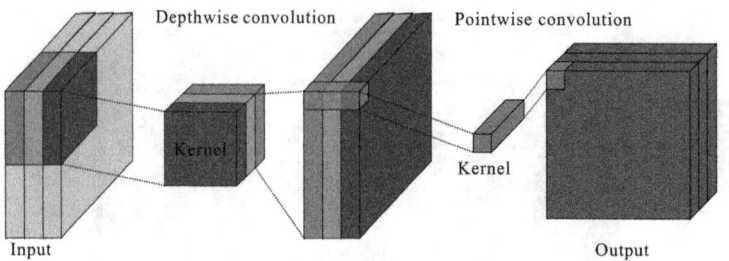

Fig. 2. Depthwise separable convolution.

create the linear combination between two layers, which is only a simple $1 \times 1 \times 1$ convolution.

Obviously, DSC can significantly reduce the parameters for the 3D U-Net. Compared with the vanilla convolution, the parameter number of DSC sharply decreases to $\frac{1}{N} + \frac{1}{T^3}$. Moreover, the training and inferencing time of our memory efficient network is also significantly reduced. Note that, such a lightweight network can avoid over fitting and improve the generalization ability, especially for the kidney and tumor segmentation under limited labeled datasets.

2.2   Non-local Context Guided Mechanism

Based on the memory efficient framework, we further apply a non-local context guided mechanism to improve the accuracy of kidney and tumor segmentation. As the kernel sizes of convolutions are fixed, the extracted feature maps can only express the local neighboring pixel-wise dependencies. To capture global context information and the long range dependencies, we employ a non-local attention mechanism [16] to enlarge the receiving fields and enhance the feature selection ability of our encoder-decoder module. Based on our non-local attention mechanism, high-level dependencies (such as positional relationships between the kidney and tumor) can be captured to improve the segmentation accuracy. Although GCNet [3] provided a non-local attention mechanism implementation for 2D image segmentation, we still cannot directly extend it to 3D kidney and tumor segmentation due to the huge number of parameters. Instead, we introduce a 2.5D non-local attention mechanism based on three directional projections.

As shown in Fig. 3, we first apply a pyramid pooling module (PPM) [18] to enlarge the receiving field of our encoder, which is composed of four max-poolings with different kernel sizes. By merging the acceptance domains from different sub-regions, we can also enrich the feature representation ability of our non-local attention mechanism. To further enhance high-level long range feature dependencies and suppress the useless local redundant relationships, we model context identification and selection process with pixel-wise dependency via channel recalibration. We use feature map $\mathbf{U} = \{\mathbf{U}_1, \ldots, \mathbf{U}_c\}$ with sizes of $H \times W \times S$ as the input of our non-local attention mechanism, where H equals W for a cube volume. Considering that it is too time-consuming by directly using

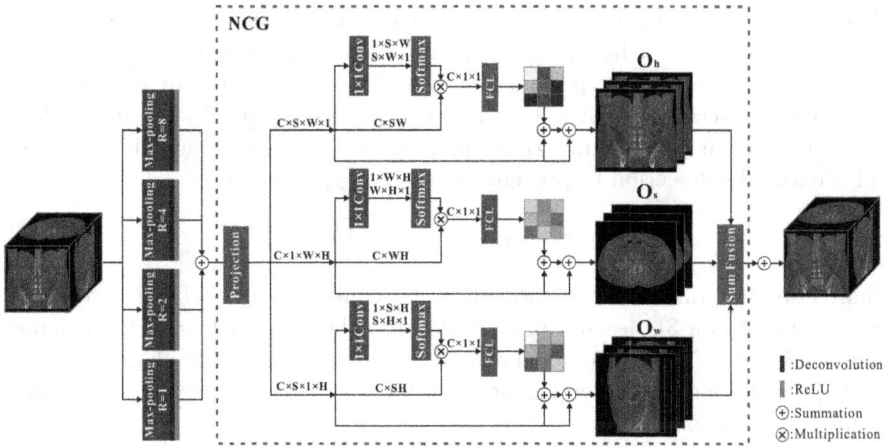

Fig. 3. Non-local context guided mechanism.

the non-local context to model all pixels in the feature cube, we implement a
2.5D non-local attention mechanism to obtain the three projection views of the
feature cube, where the projection operation can be written as,

$$\mathbf{V}_h(i) = \frac{1}{H} \sum_{i=1}^{H} \mathbf{U}_c(i,j,k), \tag{3}$$

$$\mathbf{V}_w(j) = \frac{1}{W} \sum_{j=1}^{W} \mathbf{U}_c(i,j,k), \tag{4}$$

$$\mathbf{V}_s(k) = \frac{1}{S} \sum_{k=1}^{S} \mathbf{U}_c(i,j,k). \tag{5}$$

By applying above projection operations, we can obtain three 2D feature
maps, including $\mathbf{V}_h \in \mathbb{R}^{C \times W \times S}$, $\mathbf{V}_w \in \mathbb{R}^{C \times H \times S}$, and $\mathbf{V}_s \in \mathbb{R}^{C \times H \times W}$. To model
the pairwise dependency, we further calculate the pixel correlation $\mathbf{q} \in \mathbb{R}^{C \times 1 \times 1}$,
which can be defined as follows,

$$\mathbf{q}_{t_c} = \sum_{j=1}^{N_t} \frac{e^{(W_k \mathbf{V}_{t_c}(j))}}{\sum_{m=1}^{N_t} e^{(W_k \mathbf{V}_{t_c}(m))}} \mathbf{V}_{t_c}(j), \quad t \in \{h,w,s\} \tag{6}$$

where j is the enumeration of all possible positions N_t and $N_h = S \times W, N_w = S \times H, N_s = H \times W$, respectively. W_k denotes linear transform matrices (e.g., 1×1
convolution). Three equally calculation operations are performed respectively
and defined as $t \in \{h,w,s\}$. After the weighting process, we use a fully connected
layer to generate more nonlinear features, which can be formulated as,

$$\mathbf{z_t} = \tilde{\mathbf{F}}_{fc2}(\mathbf{q_t}) = W_2 \delta(W_1(\mathbf{q_t})) \tag{7}$$

where $\mathbf{z_t} \in \mathbb{R}^{C \times 1 \times 1}$, δ is the Relu operation and W_2, W_1 denote linear transform matrices. To achieve a lightweight setting, we also use a reduction ratio r in hidden layer to reduce the parameters from C^2 to $2C^2/r$. In our experiments, we empirically set $r = 8$. Given the $\mathbf{z_t} \in \mathbb{R}^{C \times 1 \times 1}$, we use pixel-wise summations for feature fusion by applying $\mathbf{z_t}$ to different projections. In addition, we also add a residual connection to prevent network degradation as,

$$\mathbf{O}_t = \mathbf{z_t} \cdot \mathbf{V_t} + \mathbf{V_t}, \quad t \in \{h, w, s\} \tag{8}$$

Finally, we use dimension broadcasting to combine three 2D feature maps $\mathbf{O_h}, \mathbf{O_w}, \mathbf{O_s}$ into a 3D feature map, which has the same size with the original volume. Based on above non-local attention mechanism, we are able to capture the high-level long range dependencies to improve the accuracy of kidney and tumor segmentation.

3   Experimental Results

3.1   Dataset and Implementation Details

We implemented our memory efficient and non-local context guided network on a single NVIDIA RTX 2080Ti (11 GB RAM). Based on KiTS dataset [9], we trained and tested all the models with the 3D CT data scanned on a total of 210 patients. As the voxel spacing of the collected CT data is not consistent, we uniformly resampled the data to spacing of (3, 0.78, 0.78). KiTS dataset contains a variety of labeled kidney and tumor data. Based on the 210 cases, we also employed different strategies to perform data augmentations, including vertical and horizontal flipping, rotations and adding noises.

To evaluate the proposed network, we randomly divide the KiTS dataset into training set (168 cases) and validation set (42 cases). We combined both cross-entropy and dice loss[7], and used the same weighting scheme to setup our loss function. For better convergence, we further employed the Kaiming initialization [8] method to initialize all layers in our network. In addition, Adam [11] strategy is also applied as our optimizer, where an initial learning rate is set to 0.001. In our experiments, the proposed model was usually trained and terminated in about 300 epochs with a batch size of 2.

3.2   Ablation Study

To verify the effectiveness of the depthwise separable convolution (DSC) and non-local context guidance (NCG), we performed an ablation study. In our ablation experiments, we set 3D U-Net as the baseline. As shown in Table 1, we can clearly see that our DSC can significantly reduce the parameters which indicates memory efficient improvement of our proposed method. If we only added NCG to the 3D U-Net, we can obtain accuracy improvement in kidney and tumor segmentation, but with higher computational and memory cost. By combining

Table 1. Ablation experiment results. Red and right regions indicate kidney and tumor respectively.

Method	Dice(kidney)	Dice(tumor)	Param	GFLOPs
3D U-Net[6]	0.9631	0.8062	21.33M	522
3D U-Net+**DSC**	0.9646	0.8015	13.01M	132
3D U-Net+**NCG**	0.9685	0.8307	24.84M	659
Ours	**0.9710**	**0.8378**	**16.60M**	**269**

both DSC and NCG into 3D U-Net, we can not only achieve higher segmentation accuracy, but also significantly cut down the computational and memory cost. Our experimental results demonstrated that combination of DSC and NCG enables us to effectively capture the non-local global context and improve the segmentation accuracy under a network with fewer parameters.

3.3 Comparisons with State-of-the-Art Methods

To further evaluate the performances of our method, we compared our network with state-of-the-art methods, including 3D U-Net [6], 3D Res-UNet [17], 3D Att-UNet [13], DMFNet [4] and PR-Unet [2]. We have implemented the five competitors under the same computational environments. Both visual and statistical comparisons are conducted using the same data sets and with the same data argumentations.

Visual comparisons for typical challenging cases among the five competitors and our method are as shown in Fig. 4. As 3D U-Net is only a bench-mark method, it suffers limitations when kidney and tumor appear with different scales, irregular shapes or blurred contours. Based on residual structure blocks, Res-UNet obtained higher segmentation accuracy than 3D U-Net. By adding gated attention, 3D Att-UNet so outperformed 3D U-Net. Similarly, RPU-Net and DMFNet so achieved either efficiency or accuracy improvements by reducing the runtime parameters based on reversible block or constructing a multi-scale feature representation based on 3D dilated convolution. As shown in the last column of Fig. 4, we can clearly see that our network generally outperformed the five competitors even when there have different scales, irregular shapes and blurred contours for the kidney and tumor, indicating that the combination of DSC and NCG into 3D U-Net is important for kidney and tumor segmentation.

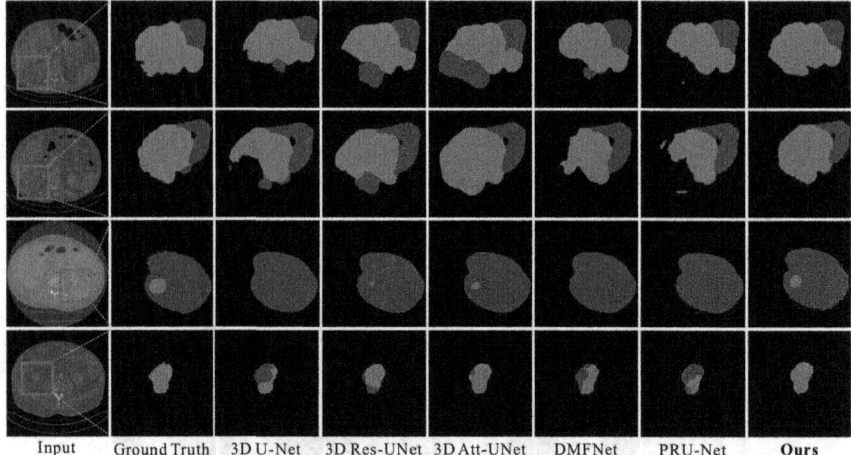

Input   Ground Truth   3D U-Net   3D Res-UNet   3D Att-UNet   DMFNet   PRU-Net   **Ours**

Fig. 4. Visualized comparisons with state-of-the-art methods. Red and right regions indicate kidney and tumor respectively. (Color figure online)

Table 2. Statistical comparisons with state-of-the-art methods.

Method	Dice(kidney)	Dice(tumor)	Param	GFLOPs
3D U-Net [6]	0.9631	0.8062	21.33M	522
3D Res-UNet [17]	0.9676	0.8306	30.04M	609
3D Att-UNet [13]	0.9693	0.8340	24.84M	438
DMFNet [4]	0.9668	0.8127	15.26M	212
PRU-Net [2]	0.9544	0.7882	7.17M	144
Ours	**0.9710**	**0.8378**	**16.60M**	**269**

In addition, we also collected the average segmentation accuracy, parameter amount and GFLOPs for different networks. Table 2 shows the statistical comparison among our method and the other five competitors. Compared with original 3D U-Net, Res-UNet and Att-UNet improve the accuracy by scarifying memory cost. Conversely, RPU-Net and DMFNet are relatively lightweight networks and more efficient, but both of them cannot guarantee the segmentation accuracy. By equipping both DSC and NCG into a 3D U-Net, our method generally outperformed all five competitors in terms of both memory efficiency and segmentation accuracy for kidney and tumor, which implies that our memory efficient and non-local context guided network is effective.

4   Conclusion

In this paper, we presented a novel approach to segmenting kidney and tumor from 3D CT volumes based on a memory efficient and non-local context guided 3D U-Net. Unlike traditional 3D U-Net, we first employ a DSC to implement a memory efficient 3D U-Net, which is able to avoid overfitting and improve the generalization ability. By encoding long range pixel-wise dependencies in features and recalibrating the weight of channels, we further implement a non-local context guided mechanism to capture global context and fully utilize the long range dependencies during the feature selections. Based on the NCG, we successfully complement high-level semantic information with the spatial information simply based on a skip connection between encoder and decoder in the 3D U-Net. Our proposed method was validated and evaluated with KiTS dataset, including a variety of kidney and tumor cases. Visualized and statistical comparisons with state-of-the-art methods were conducted to demonstrate the advantages and effectiveness of our method.

Acknowledgement. This work was supported in part by grants from the National Natural Science Foundation of China (No. 61973221), the Natural Science Foundation of Guangdong Province, China (Nos. 2018A030313381 and 2019A1515011165), the Major Project or Key Lab of Shenzhen Research Foundation, China (Nos. JCYJ2016060 8173051207, ZDSYS201707311550233, KJYY201807031540021294 and JSGG201 805081520220065), the COVID-19 Prevention Project of Guangdong Province, China (No. 2020KZDZX1174), the Major Project of the New Generation of Artificial Intelligence (No. 2018AAA0102900) and the Hong Kong Research Grants Council (Project No. PolyU 152035/17E and 15205919).

References

1. Ali, A.M., Farag, A.A., El-Baz, A.S.: Graph cuts framework for kidney segmentation with prior shape constraints. In: Ayache, N., Ourselin, S., Maeder, A. (eds.) MICCAI 2007. LNCS, vol. 4791, pp. 384–392. Springer, Heidelberg (2007). https://doi.org/10.1007/978-3-540-75757-3_47

2. Brügger, R., Baumgartner, C.F., Konukoglu, E.: a partially reversible u-net for memory-efficient volumetric image segmentation. In: Shen, D., et al. (eds.) MICCAI 2019. LNCS, vol. 11766, pp. 429–437. Springer, Cham (2019). https://doi.org/10.1007/978-3-030-32248-9_48

3. Cao, Y., Xu, J., Lin, S., Wei, F., Hu, H.: GCNet: non-local networks meet squeeze-excitation networks and beyond. In: Proceedings of the IEEE International Conference on Computer Vision (ICCV) (2019)

4. Chen, C., Liu, X., Ding, M., Zheng, J., Li, J.: 3D dilated multi-fiber network for real-time brain tumor segmentation in MRI. In: Shen, D., et al. (eds.) MICCAI 2019. LNCS, vol. 11766, pp. 184–192. Springer, Cham (2019). https://doi.org/10.1007/978-3-030-32248-9_21

5. Chollet, F.: Xception: deep learning with depthwise separable convolutions. In: Proceedings of the IEEE Conference on Computer Vision and Pattern Recognition (CVPR), pp. 1251–1258 (2017)

6. Çiçek, Ö., Abdulkadir, A., Lienkamp, S.S., Brox, T., Ronneberger, O.: 3D U-Net: learning dense volumetric segmentation from sparse annotation. In: Ourselin, S., Joskowicz, L., Sabuncu, M.R., Unal, G., Wells, W. (eds.) MICCAI 2016. LNCS, vol. 9901, pp. 424–432. Springer, Cham (2016). https://doi.org/10.1007/978-3-319-46723-8_49

7. Crum, W.R., Camara, O., Hill, D.L.: Generalized overlap measures for evaluation and validation in medical image analysis. IEEE Trans. Med. Imaging (TMI) **25**(11), 1451–1461 (2006)

8. He, K., Zhang, X., Ren, S., Sun, J.: Delving deep into rectifiers: surpassing human-level performance on ImageNet classification. In: Proceedings of the IEEE International Conference on Computer Vision (ICCV), pp. 1026–1034 (2015)

9. Heller, N., et al.: The kits19 challenge data: 300 kidney tumor cases with clinical context, CT semantic segmentations, and surgical outcomes (2019)

10. Howard, A., et al.: Searching for MobileNetV3. In: Proceedings of the IEEE International Conference on Computer Vision (ICCV), pp. 1314–1324 (2019)

11. Kingma, D.P., Ba, J.: Adam: a method for stochastic optimization. In: International Conference for Learning Representations (ICLR) (2015)

12. Lin, D.T., Lei, C.C., Hung, S.W.: Computer-aided kidney segmentation on abdominal CT images. IEEE Trans. Inf Technol. Biomed. **10**(1), 59–65 (2006)

13. Oktay, O., et al.: Attention u-net: learning where to look for the pancreas. In: Conference on Medical Imaging with Deep Learning (MIDL) (2018)

14. Rickmann, A.-M., Roy, A.G., Sarasua, I., Navab, N., Wachinger, C.: 'Project & Excite' modules for segmentation of volumetric medical scans. In: Shen, D., et al. (eds.) MICCAI 2019. LNCS, vol. 11765, pp. 39–47. Springer, Cham (2019). https://doi.org/10.1007/978-3-030-32245-8_5

15. Ronneberger, O., Fischer, P., Brox, T.: U-net: convolutional networks for biomedical image segmentation. In: Navab, N., Hornegger, J., Wells, W., Frangi, A. (eds.) MICCAI 2015. LNCS, vol. 9351, pp. 234–241. Springer, Cham (2015). https://doi.org/10.1007/978-3-319-24574-4_28

16. Wang, X., Girshick, R., Gupta, A., He, K.: Non-local neural networks. In: Proceedings of the IEEE Conference on Computer Vision and Pattern Recognition (CVPR), pp. 7794–7803 (2018)

17. Yu, L., Yang, X., Chen, H., Qin, J., Heng, P.A.: Volumetric convnets with mixed residual connections for automated prostate segmentation from 3D MR images. In: AAAI Conference on Artificial Intelligence (2017)

18. Zhao, H., Shi, J., Qi, X., Wang, X., Jia, J.: Pyramid scene parsing network. In: Proceedings of the IEEE Conference on Computer Vision and Pattern Recognition (CVPR), pp. 2881–2890 (2017)

Deep Small Bowel Segmentation with Cylindrical Topological Constraints

Seung Yeon Shin[1]([✉]), Sungwon Lee[1], Daniel Elton[1], James L. Gulley[2], and Ronald M. Summers[1]

[1] Imaging Biomarkers and Computer-Aided Diagnosis Laboratory, Radiology and Imaging Sciences, Clinical Center, National Institutes of Health, Bethesda, MD, USA
{seungyeon.shin,rms}@nih.gov
[2] Center for Cancer Research, National Cancer Institute, National Institutes of Health, Bethesda, MD, USA

Abstract. We present a novel method for small bowel segmentation where a cylindrical topological constraint based on persistent homology is applied. To address the touching issue which could break the applied constraint, we propose to augment a network with an additional branch to predict an inner cylinder of the small bowel. Since the inner cylinder is free of the touching issue, a cylindrical shape constraint applied on this augmented branch guides the network to generate a topologically correct segmentation. For strict evaluation, we achieved an abdominal computed tomography dataset with dense segmentation ground-truths. The proposed method showed clear improvements in terms of four different metrics compared to the baseline method, and also showed the statistical significance from a paired t-test.

Keywords: Small bowel segmentation · Topological constraint · Persistent homology · Inner cylinder · Abdominal computed tomography

1 Introduction

The small bowel is the longest (20–30 ft) section of the digestive tract. While surrounded by other organs including the large bowel, it is pliable and has many folds which allow it to fit into the abdominal cavity [1]. Computed tomography (CT) has become a primary imaging technique for small bowel disease diagnosis among others such as enteroclysis and endoscopy due to its diagnostic efficacy and efficiency [10]. Apart from its convenience, acquired 3D CT scans are examined by radiologists slice-by-slice in the interpretative procedure, which is very time-consuming. Also, this may be error-prone since the small bowel is close to other abdominal organs such as the large bowel and muscle, both in position and appearance.

Automatic segmentation of the small bowel may improve the procedure and thus could help precise localization of diseases and preoperative planning by

© Springer Nature Switzerland AG 2020
A. L. Martel et al. (Eds.): MICCAI 2020, LNCS 12264, pp. 207–215, 2020.
https://doi.org/10.1007/978-3-030-59719-1_21

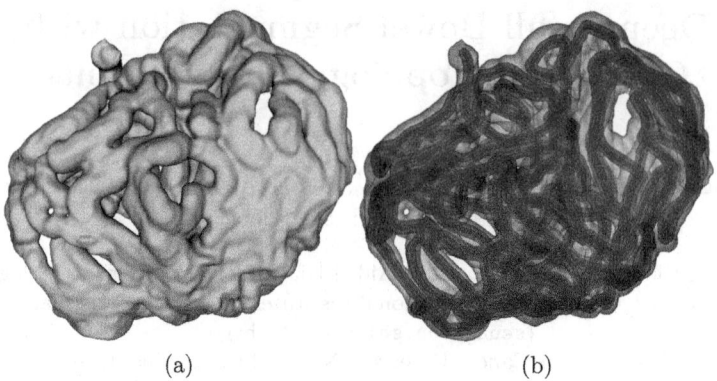

(a)   (b)

Fig. 1. An example of (a) ground-truth segmentation of the small bowel (green) and (b) corresponding path annotation (red). An inner cylinder (blue) generated by dilating the path annotation, which is used for model training, is also shown. (Color figure online)

better visualization. There have been only a few previous works on automatic small bowel segmentation [11,16]. In [16], the anatomic relationship between the mesenteric vasculature and the small bowel is used to guide the small bowel segmentation. A limitation of this method is that it requires a CT scan done in the arterial phase. Therefore, it would not work on routine contrast-enhanced CT scans which are done during the portal venous phase. Recently, in [11], the 3D U-Net [4] is trained for small bowel segmentation with sparsely annotated CT volumes (Seven axial slices for each volume) to avoid making dense annotation.

In the past decade, attempts to utilize topological features in tasks such as disease characterization [2,3], organ segmentation [5,13], and neuron image segmentation [8] have been made. Persistent homology (PH) is a method to compute such topological features underlying in a space [12]. It measures the persistencies of topological features as some threshold changes, and thus represents the robustness of each feature. Based on its differentiable property [7], PH is also incorporated into the training process of neural networks [5,8]. In [5], the method is applied to segmenting two anatomical structures, which are the myocardium of the left ventricle of the heart from short-axis view 2D cardiac magnetic resonance images and the placenta from 3D ultrasound volumes. Their topologies are clearly defined as ring-shaped and one single connected component with no loops or cavities, respectively.

The small bowel has a cylindrical shape but also has many touchings with different parts along its path, which makes it have variable topologies across patients and time. It is inappropriate to apply a constant topological constraint to such organs. Figure 1 shows an example of the small bowel path covered by the lumpy ground-truth (GT) segmentation.

Thus, we present a novel method where a cylindrical topological constraint is applied during network training while addressing the property of variable topologies of the small bowel. We propose to use a network equipped with an additional branch to predict an inner cylinder of the small bowel. The inner cylinder with a smaller diameter still maintains the whole small bowel path but is free of the touching issue. A cylindrical shape constraint applied on this augmented branch guides the network to generate a topologically correct segmentation. The proposed method is evaluated on a dataset composed of high-resolution abdominal CT scans and corresponding dense segmentation GTs, which enables stricter evaluation compared to the previous work using sparse annotation. Four evaluation metrics are used to analyze the results in diverse aspects. Paired t-tests are also conducted to show the statistical significance of the proposed method.

2 Method

2.1 Dataset

We collected 10 high-resolution abdominal CT scans which were acquired with oral administration of Gastrografin. Compared to the arterial phase CT scans used in [16], ours are routine contrast-enhanced CT scans which were done during the portal venous phase. All volumes are resampled to have isotropic voxels of 1 mm^3. The original CT scans include a wide range of body regions from chest to pelvis. We manually cropped the abdominal region to include all the small bowel to reduce the computational burden during training.

GT labels were achieved by an experienced radiologist using 3DSlicer[1] [6] based on the following steps. Firstly, the path of the small bowel is drawn as interpolated curves which connect a series of manually placed points inside the small bowel. Secondly, we grow the curves using a margin of 30 mm and threshold it again using a Hounsfield unit (HU) range of –80–200. Manually drawn air pockets, which have much lower HU values, are also added during the second step. Produced errors are manually fixed in the final step. We note that this annotation procedure took one or two full days for each volume. Finally, the dataset includes the two types of labels, which are the path and segmentation of the small bowel as shown in Fig. 1.

2.2 Persistent Homology

PH is an emerging tool in topological data analysis, where how long each topological feature of different dimensions persists is measured as some threshold changes (filtration). Data types that can be studied with PH include point clouds, networks, and images [12]. Various types of complexes are constructed from given data, and the computation of PH is conducted on top of it. Cubical complex is a more natural representation for image data than a simplicial complex. In this

---

[1] https://www.slicer.org.

section, we focus on explaining how PH is involved in our method. We refer the reader to [12] for detailed information on PH.

Voxels in a 3D volume compose elementary cubes in a cubical complex. Considering a predicted probability image Y of an input image X, we could consider a super-level set $S_Y(p)$ of Y, which is the set of voxels for which the probability value is above some threshold value p. Decreasing p from 1 to 0 makes a sequence of growing $S_Y(p)$'s:

$$S_Y(1) \subseteq S_Y(p_1) \subseteq S_Y(p_2) \subseteq ... \subseteq S_Y(0). \tag{1}$$

When $S_Y(p)$ grows, topological features, e.g., connected components, loops, hollow voids, etc., are created and destroyed as new voxels join. The life time of each feature is recorded as a bar, and a set of bars, called the barcode diagram, is achieved. The barcode diagram is exemplified in Fig. 5. We denote the birth and death values of the i-th longest bar of dimension k as $b_{k,i}$ and $d_{k,i}$, respectively. The Betti number β_k counts the number of topological features of dimension k in $S_Y(p)$. β_0, β_1, β_2 are the numbers of connected components, loops or holes, and hollow voids, respectively. Since the segmented inner cylinder of the small bowel should be all connected and has no loops or cavities within it, the values should be 1, 0, and 0.

As mentioned, the computation of PH is differentiable, thus can be incorporated into the training process of neural networks [5]. We introduce the topological loss used in [5] since it applies in our method as follows:

$$L_k(\beta_k^*) = \sum_{i=1}^{\beta_k^*}(1 - |b_{k,i} - d_{k,i}|^2) + \sum_{i=\beta_k^*+1}^{\infty} |b_{k,i} - d_{k,i}|^2, \tag{2}$$

$$L_{topo} = \sum_k L_k(\beta_k^*), \tag{3}$$

where β_k^* denotes the desired Betti numbers of the target object. Since β_k^* is given as prior knowledge, the loss requires no supervision. It is minimized when the computed barcode diagram has only β_k^* bars of length 1 for each dimension k. Therefore, the desired topology, which is specified by β_k^*, is reflected into the resulting Y after training.

In the post-processing framework used in [5], a network f trained using a supervised training set and a supervised loss is again fine-tuned for each test image with the topological loss. Since the individual fine-tuning for each test image is demanding in test time, we fine-tune the network using the training set with the loss function as follows:

$$L(X; w, w') = \frac{1}{V}|f(X, w) - f(X, w')|^2 + \lambda L_{topo}(X, w'), \tag{4}$$

where V is the number of voxels in the volume, and λ is the weight for L_{topo}. This achieves a new set of weights w', which reflects the desired topology, while minimizing the change from the pretrained weights w.

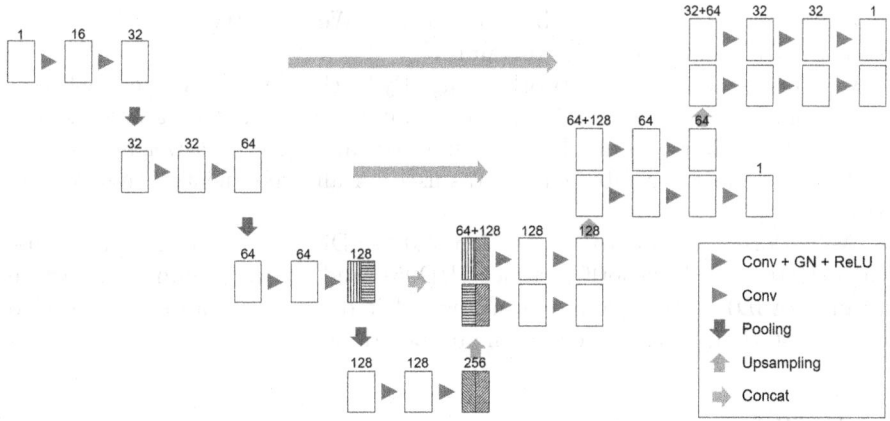

Fig. 2. Network architecture for the proposed method. Boxes represent feature maps. The number of channels is denoted on top of each feature map. GN represents the group normalization [15]. The network has two separate decoder paths for segmentation and inner cylinder prediction. While the lower level features of the encoder are mutually used in the separate decoders by skip connections, the high level features are evenly divided and separately used for each decoder in order to generate separate task-specific features without modifying the encoder structure. The decoder path for inner cylinder prediction has one side output layer which enables the application of persistent homology at the smaller spatial resolution.

2.3 Network

Figure 2 shows the network architecture for the proposed method, which is based on the structure of the 3D U-Net [4]. The differences are as follows: 1) Our network has two separate decoder paths for segmentation and inner cylinder prediction. The inner cylinder with a smaller diameter still maintains the whole small bowel path but is free of the touching issue. During network training, we apply a cylindrical topological constraint on the inner cylinder prediction instead of the segmentation. 2) The decoder path for inner cylinder prediction has one side output layer which enables the application of PH at the smaller spatial resolution. We found that the PH computation on the full resolution of a 3D volume is prohibitive in both terms of memory and time. Applying the topological loss (Eq. 3) onto the smaller spatial resolution is therefore necessary.

The added parts of the network enable the correct application of the cylindrical topological constraint for small bowel segmentation during training. Those are detachable in test time, thus do not increase the required resource.

2.4 Evaluation Details

We used a NVIDIA Tesla V100 32GB GPU to conduct experiments. The mini-batch size was set as 1, and the CT volumes were resized with a scale factor of 1/2 to make the network training fit in the GPU memory. The inner cylinder diameter was set as 3 voxels by experiments. We used the generalized Dice loss [14] for the initial supervised training.

We implemented the network using PyTorch, and used the PyTorch-compatible layers introduced in [7] to compute the PH and its gradients. For training the network, we used an AdamW optimizer [9] and a weight decay of 5×10^{-4}. The learning rate of 10^{-4} was used for all experiments. We used 0.01 for λ.

We perform a 2-fold cross validation and use Dice coefficient, Hausdorff distance (HD), 95% Hausdorff distance (HD95), and average symmetric surface distance (ASD) as our evaluation metrics. Paired t-tests are also conducted to show the statistical significance of the proposed method.

3   Results

3.1   Quantitative Evaluation

Table 1 provides quantitative results of different segmentation models. The proposed method, 'Seg + Cyl + PH', shows clear improvements for all metrics. The relative improvements are $+1.75\%$ in Dice, -12.31% in HD, -24.25% in HD95, and -14.77% in ASD, compared to the baseline, 'Seg'. Since our topological constraint takes effect globally, the improvements are more obvious with the surface distance measures than Dice. The improvements are not from augmenting the network itself with an additional branch since there is no clear improvement for 'Seg + Cyl'. Also, a comparable method where the topological constraint is directly applied on the segmentation, 'Seg + PH', shows rather worse results. This confirms the need for our sophisticated scheme for topologically better small bowel segmentation. The p-values computed by conducting paired t-tests between the baseline method and the other methods with the Dice coefficients show the statistical significance of the proposed method.

Table 1. Quantitative comparison of different segmentation models. All models are variants of that in Fig. 2. 'Seg' denotes a single decoder segmentation network trained using a supervised loss; 'Seg + PH' denotes fine-tuning a pretrained segmentation network using the topological loss, but directly on the segmentation outputs; 'Seg + Cyl' denotes the network in Fig. 2, which is trained using only supervised losses; 'Seg + Cyl + PH' denotes the proposed method. For every metric, the mean and standard deviation are presented. Refer to the text for the explanation on the evaluation metrics. P-values are computed by conducting paired t-tests between the baseline method and the other methods with the Dice coefficients.

Method	Dice	HD (mm)	HD95 (mm)	ASD (mm)	p-value
Seg [4]	0.838 ± 0.044	58.894 ± 20.423	16.081 ± 6.886	2.733 ± 0.879	-
Seg + PH [5]	0.822 ± 0.061	64.754 ± 28.825	14.666 ± 6.612	2.802 ± 1.076	0.205
Seg + Cyl	0.839 ± 0.048	63.968 ± 22.219	14.192 ± 5.494	2.644 ± 0.840	0.679
Seg + Cyl + PH	$\mathbf{0.852 \pm 0.045}$	$\mathbf{51.642 \pm 9.292}$	$\mathbf{12.180 \pm 6.232}$	$\mathbf{2.330 \pm 0.764}$	0.032

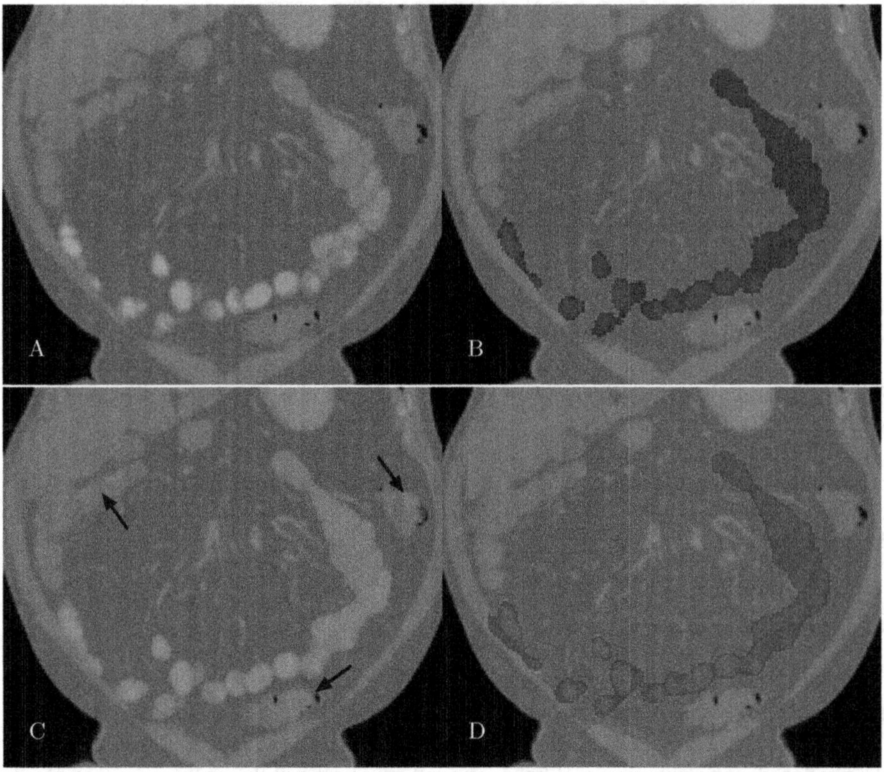

Fig. 3. Example segmentation results in coronal view. The images are: (A) an image slice of the input volume, (B) ground-truth segmentation, (C) result of the 3D U-Net [4], which corresponds to 'Seg' in Table 1, and (D) result of the proposed method. Red arrows indicate false positives. (Color figure online)

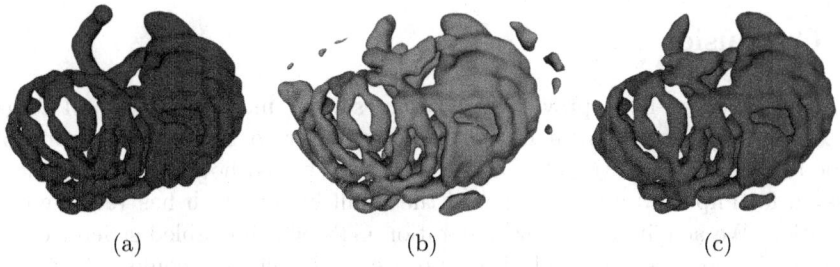

(a)   (b)   (c)

Fig. 4. Example segmentation results in 3D. (a) Ground-truth segmentation. (b) Result of the 3D U-Net [4], which corresponds to 'Seg' in Table 1. (c) Result of the proposed method.

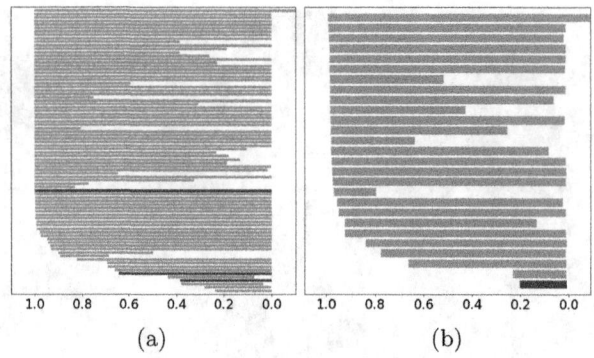

(a)   (b)

Fig. 5. Example barcode diagrams of (a) the result of the 3D U-Net [4] and (b) the result of the proposed method. The horizontal axis indicates the filtration values. The left and right ends of each bar represent the birth and death values of the corresponding feature. Red and green colors denote 0- and 1-dimensional features, respectively. 2-dimensional features, which were also considered, are not shown here due to their short life time.

3.2 Qualitative Evaluation

Figure 3 shows example segmentation results. The proposed method eliminates false positives on the large bowel by the help of the applied topological constraint. Figure 4 further clarifies the effectiveness of the proposed method by presenting 3D rendered segmentations. The proposed method produces a more topologically correct segmentation of the small bowel with fewer false positives. Figure 5 presents example barcode diagrams, which again show the reduced numbers of connected components and holes within the segmentation result of the proposed method.

4   Conclusion

Although PH has been proved effective in several medical tasks and target objects, it requires technical improvement in order to broaden its applicable scope to more complex targets. In this work, we showed how it would be incorporated for improved segmentation of the small bowel which has variable configuration. We acquired dense segmentation GTs, which enabled stricter evaluation of the proposed method. The improved segmentation could help precise localization of diseases, such as inflammatory bowel disease and carcinoid, and preoperative planning by better visualization. In future work, we plan to include CT scans with diverse constrast media to improve the clinical practicality of the proposed method.

Acknowledgments. This research was supported by the National Institutes of Health, Clinical Center and National Cancer Institute.

References

1. Small bowel obstruction (2019). https://my.clevelandclinic.org/health/diseases/15850-small-bowel-obstruction
2. Adcock, A., Rubin, D., Carlsson, G.: Classification of hepatic lesions using the matching metric. Comput. Vis. Image Understand. **121**, 36–42 (2014). https://doi.org/10.1016/j.cviu.2013.10.014
3. Belchi, F., Pirashvili, M., Conway, J., Bennett, M., Djukanovic, R., Brodzki, J.: Lung topology characteristics in patients with chronic obstructive pulmonary disease. Sci. Rep. **8**, 5341 (2018). https://doi.org/10.1038/s41598-018-23424-0
4. Çiçek, Ö., Abdulkadir, A., Lienkamp, S.S., Brox, T., Ronneberger, O.: 3D U-Net: learning dense volumetric segmentation from sparse annotation. In: Ourselin, S., Joskowicz, L., Sabuncu, M.R., Unal, G., Wells, W. (eds.) MICCAI 2016. LNCS, vol. 9901, pp. 424–432. Springer, Cham (2016). https://doi.org/10.1007/978-3-319-46723-8_49
5. Clough, J.R., Oksuz, I., Byrne, N., Zimmer, V.A., Schnabel, J.A., King, A.P.: A topological loss function for deep-learning based image segmentation using persistent homology. arXiv preprint arXiv:1910.01877 (2019)
6. Fedorov, A., et al.: 3D slicer as an image computing platform for the quantitative imaging network. Magn. Reson. Imaging **30**(9), 1323–1341 (2012). https://doi.org/10.1016/j.mri.2012.05.001
7. Gabrielsson, R.B., Nelson, B.J., Dwaraknath, A., Skraba, P., Guibas, L.J., Carlsson, G.E.: A topology layer for machine learning. arXiv preprint arXiv:1905.12200 (2019)
8. Hu, X., Li, F., Samaras, D., Chen, C.: Topology-preserving deep image segmentation. Adv. Neural Inf. Process. Syst. **32**, 5657–5668 (2019)
9. Loshchilov, I., Hutter, F.: Decoupled weight decay regularization. In: International Conference on Learning Representations (2019)
10. Murphy, K.P., McLaughlin, P.D., O'Connor, O.J., Maher, M.M.: Imaging the small bowel. Curr. Opinion Gastroenterol. **30**(2), 134–140 (2014)
11. Oda, H., et al.: Visualizing intestines for diagnostic assistance of ileus based on intestinal region segmentation from 3D CT images. arXiv preprint arXiv:2003.01290 (2020)
12. Otter, N., Porter, M.A., Tillmann, U., Grindrod, P., Harrington, H.A.: A roadmap for the computation of persistent homology. EPJ Data Sci. **6**, 17 (2017). https://doi.org/10.1140/epjds/s13688-017-0109-5
13. Ségonne, F., Fischl, B.: Integration of topological constraints in medical image segmentation. In: Paragios, N., Duncan, J., Ayache, N. (eds.) Handbook of Biomedical Imaging, pp. 245–262. Springer, Boston, MA (2015). https://doi.org/10.1007/978-0-387-09749-7_13
14. Sudre, C.H., Li, W., Vercauteren, T., Ourselin, S., Jorge Cardoso, M.: Generalised dice overlap as a deep learning loss function for highly unbalanced segmentations. In: Cardoso, M.J., et al. (eds.) DLMIA/ML-CDS -2017. LNCS, vol. 10553, pp. 240–248. Springer, Cham (2017). https://doi.org/10.1007/978-3-319-67558-9_28
15. Wu, Y., He, K.: Group normalization. arXiv preprint arXiv:1803.08494 (2018)
16. Zhang, W., et al.: Mesenteric vasculature-guided small bowel segmentation on 3-D CT. IEEE Trans. Med. Imaging **32**(11), 2006–2021 (2013). https://doi.org/10.1109/TMI.2013.2271487

Learning Sample-Adaptive Intensity Lookup Table for Brain Tumor Segmentation

Biting Yu[1]([✉]), Luping Zhou[2], Lei Wang[1], Wanqi Yang[3], Ming Yang[3], Pierrick Bourgeat[4], and Jurgen Fripp[4]

[1] University of Wollongong, Wollongong, Australia
by354@uowmail.edu.au
[2] University of Sydney, Sydney, Australia
[3] Nanjing Normal University, Nanjing, China
[4] CSIRO Health and Biosecurity, Brisbane, Australia

Abstract. Intensity variation among MR images increases the difficulty of training a segmentation model and generalizing it to unseen MR images. To solve this problem, we propose to learn a sample-adaptive intensity lookup table (LuT) that adjusts each image's contrast dynamically so that the resulting images could better serve the subsequent segmentation task. Specifically, our proposed deep SA-LuT-Net consists of an LuT module and a segmentation module, trained in an end-to-end manner: the LuT module learns a sample-specific piece-wise linear intensity mapping function under the guide of the performance of the segmentation module. We develop our SA-LuT-Nets based on two backbone networks, DMFNet and the modified 3D Unet, respectively, and validate them on BRATS2018 dataset for brain tumor segmentation. Our experiment results clearly show the effectiveness of SA-LuT-Net in the scenarios of both single and multi-modalities, which is superior over the two baselines and many other relevant state-of-the-art segmentation models.

Keywords: Brain tumor segmentation · Magnetic resonance imaging · Sample-adaptive learning

1 Introduction

Glioma is the most threatening brain tumor type to the adults worldwide [2]. Its diagnosis and treatment planning require good knowledge about the appearance and location of tumors. In clinics, a prevalent non-invasive imaging technique, magnetic resonance imaging (MRI), is commonly used to acquire this information. Automatic and accurate brain tumor segmentation on MR images is therefore in high demand to assist doctors with diagnosis and treatment. An increasing

This work is supported by ARC DP200103223.

A. L. Martel et al. (Eds.): MICCAI 2020, LNCS 12264, pp. 216–226, 2020.
https://doi.org/10.1007/978-3-030-59719-1_22

number of computer vision approaches have been explored for this purpose to directly process MR images and predict their corresponding segmentation masks. Among them, most recent works are rooted in the popular 2D convolution neural networks (CNNs) structure Unet [14] and extended to different 3D variants of Unet to capture the continuous 3D nature of MR images. For example, Isensee et al. [7,8] integrated residual learning in the 3D Unet and built more connections between shallow and deep layers to extract the location of objects; Chen et al. [6] replaced the original convolutional layer in the 3D Unet with a new three-branch block to improve the computational efficiency; Chen et al. [5] built a Unet-like structure with multi-fiber units to seize multi-scale representations. All the above works have achieved improved segmentation performance by focusing on the development of new model architectures. However, since the intensity of structural MR images is not quantitative, there may be significant differences in intensities, even for the same tissue type among different MR images [11,12]. As a result, some MR images have much weaker tumor-surrounding-contrast than others. This variation inevitably increases the difficulty of training segmentation models and affects the generalization of the trained models to unseen MR images, which is the problem of interest in this paper. To deal with the intensity variation among MR images, intensity normalization [12] was proposed as a preprocessing step to standardize MR images before they are further analyzed for recognition tasks, which has shown to be effective also in some deep learning models [13]. Methods for intensity normalization usually involve the manipulation of histograms of different MR images [4,12,15] so that their histograms could be aligned after the normalization. However, intensity normalization needs to be conducted very carefully for segmentation, as a separate processing step. Without the guide of the ultimate segmentation task, it has the risk of removing critical visual clues in MR images, which may even worsen the segmentation results. Hence, intensity normalization was not widely adopted in deep learning based segmentation methods. Instead, a simple linear intensity rescaling, like zero-mean and unit standard deviation normalization, is commonly employed to preprocess MR images, which, however, cannot resolve the above problem caused by significant intensity variation.

In this paper, we propose a framework that learns sample-adaptive intensity lookup tables (LuTs) to deal with differently contrasted MR images and improve brain tumor segmentation. Our work is underpinned by the observation that when doctors manually delineate tumors, they usually adjust the intensity values of the whole MR image, based on their expertise, in order to make the tumor portion highlighted and protruded. This suggests that they are trying to find an optimal intensity mapping function via naked (but trained) eyes. Inspired by this, we propose to learn this intensity-level mapping function (i.e., LuT) automatically and make it adaptive to different MR samples with different tumor-surrounding contrasts. Specifically, each of our intensity LuTs is associated with a piece-wise linear mapping function that is specific for each MR image. To learn this mapping, a CNN-based LuT module is designed to generate the parameters of the sample-adaptive mapping function and learned together with the subsequent segmentation module in an end-to-end manner. In this way, the learned LuT can negotiate with the segmentation task to improve the segmentation performance. It is worth mentioning that our sample-adaptive LuT is essentially different from the attention based models [16]. First, they learn weights in different spaces as attention weighs the importance of different regions in feature maps, while our method weighs the importance of intensity levels in the intensity space. For example, attention gives the similar weights to spatially neighboring pixels, while our LuT gives the same weights to pixels of the same intensity although they may be spatially distant from each other. Second, attention is usually applied at the late layers of the deep models after the feature maps have been extracted for segmentation, while our sample-adaptive LuT is applied at the very early layers of the deep model to preserve the critical visual clues from the beginning. Moreover, it can be seen that our sample-adaptive LuT and attention capture complementary information and they could be used to improve segmentation from different perspectives.

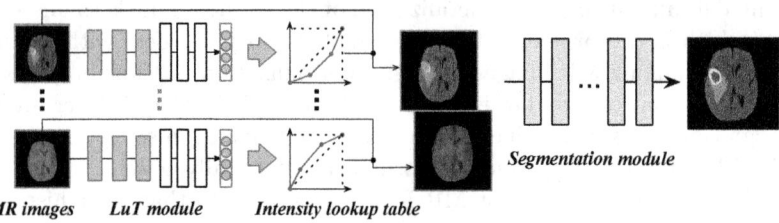

Fig. 1. Overview of SA-LuT-Net. It jointly learns: (1) a LuT module producing the sample-specific parameters of intensity LuTs, and (2) a segmentation network that processes the LuT-transformed MR images to predict the tumor labels.

The contributions of our work are summarized as follows. First, we propose a framework that jointly learns the sample-adaptive intensity LuTs and the MRI segmentation task. In this way, the proposed model can adjust the LuTs of new unseen samples so that they become optimal for the segmentation task, even if the intensity distributions of the new samples do not occur in the training set. Second, our proposed framework is developed and validated based on two backbone networks, i.e., the modified 3D Unet [7] and DMFNet [5], which achieved promising performance on brain tumor segmentation. We demonstrate the effectiveness of our proposed learning framework over the two baselines in both single and multi-modalities scenarios. Third, the proposed framework is further validated on BRATS2018 [1] validation set and achieves better results than many other relevant state-of-the-art methods, while using fewer model parameters.

2   Proposed Method

As mentioned, there could be significant intensity variation among MR images so that some of them may not contrast as well as others, making the training and generalization of the segmentation models difficult. In this paper, we propose SA-LuT-Net to explicitly handle this problem by learning sample-adaptive intensity LuTs for segmentation. An intensity LuT defines a mapping function that transfers the intensity levels from one set to another. In our case, each LuT corresponds to a mapping function whose input is the intensity levels in the original MR image. Its output is a new set of intensity levels that, when applied, changes the contrast of the original MR image so that some specific information, such as soft tissues or brain tumors, could be better segmented. Since the need of intensity adjustment varies, each MR image sample may require a different mapping function and therefore the LuTs should be sample-adaptive. In our SA-LuT-Net, we use the segmentation performance to guide the learning of the sample-adaptive LuT. An overview of our proposed SA-LuT-Net framework is given in Fig. 1. Specifically, it contains a LuT module and a segmentation module. The LuT module predicts the sample-specific parameters that determine the mapping function of the LuT. The resulting LuTs are applied to the input MR images to change their contrast. These LuT-transformed images are further used as inputs in the following segmentation module to produce the segmentation labels. The LuT and the segmentation modules are trained end-to-end so that they could negotiate with each other to produce good results.

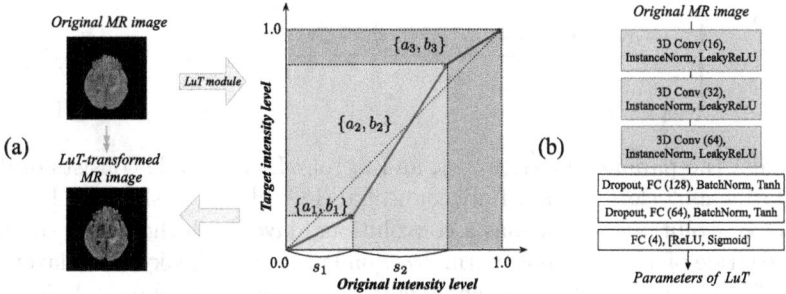

Fig. 2. (a) An intensity lookup table maps the original intensity level of an MR image to the target level by the generated sample-adaptive parameters. (b) The architecture of a LuT module.

2.1 Intensity LuT Module

Many functions could be employed to model the intensity mappings associated with LuTs. For simplicity, in our work, we use a family of piece-wise linear functions for non-linear mapping. An example of a three-segment piece-wise linear function is plotted in Fig. 2(a), and it could be written as:

$$
\hat{x} = \begin{cases} a_1 x + b_1, & 0 \leq x < s_1, \\ a_2 x + b_2, & s_1 \leq x \leq (s_1 + s_2), \\ a_3 x + b_3, & (s_1 + s_2) < x \leq 1. \end{cases} \tag{1}
$$

The two variables $\mathbf{x}$ and $\hat{\mathbf{x}}$ refer to the intensity levels in the original MR image and its corresponding LuT-transformed image, respectively. The parameters a_i and b_i ($i = 1, 2, 3$) correspond to the slope and the bias of the i-th line segment, and the parameters s_i correspond to the horizontal intervals of the i-th line segment. It needs to be noted that, the actual intensity levels in the original MR image are linearly scaled so that $\mathbf{x}$ and $\hat{\mathbf{x}}$ are in the range $[0, 1]$. As a special case, the original MR image can be associated with an identity mapping function, shown as the straight diagonal line in Fig. 2(a), whose $a_i = 1$ and $b_i = 0$, $\forall i$, indicating no intensity adjustment.

The parameters of the mapping function are estimated through the LuT module in our SA-LuT-Net. The LuT module takes an original MR image as the input and outputs the values of the parameters a_i, b_i, and s_i for this specific image. Using the three-segment piece-wise linear function as an example, the output of the LuT module is a 4-dimensional vector, consisting the elements of a_1, a_3, s_1, and s_2. The parameters $b_1 = 0$ since the first line segment passes the origin, and a_2, b_2, and b_3 could be derived from the parameters output by the LuT module. Putting all together, Eq. (1) can be rewritten as:

$$\hat{\mathbf{x}} = \begin{cases} a_1 \mathbf{x}, & 0 \leq \mathbf{x} < s_1, \\ \dfrac{a_3(s_1 + s_2 - 1) - a_1 s_1 + 1}{s_2} \mathbf{x} \\ \quad + \dfrac{(a_1 - a_3)(s_1 + s_2)s_1 + (a_3 - 1)s_1}{s_2}, & s_1 \leq \mathbf{x} \leq (s_1 + s_2), \\ a_3 \mathbf{x} - a_3 + 1, & (s_1 + s_2) < \mathbf{x} \leq 1. \end{cases} \tag{2}$$

To predict the parameters a_1, a_3, s_1, and s_2, our LuT module consists of three convolutional blocks and three fully connected (FC) blocks, as shown in Fig. 2(b). Each of convolutional blocks has a convolutional layer with the kernel size of 4^3 and the stride of 4, an instance normalization layer, and a LeakyReLU layer with slope 0.2. The number of output channel for these three convolutional blocks are 16, 32, and 64, respectively. For the first two FC blocks, a dropout layer with the rate 0.5 is first applied, and then a fully connected layer, a batch normalization layer, and a Tanh layer are following. Their numbers of output channel are set to 128 and 64. The last FC block includes a fully connected layer with 4 output channels and uses different activation functions for the four parameters to be estimated. Specifically, we require $a_1 > 0$ and $a_3 > 0$ to achieve a normal one-to-one mapping function, as well as s_1 and s_2 in $[0, 1]$ by definition. Therefore, in the last FC block, the ReLU function is applied for a_1 and a_3 to enforce positive values, while the Sigmoid function is employed to guarantee s_1 and s_2 to sit between zero and one. For single modality, our LuT module has 0.57M trainable parameters. When multi-modality MR images are available, each modality will be assigned a specific LuT module. All these LuT modules and the segmentation module are jointly trained in our SA-LuT-Net. Therefore, the learnt LuT varies with different samples and different modalities.

2.2   Segmentation Module

As illustrated in the right part of Fig. 1, our segmentation module works as a common segmentation model except that it takes the LuT-transformed MR images as the input and is trained together with the LuT module. In this work, we develop our SA-LuT-Net based on two backbone networks that represent two state-of-the-art tumor segmentation models. The first backbone is the modified 3D Unet model [7], which integrates residual connections in the 3D Unet to combine the neighboring shallow and deep features. This model won the third-place in BRATS2017 dataset [1]. The second backbone is DMFNet [5]. It replaces the ordinary convolutional layers in the residual units with adaptive dilated multi-fiber layers to capture the multi-scale features from brain images. It achieved the comparable results on BRATS2018 dataset [1] with the first-place model, NVDLMED [10], but only using about its 1/10 trainable parameters.

2.3   Training Strategy

Our SA-LuT-Net utilizes the segmentation loss to guide the end-to-end training of the entire network. Since the LuT module is located just next to the input layer, and the subsequent segmentation module is always a deep model, it is not easy to properly propagate the loss gradients to the LuT module (known as gradient vanishing). To alleviate this problem, we implement a three-stage training. At the first stage, the segmentation module is trained using the original input MR images as usual. Then at the second stage, the LuT and the segmentation modules are trained alternatively and iteratively. Specifically, in one epoch the segmentation module is fixed and only the LuT module is updated, and in the next epoch, the LuT module is fixed and only the segmentation module is updated. This will be repeated for a number of epochs to learn both LuT and segmentation modules gradually. Since the segmentation module is fixed when updating the LuT module, the gradient vanishing in the LuT module can be mitigated. However, since the segmentation module is much deeper, it needs more rounds of updating. Therefore, in the third stage, when the LuT is fully trained and stable, it is fixed and only the segmentation module is trained for a few more epochs. That completes the training process.

3   Experimental Results

3.1   Dataset and Training Settings

The proposed SA-LuT-Nets are evaluated on BRATS2018 [1] dataset, which contains 285 training subjects and 66 validation subjects with four-modality MR images, i.e., T1-weighted (T1), post-contrast T1-weighted (T1ce), T2-weighted (T2), and Fluid Attenuated Inversion Recovery (FLAIR), of size $240 \times 240 \times 155$. The training set has the segmentation ground truth with three different tumor regions: the whole tumor (WT), the tumor core (TC), and the enhancing tumor (ET). The results of the validation set are evaluated on BRATS2018 online server as its ground truth is not provided. We follow the image preprocessing steps used in the corresponding backbone models and apply the learning rates of 0.001 and 0.0001 for the LuT module and the segmentation module, respectively, in our SA-LuT-Net. The numbers of training epochs are 150 and 250 for the second and third training stages, respectively. Since SA-LuT-Nets use the same objective as the segmentation backbones, there is no new hyper-parameter involved.

Table 1. Dice scores of FLAIR segmentation results, reported by mean (std).

Methods	WT	TC	ET
Modified 3D Unet [7]	0.8437(0.1520)	0.5912(0.2104)	0.3520(0.2342)
SA-LuT-Net (3D Unet based, ours)	**0.8621(0.1258)**	**0.6450(0.1968)**	**0.3959(0.2647)**
DMFNet [5]	0.8549(0.1031)	0.5499(0.2408)	0.3696(0.3055)
DMFNet+Norm [12]	0.8494(0.0979)	0.5204(0.3110)	0.3769(0.2909)
SA-LuT-Net (DMFNet based, ours)	**0.8746(0.0864)**	**0.6459(0.2353)**	**0.3776(0.2944)**

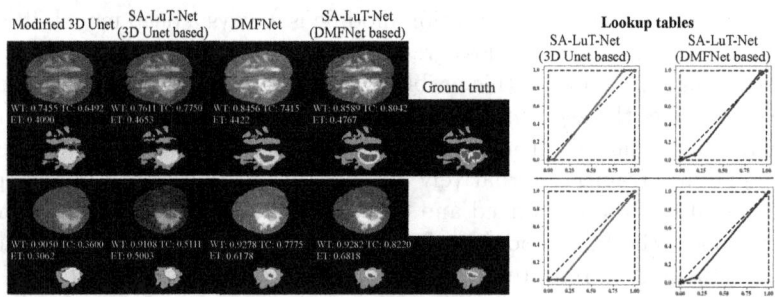

Fig. 3. Two visual comparisons between SA-LuT-Nets and baselines.

3.2   Experimental Results and Discussion

Comparison with Baselines. We investigate the effectiveness of SA-LuT-Nets over the two baseline models, the modified 3D Unet [7] and DMFNet [5], using a single modality FLAIR. A five-fold cross validation on the BRATS2018 training set is used for the evaluation. The results are reported in Table 1. As can be seen, our SA-LuT-Nets achieve significant improvements over both of their corresponding baselines: SA-LuT-Net based on 3D Unet outperforms 3D Unet by 1.8% on WT, 5.4% on TC, and 4.4% on ET, while SA-LuT-Net based on DMFNet outperforms DMFNet by 2.0% on WT, 9.6% on TC, and 0.8% on ET. It seems that by learning sample-adaptive LuT, the improvement on segmenting TC is the most salient. In addition, two visual examples are given in Fig. 3. Since the modified 3D Unet [7] and the DMFNet [5] adopt different image preprocessing approaches, their real input MR images would be visually different as shown in Fig. 3. We can see that the learnt LuTs have differently shaped curves for different samples, which adjust the image contrast based on the given samples to make them more suitable for tumor segmentation.

Moreover, we also compare the proposed SA-LuT-Net (DMFNet based) with the DMFnet that uses the intensity normalization approach [12] for preprocessing (the second last row in Table 1). As shown, the normalization approach [12] cannot improve the segmentation performance by standardizing the input MR images. This may be due to the intensity normalization being conducted as a standalone step to segmentation, therefore, it could alter some pathological details that are critical to the following segmentation. In contrast, our SA-LuT-Net (DMFNet based) can significantly increases the Dice scores. Its LuT module communicates with the segmentation module for the intensity adjustment, and therefore the LuT-transformed images suit the segmentation task.

Table 2. Four-modality segmentation results on **BRATS2018 validation set**.

Methods	Dice scores			Hausdorff95		
	WT	TC	ET	WT	TC	ET
Banerjee et al. [3]	0.8800	0.8000	0.7700	4.90	6.59	4.29
S3D-UNet [6]	0.8935	0.8309	0.7493	-	-	-
Kao et al. [9]	0.9047	0.8135	0.7875	4.32	7.56	3.81
DMFNet [5](baseline)	0.9062	0.8454	0.8012	4.66	6.44	3.06
No New-Net [8]	0.9083	0.8544	0.8101	4.27	6.52	**2.41**
NVDLMED [10] (single model)	0.9068	0.8602	**0.8173**	4.52	6.85	3.82
SA-LuT-Net (DMFNet based, ours)	**0.9116**	**0.8746**	0.8073	**3.84**	**5.16**	3.67

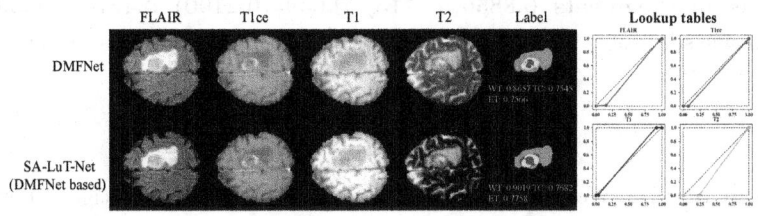

Fig. 4. A visual example result on BRATS2018 validation set.

Comparison with the State-of-the-Arts. For a wide comparison with the existing successful brain tumor segmentation models, we also test our SA-LuT-Net on the **BRATS2018 validation set** for the four-modality tumor segmentation task. Since on this task DMFNet significantly outperformed the modified 3D

Unet, we use the SA-LuT-Net (DMFNet based) in this investigation. The evaluation metric of Dice score and Hausdorff95 distance are measured and reported by BRATS2018 online server, as other methods in comparison do. Since our SA-LuT-Nets are single models, we focus on the comparison with the state-of-the-arts **single-model** based approaches. The results are reported in Table 2. Note that, for NVDLMED, it has both ensemble and single models, and we report its single-model performance from [10] for a fair comparison. For those methods on the leaderboard, we quote the results from their formally published papers [3,5,6,8,9] for comparison[2]. It is found that the proposed SA-LuT-Net (DMFNet based) achieves the best segmentation results on WT and TC regions in terms of both evaluation metrics among all the methods in comparison. It again outperforms its baseline DMFNet [5] on the segmentation of all the three tumor regions, especially with the Dice score improvement of 2.9% on TC region. Our SA-LuT-Net only performs slightly inferior to the challenge winners, i.e., the first-place NVDLMED [10] and the second-place No New-Net [8], in ET segmentation. However, our SA-LuT-Net has much fewer trainable parameters (6.14M), which is against NVDLMED (40.06M) and No New-Net (10.36M) as calculated in [5]. Overall, our proposed SA-LuT-Net performs better than other state-of-the-art single model based approaches, and uses relatively fewer parameters. A visual example is given in Fig. 4. The learnt LuTs vary with different imaging modalities. After the LuT transformation, the pathological tissues become more contrasted, and are better differentiated by the segmentation model.

Table 3. The effect of LuT line-segment numbers on FLAIR segmentation using SA-LuT-Net (DMFNet based).

Methods	WT	TC	ET
Baseline	0.8602(0.0894)	0.5219(0.3083)	0.4251(0.2964)
Two line segments	0.8594(0.1059)	0.5323(0.3079)	0.4095(0.2780)
Three line segments	**0.8856(0.0713)**	**0.6494(0.2190)**	**0.4270(0.2856)**
Four line segments	0.8825(0.0725)	0.6213(0.2458)	0.4196(0.2694)

Ablation Study. We also conduct an ablation study to investigate how the number of line segments used in LuT affects the segmentation performance. The single modality FLAIR is used in this experiment, and the training set is randomly partitioned into 80% for training and 20% for test. Two-segment, three-segment and four-segment piece-wise linear functions are tested. The results are in Table 3. The three-line-segment LuTs generate the best results, while the two-line-segment LuTs perform similarly to the baseline but inferiorly to the LuTs

---

[2] For those leaderboard results without proper documentation, there lacks essential details about the methods for fair comparison, and therefore they are excluded.

using more line segments. This is possibly because the two-segment piece-wise linear function may not be sufficiently flexible to model the required non-linear intensity mapping.

4   Conclusion

We propose a segmentation framework SA-LuT-Net that learns sample-adaptive intensity LuTs optimal for the subsequent segmentation task and realize it on two backbone networks. The proposed LuT learning is a general idea. After showing its promising performance on brain tumor segmentation, we will extend it to other MR image segmentation tasks in our future work.

References

1. Bakas, S., et al.: Advancing the cancer genome atlas glioma MRI collections with expert segmentation labels and radiomic features. Sci. Data **4**, 170117 (2017)
2. Bakas, S., et al.: Identifying the best machine learning algorithms for brain tumor segmentation, progression assessment, and overall survival prediction in the brats challenge. arXiv preprint arXiv:1811.02629 (2018)
3. Banerjee, S., Mitra, S., Shankar, B.U.: Multi-planar spatial-ConvNet for segmentation and survival prediction in brain cancer. In: Crimi, A., Bakas, S., Kuijf, H., Keyvan, F., Reyes, M., van Walsum, T. (eds.) BrainLes 2018. LNCS, vol. 11384, pp. 94–104. Springer, Cham (2019). https://doi.org/10.1007/978-3-030-11726-9_9
4. Castro, D.C., Glocker, B.: Nonparametric density flows for MRI intensity normalisation. In: Frangi, A.F., Schnabel, J.A., Davatzikos, C., Alberola-López, C., Fichtinger, G. (eds.) MICCAI 2018. LNCS, vol. 11070, pp. 206–214. Springer, Cham (2018). https://doi.org/10.1007/978-3-030-00928-1_24
5. Chen, C., Liu, X., Ding, M., Zheng, J., Li, J.: 3D dilated multi-fiber network for real-time brain tumor segmentation in MRI. In: Shen, D., et al. (eds.) MICCAI 2019. LNCS, vol. 11766, pp. 184–192. Springer, Cham (2019). https://doi.org/10.1007/978-3-030-32248-9_21
6. Chen, W., Liu, B., Peng, S., Sun, J., Qiao, X.: S3D-UNet: separable 3D U-Net for brain tumor segmentation. In: Crimi, A., Bakas, S., Kuijf, H., Keyvan, F., Reyes, M., van Walsum, T. (eds.) BrainLes 2018. LNCS, vol. 11384, pp. 358–368. Springer, Cham (2019). https://doi.org/10.1007/978-3-030-11726-9_32
7. Isensee, F., Kickingereder, P., Wick, W., Bendszus, M., Maier-Hein, K.H.: Brain tumor segmentation and radiomics survival prediction: contribution to the BRATS 2017 challenge. In: Crimi, A., Bakas, S., Kuijf, H., Menze, B., Reyes, M. (eds.) BrainLes 2017. LNCS, vol. 10670, pp. 287–297. Springer, Cham (2018). https://doi.org/10.1007/978-3-319-75238-9_25
8. Isensee, F., Kickingereder, P., Wick, W., Bendszus, M., Maier-Hein, K.H.: No new-net. In: Crimi, A., Bakas, S., Kuijf, H., Keyvan, F., Reyes, M., van Walsum, T. (eds.) BrainLes 2018. LNCS, vol. 11384, pp. 234–244. Springer, Cham (2019). https://doi.org/10.1007/978-3-030-11726-9_21
9. Kao, P.-Y., Ngo, T., Zhang, A., Chen, J.W., Manjunath, B.S.: Brain tumor segmentation and tractographic feature extraction from structural MR images for overall survival prediction. In: Crimi, A., Bakas, S., Kuijf, H., Keyvan, F., Reyes, M., van Walsum, T. (eds.) BrainLes 2018. LNCS, vol. 11384, pp. 128–141. Springer, Cham (2019). https://doi.org/10.1007/978-3-030-11726-9_12

10. Myronenko, A.: 3D MRI brain tumor segmentation using autoencoder regularization. In: Crimi, A., Bakas, S., Kuijf, H., Keyvan, F., Reyes, M., van Walsum, T. (eds.) BrainLes 2018. LNCS, vol. 11384, pp. 311–320. Springer, Cham (2019). https://doi.org/10.1007/978-3-030-11726-9_28
11. Nyúl, L.G., Udupa, J.K.: On standardizing the MR image intensity scale. Magn. Resonan. Med. Off. J. Int. Soc. Magn. Resonan. Med. **42**(6), 1072–1081 (1999)
12. Nyúl, L.G., Udupa, J.K., Zhang, X.: New variants of a method of MRI scale standardization. IEEE Trans. Med. Imaging **19**(2), 143–150 (2000)
13. Pereira, S., Pinto, A., Alves, V., Silva, C.A.: Brain tumor segmentation using convolutional neural networks in MRI images. IEEE Trans. Med. Imaging **35**(5), 1240–1251 (2016)
14. Ronneberger, O., Fischer, P., Brox, T.: U-Net: convolutional networks for biomedical image segmentation. In: Navab, N., Hornegger, J., Wells, W.M., Frangi, A.F. (eds.) MICCAI 2015. LNCS, vol. 9351, pp. 234–241. Springer, Cham (2015). https://doi.org/10.1007/978-3-319-24574-4_28
15. Shah, M., et al.: Evaluating intensity normalization on MRIs of human brain with multiple sclerosis. Med. Image Anal. **15**(2), 267–282 (2011)
16. Xu, H., Xie, H., Liu, Y., Cheng, C., Niu, C., Zhang, Y.: Deep cascaded attention network for multi-task brain tumor segmentation. In: Shen, D., et al. (eds.) MICCAI 2019. LNCS, vol. 11766, pp. 420–428. Springer, Cham (2019). https://doi.org/10.1007/978-3-030-32248-9_47

Superpixel-Guided Label Softening
for Medical Image Segmentation

Hang Li[1], Dong Wei[2], Shilei Cao[2], Kai Ma[2], Liansheng Wang[1(✉)],
and Yefeng Zheng[2]

[1] Xiamen University, Xiamen, China
`hangli@stu.xmu.edu.cn, lswang@xmu.edu.cn`
[2] Tencent Jarvis Lab, Shenzhen, China
{`donwei,eliaslcao,kylekma,yefengzheng`}`@tencent.com`

Abstract. Segmentation of objects of interest is one of the central tasks in medical image analysis, which is indispensable for quantitative analysis. When developing machine-learning based methods for automated segmentation, manual annotations are usually used as the ground truth toward which the models learn to mimic. While the bulky parts of the segmentation targets are relatively easy to label, the peripheral areas are often difficult to handle due to ambiguous boundaries and the partial volume effect, *etc.*, and are likely to be labeled with uncertainty. This uncertainty in labeling may, in turn, result in unsatisfactory performance of the trained models. In this paper, we propose superpixel-based label softening to tackle the above issue. Generated by unsupervised over-segmentation, each superpixel is expected to represent a locally homogeneous area. If a superpixel intersects with the annotation boundary, we consider a high probability of uncertain labeling within this area. Driven by this intuition, we soften labels in this area based on signed distances to the annotation boundary and assign probability values within [0, 1] to them, in comparison with the original "hard", binary labels of either 0 or 1. The softened labels are then used to train the segmentation models together with the hard labels. Experimental results on a brain MRI dataset and an optical coherence tomography dataset demonstrate that this conceptually simple and implementation-wise easy method achieves overall superior segmentation performances to baseline and comparison methods for both 3D and 2D medical images.

Keywords: Soft labeling · Superpixel · Medical image segmentation

---

H. Li, D. Wei and S. Cao—Contributed equally.

Electronic supplementary material The online version of this chapter (https://doi.org/10.1007/978-3-030-59719-1_23) contains supplementary material, which is available to authorized users.

© Springer Nature Switzerland AG 2020
A. L. Martel et al. (Eds.): MICCAI 2020, LNCS 12264, pp. 227–237, 2020.
https://doi.org/10.1007/978-3-030-59719-1_23

1   Introduction

Segmentation of objects of interest is an important task in medical image analysis. Benefiting from the development of deep neural networks and the accumulation of annotated data, fully convolutional networks (FCNs) have demonstrated remarkable performances [8,19] in this task. In general, these models assume that the ground truth is given precisely. However, for tasks with a large number of category labels, the peripheral areas are often difficult to annotate due to ambiguous boundaries and the partial volume effect (PVE) [2], etc., and are likely to be labeled with uncertainty. With a limited number of data, FCNs may have difficulties in coping with such uncertainty, which in turn affects the performance. Taking brain MRI for example, in Fig. 1, we show a slice of a multi-sequence MRI, in which the pink area shows barely or non-discernible boundaries from its surroundings, causing great difficulties in the manual annotation.

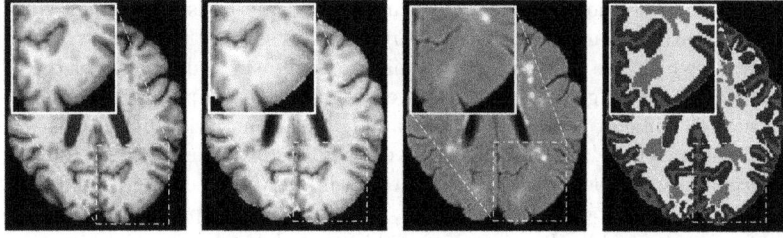

Fig. 1. Illustration of ambiguous boundaries in medical images with a slice of a multi-sequence brain MRI. The first three images show the MRI sequences, and the last shows the ground truth annotation. As we can see, the boundaries of the tissue marked in pink are barely or even not discernible from its surroundings. Best viewed in color.

To reduce the impact of imprecise boundary annotation, a potential solution is the label softening technique, and at this moment, we are only aware of few of them [5,10,11]. Based on the anatomical knowledge that the lesion-surrounding pixels may also include some lesion level information, Kats *et al.* [11] employed 3D morphological dilation to expand the binary mask of multiple sclerosis (MS) lesions and assigned a fixed pseudo probability to all pixels within the expanded region, such that these pixels can also contribute to the learning of MS lesions. Despite the improved Dice similarity coefficient in the experiments, the inherent contextual information of images was not utilized when determining the extent of dilation or exact value of the fixed pseudo probability. To account for uncertainties in the ground truth segmentation of atherosclerotic plaque in the carotid artery, Engelen *et al.* [5] proposed to blur the ground truth mask with a Gaussian filter for label softening. One limitation of this work was that, similar to [11], the creation of the soft labels was only based on the ground truth while ignoring the descriptive contextual information in the image. From another perspective, soft labels can also be obtained by fusing multiple manual annotations, e.g.., in

[10] masks of MS lesions produced by different experts were fused using a soft version of the STAPLE algorithm [22]. However, obtaining multiple segmentation annotations for medical images can be practically difficult. An alternative to label softening is the label smoothing technique [16,20] which assumes a uniform prior distribution over labels; yet again, this technique did not take the image context into consideration, either.

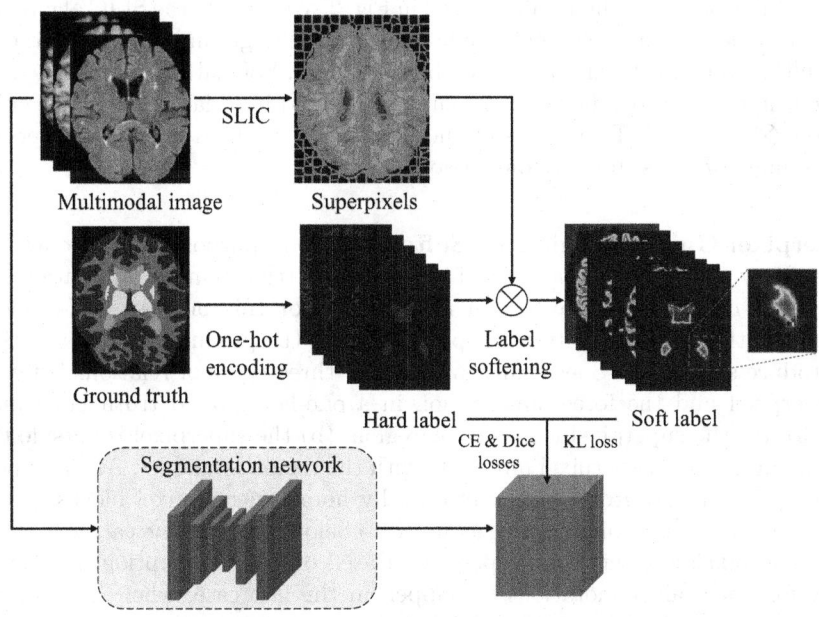

Fig. 2. Pipeline of our proposed method.

In this paper, we propose a new label softening method driven by the image contextual information, for improving segmentation performance especially near the boundaries of different categories. Specifically, we employ the concept of superpixels [1] for the utilization of local contextual information. Via unsupervised over-segmentation, the superpixels group original image pixels into locally homogeneous blocks, which can be considered as meaningful atomic regions of the image. Conceptually, if the scale of superpixel is appropriate, pixels within the same superpixel block can be assumed belonging to the same category. Based on this assumption, if a superpixel intersects with the annotation boundary of the ground truth, we consider a high probability of uncertain labeling within the area prescribed by this superpixel. Driven by this intuition, we soften labels in this area based on the signed distance to the annotation boundary, producing probability values spanning the full range of [0, 1]—in contrast to the original "hard" binary labels of either 0 or 1. The softened labels can then be used to train the segmentation models. We evaluate the proposed approach on two publicly available datasets: the Grand Challenge on MR Brain Segmentation at MICCAI 2018 (MRBrainS18) [7] dataset and an optical coherence tomography (OCT) image [3] dataset. The experimental results verify the effectiveness of our approach.

2   Method

The pipeline of our method is illustrated in Fig. 2. We employ the SLIC algorithm [1] to produce superpixels, meanwhile converting the ground truth annotation to multiple one-hot label maps (the "hard" labels). Soft labels are obtained by exploiting the relations between the superpixels and hard label maps (the cross symbol $\otimes$ in Fig. 2). Then, the soft and hard labels are used jointly to supervise the training of the segmentation network.

Superpixel-Guided Region of Softening. Our purpose is to model the uncertainty near the boundaries of categories in the manual annotation for improving model performance and robustness. For this purpose, we propose to exploit the relations between superpixels and the ground truth annotation to produce soft labels. Specifically, we identify three types of relations between a superpixel and the foreground region in a one-hot ground truth label map (Fig. 3): (a) the superpixel is inside the region, (b) the superpixel is outside the region, and (c) the superpixel intersects with the region boundary. As the superpixel algorithms [1] group pixels into locally homogeneous pixel blocks, pixels within the same superpixel can be assumed to belong to the same category given that superpixels are set to a proper size. Based on this assumption, it is most likely for uncertain annotations to happen in the last case, where the ground truth annotation indicates different labels for pixels inside the same superpixel block. Therefore, our label softening works exclusively in this case.

Formally, let us denote an image by $x \in \mathbb{R}^{W \times H}$, where W and H are the width and height, respectively. (Without loss of generalization, x can also be a 3D image $x \in \mathbb{R}^{W \times H \times T}$, where T is the number of slices, and our method still applies.) Then, its corresponding ground truth annotation can be denoted by a set of one-hot label maps: $Y = \{y^c | y^c \in \mathbb{R}^{W \times H}\}_{c=1}^C$, where C is the number of categories, and y^c is the binary label map for category c, in which any pixel $y_i^c \in \{0, 1\}$, where $i \in \{1, \dots, N\}$ is the pixel index, and N is the total number of pixels; besides, we denote the foreground area in y^c by ϕ^c. We can generate superpixel blocks $S(x) = \{s^{(j)}\}_{j=1}^M$ for x using an over-segmentation algorithm, where M is the total number of superpixels. In this paper, we adopt SLIC [1] as our superpixel-generating algorithm, which is known for computational efficiency and quality of the generated superpixels. We denote the set of soft label maps to be generated by $Q_c = \{q^c | q^c \in \mathbb{R}^{W \times H}\}$; note that $q_i^c \in [0, 1]$ is a continuous value, in contrast with the binaries in y^c. As shown in Fig. 3, the relations between any ϕ^c and $s^{(j)}$ can be classified into three categories: (a) $s^{(j)}$ is inside ϕ^c; (b) $s^{(j)}$ is outside ϕ^c; and (c) $s^{(j)}$ intersects with boundaries of ϕ^c. For the first two cases, we use the original values of y_i^c in the corresponding locations in

q^c. Whereas as for the third case, we employ label softening strategies to assign a soft label q_i^c to each pixel i based on its distance to boundaries of ϕ^c, which is described below.

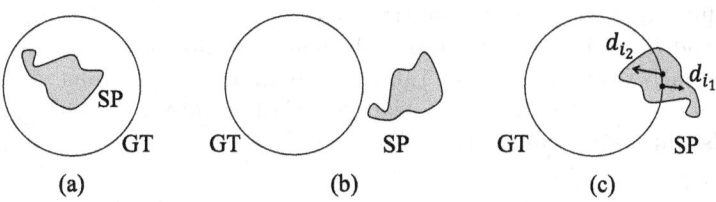

(a) (b) (c)

Fig. 3. Illustration of three types of relations between the foreground region in a binary ground truth label map (GT) and a superpixel block (SP). (a) SP is inside GT; (b) SP is outside GT; (c) SP intersects with boundaries of GT. We identity the region enclosed by the SP in the third case for label softening, based on the signed distances to GT boundaries.

Soft Labeling with Signed Distance Function. Assume a superpixel block s intersects with the boundaries of a foreground ϕ (for simplicity, the superscripts can be safely omitted here without confusion). For a pixel s_i in s, the absolute value of the distance d_i from s_i to ϕ is defined as the minimum distance among all the distances from s_i to all pixels on the boundaries of ϕ. We define $d_i > 0$ if s_i is inside ϕ, and $d_i \leq 0$ otherwise. As aforementioned, in the case of a superpixel block intersecting with the boundaries of ϕ, we need to assign each pixel in this block a pseudo-probability as its soft label according to its distance to ϕ. The pseudo-probability should be set to 0.5 for a pixel right on the boundary (i.e. $d_i = 0$), gradually approach 1 as d_i increases, and gradually approach 0 otherwise. Thus, we define the distance-to-probability conversion function as

$$q_i = f_{\text{dist}}(d_i) = \frac{1}{2}\left(\frac{d_i}{1+|d_i|}+1\right),\qquad(1)$$

where $q_i \in [0,1]$ is the obtained soft label for pixel i.

Model Training with Soft and Hard Labels. We adopt the Kullback-Leibler (KL) divergence loss [13] to supervise model training with our soft labels:

$$\mathcal{L}_{\text{KL}} = \frac{1}{N}\sum_{i=1}^{N}\sum_{c=1}^{C} q_i^c \log(q_i^c/p_i^c),\qquad(2)$$

where p_i^c is the predicted probability of the i-th pixel belonging to the class c, and q_i^c is the corresponding soft label defined with Eq. (1). Along with $\mathcal{L}_{\text{KL}}$, we also adopt the commonly used Dice loss $\mathcal{L}_{\text{Dice}}$ [15] and cross-entropy (CE) loss $\mathcal{L}_{\text{CE}}$ for medical image segmentation. Specifically, the CE loss is defined as:

$$\mathcal{L}_{\text{CE}} = -\frac{1}{N}\sum_{i=1}^{N}\sum_{c=1}^{C} w_c y_i^c \log(p_i^c),\qquad(3)$$

where w_c is the weight for class c. When $w_c = 1$ for all classes, Eq. (3) is the standard CE loss. In addition, w_c can be set to class-specific weights to counteract the impact of class imbalance [17]: $w_c = 1/\log(1.02 + \sum_{i=1}^{N} y_i^c/N)$, and we refer to this version of the CE loss as weighted CE (WCE) loss. The final loss is defined as a weighted sum of the three losses: $\mathcal{L} = \mathcal{L}_{CE} + \alpha\mathcal{L}_{Dice} + \beta\mathcal{L}_{KL}$, where α and β are hyperparameters to balance the three losses. We follow the setting in nnU-Net [8] to set $\alpha = 1.0$, and explore the proper value of β in our experiments, since it controls the relative contribution of our newly proposed soft labels which are of interest.

3   Experiments

Datasets.   To verify the effectiveness of our method on both 2D and 3D medical image segmentation, we use datasets of both types for experiments. The MRBrainS18 dataset [7] provides seven 3T multi-sequence (T1-weighted, T1-weighted inversion recovery, and T2-FLAIR) brain MRI scans with the following 11 ground truth labels: 0-background, 1-cortical gray matter, 2-basal ganglia, 3-white matter, 4-white matter lesions, 5-cerebrospinal fluid in the extracerebral space, 6-ventricles, 7-cerebellum, 8-brain stem, 9-infarction and 10-other, among which labels 9 and 10 were officially excluded from the evaluation and we follow this setting. We randomly choose five scans for training and use the rest for evaluation. For preprocessing, the scans are preprocessed by skull stripping, nonzero cropping, resampling, and data normalization. The other dataset [3] includes OCT images with diabetic macular edema (the OCT-DME dataset) for the segmentation of retinal layers and fluid regions. It contains 110 2D B-scan images from 10 patients. Eight retinal layers and fluid regions are annotated. We use the first five subjects for training and the last five subjects for evaluation (each set has 55 B-scans). Since the image quality of this dataset is poor, we firstly employ a denoising convolutional neural networks (DnCNN) [23] to reduce image noise and improve the visibility of anatomical structures. To reduce memory usage, we follow He *et al.* [6] to flatten a retinal B-scan image to the estimated Bruch's membrane (BM) using an intensity gradient method [14] and crop the retina part out.

Experimental Setting and Implementation.   For the experiments on each dataset, we first establish a baseline, which is trained without the soft labels. Then, we re-implement the Gaussian blur based label softening method [5], in which the value of σ is empirically selected, for a comparison with our proposed method. Considering the class imbalance in both datasets, we present results using the standard CE and WCE losses for all methods. We notice that the Dice loss adversely affects the performance on the OCT-DME dataset, therefore those results are not reported. We use overlap-based, volume-based, and distance-based mean metrics [21], including: Dice coefficient score, volumetric similarity (VS), 95th percentile Hausdorff distance (HD95), average surface distance (ASD), and average symmetric surface distance (ASSD) for a comprehensive evaluation of the methods. We employ a 2D U-Net [19] segmentation model (with the Xception [4] encoder) for the OCT-DME dataset, and a 3D U-Net [8] model for the MRBrainS18 dataset (patch-based training and sliding window test tricks [9] are employed in the implementation). All experiments are conducted with the PyTorch framework [18] on a standard PC with an NVIDIA GTX 1080Ti GPU. The Adam optimizer[12] is adopted with a learning rate of 3×10^{-4} and a weight decay of 10^{-5}. The learning rate is halved if the validation performance does not improve for 20 consecutive epochs. The batch size is fixed to 2 for the MRBrainS18 dataset, and 16 for the OCT-DME dataset.

Results. The quantitative evaluation results are summarized in Table 1 and Table 2 for the MRBrainS18 and OCT-DME datasets, respectively. (Example segmentation results on both datasets are provided in the supplementary material.) As expected, the weighted CE loss produces better results than the standard CE loss for most evaluation metrics on both datasets. We note that the Gaussian blur based label softening [5] does not improve upon the baselines either with the CE or WCE loss, but only obtains results comparable to those of the baselines. The reason might be that this method indiscriminately softens all boundary-surrounding pixels with a fixed standard deviation without considering the actual image context, which may potentially harm the segmentation near originally precisely annotated boundaries. In contrast, our proposed method consistently improves all metrics when using the generated soft labels with the WCE loss. In fact, with this combination of losses, our method achieves the best performances for all evaluation metrics. It is also worth mentioning that, although our method is motivated by improving segmentation near category boundaries, it also improves the overlap-based evaluation metrics (Dice) by a noticeable extent on the OCT-DME dataset. These results verify the effectiveness of our method in improving segmentation performance, by modeling uncertainty in manual labeling with the interaction between superpixels and ground truth annotations.

Table 1. Evaluation results on the MRBrainS18 dataset [7]. The KL divergence loss is used by our method for model training with our soft labels.

Method	Losses	Dice (%)↑	VS (%)↑	HD95 (mm)↓	ASD (mm)↓	ASSD (mm)↓
Baseline	CE+Dice	85.47	96.53	3.5287	0.9290	0.7722
	WCE+Dice	85.56	96.55	3.5116	0.8554	0.7371
Engelen	CE+Dice	85.16	95.44	3.6396	0.9551	0.8004
et al. [5]	WCE+Dice	85.47	95.58	3.5720	0.8432	0.7502
Ours	KL+CE+Dice	85.26	93.95	3.4684	0.9460	0.8061
	KL+WCE+Dice	**85.63**	**96.60**	**3.1194**	**0.8146**	**0.7153**

Ablation Study on Number of Superpixels. The proper scale of the superpixels is crucial for our proposed method, as superpixels of different sizes may

Table 2. Evaluation results on the OCT-DME dataset [3]. The KL divergence loss is used by our method for model training with our soft labels.

Method	Losses	Dice (%)↑	VS (%)↑	HD95 (mm)↓	ASD (mm)↓	ASSD (mm)↓
Baseline	CE	82.50	96.52	3.22	1.075	1.075
	WCE	82.82	96.44	3.27	1.082	1.087
Engelen	CE	82.69	96.38	3.24	1.092	1.092
et al. [5]	WCE	82.94	96.36	3.27	1.080	1.094
Ours	KL+CE	82.72	96.41	3.25	1.081	1.087
	KL+WCE	**83.94**	**96.73**	**3.17**	**1.058**	**1.066**

describe different levels of image characteristics, and thus may interact differently with the ground truth annotation. Since in the SLIC [1] algorithm, the size of superpixels is controlled by the total number of generated superpixel blocks, we conduct experiments to study how the number of superpixels influences the performance on the MRBrainS18 dataset. In Fig. 4, we show performances of our method with different numbers of superpixels ranged from 500 to 3500 with a sampling interval of 500. As we can see, as the number of superpixels increases, the performance first increases due to the more image details incorporated, and then decreases after reaching the peak. This is in line with our intuition, since the assumption that pixels within the same superpixel belong to the same category can hold only if the scale of superpixels is appropriate. Large superpixels can produce flawed soft labels. In contrast, as the number of superpixels grows and their sizes shrink, soft labels will degenerate into hard labels, which does not provide additional information.

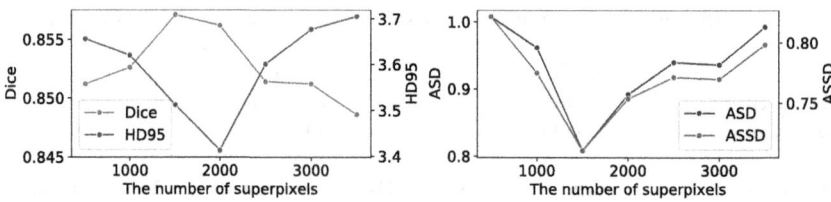

Fig. 4. Performances of our method with different numbers of superpixels on the MRBrainS18 dataset [7]. The HD95, ASD and ASSD are in mm. Best viewed in color.

Ablation Study on Weight of Soft Label Loss. The weight β controls the contribution of the soft labels in training. To explore the influence of the soft label loss, we conduct a study on the MRBrainS18 dataset to compare the performance of our method with different values of β. We set β to $1/4, 1/2, 1, 2, 4,$ and 8. The mean Dice, HD95, ASD, and ASSD of our proposed method with

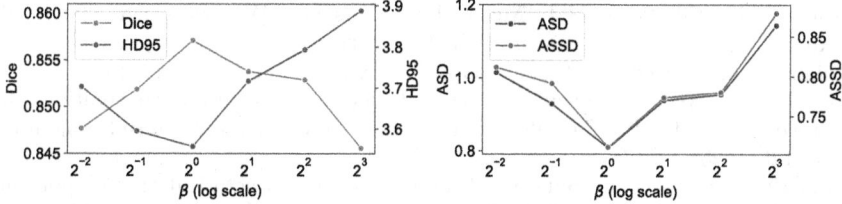

Fig. 5. Performances of our method using different values of β on the MRBrainS18 dataset [7]. The HD95, ASD and ASSD are in mm. Best viewed in color.

these values of β are shown in Fig. 5. Note that the x-axis uses a log scale since values of β differ by orders of magnitude. Improvements in performance can be observed when β increases from $1/4$ to 1. When β continues to increase, however, the segmentation performances start to drop. This indicates that the soft labels are helpful to segmentation, although giving too much emphasis to them may decrease the generalization ability of the segmentation model.

4 Conclusion

In this paper, we presented a new label softening method that was simple yet effective in improving segmentation performance, especially near the boundaries of different categories. The proposed method first employed an over-segmentation algorithm to group image pixels into locally homogeneous blocks called super-pixels. Then, the superpixel blocks intersecting with the category boundaries in the ground truth were identified for label softening, and a signed distance function was employed to convert the pixel-to-boundary distances to soft labels within $[0, 1]$ for pixels inside these blocks. The soft labels were subsequently used to train a segmentation network. Experimental results on both 2D and 3D medical images demonstrated the effectiveness of this simple approach in improving segmentation performance.

Acknowledgments. This work was supported by the National Natural Science Foundation of China (Grant No. 61671399), Fundamental Research Funds for the Central Universities (Grant No. 20720190012), Key Area Research and Development Program of Guangdong Province, China (No. 2018B010111001), National Key Research and Development Project (2018YFC2000702), and Science and Technology Program of Shenzhen, China (No. ZDSYS201802021814180).

References

1. Achanta, R., Shaji, A., Smith, K., Lucchi, A., Fua, P., Süsstrunk, S.: SLIC super-pixels compared to state-of-the-art superpixel methods. IEEE Trans. Pattern Anal. Mach. Intell. **34**(11), 2274–2282 (2012)
2. Ballester, M.A.G., Zisserman, A.P., Brady, M.: Estimation of the partial volume effect in MRI. Med. Image Anal. **6**(4), 389–405 (2002)

3. Chiu, S.J., Allingham, M.J., Mettu, P.S., Cousins, S.W., Izatt, J.A., Farsiu, S.: Kernel regression based segmentation of optical coherence tomography images with diabetic macular edema. Biomed. Opt. Express **6**(4), 1172–1194 (2015)

4. Chollet, F.: Xception: deep learning with depthwise separable convolutions. In: Proceedings of the IEEE Conference on Computer Vision and Pattern Recognition, pp. 1251–1258 (2017)

5. van Engelen, A., et al.: Supervised in-vivo plaque characterization incorporating class label uncertainty. In: IEEE International Symposium on Biomedical Imaging, pp. 246–249. IEEE (2012)

6. He, Y., et al.: Fully convolutional boundary regression for retina OCT segmentation. In: Shen, D., et al. (eds.) MICCAI 2019. LNCS, vol. 11764, pp. 120–128. Springer, Cham (2019). https://doi.org/10.1007/978-3-030-32239-7_14

7. Kuijf, H.J.: Grand challenge on MR brain segmentation at MICCAI 2018 (2018). http://mrbrains18.isi.uu.nl

8. Isensee, F., et al.: Abstract: nnU-Net: self-adapting framework for U-Net-based medical image segmentation. Bildverarbeitung für die Medizin 2019. I, pp. 22–22. Springer, Wiesbaden (2019). https://doi.org/10.1007/978-3-658-25326-4_7

9. Jin, D., et al.: Accurate esophageal gross tumor volume segmentation in PET/CT using two-stream chained 3D deep network fusion. In: Shen, D., et al. (eds.) MICCAI 2019. LNCS, vol. 11765, pp. 182–191. Springer, Cham (2019). https://doi.org/10.1007/978-3-030-32245-8_21

10. Kats, E., Goldberger, J., Greenspan, H.: A soft STAPLE algorithm combined with anatomical knowledge. In: Shen, D., et al. (eds.) MICCAI 2019. LNCS, vol. 11766, pp. 510–517. Springer, Cham (2019). https://doi.org/10.1007/978-3-030-32248-9_57

11. Kats, E., Goldberger, J., Greenspan, H.: Soft labeling by distilling anatomical knowledge for improved MS lesion segmentation. In: IEEE International Symposium on Biomedical Imaging, pp. 1563–1566. IEEE (2019)

12. Kingma, D.P., Ba, J.: Adam: a method for stochastic optimization. In: International Conference on Learning Representations (2015)

13. Kullback, S., Leibler, R.A.: On information and sufficiency. Ann. Math. Stat. **22**(1), 79–86 (1951)

14. Lang, A., et al.: Retinal layer segmentation of macular OCT images using boundary classification. Biomed. Opt. Express **4**(7), 1133–1152 (2013)

15. Milletari, F., Navab, N., Ahmadi, S.A.: V-Net: fully convolutional neural networks for volumetric medical image segmentation. In: International Conference on 3D Vision, pp. 565–571. IEEE (2016)

16. Ouyang, X., et al.: Weakly supervised segmentation framework with uncertainty: a study on pneumothorax segmentation in chest x-ray. In: Shen, D., et al. (eds.) MICCAI 2019. LNCS, vol. 11769, pp. 613–621. Springer, Cham (2019). https://doi.org/10.1007/978-3-030-32226-7_68

17. Paszke, A., Chaurasia, A., Kim, S., Culurciello, E.: ENet: a deep neural network architecture for real-time semantic segmentation. arXiv preprint arXiv:1606.02147 (2016)

18. Paszke, A., et al.: PyTorch: an imperative style, high-performance deep learning library. In: Advances in Neural Information Processing Systems, pp. 8024–8035 (2019)

19. Ronneberger, O., Fischer, P., Brox, T.: U-Net: convolutional networks for biomedical image segmentation. In: Navab, N., Hornegger, J., Wells, W.M., Frangi, A.F. (eds.) MICCAI 2015. LNCS, vol. 9351, pp. 234–241. Springer, Cham (2015). https://doi.org/10.1007/978-3-319-24574-4_28

20. Szegedy, C., Vanhoucke, V., Ioffe, S., Shlens, J., Wojna, Z.: Rethinking the Inception architecture for computer vision. In: Proceedings of the IEEE Conference on Computer Vision and Pattern Recognition, pp. 2818–2826 (2016)
21. Taha, A.A., Hanbury, A.: Metrics for evaluating 3D medical image segmentation: analysis, selection, and tool. BMC Med. Imaging **15**(1), 29 (2015)
22. Warfield, S.K., Zou, K.H., Wells, W.M.: Simultaneous truth and performance level estimation (STAPLE): an algorithm for the validation of image segmentation. IEEE Trans. Med. Imaging **23**(7), 903–921 (2004)
23. Zhang, K., Zuo, W., Chen, Y., Meng, D., Zhang, L.: Beyond a Gaussian denoiser: residual learning of deep CNN for image denoising. IEEE Trans. Image Process. **26**(7), 3142–3155 (2017)

Revisiting Rubik's Cube: Self-supervised Learning with Volume-Wise Transformation for 3D Medical Image Segmentation

Xing Tao[1], Yuexiang Li[2(✉)], Wenhui Zhou[1], Kai Ma[2], and Yefeng Zheng[2]

[1] School of Computer Science and Technology, Hangzhou Dianzi University, Hangzhou, China
vicyxli@tencent.com, zhouwenhui@hdu.edu.cn
[2] Tencent Jarvis Lab, Shenzhen, China

Abstract. Deep learning highly relies on the quantity of annotated data. However, the annotations for 3D volumetric medical data require experienced physicians to spend hours or even days for investigation. Self-supervised learning is a potential solution to get rid of the strong requirement of training data by deeply exploiting raw data information. In this paper, we propose a novel self-supervised learning framework for volumetric medical images. Specifically, we propose a context restoration task, i.e., Rubik's cube++, to pre-train 3D neural networks. Different from the existing context-restoration-based approaches, we adopt a volume-wise transformation for context permutation, which encourages network to better exploit the inherent 3D anatomical information of organs. Compared to the strategy of training from scratch, fine-tuning from the Rubik's cube++ pre-trained weight can achieve better performance in various tasks such as pancreas segmentation and brain tissue segmentation. The experimental results show that our self-supervised learning method can significantly improve the accuracy of 3D deep learning networks on volumetric medical datasets without the use of extra data.

Keywords: 3d medical image segmentation · Self-supervised learning · Rubik's cube · Volume-wise transformation

1 Introduction

The success of convolutional neural networks (CNNs) benefits from the amount of annotated data rapidly increased in the last decade. However, the high-quality medical image annotations are extremely laborious and usually hard to acquire, which require hours or even days for an experienced physician. As a result, the

---

X. Tao—This work was done when Xing Tao was an intern at Tencent Jarvis Lab.

© Springer Nature Switzerland AG 2020
A. L. Martel et al. (Eds.): MICCAI 2020, LNCS 12264, pp. 238–248, 2020.
https://doi.org/10.1007/978-3-030-59719-1_24

limited quantity of annotated medical images is the major obstacle impeding the improvement of diagnosis accuracy with the latest 3D CNN architectures [2,10].

To deal with the problem of deficient annotated data, self-supervised learning approaches, which utilize unlabelled data to train network models in a supervised manner, attract lots of attentions. The typical self-supervised learning defines a relevant pretext task to extract meaningful features from unlabelled data, where the learned representations can boost the accuracy of the subsequent target task with limited training data. Various pretext tasks have been proposed, including patch relative position prediction [4] (Jigsaw puzzles [13] can be grouped into this category), grayscale image colorization [9], and context restoration [14]. The idea of self-supervised learning was firstly brought to medical image analysis by Zhang et al. [18]. They pre-trained a 2D network for fine-grained body part recognition with a pretext task that sorted the 2D slices from the conventional medical volumes. Compared to 2D networks, 3D networks integrating more spatial context information have shown the superiority for the 3D medical data [5].

Recently, several studies have made their efforts to develop self-supervised learning frameworks for 3D neural networks [16,19]. Zhuang et al. [20] proposed a pre-train 3D networks by playing a Rubik's cube game, which can be seen as an extension of 2D Jigsaw puzzles [12]. Formulated as a classification task, however, their model only pre-trained the down-sampling layers of CNNs. When applying the pre-trained weights to a target task requiring up-sampling operations (e.g., organ segmentation), the performance improvement is neutralized by the randomly initialized up-sampling layers. To this end, we reformulate the Rubik's cube game as a context restoration task, which simultaneously pre-trains the down-sampling and up-sampling layers of fully convolutional networks (FCNs).

In this paper, we propose a novel self-supervised learning pretext task, namely Rubik's cube++[1], for volumetric medical image segmentation. Inspired by the observation that learning from a harder task often leads to a more robust feature representation [3,17], our Rubik's cube++ adopts a volume-wise transformation, e.g., 3D voxel rotation, to permute and restore the volumetric medical data, which is assumed to be much harder than the existing methods [19]. To validate our assumption that the voxel rotation is a better transformation for self-supervised learning with 3D data, we evaluate the proposed Rubik's cube++ on two medical image segmentation tasks (i.e., pancreas segmentation and brain tissue segmentation) using publicly available datasets. The experimental results demonstrate that our method can significantly boost the segmentation accuracy and achieve the state-of-the-art performance compared to other self-supervised baseline methods.

2   Method

The volumetric medical data can be seen as a high-order Rubik's cube by partitioning it into a grid of subcubes. Let the dimension of the volumetric data

---

[1] The symbol "++" represents two improvements compared to the existing Rubik's cube [20]: 1) encoder-decoder architecture, and 2) volume-wise transformation.

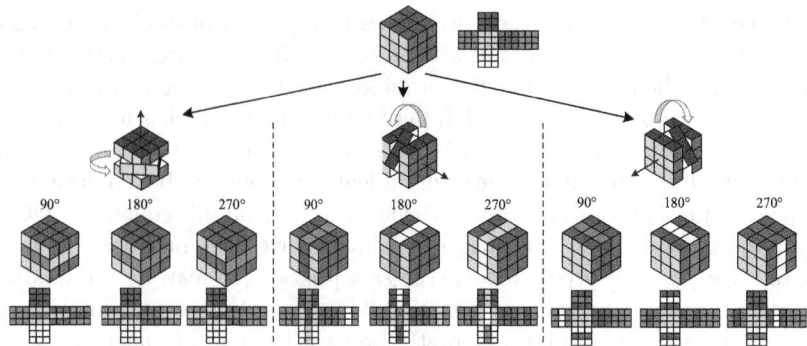

Fig. 1. The schematic diagram of the Rubik's cube++ transformations. The three-order Rubik's cube is taken as an example. There are three axes (*sagittal*, *coronal* and *axial*) and three degree (90°, 180° and 270°) for each transformation to choose. The diversely transformed results are presented on the right, which prevent trivial solutions.

be $W \times H \times L$ and the side length of the subcube be n voxels, we have a Rubik's cube with $\lfloor \frac{W}{n} \rfloor \times \lfloor \frac{H}{n} \rfloor \times \lfloor \frac{L}{n} \rfloor$ subcubes, where $\lfloor \cdot \rfloor$ is the floor function. The initial state of these subcubes, including the order and orientation, is defined as the original state of Rubik's cube. We first clarify the definition of two components: subcube and cube layer.

Subcube. It is the smallest component containing 3D anatomical information. Different from [20], the subcubes of our Rubik's cube are bound to their neighbors, which prohibits individual movement or rotation of the subcube.

Cube Layer. As shown in Fig. 1, the cube layer, consisting of a set of subcubes on the same anatomical plane along the major axis (*sagittal*, *coronal* and *axial*), is used as the unit component for the transformation of Rubik's cube++.

Our Rubik's cube++ has a set of transformations. Take the $3 \times 3 \times 3$ Rubik's cube as an example, as shown in Fig. 1, the cube layer containing nine subcubes can be rotated along a specific axis by a fixed angle. Note that if the Rubik's cube is of a cuboid shape, only 180° rotation is valid along the short axis. Compared with the image transformations used in other pretext tasks [19], the transformations of Rubik's cube++ are restricted to volume-wise rotation. Such transformations wreck the 3D information of medical data, and encourage the network to exploit useful volumetric features for restoration. Moreover, the rotation operation can generate diversely transformed results without generating image artifacts, which prevents the network from learning trivial solutions [4].

2.1   Pretext Task: Rubik's Cube Restoration

Our restoration-based pretext task is formulated to pre-train a 3D network. At the beginning of the pretext task, the Rubik's cube is permuted by a sequence of random volume-wise transformations, which results in a disarranged Rubik's cube. The original state of Rubik's cube is used as the supervision signal. A 3D network is trained to recover the original state of Rubik's cube from the disarranged state, which enforces the network to learn 3D anatomical information.

Algorithm 1. Disarrangement of Rubik's cube.

Input: Original 3D medical data $\mathbf{y}$ of shape $W \times H \times L$.
1: According to the preset parameter n, we partition the 3D medical data into a $\lfloor \frac{W}{n} \rfloor \times \lfloor \frac{H}{n} \rfloor \times \lfloor \frac{L}{n} \rfloor$ subcubes.
2: **for** axis $i \in \{sagittal, coronal, axial\}$ **do**
3:     Randomly designate m cube layers along axis i.
4:     **for** layer $j \in \{1, 2, .., m\}$ **do**
5:         Randomly select an angle $\theta \in \{90°, 180°, 270°\}$.
6:         Rotate the cube layer j along axis i by angle θ.
7:     **end for**
8: **end for**
Output: Disarranged 3D medical data $\mathbf{x}$.

The process of Rubik's cube disarrangement adopted in Rubik's cube++ is presented in Algorithm 1. Let $\mathbf{y}$ denote the 3D medical data, i.e., the original state of Rubik's cube. And, $x = T(y)$ indicates the 3D medical data in a disarranged state after a sequence of random transformations $T(\cdot)$. Note that we can easily adjust the difficulty of the pretext task by changing the parameters side length of subcube (n) and the number of rotated cube layers (m).

2.2   Network Architecture

A GAN-based architecture is used to resolve our Rubik's cube++ pretext task, which consists of two components: a generator G and a discriminator D. As shown in Fig. 2, both the generator and discriminator are of 3D neural networks. The generator adopts a 3D encoder-decoder structure with skip connections between mirrored layers in the encoder and decoder stacks, which is the same to [2]. Note that other widely used 3D FCNs, such as V-Net [10], can be easily adopted as the generator of our Rubik's cube++ for pre-training. The discriminator consists of four convolutional layers with the kernel size of $4 \times 4 \times 4$. The restored Rubik's cube $G(x)$ and original state y are respectively concatenated with the disarranged state x and fed to the discriminator for the real/fake classification.

The GAN-based framework aims to recover the original state of Rubik's cube from the disarranged state. We propose a joint loss function to supervise the Rubik's cube restoration. It consists of a reconstruction loss and an adversarial loss, which are responsible for capturing the overall structure of 3D medical data and tuning the anatomical details, respectively.

Reconstruction Loss. As shown in Fig. 2, the disarranged state x of Rubik's cube is fed to the generator for context restoration $G(x)$. The voxel-wise $\mathcal{L}_1$ loss between y and $G(x)$ is calculated to optimize the restoration quality. We also tried to use $\mathcal{L}_2$ as the reconstruction loss for our Rubik's cube++.[2] Compared to $\mathcal{L}_1$, the $\mathcal{L}_2$ loss is inclined to have blurry solutions, which may lose the boundary information of organs.

$$\mathcal{L}_1(G) = \mathbb{E}_{\mathbf{x},\mathbf{y}} \|\mathbf{y} - G(\mathbf{x})\|_1. \tag{1}$$

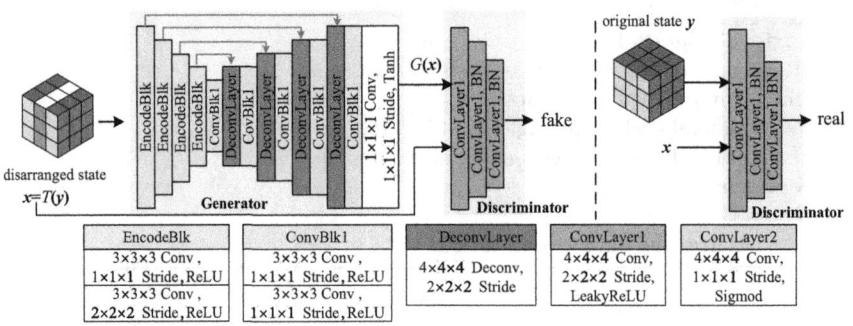

Fig. 2. The network architecture for our self-supervised learning.

Adversarial Loss. The adversarial loss derived from [6] is adopted in our pretext task to generate more real and elegant reconstruction results.[3] The generator learns a mapping from the disarranged state to the original state, $G : x \rightarrow y$. The discriminator learns to classify the fake (restored Rubik's cube produced by the generator) and the real (the original data). These two components are encouraged to compete against each other. The adversarial loss is defined as:

$$\mathcal{L}_{adv}(G, D) = \mathbb{E}_{x,y} \log D(x, y) + \mathbb{E}_x \log(1 - D(x, G(x))). \tag{2}$$

Objective. For training, the generator is encouraged to fool the discriminator, while the discriminator is required to correctly classify the real and fake data. Therefore, G tries to minimize $\mathcal{L}_{adv}$ and $\mathcal{L}_1$, while D aims to maximize $\mathcal{L}_{adv}$. The full objective for our Rubik's cube++ restoration is summarized as:

$$\mathcal{L} = \arg \min_G \max_D \left(\mathcal{L}_{adv}(G, D) + \lambda \mathcal{L}_1(G) \right), \tag{3}$$

where λ is a tuneable hyperparameter which is set to 10 in our experiments.

---

[2] An ablation study of $\mathcal{L}_1$ and $\mathcal{L}_2$ can be found in *arxiv version*.

[3] The reconstruction results are visualized in the *arxiv version*.

Transfer Learning. After the framework completes the self-supervised learning in the Rubik's cube++ restoration task, the trained generator that learns useful 3D anatomical information from raw data is adapted to the target task by replacing the last layer with the segmentation output layer. With the voxelwise annotation, the pre-trained generator can be directly fine-tuned on the target segmentation task, which alleviates the influence caused by the randomly-initialized decoder [17,20].

3   Experiments

Datasets. To evaluate the performance of our Rubik's cube++, we conduct a 4-fold cross validation on the NIH Pancreas computed tomography (CT) dataset [15], adopting the same protocol to [17]. Moreover, a leave-one-out cross validation is conducted on the MRBrainS18 dataset [11], due to its relatively small dataset size (i.e., only seven sets of brain magnetic resonance (MR) volumes). The 3D U-Net [2] is used as backbone for the generator. The Dice coefficient (DSC) [17] is used to assess the segmentation accuracy. For the multi-class task (e.g., brain tissue segmentation on MRBrainS18), we calculate the DSC for each class and average them to yield a mean DSC for performance evaluation.

Baselines. The train-from-scratch (t.f.s) strategy is involved as the baseline. We apply the video dataset (UCF101 [7]) to pre-train the 3D encoder of the generator on an action recognition task. To transfer the pre-trained weights to the target segmentation task for comparison, the decoder of the generator is randomly initialized. The recently proposed state-of-the-art approaches[4] [1,19,20] for the self-supervised and transfer learning of 3D medical data are also involved as benchmark.

Training Details. Our method is implemented using PyTorch and trained with the Adam [8] optimizer. The baselines adopt the same training protocol.

Pancreas Rubik's Cube. The pancreas CT is randomly cropped with a size of $128 \times 128 \times 128$. The side length of a subcube is set to [7,7,7]. Hence, a Rubik's cube of $18 \times 18 \times 18$ is built for each pancreas CT volume. To disarrange the cube, $m = 4$ cube layers are randomly rotated along each of the three axes. The Rubik's cube++ recovery task is trained on a GeForce GTX 1080Ti and observed to converge after about 10 h of training. To preserve the features learned by pre-training, the learning rate is set to 0.0001 while transferring the pre-trained weights to the target task (i.e., pancreas segmentation). The network converges after 250 epochs (about 5 h) of finetuning with voxel-wise annotations.

---

[4] For fair comparison, we pre-train 3D networks on the pretext tasks [19,20] using experimental datasets, instead of transferring from the publicly available weights [19] pre-trained on external data.

Brain Rubik's Cube. The brain MR volume is randomly cropped with a size of $144 \times 144 \times 32$. As the number of slice (i.e., 32) is smaller than the size of axial slices (i.e., 144×144), the side length of a subcube is set to [4,4,2], which results in a Rubik's cube with shape of $36 \times 36 \times 16$. The other training settings are similar to the prancreas Rubik's cube. As the brain MR scans are multi-modal, we apply the same transformation to each modality and concatenate them as input to the GAN-based network. Due to extremely small size of MRBrainS18, the Rubik's cube++ pre-training is completed in one hour.

Table 1. Comparison of DSC (%) and reconstruction MSE produced by Rubik's cube++ with different n values ($m = 4$). The listed results are generated via a 4-fold cross validation. (T.f.s.—train-from-scratch)

	T.f.s	$n = 3$	$n = 5$	$n = 7$	$n = 9$
recon. MSE ($1e^{-2}$)	–	0.826	1.609	2.984	4.762
10%	58.58	47.28	69.72	**73.30**	68.94
20%	70.19	65.00	75.88	**78.10**	73.34
50%	79.68	78.29	81.64	**82.80**	80.94
100%	82.90	82.10	83.72	**84.08**	83.57

3.1   Ablation Study on Pancreas Segmentation

The difficulty of Rubik's cube++ is controlled by two parameters: the subcube side length n and the number of rotated layers m in each transformation. However, the grid search of (n, m) is extremely demanding in computation. We suspect that the total number of rotated axial slices $n \times m$ largely determines the difficulty of the pretext task, we fixed one parameter $m = 4$ and varying the other (i.e., n) for the following experiments.[5]

To analyze the relationship between the difficulty of Rubik's cube++ and performance improvement to the target task, we construct the pancreas Rubik's cube with different subcube side lengths and evaluate their reconstruction mean squared error (MSE) and pancreas segmentation DSCs with different amount of training data. Table 1 shows the MSE and DSC under different settings of n. The larger subcube side length n means more slices are rotated in each transformation, which leads to a lower-order Rubik's cube and makes each cube layer contain more 3D anatomical information. Therefore, rotating such a cube layer may considerably change the inherent structure of organs, which reduces the context information and increases the difficulty for the network to solve the disarranged state.

As shown in Table 1, the reconstruction error increases from 0.00826 to 0.04762 as the subcube side length increases from 3 to 9. The experimental results

---

[5] An analysis of m can be found in *arxiv version*.

are consistent with the finding of existing works [3,17]—a harder task often leads to a more robust feature representation. The Rubik's cube++ with $n = 7$ achieves the highest DSC for pancreas segmentation with different amounts of training data. There is another finding in our experiments—the pretext is not the harder the better. A performance degradation is observed while n increases to 9, which indicates the excessive destruction of 3D structure may wreck the useful anatomical information for self-supervised learning and consequently decrease the robustness of feature representation.

Table 2. Pancreas segmentation accuracy (DSC %) of a 4-fold cross validation yielded by 3D U-Nets trained with different strategies. *The result reported in [17] using V-Net.

	10%	20%	50%	100%
Train-from-scratch	58.58	70.19	79.68	82.90
UCF101 pre-trained	62.21	71.90	77.14	82.76
Arbitrary puzzles* [17]	70.80	76.50	–	81.68
MedicalNet [1]	64.80	71.37	77.41	80.09
Rubik's cube [20]	61.07	70.43	80.30	82.76
Models genesis [19]	63.11	70.08	79.93	83.23
Rubik's cube++ (Ours)	**73.30**	**78.10**	**82.80**	**84.08**

3.2 Comparison with State-of-the-art

Pancreas Segmentation. The DSCs of 3D U-Nets trained with different strategies via a 4-fold cross validation are presented in Table 2.[6] Due to the gap between natural video and medical images, the network finetuned from UCF101 pre-trained weights gains marginal improvement or even degradation with more data used for training, compared to the t.f.s method. Due to the rich information mined from raw data, finetuning from the weights generated by self-supervised learning approaches produces a consistent improvement over the t.f.s strategy. Our method yields the largest increasement to the DSC of pancreas segmentation under all settings of the amount of training data.

Table 3. The mean DSC (%) of brain tissue segmentation of a leave-one-out cross validation yielded by frameworks trained with different strategies. (T.f.s.—train-from-scratch) The DSC for each class can be found in *arxiv version*.

	T.f.s	UCF101 pre-trained	Rubik's cube [20]	Models genesis [19]	Ours
Mean DSC	72.22	71.34	71.23	76.19	**77.56**

---

[6] For visual comparison between segmentation results, please refer to *arxiv version*.

Statistical Significance. A t-test validation is conducted on the 4-fold cross validation results (100% training data) to validate the statistical significance between our Rubik's cube++ and models genesis [19]. A p-value of 3.42% is obtained, which indicates that the accuracy improvement produced by our approach is statistically significant at the 5% significance level.

Brain Tissue Segmentation. To further validate the effectiveness of our Rubik's cube++, a leave-one-out experiment is conducted on the MRBrainS18 dataset. The mean DSC of brain tissue segmentation is listed in Table 3. The approaches only pre-training the encoder (i.e., UCF101 and Rubik's cube [20]) are observed to deteriorate the mean DSC compared to the train-from-scratch method. In contrast, the context-restoration-based self-supervised learning approaches (models genesis and Rubik's cube++), which simultaneously pre-train the encoder and decoder, generate a significant improvement (i.e., +3.97% and +5.34% in mean DSC, respectively) to the brain tissue segmentation task, compared to the train-from-scratch method. The experimental results demonstrate the merit of decoder pre-training for 3D medical image segmentation.

4   Conclusion

In this paper, we proposed a context restoration task, i.e., Rubik's cube++, to pre-train 3D neural networks for 3D medical image segmentation. Our Rubik's cube++ adopts a volume-wise transformation for context permutation, which encourages the 3D neural network to better exploit the inherent 3D anatomical information of organs. Our Rubik's cube++ is validated on two publicly available medical datasets to demonstrate its effectiveness, i.e., significantly improving the accuracy of 3D deep learning networks without the use of extra data.

Acknowledge. This work is supported by the Key Program of Zhejiang Provincial Natural Science Foundation of China (LZ14F020003), the Natural Science Foundation of China (No. 61702339), the Key Area Research and Development Program of Guangdong Province, China (No. 2018B010111001), National Key Research and Development Project (2018YFC2000702) and Science and Technology Program of Shenzhen, China (No. ZDSYS201802021814180).

References

1. Chen, S. Ma, K., Zheng, Y.: Med3D: transfer learning for 3D medical image analysis. arXiv preprint arXiv:1904.00625 (2019)
2. Çiçek, Ö., Abdulkadir, A., Lienkamp, S.S., Brox, T., Ronneberger, O.: 3D U-Net: learning dense volumetric segmentation from sparse annotation. In: Ourselin, S., Joskowicz, L., Sabuncu, M.R., Unal, G., Wells, W. (eds.) MICCAI 2016. LNCS, vol. 9901, pp. 424–432. Springer, Cham (2016). https://doi.org/10.1007/978-3-319-46723-8_49

3. Deng, J., Berg, A.C., Li, K., Fei-Fei, L.: What does classifying more than 10,000 image categories tell us? In: Daniilidis, K., Maragos, P., Paragios, N. (eds.) ECCV 2010. LNCS, vol. 6315, pp. 71–84. Springer, Heidelberg (2010). https://doi.org/10. 1007/978-3-642-15555-0_6
4. Doersch, C., Gupta, A., Efros, A.A.: Unsupervised visual representation learning by context prediction. In: IEEE International Conference on Computer Vision, pp. 1422–1430 (2015)
5. Dou, Q., et al.: 3D deeply supervised network for automated segmentation of volumetric medical images. Med. Image Anal. **41**, 40–54 (2017)
6. Isola, P., Zhu, J.Y., Zhou, T., Efros, A.A.: Image-to-image translation with conditional adversarial networks. In: IEEE Conference on Computer Vision and Pattern Recognition, pp. 1125–1134 (2017)
7. Khurram, S., Zamir, A.R., Shah, M.: UCF101: a dataset of 101 human actions classes from videos in the wild. arXiv preprint arXiv:1212.0402 (2012)
8. Kingma, D.P., Ba, J.: Adam: a method for stochastic optimization. arXiv preprint arXiv:1412.6980 (2014)
9. Larsson, G., Maire, M., Shakhnarovich, G.: Colorization as a proxy task for visual understanding. In: IEEE Conference on Computer Vision and Pattern Recognition, pp. 840–849 (2017)
10. Milletari, F., Navab, N., Ahmadi, S.A.: V-Net: fully convolutional neural networks for volumetric medical image segmentation. In: International Conference on 3D Vision, pp. 565–571 (2016)
11. MRBrainS18: Grand challenge on MR brain segmentation at MICCAI 2018 (2018). https://mrbrains18.isi.uu.nl/
12. Noroozi, M., Favaro, P.: Unsupervised learning of visual representations by solving jigsaw puzzles. In: Leibe, B., Matas, J., Sebe, N., Welling, M. (eds.) ECCV 2016. LNCS, vol. 9910, pp. 69–84. Springer, Cham (2016). https://doi.org/10.1007/978-3-319-46466-4_5
13. Noroozi, M., Vinjimoor, A., Favaro, P., Pirsiavash, H.: Boosting self-supervised learning via knowledge transfer. In: IEEE Conference on Computer Vision and Pattern Recognition, pp. 9359–9367 (2018)
14. Pathak, D., Krähenbühl, P., Donahue, J., Darrell, T., Efros, A.A.: Context encoders: Feature learning by inpainting. In: IEEE Conference on Computer Vision and Pattern Recognition, pp. 2536–2544 (2016)
15. Roth, H.R., et al.: DeepOrgan: multi-level deep convolutional networks for automated pancreas segmentation. In: Navab, N., Hornegger, J., Wells, W.M., Frangi, A.F. (eds.) MICCAI 2015. LNCS, vol. 9349, pp. 556–564. Springer, Cham (2015). https://doi.org/10.1007/978-3-319-24553-9_68
16. Spitzer, H., Kiwitz, K., Amunts, K., Harmeling, S., Dickscheid, T.: Improving cytoarchitectonic segmentation of human brain areas with self-supervised siamese networks. In: Frangi, A.F., Schnabel, J.A., Davatzikos, C., Alberola-López, C., Fichtinger, G. (eds.) MICCAI 2018. LNCS, vol. 11072, pp. 663–671. Springer, Cham (2018). https://doi.org/10.1007/978-3-030-00931-1_76
17. Wei, C., et al.: Iterative reorganization with weak spatial constraints: solving arbitrary Jigsaw puzzles for unsupervised representation learning. In: IEEE Conference on Computer Vision and Pattern Recognition, pp. 1910–1919 (2019)
18. Zhang, P., Wang, F., Zheng, Y.: Self supervised deep representation learning for fine-grained body part recognition. In: International Symposium on Biomedical Imaging, pp. 578–582 (2017)

19. Zhou, Z., et al.: Models genesis: generic autodidactic models for 3D medical image analysis. In: International Conference on Medical Image Computing & Computer Assisted Intervention, pp. 384–393 (2019)
20. Zhuang, X., Li, Y., Hu, Y., Ma, K., Yang, Y., Zheng, Y.: Self-supervised feature learning for 3D medical images by playing a Rubik's cube. In: Shen, D., et al. (eds.) MICCAI 2019. LNCS, vol. 11767, pp. 420–428. Springer, Cham (2019). https://doi.org/10.1007/978-3-030-32251-9_46

Robust Medical Image Segmentation from Non-expert Annotations with Tri-network

Tianwei Zhang[1], Lequan Yu[2], Na Hu[3], Su Lv[3], and Shi Gu[1(✉)]

[1] Department of Computer and Engineering,
University of Electronic Science and Technology of China, Chengdu, China
gus@uestc.edu.cn
[2] Department of Radiation Oncology, Stanford University, Stanford, CA 94305, USA
[3] Department of Radiology/Huaxi MR Research Center (HMRRC),
West China Hospital of Sichuan University, Chengdu, China

Abstract. Deep convolutional neural networks (CNNs) have achieved commendable results on a variety of medical image segmentation tasks. However, CNNs usually require a large amount of training samples with accurate annotations, which are extremely difficult and expensive to obtain in medical image analysis field. In practice, we notice that the junior trainees after training can label medical images in some medical image segmentation applications. These *non-expert annotations* are more easily accessible and can be regarded as a source of weak annotation to guide network learning. In this paper, we propose a novel Tri-network learning framework to alleviate the problem of insufficient accurate annotations in medical segmentation tasks by utilizing the non-expert annotations. To be specific, we maintain three networks in our framework, and each pair of networks alternatively select informative samples for the third network learning, according to the consensus and difference between their predictions. The three networks are jointly optimized in such a collaborative manner. We evaluated our method on real and simulated non-expert annotated datasets. The experiment results show that our method effectively mines informative information from the non-expert annotations for improved segmentation performance and outperforms other competing methods.

Keywords: Non-expert annotations · Tri-network · Collaborative learning · Segmentation

1 Introduction

Anatomical structure segmentation is one of the key problems in medical image analysis field. In the past years, deep convolutional neural networks (CNNs) have demonstrated promising successes in medical image segmentation tasks [2,8,13]. The high performance of CNNs often relies on a large amount of labeled training data. However, for medical image segmentation tasks, it is time-consuming

---

T. Zhang and L. Yu—Equal contribution.

© Springer Nature Switzerland AG 2020
A. L. Martel et al. (Eds.): MICCAI 2020, LNCS 12264, pp. 249–258, 2020.
https://doi.org/10.1007/978-3-030-59719-1_25

and expensive to acquire enough reliable annotations, as the annotations are needed to delineate by experienced experts in a slice-by-slice manner [6]. In clinical practice, we noticed that junior trainees can label images after training by a professional doctor. These *non-expert annotations*, which are typically more easily accessible, can be regarded as a source of weak annotation that provides coarsely spatial information but lacks accuracy in detail. Thus a natural question that arises here is whether we can utilize these non-expert annotations to train a segmentation network to alleviate the scarcity of accurate annotation in medical image segmentation tasks. As directly training neural networks with noisy annotations would severely degrade the performance of networks [17], there comes up with the demand of designing special learning strategies that can mitigate the impact of noise labels for deep network training [4,5,9,11,15].

Arpit *et al.* [1] demonstrated that deep networks could benefit by following an 'easy-to-difficult' training procedure under the assumption that the samples with small loss were more likely to be clean. Further, Han *et al.* [4] proposed a framework that co-trained two networks simultaneously and updated each network alternately by the samples with small loss in the other one. Specific for the medical image analysis tasks, Xue *et al.* [16] proposed a sample re-weighting framework for noisy-labeled skin lesion classification, where they removed the high-loss samples during the network training and employed a data re-weighting scheme to weight every reserved sample in one mini-batch. Dgani *et al.* [3] added an additional noise layer to the network for the classification of breast microcalcifications, and Lehtinen *et al.* [7] proposed a learning-from-noisy-sample method and applied it to MR image reconstruction from randomly-sampled data. Although effective on image classification and detection tasks, these methods cannot be straightforwardly applied to the segmentation task, because the noise in image segmentation stands out within the image locally in addition to its label on the global level. As an extension from global label to spatial map, Zhu *et al.* [18] introduced a label quality evaluation strategy to enable neural networks to measure the quality of labels automatically, and Mirikharaji *et al.* [10] proposed to generate a weight map to indicate the more useful pixels and alleviated the influence of the noisy pixels by re-weighting them. Most of previous works provided weight strategy on samples and spatial information partially based on the observation that lower error indicates more informative samples. However, this assumption is arguable for the segmentation task considering that the most informative locations are the boundaries, which may carry a high noise level across different samples. Thus it is necessary to refine the strategy of selecting samples and pixels for the segmentation task by balancing the choices on noise-level and informativity as they are no longer monotonously related due to the nature of segmentation.

In this paper, we aim to develop a learning framework to use noisy non-expert annotations to reduce high-quality annotation effort and combat the inherent noise in real clinical annotations. Following the inspiration of collaborative learning strategy, we propose an efficient framework by extending the Co-teaching [4] to a Tri-teaching network, where two networks jointly select

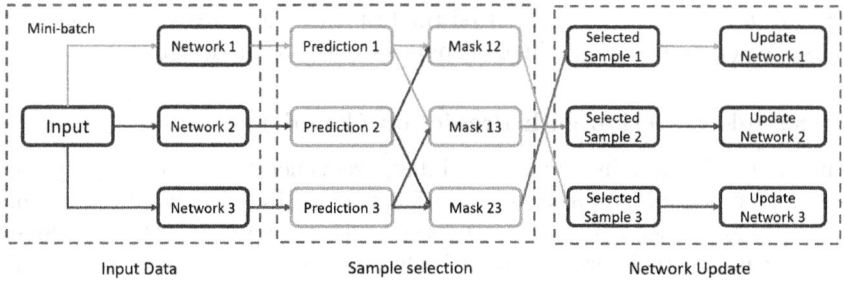

Fig. 1. The pipeline of our Tri-network framework for medical image segmentation from non-expert annotations. We show the procedure in one iteration for illustration.

samples and voxels under the novel strategies designed for two "teachers" rather than one. The introduction of an additional network here not only stabilizes the selecting procedure but also allows for the strategic space to balance noise-level and informativity. To be specific, we train three networks simultaneously and each pair of networks select informative "reliable" samples according to their predictions to guide the third network learning in each iteration. To facilitate the selection of "reliable" samples, we design two feasible strategies according to the consensus and difference between two network outputs. After that, the selected samples are fed into the third network to update its parameters. In this way, three networks jointly learn from the non-expert annotations in a collaborative manner. We evaluate our method on real and simulated non-expert annotation datasets, *i.e.*, stroke lesion segmentation dataset with real noise and public organ segmentation dataset with simulated noise. The results show that our method can effectively use non-expert annotations to improve segmentation performance and outperforms other competing methods.

2 Method

2.1 Overview

We illustrate the training procedure of Tri-network in Fig. 1. The key idea here is to train three networks simultaneously, where each pair of networks guide the third network to mine useful and reliable information from the non-expert annotations. Given a mini-batch of input data, we separately feed them into three networks (*e.g.*, U-Net) at the same time, and acquire three different prediction maps and the corresponding pixel-wise loss maps respecting to the noisy annotations. Next, for each pair of networks (*e.g.*, Network 1 and Network 2), we select those reliable pixels based on the output of two networks with the proposed sample selection strategy and generate one mask (*e.g.*, Mask 12) to represent those selected pixels. After that, we feed the mask to the third network (*e.g.*, Network 3) and guide the network to utilize that useful information for parameter updating. The same procedure is repeated for each network at each training iteration. In the testing stage, we feed the test data into three trained networks and use the ensemble of the three outputs as the final prediction.

2.2 Sample Selection with Prediction Confidence

As mentioned above, in network training, we generate a mask to represent selected pixel samples from each pair of networks. In other words, those useful samples are which two source networks consider more valuable according to the confidence of their predictions. We then use this mask to guide the training process of the third network so that it can focus more on these valuable pixels, thereby reducing the impact of noisy annotations. Here we propose two sample selection criteria, both of which prove to be effective in dealing with the segmentation problem with non-expert noisy annotations.

Consensus-Based Selection. The first sample selection strategy is based on *consensus* of network predictions. For each mini-batch data, the pair of networks produce two pixel-wise prediction maps and we further get the corresponding confidence map (or loss map) of each network by calculating loss for each pixel between network prediction and the noisy annotations. For each loss map, we sort those pixel-wise loss values and set a loss value threshold to get a binary confidence map B, where one represents T percentage of small-loss pixels (*i.e.*, high confidence) and zero indicates the loss values of corresponding pixels are greater than the specific ratio (*i.e.*, low confidence). Based on the binary confidence map B_1 and B_2 of two networks, we further calculate one binary *consensus map* $M_{cons} = (B_1 == B_2)$. There are two kinds of pixels in the consensus map: pixels with high prediction confidence (*i.e.*, low loss value) in both two networks and pixels with low prediction confidence (*i.e.*, high loss value) in both two networks. The first kind of pixels can be regarded as "clean" pixels and the second kind of pixels can be regarded as "informative" pixels. We feed both two kinds of pixels into the third network and calculate the loss for back-propagation.

Difference-Based Selection. The second sample selection strategy is based on *difference* of network predictions. Similar to the consensus strategy, we first calculate the pixel-wise confidence map (or loss map) for each network prediction. And then we calculate the loss difference map of two networks by subtracting the two loss maps and take the absolute values. In this strategy, we mine useful knowledge by choosing pixels that are greater than a specific proportion, *i.e.*, T percentage of the large-loss-difference, in the above loss difference map and generate a binary *difference map* M_{diff}. Finally, we feed the binary difference map into the third network and update its parameter with these pixels selected by the other two networks which are the same as before.

2.3 Technical Details

The framework was implemented with PyTorch on a TITAN Xp GPU. The three networks in our framework share the same network architecture, *i.e.*, U-Net [12].

The whole framework was optimized with the SGD optimizer with a momentum of 0.9 and a weight decay of 0.0001. The network was trained for 200 epochs with learning rate 0.001 until convergence. To fit the limited GPU memory for training three networks simultaneously, we set the mini-batch size as 8 and resized all the input images to 256×256 pixels. We generate the confidence map (or loss map) by calculating the cross entropy loss for each pixel, and calculate the final loss by averaging the CE loss on selected pixels for back-propagation. For the sample selection strategies, we use all pixels to update all networks at the beginning, and then gradually adjust the specific ratio T during training. Specifically, in the Consensus-based strategy, we set the ratio T as 1 at the beginning, and then linearly decreased it to 50% within 300 iterations and keep it unchanged during the remaining iterations. While in the Difference-based strategy, we set T as 0 at the beginning, and then linearly increased to 50% within the first 300 iterations.

3   Experiment

We evaluated our method on two datasets. We first validated the effectiveness of our proposed method on the stroke lesion dataset with real non-expert annotations and further analyzed the impact of noise level and ratio on a public organ segmentation dataset with simulated non-expert annotations.

3.1   Experiment Setting

Real Clinical Dataset. The clinical stroke lesion segmentation dataset was collected from a multi-modal imaging database of patients with suspected AIS in West China Hospital. This dataset contained all MRI scan sequences of 186 Stroke emergency patients, and the image modality used in our experiments is the FLAIR sequence. We randomly divided the dataset into training set (150 scans) and testing set (36 scans) for our experiments. To acquire the non-expert annotations on the training set, we recruited a junior trainee to annotate all the data after simple training. For the testing data, we invited a six-years-experienced neuroradiologist to annotate the stroke lesion regions as the ground truth.

Simulated Dataset. We employed the public dataset JSRT [14] as a multi-class classification dataset to simulate noisy annotations to further evaluate and analyze the capacity of our method. JSRT has three types of organ annotation information: Lungs, Hearts, and Clavicles. The total of 247 X-ray scans was split into 165 training scans and 82 evaluation scans. Considering that the manual noise of organ segmentation mainly is the inaccurate contours, we simulated the noisy non-expert annotations by randomly conducting morphological changes to the original clean annotations. Specifically, the simulated noise was generated by randomly eroding or dilating the contours of accurate annotations.

Table 1. Comparison with other methods on the clinical stroke dataset.

Method	Dice coefficient[%]
U-Net [12]	62.18
Ensemble U-Net	63.90
Xue *et al.* [16]	64.92
Co-teaching [4]	64.04
Tri-network (Consensus)	**68.12**
Tri-network (D-value)	67.88

Experiment Setting. We trained our framework on training data with non-expert noisy annotations and evaluated the model on testing data by the Dice coefficient score between the predicted segmentation and the accurate ground truth annotations. We compared our Tri-network with multiple recent frameworks including vanilla U-Net [12], ensemble model of U-Net, the loss re-weighting method [16] and Co-teaching [4] under the same setting. For the JSRT dataset, we reported the average results of 5 runs with random data splitting per run.

3.2   Experiments on Real Clinical Stroke Dataset

Quantitative Analysis. We first evaluated the model performance and compared with other related methods on the clinical stroke lesion segmentation dataset (see Table 1). As a baseline, the single U-Net trained with non-expert annotations achieved 62.18% Dice coefficient score on the test data. Among the compared methods, our Tri-network with Consensus-based selection achieved the highest Dice coefficient of 68.12% and Tri-network with Difference-based selection achieved a slightly lower score of 67.88%, both of which outperformed the Ensemble U-net (63.9%), Xue et al. (64.92%), and Co-teaching (64.04%). Compared to the baseline U-Net, all the other methods improved at a certain margin, demonstrating that it was feasible and effective to utilize specialized learning algorithms to train networks with noisy segmentation. For our Tri-network, its improvement over the U-Net (*Ensemble U-Net*) indicated that the selection procedures made a difference besides the ensemble of models. In addition, it also outperformed the sample re-weighting based method [16] and Co-teaching [4], supporting our claim that the training and selection procedure of Tri-network was more robust and adaptive to the segmentation problem.

To further investigate whether the improvement over Co-teaching was solely due to the increased number of networks, we re-trained the Tri-network with degenerated consensus-based sample selection strategy where we only selected small or large loss pixels rather than both. We found that the training process was difficult to converge for the small-loss selection and resulted at 64.27% Dice coefficient score for the large-loss selection. The divergence with small-loss selection was probably caused by the fact that small loss pixels were mainly in

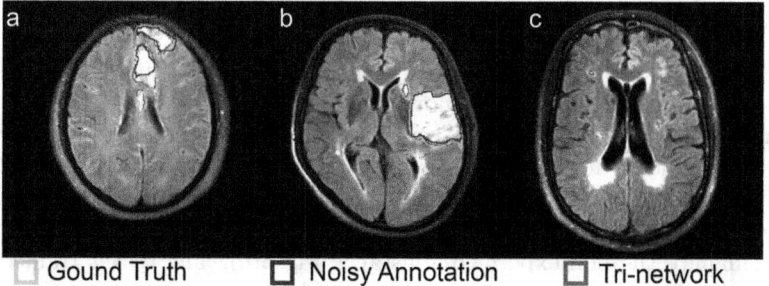

Fig. 2. Visual examples on the clinical dataset. The green, red, and blue colors denote the ground truth annotation, Tri-network, and the noisy annotation, respectively. Our method generates more accurate contours than non-expert annotation (a) and successfully identify small lesions (b & c). (Color figure online)

the center of the lesion, while the most informative samples for segmentation tasks were the pixels near the boundaries. This also supports our early claim in the introduction that the spatial information with a sample distinguishes the segmentation problem from the classification problem. The large-loss selection improved over the baseline and provided a comparable result with Co-teaching approaches, indicating that the efficiency of integrated rules of Tri-networks was beyond the degenerated rule that simply extended Co-teaching to "Tri-teaching" with model ensemble.

Overall, the comparisons we have done prove that both the extension to three network components and integrated sample section strategies and necessary and effective for segmentation with noise annotations.

Qualitative Analysis. In addition to the quantitative comparison, we showed vivid segmentation results in Fig. 2, where the green, red, and blue color denoted the ground truth annotation, Tri-network segmentation, and the non-expert annotation, respectively. Due to the lack of professional medical knowledge, the non-expert annotators often generate annotation noise, including marking areas that are not lesions, missing areas that are lesions, and delineating inaccurate contours of the marked lesions. Especially, in the task of stroke segmentation in FLAIR sequence, where the lesion area was imaged as high signals, we noticed that the non-experts often missed the tiny lesions around the demyelinating area and also delineated inaccurate contours of relative large stroke areas (compare the green v.s. the blue contours in Fig. 2). As we can see from the left panel, the contour of our segmented results was more accurate than the non-expert annotation. And the mid and right panels showed that our framework successfully recognized small lesions near demyelinating area that the non-expert could miss.

3.3 Experiments on Simulated Noisy Dataset

While we have proved the feasibility and effectiveness of our model on the stroke lesion segmentation dataset, the noise-level on this real dataset was fixed. To explore the model generalizability and its capacity to handle different levels of noise, we conducted additional experiments on another public X-ray dataset with simulated noisy label on different levels and ratios. We randomly selected 75% training samples and further randomly eroded/dilated the contour with 5–10 pixels to simulate the non-expert circumstance Fig. 3(c). The U-Net trained with clean labels (fist row in Table 2) performed fairly well and we set it as the upper bound of performance here. Compared with the U-Net trained with clean labels, the performance of U-Net trained with noise label severely decreased on all three organs, especially on the hardest small clavicle. Our method achieved 6.04% and 6.62% average dice improvement with the consensus-based and difference-based sample selection strategy, respectively, while the other learning from noisy label methods produced slightly better performance than the baseline model on this dataset with simulated noise Fig. 3(d). Especially for the clavicle segmentation, our Tri-network achieves about 11% dice score improvement. The average Hausdorff distance for lung, heart, and clavicle is 6.16, 4.83, and 6.63 pixels, respectively. These comparison results demonstrated the effectiveness of our method to utilize noisy annotations on simulated data again.

Table 2. Comparison with other methods on JSRT dataset on Dice metric [%].

Method	Lungs	Heart	Clavicles	Mean
U-Net (no noise)	97.55	94.82	92.35	94.90
U-Net	83.35	86.52	53.29	74.39
Ensemble U-Net	84.52	86.19	58.81	76.51
Xue et al. [16]	85.17	86.38	57.11	76.22
Co-teaching [4]	85.06	86.64	57.78	76.49
Tri-network (Consensus)	87.79	88.54	**64.98**	80.43
Tri-network (D-value)	**88.59**	**90.37**	64.07	**81.01**

We also studied the performance of our method under different noisy level and noisy rate. Specifically, we studied two noise levels: low noise level with morphological change within 1 to 5 pixels and high noise level with morphological change within 5 to 10 pixels. For each noisy level, we evaluated our method with noisy rate at 25%, 50%, and 75%, where we conducted random morphological operations for 25%, 50%, and 75% training samples. The clavicle segmentation results are shown in Fig. 4. Compared with U-Net baseline, our method improved the performance under different settings. Overall, our method outperforms other compared methods and the improvement is more obvious at a high noisy rate.

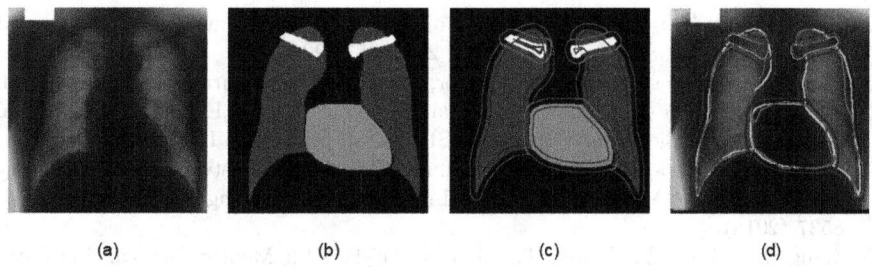

Fig. 3. Simulated noise example and visual result of JSRT Dataset. (a) Original X-ray image. (b) Ground Truth annotation. (c) Two kinds of simulated noise: red contour represents dilation and blue contour represents erosion. (d) Visual results of segmentation results: the green, red, and blue colors denote the ground truth annotation, Tri-network, and the noisy annotation, respectively. (Color figure online)

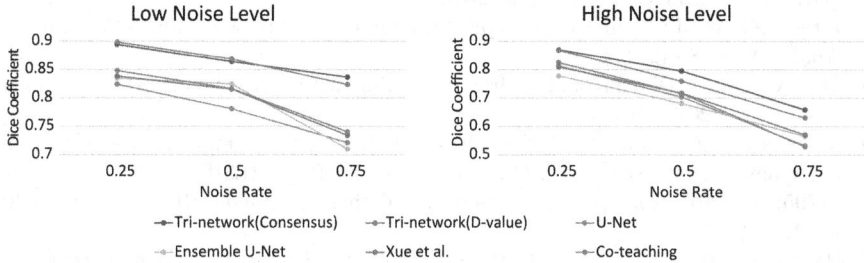

Fig. 4. The performance of clavicle segmentation of different methods on JSRT dataset with different noise settings.

4   Conclusion

In this work, we propose a Tri-network framework with integrated sample selection strategies to tackle the problem of leveraging non-expert annotations for robust medical image segmentation. The Tri-network trains three deep networks simultaneously and employs each pair of networks to guide the third network to mine useful and informative samples during training. The whole framework is optimized in a collaborative manner. As the key part of our framework, we develop two effective sample selection strategies according to the consensus or difference of two network predictions. We verify the effectiveness of our proposed framework on both real non-expert annotated dataset and simulated noisy dataset. The experimental results demonstrate that our method can improve the performance of the network trained with the non-expert annotations and outperform other competing methods.

References

1. Arpit, D., et al.: A closer look at memorization in deep networks 2017. arXiv preprint arXiv:1706.05394 (1938)

2. Ching, T., et al.: Opportunities and obstacles for deep learning in biology and medicine. J. Roy. Soc. Interf. **15**(141), 20170387 (2018)

3. Dgani, Y., Greenspan, H., Goldberger, J.: Training a neural network based on unreliable human annotation of medical images. In: 2018 IEEE 15th International Symposium on Biomedical Imaging (ISBI 2018), pp. 39–42. IEEE (2018)

4. Han, B., et al.: Co-teaching: robust training of deep neural networks with extremely noisy labels. In: Advances in Neural Information Processing Systems, pp. 8527–8537 (2018)

5. Jiang, L., Zhou, Z., Leung, T., Li, L.J., Fei-Fei, L.: MentorNet: learning data-driven curriculum for very deep neural networks on corrupted labels. arXiv preprint arXiv:1712.05055 (2017)

6. Kohli, M.D., Summers, R.M., Geis, J.R.: Medical image data and datasets in the era of machine learning–whitepaper from the 2016 C-MIMI meeting dataset session. J. Digit. Imaging **30**(4), 392–399 (2017)

7. Lehtinen, J., et al.: Noise2noise: learning image restoration without clean data. arXiv preprint arXiv:1803.04189 (2018)

8. Litjens, G., et al.: A survey on deep learning in medical image analysis. Med. Image Anal. **42**, 60–88 (2017)

9. Ma, X., et al.: Dimensionality-driven learning with noisy labels. arXiv preprint arXiv:1806.02612 (2018)

10. Mirikharaji, Z., Yan, Y., Hamarneh, G.: Learning to segment skin lesions from noisy annotations. In: Wang, Q., et al. (eds.) DART/MIL3ID - 2019. LNCS, vol. 11795, pp. 207–215. Springer, Cham (2019). https://doi.org/10.1007/978-3-030-33391-1_24

11. Patrini, G., Rozza, A., Krishna Menon, A., Nock, R., Qu, L.: Making deep neural networks robust to label noise: a loss correction approach. In: Proceedings of the IEEE Conference on Computer Vision and Pattern Recognition, pp. 1944–1952 (2017)

12. Ronneberger, O., Fischer, P., Brox, T.: U-Net: convolutional networks for biomedical image segmentation. In: Navab, N., Hornegger, J., Wells, W.M., Frangi, A.F. (eds.) MICCAI 2015. LNCS, vol. 9351, pp. 234–241. Springer, Cham (2015). https://doi.org/10.1007/978-3-319-24574-4_28

13. Shen, D., Wu, G., Suk, H.I.: Deep learning in medical image analysis. Ann. Rev. Biomed. Eng. **19**, 221–248 (2017)

14. Shiraishi, J., et al.: Development of a digital image database for chest radiographs with and without a lung nodule. Am. J. Roentgenol. **174**(1), 71–74 (2000)

15. Tanaka, D., Ikami, D., Yamasaki, T., Aizawa, K.: Joint optimization framework for learning with noisy labels. In: Proceedings of the IEEE Conference on Computer Vision and Pattern Recognition, pp. 5552–5560 (2018)

16. Xue, C., Dou, Q., Shi, X., Chen, H., Heng, P.A.: Robust learning at noisy labeled medical images: applied to skin lesion classification. In: 2019 IEEE 16th International Symposium on Biomedical Imaging (ISBI 2019), pp. 1280–1283. IEEE (2019)

17. Zhang, C., Bengio, S., Hardt, M., Recht, B., Vinyals, O.: Understanding deep learning requires rethinking generalization. arXiv preprint arXiv:1611.03530 (2016)

18. Zhu, H., Shi, J., Wu, J.: Pick-and-learn: automatic quality evaluation for noisy-labeled image segmentation. In: Shen, D., et al. (eds.) MICCAI 2019. LNCS, vol. 11769, pp. 576–584. Springer, Cham (2019). https://doi.org/10.1007/978-3-030-32226-7_64

Robust Fusion of Probability Maps

Benoît Audelan[1]([✉]), Dimitri Hamzaoui[1], Sarah Montagne[2],
Raphaële Renard-Penna[2], and Hervé Delingette[1]

[1] Université Côte d'Azur, Inria, Epione Project-Team,
Sophia Antipolis, France
benoit.audelan@inria.fr

[2] Département de Radiologie, CHU La Pitié Salpétrière/Tenon, Sorbonne Université,
Paris, France

Abstract. The fusion of probability maps is required when trying to analyse a collection of image labels or probability maps produced by several segmentation algorithms or human raters. The challenge is to weight properly the combination of maps in order to reflect the agreement among raters, the presence of outliers and the spatial uncertainty in the consensus. In this paper, we address several shortcomings of prior work in continuous label fusion. We introduce a novel approach to jointly estimate a reliable consensus map and assess the production of outliers and the confidence in each rater. Our probabilistic model is based on Student's t-distributions allowing local estimates of raters' performances. The introduction of bias and spatial priors leads to proper rater bias estimates and a control over the smoothness of the consensus map. Image intensity information is incorporated by geodesic distance transform for binary masks. Finally, we propose an approach to cluster raters based on variational boosting thus producing possibly several alternative consensus maps. Our approach was successfully tested on the MICCAI 2016 MS lesions dataset, on MR prostate delineations and on deep learning based segmentation predictions of lung nodules from the LIDC dataset.

Keywords: Image segmentation · Data fusion · Consensus · Mixture

1 Introduction

The fusion of probability maps is required to solve at least two important problems related to image segmentation. The former is to establish the underlying ground truth segmentation given several binary or multi-class segmentations provided by human raters or segmentation algorithms (e.g.. in the framework of multi-atlas segmentations). This is especially important because estimating a consensus segmentation and the inter-rater variability is the gold standard in

---

Electronic supplementary material The online version of this chapter (https://doi.org/10.1007/978-3-030-59719-1_26) contains supplementary material, which is available to authorized users.

© Springer Nature Switzerland AG 2020
A. L. Martel et al. (Eds.): MICCAI 2020, LNCS 12264, pp. 259–268, 2020.
https://doi.org/10.1007/978-3-030-59719-1_26

assessing the performance of a segmentation algorithm in the absence of physical or virtual phantoms. The second related problem is the fusion of probability maps that are outputted by several segmentation algorithms such as neural networks. Indeed, it has been shown experimentally that combining the outputs of several segmentation algorithms often leads to improved performances [11].

Prior work has mainly focused on the fusion of binary masks, one of the most well known method being the STAPLE algorithm [14]. In this case, the raters' binary segmentations are explained by Bernoulli distributions from the consensus segmentation and an Expectation-Maximization (EM) scheme allows to jointly build a consensus and estimate the raters' performances. Among known shortcomings of STAPLE, there is the constraint of having only global performance estimations of raters thus ignoring local variations [3,5]. One proposed solution [5] is to perform a STAPLE in a sliding window fashion or to extend the performance parameters to the pixel level [3]. Another limitation is that STAPLE only considers binary masks as input thus being agnostic to the image content and especially to the presence of large image gradients [4,10]. In [10], it was proposed to include in the STAPLE approach simple appearance models such as Gaussian distributions for the background and foreground, but this approach is only applicable to simple salient structures.

The extension of the STAPLE algorithm for continuous labels was proposed in [15] where raters' performances are captured by a set of biases and variances while assuming a Gaussian distribution for the raters' continuous labels. In [16], it was observed that to properly estimate raters' biases, the introduction of a prior was required. Furthermore, no spatial prior is used to regularize the consensus estimate and raters' performances are assumed to be global to the whole image.

In this paper, we introduce a comprehensive probabilistic framework that addresses many shortcomings of prior work on the fusion of continuous or categorical labels. First, we allow for a spatial assessment of raters' performances by replacing Gaussian with Student's t-likelihoods. Thus, image regions that largely differ from the consensus segmentation will be considered as outliers. Second, we introduce a bias prior and a label smoothness prior defined as a generalized linear model of spatially smooth kernels. Third, the proposed framework is posed within a proper metric, the Hellinger distance, in the space of probability maps through the introduction of a square root link function. In addition, probability maps are created from segmentation binary masks by using geodesic distance instead of Euclidean distance in order to take into account the image content. Finally, we address the unexplored issue of dissensus rather than consensus among raters. Indeed, fusing several probability maps into a single consensus map may not be meaningful when consistent patterns appear among raters. In [9], the worse performing raters' masks were removed from the consensus estimation process at each iteration. In [6], a comparison framework for the raters' maps based on the continuous STAPLE parameters was developed. In our approach, several consensus are iteratively estimated through a technique similar to variational boosting [12] and clusters of raters are identified.

We use variational Bayes (VB) inference to estimate the latent posterior distributions of variables and the unknown hyperparameters. The method has been applied on two databases of human expert segmentations of prostate and multiple sclerosis (MS) lesions and on the fusion of deep learning probability maps to segment lung nodules. We show that local variations of raters' performances were successfully identified and that improved segmentation performances were obtained after fusing probability maps.

2 Robust Estimate of Consensus Probability Map

2.1 Probabilistic Framework

We are given as input a set of P probability maps $\mathbf{D}_n^p$, each map consisting of N categorical probability values in K classes, i.e. $\mathbf{D}_n^p \in S^{K-1} \in \mathbb{R}^K$ where S^{K-1} is the K unit simplex space such that $\sum_{k=1}^K \mathbf{D}_{nk}^p = 1$. Our objective is to estimate a consensus probability map $\mathbf{T}_n \in [0,1]^K$, $\sum_{k=1}^K \mathbf{T}_{nk} = 1$ over the input maps.

Each probability map is supposed to be derived from a consensus map through a random process. We consider a link function $F(\mathbf{p}) \in \mathbb{R}^K$, $\mathbf{p} \in S^{K-1}$ mapping probability S^{K-1} space into the Euclidean space and its inverse $F^{-1}(\mathbf{r})$ such that $F^{-1}(F(\mathbf{p})) = \mathbf{p}$. We write $\tilde{\mathbf{D}}_n^p = F(\mathbf{D}_n^p)$ and $\tilde{\mathbf{T}}_n = F(\mathbf{T}_n)$.

In [15,16], the observed probability maps $\tilde{\mathbf{D}}^p$ were supposed to be Gaussian distributed. In order to get a robust estimate of the consensus, i.e. to be able to discard locally the influence of outliers , we replace the Gaussian assumption by a Student's t-distribution written as a Gaussian scale mixture:

$$p(\tilde{\mathbf{D}}_n^p|\tilde{\mathbf{T}}_n) = \int_0^\infty \mathcal{N}(\tilde{\mathbf{D}}_n^p; \tilde{\mathbf{T}}_n + \mathbf{b}_p, \frac{\mathbf{\Sigma}_p}{\tau_n^p}) \, \mathrm{Ga}(\tau_n^p; \frac{\nu_p}{2}, \frac{\nu_p}{2}) \, d\tau \,, \qquad (1)$$

where the bias $\mathbf{b}_p$ and covariance $\mathbf{\Sigma}_p$ characterize the performance of the rater p, and where $\mathrm{Ga}\left(\tau; \frac{\nu_p}{2}, \frac{\nu_p}{2}\right)$ is the Gamma distribution. The scale factors $\mathcal{T}^p = \{\tau_n^p\} \in \mathbb{R}^{+N}$ are additional latent variables that weight separately each data point $\tilde{\mathbf{D}}_n^p$ allowing to take into account local variations in the performances of rater p. ν_p^{-1} characterizes the amount of data outliers that it is necessary to discard in the estimation of the consensus. Finally, instead of the logit function as in [13], we propose to use the square root function $F_{\mathrm{sqrt}}((\mathbf{p}_1, \mathbf{p}_2)^T) = (\sqrt{\mathbf{p}_1}, \sqrt{\mathbf{p}_2})^T$, and its inverse $F_{\mathrm{sqrt}}^{-1}(\mathbf{r}) = \left(\frac{\mathbf{r}_1^2}{\mathbf{r}_1^2 + \mathbf{r}_2^2}, \frac{\mathbf{r}_2^2}{\mathbf{r}_1^2 + \mathbf{r}_2^2}\right)^T$ as a link function. By doing so, the probability $p(\mathbf{D}_n^p|\mathbf{T}_n) \propto \exp\left(-\frac{H^2(\mathbf{D}_n^p, \mathbf{T}_n)}{\sigma_p}\right)$ is related to the Hellinger distance $H^2(\mathbf{D}_n^p, \mathbf{T}_n)$ on the space of probability distributions. Maximizing the likelihood reverts to minimizing distances between probability distributions.

Bias Prior. In [16] it was showed that if no prior is provided on the bias, its estimation is undetermined. Therefore we define a zero mean Gaussian prior on the bias with precision β, i.e. $p(\mathbf{b}_p|\beta) = \mathcal{N}(\mathbf{b}; 0, \beta^{-1}\mathbf{I}_K)$.

Consensus Smoothness Prior. A reasonable assumption is that segmentation probability maps are smooth. In [14], for categorical labels, a Markov random field (MRF) was introduced to enforce the connexity of discrete label map. Yet, the MRF hyperparameter β has to be set manually because its inference cannot be done in closed form. For continuous labels, prior work [15] did not include any smoothness prior. We introduce a smoothness prior defined as a generalized linear model of a set of L spatially smooth functions $\{\Phi_l(\mathbf{x})\}$, whose hyperparameters can be estimated. If $\mathbf{x}_n \in \mathbb{R}^d$ is the position of voxel n, then the prior on the variables $\tilde{\mathbf{T}}_n$ is defined as $p(\tilde{\mathbf{T}}_n|\mathbf{W}_l) = \mathcal{N}(\tilde{\mathbf{T}}_n; \sum_{l=1}^{L} \Phi_l(\mathbf{x}_n)\mathbf{W}_l; \mathbf{\Sigma}_T\mathbf{I}_K)$ where $\mathbf{W}_l$ are vectors of size K and where $\mathbf{\Sigma}_T \in \mathbb{R}^+$ is the prior variance. For computation convenience, we write the prior using $\mathbf{W}_k \in \mathbb{R}^L$, such that $p(\tilde{\mathbf{T}}_{nk}|\mathbf{W}_k) = \mathcal{N}(\tilde{\mathbf{T}}_{nk}; \mathbf{W}_k^T\mathbf{\Phi}_n; \mathbf{\Sigma}_T)$ where $\mathbf{\Phi}_n^T = (\Phi_1(\mathbf{x}_n), \cdots, \Phi_L(\mathbf{x}_n))$. The weights $\mathbf{W}_k$ are gathered in a weight matrix $\mathbf{W} \in \mathbb{R}^{K \times L}$ such that we can write $p(\tilde{\mathbf{T}}_n|\mathbf{W}) = \mathcal{N}(\tilde{\mathbf{T}}_n; \mathbf{W}\mathbf{\Phi}_n; \mathbf{\Sigma}_T\mathbf{I}_K)$. The weights $\mathbf{W}_k$ are equipped with a zero mean Gaussian prior and precision α: $p(\mathbf{W}_k|\alpha) = \mathcal{N}(\mathbf{W}_k; 0, \alpha^{-1}\mathbf{I}_L)$. The graphical model of the framework is shown in Fig. 1a.

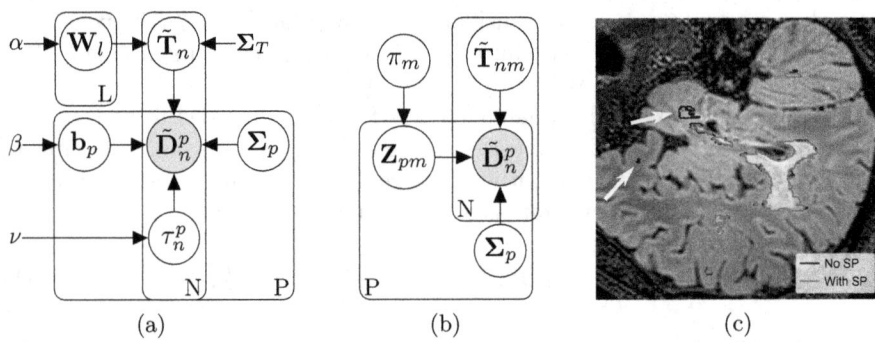

(a)   (b)   (c)

Fig. 1. Graphical model of the robust fusion framework (1a) and of the mixture of consensuses (1b). Effect of the spatial prior on the consensus smoothness (1c).

Generation of Probabilistic Maps. Probabilistic maps are typically outputted by segmentation algorithms, such as neural networks. They may be generated from binary masks using log-odds maps [13] computed as the sigmoid of signed distance maps from each binary structure. Yet, this approach ignores the underlying intensity image. We propose to compute a signed geodesic distance instead of Euclidean distance in order to take image intensity information into account, hence addressing a known shortcoming of STAPLE [4,10]. It is defined as a combination of the Euclidean distance and intensity gradient information [8].

2.2 Bayesian Inference

To estimate the consensus and learn the parameters governing raters' performances, we want to maximize the marginal log likelihood:

$$\log p(\tilde{\mathbf{D}}|\beta, \nu_p, \boldsymbol{\Sigma}_p) = \int_{\mathbb{R}^N} \left(\sum_{p=1}^{P} \int_{\mathbb{R}^K} \log p(\tilde{\mathbf{D}}_n^p, \tilde{\mathbf{T}}_n, \mathbf{b}_p | \beta, \nu_p, \boldsymbol{\Sigma}_p) \, d\mathbf{b}_p \right) d\tilde{\mathbf{T}}_n . \quad (2)$$

Previous approaches maximized this quantity using an EM algorithm requiring to compute the posterior probability $p(\tilde{\mathbf{T}}_n | \tilde{\mathbf{D}}_n^p, \mathbf{b}_p, \boldsymbol{\Sigma}_p)$. It cannot be computed in closed form when replacing Gaussians with Student's t-distributions. Instead, we use a VB approach where a factorized posterior over all latent variables is assumed: $p(\tilde{\mathbf{T}}, \mathbf{b}, \tau | \tilde{\mathbf{D}}) \approx q_{\tilde{\mathbf{T}}}(\tilde{\mathbf{T}}) q_{\mathbf{b}}(\mathbf{b}) q_\tau(\tau)$. Those approximation functions are estimated through a mean field approach which leads to closed form expressions.

The posterior approximation for the consensus map $\tilde{\mathbf{T}}_n$ can be written as a Gaussian distribution $q_{\tilde{\mathbf{T}}_n}(\tilde{\mathbf{T}}_n) = \mathcal{N}(\tilde{\mathbf{T}}_n; \mu_{\tilde{\mathbf{T}}_n}, \boldsymbol{\Sigma}_{\tilde{\mathbf{T}}_n})$ with $\boldsymbol{\Sigma}_{\tilde{\mathbf{T}}_n} = \left[\sum_{p=1}^{P} \hat{\tau}_n^p (\boldsymbol{\Sigma}_p)^{-1} + \boldsymbol{\Sigma}_T^{-1} \mathbf{I}_K \right]^{-1}$ and $\mu_{\tilde{\mathbf{T}}_n} = \boldsymbol{\Sigma}_{\tilde{\mathbf{T}}_n} \left[\sum_{p=1}^{P} \hat{\tau}_n^p \boldsymbol{\Sigma}_p^{-1} (\tilde{\mathbf{D}}_n^p - \mu_{\mathbf{b}_p}) + \boldsymbol{\Sigma}_T^{-1} \mu_{\mathbf{W}} \boldsymbol{\Phi}_n \right]$, where $\hat{\tau}_n^p = \mathbb{E}[\tau_n^p]$, $\mu_{\mathbf{b}_p} = \mathbb{E}[\mathbf{b}_p]$ and $\mu_{\mathbf{W}} = \mathbb{E}[\mathbf{W}]$. The consensus is now computed as a weighted mean of raters' values, where the weights vary spatially through $\hat{\tau}_n^p$ according to the rater's local performances. Likewise, $q_{\mathbf{b}_p}$ is found to be Gaussian distributed with covariance $\boldsymbol{\Sigma}_{\mathbf{b}_p} = \left[\beta \mathbf{I}_K + \sum_{n=1}^{N} \mathbb{E}[\tau_n^p] \boldsymbol{\Sigma}_p^{-1} \right]^{-1}$ and mean $\mu_{\mathbf{b}_p} = \boldsymbol{\Sigma}_{\mathbf{b}_p} \sum_{n=1}^{N} \mathbb{E}[\tau_n^p] \boldsymbol{\Sigma}_p^{-1} (\tilde{\mathbf{D}}_{np} - \mathbb{E}[\tilde{\mathbf{T}}_n])$. Update formula for the other variables are reported in the supplementary material.

3 Mixture of Consensuses

We now assume that the raters' maps are derived from not a single but M consensus maps. We introduce for each rater a new binary latent variable $\mathbf{Z}_{pm} \in \{0, 1\}$, $\sum_m \mathbf{Z}_{pm} = 1$, specifying from which consensus a rater map is generated. The associated component prior is given by the mixing coefficients π_m such that $p(\mathbf{Z}_{pm} = 1) = \pi_m$. We simplify the model by replacing the Student's t by Gaussian distributions and removing the bias, i.e. $p(\tilde{\mathbf{D}}_p | \tilde{\mathbf{T}}) = \prod_m \mathcal{N}(\tilde{\mathbf{T}}_m, \boldsymbol{\Sigma}_p)^{\mathbf{Z}_{pm}}$. The graphical model is presented in Fig. 1b.

Like in previous section, we use a VB to infer the consensus and model parameters. A naive solution would compute the posterior component probabilities r_{pm} (responsibilities) as a classical Gaussian mixture clustering problem with multivariate Gaussians of dimension N thus leading to dubious results due to the curse of dimensionality (high dimension, few samples). Instead, we propose first to reduce the dimension of each map by applying a principal component analysis (PCA) and then to cluster the maps in this low dimensional space. The resulting consensus maps are obtained by applying the inverse mapping from the components weights to the original space.

Variational calculus leads again to a Gaussian distribution for $q_{\tilde{\mathbf{T}}_{nm}}(\tilde{\mathbf{T}}_{nm})$, with covariance $\boldsymbol{\Sigma}_{\tilde{\mathbf{T}}_{nm}} = \left[\sum_{p=1}^{P} r_{pm} (\boldsymbol{\Sigma}_p)^{-1} \right]^{-1}$ and mean $\mu_{\tilde{\mathbf{T}}_{nm}} =$

$\Sigma_{\tilde{\mathbf{T}}_{nm}} \sum_{p=1}^{P} r_{pm} \Sigma_p^{-1} \tilde{\mathbf{D}}_n^p$. The raters' contributions to each consensus are now weighted by the responsibilities r_{pm}. Other update formulas are reported in the supplementary material.

This approach has been found experimentally to be very sensitive to the initial values. To increase its stability we follow an incremental scheme inspired by variational boosting [12]. We introduce one consensus map at a time and the distribution parameters of components included in the previous iterations are not updated. Initialization is performed at each iteration by summing the absolute value of the residuals $\text{res}_p = \sum_{n,m} |\tilde{\mathbf{D}}_n^p - \tilde{\mathbf{T}}_{nm}|$ and setting the responsibility for the new component to $\frac{\text{res}_p}{\sum_p \text{res}_p}$ for rater p. Other responsibilities are uniformly initialized such that $\sum_m r_{pm} = 1$. In practice, the algorithm is stopped when no rater is added to the newly introduced component after convergence.

4   Results

4.1   Datasets

The proposed method was tested on 3 datasets: the MICCAI 2016 dataset of MS lesions segmentations [7], prostate segmentations from a private database and lung nodule segmentations from the LIDC dataset [2]. The first two datasets include 7 (resp. 5) raters' binary delineations for 15 (resp. 18) subjects. The LIDC dataset comprises nodules delineations drawn by 4 radiologists on 888 CT images. Only nodules annotated by at least 3 radiologists were considered. The image set was split into 10 folds, one being kept separated for testing while the rest was used to train 9 different segmentation networks by 9-fold cross validation (CV). On the test set, only nodules of size above 10 mm were kept corresponding to 34 nodules. Ground truth segmentations were defined as a majority voting among raters.

4.2   Robust Consensus Estimate

We first demonstrate the estimation of a single consensus from 5 prostate delineations produced by human experts. The input binary masks are converted to probabilities using the geodesic distance transform and the sigmoid function. Figure 2a shows the 5 raters' segmentations and the associated consensus as estimated by our approach. It can be seen that rater 3 seems to be an outlier with respect to the other raters at the bottom of the image, although they agree elsewhere. This local variation of the rater's performance is captured by the scale factor τ_n^p that modulates spatially the contribution of each rater to the consensus. In areas of poor rater's performance, τ exhibits lower values which correspond to larger rater's variance. Locally, raters with weak confidence will not contribute as much as others to the consensus. This is shown in Fig. 2b and 2c, where rater 3 has smaller τ_n values than rater 1 at the bottom of the image (black arrows).

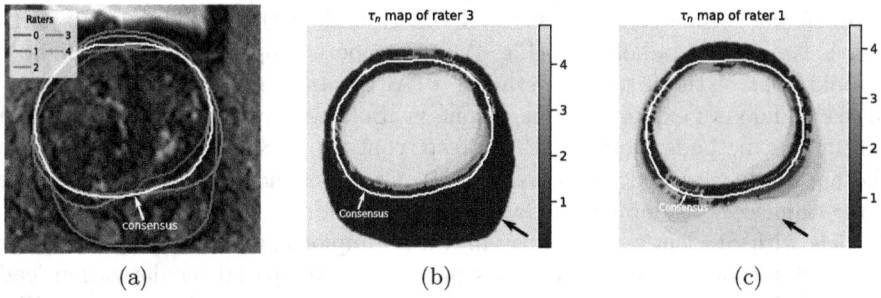

Fig. 2. Fusion of prostate segmentation binary masks (2a). The outlier rater 3 exhibits locally a higher variability linked to lower values of τ_n pointed by the black arrow (2b), whereas rater 1 (2c) shows higher τ_n values in the same area.

Converting binary masks to the continuous domain using a geodesic distance allows to take image intensity information into account and leads to consensus estimates more consistent with intensity boundaries (Fig. 3b). Moreover, the introduction of a spatial prior over the consensus allows to control the smoothness of the output (Fig. 1c). In practice, we use a dictionary of Gaussian bases centered on a regular staggered grid. Key parameters are the spacing between the bases centers, the standard deviations and the position of the origin basis. Larger spacing and scales induce smoother contours in the final map.

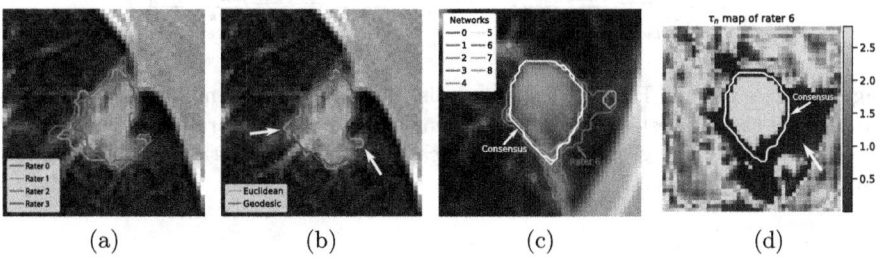

Fig. 3. Geodesic vs. Euclidean distance on radiologists' delineations from LIDC (3a and 3b). Networks probability maps fusion (3c). τ_n map for the network 6 with local variability highlighted by the arrow (3d).

Our algorithm is of specific interest when fusing probability maps outputted by segmentation algorithms. For instance, we consider lung nodules probabilistic segmentations given by 9 neural networks with a same U-Net architecture and trained with 9-fold CV. Figure 3c shows the 9 segmentations for a case with the estimated consensus segmentation. Large discrepancies can be observed locally between network 6 and the others, which is also captured by the scale factor (Fig. 3d). To assess the performance of our method, we performed a comparison study with prior works. Dice scores and Hausdorff distances were computed between the estimated consensus and the ground truth defined as a majority vote between the 4 radiologists (Fig. 4). Our proposed approaches are highlighted in bold. Out of the 9 tested methods, STAPLE and majority vote use binary masks and do not exploit the image content. Both are giving poorer results than continuous methods. Soft STAPLE (resp. continuous STAPLE) correspond to the approach proposed in [1] (resp. [15]). Gaussian models correspond to the same framework as ours, with Gaussian distributions replacing the Student's t. Models with Student's t or Gaussian are all implemented with a spatial prior unless stated otherwise. Consensuses produced with spatial regularization lead to clearly better results. In soft STAPLE [1] the regularization is done by a MRF for which the results were found to be sensitive to its parameters. Instead, our approach allows to estimate automatically the spatial prior hyperparameter.

As shown in Fig. 4, our proposed robust approach with Student's t-distribution leads to competitive results, with higher Dice scores, and lower Hausdorff distances, illustrating the relevance of our method.

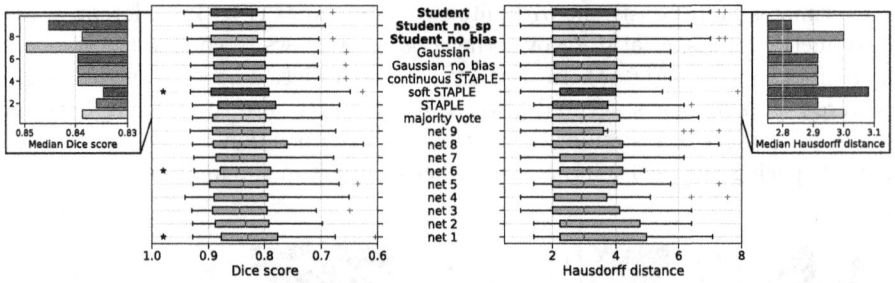

Fig. 4. Dice score and Hausdorff distance distributions over the nodule test set. Left-most values are the best results. Distributions marked with a ⋆ are found significantly different from the one given by our approach ("Student") with the Wilcoxon signed-rank test and p-value 0.05.

4.3   Mixture of Consensuses

We assume here that raters' masks can be derived from possibly several underlying ground truths rather than one. An example of mixture estimated from networks probability maps is given in Fig. 5. Three relevant components are selected which differ in the region highlighted by the white arrow in Fig. 5b. Without the mixture approach, only one consensus corresponding to the first component would have been obtained and the region pointed by the arrow would have been ignored. Thus, the mixture allows to enrich the representation and propose several possible patterns by taking into account the residuals. A case where only one component is retained in the model is shown in the supplementary material.

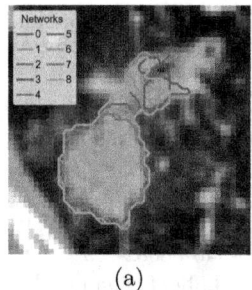 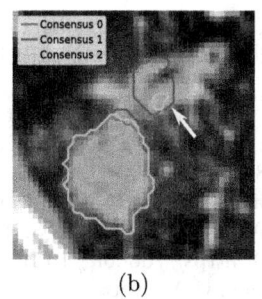 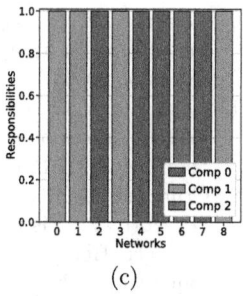

(a)   (b)   (c)

Fig. 5. Mixture of consensuses for a lung nodule. Input probabilistic masks (5a). Estimated consensuses (5b). Responsibilities with 3 relevant components (5c).

5 Conclusion

We presented a novel framework for the robust fusion of probabilistic segmentation masks. Our method relies on Student's t-distributions which allow to take rater's spatial uncertainty into account. All parameters of the model are estimated automatically using Bayesian inference. Furthermore, the concept of mixture of consensuses was explored, which allows to consider several patterns among raters. The approach was tested on several datasets and produced competitive results in comparison with other methods. We believe our method can be a useful tool to combine probabilistic masks generated by different segmentation algorithms.

Acknowledgments. This work was partially funded by the French government, through the UCA^{JEDI} "Investments in the Future" project managed by the National Research Agency (ANR) with the reference number ANR-15-IDEX-01. It was partially supported by the Clinical Data Warehouse of Greater Paris University Hospitals and by the Inria Sophia Antipolis - Méditerranée, "NEF" computation cluster.

References

1. Akhondi-Asl, A., Warfield, S.K.: Simultaneous truth and performance level estimation through fusion of probabilistic segmentations. IEEE Trans. Med. Imaging **32**(10), 1840–1852 (2013)
2. Armato III, S.G., McLennan, G., Bidaut, L., et al.: The lung image database consortium (LIDC) and image database resource initiative (IDRI): a completed reference database of lung nodules on CT scans. Med. Phys. **38**(2), 915–931 (2011)
3. Asman, A.J., Landman, B.A.: Formulating spatially varying performance in the statistical fusion framework. IEEE Trans. Med. Imaging **31**(6), 1326–1336 (2012)
4. Asman, A.J., Landman, B.A.: Non-local statistical label fusion for multi-atlas segmentation. Med. Image Anal. **17**(2), 194–208 (2013)
5. Commowick, O., Akhondi-Asl, A., Warfield, S.K.: Estimating a reference standard segmentation with spatially varying performance parameters: local MAP STAPLE. IEEE Trans. Med. Imaging **31**(8), 1593–1606 (2012)

6. Commowick, O., Warfield, S.K.: A continuous STAPLE for scalar, vector, and tensor images: an application to DTI analysis. IEEE Trans. Med. Imaging **28**(6), 838–846 (2009)
7. Commowick, O., Istace, A., Kain, M., et al.: Objective evaluation of multiple sclerosis lesion segmentation using a data management and processing infrastructure. Sci. Rep. **8**(1), 13650 (2018)
8. Criminisi, A., Sharp, T., Blake, A.: GeoS: geodesic image segmentation. In: Forsyth, D., Torr, P., Zisserman, A. (eds.) ECCV 2008. LNCS, vol. 5302, pp. 99–112. Springer, Heidelberg (2008). https://doi.org/10.1007/978-3-540-88682-2_9
9. Langerak, T.R., van der Heide, U.A., Kotte, A.N.T.J., et al.: Label fusion in atlas-based segmentation using a selective and iterative method for performance level estimation (SIMPLE). IEEE Trans. Med. Imaging **29**(12), 2000–2008 (2010)
10. Liu, X., Montillo, A., Tan, E.T., Schenck, J.F.: iSTAPLE: improved label fusion for segmentation by combining STAPLE with image intensity. In: Ourselin, S., Haynor, D.R. (eds.) Medical Imaging 2013: Image Processing, vol. 8669, pp. 727–732. International Society for Optics and Photonics, SPIE (2013)
11. Menze, B.H., Jakab, A., Bauer, S., et al.: The multimodal brain tumor image segmentation benchmark (BRATS). IEEE Trans. Med. Imaging **34**(10), 1993–2024 (2015)
12. Miller, A.C., Foti, N.J., Adams, R.P.: Variational boosting: iteratively refining posterior approximations. In: Precup, D., Teh, Y.W. (eds.) Proceedings of the 34th International Conference on Machine Learning. Proceedings of Machine Learning Research, vol. 70, pp. 2420–2429. PMLR, International Convention Centre, Sydney, Australia, 06–11 August 2017 (2017)
13. Pohl, K.M., Fisher, J., Bouix, S., et al.: Using the logarithm of odds to define a vector space on probabilistic atlases. Med. Image Anal. **11**(5), 465–477 (2007). special Issue on the Ninth International Conference on Medical Image Computing and Computer-Assisted Interventions - MICCAI 2006
14. Warfield, S.K., Zou, K.H., Wells, W.M.: Simultaneous truth and performance level estimation (STAPLE): an algorithm for the validation of image segmentation. IEEE Trans. Med. Imaging **23**(7), 903–921 (2004)
15. Warfield, S.K., Zou, K.H., Wells, W.M.: Validation of image segmentation by estimating rater bias and variance. Philosoph. Trans. Roy. Soc. A Math. Phys. Eng. Sci. **366**(1874), 2361–2375 (2008)
16. Xing, F., Prince, J.L., Landman, B.A.: Investigation of bias in continuous medical image label fusion. PLoS ONE **11**(6), 1–15 (2016)

Calibrated Surrogate
Maximization of Dice

Marcus Nordström[1,2(✉)], Han Bao[3,4], Fredrik Löfman[2], Henrik Hult[1],
Atsuto Maki[1], and Masashi Sugiyama[4,3]

[1] KTH Royal Institute of Technology, Stockholm, Sweden
marcno@kth.se
[2] RaySearch Laboratories, Stockholm, Sweden
[3] The University of Tokyo, Tokyo, Japan
[4] RIKEN, Tokyo, Japan

Abstract. In the medical imaging community, it is increasingly popular to train machine learning models for segmentation problems with objectives based on the soft-Dice surrogate. While experimental studies have showed good performance with respect to Dice, there have also been reports of some issues related to stability. In parallel with these developments, direct optimization of evaluation metrics has also been studied in the context of binary classification. Recently, in this setting, a quasi-concave, lower-bounded and calibrated surrogate for the F_1-score has been proposed. In this work, we show how to use this surrogate in the context of segmentation. We then show that it has some better theoretical properties than soft-Dice. Finally, we experimentally compare the new surrogate with soft-Dice on a 3D-segmentation problem and get results indicating that stability is improved. We conclude that the new surrogate, for theoretical and experimental reasons, can be considered a promising alternative to the soft-Dice surrogate.

Keywords: Dice · Calibration · Segmentation

1 Introduction

With the introduction of the U-net [19], it became common in the medical imaging community to train neural network models evaluated using Dice with the cross-entropy loss [5,7,13]. However, because of problems associated with handling small structures, it was later proposed that a loss based on a smoothed version of Dice, referred to as soft-Dice, would yield better predictions [18]. This was confirmed in several studies [3,6,8,21], but because of some reported problems associated with handling noisy data [4,8,16] and an increased risk of convergence issues [8], it is common for practitioners to sacrifice some performance

Electronic supplementary material The online version of this chapter (https://doi.org/10.1007/978-3-030-59719-1_27) contains supplementary material, which is available to authorized users.

© Springer Nature Switzerland AG 2020
A. L. Martel et al. (Eds.): MICCAI 2020, LNCS 12264, pp. 269–278, 2020.
https://doi.org/10.1007/978-3-030-59719-1_27

for some stability by using the sum of the soft-Dice loss and the cross-entropy loss as the objective during training [8,9,24].

In parallel with these developments, several alternative performance metrics to accuracy, i.e., the probability of correct predictions, have been investigated to tackle the class imbalance problem in binary classification [11,14,15,17]. Since these metrics do not in general reduce to a sum of per-sample scores, one cannot in general consider the classical procedure of maximizing a concave approximation of the score without loosing statistical consistency [22]. However, for the case of the fractional utility metrics, recent work showed that one can consider such a procedure without loosing statistical consistency, provided concavity is replaced with the weaker notion of quasi-concavity [1].

In this work we address the stability issues reported for soft-Dice by making use of the recent progress in binary classification. More specifically, we propose a new surrogate that is both quasi-concave and a calibrated lower bound to Dice. We then prove that soft-Dice is neither quasi-concave nor a lower bound to Dice. Finally, we compare the surrogates experimentally on a kidney segmentation problem and report some evidence for improvement on the stability issues reported for soft-Dice.

2   Surrogate Maximization

Given a pair of $\mathbb{P}$-measurable random variables (X, Y) taking values in $\mathcal{X} \times \mathcal{Y} = \mathbb{R}^D \times \{\pm 1\}$ and a set of real valued functions $\mathcal{F} \subset \mathbb{R}^{\mathcal{X}}$, the problem of binary classification is to find an $f \in \mathcal{F}$ such that $\text{sgn}(f(X))$ predicts Y as *good as possible* with respect to some score S:

$$f_* = \arg\max_{f \in \mathcal{F}} S(f, X, Y). \tag{1}$$

However, due to the discrete nature of the score functions often used, direct optimization is typically not feasible. Consequently, to simplify the problem, it is common to approximate S with a concave surrogate $\tilde{S}$. In the sequel, we will also refer to the less common situation when concavity is replaced with quasi-concavity.

Definition 1. *Let $\tilde{S}$ be some surrogate score.*

1. $\tilde{S}$ is said to be concave if

$$\tilde{S}(\alpha f_1 + (1 - \alpha)f_2, X, Y) \geq \alpha\tilde{S}(f_1, X, Y) + (1 - \alpha)\tilde{S}(f_2, X, Y), \tag{2}$$

for any measurable functions, f_1, f_2, random variables X, Y and $\alpha \in [0, 1]$.

2. $\tilde{S}$ is said to be quasi-concave if

$$\tilde{S}(\alpha f_1 + (1 - \alpha)f_2, X, Y) \geq \min\{\tilde{S}(f_1, X, Y), \tilde{S}(f_2, X, Y)\}, \tag{3}$$

for any measurable functions f_1, f_2, random variables X, Y and $\alpha \in [0, 1]$.

To ensure that a surrogate is well behaved, it needs to relate to the score in some ways. For this purpose, it is common to consider the *calibration property*, which ensures that any solution to the surrogate maximization problem is also a solution to the original score maximization problem [2,20,23]. Another property that can be considered is the lower-bound property. Note however that in order for a lower-bound to be informative, it has to approximate the score closely.

Definition 2. *Let S be a score function and $\tilde{S}$ be an associated surrogate.*

1. *$\tilde{S}$ is said to be a lower-bound to S if for any pair of random variables (X, Y) and any measurable function f, it holds that $\tilde{S}(f, X, Y) \leq S(f, X, Y)$.*

2. *$\tilde{S}$ is said to be calibrated with respect to S if for any sequence of measurable functions $\{f_l\}_{l \geq 1}$ and any pair of random variables (X, Y), it holds that $\tilde{S}(f_l, X, Y) \to \tilde{S}^* \Rightarrow S(f_l, X, Y) \to S^\dagger$ when $l \to \infty$, where $\tilde{S}^* \doteq \sup_f \tilde{S}(f, X, Y)$ and $S^\dagger \doteq \sup_f S(f)$ are the suprema taken over all measurable functions.*

The framework of surrogate maximization was initially developed for the case where the score function was taken to be accuracy:

$$S^A(f, X, Y) = \mathbb{E}_{X,Y}[\mathbf{1}_{\geq 0}(f(X)Y)], \tag{4}$$

i.e., the probability of correct predictions. For this choice of score, several surrogates have been proposed and studied in the literature [2,22] . Among them is the logistic surrogate defined by

$$\tilde{S}^A_{\log}(f, X, Y) = \mathbb{E}_{X,Y}[\log_2(2 \cdot \sigma(f(X)Y))], \tag{5}$$

where $\sigma(t) = 1/(1 + e^{-t})$ is the sigmoid function. It can be shown that the properties described above hold for this choice of score and surrogate, e.g., that $\tilde{S}^A_{\log}$ is concave and a calibrated lower-bound to S^A.

Proposition 1. *$\tilde{S}^A_{\log}$ is concave and a calibrated lower-bound to S^A.*

Proof. See [2].

When the data is very imbalanced, as when the probability $\mathbb{P}[Y = +1]$ is much higher than $\mathbb{P}[Y = -1]$ or vice versa, accuracy sometimes does not capture the essence of what practitioners want to study and other alternative scores are considered [11,14,15,17]. One such score is the F_1-score, which is commonly also referred to as Dice:

$$S^D(f, X, Y) =$$
$$\frac{\mathbb{E}_{X,Y}[2 \cdot \mathbf{1}_{\geq 0}(f(X)) \cdot \mathbf{1}_{\geq 0}(Y)]}{\mathbb{E}_{X,Y}[2 \cdot \mathbf{1}_{\geq 0}(f(X)) \cdot \mathbf{1}_{\geq 0}(Y) + \mathbf{1}_{<0}(f(X)) \cdot \mathbf{1}_{\geq 0}(Y) + \mathbf{1}_{\geq 0}(f(X)) \cdot \mathbf{1}_{<0}(Y)]}. \tag{6}$$

For this choice of score, it was recently shown in [1] that a surrogate given by

$$\tilde{S}_{\text{cal}}^{\text{D}}(f, X, Y) =$$
$$\frac{\mathbb{E}_{X,Y}[2 \cdot \phi(f(X)) \cdot \mathbf{1}_{\geq 0}(Y)]}{\mathbb{E}_{X,Y}[2 \cdot \mathbf{1}_{\geq 0}(Y) + (1 - \phi(f(X))) \cdot \mathbf{1}_{\geq 0}(Y) + (1 - \phi(-f(X))) \cdot \mathbf{1}_{<0}(Y)]},$$
$$(7)$$

where $\phi(t) = 1 + \log_2(\sigma(\max\{t, t/3\}))$, is a quasi-concave calibrated lower-bound.

Proposition 2. $\tilde{S}_{\text{cal}}^{\text{D}}$ *is quasi-concave and a calibrated lower-bound to* S^{D}.

Proof. See [1].

We refer to this surrogate as *cal-Dice*.

3   Semantic Segmentation

Let (I, S) be a pair of $\mathbb{P}$-measurable random variables taking values in $\mathcal{I} \times \mathcal{S} = \mathbb{R}^{M_1 \times \cdots \times M_D} \times \{\pm 1\}^{M_1 \times \cdots \times M_D}$ and $F : \mathbb{R}^{M_1 \times \cdots \times M_D} \to \mathbb{R}^{M_1 \times \cdots \times M_D \times K}$ be a feature extraction function, extracting K features to each D-pixel (generalized pixel in D-dimensions). Furthermore, let a pair of (conditional) random variables $(X_{|I,S}, Y_{|I,S})$ be uniform over $\{(F(I)_j, S_j)\}_{j \in \mathcal{J}}$, where $\mathcal{J} = \{1, \ldots, M_1\} \times \cdots \times \{1, \ldots, M_D\}$. Now, given a set of real valued functions $\mathcal{F} \subset \mathbb{R}^K$, the problem of segmentation can be seen as to find an $f \in \mathcal{F}$ that maximizes some average score:

$$f_* = \underset{f \in \mathcal{F}}{\arg\max} \; \mathbb{E}_{I,S}[S(f, X_{|I,S}, Y_{|I,S})]. \tag{8}$$

Here, I represents an input image and S represents the associated ground truth. Furthermore, if we consider a U-net in 3D that uses zero-padding [5], then F can be thought of as zero padded patches surrounding each voxel and f can be thought of as the convolutional-kernel to the whole U-net.

Because of the discrete nature of the score functions often considered, S is typically approximated by some surrogate $\tilde{S}$. Furthermore, since we do not have access to the full distribution $\mathbb{P}(I, S)$, we typically collect a set of samples $\{(I^i, S^i)\}_{i=1}^N \overset{\text{i.i.d.}}{\sim} \mathbb{P}(I, S)$, and use the empirical distribution for approximation. This together yields

$$\mathbb{E}_{I,S}[S(f, X_{|I,S}, Y_{|I,S})] \approx \frac{1}{N} \sum_{i=1}^N \tilde{S}(f, X_{|I=I^i, S=S^i}, Y_{|I=I^i, S=S^i}). \tag{9}$$

Classically in the segmentation community, it has been standard to train models by minimizing the cross-entropy loss [5,7,13,19]:

$$L_{\text{CE}}(f, F(I^i), S^i) =$$
$$-\frac{1}{|\mathcal{J}|} \sum_{j \in \mathcal{J}} [\mathbf{1}_{\geq 0}(S_j^i) \cdot \log_2(\sigma(f(F(I^i)_j))) + \mathbf{1}_{<0}(S_j^i) \cdot \log_2(1 - \sigma(f(F(I^i)_j)))].$$
$$(10)$$

By simple computation, it can be shown that:

$$L_{\mathrm{CE}}(f, (I^i), S^i) = 1 - \tilde{S}^{\mathrm{A}}_{\log}(f, X_{|I=I^i, S=S^i}, Y_{|I=I^i, S=S^i}), \tag{11}$$

and so we have that minimizing L_{CE} is equivalent to maximizing $\tilde{S}^{\mathrm{A}}_{\log}$. Thus, if the evaluation score considered is accuracy, then the theory from the previous section motivates the choice.

For the more common situation where Dice is used for evaluation, it has become increasingly popular during the last couple of years to consider a smoothed version of Dice referred to as soft-Dice [3,6,8–10,18,21,24]:

$$\tilde{S}^{\mathrm{D}}_{\mathrm{soft}}(f, X, Y) =$$
$$\frac{\mathbb{E}_{X,Y}[2 \cdot \sigma(f(X)) \cdot \mathbf{1}_{\geq 0}(Y)]}{\mathbb{E}_{X,Y}[2 \cdot \sigma(f(X)) \cdot \mathbf{1}_{\geq 0}(Y) + (1 - \sigma(f(X))) \cdot \mathbf{1}_{\geq 0}(Y) + \sigma(f(X)) \cdot \mathbf{1}_{<0}(Y)]}. \tag{12}$$

This choice of surrogate has been been shown to yield good results experimentally [3,6,8,10,21]. However, because of some reported problems associated with handling noisy data [4,8,16] and an increased risk of convergence issues [8], it is common for practitioners to sacrifice some performance for some stability by using the sum of the soft-Dice loss and the cross-entropy loss as the objective during training [8,9,24].

While there does not to our knowledge exist any work proving that soft-Dice is calibrated to Dice, we conjecture that this is the case because of how closely they are related. As for the other properties discussed in the previous section, we show in Theorem 1 that the surrogate in general is neither quasi-concave nor a lower bound to Dice.

Theorem 1. $\tilde{S}^{\mathrm{D}}_{\mathrm{soft}}$ *is neither quasi-concave, nor is it a lower-bound to* S^{D}.

Proof. See the supplementary document.

These theoretical considerations together with the experimental reports from the previous works motivates the following hypotheses:

1. soft-Dice could yield better experimental results than cross-entropy when evaluated with Dice because it might be calibrated to Dice,
2. soft-Dice could be less stable than cross-entropy because of properties related to concavity.

In light of this, using a linear combination of soft-Dice and cross-entropy when evaluated with Dice can informally be seen as *trading some consistency for some concavity*. However, it is easy to verify that the resulting composite surrogate in general is neither quasi-concave nor a calibrated lower bound to Dice.

To avoid sacrificing performance or stability, we propose to replace the soft-Dice surrogate with the recently studied cal-Dice surrogate. Two arguments can be made to support this. Firstly, cal-Dice has been proven to be calibrated to Dice whereas soft-Dice, to the best of our knowledge, has only been conjectured to be calibrated to Dice. Secondly, cal-Dice is a quasi-concave lower-bound to

Dice whereas soft-Dice is neither quasi-concave nor a lower bound to Dice. If the hypotheses are valid, cal-Dice will achieve similar performance to soft-Dice without sacrificing stability. To see if this is the case, we proceed by comparing cal-Dice to soft-Dice in a realistic segmentation experiment.

4   Experiments

For our experiments, we take the 100 first cases from the Kits2019 competition [7]. Volumes of $256 \times 128 \times 64$ voxels with the kidney centered are then cut out on a resolution of $0.15 \times 0.15 \times 0.35$ (cm), where the last dimension is the *slice direction*. We also pre-process the data in the same way as the winners of the competition by clipping the CT-values to the interval $(-79, 304)$, subtracting by 101 and finally dividing by 76.9 [9]. In Fig. 1 we show an illustration of a slice from one of the patients together with the associated ground truth of the kidney.

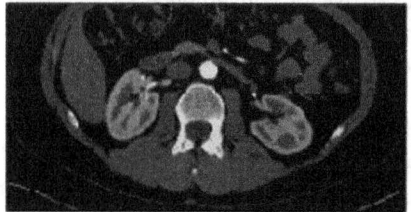 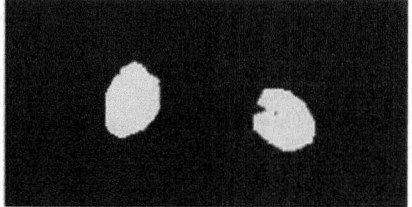

Fig. 1. Illustration of one of the 64 slices in one sample patient. To the left is the CT and to the right is the associated label map of the kidney.

The architecture used is a 3D U-net [5,19] with the following properties. Each layer but the last uses instance normalization, relu-activations and has a convolutional kernel of size $7 \times 5 \times 3$. The last layer does not use instance normalization or any activation function and furthermore has a convolutional kernel of $1 \times 1 \times 1$. The first layer uses 32 filters, then for each downsampling, the number of filters is doubled. Five downsamplings and upsamplings are performed in total using 2-strided convolutions and 2-strided transposed-convolutions, and after each downsampling and upsampling there is one regular convolutional layer.

Since we in practice often only have access to a few cases for training, we conduct a 10-fold study using only 10 patients for training and 90 for test. The model is trained using the Adam optimizer [12] with a learning rate of 10^{-3} and a batch size of 1. Furthermore, we shuffle the samples for each epoch and train for 1000 epochs in total. The result from the experiments is depicted in Fig. 2 and Fig. 3.

Based on two observations, we argue that the outcome of the experiment support the claim that cal-Dice achieves similar performance to soft-Dice without

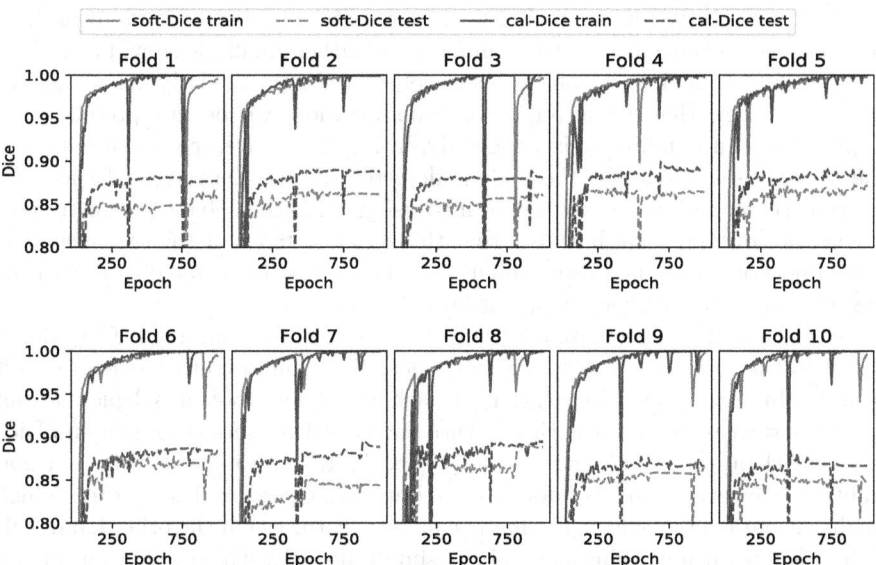

Fig. 2. Illustration of the ten fold experiments when training on 10 patients and testing on 90 patients. The whole red line illustrates the Dice score of the training data during training when using the soft-Dice surrogate and the dashed red line illustrates the Dice score of the testing data during training when using the soft-Dice surrogate. Similarly, the whole green illustrates the Dice score of the training data during training when using the cal-Dice surrogate and the dashed red line illustrates the Dice score of the testing data during training when using the cal-Dice surrogate. (Color figure online)

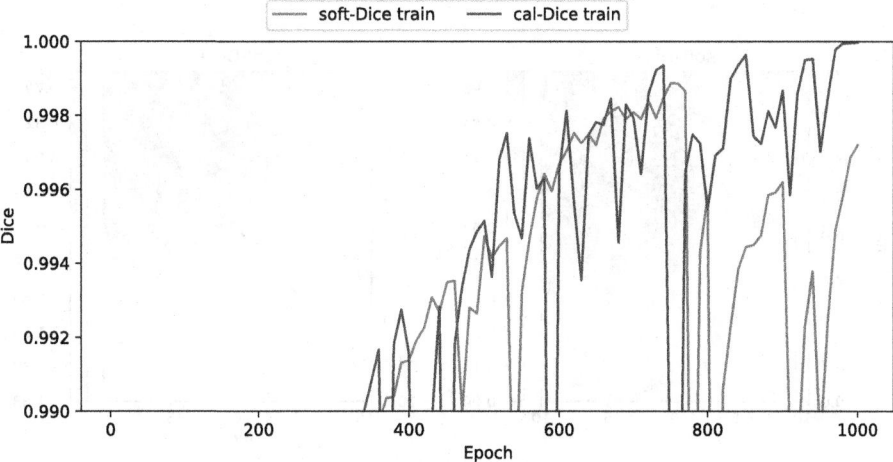

Fig. 3. Average performance on the training set over all of the folds when using soft-Dice and cal-Dice. The plot illustrates that cal-Dice pushes to perfect Dice whereas soft-Dice on average starts to get unstable when getting close to perfect Dice. (Color figure online)

sacrificing stability. Firstly, in Fig. 2, a systematic improvement in generalization is clearly visible. Since the training set is rather small, noise will affect the training even though the problem is not considered a particularly noisy segmentation problem. Hence, the improved generalization can be interpreted as an improvement in handling noise. Secondly, in Fig. 3, the average performance on the training set over all of the folds is depicted for soft-Dice and cal-Dice. We see that the neural network when trained using cal-Dice is able to perfectly represent the training data, but also, that this on average is not the case when the neural network is trained using soft-Dice. This can be interpreted as if cal-Dice has less convergence issues than soft-Dice.

We end with a speculation of why these effects are observed. Consider a segmentation problem with two pixels where the ground truth labels are both positive. In Fig. 4, the analytic gradient path for such a problem is depicted from a specific starting point for both soft-Dice and cal-Dice. Since the maximum Dice is given when $f(x_1) \geq 0$ and $f(x_2) \geq 0$, both trajectories lead to an optimal solution. However, soft-Dice focuses on improving one pixel at a time which might encourage the learning of many concrete features. On the other hand, cal-Dice, focuses on improving both pixels simultaneously, which might encourage the learning of few abstract features. This might, since making decisions based on few abstract features often is more robust to noise than making decisions based on many concrete features, be the reason to why we observe better generalization for cal-Dice than for soft-Dice. Furthermore, when learning pixels sequentially compared to learning pixels simultaneously, there might be an increased risk of getting into situations where a feature that is learnt to represent one pixel later is forgotten when focus is on another pixel. This could explain why we observe more convergence issues with soft-Dice than with cal-Dice.

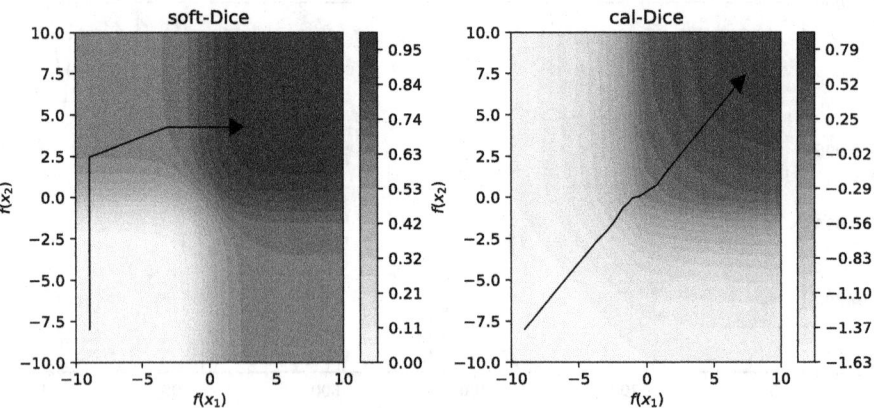

Fig. 4. Illustration of analytic gradient trajectories for soft-Dice and cal-Dice in a two pixel segmentation problem when the ground truth labels for both pixels are positive.

5 Conclusion

In this work, we have gone through the theoretical background for surrogate maximization and discussed a new surrogate for Dice that we refer to as cal-Dice. We have theoretically compared cal-Dice with soft-Dice and showed that cal-Dice has some better properties. Finally, we have shown some experimental results that support the claim that cal-Dice improves on the stability issues previously reported for soft-Dice. We conclude that cal-Dice, for theoretical and for experimental reasons, can be considered a promising alternative to soft-Dice.

Acknowledgement. Marcus Nordström, Fredrik Löfman, Henrik Hult and Atsuto Maki were supported by RaySearch Laboratories. Masashi Sugiyama was supported by the International Research Center for Neurointelligence (WPI-IRCN) at The University of Tokyo Institutes for Advanced Study.

References

1. Bao, H., Sugiyama, M.: Calibrated surrogate maximization of linear-fractional utility in binary classification. In: International Conference on Artificial Intelligence and Statistics, pp. 2337–2347 (2020)
2. Bartlett, P.L., Jordan, M.I., McAuliffe, J.D.: Convexity, classification, and risk bounds. J. Am. Stat. Assoc. **101**(473), 138–156 (2006)
3. Bertels, J., et al.: Optimizing the dice score and Jaccard index for medical image segmentation: theory and practice. In: Shen, D., et al. (eds.) MICCAI 2019. LNCS, vol. 11765, pp. 92–100. Springer, Cham (2019). https://doi.org/10.1007/978-3-030-32245-8_11
4. Bertels, J., Robben, D., Vandermeulen, D., Suetens, P.: Optimization with soft dice can lead to a volumetric bias. In: Crimi, A., Bakas, S. (eds.) BrainLes 2019. LNCS, vol. 11992, pp. 89–97. Springer, Cham (2020). https://doi.org/10.1007/978-3-030-46640-4_9
5. Çiçek, Ö., Abdulkadir, A., Lienkamp, S.S., Brox, T., Ronneberger, O.: 3D U-Net: learning dense volumetric segmentation from sparse annotation. In: Ourselin, S., Joskowicz, L., Sabuncu, M.R., Unal, G., Wells, W. (eds.) MICCAI 2016. LNCS, vol. 9901, pp. 424–432. Springer, Cham (2016). https://doi.org/10.1007/978-3-319-46723-8_49
6. Drozdzal, M., Vorontsov, E., Chartrand, G., Kadoury, S., Pal, C.: The importance of skip connections in biomedical image segmentation. In: Carneiro, G., et al. (eds.) LABELS/DLMIA - 2016. LNCS, vol. 10008, pp. 179–187. Springer, Cham (2016). https://doi.org/10.1007/978-3-319-46976-8_19
7. Heller, N., et al.: The Kits19 Challenge Data: 300 Kidney Tumor Cases With Clinical Context, CT Semantic Segmentations, and Surgical Outcomes (2019)
8. Isensee, F., Kickingereder, P., Wick, W., Bendszus, M., Maier-Hein, K.H.: No new-net. In: Crimi, A., Bakas, S., Kuijf, H., Keyvan, F., Reyes, M., van Walsum, T. (eds.) BrainLes 2018. LNCS, vol. 11384, pp. 234–244. Springer, Cham (2019). https://doi.org/10.1007/978-3-030-11726-9_21
9. Isensee, F., Maier-Hein, K.H.: An attempt at beating the 3D U-net. arXiv preprint arXiv:1908.02182 (2019)

10. Jadon, S., et al.: A comparative study of 2D image segmentation algorithms for traumatic brain lesions using CT data from the ProTECTIII multicenter clinical trial. In: Medical Imaging 2020: Imaging Informatics for Healthcare, Research, and Applications. vol. 11318, p. 11318 0Q. International Society for Optics and Photonics (2020)
11. Kar, P., Narasimhan, H., Jain, P.: Surrogate functions for maximizing precision at the top. In: International Conference on Machine Learning, pp. 189–198 (2015)
12. Kingma, D.P., Ba, J.: Adam: a method for stochastic optimization. In: Proceedings of the 3rd International Conference on Learning Representations (2015)
13. Litjens, G., et al.: A survey on deep learning in medical image analysis. Med. Image Anal. **42**, 60–88 (2017)
14. Liu, X.Y., Wu, J., Zhou, Z.H.: Exploratory undersampling for class-imbalance learning. IEEE Trans. Syst. Man Cybern. Part B (Cybern.) **39**(2), 539–550 (2008)
15. Liu, X.Y., Zhou, Z.H.: The influence of class imbalance on cost-sensitive learning: an empirical study. In: Sixth International Conference on Data Mining (ICDM 2006), pp. 970–974. IEEE (2006)
16. Mehrtash, A., Wells III, W.M., Tempany, C.M., Abolmaesumi, P., Kapur, T.: Confidence calibration and predictive uncertainty estimation for deep medical image segmentation. arXiv preprint arXiv:1911.13273 (2019)
17. Menon, A., Narasimhan, H., Agarwal, S., Chawla, S.: On the statistical consistency of algorithms for binary classification under class imbalance. In: International Conference on Machine Learning, pp. 603–611 (2013)
18. Milletari, F., Navab, N., Ahmadi, S.A.: V-net: fully convolutional neural networks for volumetric medical image segmentation. In: Fourth International Conference on 3D vision (3DV), pp. 565–571. IEEE (2016)
19. Ronneberger, O., Fischer, P., Brox, T.: U-Net: convolutional networks for biomedical image segmentation. In: Navab, N., Hornegger, J., Wells, W.M., Frangi, A.F. (eds.) MICCAI 2015. LNCS, vol. 9351, pp. 234–241. Springer, Cham (2015). https://doi.org/10.1007/978-3-319-24574-4_28
20. Steinwart, I.: How to compare different loss functions and their risks. Constr. Approximat. **26**(2), 225–287 (2007)
21. Sudre, C.H., Li, W., Vercauteren, T., Ourselin, S., Jorge Cardoso, M.: Generalised dice overlap as a deep learning loss function for highly unbalanced segmentations. In: Cardoso, M.J., et al. (eds.) DLMIA/ML-CDS - 2017. LNCS, vol. 10553, pp. 240–248. Springer, Cham (2017). https://doi.org/10.1007/978-3-319-67558-9_28
22. Vapnik, V.: The Nature of Statistical Learning Theory. Springer, New York (2013). https://doi.org/10.1007/978-1-4757-3264-1
23. Zhang, T.: Statistical behavior and consistency of classification methods based on convex risk minimization. Ann. Stat. **32**, 56–85 (2004)
24. Zhang, Y., et al.: Cascaded volumetric convolutional network for kidney tumor segmentation from CT volumes. arXiv preprint arXiv:1910.02235 (2019)

Uncertainty-Guided Efficient Interactive Refinement of Fetal Brain Segmentation from Stacks of MRI Slices

Guotai Wang[1,2(✉)], Michael Aertsen[3], Jan Deprest[4,5], Sébastien Ourselin[2], Tom Vercauteren[2], and Shaoting Zhang[1,6]

[1] School of Mechanical and Electrical Engineering,
University of Electronic Science and Technology of China, Chengdu, China
guotai.wang@uestc.edu.cn
[2] School of Biomedical Engineering and Imaging Sciences, King's College London, London, UK
[3] Department of Radiology, University Hospitals KU Leuven, Leuven, Belgium
[4] Department of Obstetrics and Gynaecology, University Hospitals KU Leuven, Leuven, Belgium
[5] Institute for Women's Health, University College London, London, UK
[6] SenseTime Research, Shanghai, China

Abstract. Segmentation of the fetal brain from stacks of motion-corrupted fetal MRI slices is important for motion correction and high-resolution volume reconstruction. Although Convolutional Neural Networks (CNNs) have been widely used for automatic segmentation of the fetal brain, their results may still benefit from interactive refinement for challenging slices. To improve the efficiency of interactive refinement process, we propose an Uncertainty-Guided Interactive Refinement (UGIR) framework. We first propose a grouped convolution-based CNN to obtain multiple automatic segmentation predictions with uncertainty estimation in a single forward pass, then guide the user to provide interactions only in a subset of slices with the highest uncertainty. A novel interactive level set method is also proposed to obtain a refined result given the initial segmentation and user interactions. Experimental results show that: (1) our proposed CNN obtains uncertainty estimation in real time which correlates well with mis-segmentations, (2) the proposed interactive level set is effective and efficient for refinement, (3) UGIR obtains accurate refinement results with around 30% improvement of efficiency by using uncertainty to guide user interactions. Our code is available online (https://github.com/HiLab-git/UGIR).

Keywords: Uncertainty · Interactive segmentation · Fetal brain

1 Introduction

Due to the good soft tissue contrast, fetal Magnetic Resonance Imaging (MRI) is an important tool for diagnosis of abnormalities of the fetal brain during

© Springer Nature Switzerland AG 2020
A. L. Martel et al. (Eds.): MICCAI 2020, LNCS 12264, pp. 279–288, 2020.
https://doi.org/10.1007/978-3-030-59719-1_28

pregnancy [6]. However, MRI is susceptible to motion of fetuses during scanning. To mitigate this problem, fast imaging techniques are often used to obtain stacks of 2D slices that have good in-plane image quality but suffer from large inter-slice motion and low 3D resolution. Segmentation of the fetal brain from stacks of fetal MRI slices plays a critical role for correcting the inter-slice motion and reconstructing a high-resolution 3D volume for fetal brain studies [2,6,12].

Despite the fact that deep learning with Convolutional Neural Networks (CNNs) has obtained state-of-the-art performance for automatic fetal brain segmentation from fetal MRI [2,12], it is still difficult for these automatic segmentation methods to obtain accurate results when dealing with images with motion artifacts, abnormal appearances due to pathologies and some challenging local regions [12]. To address this problem, an efficient interactive method to refine the automatic segmentation result is highly desirable in practice, which makes the segmentation more accurate and robust to be clinically useful [15,16].

In the literature, some recent works [16,18] use a second CNN that takes the initial automatic segmentation result and additional user interactions as input to obtain a refined result. In [15], image-specific fine-tuning and Graph Cut [1] were used for interactive refinement. Though these methods achieved higher accuracy and efficiency than traditional interactive segmentation methods [17], when used to segment a volumetric data, they require the user to carefully check the initial segmentation in 2D views slice-by-slice and manually identify mis-segmented regions to give interactions for refinement. For stacks of fetal MRI slices, automatic CNNs could obtain accurate initial segmentation for most slices [2,12], manually identifying mis-segmented regions may be unnecessary for accurately segmented slices while sometimes difficult for challenging slices. Therefore, the efficiency of such methods is limited.

To improve the efficiency for user interactions, leveraging the uncertainty information of the initial segmentation has been shown to be a promising method [13] as it can automatically identify potential mis-segmentations and guide the user to give interactions only in some uncertain regions. Despite the availability of several reliable uncertainty estimation methods for CNN-based segmentation, such as Monte Carlo (MC) dropout [3], model ensemble [5,8] and test-time augmentation [14], they require multiple forward passes at inference time and cannot provide real-time uncertainty estimation for guiding user interactions. Alternatively, a Bayesian Network has been proposed for fast uncertainty estimation with a single forward pass [4]. However, their utility for guiding interactive refinement has not been investigated.

In this paper, we propose a novel uncertainty-guided framework for interactive refinement of automatic segmentation obtained by CNNs and apply it to fetal brain segmentation from fetal MRI. The contribution is three-fold. First, to obtain real-time uncertainty estimation, we propose a novel method using Grouped Convolution (GC)-based CNNs. It obtains multiple predictions simultaneously with a single model and gives uncertainty estimation in a single forward pass, which is more suitable in the scenario of interactive refinement. Second, we propose to guide the user to give interactions more efficiently during refinement according to the uncertainty information. Thirdly, we propose a novel interactive level set method that incorporates the initial segmentation and user interactions in a uniformed framework to obtain accurate refined results efficiently. The superiority of our framework over existing methods was validated in the task of fetal brain segmentation from stacks of motion-corrupted fetal MRI slices.

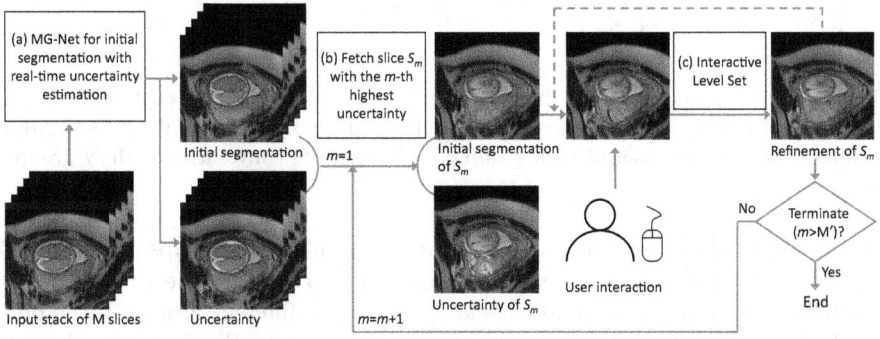

Fig. 1. The proposed Uncertainty-Guided Interactive Refinement (UGIR) framework for fetal brain segmentation. For an input stack with M slices, the user only needs to give interactions in a subset of $M'(M' < M)$ slices with the highest uncertainty.

2 Methods

Our proposed Uncertainty-Guided Interactive Refinement (UGIR) framework for efficient interactive fetal brain segmentation is shown in Fig. 1. First, a novel CNN based on convolution in Multiple Groups (MG-Net) simultaneously obtains the initial segmentation and uncertainty estimation of a stack of MRI slices in real time. Let S_m ($m = 1, 2, ...$) denote the slice with the m-th highest uncertainty. Our framework automatically and iteratively fetches slice S_m as suggestion for user interactions. After the user gives interactions in S_m, a novel interactive level set method obtains the refined result of S_m. The iterative refinement is finished when no further slice is suggested by the framework.

Simultaneous Initial Segmentation and Uncertainty Estimation. We propose MG-Net to obtain simultaneous initial segmentation and uncertainty estimation in real time with a single network and a single forward pass for inference, which is more efficient for interactive segmentation than typical uncertainty estimation methods including MC dropout [3] and model ensemble [5,8]. As shown in Fig. 2, we modify U-Net [11] by using Grouped Convolution [7].

An N-grouped convolution layer splits the input feature map along the channel dimension into N groups each with C_i channels. For each group, it uses a convolution kernel of shape $C_o \times C_i \times h \times w$ respectively, where $h \times w$ is the

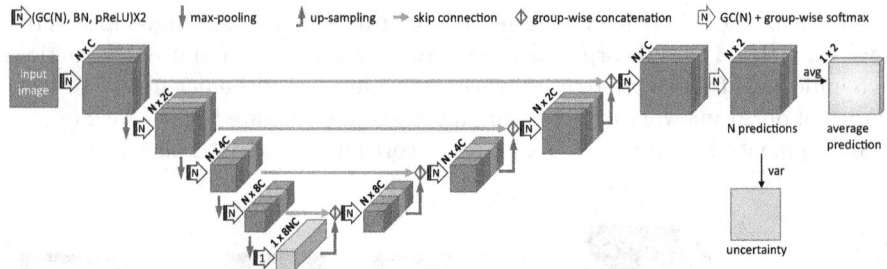

Fig. 2. The proposed MG-Net that obtains N (e.g., 4) predictions corresponding to N groups of features. The numbers over each feature map such as $N \times C$ are group number $\times$ channel number of each group. GC(N) denotes convolution with N groups.

spatial size of the kernel. Therefore, N independent feature maps are obtained each with C_o channels. They are concatenated into a single one with $N \times C_o$ channels. Note that there is no correlation between different groups in the output feature map of an N-grouped convolution layer. Similarly, we implement up-sampling layers by transposed N-grouped convolutions, and extend standard channel concatenation to group-wise concatenation to keep the N groups independent of each other. Let F_1 and F_2 represent two feature maps each with N groups. We first concatenate the n-th group of F_1 with the n-th group of F_2, and denote the result as $\hat{F}_n$. Then $\hat{F}_1$, $\hat{F}_2$, ..., and $\hat{F}_N$ are concatenated as the group-wise concatenation of F_1 and F_2. The group-wise concatenation is used for skip connection between feature maps in the encoder and their counterparts in the decoder, as shown in Fig. 2. At the last layer of the decoder, we apply softmax to each feature group respectively (i.e., group-wise softmax) to obtain N probability predictions. Therefore, MG-Net can be seen as an ensemble of N parallel sub-networks, and they are randomly initialized and trained with dropout to obtain diversity. At the lowest resolution level of MG-Net, we set group number to one to allow communication of these N sub-networks for better performance.

For training, we apply the same segmentation loss function (i.e., Dice loss [10]) to the N predictions respectively and average their loss values for back-propagation. At inference time, we take the pixel-wise mean value and variance of the N probability predictions as the final segmentation probability map and pixel-level uncertainty estimation, respectively. The mean foreground probability map is thresholded by 0.5 to obtain a binary segmentation mask.

Uncertainty-Guided User Interactions. For a stack of M slices, the CNN is able to obtain accurate segmentation for most slices and only a few slices may require manual refinement [12]. To avoid unnecessary and time-consuming manual search for mis-segmentations of each slice, we ask the user to check and refine only M' ($M' < M$) slices with the highest slice-level uncertainty. For a slice S, its binary segmentation result Y and pixel-level uncertainty map U, a naive slice-level uncertainty can be defined as $\nu^* = \sum_{\mathbf{x}} U_{\mathbf{x}}$ where $U_{\mathbf{x}}$ is the uncertainty of pixel $\mathbf{x}$. However, this may lead a slice with a small target to be neglected as it often has a low value of ν^* due to a small uncertain region. To address this problem, we alternatively define the slice-level uncertainty as $\nu = (\sum_{\mathbf{x}} U_{\mathbf{x}})/(\sum_{\mathbf{x}} Y_{\mathbf{x}} + \zeta)$, which is normalized by the segmented region size. ζ is a small number for numerical stability. We iteratively fetch the slice S_m with the m-th highest ν to ask for interactive refinement, where $m = 1, 2, ...,$ and the iteration terminates when $m > M'$, as shown in Fig. 1. M' is a predefined number, such as 60% of M according to the performance of the CNN on the validation set. We also use an early termination strategy when refinement is not needed for three consecutive fetched slices.

Interaction-Based Level Set for Fast Refinement. For interactive refinement, we use a Distance Regularized Level Set Evolution (DRLSE) [9] due to its efficiency and extend it with an interaction-constraint term, which is named as I-DRLSE. Let ϕ denote the level set function that is initialized as the signed distance transform of the initial segmentation result. We define an energy function as $E(\phi) = \alpha E_r + \beta E_u + \lambda E_l + \mu E_d$, where $\alpha, \beta, \lambda, \mu$ are weighting parameters. E_r, E_u, E_l and E_d are the region, user-interaction, length and distance regularization terms, respectively. $E_l = \int_{\Omega} \delta_{\epsilon}(\phi(\mathbf{x}))|\nabla\phi(\mathbf{x})|d\mathbf{x}$ and $E_d = \int_{\Omega} p(|\nabla\phi(\mathbf{x})|)d\mathbf{x}$, where δ_{ϵ} and $p()$ are the smoothed Dirac delta function and double-well potential function as in [9] respectively. As the target region in the fetal MRI image has an inhomogeneous appearance that brings challenges to standard intensity-based level set methods, we define the region term based on the foreground probability map P obtained by MG-Net instead of the original image:

$$E_r = \int_{\Omega} \left(|P - c_1|^2 H_{\epsilon}(\phi(\mathbf{x})) + |P - c_2|^2 (H_{\epsilon}(-\phi(\mathbf{x}))) \right) d\mathbf{x} \tag{1}$$

where H_{ϵ} is the smoothed Heaviside function as in [9]. c_1 and c_2 are the average foreground probability inside and outside the current level set contour, respectively. Our proposed user-interaction term is:

$$E_u = -\int_{\Omega} \left(H_{\epsilon}(\phi(\mathbf{x}))\log(\eta(\mathbf{x})) + H_{\epsilon}(-\phi(\mathbf{x}))\log(1 - \eta(\mathbf{x})) \right) d\mathbf{x} \tag{2}$$

where $\eta(\mathbf{x})$ is user-interaction-derived likelihood of pixel $\mathbf{x}$ being the foreground. Let $\mathcal{F}$ and $\mathcal{B}$ represent the set of pixels specified as the foreground and background by the user interactions, respectively. Inspired by [16], we use $g_{\mathbf{x}}^{\mathcal{F}}$ to represent the geodesic distance between $\mathbf{x}$ and $\mathcal{F}$, and define $\eta(\mathbf{x}) = e^{-G_{\mathbf{x}}^{\mathcal{F}}}/(e^{-G_{\mathbf{x}}^{\mathcal{F}}} + e^{-G_{\mathbf{x}}^{\mathcal{B}}})$, where $G_{\mathbf{x}}^{\mathcal{F}} = \min(g_{\mathbf{x}}^{\mathcal{F}}, D)$ and $G_{\mathbf{x}}^{\mathcal{B}} = \min(g_{\mathbf{x}}^{\mathcal{B}}, D)$ and D is a threshold value to ensure that only a local region is affected by the interactions. We set $g_{\mathbf{x}}^{\mathcal{F}}$ or $g_{\mathbf{x}}^{\mathcal{B}}$ as D when $\mathcal{F}$ or $\mathcal{B}$ is empty. E_u is infinite if the segmentation results conflict with the user interactions.

3 Experiments and Results

Data and Implementation. MRI scans of 35 fetuses in the second trimester were collected by Single Shot Fast Spin Echo (SSFSE) with pixel size 0.74 mm–1.58 mm and inter-slice spacing 3 mm–4 mm. Each fetus had three scans in axial, sagittal and coronal views respectively, leading to 105 stacks in total. We randomly selected 72 stacks from 24 patients, 9 stacks from 3 patients and 24 stacks from 8 patients for training, validation and testing, respectively. Manual segmentations of these images were used as the ground truth.

We implemented the CNNs in Pytorch on a Ubuntu desktop with an NVIDIA GTX 1080 Ti GPU and developed a PyQt GUI for user interactions. I-DRLSE was implemented in Python and it ran on the CPU. To train MG-Net, we used Dice loss [10] and Adam optimizer with weight decay 10^{-5}, mini-batch of 24 slices and learning rate 10^{-4}. The training was ended when performance on the validation set stopped to increase for 5k iterations. The group number N in MG-Net was 4 and the channel number parameter C in Fig. 2 was 16. For interactive refinement, M' was set to $0.6M$ as refinement was not needed for more than half of the slices in the validation set. For I-DRLSE, the maximal evolution step number was 200 and $\alpha = 0.1$, $\beta = 0.5$, $\lambda = 0.3$, $\mu = 0.005$, $D = 4.0$ based on grid search on the validation set. The segmentation accuracy was measured by Dice similarity and Average Symmetric Surface Distance (ASSD) between segmentation results and the ground truth.

Table 1. Quantitative evaluation of different uncertainty estimation methods for fetal brain segmentation before refinement. The values were measured at stack-level.

Method	Efficiency		Uncertainty quality		Segmentation quality	
	Param (M)	Runtime (s)	UEO (%)	RVE (%)	Dice (%)	ASSD (mm)
U-Net [11]	11.51	0.31 ± 0.09	–	–	91.54 ± 5.87	4.31 ± 2.45
MC Dropout [3]	11.51	3.12 ± 0.83	36.17 ± 5.31	42.64 ± 36.94	92.04 ± 9.27	4.16 ± 2.75
Ensemble [8]	11.51	1.56 ± 0.42	37.08 ± 7.75	40.74 ± 37.29	**92.05 ± 5.72**	4.07 ± 2.37
Bayesian Net [4]	11.51	0.31 ± 0.09	36.64 ± 5.10	26.54 ± 18.29	90.24 ± 7.39	4.87 ± 2.82
MG-Net	**4.86**	**0.29 ± 0.08**	**40.47 ± 3.58**	**21.90 ± 17.62**	91.82 ± 4.78	**4.07 ± 2.13**

Initial Segmentation and Uncertainty Estimation. Our MG-Net was compared with MC dropout [3] with 10 folds, ensemble [8] of 5 models, and a Bayesian network [4] for uncertainty estimation. We implemented all these methods using U-Net [11] as the backbone. To measure ability of the uncertainty to indicate mis-segmentation, we used Uncertainty-Error Overlap (UEO, i.e., Dice as in [5]) and Relative Volume Error (RVE) between thresholded uncertain region and mis-segmented region. The optimal threshold value for each method was determined based on the validation set. Quantitative evaluation results are shown in Table 1. Compared with ensemble of U-Net, our MG-Net obtains comparable segmentation accuracy and higher uncertainty estimation quality. MG-Net takes 0.29 s in average for simultaneous automatic segmentation and uncertainty

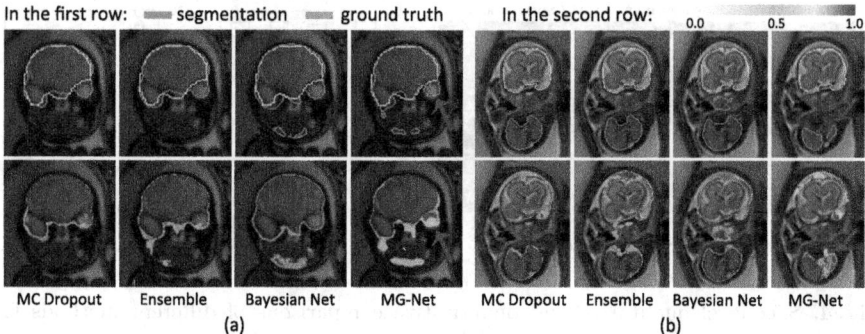

Fig. 3. Comparison of different methods for initial segmentation (1st row) and uncertainty estimation (2nd row) that is normalized to [0, 1]. Red arrows highlight the consistency between mis-segmentation (eye ball in (a) and lung in (b)) and uncertainty obtained by MG-Net. (Color figure online)

estimation of a stack, which is far more efficient than MC dropout and model ensemble and more suitable for interactive segmentation. The Bayesian network method also obtains uncertainty estimation in a fast speed, but with a reduced segmentation accuracy. Visual comparison in Fig. 3 shows that MG-Net obtains better consistency between mis-segmentation and uncertain regions than the other uncertainty estimation methods.

Refinement Using Interactive Level Set. Our I-DRLSE was firstly validated with slice-level refinement, and compared with: 1) CPU-based Graph Cut[1] as implemented in [15], and 2) training a refinement CNN (a.k.a., R-Net) [16] that takes the initial segmentation and user interactions as input. We implemented the R-Net using U-Net [11] as the backbone, and trained it with simulated interactions on initial segmentation obtained by MG-Net following [16]. As not all the slices in a stack require refinement, we randomly selected 100 obviously mis-segmented slices from the test set, and used the same set of user interactions on the initial segmentation for comparison. Figure 4(a) shows two cases where over- and under-segmentation exist in the initial segmentation respectively, which demonstrates that I-DRLSE obtains higher refinement accuracy than Graph Cut and R-Net with the same initial segmentation and interactions. Figure 4(b) shows a quantitative comparison of these refinement methods. It can be observed that I-DRLSE leads to higher Dice scores and lower ASSD values than Graph Cut and R-Net for refinement. The average slice-level machine time for CPU-based I-DRLSE was 0.45 s, which is slower than that of Graph Cut (0.07 s) and R-Net (0.12 s), but still acceptable for fast response of user interactions. The efficiency of I-DRLSE could be further improved by a GPU-optimized implementation in the future.

---

[1] Code from the maxflow-v3.01 library: https://vision.cs.uwaterloo.ca/code/.

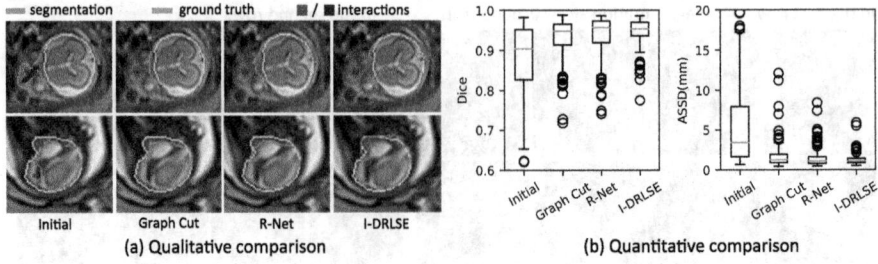

Fig. 4. Slice-level qualitative and quantitative comparisons of different methods for refinement based on the same set of initial segmentation and user interactions.

Comparison of Different Interactive Frameworks. For stack-level segmentation, our UGIR was compared with two variants: 1) UGIR(-U) denoting that the user manually searches mis-segmentation slice-by-slice to provide interactions (i.e., not guided by uncertainty) for refinement using I-DRLSE; 2) UGIR(*) that denotes using the naive slice-level uncertainty ν^* to guide user interactions. They were also compared with two existing interactive segmentation methods: using Graph Cut [1] for interactive segmentation from scratch, and DeepIGeoS [16] that uses two CNNs for initial segmentation and interactive refinement, respectively. We re-implemented DeepIGeoS following the training method in [16]. One user employed these methods to segment the fetal brain from the testing fetal MRI stacks respectively, where the interactions in a slice could be given multiple times until the result was accepted. Quantitative evaluation results are shown in Table 2. Compared with DeepIGeoS [16], our UGIR obtained similar final accuracy (p-value > 0.05 based on a paired t-test), but reduced the runtime from 75.38 s to 48.46 s. By using uncertainty-guided user interactions, UGIR improved the efficiency by near 30% from UGIR(-U). UGIR(*) and UGIR took almost the same runtime, but UGIR achieved higher accuracy.

Table 2. Quantitative comparison of different interactive methods for stack-level segmentation of the fetal brain.

	Graph cut [1]	DeepIGeoS [16]	UGIR(-U)	UGIR(*)	UGIR
Dice (%)	93.17 ± 3.15	**95.03 ± 3.07**	95.00 ± 3.09	94.65 ± 3.28	94.83 ± 3.22
ASSD (mm)	2.84 ± 1.18	2.72 ± 1.74	2.73 ± 1.12	2.75 ± 1.17	**2.70 ± 1.15**
Runtime (s)	214.54 ± 58.73	75.38 ± 42.67	68.04 ± 26.00	**48.11 ± 20.87**	48.46 ± 19.40

4 Conclusion

In this work, we propose a novel interactive segmentation framework using uncertainty to efficiently guide user interactions for refining results obtained by automatic CNNs. We introduce MG-Net based on grouped convolution to obtain multiple segmentation predictions simultaneously with real-time uncertainty estimation, which is used to suggest mis-segmented slices for user interactions, avoiding unnecessary manual check of well-segmented slices and leading to improved efficiency. A novel interactive level set I-DRLSE is also proposed to obtain refined results with spatial regularization. Experiments with fetal brain segmentation from stacks of motion-corrupted fetal MRI slices show that the proposed interactive framework achieved high accuracy with fast runtime, and the uncertainty information helped to improve the refinement efficiency by around 30%.

Acknowledgements. This work was supported by the National Natural Science Foundation of China funding [81771921, 61901084], the Wellcome Trust [WT101957, 203148/Z/16/Z], and the Engineering and Physical Sciences Research Council (EPSRC) [NS/A000027/1, NS/A000049/1]. TV is supported by a Medtronic/Royal Academy of Engineering Research Chair [RCSRF1819/7/34].

References

1. Boykov, Y.Y., Jolly, M.P.: Interactive graph cuts for optimal boundary & region segmentation of objects in N-D images. In: ICCV, pp. 105–112 (2001)
2. Ebner, M., et al.: An automated framework for localization, segmentation and super-resolution reconstruction of fetal brain MRI. Neuroimage **206**, 116324 (2020)
3. Gal, Y., Ghahramani, Z.: Dropout as a Bayesian approximation: representing model uncertainty in deep learning. In: ICML, pp. 1050–1059 (2016)
4. Jena, R., Awate, S.P.: A Bayesian neural net to segment images with uncertainty estimates and good calibration. In: Chung, A.C.S., Gee, J.C., Yushkevich, P.A., Bao, S. (eds.) IPMI 2019. LNCS, vol. 11492, pp. 3–15. Springer, Cham (2019). https://doi.org/10.1007/978-3-030-20351-1_1
5. Jungo, A., Reyes, M.: Assessing reliability and challenges of uncertainty estimations for medical image segmentation. In: Shen, D., et al. (eds.) MICCAI 2019. LNCS, vol. 11765, pp. 48–56. Springer, Cham (2019). https://doi.org/10.1007/978-3-030-32245-8_6
6. Keraudren, K., et al.: Automated fetal brain segmentation from 2D MRI slices for motion correction. Neuroimage **101**, 633–643 (2014)
7. Krizhevsky, A., Sutskever, I., Hinton, G.E.: ImageNet classification with deep convolutional neural networks. In: NeurIPS, pp. 1097–1105 (2012)
8. Lakshminarayanan, B., Pritzel, A., Blundell, C.: Simple and scalable predictive uncertainty estimation using deep ensembles. In: NeurIPS, pp. 6405–6416 (2017)
9. Li, C., Xu, C., Gui, C., Fox, M.D.: Distance regularized level set evolution and its application to image segmentation. IEEE Trans. Image Process. **19**(12), 3243–3254 (2010)
10. Milletari, F., Navab, N., Ahmadi, S.A.: V-net: fully convolutional neural networks for volumetric medical image segmentation. In: IC3DV, pp. 565–571 (2016)
11. Ronneberger, O., Fischer, P., Brox, T.: U-net: convolutional networks for biomedical image segmentation. In: Navab, N., Hornegger, J., Wells, W.M., Frangi, A.F. (eds.) MICCAI 2015. LNCS, vol. 9351, pp. 234–241. Springer, Cham (2015). https://doi.org/10.1007/978-3-319-24574-4_28
12. Salehi, S.S.M., et al.: Real-time automatic fetal brain extraction in fetal MRI by deep learning. In: ISBI, pp. 720–724 (2018)

13. Top, A., Hamarneh, G., Abugharbieh, R.: Active learning for interactive 3D image segmentation. In: Fichtinger, G., Martel, A., Peters, T. (eds.) MICCAI 2011. LNCS, vol. 6893, pp. 603–610. Springer, Heidelberg (2011). https://doi.org/10.1007/978-3-642-23626-6_74

14. Wang, G., Li, W., Aertsen, M., Deprest, J., Ourselin, S., Vercauteren, T.: Aleatoric uncertainty estimation with test-time augmentation for medical image segmentation with convolutional neural networks. Neurocomputing **338**, 34–45 (2019)

15. Wang, G., et al.: Interactive medical image segmentation using deep learning with image-specific fine-tuning. IEEE Trans. Med. Imaging **37**(7), 1562–1573 (2018)

16. Wang, G., et al.: DeepIGeoS: a deep interactive geodesic framework for medical image segmentation. IEEE Trans. Pattern Anal. Mach. Intell. **41**(7), 1559–1572 (2019)

17. Zhao, F., Xie, X.: An overview of interactive medical image segmentation. Ann. BMVA **2013**(7), 1–22 (2013)

18. Zhou, B., Chen, L., Wang, Z.: Interactive deep editing framework for medical image segmentation. In: Shen, D., et al. (eds.) MICCAI 2019. LNCS, vol. 11766, pp. 329–337. Springer, Cham (2019). https://doi.org/10.1007/978-3-030-32248-9_37

Widening the Focus: Biomedical Image Segmentation Challenges and the Underestimated Role of Patch Sampling and Inference Strategies

Frederic Madesta[1] , Rüdiger Schmitz[1,2](✉), Thomas Rösch[2],
and René Werner[1]

[1] Department of Computational Neuroscience,
University Medical Center Hamburg-Eppendorf, Hamburg, Germany
[2] Department for Interdisciplinary Endoscopy,
University Medical Center Hamburg-Eppendorf, Hamburg, Germany
{f.madesta,r.schmitz}@uke.de

Abstract. Image analysis challenges have considerably influenced the recent years in natural and biomedical computer vision. With several important architectures and training strategies having emerged from image analysis challenges, they are often interpreted as contests in model design and training, and much effort is put into optimization of these aspects.

This paper is to widen the focus beyond model architecture and training pipeline design by shedding a light on inference efficiency and the underestimated role of patch sampling strategies. A notable influence of the patch overlap on the challenge scores for successful MICCAI challenges of the previous year is found, in contrast to this parameter being systematically reported in rarely any challenge paper. These edge-overlap effects are shown to be etiologically related to varying dataset-specific intra-patch accuracies. Finally, novel strategies for inference-time patch sampling – other than strided cropping and including Monte Carlo - and uncertainty-based strategies – are proposed and examined, where special focus is put on effects that overarch the single-dataset level and, amongst other effects, an improved performance in the low patch number regimen is achieved.

Drawing on these findings, practical guidance is provided to the reader, and potential challenge participant, on how inference strategies can be optimized experimentally. Moreover, implications on the ongoing best practice debate with respect to challenge design and reporting are discussed. In the hope it may stipulate interest in the undervalued topic of optimized sampling strategies, our inference framework and the

---

F. Madesta and R. Schmitz—Equal contribution.

Electronic supplementary material The online version of this chapter (https://doi.org/10.1007/978-3-030-59719-1_29) contains supplementary material, which is available to authorized users.

© Springer Nature Switzerland AG 2020
A. L. Martel et al. (Eds.): MICCAI 2020, LNCS 12264, pp. 289–298, 2020.
https://doi.org/10.1007/978-3-030-59719-1_29

source codes for the patch sampling strategies are made publicly available (https://github.com/IPMI-ICNS-UKE/inference-patch-sampling).

Keywords: Inference · Patch sampling · Segmentation · Biomedical image analysis challenges

1   Introduction

1.1   Background

From the 2012 ImageNet challenge won by AlexNet [10] through U-Net [16] at the ISBI 2015 cell tracking challenge to today - image analysis challenges have visibly shaped the fields of computer vision and medical image analysis in the recent years. They have thus acquired a reputation of innovators in terms of model architectures and training strategies and many of them have a continuing influence as benchmarks, lasting much beyond their official end. What is reported and compared in challenges hence also influences the technical literature relying on them as benchmarks.

Two properties (amongst others) are common for many biomedical image analysis challenges: (i) the task or a sub-task of it is segmentation or effectively boils down to it and (ii) a single image, being from the domain of medical images that are typically large, needs to be divided into patches for processing.

1.2   Related Works

From various challenges, benchmarks and technical papers, it is known that patch sampling strategies, such as task-adapted loss functions [3] or specific hard negative mining techniques [4], as well the choice of input patch shapes, e.g. 2.5D versus 3D patches [6–8] or the use of multi-scale patches [9,17] influence model performance. Accordingly, these are commonly reported in the challenge and benchmark papers and topics of ongoing optimization and research.

Given their scientific influence, there logically arose a debate on what shall be reported in challenge tasks and papers and how. Systematic and meta analyses of challenge tasks have brought important stimuli to this debate and helped draw practical consequences [12,15]. For example, the high influence of different ranking schemes or missing cases handling [12] have been contrasted with the low coverage with which these parameters had been reported by the challenge organizers. This let the authors not only generally advocate for the development of common best practice guidelines for challenge design and reporting, but also enabled them to identify specific issues with respect to which design and reporting shall be improved.

Before the widespread introduction of U-Net [16] and Fully-Convolutional Neural Networks [13] and since the Ciresan win at ISBI 2012 [5], the sliding window application of (classification) CNNs was state of the art for biomedical image segmentation. Even after U-Net, sliding window as an idea survived when using U-Nets, its variants and alike for segmentation of large images. Therefore, the de-facto standard for inference on large images is the use of ordered, strided image crops.

1.3 Contributions

However, patches need not only to be sampled at training time, but also when predicting testing data (and, notably, when practically applying the trained model for clinical use).

Taking recent challenges arching over a diverse set of different imaging modalities as examples, this work shows that

- when using strided crops for sliding window inference, the stride width can have a decisive influence on the challenge metrics.
- However, taking challenge reports of the years 2016–2019 as examples, this is contrasted by how patch sampling strategies are usually reported: not. We argue that challenge reports by best practices should include the systematic reporting of evaluation time patch sampling.
- Having said that stride width *can* decisively influence challenge results, we also show that is does not have to. The differences between the scenarios are tracked back to fundamental properties of the model and dataset.
- Based on this, we propose a scheme of how to infer experimentally information on the optimal inference strategy 'on the go' when training the model.

In addition, we propose novel strategies for evaluation-time patch sampling, namely

- guided random sampling (Monte Carlo) as well as
- generalized entropy - and
- uncertainty-based inference patch sampling

and show that these can beat standard sliding window techniques in certain scenarios.

We therefore conclude that design of patch sampling strategies beyond the de-facto standard of ordered crops opens up a rich potential for inference step optimization. The focus should be widened to include it into biomedical challenge participation, analysis and beyond.

2   Materials and Methods

2.1 Datasets

We perform our experiments on three different challenge datasets that are selected in order to span a wide range of imaging modalities. These are: (i) the StructSeg 2019 challenge on organ and tumor segmentation in CT scans, (ii) the DRIVE challenge for vessel segmentation in fundoscopy images, and (iii) the PAIP 2019 challenge focusing on liver cancer segmentation in histopathology images. A detailed description is provided in the Supplementary Materials.

2.2 Segmentation Models

For our experiments in this work, we employ pre-trained segmentation models for the datasets described above. The models have either competed directly in the respective challenges and reached top-10 results or have achieved superb results when being evaluated against the challenge dataset used as a benchmark later. Details can be found in the Supplementary Materials.

2.3 Challenge Analysis

In order to assess how evaluation strategies are reported in segmentation challenge papers, we searched and filtered recent years' challenges as described in the Supplementary Materials. This procedure resulted in $N = 27$ segmentation challenges with a total of $N = 170$ different models for analysis.

2.4 Inference Framework and Experimental Setup

The evaluated segmentation models are implemented in different frameworks, namely Tensorflow 2.1.0 [2] and PyTorch 1.2.0 [14]. Using Python 3.7, we have implemented a generic evaluation framework which can load models from both frameworks and handles data loading, patch sampling, prediction stitching and metric evaluations in a framework-independent manner. Performance scores reported in this paper are based on the Dice coefficient (DC). Complementary results for the 95% Hausdorff distance (95HD) are provided in the Supplementary Materials.

2.5 Patch Sampling Strategies

Let $I : \Omega \to V^C$ be a D-dimensional image with $\Omega = [1, N_i] \times \cdots \times [1, N_D]$ and $V \subset \mathbb{R}^C$, where $C \in \mathbb{N}_+$ denotes the number of channels. An image patch P_φ of size $(s_1, \ldots, s_D)^\top$ centered at $c \in \Omega$ can then be described as the restriction of I to $\varphi(c) = [c_1 - s_1/2, c_1 + s_1/2] \times \cdots \times [c_D - s_D/2, c_D + s_D/2]$, i.e., $P_\varphi = I|_{\varphi(c)}$. The corresponding D'-class prediction for this patch can be analogously defined as $P_\varphi^{\text{pred}} : \varphi(c) \to [0, 1]^{D'}$. While sampling patches by any of the strategies below, both the areas φ that have already been sampled as well as corresponding predictions P_φ^{pred} are tracked using the multisets Φ_{area} and Φ_{pred}. In contrast to sets, multisets allow for multiple instances for each element thus enable stitching potentially overlapping and duplicate patches back together.

Ordered Crops: Starting from $c = (s_1/2, \ldots, s_D/2)^\top$, the central coordinate c is shifted by some stride $\mathbf{d} = (d_1, \cdots, d_D)^\top$. Without loss of generality, the iteration is started with the first dimension. After a full loop regarding this dimension, one step is taken into the direction of the second dimension, et cetera, until the whole image is covered.

Monte Carlo Sampling: Random Cropping with Guidance: For this strategy, the central coordinate c of a patch to be cropped is taken as a random variable X. Using a well-defined probability mass function $p_X(c) = \mathbb{P}(X = c)$, random center points and thus random patches can be sampled. Initially, p_X is set to a uniform distribution $p_X(c) = |\Omega|^{-1}$. Employing Φ, the so-called coverage can be defined by counting how often each pixel/voxel has already been covered by randomly sampled patches

$$N(r) = \sum_{\varphi \in \Phi_{\text{area}}} \mathbb{1}_\varphi(r), \quad r \in \Omega. \tag{1}$$

While sampling, p_X gets updated according to

$$p_X(c) = \frac{1}{\mathcal{N}} \frac{|\Omega|^{-1}}{N(c) + \delta}, \quad \delta \in \mathbb{R}_+. \tag{2}$$

We refer to this term as *coverage-guidance* as it encourages sampling of patches that have a relatively low coverage. The resulting strategy is called *coverage-guided Monte Carlo sampling*. In order to obtain a valid probability mass function, we employ a variable normalization factor $\mathcal{N}^{-1} \in \mathbb{R}_+$, so that p_X sums to one.

Dynamic Uncertainty and Entropy-Inspired Sampling: The above formalism (and so the corresponding implementation) can easily be adopted in order to accommodate other ideas than coverage-guidance, just by alteration of the probability map. Exemplarily, this can be used to host dynamic, online uncertainty-dependent strategies or to make use of a generalized entropy for putting emphasis on "interesting" image regions:

To focus the sampling on more relevant areas, we base the calculation of p_X on the probability map

$$E(r) = \frac{1}{\sum_{r \in \Omega} \|\nabla I(r)\|_2^2} \|\nabla I(r)\|_2^2, \tag{3}$$

inspired by the gradient-based extension of Shannon's entropy for multi-dimensional images [11]. The gradient operation is discretized and approximated by second-order central differences. Additionally, we increase the re-sampling likelihood in areas where overlapping predictions differ significantly (in the sense of an overlap uncertainty). To this end, we calculate the variance for every pixel/voxel with non-zero coverage

$$\sigma^2(r) = \frac{\sum_{P_\varphi^{\text{pred}} \in \Phi_{\text{pred}}} \left(P_\varphi^{\text{pred}}(r)\right)^2 - \frac{1}{N(r)} \left(\sum_{P_\varphi^{\text{pred}} \in \Phi_{\text{pred}}} P_\varphi^{\text{pred}}(r)\right)^2}{N(r)}. \tag{4}$$

In order to keep σ^2 independent of the number of classes D' and make the sampling method applicable to arbitrary segmentation tasks, σ^2 is divided by the maximum possible variance $\max\{\sigma^2\} = 1/4$ and averaged over all classes. This results in the normalized uncertainty measure σ_n^2. Using the guidance technique (c.f. Eq. 2), the final probability mass function for patch sampling is computed by

$$p_X(\boldsymbol{c}) = \frac{1}{\mathcal{N}}\left(\frac{E(\boldsymbol{c})}{N(\boldsymbol{c})+\delta} + \sigma_n^2(\boldsymbol{c})\right), \quad \delta \in \mathbb{R}_+. \tag{5}$$

2.6   Measuring Intra-patch Performance on the Go

In order to get an estimate of how the model performance varies within a patch, we calculate a pixel/voxel-wise cross entropy loss for each prediction/ground truth patch tuple in our test sets. The resulting accumulated loss map can be interpreted as the global spatially resolved performance of the predicted patches. It can, as we show below, be employed to set an optimal stride width for a sliding window evaluation strategy. In addition, it signals when other strategies might be beneficial.

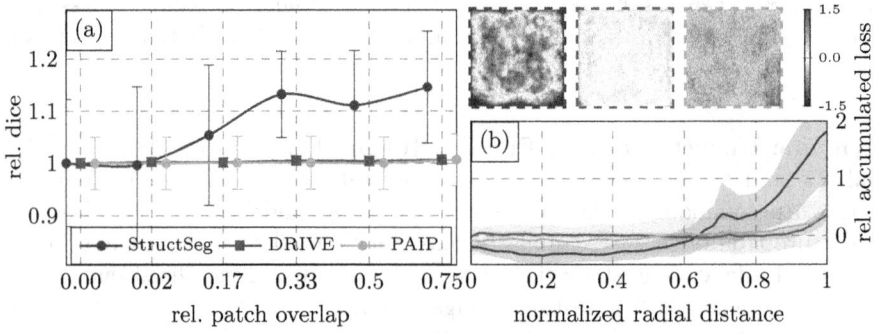

Fig. 1. (a): relative increase of the Dice score with increasing patch overlap for sliding window evaluation (mean ±95% confidence intervals). The insets give the accumulated intra-patch performances for the respective models (normalized by their means). (b) depicts the mean relative patch performances as functions of the radial distance. Lower values correspond to a better performance.

3   Results

3.1   The Stride-Width May Determine Your Challenge Performance - and Will Most Probably Not Be Reported in the Challenge Paper

Our first experiments seeks to examine whether and how variations in the stride width influence the segmentation quality as measured by the Dice coefficient (cf. Supplementary Materials for a complementary analysis using the 95HD).

In order to compare how different models and datasets benefit from increasing patch overlap, we analyse the DC relative to its value for 0 overlap (stride width equal to patch width). As depicted in Fig. 1(a), DRIVE and PAIP models do not benefit from increasing overlap. This is opposed to StructSeg, for which a relative patch overlap of 33% achieves a rise of 13.2% (in absolute terms and for our model: Dice 0.715 at zero overlap vs. 0.809 at 33% overlap). Taking the original DC scores for this challenge task as an example [1] and assuming equal sampling strategies, that relative increase would have made the 4th (0.4857) beat the original winner (0.5447) of this task without any changes to the model or training pipeline.

Figure 1(a) shows that variations in the stride width may have an enormous influence on segmentation performance in certain cases. Irrespective of this, neither sampling strategies nor stride widths are systematically reported in the challenge literature: The patch sampling strategies for all models can be inferred in 30% of the cases (6/20). The stride width, however, is not given for more then 4.1% of the models (7/170). We have not found a single challenge that reports all stride widths for all competing models.

3.2 Experimentally Determining the Optimal Patch Overlap

With the strikingly different patch-overlap effects in PAIP and DRIVE on the one hand and StructSeg on the the hand, we asked for the underlying reasons for this. The insets of Fig. 1 show the accumulated intra-patch performances for StructSeg, DRIVE and PAIP (left to right). When viewed as functions of the radial distance (Fig. 1(b)) the relative intra-patch accumulated loss reflects the behaviour that we had seen in panel (a). In fact, the StructSeg model is characterised by a relatively poor patch performance at its margin versus at its center. As compared to DRIVE and PAIP, the lateral performance slip is stronger and occurs at much smaller radii for StructSeg. The radial coordinate at which the relative patch performance deteriorates for StructSeg corresponds to a relative patch overlap of 33–50%, again suggesting an etiological relation between intra-patch performance and stride effects.

The intra-patch performance can be computed on the go via training. Therefore, it allows us to infer the necessity for a strong evaluation patch overlap already at training time. Likewise, it allows the challenge organizers to estimate the importance of stride width effects in their dataset.

It is worth noting that, by the nature of fully-convolutional neural networks, one can always find a center sub-region of the input patch for which no edge-effects occur because individual pixels are processed equally. Hence, one can theoretically compute a stride width which safely prevents edge-effects. This center region, however, is usually very small (particularly modern architectures that are designed for leveraging context information). In contrast to this conservative estimate, intra-patch performance provides a framework to experimentally determine the *necessary*, hence *optimal* overlap.

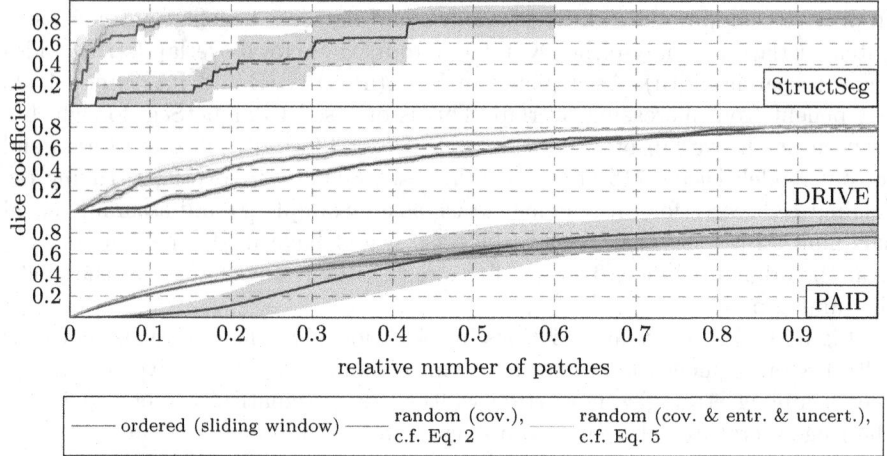

Fig. 2. Dice convergence curves for all applied patch sampling strategies and datasets/models (mean ± standard deviation).

3.3 An Attempt at Beating Sliding Window Patch-Sampling

We next evaluate the alternative patch sampling strategies (cf. Sect. 2.5) against the sliding window technique as the baseline. For the latter, we choose an optimal stride width as described in Sect. 3.1, resulting in 67% of the patch size for StructSeg. For DRIVE and PAIP, where patch overlap is of lesser influence, we chose 33% and 16.7% as examples. Figure 2 shows the Dice scores for the strategies as depending on the number of predicted patches. To allow for an inter-dataset comparison despite their different image sizes, the number of patches is given as a relative number (with one being the number of strided patches needed to cover the whole image).

First, it is evident that our proposed strategies achieve a much faster performance increase in the early patches, independent of the dataset. This has, of course, to be weighed against the computational overhead by sampling patches from the corresponding probability distribution and by updating the probability distribution itself, which we observed to be very moderate, however. On the PAIP dataset, for instance, our costliest strategy including a coverage-dependent plus and uncertainty term results in 3% overhead, when updating the probability distribution every 1% of the image. Second, the convergence curves for these strategies are stable between cases, as opposed to the sliding window approach. The latter is stable only for DRIVE, where the blood vessels as the segmented class are spread over the entire image. For localized classes, as in PAIP or Struct-Seg, the sliding window technique results in a much more unstable convergence curve as judged by the relatively large standard deviations. Third, entropy guidance leads to a particularly steep increase at the very first patches. The fact that this effect is independent of the specific dataset suggests that entropy guidance can robustly select the most meaningful image regions. This is opposed to alternative, 'handcrafted' techniques for thresholding the most relevant image regions, which are specific for a single dataset. Lastly, it should be noted that the proposed strategies are more flexible: in that one can proceed arbitrarily if time permits and in that one can easily adopt further strategies. For example, the uncertainty, being an overlap uncertainty in this case, can easily be replaced by e.g. an uncertainty term from Bayesian inference.

4   Conclusions

Patch sampling strategies play an important role not only at training, but also at inference time. Therefore, reporting of evaluation time patch sampling strategies in challenge reports needs to be systematized and improved.

Patch sampling other than by strided crops holds potential in a variety of scenarios: If fast convergence is needed, strided crop strategies can easily be outperformed by a variety of strategies. Other than that, non-strided strategies allow for combination with uncertainty and Bayesian evaluation methods, and a flexible stopping or continuation of inference runs.

Generalized entropy can be used for additional guidance in order to sample informative regions. It achieves this in a dataset-independent manner, as opposed to "handcrafted" pre-segmentation by thresholds and alike.

Intra-patch performance should be monitored at training time. It provides clues about the ideal patch sampling strategy as well as the optimal stride width and can be computed on the go while training, hence *before* any evaluations and without any extra cost.

Acknowledgments. This work was supported by DFG grant WE 6197/2-1, the European Fund for Regional Development (ERDF), the Free and Hanseatic City of Hamburg, the Forschungszentrum Medizintechnik Hamburg (02fmthh2017), and Olympus Co. Hamburg. Furthermore, RS gratefully acknowledges funding by the Studienstiftung des deutschen Volkes and the Günther Elin Krempel foundation. The authors would like to thank NVIDIA for the donation of graphics cards under the GPU Grant Program.

References

1. StructSeg 2019: Automatic Structure Segmentation for Radiotherapy Planning Challenge 2019, August 2019. https://structseg2019.grand-challenge.org/Home/
2. Abadi, M., et al.: TensorFlow: large-scale machine learning on heterogeneous distributed systems, March 2016. arXiv:1603.04467
3. Abraham, N., Khan, N.M.: A novel focal Tversky loss function with improved attention U-net for lesion segmentation. In: 2019 IEEE 16th International Symposium on Biomedical Imaging (ISBI 2019), pp. 683–687. IEEE, Venice, April 2019
4. Bian, C., et al.: Pyramid network with online hard example mining for accurate left atrium segmentation. In: Pop, M., et al. (eds.) STACOM 2018. LNCS, vol. 11395, pp. 237–245. Springer, Cham (2019). https://doi.org/10.1007/978-3-030-12029-0_26

5. Ciresan, D., Giusti, A., Gambardella, L.M., Schmidhuber, J.: Deep neural networks segment neuronal membranes in electron microscopy images. In: Pereira, F., Burges, C.J.C., Bottou, L., Weinberger, K.Q. (eds.) Advances in Neural Information Processing Systems, vol. 25, pp. 2843–2851. Curran Associates, Inc. (2012)

6. Han, X.: Automatic liver lesion segmentation using a deep convolutional neural network method. Med. Phys. **44**(4), 1408–1419 (2017)

7. Isensee, F., Jaeger, P., Full, P.M., Wolf, I., Engelhardt, S., Maier-Hein, K.H.: Automatic cardiac disease assessment on cine-MRI via time-series segmentation and domain specific features. arXiv:1707.00587 (2018)

8. Isensee, F., Maier-Hein, K.H.: An attempt at beating the 3D U-Net. arXiv:1908.02182, October 2019

9. Kamnitsas, K., et al.: Efficient multi-scale 3D CNN with fully connected CRF for accurate brain lesion segmentation. Med. Image Anal. **36**, 61–78 (2017)

10. Krizhevsky, A., Sutskever, I., Hinton, G.E.: ImageNet classification with deep convolutional neural networks. In: Pereira, F., Burges, C.J.C., Bottou, L., Weinberger, K.Q. (eds.) Advances in Neural Information Processing Systems, vol. 25, pp. 1097–1105. Curran Associates, Inc. (2012)

11. Larkin, K.G.: Reflections on shannon information: In search of a natural information-entropy for images. arXiv:1609.01117 (2016)

12. Maier-Hein, L., et al.: Why rankings of biomedical image analysis competitions should be interpreted with care. Nat. Commun. **9**(1), 1–13 (2018)

13. Long, J., Shelhamer, E., Darrell, T.: Fully convolutional networks for semantic segmentation. In: Proceedings of the IEEE Conference on Computer Vision and Pattern Recognition, pp. 3431–3440 (2015)

14. Paszke, A., et al.: Automatic differentiation in PyTorch. NIPS 2017. https://openreview.net/pdf?id=BJJsrmfCZ

15. Reinke, A., et al.: How to exploit weaknesses in biomedical challenge design and organization. In: Frangi, A.F., Schnabel, J.A., Davatzikos, C., Alberola-López, C., Fichtinger, G. (eds.) MICCAI 2018. LNCS, vol. 11073, pp. 388–395. Springer, Cham (2018). https://doi.org/10.1007/978-3-030-00937-3_45

16. Ronneberger, O., Fischer, P., Brox, T.: U-net: convolutional networks for biomedical image segmentation. In: Navab, N., Hornegger, J., Wells, W.M., Frangi, A.F. (eds.) MICCAI 2015. LNCS, vol. 9351, pp. 234–241. Springer, Cham (2015). https://doi.org/10.1007/978-3-319-24574-4_28

17. Schmitz, R., Madesta, F., Nielsen, M., Werner, R., Rösch, T.: Multi-scale fully convolutional neural networks for histopathology image segmentation: from nuclear aberrations to the global tissue architecture. arXiv:1909.10726, September 2019

Voxel2Mesh: 3D Mesh Model Generation from Volumetric Data

Udaranga Wickramasinghe[1(✉)], Edoardo Remelli[1], Graham Knott[2], and Pascal Fua[1]

[1] Computer Vision Laboratory, École Polytechnique Fédérale de Lausanne, Lausanne, Switzerland
`udaranga.wickramasinghe@epfl.ch`
[2] BioEM Laboratory, École Polytechnique Fédérale de Lausanne, Lausanne, Switzerland

Abstract. CNN-based volumetric methods that label individual voxels now dominate the field of biomedical segmentation. However, 3D surface representations are often required for proper analysis. They can be obtained by post-processing the labeled volumes which typically introduces artifacts and prevents end-to-end training. In this paper, we therefore introduce a novel architecture that goes directly from 3D image volumes to 3D surfaces without post-processing and with better accuracy than current methods. We evaluate it on Electron Microscopy and MRI brain images as well as CT liver scans. We will show that it outperforms state-of-the-art segmentation methods.

Keywords: Volumetric segmentation · 3D surfaces · Deep learning

1 Introduction

State-of-the-Art volumetric segmentation techniques rely on Convolutional Neural Networks (CNNs) operating on an image volume [3,13,17]. However in clinical and research practice, a mesh representation is often required to model the surface morphology and to compute area-based statistics. Unfortunately, converting volumes into surfaces relies on algorithms such as Marching Cubes [10] followed by mesh smoothing, which is not differentiable, prevents end-to-end training, and introduces artifacts.

We therefore introduce an end-to-end trainable architecture that goes directly from volumetric images to 3D surface meshes. Our **Voxel2Mesh** architecture is depicted by Fig. 1 (b). It comprises a voxel encoder, voxel decoder and a mesh decoder. The two decoders communicate at all resolution levels and our approach incorporates two innovative features that are key to performance.

Electronic supplementary material The online version of this chapter (https://doi.org/10.1007/978-3-030-59719-1_30) contains supplementary material, which is available to authorized users.

© Springer Nature Switzerland AG 2020
A. L. Martel et al. (Eds.): MICCAI 2020, LNCS 12264, pp. 299–308, 2020.
https://doi.org/10.1007/978-3-030-59719-1_30

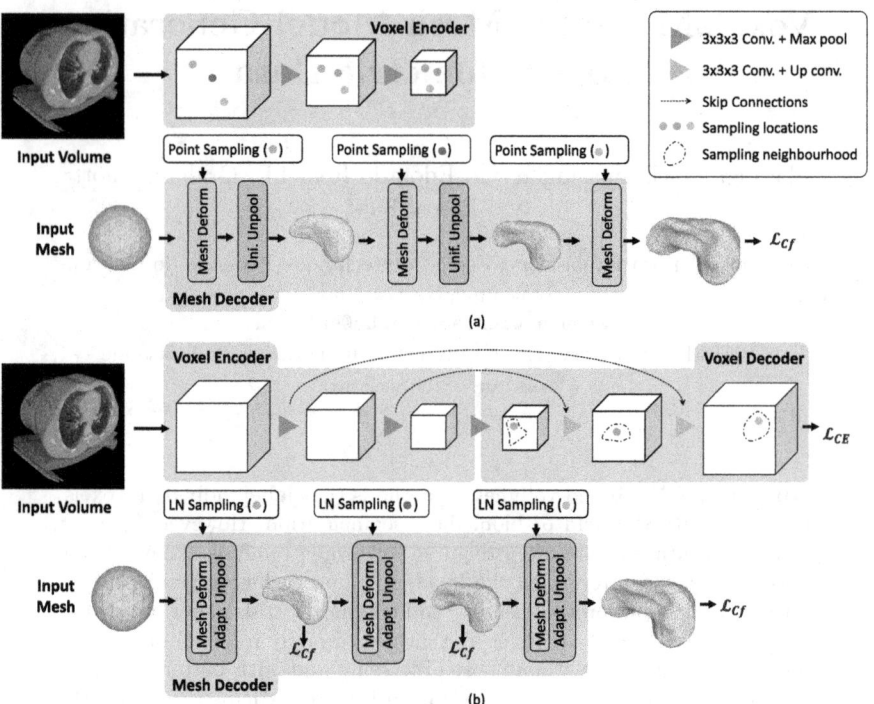

Fig. 1. Architectures (a) The **Pixel2Mesh-3D** architecture, a straightforward extension of [19], uses a surface decoder but no voxel decoder. (b) By contrast, our **Voxel2Mesh** architecture takes as input an image and spherical mesh. They are jointly encoded and then decoded into cubes and meshes of increasing resolution. At each mesh decoding stage, the decoder first receives as input the current mesh and a set of features sampled from the cube of corresponding resolution. Then the mesh is deformed and refined non-uniformly by adding vertices only where they are needed.

- **Learned Neighborhood Sampling.** The mesh decoder learns to sample the output of the volume decoder only where needed, that is, in the neighborhood of output vertices.
- **Adaptive Mesh Unpooling.** Accurately representing the surface requires densely sampled mesh vertices in high-curvature areas but not elsewhere. We introduce an adaptive mesh unpooling scheme that achieves this results and eliminates the need for exponentially large amounts of memory that uniform unpooling requires.

Our contribution therefore is a novel architecture that takes a 3D volume as input and yields an accurate 3D surface without any post-processing. We evaluate it on Electron Microscopy and MRI brain images as well as CT liver scans. We will show that it outperforms state-of-the-art segmentation methods, especially when the training set is relatively small.

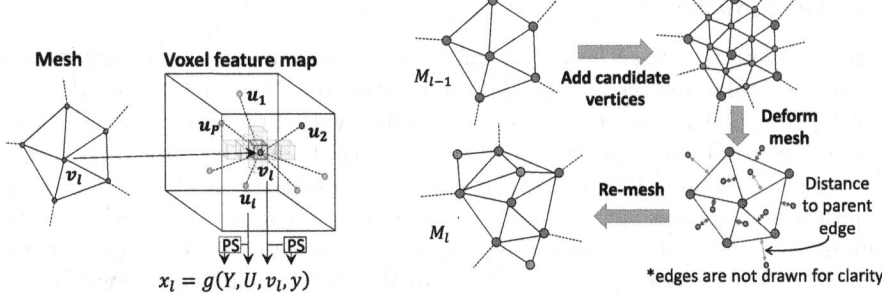

Fig. 2. Approach. (a) Learned Neighborhood Sampling. (b) Adaptive Mesh Unpooling.

2 Related Work

CNN-based volumetric methods such as U-Net and its variants [3,6,13,17] now dominate biomedical image segmentation. This is evident from the CHAOS challenge [2] and Medical Segmentation Decathlon [7] results. The winners of both competitions used ensembles of methods relying on volumetric CNNs.

2.1 Importance of Surface Models

Many biological imaging tools are designed to study the morphology of structures such as cells, organs, or tissues. Researchers usually prefer to visualize them as 3D surfaces at the required level of detail everywhere and are not limited by the voxels resolution. Even though volumes and distances can be estimated using voxels, analyzing surfaces is best accomplished using meshes.

But, state-of-the-art methods produce volumetric descriptions and therefore must be converted to surface meshes. This conversion typically relies on algorithms such as Marching Cubes [10] followed by mesh smoothing. This introduces artifacts and prevents end-to-end training. We now turn to existing approaches that mitigate these difficulties.

2.2 Deformable Models

Deformable surface models became popular in the 1990s to model biological structures in volumetric data [5,12] and are still being developped [8,9,16]. They are now used in conjunction with deep networks [11] trained to return the energy function the deformed models should minimize.

While they can remove some of the artifacts introduced by converting volumes to surfaces, their use makes the processing pipeline more complex and still prevents end-to-end training. Furthermore, they are not well-suited to segmenting structures that exhibit high inter-sample shape variations, such as the synaptic junctions used in our experiments.

2.3   Deep Surfaces

In this context, the Pixel2Mesh [19] approach and its more recent variants [15,20] are of particular interest. They are among the very few approaches that go *directly* from 2D images to 3D surface meshes without resorting to an intermediate stage. They take an image and encodes it into a set of progressively smaller feature maps. This set is then used at each stage of the decoding process to produce an increasingly accurate mesh. This approach is easily extended to handle 3D image volumes using the architecture depicted by Fig. 1(a) and we will refer to this extension as **Pixel2Mesh-3D**. Unfortunately, as we will see, it was conceived for a different purpose and its design choices makes it suboptimal for handling 3D image volumes.

3   Method

Our **Voxel2Mesh** architecture is depicted by Fig. 1(b). It takes an image volume as input and returns a 3D surface mesh. The image volume is first encoded into smaller latent volumes that serves as input to the *voxel decoder*. Then the voxel decoder generates a pyramid of cubes of increasing resolution whose voxels contain feature vectors. Finally the *mesh decoder* generates increasingly precise deformations of an initial spherical mesh using feature vectors extracted from voxel decoder. The voxel encoder and voxel decoder pictured at the top of Fig. 1(b) are based on a standard U-Net [3] architecture.

A key specificity of our approach is that both the sampling of the voxel features and the location and number of the new vertices needed to refine the mesh are adaptive so that the final mesh is refined where it needs to be, and only there.

3.1   Mesh Decoder

The input to the mesh decoder is a sphere mesh with 3D vertices forming facets whose edges we use to perform graph convolutions. It learns to iteratively refine the sphere mesh to match the target object.

Let us denote by $l = 0$ the input to the decoders and by $1 \leq l \leq L$ the output of subsequent blocks. For each mesh vertex, we write

$$\mathbf{z}_l = h_l(\mathbf{x}_l, \mathbf{z}_{l-1}, \mathbf{v}_{l-1}) \text{ and } \mathbf{v}_l = \mathbf{v}_{l-1} + \Delta_l(\mathbf{z}_l), \tag{1}$$

where $\mathbf{v}_l$ are the 3D vertex coordinates after block l; $\mathbf{x}_l$ and $\mathbf{z}_{l-1}$ are the feature vectors produced by blocks l and $l-1$ in the voxel and mesh decoder, respectively; h_l and Δ_l are two functions implemented by 4 graph convolution layers each, whose weight we learn during training. By convention, we take $\mathbf{z}_0$ to be an empty feature vector. We write the graph convolutions as

$$\mathbf{f}' = w_1 \mathbf{f} + \frac{1}{|\mathcal{N}(\mathbf{v}_l)|} \sum_{\mathbf{v}_l^i \in \mathcal{N}(\mathbf{v}_l)} \mathbf{f}^i w_2 e^{-d_i^2/\sigma^2}, \tag{2}$$

where $\mathbf{f}'$ and $\mathbf{f}$ are the feature vector associated with the vertex $\mathbf{v}_l$ before and after the convolution. $\mathcal{N}(\mathbf{v}_l)$ is the set of neighborhood vertices of $\mathbf{v}_l$ and $\mathbf{y}^{\,i}$ is the feature vector corresponding to the neighboring vertex $\mathbf{v}_l^i$. $d_i = \sqrt{\|\mathbf{v}_l^i - \mathbf{v}_l\|}$. $\mathbf{w}_1, \mathbf{w}_2$ and σ are weights learned during training.

Learned Neighborhood Sampling (LNS). The feature vector x_l in Eq. 1 is extracted from voxel features by feature sampling at locations that are functions of the mesh vertices. Since voxel features lie on a discrete grid, we use tri-linear interpolation to sample features and refer to this as *point sampling*. Current approaches only sample at exact vertex locations [19] or in pre-determined neighborhoods around the vertex [20]. This restricts the sampler's ability to pool information from its neighborhood.

Instead, we introduce our LNS strategy that learns optimum sampling locations. It first samples feature vector $\mathbf{y}$ at a given vertex $\mathbf{v}_l$ using point sampling. We then train a neural function to return the set of neighborhood points to sample

$$\mathbf{U} = \{u_i\}_{i=1}^{P} = f(\mathbf{y}, \mathbf{v}_l). \tag{3}$$

Next, the set of features $\mathbf{Y} = \{\mathbf{y}_i\}_{i=1}^{P}$ are sampled at $\{u_i\}_{i=1}^{P}$, again using point sampling. Finally, the feature vector $\mathbf{x}_l$ corresponding to vertex $\mathbf{v}_l$ is given by another neural function

$$\mathbf{x}_l = g(\mathbf{Y}, \mathbf{U}, \mathbf{y}, \mathbf{v}_l). \tag{4}$$

As shown in Fig. 2 (a), LNS only samples from the voxel feature map corresponding to the mesh deformation stage. This is in contrast to earlier sampling strategies, that samples from all feature maps at each stage which yields graph convolution networks with many more weights in their mesh deforming module and thus over-fitting when trained with smaller datasets.

Adaptive Mesh Unpooling. High accuracy requires enough vertices to properly fit the underlying surface. We could start with a sphere with many vertices but this is neither computationally nor memory efficient. Therefore, **Pixel2Mesh-3D** and its variants use an uniform unpooling strategy that gradually increase the vertex count. Unfortunately, the vertex count still increases exponentially.

To prevent this, we introduce the adaptive unpooling strategy depicted by Fig. 2 (b). First, we add candidate vertices using uniform unpooling strategy. Then the mesh is deformed and we compute the shortest distance from each candidate vertex to its parent edge as indicated by red and green arrows in Fig. 2 (b). If the distance is greater than a threshold, we keep them, otherwise we discard them. This looses edge connectivity making re-meshing necessary. To this end, we exploit the fact that the mesh decoder learns a continuous mapping from the surface points on the input sphere to those on the object surface. This relationship enables us to find the corresponding points on the sphere's surface for each mesh vertex. We compute the convex hull to restore edge connectivity $\mathcal{E}'$ between the points on the sphere. $\mathcal{E}'$ can then be directly transferred to the target mesh because the mapping is continuous. Since our remeshing only recomputes the neighbors of each vertex and does not perform any non-differentiable operations on vertex variables, it preserves overall differentiability.

3.2   Loss Function

We use the cross entropy loss $\mathcal{L}_{ce}$ with ground-truth volumes and the Chamfer distance $\mathcal{L}_{cf}$ to points at the boundary of the same ground-truth volumes to train the voxel and mesh decoders, respectively. Instead of using mesh vertices when evaluating $\mathcal{L}_{cf}$, we randomly sample points from the 3D mesh [14]. We also introduce three regularization terms normal loss $\mathcal{L}_n$, laplacian loss $\mathcal{L}_{lap}$, and edge length loss $\mathcal{L}_{el}$ to improve convergence and smooth the output mesh [19]. We write the complete loss as

$$\mathcal{L} = \sum_{l=1}^{L} \mathcal{L}_{cf}^{l} + \lambda_1 \mathcal{L}_{ce} + \lambda_2 \mathcal{L}_n + \lambda_3 \mathcal{L}_{lap} + \lambda_4 \mathcal{L}_{el}, \tag{5}$$

where L is the number of stages in the mesh decoder.

4   Experiments

4.1   Datasets

We tested our approach on 3 datasets. We describe them below briefly and provide more details on the training and testing splits in the supplementary material.

Synaptic Junction Dataset. It comprises a $500 \times 500 \times 200$ FIB-SEM image stack of a mouse cortex. We extracted 13 volumes roughly centered around a synapse for training and 13 for testing. The task is to segment the pre-synaptic region, post-synaptic region, and synaptic cleft. They are shown in blue, green, and red respectively in the first two rows of Fig. 4.

Hippocampus Dataset. It consists of 260 labeled MRI image cubes from the Medical Segmentation Decathlon [18]. The task is to segment the hippocampus, as depicted by the fourth row of Fig. 4.

Liver Dataset. It consists of 20 labeled CT image cubes from the CHAOS challenge [2]. The task is to segment the liver as shown in the third row of Fig. 4.

4.2   Baselines

As the architecture of **Voxel2Mesh** borrows from **U-NET** and **Pixel2Mesh-3D**, they both constitute natural baselines. As state-of-the-art CNN based approaches, we use **TernausNet, LinkNet34, ResNet50** and **ResNet50-SE**,

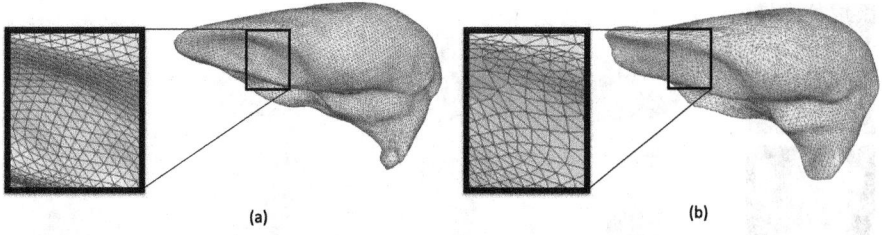

(a)   (b)

Fig. 3. Levels of resolution. (a) **Pixel2Mesh-3D** result (10422 vertices). (b) **Voxel2Mesh** result (7498 vertices). With our adaptative unpooling, we obtain better results with fewer vertices.

Table 1. Comparative results on three datasets using the IoU metric.

	Liver	Hippo.	Synaptic junction		
			Pre-synap	Synapse	Post-synap
TernausNet [6]	*84.4 ± 1.3*	78.4 ± 1.2	73.5 ± 1.3	64.4 ± 0.5	*78.4 ± 1.3*
LinkNet34 [17]	82.8 ± 1.4	79.4 ± 0.8	72.3 ± 0.5	63.2 ± 1.2	78.2 ± 1.1
ResNet50 [1]	82.1 ± 0.7	80.7 ± 0.2	70.3 ± 0.8	63.3 ± 0.6	76.2 ± 1.4
ResNet50-SE [1]	82.6 ± 1.2	80.5 ± 1.3	71.3 ± 0.6	63.6 ± 0.7	76.3 ± 0.9
V-NET [13]	81.5 ± 1.4	75.3 ± 1.4	64.3 ± 0.7	65.2 ± 1.3	74.1 ± 0.7
U-NET [3]	84.2 ± 1.6	*80.9 ± 1.5*	*73.6 ± 1.3*	*67.2 ± 0.8*	78.2 ± 0.9
Best CNN + **CLN**	84.6 ± 1.7	81.1 ± 1.5	74.5 ± 1.2	67.6 ± 0.8	79.5 ± 0.9
Best CNN + **FPP**	84.3 ± 1.7	80.8 ± 1.5	74.2 ± 1.2	**67.4 ± 0.8**	79.3 ± 0.9
Voxel2Mesh	**86.9 ± 1.1**	**82.3 ± 0.9**	**77.3 ± 1.2**	65.3 ± 1.2	**83.2 ± 1.6**

Table 2. Comparative results against CNN based mesh deforming baselines.

	Liver		Hippocampus	
	IoU	Cf.	IoU	Cf.
PS + UMU	83.3 ± 0.8	3.3 ×10⁻³	78.8 ± 1.1	2.9 ×10⁻³
HS + UMU	84.2 ± 0.6	2.8 ×10⁻³	79.9 ± 0.9	2.3 ×10⁻³
LNS + UMU	85.6 ± 0.9	2.1 ×10⁻³	81.2 ± 1.2	1.8 ×10⁻³
LNS + AMU (Voxel2Mesh)	**86.9 ± 1.1**	**1.3 × 10⁻³**	**82.3 ± 0.9**	**1.1 × 10⁻³**

which belong to the ensemble of architectures that won the CHAOS challenge. **U-NET** was used as the base architecture by the winner of Medical Segmentation Decathlon. We also use **V-NET**, a widely used variant of **U-NET**, as a baseline. Since we are working with volumetric data, we use 3D variants of all these architectures.

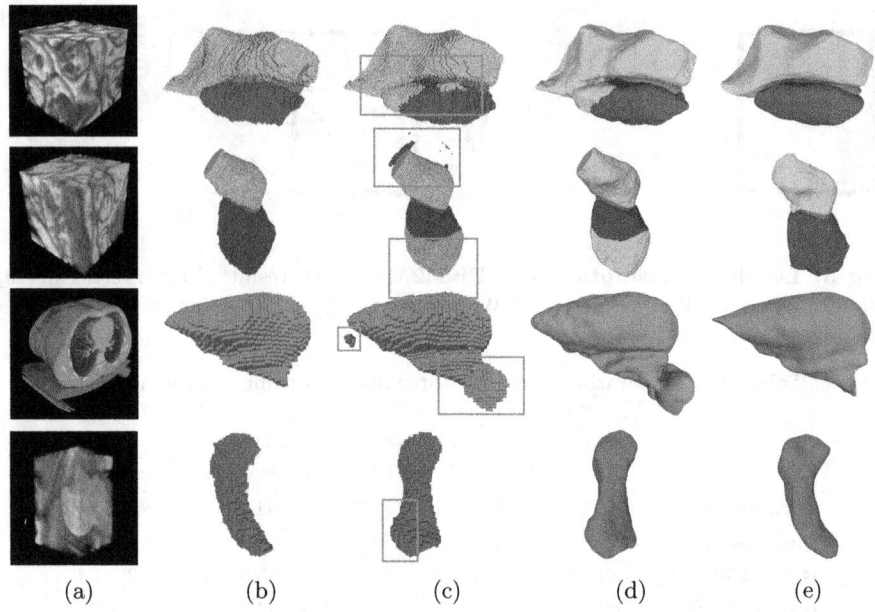

Fig. 4. Qualitative results. (a) Input volumes. EM (row 1,2), CT (row 3), MRI (row 4) (b) Ground truth (c) CNN baseline (d) CNN baseline + post processing (e) **Voxel2Mesh**. The orange boxes highlight false positive regions. (Color figure online)

4.3   Comparative Results

Figure 4 and Fig. 3 depict our results qualitatively and we report quantitative ones in Table 1. As all the baselines shown above the first thick line return volumetric descriptions, we rasterize the mesh that **Voxel2Mesh** returns and use intersection over union (IoU) score to compare all the results against the ground truth. In all cases, we trained the networks three times with different initializations and we report the mean IoU and its standard deviation.

For completeness, we simulated a post-processing pipeline by selecting the best performing baseline for each of the three datasets, removing small false positive regions outside the object by connected component analysis, running Marching Cubes followed by smoothing using Algebraic Point Set Surfaces [4]. We refer to the result obtained by only removing the false positives as *Best CNN* + **CLN** and the one with full post-processing as *Best CNN* + **FPP**.

Voxel2Mesh performs best in all cases except the synaptic cleft, where it comes second. This can ascribed to the fact that synaptic clefts sometimes have holes in them, which a spherical mesh cannot capture. The improvement is most significant in the two datasets—liver and synaptic junction—with fewer training samples compared to the hippocampus dataset that features more training data.

The key challenge when training **Voxel2Mesh** is finding the correct amount of regularization. If the regularization is not sufficient, it can result in vertices with large movements and faces with large area. If it is too much, it can result in meshes that are over-smoothed. Therefore, the regularization coefficients should be found using hyperparameter grid search.

4.4 Ablation Study

Pixel2Mesh-3D is the baseline closest to our approach because it directly outputs a 3D surface. Point Sampling (**PS**) and Uniform Mesh Unpooling (**UMU**) are the two modules in that play the same role as our Learned Neighborhood Sampling (**LNS**) and adoptive mesh unpooling (**AMU**). To check the importance of these strategies, we replaced them in our **Voxel2Mesh** pipeline by the equivalent ones in **Pixel2Mesh-3D**. We also evaluate the performance of Hypothesis Sampling (**HS**), the sampling strategy of [20] that relies on a fixed neighborhood sampling. We report the results in Table 2 in Chamfer distance terms. They demonstrate that our adaptative strategies **LNS+AMU** deliver a clear benefit.

5 Conclusion

We have proposed an end-to-end trainable architecture that takes an image volume as input and outputs a 3D surface mesh. This makes the post processing steps usually required to obtain such a mesh from a volumetric representation unnecessary, while preserving accuracy. Our adaptive sampling and unpooling strategies are key to this result. Not only does our architecture deliver good results, it also bridges the gap between voxel-based and surface-based representations. In future work, we plan to extend our approach to structures with more complex topologies, such as the synaptic cleft and its potential holes.

Acknowledgments. This work was supported in part by a Swiss National Science Foundation grant.

References

1. Kavur, A., et al.: CHAOS Challenge - Combined (CT-MR) Healthy Abdominal Organ Segmentation. arXiv Preprint (2020)
2. CHAOS: Combined (CT-MR) Healthy Abdominal Organ Segmentation. In: International Symposium on Biomedical Imaging (2019)
3. Çiçek, Ö., Abdulkadir, A., Lienkamp, S.S., Brox, T., Ronneberger, O.: 3D U-Net: learning dense volumetric segmentation from sparse annotation. In: Ourselin, S., Joskowicz, L., Sabuncu, M.R., Unal, G., Wells, W. (eds.) MICCAI 2016. LNCS, vol. 9901, pp. 424–432. Springer, Cham (2016). https://doi.org/10.1007/978-3-319-46723-8_49
4. Guennebaud, G., Gross, M.: Algebraic point set surfaces. In: ACM SIGGRAPH (2007)
5. He, L., et al.: A comparative study of deformable contour methods on medical image segmentation. Image Vis. Comput. **26**(2), 141–163 (2008)

6. Iglovikov, V., Shvets, A.: Ternausnet: U-net with vgg11 encoder pre-trained on imagenet for image segmentation. arXiv Preprint (2018)
7. IsenseeEmail, F., Petersen, J., Zimmerer, A.K., Jaeger, P., Kohl, S., Wasserthal, J.: nnU-Net: Self-adapting Framework for U-Net-Based Medical Image Segmentation. arXiv Preprint (2018)
8. Jorstad, A., Nigro, B., Cali, C., Wawrzyniak, M., Fua, P., Knott, G.: Neuromorph: a toolset for the morphometric analysis and visualization of 3D models derived from electron microscopy image stacks. Neuroinformatics 13(1), 83–92 (2014)
9. Leventon, M.E., Grimson, W.E., Faugeras, O.: Statistical shape influence in geodesic active contours. In: Conference on Computer Vision and Pattern Recognition, pp. 316–323 (2000)
10. Lorensen, W., Cline, H.: Marching cubes: a high resolution 3D surface construction algorithm. In: ACM SIGGRAPH (1987)
11. Marcos, D., Tuia, D., Kellenbergerg, B., Urtasun, R.: Learning deep structured active contours end-to-end. In: Conference on Computer Vision and Pattern Recognition (2018)
12. Mcinerney, T., Terzopoulos, D.: Deformable models in medical image analysis: a survey. Med. Image Anal. 1, 91–108 (1996)
13. Milletari, F., Navab, N., Ahmadi, S.A.: V-Net: Fully Convolutional Neural Networks for Volumetric Medical Image Segmentation. arXiv Preprint, June 2016
14. Osada, R., Funkhouser, T., Chazelle, B., Dobkin, D.: Shape distributions. ACM Trans. Graph. 21(4), 807–832 (2002)
15. Pan, J., Jia, K.: Deep mesh reconstruction from single rgb images via topology modification networks. In: International Conference on Computer Vision (2019)
16. Prevost, R., Cuingnet, R., Mory, B., Cohen, L.D., Ardon, R.: Incorporating shape variability in image segmentation via implicit template deformation. In: Mori, K., Sakuma, I., Sato, Y., Barillot, C., Navab, N. (eds.) MICCAI 2013. LNCS, vol. 8151, pp. 82–89. Springer, Heidelberg (2013). https://doi.org/10.1007/978-3-642-40760-4_11
17. Shvets, A., Rakhlin, A., Kalinin, A., Iglovikov, V.: Automatic Instrument Segmentation in Robot-Assisted Surgery Using Deep Learning. arXiv Preprint (2018)
18. Simpson, A., Cardoso, M.: A large annotated medical image dataset for the development and evaluation of segmentation algorithms. arXiv Preprint (2019)
19. Wang, N., Zhang, Y., Li, Z., Fu, Y., Liu, W., Jiang, Y.: Pixel2mesh: generating 3D mesh models from single RGB images. In: European Conference on Computer Vision (2018)
20. Wen, C., Zhang, Y., Li, Z., Fu, Y.: Pixel2mesh++: multi-view 3D mesh generation via deformation. In: International Conference on Computer Vision (2019)

Unsupervised Learning for CT Image Segmentation via Adversarial Redrawing

Youyi Song[1(✉)], Teng Zhou[2], Jeremy Yuen-Chun Teoh[3], Jing Zhang[4],
and Jing Qin[1]

[1] Center for Smart Health, School of Nursing, The Hong Kong Polytechnic
University, Hong Kong, China
youyisong.song@connect.polyu.hk
[2] Department of Compute Science, Shantou University, Shantou, China
[3] Department of Surgery, The Chinese University of Hong Kong,
Hong Kong SAR, China
[4] College of Electrical Engineering, Sichuan University, Chengdu, China

Abstract. We propose a novel adversarial learning framework for unsupervised training of CNNs in CT image segmentation. It is motivated by difficulties in collecting voxel-wise annotations, which is laborious, time-consuming and expensive. It is conceptually simple, allowing us to train an effective segmentation network without any human annotation. Specifically, we design the generator with a CNN producing the segmentation results and a decoder redrawing the CT volume based on the segmentation results. The CNN is then implicitly trained in the adversarial learning framework where a discriminator gradually enforcing the generator to generate CT volumes whose distribution well matches the distribution of the training data. We further propose two constrains as regularization schemes for the training procedure to drive the model towards optimal segmentation by avoiding some unreasonable results. We conducted extensive experiments to evaluate the proposed method on a famous publicly available dataset, and the experimental results demonstrate the effectiveness of the proposed method.

Keywords: Unsupervised learning · Adversarial redrawing · CNNs · CT image segmentation.

1 Introduction

Computed tomography (CT) image segmentation is a fundamental task in medical image analysis, allowing us to measure or extract quantitative information of objects in the images. These quantitative measurements are essential for a wide range of applications, e.g. diseases diagnosis, therapeutic assistance, radiotherapy planning, surgery simulation, and injury prediction, to mention a few [1]. Among all available segmentation algorithms to date, deep convolutional neural networks (CNNs) [2,3] are shown to be the best choice, having exhibited excellent performance in a large variety of CT image segmentation tasks [4–7].

© Springer Nature Switzerland AG 2020
A. L. Martel et al. (Eds.): MICCAI 2020, LNCS 12264, pp. 309–320, 2020.
https://doi.org/10.1007/978-3-030-59719-1_31

However, CNNs are rather expensive to use in practice. In order to properly train a CNN for segmentation, we usually have to collect a large number of ground truth images with voxel-wise annotations by clinical experts, which is laborious, time-consuming and costly. Although currently there are pre-trained CNNs and public CT datasets available, evidence [8,9] shows that re-training or at least fine-tuning is still required when applying a trained CNN to a new dataset, which means that we still need to collect the ground truth images with voxel-wise annotations for the new dataset.

In order to alleviate the workload on collecting voxel-wise annotations, there are two main types of methods: training with (1) fewer ground truth images [10–13] and (2) weaker supervision [14–17]. In the first type, two commonly-used strategies are data augmentation [10,11] and transfer learning [12,13], creating ground truth images for training either by rotating, cropping, and flipping the 'real' ground truth images [10,11] or resorting to other available CT datasets [12,13]. In the second type, weakly supervised [14,15] and semi-supervised [16,17] methods are two promising ways, training the CNN respectively by 'image'-level annotations (e.g. object's center) [14,15] or a few images with voxel-level annotations and a lot of images without any annotation information [16,17].

In recent years, there are studies that train CNNs without any human annotation, by exploiting (1) domain adaption [18–21] and (2) unsupervised training [22–24]. In the first category, the CNN is trained by another domain images in a supervised manner, and then is directly applied to CT images. The underlying idea is to exploit features' similarity in different domains. In the second category, the key is to design a training mechanism with a powerful loss function so that it can express the desired property of the targeting objects without any supervision from human annotations. Existing unsupervised methods, however, face great challenges in modeling the statistical properties that can lead to a meaningful segmentation [22–24].

In this paper, we propose a novel unsupervised technique to train CNNs for CT image segmentation. The key idea is in spirit similar to [25], leveraging adversarial learning paradigm [26] to provide CNNs' supervision by generating CT volumes based on CNNs' segmented results. It is conceptually simple, allowing us to train an effective CNN without using any human annotations. Specifically, we first design the generator with a CNN producing the segmentation results and a decoder redrawing the CT volume based on the segmentation results. The CNN is then implicitly trained to learn how to yield better segmentation results when the discriminator enforcing the generator to generate CT volumes whose distribution well matches the distribution of the training data. We further propose two constraints as regularization terms to manage the training procedure towards optimal segmentation results by avoiding unreasonable results. We conduct extensive experiments to evaluate the proposed method on a publicly available dataset, and the experimental results demonstrate its effectiveness.

2   Methodology

Figure 1 illustrates the pipeline of the proposed unsupervised learning model via adversarial redrawing. First, a CNN (we employ the widely used U-Net in our implementation) is developed as a part of the generator, which generates a CT volume by redrawing the segmented objects obtained from the CNN via a decoder given random noise. The CNN is then implicitly trained by using a discriminator to enforce the generator to generate CT volumes whose distribution matches that of the training data. Technique details are presented below.

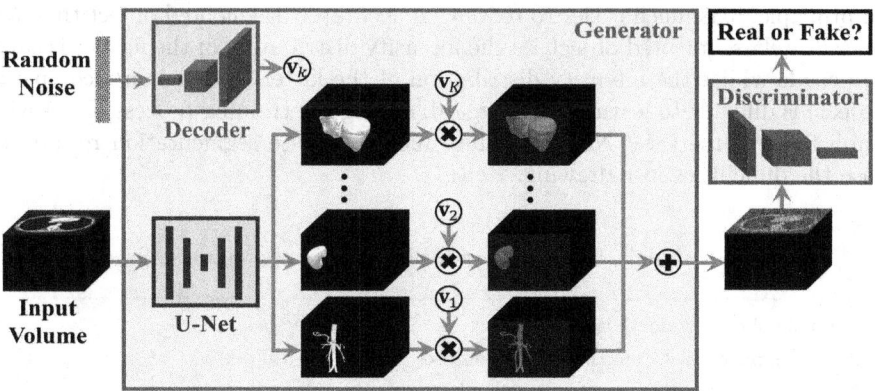

Fig. 1. The pipeline of the proposed unsupervised learning model for CT image segmentation; we choose U-Net as the backbone.

2.1   The Proposed Unsupervised Learning Model

Suppose that there are K objects to be segmented in a given CT volume $\mathbf{v} \in \mathbb{R}^{W \times L \times H}$, where W, L, and H denote the width, length, and height of the volume, respectively. We first employ a CNN to produce the segmentation result. We use $\mathbf{M}_k \in \{0,1\}^{W \times L \times H}$ to denote the segmentation map of the object $k \in \{0, 1, 2, \cdots, K\}$, where $\mathbf{M}_k(x, y, z) = 1$ means that the voxel at the position (x, y, z) to be segmented as object k. Here $\mathbf{M}_0$ is the background map, and it can be directly computed as $\mathbf{M}_0(x, y, z) = 1 - \sum_{k=1}^{K} \mathbf{M}_k(x, y, z)$.

We employ adversarial learning paradigm [26] for unsupervised training of the CNN. First, we design the generator as follows. In each segmentation map $\mathbf{M}_k$, $k \in \{0, 1, 2, \cdots, K\}$, we employ a decoder to estimate the intensity value of its foreground voxels in order to learn the underlying imaging process of the object k. We call this process as redrawing. The redrawing is conducted by decoding a random noise $\mathbf{z}_k \sim p(\mathbf{z})$ into a volume $\mathbf{v}_k \in \mathbb{R}^{W \times L \times H}$ and then gating it by $\mathbf{v}_k \otimes \mathbf{M}_k$, where $\otimes$ stands for the element-wise multiplication. We then generate the CT volume $\tilde{\mathbf{v}} \in \mathbb{R}^{W \times L \times H}$ by aggregating all of them (element-wise summation), that is, $\tilde{\mathbf{v}} = \sum_{k=0}^{K} \mathbf{v}_k \otimes \mathbf{M}_k$. We next develop a discriminator to compare the generated CT volume with the input volume and enforce the generator to produce better segmentation results to redraw the CT volume with similar intensity distribution to the input data.

To this end, the CNN now can be trained with unsupervised by solving the below adversarial learning problem:

$$\min_{\mathbf{G}} \max_{\mathbf{D}} \left(\mathbb{E}_{\mathbf{v}} \big[\log \mathbf{D}(\mathbf{v}) \big] + \mathbb{E}_{\mathbf{v}, \mathbf{z}_0, \cdots, \mathbf{z}_K} \big[1 - \log \mathbf{D}\big(\mathbf{G}(\mathbf{v}|\mathbf{z}_0, \cdots, \mathbf{z}_K)\big)\big]\right), \quad (1)$$

where $\mathbf{G}$ and $\mathbf{D}$ stand for the generator and discriminator, respectively. We now inspect why it works? Eq. 1 is able to guarantee that the generated CT volumes are indistinguishable from the input CT volumes by the discriminator. In principle, it is much easier to redraw an accurately segmented object than an inaccurately segmented object, as the intensity distribution of the former is easy to decode whilst the intensity distribution of the latter (even as an incomplete object) is difficult to learn. In this regard, during the training process, Eq. 1 will implicitly enforce the CNN to produce more accurate segmentation results to ease the difficulties in redrawing.

Table 1. The pseudo code of the training procedure

1: **for** number of training iterations **do**
2:     sample data $\mathbf{v}$ from the training dataset
3:     sample object's index $k \sim \text{Uniform}(\{0, 1, 2, \cdots, K\})$
4:     sample noise vector $\mathbf{z}_k \sim \mathcal{N}(\mathbf{0}, \mathbf{I})$ ▷ Normal distribution
5:     $\widetilde{\mathbf{v}} \leftarrow \mathbf{G}(\mathbf{v}|k, \mathbf{z}_k)$ ▷ Generating CT volume
6:     $\mathcal{L}_{\mathbf{R}} \leftarrow ||\mathbf{R}(\widetilde{\mathbf{v}}) - \mathbf{z}_k||_2^2$ ▷ Computing regressor' loss
7:     $\mathcal{L}_{\mathbf{G}} \leftarrow \mathbf{D}(\widetilde{\mathbf{v}})$ ▷ Computing discriminator's prediction on $\widetilde{\mathbf{v}}$
8:     $\mathcal{L}_{\mathbf{D}} \leftarrow \min(0, \mathbf{D}(\mathbf{v}) - 1) + \min(0, -\mathbf{D}(\widetilde{\mathbf{v}}) - 1)$ ▷ Computing adversarial loss
9:     $\theta_{\mathbf{G}} \leftarrow \theta_{\mathbf{G}} - \ell \cdot \nabla_{\theta_{\mathbf{G}}}(\mathcal{L}_{\mathbf{G}} - \alpha \mathcal{L}_{\mathbf{R}})$ ▷ Updating generator with learning rate ℓ
10:     $\theta_{\mathbf{R}} \leftarrow \theta_{\mathbf{R}} - \ell \cdot \nabla_{\theta_{\mathbf{R}}} \mathcal{L}_{\mathbf{R}}$ ▷ Updating regressor with learning rate ℓ
11:     $\theta_{\mathbf{D}} \leftarrow \theta_{\mathbf{D}} - \ell \cdot \nabla_{\theta_{\mathbf{D}}} \mathcal{L}_{\mathbf{D}}$ ▷ Updating discriminator with learning rate ℓ
12: **end for**

2.2   Regularization with Segmentation Constraints

In such an unsupervised training scheme, the CNN's performance cannot be strictly guaranteed, particularly when the training data are limited. There are three possible cases of the CNN's output: (1) a reasonable segmentation, under the assumption that the global optimizer of generator and discriminator can be attained, (2) an arbitrary segmentation, randomly splitting the input volume $\mathbf{v}$ into $K + 1$ regions, and (3) an 'empty' segmentation, splitting $\mathbf{v}$ into k regions where $1 \leq k \leq K$. In this regard, we further propose two constraints: (1) non-arbitrary and (2) non-empty, as regularization schemes to exclude the two wrong cases, driving the model towards reasonable and optimal segmentation results.

Non-arbitrary: In order to prevent the CNN from producing an arbitrary segmentation, we control the model to redraw only one object at each iteration when solving Eq. 1. By doing so, the generator is enforced to focus on just the corresponding region. In the generated volume, voxels outside the corresponding region still have the same intensity value as that at the last iteration. In such a case, in order to continually decrease the adversarial loss, the generator is enforced to yield optimal segmentation results when updating the corresponding decoder no longer helps.

Non-empty: In order to prevent the CNN from producing an 'empty' segmentation, we add a regularization term $||\mathbf{R}(\tilde{\mathbf{v}}) - \mathbf{z}_k||_2^2$ in the loss function, where $\mathbf{R}$ is a regressor to regress the random noise $\mathbf{z}_k$ from the generated CT volume $\tilde{\mathbf{v}}$. By doing so, if the object modeled at this iteration is segmented to be empty, $\tilde{\mathbf{v}}$ is the same as last iteration, and so does $\mathbf{R}(\tilde{\mathbf{v}})$. However, $\mathbf{z}_k$ is almost impossible still equal to the value at the last iteration, and hence the regularization term will yield a large value to militate against this case.

We choose the hinge version of the adversarial loss, as suggested in the recent studies [27–30], for alleviating the training difficulty, and the loss function is

$$\max_{\mathbf{G},\mathbf{R}} \mathbb{E}_{\mathbf{v},k,\mathbf{z}_k} \big[\mathbf{D}\big(\mathbf{G}(\mathbf{v}|k,\mathbf{z}_k)\big) - \alpha \big|\big|\mathbf{R}\big(\mathbf{G}(\mathbf{v}|k,\mathbf{z}_k)\big) - \mathbf{z}_k\big|\big|_2^2 \big],$$
$$\max_{\mathbf{D}} \big(\mathbb{E}_{\mathbf{v}}\big[\min\big(0, \mathbf{D}(\mathbf{v}) - 1\big)\big] + \mathbb{E}_{\mathbf{v},k,\mathbf{z}_k}\big[\min\big(0, -\mathbf{D}\big(\mathbf{G}(\mathbf{v}|k,\mathbf{z}_k)\big) - 1\big)\big] \big), \quad (2)$$

where α is a balance parameter to control regularization term's importance in the loss; details of how to solve Eq. 2 are presented in Table 1.

3   Experiments

3.1   Dataset

The proposed method is assessed on a publicly available CT dataset [31][1]. It contains 90 CT volumes, 43 from TCIA Pancreas-CT dataset [32,33] and 47 from BTCV Abdomen dataset [34,35]. There are 8 organs to be segmented: (1) liver, (2) spleen, (3) left kidney, (4) stomach, (5) pancreas, (6) gallbladder, (7) esophagus, and (8) duodenum. The spacing resolution of CT volumes at three directions are varying hugely, from 0.6 to 0.9 mm of in-plane and from 0.5 to 5.0 mm of inter-slice spacing.

---

[1] Available on https://zenodo.org/record/1169361#.XSFOm-gzYuU.

3.2 Evaluation Metric

We employ two metrics to evaluate the segmentation accuracy: (1) Dice similarity coefficient (DSC) and (2) average surface distance (ASD). DSC is to measure the match of the segmentation result and the ground truth by normalizing voxels' number in their intersection over the average of voxels' number in them. ASD is to measure the average of the minimal Euclidean distance of boundary voxels of the segmentation result to boundary voxels of the ground truth and boundary voxels of the ground truth to boundary voxels of the segmentation result. Note that DSC has its value in $[0, 1]$ while ASD in $[0, \infty)$, and a better segmentation algorithm has a larger value of DSC while a smaller value of ASD.

3.3 Implementation Details

We first align the CT volume to have the same spacing resolution by linear interpolation. We then search the network's architecture automatically by employing [36]. Specifically, we allocate 15% of GPU memory for searching the U-Net. 8 decoders for 8 objects to be segmented have the same architecture as the searched U-Net's decoder (hence, n, the size of the random noise is also decided by it). The discriminator and the regressor have the same architecture as the searched U-Net's encoder, plus a linear layer with the output size of 1 and n, respectively. We use orthogonal initialization [37] for the whole network and optimize it by Adam [38] with the initial learning rate as 0.0003 and the balance parameter α in Eq. 2 as $3/n$. In addition, we re-start the training process when the model collapses to generate empty segmentation results; this is often encountered at the early stage of the training.

Table 2. Segmentation accuracy of different methods; DSC: % and ASD: mm.

		2D		3D	
		DSC	ASD	DSC	ASD
Fully	Dice Loss	83.7 ± 6.8	1.72 ± 1.43	84.6 ± 6.3	1.67 ± 1.24
Supervised	CE Loss	84.2 ± 6.6	1.68 ± 1.31	85.3 ± 6.2	1.62 ± 1.19
Weakly	CL-Cen [14]	78.4 ± 7.1	2.01 ± 1.93	79.6 ± 6.2	1.94 ± 1.97
Supervised	CL-RanP [14]	75.2 ± 7.7	2.41 ± 2.07	76.0± 6.6	2.13 ± 2.16
	SP [15]	76.8 ± 7.4	2.31 ± 2.22	77.2 ± 6.8	2.16 ± 2.09
Unsupervised	W-net [22]	60.2 ± 9.4	4.04 ± 3.84	61.7± 8.6	3.82 ± 3.46
	BP [23]	64.3 ± 8.8	3.72 ± 3.71	62.4 ± 8.1	3.78 ± 3.66
	IIC [24]	65.2 ± 8.9	3.48 ± 3.67	64.2 ± 8.4	3.54 ± 3.84
Ablation	Ours–RA	62.4 ± 9.2	3.79 ± 3.38	61.7 ± 9.4	3.86 ± 3.47
Study	Ours–RF	68.2 ± 8.2	3.01 ± 3.24	67.4 ± 7.6	3.17 ± 3.08
	Ours	74.7 ± 7.1	2.47 ± 2.72	73.2 ± 6.8	2.64 ± 2.57

3.4 Experimental Results

Comparison with Unsupervised Models: We first compared the proposed model with three state-of-the-art unsupervised methods: (1) W-net [22], (2) BP [23], and (3) IIC [24]. They train U-Nets by 'soft' normalized cut loss function, back-propagating self-constrained feature similarity, and information invariant clustering, respectively; refer to [22–24] for technical details. In the experiment, we used the same architecture of the U-Net and the same learning setting, and evaluated on both 2D and 3D versions. The results were obtained based on a 5-fold cross-validation, and are presented in Table 2; for unsupervised methods, we cannot control which output segmentation mask corresponds to which object, so the evaluation results are obtained by using regions' permutation that matches the ground truth the best. It is observed in Table 2 that our method, compared with other unsupervised models, yielded the most accurate segmentation results in both 2D and 3D versions, with improvement about 11.5% for DSC and 1.18 mm for ASD on average, demonstrating the effectiveness of our method.

The Gap with Fully Supervised Training: In order to evaluate the proposed unsupervised model more objectively, we also investigated the performance gap between the proposed model and fully supervised models. To do so, we trained two U-Nets in the supervised manner, by Dice and CE (cross-entropy) loss functions, respectively. Two U-Nets have the same architecture as our method and are trained with the same learning setting. We tested both 2D and 3D versions. The results were obtained based on the same 5-fold cross-validation and are presented in Table 2. It is observed that there is a segmentation accuracy gap of 10.5% for DSC and 0.88 mm for ASD on average.

The Gap with Weakly Supervised Training: We further evaluated the segmentation accuracy gap of the proposed unsupervised method with some weakly supervised models. We hence trained three U-Nets: (1) CL-Cen, (2) CL-RanP, and (3) SP. CL-Cen and CL-RanP are trained by the constrained loss [14], with the supervision being the object's centroid and a randomly sampled point in the object, respectively; the centroid and point are represented by several voxels such that their size (volume) is about 0.1% of the object, as suggested by [14]. SP trains the U-Net by slice propagated mask [15], with the supervision being the minimal box that covers the object; refer to [14,15] for technical details. Three U-Nets have the same architecture and are trained with the same learning setting. The results were acquired based on the same 5-fold cross-validation and are presented in Table 2. We can see from Table 2 that our method is nearly comparable with weakly trained methods; it only has a segmentation accuracy gap of 2.1% for DSC and 0.39 mm for ASD on average.

While there is still a performance gap between the proposed unsupervised model and the fully/weakly supervised models, the gap is reasonable and acceptable considering that there is no supervision information for the proposed model. To more comprehensively evaluate the proposed model, we compared our model with semi-supervised and transfer learning approaches under the same amount of supervision information.

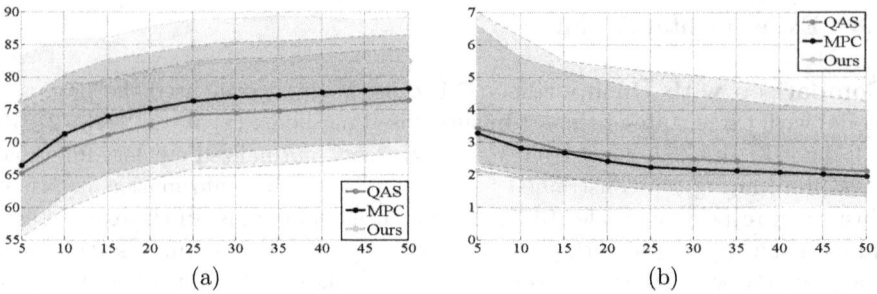

Fig. 2. Comparison with semi-supervised models under the same amount of supervision information: (a) results of *DSC* (%) and (b) results of *ASD* (*mm*).

Comparison with Semi-supervised Methods: We first compare the proposed method with state-of-the-art semi-supervised methods under the same amount of supervision information. We randomly select a certain amount of data (from 5% to 50% of the training dataset split by the 5-fold cross-validation) to train the U-Net (supervised) and then use the trained U-Net to initialize the proposed model (except for the U-Net, other parts still use orthogonal initialization). We compared this improved version with two semi-supervised methods: (1) QAS [16] and (2) MPC [17]. They train the U-Net in a semi-supervised manner by quality assurance supervision and multi-planar co-training, respectively; for more technical details please refer to [16,17]. We tested both 2D and 3D versions, and reported their mean results in Fig. 2, (a) for *DSC* and (b) for *ASD*. It is observed that our method consistently outperforms the semi-supervised approaches, demonstrating that the proposed adversarial redrawing and regularization schemes are capable of driving the model towards better segmentation results under certain supervision.

Comparison with Transfer Learning: We now conduct a set of experiments to compare our model with transfer learning schemes under the same amount of supervision information. We train the U-Net in the TCIA dataset and then transfer it to the BTCV dataset, and vice visa. We further fine-tune the U-Net, using 0% to 50% data (randomly selected) of the training dataset split by a 5-fold cross-validation. We denote this U-Net by 'Transfer' in Fig. 3. This method is compared to two variants of the proposed method: (1) 'Ours' and (2) 'Ours-Transfer'. 'Ours' is without the transfer learning, using just the selected data to train the U-Net for the initialization, while 'Ours-Transfer' uses the fine-tuned U-Net as the initialization. Both 2D and 3D versions were tested, and the results are presented in Fig. 3. It is observed that 'Ours-Transfer' achieve the best accurate segmentation accuracy, demonstrating the effectiveness of the proposed model. Also, even though there is no knowledge transfer, the proposed method still works better when the transferred U-Net is fine-tuned by the data less than 10% of the training data.

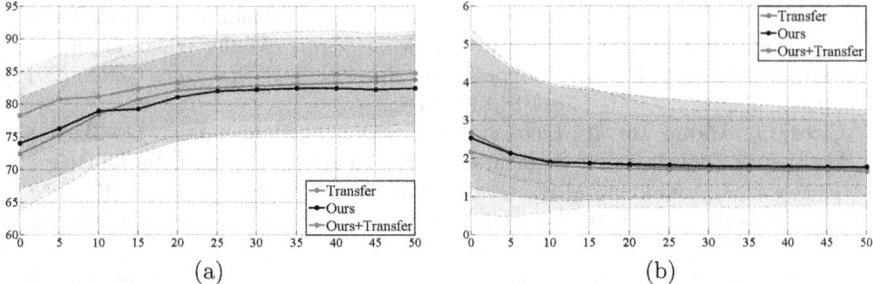

Fig. 3. Comparison with transfer learning schemes: (a) results of DSC (%) and (b) results of ASD (mm).

Ablation Study: We finally evaluate the effect of the two segmentation constraints: (1) Non-arbitrary and (2) Non-empty, on the segmentation accuracy. We denote 'Ours-RA' as the variant that is without both two constraints (redrawing all objects), and 'Ours-RF' as the variant that is without Non-empty constraint (regularization term free). Note that the Non-empty constraint depends on the Non-arbitrary constraint, and hence there is no variant that puts just the Non-empty constraint. The results were obtained based on the same 5-fold cross-validation, and are presented in Table 2. The results demonstrate that both the constraints are helpful in improving the segmentation accuracy.

4 Conclusion

We propose a novel unsupervised model for automated segmentation of CT images and extensive experiments demonstrated its effectiveness and advantages over existing unsupervised models. The proposed model is of great practical significance since manually annotating CT volumes and acquiring voxel-wise annotations are notoriously laborious and time-consuming. The proposed unsupervised learning mechanism is general enough and can be readily applied to the segmentation of other image modalities where acquiring sufficient high-quality annotations is also a difficult task.

Acknowledgement. The work described in this paper is supported by grants from the Hong Kong Research Grants Council (Project No. PolyU 152035/17E and Project No. 15205919), a grant from the Natural Foundation of China (Grant No. 61902232), a grant from the Hong Kong Innovation and Technology Commission (Project No. ITS/398/17FP), and a grant from the Li Ka Shing Foundation Cross-Disciplinary Research (Grant no. 2020LKSFG05D).

References

1. Cerrolaza, J., Picazo, M., Humbert, L., et al.: Computational anatomy for multi-organ analysis in medical imaging: a review. Med. Image Anal. **56**, 44–67 (2019)

2. Ronneberger, O., Fischer, P., Brox, T.: U-Net: convolutional networks for biomedical image segmentation. In: Navab, N., Hornegger, J., Wells, W.M., Frangi, A.F. (eds.) MICCAI 2015. LNCS, vol. 9351, pp. 234–241. Springer, Cham (2015). https://doi.org/10.1007/978-3-319-24574-4_28

3. Çiçek, Ö., Abdulkadir, A., Lienkamp, S.S., Brox, T., Ronneberger, O.: 3D U-Net: learning dense volumetric segmentation from sparse annotation. In: Ourselin, S., Joskowicz, L., Sabuncu, M.R., Unal, G., Wells, W. (eds.) MICCAI 2016. LNCS, vol. 9901, pp. 424–432. Springer, Cham (2016). https://doi.org/10.1007/978-3-319-46723-8_49

4. Litjens, G., Kooi, T., Bejnordi, B., et al.: A survey on deep learning in medical image analysis. Med. Image Anal. **42**, 60–88 (2017)

5. Shen, D., Wu, G., Suk, H.: Deep learning in medical image analysis. Annu. Rev. Biomed. Eng. **19**, 221–248 (2017)

6. Li, X., Chen, H., Qi, X., et al.: H-DenseUNet: hybrid densely connected UNet for liver and tumor segmentation from CT volumes. IEEE Trans. Med. Imaging **37**(12), 2663–2674 (2018)

7. Kakeya, H., Okada, T., Oshiro, Y.: 3D U-JAPA-Net: mixture of convolutional networks for abdominal multi-organ CT segmentation. In: Frangi, A.F., Schnabel, J.A., Davatzikos, C., Alberola-López, C., Fichtinger, G. (eds.) MICCAI 2018. LNCS, vol. 11073, pp. 426–433. Springer, Cham (2018). https://doi.org/10.1007/978-3-030-00937-3_49

8. Zhou, Z., Shin, J., Zhang, L., et al.: Fine-tuning convolutional neural networks for biomedical image analysis: actively and incrementally. In: IEEE International Conference on Computer Vision, pp. 7340–7351 (2017)

9. Wang, Yu., Ramanan, D., Hebert, M.: Growing a brain: fine-tuning by increasing model capacity. In: IEEE International Conference on Computer Vision, pp. 2471–2480 (2017)

10. Zhong, Z., Zheng, L., Kang, G., et al.: Random erasing data augmentation. In: AAAI Conference on Artificial Intelligence, pp. 1–8 (2020)

11. Cubuk, E., Zoph, B., Mane, D., et al.: Autoaugment: learning augmentation strategies from data. In: IEEE International Conference on Computer Vision, pp. 113–123 (2019)

12. Van Opbroek, A., Achterberg, H., Vernooij, M., et al.: Transfer learning for image segmentation by combining image weighting and kernel learning. IEEE Trans. Med. Imaging **38**(1), 213–224 (2018)

13. Sun, R., Zhu, X., Wu, C., et al.: Not all areas are equal: transfer learning for semantic segmentation via hierarchical region selection. In: IEEE International Conference on Computer Vision, pp. 4360–4369 (2019)

14. Kervadec, H., Dolz, J., Tang, M., et al.: Constrained-CNN losses for weakly supervised segmentation. Med. Image Anal. **54**, 88–99 (2019)

15. Cai, J., et al.: Accurate weakly-supervised deep lesion segmentation using large-scale clinical annotations: slice-propagated 3d mask generation from 2D RECIST. In: Frangi, A.F., Schnabel, J.A., Davatzikos, C., Alberola-López, C., Fichtinger, G. (eds.) MICCAI 2018. LNCS, vol. 11073, pp. 396–404. Springer, Cham (2018). https://doi.org/10.1007/978-3-030-00937-3_46

16. Lee, H., Tang, Y., Tang, O., et al.: Semi-supervised multi-organ segmentation through quality assurance supervision. arXiv preprint arXiv:1911.05113 (2019)

17. Zhou, Y., Wang, Y., Tang, P., et al.: Semi-supervised 3D abdominal multi-organ segmentation via deep multi-planar co-training. In: IEEE Winter Conference on Applications of Computer Vision, pp. 121–140 (2019)

18. Wilson, G. and Cook, D.: A survey of unsupervised deep domain adaptation. arXiv preprint arXiv:1812.02849 (2018)
19. Chen, C., Dou, Q., Chen, H., et al.: Synergistic image and feature adaptation: Towards cross-modality domain adaptation for medical image segmentation. In: AAAI Conference on Artificial Intelligence, pp. 865–872 (2019)
20. Tajbakhsh, N., Jeyaseelan, L., Li, Q., et al.: Embracing imperfect datasets: A review of deep learning solutions for medical image segmentation. arXiv preprint arXiv:1908.10454 (2019)
21. Ouyang, C., Kamnitsas, K., Biffi, C., Duan, J., Rueckert, D.: Data efficient unsupervised domain adaptation for cross-modality image segmentation. In: Shen, D., et al. (eds.) MICCAI 2019. LNCS, vol. 11765, pp. 669–677. Springer, Cham (2019). https://doi.org/10.1007/978-3-030-32245-8_74
22. Xia, X. and Kulis, B.: W-net: A deep model for fully unsupervised image segmentation. arXiv preprint arXiv:1711.08506 (2017)
23. Kanezaki, A.: Unsupervised image segmentation by backpropagation. In: IEEE International Conference on Acoustics, Speech and Signal Processing, pp. 1543–1547 (2018)
24. Ji, X., Henriques, J. and Vedaldi, A.: Invariant information clustering for unsupervised image classification and segmentation. In: IEEE International Conference on Computer Vision, pp. 9865–9874 (2019)
25. Chen, M., Artières, T.,Denoyer, L.: Unsupervised object segmentation by redrawing. In: Advances in Neural Information Processing Systems, pp. 12826–12737 (2019)
26. Goodfellow, I., Pouget-Abadie, J., Mirza, M., et al.: Generative adversarial nets. In: Advances in Neural Information Processing Systems, pp. 2672–2680 (2014)
27. Tran, D., Ranganath, R., Blei, D.M.: Deep and hierarchical implicit models. arXiv preprint arXiv:1702.08896 (2017)
28. Zhang, H., Goodfellow, I., Metaxas, D., et al.: Self-attention generative adversarial networks. arXiv preprint arXiv:1805.08318 (2018)
29. Brock, A., Donahue, J. and Simonyan, K.: Large scale gan training for high fidelity natural image synthesis. In: International Conference on Learning Representations, pp. 1–11 (2019)
30. Lucic, M., Tschannen, M., Ritter, M., et al.: High-fidelity image generation with fewer labels. arXiv preprint arXiv:1903.02271 (2019)
31. Gibson, E., Giganti, F., Hu, Y., et al.: Automatic multi-organ segmentation on abdominal CT with dense v-networks. IEEE Trans. Med. Imaging 37(8), 1822–1834 (2018)
32. Clark, K., Vendt, B., Smith, K., et al.: The cancer imaging archive (TCIA): maintaining and operating a public information repository. J. Digit. Imaging 26(6), 1045–1057 (2013). https://doi.org/10.1007/s10278-013-9622-7
33. Roth, H., Farag, A., Turkbey, E., et al.: Data from pancreas-CT. The cancer imaging archive. (2015)
34. Landman, B., Xu, Z., Eugenio, I., et al.: MICCAI multi-atlas labeling beyond the cranial vault-workshop and challenge (2015)
35. Xu, Z., Lee, C., Heinrich, M., et al.: Evaluation of six registration methods for the human abdomen on clinically acquired CT. IEEE Trans. Biomed. Eng. 63(8), 1563–1572 (2016)
36. Isensee, F., Petersen, J., Klein, A., et al.: nnu-net: Self-adapting framework for u-net-based medical image segmentation. arXiv preprint arXiv:1809.10486 (2018)

37. Saxe, A., McClelland, J. and Ganguli, S.: Exact solutions to the nonlinear dynamics of learning in deep linear neural networks. In: International Conference on Learning Representations, pp. 1–15 (2014)
38. Kingma, D. and Ba, J.: Adam: A method for stochastic optimization. arXiv preprint arXiv:1412.6980 (2014)

Deep Active Contour Network
for Medical Image Segmentation

Mo Zhang[1,2,3], Bin Dong[1,4,5], and Quanzheng Li[6(✉)]

[1] Center for Data Science, Peking University, Beijing 100871, China
[2] Center for Data Science in Health and Medicine, Peking University,
Beijing 100871, China
[3] Laboratory for Biomedical Image Analysis, Beijing Institute of Big Data Research,
Beijing 100871, China
[4] Beijing International Center for Mathematical Research (BICMR),
Peking University, Beijing 100871, China
[5] Institute for Artificial Intelligence, Peking University, Beijing 100871, China
[6] Department of Radiology, Center for Advanced Medical Computing and Analysis,
MGH/BWH Center for Clinical Data Science, Massachusetts General Hospital,
Harvard Medical School, Boston, MA 02115, USA
li.quanzheng@mgh.harvard.edu

Abstract. Image segmentation is vital to medical image analysis and clinical diagnosis. Recently, convolutional neural networks (CNNs) have achieved tremendous success in this task, however, it performs poorly at recognizing precise object boundary due to the information loss in the successive downsampling layers. To overcome this problem, we integrate an active contour model (convexified Chan-Vese model) into the CNN structure (DenseUNet), forming a new framework called deep active contour network (DACN). Instead of manual setting, DACN applies a CNN backbone to learn the initialization and parameters of active contour model (ACM) automatically. The proposed DACN leverages the advantage of ACM to detect object boundaries accurately, which can be trained in an end-to-end differential manner. The experimental results on two public datasets demonstrate the effectiveness of DACN, and the trimap experiment confirms the superior ability of DACN to obtain precise boundary delineation.

Keywords: Active contour model · Boundary delineation · Semantic segmentation

1 Introduction

Semantic segmentation is a central theme in the area of medical image processing. It is a process of splitting an image into several sub regions. In the past decades, various algorithms have been implemented for this topic ranging from thresholding [21], region growing [1], clustering [20] to active contour models

© Springer Nature Switzerland AG 2020
A. L. Martel et al. (Eds.): MICCAI 2020, LNCS 12264, pp. 321–331, 2020.
https://doi.org/10.1007/978-3-030-59719-1_32

(ACMs) [2,3,14]. Nowadays, convolutional neural networks (CNN) have significantly improved the performance of many segmentation tasks, mainly benefiting from its powerful ability to learn informative hierarchical features directly from data. However, as illustrated in [10,25], it is rather difficult for CNN to recognize the object boundary precisely. On the other hand, active contour models (ACMs) are a series of approaches to fit a curve for the object contour in the image, which tend to generate accurate localization of boundaries. In this circumstance, an intuitive idea is to leverage the advantage of ACM to compensate for the defects of deep learning models.

Recently, researchers have developed many techniques to combine ACM with CNN. Some works presented a novel loss function based on the energy functional of ACM, such as Mumford-Shah loss [16], AC loss [5], level set loss [17] and active contour loss [9]. At the meantime, some investigators attempted to incorporate ACM into deep learning methods in an end-to-end fashion. For instance, the work [11] utilized level set method to assist networks in detecting salient objects more precisely, however, its performance depends heavily on the fine tuning of parameters γ and λ in the level set formulation. In contrast, in order to avoid parameter tuning, DSAC [23] and DARNet [5] trained a CNN to learn ACM parameterizations automatically, nevertheless, they still lack robustness and efficiency as the result is sensitive to the manual initialization of target contours. In addition, Hatamizadeh *et al.* [10] presented a new architecture named DALS combining ACM and CNN to segment various lesions in medical imaging, however, the ACM module in DALS is not trainable only working as a post-processing step.

In this work, to overcome these limitations, we propose an end-to-end deep active contour network (DACN) for segmentation in medical imaging. In the proposed DACN, both the pixel-wise parameter maps and initial contours of ACM are learned directly from data by a CNN. It is a completely automatical and differentiable framework. More specifically, we use the classic DenseUNet as the CNN backbone, and select an improved active contour model (convexified Chan-Vese model) which reduces the original energy functional to a convex minimization. We evaluate our DACN method on two public datasets: Herlev dataset and ISIC 2017 Skin Lesion dataset, where the new framework yields superior results compared to UNet, DenseUNet as well as other competitive models. Moreover, segmentation maps obtained by DACN have more sophisticated delineation of object edges, demonstrated by the additional trimap experiment.

The main contributions of this paper are listed as follows:

1) We present deep active contour network (DACN) for image segmentation, taking advantage of ACM to detect precise boundaries in CNN architecture.
2) We choose an improved Chan-Vese model as the ACM module, and utilize a auxiliary CNN loss function to enhance feature extraction.
3) DACN obtains good performance on Herlev and ISIC dataset, more generally, it can also be used in other segmentation tasks to improve boundary accuracy.

There are 3 main differences between the recent DALS and our DACN: 1) The ACM exploited in DALS is the classic Chan-Vese model [3] with local evolution

---

Algorithm 1. Split Bregman for model (2)

Given an input image f, select the parameter λ and μ.

Initialize the algorithm by choosing $u^0 = 0, d^0 = 0, b^0 = 0, c_1^0 = 1, c_2^0 = 0$, and $k = 0$.

while stopping criteria are not met **do**

    1: Define $r^k = \left(c_1^k - f\right)^2 - \left(c_2^k - f\right)^2$

    2: $u^{k+1} = GS_{GCS}\left(r^k, d^k, b^k\right)$

    3: $d^{k+1} = shrink\left(\nabla u^{k+1} + b^k, \frac{1}{\lambda}\right)$

    4: $b^{k+1} = b^k + \nabla u^{k+1} - d^{k+1}$

    5: Find $\Omega^k = \left\{x : u^k(x) \geq \gamma\right\}$

    6: Update $c_1^{k+1} = \int_{\Omega^k} f dx$, and $c_2^{k+1} = \int_{(\Omega^k)^c} f dx$

    7: k=k+1

end while

---

[19], while the proposed DACN adopts an improved model of Chan-Vese which can find the global minimizer; 2) The ACM used in DALS is not involved into the training process, only serving as a post-processing step, however, our DACN is a fully end-to-end trainable framework; 3) In DALS, parameters of ACM are estimated from the network output by an exponential transformation, while that of DACN are learned directly via the CNN backbone.

2 Method

2.1 Convexified Chan-Vese Model

Active contour models (ACMs), also referred as snakes, are firstly proposed by Kass et al. [14] to evolve the contours by solving an energy minimization problem. In contrast to parametric snakes, level set based ACMs define contours implicitly via a level set function in a higher dimension, where the object contours are denoted by the zero level set. In the past decades, a variety of ACMs have been developed to improve the performance of image segmentation, among which the region-based Chan-Vese model [3] is widely used. The energy functional of Chan-Vese model is formulated as:

$$
\begin{aligned}
F\left(c_1, c_2, C\right) =& \mu \cdot \text{Length}(C) + \nu \cdot \text{Area}(inside(C)) \\
&+ \lambda_1 \int_{inside(C)} \left|u_0(x, y) - c_1\right|^2 dxdy \\
&+ \lambda_2 \int_{outside(C)} \left|u_0(x, y) - c_2\right|^2 dxdy,
\end{aligned}
\tag{1}
$$

where $u_0(x, y)$ is the raw image, C is a closed curve, the first term $Length(C)$ represents the length of C, the second term denotes the area inside C, and $\mu, \nu, \lambda_1, \lambda_2$ are scalar parameters to be regulated. Moreover, c_1, c_2 represent the mean values of image $u_0(x, y)$ inside and outside the curve C respectively.

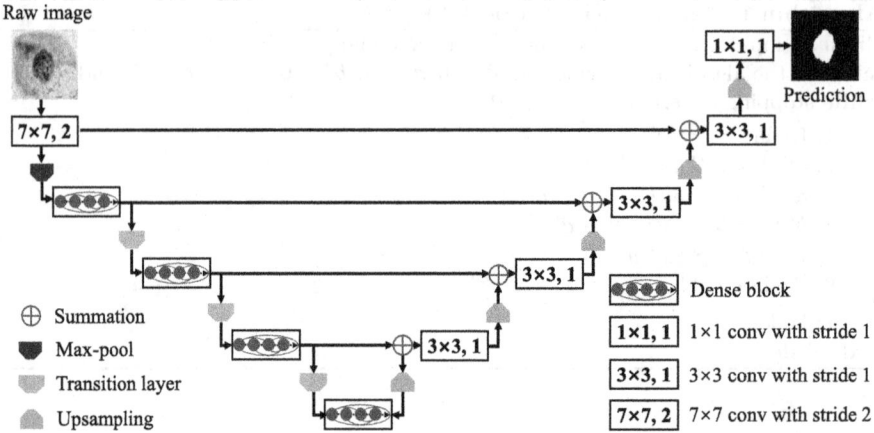

Fig. 1. The structure of DenseUNet. The raw image has a resolution of 256×256, and the setting of channels follows the original work [22].

In order to solve the minimal partition problem, the level set method was introduced and the problem amounted to solving a partial differential equation (PDE) by gradient descent [3]. More recently, Chan et al. [2] proposed a convexified version of Chan-Vese model to obtain the global minimizer, which significantly improved the efficiency of computation. Following [2,8], the original problem can be reduced to a simple convex minimization:

$$\min_{0 \leq u \leq 1} |\nabla u|_1 + \mu \langle u, r \rangle, \quad r = (f - c_1)^2 - (f - c_2)^2. \tag{2}$$

Here f is the image to be segmented, c_1, c_2 are arbitrary fixed scalars, μ is the parameter balancing the regularization process and data term. Finally, the segmentation output can be defined as:

$$\Omega = \{x : u(x) \geq \gamma\}, \text{ for a.e. } \gamma \in [0, 1]. \tag{3}$$

The work [8] applied the split Bregman algorithm to solve the above problem, while the procedure is summarized in Algorithm 1. GS_{GCS} represents one iteration of the Gauss-Seidel method:

$$\alpha_{i,j} = d_{i-1,j}^x - d_{i,j}^x - b_{i-1,j}^x + b_{i,j}^x + d_{i,j-1}^y - d_{i,j}^y - b_{i,j-1}^y + b_{i,j}^y,$$
$$\beta_{i,j} = \frac{1}{4} \left(u_{i-1,j} + u_{i+1,j} + u_{i,j-1} + u_{i,j+1} - \frac{\mu}{\lambda} r + \alpha_{i,j} \right), \tag{4}$$
$$u_{i,j} = \max \{\min \{\beta_{i,j}, 1\}, 0\},$$

where $b_{i,j}^x$ ($d_{i,j}^x$) denotes the value of the X-direction component of $\boldsymbol{b}$ ($\boldsymbol{d}$) at pixel (i, j), $\boldsymbol{b}$ and $\boldsymbol{d}$ are the intermediate variables in Algorithm 1. In the third step, *shrink* denotes the shrinkage operator. For more details about Algorithm 1, we refer the reader to [8].

2.2 The CNN Backbone

In this paper, we choose DenseUNet [22] as our CNN backbone. As shown in Fig. 1, DenseUNet is an encoder-decoder framework which integrates the dense block [12] into the classic UNet. More specifically, in the dense block, output feature maps of each layer are transmitted to all subsequent layers as inputs, making it competent in enhancing feature propagation and alleviating gradient vanishing. The transition layer is composed of a 1×1 convolution followed by an average pooling operation with stride of 2. More details about DenseUNet can be found in the original work [22].

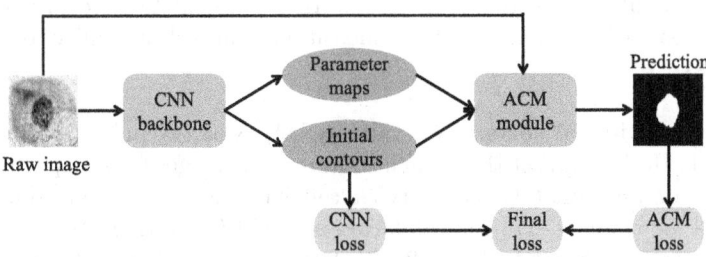

Fig. 2. The architecture of DACN. DACN is an end-to-end trainable framework with a differential ACM module. In contrast to the traditional ACM algorithm, parameters learned by the CNN backbone are pixel-wise functions $\mu(x, y), \lambda(x, y)$ rather than scalars (μ, λ in Algorithm 1).

2.3 The DACN Architecture

In this section, we present deep active contour network (DACN) to deal with medical image segmentation. As shown in Fig. 2, the proposed DACN integrates the classic ACM (convexified Chan-Vese model) with a CNN backbone (Dense-UNet) in an end-to-end differentiable manner. Firstly, the initial contours and pixel-level parameter maps $(\mu(x, y), \lambda(x, y))$ of ACM are learned from data by the CNN backbone. Secondly, these contours, maps as well as raw image are transmitted to ACM to evolve the curve iteratively via Algorithm 1. Finally, the output of ACM is compared with ground truth to produce a cross-entropy loss function (named ACM loss). In the same way, the initial contours can also yield a loss function (named CNN loss) to provide auxiliary supervision for the CNN backbone. As shown in Fig. 2, the final loss is established by the CNN loss and ACM loss as follow:

$$\mathcal{L}_{final} = \alpha \cdot \mathcal{L}_{CNN} + \mathcal{L}_{ACM}, \tag{5}$$

where α is a balancing parameter. By minimizing the final loss, the error can be back-propagated through the entire DACN architecture to guide the weights updating in the CNN backbone.

3   Experiments

We compare DACN with the widely used UNet, the baseline DenseUNet as well as recent state-of-the-art methods. To quantify the performance, we utilize several metrics including Dice, Precision, Recall, Accuracy and Hausdorff Distance. Furthermore, in order to evaluate the boundary accuracy, we also conduct the trimap experiment [4,18]. In the trimap experiment, evaluation metrics are not computed over the entire image, but only in the region surrounding the object boundary. Specifically, the evaluation region is generated by taking a w pixel band around the edges of objects, where w denotes the width of the target region. Trimap experiment is a more appropriate measurement for users concerned about fine contours. In this work, we calculate Dice in such edge-adjacent area with different widths to measure the model capability to delineate boundaries.

Data Description. We extensively validate DACN on two public medical image datasets: 1) Herlev dataset [13], which contains 917 images from Pap smear tests and corresponding annotations of cervical cell. The entire set is divided into three parts: 562 for training, 171 for validation and 184 for testing; 2) International Skin Imaging Collaboration (ISIC-2017) dataset [6], which aims to segment the skin lesion in dermatoscope images. The training, validation, and testing sets comprise 2000, 150, and 600 images respectively with various resolutions. As for image preprocessing, all images are resized to 256×256, followed by normalization and Contrast Limited Adaptive Histogram Equalization (CLAHE).

Table 1. Quantitative analysis of different methods on Herlev dataset.

Model	Dice	Precision	Recall	Accuracy	Hausdorff distance
SP-CNN [7]	0.9000	0.8900	0.9100	–	–
PSPNet [24]	0.9070	0.9280	0.9090	–	–
DeeplabV3 [24]	0.9130	0.9170	0.9260	–	–
ASCNet [24]	0.9150	0.9100	0.9380	–	–
UNet	0.9042	0.9053	0.9308	0.9588	36.4990
DenseUNet	0.9327	0.9308	0.9459	0.9731	17.3826
DACN	**0.9454**	**0.9474**	**0.9508**	**0.9763**	**15.5814**

Table 2. Quantitative analysis of different methods on ISIC dataset.

Model	Dice	Precision	Recall	Accuracy	Hausdorff distance
FocusNetAlpha [15]	0.8404	0.8002	0.8222	**0.9349**	–
UNet	0.7826	0.8766	0.7683	0.9135	39.1774
DenseUNet	0.8403	**0.9364**	0.8087	0.9316	26.1643
DACN	**0.8463**	0.9076	**0.8432**	0.9319	**24.4691**

Implementation Details. Our implementation is based on the TensorFlow framework and all experiments are carried out on a single NVIDIA GTX1080ti GPU. We apply the Adam algorithm with default parameters to minimize the cross entropy loss function. All models are trained for 30000 epochs with batch size of 4. Each convolutional layer is followed by RELU activation and batch normalization. The hyperparameter α in the loss function is set to 0.01. Both parameter maps $(\mu(x, y), \lambda(x, y))$ of ACM are initialized to null matrix.

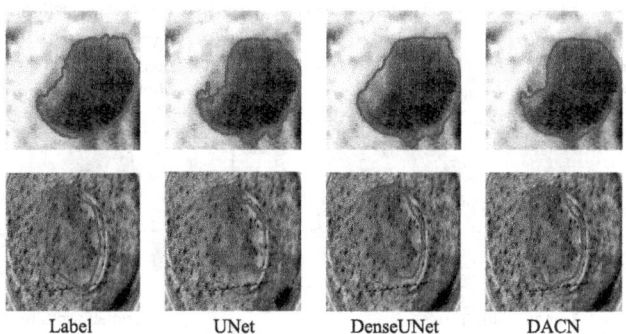

| Label | UNet | DenseUNet | DACN |

Fig. 3. Comparison of segmentation maps of different models. Top row: an example on Herlev dataset. Bottom row: an example on ISIC dataset. Compared to UNet and DenseUNet, DACN produces more accurate prediction maps.

4   Results

Evaluation of the Performance of DACN. Table 1 shows the quantitative comparison of different approaches on Herlev dataset. The proposed DACN outperforms all other models including the CNN backbone DenseUNet and existing state-of-the-art frameworks on this dataset. Table 2 shows the experimental results on ISIC dataset. DACN performs best in Dice (0.8463), Recall (0.8432) and Hausdorff Distance (24.4691). Compared to the baseline DenseUNet, DACN yields a higher Recall (0.8432) with a considerable improvement (3.45%), suggesting that DACN produces less false negatives (FN). Accuracy (0.9319) of DACN is close to the optimal one (0.9349). Although Precision of DACN is lower than that of DenseUNet, it is still at a high level. Besides, it is worth mentioning that DACN gets good performance in Hausdorff Distance on both datasets. Hausdorff Distance measures the boundary distance between two surfaces, indicating that DACN tends to produce more precise localization of object boundary. Segmentation results of different methods are shown in Fig. 3. It can be observed that the target boundaries are really complex and low-contrast to background, thus resulting in the failure of UNet and DenseUNet. However, in such case, DACN still generates relatively accurate prediction maps.

Evaluation of the Edge Location Precision. Specifically, we make trimap experiment to quantify the performance of boundary delineation. In order to compare the property of different models, we display the bar charts about related results in Fig. 4. Compared to the CNN backbone (DenseUNet), DACN gains higher Dice in all settings on both datasets. When the band widths of evaluation region are 5, 10, 15, 20 pixels, on ISIC dataset, the improvements of DACN across Dice coefficient are 4.40%, 3.59%, 3.12% and 2.45% respectively. With

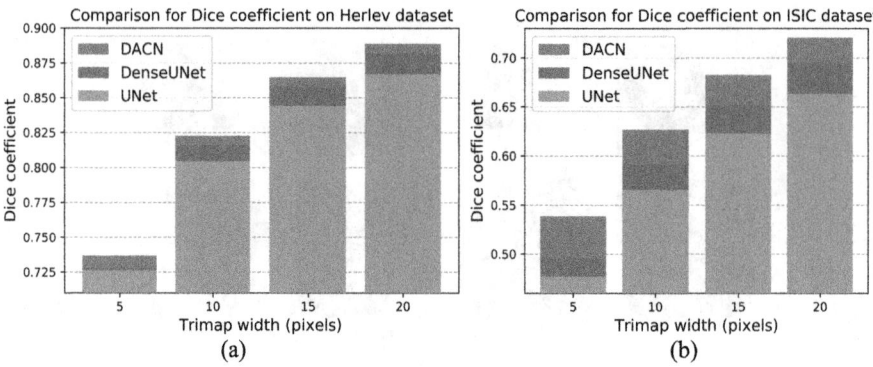

Fig. 4. The results of trimap experiment on two datasets. (a) The bar chart about trimap experiment on Herlev dataset. (b) The same bar chart on ISIC dataset. Dice is calculated in the region surrounding the object boundaries, where trimap width represents the band of this region.

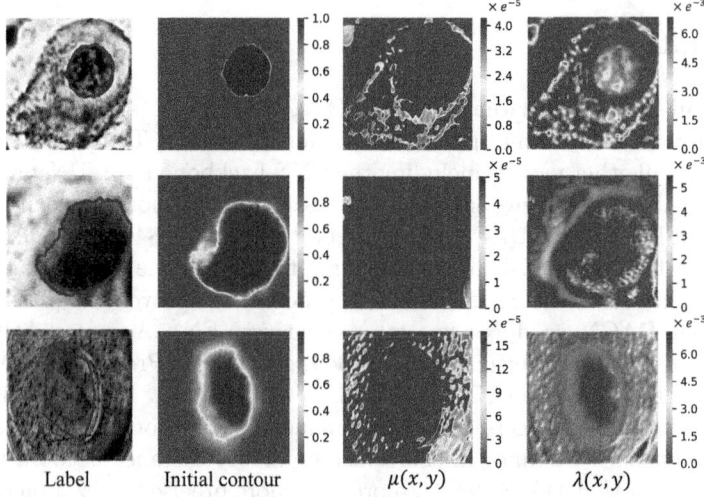

Fig. 5. Illustrations of the learned initial contours and pixel-wise parameter maps by the CNN backbone. The top two rows: examples on Herlev dataset. Bottom row: an example on ISIC dataset.

the increasing of band width, the gap between the CNN backbone and DACN reduces gradually, which may account for the slight improvement of Dice computed over the entire image. The above results demonstrate that DACN has strong capability to identify accurate boundaries, benefiting from the utilization of active contour models (ACMs).

For the sake of exploring the working mechanism of DACN, we show the learned initial contours and pixel-level parameter maps $\mu(x, y)$, $\lambda(x, y)$ in Fig. 5. In the initial contours, some pixels around the object boundary are difficult samples with weak confidence, making it necessary to evolve the contour more accurately by ACMs. In addition, in the $\mu(x, y)$ map, locations which have similar intensity with the target in raw image are inclined to generate higher μ values. One possible explanation is that the learned parameter maps can provide additional guidance for DACN to evolve towards the object boundary, which compensates for the faults of CNN.

5   Conclusion

In this paper, we present a novel deep active contour network (DACN) for medical image segmentation, which integrates ACM (convexified Chan-Vese model) into the DenseUNet architecture in an end-to-end differential manner. By leveraging the advantage of ACM to locate object edges, the proposed DACN tends to generate more accurate segmentation of contours. Our DACN has better performance on two public datasets compared to UNet, DenseUNet as well as several state-of-the-art models, especially for boundary delineation. Additionally, DACN can also be applied to multi-class semantic segmentation, where the issue of multi-class semantic segmentation should be decomposed into several single-class segmentations. In the future, it is worth further investigation about the working mechanism of DACN.

References

1. Adams, R., Bischof, L.: Seeded region growing. IEEE Trans. Pattern Anal. Mach. Intell. **16**(6), 641–647 (1994)
2. Chan, T.F., Esedoglu, S., Nikolova, M.: Algorithms for finding global minimizers of image segmentation and denoising models. SIAM J. Appl. Math. **66**(5), 1632–1648 (2006)
3. Chan, T.F., Vese, L.A.: Active contours without edges. IEEE Trans. Image Process. **10**(2), 266–277 (2001)
4. Chen, L.C., Zhu, Y., Papandreou, G., Schroff, F., Adam, H.: Encoder-decoder with atrous separable convolution for semantic image segmentation. In: Proceedings of the European Conference on Computer Vision (ECCV), pp. 801–818 (2018)
5. Chen, X., Williams, B.M., Vallabhaneni, S.R., Czanner, G., Williams, R., Zheng, Y.: Learning active contour models for medical image segmentation. In: Proceedings of the IEEE Conference on Computer Vision and Pattern Recognition, pp. 11632–11640 (2019)

6. Codella, N.C., et al.: Skin lesion analysis toward melanoma detection: a challenge at the 2017 international symposium on biomedical imaging (isbi), hosted by the international skin imaging collaboration (isic). In: 2018 IEEE 15th International Symposium on Biomedical Imaging (ISBI 2018), pp. 168–172. IEEE (2018)

7. Gautam, S., Bhavsar, A., Sao, A.K., Harinarayan, K.: CNN based segmentation of nuclei in pap-smear images with selective pre-processing. In: Medical Imaging 2018: Digital Pathology, vol. 10581, p. 105810X. International Society for Optics and Photonics (2018)

8. Goldstein, T., Bresson, X., Osher, S.: Geometric applications of the split bregman method: segmentation and surface reconstruction. J. Sci. Comput. **45**(1–3), 272–293 (2010). https://doi.org/10.1007/s10915-009-9331-z

9. Gur, S., Wolf, L., Golgher, L., Blinder, P.: Unsupervised microvascular image segmentation using an active contours mimicking neural network. In: Proceedings of the IEEE International Conference on Computer Vision, pp. 10722–10731 (2019)

10. Hatamizadeh, A., et al.: Deep active lesion segmentation. In: Suk, H.-I., Liu, M., Yan, P., Lian, C. (eds.) MLMI 2019. LNCS, vol. 11861, pp. 98–105. Springer, Cham (2019). https://doi.org/10.1007/978-3-030-32692-0_12

11. Hu, P., Shuai, B., Liu, J., Wang, G.: Deep level sets for salient object detection. In: Proceedings of the IEEE Conference on Computer Vision and Pattern Recognition, pp. 2300–2309 (2017)

12. Huang, G., Liu, Z., Van Der Maaten, L., Weinberger, K.Q.: Densely connected convolutional networks. In: Proceedings of the IEEE Conference on Computer Vision and Pattern Recognition, pp. 4700–4708 (2017)

13. Jantzen, J., Norup, J., Dounias, G., Bjerregaard, B.: Pap-smear benchmark data for pattern classification. In: Nature Inspired Smart Information Systems (NiSIS 2005), pp. 1–9 (2005)

14. Kass, M., Witkin, A., Terzopoulos, D.: Snakes: active contour models. Int. J. Comput. Vis. **1**(4), 321–331 (1988). https://doi.org/10.1007/BF00133570

15. Kaul, C., Pears, N., Manandhar, S.: Divided we stand: A novel residual group attention mechanism for medical image segmentation. arXiv preprint arXiv:1912.02079 (2019)

16. Kim, B., Ye, J.C.: Mumford-shah loss functional for image segmentation with deep learning. IEEE Trans. Image Process. **29**, 1856–1866 (2019)

17. Kim, Y., Kim, S., Kim, T., Kim, C.: Cnn-based semantic segmentation using level set loss. In: 2019 IEEE Winter Conference on Applications of Computer Vision (WACV), pp. 1752–1760. IEEE (2019)

18. Kohli, P., Torr, P.H., et al.: Robust higher order potentials for enforcing label consistency. Int. J. Comput. Vis. **82**(3), 302–324 (2009). https://doi.org/10.1007/s11263-008-0202-0

19. Lankton, S., Tannenbaum, A.: Localizing region-based active contours. IEEE Trans. Image Process. **17**(11), 2029–2039 (2008)

20. Lee, T.H., Fauzi, M.F.A., Komiya, R.: Segmentation of CT brain images using k-means and em clustering. In: 2008 Fifth International Conference on Computer Graphics, Imaging and Visualisation, pp. 339–344. IEEE (2008)

21. Li, J., Zhu, S., Bin, H.: Medical image segmentation techniques. Sheng wu yi xue gong cheng xue za zhi= Journal of biomedical engineering = Shengwu yixue gongchengxue zazhi **23**(4), 891–894 (2006)

22. Li, X., Chen, H., Qi, X., Dou, Q., Fu, C.W., Heng, P.A.: H-denseunet: hybrid densely connected UNet for liver and tumor segmentation from CT volumes. IEEE Trans. Med. Imaging **37**(12), 2663–2674 (2018)

23. Marcos, D., Tuia, D., Kellenberger, B., Zhang, L., Bai, M., Liao, R., Urtasun, R.: Learning deep structured active contours end-to-end. In: Proceedings of the IEEE Conference on Computer Vision and Pattern Recognition, pp. 8877–8885 (2018)

24. Zhang, M., Zhao, J., Li, X., Zhang, L., Li, Q.: Ascnet: Adaptive-scale convolutional neural networks for multi-scale feature learning. arXiv preprint arXiv:1907.03241 (2019)

25. Zhang, Y., Chung, A.C.S.: Deep supervision with additional labels for retinal vessel segmentation task. In: Frangi, A.F., Schnabel, J.A., Davatzikos, C., Alberola-López, C., Fichtinger, G. (eds.) MICCAI 2018. LNCS, vol. 11071, pp. 83–91. Springer, Cham (2018). https://doi.org/10.1007/978-3-030-00934-2_10

Learning Crisp Edge Detector Using Logical Refinement Network

Luyan Liu$^{(\boxtimes)}$, Kai Ma, and Yefeng Zheng

Tencent Jarvis Lab, Shenzhen, China
lly2111101@163.com

Abstract. Edge detection is a fundamental problem in different computer vision tasks. Recently, edge detection algorithms achieve satisfying improvement built upon deep learning. Although most of them report favorable evaluation scores, they often fail to accurately localize edges and give thick and blurry boundaries. In addition, most of them focus on 2D images and the challenging 3D edge detection is still under-explored. In this work, we propose a novel logical refinement network for crisp edge detection, which is motivated by the logical relationship between segmentation and edge maps and can be applied to both 2D and 3D images. The network consists of a joint object and edge detection network and a crisp edge refinement network, which predicts more accurate, clearer and thinner high quality binary edge maps without any post-processing. Extensive experiments are conducted on the 2D nuclei images from Kaggle 2018 Data Science Bowl and a private 3D microscopy images of a monkey brain, which show outstanding performance compared with state-of-the-art methods.

Keywords: Crisp edge detection · Logical gate · Logical refinement · Deep learning

1 Introduction

Edge detection is a fundamental and important task in computer vision which provides ample supplementary cues to other tasks like semantic and instance segmentation [22], object detection [14] and recognition [8], scene understanding [20], etc. Until now, there are numerous works about edge detection. Most of the early works usually detect edges based on color, intensity, texture [6] and other low-level learning features [13]. Benefiting from the recent prevailing trend of deep learning algorithms, the edge detection methods have been greatly improved from the earlier traditional handcrafted feature based methods [6,7], to the deep learning based methods [11,12,19]. DeepEdge [3], DeepContour [17] and DeepCrisp [18] were proposed to leverage deep convolutional neural networks to facilitate the exploration of more discriminative features for edge detection. Bertasius et al. [4] showed that the low-level boundary detection process could benefit from the high-level object features. A simultaneous edge alignment and

© Springer Nature Switzerland AG 2020
A. L. Martel et al. (Eds.): MICCAI 2020, LNCS 12264, pp. 332–341, 2020.
https://doi.org/10.1007/978-3-030-59719-1_33

learning method [21] was proposed to improve edge quality by addressing the label misalignment problem. Hierarchical multiscale and multilevel information was exploited in [9,11,12,15,19] to make full use of rich features for edge detection. Even though the existing methods are propitious to generate edge maps with high scores, they may confront problems of having low quality edge maps due to blurry and deviating from actual image boundaries [10,18]. The shortcoming may be adversarial for tasks required crisper and sharper boundaries like optical flow and image segmentation. Additionally, and importantly, most of the recent methods are designed for 2D images, leaving the 3D edge detection an open problem. In this paper, we propose a novel coarse-refine framework to address the challenging problems above, which can be applied to both 2D and 3D images.

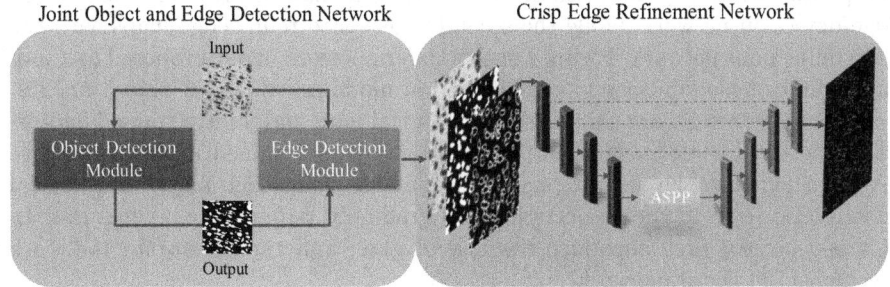

Fig. 1. The framework of our proposed logical refinement network. (Color figure online)

By exploring the relationship between binary segmentation and edge maps, it is not difficult to find out that the segmentation map contains ample edge information and the edge map is a subset of segmentation. Inspired by this observation, we propose a novel logical refinement network and a novel logical gate to generate accurate and crisp edges. The logical gate leverages the relationship between edge and segmentation maps to refine edge features. When it works in conjunction with logical refinement network, the quality of edge maps can be gradually improved. Our contributions can be summarized into the following two parts: 1) We propose a simple yet efficient logical gate, which passes feature maps between object and edge detection tasks, to simultaneously refine edge features. 2) We propose a novel coarse-refine framework for crisp edge detection, named logical refinement network, which utilizes the interrelation between object and edge maps to detect crisper and thinner image edges. Extensive experiments show that our proposed framework is effective on both 2D and 3D images.

2 Methodology

Our method leverages a coarse-refine manner to capture both coarse (global) and fine (local) information to produce finer image boundaries, and it includes

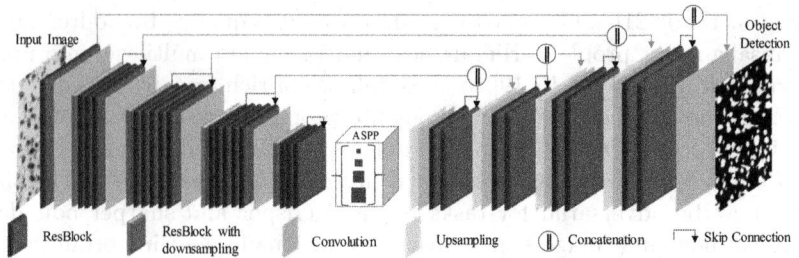

Fig. 2. The architecture of the object detection module (cf. the blue box in Fig. 1). (Color figure online)

two phases: the first phase is to detect coarse edge maps using a joint object and edge detection network, while the second phase is to refine edge maps with the edge refinement network. Figure 1 shows the framework of our proposed method. In the first phase, object and edge detection modules, which are shown in Figs. 2 and 3 respectively, are connected with logical gate and jointly trained end-to-end. The object information and coarse edge maps obtained in the first phase are then fed into the second phase to refine the final edge maps. The logical gate is also used in the second phase to gradually refine the edge features. In this section, we first introduce the logical gate, and then illustrate the work mechanism of the framework.

Logical Gate. Both edge and object detection can be treated as a pixel-wise binary classification task. An object detection map can be defined as D_O that highlights the full semantic areas of the target object. Then, the edge detection map can be defined as D_E, which highlights the edge of objects only. Under this definition, the pixels in D_E belong to a subset of the pixels in D_O, in which the logical relationship between edge and object maps can be reformulated as $D_E \cap D_O = D_E$, and $D_E \cup D_O = D_O$, where $\cap$ is Boolean AND operation and $\cup$ is Boolean OR operation. In this paper, we exploit such interrelation with a logical gate to refine edge features.

The object (D_O) and edge (D_E) maps are integrated by the logical gate operation G (cf. the light-green box in Figs. 3 and 4), which is formulated as $G = Conv(D_E \bigoplus (D_O \bigotimes D_E))$, where $\bigoplus$ is element-wise addition, $\bigotimes$ is element-wise multiplication and $Conv$ is a 3×3 convolutional layer. In Fig. 3, the feature map F also plays a role as edge map, since there are plenty of edge contexts contained in F. In Fig. 4, the object and edge maps obtained in the first phase are used as D_O and D_E to refine final edge maps. After applying the logical gate operation in the networks, the edge features will become clearer and crisper. It is because that the object features contain complete edge information and can be utilized to improve edge features by multiplication operation, and the distractors in the segmentation features can be suppressed by adding the edge features.

Joint Object and Edge Detection Network. The joint object and edge detection network includes edge and object detection modules. Inspired by

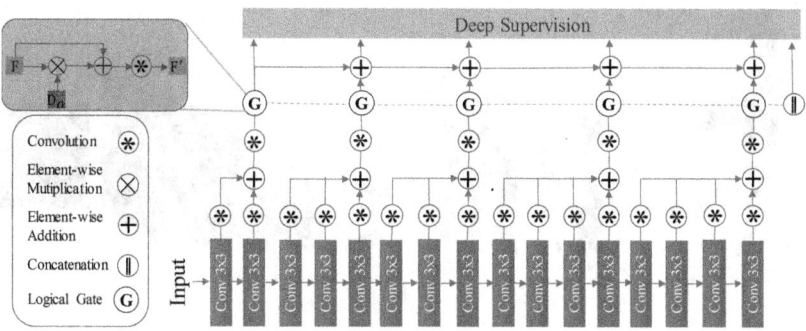

Fig. 3. The architecture of the edge detection module (cf. the orange box in Fig. 1). (Color figure online)

U-Net [16] and SegNet [2], the object detection module is designed as an encoder-decoder architecture, which is shown in Fig. 2, since this kind of architecture can capture high level global contexts and low level local details at the same time. The encoder part has an input residual convolution block and four stages with 4, 6, 6, 4 residual blocks, respectively. The input and output of each stage is element-wise added in skip connection. To further capture local details and explore sufficient multiscale features, an Atrous Spatial Pyramid Pooling (ASPP) block is used after the last stage of the encoder. The decoder includes four stages and an output convolutional filter, and there are two residual blocks in each stage. The output of object detection module can be defined as D_O, which is exploited by the logical gate in the edge detection module to improve the edge features in the first phase.

The 2D edge detection module is a simple yet efficient network, which is shown in Fig. 3. The network is composed of 16 convolutional layers which are divided into five stages. Each convolutional layer is connected to another convolutional layer and all resulting feature maps are element-wise accumulated to fuse feature maps into five stages. Each stage is followed by a convolutional layer. The feature map (F) after the convolutional layer, which also plays a role as edge map (D_E), is fed into logical gate G along with the object map (D_O) generated from the object detection module. Specifically, the input feature map will be element-wise multiplied by the object map (D_O) and then element-wise added by the edge map (D_E), after which a convolutional layer is followed. The output of each logical gate operation (F') is layer-specifically and deeply supervised. The obtained edge and object maps are then passed to the next phase to refine the coarse and thick edge maps obtained in this phase.

Crisp Edge Refinement Network. The edge maps obtained from the first phase is usually coarse and unsharp. Such "coarse" appears in the following two aspects: one is the blurry and noisy boundaries, and the other one is the unevenly predicted probabilities. To address drawbacks in the edge maps, we develop a novel crisp edge refinement network with an encoder-decoder architecture, which

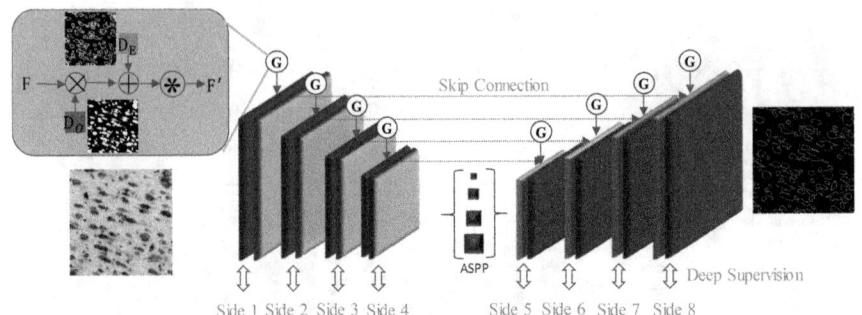

Fig. 4. The architecture of the crisp edge refinement network (cf. the green box in Fig. 1). (Color figure online)

is shown in Fig. 4. Both encoder and decoder have four stages. Each stage has two convolutional layers followed by ReLU and group normalization. In the last stage of the encoder, an ASPP block is also added to enrich hierarchical features. The output feature map (F) of each stage is passed to logical gate G with edge (D_E) and object (D_O) maps obtained from the first phase, and the updated feature map (F') is input to the next stage. All stages are fused together and thus result in nine outputs, which are deeply supervised by ground truth.

Hybrid Loss Function. The object detection module is trained with a cross-entropy loss. To address the class imbalance problem in edge detection and obtain high quality edge maps, we define a hybrid loss, including a focal loss and a cross-entropy loss, as the training loss of the edge detection module and the crisp edge refinement network. It is defined as the summation over all outputs:

$$\mathcal{L} = \sum_{k=1}^{K} \alpha_k \ell^k = \sum_{k=1}^{K} \alpha_k (\ell_{ce}^k + \ell_{focal}^k) \tag{1}$$

where ℓ^k is the loss of k-th side output, K is the total number of outputs, and α_k is the weight of each loss. As described above, the edge detection module and crisp edge refinement network are deeply supervised with six (K=6) and nine (K=9) outputs, respectively.

Table 1. Evaluation of the effectiveness of the proposed logical gate.

	Phase 1				Phase 2			
	ODS (%)	OIS (%)	DSC (%)	HD	ODS (%)	OIS (%)	DSC (%)	HD
W/O G	80.84	81.20	35.23	22.298	–	–	–	–
With G	82.11	83.52	32.08	18.572	85.05	85.05	50.27	12.811

3   Experiments

Datasets and Implementation Details. We evaluate our method on a 3D monkey brain cell dataset acquired from a special 3D light-sheet microscopy imaging equipment and a 2D nuclei detection dataset from Kaggle 2018 Data Science Bowl [5]. The 3D dataset contains six patches with size of $300 \times 300 \times 100$ voxels sampled from different regions of monkey brain images. The 2D dataset includes 634 images from training set of Kaggle 2018 Data Science Bowl which are resized to 256×256 pixels. Both datasets are originally designed for instance segmentation and very challenging since most of the images contain dense objects with overlapping image boundaries. We randomly select 20% of data for testing, and the rest for training. Our network is implemented on the PyTorch framework and a Tesla P40 GPU with 24 GB memory is used.

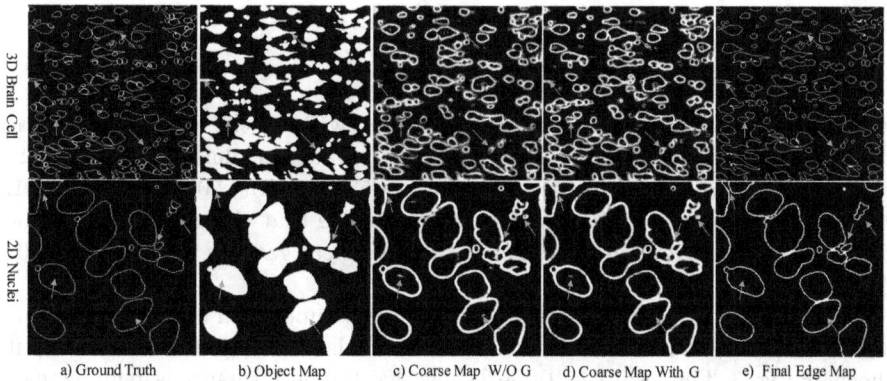

| a) Ground Truth | b) Object Map | c) Coarse Map W/O G | d) Coarse Map With G | e) Final Edge Map |

Fig. 5. The evaluation results with and without the proposed logical gate (Coarse Map: edge map predicted in the first phase).

Optimal Dataset Scale (ODS) and Optimal Image Scale (OIS) [1] are two common used metrics in edge detection tasks. ODS uses a fixed threshold, which is calibrated globally for the whole dataset, to provide optimal performance. OIS evaluates the performance with the optimal threshold selected in a per-image basis. During quantitative evaluation, a maximum tolerance distance d is used to match ground-truth edges, which is 0.0075 by default. In addition, to show the localization ability of different methods, we also leverage Dice Score Coefficient (DSC) and Hausdorff Distance (HD) as evaluation metrics. Notably, our proposed method can predict final binary edge maps without any post-processing. To be fair, for other compared methods, we evaluate the DSC and HD with a fixed optimal threshold calibrated globally for the whole dataset.

Ablation Study. To evaluate the effectiveness of our proposed logical gate operation, we conduct a set of experiments with and without the logical gate. Table 1 shows that the logical gate improves the performance in the coarse phase

Table 2. Evaluation of the effectiveness of hierachical boosting.

Metric	Side 1	Side 2	Side 3	Side 4	Side 5	Side 6	Side 7	Side 8	Fusion
ODS (%)	65.78	68.08	73.53	80.44	81.50	82.83	84.49	84.94	**85.05**
OIS (%)	66.10	68.20	73.60	80.44	81.50	82.90	84.60	84.97	**85.05**
DSC (%)	50.21	50.19	50.19	50.20	50.22	50.22	51.75	**51.24**	50.27
HD	12.832	12.832	12.832	12.832	12.826	12.815	**12.088**	12.447	12.811

Table 3. Comparison with the state-of-the-art methods on 3D and 2D datasets.

	3D Brain Cell				2D Nuclei			
	ODS (%)	OIS (%)	DSC (%)	HD	ODS (%)	OIS (%)	DSC (%)	HD
HED [19]	68.52	69.13	28.04	22.811	82.28	82.66	39.54	44.981
RCF [11]	80.84	81.20	35.23	22.298	87.25	88.12	40.03	31.601
BDCN [9]	**85.43**	**85.43**	43.83	18.341	88.08	**88.76**	50.76	**23.340**
Proposed	85.05	85.05	**50.27**	**12.811**	**88.68**	88.68	**51.65**	30.252

distinctly, while the model cannot converge well without the logical gate in the refinement phase. With the logical gate in the refinement phase, the ODS, OIS, DSC and HD can be further improved to 85.05%, 85.05%, 50.27% and 12.811, respectively. From the arrows in Fig. 5, we can see that the edge maps can be improved to be clearer and thinner with the logical gate on both 3D and 2D datasets.

We also evaluate the effectiveness of the deeply supervised hierarchical boosting in crisp edge refinement network. Each side is corresponding to an output shown in Fig. 3. The results in Table 2 show that the performance is in an increasing trend with the helpful hierarchical information. With all convolutional layers combined to employ ample features, it achieves a boost in performance.

Comparisons with State of the Art. We compare the proposed method with state-of-the-art methods including HED [19], RCF [11,12], and BDCN [9], and conduct extensive experiments on those two datasets. The results shown in Table 3 indicate that the performance of our proposed method is comparable with BDCN, which is on the cutting edge. It is worth to note that BDCN, as well as all other compared methods, need an optimal threshold to get the binary edge map, while our proposed method can predict final edge map with crisp boundaries directly. Last but not least, the DSC of the proposed method outperforms all other methods, which indicates the superior "correctness" of our proposed method in distinguishing edge and non-edge pixels. Figure 6 shows the edge detection results of different methods. As indicated by the arrows, the edge response of our proposed method is more precise, sharper and clearer than compared methods.

We further evaluate the "crispness" of edges from the proposed method by varying the maximum tolerance distance d when matching ground-truth edges during evaluation, which is shown in Fig. 7. The performance of all methods

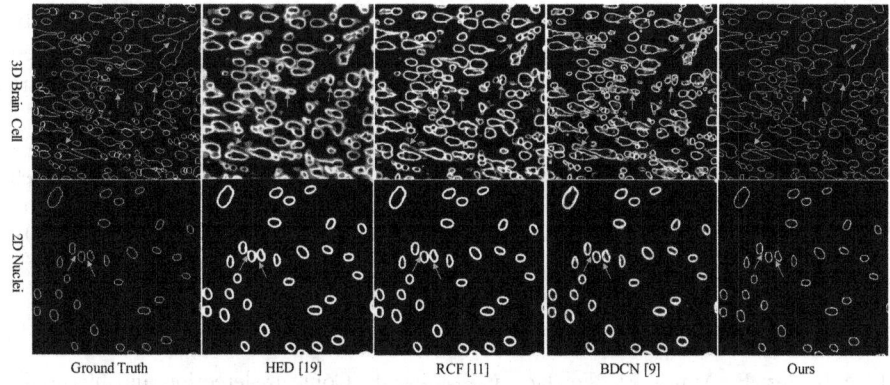

Fig. 6. The results of different edge detection methods.

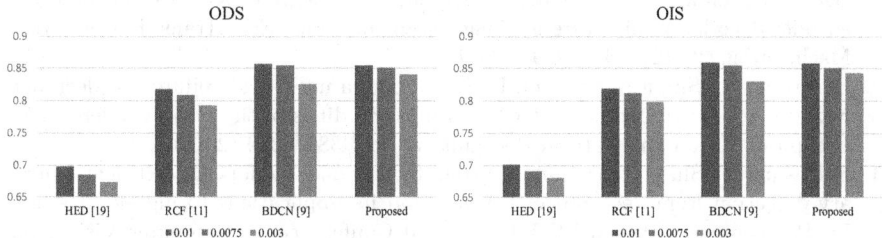

Fig. 7. Performance (ODS and OIS) as a function of the maximum tolerance distance for edge matching to evaluate the "crispness" of edges.

decreases when tightening the evaluation criterion from 0.01 to 0.003. The performance of our proposed method decreases slowly when d decreases. In contrast, the performance of compared methods drops quickly. In fact, the ODS gap between the proposed method and RCF increases from 3.68% to 4.80%, and the OIS gap increases from 3.87% to 4.39%. However, the gaps between BDCN and CRF become closer with a smaller d, decreasing from 3.85% to 3.32% in the ODS gap and from 3.94% to 3.22% in the OIS gap, respectively. The results suggest that our proposed method produces a crisp edge.

4   Conclusion

In this paper, we proposed a novel coarse-refine framework for crisp edge detection, called logical refinement network. Motivated by the logical relationship between binary segmentation and edge maps, we proposed a logical gate in which the segmentation and edge features are utilized to gradually improve the quality of edge maps. In conjunction with logical gate, the proposed method detects crisp and clear edges, which stick to the actual image boundaries. Experiments show that the proposed method is able to detect accurate and crisp 2D and 3D image edges, and it is also the first attempt to address the 3D edge detection problem with deep learning. In terms of the correctness and crispness of detected edges, our proposed method significantly outperforms existing state-of-the-art algorithms in both 2D and 3D.

Acknowledegments. This work was supported by the grants from Key Area Research and Development Program of Guangdong Province, China (No. 2018B010111001) and the Science and Technology Program of Shenzhen, China (No. ZDSYS201802021814180).

References

1. Arbelaez, P., Maire, M., Fowlkes, C., Malik, J.: Contour detection and hierarchical image segmentation. IEEE Trans. Pattern Anal. Mach. Intell. **33**(5), 898–916 (2010)
2. Badrinarayanan, V., Kendall, A., Cipolla, R.: SegNet: a deep convolutional encoder-decoder architecture for image segmentation. IEEE Trans. Pattern Anal. Mach. Intell. **39**(12), 2481–2495 (2017)
3. Bertasius, G., Shi, J., Torresani, L.: DeepEdge: a multi-scale bifurcated deep network for top-down contour detection. In: Proceedings of the IEEE Conference on Computer Vision and Pattern Recognition, pp. 4380–4389 (2015)
4. Bertasius, G., Shi, J., Torresani, L.: High-for-low and low-for-high: efficient boundary detection from deep object features and its applications to high-level vision. In: Proceedings of the IEEE International Conference on Computer Vision, pp. 504–512 (2015)
5. Caicedo, J.C., et al.: Nucleus segmentation across imaging experiments: the 2018 data science bowl. Nat. Methods **16**(12), 1247–1253 (2019)
6. Canny, J.: A computational approach to edge detection. IEEE Trans. Pattern Anal. Mach. Intell. **6**, 679–698 (1986)
7. Dollár, P., Zitnick, C.L.: Structured forests for fast edge detection. In: Proceedings of the IEEE International Conference on Computer Vision, pp. 1841–1848 (2013)
8. Girshick, R., Donahue, J., Darrell, T., Malik, J.: Rich feature hierarchies for accurate object detection and semantic segmentation. Proceedings of the IEEE Conference on Computer Vision and Pattern Recognition, pp. 580–587 (2014)
9. He, J., Zhang, S., Yang, M., Shan, Y., Huang, T.: Bi-directional cascade network for perceptual edge detection. In: Proceedings of the IEEE Conference on Computer Vision and Pattern Recognition, pp. 3828–3837 (2019)
10. Hu, Y., Chen, Y., Li, X., Feng, J.: Dynamic feature fusion for semantic edge detection. arXiv preprint arXiv:1902.09104 (2019)
11. Liu, Y., Cheng, M.M., Hu, X., Bian, J.W., Zhang, L., Bai, X., Tang, J.: Richer convolutional features for edge detection. IEEE Trans. Pattern Anal. Mach. Intell. **41**(8), 1939–1946 (2019)
12. Liu, Y., Cheng, M.M., Hu, X., Wang, K., Bai, X.: Richer convolutional features for edge detection. In: IEEE Conference on Computer Vision and Pattern Recognition, pp. 3000–3009 (2017)
13. Maire, M., Yu, S.X., Perona, P.: Reconstructive sparse code transfer for contour detection and semantic labeling. In: Cremers, D., Reid, I., Saito, H., Yang, M.-H. (eds.) ACCV 2014. LNCS, vol. 9006, pp. 273–287. Springer, Cham (2015). https://doi.org/10.1007/978-3-319-16817-3_18

14. Pont-Tuset, J., Arbelaez, P., Barron, J.T., Marques, F., Malik, J.: Multiscale combinatorial grouping for image segmentation and object proposal generation. IEEE Trans. Pattern Anal. Mach. Intell. **39**(1), 128–140 (2016)

15. Qin, X., Zhang, Z., Huang, C., Gao, C., Dehghan, M., Jagersand, M.: BASNet: Boundary-aware salient object detection. In: The IEEE Conference on Computer Vision and Pattern Recognition, June 2019

16. Ronneberger, O., Fischer, P., Brox, T.: U-Net: convolutional networks for biomedical image segmentation. In: Navab, N., Hornegger, J., Wells, W.M., Frangi, A.F. (eds.) MICCAI 2015. LNCS, vol. 9351, pp. 234–241. Springer, Cham (2015). https://doi.org/10.1007/978-3-319-24574-4_28

17. Shen, W., Wang, X., Wang, Y., Bai, X., Zhang, Z.: DeepContour: a deep convolutional feature learned by positive-sharing loss for contour detection. In: Proceedings of the IEEE Conference on Computer Vision and Pattern Recognition, pp. 3982–3991 (2015)

18. Wang, Y., Zhao, X., Huang, K.: Deep crisp boundaries. In: Proceedings of the IEEE Conference on Computer Vision and Pattern Recognition, pp. 3892–3900 (2017)

19. Xie, S., Tu, Z.: Holistically-nested edge detection. In: Proceedings of the IEEE International Conference on Computer Vision, pp. 1395–1403 (2015)

20. Yu, Z., Feng, C., Liu, M.Y., Ramalingam, S.: CaseNet: deep category-aware semantic edge detection. In: Proceedings of the IEEE Conference on Computer Vision and Pattern Recognition, pp. 5964–5973 (2017)

21. Yu, Z., et al.: Simultaneous edge alignment and learning. In: European Conference on Computer Vision (2018)

22. Zimmermann, R.S., Siems, J.N.: Faster training of Mask R-CNN by focusing on instance boundaries. Comput. Vis. Image Underst. **188**, 102795 (2019)

Defending Deep Learning-Based Biomedical Image Segmentation from Adversarial Attacks: A Low-Cost Frequency Refinement Approach

Qi Liu[1]([✉]), Han Jiang[1], Tao Liu[2], Zihao Liu[2], Sicheng Li[3], Wujie Wen[1], and Yiyu Shi[4]

[1] Lehigh University, Bethlehem, PA 18015, USA
{qil219,haj219,wuw219}@lehigh.edu
[2] Florida International University, Miami, FL 33199, USA
{tliu023,zliu021}@fiu.edu
[3] Alibaba DAMO Academy, Sunnyvale, CA, USA
sicheng.li@alibaba-inc.com
[4] University of Notre Dame, Notre Dame, IN 46556, USA
yshi4@nd.edu

Abstract. Deep learning has demonstrated superb performance and efficiency in medical image segmentation. However, recently the community has also found the first practical adversarial example crafting algorithm dedicated to misleading deep learning-based biomedical image segmentation models. The generated segmentation-oriented adversarial examples, while almost indistinguishable by human eyes, can always produce target incorrect segmentation prediction with high intersection-over-union (IoU) rate, significantly concerning the safe use of such an emerging technique in medical diagnosis tasks. On the other hand, research on defending such an emerging attack in the context of medical image segmentation is lacking. In this work, we make the very first attempt to develop a low-cost and effective input-transformation based defense technique. To maximize the defense efficiency (or recovered segmentation results) of adversarial samples while minimizing the segmentation performance loss of benign samples after applying defense, we propose a novel low-cost image compression-based defense approach guided by fine-grained frequency refinement (FR). Extensive experimental results on various deep learning segmentation models show that our defense can offer very high defense efficiency against adversarial examples with very marginal segmentation performance loss of benign images on both ISIC skin lesion segmentation challenge and the problem of glaucoma optic disc segmentation. To further validate our method's effectiveness, we also extend our evaluation to the image classification model. We show the influence of our recovered segmentation prediction by our defense on disease prediction in adversarial settings. The code is released at: https://github.com/qiliu08/frequency-refinement-defense.

© Springer Nature Switzerland AG 2020
A. L. Martel et al. (Eds.): MICCAI 2020, LNCS 12264, pp. 342–351, 2020.
https://doi.org/10.1007/978-3-030-59719-1_34

1   Introduction

Recently, deep learning has been widely applied to a variety of medical imaging tasks to assist doctors in making a more precise medical diagnosis at significantly reduced labor expenses. [4,13]. As the state-of-the-art deep learning solution continues advancing the performance in medical field, a question that naturally arises would be whether the adversarial examples could also compromise deep learning medical diagnosis results. The so-called adversarial example is a type of malicious inputs that possesses an indistinguishable visualization with benign inputs for human beings [3,8,11]. It has proved to be a significant security concern for deep learning-based image recognition and segmentation in computer vision. As expected, the latest study discovered the very first practical adversarial example in the context of medical image segmentation, namely Adaptive Segmentation Mask Attack (ASMA). It confirmed its high effectiveness to mislead the segmentation prediction to any target adversarial mask with a very high intersection-over-union (IoU) rate [14]. Distinct from existing segmentation attack algorithms for computer vision tasks, which are nontarget thus unrealistic in the medical field, ASMA is a targeted adversarial example generating algorithm that could lead to a convincing prediction shape of choice with subtle input modifications that are invisible to the bare eye. As a result, there is no doubt that such an emerging security flaw, if left unchecked, will cause severe consequences in the near future, especially considering that the doctors may ever-increasingly rely on deep learning predicted results for the treatment to patients. From an economic aspect, many fraud insurance claims could happen just because of the false breast cancel classification result incurred by these adversarial examples [7].

Rather than treating such an ever-increasing threat as an "after-thought" factor in deep learning-based medical imaging, in this paper, we make the very first attempt to mitigate such a new attack. Our approach is inspired by JPEG– a popular low-cost image compression framework [12,18]. We found that JPEG cannot balance the defense efficiency against adversarial examples and accuracy on benign images because of the human vision-centered quantization. To overcome this limitation, we propose the frequency refinement (FR) approach to redesign quantization based on the unique statistical pattern of adversarial perturbations in frequency domain. Our FR can almost recover the low IoU of segmentation prediction under adversarial settings to the original level without scarifying the accuracy of benign images (see the example on Fig. 2 column 1 and 4). We also extend our elevation to classification-based disease diagnosis. Experiments show that the false segmentation prediction incurred by adversarial examples would hurt the accuracy of disease classification significantly, e.g. increasing misdiagnosis risk (sensitivity: 50.6%). However, the recovered segmentation prediction by our FR can improve the sensitivity to the level comparable to the original model (68.2% vs. 71%). *To the best of our knowledge, this is the first study that targets the defense against the state-of-the-art adversarial examples in the context of medical imaging.*

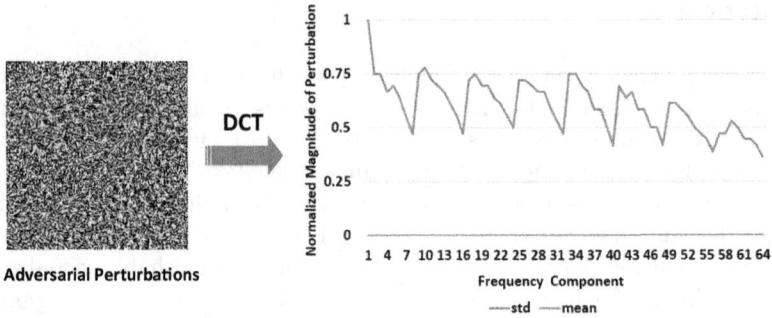

Fig. 1. Statistical information of adversarial perturbations in frequency domain

2   Background and Motivation

2.1   Adversarial Examples for Medical Image Segmentation

Ozbulak et al. [14] proposed a gradient descent-based targeted adversarial example generating algorithm, namely Adaptive Segmentation Mask Attack (ASMA). It is the first attack algorithm to accurately produce targeted adversarial masks meaningful in the sense of medical image segmentation. The basic idea of ASMA is to increase the prediction likelihood of the selected foreground pixels in the target adversarial mask for a specific class c except for pixels that are already predicted as class c by the segmentation model $f(\theta, X)$, while reducing the prediction likelihood of all other pixels outside the target adversarial mask for other classes except for those classified as other classes already. The input X can be iteratively updated as follows:

$$X_{i+1} = X_i + \alpha_i \cdot \sum_{c=1}^{m} \nabla_x \left(\mathbb{1}_{Y_{AE}=c} \odot \mathbb{1}_{\arg\max(f(\theta, X_i)) \neq c} \odot f_c(\theta, X_i) \right) \qquad (1)$$

where α_i is an adaptive perturbation multiplier and controlled by $\alpha_i = \beta \times IoU(Y_{AE}, Y_i) + \tau$, by considering the IoU score at the i-th iteration. β and τ are hyper-parameters to decide the final perturbation multiplier. $\odot$ is the element-wised matrix multiplication. Y_{AE} and X_0 are the desired prediction mask for adversarial example that contains class labels, and an input image, respectively.

2.2   JPEG Image Compression

JPEG [18] is a popular lossy image compression framework that mainly consists of image partitioning, Discrete Cosine Transform (DCT), quantization and lossless encoding etc. A 8×8 quantization table (Q-Table) with different quantization steps are used to scale DCT coefficients in frequency domain to achieve image compression. Based on the fact that human visual system (HVS) cares more about the low frequency features, larger (smaller) quantization steps are assigned to higher (lower) frequency components in Q-table. The trade-off

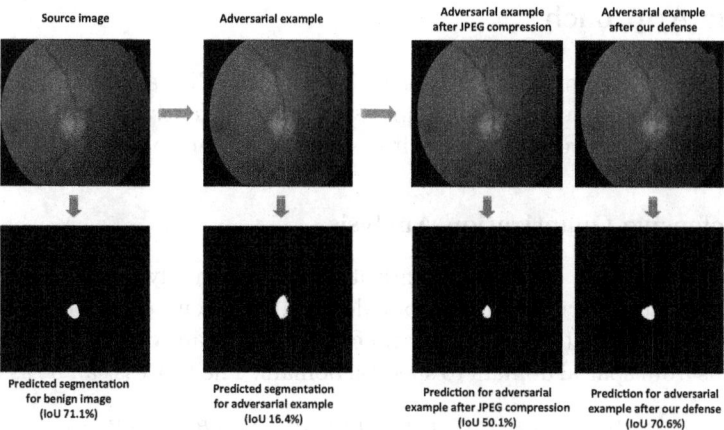

Fig. 2. The visualization of predicted segmentation for source and adversarial images with/without our defense and JPEG compression on the glaucoma optic disc dataset.

between image quality and compression rate can be realized by scaling Q-table with a parameter–"Quantization Factor (QF)". A higher QF indicates better image quality but a lower compression rate.

Limitation of JPEG on Defense. We select JPEG for our initial exploration of defense solutions against ASMA, considering its low-cost and popularity for medical image compression. Figure 1 illustrates the ASMA-based adversarial perturbations of a representative image from glaucoma optic dis dataset [17], as well as the statistical information (mean and standard deviations) of the perturbations' DCT coefficients across 64 frequency bands. We observe that such adversarial perturbations could appear at any frequency band, with maximized distortions introduced in the lowest frequency band. However, JPEG compression always quantizes less on low frequency features (more on high frequency features) to preserve the visual quality for human eyes. Thus, standard JPEG can not effectively filter these perturbations in the whole spectral domain. As Fig. 2 shows, ASMA-based adversarial example drops IoU from 71.1% (benign image) to 16.4% on segmentation prediction (see the first two columns). However, JPEG-based defense only recovers IoU from 16.4% to 50.1% for adversarial example to maintain a high IoU for the benign image after defense given that such defense will be applied to any image in practice (see the third column). It confirms that standard JPEG is not an effective defense method against such adversarial examples and prompts the need to explore better low-cost defense solutions in the context of medical image segmentation.

3   Our Approach

In this section, we propose a frequency refinement (FR) approach to redesign the quantization table in JPEG compression, a.k.a. defensive quantization table (DQ-Table), to achieve both competitive testing accuracy and defense efficiency.

3.1   Defensive Quantization Analysis

To better explore the defensive quantization, we first analyze why quantization can mitigate adversarial examples but degrade the accuracy of benign images. The DCT transformation is a linear function which transforms adversarial perturbations from spatial domain to spectral domain. The process can be as follows:

$$DCT(X + P) = DCT(X) + DCT(P) = C_X \cdot B + C_P \cdot B \qquad (2)$$

Where P is the adversarial perturbation. C_X (C_P) and B are the DCT coefficients of input X (P) and DCT basis function, respectively. Here, $C_P \ll C_X$. The quantization function can be represented as:

$$q(X, QS) = \begin{cases} 0 & \text{if } \frac{|X|}{QS} < 0.5 \\ 1 & \text{otherwise} \end{cases} \qquad (3)$$

where QS is the quantization step. As a result, the quantization process in spectral domain can be approximated as:

$$q(C_X + C_P, QS) \approx q(C_X, QS) + q(C_P, QS) \qquad (4)$$

Ideally, if $QS > 2 \cdot |C_P|$, the malicious perturbation can be filtered. However, in practice, it is impossible to know the actual magnitude of the adversarial perturbation in different frequency bands. Instead, a possible solution is to use a large quantization step as much as possible. However, this can easily lead to prominent segmentation accuracy reduction due to introducing quantization errors to many important benign features $\sigma < \frac{QS}{2}$. Note a larger QS will increase the upper bound of quantization error, resulting in a more significant accuracy drop. To solve this issue, we propose to balance this by designing the defensive quantization table (DQ-Table) through fine-grained frequency analysis.

3.2   Frequency Component Analysis

To design an effective DQ-Table, we need to identify which frequency components are more critical for a deep learning-based segmentation model. For a single-pixel x, the 8×8 DCT can be expressed as:

$$x = \sum_{i=1}^{8} \sum_{j=1}^{8} c_{ij} \cdot b_{ij} \qquad (5)$$

where c_{ij} and b_{ij} are the DCT coefficient and DCT transformation basis at 64 frequency bands, respectively. The contribution of a frequency component b_{ij}

to the segmentation model is associated with the gradient of the segmentation model function f with respect to b_{ij}, which can be calculated as:

$$\frac{\partial f}{\partial b_{ij}} = \frac{\partial f}{\partial x} \times \frac{\partial x}{\partial b_{ij}} = \frac{\partial f}{\partial x} \times c_{ij} \qquad (6)$$

Eq. 6 means that the output of the segmentation model f will be mainly decided by the importance of pixel x-$\frac{\partial f}{\partial x}$ and the magnitude of DCT coefficient (c_{ij}). Since $\frac{\partial f}{\partial x}$ varies from one pixel to another, for each benign image, the importance of a frequency component for segmentation should be characterized from the statistics information of DCT coefficients. The study [15] has proved that the DCT coefficients approximately obey a Laplace distribution with zero mean and various standard deviations (δ_{ij}). A larger δ_{ij} means a more critical contribution to the segmentation model. A simple solution to design the DQ-Table is to apply a larger (or smaller) QS at frequency bands with a larger (or smaller) δ_{ij}, so as to prevent the accuracy reduction induced by quantization errors. However, in our exploration, we also observe that a few frequency bands carrying the largest δ_{ij} suffer from more significant adversarial perturbation than others. This finding indicates that the frequency band with a larger δ_{ij}, which makes more essential contributions to the segmentation model, is also more prone to adversarial attacks. Thus, we further propose the frequency refinement approach (FR) for creating effective DQ-Table.

3.3   DQ-Table Design

Based on the above analysis, our proposed frequency refinement will guide the DQ-Table design based on the following two strategies: defense priority strategy and accuracy compensation strategy. According to two strategies, the 64 frequency bands will be roughly divided into three groups: priority defense (PD) band, accuracy compensation (AC) band and global defense (GD) band. Each group of bands will be assigned with an optimized quantization step (QS) constraint. We first sort the standard deviations (δ_{ij}). Then we set two thresholds T_1 and T_2 to categorize the 64 frequency bands into three bands. To simplify our design, we design a step function to assign QS constraint to the three divided bands based on the following strategies:

Defense Priority Strategy – We observe that adversarial perturbations are largely distributed in a few frequency bands with the first several largest δ_{ij}. For those frequency bands, we need to prioritize defense efficiency by setting a moderate QS_1, e.g. 20–50, to properly filter adversarial perturbations without distorting benign features. We name those frequency bands as priority defense (PD) band ($\delta_{ij} < T_1$). Besides, we find that the PD band usually consists of a few lowest frequency bands (see Fig. 1). This is because the test medical image sample usually carries adequate low-frequency information (e.g., a large number of similar pixels in the skin or blood image) compared with other types of image samples (e.g., ImageNet dataset [6]). Note that, the traditional JPEG compression will always set a smaller QS for lower frequency components, and hence is incapable of eliminating adversarial perturbations in these components, which is often the case for adversarial images targeting medical segmentation.

Accuracy Compensation Strategy – To compensate the accuracy reduction induced by quantization errors on PD band, we need to set a tiny QS_2, e.g. $QS_2 \leq 20$, in some of the sub-important frequency bands, namely accuracy compensation (AC) band ($T_1 < \delta_{ij} < T_2$). For other frequency bands, we adopt a large QS_3, e.g. 50–100, to eliminate perturbation as much as possible, namely global defense (GD) band ($\delta_{ij} > T_2$). As a result, the step function can be represented as:

$$f_s(\delta_{ij}) = \begin{cases} QS_1 & \text{if } \delta_{ij} < T_1 \\ QS_2 & \text{if } T_1 < \delta_{ij} < T_2 \\ QS_3 & \text{if } \delta_{ij} > T_2 \end{cases} \tag{7}$$

where $QS_1 \geq QS_2$ and $QS_2 \leq QS_3$. To simplify our design, we fix the number of frequency bands in each group band. Specifically, for the PD band, it includes three frequency bands with top-3 of sorted δ_{ij}. The AC band has 12 frequency bands (rank 4th – 15th of sorted δ_{ij}). The remaining frequency bands (rank 16th – 64th of sorted δ_{ij}) will be allocated to the GD band.

Table 1. Testing accuracy (IoU (%) on benign images) of JPEG v.s. our FRs.

	Original model	JPEG(85)	JPEG(50)	FR(20,10,60)	FR(30,5,80)
ISIC skin lesion [5]	87.1 ± 4.5	**86.5 ± 7.5**	86 ± 8.1	86.3 ± 7.3	**86.5 ± 7.2**
Glaucoma [17]	70.5 ± 7.1	69.2 ± 10.1	67.3 ± 10	69.1 ±9 .8	**69.3 ± 9.6**

Table 2. Defense efficiency (IoU (%) on adversarial examples) of JPEG v.s. our FRs.

	No defense	JPEG(85)	JPEG(50)	FR(20,10,60)	FR(30,5,80)
ISIC skin lesion [5]	46.6 ± 9.2	84.3 ± 8.4	85.3 ± 8.9	84.9 ± 8.5	**85.5 ± 8.3**
Glaucoma [17]	28.6 ± 16.8	63.4 ± 11.8	65.9 ± 11	67.3 ± 10.9	**68 ± 10.1**

4 Evaluation

In this section, we comprehensively evaluate the defense efficiency (or accuracy recovery) against ASMA-based adversarial examples, as well as the segmentation accuracy of benign medical images for our proposed frequency refinement (FR) method. The advantage of segmentation prediction recovery on disease diagnosis (classification) using our defense is also discussed.

Datasets and Models – We used the two datasets in [14] to reproduce ASMA-based adversarial examples for a fair evaluation of our defense, which includes ISIC skin lesion segmentation dataset [5] and glaucoma optic disc dataset [17]. For segmentation task, two state-of-the-art segmentation models are selected, including Resnet-50 [2,9] for ISIC skin lesion dataset and U-Net [1,16] for glaucoma optic disc dataset. For disease diagnosis on glaucoma dataset, an ensemble of deep learning models [1], which consist of DenseNet [10] and ResNet[9], is adopted for disease classification purpose.

Evaluation Metrics – We characterize the intersection over union (IoU) of the label mask and the predicted segmentation mask on the given 100 benign and adversarial images. For the classification task, we evaluate the sensitivity of disease diagnosis. In our experiment, the disease diagnosis is a simple two-class classification problem: with or without the disease.

Evaluated Designs and Settings – To optimize DQ-Table of our FR approach, we designed multiple sets of (QS_1, QS_2, QS_3) to search for optimized results. Specifically, we set the following QS constraints (see Sect. 3.3) in our optimization process: $QS_1 \in \{20, 30, 40, 50\}$, $QS_2 \in \{5, 10, 15, 20\}$, $QS_3 \in \{50, 60, 80, 100\}$. Among them, we selected two representative solutions – $FR(20, 10, 60)$ and $FR(30, 5, 80)$ as our defense candidates. We compare these two candidates with the JPEG compression approach with two representative QF configurations: 85 and 50, i.e., JPEG(85) and JPEG(50). JPEG(85) is a high quality baseline as it incurs a very marginal accuracy reduction for benign images, which is similar to our approach. JPEG(50) is a low quality baseline, which provides better defense efficiency at the cost of a more severe accuracy reduction.

Table 3. Defense efficiency (sensitivity (%)) of JPEG v.s. our FR for disease diagnosis.

	No defense	JPEG(85)	JPEG(50)	FR(20,10,60)	FR(30,5,80)	Baseline
Glaucoma [17]	50.6%	54.6%	59.1%	65.5%	**68.2%**	71%

4.1 Evaluation Results

Testing Accuracy – As Table 1 shows, our two FR candidates show only marginal accuracy (IoU) degradation (i.e., ~1%) on benign images for both ISIC and Glaucoma datasets. Due to the simplicity of ISIC dataset (i.e., a high IoU 87.1% on the original model), we also found that the low quality JPEG(50) compression can still achieve a competitive IoU, i.e., 86%. However, for a more complex Glaucoma dataset, JPEG(50) exhibits a prominent IoU degradation (~3%). Considering that defense will be applied to any benign or adversarial image in practice and the achievable defense efficiency makes more sense if the defense does not degrade the IoU of benign images, we focus on the JPEG(85) baseline for defense efficiency comparison.

Defense Efficiency – As listed in Table 2, our two FR candidates offer the most significant IoU improvement (or recover) on adversarial examples for both ISIC and Glaucoma datasets. In particular, FR(30,5,80) delivers better defense efficiency comparing with FR(20,10,60). This is because larger quantization steps

(QS) used in the PD band and GD band can eliminate adversarial perturbations more effectively while smaller QS in the AC band can still compensate for the incurred accuracy reduction. Compared with JPEG baselines, our FRs achieve a slight improvement of defense efficiency for the simple ISIC dataset. However, for the more complex Glaucoma dataset, our two FRs significantly outperform the JPEG compression for the similar high IoU on benign images, e.g. 63.4% (JPEG(85)) vs. 67.3% (FR(20,10,60)) and 68% (FR(30,5,80)). Moreover, we also observe that even the more defensive JPEG(50) is still worse than any of the two FRs. These results indicate that our defense can better mitigate such adversarial examples with almost no accuracy loss, which is practically useful.

Further Evaluation on Disease Diagnosis – While ASMA-based segmentation adversarial examples do not directly target classification models, the generated false segmentation predictions can also impact the disease diagnosis accordingly. As Table 3 reports, the original disease classification sensitivity drops from 71% (basline) to 50.6% for images under adversarial settings on the segmentation task. We also observe that the IoU difference between our FR and JPEG on the segmentation task is further enlarged in disease diagnosis for defending against adversarial examples. For example, our FR(30,5,80) candidate surpasses JPEG(85) by 4.5% on segmentation adversarial examples, while such difference is increased to 13.6% (sensitivity) in classification. A possible explanation is that our defense, compared with JPEG, provides a more precise focus on extracting important features for classification. Therefore, our higher defense efficiency on segmentation can translate into better sensitivity on classification.

5   Conclusion

Deep learning has demonstrated tremendous performance improvement in fields like medical image segmentation. However, a recent study revealed that deep learning-based segmentation models could be misled by the very first practical adversarial examples in the context of medical image segmentation. Our work is the first to explore and design defense solutions to mitigate such an emerging threat. According to the unique property of adversarial examples of medical images in spectral domain, we develop a frequency refinement (FR) approach to effectively eliminate malicious perturbations of adversarial examples without distorting benign features essential for segmentation. Experiments show that our FR can achieve high testing accuracy and defense efficiency simultaneously, serving as a reference design for future defense development in medical domain.

Acknowledgements. This work was supported in part by NSF Grants CNS-2011260 and SPX-2006748.

References

1. Agrawal, V., Kori, A., Alex, V., Krishnamurthi, G.: Enhanced optic disk and cup segmentation with glaucoma screening from fundus images using position encoded CNNs. arXiv preprint arXiv:1809.05216 (2018)

2. Anand: isic 2018 github (2019). https://github.com/cygnus77/isic-2018
3. Carlini, N., Wagner, D.: Towards evaluating the robustness of neural networks. In: 2017 IEEE Symposium on Security and Privacy (SP), pp. 39–57. IEEE (2017)
4. Chen, H., Dou, Q., Yu, L., Qin, J., Heng, P.A.: Voxresnet: deep voxelwise residual networks for brain segmentation from 3D MR images. NeuroImage **170**, 446–455 (2018)
5. Codella, N.C., et al.: Skin lesion analysis toward melanoma detection: a challenge at the 2017 international symposium on biomedical imaging (isbi), hosted by the international skin imaging collaboration (isic). In: 2018 IEEE 15th International Symposium on Biomedical Imaging (ISBI 2018), pp. 168–172. IEEE (2018)
6. Deng, J., Dong, W., Socher, R., Li, L.J., Li, K., Fei-Fei, L.: Imagenet: a large-scale hierarchical image database. In: 2009 IEEE Conference on Computer Vision and Pattern Recognition, pp. 248–255. IEEE (2009)
7. Finlayson, S.G., Chung, H.W., Kohane, I.S., Beam, A.L.: Adversarial attacks against medical deep learning systems. arXiv preprint arXiv:1804.05296 (2018)
8. Goodfellow, I.J., Shlens, J., Szegedy, C.: Explaining and harnessing adversarial examples. arXiv preprint arXiv:1412.6572 (2014)
9. He, K., Zhang, X., Ren, S., Sun, J.: Deep residual learning for image recognition. In: Proceedings of the IEEE Conference on Computer Vision and Pattern Recognition, pp. 770–778 (2016)
10. Huang, G., Liu, Z., Van Der Maaten, L., Weinberger, K.Q.: Densely connected convolutional networks. In: Proceedings of the IEEE Conference on Computer Vision and Pattern Recognition, pp. 4700–4708 (2017)
11. Liu, Q., Liu, T., Liu, Z., Wang, Y., Jin, Y., Wen, W.: Security analysis and enhancement of model compressed deep learning systems under adversarial attacks. In: 2018 23rd Asia and South Pacific Design Automation Conference (ASP-DAC), pp. 721–726. IEEE (2018)
12. Liu, Z., et al.: Machine vision guided 3d medical image compression for efficient transmission and accurate segmentation in the clouds. In: Proceedings of the IEEE Conference on Computer Vision and Pattern Recognition, pp. 12687–12696 (2019)
13. Milletari, F., Navab, N., Ahmadi, S.A.: V-net: fully convolutional neural networks for volumetric medical image segmentation. In: 2016 Fourth International Conference on 3D Vision (3DV), pp. 565–571. IEEE (2016)
14. Ozbulak, U., Van Messem, A., De Neve, W.: Impact of adversarial examples on deep learning models for biomedical image segmentation. In: Shen, D., et al. (eds.) MICCAI 2019. LNCS, vol. 11765, pp. 300–308. Springer, Cham (2019). https://doi.org/10.1007/978-3-030-32245-8_34
15. Reininger, R., Gibson, J.: Distributions of the two-dimensional DCT coefficients for images. IEEE Trans. Commun. **31**(6), 835–839 (1983)
16. Ronneberger, O., Fischer, P., Brox, T.: U-Net: convolutional networks for biomedical image segmentation. In: Navab, N., Hornegger, J., Wells, W.M., Frangi, A.F. (eds.) MICCAI 2015. LNCS, vol. 9351, pp. 234–241. Springer, Cham (2015). https://doi.org/10.1007/978-3-319-24574-4_28
17. Sivaswamy, J., Krishnadas, S., Chakravarty, A., Joshi, G., Tabish, A.S., et al.: A comprehensive retinal image dataset for the assessment of glaucoma from the optic nerve head analysis. JSM Biomed. Imaging Data Papers **2**(1), 1004 (2015)
18. Wallace, G.K.: The jpeg still picture compression standard. IEEE Trans. Consum-Electron. **38**(1), xviii–xxxiv (1992)

CNN-GCN Aggregation Enabled Boundary Regression for Biomedical Image Segmentation

Yanda Meng[1], Meng Wei[1], Dongxu Gao[1], Yitian Zhao[2], Xiaoyun Yang[3], Xiaowei Huang[4], and Yalin Zheng[1(✉)]

[1] Department of Eye and Vision Science, Institute of Life Course and Medical Sciences, University of Liverpool, Liverpool, UK
yalin.zheng@liverpool.ac.uk
[2] Cixi Institute of Biomedical Engineering, Ningbo Institute of Industrial Technology, Chinese Academy of Sciences, Ningbo, China
[3] China Science IntelliCloud Technology Co., Ltd., Shanghai, China
[4] Department of Computer Science, University of Liverpool, Liverpool, UK

Abstract. Accurate segmentation of anatomic structure is an essential task for biomedical image analysis. Recent popular object contours regression based segmentation methods have increasingly attained researchers' attentions. They made a new starting point to tackle segmentation tasks instead of commonly used dense pixels classification methods. However, because of the nature of CNN based network (lack of spatial information) and the difficulty of this methodology itself (need of more spatial information), these methods needed extra process to maintain more spatial features, which may cause longer inference time or tedious design and inference process. To address the issue, this paper proposes a simple, intuitive deep learning based contour regression model. We develop a novel multi-level, multi-stage aggregated network to regress the coordinates of the contour of instances directly in an end-to-end manner. The proposed network seamlessly links convolution neural network (CNN) with Attention Refinement module (AR) and Graph Convolution Network (GCN). By hierarchically and iteratively combining features over different layers of the CNN, the proposed model obtains sufficient low-level features and high-level semantic information from the input image. Besides, our model pays distinct attention to the objects' contours with the help of AR and GCN. Primarily, thanks to the proposed aggregated GCN and vertices sampling method, our model benefits from direct feature learning of the objects' contour locations from sparse to dense and the spatial information propagation across the whole input image. Experiments on the segmentation of fetal head (FH) in ultrasound images and of the optic disc (OD) and optic cup (OC) in color fundus images demonstrate that our method outperforms state-of-the-art methods in terms of effectiveness and efficiency.

Electronic supplementary material The online version of this chapter (https://doi.org/10.1007/978-3-030-59719-1_35) contains supplementary material, which is available to authorized users.

© Springer Nature Switzerland AG 2020
A. L. Martel et al. (Eds.): MICCAI 2020, LNCS 12264, pp. 352–362, 2020.
https://doi.org/10.1007/978-3-030-59719-1_35

Keywords: Regression · Segmentation · GCN · Attention · Aggregation

1 Introduction

The accurate assessment of anatomic structures in biomedical images plays an essential role in the care of many medical conditions or diseases. For instance, fetal head (FH) circumference in ultrasound images can be used to estimate the gestational age and to monitor the growth of the fetus [14]. Likewise, the size of the optic disc (OD) and optic cup (OC) in color fundus images is important for the management of glaucoma [19]. However, manual annotation is time-consuming and costly, so an automatic accurate segmentation method is demanded.

The (biomedical) image segmentation task is a fundamental problem in the field of computer vision. Previous Convolution Neural Network (CNN) based methods [6,7,22,27] regarded segmentation as a pixel-wise classification problem and classified each pixel of an image into a class. Benefit from CNN's excellent ability to extract high-level semantic features, they obtained promising results in various segmentation tasks. For example, M-Net [6] obtained state-of-the-art performance in OD and OC segmentation task, but it needed additional process, e.g. multi-scale input and ellipse fitting. To maintain enough semantic and spatial information from biomedical images, U-Net++ [27] proposed an aggregated CNN to fuse and reuse multi-level features across different layers, but it may result in overuse of information flow as some low-level features are unnecessarily over-extracted while object boundaries are simultaneously under-sampled. To address this issue, we apply an Attention Refinement module (AR) working as a filter between CNN encoder and Graph Convolution Network (GCN) decoder, which cooperates with the GCN to gain more useful and representative semantic and spatial features, especially the boundary location information from the CNN.

Instead of dense pixels classification, recent works [3,24,25] exploited object contours for efficient segmentation and achieved comparable performance with pixel-based segmentation methods. Specifically, DARNet [3] exploited the combination of Fully Convolution Networks (FCNs) [18] and Active Contour Models (ACMs) [16]. Nevertheless, these methods need initialize object contour and iteratively optimize it to predict objects' contour during inference, which requires a relatively long running time. Other methods [24,25] represented object boundary with polar space coordinate, then regressed the distances between the center point and the boundary points with CNN. Besides, they found that CNN cannot regress the Euclidean space coordinate representation of the boundary well, as some noise may be added, and the CNN may not maintain enough spatial information [24,25]. Our proposed aggregation GCN can handle this issue well as confirmed by our experiment results. Besides, those methods' performance suffers from the low-quality of the center point, Xie *et al.* [24] utilized center sampling methods to predict and select high-quality center points to improve the segmentation result. In contrast, our boundary representation method is not sensitive to the center point as the boundary does not have too many correlations with the center point.

Although the above methods achieved state-of-the-art performance on many segmentation tasks, they inevitably necessitate sophisticated network design and tedious inference process. Conversely, inspired by the manner that clinicians annotate images, our method takes a simple but effective way to directly regress the boundary location without any further bells and whistles (multi-scale input, ellipse fitting, iterative optimization inference, center selection process). In summary, this work has the following contributions:

- We propose a simple and intuitive approach to (biomedical) image semantic segmentation and regard it as a vertex-wise boundary regression problem in an end-to-end fashion.
- We propose aggregated mechanisms on both CNN and GCN (with vertices sampling methods), which iteratively and hierarchically reuse the contextual and spatial information. The additional attention module filters out the redundant information and helps the GCN decoder obtain useful location information from the CNN encoder.
- We propose a new loss function suitable for object boundary localization, which helps prevent taking a large update step when approaching a small range of errors in the late training stage.

2   Method

2.1   Data Representation

The object boundaries, such as FH, are extracted from the binary masks of images and uniformly divided into N vertices with the same interval $\Delta \theta$ (e.g. N = 360, $\Delta \theta = 1°$ or N = 180, $\Delta \theta = 2°$) . The geometric center of a contour is defined as the center vertex. We represent the object boundary with vertices and edges as $B = (V, E)$, where V has $N + 1$ vertices in the Euclidean space, $V \in \mathbb{R}^{N \times 2}$, and $E \in \{0, 1\}^{(N+1) \times (N+1)}$ is a sparse adjacency matrix, representing the edge connections between vertices, where $E_{i,j} = 1$ means vertices V_i and V_j are connected by an edge, and $E_{i,j} = 0$ otherwise. In our work, every two consecutive vertices on the boundary and the center vertex are connected to form a triangle. For the OD and OC segmentation task, the OD and OC are divided separately while the center of the OC is shared as the center vertex. More details are shown in Fig. 1.

2.2   Graph Convolution and Vertices Sampling

Following [4], the graph convolution used in this work is defined in Fourier space by formulating spectral filtering with a kernel g_θ using a recursive 3rd order Chebyshev polynomial [4].

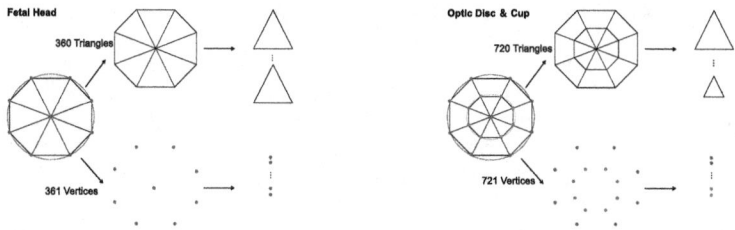

Fig. 1. Illustration of how object contours are represented to make it compatible for GCN. Left: Fetal Head; Right: Optic Disc and Cup. The boundary is represented by equally sampled vertices along it and the geometric center is defined as the center vertex. Each triangle consists of three vertices and three edges where two vertices are from the boundary and the other is the center vertex. Then, the vertices locations and their geometric relationships are defined by an adjacency matrix from the triangulations, which can be used by GCN. For the OD and OC segmentation, the center of the OC is shared as the center vertex for OD and OC. However, triangulations are made for both the OD and OC respectively.

To achieve multi-scale aggregated graph convolutions on different vertex resolutions, inspired by [20], we employ the permutation matrix $Q_d \in \{0,1\}^{m \times n}$ to down-sample m vertices, m = 360 for FH or 720 for DO and OC in our work. Q_d is obtained by iteratively contracting vertex pairs, which uses a quadratic matrix to maintain surface error approximations [9]. The down-sampling can be regarded as a pre-processing, and the discarded vertices are saved with Barycentric coordinates so that the up-sampling can map the discarded vertices back with the same Barycentric location. The up-sampled vertices V_u can be obtained by a sparse matrix multiplication, i.e., $V_u = Q_u V_d$, where $Q_u \in \mathbb{R}^{m \times n}$ is another transformation matrix, V_d are down-sampled vertices. The up-sampling is applied during learning, and it operates convolution transformations on retained vertices.

2.3 Proposed Aggregation Network

Semantic Encoder: Figure 2(a) shows the structure of our image context encoder, which aims to lessen the location information loss and gain more semantic features through different receptive fields. The encoder takes input images of shape $314 \times 314 \times 3$ (Fundus OD and OC images) or $140 \times 140 \times 1$ (Ultrasound FH images), with up-sampling and down-sampling. Our proposed encoder has five output features, for each, the shape is $5 \times 5 \times 128$, and then those intermediate features will be input to the attention refinement module (AR).

Attention Refinement Module: We propose an AR to purify the output features of each level (row) in the encoder, which easily integrates the global context information. As Fig. 2 shows, AR contains five attention blocks, and each block employs global channels average pooling to capture global context through the different channels, and computes an attention vector to guide the feature learning

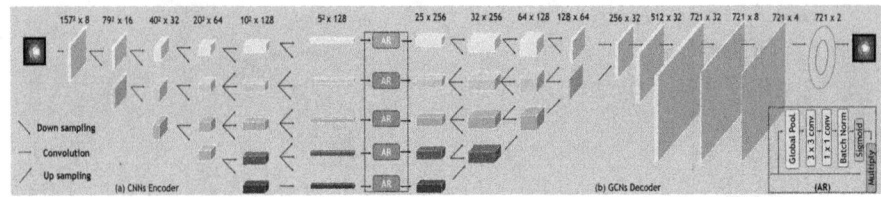

Fig. 2. Overview of the network architecture. The feature maps size of the CNN encoder and vertex maps size of the GCN decoder for each stage (columns) are shown. In the CNN encoder, the horizontal arrow represents a CNN Residual Block [13] with kernel size 3 × 3, stride 2, followed by a Batch Normalization (BN) layer [15] and ReLU as the activation function. The lower resolution level feature is bi-linearly up-sampled by a factor 2. In the GCN decoder, down-sampling and up-sampling are conducted by graph vertices sampling, which is in Sect. 2.1. The horizontal arrow represents residual graph convolution (ResGCN) blocks [17] with polynomial of order 3. The example here is for OD and OC segmentation, and for FH segmentation, the convolution operations will be the same.

through two convolution layer followed by a batch normalization layer and sigmoid as the activation function. For the filter, the kernel size is 3 × 3 and 1 × 1.

Spatial Decoder: The decoder takes processed multi-paths outputs from the attention module, then decodes with ResGCN blocks [17] through different levels. Benefits from the graph sampling, our decoder can regress the location of the object contour from sparse to dense. For each ResGCN Block, it has 4 graph convolution layers, followed by a BN layer [15] and ReLU as the activation function. After going through ResGCN blocks and graph vertices up-samplings, the number of vertices is up-sampled from 25 to 721, and each vertex is represented by a vector of length 32. At last, three additional graph convolution layers are added to generate 2D object contour vertices, which reduces the vertex feature map channels to 2, as each contour vertex has two dimensions: x and y.

2.4 Loss Function

We regard segmentation as a vertices location regression problem. L2 and L1 loss have been used in regression tasks by CNN based networks [11,12]. However, it is difficult for the L1 loss to find the global minimization in the late training stage without careful tuning the learning rate. Besides, it is commonly known that the L2 loss is sensitive to outliers which may lead to unstable training.

Inspired by Wing-loss [5] and Smooth-L1 loss [10], we propose a new loss function that can recover quickly when dealing with large errors during the early training stage and can prevent from taking large update steps when approaching small range errors in the late training stage. Our loss function is defined as:

$$L(x) = \begin{cases} W[e^{(\epsilon \times |x|)} - 1] & if \quad |x| < W \\ |x| - C & otherwise \end{cases} \quad (1)$$

Where W should be positive and limit the range of the non-linear part, ϵ decides the curvature between $(-W, W)$ and $C = W - W[e^{(|w|/\epsilon)} - 1]$ connects the linear and non-linear parts. For the OD and OC segmentation task, we apply a weight mask and assign more weights to the vertices that belong to the OC, as the OC is usually difficult to segment due to the poor image quality or poor color contrast.

3 Experiments

3.1 Datasets

We evaluate the proposed approach with two types of biomedical images on two segmentation tasks respectively: OD and OC segmentation from fundus images and segmentation of FH in ultrasound images.

Fudus OD and OC Images: 2068 images from five datasets (Refuge [19], Drishti-GS [23], ORIGA [26], RIGA [1], RIM-ONE [8]) are pooled together. 190 fundus images are randomly selected as the test dataset, the rest 1878 fundus images are used for the training and validation. Considering the negative influence of non-target areas in fundus retina images, we first localize the disc centers by a detector [21] and then crop a subimage of 314×314 pixels centered at the disc center for the subsequent analysis.

Ultrasound FH Images: The HC18-Challenge dataset[1] [14], contains 999 two-dimensional (2D) ultrasound images most with size of 800×540 pixels. We zero-padded each image to shape of 840×840 pixels, and then resize into 140×140 as the input image of our CNN-GCN network. 94 images are randomly selected as the test dataset whilst the rest 905 images for training.

3.2 Implementation Details

To augment our dataset, we perturb the input image of training dataset by randomly rotating images for both segmentation tasks. Specifically, the rotation ranges from -10 to $10°$. 10% of the training dataset are randomly selected as the validation dataset. We use stochastic gradient descent with a momentum of 0.99 to optimize our loss function. The number of graph vertices for OC and OD is sampled to 721, 512, 256, 128, 64, 32, 25 crosses seven stages with graph vertices sampling method. We trained our model 300 epochs for both datasets, with a learning rate of 1e–2 and decay rate of 0.995 every epoch. The batch size is set as 48. All the training processes are conducted on a server with 8 TESLA V100 and 4 TESLA P100, and all the test experiments are performed on a local machine Geforce RTX 2080Ti.

---

[1] https://hc18.grand-challenge.org/.

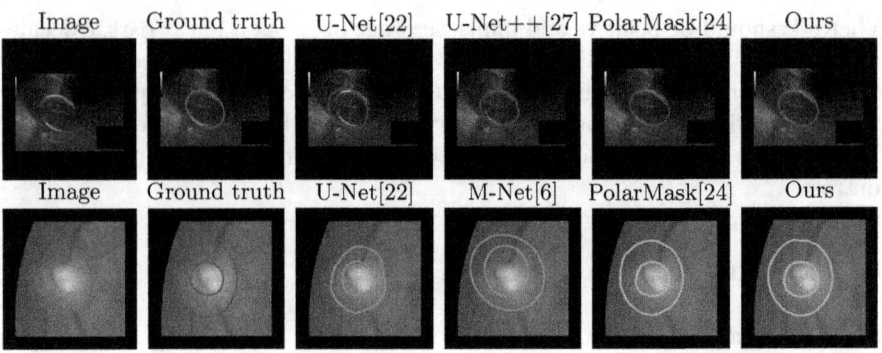

Fig. 3. Qualitative results of segmentation on example images of the two testing datsets. Top row: FH segmentation results; Bottom row: results on OD and OC segmentation.

Table 1. Segmentation results on the fundus images for OD and OC segmentation and on HC18-Challenge [14] for FH. The performance is reported as Dice score (%) and AUC (%). The best result in each category is highlighted in bold.

Tasks						
Methods	OC		OD		FH	
	Dice score	AUC	Dice score	AUC	Dice score	AUC
U-Net [22]	0.9016	0.9186	0.9522	0.9648	0.9625	0.9688
M-Net[6]	**0.9335**	**0.9417**	0.9230	0.9332	–	–
U-Net++ [27]	0.9198	0.9285	0.9626	0.9777	0.9701	0.9789
DANet [7]	0.9232	0.9327	0.9654	0.9726	0.9719	0.9786
DARNet [3]	0.9235	0.9339	0.9617	0.9684	0.9719	0.9790
PolarMask [24]	0.9238	0.9366	0.9670	0.9782	0.9723	0.9780
Our method	0.9246	0.9376	**0.9688**	**0.9784**	**0.9738**	**0.9796**

4   Results

In this section, we show our qualitative (Fig. 3) and quantitative results (Table 1) of the OD and OC and FH segmentation tasks. We compare our model with other state-of-the-art methods, including U-Net [22], PolarMask [24], M-Net [6], U-Net++ [27], DANet [7], DARNet [3], DeepLabv3+ [2] through running their open public source code. Dice score and Area Under the Curve (AUC) are used as the segmentation accuracy metrics.

Optic Disc and Cup Segmentation: We perform evaluation experiments on the retina testing dataset. Figure 3 and Table 1 show qualitative and quantitative results respectively. We achieve 96.88% and 92.46% Dice score on the OD and OC segmentation respectively. There are no any bells and whistles (multi-scale training, ellipse fitting, longer training epochs, etc.) As for the inference speed, our model achieves faster result at 66.6 milliseconds (ms) per image than PolarMask [24] (72.1 ms) and DARNet [3] (1239.2 ms).

Fetal Head Segmentation: Table 1 and Fig. 3 shows the quantitative and qualitative results respectively. Our model achieves 0.9738 Dice score and 0.9796 AUC, which outperforms U-Net [22] by 1.2% in terms of Dice score. In terms of efficiency for image inference, our model (60.2 ms) is faster than PolarMask [24] (65.5 ms) and DARNet [3] (1011.9 ms) per image.

Table 2. Performance comparisons (%) of different loss functions and weight mask settings on the OD and OC and FH segmentation, respectively. For weight mask = 5, our model achieves best performance on the OD and OC segmentation.

Tasks						
Loss function	OC		OD		FH	
	Dice score	AUC	Dice score	AUC	Dice score	AUC
L1	0.9108	0.9256	0.9543	0.9636	0.9503	0.9684
L2	0.9103	0.9208	0.9553	0.9668	0.9442	0.9571
Smooth-L1 [10]	0.9086	0.9112	0.9521	0.9652	0.9395	0.9452
Our proposed loss						
Weight mask = 0	0.9183	0.9218	0.9616	0.9738	**0.9738**	**0.9796**
Weight mask = 3	0.9223	0.9338	0.9646	0.9768		
Weight mask = 5	**0.9246**	**0.9376**	**0.9688**	**0.9784**		
Weight mask = 7	0.9173	0.9238	0.9623	0.9718		
Weight mask = 9	0.9109	0.9215	0.9603	0.9708		

5 Ablation Study

We conduct several experiments on ablation studies to investigate the effectiveness of our model. The ablation results on different loss function are shown in Table 2. Due to the space limitation, ablation experiment results on other factors (e.g. the network structure components, the interval angle for vertices sampling, the parameter settings for proposed loss function) are shown in the supplementary material.

Parameters of Loss Function: We perform experiments to evaluate the effect of parameter settings of our proposed loss function (figure in supplementary material). When $w = 6$, $\epsilon = 5$, our model achieve the best performance for the OD and OC segmentation on the test dataset; and $w = 8$, $\epsilon = 5$, for the FH segmentation on the test dataset.

Loss Function: We conduct experiments to evaluate the effectiveness of our proposed loss function. We compare with L1, L2, Smooth-L1 [10] loss functions. Table 2 shows the quantitative results on OD and OC and FH segmentation tasks respectively. As illustrated, our loss function achieves a mean Dice score that is 1.5% relatively better than that of L1 loss function on OD and OC and 2.5% relatively better than L1 loss function on FH segmentation. It also shows comparing with no-weight mask loss function, our proposed weight mask helps to improve OD and OC segmentation results by 0.7% when weight mask = 5.

6 Conclusion

We propose a simple and intuitive regression methodology to tackle segmentation tasks through directly regressing the contour of the objects instead of dense pixel predictions. We have demonstrated its effectiveness and efficiency over other state-of-the-art methods on the segmentation problems of the fetal head and optic disc and cup. It is anticipated that our approach can be widely applicable to real world biomedical applications.

Acknowledgement. Y. Meng thanks the China Science IntelliCloud Technology Co., Ltd for the studentship. Dr D. Gao is supported by EPSRC Grant (EP/R014094/1). We thank NVIDIA for the donation of GPU cards. This work was undertaken on Barkla, part of the High Performance Computing facilities at the University of Liverpool, UK.

References

1. Almazroa, A., et al.: Retinal fundus images for glaucoma analysis: the RIGA dataset. In: Medical Imaging 2018: Imaging Informatics for Healthcare, Research, and Applications, vol. 10579, p. 105790B. International Society for Optics and Photonics (2018)
2. Chen, L.C., Zhu, Y., Papandreou, G., Schroff, F., Adam, H.: Encoder-decoder with atrous separable convolution for semantic image segmentation. In: ECCV (2018)
3. Cheng, D., Liao, R., Fidler, S., Urtasun, R.: DARNet: deep active ray network for building segmentation. In: Proceedings of the IEEE Conference on Computer Vision and Pattern Recognition, pp. 7431–7439 (2019)
4. Defferrard, M., Bresson, X., Vandergheynst, P.: Convolutional neural networks on graphs with fast localized spectral filtering. In: Advances in Neural Information Processing Systems, pp. 3844–3852 (2016)
5. Feng, Z.H., Kittler, J., Awais, M., Huber, P., Wu, X.J.: Wing loss for robust facial landmark localisation with convolutional neural networks. In: Proceedings of the IEEE Conference on Computer Vision and Pattern Recognition, pp. 2235–2245 (2018)
6. Fu, H., Cheng, J., Xu, Y., Wong, D.W.K., Liu, J., Cao, X.: Joint optic disc and cup segmentation based on multi-label deep network and polar transformation. IEEE Trans. Med. Imaging **37**(7), 1597–1605 (2018)
7. Fu, J., et al.: Dual attention network for scene segmentation. In: Proceedings of the IEEE Conference on Computer Vision and Pattern Recognition, pp. 3146–3154 (2019)
8. Fumero, F., Alayón, S., Sanchez, J.L., Sigut, J., Gonzalez-Hernandez, M.: RIM-ONE: an open retinal image database for optic nerve evaluation. In: 24th International Symposium on Computer-Based Medical Systems (CBMS), pp. 1–6. IEEE (2011)

9. Garland, M., Heckbert, P.S.: Surface simplification using quadric error metrics. In: Proceedings of the 24th Annual Conference on Computer Graphics and Interactive Techniques, pp. 209–216. ACM Press/Addison-Wesley Publishing Co. (1997)

10. Girshick, R.: Fast R-CNN. In: Proceedings of the IEEE International Conference on Computer Vision, pp. 1440–1448 (2015)

11. Girshick, R., Donahue, J., Darrell, T., Malik, J.: Rich feature hierarchies for accurate object detection and semantic segmentation. In: Proceedings of the IEEE Conference on Computer Vision and Pattern Recognition, pp. 580–587 (2014)

12. He, K., Zhang, X., Ren, S., Sun, J.: Spatial pyramid pooling in deep convolutional networks for visual recognition. IEEE Trans. Pattern Anal. Mach. Intell. **37**(9), 1904–1916 (2015)

13. He, K., Zhang, X., Ren, S., Sun, J.: Deep residual learning for image recognition. In: Proceedings of the IEEE Conference on Computer Vision and Pattern Recognition, pp. 770–778 (2016)

14. van den Heuvel, T.L., de Bruijn, D., de Korte, C.L., van Ginneken, B.: Automated measurement of fetal head circumference using 2D ultrasound images. PLoS ONE **13**(8), e0200412 (2018)

15. Ioffe, S., Szegedy, C.: Batch normalization: accelerating deep network training by reducing internal covariate shift. arXiv preprint arXiv:1502.03167 (2015)

16. Kass, M., Witkin, A., Terzopoulos, D.: Snakes: active contour models. Int. J. Comput. Vis. **1**(4), 321–331 (1988)

17. Li, G., Müller, M., Thabet, A., Ghanem, B.: Can GCNs go as deep as CNNs? arXiv preprint arXiv:1904.03751 (2019)

18. Long, J., Shelhamer, E., Darrell, T.: Fully convolutional networks for semantic segmentation. In: Proceedings of the IEEE Conference on Computer Vision and Pattern Recognition, pp. 3431–3440 (2015)

19. Orlando, J.I., et al.: REFUGE challenge: a unified framework for evaluating automated methods for glaucoma assessment from fundus photographs. Med. Image Anal. **59**, 101570 (2020)

20. Ranjan, A., Bolkart, T., Sanyal, S., Black, M.J.: Generating 3D faces using convolutional mesh autoencoders. In: Proceedings of the European Conference on Computer Vision (ECCV), pp. 704–720 (2018)

21. Ren, S., He, K., Girshick, R., Sun, J.: Faster r-cnn: towards real-time object detection with region proposal networks. In: Advances in Neural Information Processing Systems, pp. 91–99 (2015)

22. Ronneberger, O., Fischer, P., Brox, T.: U-Net: convolutional networks for biomedical image segmentation. In: Navab, N., Hornegger, J., Wells, W.M., Frangi, A.F. (eds.) MICCAI 2015. LNCS, vol. 9351, pp. 234–241. Springer, Cham (2015). https://doi.org/10.1007/978-3-319-24574-4_28

23. Sivaswamy, J., Krishnadas, S., Joshi, G.D., Jain, M., Tabish, A.U.S.: Drishti-GS: retinal image dataset for optic nerve head (ONH) segmentation. In: 2014 IEEE 11th International Symposium on Biomedical Imaging (ISBI), pp. 53–56. IEEE (2014)

24. Xie, E., et al.: Polarmask: Single shot instance segmentation with polar representation. arXiv preprint arXiv:1909.13226 (2019)

25. Xu, W., Wang, H., Qi, F., Lu, C.: Explicit shape encoding for real-time instance segmentation. In: Proceedings of the IEEE International Conference on Computer Vision, pp. 5168–5177 (2019)

26. Zhang, Z., et al..: ORIGA-light: an online retinal fundus image database for glaucoma analysis and research. In: 2010 Annual International Conference of the IEEE Engineering in Medicine and Biology, pp. 3065–3068. IEEE (2010)

27. Zhou, Z., Rahman Siddiquee, M.M., Tajbakhsh, N., Liang, J.: UNet++: a nested u-net architecture for medical image segmentation. In: Stoyanov, D., et al. (eds.) DLMIA/ML-CDS - 2018. LNCS, vol. 11045, pp. 3–11. Springer, Cham (2018). https://doi.org/10.1007/978-3-030-00889-5_1

KiU-Net: Towards Accurate Segmentation of Biomedical Images Using Over-Complete Representations

Jeya Maria Jose Valanarasu[1]([✉]), Vishwanath A. Sindagi[1], Ilker Hacihaliloglu[2], and Vishal M. Patel[1]

[1] Johns Hopkins University, Baltimore, MD, USA
jeyamariajose7@gmail.com
[2] The State University of New Jersey, Rutgers, NJ, USA

Abstract. Due to its excellent performance, U-Net is the most widely used backbone architecture for biomedical image segmentation in the recent years. However, in our studies, we observe that there is a considerable performance drop in the case of detecting smaller anatomical structures with blurred noisy boundaries. We analyze this issue in detail, and address it by proposing an over-complete architecture (Ki-Net) which involves projecting the data onto higher dimensions (in the spatial sense). This network, when augmented with U-Net, results in significant improvements in the case of segmenting small anatomical landmarks and blurred noisy boundaries while obtaining better overall performance. Furthermore, the proposed network has additional benefits like faster convergence and fewer number of parameters. We evaluate the proposed method on the task of brain anatomy segmentation from 2D Ultrasound (US) of preterm neonates, and achieve an improvement of around 4% in terms of the DICE accuracy and Jaccard index as compared to the standard-U-Net, while outperforming the recent best methods by 2%. Code: https://github.com/jeya-maria-jose/KiU-Net-pytorch

Keywords: Over-complete representations · Ultrasound · Brain · Deep learning · Segmentation · Preterm neonate

1 Introduction

Preterm birth is among the leading public health problems in the USA and Europe [14]. The reported annual cost of care for preterm neonates exceeds $18 billion dollars every year in the USA alone [14]. Although, advancements made in neonatal care have increased the survival rates, majority of these infants are at risk for adverse neuro-developmental outcomes. Among the different types of preterm brain injury, intraventricular hemorrhage (IVH) remains the most common cause of acquired hydrocephalus resulting in the enlargement of ventricles. On the other hand, absence of septum pellucidum is used as a biomarker for the diagnosis of other brain disorders such as septo-optic dysplasia. Cranial

© Springer Nature Switzerland AG 2020
A. L. Martel et al. (Eds.): MICCAI 2020, LNCS 12264, pp. 363–373, 2020.
https://doi.org/10.1007/978-3-030-59719-1_36

ultrasound (US) remains the main imaging modality used to diagnose brain disorders in preterm neonates due to its real-time, safe, and cost effective imaging capabilities. Current clinical evaluation involves qualitative investigation of the collected US scans or quantitative manual measurement of landmarks such as ventricular index (VI), anterior horn width (AHW), frontal and temporal horn ratio (FTHR) [4]. Qualitative evaluation is subjective and manual measurement involves intra and inter-user variability errors. The diagnostic accuracy is further affected by the unclear boundary of the ventricles, due to build up of bleeding pressure, or sub-optimal orientation of the transducer during imaging. Additionally, shading artifacts causes incomplete boundaries in the acquired US data. Depending on the bleeding extend, the shape of the ventricle varies for different subjects. Finally, manual measurement is also problematic for normal preterm neonates without any brain injury due to very small ventricle size and blurred boundaries. Similar problems are also faced for identifying septum pellucidum due to its small size and unclear boundary. In order to overcome these challenges, precise and automatic segmentation of ventricles and septum pellucidum is critical for accurate diagnosis and prognosis.

Several groups have proposed semi-automatic and fully automatic methods for segmentation of ventricles from 2D/3D US scans. Methods based on traditional medical image analysis are time consuming or not robust enough to the previously mentioned challenging scan conditions [2,16,19]. The reported DICE similarity coefficient values were 70.8% [2], 80% [19], and 76.5% [16]. The reported computation times were 54 min for [16]. The other methods did not report any computation time. Most recently, methods based on deep learning were also investigated by various groups to improve the robustness and computation time of segmentation [13,20,21]. Since the introduction of U-Net [17] in 2015, it has been the leading deep learning-based network of any method that deals with biomedical image segmentation [3,7,8,12,15,23,24]. In [13], a U-Net architecture was used for segmentation of ventricles.

Based on the observations that the existing approaches do not achieve optimal performance (especially in the case of segmenting out small anatomical structure), we analyze this issue in detail. Specifically, we conducted experiments with the standard U-Net architecture which is a leading backbone in several segmentation algorithms. In spite of the skip connections that enable the propagation of information from shallower layers to deeper layers, the network is unable to capture finer details (see Fig. 1) for the following reasons. The standard encoder-decoder architecture of U-Net belongs to the family of under-complete convolutional autoencoders, where the dimensionality of data is reduced near the bottleneck. The initial few blocks of the encoder learn low-level features of the data while the later blocks learn the high-level features. Eventually, the encoder learns to map the data to lower dimensionality (in the spatial sense). The increasing receptive field size over the depth of the network, constrains the network to focus more on the higher-level features. However, it is important to note that tiny structures require smaller receptive fields. In the case of standard U-Net, even with skip connections, the smallest receptive field is limited by that of the first layer. Hence, under-complete architectures are essentially limited in their abilities to capture finer details.

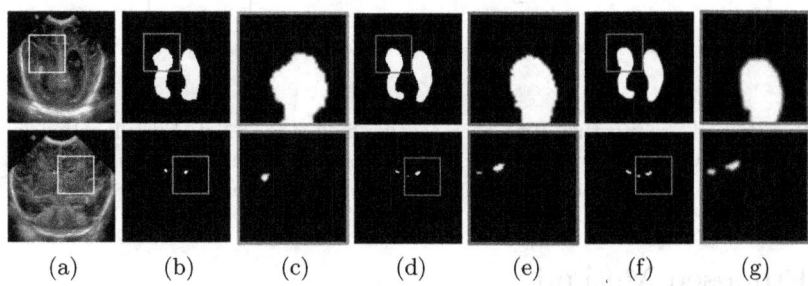

Fig. 1. (a) Input B-Mode Ultrasound Image. Predictions from (b) U-Net, (d) KiU-Net (ours), (f) Ground Truth. (c), (e) and (g) are the zoomed in patches from (b), (d) and (f) respectively. The boxes in the original images correspond to the zoomed in portion for the zoomed images. It can be seen that our proposed network captures edges and small masks better than U-Net.

Considering the aforementioned drawback of under-complete representations, we resort to over-complete architectures where the data is projected onto a higher dimension in the intermediate layers. In the literature, over-complete representations have been shown to be more robust and stable, especially in the presence of noise [11]. However, such architectures have been relatively unexplored for segmentation tasks in both the computer vision and medical imaging communities [6]. In this paper, we explore the use of such an over-complete network for segmentation to address the issue of lack of smaller receptive field in the standard U-Net. We refer to the over-complete network as Kite-Net (Ki-Net) as it's shape is similar to that of a kite. In the following sections, we show how the information learned by Ki-Net actually helps in capturing finer shape structures and edges better than the generic under-complete networks. Furthermore, we propose to effectively combine the benefits of the proposed Ki-Net with that of the standard U-Net using a novel cross-scale fusion strategy. We show that this novel network (KiU-Net) achieves state-of-the-art performance on the brain anatomy segmentation task from US images when compared with the latest methods.

In summary, this paper (1) explores over-complete deep networks (Ki-Net) for the task of segmentation, (2) proposes a novel architecture (KiU-Net) combining the features of both under-complete and over-complete deep networks which captures finer details better than the standard encoder-decoder architecture of U-Net thus aiding in precise segmentation, and (3) achieves faster convergence and better performance metrics than recent methods for segmentation.

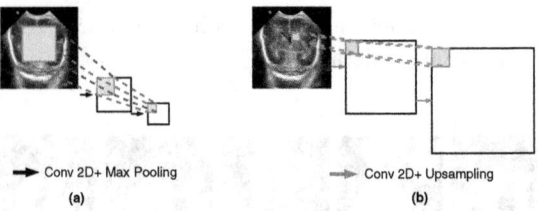

Fig. 2. Effect of architecture type on receptive field. (a) U-Net: Each location in the intermediate layers focuses on a much larger region in the input. (b) Ki-Net: Each location in the intermediate layers focuses on a much smaller region in the input.

2 Proposed Method

Over-Complete Representations: As illustrated in Fig. 2, the receptive field of the filters in a generic "encoder-decoder" architecture increases as we go deeper in the network. This increase in receptive field size can be attributed to two reasons: (i) every conv layer filter gathers information from a surrounding window, and (ii) the use of max-pooling layer after every conv layer. The max-pooling layers essentially double the receptive field size after every conv layer. The increasing receptive field reasons is critical for CNNs to learn high-level features like objects, shapes or blobs. However, a side effect of this is that it reduces the focus of the filters. That is, except the first layer, filters in the other layers have reduced abilities to learn features that correspond to fine details like edges and their texture. This causes any network with the standard under-complete architecture to not produce sharp predictions around the edges in tasks like segmentation.

To overcome this issue, we propose Ki-Net which is over-complete in the spatial sense. That is, the spatial dimensions of the intermediate layers is more than that of the input data. We achieve this by employing an upsampling layer after every conv layer in the encoder. Furthermore, we employ a max pooling layer after every conv layer in the decoder in order to reduce the dimensionality back to that of the input. This forces the over-complete conv architecture to behave differently than the standard under-complete conv architecture. The filters in this type of architecture learn finer low-level features due to the decreasing size of receptive field even as we go deeper in the encoder network.

Figure 2(a) illustrates how the receptive field is large for U-Net. Figure 2(b) illustrates how the use of over-complete architecture like Ki-Net restricts the receptive field size to a smaller region. Hence, by constricting the receptive field size, we force the filters in the deeper layers to learn very fine edges as it tries to focus heavily on smaller regions. To illustrate this, we show how the filters of encoder fire in a Ki-Net when compared to U-Net in Fig. 3. It can be observed that the filters in U-Net become smaller as we go deeper and fire across high-level shapes where as the filters become bigger as we go deeper in Ki-Net and the features captured are fine edges across all layers with an increased resolution.

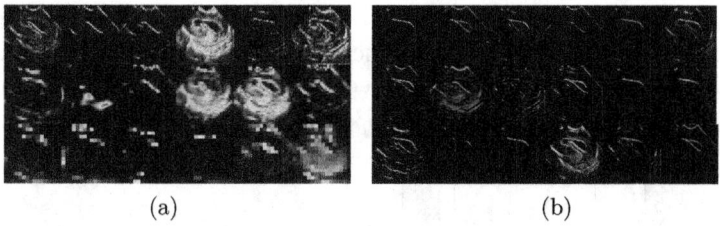

(a)   (b)

Fig. 3. Visualization of filter responses for (a) U-Net, and (b) Ki-Net. Top row: Feature maps from the first layer of encoder. Middle row: Feature maps from the second layer of encoder. Bottom row: Feature maps from the third layer of encoder. By restricting the receptive field, Ki-Net is able to focus on edges and smaller regions.

KiU-Net: As we have established that our proposed Ki-Net has better abilities to captures edges compared to U-Net, we combine it with the standard U-Net in order to improve the overall segmentation accuracy as Ki-Net if used separately will only capture the edges. The combined network, KiU-Net, exploits the low-level fine edges capturing feature maps of Ki-Net as well as the high-level shape capturing feature maps of U-Net. We propose using a parallel network architecture where one branch is a Ki-Net and the other a U-Net as seen in Fig. 4(a). The input image is forwarded through both the branches simultaneously. In both the branches, we have 3 layers of conv blocks in the encoder as well as the decoder. Each conv block in the encoder of Ki-Net branch consists of a 2D conv layer followed by a bilinear interpolation with a scale factor of 2 and ReLU non-linearity. Similarly, each conv block in the decoder of Ki-Net branch consists of a 2D conv layer followed by a max-pooling layer with a pooling coefficient of two. In addition, we use skip connections between the blocks of encoder and decoder similar to U-Net to enhance the localization. In the U-Net branch, we adopt the "encoder-decoder" architecture of a U-Net.

In order to augment the two networks, one can perform simple concatenation of features at the final layer. However, this may not be necessarily optimal. Instead, we combine the feature maps at each block and this results in better convergence as the flow of gradients during back propagation is across both the branches at each block level [18]. Furthermore, in order to combine the features at each block level more effectively, we propose a cross residual fusion block (CRFB). This block extracts complementary features from both network branches and forwards to both of them respectively. Specifically, the CRFB consists of residual connections, followed by a set of conv layers (see Fig. 4 (b)). In order to combine the feature maps from the two networks F_U^i (U-Net) and F_{Ki}^i (Ki-Net) after the ith block, cross-residual features R_U^i and R_{Ki}^i are first estimated through a set of conv layers. These cross-residual feature are then added to the original features F_U^i (U-Net) and F_{Ki}^i to obtain the complementary features $\hat{F}_U^i$ and $\hat{F}_{Ki}^i$, $i.e$, $\hat{F}_U^i = F_U^i + R_{Ki}^i$ and $\hat{F}_{Ki}^i = F_{Ki}^i + R_U^i$. This strategy is more effective compared to simple feature fusion schemes like addition or concatenation. Finally, the features from decoder in both the branches are added and forwarded through 1×1 conv layer to produce the final segmentation mask. The complete details of the network such as the kernel size, number of filters, etc. are included in supplementary material.

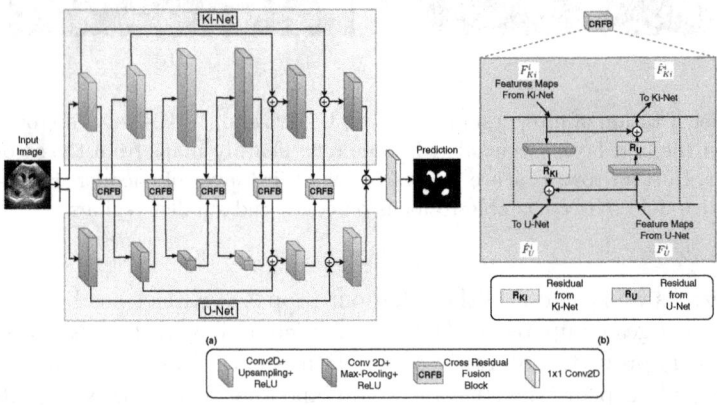

Fig. 4. (a) An overview of the proposed KiU-Net architecture. (b) Cross Residual Fusion block architecture.

We train the network using pixel-wise binary cross entropy loss between the prediction and ground-truth. The loss function between the prediction p and the ground truth $\hat{p}$ is defined as follows:

$$\mathcal{L}_{CE(p,\hat{p})} = -\frac{1}{wh} \sum_{x=0}^{w-1} \sum_{y=0}^{h-1} (p(x,y) \log(\hat{p}(x,y))) + (1 - p(x,y))log(1 - \hat{p}(x,y)),$$

where w and h are the dimensions of image, $p(x,y)$ and $\hat{p}(x,y)$ denote the output at a specific location (x,y) of the prediction and ground truth, respectively.

3   Experiments and Results

Dataset Acquisition and Details: After obtaining institutional review board (IRB) approval, US scans were collected from 20 different premature neonates (age < 1 year). The dataset contains subjects with IVH as well as healthy ones. The US scans were collected using a Philips US machine (Philips iE33) with a C8-5 broadband curved array transducer using coronal and sagittal scan planes. Imaging depth and resolution varied between 6–8 cm and 0.1–0.15 mm, respectively. Ventricles and septum pellecudi were manually segmented by an expert ultrasonographer. A total of 1629 images with annotations were obtained in total. The scans were randomly divided into 1300 images for training and 329 images for testing. This process was repeated 3 times. During random split the training and testing data did not include scans from the same patient. Before processing the resolution of each image was changed to 128×128.

Implementation Details: KiU-Net is trained using cross-entropy loss $\mathcal{L}_{CE(p,\hat{p})}$ with the Adam optimizer [10] and a batch-size of 1. The learning rate was set equal to 0.001. The network was built in PyTorch framework and trained using Nvidia-RTX 2080Ti GPUs. The network was trained for a total of 100 epochs.

Comparison with Recent Methods: Since the main focus of this work is to augment the U-Net architecture with additional capabilities, we compare our method with U-Net and other recent methods. Table 1 shows that the proposed method performs better than other recent methods like Seg-Net [1], pix2pix [9], and Wang et al. [21]. Seg-Net [1] has been most recently investigated for segmentation of kidneys from US data [22], pix2pix [9] has been used for multi-task organ segmentation from chest x-ray radiography [5], and Wang *et al.* [21] has been previously used for segmentation of ventricles from brain US data. We run the experiments 3 times for different random folds of training and testing data and report the mean metrics with the variance.

It can be observed that the proposed method achieves an improvement of 4% in DICE accuracy with respect to U-Net and a 2% improvement with respect to state-of-the-art [21] (see Table 1). Figure 5 illustrates the prediction of segmentation masks using different methods along with the input and ground truth. From the first row in Fig. 5, we can observe that KiU-Net (our method) is able to predict even very small masks precisely, whereas all the other methods fail. Similarly, from the second row we can observe that our network detects the edges better than other methods. This demonstrates that the intuition of constricting the receptive field size by following the over-complete representation served its purpose as the smaller masks are not missed in our method. Additionally, it may be noted that the proposed method performs well irrespective of the size of the anatomy structures. Furthermore, the proposed network has the following additional benefits. First, it uses much fewer number of parameters in comparison to the other methods. Note that U-Net used in KiU-Net has less number of blocks and filters compared to the original U-Net as in [17], thus resulting in less number of parameters. Second, it converges much faster compared to the standard U-net (see Fig. 6). Its inference time is 8 ms for one test image.

Table 1. Comparison of results. Proposed method outperforms existing approaches.

Method	DICE Acc (%)	Jaccard Idx (%)	Parameters
Seg-Net [1]	82.79 ± 0.320	75.02 ± 0.570	12.5M
U-Net [17]	85.37 ± 0.002	79.31 ± 0.065	3.1M
pix2pix [9]	85.46 ± 0.022	77.45 ± 0.56	54.4M
Wang et al. [21]	87.47 ± 0.080	80.51 ± 0.190	6.1M
KiU-Net (ours)	**89.43 ± 0.013**	**83.26 ± 0.047**	**0.29M**

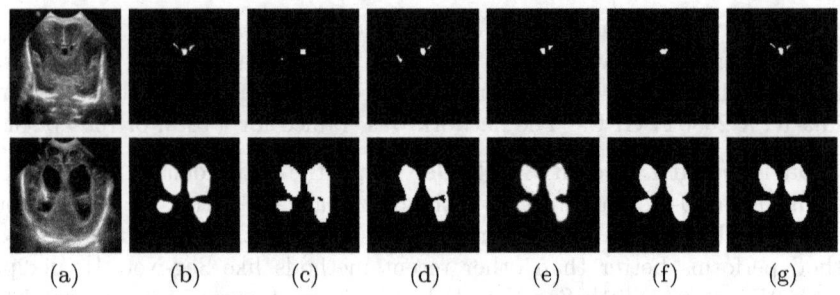

(a)   (b)   (c)   (d)   (e)   (f)   (g)

Fig. 5. Qualitative results on sample test images. (a) B-mode input US image. (b) Ground truth. (c) Seg-Net [1]. (d) U-Net [17] (e) pix2pix [9]. (f) Wang et al. [21]. (g) KiU-Net (ours).

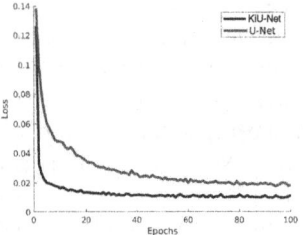

Method	DICE	Jaccard
UC	82.79	75.02
OC	56.04	43.97
OC+UC	84.80	76.48
UC with SK	85.37	79.31
OC with SK	60.38	47.86
OC+UC with SK	86.24	78.11
KiU-Net (ours)	**89.43**	**83.26**

Fig. 6. Comparison of convergence of the loss between KiU-Net and U-Net.

Fig. 7. Ablation study.

Ablation Study: We study the performance of each block's contribution to our KiU-Net by conducting a detailed ablation study. The results are shown in Fig. 7. We start with the standard under-complete architecture (UC) and the over-complete architecture (OC). It can be noted here that the performance of OC is lesser than UC because even though OC captures the edges properly it does not capture most high level features like UC. Then, we show that fusing both the networks (OC+UC) just by combining the feature maps at the final layer helps in improving the performance. This is followed by an experiment where we use skip connections (SK). It may be noted that UC with SK is basically the U-Net. Finally, we incorporate the cross residual fusion block (CRFB) at each block level in our KiU-Net, resulting in further improvements which demonstrates the effectiveness of our novel cross fusion strategy. Figure 8 illustrates the qualitative improvements after adding each major block.

More results on different datasets can be found in supplementary material.

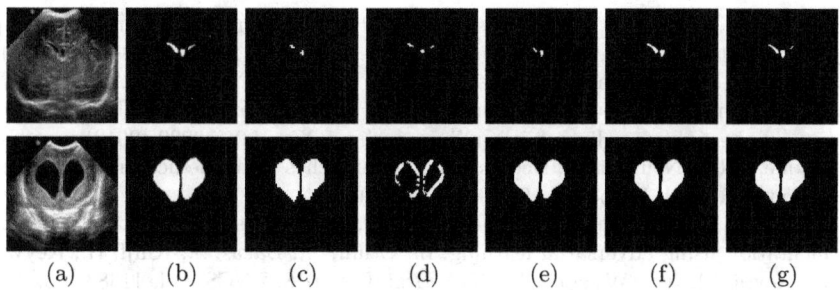

(a)   (b)   (c)   (d)   (e)   (f)   (g)

Fig. 8. Qualitative results of ablation study on test images. (a) B-Mode input US image. (b) Ground Truth annotation. Prediction of segmentation masks by (c) UC - Under-complete architecture (d) OC - Over-complete architecture (e) UC + SK (under-complete architecture with skip connections) (f) UC + OC with SK (combined architecture with skip connections) (g) KiU-Net (ours)

4 Conclusion

We proposed a novel network called KiU-Net which is constructed by augmenting the standard under-complete architecture based U-Net with an over-complete structure (Ki-Net). The purpose of Ki-Net is to specifically capture fine edges and small anatomical structures which are typically missed out in the other methods. Further, we incorporate a new fusion strategy that is based on cross-scale residual blocks which results in a more effective use of information from the two networks. The proposed network has additional benefits like it uses much fewer number of parameters and results in faster convergence. The proposed method achieves better performance as compared to recent methods on a relatively complex dataset which has both small and big segmentation masks.

Acknowledgement. This work was supported by the NSF grant 1910141.

References

1. Badrinarayanan, V., Kendall, A., Cipolla, R.: Segnet: a deep convolutional encoder-decoder architecture for image segmentation. IEEE Trans. Pattern Anal. Mach. Intell. **39**(12), 2481–2495 (2017)
2. Boucher, M.-A., Lippé, S., Damphousse, A., El-Jalbout, R., Kadoury, S.: Dilatation of lateral ventricles with brain volumes in infants with 3D transfontanelle us. In: Frangi, A.F., Schnabel, J.A., Davatzikos, C., Alberola-López, C., Fichtinger, G. (eds.) MICCAI 2018. LNCS, vol. 11072, pp. 557–565. Springer, Cham (2018). https://doi.org/10.1007/978-3-030-00931-1_64
3. Çiçek, Ö., Abdulkadir, A., Lienkamp, S.S., Brox, T., Ronneberger, O.: 3D U-Net: learning dense volumetric segmentation from sparse annotation. In: Ourselin, S., Joskowicz, L., Sabuncu, M.R., Unal, G., Wells, W. (eds.) MICCAI 2016. LNCS, vol. 9901, pp. 424–432. Springer, Cham (2016). https://doi.org/10.1007/978-3-319-46723-8_49

4. El-Dib, M., Massaro, A.N., Bulas, D., Aly, H.: Neuroimaging and neurodevelopmental outcome of premature infants. Am. J. Perinatol. **27**(10), 803–818 (2010)
5. Eslami, M., Tabarestani, S., Albarqouni, S., Adeli, E., Navab, N., Adjouadi, M.: Image to images translation for multi-task organ segmentation and bone suppression in chest x-ray radiography. arXiv preprint arXiv:1906.10089 (2019)
6. Haque, I.R.I., Neubert, J.: Deep learning approaches to biomedical image segmentation. Inf. Med. Unlocked **18**, 100297 (2020)
7. Islam, M., Vaidyanathan, N.R., Jose, V.J.M., Ren, H.: Ischemic stroke lesion segmentation using adversarial learning. In: Crimi, A., Bakas, S., Kuijf, H., Keyvan, F., Reyes, M., van Walsum, T. (eds.) BrainLes 2018. LNCS, vol. 11383, pp. 292–300. Springer, Cham (2019). https://doi.org/10.1007/978-3-030-11723-8_29
8. Islam, M., Vibashan, V.S., Jose, V.J.M., Wijethilake, N., Utkarsh, U., Ren, H.: Brain tumor segmentation and survival prediction using 3D attention UNet. In: Crimi, A., Bakas, S. (eds.) BrainLes 2019. LNCS, vol. 11992, pp. 262–272. Springer, Cham (2020). https://doi.org/10.1007/978-3-030-46640-4_25
9. Isola, P., Zhu, J.Y., Zhou, T., Efros, A.A.: Image-to-image translation with conditional adversarial networks. In: Proceedings of the IEEE Conference on Computer Vision and Pattern Recognition, pp. 1125–1134 (2017)
10. Kingma, D.P., Ba, J.: Adam: a method for stochastic optimization. arXiv preprint arXiv:1412.6980 (2014)
11. Lewicki, M.S., Sejnowski, T.J.: Learning overcomplete representations. Neural Comput. **12**(2), 337–365 (2000)
12. Li, X., Chen, H., Qi, X., Dou, Q., Fu, C.W., Heng, P.A.: H-denseunet: hybrid densely connected Unet for liver and tumor segmentation from CT volumes. IEEE Trans. Med. Imaging **37**(12), 2663–2674 (2018)
13. Martin, M., Sciolla, B., Sdika, M., Wang, X., Quetin, P., Delachartre, P.: Automatic segmentation of the cerebral ventricle in neonates using deep learning with 3d reconstructed freehand ultrasound imaging. In: 2018 IEEE International Ultrasonics Symposium (IUS), pp. 1–4. IEEE (2018)
14. Ment, L.R., Hirtz, D., Hüppi, P.S.: Imaging biomarkers of outcome in the developing preterm brain. Lancet Neurol. **8**(11), 1042–1055 (2009)
15. Milletari, F., Navab, N., Ahmadi, S.A.: V-net: fully convolutional neural networks for volumetric medical image segmentation. In: 2016 Fourth International Conference on 3D Vision (3DV), pp. 565–571. IEEE (2016)
16. Qiu, W., et al.: Automatic segmentation approach to extracting neonatal cerebral ventricles from 3D ultrasound images. Med. Image Anal. **35**, 181–191 (2017)
17. Ronneberger, O., Fischer, P., Brox, T.: U-Net: convolutional networks for biomedical image segmentation. In: Navab, N., Hornegger, J., Wells, W.M., Frangi, A.F. (eds.) MICCAI 2015. LNCS, vol. 9351, pp. 234–241. Springer, Cham (2015). https://doi.org/10.1007/978-3-319-24574-4_28
18. Sindagi, V.A., Patel, V.M.: Multi-level bottom-top and top-bottom feature fusion for crowd counting. In: Proceedings of the IEEE International Conference on Computer Vision, pp. 1002–1012 (2019)
19. Tabrizi, P.R., Obeid, R., Cerrolaza, J.J., Penn, A., Mansoor, A., Linguraru, M.G.: Automatic segmentation of neonatal ventricles from cranial ultrasound for prediction of intraventricular hemorrhage outcome. In: 2018 40th Annual International Conference of the IEEE Engineering in Medicine and Biology Society (EMBC), pp. 3136–3139. IEEE (2018)
20. Valanarasu, J.M.J., Yasarla, R., Wang, P., Hacihaliloglu, I., Patel, V.M.: Learning to segment brain anatomy from 2D ultrasound with less data. IEEE J. Selected Topics Signal Process. 1 (2020)

21. Wang, P., Cuccolo, N.G., Tyagi, R., Hacihaliloglu, I., Patel, V.M.: Automatic real-time CNN-based neonatal brain ventricles segmentation. In: 2018 IEEE 15th International Symposium on Biomedical Imaging (ISBI 2018), pp. 716–719. IEEE (2018)
22. Yin, S., et al.: Automatic kidney segmentation in ultrasound images using subsequent boundary distance regression and pixelwise classification networks. Med. Image Anal. **60**, 101602 (2020)
23. Zhao, N., Tong, N., Ruan, D., Sheng, K.: Fully automated pancreas segmentation with two-stage 3D convolutional neural networks. In: Shen, D., et al. (eds.) MICCAI 2019. LNCS, vol. 11765, pp. 201–209. Springer, Cham (2019). https://doi.org/10.1007/978-3-030-32245-8_23
24. Zhou, Z., Siddiquee, M.M.R., Tajbakhsh, N., Liang, J.: Unet++: redesigning skip connections to exploit multiscale features in image segmentation. IEEE Trans. Med. Imaging **39**(6), 1856–1867 (2019)

LAMP: Large Deep Nets with Automated Model Parallelism for Image Segmentation

Wentao Zhu$^{(\boxtimes)}$, Can Zhao, Wenqi Li, Holger Roth, Ziyue Xu, and Daguang Xu

NVIDIA, Bethesda, USA
wentaozhu1991@gmail.com

Abstract. Deep Learning (DL) models are becoming larger, because the increase in model size might offer significant accuracy gain. To enable the training of large deep networks, data parallelism and model parallelism are two well-known approaches for parallel training. However, data parallelism does not help reduce memory footprint per device. In this work, we introduce Large deep 3D ConvNets with Automated Model Parallelism (LAMP) and investigate the impact of both input's and deep 3D ConvNets' size on segmentation accuracy. Through automated model parallelism, it is feasible to train large deep 3D ConvNets with a large input patch, even the whole image. Extensive experiments demonstrate that, facilitated by the automated model parallelism, the segmentation accuracy can be improved through increasing model size and input context size, and large input yields significant inference speedup compared with sliding window of small patches in the inference. Code is available (https://monai.io/research/lamp-automated-model-parallelism).

Keywords: Automated model parallelism · Large deep ConvNets · Large image segmentation · Parallel U-Net

1 Introduction

Currently, deep learning models have been becoming larger. More and more studies demonstrate that, the increase in model size offers significant accuracy gain. In the natural language processing (NLP), transformers have paved the way for large models. For instance, the Bert-large model [7] consumes 0.3 billion (B) parameters and GPT-2 [18] has 1.5B parameters. In the image classification of computer vision, AmoebaNet (B) [10] consists of 550 million (M) parameters and achieves the best top-1 accuracy of 84.4% on ImageNet 2012 validation dataset [6]. As the model size continues to grow, training these large models becomes challenging because it is difficult to fit the training within the memory limit of one single GPU.

© Springer Nature Switzerland AG 2020
A. L. Martel et al. (Eds.): MICCAI 2020, LNCS 12264, pp. 374–384, 2020.
https://doi.org/10.1007/978-3-030-59719-1_37

There are several ways to train large models on GPUs. Model compression, such as mixed precision training [16], tries to use less bits to represent the network. It can reduce GPU memory consumption to some extent, however, might affect accuracy and can only fit a slightly or moderately large model to one GPU. Checkpointing [4,15] reduces the memory of the intermediate feature maps and gradients during training, such that the memory consumption can be reduced to $O(\log n)$ with $O(n \log n)$ extra time for forward computation in the network of n layers theoretically. Invertible networks [2,3,8,34] further reduce memory consumption to $O(1)$ by modifying the networks to be invertible which recalculate the feature maps in the back-propagation and might impact accuracy for discriminative models such as commonly used U-Net for segmentation [21].

Facilitated by the high speed communication tools such as NVLINK, parallel training across devices is a popular direction for this challenge. Generally, there are two common parallelisms to fit large models into GPUs without information loss and re-calculation, data parallelism and model parallelism [10,17,19]. Data parallelism duplicates the model and runs split batch in multiple devices. It does not reduce model's memory footprint per device and cannot address out of memory issue faced by training large models. Model parallelism splits a model into multiple partitions and naturally handles this issue. For instance, a state-of-the-art model parallelism, Megatron, can scale up to 20B parameter models by using 16 GPUs. Advanced model parallelism executes partitions concurrently across devices for efficient training, and multiple model parallelisms have emerged, e.g., pipeline parallelism in GPipe [10] and PipeDream [17], and TensorSlicing [22] in Megatron [23] and Mesh Tensorflow [22]. However, model parallelisms, such as Megatron [23], only support a limited set of operators and models. For example, in medical image analysis, the most widely used model, U-Net [21], is not supported by these existing parallelisms. In medical domain, it is a common need to be able to handle 3D volumetric image, which essentially consumes more memory with 3D ConvNets than their 2D counterparts. Unfortunately, current medical image computing is still limited by GPU memory size. A lot of techniques, such as sliding window and resampling, are utilized to get around the problem. Moreover, the designed 3D models often use much less filters than advanced 2D models in each convolution [11]. Therefore, insightful investigations of large models and large context, i.e., large input, might be extremely useful for the current research by leveraging automated model parallelism.

Training large models with large input is especially challenging for medical images due to limited number of training data. Large input increases context which is critical for image understanding [11]. However, it reduces the variation of training input and aggravates the extremely imbalance issue among background and relatively small subjects (e.g., small organs and lesions) commonly existed in medical image computing [25,29]. Various loss functions have been proposed to alleviate this challenge. For example, adaptive weighted loss is proposed with a hybrid loss between dice loss of class-level loss and focal loss of voxel-level loss for small organ segmentation [29]. The second example is the boundary loss [13], which is different from previous approaches using unbalanced integrals over the regions. It uses integrals over the boundary (interface) between the regions, which can be implemented by a level set distance map weighted cross entropy loss leveraging an integral approach to computing boundary variations. Transfer learning by fine-tuning from a pretrained model is another way to reduce the training difficulty of specially designed medical image models [26]. Based on learning theory such as curriculum learning [1,12], a model can be well trained by firstly being fit easy samples/tasks and later being fit hard samples/tasks.

Contributions. In this work, we investigate the impact of model size and input size in medical image analysis. We choose 3D U-Net [21] and the other advanced U-Net, 3D Squeeze-and-Excitation U-Net (SEU-Net) [9] in AnatomyNet [29], and validate them on large image segmentation tasks, i.e., head and neck (HaN) multi-organ segmentation [29] and decathlon liver and tumor segmentation [24]. Considering the flexibility and efficiency, we design a parallel U-Net based on GPipe [10] as the back-end parallelism. In the training, we employ existing well-designed adaptive weighted loss in [29] and design a curriculum training strategy based on different input sizes. Specifically, we sequentially fit the model with small patches for training in the first stage, medium patches thereafter, and large input lastly. We conduct extensive experiments, and conclude that, employing large models and input context increases segmentation accuracy. Large input also reduces inference time significantly by leveraging automated model parallelism in Fig. 1.

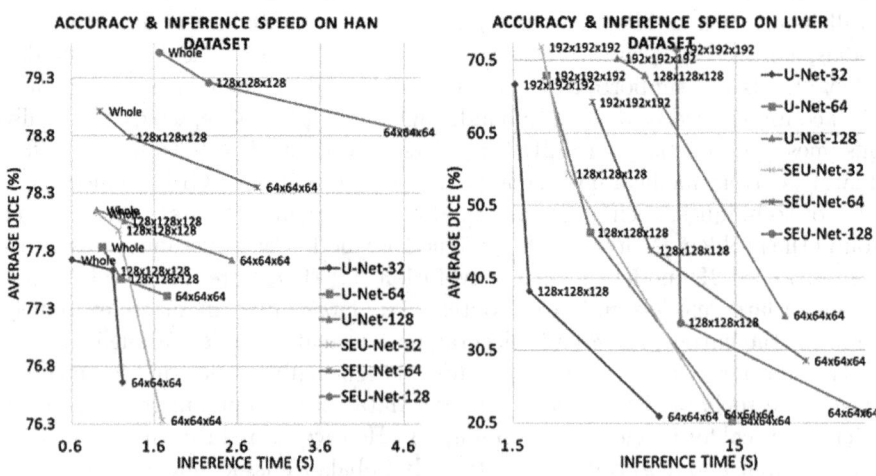

Fig. 1. Segmentation accuracy (Dice coefficient, %) and inference time (s) comparisons among 3D U-Net and 3D SEU-Net of different sizes (#filters in the first convolutional layer: 32, 64, 128) and different input sizes ($64 \times 64 \times 64$, $128 \times 128 \times 128$, whole image or $192 \times 192 \times 192$) on HaN nine organ auto-segmentation and decathlon liver and tumor segmentation datasets. Large model and input yield better segmentation accuracy consistently, and large input significantly decreases inference time.

2   Method

Considering flexibility and efficiency, we employ GPipe [10] as the backend parallelism. The model parallelism is introduced in Sect. 2.1. We describe how to design a parallel U-Net in Sect. 2.2. How to train the large models with large context input is introduced in Sect. 2.3.

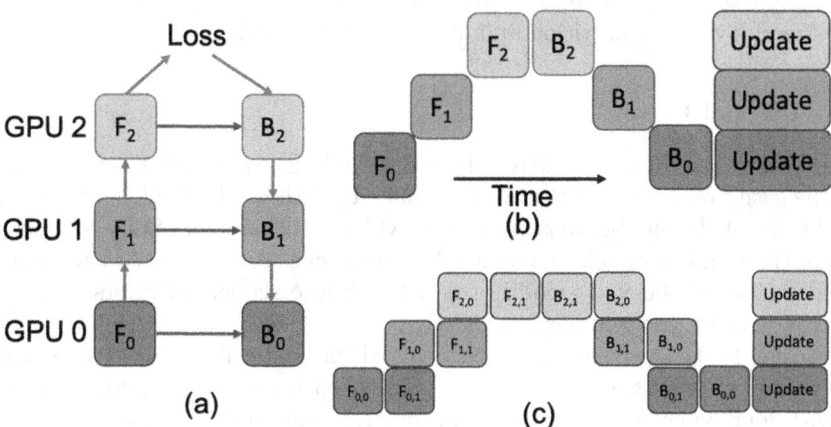

Fig. 2. (a) A deep model is partitioned across three GPUs. F_k is the forward function of the k-th cell. B_k is the back-propagation function which relies on both B_{k+1} from upper layer and feature F_k. (b) Conventional model parallelism has low device utilization because of dependency of the model. (c) Pipeline parallelism splits the input minibatch to smaller micro-batches (two micro-batches in the figure) and enables different devices to run micro-batches simultaneously. Synchronized gradient calculation can be applied lastly.

2.1   Automated Model Parallelism

Deep networks can be defined as a sequential model of L layers. Each layer L_i can be modeled by a forward computation function f_i with parameters w_i. Given the number of partitions K, i.e., the number of GPUs typically, the model can be partitioned into K parts as illustrated in Fig. 2(a). Specifically, let part p_k consist of consecutive layers from layer L_i to layer L_j. The parameters of part p_k is the union of parameters $w_i, w_{i+1}, \ldots, w_j$, and the forward function can be derived sequentially

$$F_k = f_j \circ f_{j-1} \circ \cdots \circ f_i. \tag{1}$$

According to the chain rule in the gradient calculation, the back-propagation function B_k can be derived from F_k by automated symbolic differentiation in the existing deep learning packages, e.g., PyTorch.

In the forward pass, GPipe [10,14] first splits the input mini-batch of size N to M micro-batches as illustrated in Fig. 2(c). Micro-batches are pipelined through K devices by model parallelism sequentially as illustrated in Fig. 2(b). This micro-batch splitting in Fig. 2(c) has a higher device utilization than conventional model parallelism in Fig. 2(b). After forward pass of all the micro-batches in the current mini-batch, gradients from all M micro-batches are accumulated synchronously and back-propagation is applied to update model parameters. GPipe reduces space complexity from $O(N \times L)$ to $O(N + \frac{L}{K} \times \frac{N}{M})$, where $\frac{L}{K}$ is the size of layers per partition and $\frac{N}{M}$ is the micro-batch size [10].

2.2   Parallel U-Net

The pipeline parallelism is extremely simple and intuitive, and it is flexible and can be easily used to design various parallel algorithms. To use GPipe, we only need to 1) set the number of partitions K, which is the number of GPUs typically, 2) set the number of micro-batches M, which can also be set as the number of GPUs for efficiency, 3) modify the network into sequential layers. Next, we describe how to design a parallel U-Net.

We employ the conventional U-Net [21], which can be divided into three parts: an encoder E with five blocks $e_1, e_2, \ldots, e_5$ from input sequentially, a decoder D with four blocks $d_5, d_4, \ldots, d_1$, and four skip connections $s_1, s_2, \ldots, s_4$. The U-Net can be formulated

$$E = e_5 \circ e_4 \circ \cdots \circ e_1, \quad d_i = s_i(e_i, d_{i+1}), i = 1, 2, \ldots, 4,$$
$$D = d_1 \circ d_2 \circ \cdots \circ d_5, \tag{2}$$

where s_i is typically a concatenation along channel dimension. The input of encoder E is the image, and the input of decoder block d_5 is the output of encoder. We can then add a softmax function after decoder D for segmentation.

The main challenge of pipeline-based parallel U-Net is the dependency of intermediate encoder in the skip connection s_i. GPipe requires that the model needs to be implemented in a sequential way. However, each $e_i, i = 1, 2, \ldots, 4$, is used in both encoder and decoder, which affects automated partition in GPipe. We can remove the dependency and modify U-Net by duplicating the output of each encoder $e_i = \{e_{i,0}, e_{i,1}\}, i = 1, 2, \ldots, 4$. Specifically, the sequential U-Net can be derived

$$E = e_5 \circ e_{4,0} \cdots \circ e_{2,0} \circ e_{1,0}, \quad d_i = s_i(e_{i,1}, d_{i+1}), i = 1, 2, \ldots, 4,$$
$$D = d_1 \circ d_2 \circ \cdots \circ d_5. \tag{3}$$

The temporary variable $e_{i,1}$ breaks the dependency in the skip connection and facilitates the automated partition in automated parallelism of GPipe. We can employ the existing GPipe algorithm to implement parallel U-Net based on the designed sequential U-Net.

2.3 Learning Large Models

Leveraging the powerful tool of parallel U-Net, we investigate the impact of model size and input context size. Although previous study demonstrates large input size increases segmentation accuracy because of large context [11], it also decreases the variation of training input and aggravates the extremely imbalance issue between background and the small subjects. From model size's perspective, large model consists of more parameters which typically require more various data to fit. Therefore, designing a learning strategy is essential to fully exploit the power of large input with more context information.

Inspired by the learning theory, i.e. curriculum learning [1], we can fit easy data/task into the network first and let the network to solve hard task later. Learning from smaller patches is easier, because smaller patches can be sampled with less imbalance and the lower dimension of smaller patches consists of less structures to learn for structured tasks, e.g., image segmentation. In practice, we firstly sample small positive patches (size of $64 \times 64 \times 64$) to train the model in the initial stage. In the second stage, we sample medium positive patches (size of $128 \times 128 \times 128$) to train the model. Finally, we use the largest patch to train the model. In this way, we can fully train models with large input patches in a practical way.

Table 1. Dice coefficient (%) achieved on the HaN test set using different sizes of U-Nets and inputs.

Models	BS	CH	MA	OL	OR	PL	PR	SL	SR	Average ↑
U-Net-32 (64^3)	84.23	48.87	89.75	69.11	68.28	87.43	85.48	79.36	77.41	76.66
U-Net-64 (64^3)	84.28	46.21	91.55	70.34	69.92	87.76	85.98	81.46	79.23	77.41
U-Net-128 (64^3)	84.58	48.52	91.12	71.04	69.28	87.76	85.78	81.34	80.03	77.72
U-Net-32 (128^3)	84.23	53.30	91.97	70.29	68.40	87.43	85.48	79.36	78.17	77.63
U-Net-64 (128^3)	84.71	46.21	92.47	70.34	69.92	87.76	85.98	81.46	79.23	77.56
U-Net-128 (128^3)	84.84	48.52	93.71	71.04	69.28	87.76	85.78	81.57	80.03	78.06
U-Net-32 (Whole)	84.23	53.30	91.97	70.29	68.40	87.43	85.48	79.36	79.02	77.72
U-Net-64 (Whole)	84.71	48.59	92.47	70.34	69.92	87.76	85.98	81.46	79.23	77.83
U-Net-128 (Whole)	84.84	48.52	93.71	71.04	70.09	87.76	85.78	81.57	80.03	78.15

Table 2. Dice coefficient (%) achieved on the HaN test set using different sizes of SEU-Nets and inputs.

Models	BS	CH	MA	OL	OR	PL	PR	SL	SR	Average ↑
AnatomyNet [29]	86.65	53.22	92.51	72.10	70.64	88.07	87.35	81.37	81.30	79.25
SEU-Net-32 (64^3)	84.07	47.09	90.12	68.58	69.73	87.14	85.21	79.20	75.81	76.33
SEU-Net-64 (64^3)	85.49	50.32	92.45	71.93	69.94	88.24	86.27	81.15	79.37	78.35
SEU-Net-128 (64^3)	86.38	51.85	93.55	70.62	70.08	88.11	85.99	81.79	81.13	78.83
SEU-Net-32 (128^3)	85.76	50.52	92.91	70.76	69.73	87.31	85.86	81.03	77.95	77.98
SEU-Net-64 (128^3)	85.73	50.37	94.26	71.97	71.09	88.34	86.58	81.15	79.64	78.79
SEU-Net-128 (128^3)	86.38	51.85	93.87	71.63	70.44	88.11	86.75	81.79	82.48	79.26
SEU-Net-32 (Whole)	85.76	51.27	92.91	70.76	69.73	87.31	85.86	81.03	78.43	78.12
SEU-Net-64 (Whole)	85.73	52.29	94.26	71.97	71.09	88.34	86.58	81.15	79.64	79.01
SEU-Net-128 (Whole)	86.38	51.85	93.87	73.70	70.44	88.26	86.75	81.96	82.48	**79.52**

Table 3. Average inference time (s) per test image achieved on the HaN test set using different sizes of networks and inputs.

Models	Inference time ↓	Models	Inference time ↓
U-Net-32 (64^3) 2 × 16G	1.21 ± 0.07	SEU-Net-32 (64^3) 2 × 16G	1.69 ± 0.17
U-Net-64 (64^3) 4 × 16G	1.75 ± 0.08	SEU-Net-64 (64^3) 2 × 32G	2.85 ± 0.13
U-Net-128 (64^3) 2 × 32G	2.53 ± 0.04	SEU-Net-128 (64^3) 4 × 32G	4.73 ± 0.69
U-Net-32 (128^3)	1.09 ± 0.28	SEU-Net-32 (128^3)	1.16 ± 0.36
U-Net-64 (128^3)	1.19 ± 0.16	SEU-Net-64 (128^3)	1.29 ± 0.18
U-Net-128 (128^3)	1.23 ± 0.16	SEU-Net-128 (128^3)	2.25 ± 0.13
U-Net-32 (Whole)	0.61 ± 0.07	SEU-Net-32 (Whole)	0.92 ± 0.07
U-Net-64 (Whole)	0.96 ± 0.22	SEU-Net-64 (Whole)	0.94 ± 0.07
U-Net-128 (Whole)	0.90 ± 0.14	SEU-Net-128 (Whole)	1.66 ± 0.14

3   Experiments

We use two datasets to investigate the impact of large models and large input context for segmentation, the head and neck (HaN) and decathlon liver datasets. The HaN dataset consists of whole-volume computed tomography (CT) images with manually generated binary masks of nine anatomies, i.e., brain stem (BS), chiasm (CH), mandible (MD), optic nerve left (OL), optic nerve right (OR), parotid gland left (PL), parotid gland right (PR), submandibular gland left (SL), and submandibular gland right (SR). We download the publicly available pre-processed data from AnatomyNet [29], which includes three public datasets: 1) MICCAI Head and Neck Auto Segmentation Challenge 2015 [20]; 2) the Head-Neck Cetuximab collection from The Cancer Imaging Archive (TCIA) [5]; 3) the CT images from four different institutions in Québec, Canada [28], also from TCIA. We use the dataset directly for fair comparison with benchmark methods. The dataset consists of 261 training images with missing annotations and ten test samples consisting of all annotations of nine organs. The largest image size can be 352 × 256 × 288. We use the same data augmentation techniques in [29].

The other dataset is 3D liver and tumor segmentation CT dataset from the medical segmentation decathlon [24]. We randomly split the dataset into 104 training images and 27 test images. We re-sample the CT images to 1 × 1 × 1 mm³ spacing. To focus on the liver region, we clip the voxel value within range [−21, 89] and linearly transform each 3D image into range [0, 1]. In the training, we randomly flip and rotation 90° in XY space with probability 0.1. We further add uniform random noise [−0.2, 0.2] to augment the training data. The largest image size can be 512 × 512 × 704. We will release the script and data splitting for reproducibility.

In the training, for the largest input, we use batch size of one and RMSProp optimizer [27] with 300 epochs and learning rate of 1 × 10⁻³. For training with patch size 128 × 128 × 128, we use batch size of four and 1200 epochs. For training with patch size 64 × 64 × 64, we use batch size of 16 and 4800 epochs. For U-Net-32 and Squeeze-and-Excitation U-Net (SEU-Net-32), the number of filters in each convolution of the first encoder block is 32. We increase the number of filters to 64 and 128 to investigate the impact of increasing model size. In the encoder of each model, the number of filters are doubled with the increase of encoder blocks accordingly. The decoder is symmetric with the encoder.

We employ two networks, 3D U-Net and 3D SEU-Net, to investigate the impact of model size and input context size in Table 1 and 2 on HaN dataset. With the increase of model size and input size, the segmentation accuracy increases consistently for both U-Net and SEU-Net. The SEU-Net-128 with whole image as input achieves better performance than AnatomyNet searching different network structures [29]. The reason for the accuracy improvement is that large input and model yield big context and learning capacity, respectively. We investigate the impact of large input on inference time by averaging three rounds of inferences in Table 3. Using large input in the inference reduces the inference time significantly because it reduces the number of inference rounds. Results on liver and tumor segmentation task validate large input increases segmentation accuracy and reduces the inference time in Table 4 and 5.

Table 4. Dice coefficientt (%) achieved on the Decathlon liver segmentation test set using different sizes of inputs and U-Nets and SEU-Nets.

Models	Liver	Tumor	Average ↑	Models	Liver	Tumor	Aevage ↑
U-Net-32 (64^3)	4.76	38.06	21.41	SEU-Net-32 (64^3)	0.73	42.56	21.65
U-Net-64 (64^3)	9.70	31.96	20.83	SEU-Net-64 (64^3)	11.90	46.19	29.05
U-Net-128 (64^3)	34.52	35.99	35.26	SEU-Net-128 (64^3)	0.34	43.44	21.89
U-Net-32 (128^3)	26.23	51.12	38.68	SEU-Net-32 (128^3)	58.88	50.83	54.86
U-Net-64 (128^3)	40.95	52.63	46.79	SEU-Net-64 (128^3)	38.38	50.25	44.32
U-Net-128 (128^3)	84.83	51.98	68.41	SEU-Net-128 (128^3)	20.20	48.44	34.32
U-Net-32 (192^3)	82.83	51.57	67.20	SEU-Net-32 (192^3)	89.25	55.38	72.32
U-Net-64 (192^3)	91.58	45.29	68.44	SEU-Net-64 (192^3)	77.66	51.93	64.80
U-Net-128 (192^3)	90.99	50.67	70.83	SEU-Net-128 (192^3)	87.61	56.48	72.05

Table 5. Average inference time (s) per test image achieved on the Decathlon liver segmentation test set using different sizes of networks and inputs.

Models	Inference time ↓	Models	Inference time ↓
U-Net-32 (64^3) 2 × 16G	6.78 ± 0.06	SEU-Net-32 (64^3) 4×16G	12.23 ± 0.08
U-Net-64 (64^3) 4 × 16G	14.52 ± 0.02	SEU-Net-64 (64^3) 2×32G	31.47 ± 0.16
U-Net-128 (64^3) 4 × 32G	25.37 ± 1.10	SEU-Net-128 (64^3) 8 × 32G	57.99 ± 11.08
U-Net-32 (128^3)	1.77 ± 0.42	SEU-Net-32 (128^3)	2.64 ± 0.06
U-Net-64 (128^3)	3.30 ± 0.52	SEU-Net-64 (128^3)	6.23 ± 0.17
U-Net-128 (128^3)	5.84 ± 0.21	SEU-Net-128 (128^3)	8.49 ± 0.08
U-Net-32 (256^3)	1.52 ± 0.58	SEU-Net-32 (256^3)	2.00 ± 0.20
U-Net-64 (256^3)	2.11 ± 0.10	SEU-Net-64 (256^3)	3.37 ± 0.10
U-Net-128 (256^3)	4.39 ± 0.25	SEU-Net-128 (256^3)	8.10 ± 0.50

4   Conclusion

In this work, we try to investigate the impact of model size and input context size on two medical image segmentation tasks. To run large models and large input in the GPUs, we design a parallel U-Net with sequential modification based on an automated parallelism. Extensive results demonstrate that, 1) large model and input increases segmentation accuracy, 2) large input reduces inference time significantly. The Large deep networks with Automated Model Parallelism (LAMP) can be a useful tool for many medical image analysis tasks such as large image registration [30,31], detection [32,33] and neural architecture search.

References

1. Bengio, Y., Louradour, J., Collobert, R., Weston, J.: Curriculum learning. In: Proceedings of the 26th Annual International Conference on Machine Learning, pp. 41–48 (2009)
2. Blumberg, S.B., Tanno, R., Kokkinos, I., Alexander, D.C.: Deeper image quality transfer: training low-memory neural networks for 3D images. In: Frangi, A.F., Schnabel, J.A., Davatzikos, C., Alberola-López, C., Fichtinger, G. (eds.) MICCAI 2018. LNCS, vol. 11070, pp. 118–125. Springer, Cham (2018). https://doi.org/10.1007/978-3-030-00928-1_14
3. Brügger, R., Baumgartner, C.F., Konukoglu, E.: A partially reversible U-net for memory-efficient volumetric image segmentation. In: Shen, D., et al. (eds.) MICCAI 2019. LNCS, vol. 11766, pp. 429–437. Springer, Cham (2019). https://doi.org/10.1007/978-3-030-32248-9_48
4. Chen, T., Xu, B., Zhang, C., Guestrin, C.: Training deep nets with sublinear memory cost. arXiv preprint arXiv:1604.06174 (2016)
5. Clark, K., et al.: The cancer imaging archive (TCIA): maintaining and operating a public information repository. J. Digit. Imaging **26**(6), 1045–1057 (2013)
6. Deng, J., Dong, W., Socher, R., Li, L.J., Li, K., Fei-Fei, L.: ImageNet: a large-scale hierarchical image database. In: 2009 IEEE Conference on Computer Vision and Pattern Recognition, pp. 248–255. IEEE (2009)
7. Devlin, J., Chang, M.W., Lee, K., Toutanova, K.: BERT: pre-training of deep bidirectional transformers for language understanding. arXiv preprint arXiv:1810.04805 (2018)
8. Gomez, A.N., Ren, M., Urtasun, R., Grosse, R.B.: The reversible residual network: backpropagation without storing activations. In: Advances in Neural Information Processing Systems, pp. 2214–2224 (2017)
9. Hu, J., Shen, L., Sun, G.: Squeeze-and-excitation networks. In: Proceedings of the IEEE Conference on Computer Vision and Pattern Recognition, pp. 7132–7141 (2018)
10. Huang, Y., et al.: GPipe: efficient training of giant neural networks using pipeline parallelism. In: Advances in Neural Information Processing Systems, pp. 103–112 (2019)
11. Isensee, F., et al.: Abstract: nnU-Net: self-adapting framework for U-net-based medical image segmentation. In: Handels, H., Deserno, T., Maier, A., Maier-Hein, K., Palm, C., Tolxdorff, T. (eds.) Bildverarbeitung für die Medizin 2019. I, p. 22. Springer, Wiesbaden (2019). https://doi.org/10.1007/978-3-658-25326-4_7

12. Jesson, A., Guizard, N., Ghalehjegh, S.H., Goblot, D., Soudan, F., Chapados, N.: CASED: curriculum adaptive sampling for extreme data imbalance. In: Descoteaux, M., Maier-Hein, L., Franz, A., Jannin, P., Collins, D.L., Duchesne, S. (eds.) MICCAI 2017. LNCS, vol. 10435, pp. 639–646. Springer, Cham (2017). https://doi.org/10.1007/978-3-319-66179-7_73

13. Kervadec, H., Bouchtiba, J., Desrosiers, C., Granger, E., Dolz, J., Ayed, I.B.: Boundary loss for highly unbalanced segmentation. In: International Conference on Medical Imaging with Deep Learning, pp. 285–296 (2019)

14. Lee, H., et al.: torchgpipe, A GPipe implementation in PyTorch (2019). https://github.com/kakaobrain/torchgpipe

15. Martens, J., Sutskever, I.: Training deep and recurrent networks with Hessian-free optimization. In: Montavon, G., Orr, G.B., Müller, K.-R. (eds.) Neural Networks: Tricks of the Trade. LNCS, vol. 7700, pp. 479–535. Springer, Heidelberg (2012). https://doi.org/10.1007/978-3-642-35289-8_27

16. Micikevicius, P., et al.: Mixed precision training. arXiv preprint arXiv:1710.03740 (2017)

17. Narayanan, D., et al.: Pipedream: generalized pipeline parallelism for DNN training. In: Proceedings of the 27th ACM Symposium on Operating Systems Principles, pp. 1–15 (2019)

18. Radford, A., Wu, J., Child, R., Luan, D., Amodei, D., Sutskever, I.: Language models are unsupervised multitask learners. OpenAI Blog 1(8), 9 (2019)

19. Rajbhandari, S., Rasley, J., Ruwase, O., He, Y.: Zero: Memory optimization towards training a trillion parameter models. arXiv preprint arXiv:1910.02054 (2019)

20. Raudaschl, P.F., et al.: Evaluation of segmentation methods on head and neck CT: Auto-segmentation challenge 2015. Med. Phys. 44, 2020–2036 (2017)

21. Ronneberger, O., Fischer, P., Brox, T.: U-Net: convolutional networks for biomedical image segmentation. In: Navab, N., Hornegger, J., Wells, W.M., Frangi, A.F. (eds.) MICCAI 2015. LNCS, vol. 9351, pp. 234–241. Springer, Cham (2015). https://doi.org/10.1007/978-3-319-24574-4_28

22. Shazeer, N., et al.: Mesh-TensorFlow: deep learning for supercomputers. In: Advances in Neural Information Processing Systems, pp. 10414–10423 (2018)

23. Shoeybi, M., Patwary, M., Puri, R., LeGresley, P., Casper, J., Catanzaro, B.: Megatron-LM: training multi-billion parameter language models using gpu model parallelism. arXiv preprint arXiv:1909.08053 (2019)

24. Simpson, A.L., et al.: A large annotated medical image dataset for the development and evaluation of segmentation algorithms. arXiv preprint arXiv:1902.09063 (2019)

25. Sudre, C.H., Li, W., Vercauteren, T., Ourselin, S., Jorge Cardoso, M.: Generalised dice overlap as a deep learning loss function for highly unbalanced segmentations. In: Cardoso, M.J., et al. (eds.) DLMIA/ML-CDS - 2017. LNCS, vol. 10553, pp. 240–248. Springer, Cham (2017). https://doi.org/10.1007/978-3-319-67558-9_28

26. Tajbakhsh, N., et al.: Convolutional neural networks for medical image analysis: full training or fine tuning? IEEE Trans. Med. Imaging 35(5), 1299–1312 (2016)

27. Tieleman, T., Hinton, G.: Lecture 6.5-rmsprop: Divide the gradient by a running average of its recent magnitude. COURSERA: Neural Netw. Mach. Learn. 4(2), 26–31 (2012)

28. Vallières, M., et al.: Radiomics strategies for risk assessment of tumour failure in head-and-neck cancer. Sci. Rep. 7(1), 10117 (2017)

29. Zhu, W., et al.: AnatomyNet: deep learning for fast and fully automated whole-volume segmentation of head and neck anatomy. Med. Phys. 46(2), 576–589 (2019)

30. Zhu, W., et al.: NeurReg: Neural registration and its application to image segmentation. In: The IEEE Winter Conference on Applications of Computer Vision, pp. 3617–3626 (2020)

31. Zhu, W., et al.: Neural multi-scale self-supervised registration for echocardiogram dense tracking. arXiv preprint arXiv:1906.07357 (2019)

32. Zhu, W., Liu, C., Fan, W., Xie, X.: Deeplung: deep 3D dual path nets for automated pulmonary nodule detection and classification. In: WACV, pp. 673–681. IEEE (2018)

33. Zhu, W., Vang, Y.S., Huang, Y., Xie, X.: DeepEM: deep 3D ConvNets with EM for weakly supervised pulmonary nodule detection. In: Frangi, A.F., Schnabel, J.A., Davatzikos, C., Alberola-López, C., Fichtinger, G. (eds.) MICCAI 2018. LNCS, vol. 11071, pp. 812–820. Springer, Cham (2018). https://doi.org/10.1007/978-3-030-00934-2_90

34. Zhuang, J., Dvornek, N.C., Li, X., Ventola, P., Duncan, J.S.: Invertible network for classification and biomarker selection for ASD. In: Shen, D., et al. (eds.) MICCAI 2019. LNCS, vol. 11766, pp. 700–708. Springer, Cham (2019). https://doi.org/10.1007/978-3-030-32248-9_78

INSIDE: Steering Spatial Attention with Non-imaging Information in CNNs

Grzegorz Jacenków[1]([✉]), Alison Q. O'Neil[1,2], Brian Mohr[2],
and Sotirios A. Tsaftaris[1,2,3]

[1] The University of Edinburgh, Edinburgh, UK
g.jacenkow@ed.ac.uk
[2] Canon Medical Research Europe, Edinburgh, UK
[3] The Alan Turing Institute, London, UK

Abstract. We consider the problem of integrating non-imaging information into segmentation networks to improve performance. Conditioning layers such as FiLM provide the means to selectively amplify or suppress the contribution of different feature maps in a linear fashion. However, spatial dependency is difficult to learn within a convolutional paradigm. In this paper, we propose a mechanism to allow for spatial localisation conditioned on non-imaging information, using a feature-wise attention mechanism comprising a differentiable parametrised function (e.g. Gaussian), prior to applying the feature-wise modulation. We name our method INstance modulation with SpatIal DEpendency (INSIDE). The conditioning information might comprise any factors that relate to spatial or spatio-temporal information such as lesion location, size, and cardiac cycle phase. Our method can be trained end-to-end and does not require additional supervision. We evaluate the method on two datasets: a new CLEVR-Seg dataset where we segment objects based on location, and the ACDC dataset conditioned on cardiac phase and slice location within the volume. Code and the CLEVR-Seg dataset are available at https://github.com/jacenkow/inside.

Keywords: Attention · Conditioning · Non-imaging · Segmentation

1 Introduction

Acquisition of medical images often involves capturing non-imaging information such as image and patient metadata which are a source of valuable information yet are frequently disregarded in automatic segmentation and classification. The useful information should expose correlation with the task such as body mass index (BMI) with ventricular volume [1], or symptom laterality with stroke lesion laterality [19], and these correlations can be exploited to improve the quality

Electronic supplementary material The online version of this chapter (https://doi.org/10.1007/978-3-030-59719-1_38) contains supplementary material, which is available to authorized users.

© Springer Nature Switzerland AG 2020
A. L. Martel et al. (Eds.): MICCAI 2020, LNCS 12264, pp. 385–395, 2020.
https://doi.org/10.1007/978-3-030-59719-1_38

of the structure segmentation. Nevertheless, combining both imaging and non-imaging information in the medical domain remains challenging, with dedicated workshops to approach this problem [21].

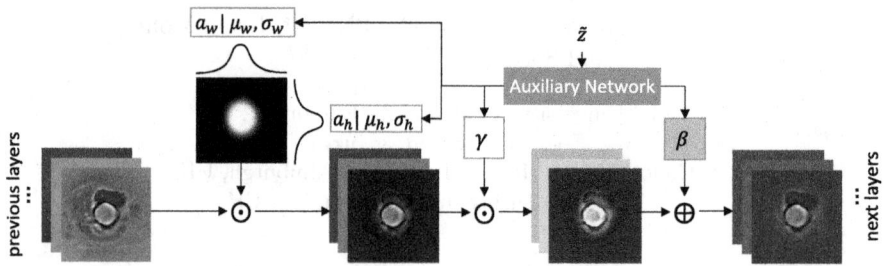

Fig. 1. Visualisation of the method. Given a feature map F_c and conditioning vector $\tilde{z}$, the method first applies spatial attention (a) with scale (γ) and shift (β) factors to F_c respectively. The attention matrix (a) is the product of two Gaussian vectors (a_h, a_w). Therefore, for a single feature map, the auxiliary network predicts six parameters $(\gamma, \beta, \mu_h, \sigma_h, \mu_w, \sigma_w)$. We denote Hadamard product with $\odot$ symbol.

Conditioning layers have become the dominant method to tackle this challenge, finding application in image synthesis [3], style transfer [7] and visual question answering (VQA) [16]. In this setup, the network is conditioned on non-imaging information via a learned set of scalar weights which affinely transform feature maps to selectively amplify or suppress each feature, thus controlling its contribution to the final prediction. However, this method has limited capability to adjust channels spatially, and is less suited to conditioning on information relating to spatial or spatio-temporal prior knowledge. Consider a problem where we expect to produce a segmentation only on one side of the image (left or right) indicated by the laterality of the patient's symptoms. To accomplish this task, the network would require to learn how to encode relative spatial relationships and split them into channels. We show that spatial conditioning can be challenging and propose a method to overcome this limitation.

We present a new conditioning layer which uses non-imaging information to steer spatial attention before applying the affine transformation. We choose a Gaussian for the attention mechanism due to its parameter-efficiency, allowing us to learn a separate attention per channel. However, other differentiable functions can also be used. We first test our method on a simulated dataset, our extension of the CLEVR[1] dataset [10], where we segment objects based on their location within the image space. To prove the method is applicable in a clinical setting, we use the ACDC[2] dataset [2] with the task to segment anatomical structures from cardiac cine-MR images. We perform 2D segmentation, and provide slice position and cardiac cycle phase as the non-imaging information to our method.

---

[1] Diagnostic Dataset for Compositional Language and Elementary Visual Reasoning.

[2] Automated Cardiac Diagnosis Challenge (ACDC), MICCAI Challenge 2017.

Contributions: (1) we propose a new conditioning layer capable of handling spatial and spatio-temporal dependency given a conditioning variable; (2) we extend the CLEVR dataset for segmentation tasks and several conditioning scenarios, such as shape-, colour-, or size-based conditioning in the segmentation space; (3) we evaluate different conditioning layers for the task of segmentation on the CLEVR-Seg and ACDC datasets.

2   Related Work

An early work on adapting batch normalisation for conditioning was in style transfer. The conditional instance normalisation layer [6] (Eq. 1) applied a pair of scale (γ_s) and shift (β_s) vectors from the style-dependent parameter matrices, where each pair corresponded to a single style s such as Claude Monet or Edvard Munch. This allowed several styles to be learned using a single network and proved that affine transformations were sufficient for the task. However, the method is restricted to the discrete set of styles seen during training. In Adaptive Instance Normalisation (AdaIN) [7], the authors proposed to instead use a network to predict the style-dependent vectors (as in hypernetworks), allowing parameters to be predicted for arbitrary new styles at inference time.

$$z = \gamma_s \frac{x - \mu_x}{\sigma_x} + \beta_s \qquad (1)$$

AdaIN has been applied outside of the style transfer domain, for instance to image synthesis using face landmarks where the method is used to inpaint the landmark with face texture [23], and to conditional object segmentation given its coordinates [20]. A similar method to AdaIN was applied to visual question-answering (VQA); the authors used feature-wise linear modulation layer (FiLM) [16] to condition the network with questions. FiLM is identical to AdaIN but omits the instance *normalisation* step (μ_x, σ_x in Eq. 1), which the authors found to be unnecessary. FiLM has found application in medical image analysis for disentangled representation learning [4] and for segmentation [9].

A drawback of both AdaIN and FiLM is that they manipulate whole feature maps in an affine fashion, making the methods insensitive to spatial processing. To overcome this limitation, SPADE [15] was proposed, where a segmentation mask is used as a conditioning input in the task of image synthesis, leading to both feature-wise and class-wise scale and shift parameters at each layer. This method is not suitable if the non-imaging information cannot be conveniently expressed in image space.

The closest method to ours is [18]. The authors proposed to extend FiLM with spatial attention, creating a Guiding Block layer, in which the spatial attention is defined as two vectors $\alpha \in \mathbb{R}^H$ and $\beta \in \mathbb{R}^W$ which are replicated over the H and W axes and added to the global scale factor ($\gamma_c^{(s)}$) as shown in Eq. 2 (the authors call the shifting factor as $\gamma_c^{(b)}$). This spatial conditioning is expensive as there are an additional $H + W$ parameters to learn; perhaps for this reason, a single attention mechanism is learned for each layer and applied across all feature maps.

$$F'_{h,w,c} = (1 + \alpha_h + \beta_w + \gamma_c^{(s)})F_{h,w,c} + \gamma_c^{(b)} \tag{2}$$

In our work, we utilise a learned attention mechanism for each feature map. Our mechanism is similar to [12], where the product of two Gaussian matrices parametrised by mean (μ), standard deviation (σ) and stride (γ) between consecutive Gaussians (one Gaussian per row, one matrix per axis) is constructed. However, the relation between standard deviations and strides is estimated before the training and kept fixed. Our method applies a single Gaussian vector per axis (no stride) and we train the whole method end-to-end. Further, the parameters in [12] are estimated using consecutive input images whilst we use an auxiliary conditioning input, and we combine with a FiLM layer.

3   Method

3.1   INstance Modulation with SpatIal DEpendency (INSIDE)

Our method adopts the formulation of previous conditioning layers [22] where, given a feature map F_c, we apply an affine transformation using scale (γ) and shift (β) factors. However, to facilitate spatial manipulation we propose to apply a Gaussian attention mechanism prior to feature-wise linear modulation (FiLM) to process only a (spatially) relevant subset of each feature map. The choice of the attention mechanism, where each matrix is constructed with two Gaussian vectors $[(a_h|\mu_h, \sigma_h), (a_w|\mu_w, \sigma_w)]$ is motivated by parameter efficiency. Therefore, the method can learn one attention mechanism per feature map by adding four additional parameters for each channel (six parameters in total, including the scale and shift factors).

We illustrate the method in Fig. 1. Given a feature map $F_c \in \mathbb{R}^{H \times W}$ as input, where c is the channel, we first apply Gaussian attention similar to [12]. We define two vectors $a_{c,h} \in \mathbb{R}^H$ and $a_{c,w} \in \mathbb{R}^W$ following the Gaussian distribution parametrised by mean and standard deviation to construct an attention matrix $a_c = a_{c,h}a_{c,w}^T$. The attention is applied to the feature map prior to feature-wise modulation, i.e.

$$\text{INSIDE}(F_c|\gamma_c, \beta_c, a_c) = F_c \odot a_c \odot \gamma_c + \beta_c. \tag{3}$$

To construct the Gaussian vectors, we normalise the coordinate system, transforming each axis to span the interval $[-1, 1]$. We apply a similar transformation to the standard deviation; the value (the output of a sigmoid activation) lies within the $[0, 1]$ range. We set the maximum width to 3.5 standard deviations to cover (at maximum) 99.95% of the image width, thus constraining by design the allowable size of the Gaussian.

3.2   Auxiliary Network

We use a separate auxiliary network (a hypernetwork) for each layer to predict the parameters of INSIDE (see Eq. 3). The network takes a conditional input $\tilde{z}$ to control the Gaussian attention and affine transformation. The information is encoded using a 3-layer MLP arranged as $(\frac{c}{2} - \frac{c}{2} - 6c)$ where c is the number of channels feeding into the INSIDE layer. We use $tanh$ activation functions except for the last layer where scale (γ) and shift (β) factors are predicted with no activation (identity function). The Gaussian's mean is bounded between $[-1, 1]$ (relative position along the axis from the centre), enforced with a $tanh$ function, and we use $sigmoid$ activations to predict the standard deviation of the Gaussian vectors.

3.3   Loss Function

To avoid the network defaulting to a general solution with a large diffuse Gaussian [14], we add an L_2 regularisation penalty η to the cost function to encourage learning of localisation, as in the equation below:

$$\mathcal{L} = \mathcal{L}_{\text{Dice}} + 0.1 \cdot \mathcal{L}_{\text{Focal}} + \eta||\sigma||_2^2 .$$

The first part of the cost function relates to the segmentation task and involves a combination of Dice loss [5] (evaluated on the task foreground classes) and Focal loss [13] (evaluated on every class including background). The second part is the penalty applied to our conditioning layer. Throughout the training, we keep $\eta = 0.0001$ and the Focal loss focusing parameter $\gamma = 0.5$. The coefficients were selected using a grid search giving reasonable performance across all tested scenarios. We optimise every model with Adam [11] with learning rate set to 0.0001, and $\beta_1 = 0.9$, $\beta_2 = 0.999$. We apply early stopping criterion evaluated on validation set using Dice score only.

4   Experiments

We evaluate our method on two datasets and report the Dice coefficient on 3-fold cross validation. Each experiment was further repeated three times using different seeds to avoid variance due to the weight initialisation. We compare our method against the following techniques, as discussed earlier in Sect. 2:

– Baseline - a vanilla CNN network without conditioning
– FiLM [16] - feature-wise affine transformation (also component of INSIDE)
– Guiding Block [18] - extension of FiLM with spatial attention.

4.1 CLEVR-Seg Dataset

We present a novel dataset based on the CLEVR dataset [10], which we name CLEVR-Seg. We have extended the original dataset with segmentation masks and per-object attributes, such as colour (yellow, red, green), location (quadrant containing the centre of mass), shape (cubes, spheres, prisms), and size (small, medium, large). The attributes determine the segmentation task, i.e. *segment red objects*, *segment objects in the bottom left quadrant*, etc. The network must thus use the non-imaging information to produce an accurate result. In contrast to the original work, conditioning is provided as categorical one-hot encoded vectors, rather than as natural language questions since VQA is not our primary focus. We generated 4000 random images with 3 to 5 objects each (containing at least one of each shape, size and colour), paired with segmentation masks for which each conditioning factor was drawn at random with equal probability. We split the dataset into training (2880 samples), validation (320), and test (800) subsets which we kept fixed throughout the evaluation. The intensities in each image were normalised to fit the [0, 1] range.

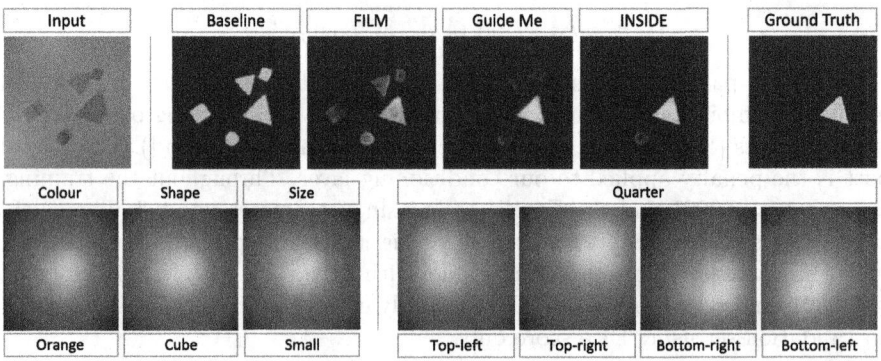

Fig. 2. Top: Segmentations produced by the conditioning methods on CLEVR-Seg dataset where we condition objects based on the location (bottom-right quadrant). **Bottom:** Learned Gaussians from INSIDE (averaged across all feature maps) for different conditioning scenarios. The first three scenarios are spatially independent and thus, the attentions default to general solutions with diffuse Gaussians.

Network: We use a simple fully-convolutional encoder-decoder with 3 down- and 3 up-sample blocks. Each block consists of (3×3) kernels followed by ReLU activation function and max-pooling/up-sampling, starting with 16 kernels and doubling/halving at each subsequent step. We test each conditional layer by placing it between the encoder and the decoder, i.e. at the network bottleneck.

Results: We first evaluate the spatial conditioning scenario. Quantitative results are shown in Table 1 and qualitative examples are presented in Fig. 2 top. We observe that FiLM has poor performance, achieving a Dice score of 0.487 ($\pm$0.007). This result confirms our hypothesis that spatial conditioning is difficult to disentangle into separate channels, otherwise FiLM would achieve satisfactory performance. On the other hand, the Guiding Block achieves adequate performance with a Dice score of 0.819 ($\pm$0.033). When we use only one Gaussian attention, INSIDE performs worse than the Guiding Block, however when we use one learned attention per channel, INSIDE performs best, with a Dice score of 0.857 ($\pm$0.025). We further evaluate our attention mechanisms without feature-wise modulation ("Single Attention", "Multiple Attentions"). These methods yield satisfactory results, although with higher variance. The combination of both gives the highest Dice score and lowest variance across all evaluation scenarios. The use of feature-wise attention mechanisms give more flexibility to learn shape- and size-dependent positional bias. Similar patterns are seen on other conditioning scenarios, i.e. colour, shape and size.

Table 1. Quantitative results on our CLEVR-Seg dataset where we condition on a quadrant (spatial conditioning), object colour, shape and size. We report Dice scores (multiplied by 100) with standard deviations shown as subscripts. The method with highest average result is presented in **bold**. We use the Wilcoxon test to assess statistical significance between INSIDE (with multiple attentions) and the best baseline method. We denote two (**) asterisks for $p \leqslant 0.01$.

Method	Quadrant	Colour	Shape	Size
Baseline	$29.3_{0.7}$	$28.5_{0.2}$	$27.6_{0.2}$	$27.3_{1.2}$
FiLM	48.7_2	89.8_2	$87.7_{1.2}$	84.2_2
Guiding block	$81.9_{3.3}$	89.3_5	89.9_2	84.3_3
Single attention (w/o FiLM)	$50.2_{0.7}$	$81.5_{7.5}$	$79.2_{6.9}$	$80.8_{2.5}$
Multiple attentions (w/o FiLM)	$82.4_{3.8}$	$90.1_{2.9}$	$88.3_{5.9}$	$\mathbf{85.4_{2.1}}$
INSIDE (single attention)	$77.9_{2.5}$	$87.8_{0.6}$	$89.8_{0.7}$	$\mathbf{85.4_{0.8}}$
INSIDE (multiple attentions)	$\mathbf{85.7^{**}_{2.5}}$	$\mathbf{90.7^{**}_{1.9}}$	$\mathbf{90.7^{**}_{1.9}}$	$\mathbf{85.4^{**}_{1.2}}$

4.2   ACDC Dataset

The ACDC dataset [2] contains cine-MR images of 3 cardiac structures, the myocardium and the left and right ventricular cavities, with the task to segment these anatomies. The annotated dataset contains images at end-systolic and -diastolic phases from 100 patients, at varying spatial resolutions. We resample the volumes to the common resolution of $1.37\,\mathrm{mm}^2$ per pixel, resize each slice to 224×224 pixels, clip outlier intensities within each volume outside the range $[5\%, 95\%]$, and finally standardise the data to be within the $[0, 1]$ range.

Conditioning. We evaluate two conditioning scenarios: slice position and phase. Slice position is normalised between $[0, 1]$ (from apical slice to basal slice), and cardiac cycle phase, i.e. end-systolic or -diastolic, is encoded as a one-hot vector.

Network. To segment the images, we train a U-Net [17] network with 4-down and 4-up sampling blocks, Batch Normalisation [8] and ReLU activations, with a softmax for final classification. The architecture selection was motivated by its state-of-the-art results on the ACDC dataset [2]. The conditional layers are placed along the decoding path between consecutive convolutional blocks (each stage has two convolutional blocks). The diagrams can be found in the supplemental material.

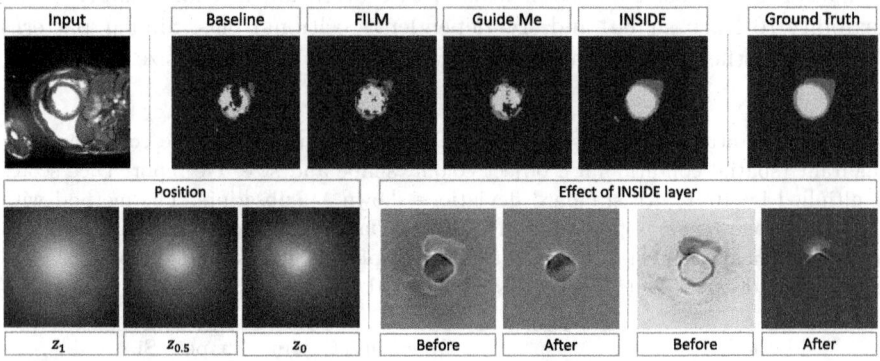

Fig. 3. Top: Segmentation produced on 25% dataset, conditioning on slice position (z-axis). **Bottom-left:** Visualisation of the Gaussian attentions (averaged across channels) from the final INSIDE layer. Moving from the basal slice (denoted as z_1) along the z-axis to the apical slice (denoted as z_0), we observe the spread of the Gaussians to contract. **Bottom-right:** Visualisation of applying INSIDE layer.

Results. The empirical results on the ACDC dataset are presented in Table 2, with varying fractions of the training set, i.e. at 100%, 25%, and 6%. Overall, our method achieves consistent improvement over the baseline (when no conditioning information is provided) with better relative performance as the size of the training dataset decreases (+0.9%, +2.6%, +16% Dice respectively). We argue the networks rely more on non-imaging information when the number of training examples is reduced. We further present selected segmentation results and visualise how the attention changes depending on the conditioning information (Fig. 3). Across the evaluation scenarios, we notice conditioning on slice position generally yields the highest improvement, which is expected as there is a clear link between position and heart size (expressed by the Gaussian's standard deviation). The proposed method achieved the highest average Dice score across all

Table 2. Quantitative results on ACDC dataset where each image is provided with slice position within the heart volume or phase (end-systolic or end-diastolic). We report average Dice score (multipled by 100) across all anatomical structures evaluated on whole volumes. The method with highest Dice score is presented in **bold**. We use the Wilcoxon test to assess statistical significance between INSIDE and the second best method. We denote one (*) and two (**) asterisks for $p \leqslant 0.1$ and $p \leqslant 0.01$ respectively. We apply Bonferroni correction ($m = 2$) to account for multiple comparisons (when comparing to "Baseline").

Method	100% dataset		25% dataset		6% dataset	
	Position	Phase	Position	Phase	Position	Phase
Baseline	$87_{1.9}$		$78.2_{2.5}$		53.6_6	
FiLM	$84.7_{4.5}$	$85.4_{3.9}$	$73.4_{16.3}$	$76_{5.4}$	$59.9_{5.4}$	$55.7_{7.6}$
Guiding block	83.7_4	$76.2_{21.4}$	77.8_2	$77.6_{2.4}$	$53.7_{5.5}$	54.8_5
INSIDE	$\mathbf{87.8^{**}_{1.5}}$	$\mathbf{87.7^*_{1.6}}$	$\mathbf{80.2^{**}_{1.4}}$	$\mathbf{78.9^*_{1.8}}$	$\mathbf{62.2^*_{5.2}}$	$\mathbf{61.4^{**}_{3.8}}$

tested scenarios. The Guiding Block underperforms in most experiments, and we argue that our choice of Gaussian attention imposes a beneficial shape prior for the heart. FiLM performs well (at 6% training data) when position is provided as the conditioning information, but underperforms comparing to our method; this is logical since non-imaging information helps to inform the network about the expected size of segmentation masks, but does not have enough flexibility to spatially manipulate features maps as our method.

5 Conclusion

Endowing convolutional architectures with the ability to peruse non-imaging information is an important problem for our community but still remains challenging. In this work, we have proposed a new conditional layer which extends FiLM with Gaussian attention that learns spatial dependencies between image inputs and non-imaging information when provided as condition. We have shown the attention mechanism allows spatial-dependency to be modelled in conditional layers. Our method is low in parameters, allowing efficient learning of feature-wise attention mechanisms which can be applied to 3D problems by adding an additional orthogonal 1D Gaussian for each channel.

Acknowledgment. This work was supported by the Engineering and Physical Sciences Research Council [grant number EP/R513209/1]; and Canon Medical Research Europe Ltd. S.A. Tsaftaris acknowledges the support of the Royal Academy of Engineering and the Research Chairs and Senior Research Fellowships scheme.

References

1. Bai, W., et al.: Automated cardiovascular magnetic resonance image analysis with fully convolutional networks. J. Cardiovasc. Magn. Reson. **20**(1), 65 (2018)

2. Bernard, O., et al.: Deep learning techniques for automatic MRI cardiac multi-structures segmentation and diagnosis: is the problem solved? IEEE Trans. Med. Imaging **37**(11), 2514–2525 (2018)

3. Brock, A., Donahue, J., Simonyan, K.: Large scale GAN training for high fidelity natural image synthesis. arXiv preprint arXiv:1809.11096 (2018)

4. Chartsias, A., et al.: Disentangled representation learning in cardiac image analysis. Med. Image Anal. **58**, 101535 (2019)

5. Dice, L.R.: Measures of the amount of ecologic association between species. Ecology **26**(3), 297–302 (1945)

6. Dumoulin, V., Shlens, J., Kudlur, M.: A learned representation for artistic style. arXiv preprint arXiv:1610.07629 (2016)

7. Huang, X., Belongie, S.: Arbitrary style transfer in real-time with adaptive instance normalization. In: Proceedings of the IEEE International Conference on Computer Vision, pp. 1501–1510 (2017)

8. Ioffe, S., Szegedy, C.: Batch normalization: accelerating deep network training by reducing internal covariate shift. arXiv preprint arXiv:1502.03167 (2015)

9. Jacenków, G., Chartsias, A., Mohr, B., Tsaftaris, S.A.: Conditioning convolutional segmentation architectures with non-imaging data. In: International Conference on Medical Imaging with Deep Learning–Extended Abstract Track (2019)

10. Johnson, J., Hariharan, B., van der Maaten, L., Fei-Fei, L., Lawrence Zitnick, C., Girshick, R.: CLEVR: a diagnostic dataset for compositional language and elementary visual reasoning. In: Proceedings of the IEEE Conference on Computer Vision and Pattern Recognition, pp. 2901–2910 (2017)

11. Kingma, D.P., Ba, J.: Adam: a method for stochastic optimization. arXiv preprint arXiv:1412.6980 (2014)

12. Kosiorek, A., Bewley, A., Posner, I.: Hierarchical attentive recurrent tracking. In: Advances in Neural Information Processing Systems, pp. 3053–3061 (2017)

13. Lin, T.Y., Goyal, P., Girshick, R., He, K., Dollár, P.: Focal loss for dense object detection. In: Proceedings of the IEEE International Conference on Computer Vision, pp. 2980–2988 (2017)

14. Nibali, A., He, Z., Morgan, S., Prendergast, L.: Numerical coordinate regression with convolutional neural networks. arXiv preprint arXiv:1801.07372 (2018)

15. Park, T., Liu, M.Y., Wang, T.C., Zhu, J.Y.: Semantic image synthesis with spatially-adaptive normalization. In: Proceedings of the IEEE Conference on Computer Vision and Pattern Recognition, pp. 2337–2346 (2019)

16. Perez, E., Strub, F., De Vries, H., Dumoulin, V., Courville, A.: FiLM: visual reasoning with a general conditioning layer. In: Thirty-Second AAAI Conference on Artificial Intelligence (2018)

17. Ronneberger, O., Fischer, P., Brox, T.: U-Net: convolutional networks for biomedical image segmentation. In: Navab, N., Hornegger, J., Wells, W.M., Frangi, A.F. (eds.) MICCAI 2015. LNCS, vol. 9351, pp. 234–241. Springer, Cham (2015). https://doi.org/10.1007/978-3-319-24574-4_28

18. Rupprecht, C., Laina, I., Navab, N., Hager, G.D., Tombari, F.: Guide me: interacting with deep networks. In: Proceedings of the IEEE Conference on Computer Vision and Pattern Recognition, pp. 8551–8561 (2018)

19. Sato, S., et al.: Conjugate eye deviation in acute intracerebral hemorrhage: stroke acute management with urgent risk-factor assessment and improvement-ich (samurai-ich) study. Stroke **43**(11), 2898–2903 (2012)

20. Sofiiuk, K., Barinova, O., Konushin, A.: AdaptIS: adaptive instance selection network. In: Proceedings of the IEEE International Conference on Computer Vision, pp. 7355–7363 (2019)

21. Arslan, S., Ktena, S.I., Glocker, B., Rueckert, D.: Graph saliency maps through spectral convolutional networks: application to sex classification with brain connectivity. In: Stoyanov, D., et al. (eds.) GRAIL/Beyond MIC -2018. LNCS, vol. 11044, pp. 3–13. Springer, Cham (2018). https://doi.org/10.1007/978-3-030-00689-1_1
22. Ulyanov, D., Vedaldi, A., Lempitsky, V.: Instance normalization: the missing ingredient for fast stylization. arXiv preprint arXiv:1607.08022 (2016)
23. Zakharov, E., Shysheya, A., Burkov, E., Lempitsky, V.: Few-shot adversarial learning of realistic neural talking head models. arXiv preprint arXiv:1905.08233 (2019)

SiamParseNet: Joint Body Parsing and Label Propagation in Infant Movement Videos

Haomiao Ni[1], Yuan Xue[1], Qian Zhang[2], and Xiaolei Huang[1(✉)]

[1] College of Information Sciences and Technology,
The Pennsylvania State University, University Park, PA, USA
sharon.x.huang@psu.edu
[2] School of Information and Control Engineering,
Xi'an University of Architecture and Technology, Xi'an, China

Abstract. General movement assessment (GMA) of infant movement videos (IMVs) is an effective method for the early detection of cerebral palsy (CP) in infants. Automated body parsing is a crucial step towards computer-aided GMA, in which infant body parts are segmented and tracked over time for movement analysis. However, acquiring fully annotated data for video-based body parsing is particularly expensive due to the large number of frames in IMVs. In this paper, we propose a semi-supervised body parsing model, termed *SiamParseNet* (SPN), to jointly learn single frame body parsing and label propagation between frames in a semi-supervised fashion. The Siamese-structured SPN consists of a shared feature encoder, followed by two separate branches: one for intra-frame body parts segmentation, and one for inter-frame label propagation. The two branches are trained jointly, taking pairs of frames from the same videos as their input. An adaptive training process is proposed that alternates training modes between using input pairs of only labeled frames and using inputs of both labeled and unlabeled frames. During testing, we employ a multi-source inference mechanism, where the final result for a test frame is either obtained via the segmentation branch or via propagation from a nearby *key* frame. We conduct extensive experiments on a partially-labeled IMV dataset where SPN outperforms all prior arts, demonstrating the effectiveness of our proposed method.

1 Introduction

Early detection of cerebral palsy (CP), a group of neurodevelopmental disorders which permanently affect body movement and muscle coordination [17], enables early rehabilitative interventions for high-risk infants. One effective CP detection method is general movement assessment (GMA) [2], where qualified clinicians observe the movement of infant body parts from captured videos and provide evaluation scores. For computer-assisted GMA, accurate segmentation of infant body parts is a crucial step. Among different sensing modalities [9,15], RGB camera-based approaches [1,21] have numerous advantages, such as easy access

---

H. Ni and Y. Xue—These authors contributed equally to this work.

© Springer Nature Switzerland AG 2020
A. L. Martel et al. (Eds.): MICCAI 2020, LNCS 12264, pp. 396–405, 2020.
https://doi.org/10.1007/978-3-030-59719-1_39

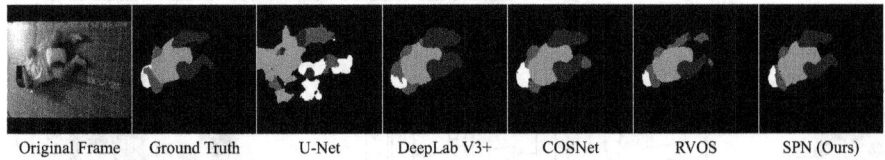

Original Frame   Ground Truth   U-Net   DeepLab V3+   COSNet   RVOS   SPN (Ours)

Fig. 1. Comparison between different body parsing methods on IMVs.

to the capturing device and better recording of spontaneous infant movements. Therefore, in this paper, we focus on parsing body parts in infant movement videos (IMVs) captured by RGB cameras.

Parsing infant bodies in IMVs is closely related to the video object segmentation task (VOS), which has been widely explored in natural scenes. However, challenges arise when directly applying existing VOS methods to infant body parsing, such as frequent occlusion among body parts due to infant movements. Among current state-of-the-art methods, Lu *et al.* [14] introduced a CO-attention Siamese Network (COSNet) to capture the global-occurrence consistency of primary objects among video frames for VOS. Ventura *et al.* [19] proposed a recurrent network RVOS to integrate spatial and temporal domains for VOS by employing uni-directional convLSTMs [20]. Zhu *et al.* [22] proposed Deep Feature Flow to jointly learn image recognition and flow networks, which first runs the convolutional sub-network on key frames and then propagates their deep feature maps to other frames via optical flow. Also using optical flow, in the medical video field, Jin *et al.* [11] proposed MF-TAPNet for instrument segmentation in minimally invasive surgery videos, which incorporates motion flow-based temporal prior with an attention pyramid network. Optical flow-based methods aim to find point-to-point correspondences between frames and have achieved promising results. However, for infant videos with frequent occlusions, it can be challenging to locate corresponding points on occluded body parts. Moreover, few previous methods have investigated the semi-supervised training setting. As the majority of IMV frames are unlabeled due to the high cost of annotation, semi-supervised methods have great potential in IMV body parsing and deserve further research.

In this paper, we aim to address the aforementioned challenges by proposing *SiamParseNet* (SPN), a semi-supervised framework based on a siamese structure [3] that automatically segments infant body parts in IMVs. The SPN consists of one shared feature encoder Δ_{enc}, one intra-frame body part segmentation branch Γ_{seg}, and one inter-frame label propagation branch Γ_{prop}. Γ_{prop} is designed to take into consideration multiple possible correspondences when calculating the label probabilities for one point to mitigate the occlusion issue. To encourage consistent outputs from Γ_{seg} and Γ_{prop}, we further introduce a consistency loss between their outputs as a mutual regularization. During testing, we propose a multi-source inference (MSI) scheme to further improve body parsing performance. MSI splits the whole video into multiple short clips and selects a *key* frame to represent each clip. Since propagations from key frames are often more accurate, MSI utilizes the trained segmentation branch to generate results for

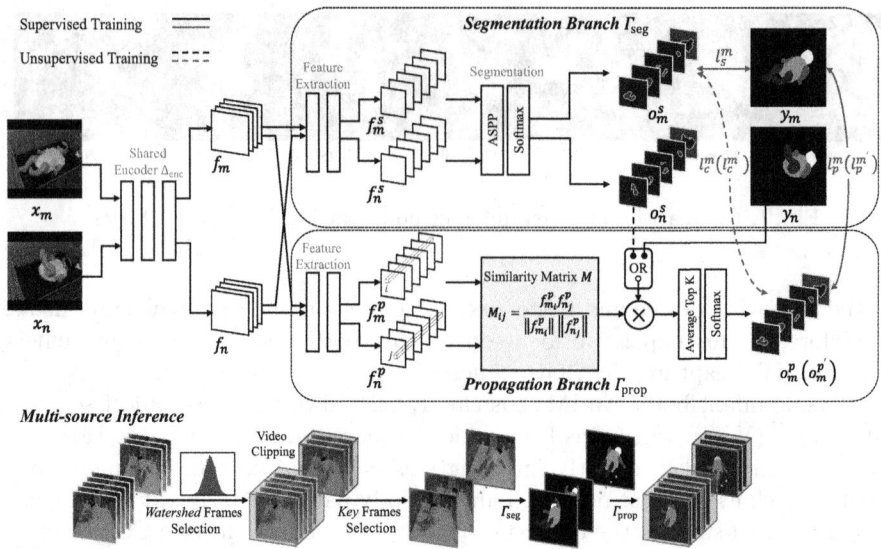

Fig. 2. The overall framework of SiamParseNet (SPN). Top: semi-supervised training framework. Bottom: multi-source Inference for generating test results.

key frames and the trained propagation branch to generate results for other non-key frames. Our proposed methods are validated on an IMV dataset [21] and have shown noticeably better performances when compared with several other state-of-the-art image/video segmentation methods [5,14,18,19]. An example of comparing the result of SPN with other methods is shown in Fig. 1. We also conduct various ablation studies to show the importance of our proposed joint training, consistency loss, adaptive semi-supervised training process, and multi-source inference. To the best of our knowledge, our work is the first attempt towards solving the IMV infant body parsing problem under the semi-supervised learning setting.

2   Methodology

Figure 2 shows the overall framework of our proposed SiamParseNet (SPN). The training of SPN takes as input a pair of frames from the same video, and the inherent siamese structure of SPN enables its training with any pair of frames regardless of the availability of annotation. The flexibility of the siamese structure of SPN significantly augments the number of available training examples as well as maximizes the utilization of partially labeled data. More specifically, we consider three different training modes according to the availability of labels for a paired input: the fully supervised mode which takes as input a pair of frames that are both annotated, the semi-supervised mode which has one frame in the input pair annotated, and the unsupervised mode which takes a pair of input frames that are both unannotated. During training, we adopt an adaptive alternative training (AAT) process that relies more on the supervised mode at the early stages and then gradually incorporate more semi-supervised and unsupervised training at later stages. During testing, a multi-source inference mechanism is utilized to achieve robust segmentation taking advantage of both the trained segmentation branch Γ_{seg} and propagation branch Γ_{prop}. Next, we explain the SPN semi-supervised training framework, the adaptive alternative training process, and the multi-source inference procedure in more details.

2.1 Semi-supervised Learning

Given a pair of input frames x_m and x_n, we first employ the shared encoder Δ_{enc} to extract their visual feature maps f_m and f_n. We then feed this pair of feature maps to branch Γ_{seg} and Γ_{prop}. Γ_{seg} further processes f_m and f_n as f_m^s and f_n^s and generates segmentation probability maps o_m^s and o_n^s with a segmentation network. Γ_{prop} encodes f_m and f_n as f_m^p and f_n^p to calculate a similarity matrix M in feature space. Using M, Γ_{prop} can generate the final segmentation maps o_n^p and o_m^p through different paths, depending on the availability of ground truth labels for x_m and x_n.

Case 1: When both frames x_m and x_n are annotated with ground truth label maps y_m and y_n, we have the fully supervised training mode. In this mode, Γ_{prop} takes the ground truth segmentation map from one frame and propagates it to another frame (solid line in Fig. 2). The overall loss l_{sup} is calculated as:

$$l_{\text{sup}} = l_s^m + l_s^n + l_p^m + l_p^n + \lambda \left(l_c^m + l_c^n \right), \tag{1}$$

where all losses are cross-entropy losses between one-hot vectors. More specifically, l_s^m and l_s^n are segmentation losses of Γ_{seg} between o_m^s and y_m, o_n^s and y_n, respectively. l_p^m and l_p^n are losses of Γ_{prop} between o_m^p and y_m, o_n^p and y_n. The consistency loss l_c measures the degree of overlapping between outputs of the two branches Γ_{seg} and Γ_{prop}, where λ is a scaling factor to ensure l_c have roughly the same magnitude as l_s and l_p.

Case 2: When none of the input frames are labeled, which is the unsupervised training mode, Γ_{prop} propagates the segmentation map of one frame generated by Γ_{seg} to another (dotted line in Fig. 2). More specifically, Γ_{prop} utilizes the outputs of Γ_{seg}, o_m^s and o_n^s, and transforms them to obtain its probabilistic maps $o_n^{p'}$ and $o_m^{p'}$. Since no ground truth label is available, the loss is calculated as the consistency loss between the two branches:

$$l_{\text{un}} = \lambda \left(l_c^{m'} + l_c^{n'} \right). \tag{2}$$

Case 3: If only one input frame is annotated, we have the semi-supervised training mode. Without loss of generality, let us assume that y_m is available and y_n is not. Then, Γ_{prop} propagates from Γ_{seg}'s output o_n^s instead of y_n to generate the probability map $o_m^{p'}$, as the dotted line in Fig. 2 shows. We compute the losses $l_p^{m'}$ and $l_c^{m'}$, which measure the loss between $o_m^{p'}$ and y_m, $o_m^{p'}$ and o_m^s, respectively. We also calculate l_s^m and l_c^n, which measure the loss between o_m^s and y_m, o_n^p and o_n^s, respectively. Thus, the overall loss is:

$$l_{\text{semi}} = l_s^m + l_p^{m'} + \lambda \left(l_c^{m'} + l_c^n \right). \tag{3}$$

As a general framework, SPN can employ various networks as its backbone. Without loss of generality, we follow DeepLab [4,5] and choose the first three blocks of ResNet101 [8] as encoder Δ_{enc}. For branch Γ_{seg}, we employ the 4th block of ResNet101 to further extract features with the ASPP [4] module. Branch Γ_{prop} also utilizes the 4th block of ResNet101 for feature representation. Note that the two branches do not share the same weights and the weights are updated separately during training.

To propagate a given source segmentation map to a target frame, similar to [10], we first calculate the cosine similarity matrix M of f_m^p and f_n^p as

$$M_{ij} = \frac{f_{m_i}^p \cdot f_{n_j}^p}{\|f_{m_i}^p\| \, \|f_{n_j}^p\|}, \tag{4}$$

where M_{ij} is the affinity value between $f_{m_i}^p$, point i in map f_m^p, and $f_{n_j}^p$, point j in map f_n^p. $\|\cdot\|$ indicates the L2 norm. Then, given the source segmentation map $\hat{y}_n$ (either ground truth y_n or Γ_{seg} generated o_n^s), and the similarity matrix M, Γ_{prop} produces $o_{m_i}^p$, point i in output map o_m^p as

$$o_{m_i}^p = \text{softmax} \left(\frac{1}{K} \sum\nolimits_{j \in \text{Top}(M_i, K)} M_{ij} \hat{y}_{n_j} \right), \tag{5}$$

where $\text{Top}(M_i, K)$ contains the indices of the top K most similar scores in the ith row of M. Since Γ_{prop} considers multiple correspondences for a point rather than one-to-one point correspondences as in optical flow [11,16,22], SPN can naturally better handle occlusions in IMVs than optical flow based methods.

2.2   Adaptive Alternative Training

As mentioned briefly in the beginning of Sect. 2, during the training of SPN, we adopt an adaptive alternative training (AAT) process to alternatively use different training modes to achieve optimal performance. Intuitively, SPN should rely more on the supervised mode at early stages and then gradually incorporate more semi-supervised and unsupervised training at later stages of training. To dynamically adjust the proportion of different training modes, we propose AAT to automatically sample training data among the three cases. Assume that the probabilities of selecting case 1, case 2, and case 3 for any iteration/step of training are p_1, p_2, and p_3, respectively. Considering case 2 and case 3 both involve utilizing unlabeled frames, we set $p_2 = p_3 = \frac{1-p_1}{2}$. Thus we only need to control the probability of choosing case 1 training and the other two cases are automatically determined. For AAT, we use an annealing temperature t to gradually reduce p_1 as training continues, where p_1 is computed as

$$p_1 = \max \left(1 - (1 - \mathbb{P}_1) \left(\frac{i}{i_{\max}} \right)^t, \mathbb{P}_1 \right), \tag{6}$$

where i is the training step, $\mathbb{P}_1$ is the pre-defined lower bound probability of p_1, $i_{\max}$ is the maximum number of steps of using AAT.

2.3 Multi-source Inference for Testing

To further mitigate the occlusion issue during testing, we exploit the capabilities of both trained branches in SPN by a multi-source inference (MSI) mechanism, as illustrated in the bottom part of Fig. 2. While the propagation branch could generate more desirable results than the segmentation branch, an appropriate source frame needs to be chosen to alleviate the occlusion issue during propagation. To this end, we propose to choose *key* frames as source frames for propagation. For each testing IMV, we calculate the pixel differences between consecutive frames. The differences are modeled by a Gaussian distribution, and its α-th percentile is chosen as the threshold to sample a series of *watershed* frames, whose pixel differences are higher than the threshold. We then segment the video into multiple clips delimited by watershed frames, so that infant poses and appearances are similar within the same clip. Then, we choose the middle frame of each clip as the *key* frame for that clip. The intuition behind the choice is that middle frames have the least cumulative temporal distance from other frames [7] and thus can better represent the clip that it is in. During inference, Γ_{seg} first segments the selected key frames to provide propagation sources. Then, for other non-key frames within a clip, Γ_{prop} takes the corresponding key frame's segmentation output and propagates it to all other non-key frames in the clip. By splitting a long video into short video clips and using key frames to provide local context and source of propagation within each short clip, the proposed MSI can effectively mitigate the occlusion problem in IMVs.

3 Experiments

We conduct extensive experiments on an IMV dataset collected from a GMA platform [21]. 20 videos with infants' ages ranging from 0 to 6 months are recorded by either medical staff in hospitals or parents at home. The original videos are very long and they are downsampled every 2 to 5 frames to remove some redundant frames. All frames are resized to the resolution of 256×256 and some of the frames are annotated with five categories: background, head, arm, torso, and leg. This challenging dataset covers large varieties of video content, including different infant poses, body appearance, diverse background, and viewpoint changes. We randomly divide the dataset into 15 training videos and 5 testing videos, resulting in $1,267$ labeled frames and $21,154$ unlabeled frames in the training set, and 333 labeled frames and $7,246$ unlabeled frames in the testing set. We evaluate all methods with Dice coefficient on labeled testing frames. We represent each pixel label in the segmentation map as a one-hot vector, where background pixels are ignored when calculating Dice to focus on the body parts. Dice scores of each labeled testing frame are averaged to get the final mean Dice.

Table 1. Quantitative comparison of different methods.

Methods	Dice
U-Net [18]	46.12
DeepLab V3+ [5]	73.32
COSNet [14]	79.22
RVOS [19]	**81.98**
SPN w/o SSL	82.31
SPN	**83.43**

(a) Comparison between SPN and current state-of-the-art methods.

Methods	Dice
Single-Γ_{seg}	71.82
SPN-Γ_{seg}	**81.33**
SPN w/o l_c	81.38
SPN w/o SSL	**82.31**
SPN $t = 1.4$	82.88
SPN $t = 0.9$	82.79
SPN $t = 0.4$	**83.43**

(b) Ablation study of SPN.

Methods	0/15	8/15	10/15
SPN w/o SSL	82.31	77.83	72.93
SPN	83.43	80.50	78.56
Dice Gain	1.12	2.67	**5.63**

(c) SPN without and with SSL trained using different numbers of completely unlabeled videos, out of the 15 training videos.

3.1 Implementation Details

To accelerate training and reduce overfitting, similar to [4,5,14,19], we initialize the network parameters using weights from DeepLab V3+ [5] pretrained on the COCO dataset [13] for shared encoder Δ_{enc}, segmentation branch Γ_{seg} and propagation branch Γ_{prop}. For Γ_{prop}, we set K to be 20, after grid searching over the values of K from 5 to 20 with interval 5. The scaling factor λ in Eq. 1 is set to be 10^{-6}. To build the training set for SPN that consists of pairs of frames from the same videos, we collect input pairs for the three training modes separately. For training case 1 (*i.e.*, fully supervised mode), we take two randomly selected labeled frames and repeat the operation until $10,000$ image pairs are selected from $1,267$ labeled training frames, with $20,000$ images in total. For case 2 (*i.e.*, unsupervised mode), we randomly select two unlabeled frames and repeat until we have $10,000$ image pairs. For case 3 (*i.e.*, semi-supervised mode), we randomly choose one labeled frame and one unlabeled frame in the same video and repeat until we have $10,000$ image pairs. Then, the sampling of training input pairs from the built set follows Eq. 6, where we set $\mathbb{P}_1$ to be $1/3$ and $i_{\max}$ to be 20 epochs. Unless otherwise specified, t is set to be 0.4 in all experiments. We use the SGD optimizer with momentum 0.9. We set the initial learning rate to be 2.5×10^{-4} and adopt the poly learning rate policy [4] with power of 0.9. The training batch size is set to be 20. Traditional data augmentation techniques, such as color jittering, rotation, flipping, are also applied. We terminate the training until the pixel-level accuracy of both branches remains mostly unchanged for 2 epochs. During inference, we set α in the key frame selection algorithm to be 0.98.

3.2 Result Analysis

We compare our proposed SPN with current state-of-the-art methods, including single frame based U-Net [18] and DeepLab V3+ [5], and video based COS-Net [14] and RVOS [19] in Fig. 1 and Table 1(a). For fair comparison, except U-Net, all methods employ pretrained models from ImageNet [6] or COCO dataset [13]. DenseCRF [12] is also adopted as post-processing for all methods. From Fig. 1, one can observe that SPN clearly handles occlusion better than other

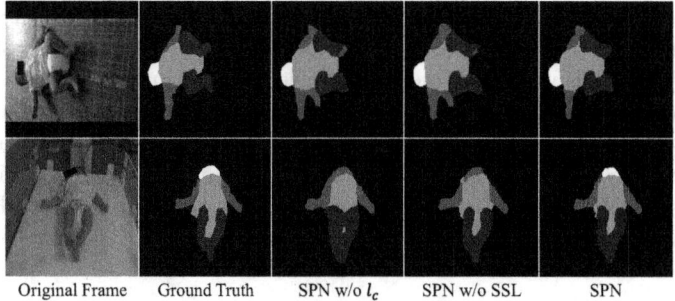

Original Frame   Ground Truth   SPN w/o l_c SPN w/o SSL   SPN

Fig. 3. Qualitative comparison of ablation study.

methods and shows better qualitative results. As Table 1(b) shows, SPN without semi-supervised learning (*i.e.*, fully supervised mode only) and the full SPN model with SSL have achieved substantially better quantitative performance when compared with previous state-of-the-art methods.

To validate the effect of joint training of Γ_{seg} and Γ_{prop}, we compare two variants of SPN under fully supervised training mode: [Single-Γ_{seg}] which is trained using only segmentation branch and [SPN-Γ_{seg}] which is trained jointly but only Γ_{seg} is used for all testing frames. Since Γ_{prop} is not available, multi-source inference is not used during test. As Table 1(b) shows, compared with [Single-Γ_{seg}], joint training of SPN greatly boosts the mean dice of Γ_{seg} by over 9%, which can be contributed to the siamese structure, the shared encoder, the consistency loss, among others. To further validate the effect of the consistency loss, we also compare two variants of the SPN model: [SPN w/o l_c] which is SPN trained without using consistency loss and SSL, and [SPN w/o SSL] which is SPN trained with consistency loss but without SSL. For both variants, MSI is used for testing. As shown in Table 1(b), [SPN w/o SSL] gives better mean Dice than [SPN w/o l_c], which demonstrates the usefulness of the consistency loss, even in the fully supervised setting. In addition, by comparing the results of [SPN-Γ_{seg}] and [SPN w/o SSL], one can see the effectiveness of MSI since the only difference between those two models is the multi-source inference.

For full SPN model with SSL, we experiment with different values of the annealing temperature t in AAT (Eq. 6). From Table 1(b), one can observe that [SPN w/ SSL] outperforms all other variants including the one without SSL, and the best model comes with $t = 0.4$, which we set as the default value in all other experiments. Qualitatively, from Fig. 3, one can see that different from other variants of SPN, our full SPN model avoids mis-segmentation of shadows and occluded head region, giving the best segmentation performance.

To further demonstrate the power of semi-supervised learning in our proposed SPN, we experiment with a *video-level* SSL setting: we randomly choose a certain number of training videos and remove **ALL** annotations from those videos. This setting is more stringent than the one used in [11], which showed promising results with a *frame-level* SSL setting: they removed labels of some frames in each video but all training video are still partially labeled. For our experiment using the *video-level* SSL, we compare the performances of the [SPN w/o SSL] and the full SPN models when only keeping labeled frames in 7 training videos (and using 8 training videos without labels), and when only keeping labels in 5 videos (and using 10 without labels). As shown in Table 1(c), with fewer annotated videos, the full SPN with SSL clearly shows significant performance gains (up to 5.63%) than [SPN w/o SSL]. Such results indicate the potential of SPN under various semi-supervised learning scenarios.

4   Conclusions

In this paper, we propose SiamParseNet, a novel semi-supervised framework for joint learning of body parsing and label propagation in IMVs toward computer-assisted GMA. Our proposed SPN exploits a large number of unlabeled frames in IMVs via adaptive alternative training of different training modes and shows superior performance under various semi-supervised training settings. Combined with multi-source inference for testing, SPN not only has great potential in infant body parsing but can also be easily adapted to other video based segmentation tasks such as instrument segmentation in surgical videos.

References

1. Adde, L., Helbostad, J., Jensenius, A., Taraldsen, G., Støen, R.: Using computer-based video analysis in the study of fidgety movements. Early Hum. Dev. **85**, 541–547 (2009)
2. Adde, L., Rygg, M., Lossius, K., Øberg, G.K., Støen, R.: General movement assessment: predicting cerebral palsy in clinical practise. Early Hum. Dev. **83**, 13–18 (2007)
3. Bertinetto, L., Valmadre, J., Henriques, J.F., Vedaldi, A., Torr, P.H.S.: Fully-convolutional siamese networks for object tracking. In: Hua, G., Jégou, H. (eds.) ECCV 2016. LNCS, vol. 9914, pp. 850–865. Springer, Cham (2016). https://doi.org/10.1007/978-3-319-48881-3_56
4. Chen, L.C., Papandreou, G., Kokkinos, I., Murphy, K., Yuille, A.L.: DeepLab: semantic image segmentation with deep convolutional nets, atrous convolution, and fully connected CRFs. IEEE Trans. Pattern Anal. Mach. Intell. **40**(4), 834–848 (2017)
5. Chen, L.-C., Zhu, Y., Papandreou, G., Schroff, F., Adam, H.: Encoder-decoder with atrous separable convolution for semantic image segmentation. In: Ferrari, V., Hebert, M., Sminchisescu, C., Weiss, Y. (eds.) ECCV 2018. LNCS, vol. 11211, pp. 833–851. Springer, Cham (2018). https://doi.org/10.1007/978-3-030-01234-2_49
6. Deng, J., Dong, W., Socher, R., Li, L.J., Li, K., Fei-Fei, L.: ImageNet: a large-scale hierarchical image database. In: Proceedings of the IEEE Conference on Computer Vision and Pattern Recognition (CVPR), pp. 248–255 (2009)
7. Griffin, B.A., Corso, J.J.: BubbleNets: Learning to select the guidance frame in video object segmentation by deep sorting frames. In: Proceedings of the IEEE Conference on Computer Vision and Pattern Recognition (CVPR), pp. 8914–8923 (2019)

8. He, K., Zhang, X., Ren, S., Sun, J.: Deep residual learning for image recognition. In: Proceedings of the IEEE Conference on Computer Vision and Pattern Recognition (CVPR), pp. 770–778 (2016)

9. Hesse, N., et al.: Learning an infant body model from RGB-D data for accurate full body motion analysis. In: Frangi, A.F., Schnabel, J.A., Davatzikos, C., Alberola-López, C., Fichtinger, G. (eds.) MICCAI 2018. LNCS, vol. 11070, pp. 792–800. Springer, Cham (2018). https://doi.org/10.1007/978-3-030-00928-1_89

10. Hu, Y.-T., Huang, J.-B., Schwing, A.G.: VideoMatch: matching based video object segmentation. In: Ferrari, V., Hebert, M., Sminchisescu, C., Weiss, Y. (eds.) ECCV 2018. LNCS, vol. 11212, pp. 56–73. Springer, Cham (2018). https://doi.org/10.1007/978-3-030-01237-3_4

11. Jin, Y., Cheng, K., Dou, Q., Heng, P.-A.: Incorporating temporal prior from motion flow for instrument segmentation in minimally invasive surgery video. In: Shen, D., et al. (eds.) MICCAI 2019. LNCS, vol. 11768, pp. 440–448. Springer, Cham (2019). https://doi.org/10.1007/978-3-030-32254-0_49

12. Krähenbühl, P., Koltun, V.: Efficient inference in fully connected CRFs with gaussian edge potentials. In: Advances in Neural Information Processing Systems, pp. 109–117 (2011)

13. Lin, T.-Y., et al.: Microsoft COCO: common objects in context. In: Fleet, D., Pajdla, T., Schiele, B., Tuytelaars, T. (eds.) ECCV 2014. LNCS, vol. 8693, pp. 740–755. Springer, Cham (2014). https://doi.org/10.1007/978-3-319-10602-1_48

14. Lu, X., Wang, W., Ma, C., Shen, J., Shao, L., Porikli, F.: See more, know more: unsupervised video object segmentation with co-attention siamese networks. In: Proceedings of the IEEE Conference on Computer Vision and Pattern Recognition (CVPR), pp. 3623–3632 (2019)

15. Marcroft, C., Khan, A., Embleton, N.D., Trenell, M., Plötz, T.: Movement recognition technology as a method of assessing spontaneous general movements in high risk infants. Front. Neurol. 5, 284 (2014)

16. Meister, S., Hur, J., Roth, S.: UnFlow: unsupervised learning of optical flow with a bidirectional census loss. In: Thirty-Second AAAI Conference on Artificial Intelligence (2018)

17. Richards, C.L., Malouin, F.: Cerebral palsy: definition, assessment and rehabilitation. In: Handbook of Clinical Neurology, vol. 111, pp. 183–195. Elsevier (2013)

18. Ronneberger, O., Fischer, P., Brox, T.: U-Net: convolutional networks for biomedical image segmentation. In: Navab, N., Hornegger, J., Wells, W.M., Frangi, A.F. (eds.) MICCAI 2015. LNCS, vol. 9351, pp. 234–241. Springer, Cham (2015). https://doi.org/10.1007/978-3-319-24574-4_28

19. Ventura, C., Bellver, M., Girbau, A., Salvador, A., Marques, F., Giro-i Nieto, X.: RVOS: end-to-end recurrent network for video object segmentation. In: Proceedings of the IEEE Conference on Computer Vision and Pattern Recognition (CVPR), pp. 5277–5286 (2019)

20. Xingjian, S., Chen, Z., Wang, H., Yeung, D.Y., Wong, W.K., Woo, W.C.: Convolutional LSTM network: a machine learning approach for precipitation nowcasting. In: Advances in Neural Information Processing Systems, pp. 802–810 (2015)

21. Zhang, Q., Xue, Y., Huang, X.: Online training for body part segmentation in infant movement videos. In: 2019 IEEE 16th International Symposium on Biomedical Imaging (ISBI 2019), pp. 489–492. IEEE (2019)

22. Zhu, X., Xiong, Y., Dai, J., Yuan, L., Wei, Y.: Deep feature flow for video recognition. In: Proceedings of the IEEE Conference on Computer Vision and Pattern Recognition (CVPR), pp. 2349–2358 (2017)

Orchestrating Medical Image Compression and Remote Segmentation Networks

Zihao Liu[1,2(✉)], Sicheng Li[2], Yen-kuang Chen[2], Tao Liu[1], Qi Liu[3], Xiaowei Xu[4], Yiyu Shi[4], and Wujie Wen[3]

[1] FIU, Miami, FL, USA
zliu021@fiu.edu
[2] Alibaba DAMO Academy, Hangzhou, China
[3] Lehigh University, Bethlehem, PA, USA
[4] University of Notre Dame, Notre Dame, IN, USA

Abstract. Deep learning-based medical image segmentation on the cloud offers superb performance by harnessing the recent model innovation and hardware advancement. However, one major factor that limits its overall service speed is the long data transmission latency, which could far exceed the segmentation computation time. Existing image compression techniques are unable to achieve an efficient compression to dramatically reduce the data offloading overhead, while maintaining a high segmentation accuracy. The underlying reason is that they are all developed upon human visual system, whose image perception pattern could be fundamentally different from that of deep learning-based image segmentation. Motivated by this observation, in this paper, we propose a generative segmentation architecture consisting of a compression network, a segmentation network and a discriminator network. Our design orchestrates and coordinates segmentation and compression for simultaneous improvements of segmentation accuracy and compression efficiency, through a dedicated GAN architecture with novel loss functions. Experimental results on 2D and 3D medical images demonstrate that our design can reduce the bandwidth requirement by 2 orders-of-magnitude comparing with that of uncompressed images, and increase the accuracy of remote segmentation remarkably over the state-of-the-art solutions, truly accelerating the cloud-based medical imaging service.

1 Introduction

Recent advances in deep learning have significantly boosted the performance of automatic medical image segmentations [6,7,9,13,22,26,31]. However, such methods usually incur extremely high computational cost [36]. For example, segmenting a 3D Computed Tomography (CT) volume with a typical neural

Electronic supplementary material The online version of this chapter (https://doi.org/10.1007/978-3-030-59719-1_40) contains supplementary material, which is available to authorized users.

A. L. Martel et al. (Eds.): MICCAI 2020, LNCS 12264, pp. 406–416, 2020.
https://doi.org/10.1007/978-3-030-59719-1_40

network [5] involves 2.2 Tera floating-point operations (TFLOPs), making the real-time service impossible with a resource-constraint local computing device. The problem becomes more prominent considering the exponentially growing number of medical images in the past decade [12]. A viable solution is to have the cloud computing platforms to conduct the deep learning-based analyses [21,38,39].

However, the modern medical imaging requires significantly large data volume to represent high resolution and graphical fidelity, posing severe challenges on the data transmission from the local to the cloud. The latency overhead brought by such data transmission could be much longer than that of deep learning computations which are accelerated by clusters of GPUs, hence dominates the overall service time [18]. For example, as long as 13 s are required to transmit one 3D CT image of size 300 MB [24], whereas the state-of-the-art segmentation network only takes about a hundred milliseconds to process on the cloud [11,16,20].

A common practice to lower such excessive data transfer overhead would be image compression. While many popular standards like JPEG [34], JPEG-2000 [2,3], MPEG [15], as well as their enhanced versions [4,19,27,28,35], can partially address this issue, the achievable compression rate improvement is limited because all the solutions need to guarantee the image's visual quality for human eyes, rather than deep learning systems. Image compression using neural network-based auto-encoders [1,8,17,23,33] can surpass aforementioned standards, however, the underlying constraint is still the human perceived image quality measurement like PNSR and SSIM, instead of deep learning accuracy. The most recent work [33] proposed to directly use the compressed representation from the encoder to accelerate the computation of image classification and segmentation, unfortunately, there exist two drawbacks which make such a solution very impractical on medical imaging: 1) limited compression rate due to its focus on minimizing the pixel-wise difference between original image and reconstruct image; 2) unacceptable accuracy loss comparing with that of uncompressed images. Apparently, almost all the above compression methods are designed to minimize the human visual distortion, however, when processing image at the cloud side the image quality is usually judged by network performance (e.g., segmentation accuracy) rather than human vision. As a result, it naturally brings up several interesting questions: *1) Can we design a compression method optimal for deep learning-based image segmentation instead of human vision? 2) If so, how should we design that? Is it possible to design a* **matched** *pair of compression and segmentation network for the whole process? Will the achievable compression rate and segmentation quality under such a method outperform the existing solutions significantly?*

In this work, we propose to orchestrate medical image compression and segmentation networks for efficient data transmission as well as high segmentation accuracy. Particularly, our end-to-end method trains multiple neural networks simultaneously for both image compression locally and segmentation in the cloud using adversarial learning, thus to make the two steps matched to extract and retain the most important features for segmentation. The neural network for image compression is designed to be light-weighted, which fits well for local processing. The main contributions of our work are as follows: 1) We propose a joint method to integrate the compression network and the generative segmentation network (with a discriminator network), so as to fully unleash the compression potential on medical imaging; 2) We design a series of training loss functions to optimize the compressive segmentation in the proposed network architecture, to achieve high compression rate while maintaining the segmentation accuracy; 3) We conduct comprehensive evaluations on 2D and 3D medical images and report that our method outperforms latest solutions in two aspects: for the same compression rate, our method achieves better segmentation accuracy; for the same level of segmentation accuracy, it offers remarkable compression rate improvement compared with the state-of-the-art designs. These advantages demonstrate great potentials for its applications in today's deep neural network assisted medical image segmentation.

2   Method

Figure 1 depicts an overview of our proposed design, which consists of three integrated components: the compression network (C), the segmentation network (S) and the discrimination network (D). Specifically, 1) C functions as a lossy image compression engine to ensure efficient data transmission. Also, the compression network should be light-weighted for fast processing on resource-constraint local computing devices; 2) The segmentation network S could be any commonly-used segmentor s with feature reconstruction layers g. Instead of reconstructing the whole image, g only reconstructs the essential feature maps that will be used to generate a probability label map by segmentor. 3) The discriminator D aims to capture any difference between the predicted label map from S and the corresponding ground truth label map. C, S and D are alternatively trained in an adversarial fashion by solving a min-max optimization problem. The goal is to achieve a high compression ratio, under the guidance of DNN-based segmentation quality measurement (NOT human perceived image quality), so as to facilitate data transmission while providing similar or even higher segmentation accuracy for better Quality-of-Service (QoS).

Note that the compressed bitstream sent to the cloud will be only used by segmentation networks in order to generate accurate segmentation label maps. Such predicted label maps, together with the local stored high-resolution image copies, will assist doctors for medical diagnosis, surgical planning/treatment etc. Therefore, the compression network does not necessarily preserve high image visual quality, but to guarantee the correct segmentation results.

2.1   Network Architecture Design

Compression Network (C): Unlike the existing neural network-based compression methods which attempt to minimize the pixel-wise visual distortions between original image and reconstructed image, our compression network focuses on minimizing the difference between the predict label from S and ground truth label y for an input x, as well as the number of required bits $(-log_2 Q(C(x))$, where Q is a probabilistic model described in Sect. 2.2). This indicates that C is dedicated to compress images in an DNN-favorable manner to filter out the undesired features and aggressively improve the compression ratio. Figure 2(a) shows the detailed network architecture to compress 2D medical images. The compression network for 3D images is designed following the similar approach. To generate a lightweight network for efficient local processing, we limit model parameters by reducing the number of feature maps at each layer or directly dropping some convolutional layers The network profiling on the number of parameters and the number of computations required by C is 1.3 M and 8.1 GFLOPs, which are only 0.83% and 0.79% as that of a segmentation network [37]. For more details, please see our supplemental material.

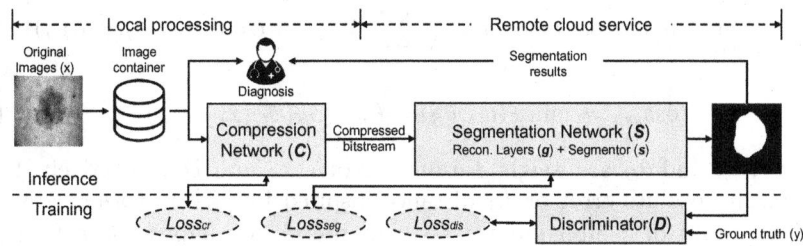

Fig. 1. Orchestrated medical image compression and remote segmentation networks.

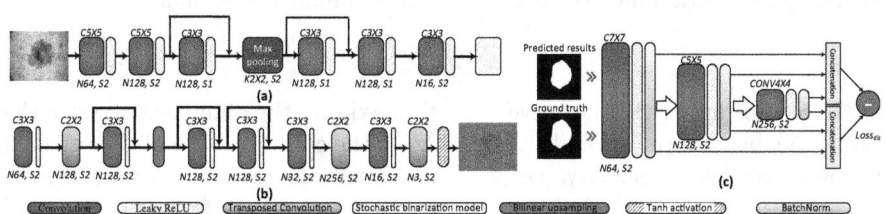

Fig. 2. Illustrations of (a) Compression network; (b) Feature reconstruction layers and (c) Discriminator network in our design.

Segmentation Network (S) and Discriminator (D): We do not intentionally design new segmentors, instead, we adopt existing representative networks for 2D and 3D segmentation tasks [14,37] so as to demonstrate the scalability of our design. For this purpose, we add the feature reconstruction layers (g) to ensure the output from compression network is compatible with any s. Note that our g does not try to reconstruct the whole detailed image, but features required information for s. Figure 2(b) illustrates the detail network structure. To further compensate the potential accuracy loss caused by the joint training of S and C, our method incorporates a discriminator D after the S, shown as

Fig. 2(c). The ground truth label map and predicted label map from S will be fed into D one by one, the output from each layer will concatenate together and then their difference will be used as the label feature loss to train C, S and D. One thing we'd emphasise is that the D is also segmentation accuracy guided, it only distinguish the label maps rather than the image quality, which is totally different from the previous works.

2.2   Training Loss Design

After determining the network architectures, we now design the loss function dedicated to each network for jointly training. Given a dataset with N training images x_n, and y_n as the corresponding ground truth label map, the multi-scale label feature loss ($loss_{dis}$) and segmentation loss ($loss_{seg}$) can be defined as follows:

$$loss_{dis} = \min_{\theta_C, \theta_S} \max_{\theta_D} \zeta(\theta_C, \theta_S, \theta_D) = \frac{1}{N} \sum_{n=1}^{N} \ell_{mae}(\phi_D(\phi_S(\phi_C(x_n))), \phi_D(y_n)) \quad (1)$$

$$loss_{seg} = \min_{\theta_C, \theta_S} \xi(\theta_C, \theta_S) = \ell_{mse}(\phi_S(\phi_C(x_n)), y_n) \quad (2)$$

where θ_C, θ_S and θ_D are weight parameters of C, S and D, respectively. ℓ_{mae} is the mean absolute error or L_1 distance inspired by [37], $\phi_S(\phi_C(x_n))$ is the prediction result of S after input x_n is compressed by compression network C and $\phi_D(\cdot)$ represents the multi-scale hierarchical features extracted from each convolutional layer in D. ℓ_{mse} is the MSE between predicted label from S and ground truth label. $\phi_C(\cdot)$, $\phi_S(\cdot)$ and $\phi_D(\cdot)$ represent the functionality of C, S and D, respectively. Thus, the loss for the discriminator is formulated as:

$$- loss_{dis} = - \min_{\theta_C, \theta_S} \max_{\theta_D} \zeta(\theta_C, \theta_S, \theta_D) \quad (3)$$

We set this loss with a negative value to maximize the difference between the predicted label and the ground truth label. On the contrary, we add the reserved version of this loss (positive value) to C and S, with the goal of minimizing such loss for the combined C and S. Therefore, the total loss for segmentor and compression network is:

$$loss_{total} = loss_{dis} + loss_{seg} = \min_{\theta_C, \theta_S} \xi(\theta_C, \theta_S) + \min_{\theta_C, \theta_S} \max_{\theta_D} \zeta(\theta_C, \theta_S, \theta_D) \quad (4)$$

Finally, we introduce a compression loss ($loss_{cr}$) to optimize the output of C for achieving the best compression rate. We use e to estimate the number of bits for the representation after C, e.g. entropy coding. Since this coding process is non-differentiable, we adopt a continuous differentiable Jensen's inequality [29] to estimate the upper bound of the number of required bits. This estimation is used to train the compression network [30]. Then the total loss for C is:

$$loss_{cr} + loss_{seg} + loss_{dis} = \underbrace{min(e(f(x_n)))}_{\text{\# of bits}} + \underbrace{\min_{\theta_C, \theta_S} \max_{\theta_D} \zeta(\theta_C, \theta_S, \theta_D) + \min_{\theta_C, \theta_S} \xi(\theta_C, \theta_S)}_{\text{Segmentation distortion}} \quad (5)$$

2.3   Training and Testing

Our training process follows an alternating fashion: for each training epoch, **1)** we fix the parameters of D and only train that of C and S for one step using above designed loss functions, i.e. $loss_{total}$ (Eq. 4) for g and segmentor s, and C has an extra loss $loss_{cr}$ (Eq. 5) to optimize the compression rate; Note that a stochastic binarization algorithm [32] is applied to the encoded data, i.e. the compressed representation is in binary format. **2)** We fix the parameters of C and S then train D by the gradients computed from its loss function ($loss_{dis}$). As Eq. 1 shows, this training process behaves more like a min-max game: while C and S try to minimize $loss_{dis}$, D attempts to maximize it. As a result, the network training gradually improves the segmentation results of S, as well as the compression efficiency of C after each epoch until reaching convergence. At the testing process, only C and S are used to predict the segmentation label maps and D is not involved.

3   Experiments and Results

3.1   Experimental Setup

Dataset. We use ISIC 2017 challenge dataset [10] to evaluate the 2D image segmentation. This fully annotated dataset provides 2000 training images, 150 validation images for the Lesion segmentation task. For 3D image segmentation, we select the HVSMR 2016 challenge dataset [25], which consists of 5 3D cardiac MR scans for training and 5 scans for testing. Each image includes three segmentation labels: myocardium, blood pool and background. Note that directly training with the large-size 3D medical images is not feasible, instead, we randomly crop the original image to many smaller pieces of data to facilitate training and overcome the overfitting, which is consistent with [18].

Target Designs. Our network architectures are realized by heavily modifying the adversarial segmentation network from SegAN [37] and incorporating our compression network, replacing the discriminator network, etc. Specifically, our networks include: **D1** with only segmentator S and discriminator D; **D2** with compression network C and segmentation network S but no discriminator; **D3** with all of the compression network C, segmentation network S and discriminator D, without considering the compression loss. This design is expected to offer the best segmentation accuracy, but limited compression efficiency; **D4** with compression loss upon **D3**. This design should achieve aggressive compression rate with slightly degraded segmentation accuracy. For a fair comparison, we adopt the traditional JPEG-2000, H.264, the auto encoder-based and the latest machine vision-based compression [18] in our evaluations. Note that the auto encoder-based compression (Auto/Seg) is implemented to reconstruct original image for segmentor. As such, we expect Auto/Seg should suffer from prominent segmentation accuracy loss at high compression rates. All the methods are evaluated under four aspects: *segmentation performance, compression efficiency, cloud-based service latency and visual analysis.*

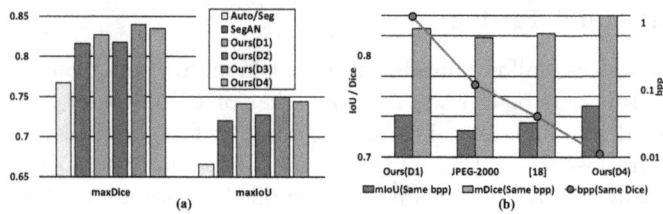

Fig. 3. (a) Segmentation results under different network configurations. (b) Segmentation accuracy and bpp comparisons with prior methods.

Table 1. 3D segmentation results on HVSMR 2016 challenge dataset [25]

	Myocardium						Blood pool					
	Dice			IoU			Dice			IoU		
	Uncomp.	[18]	Ours	Uncomp.	[18]	Ours	Uncomp.	[18]	Ours	Uncomp.	[18]	Ours
Img.1	0.895	0.868	0.899	0.809	0.756	0.817	0.915	0.876	0.927	0.844	0.818	0.864
Img.2	0.829	0.798	0.831	0.708	0.681	0.711	0.951	0.903	0.948	0.916	0.875	0.921
Img.3	0.811	0.782	0.815	0.672	0.652	0.674	0.883	0.858	0.888	0.807	0.754	0.808
Img.4	0.877	0.853	0.874	0.780	0.758	0.776	0.955	0.906	0.956	0.913	0.872	0.915
Img.5	0.809	0.778	0.810	0.679	0.647	0.681	0.883	0.849	0.881	0.806	0.779	0.788
Average	0.844	0.816	**0.846**	0.729	0.699	**0.732**	0.918	0.878	**0.920**	0.857	0.820	**0.859**
bpp	Uncompressed (~1.1)			H.264 (~0.15)			[18](~0.04)			**Ours(~0.014)**		

3.2 Evaluation Results

2D Segmentation. Figure 3(a) reports the Dice/IoU score of 2D segmentation on the selected designs with different architectures and component combinations. Our methods, instead of degrading any accuracy, can even improve the segmentation performance after image compression. In particular, **D1** achieves higher score over SegAN, indicating that the proposed predict-oriented discriminator can better improve the segmentation accuracy with the combination of $Loss_{seg}$ and $Loss_{dis}$ than the baseline adversarial segmentation network on uncompressed images. With the consideration of compression, **D3** and **D4** shows the best Dice and IoU. This is because our joint training process attempts to learn as many features as possible with the compression network, segmentation network and discriminator. As expected, Auto/Seg, which is designed under the guidance of human visual quality loss (e.g. MSE), achieves the lowest Dice/IoU among all the methods. Figure 3(b) shows the average bpp (bits per pixel) of each compression approaches. **D4** which is trained with additional compression loss $Loss_{cr}$, gives the best average bpp of 0.012. That is to say, our method significantly improves the image compression rate by almost two orders of magnitude than that of uncompressed images (average bpp of 1.24), by one order of magnitude than that of JPEG-2000 (average bpp of 0.12) and >3× than that of the latest [18] (average bpp of 0.04).

3D Segmentation. Table 1 shows the evaluation results on 3D image segmentation. We test 3D CMR volumes with segmentation targets "Myocardium" and

"Blood Pool", and compare the Dice/IoU scores with the uncompressed design and the method in [18]. For a fair comparison, we keep the compression rate at the same level as ours (bpp = 0.014). Compared with the uncompressed image segmentation, our design improves the average Dice/IoU score by 0.002/0.003 and 0.002/0.002 on "Myocardium" and "Blood Pool", respectively. Moreover, we demonstrate a significant improvement on Dice/IoU score comparing with the latest work [18], for the reason that this method cannot keep high segmentation accuracy at a high compression rate. These results show great scalability and outstanding segmentation performance of our design for 3D images.

Cloud-Based Service Latency. Table 2 shows a detailed latency breakdown to process a 3D CT image of size 300 MB. The computation latency on the cloud is evaluated by Nvidia GeForce GTX 1080 GPUs, while the image compression runs on an Intel Core i7-6850 CPU to emulate a resource-constraint local computing device and the data transmission speed is retrieved from [24]. Putting them together, our design only takes a total latency of 0.26s, which achieves 5.7× and 2.4× speedup over the JPEG-based design and [18], respectively. Since the data transmission time dominates the total service latency, significantly improving compression rate with our solution is essential for service speedup. Considering the impressive performance and low compression overhead, our solution will be very attractive for ever-increasing DNN based medical image analyses.

Table 2. Latency breakdown of the cloud-based service

	Volume(MB)	Trans.(s)	Compression(s)	Reconstruction(s)	Segmentation(s)	Total(s)
JPEG	30	1.4	0.0013	0.0013	0.1	1.5026
[18]	10	0.53	0.0015	0.0015	0.1	0.633
Ours	3.3	0.16	0.003	0.0003	0.1	0.2633

Visual Analysis. The second row from Fig. 4 represents the visualization results from feature reconstruction layers g before feeding into a segmentor s. Compared with original images, the reconstructed feature maps preserve limited visual quality for human vision, however guarantee a correct segmentation. These results also indicate that: 1) the original images with RGB channels or with an intensity channel are not always the optimal, instead, our single-channel reconstructed feature maps fit well with the segmentation tasks. 2) some undesired features have been removed. For example, the hairs in the original image of first column are eliminated, which actually make the segmentations more accurate. 3) all the reconstructed feature maps from both 2D or 3D images, are formed by many small blocks with the same patterns and such patterns can further improve compression rate.

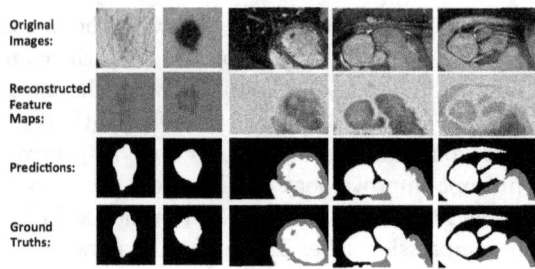

Fig. 4. The comparison between original images from 2D RGB dataset (left 2 columns) and 3D cardiovascular magnetic resonance (CMR) dataset (right 3 columns), reconstructed feature maps from feature reconstruction layers and the corresponding predicted label maps and ground truth label maps.

4   Conclusion

This work presents a generative segmentation architecture for compressed medical images. We propose to leverage the compression network and different loss function designs to enhance the cloud-based segmentation performance and efficiency by synthetically considering segmentation accuracy and compression rate. We conducted comprehensive evaluations on both 2D RGB and 3D CMR images and compared our design with state-of-the-art solutions. Experimental results show that our design not only significantly improves compression rate, but also increases the segmentation accuracy, outperforming the existing solutions by offering better efficiency on cloud-based image segmentation.

Acknowledgement. This work was supported in part by NSF Grants SPX-2006748 and SHF-2011236.

References

1. Agustsson, E., et al.: Generative adversarial networks for extreme learned image compression. arXiv:1804.02958 (2018)
2. Boliek, M.: Information technology JPEG 2000 image coding system: extensions for three-dimensional data. ISO/IEC 15444-10, ITU-T Rec. T.809 (2002)
3. Boliek, M.: JPEG 2000 image coding system: core coding system. ISO/IEC (2002)
4. Bruylants, T., et al.: Wavelet based volumetric medical image compression. Signal Process. Image Commun. **31**, 112–133 (2015)
5. Chen, J., et al.: Combining fully convolutional and recurrent neural networks for 3D biomedical image segmentation. In: Advances in Neural Information Processing Systems, pp. 3036–3044 (2016)
6. Chen, H., et al.: Deep contextual networks for neuronal structure segmentation. In: AAAI, pp. 1167–1173 (2016)
7. Chen, H., et al.: VoxResNet: deep voxelwise residual networks for brain segmentation from 3D MR images. NeuroImage **170**, 446–455 (2017)

8. Cheng, Z., Sun, H., Takeuchi, M., Katto, J.: Learning image and video compression through spatial-temporal energy compaction. In: Proceedings of the IEEE Conference on Computer Vision and Pattern Recognition, pp. 10071–10080 (2019)
9. Çiçek, Ö., Abdulkadir, A., Lienkamp, S.S., Brox, T., Ronneberger, O.: 3D U-Net: learning dense volumetric segmentation from sparse annotation. In: Ourselin, S., Joskowicz, L., Sabuncu, M.R., Unal, G., Wells, W. (eds.) MICCAI 2016. LNCS, vol. 9901, pp. 424–432. Springer, Cham (2016). https://doi.org/10.1007/978-3-319-46723-8_49
10. Codella, N.C., et al.: Skin lesion analysis toward melanoma detection: a challenge at the 2017 international symposium on biomedical imaging (ISBI), hosted by the international skin imaging collaboration (ISIC). In: 2018 IEEE 15th International Symposium on Biomedical Imaging (ISBI 2018), pp. 168–172. IEEE (2018)
11. Coomans, W., et al.: XG-fast: the 5th generation broadband. IEEE Commun. Mag. **53**(12), 83–88 (2015)
12. Dinov, I.D.: Volume and value of big healthcare data. J. Med. Stat. Inf. **4** (2016)
13. Dou, Q., Chen, H., Jin, Y., Yu, L., Qin, J., Heng, P.-A.: 3D deeply supervised network for automatic liver segmentation from CT volumes. In: Ourselin, S., Joskowicz, L., Sabuncu, M.R., Unal, G., Wells, W. (eds.) MICCAI 2016. LNCS, vol. 9901, pp. 149–157. Springer, Cham (2016). https://doi.org/10.1007/978-3-319-46723-8_18
14. Isensee, F., et al.: NNU-net: breaking the spell on successful medical image segmentation. arXiv preprint arXiv:1904.08128 (2019)
15. ITU-T, JTC: Generic coding of moving pictures and associated audio information-part 2: video (1995)
16. Kang, Y., et al.: Neurosurgeon: collaborative intelligence between the cloud and mobile edge. ACM SIGPLAN Notices **52**(4), 615–629 (2017)
17. Lee, J., Cho, S., Beack, S.K.: Context-adaptive entropy model for end-to-end optimized image compression. arXiv preprint arXiv:1809.10452 (2018)
18. Liu, Z., et al.: Machine vision guided 3d medical image compression for efficient transmission and accurate segmentation in the clouds. In: Conference on Computer Vision and Pattern Recognition (2019)
19. Liu, Z., et al.: DeepN-JPEG: a deep neural network favorable JPEG-based image compression framework. In: Proceedings of the 55th Annual Design Automation Conference, pp. 1–6 (2018)
20. Ma, Y., Jia, Z.: Evolution and trends of broadband access technologies and fiber-wireless systems. In: Tornatore, M., Chang, G.-K., Ellinas, G. (eds.) Fiber-Wireless Convergence in Next-Generation Communication Networks, pp. 43–75. Springer, Cham (2017). https://doi.org/10.1007/978-3-319-42822-2_2
21. Marwan, M., et al.: Using cloud solution for medical image processing: issues and implementation efforts. In: 2017 3rd International Conference of Cloud Computing Technologies and Applications (CloudTech), pp. 1–7. IEEE (2017)
22. Milletari, F., et al.: V-net: fully convolutional neural networks for volumetric medical image segmentation. In: 2016 Fourth International Conference on 3D Vision (3DV), pp. 565–571. IEEE (2016)
23. Minnen, D., et al.: Joint autoregressive and hierarchical priors for learned image compression. In: Advances in Neural Information Processing Systems, pp. 10771–10780 (2018)
24. Molla, R.: Fixed broadband speeds are getting faster - what's fastest in your city? (2017)

25. Pace, D.F., Dalca, A.V., Geva, T., Powell, A.J., Moghari, M.H., Golland, P.: Interactive whole-heart segmentation in congenital heart disease. In: Navab, N., Hornegger, J., Wells, W.M., Frangi, A.F. (eds.) MICCAI 2015. LNCS, vol. 9351, pp. 80–88. Springer, Cham (2015). https://doi.org/10.1007/978-3-319-24574-4_10

26. Ronneberger, O., Fischer, P., Brox, T.: U-Net: convolutional networks for biomedical image segmentation. In: Navab, N., Hornegger, J., Wells, W.M., Frangi, A.F. (eds.) MICCAI 2015. LNCS, vol. 9351, pp. 234–241. Springer, Cham (2015). https://doi.org/10.1007/978-3-319-24574-4_28

27. Sanchez, V., et al.: 3-D scalable medical image compression with optimized volume of interest coding. IEEE Trans. Med. Imaging **29**(10), 1808–1820 (2010)

28. Sanchez, V., Abugharbieh, R., Nasiopoulos, P.: Symmetry-based scalable lossless compression of 3D medical image data. IEEE Trans. Med. Imaging **28**(7), 1062–1072 (2009)

29. Theis, L., et al.: A note on the evaluation of generative models. arXiv preprint arXiv:1511.01844 (2015)

30. Theis, L., et al.: Lossy image compression with compressive autoencoders. arXiv preprint arXiv:1703.00395 (2017)

31. Wang, T., et al.: SCNN: a general distribution based statistical convolutional neural network with application to video object detection. In: The Thirty-Third AAAI Conference on Artificial Intelligence (AAAI 2019) (2019)

32. Toderici, G., et al.: Variable rate image compression with recurrent neural networks. arXiv preprint arXiv:1511.06085 (2015)

33. Torfason, R., et al.: Towards image understanding from deep compression without decoding. arXiv preprint arXiv:1803.06131 (2018)

34. Wallace, G.K.: The JPEG still picture compression standard. IEEE Trans. Consum. Electron. **38**(1), xviii–xxxiv (1992)

35. Xu, Z., et al.: Diagnostically lossless coding of X-ray angiography images based on background suppression. Comput. Electr. Eng. **53**, 319–332 (2016)

36. Xu, X., et al.: Scaling for edge inference of deep neural networks. Nat. Electron. **1**(4), 216 (2018)

37. Xue, Y., et al.: Segan: adversarial network with multi-scale L1 loss for medical image segmentation. Neuroinformatics **16**(3–4), 383–392 (2018)

38. Zhao, T., et al.: Cloud-based medical image processing system with anonymous data upload and download, US Patent 8,553,965, 8 October 2013

39. Zhao, T., et al.: Cloud-based medical image processing system with access control, US Patent 8,682,049, 25 March 2014

Bounding Maps for Universal Lesion Detection

Han Li[1,2], Hu Han[1,3(✉)], and S. Kevin Zhou[1,3(✉)]

[1] Medical Imaging, Robotics, Analytic Computing Laboratory/Engineering (MIRACLE), Key Laboratory of Intelligent Information Processing of Chinese Academy of Sciences (CAS), Institute of Computing Technology, CAS, Beijing, China
{hanhu,zhoushaohua}@ict.ac.cn
[2] University of Chinese Academy of Sciences, Beijing, China
[3] Peng Cheng Laboratory, Shenzhen, China

Abstract. (ULD) in computed tomography plays an essential role in computer-aided diagnosis systems. Many detection approaches achieve excellent results for ULD using possible bounding boxes (or anchors) as proposals. However, empirical evidence shows that using anchor-based proposals leads to a high false-positive (FP) rate. In this paper, we propose a **box-to-map** method to represent a bounding box with three soft continuous maps with bounds in x-, y- and xy-directions. The **bounding maps (BMs)** are used in two-stage anchor-based ULD frameworks to reduce the FP rate. In the 1st stage of the region proposal network, we replace the sharp binary ground-truth label of anchors with the corresponding xy-direction BM hence the positive anchors are now graded. In the 2nd stage, we add a branch that takes our continuous BMs in x- and y-directions for extra supervision of detailed **locations**. Our method, when embedded into three state-of-the-art two-stage anchor-based detection methods, brings a free detection accuracy improvement (e.g., a 1.68% to 3.85% boost of sensitivity at 4 FPs) without extra inference time.

Keywords: Universal Lesion Detection · Bounding box · Bounding map

1 Introduction

Universal Lesion Detection (ULD) in computed tomography (CT) images [1–8], which aims to localize different types of lesions instead of identifying lesion types [9–20], plays an essential role in computer-aided diagnosis (CAD) systems. Recently, deep learning-based detection approaches achieve excellent results for ULD [21,22] using possible bounding boxes (BBoxs) (or anchors) as proposals. However, empirical evidence shows that using anchor-based proposals leads to severe data imbalance (e.g., class and spatial imbalance) [23], which leads to

This work is supported in part by the Natural Science Foundation of China (grants 61672496), Youth Innovation Promotion Association CAS (grant 2018135) and Alibaba Group through Alibaba Innovative Research Program.

A. L. Martel et al. (Eds.): MICCAI 2020, LNCS 12264, pp. 417–428, 2020.
https://doi.org/10.1007/978-3-030-59719-1_41

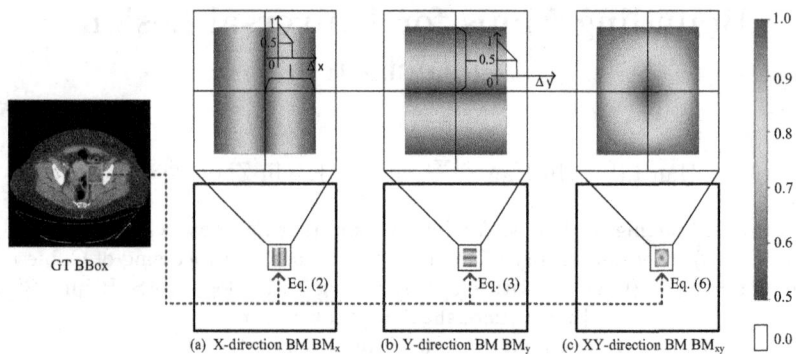

Fig. 1. The sharp GT BBox of an image is represented by three continuous 2D bounding maps (BMs) in (along) different directions (axes): (a) BM_x, (b) BM_y, (c) BM_{xy}.

a high false-positive (FP) rate in ULD. Therefore, there is an urgent need to reduce the FP proposals and improve the lesion detection performance.

Most existing ULD methods are mainly inspired by the successful deep models in object detection from natural images. Tang et al. [6] constructed a pseudo mask for each lesion region as the extra supervision information to adapt a Mask-RCNN [24] for ULD. Yan et al. [7] proposed a 3D Context Enhanced (3DCE) R-CNN model based on the model [25] pre-trained from ImageNet for 3D context modeling. Li et al. [8] proposed the so-called MVP-Net, which is a multi-view feature pyramid network (FPN) [26] with position-aware attention to incorporate multi-view information for ULD. Han et al. [27] leveraged cascaded multi-task learning to jointly optimize object detection and representation learning.

All the above approaches proposed for ULD are designed based on a two-stage anchor-based framework, i.e., proposal generation followed by classification and regression like Faster R-CNN [28]. They achieve good performance because: i) The anchoring mechanism is a good reception field initialization for limited-data and limited-lesion-category datasets. ii) The two-stage mechanism is a coarse-to-fine mechanism for the CT lesion dataset that only contains two categories ('lesion' or not), i.e., first finds lesion proposals and then removes the FP proposals. However, such a framework has two main limitations for effective ULD: (i) *The imbalanced anchors in stage-1.* (e.g., class, spatial imbalance [23]). In the first stage, anchor-based methods first find out the positive (lesion) anchors and use them as the region of interest (ROI) proposals according to the intersection over union (IoU) between anchors and ground-truth (GT) BBoxs. Hence, the number of positive anchors is decided by the IoU threshold and the amount of GT BBoxs per image. Specifically, an anchor is considered positive if its IoU with a GT BBox is greater than the IoU threshold and negative otherwise. This idea helps natural images to get enough positive anchors because they may have a lot of GT BBoxs per image, but it isn't suitable for ULD. Most CT slices only have one or two GT lesion BBox(s), so the amount of positive anchors is rather limited. This limitation can cause severe data imbalance and influence the training convergence of the whole network. Using a lower IoU threshold is a simple way

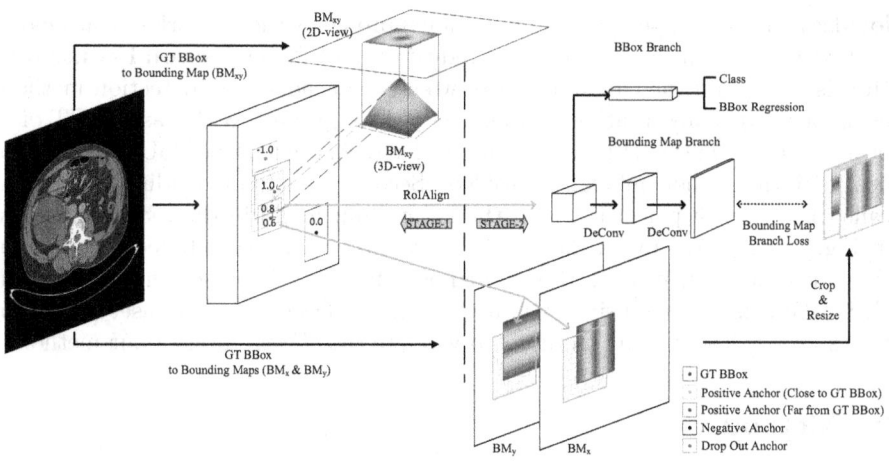

Fig. 2. The network architecture of the proposed ULD approach, in which, three proposed BMs in x-, y- and xy-directions are used in its two stages.

to get more positive anchors, but a lot of low-IoU anchors are labeled as positive can also lead to a high FP rate in ULD. (ii) *The insufficient supervision in stage-2.* In the second stage, each ROI proposal (selected anchor) from the first stage has one corresponding classification score to represent the possibility of containing lesions. The ROI proposals with high classification scores are chosen to obtain the final BBox prediction. ULD is a challenging task due to the similar appearances (e.g., intensity and texture) between lesions and other tissues; the non-lesion regions can also get very high scores. Hence, a single classification score can easily lead to FPs in ULD.

To address the anchor-imbalance problem, anchor-free methods [29,30] solve detection in a per-pixel prediction manner and achieve success in natural images with sufficient data and object categories. But for lesion detection (lesion or not) with limited data, they lack needed precision. To overcome the supervision-insufficient problem, Mask R-CNN-like [24] methods add a mask branch to introduce extra segmentation supervision and hence improve the detection performance. But it needs training segmentation masks that are costly to obtain.

In this paper, we present a continuous bounding map (BM) representation to enable the per-pixel prediction in the 1st stage and introduce extra-supervision in the 2nd stage of any anchor-based detection method. Our **first contribution** is a new box-to-map representation, which represents a BBox by three 2D bounding maps (BMs) in (along) three different directions (axes): x-direction (BM_x), y-direction (BM_y), and xy-direction (BM_{xy}), as shown in Fig. 1. The pixel values in BM_x and BM_y decrease from the centerline to the BBox borders in x and y directions respectively with a linear fashion, while the pixel values in BM_{xy} decrease from both two directions. Compared with a sharp binary representation (e.g., binary anchors label in RPN, binary segmentation mask in Mask R-CNN [24]), such a soft continuous map can provide a more detailed representation of

location. This (i.e., per-pixel & continuous) promotes the network to learn more contextual information [30], thereby reducing the FPs. Our **second contribution** is to expand the capability of a two-stage anchor-based detection method using our BM representation in a light way. First, we use BM_{xy} as the GT of a positive anchor in the first stage as in Fig. 2 and choose a proper IoU threshold to deal with the anchor imbalance problem. Second, we add one additional branch called BM branch paralleled with the BBox branch [28] in the second stage as in Fig. 3. The BM branch introduces extra supervision of detailed location to the whole network in a pixel-wise manner and thus decreases the FP rate in ULD. We conduct extensive experiments on the DeepLesion Dataset [31] with four state-of-the-art ULD methods to validate the effectiveness of our method.

2   Method

As shown in Fig. 2, we utilize BMs to reduce the ULD FP rate by replacing the original positive anchor class labels in stage-1 and adding a BM branch to introduce extra pixel-wise location supervision in stage-2. Section 2.1 details the BM representation and Sect. 2.2 defines the anchor labels for RPN training based on our BMs. Section 2.3 explains the newly introduced BM branch.

2.1   Bounding Maps

Motivated by [30], the BMs are formed in all-zero maps by only changing the value of pixels located within the BBox(s) as in Fig. 1. Let $(x_1^{(i)}, y_1^{(i)}, x_2^{(i)}, y_2^{(i)})$ be the ith lesion GT BBox of one CT image $I_{ct} \in \mathcal{R}^{W \times H}$, the set of coordinates within i^{th} BBox can be denoted as:

$$S_{BBox}^{(i)} = \{(x,y)|x_1^{(i)} \leq x \leq x_2^{(i)} \ \& \ y_1^{(i)} \leq y \leq y_2^{(i)}\}, \tag{1}$$

and the center point of this BBox lies at $(x_{ctr}^{(i)}, y_{ctr}^{(i)}) = (\frac{x_1^{(i)}+x_2^{(i)}}{2}, \frac{y_1^{(i)}+y_2^{(i)}}{2})$.

Within each BBox $S_{BBox}^{(i)}$, the pixel values in $BM_x^{(i)} \in \mathcal{R}^{W \times H}$ and $BM_y^{(i)} \in \mathcal{R}^{W \times H}$ decrease from 1 (center line) to 0.5 (border) in a linear fashion:

$$BM_x^{(i)}(x,y) = \begin{cases} 0 & (x,y) \notin S_{BBox}^{(i)} \\ 1 - k_x^{(i)} \left| x^{(i)} - x_{ctr}^{(i)} \right| & (x,y) \in S_{BBox}^{(i)} \end{cases}, \tag{2}$$

$$BM_y^{(i)}(x,y) = \begin{cases} 0 & (x,y) \notin S_{BBox}^{(i)} \\ 1 - k_y^{(i)} \left| y^{(i)} - y_{ctr}^{(i)} \right| & (x,y) \in S_{BBox}^{(i)} \end{cases}, \tag{3}$$

where $k^{(i)}$ is the slope of linear function in x-direction or y-direction, which is calculated according to the GT BBox's width $(x_2^{(i)} - x_1^{(i)})$ or height $(y_2^{(i)} - y_1^{(i)})$:

$$k_x^{(i)} = \frac{1}{x_2^{(i)} - x_1^{(i)}}, \quad k_y^{(i)} = \frac{1}{y_2^{(i)} - y_1^{(i)}}. \tag{4}$$

We take the sum of all the $BM_x^{(i)}$s and $BM_y^{(i)}$s to obtain the total $BM_x \in \mathcal{R}^{W \times H}$ and $BM_y \in \mathcal{R}^{W \times H}$ of one input image, respectively.

$$BM_x = \min \Big[\sum_{i=1}^{I} BM_x^{(i)}, 1 \Big], BM_y = \min \Big[\sum_{i=1}^{I} BM_y^{(i)}, 1 \Big], \tag{5}$$

where I is the number of GT BBox(s) of one CT image. Then the xy-direction BM $BM_{xy} \in \mathcal{R}^{W \times H}$ can be generated by calculating the square root of the product between BM_x and BM_y:

$$BM_{xy} = \sqrt[2]{BM_x \odot BM_y}, \tag{6}$$

where $\odot$ denotes the element-wise multiplication.

By introducing the above BMs, we expect they can promote network training and reduce FPs. Because the proposed BMs offer a soft continuous map about the lesion other than a sharp binary mask, which can convey more contextual information about the lesion, not only its location but also guidance of confidence. These properties are favourable for object detection task with irregular shapes and limited-amount GT BBox(s) like ULD.

2.2 Anchor Label in RPN

In the original two-stage anchor-based detection frameworks, RPN is trained to produce object bounds and objectness classification scores $\hat{C}_{ct} \in \mathcal{R}^{\frac{W}{R} \times \frac{H}{R} \times 1}$ at each position (or anchors' centerpoint), where R is the output stride. During training, all the anchors are first divided into three categories of positive (lesion), negative and drop-out anchors based on their IoUs with the GT BBoxs. Then the GT labels of positive, negative and drop-out anchors are set as 1, 0, -1 respectively and only the positive and negative anchors are used for loss calculation in RPN training.

In our proposed method, we still use 0 and -1 as the GT class labels of negative and drop-out anchors, but we set the class label of positive anchors as their corresponding value in $BM_{xy} \in \mathcal{R}^{W \times H}$. For size consistency, we first resize $BM_{xy} \in \mathcal{R}^{W \times H}$ to $BM_{xy}^r \in \mathcal{R}^{\frac{W}{R} \times \frac{H}{R} \times 1}$ to match the size of $\hat{C}_{ct} \in \mathcal{R}^{\frac{W}{R} \times \frac{H}{R} \times 1}$. Therefore, the GT label of anchor C_{anc} is given as:

$$C_{anc}(x, y, IoU_{anc}) = \begin{cases} 0 & IoU_{anc} \leq IoU_{min} \\ -1 & IoU_{min} < IoU_{anc} < IoU_{max} \\ BM_{xy}^r[x, y] & IoU_{anc} \geq IoU_{max} \end{cases}, \tag{7}$$

where (x, y) is the centerpoint coordinates of an anchor in $\hat{C}_{ct} \in \mathcal{R}^{\frac{W}{R} \times \frac{H}{R} \times 1}$ and IoU_{anc} denotes the IoU between the anchor and GT BBox.

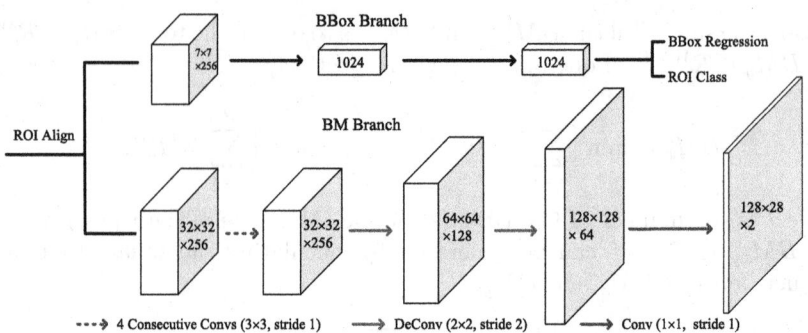

Fig. 3. BM branch is in parallel with BBox branch and applied separately to each ROI.

Anchor Classification Loss Function: For each anchor, the original RPN loss is the sum of anchor classification loss and BBox regression loss. However, the amount of GT BBox in one CT slice is usually more limited than one natural image. Hence a proper RPN IoU threshold is hard to find in ULD task: a higher IoU threshold can cause imbalanced anchors problem while a lower IoU threshold which causes too many low-IoU anchors' GT label are set as 1 can lead to a high FP rate. Therefore, we replace the original anchor classification loss with our proposed anchor classification loss:

$$\mathcal{L}_{anc} = \begin{cases} \mathcal{L}_2(\hat{C}_{anc}, C_{anc}) & IoU_{anc} \leq IoU_{min} \ \& IoU_{anc} \geq IoU_{max} \\ 0 & IoU_{min} < IoU_{anc} < IoU_{max} \end{cases}, \quad (8)$$

where $\mathcal{L}_2$ is the norm-2 loss, IoU_{min} and IoU_{max} denote the negative and positive anchor thresholds, respectively.

2.3   Bounding Map Branch

As shown in Fig. 3, the BM branch is similar to the mask branch in Mask R-CNN [24]. It is paralleled with the BBox branch and applied separately to each ROI. The branch consists of four 3×3 convolution, two 2×2 deconvolution and one 1×1 convolution layers. It takes ROI proposal feature map $F_{ROI} \in \mathcal{R}^{32 \times 32 \times 256}$ as input and aims to obtain the BM_x and BM_y proposals, denoted by $BM_x^{ROI} \in \mathcal{R}^{128 \times 128 \times 1}$ and $BM_y^{ROI} \in \mathcal{R}^{128 \times 128 \times 1}$, respectively:

$$[\hat{BM}_x^{ROI}, \hat{BM}_y^{ROI}] = H_{BM}(F_{ROI}), \quad (9)$$

where H_{BM} is the function of BM branch.

BM Branch Loss Function: For each ROI, BM_x and BM_y are first cropped based on the ROI BBox and resized to the size of the BM branch output to obtain $BM_x^{ROI} \in \mathcal{R}^{128 \times 128 \times 1}$ and $BM_y^{ROI} \in \mathcal{R}^{128 \times 128 \times 1}$. Then we concatenate

Table 1. Sensitivity (%) at various FPPI on the testing set of DeepLesion [31].

FPPI	@0.5	@1	@2	@3	@4
Faster R-CNN [28]	57.17	68.82	74.97	78.48	82.43
Faster R-CNN w/Ours	63.96 (**6.79**↑)	74.43 (**5.61**↑)	79.80 (**4.83**↑)	82.55 (**4.07**↑)	86.28 (**3.85**↑)
3DCE (9 slices) [7]	59.32	70.68	79.09	-	84.34
3DCE (9 slices) w/Ours	64.38 (5.06↑)	75.55 (4.87↑)	82.74 (3.65↑)	83.77 (-)	87.78 (3.44↑)
3DCE (27 slices) [7]	62.48	73.37	80.70	-	85.65
3DCE (27 slices) w/Ours	66.75 (4.27↑)	76.71 (3.34↑)	83.75 (3.05↑)	86.01 (-)	88.59 (2.94↑)
FPN-3DCE (9 slices) [26]	64.25	74.41	81.90	85.02	87.21
FPN-3DCE (9 slices) w/Ours	69.09 (4.84↑)	78.02 (3.61↑)	85.35 (3.45↑)	88.59 (3.57↑)	90.49 (3.28↑)
MVP-Net (3 slices) [8]	70.01	78.77	84.71	87.58	89.03
MVP-Net (3 slices) w/Ours	**73.32** (3.31↑)	**81.24** (2.47↑)	**86.75** (2.04↑)	**89.54** (1.96↑)	**90.71** (1.68↑)
FCOS (anchor-free) [29]	37.78	54.84	64.12	69.41	77.84
Objects as points (anchor-free) [30]	34.87	43.58	52.41	59.13	64.01

the two BMs into a multi-channel map and use it as the ground-truth for our BM branch. Therefore, the loss function of BM branch for each ROI can be defined as a norm-2 loss:

$$\mathcal{L}_{BM} = \mathcal{L}_2([\hat{BM}_x^{ROI}, \hat{BM}_y^{ROI}], [BM_x^{ROI}, BM_y^{ROI}]). \tag{10}$$

Full Loss Function: The full loss function of our method is given as:

$$\mathcal{L}_{full} = \frac{1}{M} \sum_{m=1}^{M} (\mathcal{L}_{reg}^{(m)} + \mathcal{L}_{anc}^{(m)}) + \frac{1}{N} \sum_{n=1}^{N} (\mathcal{L}_B^{(n)} + \mathcal{L}_{BM}^{(n)}), \tag{11}$$

where $\mathcal{L}_{reg}^{(m)}$ and $\mathcal{L}_B^{(n)}$ are the original box regression loss (in RPN) of the mth training (negative & positive) anchor and BBox branch loss of nth positive ROI in Faster R-CNN [28]. $\mathcal{L}_{anc}^{(m)}$ and $\mathcal{L}_{BM}^{(n)}$ denote our anchor classification loss and BM branch loss for m^{th} training anchors and n^{th} positive ROI. M and N are the number of training anchors and positive ROIs, respectively.

3   Experiments

3.1   Dataset and Setting

We conduct experiments using the DeepLesion dataset [31]. The dataset is a large-scale CT dataset with 32,735 lesions on 32,120 axial slices from 10,594 CT studies of 4,427 unique patients. Different from existing datasets that typically focus on one type of lesion, DeepLesion contains a variety of lesions with a variety of diameters ranges (from 0.21 to 342.5 mm). We rescale the 12-bit CT intensity range to [0, 255] with different window ranges proposed in different frameworks. Every CT slice is resized to 800 × 800, and the slice intervals are interpolated to 2 mm.[1] We conducted experiments on the official training (70%),

---

[1] We use a CUDA toolkit in [32] to speed up this process.

validation (15%), testing (15%) sets. The number of FPs per image (FPPI) is used as the evaluation metric, and we mainly compare the sensitivity at 4 FPPI for WRITING briefness, just as in [8].

We only use the horizontal flip as the training data augmentation and train them with stochastic gradient descent (SGD) for 15 epochs. The base learning rate is set as 0.002, and decreased by a factor of 10 after the 12th and 14th epoch. The models with our method utilize a lower positive anchor IoU threshold of 0.5, and the other network settings are the same as the corresponding original models.

3.2   Detection Performance

We perform experiment with three state-of-the-art two-stage anchor-based detection methods to evaluate the effectiveness of our approach. We also use two state-of-the-art anchor-free natural image detection methods for comparison.

- **3DCE.** The 3D context enhanced region-based CNN (3DCE) [7] is trained with 9 or 27 CT slices to form the 9-slice or 27-slice 3DCE.
- **FPN-3DCE.** The 3DCE [7] is re-implemented with the FPN backbone [26] and trained with 9 CT slices to form the 9-slice FPN-3DCE. The other network setting is consistent with the baseline 3DCE.
- **MVP-Net.** The multi-view FPN with position-aware attention network (MVP-Net) [8] is trained with 3 CT slices to form the 3-slice MVP-Net.
- **Faster R-CNN.** Similar to MVP-Net [8], we rescale an original 12-bit CT image with window ranges of [50, 449], [−505, 1980] and [446, 1960] to generate three rescaled CT images. Then we concatenate the three rescaled CT images into three channels to train a Faster R-CNN. The other network settings are the same as the baseline MVP-Net.
- **FCOS & Objects as points.** The experiment settings for the anchor-free methods, namely Fully Convolutional One-Stage Object Detection (FCOS) [29] and objects as points [30], are the same as the baseline Faster R-CNN.

As shown in Table 1, our method brings promising detection performance improvements for all baselines uniformly at different FPPIs. The improvement of Faster R-CNN [28], 9-slice 3DCE, 27-slice 3DCE and 9-slice FPN-3DCE are more pronounced than that of MVP-Net. This is because the MVP-Net is designed for reducing the FP rate in UDL and has achieved relatively high performance. Also, the anchor-free methods yields unsatisfactory results, and we think the main reason is that they completely discard the anchor and two-stage mechanism. Figure 4 presents a case to illustrate the effectiveness of our method in improving the performance of Faster-R-CNN.

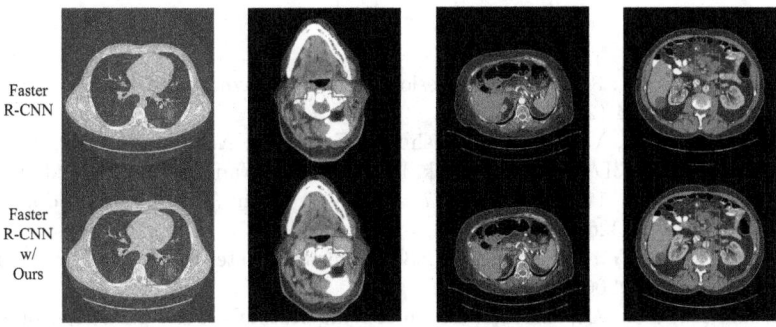

Fig. 4. High-classification-score results (above 0.9) of Faster R-CNN with or without our method on a test image. Green and red boxes corresponded to GT BBox and predicted BBox, respectively. The classification scores are marked in the images.

3.3 Ablation Study

We provide an ablation study about the two key components of the proposed approach, e.g., with vs. without using BM_{xy} in stage-1 and with vs. without using BM branch (BM_x & BM_y) in stage-2. We also perform a study to compare the efficiency between linear BMs and Gaussian BMs. As shown in Table 2, using BM_{xy} as the class label for positive anchors, we obtain a 2.27% improvement over the Faster R-CNN [28] baseline. Further adding a BM branch for introducing extra pixel-wise supervision accounts for another 1.14% improvement. Using both BM_{xy} and BM branch gives the best performance. Taking Gaussian BM instead linear BM does not bring improvement. The use of our method causes a minor influence to the inference time measured on a Titan XP GPU.

Table 2. Ablation study of our method at various FPs per image (FPPI).

Faster R-CNN [28]	BM_{xy}	BM_x&BM_y	Gaussian BM	$FPPI=2$	$FPPI=4$	Inference (s/img)
✓				74.97	78.48	0.3912
✓	✓			77.47	80.69	0.3946
✓	✓	✓		**79.80**	**82.55**	0.3946
✓	✓	✓	✓	78.44	82.37	0.4004

4 Conclusion

In this paper, we study how to overcome the two limitations of two-stage anchor-based ULD methods: the imbalanced anchors in the first stage and the insufficient supervision information in the second stage. We first propose BMs to represent a BBox in three different directions and then use them to replace the original binary GT labels of positive anchors in stage-1 introduce additional supervision through a new BM branch in stage-2. We conduct experiments based on several state-of-the-art baselines on the DeepLesion dataset, and the results show that the performances of all the baselines are boosted with our method.

References

1. Zhang, N., et al.: 3d anchor-free lesion detector on computed tomography scans. arXiv:1908.11324 (2019)
2. Zhang, Z., Zhou, Y., Shen, W., Fishman, E., Yuille, A.: Lesion detection by efficiently bridging 3D context. In: Suk, H.-I., Liu, M., Yan, P., Lian, C. (eds.) MLMI 2019. LNCS, vol. 11861, pp. 470–478. Springer, Cham (2019). https://doi.org/10.1007/978-3-030-32692-0_54
3. Zhang, N., Cao, Y., Liu, B., Luo, Y.: 3d aggregated faster R-CNN for general lesion detection. arXiv:2001.11071 (2020)
4. Zlocha, M., Dou, Q., Glocker, B.: Improving RetinaNet for CT lesion detection with dense masks from weak RECIST labels. In: Shen, D., et al. (eds.) MICCAI 2019. LNCS, vol. 11769, pp. 402–410. Springer, Cham (2019). https://doi.org/10.1007/978-3-030-32226-7_45
5. Tao, Q., Ge, Z., Cai, J., Yin, J., See, S.: Improving deep lesion detection using 3D contextual and spatial attention. In: Shen, D., et al. (eds.) MICCAI 2019. LNCS, vol. 11769, pp. 185–193. Springer, Cham (2019). https://doi.org/10.1007/978-3-030-32226-7_21
6. Tang, Y., Yan, K., Tang, Y., Liu, J., Xiao, J., Summers, R.M.: ULDor: a universal lesion detector for CT scans with pseudo masks and hard negative example mining. In: IEEE ISBI, pp. 833–836 (2019)
7. Yan, K., Bagheri, M., Summers, R.M.: 3D context enhanced region-based convolutional neural network for end-to-end lesion detection. In: Frangi, A.F., Schnabel, J.A., Davatzikos, C., Alberola-López, C., Fichtinger, G. (eds.) MICCAI 2018. LNCS, vol. 11070, pp. 511–519. Springer, Cham (2018). https://doi.org/10.1007/978-3-030-00928-1_58
8. Li, Z., Zhang, S., Zhang, J., Huang, K., Wang, Y., Yu, Y.: MVP-Net: multi-view FPN with position-aware attention for deep universal lesion detection. In: Shen, D., et al. (eds.) MICCAI 2019. LNCS, vol. 11769, pp. 13–21. Springer, Cham (2019). https://doi.org/10.1007/978-3-030-32226-7_2
9. Liao, F., Liang, M., Li, Z., Hu, X., Song, S.: Evaluate the malignancy of pulmonary nodules using the 3-d deep leaky noisy-or network. IEEE Trans. Neural Netw. Learn. Syst. 30(11), 3484–3495 (2019)
10. Lin, Y., et al.: Automated pulmonary embolism detection from CTPA images using an end-to-end convolutional neural network. In: Shen, D., et al. (eds.) MICCAI 2019. LNCS, vol. 11767, pp. 280–288. Springer, Cham (2019). https://doi.org/10.1007/978-3-030-32251-9_31
11. Wang, X., Han, S., Chen, Y., Gao, D., Vasconcelos, N.: Volumetric attention for 3D medical image segmentation and detection. In: Shen, D., et al. (eds.) MICCAI 2019. LNCS, vol. 11769, pp. 175–184. Springer, Cham (2019). https://doi.org/10.1007/978-3-030-32226-7_20
12. Yan, K., et al.: MULAN: multitask universal lesion analysis network for joint lesion detection, tagging, and segmentation. In: Shen, D., et al. (eds.) MICCAI 2019. LNCS, vol. 11769, pp. 194–202. Springer, Cham (2019). https://doi.org/10.1007/978-3-030-32226-7_22
13. Astaraki, M., Toma-Dasu, I., Smedby, Ö., Wang, C.: Normal appearance autoencoder for lung cancer detection and segmentation. In: Staib, L.H., et al. (eds.) MICCAI 2019. LNCS, vol. 11769, pp. 249–256. Springer, Cham (2019). https://doi.org/10.1007/978-3-030-32226-7_28

14. Tang, H., Zhang, C., Xie, X.: NoduleNet: decoupled false positive reduction for pulmonary nodule detection and segmentation. In: Shen, D., et al. (eds.) MICCAI 2019. LNCS, vol. 11769, pp. 266–274. Springer, Cham (2019). https://doi.org/10.1007/978-3-030-32226-7_30

15. Shao, Q., Gong, L., Ma, K., Liu, H., Zheng, Y.: Attentive CT lesion detection using deep pyramid inference with multi-scale booster. In: Shen, D., et al. (eds.) MICCAI 2019. LNCS, vol. 11769, pp. 301–309. Springer, Cham (2019). https://doi.org/10.1007/978-3-030-32226-7_34

16. Liu, J., Cao, L., Akin, O., Tian, Y.: 3DFPN-HS^2: 3D feature pyramid network based high sensitivity and specificity pulmonary nodule detection. In: Shen, D., et al. (eds.) MICCAI 2019. LNCS, vol. 11769, pp. 513–521. Springer, Cham (2019). https://doi.org/10.1007/978-3-030-32226-7_57

17. Wang, B., Qi, G., Tang, S., Zhang, L., Deng, L., Zhang, Y.: Automated pulmonary nodule detection: high sensitivity with few candidates. In: Frangi, A.F., Schnabel, J.A., Davatzikos, C., Alberola-López, C., Fichtinger, G. (eds.) MICCAI 2018. LNCS, vol. 11071, pp. 759–767. Springer, Cham (2018). https://doi.org/10.1007/978-3-030-00934-2_84

18. Zhu, W., Vang, Y.S., Huang, Y., Xie, X.: DeepEM: deep 3D ConvNets with EM for weakly supervised pulmonary nodule detection. In: Frangi, A.F., Schnabel, J.A., Davatzikos, C., Alberola-López, C., Fichtinger, G. (eds.) MICCAI 2018. LNCS, vol. 11071, pp. 812–820. Springer, Cham (2018). https://doi.org/10.1007/978-3-030-00934-2_90

19. Li, H., et al.: High-resolution chest x-ray bone suppression using unpaired CT structural priors. IEEE Trans. Med. Imag. (2020)

20. Liu, S., et al.: 3D anisotropic hybrid network: transferring convolutional features from 2D images to 3D anisotropic volumes. In: Frangi, A.F., Schnabel, J.A., Davatzikos, C., Alberola-López, C., Fichtinger, G. (eds.) MICCAI 2018. LNCS, vol. 11071, pp. 851–858. Springer, Cham (2018). https://doi.org/10.1007/978-3-030-00934-2_94

21. Kevin Zhou, S.: Medical Image Recognition, Segmentation and Parsing: Machine Learning and Multiple Object Approaches. Academic Press (2015)

22. Kevin Zhou, S., Greenspan, H., Shen, D.: Deep Learning for Medical Image Analysis. Academic Press (2017)

23. Oksuz, K., Cam, B.C., Kalkan, S., Akbas, E.: Imbalance problems in object detection: a review. Trans. Pattern Anal. Mach. Intell. (2020)

24. He, K., Gkioxari, G., Dollár, P., Girshick, R.: MASK R-CNN. In: IEEE ICCV, pp. 2961–2969 (2017)

25. Deng, J., Dong, W., Socher, R., Li, L., Li, K., Fei-Fei, L.: ImageNet: a large-scale hierarchical image database. In: IEEE CVPR, pp. 248–255 (2009)

26. Lin, T., Dollár, P., Girshick, R., He, K., Hariharan, B., Belongie, S.: Feature pyramid networks for object detection. In: IEEE CVPR, pp. 2117–2125 (2017)

27. Han, H., Li, J., Jain, A.K., Shan, S., Chen, X.: Tattoo image search at scale: joint detection and compact representation learning. IEEE Trans. Pattern Anal. Mach. Intell. 41(10), 2333–2348 (2019)

28. Ren, S., He, K., Girshick, R., Sun, J.: Faster R-CNN: towards real-time object detection with region proposal networks. In: NIPS, pp. 91–99 (2015)

29. Tian, Z., Shen, C., Chen, H., He, T:. FCOS: fully convolutional one-stage object detection. In: IEEE ICCV, pp. 9627–9636 (2019)

30. Zhou, X., Wang, D., Krähenbühl, P.: Objects as points. arXiv:1904.07850 (2019)

31. Yan, K., et al.: Deep lesion graphs in the wild: relationship learning and organization of significant radiology image findings in a diverse large-scale lesion database. In: IEEE CVPR, pp. 9261–9270 (2018)

32. Huang, C., Han, H., Yao, Q., Zhu, S., Zhou, S.K.: 3D U^2-Net: a 3D universal U-Net for multi-domain medical image segmentation. In: Shen, D., et al. (eds.) MICCAI 2019. LNCS, vol. 11765, pp. 291–299. Springer, Cham (2019). https://doi.org/10. 1007/978-3-030-32245-8_33

Multimodal Priors Guided Segmentation of Liver Lesions in MRI Using Mutual Information Based Graph Co-Attention Networks

Shaocong Mo[1], Ming Cai[1(✉)], Lanfen Lin[1], Ruofeng Tong[1], Qingqing Chen[2],
Fang Wang[2], Hongjie Hu[2], Yutaro Iwamoto[3], Xian-Hua Han[5],
and Yen-Wei Chen[3,4,1]

[1] College of Computer Science and Technology, Zhejiang University,
Hangzhou, China
cm@zju.edu.cn
[2] Department of Radiology, Sir Run Run Shaw Hospital, Hangzhou, China
[3] College of Information Science and Engineering, Ritsumeikan University,
Kusatsu, Japan
[4] Research Center for Healthcare Data Science, Zhejiang Lab, Hangzhou, China
[5] Artificial Intelligence Research Center, Yamaguchi University, Yamaguchi, Japan

Abstract. Segmentation of focal liver lesions serves as an essential preprocessing step for initial diagnosis, stage differentiation, and post-treatment efficacy evaluation. Multimodal MRI scans (e.g., T1WI, T2WI) provide complementary information on liver lesions and is widely used for diagnosis. However, some modalities (e.g., T1WI) have high resolution but lack of important visual information (e.g., edge) belonged to other modalities (T2WI), it is significant to enhance tissue lesion quality in T1WI using other modality priors (T2WI) and improve segmentation performance. In this paper, we propose a graph learning based approach with the motivation of extracting modality-specific features efficiently and establishing the regional correspondence effectively between T1WI and T2WI. We first project deep features into a graph domain and employ graph convolution to propagate information across all regions for extraction of modality-specific features. Then we propose a mutual information based graph co-attention module to learn weight coefficients of one bipartite graph, which is constructed by the fully-connection of graphs with different modalities in the graph domain. At last, we get the final refined features for segmentation by re-projection and residual connection. We validate our method on a multimodal MRI liver lesion dataset. Experimental results show that the proposed approach achieves improvement of liver lesion segmentation in T1WI by learning guided features from multimodal priors (T2WI) compared to existing methods.

Keywords: Multi-modal · Liver lesion segmentation · Graph mutual information

© Springer Nature Switzerland AG 2020
A. L. Martel et al. (Eds.): MICCAI 2020, LNCS 12264, pp. 429–438, 2020.
https://doi.org/10.1007/978-3-030-59719-1_42

1 Introduction

Liver cancer is the second most common cause of cancer-related deaths worldwide among men, and the sixth among women. Liver lesion segmentation is a critical preprocessing step for liver cancer diagnosis, stage estimation, and post-operative treatment [1,6]. Magnetic Resonance Imaging (MRI) has been a standard imaging technology over the past decades, and multimodal MRI images with different tissue contrast such as T1-weighted images (T1WI) and T2-weighted images (T2WI) provide complementary information for diagnosis of liver lesions.

Different modality imaging preforms variably with diverse visual information and meta-attributes. For instance, T1WI modality provides anatomical structure information of organs and T2WI modality discovers lesions more easily. The accumulation of water molecules in most lesions resulting in obviously higher signals than normal tissue around in T2WI modality while showing equal/lower signal appearances of the lesion in contrast with background tissue in T1WI modality. However, the image resolution of T2WI modality is lower than T1WI modality. It is important to enhance the quality of tissue lesion in main modality (e.g., T1WI) with higher image resolution using other modality priors (e.g., T2WI). Another issue is how to extract modality-specific feature efficiently and model connection effectively between main modality and other modalities. Current deep learning methods with slow growth receptive fields and traditional *late-fusion* strategy hardly capture implicit relationships within or between modalities.

Many works have been proposed for liver or liver lesion segmentation in MRI [8,14,19,20]. However, most of the existing works are performed without considering implicit relationships within the single modality and hardly to utilize complementary features of multimodal MRI images effectively. As for multimodal methods, most of them applied to other sites like brain prefer *early/late-fusion* strategy [2,4,5,21]. These works focus on feature fusion densely or crossly along a deep path but ignore modality-specific feature extraction.

In this paper, we aim to strengthen liver lesion segmentation performance in one modality by jointly learning complementary information from another modality that provides guided priors. We present a graph learning based network and utilize graph convolution networks to extract modality-specific feature and capture long-range contextual correlation in graph domain. Then we propose an attention mechanism to model the connections between modalities. To establish the relationships effectively, considering modality-specific intensity distribution and appearance, we propose to use mutual information to estimate the similarity numerically in our attention mechanism between two modality graphs. In this way, the main modality graph could selectively propagate guided information from auxiliary modality with attention weight and achieve feature fusion. Note that we called the target modality (T1WI) as the main modality and the other modality (T2WI) used for guidance as the auxiliary modality.

Our contributions can be summarized as follows, (1) We proposed a T2WI guided T1WI segmentation framework to enhance the lesion segmentation accuracy in T1WI modality. (2) We propose a graph-based method for modality-specific feature extraction and modality fusion. (3) We propose a graph co-attention module based on mutual information for feature propagation cross modalities in graph domain, which build the correlations between modalities.

2 Methodology

In this section, we present our proposed method with the motivation of capturing modality-specific information and establishing the node-to-node correspondence between modalities' structure data for multimodal feature fusion. As shown in Fig. 1(a), the proposed framework includes four components: (1) A regular backbone to extract deep features of input multimodal MRI pairs, (2) Projection of feature maps into graph domain and re-project back into the original feature space, (3) Reasoning with graph convolution to extract the modality-specific features, (4) Mutual information based graph co-attention module to capture information between modalities.

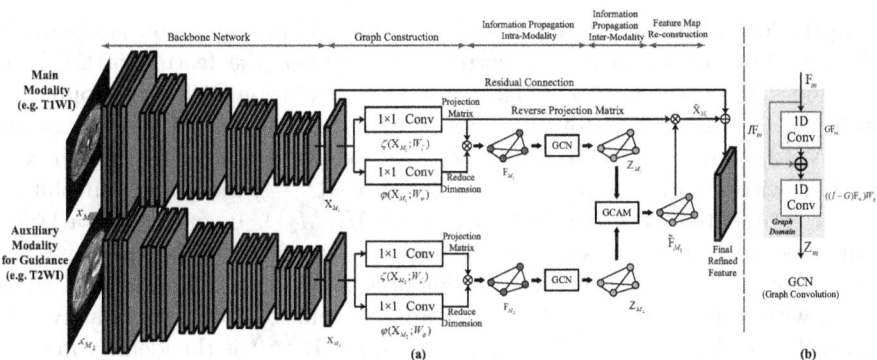

Fig. 1. (a) The pipeline of our proposed approach. Pairs of slices that belong to main modality and auxiliary modality respectively are input to extract deep features by non-shared backbone network, then are projected into graph domain as fully-connected graphs, propagate information and main modality graph fuse auxiliary modality graph feature in turn, finally main modality graph is re-projected back and residually connected with original feature map to final refined feature. (b) The process of graph convolution in graph domain, including two 1D convolution with the learnable adjacency matrix G and parameters W_g.

2.1 Graph Construction and Graph Convolution

Given pair images of two MRI modalities, the main modality M_1(T1WI) and the auxiliary modality M_2(T2WI, provides guided information), denoted as x_{M_1},

x_{M_2}, a non-shared fully connection convolutional neural backbone network is employed to extract deep features for each image. Assume the feature maps $\mathbf{X}_m \in \mathbf{R}^{C \times H \times W}$, $m \in \{M_1, M_2\}$, where C is the number of channels (feature dimension for each pixel), and $H \times W$ is the deep feature size, which is defined on a regular grid coordinates system $\Omega = \{1, ..., H\} \times \{1, ..., W\}$(spatial domain).

Graph Projection. Inspired by region based recognition and following [3,11], we first project the feature map $\mathbf{X}_m(m \in \{M_1, M_2\})$ from the regular grid coordinates Ω into $\mathbf{F}_m \in \mathbf{R}^{N \times D}(m \in \{M_1, M_2\})$ in graph domain Ω', where N is the number of nodes and D represents the dimension of node representation (node feature in graph domain). The entire projected $\mathbf{F}_m$ can be built as a lightweight *fully-connected* graph. Each node of the graph represents a group of features in the partial region of the original regular grid coordinates. In this way, modality-specific features can be easily extracted, even for disjoint or distant regions. We can also easily fuse the effective multimodal features together. In detail, the project function $f(\cdot)$ can be formulated as a linear combination with learnable weights. And the projection $f(\cdot)$ is represented as $\mathbf{F}_m = f(\varphi(\mathbf{X}_m; W_\varphi)) = \zeta(\mathbf{X}_m; W_\zeta) \times \varphi(\mathbf{X}_m; W_\varphi)$ on the practical level, where $\zeta(\cdot)$ and $\varphi(\cdot)$ are two convolution layers for graph projection and feature dimension reduction, respectively.

Graph Convolution. After projecting, a fully connected graph is obtained, which make it easier to exploit correlations between the feature of the relative nodes by learning edge weights. Graph convolution [9,10] is adopted to propagate representations of all nodes further. Specifically, let G denotes the $N \times N$ adjacency matrix of graph for cross-nodes diffusion. For a graph convolution with its state update parameter $W_g \in \mathbf{R}^{D \times D}$, the graph convolution can be formulated as $\mathbf{Z}_m = G\mathbf{F}_m W_g(m \in \{M_1, M_2\})$. In particular, a laplacian smoothing operator is performed to propagate the node features over the graph. Considering its own representation of each node, the adjacency matrix is added with self-connection. Thus the graph convolution formulation arrives at $\mathbf{Z}_m = ((I - G)\mathbf{F}_m)W_g(m \in \{M_1, M_2\})$, where $I \in \mathbf{R}^{N \times N}$ is the identity matrix. In practice, the graph convolution is implemented by two 1D convolution layers along with channel-wise and node-wise directions as shown in Fig. 1(b). Besides, the identity matrix I is a residual connection for every node. In end-to-end trainable fashion, the adjacency matrix G and state update parameter W_g can be optimized by gradient descent.

2.2   Graph Mutual Information and Graph Re-projection

In this section, we introduce our proposed mutual information based graph co-attention module. The proposed module takes inspiration from Attention Based Graph Neural Network [16] and Graph Attention Network [18]. Both of these two state-of-the-art methods update each node by learning weight coefficients of its neighboring nodes and weighted sum up. The proposed method shares same idea but combines two graphs into one bipartite graph to construct a relationship between two graphs. The main idea of this module is that each node in main modality graph $\mathbf{Z}_{M_1}$ is reconstructed by fusing all neighboring nodes in auxiliary modality graph $\mathbf{Z}_{M_2}$ with learning weight coefficients. The architecture of our Graph Co-Attention Module is shown in Fig. 2.

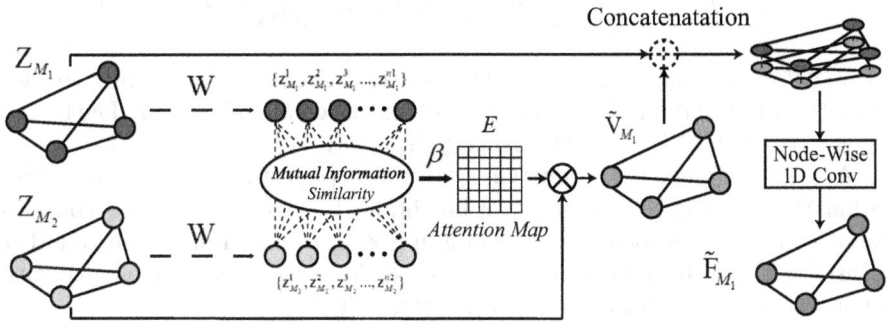

Fig. 2. The architecture of the Mutual Information Based Graph Co-attention Module (GCAM). Taken the main modality graph $\mathbf{Z}_{M_1}$ (red) and the auxiliary modality graph $\mathbf{Z}_{M_2}$ (yellow) as input, after linear transformation with trainable weight $\mathbf{W}$, mutual information is computed between all nodes. The auxiliary modality graph is selectively accumulated by attention map E. Finally, the main modality graph concatenated with selected graph passes through a 1D convolution into fused graph $\tilde{\mathbf{F}}_{M_1}$ (green) (Color figure online).

Assume we have main modality M_1 node representations $\{\mathbf{z}_{M_1}^1, \mathbf{z}_{M_1}^2, \mathbf{z}_{M_1}^3, ...,$ $\mathbf{z}_{M_1}^{n_1}\}$ and auxiliary modality M_2 node representations $\{\mathbf{z}_{M_2}^1, \mathbf{z}_{M_2}^2, \mathbf{z}_{M_2}^3, ..., \mathbf{z}_{M_2}^{n_2}\}$, where $\mathbf{z}_m^t \in \mathbf{R}^d (t \in \{n_1, n_2\}, m \in \{M_1, M_2\}, d \in \{D_1, D_2\})$. n_1 and n_2 are the number of all nodes in the graph M_1 and the graph M_2 respectively, and d is the feature dimension, as mentioned in Sect. 2.1. The Graph Co-Attention Module updates node representations in graph $\mathbf{Z}_{M_1}$ by selectively accumulating information from node features in graph $\mathbf{Z}_{M_2}$. In the end, a pair-wise function $y(\cdot)$ should be built that can quantitatively estimate correlation score e_{ij} between the nodes of two graphs,

$$e_{ij} = y(\mathbf{z}_{M_1}^i, \mathbf{z}_{M_2}^j), i \in [1, n_1], j \in [1, n_2] \tag{1}$$

The original formulation in Attention Based Graph Neural Network [16] to estimate correlation score is to compute cosine similarity between the target nodes, then apply linear transformation with a weighted vector β, like that, $y(\mathbf{z}_{M_1}^i, \mathbf{z}_{M_2}^j) = \beta \cdot \mathrm{COS}(\mathbf{z}_{M_1}^i, \mathbf{z}_{M_2}^j)(i \in [1, n_1], j \in [1, n_2])$, where $\mathrm{COS}(x, y) = x^T y / (\|x\| \cdot \|y\|)$ with L_2 normalization. However, considering many differences between two modality M_1 and M_2 (e.g., intensity distribution, contrast), we use mutual information to estimate the correlation score. Mutual information has been widely used in medical image registration [12,15] and achieved great success. Mutual information measures the statistical relationship among pixels of two images. Thus, mutual information is utilized to measure the statistical correlation among scalars of two node vectors as following,

$$
\begin{aligned}
y(\mathbf{z}_{M_1}^i, \mathbf{z}_{M_2}^j) &= \beta \cdot exp(-MI(\mathbf{Wz}_{M_1}^i, \mathbf{Wz}_{M_2}^j)) \\
&= \beta \cdot exp(-(\sum_{d_1=1}^{D_1} \sum_{d_2=1}^{D_2} p(\mathbf{Wz}_{M_1}^i, \mathbf{Wz}_{M_2}^j) \log(\frac{p(\mathbf{Wz}_{M_1}^i, \mathbf{Wz}_{M_2}^j)}{p(\mathbf{Wz}_{M_1}^i)p(\mathbf{Wz}_{M_2}^j)})))
\end{aligned}
\tag{2}
$$

where $\mathbf{W}, \beta$ are the trainable weights, $p(\cdot)$ is probability density function for discrete vector, and D_1, D_2 are the feature dimension of node vector. The reason using $exp(-MI(\cdot))$ is to avoid $\log(p(x,y)/(p(x)p(y))) = 0$ situation.

After we obtained the correlation matrix $E = \{e_{ij}\}$, the fused node representation $\tilde{\mathbf{V}}_{M_1} = \{\tilde{\mathbf{v}}_{M_1}^i\}(i \in [1, n_1])$ can be obtained by Eq. (3), which is concatenated with the corresponding node in graph $\mathbf{Z}_{M_1}$ and then merged by another transformation, which implemented as a 1D node-wise convolution followed with a non-linear activation function, get a new graph $\tilde{\mathbf{F}}_{M_1}$.

$$
\forall i \in [1, n_1], a_{ij} = \exp(e_{ij}) \Big/ \sum_{k=1}^{n_2} \exp(e_{ik}), \tilde{\mathbf{v}}_{M_1}^i = \sum_{j=1}^{n_2} a_{ij} \cdot \mathbf{z}_{M_2}^j
\tag{3}
$$

Graph Re-projection. We use the projection matrix $\zeta(\cdot)$, which was obtained in the previous graph projection step, to re-project the fused graph $\tilde{\mathbf{F}}_{M_1}$ into the original feature space, leading to a new feature map $\tilde{\mathbf{X}}_{M_1}$ in the original regular grid coordinates Ω. In the end, the new feature map is added with a residual connection of original feature $\mathbf{X}_{M_1}$ as final refined feature for main modality M_1.

3   Experiments

3.1   Dataset, Preprocessing and Experimental Setting

Dataset. We built an internal MRI liver lesion image dataset composed of 203 distinct subjects. Each patient was scanned by a standard clinical abdomen MRI examination with standard imaging protocols including T2FS and T1-Post Contrast in the arterial phase. All T2FS and T1-Post Contrast images have a size of 512 × 512, but they have a gap with thickness in the axial dimension. The thickness of T1-Post Contrast imaging is 2.20 mm and the thickness of T2FS imaging varies from 7.99 mm to 11.00 mm. The multimodal MR images have manual lesion labels, which are drawn and verified by two experienced radiologists.

Preprocessing. All images are processed by N4 bias field correction [17]. The T2FS images are registered as moving images to the corresponding T1-Post Contrast images using a rigid registration algorithm supported by SimpleElastix registration toolbox [13]. Then we remove from the abdomen regions of each image the 2.5% top and 0.5% bottom in terms of intensity. Image intensities are normalized by subtracting the mean and dividing by the standard deviation.

Experimental Setting. Adam optimizer is used with momentum parameters β setting to 0.9 and 0.999. In training phase, the learning rate is initially set to

$1e^{-4}$ and the model is trained for 100 epochs with batch size of 4. 80% subjects in dataset are used for training, and the ratio of positive training slice pairs and negative ones is 1:1. The network is fed by pairs of the whole MRI slice images (not segmented liver images). Since we focus on T1 segmentation, the T1 ground truth is used for training. As for network hyper-parameters, the number of graph node is set to be 64 and the feature dimension of every node is set to be 128. Dice loss is employed to optimize our network, and we evaluate the performance of our proposed model using dice score metrics on patient level. Since the size of lesions varies from several millimeters to several centimeters, we separately evaluated the segmentation accuracy of lesions equal or larger than 5 cm ($\geq$5 cm) and smaller than 5 cm (<5 cm).

3.2   Experiment Results

We choose fully convolution network (FCN) with ResNet50 backbone as our baseline model. Liver lesion segmentation under single modality is evaluated firstly, including T1 Post-Contrast (Arterial Phase) and T2FS. For all testing cases, baseline model achieves dice coefficient 53.09% and 58.08% in T1 Post-Contrast and T2FS, respectively. We assess the impact of auxiliary modality T2FS, which offers guided information.

Table 1. Dice Coefficient results of ablation experiments for liver lesion segmentation in T1-Post Contrast modality.

Method	$\geq$5 cm	<5 cm	All
Single-modality (T1 only)	68.06%	42.49%	53.09%
Multimodal priors guided FCN (w/o attention)	74.24%	46.29%	57.58%
Multimodal priors guided FCN+GCN (w/o attention)	75.00%	46.27%	58.18%
Multimodal priors guided FCN+GCN (Attention with Inner Product Similarity)	76.28%	46.54%	58.87%
Multimodal priors guided FCN+GCN (Attention with Mutual Information)	**76.47%**	**47.12%**	**59.29%**

Ablation Study. In order to verify the rationality of our method, we experimented with each component. Since our proposed method is mainly in *late-fusion* style, we evaluate our method by comparing to *late-fusion* strategy employed baseline models. In detail, multiple streams' feature maps are concatenated in channel dimension and then pass through skip architecture of FCN (Multimodal priors guided FCN). As for graph-based method, after respective modality-specific feature extraction, two streams final features are concatenated in channel dimension (Multimodal priors guided FCN+GCN). We also compared the proposed mutual information based attention module with the conventional inner product (cos similarity without normalization) based attention.

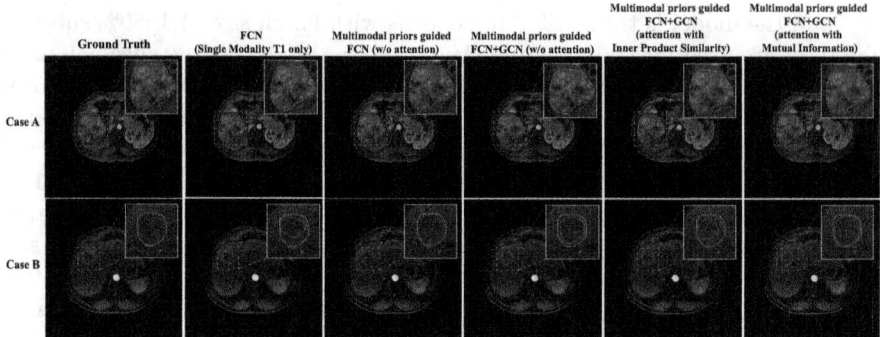

Fig. 3. Qualitative segmentation results from the testing set in ablation study. **The green contour is the ground truth and the red contour is the inference.** All result regions are partially enlarged in white box. Case A is the typical case with large lesion while Case B is the typical case with small lesion (Color figure online).

The ablation experimental results are summarized in Table 1. As shown in Table 1, compared with the single-modality segmentation, the proposed multimodal priors guided method improved the segmentation accuracy. The proposed graph CNN (GCN) further improved the segmentation accuracy. The mutual information based co-attention GCN achieved the highest dice score of lesion in main modality T1-Post Contrast for all testing cases, not only large lesions but also smaller lesions. Note that the mutual information based co-attention GCN achieved better performance than conventional inner product based co-attention GCN. The mutual information based graph co-attention module not only extracts modality-specific feature effectively, but also achieves feature fusion efficiently between modalities, which means that the design of our method is reasonable and suitable for multimodal fusion. We also present two typical inference cases of different patients with different size lesions in ablation study shown in Fig. 3. The lesion segmentation edges are more smoothing when using mutual information based method for large lesions and edges in small lesions can be better learned from another modality by our method.

Comparison with State-of-the-arts Methods. We evaluate our proposed method by comparing to some existing works with different *late-fusion* structure, including 2D version HyperDenseNet [5], HeMIS-UNet [7] and IVDNet [4]. In addition, we also show the accuracy by simply registering the segmentation mask of T2FS to T1 domain for comparison.

As shown in Table 2, by comparing with other existing methods, our mutual information based co-attention GCN method achieved better results than existing methods for both large-size lesions and small-size lesions. The segmentation accuracy (dice score) of the proposed method are 76.47% and 47.12% for the large-size lesions and small-size lesions, respectively. From the above experimental results, we can conclude that (1) Effective modality-specific feature extraction can help model learn implicit intensity relationship in graph domain. (2) Efficient

Table 2. Dice Coefficient comparison with state-of-the-art multimodal segmentation methods for liver lesion segmentation in T1-Post Contrast modality.

Method	$\geq$5 cm	<5 cm	All
HyperDenseNet-2D [5]	36.18%	3.33%	16.95%
HeMIS-UNet [7]	67.39%	26.11%	43.23%
IVDNet [4]	70.42%	26.30%	44.59%
Registration-based method	68.74%	40.93%	52.46%
Proposed method (**Attention with Mutual Information**)	**76.47%**	**47.12%**	**59.29%**

feature fusion by capturing the guided information selectively from the auxiliary modality in graph domain is better than concatenation with complex rules in spatial domain.

4   Conclusion

In this paper, we propose a graph learning based method for extracting modality-specific feature efficiently and establishing a correlation effectively between main modality and auxiliary modality in graph domain. Graph convolution is utilized after projecting feature maps into graph domain and propagate information within a modality. Then mutual information based graph co-attention module is proposed to compute relation-aware representation cross modalities and fuse features in graph domain. The proposed method is especially useful for multimodal image fusion based tasks.

Acknowledgements. This work was supported in part by Major Scientific Research Project of Zhejiang Lab under the Grant No. 2018DG0ZX01, and in part by the Grant-in Aid for Scientific Research from the Japanese Ministry for Education, Science, Culture and Sports (MEXT) under the Grant No. 18H03267 and No.17H00754.

References

1. Forner, A., Reig, M., Bruix, J.: Hepatocellular carcinoma. Lancet (London, England) **391**, 1301–1314 (2018). https://doi.org/10.1016/s0140-6736(18)30010-2
2. Chen, C., Dou, Q., Jin, Y., Chen, H., Qin, J., Heng, P.-A.: Robust multimodal brain tumor segmentation via feature disentanglement and gated fusion. In: Shen, D., et al. (eds.) MICCAI 2019. Robust multimodal brain tumor segmentation via feature disentanglement and gated fusion, vol. 11766, pp. 447–456. Springer, Cham (2019). https://doi.org/10.1007/978-3-030-32248-9_50
3. Chen, Y., Rohrbach, M., Yan, Z., Shuicheng, Y., Feng, J., Kalantidis, Y.: Graph-based global reasoning networks. In: Proceedings of the IEEE Conference on Computer Vision and Pattern Recognition, pp. 433–442 (2019)
4. Dolz, J., Desrosiers, C., Ayed, I.B.: IVD-Net: intervertebral disc localization and segmentation in MRI with a multi-modal UNet. In: Zheng, G., Belavy, D., Cai, Y., Li, S. (eds.) CSI 2018. LNCS, vol. 11397, pp. 130–143. Springer, Cham (2019). https://doi.org/10.1007/978-3-030-13736-6_11

5. Dolz, J., Gopinath, K., Yuan, J., Lombaert, H., Desrosiers, C., Ayed, I.B.: HyperDense-Net: a hyper-densely connected CNN for multi-modal image segmentation. IEEE Trans. Med. Imaging **38**(5), 1116–1126 (2018)
6. El-Serag, H.B.: Epidemiology of hepatocellular carcinoma. In: The Liver: Biology and Pathobiology, pp. 758–772 (2020)
7. Havaei, M., Guizard, N., Chapados, N., Bengio, Y.: HeMIS: hetero-modal image segmentation. In: Ourselin, S., Joskowicz, L., Sabuncu, M.R., Unal, G., Wells, W. (eds.) MICCAI 2016. LNCS, vol. 9901, pp. 469–477. Springer, Cham (2016). https://doi.org/10.1007/978-3-319-46723-8_54
8. Jansen, M.J., et al.: Liver segmentation and metastases detection in MR images using convolutional neural networks. J. Med. Imaging **6**(4), 044003 (2019)
9. Kipf, T.N., Welling, M.: Semi-supervised classification with graph convolutional networks. In: 5th International Conference on Learning Representations, ICLR 2017, Toulon, France, April 24–26, 2017, Conference Track Proceedings. OpenReview.net (2017). https://openreview.net/forum?id=SJU4ayYgl
10. Li, Q., Han, Z., Wu, X.M.: Deeper insights into graph convolutional networks for semi-supervised learning. In: Thirty-Second AAAI Conference on Artificial Intelligence (2018)
11. Liang, X., Hu, Z., Zhang, H., Lin, L., Xing, E.P.: Symbolic graph reasoning meets convolutions. In: Advances in Neural Information Processing Systems, pp. 1853–1863 (2018)
12. Maes, F., Vandermeulen, D., Suetens, P.: Medical image registration using mutual information. Proc. IEEE **91**(10), 1699–1722 (2003)
13. Marstal, K., Berendsen, F., Staring, M., Klein, S.: SimpleElastix: a user-friendly, multi-lingual library for medical image registration. In: Proceedings of the IEEE Conference on Computer Vision and Pattern Recognition Workshops, pp. 134–142 (2016)
14. Mazurowski, M.A., Buda, M., Saha, A., Bashir, M.R.: Deep learning in radiology: an overview of the concepts and a survey of the state of the art with focus on MRI. J. Magn. Reson. Imaging **49**(4), 939–954 (2019)
15. Sedghi, A., et al.: Semi-supervised image registration using deep learning. In: Medical Imaging 2019: Image-Guided Procedures, Robotic Interventions, and Modeling, vol. 10951, p. 109511G. International Society for Optics and Photonics (2019)
16. Thekumparampil, K.K., Wang, C., Oh, S., Li, L.J.: Attention-based graph neural network for semi-supervised learning. arXiv preprint arXiv:1803.03735 (2018)
17. Jansen, M.J., et al.: Liver segmentation and metastases detection in MR images using convolutional neural networks. J. Med. Imaging **6**(4), 044003 (2019)
18. Velickovic, P., Cucurull, G., Casanova, A., Romero, A., Liò, P., Bengio, Y.: Graph attention networks. In: 6th International Conference on Learning Representations, ICLR 2018, Vancouver, BC, Canada, April 30–May 3, 2018, Conference Track Proceedings. OpenReview.net (2018). https://openreview.net/forum?id=rJXMpikCZ
19. Xiao, X., et al.: Radiomics-guided GAN for segmentation of liver tumor without contrast agents. In: Shen, D., et al. (eds.) MICCAI 2019. LNCS, vol. 11765, pp. 237–245. Springer, Cham (2019). https://doi.org/10.1007/978-3-030-32245-8_27
20. Zeng, Q., et al.: Liver segmentation in magnetic resonance imaging via mean shape fitting with fully convolutional neural networks. In: Shen, D., et al. (eds.) MICCAI 2019. LNCS, vol. 11765, pp. 246–254. Springer, Cham (2019). https://doi.org/10.1007/978-3-030-32245-8_28
21. Zhou, T., Ruan, S., Canu, S.: A review: deep learning for medical image segmentation using multi-modality fusion. Array, p. 100004 (2019)

Mt-UcGAN: Multi-task Uncertainty-Constrained GAN for Joint Segmentation, Quantification and Uncertainty Estimation of Renal Tumors on CT

Yanan Ruan[1], Dengwang Li[1(✉)], Harry Marshall[2], Timothy Miao[3], Tyler Cossetto[3], Ian Chan[3], Omar Daher[3], Fabio Accorsi[3], Aashish Goela[3], and Shuo Li[4(✉)]

[1] Shandong Key Laboratory of Medical Physics and Image Processing, Shandong Institute of Industrial Technology for Health Sciences and Precision Medicine, School of Physics and Electronics, Shandong Normal University, Jinan, Shandong 250358, China
dengwang@sdnu.edu.cn
[2] Department of Radiology, David Geffen School of Medicine at the University of California, Los Angeles, CA 90095, USA
[3] Department of Medical Imaging, Western University Schulich School of Medicine and Dentistry, London, ON, Canada
[4] University of Western Ontario, London, ON, Canada
slishuo@gmail.com

Abstract. The segmentation of renal tumor, quantification of tumor indices (i.e., the center point coordinates, diameter, circumference, and cross-sectional area) and uncertainty estimation of segmentation are the key processes for clinical tumor disease diagnosis. However, these tasks have been studied independently so far. Because segmentation and quantification tasks have different optimization types, representing two different tasks as a unified optimization framework is a severe challenge. In this paper, we propose a unified framework (i.e., Mt-UcGAN: multi-task uncertainty-constrained generative adversarial network) for joint segmentation, quantification, and uncertainty estimation of renal tumors on CT. Mt-UcGAN includes a multitasking integrated generator (MtIG) and an uncertainty-constrained discriminator (UcD). MtIG achieves multi-task joint learning by novelly merging skip connections and Monte Carlo sampling. UCD guides the learning of segmentation and quantification networks by innovatively feeding prior information with high uncertainty constraints. Mt-UcGAN effectively corrects tumor prediction errors and improves network performance through continuous adversarial learning and alternate training. Experiments are performed on CT of 113 renal tumor patients. The dice coefficient of Mt-UcGAN is 92.1%, and the R^2 coefficient of tumor circumference is 0.9513. The results show that this method has great potential to be extended to other medical image analysis tasks and clinical application value.

Keywords: Segmentation · Quantification · Uncertainty estimation

© Springer Nature Switzerland AG 2020
A. L. Martel et al. (Eds.): MICCAI 2020, LNCS 12264, pp. 439–449, 2020.
https://doi.org/10.1007/978-3-030-59719-1_43

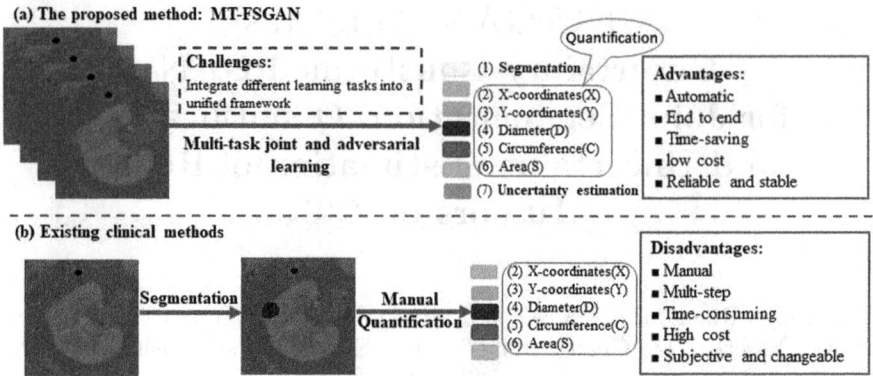

Fig. 1. (a) Our method simultaneously implements pixel-level semantic segmentation, quantification of five tumor indices (tumor diameter (D), circumference (C), cross-sectional area (S), and center point coordinates (X, Y)) and uncertainty estimation through joint learning and adversarial learning, which are time-saving, end-to-end, reliable and stable. (b) The existing clinical method is to segment through algorithm first and then the doctors manual quantify by visual observation and experience, which is time-consuming, multi-step, subjective and changeable because quantification accuracy depends on segmentation accuracy. And so far there has been no research on uncertainty estimation.

1   Introduction

The segmentation, quantification, and uncertainty estimation of renal tumors on CT images are key processes in clinical tumor disease diagnosis. Some important renal tumor indices, such as tumor diameter, perimeter, cross-sectional area, and center point coordinates, are an important basis for tumor diagnosis [1,2]. Therefore, accurate quantification of the tumor indices is essential for accurate diagnosis of tumors. However, manual segmentation and quantification are challenging and time-consuming in practice and show high intra- and inter-operator variability [3]. The advantage of the renal tumor segmentation method is that it can provide physicians with visual inspection and pixel-level semantic interpretation based on the segmentation results [4–7]. However, due to the need for additional geometric calculations, the final quantification result of tumor indices is usually affected by the segmentation accuracy.

Direct quantification methods of tumor indices cannot provide a visual examination and pixel-level semantic interpretation for clinicians, which limits the potential clinical use of this method [8]. So far, the two tasks of segmentation and quantification have been studied independently [9–15]. The segmentation task is a discrete pixel-level classification problem, while direct exponential quantification is a global regression problem. These two tasks have different optimization types. Therefore, representing two different tasks as a unified optimization framework is a serious challenge. However, these two tasks are common in nature and have a strong complementary relationship [16–18]. By modeling these two tasks into a unified framework, joint and efficient optimization can be achieved, and the performance of automatic quantification of tumor indices can be improved.

Uncertainty is the feedback of clinical diagnosis. Specifically, uncertainty estimation can avoid overconfidence and erroneous quantification, and allow clinicians to further modify cases with higher uncertainty [19–21]. And it can also provide clinicians with feedback on the reliability of the results, which helps doctors to conduct subsequent visual inspections and revisions on the results to further improve the accuracy of the diagnosis. This is crucial for clinical diagnosis, especially with the popularization of automatic tumor segmentation algorithms. More importantly, uncertainty estimation can feed important prior information to deep learning networks to guide the learning of the network. However, current research on renal tumors ignores this vital task.

In this paper, the multi-task uncertainty-constrained generative adversarial network (Mt-UcGAN) is proposed for joint segmentation, quantification, and uncertainty estimation of renal tumors. We creatively proposed an adversarial mechanism with uncertainty constraints, consisting of two competing modules: 1) Multitasking integrated generator, which novelly integrates skip connections to force the integration of segmentation and quantification tasks that share the same encoder into a unified optimization framework, thereby learning the shared representation of segmentation and quantification to generate beneficial interactions. 2) Uncertainty-constrained discriminator, which creatively feeds prior knowledge of the prediction result with high uncertainty to the generator, and guides the learning of segmentation and quantification networks through a multi-task comprehensive loss function.

Our contributions are: 1) For the first time, a unified framework for joint segmentation, quantification, and uncertainty estimation of renal tumors was proposed. It provides clinicians with direct assessment of the clinically necessary indicators of renal tumors while segmenting tumors, and the reliability of segmentation. 2) A novel multitasking integrated generator is proposed, which incorporates skip connections to effectively reduce the interference of unified optimization of segmentation and quantification on segmentation. 3) An innovative uncertainty-constrained adversarial mechanism is proposed, which effectively feedbacks the prior knowledge of high uncertainty constraints to guide the learning of segmentation and quantification networks.

2 Methodology

Our Mt-UcGAN simultaneously segments and quantifies renal tumors, and estimates the uncertainty of the segmentation results through multi-task uncertainty-constrained GAN mechanism (see Fig. 2). It is implemented through two collaborative modules: 1) Multitasking integrated generator (Sect. 2.1) consists of a region of interest extractor (see Fig. 2(a)) for the extraction of tumor regions of interest to reduce the input noise and the post-processing amount of data, an encoder-decoder with MC-dropout (see Fig. 2(b)) for joint segmentation and uncertainty estimation by fusing Monte Carlo sampling to better preserves class boundary information, and a regressor that shares the same encoder with the encoder-decoder (see Fig. 2(c)) for the quantification of five tumor indices (i.e., the center point coordinates, diameter, circumference, and cross-sectional area) by fusing skip connections to interact with the segmentation network. 2) Uncertainty-constrained discriminator (Sect. 2.2) for guidance on the learning of segmentation and quantification network by feeding back the prior knowledge of high uncertainty to the generator to monitor and encourage the generative model to generate correct predictions.

2.1   Multitasking Integrated Generator (MtIG) for Joint Learning

The MtIG integrates region of interest extractor, encoder-decoder with MC-dropout and end-to-end regressor into the generator, which simultaneously implements pixel-level semantic segmentation, indices quantification, and uncertainty estimation of segmentation through joint learning.

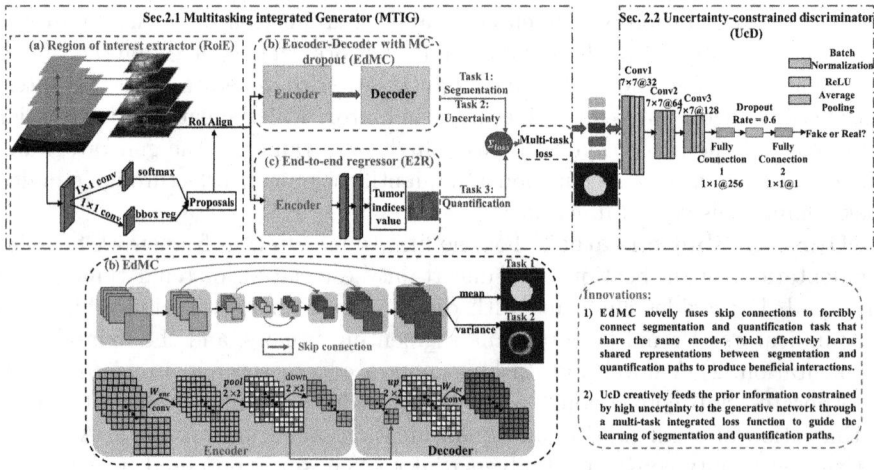

Fig. 2. Our proposed Mt-UcGAN achieves segmentation, quantification, and uncertainty estimation of renal tumors. An innovative adversarial mechanism of uncertainty constraints effectively integrates multiple tasks through joint learning and learns the prior information of uncertainty constraint feedback.

Region of interest extractor (RoiE) connects hierarchical pyramid feature extraction network and region proposal network for extraction of the tumor regions of interest (see Fig. 2(a)). The hierarchical pyramid feature extraction network effectively detects early small renal tumor targets. This combines low-resolution but semantically strong features with high-resolution but semantically weak features through top-down paths and horizontal connections based on the principle of the pyramid structure. The result is high-level semantic information at all scales. The extraction of the region of interest reduces the amount of post-processing data, while eliminating some noise by determining the general location of the tumor, reduces the time complexity of the network, and increases accuracy.

Encoder-decoder with MC-dropout (EdMC) novelly incorporates Monte-Carlo sampling for joint segmentation and uncertainty estimation of the renal tumor (see Fig. 2(b)). It includes a series of encoders and a corresponding set of decoders, followed by a per-pixel classifier. Each encoder consists of one or more non-linear convolutional layers with batch normalization and ReLU, followed by non-overlapping maximum pooling or subsampling. Each decoder contains multiple convolutional layers and then up-samples the sparse encoding due to the merging process using the largest pool index in the encoding sequence. Each encoder corresponds to a decoder by skip connections. This effectively preserves class boundary details and reduces the total number of model parameters. A dropout layer is then inserted after each encoder and each decoder unit. Multiple sampling is achieved through the dropout layer. The average of multiple samples is the final output corresponding to the image semantic segmentation, and the sample variance represents the uncertainty of the model prediction. The mask loss L_m are derived from the following formulas:

$$L_m\left(m_{it}, m_{ip}\right) = -\left(m_{ip}\log\left(m_{ip}\right) + \left(1 - m_{it}\right)\log\left(1 - m_{ip}\right)\right) \qquad (1)$$

where the variable m_{it} represents the mask binary matrices from the prediction and m_{ip} represents ground-truth label.

End-to-end regressor (E_2R) that shares encoder with the segmentation network novelly merges skip connections to force learning of the shared representation of segmentation and quantification to produce beneficial interactions for the prediction of the tumor indices (i.e., the center point coordinates, diameter, circumference, and cross-sectional area) (see Fig. 2(c)), which reduces the interference of unified optimization of segmentation and quantification on segmentation. The error function is based on the difference between the predicted and actual values, and the mapping relationship is derived from the following formula:

$$L_\mathrm{r}\left(x_{i_i}, \mathrm{x}_{ip}\right) = \mathrm{smooth}_{L1}\left(v_{it} - v_{ip}\right), \mathrm{smooth}_{L1}(x) = \begin{cases} 0.5x^2 & \text{if } |x| < 1 \\ |x| - 5 & \text{otherwise} \end{cases} \qquad (2)$$

Where x_{ip} variable represents the predicted value of five indices (i.e., the center point coordinates (X, Y), diameter (D), circumference (C), and cross-sectional area (S) of the tumor), and x_{it} represents the measured value of the real label.

The global loss function of multitasking integrated generator (MtIG) incorporating dual paths is defined as:

$$
\begin{aligned}
L_{MtIG}\left(m_{it}, m_{ip}, b_{it}, b_{ip}, v_{it}, v_{ip})\right) = \underbrace{\gamma \frac{1}{N_{r2}} \sum_{i} p_{it} L_r\left(b_{ip}, b_{it}\right)}_{\text{Object Detection}} \\
+ \underbrace{\beta \frac{1}{N_{mask}} L_m\left(m_{it}, m_{ip}\right)}_{\text{Segmentation path}} + \underbrace{\delta \frac{1}{N_{r3}} \sum_{i} p_{it} L_r\left(v_{ip}, v_{it}\right)}_{\text{Quantification path}}
\end{aligned}
\tag{3}
$$

where constant N represents the number of corresponding bounding boxes. These hyperparameters β, γ and δ are set to 0.2, 0.3 and 0.5 respectively according to experience and practice to balance the training losses of different tasks.

Summarized Advantage: The multitasking integrated generator novelly merges skip connection and Monte Carlo sampling to represent different tasks as a unified framework, thereby generating beneficial interactions, reducing the interference of unified optimization of segmentation and quantification networks on segmentation.

2.2 Uncertainty-constrained Discriminator (UcD) for Adversarial Guided Learning

The UcD module monitors and encourages generative models to generate correct predictions through adversarial learning guided by the high uncertainty of the generative model (see Fig. 2). Under the adversarial mechanism, the UcD module receives prediction maps with high uncertainty from the generator or manual maps from ground truth as input and then outputs a single scalar indicating whether the input is from the generative network or ground truth. Then it feeds the prior information of uncertainty constraints to the generator through the multi-task comprehensive loss function to guide the learning of segmentation and quantification networks. When strong adversarial learning occurs, the discriminative network eagerly causes the generative model to look for mismatches in various high-order statistics between the predicted segmentation map and the ground truth. The hybrid loss function of Mt-UcGAN is defined as:

$$
\begin{aligned}
L_{Mt-UcGAN}\left(\theta_s, \theta_d\right) = \underbrace{\frac{1}{N_m} \sum_{i} L_{MtIG}\left(\mathrm{m}_{it}, \mathrm{m}_{it}, \mathrm{m}_{ip}, \mathrm{b}_{it}, \mathrm{b}_{ip}, \mathrm{v}_{it}, \mathrm{v}_{ip}\right)}_{\text{Multitasking Integrated generator}} \\
\underbrace{- \lambda\left[L_{UcD}\left(D\left(m_{it}\right), 1\right) + L_{UcD}\left(m_{ip}, 0\right)\right]}_{\text{Uncertainty-constrained Discriminator}}
\end{aligned}
\tag{4}
$$

λ is set to one to maintain the balance of adversarial learning. The weighted two-class cross-entropy loss of UcD is defined as:

$$
L_{UcD}\left(\mathrm{m}_{it}, UcD\left(\mathrm{m}_{it}\right)\right) = -\left[m_{it} \log UcD\left(m_{it}\right) + \left(1 - m_{it}\right) \log\left(1 - UcD\left(m_{it}\right)\right)\right]
\tag{5}
$$

where m_{it} is the input labels (fake maps are zeros and ground maps are ones), while $UcD\,(\mathrm{m}_{it})$ are the single scalar of the output of the discriminative network.

Summarized Advantage: The uncertainty-constrained discriminator creatively feeds the prior knowledge of prediction results with high uncertainty to the generative network to guide the learning of segmentation and quantification path.

3   Experiments and Results

The Mt-UcGAN demonstrates high segmentation performance with a pixel accuracy of 97.3%, high quantification performance with the R^2 coefficients of tumor circumference is 0.9513 and low uncertainty (see Fig. 3). Experimental results demonstrate the effectiveness of this method in segmentation, quantification, and uncertainty estimation of renal tumors on CT.

Dataset and Configuration. A total of 3000 2D axial slices composed of 113 subjects with renal tumors is selected as the experiment. Two radiologists with more than ten years of experience manually segmented and quantified renal tumors on CT images. If there are differences, a consensus must be reached between the two experts. Our deep learning model was implemented using TensorFlow 1.3.0, Keras 2.0.8 on an Ubuntu 16.04 machine, and was trained and tested on an NVIDIA Titan Xp 12GB GPU. All experiments were assessed with a 10-fold cross-validation test. Divide the data set into ten parts, taking nine of them as training data and one part as test data in turn. The average value of the accuracy of the ten results is used as an estimate of the accuracy of the algorithm. We alternately optimize the hybrid loss function of the segmentation network and the loss function of the discriminant network in the Mt-UcGAN. First, the parameters of the discriminant network are fixed to optimize the generation network, and then the discriminative network is optimized according to the updated parameters. It alternates until the network converges.

Accurate Segmentation. The experimental results show that Mt-UcGAN has high segmentation performance with a pixel accuracy of 97.3%, a dice coefficient of 92.1%, a sensitivity of 95.7%, a specificity of 93.4%, as shown in Tables 2 and 3.

Precise Quantification. The proposed Mt-UcGAN has high quantitative performance as shown in Table 1. The R^2 coefficients predicted by our method for the five tumor indices are 0.9321 in X-coordinate of tumor center point, 0.9402 in Y-coordinate of tumor center point, 0.9289 in diameter, 0.9513 in circumference and 0.9485 in area. It shows that the values of the tumor indices predicted by our method are very close to the actual values, and the fitting effect is very well.

Advantage of Mt-UcGANs Architecture (Ablation Study). Table 2 demonstrates that each of our technological innovations in Mt-UcGANs has effectively improved the accuracy of the renal tumor segmentation. The third row is about 8% higher than the second row in pixel accuracy, indicating that skip connection can significantly reduce the interference on segmentation caused

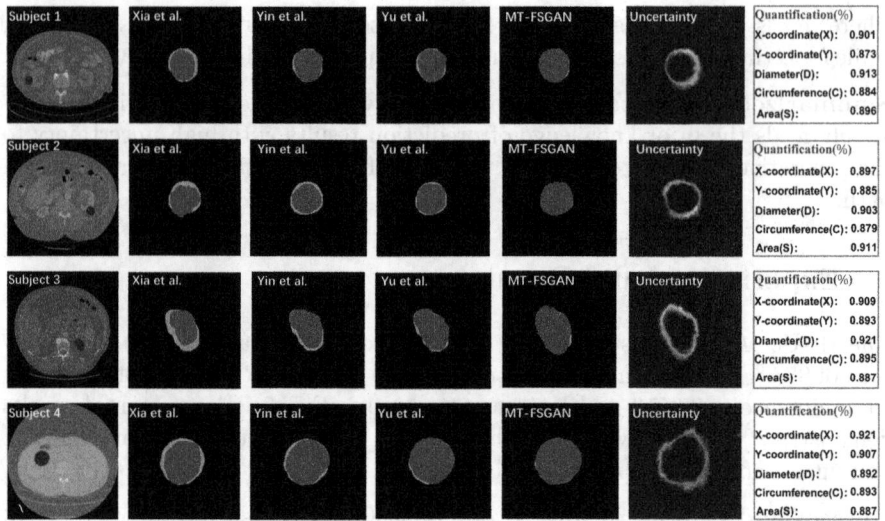

Fig. 3. The comparison of segmentation results between the proposed method and three typical deep learning networks indicates that the performance of the network is superior. The first column is Groundtruth, and the second to fifth columns are the latest deep learning methods [22–24] and our method for renal tumor lesion segmentation comparison. The last column is uncertainty estimation of our segmentation results.

Table 1. Mt-UcGAN yielded higher quantitative performance on the five indexes of tumors. The R^2 coefficients are all close to 1.

Metrics	X-coordinate	Y-coordinate	Diameter (D)	Circumference (C)	Area (S)
R^2 coefficient	0.9321	0.9402	0.9289	0.9513	0.9485

by the unified optimization of segmentation and quantification. The fourth row is about 5% higher than the third row in pixel accuracy, indicating that Monte Carlo sampling can improve the accuracy of the network. The fifth row is about 5% higher than the fourth row in pixel accuracy, indicating that the constraint of uncertainty can improve the accuracy of the network.

Comparison with State-of-the-art Methods. This paper tracks a comparison of segmentation performance among the proposed method and state-of-the-art method [22–24] by pixel accuracy, dice coefficient, specificity, sensitivity as shown in Table 3. The segmentation result of our proposed method is closest to ground truth compared with the state-of-art deep learning methods (see Fig. 3). To directly evaluate the quality of the segmentation process, Fig. 3 shows the cross-sectional images from the same cube.

Table 2. Each of our technological innovations in Mt-UcGANs effectively improved the segmentation accuracy of network.

Method	Pixel accuracy	Dice coefficient	Specificity	Sensitivity
Ed	83.5%	79.6%	80.7%	81.8%
$Ed + E_2R$	74.3%	71.9%	73.5%	74.4%
$Ed + E_2R + skip$	87.5%	82.6%	83.7%	84.8%
$EdMC + E_2R + skip$	92.3%	87.1%	88.6%	89.1%
$EdMC + E_2R + skip + UcD$	**97.3%**	**92.1%**	**95.7%**	**93.4%**

Table 3. Mt-UcGAN yielded higher performance than state-of-art segmentation methods on renal tumors.

Method	Pixel accuracy	Dice coefficient	Specificity	Sensitivity
Proposed method	**97.3%**	**92.1%**	**95.7%**	**93.4%**
Yin, Kevin, et al. [22]	92.1%	79.6%	86.7%	83.4%
Xia, Kai-jian, et al. [23]	89.4%	83.8%	81.1%	85.4%
Yu, Qian, et al. [24]	87.7%	80.4%	83.4%	82.2%

4 Conclusion

For the first time, a multi-task uncertainty-constrained generative adversarial network (Mt-UcGAN) was proposed for joint segmentation, quantification, and uncertainty estimation of renal tumors. We creatively proposed an adversarial mechanism with uncertainty constraints. Experiment results demonstrate that Mt-UcGAN can aid in the clinical diagnosis of tumor assessments. And it can also provide clinicians with feedback on the reliability of the results, which helps doctors to conduct subsequent visual inspections and revisions on the results to further improve the accuracy of the diagnosis.

Acknowledgments. This work was funded by the National Natural Science Foundation of China (61971271), the Taishan Scholars Project of Shandong Province (Tsqn20161023) and the Primary Research and Development Plan of Shandong Province (No. 2018GGX101018, No. 2019QYTPY020).

References

1. Mehrazin, R., et al.: Impact of tumour morphology on renal function decline after partial nephrectomy. BJU Int. **111**(8), E374–E382 (2013)
2. Greene, F.L., et al.: AJCC Cancer Staging Handbook: TNM Classification of Malignant Tumors. Springer Science & Business Media, New York (2002)
3. Spaliviero, M., et al.: Interobserver variability of RENAL, PADUA, and centrality index nephrometry score systems. World J. Urol. **33**(6), 853–858 (2015)

4. Kutikov, A., Uzzo, R.G.: The renal nephrometry score: a comprehensive standardized system for quantitating renal tumor size, location and depth. J. Urol. **182**(3), 844–853 (2009)
5. Ficarra, V., et al.: Preoperative aspects and dimensions used for an anatomical (PADUA) classification of renal tumours in patients who are candidates for nephron-sparing surgery. Eur. Urol. **56**(5), 786–793 (2009)
6. Taha, A., Lo, P., Li, J., Zhao, T.: Kid-Net: convolution networks for kidney vessels segmentation from CT-volumes. In: Frangi, A.F., Schnabel, J.A., Davatzikos, C., Alberola-López, C., Fichtinger, G. (eds.) MICCAI 2018. LNCS, vol. 11073, pp. 463–471. Springer, Cham (2018). https://doi.org/10.1007/978-3-030-00937-3_53
7. Yang, G., et al.: Automatic segmentation of kidney and renal tumor in CT images based on 3d fully convolutional neural network with pyramid pooling module. In: 2018 24th International Conference on Pattern Recognition (ICPR), pp. 3790–3795. IEEE (2018)
8. Edge, S.B., et al.: AJCC Cancer Staging Manual, vol. 649. Springer, New York (2010)
9. Afshin, M., Ayed, I.B., Islam, A., Goela, A., Peters, T.M., Li, S.: Global assessment of cardiac function using image statistics in MRI. In: Ayache, N., Delingette, H., Golland, P., Mori, K. (eds.) MICCAI 2012. LNCS, vol. 7511, pp. 535–543. Springer, Heidelberg (2012). https://doi.org/10.1007/978-3-642-33418-4_66
10. Zhen, X., Wang, Z., Yu, M., Li, S.: Supervised descriptor learning for multi-output regression. In: Proceedings of the IEEE Conference on Computer Vision and Pattern Recognition, pp. 1211–1218 (2015)
11. Zhen, X., Zhang, H., Islam, A., Bhaduri, M., Chan, I., Li, S.: Direct and simultaneous estimation of cardiac four chamber volumes by multioutput sparse regression. Med. Image Anal. **36**, 184–196 (2017)
12. Wu, H., Bailey, C., Rasoulinejad, P., Li, S.: Automatic landmark estimation for adolescent idiopathic scoliosis assessment using BoostNet. In: Descoteaux, M., Maier-Hein, L., Franz, A., Jannin, P., Collins, D.L., Duchesne, S. (eds.) MICCAI 2017. LNCS, vol. 10433, pp. 127–135. Springer, Cham (2017). https://doi.org/10.1007/978-3-319-66182-7_15
13. Sun, H., Zhen, X., Bailey, C., Rasoulinejad, P., Yin, Y., Li, S.: Direct estimation of spinal cobb angles by structured multi-output regression. In: Niethammer, M., et al. (eds.) IPMI 2017. LNCS, vol. 10265, pp. 529–540. Springer, Cham (2017). https://doi.org/10.1007/978-3-319-59050-9_42
14. Zhen, X., Yu, M., Islam, A., Bhaduri, M., Chan, I., Li, S.: Descriptor learning via supervised manifold regularization for multioutput regression. IEEE Trans. Neural Netw. Learn. Syst. **28**(9), 2035–2047 (2016)
15. Bray, F., Ferlay, J., Soerjomataram, I., Siegel, R. L., Torre, L. A., Jemal, A.: Global cancer statistics 2018: GLOBOCAN estimates of incidence and mortality worldwide for 36 cancers in 185 countries. CA Cancer J. Clin. **68**(6), 394–424 (2018)
16. Xu, C., Howey, J., Ohorodnyk, P., Roth, M., Zhang, H., Li, S.: Segmentation and quantification of infarction without contrast agents via spatio temporal generative adversarial learning. Med. Image Anal., 101568 (2019)
17. Luo, G., et al.: Commensal correlation network between segmentation and direct area estimation for bi-ventricle quantification. Med. Image Anal., 101591 (2019)
18. Ruan, Y., et al.: MB-FSGAN: joint segmentation and quantification of kidney tumor on CT by the multi-branch feature sharing generative adversarial network. Med. Image Anal. (2020)

19. Jungo, A., Reyes, M.: Assessing reliability and challenges of uncertainty estimations for medical image segmentation. In: Shen, D., et al. (eds.) MICCAI 2019. LNCS, vol. 11765, pp. 48–56. Springer, Cham (2019). https://doi.org/10.1007/978-3-030-32245-8_6

20. Raghu, M., et al.: Direct uncertainty prediction for medical second opinions. arXiv preprint arXiv:1807.01771 (2018)

21. Wang, G., Li, W., Aertsen, M., Deprest, J., Ourselin, S., Vercauteren, T.: Aleatoric uncertainty estimation with test-time augmentation for medical image segmentation with convolutional neural networks. Neurocomputing **338**, 34–45 (2019)

22. Xia, K.J., Yin, H.S., Zhang, Y.D.: Deep semantic segmentation of kidney and space-occupying lesion area based on SCNN and ResNet models combined with SIFT-flow algorithm. J. Med. Syst. **43**(1), 2 (2019)

23. Yin, K., Liu, C., Bardis, M., Martin, J., Liu, H., Ushinsky, A., Glavis-Bloom, J., Chantaduly, C., Chow, D.S., Houshyar, R., et al.: Deep learning segmentation of kidneys with renal cell carcinoma. J. Clin. Oncol. **37**, e16098–e16098 (2019)

24. Yu, Q., Shi, Y., Sun, J., Gao, Y., Zhu, J., Dai, Y.: Crossbar-Net: a novel convolutional neural network for kidney tumor segmentation in CT images. IEEE Trans. Image Process. **28**(8), 4060–4074 (2019)

Weakly Supervised Deep Learning for Breast Cancer Segmentation with Coarse Annotations

Hao Zheng[1,2,3], Zhiguo Zhuang[4], Yulei Qin[1,3], Yun Gu[1,3(✉)], Jie Yang[1,3(✉)], and Guang-Zhong Yang[2,3]

[1] Institute of Image Processing and Pattern Recognition,
Shanghai Jiao Tong University, Shanghai, China
{geron762,jieyang}@sjtu.edu.cn
[2] School of Biomedical Engineering, Shanghai Jiao Tong University, Shanghai, China
[3] Institute of Medical Robotics, Shanghai Jiao Tong University, Shanghai, China
[4] Department of Radiology, Renji Hospital,
Shanghai Jiao Tong University School of Medicine, Shanghai, China

Abstract. Cancer lesion segmentation plays a vital role in breast cancer diagnosis and treatment planning. As creating labels for large medical image datasets can be time-consuming, laborious and error prone, a framework is proposed in this paper by using coarse annotations generated from boundary scribbles for training deep convolutional neural networks. These coarse annotations include locations of lesions but are lack of accurate information about boundaries. To mitigate the negative impact of annotation errors, we propose an adaptive weighted constrained loss that can change the weight of the task-specific penalty term according to the learning process. To impose further supervision about the boundaries, uncertainty-based boundary maps are generated, which can provide better descriptions for the blurry boundaries. Validation on a dataset containing 154 MRI scans has shown an average Dice coefficient of 82.25%, which is comparable to results from fine annotations, demonstrating the efficacy of the proposed approach.

Keywords: Coarse annotations · Adaptive weighted constrained loss · Uncertainty-based boundary map

1 Introduction

Dynamic contrast-enhanced magnetic resonance imaging (DCE-MRI) has been a popular and versatile technique for the evaluation of breast cancer staging and treatment planning [14]. In these applications, accurate lesion delineation

This research was partly supported by National Key R&D Program of China (No. 2019YFB1311503), Committee of Science and Technology, Shanghai, China (No. 19510711200), and Shanghai Sailing Program (No. 20YF1420800).

ⓒ Springer Nature Switzerland AG 2020
A. L. Martel et al. (Eds.): MICCAI 2020, LNCS 12264, pp. 450–459, 2020.
https://doi.org/10.1007/978-3-030-59719-1_44

is essential for quantifying the progression of the tumor mass, as well as surgical planning and margin definition. Over the years, deep learning methods have achieved promising performance in many medical image analysis tasks. However, training deep neural networks requires a large number of annotated data which are hard to achieve in practice. For DCE-MRI, for example, it is also too time-consuming to delineate for senior clinicians. As the breast cancer lesions in DCE-MRI exhibit variable contrast, size, shape, and enhancement patterns, only experienced observers are able to accurately annotate these lesions. Due to the significant cost of creating annotations for big medical image datasets, it is of great clinical relevance to explore the potential of weak supervision for deep learning.

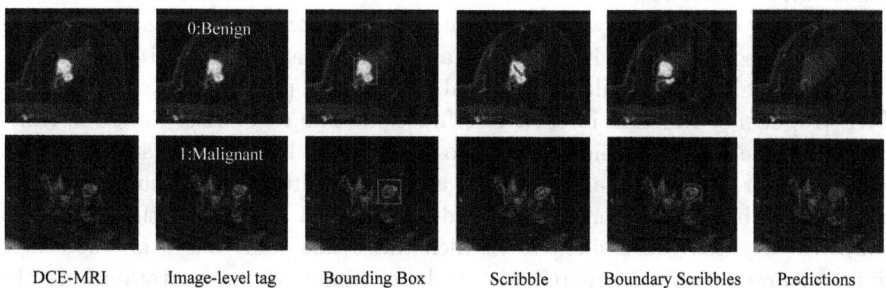

DCE-MRI   Image-level tag   Bounding Box   Scribble   Boundary Scribbles   Predictions

Fig. 1. Examples of different weak annotations on two small breast cancer lesions. Image-level tags are binary labels (benign or malignant) of cancer lesions. Bounding boxes are squares or cubes which include the entire lesion. Scribbles are points or lines inside the lesion. Boundary scribbles are coarse lesion edges and predictions are our segmentation results.

As shown in Fig. 1, existing common weak supervisions include image-level tags [12,16], bounding boxes [4,9] and scribbles [11,15]. However, the performance of the state-of-the-art weak supervision-based approaches is limited by a phenomenon named background enhancement [14] (BE) in DCE-MRI. After the injection of Gd-DTPA contrast agent, not only the intensity of cancer lesion, but also the intensity of mammary gland can increase. Sometimes the intensity of mammary gland rises significantly, affecting the detection and staging of cancerious regions [14]. When the image background is complicated due to BE, image-level tag-based methods can result in high false positives as they cannot distinguish the cancer lesions from the surrounding gland. Most bounding-box and scribble based methods adopt the framework that generates proposals in the first step followed by network training. However, generating proposals relies on prior knowledge and classical segmentation approaches such as GrabCut [1], which can be easily confused by the background enhancement and inhomogeneity of the lesions. When training a model using these proposals with inaccurate patterns, the model tends to learn inaccurate information. Thus, weak annotation that can not only simplify expert annotation but also provide stronger supervision is needed.

When making lesion annotations, localization and boundary refinement are two main steps that experienced observers tend to spend most of their time on. Accurate location of the lesions plays a critical role in overcoming the BE problem, so this step cannot be omitted. In contrast, many lesions show distinguishable edges and algorithm could learn to correct small errors or boundary deviations. Thus, we propose in this paper to use boundary scribble as shown in Fig. 1 for weak annotation. To further speed up the process, annotators could skip some slices in which the appearances of cancer lesions are similar to their adjacent slices. Filling the holes in boundary scribbles and interpolating skipped slices generates coarse annotations. For this method to work, the learning process needs extra constrains.

Enforcing extra penalty in the loss function is a common approach in weakly supervised segmentation. Kervadec et al. [8] formulate a regularizer based on the target-region size, while Zhang et al. [6] add the pairwise potential term of CRF [10] energy function in their loss function. The regularizer design is task-specific, and a constant weight is used to combine it with the basic segmentation loss. However, such manually designed constrains can be problematic in terms of generalizability. To over come this drawback, we propose in this paper an adaptive weighted constrained loss which tunes this value based on the sensitivity of predictions. Compared to fine labels, our coarse annotations mainly lack the accurate boundary information. As the edge pattern of the lesion is an important image feature in cancer classification, the learning process should focus more on this area. In previous work, Yoo et al. [17] generate edge maps from weak annotations through unsupervised segmentation approach and edge information. However, for breast cancer, malignant lesions usually show irregular and ambiguous edges as they invade the surrounding tissues. In this situation, the edges of unsupervised segmentation results tend to be inaccurate, bringing wrong patterns into the learning. To resolve this problem, we resort to generating the boundary maps based on the uncertainties during training. These maps are used in an auxiliary task to assist the learning of boundary representations.

The main aims and contributions of this work include:

1. To reduce manual annotation efforts, we use coarse annotations generated from boundary scribbles to train deep neural networks, and design the corresponding framework.
2. To add further constrains for learning from coarse annotations, we propose an adaptive weighted constrained loss which can change the extent of penalty based on the sensitivity of predictions.
3. To make up for the lack of accurate boundary information, we generate uncertainty-based boundary maps that can provide a better description for inconspicuous edges.

2 Method

Figure 2 provides a schematic illustration of the proposed framework. The process is divided into two stages, each containing two steps. In the first step, the coarse annotations are directly used to train the network with an adaptive weighted constrained loss. We compare the predictions in different epochs and generate the uncertainty-based boundary maps. These maps provide extra supervision through an auxiliary task in the second step. In this phase, the network effectively acts as a refining machine, whose outputs are used as the new coarse annotations in the subsequent stage. The same process is repeated in the second stage. During testing, only the final trained network is required. The following sections provide a detailed explanation of the method proposed.

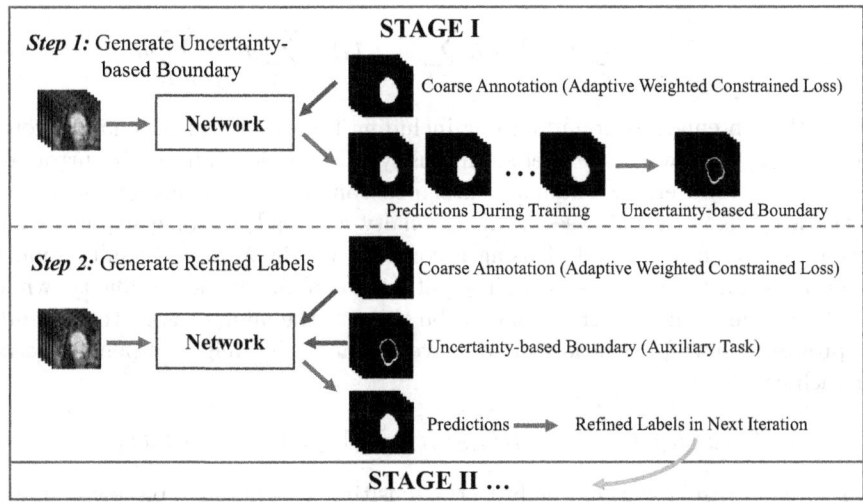

Fig. 2. Schematic illustration of the framework to learn from coarse annotations. The whole process is divided into two stages, each containing two steps. In the first step, the coarse annotations are directly used to train the network with adaptive weighted constrained loss. The predictions in different epochs are analyzed and used to generate the uncertainty-based boundary maps. These maps provide extra supervision in the second step. And the outputs in this stage are used as the new coarse annotations in the subsequent stage. The process of the second stage is same as the former.

2.1 Adaptive Weighted Constrained Loss

In weakly supervised segmentation, a common formulation of the loss function is

$$\ell_{total}\left(\bar{y}, y, x\right) = \ell_{seg}\left(\bar{y}, y\right) + \lambda \ell_r\left(\bar{y}, y, x\right), \tag{1}$$

where $\bar{y}$ is the prediction, y is the label and x is the input image. The total loss ℓ_{total} is composed of a basic segmentation loss ℓ_{seg} as well as a penalty term ℓ_r. The selection of ℓ_{seg} relies on the properties of the weak annotation. For scribbles inside the foreground or background, partial cross entropy loss is widely adopted in previous studies [6,8]. However, our coarse annotations include errors especially in the boundary areas. So we use Tversky loss [13] as the basic segmentation loss to reach a high recall rate,

$$\ell_{Tversky}\left(\bar{y}, y\right) = 1 - \frac{\sum_{i=1}^{N} \bar{y}_i y_i}{\sum_{i=1}^{N} \bar{y}_i y_i + \alpha \sum_{i=1}^{N} \bar{y}_i \left(1 - y_i\right) + \beta \sum_{i=1}^{N} \left(1 - \bar{y}_i\right) y_i}, \quad (2)$$

where $\alpha + \beta = 1$ and higher β leads to higher sensitivity. The choice of penalty term ℓ_r depends on the prior knowledge (e.g. shape and size) of the target. In DCE-MRI, a typical image feature is the intensity change of lesions after the injection of contrast agent. Thus we design the penalty term based on image intensities,

$$\ell_r\left(\bar{y}, x\right) = \sum_{i \in B}\left(1 - \bar{y}_i\right) x_i / \sum_{i \in B}\left(1 - \bar{y}_i\right) - \sum_{i \in B} \bar{y}_i x_i / \sum_{i \in B} \bar{y}_i, \quad (3)$$

where B is an enlarged bounding box including the target. Such penalty allows a large margin between the average intensity of the lesions and their surrounding tissues. However, the manually designed constrain is not always beneficial to the learning. In some cases, a high penalty can lead to worse segmentation performance. Thus, instead of using a constant weight λ, more penalty should be imposed on the samples of high sensitivity to improve the specificity, while small penalties or no constrains should be given to the failure cases. To this end, we propose a new formulation to adaptively change the weight of penalty term for each case,

$$\ell_{total}\left(\bar{y}, y, x\right) = \omega\left(\bar{y}, y\right) \ell_{seg}\left(\bar{y}, y\right) + \left(1 - \omega\left(\bar{y}, y\right)\right) \ell_r\left(\bar{y}, x\right). \quad (4)$$

To relate the regularization weight to the sensitivity, we design a piecewise linear function,

$$\omega\left(\bar{y}, y\right) = \begin{cases} 1, & 0 \leq s\left(\bar{y}, y\right) < t_L \\ \frac{1-m}{t_L - t_R} s\left(\bar{y}, y\right) + \frac{m t_L - t_R}{t_L - t_R}, & t_L \leq s\left(\bar{y}, y\right) < t_R \\ m, & t_R \leq s\left(\bar{y}, y\right) \leq 1 \end{cases} \quad (5)$$

where $s\left(\bar{y}, y\right) = \sum_i \bar{y}_i y_i / \sum_i y_i$ is the sensitivity, m is the minimal weight of ℓ_{seg}, and t_L and t_R are two thresholds dividing the domain of adaptive weight. This loss function can keep a high sensitivity by Tversky loss, and improve the precision via adaptively changing the weights of regularizer in the meanwhile.

2.2   Uncertainty-Based Boundary Map

Compared to fine labels, our coarse annotations mainly lack accurate boundary information. As a result, the segmentation tends to have a smooth outline instead of an elaborate edge. To drive the model to learn the concept of boundary, Yoo et al. [17] design their PseudoEdgeNet which adds the supervision about edge through an auxiliary task. They incorporate sobel filter into the results of an unsupervised segmentation approach to generate the boundary maps. These edges are highly related to the gradient of image intensity. However, for breast cancer, malignant lesions invading their surrounding tissues usually present ambiguous edges. For these cases, relying too much on image intensities can negatively affect the sensitivity of the method. Thus, it is essential for the boundary maps to be capable of dealing with these indistinct edges.

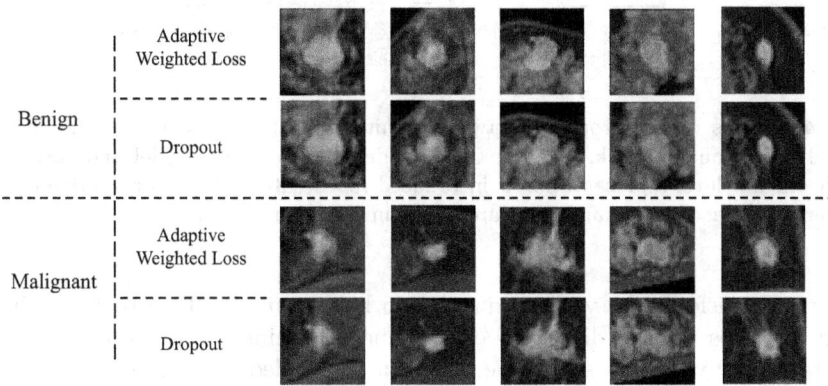

Fig. 3. Uncertainty maps generated by adaptive weighted constrained loss and dropout.

In this paper, uncertainty-based boundary maps are proposed for two reasons. First is the observation that the distribution of uncertain predictions concentrates near the edge of the target. This makes it feasible to extract boundary regions from the uncertainty map. The second reason is that the uncertainty maps can provide a better description for blurry edges. Figure 3 illustrates the uncertainty maps both for benign and malignant lesions. Dropout [5] is a widely adopted approach to evaluate the uncertainty in deep learning. However, when the network has learned strong and repeated feature representations for the cases in training set, the distribution of the uncertain voxels is sparse. These sparse edge points do not contribute to the learning of boundary representations, so we explore another way to evaluate the uncertainty. During training, because of the shuffled input order, the different batch composition and the random data augmentation, the predictions keep changing near the edge of lesions. Such an uncertainty within the training process is amplified by our adaptive weighted constrained loss when the weight of penalty term varies with the segmentation performance. Since the predictions in blurry edge regions are more sensitive to the weight of regularizer, these areas can be all highlighted in the uncertainty maps. To this end, we generate the boundary annotations from these uncertainty maps by three steps. Firstly, the predictions in the last 20 epochs during training are saved before their variance maps are calculated. Secondly, a threshold

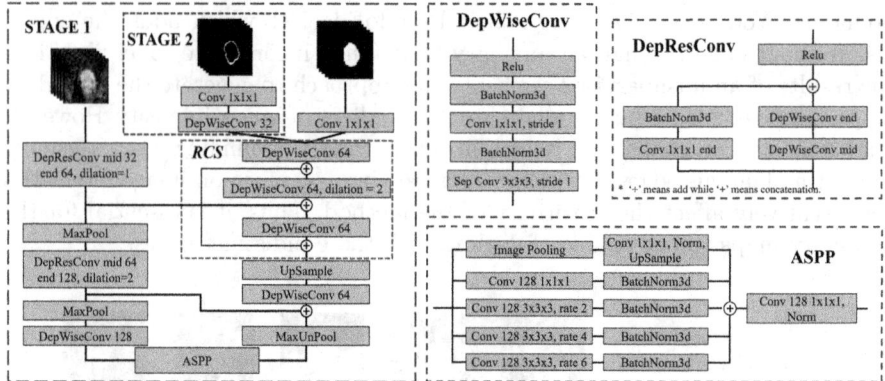

Fig. 4. Details of the proposed network architecture. There are three fundamental structures in our network, DepWiseConv model, DepResConv model and ASPP. In RCS, the low-level representation is introduced repeatedly in three consecutive layers. Uncertainty-based boundary maps are added in the second stage.

is set to transform the variance maps into binary images. Finally, a relatively large kernel is used to dilate the coarse labels, forming the lesion regions, and the boundary voxels outside these regions are excluded.

The boundary supervision is imposed on the model through an auxiliary task. The detailed architecture of our network is shown in Fig. 4. After generating the boundary maps, they are used as labels in another prediction. A weighted cross entropy loss is adopted here because of the class imbalance. A much higher weight (8) is given to the foreground. Besides, to enhance the capability of network, we build it with depthwise separable convolution [3], atrous spatial pyramid pooling (ASPP) [2] and a repeated consideration structure (RCS).

3   Experiments and Results

In this study, DCE-MRI scans from 154 female patients were included. The dataset were randomly split into training set, validation set and test set with 90, 24 and 40 cases respectively. The boundary scribbles were drawn by one senior radiologist, while the ground truth was annotated by other two experienced radiologists. During preprocessing, all images were interpolated to 0.5 mm × 0.5 mm × 0.5 mm. The third subtraction sequence was the input to network, which was obtained by subtracting the pre-contrast sequence from the forth post-contrast sequence on DCE-MRI.

During training, all the networks were trained 100 epochs using SGD optimizer with a momentum of 0.9 and a weight decay of 0.0001. The initial learning rate was 0.1, and it was divided by 10 in the 40th and 80th epochs. The hyperparameters were tuned in validation set. We fixed the others when optimizing one parameter.

After two iterations, we chose the optimal combination and evaluated the performance in the test set. In the first segmentation iteration, the used hyperparameters were $\alpha = 0.3$, $\beta = 0.7$, $m = 0.4$, $t_L = 0.5$ and $t_R = 0.7$. As the quality of coarse annotations was refined in the second iteration, the changed parameters were $\alpha = 0.4$ and $\beta = 0.6$. During inference, the average time is 0.8s per case after extracting the breast parts based on the location of sternum and the edge of chest in preprocessing. The preprocessing for one case takes about 10 s.

Table 1. Comparison of different methods for training and test set. 'Coarse', 'Refined' and 'Fine' mean training the network with coarse, refined and fine annotations respectively. 'Two-Stage' means that the refinement process was also adopted to this method. 'Dice' denotes Dice loss while 'AWCL' means adaptive weighted constrained loss. 'Edge_c' and 'Edge_g' are boundary maps generated from the coarse annotations and Graphcut refined annotations respectively. 'UB' denotes the proposed uncertainty-based boundary and 'Drop' means the uncertainty evaluated by dropout method.

	Method	DSC (%)	Sensitivity (%)	Specificity (%)
Training set	Coarse annotation	76.58	79.30	76.50
	GraphCut	73.38	89.94	63.42
	GraphCut+CRF	76.28	86.43	71.39
	Proposed	79.96	86.03	76.71
Test set	Kervadec et al. [8] MedIA2019	76.30	84.80	74.41
	Zhang et al. [6] MICCAI2019	78.07	85.10	76.70
	Yoo et al. [17] MICCAI2019	78.39	83.38	80.19
	Kervadec et al. [8] two-Stage	78.15	85.08	76.79
	Zhang et al. [6] two-stage	79.69	84.48	80.63
	Yoo et al. [17] two-stage	80.26	81.88	83.92
	Coarse+Dice	75.21	78.98	77.04
	Coarse+Tversky	71.94	88.67	64.67
	Coarse+AWCL	78.51	84.86	78.27
	Coarse+AWCL+Edge_c	78.13	84.93	78.12
	Coarse+AWCL+Edge_g	78.00	83.59	79.65
	Coarse+AWCL+UB	79.22	85.19	78.56
	Coarse+AWCL+Drop	77.96	84.25	76.21
	Refined+AWCL	81.15	83.98	82.47
	Refined+AWCL+UB	82.25	**85.28**	83.61
	Fine+Dice	**82.64**	85.23	**84.43**

Dice similarity coefficient (DSC), sensitivity and specificity were used to evaluate different methods. The quantitative results are shown in Table 1. We first compared our coarse annotations with fine labels. And it is shown that all the evaluation metrics are less than 80%. Directly training the network with these coarse annotations only achieves a DSC of 75.21%. Performing Tversky loss can significantly improve the sensitivity to 88.67%, but the decrease in precision hurts the overall performance. Adding a penalty term in the loss function like Kervadec et al. [8] can increase the DSC to 76.30%. By using adaptive weighted constrained loss, the DSC can be further improved to 78.51%. Following previous studies [6,17], we refined the coarse annotations by unsupervised approaches. GraphCut can improve the sensitivity from 79.30% to 89.94%, but the decrease in specificity is also significant. So we implemented dense CRF [7,10] followed the GraphCut for further refinement. However, no obvious differences is seen after adopting these refined annotations. We also applied sobel filter to generate the boundary maps and performed PseudoEdgeNet for segmentation. Imposing extra supervision about boundary increases the specificity from 76.70% to 80.19%, with a decrease of 1.72% in sensitivity. In comparison, using our proposed uncertainty-based boundary maps do not hurt the sensitivity. We also generated the uncertainty-based boundary maps by using the dropout approach. However, results show that these maps negatively affect the segmentation performance. To further evaluate the effectiveness of boundary supervision, we generated boundary maps from the coarse annotations and Graphcut refined annotations respectively, and trained the network with these maps and coarse annotations. It is seen that these results are even worse than the performance without boundary supervision, which demonstrates the importance of a suitable boundary description. In our proposed framework, the segmentation results in the first iteration were used as the refined annotations in the subsequent stage. These results can be of a high sensitivity while the specificity is much higher than that of unsupervised methods. Using these refined annotations improves the DSC to 82.25%, only a slight lower than the results of fine labels (82.64%). We also adopted the refinement process to other methods [6,8,17]. They all benefit from the refinement while the increase is not as significant as the proposed method, demonstrating that a more accurate refinement leads to more improvement. We also tried more iterations but the improvement is insignificant. Thus, in this paper, our framework only includes two iterations, which is enough for the refinement.

4   Conclusion

In conclusion, a multi-stage framework is proposed for weakly supervised breast cancer segmentation. Coarse annotations are obtained from boundary scribbles which can save a lot of manual efforts. To make up for the inaccurate information in coarse annotations, we adaptively add task-specific penalties in the loss function and generate uncertainty-based boundary maps for extra supervision. The segmentation performance achieved is comparable to the results of using fine labels, thus demonstrating the potential clinical value of the proposed framework.

References

1. Carsten, R., Vladimir, K., Andrew, B.: "GrabCut": interactive foreground extraction using iterated graph cuts. ACM Trans. Graph. **23**(3), 309–314 (2004). https://doi.org/10.1145/1015706.1015720

2. Chen, L., Papandreou, G., Kokkinos, I., Murphy, K., Yuille, A.L.: DeepLab: semantic image segmentation with deep convolutional nets, atrous convolution, and fully connected crfs. IEEE Trans. Pattern Anal. Mach. Intell. **40**(4), 834–848 (2018). https://doi.org/10.1109/TPAMI.2017.2699184
3. Chollet, F.: Xception: deep learning with depthwise separable convolutions. In: The IEEE Conference on Computer Vision and Pattern Recognition (CVPR), July 2017
4. Dai, J., He, K., Sun, J.: BoxSup: exploiting bounding boxes to supervise convolutional networks for semantic segmentation. In: The IEEE International Conference on Computer Vision (ICCV), December 2015
5. Gal, Y., Ghahramani, Z.: Dropout as a Bayesian approximation: representing model uncertainty in deep learning. In: International Conference on International Conference on Machine Learning (2016)
6. Ji, Z., Shen, Y., Ma, C., Gao, M.: Scribble-based hierarchical weakly supervised learning for brain tumor segmentation. In: International Conference on Medical Image Computing and Computer-Assisted Intervention (2019)
7. Kamnitsas, K., et al.: Efficient multi-scale 3D CNN with fully connected CRF for accurate brain lesion segmentation. Med. Image Anal. **36**, 61–78 (2016)
8. Kervadec, H., Dolz, J., Tang, M., Granger, E., Boykov, Y., Ayed, I.: Constrained-CNN losses for weakly supervised segmentation. Med. Image Anal. **54**, 88–99 (2019). https://doi.org/10.1016/j.media.2019.02.009
9. Khoreva, A., Benenson, R., Hosang, J., Hein, M., Schiele, B.: Simple does it: weakly supervised instance and semantic segmentation. In: 30th IEEE Conference on Computer Vision and Pattern Recognition (CVPR), June 2017
10. Krähenbühl, P., Koltun, V.: Efficient inference in fully connected CRFs with Gaussian edge potentials. In: Conference and Workshop on Neural Information Processing Systems (2011)
11. Lin, D., Dai, J., Jia, J., He, K., Sun, J.: ScribbleSup: scribble-supervised convolutional networks for semantic segmentation. In: The IEEE Conference on Computer Vision and Pattern Recognition (CVPR), June 2016
12. Saleh, F.S., Aliakbarian, M.S., Salzmann, M., Petersson, L., Alvarez, J.M., Gould, S.: Incorporating network built-in priors in weakly-supervised semantic segmentation. IEEE Trans. Pattern Anal. Mach. Intell. **40**(6), 1382–1396 (2018). https://doi.org/10.1109/TPAMI.2017.2713785
13. Salehi, S., Erdogmus, D., Gholipour, A.: Tversky loss function for image segmentation using 3D fully convolutional deep networks. CoRR abs/1706.05721 (2017). http://arxiv.org/abs/1706.05721
14. Takayoshi, U., Masako, K., Junichiro, W.: Does the degree of background enhancement in breast mri affect the detection and staging of breast cancer? Eur. Radiol. **21**(11), 2261–2267 (2011). https://doi.org/10.1007/s00330-011-2175-6
15. Tang, M., Djelouah, A., Perazzi, F., Boykov, Y., Schroers, C.: Normalized cut loss for weakly-supervised CNN segmentation. ArXiv e-prints, April 2018
16. Wei, Y., et al.: STC: a simple to complex framework for weakly-supervised semantic segmentation. IEEE Trans. Pattern Anal. Mach. Intell. **39**(11), 2314–2320 (2017). https://doi.org/10.1109/TPAMI.2016.2636150
17. Yoo, I., Yoo, D., Paeng, K.: PseudoEdgeNet: nuclei segmentation only with point annotations. In: International Conference on Medical Image Computing and Computer-Assisted Intervention (2019)

Multi-phase and Multi-level Selective Feature Fusion for Automated Pancreas Segmentation from CT Images

Xixi Jiang[1], Qingqing Luo[1], Zhiwei Wang[2], Tao Mei[3], Yu Wen[4], Xin Li[4], Kwang-Ting Cheng[2], and Xin Yang[1,5(✉)]

[1] School of Electronic Information and Communication,
Huazhong University of Science and Technology, Wuhan, China
xinyang2014@hust.edu.cn
[2] Hong Kong University of Science and Technology, Hong Kong, China
[3] JD AI Research, Mountain View, USA
[4] Union hospital, Tongji Medical College, Huazhong University of Science and Technology, Wuhan, China
[5] Wuhan National Laboratory of Optoelectronics, Huazhong University of Science and Technology, Wuhan, China

Abstract. CT images scanned in arterial and venous phases have been demonstrated to provide complementary information for accurate pancreas segmentation. In this paper, we propose a novel multi-phase and multi-level selective feature fusion network (MMNet) with a core component named adaptive cross refinement (ACR) module. Specifically, MMNet adopts two parallel encoders to extract features of the two phases respectively, which are then fused by ACR to excel each complementarity advantage. Unlike most existing fusion methods which only exchange and combine features of a single level with the same resolution between two phases/modalities, ACR module intelligently aggregates features of all levels in one phase as a multi-level prior, and then adaptively selects the most effective information from the multi-level prior to refine features at each level of the other phase. Such multi-phase, multi-level selective feature exchange and fusion strategy is bi-directional to mutually benefit segmentation of both phases. Experimental results on 141 cases of our private dataset demonstrate the effectiveness of our ACR module and superior performance to the state-of-the-art fusion methods.

Keywords: Multi-phase image segmentation · Multi-level features · Selective feature fusion

This work was supported by the National Natural Science Foundation of China (61872417), JD AI Research (the grapevine scholar plan), the Fundamental Research Funds for the Central Universities (2019kfyRCPY118, 2020kfyXGYJ026), the Open Project of Wuhan National Laboratory for Optoelectronics (2018WNLOKF025).

© Springer Nature Switzerland AG 2020
A. L. Martel et al. (Eds.): MICCAI 2020, LNCS 12264, pp. 460–469, 2020.
https://doi.org/10.1007/978-3-030-59719-1_45

1 Introduction

Pancreatic cancer is one of the leading causes of cancer mortality [7]. Accurately segmenting pancreas from CT images is a prerequisite for quantitative and qualitative analysis, and for surgical assistance. Recently many researches have been conducted to automate this task for better accuracy. Despite great progress have been made due to the development of deep learning techniques [14,15], accurate pancreas segmentation remains very challenging due to its small volume in CT scan, the ambiguous boundary and the large variability in pancreas' shape. Most existing methods rely on only CT images of the venous phase for pancreas segmentation. Recently, some studies [12,17] demonstrate that combining images from both venous and arterial phases is a promising solution to improve pancreas segmentation due to the complementary visual cues from the two phases. As shown in Fig. 1, pancreas and the splenic vein (marked in green) are easier to distinguish in the venous phase, while the pancreas and duodenum (marked in blue) are easier to separate in the arterial phase.

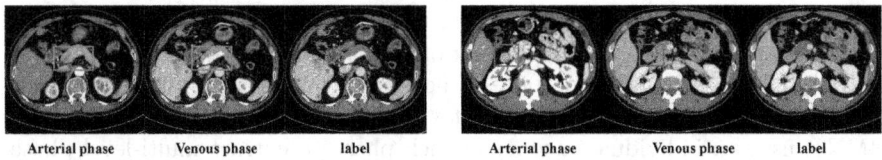

Fig. 1. Two examples for illustration of the complementarity between the arterial and venous phases. (Color figure online)

Existing methods for combining multiple phases, or more broadly multiple modalities, can be categorized into three classes [1]: early fusion, late fusion and hybrid fusion. Early fusion integrates multi-modal features at the low-level stage or input stage, while the late fusion performs aggregation at the decision stage. Hybrid fusion typically utilizes modal-specific encoders to extract features for each modality, and then fuses the features through multiple intermediate layers. Common hybrid fusion methods adopt simple strategies such as concatenation [3], pixel-wise addition [6], which cannot learn the complex relations between different modalities. To address this issue, Dolz et al. [5] and Zhou et al. [17] further introduced skip connections across modalities for intensive information exchange. However, as each modality could provide both useful information and irrelevant noises, fusing multi-modal features without effectively suppressing noises in [5,17] could hardly achieve consistent improvements based on fusion for arbitrary cases. Li et al. [8] and Chen et al. [2] proposed to use attention blocks to suppress noises and emphasize task-related areas in the fusion process. Despite promising results that have been demonstrated, [2,8,17] only fused multi-modal features of the same scale, ignoring effective mutual guidance from different levels. The improvements in these methods are sometimes limited.

On the other hand, some recent studies [4,11,16] concurrently exploited high-level semantics and low-level details for segmentation on single modal images and have demonstrated promising improvements, evidencing the potential of fusing multi-level features.

In this study, we aim at making full use of bi-phase complementary information from multiple levels for accurate pancreas segmentation. Such a task is quite challenging due to the large statistical discrepancies among features of different levels and different phases. Specifically, features of different phases play quite different roles in distinguishing different pancreas regions from the surrounding organs. Similarly, features of different levels have different contribution weights. Low-level features have richer details while high-level features contain more abundant semantic information. Moreover, when image quality degrades in one phase, such as abnormal lighting, the information provided by the phase would become more misleading than usual. Therefore, the impacts of features could vary a lot according to their locations, levels and phases. Simply combining these features without carefully analyze their respective impacts could inevitably incur nontrivial noises, significantly attenuating the benefits arising from complementary information fusion. To handle the varying predictive power of different features of the two phases, the fusion method should be selective, that is, adaptively select the useful information and suppress task-irrelevant noises.

To this end, this paper proposes a novel multi-phase and multi-level selective feature fusion network (MMNet) for accurate pancreas segmentation. Our MMNet uses an individual encoder in each phase to extract multi-level phase-related features. Then an adaptive cross refinement module is designed to first aggregate multi-level features and then adaptively select the most effective information from the aggregated features of one phase to refine each single-level features of the other phase. The selective feature fusion and refinement process is performed bi-directionally between the two phases to enable mutual benefits. Extensive experiments on our private dataset demonstrate that the proposed MMNet is superior to the single-phase baseline and the state-of-the-art fusion methods [8,17].

2   Method

This section first provides an overview of MMNet, followed by a detailed description of the ACR module. For convenience, we denote the venous phase and arterial phase as V-phase and A-phase respectively.

2.1   Overall Architecture

Figure 2 illustrates the framework of MMNet which takes a pair of spatially-aligned CT scans of the same subject as input, extracts single-phase multi-level features using the respective encoder (i.e. UE), fuses multi-level multi-phase features via the ACR module, and finally decodes the refined features for each phase using a decoder (i.e. UD). We denote multi-level features extracted from

V-phase and A-phase as $V = \{V^i, i = 1, 2, 3, 4\}$ and $A = \{A^j, j = 1, 2, 3, 4\}$ respectively. The encoders and decoders can be any convolutional neural network. In this study, we employ a shallow version of UNet [10] for both phases (with three downsampling layers in the encoder and three upsampling layers in the decoder).

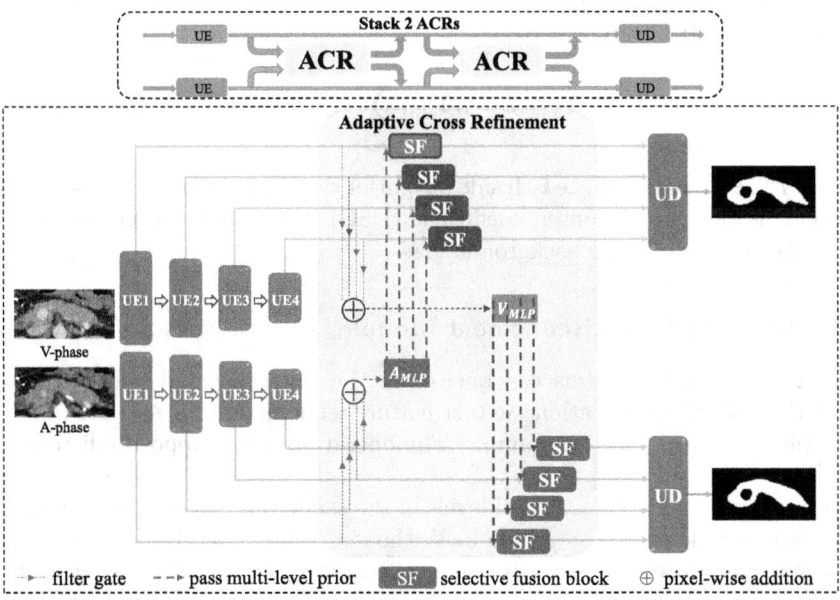

Fig. 2. The framework of the proposed MMNet. The dotted lines with arrows indicate the information exchange between the two phases. UE denotes the UNet encoder, UD denotes the UNet decoder. MLP denotes the multi-level prior.

After obtaining the multi-level features of each phase, the proposed ACR module exchanges features across two phases and fully integrates their advantages. The ACR module has two different direction-specific operations, that is, A-to-V and V-to-A information integrations. In the one-direction information flow, all feature maps of different levels in one phase (i.e. sender) are firstly aggregated as a multi-level prior, and then it is used to refine features at each level of the other phase (i.e. receiver). To suppress noises and select the most effective information from the multi-level prior of the sender, we introduce a filter gate at each layer of the sender before aggregation. Meanwhile, at each layer of the receiver, a selective fusion (SF) block is used to automatically learn weights to balance the amount of new information from the multi-level prior of the sender being integrated into the receiver. Through SF, the receiver learns the complementary semantics and details from the sender to suppress the non-pancreas noises at shallow layers and increase more boundary details into features at deep layers. Moreover, we stack two ACRs to progressively take full advantage of multi-level features of the two phases. In this case, the output of the first ACR is directly passed to the second ACR as its input.

Through the mutual enhancement between the two phases, we obtain refined features with greater distinctiveness. Then the refined features of each phase are passed to the respective decoders for segmentation maps. The parameters of the two decoders are shared. Each decoder is deeply supervised with four side outputs. Given the ground truth Y and segmentation maps (P_v, P_a), the loss of our framework is formulated as:

$$L_{total} = L(P_v, Y) + L(P_a, Y) + \sum_{i=1}^{4} (L(P_v^i, Y) + L(P_a^i, Y)) \tag{1}$$

Where P_v^i, P_a^i represents the i-th side output of the V-phase and A-phase respectively, L is the Dice-Sørensen coefficient (DSC) loss, which prevent the model from biasing towards the background class.

2.2 Adaptive Cross Refinement Module

The ACR module performs two operations, i.e. filtration and selective fusion (SF). For a simple explanation, we take feature refinement from A-phase (sender) to V-phase (receiver) as an example. The operation of the opposite direction is identical.

Filtration: Feature maps of all levels in the sender are aggregated as a multi-level prior by element-wise addition. Without careful supervision, useful information will be drowned in massive noises. To address the problem, we set a filter gate for features of each level before aggregation. The filter gate is a weight map in the range $[0, 1]$, and each pixel controls the filtering rate of the corresponding pixel position. The filter gate is set to 1 if the feature is helpful to the receiver; otherwise, the filter gate is to 0. The filter gate G_{out}^j and the multi-level prior A_{MLP}^i send to layer i of the receiver is defined as:

$$G_{out}^j = sigmoid(W_j A^j) \tag{2}$$

$$A_{MLP}^i = \sum_{j=1}^{4} S(G_{out}^j * A^j) \tag{3}$$

where W_j is the parameter of 1*1 convolution with a 1-channel output, A^j denotes the features of j-th layer of A-phase, S function is up or down sampling and a 1*1 convolution which makes the number of channels of the filtered features same as that of the receiver, and * is the element-wise multiplication.

Selective Fusion (SF): The basic idea of SF is to automatically learn weight maps to determine the pixel-wise feature importance and the amount of new information from the sender that the receiver should take into account. As shown in Fig. 3, at layer i of the receiver, SF block first fuses the input features $\{V^i, A_{MLP}^i\}$ via channel-wise concatenation, then we process the fused results using four convolutional layers. The first 1*1 convolution is to reduce

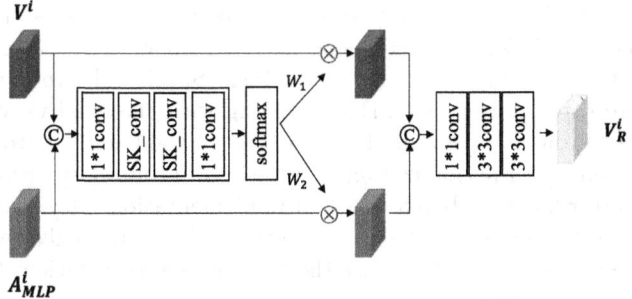

Fig. 3. The schematic illustration of the selective feature fusion block.

the number of channels, and the following two layers use selective kernel convolution [9], which can dynamically aggregate features obtained from kernels of different sizes. Through the last 1*1 convolution with a 2-channel output and softmax activation, two weight maps are produced to indicate the pixel-wise importance of each input. Then we reweight the input features by element-wise multiplication. Finally, the reweighted features are fused by concatenation and three convolutional layers, including one 1*1 convolution and two 3*3 convolutions, to produce the refined features V_R^i. The SF block adaptively learns weight maps of the two inputs according to their contributions. When the information provided by one phase is not good enough for the target task, it dynamically learns the complementary information from the other phase.

3   Experiment Results

3.1   Dataset and Implementation Details

We evaluate our method on a locally-collected dataset, which contains CT scans of 141 subjects. Each subject has images of both the venous and arterial phases. The subjects collected exclude pancreatitis, any pancreatic tumors, and other pancreatic lesions. We split the dataset into three parts, 71 cases in the training set, 16 cases in the validation set, and the rest 54 for testing. In particular, the testing set consists of 26 normal cases and 28 fatty cases. Subjects with fatty pancreas are more challenging since the inhomogeneous intensity distribution of the low-density areas makes it difficult to segment the pancreas as a whole (as shown in Fig. 4(a)).

We spatially align 3D CT images of the two phases via mutual information and the registration performance is 82.48% for DSC and 6.54 mm for the Hausdorff distance. The proposed multi-phase fusion aims at improving the fine stage of a coarse-to-fine framework [14,15], in which the coarse stage identifies a region of interest (ROI) containing a pancreas, and the fine stage produces accurate segmentation within the ROI. We observe that even if the ground-truth bounding box is used to crop the ROI, the fine stage can't achieve perfect segmentation

[14,15]. Therefore, improving the performance of the fine stage is important for improving the overall segmentation accuracy. We follow the methods in [14,15] to train 2D networks for the segmentation task. Specifically, the input images of MMNet are three consecutive 2D slices along with the axial view, which are cropped by the ground-truth bounding box. We set the batch size to 1 for training. We replaced batch normalization in UNet with group normalization [13] as it performs better for small batch size. Our implementation is based on PyTorch. The models are trained using Adam optimizer and we gradually decreased the learning rate starting at 1e−4. We use the Dice-Sørensen coefficient (DSC) metric to measure the segmentation accuracy.

3.2 Results

Table 1 shows the results of a single-phase baseline, four known and/or state-of-the-art fusion methods, MMNet and its variants. Since these fusion methods are model-agnostic, for a fair comparison, we implement all comparison methods based on our backbone. To analyze the impacts of each component in ACR, we have conducted an ablation study to compare our MMNet (having two ACRs) with its variants, including MMNet with only one ACR module (i.e. w/one ACR), MMNet without selective fusion (i.e. w/o SF), MMNet without deep supervision (i.e. w/o ds). To evaluate the performance of the proposed multi-level prior, we apply the ACR module to merge single-level features (i.e. w/o MLP). Specifically, in the information flow in one direction, MNet only sends features of the same resolution from one phase to the other phase.

Table 1. Quantitative comparison of different methods. We report DSC (%) results in the format of mean ± standard deviation.

Methods	Normal pancreas	Fatty pancreas	Testing set
Single-phase (V-phase)	90.14 ± 3.16	87.59 ± 6.38	88.82 ± 5.25
Concatenation	90.72 ± 3.15	86.88 ± 8.82	88.73 ± 6.98
Addition	90.61 ± 3.72	86.78 ± 8.89	88.63 ± 7.16
Hyper-connections (HPN [17])	91.41 ± 2.44	87.36 ± 9.10	89.31 ± 7.06
Spatial attention (FuseUNet [6])	91.26 ± 2.37	88.35 ± 7.15	89.75 ± 5.60
MMNet (proposed)	**91.88 ± 2.38**	**89.61 ± 6.67**	**90.70 ± 5.20**
MMNet w/ one ACR	91.65 ± 2.56	88.94 ± 7.47	90.24 ± 5.82
MMNet w/o SF	91.46 ± 2.54	86.80 ± 9.41	89.04 ± 7.38
MMNet w/o ds	91.61 ± 2.04	88.89 ± 7.63	90.20 ± 5.83
MMNet w/o MLP	91.80 ± 2.08	88.44 ± 8.92	90.06 ± 6.80

Three observations can be made from the results. First, all methods with multi-phase fusion (rows 2–6) outperform the single-phase method for the normal pancreas. For the fatty cases, among the four popular fusion methods (rows 2–5), only spatial attention (row 5) can achieve superior performance to the single-phase method. It shows that, by suppressing interference, the complementary information of different phases can be better utilized. Second, experimental results show that excluding an ACR module (i.e. w/one ACR), selective fusion (i.e. w/o SF), and deep supervision (i.e. w/o ds) from our MMNet decreases the DSC by 0.23%, 0.42%, 0.27% respectively for the normal cases, by 0.67%, 2.81%, 0.72% respectively for the fatty cases and by 0.46%, 1.66%, 0.50% respectively for the entire test cases. It is clear that selective fusion plays the most important role in improving the performance, in particular for the fatty cases (i.e. 2.81% improvement). Deep supervision and adding more ACR modules could provide additional improvements as well. Third, by introducing multi-level prior, there is a significant improvement in the fatty pancreas (from 88.44% to 89.61%), which validates the effectiveness of the mutual guidance between features at different levels of different phases.

Furthermore, we have calculated statistical significance using the paired t-test between MMNet and the other competing methods. The p-values of single-phase, concatenation, addition, HPN, FuseUNet are 5.59E−4, 2.31E−5, 3.32E−5, 1.15E−3 and 1.97E−5 respectively for the fatty pancreas, 2.63E−8, 4.85E−8, 1.75E−7, 1.71 E−4, 2.73E−8 respectively for the entire testing set. The results demonstrate that improvements achieved by our MMNet is statistically significant for both the fatty cases and the entire testing set (i.e. the p-values are all smaller than 5.00E−2). It is noteworthy that accurate segmentation of fatty pancreas is even more clinically meaningful than normal cases as it can not only predict the risk of glucose metabolism disorder, but also help preoperative prediction for pancreatectomy patients.

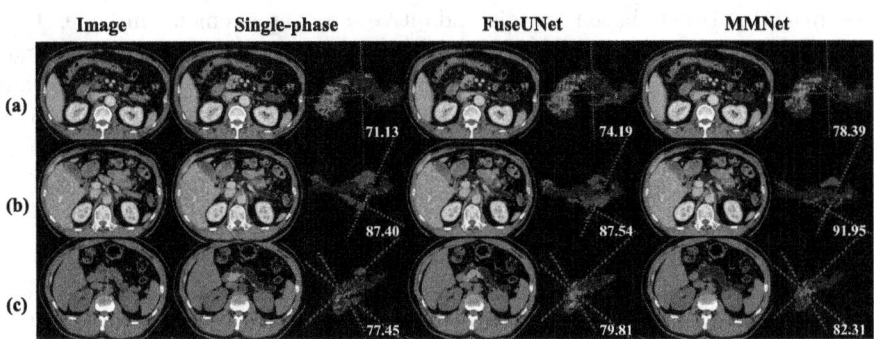

Fig. 4. Qualitative comparison of different methods. Blue, green and red voxels indicate true positives, false negatives and false positives respectively. For left to right, we show the input images of V-phase and the segmentation results of one slice and 3d segmentation results for different methods. The values report the DSC results (%) (Color figure online).

We display the segmentation results of three examples in Fig. 4. It can be observed that the proposed MMNet achieves better results in terms of fewer false negatives (a, c) and false positives (b, c). To further illustrate the effectiveness of the proposed method, Fig. 5 shows exemplar feature maps of each layer before and after the ACR module. As can be seen in Fig. 5, low-level features have rich details and clear boundaries, while they also contain massive background noises due to the limitation of the receptive field. Conversely, high-level features contain abundant semantic information and little background clutters, while they lack sufficient boundary details due to multiple downsampling operations. Through adaptively exchanging information between the two phases by ACR, the shallow features can take advantage of semantic information from deep features and vice versa.

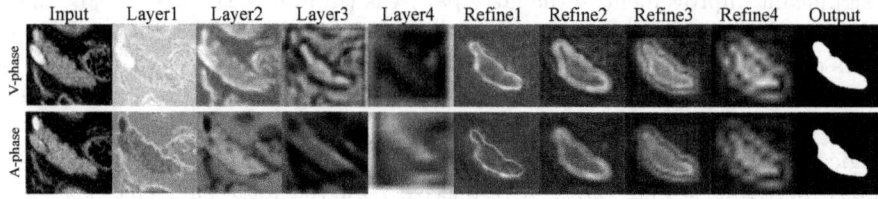

Fig. 5. The visualization of multi-level features of two phases before (columns 2–5) and after the ACR module (columns 6–9).

4   Conclusions

In this paper, we propose a novel multi-modal and multi-level selective feature fusion network based on the adaptive cross refinement module. Our method focuses on fully exploiting and effectively selecting multi-phase information. Experimental results demonstrate the effectiveness of the proposed fusion method MMNet for accurate pancreas segmentation. The future work includes integrating the proposed MMNet into a coarse-to-fine segmentation framework.

References

1. Baltrušaitis, T., Ahuja, C., Morency, L.P.: Multimodal machine learning: a survey and taxonomy. IEEE Trans. Pattern Anal. Mach. Intell. **41**(2), 423–443 (2018)
2. Chen, T., et al.: Multi-view learning with feature level fusion for cervical dysplasia diagnosis. In: Shen, D., et al. (eds.) MICCAI 2019. LNCS, vol. 11764, pp. 329–338. Springer, Cham (2019). https://doi.org/10.1007/978-3-030-32239-7_37
3. Chen, Yu., Chen, J., Wei, D., Li, Y., Zheng, Y.: OctopusNet: a deep learning segmentation network for multi-modal medical images. In: Li, Q., Leahy, R., Dong, B., Li, X. (eds.) MMMI 2019. LNCS, vol. 11977, pp. 17–25. Springer, Cham (2020). https://doi.org/10.1007/978-3-030-37969-8_3
4. Deng, Z., et al.: R3Net: recurrent residual refinement network for saliency detection. In: Proceedings of the 27th International Joint Conference on Artificial Intelligence, pp. 684–690. AAAI Press (2018)

5. Dolz, J., Gopinath, K., Yuan, J., Lombaert, H., Desrosiers, C., Ayed, I.B.: HyperDense-Net: a hyper-densely connected CNN for multi-modal image segmentation. IEEE Trans. Med. Imaging **38**(5), 1116–1126 (2018)

6. Hazirbas, C., Ma, L., Domokos, C., Cremers, D.: FuseNet: incorporating depth into semantic segmentation via fusion-based CNN architecture. In: Lai, S.-H., Lepetit, V., Nishino, K., Sato, Y. (eds.) ACCV 2016. LNCS, vol. 10111, pp. 213–228. Springer, Cham (2017). https://doi.org/10.1007/978-3-319-54181-5_14

7. Ilic, M., Ilic, I.: Epidemiology of pancreatic cancer. World J. Gastroenterol. **22**(44), 9694 (2016)

8. Li, C., Sun, H., Liu, Z., Wang, M., Zheng, H., Wang, S.: Learning cross-modal deep representations for multi-modal MR image segmentation. In: Shen, D., et al. (eds.) MICCAI 2019. LNCS, vol. 11765, pp. 57–65. Springer, Cham (2019). https://doi.org/10.1007/978-3-030-32245-8_7

9. Li, X., Wang, W., Hu, X., Yang, J.: Selective kernel networks. In: Proceedings of the IEEE Conference on Computer Vision and Pattern Recognition, pp. 510–519 (2019)

10. Ronneberger, O., Fischer, P., Brox, T.: U-Net: convolutional networks for biomedical image segmentation. In: Navab, N., Hornegger, J., Wells, W.M., Frangi, A.F. (eds.) MICCAI 2015. LNCS, vol. 9351, pp. 234–241. Springer, Cham (2015). https://doi.org/10.1007/978-3-319-24574-4_28

11. Wang, Y., et al.: Deep attentive features for prostate segmentation in 3d transrectal ultrasound. IEEE Trans. Med. Imaging **38**(12), 2768–2778 (2019)

12. Wen, Y., Jiang, X., Li, X., Yang, X., Han, P.: Automated pancreas segmentation based on multi-modal fusion of dual-energy CT images. In: The Radiological Society of North America Annual Meeting (RSNA) (2019)

13. Wu, Y., He, K.: Group normalization. In: Ferrari, V., Hebert, M., Sminchisescu, C., Weiss, Y. (eds.) ECCV 2018. LNCS, vol. 11217, pp. 3–19. Springer, Cham (2018). https://doi.org/10.1007/978-3-030-01261-8_1

14. Xie, L., Yu, Q., Zhou, Y., Wang, Y., Fishman, E.K., Yuille, A.L.: Recurrent saliency transformation network for tiny target segmentation in abdominal CT scans. IEEE Trans. Med. Imaging **39**(2), 514–525 (2019)

15. Yu, Q., Xie, L., Wang, Y., Zhou, Y., Fishman, E.K., Yuille, A.L.: Recurrent saliency transformation network: incorporating multi-stage visual cues for small organ segmentation. In: Proceedings of the IEEE Conference on Computer Vision and Pattern Recognition, pp. 8280–8289 (2018)

16. Zhang, L., Dai, J., Lu, H., He, Y., Wang, G.: A bi-directional message passing model for salient object detection. In: Proceedings of the IEEE Conference on Computer Vision and Pattern Recognition, pp. 1741–1750 (2018)

17. Zhou, Y., et al.: Hyper-pairing network for multi-phase pancreatic ductal adenocarcinoma segmentation. In: Shen, D., et al. (eds.) MICCAI 2019. LNCS, vol. 11765, pp. 155–163. Springer, Cham (2019). https://doi.org/10.1007/978-3-030-32245-8_18

Asymmetrical Multi-task Attention U-Net for the Segmentation of Prostate Bed in CT Image

Xuanang Xu[1], Chunfeng Lian[1], Shuai Wang[1], Andrew Wang[2], Trevor Royce[2], Ronald Chen[2], Jun Lian[2(✉)], and Dinggang Shen[1]

[1] Department of Radiology and BRIC, University of North Carolina at Chapel Hill, Chapel Hill, NC 27599, USA
dinggang.shen@gmail.com
[2] Department of Radiation Oncology, University of North Carolina at Chapel Hill, Chapel Hill, NC 27599, USA
jun_lian@med.unc.edu

Abstract. Segmentation of the prostate bed, the residual tissue after the removal of the prostate gland, is an essential prerequisite for post-prostatectomy radiotherapy but also a challenging task due to its non-contrast boundaries and highly variable shapes relying on neighboring organs. In this work, we propose a novel deep learning-based method to automatically segment this "invisible target". As the main idea of our design, we expect to get reference from the surrounding normal structures (bladder&rectum) and take advantage of this information to facilitate the prostate bed segmentation. To achieve this goal, we first use a U-Net as the backbone network to perform the bladder&rectum segmentation, which serves as a low-level task that can provide references to the high-level task of the prostate bed segmentation. Based on the backbone network, we build a novel attention network with a series of cascaded attention modules to further extract discriminative features for the high-level prostate bed segmentation task. Since the attention network has one-sided dependency on the backbone network, simulating the clinical workflow to use normal structures to guide the segmentation of radiotherapy target, we name the final composition model asymmetrical multi-task attention U-Net. Extensive experiments on a clinical dataset consisting of 186 CT images demonstrate the effectiveness of this new design and the superior performance of the model in comparison to the conventional atlas-based methods for prostate bed segmentation. The source code is publicly available at https://github.com/superxuang/amta-net.

Keywords: CT image segmentation · Fully convolutional networks · Multi-task learning

This work was supported in part by NIH Grant CA206100.

Electronic supplementary material The online version of this chapter (https://doi.org/10.1007/978-3-030-59719-1_46) contains supplementary material, which is available to authorized users.

1   Introduction

Radical prostatectomy is an effective treatment for prostate cancer when the cancer is confined to the prostate. However, after the resection of the prostate gland, residual cancerous tissue may yet be hiding in the remaining part of the surgical bed and the surrounding tissues, where the region is known as the prostate bed (or prostatic fossa). Without treatment, this can increase the risk of cancer recurrence even metastasis substantially. To irradiate the cancerous tissue, postoperative radiotherapy on the prostate bed is regarded as a standard adjuvant or salvage setting for the radical prostatectomy. As a prerequisite for the postoperative radiotherapy, accurate prostate bed segmentation in planning computed tomography (CT) images is vital to the success of the disease control.

However, accurate contouring of the prostate bed from CT image is a highly challenging and unique task. As shown in Fig. 1, the prostate bed, an anatomical region in the male pelvis situated between the bladder and rectum, mainly consists of the residual prostatic tissue after the removal of the prostate gland and some adjacent volume of the bladder. It is not an intact structure with boundary like the prostate gland so often referred to as a "virtual" volume [1,3,4] in the literature. This made the segmentation of the prostate bed a unique problem and much harder than the segmentation of most other structures. The boundary of the prostate bed is mainly defined by the shape of neighboring organs and a series of consensus guidelines [9,10,12,14] rather than the local intensity contrast. Therefore, it is difficult to distinguish the prostate bed in CT image merely considering the difference in gray level without any anatomical knowledge. Moreover, since the prostate bed mainly consists of soft tissues, its shape and size are highly variable across different patients. The status (full or empty) of the neighboring bladder and rectum could significantly change the volume of the prostate bed.

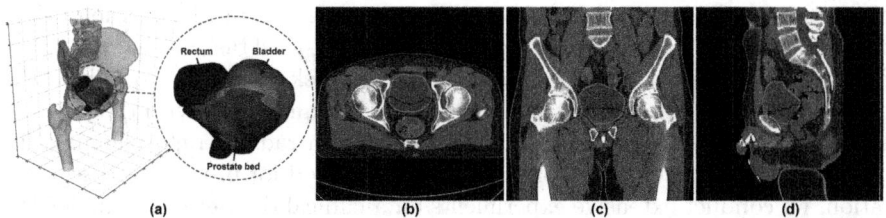

Fig. 1. An exampled post-prostatectomy case displaying the prostate bed (red), bladder (yellow), and rectum (cyan) in 3D (a) and 2D (b, c, d) views (Color figure online).

In clinical practice, this challenging task is commonly carried out by the physicians using manual contouring tools, which is time-consuming and prone to inter-observer variation. Although automated workflows are highly desired, there are only a few methods proposed for the prostate bed segmentation using the atlas-based methods [1,3]. Hwee et al. [3] firstly tried to segment the prostate bed automatically using a commercial atlas-based segmentation (ABS) software with

75 atlas images. Although their method could achieve significantly faster speed than the manual contouring procedure, the accuracy of the generated contours are not adequate for clinical use (with a mean Dice similarity coefficient (DSC) of 0.47). Similar conclusion was drawn in a later research by Delpon et al. [1] They compared the performance of five commercial ABS systems for prostate bed and neighboring organs-at-risk (OAR) segmentation. The results showed that the ABS methods were very efficient and accurate for high-contrast organs (e.g.., the femoral heads) but insufficient for the prostate bed. Overall, the atlas-based methods are not accurate enough for the prostate bed segmentation due to (1) over-reliance on local intensity contrast and (2) less consideration of the geometric correlation between the prostate bed and the neighboring organs.

In this paper, to address the issues above, we present a novel asymmetrical multi-task attention U-Net (AMTA-U-Net) to perform accurate segmentation of the prostate bed in CT image. Deep learning-based methods, specifically the fully convolutional networks (FCNs) [5, 6, 8], have significantly improved the accuracy of medical image segmentation, especially for the organs suffering highly variable shapes and ambiguous boundaries (e.g., pelvic organs [2, 13, 15]). Thus, we propose to use the FCN as the framework to handle the difficult prostate bed segmentation. Considering the strong geometric correlation between the prostate bed and bladder&rectum, we formulate the prostate bed segmentation as a high-level task depending on the low-level task of bladder&rectum segmentation, finally resulting in a novel multi-task network with asymmetrical attention mechanism to derive the prostate bed mask from the structural information of bladder&rectum.

In summary, the main contribution of this work is three-fold: (1) To achieve robust segmentation of the prostate bed, a treatment target with no clear margin, we leverage the power of deep learning to handle this challenging problem. To the best of our knowledge, this is the first attempt using deep learning-based methods to solve this clinical problem. (2) To further improve the segmentation accuracy of the prostate bed, we propose a novel asymmetrical multi-task attention U-Net to formulate the prostate bed segmentation as a high-level task getting references from the low-level bladder&rectum segmentation task. (3) As a by-product, the proposed method can segment the bladder and rectum jointly with the prostate bed, which is meaningful for the OAR definition in radiotherapy planning. To demonstrate the effectiveness of the proposed method for prostate bed segmentation, we conduct extensive experiments on a clinical dataset consisting of 186 CT images from 186 real post-prostatectomy subjects. The experimental results show that the proposed AMTA-U-Net achieves higher accuracy than the baseline U-Net and other multi-task deep models and significantly outperforms the conventional atlas-based methods.

2   Method

In this section, we will introduce in details the proposed AMTA-U-Net for prostate bed segmentation. The top part of Fig. 2 gives a schematic representation of this method. It mainly consists of two components: (1) a backbone network with U-Net architecture used for the low-level bladder&rectum segmentation task, and (2) an attention network built with a series of cascaded attention modules (AM) on the backbone network used for the high-level prostate bed segmentation task. The inner structure of the attention module is shown at the bottom of Fig. 2.

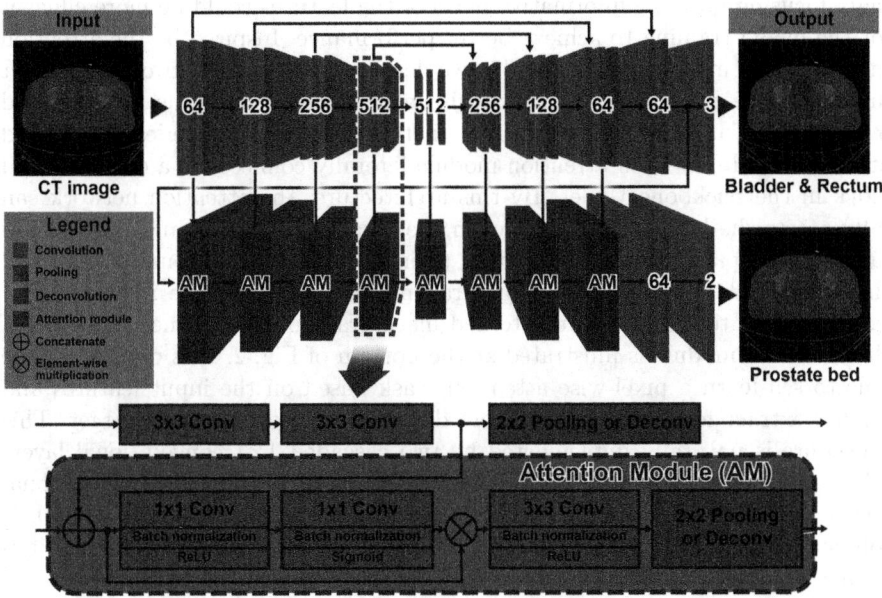

Fig. 2. Schematic representation of the proposed asymmetrical multi-task attention U-Net (top) and the inner structure of the attention module (bottom).

2.1 Backbone Network for Bladder&Rectum Segmentation

The shape of the bladder&rectum is an essential reference for human physicians when they delineate the prostate bed. It would also be a prerequisite for the proposed method to segment the bladder&rectum first. To achieve this goal, we exploit the U-Net[11], which is a classical and powerful FCN architecture for medical image segmentation, as the backbone network to predict a pixel-wise mask of the bladder&rectum. The detailed architecture of the backbone U-Net is illustrated at the top of Fig. 2. The number labeled on each convolutional block denotes the corresponding output channels. As the input image propagates through the backbone network, we can get not only the segmentation mask of the bladder&rectum but also a series of hierarchical feature maps with gradually increased bladder&rectum structural information. These feature maps will serve as the reference to be further inferred in the subsequent attention network to predict the final prostate bed mask.

2.2   Attention Network for Prostate Bed Segmentation

Since the prostate bed boundary largely depends on the shape of the bladder&rectum, it is intuitive that the hierarchical features used for the bladder&rectum segmentation can also be used as the reference for the prostate bed segmentation. However, instead of directly learning from the entire feature map, focusing on some informative parts of the features could be more efficient for the model training to achieve better performance. Inspired by the attention mechanism in multi-task learning [7], we design an attention network to extract discriminative features from the backbone network to infer the prostate bed mask. As shown in Fig. 2, the attention network consists of a series of cascaded attention modules. Each attention module laterally connects to a convolutional block in the backbone U-Net. By this architecture, the attention network can fully access the hierarchical features in the backbone network and take advantages of the spatial image information (from the left convolutional blocks) and the semantic bladder&rectum structural information (from the right convolutional blocks) to infer the prostate bed mask gradually. The inner structure of the attention module is illustrated at the bottom of Fig. 2. It is designed to be able to self-learn a pixel-wise attention mask based on the input features and further extract features that are more discriminative for the final target. This procedure is naturally implemented by two cascaded 1×1 convolutional layers followed by another 3×3 convolutional layer. The first two 1×1 convolutional layers act as a feature selector, which is used to self-learn an element-wise $[0, 1]$ soft mask to tailor the input features by element-wise multiplication. The following 3×3 convolutional layer acts as a feature extractor to further adapt the masked feature map to the final target. To keep the spatial consistency, a 2×2 pooling/deconvolutional layer is used to down-/up-sample the extracted feature map at the end of the attention module.

2.3   Implementation Details

The proposed AMTA-U-Net takes 2D CT slices as the input. To take more spatial context into consideration, we combine two adjacent slices with the center slice to compose a 3-channel input image. All the CT slices are center-cropped and resampled to a uniform size of 128×128 with a spatial resolution of $2\,\mathrm{mm}\times2\,\mathrm{mm}$. Pixel intensities are rescaled from $[-200, 800]$ Hounsfield Unit (HU) to $[0, 1]$. To mitigate overfitting in the training stage, we randomly translate and rotate the input CT slices in a range of $[-5.00, 5.00]$mm and $[-0.05, 0.05]$rad, respectively. We train the models for 100 epochs with a base learning rate of 10^{-3} and a batch size of 144. For all training epochs, the model achieving the best performance on the validation set is used as the final model to be evaluated with the testing set. The implementation of the proposed method has been made publicly available at https://github.com/superxuang/amta-net.

3   Experiments

3.1   Dataset

We conduct experiments on a dataset that consists of 186 post-prostatectomy patients collected in one clinical site from the year 2009 to 2019. Each subject contains one planning CT image and three segmentation masks corresponding to the prostate bed, bladder, and rectum, respectively. We randomly divide the dataset into five-folds and use cross-validation to evaluate the performance of different models (three for training, one for validation, and one for testing). DSC and average symmetric surface distance (ASD) are used as the metrics for the evaluation.

3.2   Contribution Role of the Bladder&Rectum in Prostate Bed Segmentation

As we aforementioned, the contour of the bladder&rectum is an essential reference to help physicians in the manual delineation of the prostate bed. Thus, the reference contour may serve as a prerequisite for automatic methods as well. To verify the contribution of the bladder&rectum structures in the prostate bed segmentation, we consider the ground-truth mask of the bladder&rectum as prior knowledge. We combine it with the input CT slices to compose a multi-channel image, which is used to predict the prostate bed mask through a standard U-Net. As the experimental results show in Table 1, when using the prior knowledge of the bladder&rectum, the U-Net achieves an average DSC of 75.54%, which is 2.25% higher than that of a U-Net does not use the prior knowledge of the bladder&rectum (DSC = 73.29%). This result demonstrates that the bladder&rectum structural information can help to improve the segmentation accuracy of the prostate bed. Based on this finding, in the design of our proposed method, we consider the prostate bed and the bladder&rectum jointly, and reform the prostate bed segmentation as a high-level task based on the low-level task of the bladder&rectum segmentation.

Table 1. Comparison of prostate bed segmentation with/without bladder&rectum structural prior knowledge.

Using prior knowledge of bladder& rectum	DSC [mean(std) %]	ASD [mean(std) mm]
No	73.29(7.43)	2.79(1.27)
Yes	**75.54**(6.92)	**2.47**(1.12)

3.3   Comparison with Different Deep Learning Models

For the proposed method, there are three key properties contributing to the final improvement of the prostate bed segmentation when compared with the baseline U-Net: (1) the multi-task learning strategy improving model generalization by parameter sharing, (2) the asymmetrical network architecture underlining the geometric dependency between the prostate bed and the bladder&rectum, and (3) the attention mechanism selecting discriminative features for the specific target. To verify the effectiveness of these designs, in this experiment, we compare the proposed method with other deep models which are related to different combinations of the above properties. The experimental results are summarized in Table 2.

Table 2. Comparison of different deep learning-based models.

Models	DSC [mean(std) %]			ASD [mean(std) mm]		
	PB	Bladder	Rectum	PB	Bladder	Rectum
U-Net	73.29(7.43)	-	-	2.79(1.27)	-	-
Multi-task U-Net	74.41(7.23)	87.84(10.04)	80.22(7.82)	2.58(1.21)	1.62(2.12)	**2.50**(1.85)
Cascaded U-Net	75.03(7.41)	87.93(8.95)	79.68(9.54)	2.54(1.23)	1.53(1.47)	2.78(2.97)
MTA-U-Net[7]	75.03(7.11)	**88.46**(8.08)	80.31(9.23)	2.51(1.13)	**1.44**(1.30)	2.56(2.91)
Proposed	**75.67**(6.56)	88.40(8.72)	**80.35**(9.36)	**2.42**(1.03)	1.47(1.22)	2.60(3.00)

As shown in Table 2, all the multi-task models (Multi-task U-Net, Cascaded U-Net, MTA-U-Net, and our method) outperform the single-task model (U-Net), demonstrating the effectiveness of the multi-task learning strategy for the prostate bed segmentation. Among the multi-task models, the proposed method achieves the highest accuracy on the prostate bed, outperforming the models without consideration of the dependency between the prostate bed and bladder&rectum (Multi-task U-Net and MTA-U-Net), nor the attention mechanism (Multi-task U-Net and Cascaded U-Net). This result indicates that an attention mechanism to include the geometric dependency between the prostate bed and bladder&rectum can help improve the prostate bed segmentation.

3.4   Comparison with Atlas-Based Method

As we introduced in Sect. 1, the topic of automated prostate bed segmentation has been rarely studied in the past except for a few attempts using some commercial atlas-based segmentation (ABS) software. Hence, to demonstrate the superior performance of the proposed method, we conduct a comparison between these commercial ABS software and the proposed method. In this comparison, we not only list the results of the commercial ABS software that are conducted from different datasets but also evaluate one of the high-performance ABS software on our dataset using the same 5-folds cross-validation strategy

Table 3. Comparison with commercial atlas-based segmentation (ABS) software.

Method	Dataset (Train/test)	DSC [mean (std) %]			ASD [mean (std) mm]		
		PB	Bladder	Rectum	PB	Bladder	Rectum
ABS(MIM)[3]	80(75/5)	47.0(16.0)	67.0(18.0)	58.0(9.0)	-	-	-
ABS(WFB)[1]	20(10/10)	56.0(10.0)	76.0(12.0)	73.0(7.0)	-	-	-
ABS(MIM)[1]	20(10/10)	61.0(9.0)	80.0(14.0)	75.0(7.0)	-	-	-
ABS(ABAS)[1]	20(10/10)	67.0(13.0)	81.0(13.0)	75.0(9.0)	-	-	-
ABS(SPICE)[1]	20(10/10)	37.0(9.0)	76.0(26.0)	68.0(12.0)	-	-	-
ABS(RS)[1]	20(10/10)	51.0(17.0)	59.0(15.0)	49.0(12.0)	-	-	-
ABS(MIM)	186(5-fold CV)	64.2(11.9)	64.1(17.5)	61.8(11.5)	4.8(11.4)	7.7(15.3)	5.9(11.0)
Proposed	186(5-fold CV)	**75.7**(6.6)	**88.4**(8.7)	**80.4**(9.4)	**2.4**(1.0)	**1.5**(1.2)	**2.6**(3.0)

as our proposed method (four folds for atlas building and one fold for testing). As the results show in Table 3, the proposed method significantly outperforms the atlas-based method on both the prostate bed segmentation task and the bladder&rectum segmentation task, demonstrating the superior performance of the proposed method when compared with the conventional atlas-based method. Figure 3 gives a visualization of some cases in this comparison.

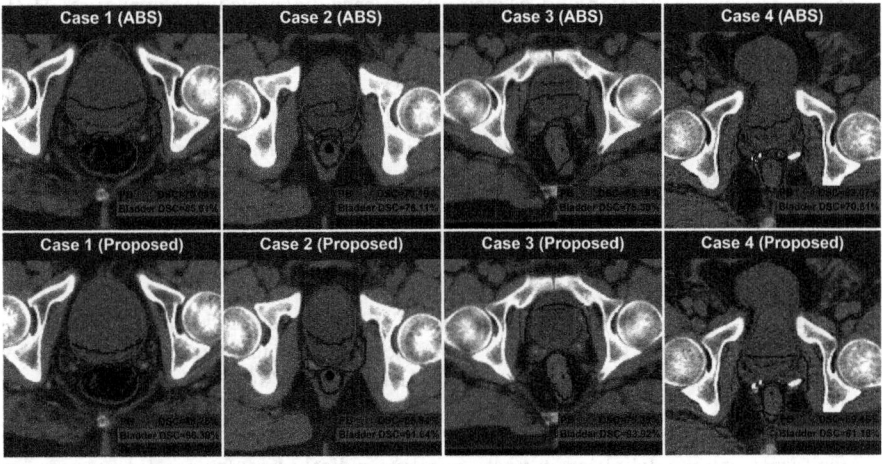

Fig. 3. Contours generated by the ABS method and the proposed method. The predicted and the ground-truth contours are denoted by solid and dash lines, respectively.

4   Conclusion

In this work, we present a novel multi-task deep learning-based method, the asymmetrical multi-task attention U-Net, to handle the highly challenging problem of the "invisible target"—prostate bed segmentation in CT images. The proposed method performs the prostate bed segmentation jointly with the bladder&rectum segmentation in a multi-task manner. The high-level task of prostate bed segmentation is accomplished by an attention network that can extract discriminative features from a backbone U-Net used for the low-level task of bladder&rectum segmentation. Extensive experiments on a clinical dataset consisting of 186 CT images demonstrate the effectiveness of the designs in the proposed method and the superior performance of the deep learning-based methods in comparison to the conventional atlas-based methods for prostate bed segmentation.

References

1. Delpon, G., et al.: Comparison of automated atlas-based segmentation software for postoperative prostate cancer radiotherapy. Front. Oncol. **6**, 178 (2016)
2. He, K., Cao, X., Shi, Y., Nie, D., Gao, Y., Shen, D.: Pelvic organ segmentation using distinctive curve guided fully convolutional networks. IEEE Trans. Med. Imaging **38**(2), 585–595 (2018)
3. Hwee, J., et al.: Technology assessment of automated atlas based segmentation in prostate bed contouring. Radiat. Oncol. **6**(1), 110 (2011)
4. Latorzeff, I., Sargos, P., Loos, G., Supiot, S., Guerif, S., Carrie, C.: Delineation of the prostate bed: the "invisible target" is still an issue? Front. Oncol. **7**, 108 (2017)
5. Lian, C., Liu, M., Zhang, J., Shen, D.: Hierarchical fully convolutional network for joint atrophy localization and Alzheimer's disease diagnosis using structural MRI. IEEE Trans. Pattern Anal. Mach. Intell. **42**(4), 880–893 (2020)
6. Lian, C., Zhang, J., Liu, M., Zong, X., Hung, S.C., Lin, W., Shen, D.: Multi-channel multi-scale fully convolutional network for 3D perivascular spaces segmentation in 7T MR images. Med. Image Anal. **46**, 106–117 (2018)
7. Liu, S., Johns, E., Davison, A.J.: End-to-end multi-task learning with attention. In: Proceedings of the IEEE Conference on Computer Vision and Pattern Recognition, pp. 1871–1880 (2019)
8. Long, J., Shelhamer, E., Darrell, T.: Fully convolutional networks for semantic segmentation. In: Proceedings of the IEEE Conference on Computer Vision and Pattern Recognition, pp. 3431–3440 (2015)
9. Michalski, J.M., et al.: Development of RTOG consensus guidelines for the definition of the clinical target volume for postoperative conformal radiation therapy for prostate cancer. Int. J. Radiat. Oncol. Biol. Phys. **76**(2), 361–368 (2010)
10. Poortmans, P., Bossi, A., Vandeputte, K., Bosset, M., Miralbell, R., Maingon, P., Boehmer, D., Budiharto, T., Symon, Z., Van den Bergh, A.C., et al.: Guidelines for target volume definition in post-operative radiotherapy for prostate cancer, on behalf of the EORTC radiation oncology group. Radiother. Oncol. **84**(2), 121–127 (2007)
11. Ronneberger, O., Fischer, P., Brox, T.: U-Net: convolutional networks for biomedical image segmentation. In: Navab, N., Hornegger, J., Wells, W.M., Frangi, A.F. (eds.) MICCAI 2015. LNCS, vol. 9351, pp. 234–241. Springer, Cham (2015). https://doi.org/10.1007/978-3-319-24574-4_28
12. Sidhom, M.A., Kneebone, A.B., Lehman, M., Wiltshire, K.L., Millar, J.L., Mukherjee, R.K., Shakespeare, T.P., Tai, K.H.: Post-prostatectomy radiation therapy: consensus guidelines of the Australian and New Zealand radiation oncology genitourinary group. Radiother. Oncol. **88**(1), 10–19 (2008)

13. Wang, S., He, K., Nie, D., Zhou, S., Gao, Y., Shen, D.: Ct male pelvic organ segmentation using fully convolutional networks with boundary sensitive representation. Med. Image Anal. **54**, 168–178 (2019)
14. Wiltshire, K.L., et al.: Anatomic boundaries of the clinical target volume (prostate bed) after radical prostatectomy. Int. J. Radiat. Oncol. Biol. Phys. **69**(4), 1090–1099 (2007)
15. Xu, X., Zhou, F., Liu, B.: Automatic bladder segmentation from CT images using deep CNN and 3d fully connected CRF-RNN. Int. J. Comput. Assist. Radiol. Surg. **13**(7), 967–975 (2018)

Learning High-Resolution and Efficient Non-local Features for Brain Glioma Segmentation in MR Images

Haozhe Jia[1,2,4], Yong Xia[1,2(✉)], Weidong Cai[3], and Heng Huang[4,5]

[1] Research and Development Institute of Northwestern Polytechnical University in Shenzhen, Shenzhen 518057, China
yxia@nwpu.edu.cn
[2] National Engineering Laboratory for Integrated Aero-Space-Ground-Ocean Big Data Application Technology, School of Computer Science and Engineering, Northwestern Polytechnical University, Xi'an 710072, China
[3] School of Computer Science, University of Sydney, Sydney, NSW 2006, Australia
[4] Department of Electrical and Computer Engineering, University of Pittsburgh, Pittsburgh, PA 15261, USA
[5] JD Finance America Corporation, Mountain View, CA 94043, USA

Abstract. Brain glioma segmentation using multi-parametric magnetic resonance (MR) imaging has significant clinical value. Although 3D convolutional neural networks (CNNs) have become increasingly prevalent in delivering this segmentation task, these models still suffer from an insufficient ability to high-resolution feature representation for small and irregular regions, limited local receptive fields, and poor long-range dependencies. In this paper, we propose a 3D High-resolution and Non-local Feature Network (HNF-Net) for brain glioma segmentation using multi-parametric MR imaging. We construct HNF-Net based mainly on the parallel multi-scale fusion (PMF) module, which helps produce strong high-resolution feature representation and aggregate multi-scale contextual information. We also introduce the expectation-maximization attention (EMA) module to HNF-Net, aiming to capture the long-range dependent contextual information and reduce the feature redundancy in a lightweight fashion. We evaluated our HNF-Net on the BraTS 2019 Challenge dataset against eight top-ranking methods listed on the challenge leaderboard. Our results suggest that the proposed HNF-Net achieves improved overall performance over these methods, and our ablation study demonstrates the effectiveness of the PMF module and EMA module.

Keywords: Brain glioma segmentation · High-resolution feature representation · Lightweight non-local module

1 Introduction

As the most common primary brain malignancy, gliomas generally contain heterogeneous histological sub-regions, i.e. edema/invasion, active tumor structures,

© Springer Nature Switzerland AG 2020
A. L. Martel et al. (Eds.): MICCAI 2020, LNCS 12264, pp. 480–490, 2020.
https://doi.org/10.1007/978-3-030-59719-1_47

cystic/necrotic components, and non-enhancing gross abnormality. Accurate and automated segmentation of these intrinsic sub-regions using multi-parametric magnetic resonance (MR) imaging is critical for the potential diagnosis and treatment of this disease. This task, however, remains challenging, due to the heterogeneity of gliomas in shape, appearance, and location [2].

With deep learning being widely applied to computer vision applications, convolutional neural networks (CNNs) have been designed for this segmentation task and have shown convincing performance. In [8], Havaei et al. proposed a 2D CNN to exploit both local features and global contextual features simultaneously, which outperforms the previous methods while being over 30 times faster. Dong et al. [6] utilized a 2D U-Net [16] to segment brain gliomas in a fully convolutional fashion and introduced a soft Dice loss [13] to further improve the accuracy. However, the performance of these models remains limited, since they only focus on 2D intra-slice features and ignore 3D global contextual information.

Kamnitsas et al. [10] constructed a 3D dual pathway CNN, namely DeepMedic, which simultaneously processes the input image at multiple scales with a dual pathway architecture so as to exploit both local and global contextual information. DeepMedic also uses a 3D fully connected conditional random field to remove false positives. This model, however, tends to lose the global structural information since it uses small local image patches as its input, and the inference is inefficient for the same reason. To jointly use the 3D contextual information and global structural information, a recent popular practice is to construct segmentation models based on 3D U-Net [4]. In [9], Isensee et al. achieved outstanding segmentation performance using a 3D U-Net with instance normalization and leaky ReLU activation, in conjunction with a combination loss function and a region-based training strategy. Chen et al. [3] proposed a highly efficient 3D U-Net, which leverages the 3D multi-fiber unit to reduce the computational cost and uses 3D dilated convolutions to build multi-scale feature representation, and achieved satisfactory accuracy in the real-time segmentation of brain gliomas. In [14], Myronenko et al. incorporated a variational auto-encoder (VAE) based reconstruction decoder into a 3D U-Net to regularize the shared encoder, and achieved the state-of-the-art segmentation performance at that time.

Despite their performance gains over previous approaches, these 3D U-Net based methods still have two major limitations. First, the encoders of these models have limited convolutional layers and parameters in high-resolution stages to avoid high GPU memory usage, and the decoder may lose some detailed contextual information when low-resolution features are upsampled to form high-resolution features. Consequently, these models usually have insufficient high-resolution feature representation ability for small and irregular regions such as the enhancing tumor and tumor core. Second, these models can hardly overcome the difficulties caused by the highly variable locations, morphology, and sub-structures of gliomas, since they usually extract features with fixed geometric structures which result in limited local receptive fields and poor long-range dependencies. Although Non-local self-attention modules [7,20,21] have been proposed to build long-range dependencies of spatial contextual information for computer vision tasks, the high computation complexity and GPU memory occupation make it hard to be applied to volumetric medical image segmentation.

In this paper, we propose a 3D High-resolution and Non-local Feature Network (HNF-Net) for brain glioma segmentation using multi-parametric MR imaging. We construct HNF-Net based mainly on the parallel multi-scale fusion (PMF) module, which maintains strong high-resolution feature representation and aggregates multi-scale contextual information. We further reformulate the Non-local self-attention mechanism in a light-weight expectation-maximization iteration manner, and thus introduce the expectation-maximization attention (EMA) module [11] to HNF-Net to enhance the long-range dependent spatial contextual information at the cost of acceptable computational complexity. We evaluated the proposed HNF-Net on the BraTS 2019 dataset against eight top-tier solutions. Our results demonstrate the effectiveness of the proposed PMF and EMA modules and the superior performance of our HNF-Net.

The contributions of this work are two-fold: (1) we construct HNF-Net with the PMF module to learn high-resolution feature representation and aggregate multi-scale contextual information; and (2) we introduce the EMA module to capture Non-local long-range dependent spatial contextual information in a lightweight fashion.

2   Dataset

We used the BraTS 2019 Challenge database [1,2,12] for this research, which contains 335 training and 125 validation multi-parametric brain MR studies. Each study has four MR images, including T1-weighted (T1), post-contrast T1-weighted (T1ce), T2-weighted (T2), and fluid attenuated inversion recovery (Flair) sequences. All MR images have the same size of $240 \times 240 \times 155$ and the same voxel spacing of $1 \times 1 \times 1\,\mathrm{mm}^3$. For each study, the enhancing tumor (ET), peritumoral edema (ED), and necrotic and non-enhancing tumor core (NCR/NET) were annotated on a voxel-by-voxel basis by experts. The annotations for training studies are publicly available, and the annotations for validation studies are withheld for online evaluation.

3   Method

The proposed HNF-Net has an encoder-decoder structure. For each study, four multi-parametric brain MR sequences are first concatenated to form a four-channel input and then processed at five scales i.e., r, $1/2r$, ... $1/16r$, highlighted in green, yellow, blue, pink, and orange in Fig. 1, respectively. At the original scale r, there are four convolutional blocks, two for encoding and the other two for decoding. The connection from the encoder to the decoder skips the processing at other scales so as to maintain the high resolution and spatial information in a long-range residual fashion. At other four scales, four PMF modules are jointly used as a high-resolution and multi-scale aggregated feature extractor.

At the end of the last PMF module, the output feature maps at four scales are first recovered to the $1/2r$ scale and then concatenated as mixed features. Next, the EMA module is used to efficiently capture long-range dependent contextual information and reduce the redundancy of the obtained mixed features. Finally, the output of the EMA module is recovered to original scale r and 32 channels via $1 \times 1 \times 1$ convolutions and upsampling and then added to the full-resolution feature map produced by the encoder for the dense prediction of voxel labels. We adopt a combination of generalized Dice loss [18] and cross-entropy loss as the loss function. We now delve into the details of the PMF module and EMA module.

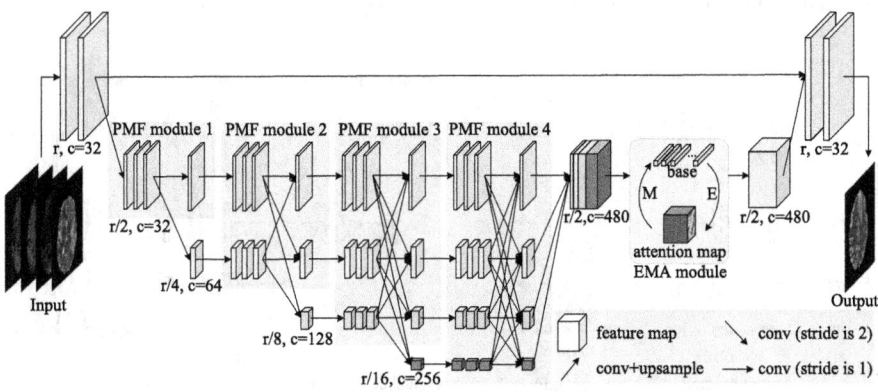

Fig. 1. Diagram of the proposed HNF-Net. r denotes the original resolution and c denotes the channel number of feature maps.

3.1   PMF Module for High-Resolution Feature Representation

It has been observed that the high-resolution low-level features produced at the early stages of CNNs reveal fine spatial information but have weak semantic guidance, whereas the low-resolution high-level features have strong semantic consistency but give coarse spatial predictions. Given that learning strong high-resolution representation is essential for small object segmentation, high-resolution features are maintained throughout the segmentation process in recent solutions [15,17,19], and it has been shown that this strategy contributes to convincing performance.

For this study, we construct the PMF module as the main component of our HNF-Net. The PMF module has two parts, the parallel multi-scale convolutional block and fully connected fusion block, as shown in Fig. 2(a) and Fig. 2(b), respectively. The former has a set of parallel branches similar to the group convolution, and each branch is built with repeated residual convolutional blocks at a specific scale. The latter fuses all output features of the parallel multi-scale convolutional block in a parallel but fully connected fashion, where each branch is the summation of the output features of all resolution branches. Thus, in each PMF Module, the parallel multi-scale convolutional block can fully exploit multi-resolution features but maintain high-resolution feature representation, and the fully connected fusion block can aggregate rich multi-scale contextual information.

Moreover, we cascade multiple PMF modules, in which the number of branches increases progressively with depth, as shown in Fig. 2(c). As a result, from the perspective of the highest resolution stage, its high-resolution feature representation is boosted with repeated fusion of multi-scale low-resolution representations. Meanwhile, the cascade network can be regarded as an ensemble of several U-shape sub-networks with different depths and widths, which tends to further reduce the semantic gap of the features at different depths.

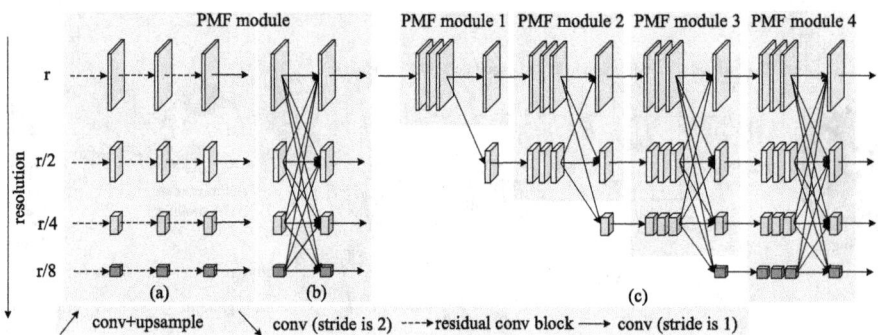

Fig. 2. Architecture of the PMF module. The PMF module has two parts, the parallel multi-scale convolutional block and fully connected fusion block, as shown in (a) and (b), respectively. In our proposed HNF-Net, we cascade multiple PMF modules together with the structure shown in (c). All downsample operations are achieved with 2-stride convolutions, and all upsample operations are achieved with joint $1 \times 1 \times 1$ convolutions and trilinear interpolation. It is noted that, since it is inconvenient to show 4D feature maps $(C \times D \times H \times W)$ in the figure, we show all feature maps without depth information, and the thickness of each feature map reveals its channel number.

3.2   EMA Module for Non-local Features

The Non-local self-attention mechanism can help to aggregate contextual information from all spatial positions and capture long-range dependencies, and hence has been widely used for semantic image segmentation [7,20,21]. However, when incorporating this mechanism into a CNN with 3D convolutions, the spatial and computational complexity of the model increases dramatically, since it requires the calculation of point-wise spatial attention and generation of large attention maps, which are extremely time and memory consuming. Hence, we introduce the EMA module [11] to our glioma segmentation model, aiming to incorporate a lightweight Non-local attention mechanism into our model.

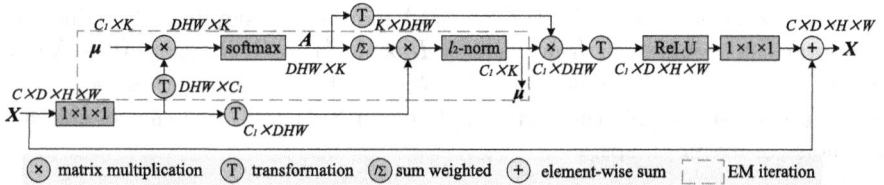

Fig. 3. The structure of EMA module. The shape of the input feature maps X are $C \times D \times H \times W$, where C is the channel number. The dotted box denotes the EM algorithm operation, where the Non-local spatial attention maps A and the bases μ are generated alternately as the E step and M step, respectively. After convergence, we can use the obtained A and μ to generate reconstructed feature maps $\widetilde{X}$. At both the beginning and ending of the EM algorithm operation, the $1 \times 1 \times 1$ convolutions are adopted to change the channel number. In addition, to avoid overfitting, we further sum $\widetilde{X}$ with X in a residual fashion.

The main concept of the EMA module is operating the Non-local attention on a set of feature reconstruction bases rather than directly achieving this on the high-resolution feature maps. Since the reconstruction bases have much less elements than the original feature maps, the computation cost of the Non-local attention can be significantly reduced. The pipeline of the EMA module is illustrated in Fig. 3. Given the input feature maps $X \in R^{C \times D \times H \times W}$ and the reconstruction bases $\mu \in R^{C \times K}$, where C is the number of channels and K is the number of bases, we regard the reconstruction bases μ and Non-local self-attention $A \in R^{D \times H \times W \times K}$ as the learned parameters and latent variables, respectively. The expectation-maximization (EM) algorithm [5] aims to find the optimal learnable parameters, which maximize the complete data likelihood. Specifically, the expectation (E) step estimates the expectation of A and the maximization (M) step updates μ by maximizing the likelihood, shown as follows:

$$A^t = softmax(X^T(\mu^{t-1})) \qquad (1)$$

$$\mu_k^t = \frac{\sum_{n=1}^{N}(A_{nk}^t X_n)}{\sum_{m=1}^{N} A_{mk}^t} \qquad (2)$$

where t denotes the t-th iteration, $N = D \times H \times W$, μ^k is the k-th base, and A_{nk} is the attention vector in the k-th channel at location n. As suggested by [11], we alternatively execute the E step and M step for three iterations. Then, we use the normalized attention A and bases μ to obtain the reconstructed feature maps $\widetilde{X}$, which have long-range dependencies and can be formulated as:

$$\widetilde{X} = \mu A^T \qquad (3)$$

Since we set $K \ll D \times H \times W$, the EMA module can significantly reduce the computational complexity from $O((D \times H \times W)^2)$ to $O(D \times H \times W \times K)$, as compared to the traditional point-wise Non-local mechanism. Moreover, as $\widetilde{X}$ lies in a subspace of X, the EMA module can further reduce the redundancy and noise of feature maps.

Table 1. Segmentation performances of the proposed HNF-Net and eight top-ranking methods on the BraTS 2019 validation set. All results were directly adopted from the BraTS 2019 Challenge leaderboard.

Method	Dice (%)			95%HD (mm)			Mean-rank
	ET	WT	TC	ET	WT	TC	
HNF-Net (**ours**)	$81.16_{(3)}$	$91.12_{(2)}$	$84.52_{(6)}$	$3.49_{(2)}$	$4.13_{(2)}$	$\mathbf{5.25}_{(1)}$	**2.67**
Questionmarks	$80.21_{(5)}$	$90.94_{(4)}$	$\mathbf{86.47}_{(1)}$	$\mathbf{3.15}_{(1)}$	$4.26_{(3)}$	$5.44_{(3)}$	2.83
NVDLMED [14]	$\mathbf{82.28}_{(1)}$	$91.01_{(3)}$	$86.22_{(2)}$	$3.62_{(3)}$	$4.42_{(5)}$	$5.46_{(4)}$	3.00
SVIG1	$81.33_{(2)}$	$\mathbf{91.16}_{(1)}$	$85.79_{(3)}$	$4.21_{(6)}$	$\mathbf{4.10}_{(1)}$	$5.92_{(6)}$	3.17
lfn [9]	$80.24_{(4)}$	$90.91_{(5)}$	$85.49_{(4)}$	$3.88_{(5)}$	$4.36_{(4)}$	$5.32_{(2)}$	4.00
NWPU_ASGO	$73.54_{(9)}$	$90.71_{(7)}$	$84.92_{(5)}$	$3.63_{(4)}$	$5.27_{(6)}$	$5.81_{(5)}$	6.00
GHcheng	$78.69_{(8)}$	$90.80_{(6)}$	$83.31_{(8)}$	$4.33_{(7)}$	$5.36_{(7)}$	$6.97_{(8)}$	7.33
ANSIR	$80.06_{(6)}$	$90.09_{(8)}$	$84.38_{(7)}$	$4.52_{(8)}$	$6.94_{(9)}$	$6.00_{(7)}$	7.50
deecamp	$79.22_{(7)}$	$89.40_{(9)}$	$80.27_{(9)}$	$6.08_{(9)}$	$5.61_{(8)}$	$8.68_{(9)}$	8.50

4   Experiments and Results

Implementation Details: Suggested by some previous works [3,9], we preprocessed each brain MR sequence, including brain stripping, clipping voxel intensity with a window of [0.5%–99.5%], and normalizing voxel values into zero mean and unit variance. To reduce the potential overfitting, we further employed several online data augmentation techniques, including random flipping (on all three planes independently), random rotation ($\pm 10°$ on all three planes independently), and random intensity shift of [± 0.1]. In the training phase, we concatenated four MR sequences along the channel dimension and randomly cropped the input image into a fixed size of $128 \times 128 \times 128 \times 4$. We adopted the Adam optimizer with an initial learning rate of 0.001 and a batch size of 4 with synchronized batch normalization. All experiments were performed using the Pytorch on a workstation with 4 NVIDIA Geforce GTX 2080Ti GPUs.

Comparison with State-of-the-Art Methods: We trained our HNF-Net on the BraTS 2019 training set and submitted the segmentation results of the validation set for the online evaluation. In the BraTS 2019 challenge, the segmentation performance of three sub-regions, namely enhancing tumor (ET), tumor core (TC), and whole tumor (WT), are evaluated by the Dice score and 95% Hausdorff distance (%95HD). Since there are a total of 140 valid entries on the validation leaderboard, we present the segmentation performance of the HNF-Net and the performance of eight top-ranking methods in Table 1. It is shown that the proposed HNF-Net achieves a Dice score of 81.16% for ET, 91.12% for WT, and 84.52% for TC, which ranks the 3rd, 2nd, and 6th among nine competing methods, respectively, and achieves a %95HD of 3.49 for ET, 4.13 for WT, and 5.25 for TC, which ranks the 2nd, 2nd, and 1st among nine methods, respectively. Since no method achieves the best performance in terms of all metrics, we use the average of the six ranks (mean-rank) as the overall performance indicator. A lower mean-rank value means better segmentation accuracy. Thus, the mean-rank of our HNF-Net is 2.67, which is the lowest among nine competing methods. Therefore, we believe that our HNF-Net is very competitive with respective to those eight top-ranking methods, particularly with less outliers even in those small and irregular ET and TC regions as indicated by low %95HD values.

Table 2. Segmentation performances of 3D U-Net (baseline1), 3D U-Net++ (baseline2), HNF-Net but without & with original Non-local modules [20], and our proposed HNF-Net on the BraTS 2019 training set. All results were obtained using the same five-fold cross-validation.

Method	Params (M)	FLOPs (G)	Dice (%)		
			ET	WT	TC
3D U-Net++ [22]	**27.47**	**2019.31**	74.80	89.53	82.91
3D U-Net [4]	15.80	1240.27	74.82	88.35	80.74
HNF-Net (w/o Non-local)	16.79	420.36	79.93	90.30	84.25
HNF-Net (w Non-local [20])	17.31	558.01	80.43	90.64	85.77
HNF-Net (ours)	16.82	420.49	**80.96**	**91.12**	**86.40**

Ablation Study: To evaluate the effectiveness of the PMF module and EMA module in HNF-Net, we conducted an ablation study on the BraTS 2019 training set using five-fold cross-validation. We chose 3D U-Net [4] and 3D U-Net++ [22] as two baseline models, which uses neither the PMF module nor the EMA module. Besides the propsoed HNF-Net, we also tested its two variants where the first one has no Non-local module and the second one uses the original Non-local module [20]. The experiments were performed under the same settings and the results were given in Table 2. It shows that (1) compared to 3D U-Net [4], using the PMF module not only dramatically improved the Dice score by 5.11% for ET, 1.95% for WT, and 3.51% for TC but also reduced the computations significantly with 1/3 of the FLOPs, though having moderately increased parameters; (2) incorporating the EMA module into the segmentation model further improves the Dice score by 1.03% for ET, 0.82% for WT, and 2.15% for TC but only increases the parameters and FLOPs slightly; (3) compared to 3D U-Net++ [22], another U-shape baseline model also with denser layer-forwarding policy,

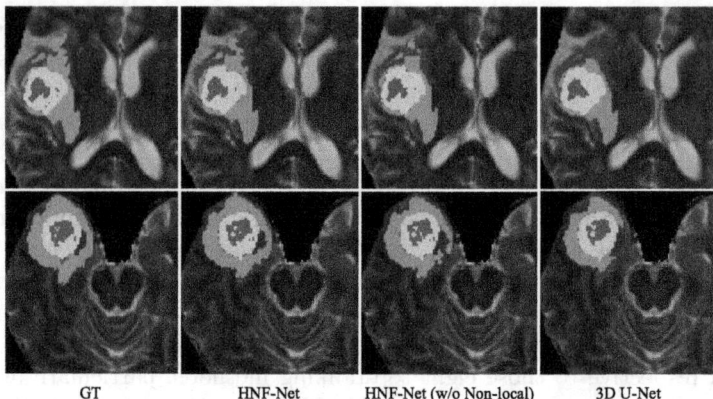

GT   HNF-Net   HNF-Net (w/o Non-local)   3D U-Net

Fig. 4. The visual comparison of the segmentation results of HNF-Net, HNF-Net (w/o Non-local), and 3D U-Net. GT represents ground truth. The NCR/NET, ED, and ET regions are highlighted in red, green, and yellow, respectively. (Color figure online)

the proposed HNF-Net also significantly improves the Dice score by 6.16% for ET, 1.59% for WT, and 3.49% for TC but only with around 60% parameters and 20% FLOPs; (4) Using EMA module to replace the original Non-local module [20] can obtain a slight performance gain but has obviously smaller computation cost, especially for FLOPs. The results suggest that the high-resolution feature representation produced by the PMF module is beneficial to the glioma segmentation and that the EMA module is effective in improving segmentation accuracy via capturing long-range dependencies. In addition, the segmentation results of 3D U-Net [4], HNF-Net (w/o Non-local), and HNF-Net were visualized in Fig. 4. It is shown that both HNF-Net and HNF-Net (w/o Non-local) obtained obviously better segmentation results than 3D U-Net, and HNF-Net achieved best segmentation results. The conclusion drawn from this table is consistent with the conclusions drawn from quantitative evaluation.

5   Conclusion

In this paper, we have proposed HNF-Net for brain glioma segmentation using multi-parametric MR imaging, which uses the PMF module to exploit multi-resolution feature representation and employs the EMA module to capture long-range dependent contextual information in a lightweight fashion. Our results on the BraTS 2019 dataset show that the proposed HNF-Net achieves the state-of-the-art performance and also suggest the effectiveness of the proposed PMF and EMA modules. One of our potential future works is to extend the proposed HNF-Net to the segmentation of other small and irregular lesions and organs such as kidney tumors or hippocampus.

Acknowledgement. Haozhe Jia and Yong Xia were partially supported by the Science, Technology and Innovation Commission of Shenzhen Municipality, China under

Grant JCYJ20180306171334997, the National Natural Science Foundation of China under Grant 61771397, and the Innovation Foundation for Doctor Dissertation of Northwestern Polytechnical University under Grant CX202042.

References

1. Bakas, S., et al.: Advancing the cancer genome atlas glioma MRI collections with expert segmentation labels and radiomic features. Sci. Data **4**, 170117 (2017)
2. Bakas, S., et al.: Identifying the best machine learning algorithms for brain tumor segmentation, progression assessment, and overall survival prediction in the BRATS challenge. arXiv preprint arXiv:1811.02629 (2018)
3. Chen, C., Liu, X., Ding, M., Zheng, J., Li, J.: 3D dilated multi-fiber network for real-time brain tumor segmentation in MRI. In: Shen, D., et al. (eds.) MICCAI 2019. LNCS, vol. 11766, pp. 184–192. Springer, Cham (2019). https://doi.org/10. 1007/978-3-030-32248-9_21
4. Çiçek, Ö., Abdulkadir, A., Lienkamp, S.S., Brox, T., Ronneberger, O.: 3D U-Net: learning dense volumetric segmentation from sparse annotation. In: Ourselin, S., Joskowicz, L., Sabuncu, M.R., Unal, G., Wells, W. (eds.) MICCAI 2016. LNCS, vol. 9901, pp. 424–432. Springer, Cham (2016). https://doi.org/10.1007/978-3-319-46723-8_49
5. Dempster, A.P., Laird, N.M., Rubin, D.B.: Maximum likelihood from incomplete data via the EM algorithm. J. Roy. Stat. Soc.: Ser. B (Methodol.) **39**(1), 1–22 (1977)
6. Dong, H., Yang, G., Liu, F., Mo, Y., Guo, Y.: Automatic brain tumor detection and segmentation using U-Net based fully convolutional networks. In: Valdés Hernández, M., González-Castro, V. (eds.) MIUA 2017. CCIS, vol. 723, pp. 506–517. Springer, Cham (2017). https://doi.org/10.1007/978-3-319-60964-5_44
7. Fu, J., et al.: Dual attention network for scene segmentation. In: Proceedings of the IEEE Conference on Computer Vision and Pattern Recognition, pp. 3146–3154 (2019)
8. Havaei, M., et al.: Brain tumor segmentation with deep neural networks. Med. Image Anal. **35**, 18–31 (2017)
9. Isensee, F., Kickingereder, P., Wick, W., Bendszus, M., Maier-Hein, K.H.: No new-net. In: Crimi, A., Bakas, S., Kuijf, H., Keyvan, F., Reyes, M., van Walsum, T. (eds.) BrainLes 2018. LNCS, vol. 11384, pp. 234–244. Springer, Cham (2019). https://doi.org/10.1007/978-3-030-11726-9_21
10. Kamnitsas, K., et al.: Efficient multi-scale 3D CNN with fully connected CRF for accurate brain lesion segmentation. Med. Image Anal. **36**, 61–78 (2017)
11. Li, X., Zhong, Z., Wu, J., Yang, Y., Lin, Z., Liu, H.: Expectation-maximization attention networks for semantic segmentation. In: Proceedings of the IEEE International Conference on Computer Vision, pp. 9167–9176 (2019)
12. Menze, B.H., et al.: The multimodal brain tumor image segmentation benchmark (BRATS). IEEE Trans. Med. Imaging **34**(10), 1993–2024 (2014)
13. Milletari, F., Navab, N., Ahmadi, S.A.: V-net: fully convolutional neural networks for volumetric medical image segmentation. In: 2016 fourth International Conference on 3D Vision (3DV), pp. 565–571. IEEE (2016)
14. Myronenko, A.: 3D MRI brain tumor segmentation using autoencoder regularization. In: Crimi, A., Bakas, S., Kuijf, H., Keyvan, F., Reyes, M., van Walsum, T. (eds.) BrainLes 2018. LNCS, vol. 11384, pp. 311–320. Springer, Cham (2019). https://doi.org/10.1007/978-3-030-11726-9_28

15. Pohlen, T., Hermans, A., Mathias, M., Leibe, B.: Full-resolution residual networks for semantic segmentation in street scenes. In: Proceedings of the IEEE Conference on Computer Vision and Pattern Recognition, pp. 4151–4160 (2017)

16. Ronneberger, O., Fischer, P., Brox, T.: U-net: convolutional networks for biomedical image segmentation. In: Navab, N., Hornegger, J., Wells, W.M., Frangi, A.F. (eds.) MICCAI 2015. LNCS, vol. 9351, pp. 234–241. Springer, Cham (2015). https://doi.org/10.1007/978-3-319-24574-4_28

17. Saxena, S., Verbeek, J.: Convolutional neural fabrics. In: Advances in Neural Information Processing Systems, pp. 4053–4061 (2016)

18. Sudre, C.H., Li, W., Vercauteren, T., Ourselin, S., Jorge Cardoso, M.: Generalised dice overlap as a deep learning loss function for highly unbalanced segmentations. In: Cardoso, M.J., et al. (eds.) DLMIA/ML-CDS -2017. LNCS, vol. 10553, pp. 240–248. Springer, Cham (2017). https://doi.org/10.1007/978-3-319-67558-9_28

19. Sun, K., et al.: High-resolution representations for labeling pixels and regions. arXiv preprint arXiv:1904.04514 (2019)

20. Wang, X., Girshick, R., Gupta, A., He, K.: Non-local neural networks. In: Proceedings of the IEEE Conference on Computer Vision and Pattern Recognition, pp. 7794–7803 (2018)

21. Zhao, H., et al.: PsaNet: Point-wise spatial attention network for scene parsing. In: Proceedings of the European Conference on Computer Vision (ECCV), pp. 267–283 (2018)

22. Zhou, Z., Rahman Siddiquee, M.M., Tajbakhsh, N., Liang, J.: UNet++: a nested U-net architecture for medical image segmentation. In: Stoyanov, D., et al. (eds.) DLMIA/ML-CDS -2018. LNCS, vol. 11045, pp. 3–11. Springer, Cham (2018). https://doi.org/10.1007/978-3-030-00889-5_1

Robust Pancreatic Ductal Adenocarcinoma Segmentation with Multi-institutional Multi-phase Partially-Annotated CT Scans

Ling Zhang[1]($\boxtimes$), Yu Shi[2], Jiawen Yao[1], Yun Bian[3], Kai Cao[3], Dakai Jin[1], Jing Xiao[4], and Le Lu[1]

[1] PAII Inc., Bethesda, MD 20817, USA
zhangling300@paii-labs.com
[2] Shengjing Hospital of China Medical University, Shenyang, China
[3] Department of Radiology, Changhai Hospital, Shanghai 200433, China
[4] Ping An Technology Co., Ltd., Shenzhen, China

Abstract. Accurate and automated tumor segmentation is highly desired since it has the great potential to increase the efficiency and reproducibility of computing more complete tumor measurements and imaging biomarkers, comparing to (often partial) human measurements. This is probably the only viable means to enable the large-scale clinical oncology patient studies that utilize medical imaging. Deep learning approaches have shown robust segmentation performances for certain types of tumors, e.g., brain tumors in MRI imaging, when a training dataset with plenty of pixel-level fully-annotated tumor images is available. However, more than often, we are facing the challenge that only (very) limited annotations are feasible to acquire, especially for hard tumors. Pancreatic ductal adenocarcinoma (PDAC) segmentation is one of the most challenging tumor segmentation tasks, yet critically important for clinical needs. Previous work on PDAC segmentation is limited to the moderate amounts of annotated patient images ($n < 300$) from venous or venous+arterial phase CT scans. Based on a new self-learning framework, we propose to train the PDAC segmentation model using a much larger quantity of patients ($n \approx 1,000$), with a mix of annotated and un-annotated venous or multi-phase CT images. Pseudo annotations are generated by combining two teacher models with different PDAC segmentation specialties on unannotated images, and can be further refined by a teaching assistant model that identifies associated vessels around the pancreas. A student model is trained on both manual and pseudo annotated multi-phase images. Experiment results show that our proposed method provides an absolute improvement of 6.3% Dice score over the strong baseline of nnUNet trained on annotated images, achieving the performance (Dice = 0.71) similar to the inter-observer variability between radiologists.

Keywords: Pancreatic tumor segmentation · Unannotated data · Deep learning

© Springer Nature Switzerland AG 2020
A. L. Martel et al. (Eds.): MICCAI 2020, LNCS 12264, pp. 491–500, 2020.
https://doi.org/10.1007/978-3-030-59719-1_48

1   Introduction

For all machine learning-based tumor detection, characterization, and monitoring problems in cancer imaging, the volumetric segmentation of critical tumors plays an essential role [4]. It serves the core for downstream processes of quantification, diagnosis, staging, prognosis, radiation planning, and treatment response prediction, all requiring a separate tumor segmentation step. In most of current clinical practices, tumor segmentation is still manually performed by clinicians, resulting in the consumption of labor, and low reproducibility of the derived biomarkers due to subjectivity. The tumor-related computerized models have been evaluated using relatively small-sized or moderate scale tumor datasets with expert annotations [4,16]. Deep learning methods can potentially increase the efficiency and reproducibility and make clinical/oncology patient studies scalable. For example, UNet [11] has recently been adopted for the objective and automated assessment of brain tumor treatment response in a multicentre study [9]. However, it is usually infeasible and unconventional to construct such a large, well-organized, and volumetric-annotated tumor imaging dataset of 455 MRI scans by experts to train a fully-supervised deep model. We face a situation that the private and/or publicly existing full annotations are moderate to small-sized, while the unannotated imaging data can be huge. Furthermore, smaller-sized tumors are more difficult to segment, especially in CT scans with lower contrast than in MRI. Therefore fully automated and accurate (small) tumor segmentation in CT/MRI is still a challenging task to tackle.

Pancreatic ductal adenocarcinoma (PDAC), which constitutes 90% of pancreatic cancers, is a dismal disease, with a 5-year overall survival rate only at 9%. Less than 20% of patients are eligible for the initial surgical resection. However, outcomes vary significantly even among the resected patients of the same TNM (tumor, node, and metastasis) stage receiving similar treatments. There is a critical and urgent need for additional predictive disease biomarkers to permit more personalized treatment. Radiological imaging provides the valuable non-invasive and informative information of the entire tumor. Subsequently, there are great interests in developing effective imaging-based biomarkers to stratify the group of resectable PDAC patients [2] and predict gene mutation status from CT imaging [3], etc. Making these biomarkers to reach the clinical practices, a robust fully-automated PDAC segmentation model is desirable, as it can improve the objectiveness and enable the multicentre validation on a large-scale patient cohort. For the borderline resectable and locally-advanced PDACs, chemoradiation therapy is the suggested treatment option. One key step before each chemoradiation treatment is the manual segmentation and assessment of gross tumor volume, as a time-consuming and complex task requiring special expertise [10].

Fully-automated segmentation of pancreatic tumor in CT scans is one of the most challenging tumor segmentation tasks, where previous state-of-the-art methods produce the Dice scores between 0.52 and 0.64 [8,13,19,20], depending on the factors of tumor types (PDAC and others), utilized CT phases (arterial, venous), image quality, and consistency of annotations, and so on. Besides the complex abdominal structures, PDACs are quite variable in their shape, size, location, and enhancement patterns, demonstrating hypo-, iso-, or even hyper-enhancement. The heterogeneity of pancreas regions (i.e., pancreas tissue, duct, veins, and arteries) and the ill-defined tumor boundary make PDAC segmentation highly complicated even for radiologists. The inter-observer variability of this task is ∼0.71 in the Dice score, as reported in [10,16].

In this paper, we propose a fully-automated and highly accurate PDAC segmentation method. Previous PDAC segmentation approaches [8,19,20] are limited to the small to moderate amounts of annotated patients (patient number n < 300) using venous or venous+arterial phase CT scans. In contrast, we train a model from a significantly larger patient population of n≈1,000, including both (self-collected and publicly available) annotated and unannotated CT images covering multiple imaging phases, via the framework of self-learning [12,14,17]. Self-learning assumes that a deep model (student) trained from noisy annotations (teacher) has the potential to surpass the teacher [17]. Recent work finds new effective strategies to improve the student performance further, including adding regularization [12] or noises [14] to perturb the noisy annotations and generate noisy but informative annotations on a large unannotated external dataset [14]. Specifically, (1) Our PDAC segmentation model is built upon a state-of-the-art medical image (particularly tumor) segmentation backbone nnUNet [8], augmented using a new self-learning strategy that generates pseudo annotations on unannotated images by two teachers with different specialties, instead of traditionally by one teacher [12,14,17]. (2) We incorporate the semantic parsing of organs and vessels around the pancreas to further refine the pseudo annotations. (3) We demonstrate that our proposed method provides an absolute improvement of 6.3% Dice score over the strong baseline of nnUNet [8] on multi-phase CT, achieving the highest fully-automated PDAC segmentation Dice score of 0.71 to date. Our results are substantially higher than the Dice scores of [0.52, 0.64] in [8,13,19,20] and comparable with the inter-observer variability [10,16].

2 Methods

Figure 1 illustrates our proposed self-learning framework for PDAC segmentation using multi-phase CT scans. Given the self-collected Dataset A with only a moderate number of PDAC annotations available, our framework can effectively incorporate and utilize three other datasets (B, C, D) to significantly improve the PDAC segmentation performance, described as follows.

In details, *firstly*, we train a multi-phase pancreas and PDAC segmentation model on the private Dataset A with the registered non-contrast, arterial and venous phases CTs, denoted as Teacher A. *Secondly*, Dataset B [13] is a public venous phase CT dataset including manual pixel-level annotations of pancreas and tumor and is used to train a segmentation model Teacher B. Note that since there is no pancreas annotations in our Dataset A, we use teacher B to segment the pancreas in the venous phase CT images in Dataset A to assist the training

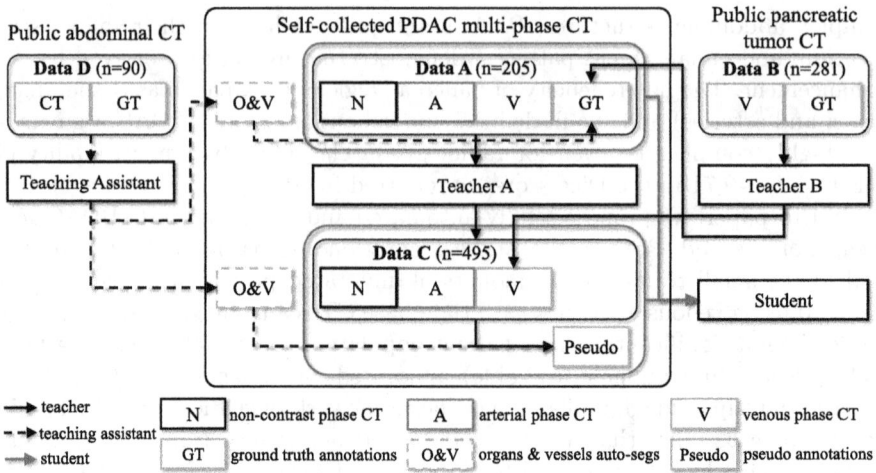

Fig. 1. The proposed learning framework for pancreatic ductal adenocarcinoma (PDAC) segmentation on multi-phase CT scans. **Data A** and **Data C**: self-collected multi-phase CT datasets from two hospitals with and without PDAC annotations, respectively. **Data B**: a public venous phase CT dataset with pancreas and tumor annotations. **Data D**: public CT datasets with abdominal organ and vessel annotations. Pseudo annotations are generated by the teacher model A and B with different specialties. The student model is trained with the combined Data A and Data C and guided by the teaching assistant, which further corrects the pseudo pancreas annotations.

of teacher A[1]. Teachers A and B have their specialized expertise depending on the different characteristics of Data A and B. *Thirdly*, teacher A and teacher B respectively apply to segment the registered multi-phase CTs and the venous phase CTs in the self-collected Dataset C (a large scale but un-annotated multi-phase CT imaging study with PDACs). The resulted segmentation probability maps are adaptively combined to generate pseudo annotations of the pancreas and PDAC in Dataset C. *Fourthly*, Dataset D [5] is a public abdominal CT dataset with annotations of the major abdominal organs & vessels, and is employed here to train a Teaching Assistant to refine the pancreas annotations in Datasets A and C. *Last*, we train a Student model on both Datasets A and C with manual and pseudo annotations (generated as above) of the pancreas and PDAC. For the multi-phase CT imaging registration as preprocessing, we use DEEDS [6], which performs the best in a recent evaluation of abdominal CT imaging registration algorithms [15].

nnUNet. For the training of our segmentation models mentioned above, we use the nnUNet backbone [8] due to its high accuracy on several medical image segmentation tasks, such as abdominal organs, vessels, and tumors [7–9]. The 3D UNet stage-1, which trains UNet on downsampled images, is used as the network architecture for a trade-off between the training efficiency and tumor

---

[1] We empirically find that a combined pancreas and tumor model segments PDAC tumors noticeably better than a single standalone tumor model.

segmentation accuracy. A combination of Dice and cross-entropy loss is utilized. We train the model to optimize the loss of both pancreas and PDAC. The model that produces the best Dice score of PDAC on the validation set is selected as the best PDAC segmentation model. In inference, we keep the non-background maximal connected component to remove false positives. For organ and vessel segmentation, we train a model to optimize the overall loss of all 17 classes [5].

Self-learning. Compared to previous self-learning methods of having one teacher, we introduce **an additional teacher B to benefit from the knowledge** in the annotated public Dataset B [13]. While our self-collected Dataset A includes PDACs (mostly small size) located at the pancreas head and uncinate regions, Dataset B consists of a variety of size distributions of pancreatic tumors spanning over the whole pancreas. However, for Dataset B, (1) the pancreatic ducts, especially abnormal ones, can show similar appearances with PDACs in the venous phase CT; Other types of tumors in Dataset B, such as pancreatic neuroendocrine tumors, demonstrates different image enhancement patterns with PDACs. As a result, **teacher B tends to identify some pancreatic ducts and normal pancreas tissues as tumors.** (2) On the other hand, the multi-phase (non-contrast, arterial, and venous) CT images in Dataset A can alleviate these difficulties by providing additional cues, such as the dynamic enhancement patterns of different structures. (3) By counting in all aspects, we generate the pseudo annotations for Dataset C by a weighted combining operator on the two teachers' segmentation probability maps. At the pancreas' head and uncinate, we assign a higher weight ω_0 to teacher A (i.e., $1 - \omega_0$ to teacher B), and at other regions, a higher weight ω_1 to teacher B (i.e., $1 - \omega_1$ to teacher A). As such, the teachers behave collaboratively like an ensemble when generating the pseudo annotations, which subsequently forces the student to learn from the reinforced ensemble model. (4) Moreover, the student's knowledge is expanded through learning on the large Dataset C that demonstrates more PDAC variations, allowing the student to learn beyond his teachers to be capable of segmenting more challenging images desirably.

Note that we train the student model from scratch on the combination of Datasets A and C with manual and pseudo annotations. Such a strategy is found to be more effective than initializing the student with the teacher or first pretraining on un-annotated dataset and then finetuning on annotated dataset [14]. Our overall self-learning training framework utilizing four datasets with different levels of annotations and patient distributions is shown in Fig. 1. In summary, the proposed teacher-student self-learning representation and training strategies enable our work and demonstrate the feasibility, as the largest study of this kind: utilizing three multi-institutional multi-phase PDAC CT imaging datasets.

Organ and Vessel Parsing. The semantic image parsing (of organs and vessels) component acts as a teaching assistant. It corrects and refines the pseudo annotations of the pancreas in Datasets A and C by masking out the (previously produced) pancreas annotations that belong to different vessel classes (i.e., portal and splenic vein, superior mesenteric vein and artery, and truncus coeliacus). As such, the final student model of pancreas+PDAC segmentation is encouraged to be more focused on learning the pancreas region (with reinforced and corrected pseudo annotation) and distinguishing Pancreas and PDAC from vessels. We observe that without the teaching assistant, some vessel regions around the pancreas tend to be segmented as the pancreas or PDAC even after self-learning.

3   Experimental Results

Datasets. Four multi-institutional datasets (total $n = 1,071$) are used in this work. **Dataset A**, including 205 patients with PDACs (the mean tumor size is 2.5 cm), is collected from hospital A with non-contrast, pancreatic (late arterial), and venous phases of CT scans. Such a multi-phase CT imaging setting is the standardized protocol for depiction, staging, and resectability evaluations of PDAC, specified in the National Comprehensive Cancer Network (NCCN) guidelines [1]. The median imaging spacing is $0.70 \times 0.70 \times 3$ mm in [X, Y, Z]. PDAC tumors are manually traced and annotated on the pancreatic phase slice by slice by one radiologist with 18 years of experience in pancreatic imaging. **Dataset B**, including 281 patients with pancreatic tumor annotations, is a public dataset provided by Memorial Sloan Kettering Cancer Center [13]. The median imaging spacing is $0.80 \times 0.80 \times 2.5$ mm. **Dataset C**, including 495 patients with PDACs (no manual annotations), is collected from hospital C with non-contrast, early arterial, and venous phase CTs used in this work. The median imaging spacing is $0.68 \times 0.68 \times 3$ mm. **Dataset D** is a combination of two public datasets (described in [5]), including 90 patients' abdominal CTs with annotated organs and vessels up to 14 classes. An engineer manually annotates three additional vessel classes (superior mesenteric vein and artery, and truncus coeliacus) in 46 CTs and completes some CTs without annotations of the portal and splenic veins under the supervision of a board-certified radiologist. An initial nnUNet network is trained to segment the remaining CTs; the segmented pseudo masks of the four classes of vessels are manually corrected by the engineer. Finally, the second nnUNet (as teaching assistant) is trained on all 90 CTs with 17 classes of annotations.

Implementation Details. For the nnUNet [8] training, most parameters are set by default. We find that increasing the batch size or changing the optimizer produces similar performance. Multi-phase CT images are directly concatenated as input channels to feed the network. The input-level fusion is widely adopted in the multi-modality tumor segmentation tasks [18]. We compare the input-level fusion with a layer-level fusion, i.e., the hyper-pairing network [19], which previously shows the state-of-the-art PDAC segmentation performance for multi-phase CTs. The implementations remain the same with the nnUNet framework except that the backbone network is replaced with the hyper-pairing UNet. Only arterial and venous phases are used as in [19], and our GPU cannot feed in the hyper-pairing UNet with three CT phases. The phase augmentation and pairing loss in [19] are not implemented. The weights for combining the two teachers' segmentation probability maps are set as $\omega_0 = 0.8$ and $\omega_1 = 0.6$, with the first 60% pancreas volume (starting from the left-most slice occupied by the pancreas

Table 1. PDAC segmentation results on Data A by 5-fold cross-validation. TA: teaching assistant model trained on Data D. Results are reported as mean±std. * is an average value of the two inter-observer variability values in [16] which are median Dice scores. As a comparison, our final student model has a median Dice of 0.755.

Methods: CT phases	Training data	Dice
nnUNet: venous (Teacher B)	Data B	0.395 ± 0.290
nnUNet: non-contrast	Data A	0.476 ± 0.221
nnUNet: pancreatic	Data A	0.630 ± 0.230
nnUNet: venous	Data A	0.522 ± 0.250
nnUNet: pancreatic+venous	Data A	0.629 ± 0.222
Hyper-pairing [19] nnUNet: pancreatic+venous	Data A	0.604 ± 0.230
nnUNet: 3-phases (Teacher A)	Data A	0.646 ± 0.199
nnUNet+Self-learn: 3-phases (Student)	Data A, B, C	0.698 ± 0.174
nnUNet+Self-learn+TA: 3-phases (Student)	Data A, B, C, D	$\mathbf{0.709 \pm 0.159}$
Inter-observer (CT [16]/MRI [10])		0.697*/0.710

annotations in the sagittal direction) being roughly treated as the head and uncinate; and the remaining 40% as other locations. The teacher models are trained with 200 epochs (250 batches per epoch), and the student models with 33 epochs (1500 batches per epoch). Each training process takes one day on a NVIDIA Titan RTX-6000 GPU. For training the teacher and teaching assistant models, a random training-validation splitting is used. For comparing the models' performance, five-fold cross-validation is used. The results on Dataset A are reported, and Dice coefficient is used as the evaluation metric.

Quantitative Results and Discussion. Table 1 shows the PDAC segmentation results on Dataset A by different methods. The nnUNet trained on a single venous phase CT has a mean Dice score of 0.522, comparable with the performances reported in [8,19] when evaluating UNet only on the venous phase CT. A single pancreatic (late arterial) phase substantially improves the performance to 0.630. This is consistent with the clinical guideline [1] that PDACs are best visible in the pancreatic phase. Non-contrast phase has the lowest performance. But when it is combined with the other two phases, the PDAC segmentation performance can be further increased to 0.646, surpassing the previous reported highest Dice score of 0.639 [19]. This is likely because the heterogeneity of the pancreas regions (e.g., tissue, pancreas duct, vessels) showing in the contrast-enhanced CT phases becomes more homogeneous in the non-contrast phase. The hyper-pairing [19] nnUNet does not improve the accuracy in our experiment. However, we acknowledge that our implementation may not be fully delicately optimized, e.g., it may need to be trained for more epochs, given that the hyper-pairing network is twice larger than a single network.

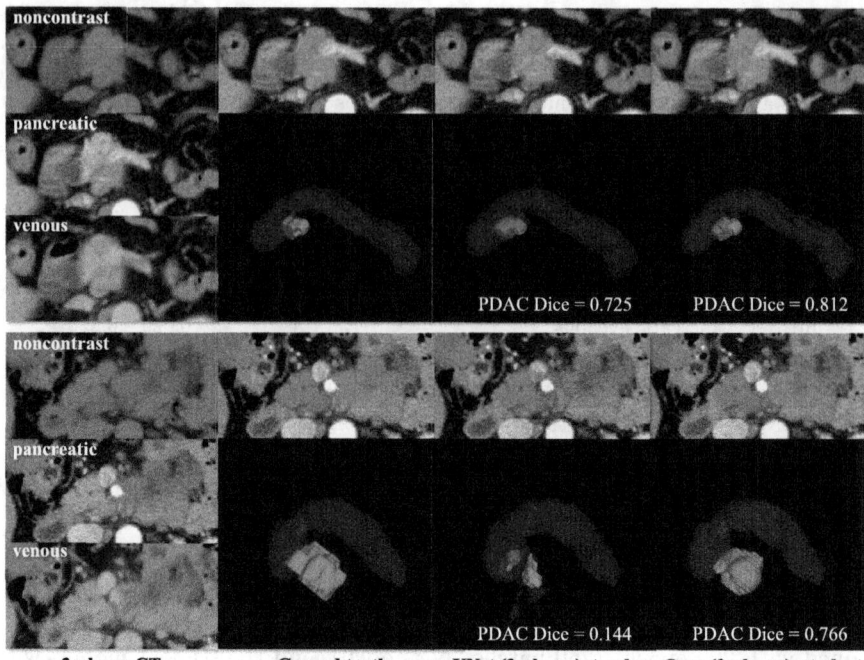

Fig. 2. Two qualitative examples of Pancreas (red) and PDAC (green) segmentation on multi-phase CT images. Upper panel: The student model further improves the teacher's accuracy by identifying/delineating more accurate PDAC boundaries. Lower panel: The student model substantially outperforms its teacher in segmenting a large tumor with irregular shape located at the pancreas uncinate. In both cases, the student model successfully identifies vessels around the pancreas (i.e., portal and splenic veins, superior mesenteric vein and artery) by excluding them from segmentation. (Color figure online)

More importantly, compared to the above strong baselines of nnUNet trained on three phases, our proposed self-learning approach substantially improves the PDAC segmentation performance in Dice scores from 0.646 to 0.698. By training with the pseudo annotations further corrected by the teaching assistant, the student model reaches a Dice score of 0.709 (roughly 10.5% absolute Dice improvement than the previous state-of-the-art work [19]). This also achieves a similar performance compared to the inter-observer variability between radiologists [10,16]. The learned student model can improve the teacher's performance in general and is especially better in some cases, which are difficult for the teacher, e.g., large tumors with irregular shape, veins. Two illustrative pancreas and PDCA segmentation examples are shown in Fig. 2.

4   Conclusion

Fully automated and accurate segmentation of pancreatic ductal adenocarcinoma (PDAC) is one of the most challenging tumor segmentation tasks, in the aspects of complex abdominal structures, large variations in morphology and appearance, low image contrast and fuzzy/uncertain boundary, etc. Previous studies introduce the cascade UNet for segmenting venous phase CT and hyperpairing network for segmenting venous+arterial phases CT and achieving mean Dice scores of 0.52 and 0.64, respectively. By incorporating nnUNet into a new self-learning framework with two teachers and one teaching assistant to segment three-phases of CT scans, our method reaches a Dice coefficient of 0.71, similar to the inter-observer variability between radiologists. This provides promise that a radiologist-level performance for accurate PDAC tumor segmentation in multi-phase CT imaging can be achieved through our computerized method.

References

1. NCCN Clinical Practice Guidelines in Oncology (NCCN Guidelines®) Pancreatic Adenocarcinoma. https://www2.tri-kobe.org/nccn/guideline/pancreas/english/pancreatic.pdf
2. Attiyeh, M.A., et al.: Survival prediction in pancreatic ductal adenocarcinoma by quantitative computed tomography image analysis. Ann. Surg. Oncol. **25**(4), 1034–1042 (2018)
3. Attiyeh, M.A., et al.: CT radiomics associations with genotype and stromal content in pancreatic ductal adenocarcinoma. Abdom. Radiol. **44**(9), 3148–3157 (2019)
4. Bi, W.L., et al.: Artificial intelligence in cancer imaging: clinical challenges and applications. CA Cancer J. Clin. **69**(2), 127–157 (2019)
5. Gibson, E., et al.: Automatic multi-organ segmentation on abdominal CT with dense v-networks. TMI **37**(8), 1822–1834 (2018)
6. Heinrich, M.P., Jenkinson, M., Papież, B.W., Brady, S.M., Schnabel, J.A.: Towards realtime multimodal fusion for image-guided interventions using self-similarities. In: Mori, K., Sakuma, I., Sato, Y., Barillot, C., Navab, N. (eds.) Medical Image Computing and Computer-Assisted Intervention - MICCAI 2013, pp. 187–194. Springer, Heidelberg (2013)
7. Isensee, F., Maier-Hein, K.H.: An attempt at beating the 3D U-Net. arXiv preprint arXiv:1908.02182 (2019)
8. Isensee, F., et al.: nnU-Net: self-adapting framework for U-net-based medical image segmentation. arXiv preprint arXiv:1809.10486 (2018)
9. Kickingereder, P., et al.: Automated quantitative tumour response assessment of MRI in neuro-oncology with artificial neural networks: a multicentre, retrospective study. Lancet Oncol. **20**(5), 728–740 (2019)
10. Liang, Y., et al.: Auto-segmentation of pancreatic tumor in multi-parametric MRI using deep convolutional neural networks. Radiother. Oncol. **145**, 193–200 (2020)
11. Ronneberger, O., Fischer, P., Brox, T.: U-Net: convolutional networks for biomedical image segmentation. In: Navab, N., Hornegger, J., Wells, W.M., Frangi, A.F. (eds.) MICCAI 2015. LNCS, vol. 9351, pp. 234–241. Springer, Cham (2015). https://doi.org/10.1007/978-3-319-24574-4_28

12. Roth, H., et al.: Weakly supervised segmentation from extreme points. In: Zhou, L., et al. (eds.) LABELS/HAL-MICCAI/CuRIOUS -2019. LNCS, vol. 11851, pp. 42–50. Springer, Cham (2019). https://doi.org/10.1007/978-3-030-33642-4_5
13. Simpson, A.L., et al.: A large annotated medical image dataset for the development and evaluation of segmentation algorithms. arXiv preprint arXiv:1902.09063 (2019)
14. Xie, Q., Hovy, E., Luong, M.T., Le, Q.V.: Self-training with noisy student improves imagenet classification. arXiv preprint arXiv:1911.04252 (2019)
15. Xu, Z., et al.: Evaluation of six registration methods for the human abdomen on clinically acquired CT. IEEE Trans. Biomed. Eng. **63**(8), 1563–1572 (2016)
16. Yamashita, R., et al.: Radiomic feature reproducibility in contrast-enhanced CT of the pancreas is affected by variabilities in scan parameters and manual segmentation. Eur. Radiol. **30**(1), 195–205 (2020)
17. Zhang, L., Gopalakrishnan, V., Lu, L., Summers, R.M., Moss, J., Yao, J.: Self-learning to detect and segment cysts in lung CT images without manual annotation. In: ISBI 2018, pp. 1100–1103 (2018)
18. Zhou, T., Ruan, S., Canu, S.: A review: deep learning for medical image segmentation using multi-modality fusion. Array **3**, 100004 (2019)
19. Zhou, Y., et al.: Hyper-pairing network for multi-phase pancreatic ductal adenocarcinoma segmentation. In: Shen, D., et al. (eds.) MICCAI 2019. LNCS, vol. 11765, pp. 155–163. Springer, Cham (2019). https://doi.org/10.1007/978-3-030-32245-8_18
20. Zhu, Z., Xia, Y., Xie, L., Fishman, E.K., Yuille, A.L.: Multi-scale coarse-to-fine segmentation for screening pancreatic ductal adenocarcinoma. In: Shen, D., et al. (eds.) MICCAI 2019. LNCS, vol. 11769, pp. 3–12. Springer, Cham (2019). https://doi.org/10.1007/978-3-030-32226-7_1

Generation of Annotated Brain Tumor MRIs with Tumor-induced Tissue Deformations for Training and Assessment of Neural Networks

Hristina Uzunova$^{(\boxtimes)}$, Jan Ehrhardt, and Heinz Handels

Institute of Medical Informatics, University of Lübeck, Lübeck, Germany
uzunova@imi.uni-luebeck.de

Abstract. Machine learning methods heavily rely on the availability of large annotated datasets of a certain domain for training. However, freely available datasets of patients with pathologies rarely contain annotations of normal structures, thus cannot be used as ground truth for various image processing methods. To overcome this issue, we propose a topology preserving unpaired domain translation method, including an explicit pathology integration to generate annotated ground truth data of pathological domains. Moreover, we integrate a novel inverse probabilistic approach to generate deformations of the surrounding caused by pathological tissue. Our experiments show the necessity for annotated pathological data for algorithm evaluation. Furthermore, when training neural networks on healthy data and testing on real pathological images, the results are strongly impaired. By generating training data with pathologies using the proposed method, the performance of segmentation and registration methods increases significantly. The best results are achieved by also integrating pathology-induced tissue deformations.

Keywords: Tumor generation · Transfer learning · Domain translation

1 Introduction

Machine learning methods, especially neural networks, have proven to excel at many image processing and analysis methods in the medical image domain. Yet, their success strongly relies on the availability of large training data sets with high quality ground truth annotations, e.g. expert segmentation of anatomical/pathological structures. Therefore, generating realistic synthetic data with ground truth labels has become crucial to boost the performance of neural networks. In [21], the authors generate brain and heart MRIs with corresponding ground truth displacement fields for the augmentation of a registration network

Electronic supplementary material The online version of this chapter (https://doi.org/10.1007/978-3-030-59719-1_49) contains supplementary material, which is available to authorized users.

© Springer Nature Switzerland AG 2020
A. L. Martel et al. (Eds.): MICCAI 2020, LNCS 12264, pp. 501–511, 2020.
https://doi.org/10.1007/978-3-030-59719-1_49

using a statistical shape and appearance model. In [14], GAN-based image generation is used as an augmentation technique for a cell segmentation network.

Other methods enable the generation of pathological data to boost the segmentation or classification of pathologies [8,24]. In [19], synthetic tumors are simulated on normal-appearance brain MRIs using conditional GANs, leading to an improved performance of a tumor segmentation network. Further approaches generate normal appearance images from pathological data to enable unsupervised pathology segmentation or dataset balancing [2,23]. Those methods address certain pathological objects, yet the presence of pathologies in medical images strongly influences image analysis tasks targeting normal anatomical structures [13]. Data with ground truth annotations of both the normal and the abnormal structures would be required for the training of machine learning methods engaging with such tasks. However, most of the large publicly available datasets containing some type of pathologies are commonly designed for the segmentation (detection/localization) of the particular pathological structure and thus only contain expert segmentations of the latter, e.g. [15]. On the other hand, datasets containing ground truth annotations of normal anatomy (as used for e.g. atlas generation) are usually generated from healthy populations [18]. This induces two main problems: 1) the lack of ground truth annotation to evaluate the accuracy of standard algorithms on pathological data, and 2) the lack of data to train algorithms that target anatomical structures in pathological data.

In this work, we propose a method for the generation of realistic pathological data with ground truth labels of both anatomical and pathological structures. This is achieved by a GAN-based domain translation approach, that retains the topology of a healthy source domain, whereas the appearance of a target pathological domain is recreated. This way, the anatomic annotations of the source domain, can be directly applied to the generated images. Our method also includes an explicit pathology simulation such that tumors can be injected in the images in a controlled manner and their ground truth segmentations are available. Still, simply overlaying pathological tissue over the healthy structures as in [19] is not sufficient for a realistic appearance since brain tumors cause distortions of their surrounding tissue due to the tumor mass effect. For this reason, a novel inverse probabilistic approach to simulate tumor-induced deformations is proposed here. The feasibility of the method is demonstrated on brain MRIs by generating images containing brain tumors based on the topology of healthy brains. In our experiments the generated images serve as training datasets for segmentation and registration neural networks. The results show a significant improvement on both tasks when using our synthetic pathological data and underline the importance of mass effect simulation.

2   Methods

Generative adversarial networks (GANs) are models able to generate realistic images of high quality [9]. GANs learn to map a random noise vector $\mathbf{z}$ to an output image y using a generator function $G : \mathbf{z} \rightarrow y$. To ensure that the generator produces realistically looking images that cannot be distinguished from real

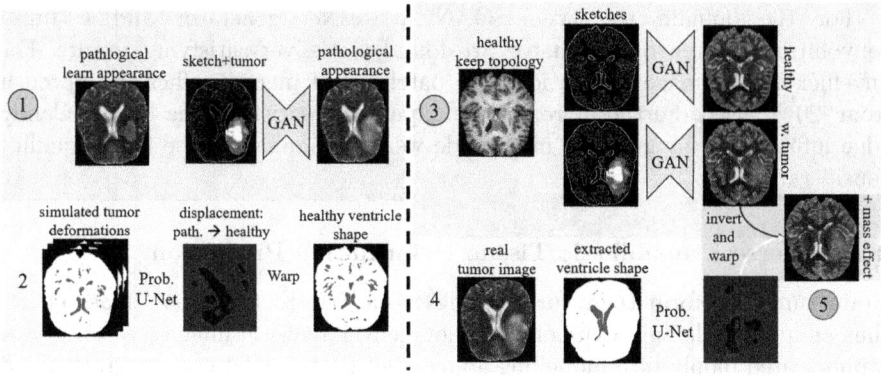

Fig. 1. Method overview. Left: training; right: inference. 1) Learn pathological appearance; 2) Learn inverse tumor deformations; 3) Generate pathological appearance from the topology of a healthy image (pathology injection possible); 4) Extract the inverse pathology displacement from a real pathological image; 5) Warp a generated tumor image with the inverse predicted displacement.

ones, an adversarial discriminator D is enclosed in the training process, aiming to perfectly distinguish between real images and generator's fakes. An extension of regular GANs are conditional GANs (cGANs), that learn the mapping from an observed image x additionally, $G : \{x, \mathbf{z}\} \rightarrow y$. A widespread application of cGANs is style and domain transfer [22].

2.1   Topology-aware Domain Translation with Pathology Integration

To preserve the ground truth annotations of labelled images but mimic the appearance of unlabelled (e.g pathological) images, a domain translation method that preserves the topology of the source is required. However, with no paired data available, this might be a significant hurdle. Here, we pursue the approach proposed in [20] to establish unpaired domain translation by considering intensity-independent shapes as a condition for a cGAN, while learning to generate the appearance of the target image domain (Fig. 1, step 1). This way, in the inference phase the shape of a source image can be translated to the domain of the training data, while preserving the topology of the input (Fig. 1, step 3). The shape information needs to be as accessible and easy to generate as possible for any source and target domain, so the extracted image edges are used based on [20].

When translating from a healthy to a pathological appearance, the training data is (mostly) strictly pathological. Thus, simply extracting the edges of tumors leads to pathology hallucination [3], making it impossible to control the presence and position of the latter. Hence, in this work, the masks of the pathological structures are considered as a second condition to the cGAN. In this way it is possible to inject pathologies to healthy tissue of a desired size, position and form, as well as generate images without pathological structures.

For the domain translation GAN a ResNet generator and a fully-convolutional patch discriminator are found to deliver satisfying results. For an efficient 3D image generation, the patch-based memory-efficient approach from [20] is used. Furthermore, in our experience enriching the binary Canny edge information by gradient magnitude weighting enhances the image quality considerably.

2.2 Inverse Probabilistic Tissue Deformation Prediction

Brain tumors deform their surrounding tissue due to the tumor mass effect, thus simply overlaying a tumor does not deliver realistic images. A variety of sophisticated biophysical modelling approaches that simulate tumor growth and its mass effect like [6,11] exist, however they are typically time-consuming and have limited accuracy due to unknown parameters. Still, such distortions might be of a crucial importance for further image processing methods. Here, a novel idea to simulate pathology-induced tissue deformations is presented. Determining the deformation of a pathological image at a given state is a challenging task due to the typical lack of corresponding healthy images. Furthermore, different pathologies at different stages have strongly varying influence on their surroundings. Thus, a straight-forward learning of the deformation is not feasible.

The key idea in this work is based on deducing the inverse tissue deformation of a pathological image by learning the healthy tissue shape distribution. Thus, a network is designed such that it directly predicts a displacement field from a given deformed shape (marked red in Fig. 1). Formally, $S_p \in \mathbb{R}^n$ is the shape describing a pathological image and $S_{h_i} \in \mathbb{R}^n$ is a possible healthy shape. Assume that S_p is a deformed version of S_{h_i}. Then $f : \mathbb{R}^n \to \mathbb{R}^{n \times d}$ is a probabilistic neural network such that $f(S_p) = \varphi_i$ and $S_p \circ \varphi_i \approx S_{h_i}$, where φ_i represents a displacement field and d is the image dimension. A probabilistic U-Net approach [12] is used to estimate a distribution of the unknown deformation parameters and allow for many possible normal shapes corresponding to a deformed one. Also, some biophysical properties are captured into a regularisation function in addition to the network loss: firstly, we assume constant tissue diffusivity and apply a global diffusion regularizer, secondly the locality of the mass effect is ensured with a weighted sparsity regularisation with increasing weights proportional to the distance from the tumor center.

More specifically, simplified shape representations that capture deformations are required for training. Here, the threshold-based ventricle segmentation of healthy patients are considered and deformed with a naive approach [16]. A probabilistic U-Net is then trained to learn the displacement field that transforms a deformed shape into a normal one (Fig. 1, step 2). The tumor deformation is therefore the inverse of the learned displacement field. To be able to easily invert the displacements and ensure diffeomorphism, the network learns velocity fields [17] and, based on them, the displacement fields are approximated. The diffeomorphic method used here is based on static velocity fields described in [1], where given the velocities v, the displacement fields φ are calculated as $\varphi = \exp(v)$ and $\varphi^{-1} = \exp(-v)$. Thus, inverse deformations are simply computed by inverting the velocities and using the scaling-squaring algorithm to approximate the $exp(\cdot)$ function. This strategy enables deducing a possible displacement from the shape of a real pathological image in the inference phase, and applying its inverse on the generated domain-translated image (Fig. 1, step 4)[1].

3 Experiments and Results

3.1 Data

Pathological: 220 3D brain T2 MRIs of patients with high grade glioblastomas and their ground truth segmentation masks from the BRATS challenge [15]. For evaluation purposes, well visible anatomical structures (ventricles and caudate nuclei) of 20 randomly selected images are manually segmented and used for testing exclusively.

Healthy: 3D brain MRI T1 scans of healthy patients with labelled anatomic regions from two freely available datasets: 30 images from the IXI dataset[2] [10] and 40 from the LONI LPBA40 [18]. However, only the segmentations of the structures available in the pathological test set are considered.

Atlas: T1 and T2 sequences of the ICBM 152 brain atlas [7].

3.2 Experimental Setup

Our experimental setup represents the following scenario: Given a set of images containing pathologies and labelled images of some other healthy patients' domain, generate labelled images similar to the pathological domain in order to, firstly, estimate the performance (exp. 1), and secondly, train (exp. 2 and 3) algorithms applied on the pathological dataset. For all experiments, synthetic data is generated according to the pipeline shown in Fig. 1. In the first step, a GAN is trained on T2 images from the BRATS dataset, in order to empha-size the difference between the healthy and pathological domain and show the possibility for domain translation between different MRI acquisition parameters. In the second step, a probabilistic U-Net is trained on ca. 350 deformed shapes of IXI images to learn the deformation from pathological to healthy shapes. The inference in step 3 and 4 results in three kinds of images that are used as training or testing data in our experiments: domain translated healthy, domain translated with an overlayed tumor, and the latter combined with a predicted tumor deformation (ca. 440 images of each type, examples in Fig. 2 and Fig. 3).

1) Evaluation of algorithm accuracy. Missing ground truth annotations of pathological data inhibit the assessment of image processing methods. On the example of atlas-based segmentation using a pre-trained 3D registration neural

---

[1] For more details, see our code at: https://github.com/hristina-uzunova/TumorMassEffect.

[2] http://brain-development.org/.

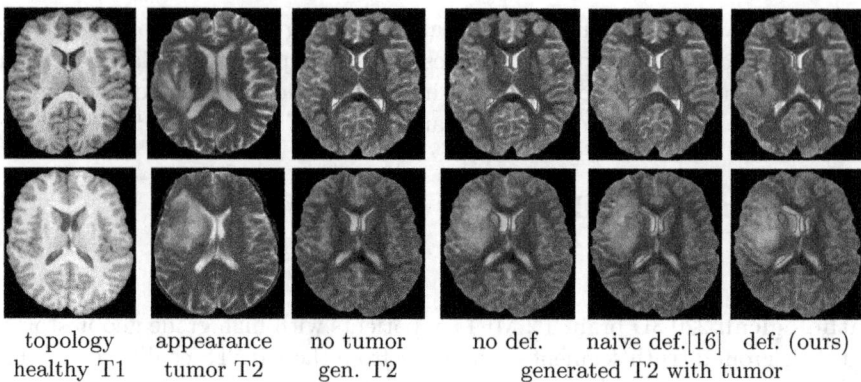

| topology | appearance | no tumor | no def. | naive def.[16] | def. (ours) |
| healthy T1 | tumor T2 | gen. T2 | | generated T2 with tumor | |

Fig. 2. Example of 2D generated images. From left to right: real T1 healthy patients MRI depicting the source topology; real T2 MRI containing the target tumor (and appearance); generated T2 images: without tumor; with a tumor and no deformation; deformation created with the naive approach; predicted deformation by our approach. For better visibility the edges of the non-deformed segmentations are overlayed.

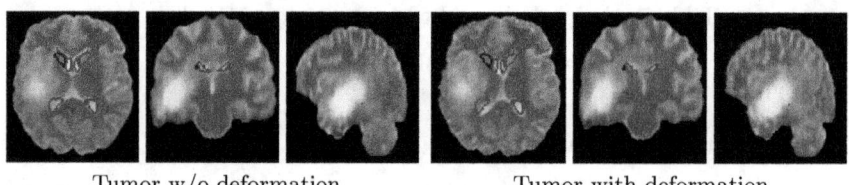

Tumor w/o deformation   Tumor with deformation

Fig. 3. Example of 3D generated images: axial, coronar and sagittal slices. Left: Injected tumor without a deformation; Right: applied tumor-induced deformation. For better visibility the edges of the non-deformed segmentations are overlayed.

network [25], we hypothesize that its usage yields comparable results on our synthetic data set and on real pathological data, making it possible to estimate the algorithms accuracy for real data.

2) Image registration. Here, the impact of tumors and tumor mass effect in the training and testing data are explored for the use-case registration. A supervised method is required to underline the necessity of ground truth data from pathological domains. Hence, the architecture of our choice is FlowNet [4], where a registration displacement field is predicted from an input image pair. The ground-truth displacements are generated using a pairwise registration [5] of the LPBA40 data and directly transferred to the domain translated images. Since the registration of two pathological images is infeasible, a fixed image of a healthy appearance is chosen if the moving image contains tumors. Predicted tumor-induced deformations are directly integrated into the ground-truth displacement when applicable. In the test phase an image-to-atlas registration is established, registering the test BRATS images to the T2 atlas. As the FlowNet architecture is extremely memory consuming, this experiment is realized for 2D image slices only.

3) Semantic segmentation. In this experiment, the influence of pathologies on the semantic segmentation of 2D and 3D data is explored. For this purpose a 2D and a 3D U-Net are trained on the different synthetic datasets. The training is established in a strictly supervised manner, where the labels of the original healthy IXI data are directly used as ground truth for the domain translated images. However, when using deformations the labels are transformed accordingly, also anatomical labels overlayed by tumor tissue are not considered.

Additionally, for experiments 2) and 3), the influence of random elastic data augmentation of the datasets containing tumors is explored.

3.3   Results

Some examples of the generated images are shown in Fig. 2 and in Fig. 3 for 2D and 3D respectively. Consistent with [20], the resulting 2D and 3D images are of a sufficiently realistic appearance and high quality. The first experi-

Table 1. Results of the 3D segmentation and 2D registration experiments measured in mean Dice coefficients. Training and testing datasets: real healthy (real IXI/LPBA40 T1 MRIs of healthy patients); real tumor (real BRATS images with manual anatomical annotations); gen. healthy (generated T2 MRIs with no tumors); gen. tumor (generated T2 MRIs with tumors); gen. tumor def. (generated T2 MRIs with tumors and predicted tumor-induced deformations); subscript ^{A} indicates random elastic data augmentation. Italic numbers correspond to the baseline; bold marks the best and statistically significant ($p < 0.005$ in a two-tailed paired t-test) result for each experiment.

	Train on	Test on	Ventricles	Caudate n.
			Dice mean ($\pm$ std)	
Seg.	Real T1 healthy	Real T1 healthy	_0.80($\pm$0.10)_	_0.61($\pm$0.37)_
	Real T1 healthy	Real T2 tumor	0.01($\pm$0.01)	0.00($\pm$0.01)
	Gen. T2 healthy	Real T2 tumor	0.59($\pm$0.14)	0.47($\pm$0.17)
	Gen. T2 tumor	Real T2 tumor	0.53($\pm$0.19)	0.51($\pm$0.20)
	Gen. T2 tumor^A	Real T2 tumor	0.64($\pm$0.14)	0.56($\pm$0.16)
	Gen. T2 tumor, def	Real T2 tumor	0.63($\pm$0.16)	0.56($\pm$0.16)
	Gen. T2 tumor, def.^{A}	Real T2 tumor	**0.70($\pm$0.11)**	**0.57($\pm$0.17)**
Reg.	None (init)	Real T1 healthy	0.52($\pm$0.19)	0.52($\pm$0.19)
	Real T1 healthy	Real T1 healthy	_0.62($\pm$0.17)_	_0.62($\pm$0.17)_
	None (init)	Real T2 tumor	0.38($\pm$0.16)	0.39($\pm$0.16)
	Real T1 healthy	Real T2 tumor	0.48($\pm$0.15)	0.49($\pm$0.15)
	Gen. T2 healthy	Real T2 tumor	0.52($\pm$0.16)	0.52($\pm$0.16)
	Gen. T2 tumor	Real T2 tumor	0.50($\pm$0.16)	0.49($\pm$0.16)
	Gen. T2 tumor^A	Real T2 tumor	0.44($\pm$0.18)	0.43($\pm$0.18)
	Gen. T2 tumor, def	Real T2 tumor	**0.55($\pm$0.14)**	**0.55($\pm$0.14)**
	Gen. T2 tumor, def.^{A}	Real T2 tumor	0.41($\pm$0.19)	0.41($\pm$0.19)

ment shows the capability of the images to be used for assessment of a registration network pre-trained on healthy T1 images. When used for atlas registration on real pathological T2 data, the registration yields mean Dice values of $0.43(\pm0.14)/0.40(\pm0.20)$ (ventricles/caudate nuclei) and for the generated deformed tumor images $0.47(\pm0.19)/0.47(\pm0.21)$. Those results are comparable and show no significant difference in an unpaired t-test ($p > 0.1$), which implicates plausibility of the generated data and induces its suitability to evaluate the accuracy of pretrained neural networks. When testing the registration network on the generated T2 tumor images without deformations, mean Dices of $0.62(\pm0.11)/0.63(\pm0.10)$ are achieved (see supplementary). This emphasizes the importance to integrate tumor-induced deformations into synthetic images.

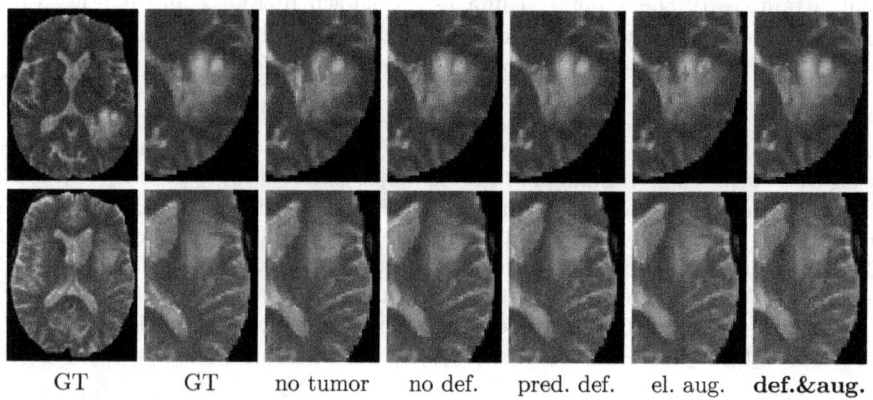

GT   GT   no tumor   no def.   pred. def.   el. aug.   **def.&aug.**

Fig. 4. Example segmentations of 3D pathological images. Column 1–2: ground truth whole image and zoomed to the tumor region; Column 3–7: segmentations of U-Net trained differently with fake images (the best setup is marked bold). Note that when tumors do not directly impact the target tissue, the influence of the different training types is marginal (second row).

For experiments 2) and 3), each training setup is executed ten times with different random seeds to ensure the stability of the results. All methods are evaluated in terms of Dice overlaps of the ventricles and caudate nuclei averaged over all 20 test BRATS images and seeds. The segmentation and registration results are shown in Table 1. The 2D segmentation results are analogous to the 3D results with the best setup yielding $0.71(\pm0.12)/0.64(\pm0.24)$. Also, deformations with the naive approach [16] do not deliver significantly better results compared to using no deformations (see supplementary). The results clearly show that generated domain-translated images with pathologies and their corresponding deformations improve training by far. Adding tumors to the generated images enhances the segmentation of smaller structures, yet, the segmentation of the larger ventricles is impaired. This is due to subtle tumors in the test images that do not impact the segmentation of the ventricles (Fig. 4), thus it might be useful to mix the training datasets with and without tumors. However, by extending the training dataset by our proposed deformation method, significantly better results are achieved for all experiments. This shows that pathological tissue deformations are crucial for both image registration and segmentation. Adding random elastic augmentation significantly enhances the segmentation results. Contrary to that, this type of augmentation disrupts the training process of the registration network strongly, which is consistent with [21]. Overall, the best setups for registration and segmentation deliver Dice coefficients in a reasonable range compared to the baseline training and testing on the real healthy T1 MRIs.

4   Discussion and Conclusion

In this work we propose a method to generate images from pathological domains with ground truth anatomical annotations directly transferred from healthy patients. Our approach includes a tumor synthesizing technique and a novel idea to simulate the tumor mass effect. In the performed experiments, the necessity for generating ground truth pathological data is emphasized and we show that the synthesized data is suitable for the training of neural networks applied for real pathological data. Moreover, a significant improvement of the networks' performance is achieved by additionally considering tumor-induced deformations. Future work could gain improvement by mixing healthy and pathological images in a single dataset and a more elaborate assessment of the tissue deformations.

References

1. Arsigny, V., Commowick, O., Pennec, X., Ayache, N.: A log-Euclidean framework for statistics on diffeomorphisms. In: Larsen, R., Nielsen, M., Sporring, J. (eds.) MICCAI 2006. LNCS, vol. 4190, pp. 924–931. Springer, Heidelberg (2006). https://doi.org/10.1007/11866565_113
2. Astaraki, M., Toma-Dasu, I., Smedby, Ö., Wang, C.: Normal appearance autoencoder for lung cancer detection and segmentation. In: Shen, D., et al. (eds.) MICCAI 2019. LNCS, vol. 11769, pp. 249–256. Springer, Cham (2019). https://doi.org/10.1007/978-3-030-32226-7_28
3. Cohen, J.P., Luck, M., Honari, S.: Distribution matching losses can hallucinate features in medical image translation. In: Frangi, A.F., Schnabel, J.A., Davatzikos, C., Alberola-López, C., Fichtinger, G. (eds.) MICCAI 2018. LNCS, vol. 11070, pp. 529–536. Springer, Cham (2018). https://doi.org/10.1007/978-3-030-00928-1_60
4. Dosovitskiy, A., et al.: FlowNet: learning optical flow with convolutional networks. In: Proceedings of the IEEE International Conference on Computer Vision, pp. 2758–2766 (2015)
5. Ehrhardt, J., Schmidt-Richberg, A., Werner, R., Handels, H.: Variational registration: a flexible open-source ITK toolbox for nonrigid image registration. In: Handels, H., Deserno, T.M., Meinzer, H.-P., Tolxdorff, T. (eds.) Bildverarbeitung für die Medizin 2015. I, pp. 209–214. Springer, Heidelberg (2015). https://doi.org/10.1007/978-3-662-46224-9_37

6. Ezhov, I., et al.: Neural parameters estimation for brain tumor growth modeling. In: Shen, D., et al. (eds.) MICCAI 2019. LNCS, vol. 11765, pp. 787–795. Springer, Cham (2019). https://doi.org/10.1007/978-3-030-32245-8_87

7. Fonov, V., Evans, A.C., Botteron, K., Almli, C.R., McKinstry, R.C., Collins, D.L.: Unbiased average age-appropriate atlases for pediatric studies. NeuroImage 54(1), 313–327 (2011)

8. Frid-Adar, M., Klang, E., Amitai, M., Goldberger, J., Greenspan, H.: Synthetic data augmentation using GAN for improved liver lesion classification. In: 2018 IEEE 15th International Symposium on Biomedical Imaging (ISBI 2018), pp. 289–293 (2018)

9. Goodfellow, I., et al.: Generative adversarial nets. In: Advances in Neural Information Processing Systems 27, pp. 2672–2680 (2014)

10. Hammers, A., et al.: Three-dimensional maximum probability atlas of the human brain, with particular reference to the temporal lobe. Hum. Brain Mapp. 19(4), 224–247 (2003)

11. Hogea, C., Davatzikos, C., Biros, G.: Modeling glioma growth and mass effect in 3D MR images of the brain. In: Ayache, N., Ourselin, S., Maeder, A. (eds.) MICCAI 2007. LNCS, vol. 4791, pp. 642–650. Springer, Heidelberg (2007). https://doi.org/10.1007/978-3-540-75757-3_78

12. Kohl, S., et al.: A Probabilistic U-Net for segmentation of ambiguous images. In: Advances in Neural Information Processing Systems 31, pp. 6965–6975 (2018)

13. Kwon, D., Niethammer, M., Akbari, H., Bilello, M., Davatzikos, C., Pohl, K.M.: PORTR: pre-operative and post-recurrence brain tumor registration. IEEE Trans. Med. Imaging 33(3), 651–667 (2014)

14. Liu, J., Shen, C., Liu, T., Aguilera, N., Tam, J.: Active appearance model induced generative adversarial network for controlled data augmentation. In: Shen, D., et al. (eds.) MICCAI 2019. LNCS, vol. 11764, pp. 201–208. Springer, Cham (2019). https://doi.org/10.1007/978-3-030-32239-7_23

15. Menze, B.H., Jakab, A., Bauer, S., et al.: The multimodal brain tumor image segmentation benchmark (BRATS). IEEE Trans. Med. Imaging 34(10), 1993–2024 (2015)

16. Pfarrkirchner, B., Gsaxner, C., Schmalsteig, D., Egger, J., Lindner, L.: TuMore: generation of synthetic brain tumor MRI data for deep learning based segmentation approaches. In: Medical Imaging 2018: Imaging Informatics for Healthcare, Research, and Applications, p. 63 (2018)

17. Rohé, M.-M., Datar, M., Heimann, T., Sermesant, M., Pennec, X.: SVF-Net: learning deformable image registration using shape matching. In: Descoteaux, M., Maier-Hein, L., Franz, A., Jannin, P., Collins, D.L., Duchesne, S. (eds.) MICCAI 2017. LNCS, vol. 10433, pp. 266–274. Springer, Cham (2017). https://doi.org/10.1007/978-3-319-66182-7_31

18. Shattuck, D.W., et al.: Construction of a 3D probabilistic atlas of human cortical structures. Neuroimage 39(3), 1064–1080 (2008)

19. Shin, H.-C., et al.: Medical image synthesis for data augmentation and anonymization using generative adversarial networks. In: Gooya, A., Goksel, O., Oguz, I., Burgos, N. (eds.) SASHIMI 2018. LNCS, vol. 11037, pp. 1–11. Springer, Cham (2018). https://doi.org/10.1007/978-3-030-00536-8_1

20. Uzunova, H., Ehrhardt, J., Jacob, F., Frydrychowicz, A., Handels, H.: Multi-scale GANs for memory-efficient generation of high resolution medical images. In: Shen, D., et al. (eds.) MICCAI 2019. LNCS, vol. 11769, pp. 112–120. Springer, Cham (2019). https://doi.org/10.1007/978-3-030-32226-7_13

21. Uzunova, H., Wilms, M., Handels, H., Ehrhardt, J.: Training CNNs for image registration from few samples with model-based data augmentation. In: Descoteaux, M., Maier-Hein, L., Franz, A., Jannin, P., Collins, D.L., Duchesne, S. (eds.) MICCAI 2017. LNCS, vol. 10433, pp. 223–231. Springer, Cham (2017). https://doi.org/10.1007/978-3-319-66182-7_26

22. Wang, T.C., Liu, M.Y., Zhu, J.Y., Tao, A., Kautz, J., Catanzaro, B.: High-resolution image synthesis and semantic manipulation with conditional GANs. In: 2018 IEEE/CVF Conference on Computer Vision and Pattern Recognition, pp. 8798–8807 (2018)

23. Wu, E., Wu, K., Cox, D., Lotter, W.: Conditional infilling GANs for data augmentation in mammogram classification. In: Image Analysis for Moving Organ, Breast, and Thoracic Images, pp. 98–106 (2018)

24. Xing, Y., et al.: Adversarial pulmonary pathology translation for pairwise chest X-ray data augmentation. In: Shen, D., et al. (eds.) MICCAI 2019. LNCS, vol. 11769, pp. 757–765. Springer, Cham (2019). https://doi.org/10.1007/978-3-030-32226-7_84

25. Yang, X., Kwitt, R., Styner, M., Niethammer, M.: Quicksilver: fast predictive image registration – a deep learning approach. NeuroImage **158**, 378–396 (2017)

E²Net: An Edge Enhanced Network for Accurate Liver and Tumor Segmentation on CT Scans

Youbao Tang[1(✉)], Yuxing Tang[1], Yingying Zhu[1], Jing Xiao[2], and Ronald M. Summers[1]

[1] Imaging Biomarkers and Computer-Aided Diagnosis Laboratory, Radiology and Imaging Sciences, National Institutes of Health Clinical Center, Bethesda, MD 20892-1182, USA
{youbao.tang,rms}@nih.gov
[2] Ping An Insurance Company of China, Shenzhen 510852, China

Abstract. Developing an effective liver and liver tumor segmentation model from CT scans is very important for the success of liver cancer diagnosis, surgical planning and cancer treatment. In this work, we propose a two-stage framework for 2D liver and tumor segmentation. The first stage is a coarse liver segmentation network, while the second stage is an edge enhanced network (E²Net) for more accurate liver and tumor segmentation. E²Net explicitly models complementary objects (liver and tumor) and their edge information within the network to preserve the organ and lesion boundaries. We introduce an edge prediction module in E²Net and design an edge distance map between liver and tumor boundaries, which is used as an extra supervision signal to train the edge enhanced network. We also propose a deep cross feature fusion module to refine multi-scale features from both objects and their edges. E²Net is more easily and efficiently trained with a small labeled dataset, and it can be trained/tested on the original 2D CT slices (resolve resampling error issue in 3D models). The proposed framework has shown superior performance on both liver and liver tumor segmentation compared to several state-of-the-art 2D, 3D and 2D/3D hybrid frameworks.

Keywords: Edge enhanced network · Cross feature fusion · Liver segmentation · Tumor segmentation · CT scans

1 Introduction

The liver is the body's largest internal organ and liver cancer is the leading cause of cancer deaths worldwide, accounting for more than 700,000 deaths each year[1]. Computed tomography (CT) is commonly adopted for imaging abdominal organs including liver. Developing accurate, robust and automated techniques

---

[1] https://www.cancer.org/cancer/liver-cancer.html.

A. L. Martel et al. (Eds.): MICCAI 2020, LNCS 12264, pp. 512–522, 2020.
https://doi.org/10.1007/978-3-030-59719-1_50

for liver and its tumor segmentation from CT scans is of high demand to assist clinicians in liver cancer diagnosis, surgical planning and precision medicine in clinical practice. However, liver and liver tumor segmentation is very challenging due to low contrast or blurry/unclear boundaries between the liver, tumor and nearby organ tissues. Moreover, the pathology of liver tumor is inherently heterogeneous on population, which leads to large variations on the size, shape, location, appearance/textures and numbers of tumors within one patient. In the last decade, deep learning has been successfully and widely used in many tasks of medical image analysis [1, 3, 13, 19–22, 25, 27]. Also, researchers have developed various computer-aided diagnosis (CADx) techniques to tackle liver and tumor segmentation. Recently, 2D and 3D fully convolutional neural network (FCN) based methods [7, 10, 14, 23, 24] have achieved state-of-the-art performance. 3D FCN models are supposed to consider the contexts on the z-axis, which would lead to better segmentation accuracy than 2D models. Nevertheless, the current 3D segmentation models have an excessive number of parameters with extremely high complexity, which are difficulty to train. Notably, 3D models require large size labeled training data and rich computational resources for optimization. Furthermore, many CT scan shows a large variation on the z-axis slice spacing ranges since it consists of anisotropic dimensions. For example, the slice spacing ranges are 0.45 mm to 6.0 mm in the LiTS challenge dataset [2]. A popular solution is to sample the scans into a fixed spacing (e.g. 1.0 mm) during training 3D or 2D/3D hybrid models. However, for cases with a fine spacing of less than 1.0 mm, some important inter-slice information will be lost. For cases with a coarse spacing of larger than 1.0 mm, extra errors will be introduced by sampling. To the best of our knowledge, the existing deep learning based methods [7, 10, 14, 23, 24] did not explicitly model the edges of objects (liver and tumor). The complementarity between the objects and their edges has not been explored, which might boost the segmentation performance.

To address these problems, we propose a powerful 2D segmentation model for liver and tumor segmentation by leveraging and emphasizing their edge information as complementary information. We investigate the correlation between liver/tumor segmentation and edge prediction. The proposed model has three main contributions: 1) Our segmentation model is trained with an edge enhanced cost function, which explicitly models complementary and discriminative feature information within the network to preserve the liver and tumor boundaries. 2) A deep cross feature fusion module is proposed to bidirectionally refine multi-scale features from both objects (*i.e.*, liver and tumor) and their edges. 3) Extensive experiments on the publicly available LiTS and 3DIRCADb datasets show the superiority of the proposed method as compared to several state-of-the-art 2D, 3D and hybrid models for liver and tumor segmentation.

2 Methodology

Figure 1 shows an overview of the proposed framework, which consists of two stages. In the first stage, given a CT image, we coarsely segment the liver region

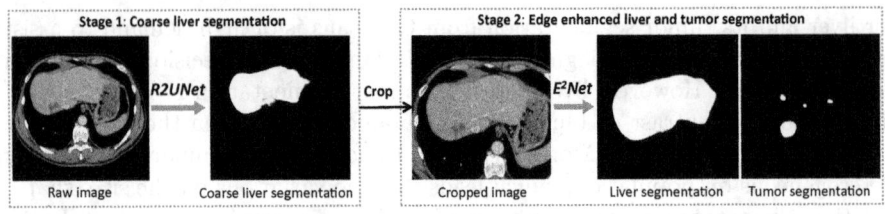

Fig. 1. Overview of the proposed framework.

using a fully convolutional neural network (denoted R2UNet) if a liver appears. Based on the segmented region, a CT sub-image is cropped as the input of the second stage, wherein we propose an edge enhanced network (E²Net) that is used to simultaneously segment the liver and tumor regions more accurately.

Coarse Liver Segmentation. We use Res2Net-50 [9] as the backbone to extract multi-scale features from CT images. Res2Net [9] can represent multi-scale features at a granular level and increase the range of receptive fields for each network layer. It has been demonstrated that Res2Net blocks brought consistent performance gains over baseline models, *e.g.*, ResNet [11], for various tasks such as semantic segmentation. For an input CT image with a size of $H \times W$, the multi-scale features extracted using Res2Net-50 are denoted as $F = \{F^i | i = 1, 2, 3, 4, 5\}$. The size of F^i is $\frac{H}{2^i} \times \frac{W}{2^i} \times C_i$, where C_i is the number of channels. To reduce the computational cost, we pad two convolutional layers with 32 1×1 and 3×3 kernels to each feature F^i to compress it to 32 channels. All compressed features are sent to a decoder similar to UNet [17] except all convolutional layers having 32 kernels for coarse liver segmentation. We denote this network as R2UNet. Please refer to Fig. 2(a) for its architecture illustration.

Accurate Liver and Tumor Segmentation Using E²Net. Based on the coarse liver segmentation result, a sub-image is cropped, where most of the irrelevant regions are removed. Using the sub-image as input, the network used in the second stage can focus on learning discriminative features for accurate liver and tumor segmentation. A baseline method is to use R2UNet with two output channels, one for liver and the other for tumor segmentation. We empirically find that this baseline cannot well segment the areas near the boundaries of the liver and tumor when the boundaries are blurry. To alleviate this issue, we introduce an extra branch to explicitly learn features for edge prediction. This branch has the same architecture as the aforementioned R2UNet segmentation model. We observe that the features extracted by these two branches retain complementary information. A straightforward strategy is to fuse these features by concatenating them channel-wisely for the final liver and tumor segmentation. Please refer to Fig. 2(b) for the illustration of this improved architecture.

Using edge as supervision, the heavy imbalance between edge and other pixels hinders the model from learning highly discriminative features for high-quality edge prediction. A weighted loss can be used to alleviate this issue. But we provide a new solution from a totally different perspective. We first perform

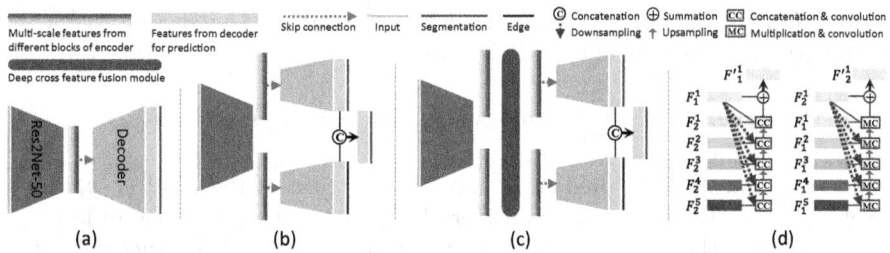

Fig. 2. Illustration of different architecture configurations: (a) R2UNet with a single branch used as a baseline, using liver mask as supervision; (b) Adding an extra branch using edge as supervision, performing feature fusion with concatenation; (c) Adding the proposed deep cross feature fusion (DCFF) module for feature refinement, *i.e.*, the proposed E²Net; (d) Illustration of a single scale feature refinement using DCFF.

distance transformation on the edge image to get a distance map. Then we multiply it with the binary liver or tumor mask and normalize it to $[0, 1]$. Finally, the result of 1 minus the normalized distance map is used as supervision, where the pixels closer to the edge have larger values. The intuition behind is that the pixels closer to the edge are more difficult to segment.

As shown in Fig. 2(b), there is no interaction between the features from two branches except the final fusion step. However, there should be some interrelations between the compressed multi-scale features extracted by the segmentation branch (denoted $F_1 = \{F_1^i | i = 1, 2, 3, 4, 5\}$) and that extracted by the edge prediction branch (denoted $F_2 = \{F_2^i | i = 1, 2, 3, 4, 5\}$). For example, compared with F_2^i, $F_1^i * F_2^i$ could better represent the edge information by suppressing the features from non-edge areas. Compared with F_1^i, $F_1^i + F_2^i$ could better represent the liver or tumor region by suppressing the features from the background. To introduce these interrelations, we propose a deep cross feature fusion (DCFF) module to refine the multi-scale features F_1 and F_2. Our final model E²Net for accurate liver and tumor segmentation in the second stage is shown in Fig. 2(c).

In the DCFF module, for feature of each scale from one branch, we use all equal and larger scale features from the other branch to refine it. Let's take F_1^1 and F_2^1 as examples. For F_1^1, its refined feature F'_1^1 is obtained based on F_1^1 itself and all features $F_2 = \{F_2^i | i = 1, 2, 3, 4, 5\}$. As shown in Fig. 2(d), for each F_2^i, we first downsample F_1^1 to the same size as F_2^i and concatenate them. Then a series of operations including concatenation, convolution and upsampling are performed like the behavior of R2UNet's decoder. Finally, the above resulted feature and F_1^1 are summed together to obtain F'_1^1. For $F_2^1 \Rightarrow F'_2^1$, it is similar to $F_1^1 \Rightarrow F'_1^1$ except replacing all concatenation operations with element-wise multiplication. The discriminability of the multi-scale features is supposed to be improved by this inter-relational refinement.

Note that although the encoders and decoders in both stages have the same structures, their weights are not shared so that each model will avoid learning highly correlated information. This is also validated by experiments.

Model Optimization. For both segmentation and edge prediction tasks, we use binary cross entropy (BCE). It is defined as:

$$\ell_{BCE}(g,p) = -\sum\nolimits_{(x,y)}[g_{x,y}\log(p_{x,y}) + (1-g_{x,y})\log(1-p_{x,y})] \tag{1}$$

where $p_{x,y}$ and $g_{x,y}$ are prediction and ground truth of the pixel (x,y). As a pixel-wise loss, BCE does not consider the global structure of the object. To deal with this, the IoU loss [16] aims to optimize the global structure of the segmented object rather than focusing on a single pixel. It is defined as:

$$\ell_{IoU}(g,p) = 1 - \frac{\sum_{(x,y)}[g_{x,y} * p_{x,y}]}{\sum_{(x,y)}[g_{x,y} + p_{x,y} - g_{x,y} * p_{x,y}]} \tag{2}$$

Hence, the objective of the first stage is defined as the summation of the IoU loss and the BCE loss. It is formulated as $\ell_{1^{st}} = \ell_{IoU}(g,s) + \ell_{BCE}(g,s)$, where g/s is the liver ground truth mask/segmentation result. The second stage has three outputs, *i.e.*, s^1, e and s^2, from the segmentation branch, the edge prediction branch, and the fusion step. The objective of this stage is defined as:

$$\ell_{2^{nd}} = \ell_{IoU}(g_m,s^1) + \ell_{BCE}(g_m,s^1) + \ell_{IoU}(g_m,s^2) + \ell_{BCE}(g_m,s^2) + 4*\ell_{BCE}(g_e,e) \tag{3}$$

where g_m/g_e is the liver and tumor ground truth masks/edge distance maps.

The models in the two stages are trained separately. We use stochastic gradient descent with a momentum of 0.9, an initial learning rate of 0.01, which is divided by 10 once the validation loss is stable. After decreasing the learning rate twice, we stop training. The training batch size is 32. For the first stage, we randomly cropped 448×448 sub-images from the whole CT images during training. For the second stage, we randomly pad the liver regions with 10 to 60 pixels and resize them into 256×256. During inference, we segment all 2D slices of the input CT scan and stack the results to get the 3D segmentation. The whole training process costs about 80 h with an Intel Xeon Gold 6230 CPU and a Tesla V100 GPU. The average inference time is about 12 s per case on the 3DIRCADb dataset [18] when the test batch size is 1.

3   Experimental Results

Datasets. We tested the proposed method on the MICCAI 2017 Liver Tumor Segmentation Challenge [2] (LiTS dataset) and 3DIRCADb dataset [18]. The LiTS dataset contains 131 and 70 contrast-enhanced 3D abdominal CT scans for training and testing, respectively. The pixel-wise liver and tumor ground truths are publicly available for the training set while they are withheld for the test set for online evaluation. The 3DIRCADb dataset contains 20 venous phase enhanced CT scans, where 15 scans have hepatic tumors in the liver. The range of the original Hounsfield Unit (HU) values in these CT scans is from less than −3,000 to more than +3,000. We truncated the image intensity values of

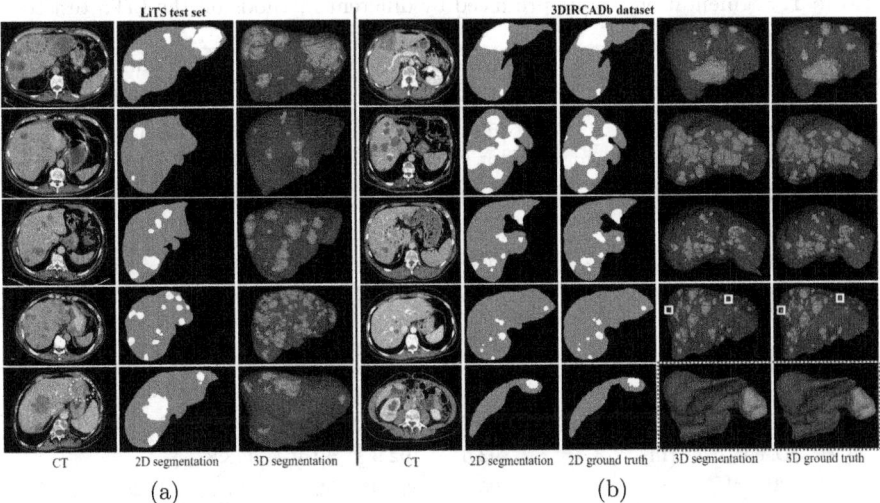

Fig. 3. Visual examples of segmentation results produced by the proposed method on (a) LiTS test set and (b) 3DIRCADb dataset. The ground truths are unavailable in the LiTS test set. To make the tumors visible, we set a larger transparency to livers in all 3D examples except the ones indicated by a purple box where the livers' 3D shapes are well visualized. The yellow/red dashed circles indicate some cases where the livers/tumors' boundaries are blurry. The white boxes in last two columns indicate two cases where the small tumors cannot be well segmented. Best viewed in color. (Color figure online)

all scans to the range of $[-100, 240]$ HU to remove the irrelevant details, and then normalized them to $[-1, 1]$. The 131 LiTS training samples were randomly split into a training set (111) and a validation set (20) for model training and selection. The 3DIRCADb dataset was used for independent hold-out evaluation.

Evaluation Criteria. The output of the fusion step (s^2) is used as the final liver and tumor segmentation result for performance evaluation. Following the evaluation of the LiTS challenge and other approaches [6,7,14], we used the Dice per case score and the global Dice score (Dice global) to evaluate the segmentation performance, and also used the root mean square error (RMSE) to measure the tumor burden that is defined as the liver/tumor ratio [12]. Dice per case score refers to an average Dice score per CT scan/volume while global Dice score is the Dice score evaluated by combining all CT scans into one.

Qualitative Segmentation Results. Figure 3 shows five visual examples of liver and tumor segmentation results produced by the proposed E^{2}Net on both LiTS test set and 3DIRCADb dataset. From Fig. 3, the liver and tumor regions can be well segmented by our E^{2}Net, even for some cases where the boundaries of the livers (the yellow dashed circle) or tumors (the red dashed circles) are very blurry. This is an advantage of E^{2}Net that models edge information within the network training to preserve liver and tumor boundaries. In Fig. 3(b), the

Table 1. Segmentation results produced by different methods on the LiTS test set.

Methods		Liver dice (%)		Tumor dice (%)		Tumor burden
		Per case	Global	Per case	Global	RMSE
2D	TwoFCNs [23]	95.1	95.1	66.1	78.3	0.023
	DeeplabV3+ [5]	95.7	96.1	66.6	80.4	0.016
	2.5DResUNet [10]	-	-	67.0	-	-
	UNet+SP [7]	96.0	96.5	67.6	79.6	0.020
	DenseNet (pre-trained) [14]	95.3	95.9	68.3	81.8	-
	DenseUNet (pre-trained) [14]	95.8	96.3	70.2	82.1	-
	E^{2}Net (Ours)	96.4	**96.8**	72.4	**82.9**	**0.015**
2&3D	UNet [6]	-	-	65.0	-	-
	H-DenseUNet [14]	96.1	96.5	72.2	82.4	**0.015**
	LW-HCN [28]	**96.5**	**96.8**	**73.0**	82.0	**0.015**
3D	DenseUNet [14]	93.6	92.9	59.4	78.8	-
	I3D [4]	95.7	96.0	62.4	77.6	0.025
	I3D (pre-trained) [4]	95.6	96.2	66.6	79.9	0.023

automatic segmentation results are very close to the ground truths. From the example indicated by a purple box, the 3D surface of our segmentation is smoother than the ground truth, suggesting that E^{2}Net is able to correct some inaccuracies of the human annotations. Therefore, the annotators can simply refine the automatic segmentations to get high-quality annotations. As such, E^{2}Net has the potential to speed up the manual annotation process. In the last two columns of Fig. 3, some small tumors indicated by white boxes cannot be well segmented. Through investigation, we find that these tumors are small and have low contrast with their surrounding liver regions. For such cases, providing only the 2D in-plane information might be insufficient for E^{2}Net to learn discriminative features to distinguish them. One possible solution is to incorporate 3D spatial and contextual information between sequential slices, which is left as future work.

Quantitative Segmentation Results. Table 1 lists the liver and tumor segmentation results of the proposed E^{2}Net and other state-of-the-art methods published in the existing literature on the LiTS test set. As a 2D model, our method is first compared with the other 2D models. We can see from the table that it outperforms the others by a large margin. For instance, the tumor Dice per case score is improved from 70.2% to 72.4%, suggesting that our model is capable of learning more discriminative features from 2D CT slices for better segmentation. Although 3D models can consider the 3D spatial information from the CT scans, they have much more trainable parameters than 2D models that require a lot more training data for optimization. However, the amount of annotated training data is insufficient in practice for this task. Therefore, it is not surprising that the 3D models even perform worse than the existing 2D models, as shown in Table 1. To address this problem, researchers have developed some hybrid

Table 2. Results produced by different methods in terms of Dice per case (%) on the 3DIRCADb dataset.

Methods	Liver	Tumor
Moghbel et al. [15]	91.1	75.0
Foruzan et al. [8]	-	82.0
Wu et al. [26]	-	83.0
H-DenseUNet [14]	98.2	93.7
LW-HCN [28]	98.1	94.1
E^{2}Net (Ours)	**98.9**	**95.7**

Table 3. Results of different configurations of our method in terms of Dice per case (%) on the LiTS validation set.

Configurations	Liver	Tumor
1st stage	95.3	-
Baseline (2nd stage)	96.1	71.4
+ edge	96.6	72.2
+ dist	97.1	72.9
+ edge + DCFF	97.5	73.7
+ dist + DCFF	**97.8**	**74.8**

models to consider both 2D in-plane and 3D spatial information, which achieved better performance than a single 2D or 3D model, such as H-DenseUNet [14] and LW-HCN [28]. As shown in Table 1, our E^{2}Net is better than H-DenseUNet in terms of all evaluation metrics and gets comparable performance with LW-HCN. This demonstrates that a powerful and well-designed 2D model, such as the proposed method, still can compete with the hybrid models, even without using 3D information. For tumor segmentation, the global Dice score of our method is better than the one of LW-HCN, but the Dice per case score is worse. One possible reason we find is that there are some CT scans only having small tumors while our method cannot well segment small tumors sometimes as described in Sect. 3. For such CT scans, our method gets low Dice scores that heavily reduce the average Dice score per case. However, these small tumor segmentations only make a small contribution to the global Dice score computation.

Table 2 lists the liver and tumor segmentation results of different methods in terms of Dice per case score on the 3DIRCADb dataset. Our method is trained using the LiTS training set and directly tested on the 3DIRCADb dataset, meaning that the CT scans of 3DIRCADb dataset are totally unseen by our E^{2}Net and different from the LiTS dataset. From Table 2, we can see that E^{2}Net obtains the best performance on both liver and tumor segmentation. Compared with the hybrid model LW-HCN [28] that has the highest tumor Dice per case score of 94.1% in the literature, our 2D model improves this score to 95.7% with a large margin. These remarkable results demonstrate that our method has strong generalizability to accurately segment the livers and their tumors.

Ablation Study. To explore the effect of different design components in the proposed method, we set up the following different experimental configurations and test them on the LiTS validation set: 1) only using the first stage for liver segmentation, 2) using the model (R2UNet) of the first stage as the baseline in the second stage, 3) adding another branch and using edge or distance map (dist) as extra supervision, 4) using the proposed deep cross feature fusion (DCFF) module. Table 3 lists the liver and tumor segmentation performance of different configurations in terms of the Dice per case score. From this table, we can see that

(1) the second stage is essential to get better performance, meaning that such a coarse-to-fine strategy is effective for liver and tumor segmentation. (2) *Baseline + edge/dist* is better than *Baseline*, suggesting that the added branch can learn complementary features to the baseline for performance improvement. (3) As extra supervision, the distance map performs better than the edge, demonstrating the effectiveness of our designed distance map. (4) The largest performance boost is obtained when using DCFF, suggesting that the proposed DCFF can fuse and refine the multi-scale features from both branches effectively and simultaneously. We observed the same findings as above when using E^2Net in both stages. Hence, in our experiment, we used a simpler R2UNet model in the first stage.

4   Conclusions

This paper proposes an edge enhanced deep learning network for robust and accurate liver/tumor segmentation. Operating on original 2D CT slices, the proposed method eliminates the z-axis re-sampling errors caused by different CT slice thickness in other 3D segmentation models. Moreover, our model is easier to train/apply with less computational resources compared to 3D models. By enhancing the edge information, the proposed method improves the performance of liver and tumor segmentation significantly, especially when poor boundaries exist in CT images. Extensive experiments on the challenging LiTS and 3DIRCADb datasets demonstrate the power and effectiveness of our method. Future work will explore the possibility of developing low cost and fast segmentation method which can be used in an embedded system on CT scanner.

Acknowledgments. This research was supported by the Intramural Research Program of the National Institutes of Health Clinical Center and by the Ping An Insurance Company through a Cooperative Research and Development Agreement. We thank Nvidia for GPU card donation.

References

1. Agarwal, V., Tang, Y., Xiao, J., Summers, R.M.: Weakly supervised lesion co-segmentation on CT scans. In: International Symposium on Biomedical Imaging, pp. 203–206 (2020)
2. Bilic, P., et al.: The liver tumor segmentation benchmark (LiTS). arXiv preprint arXiv:1901.04056 (2019)
3. Cai, J., et al.: Accurate weakly-supervised deep lesion segmentation using large-scale clinical annotations: slice-propagated 3D mask generation from 2D RECIST. In: Frangi, A.F., Schnabel, J.A., Davatzikos, C., Alberola-López, C., Fichtinger, G. (eds.) MICCAI 2018. LNCS, vol. 11073, pp. 396–404. Springer, Cham (2018). https://doi.org/10.1007/978-3-030-00937-3_46
4. Carreira, J., Zisserman, A.: Quo vadis, action recognition? A new model and the kinetics dataset. In: IEEE Conference on Computer Vision and Pattern Recognition, pp. 6299–6308 (2017)

5. Chen, L.C., Zhu, Y., Papandreou, G., Schroff, F., Adam, H.: Encoder-decoder with atrous separable convolution for semantic image segmentation. In: European Conference on Computer Vision, pp. 801–818 (2018)
6. Chlebus, G., Meine, H., Moltz, J.H., Schenk, A.: Neural network-based automatic liver tumor segmentation with random forest-based candidate filtering. arXiv preprint arXiv:1706.00842 (2017)
7. Chlebus, G., et al.: Automatic liver tumor segmentation in CT with fully convolutional neural networks and object-based postprocessing. Sci. Rep. **8**(1), 1–7 (2018)
8. Foruzan, A.H., Chen, Y.W.: Improved segmentation of low-contrast lesions using sigmoid edge model. Int. J. Comput. Assist. Radiol. Surg. **11**(7), 1267–1283 (2016)
9. Gao, S., Cheng, M.M., Zhao, K., Zhang, X.Y., Yang, M.H., Torr, P.H.: Res2Net: a new multi-scale backbone architecture. IEEE Trans. Pattern Anal. Mach. Intell. 1 (2019)
10. Han, X.: Automatic liver lesion segmentation using a deep convolutional neural network method. arXiv preprint arXiv:1704.07239 (2017)
11. He, K., Zhang, X., Ren, S., Sun, J.: Deep residual learning for image recognition. In: IEEE Conference on Computer Vision and Pattern Recognition, pp. 770–778 (2016)
12. Jagannath, S., et al.: Tumor burden assessment and its implication for a prognostic model in advanced diffuse large-cell lymphoma. J. Clin. Oncol. **4**(6), 859–865 (1986)
13. Jin, D., Xu, Z., Tang, Y., Harrison, A.P., Mollura, D.J.: CT-realistic lung nodule simulation from 3D conditional generative adversarial networks for robust lung segmentation. In: Frangi, A.F., Schnabel, J.A., Davatzikos, C., Alberola-López, C., Fichtinger, G. (eds.) MICCAI 2018. LNCS, vol. 11071, pp. 732–740. Springer, Cham (2018). https://doi.org/10.1007/978-3-030-00934-2_81
14. Li, X., Chen, H., Qi, X., Dou, Q., Fu, C.W., Heng, P.A.: H-DenseUNet: hybrid densely connected UNet for liver and tumor segmentation from CT volumes. IEEE Trans. Med. Imaging **37**(12), 2663–2674 (2018)
15. Moghbel, M., Mashohor, S., Mahmud, R., Saripan, M.I.B.: Automatic liver segmentation on computed tomography using random walkers for treatment planning. EXCLI J. **15**, 500 (2016)
16. Rahman, M.A., Wang, Y.: Optimizing intersection-over-union in deep neural networks for image segmentation. In: Bebis, G., et al. (eds.) ISVC 2016. LNCS, vol. 10072, pp. 234–244. Springer, Cham (2016). https://doi.org/10.1007/978-3-319-50835-1_22
17. Ronneberger, O., Fischer, P., Brox, T.: U-Net: convolutional networks for biomedical image segmentation. In: Navab, N., Hornegger, J., Wells, W.M., Frangi, A.F. (eds.) MICCAI 2015. LNCS, vol. 9351, pp. 234–241. Springer, Cham (2015). https://doi.org/10.1007/978-3-319-24574-4_28
18. Soler, L., et al.: 3D image reconstruction for comparison of algorithm database: a patient-specific anatomical and medical image database. IRCAD, Strasbourg, France, Technical report (2010)
19. Tang, Y.B., Yan, K., Tang, Y.X., Liu, J., Xiao, J., Summers, R.M.: ULDor: a universal lesion detector for CT scans with pseudo masks and hard negative example mining. In: International Symposium on Biomedical Imaging, pp. 833–836 (2019)
20. Tang, Y., Harrison, A.P., Bagheri, M., Xiao, J., Summers, R.M.: Semi-automatic RECIST labeling on CT scans with cascaded convolutional neural networks. In: Frangi, A.F., Schnabel, J.A., Davatzikos, C., Alberola-López, C., Fichtinger, G. (eds.) MICCAI 2018. LNCS, vol. 11073, pp. 405–413. Springer, Cham (2018). https://doi.org/10.1007/978-3-030-00937-3_47

21. Tang, Y.X., et al.: Automated abnormality classification of chest radiographs using deep convolutional neural networks. NPJ Digit. Med. **3**(1), 1–8 (2020)
22. Tang, Y., Tang, Y., Sandfort, V., Xiao, J., Summers, R.M.: TUNA-Net: task-oriented UNsupervised adversarial network for disease recognition in cross-domain chest X-rays. In: Shen, D., et al. (eds.) MICCAI 2019. LNCS, vol. 11769, pp. 431–440. Springer, Cham (2019). https://doi.org/10.1007/978-3-030-32226-7_48
23. Vorontsov, E., Tang, A., Pal, C., Kadoury, S.: Liver lesion segmentation informed by joint liver segmentation. In: International Symposium on Biomedical Imaging, pp. 1332–1335 (2018)
24. Wang, X., Han, S., Chen, Y., Gao, D., Vasconcelos, N.: Volumetric attention for 3D medical image segmentation and detection. In: Shen, D., et al. (eds.) MICCAI 2019. LNCS, vol. 11769, pp. 175–184. Springer, Cham (2019). https://doi.org/10.1007/978-3-030-32226-7_20
25. Wang, Y., et al.: Weakly supervised universal fracture detection in pelvic X-rays. In: Shen, D., et al. (eds.) MICCAI 2019. LNCS, vol. 11769, pp. 459–467. Springer, Cham (2019). https://doi.org/10.1007/978-3-030-32226-7_51
26. Wu, W., Wu, S., Zhou, Z., Zhang, R., Zhang, Y.: 3D liver tumor segmentation in CT images using improved fuzzy C-means and graph cuts. BioMed Res. Int. **2017**, 1–11 (2017)
27. Yan, K., et al.: MULAN: multitask universal lesion analysis network for joint lesion detection, tagging, and segmentation. In: Shen, D., et al. (eds.) MICCAI 2019. LNCS, vol. 11769, pp. 194–202. Springer, Cham (2019). https://doi.org/10.1007/978-3-030-32226-7_22
28. Zhang, J., Xie, Y., Zhang, P., Chen, H., Xia, Y., Shen, C.: Light-weight hybrid convolutional network for liver tumour segmentation. In: International Joint Conference on Artificial Intelligence, pp. 10–16 (2019)

Universal Loss Reweighting to Balance Lesion Size Inequality in 3D Medical Image Segmentation

Boris Shirokikh[1,2,3]([✉]), Alexey Shevtsov[2,3], Anvar Kurmukov[2,4], Alexandra Dalechina[5], Egor Krivov[2,3], Valery Kostjuchenko[5], Andrey Golanov[6], and Mikhail Belyaev[1]

[1] Skolkovo Institute of Science and Technology, Moscow, Russia
boris.shirokikh@phystech.edu
[2] Kharkevich Institute for Information Transmission Problems, Moscow, Russia
[3] Moscow Institute of Physics and Technology, Moscow, Russia
[4] Higher School of Economics, Moscow, Russia
[5] Moscow Gamma-Knife Center, Moscow, Russia
[6] Burdenko Neurosurgery Institute, Moscow, Russia

Abstract. Target imbalance affects the performance of recent deep learning methods in many medical image segmentation tasks. It is a twofold problem: class imbalance – positive class (lesion) size compared to negative class (non-lesion) size; lesion size imbalance – large lesions overshadows small ones (in the case of multiple lesions per image). While the former was addressed in multiple works, the latter lacks investigation. We propose a loss reweighting approach to increase the ability of the network to detect small lesions. During the learning process, we assign a weight to every image voxel. The assigned weights are inversely proportional to the lesion volume, thus smaller lesions get larger weights. We report the benefit from our method for well-known loss functions, including Dice Loss, Focal Loss, and Asymmetric Similarity Loss. Additionally, we compare our results with other reweighting techniques: Weighted Cross-Entropy and Generalized Dice Loss. Our experiments show that *inverse weighting* considerably increases the detection quality, while preserves the delineation quality on a state-of-the-art level. We publish a complete experimental pipeline (https://github.com/neuro-ml/inverse_weighting) for two publicly available datasets of CT images: LiTS and LUNA16. We also show results on a private database of MR images for the task of multiple brain metastases delineation.

Keywords: Segmentation · CNN · Lung nodules · Brain metastases · CT · MRI

Electronic supplementary material The online version of this chapter (https://doi.org/10.1007/978-3-030-59719-1_51) contains supplementary material, which is available to authorized users.

1   Introduction

In recent years, convolutional neural networks (CNNs) have become the dominant approach to solve medical image segmentation tasks [14]. A wide variety of CNN models, training procedures and loss functions were built under the BRATS [16] and ISLES [15] competitions. The most common way to measure the performance of such a new method is to use segmentation voxel-wise metrics, e.g. Dice Score [2]. However, in the case of multiple lesions per image, clinical tasks also require analyzing algorithm in terms of the detection quality. For instance, all tumors, including the smallest ones, should be found and delineated in the brain stereotactic radiosurgery or in the lung cancer screening process. But since the Dice Score is a voxel-wise metric, it does not differentiate between missing several True Positives in a large lesion or in a small one.

Learning a model under the presence of extremely small targets is challenging. This is especially the problem for 3D medical image segmentation tasks. The total fraction of voxels with lesion is about 0.1% in the case of lung nodules and about 1% in case of multiple brain metastases. Moreover, in a series of medical image segmentation tasks we have a problem with the size imbalance. In some cases, large lesions could be up to 50 times bigger than the small ones (see typical lesion diameters distribution on Fig. 2).

Several approaches have been suggested to tackle the problem of target imbalance. The main idea is to add weight to a loss function to equally represent each class (lesion vs non-lesion or different lesion types in a multi-class problem). It is implemented, for example, in Weighted Cross-Entropy [18] and Generalized Dice Loss [19]. The shortcoming of this approach is that it pays attention only to the lesion type, but not the lesion size (see Fig. 1). Besides, most of the research focuses on the delineation quality and lacks an investigation into the detection performance. Ideal segmentation implies perfect detection, however, due to the substantial differences between large and small lesions, almost a perfect delineation could have poor detection quality. Here we address this problem by applying the idea of weighting a loss function with respect to target sizes.

Our contribution is twofold:

- We propose a loss function reweighting strategy, that balances the lesions of different sizes. We call our approach **inverse weighting**, since the generated weights are inversely proportional to the lesion size.
- We evaluate the effect of using the most popular segmentation loss functions on segmentation quality and network's ability to detect lesions of different sizes. On a series of medical image segmentation tasks, we show how our approach improves the detection quality, especially for small lesions (Fig. 3), while preserving delineation performance.

2   Related Work

A large number of neural network architectures, improved training procedures, and loss functions have been proposed in recent years. We extensively investigate

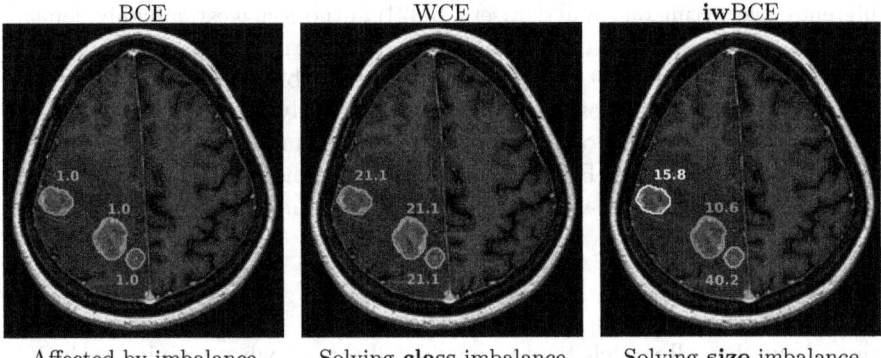

Fig. 1. The effect of inverse weighting. No reweighting applied (left), class balancing via weighted-cross entropy (center), **inverse weighting** (right). Weights for every tumor are calculated using formulas in Table 1 and placed near the tumors.

the behavior of loss functions keeping the rest of the deep learning pipeline on the state-of-the-art level without diving into details.

The *Binary Cross-Entropy* (BCE) is the standard loss function commonly used for segmentation tasks. It does not handle the problem of class imbalance and differently sized objects thus often yielding poor results. Authors of [13] suggested using *Focal Loss* as an extension of BCE in highly class imbalanced detection tasks and it is widely used in segmentation tasks as well [8]. Focal Loss does not apply any type of reweighting but automatically focuses the network attention on difficult examples. *Dice Loss* [17] has recently become one of the state-of-the-art losses for medical image segmentation tasks. The authors claim that Dice Loss establishes the right balance between classes without assigning any weights. But for the tasks with multiple targets, a large object overshadows the small one, hence the network tends to miss small lesions. Recent work [8] proposed *Asymmetric Similarity Loss* (ASL) based on F_β score. ASL extends Dice Loss (the special case with $\beta = 1$) and allows training a network with a better balance between precision and recall. But it shares the same drawback with Dice Loss: differently sized overshadowing objects. Authors of [5] proposed Sensitivity-Specificity loss which we left without consideration. It performs worse than Dice Loss on a 3D medical image segmentation task in [19] and utilizes a similar idea with ASL.

Several approaches reweight BCE and Dice Loss to improve network performance in medical image segmentation tasks. In [18] authors use *Weighted Cross-Entropy* (WCE) loss and [19] suggest Generalized Dice Loss (GDL) to tackle the problem of class imbalance. Both approaches utilize the same idea of reweighting the corresponding losses with weights inverse to the sizes of classes (see Table 1). Our approach simultaneously solves class imbalance problem and imbalance between differently sized objects. A deeper modification of Cross-Entropy loss to handle class imbalance is evaluated in [11], but the goal is quite different – overfitting on small datasets. In [21] authors suggest, a highly dependable on hyperparameters, a combination of Cross-Entropy and logarithmic Dice Loss to solve multiclass (19 classes) segmentation problem. In our work, we show an improvement for both of these losses independently.

We focus our attention on the most relevant loss functions and their explicitly reweighted modifications. Below we detail how our method is applied to state-of-the-art losses and compare it with WCE and GDL.

3   Method

We find out that all models tend to miss small targets when training with BCE or Focal Loss. We assume poor performance comes from the inability of these losses to equally represent differently sized targets. Dice Loss and ASL have the same drawback: large targets overshadow the small ones. Moreover, already developed losses handle only the imbalance between classes, not between lesion sizes. We aim to close the gap and propose a simple methodology to reweight loss functions in the way that all targets contribute equally, e.g. small targets have greater weights.

During the training stage, we generate a tensor of weights for every incoming patch. To form such a tensor we split the corresponding ground-truth patch into $K + 1$ connected components $L_0, \ldots, L_K$, where L_0 is the non-lesion component (background) and K is the number of lesions in the current patch. Next, we assign the weight to every component which is inverse to the component's volume:

$$w_j = \frac{\sum_{k=0}^{K} |L_k|}{(K+1) \cdot |L_j|}, \tag{1}$$

here w_j is the weight, assigned to every voxel inside the corresponding component L_j. The constant in the denominator ensures that the sum of our weights is equal to the sum of the unit tensor of the same size (see derivation details in Supplementary Materials). We call this method **inverse weighting (iw)**. Note, how our approach assigns greater weights to the smaller tumors (Fig. 1). At this point, we can modify any of the discussed loss functions with our reweighting. Since WCE and GDL explicitly reweight state-of-the-art losses, we do not apply reweighting twice. Corresponding modifications for BCE, Focal Loss, Dice Loss, and ASL are shown in the Table 1.

4   Experiments

4.1   Data

We report our results on three datasets. Two publicly available datasets that include 3D CT images: LUNA16 [10] with lung cancerous nodules and LiTS [4] with liver tumors; and one private dataset with MR images of multiple brain metastases.

Table 1. Loss functions and their modifications. Here y_i denotes the ith element of the ground truth binary mask, p_i is the corresponding predicted probability, and $\mathbf{w_i}$ is the proposed inverse weight.

Loss	Original expression	Proposed modification (**iw**)
BCE	$-(y_i \log p_i + (1-y_i)\log(1-p_i))$	$-\mathbf{w_i}(y_i \log p_i + (1-y_i)\log(1-p_i))$
Focal Loss$_{\gamma,\alpha}$	$-(\alpha(1-p_i)^\gamma y_i \log p_i$ $+(1-\alpha)p_i^\gamma(1-y_i)\log(1-p_i))$	$-\mathbf{w_i}(\alpha(1-p_i)^\gamma y_i \log p_i$ $+(1-\alpha)p_i^\gamma(1-y_i)\log(1-p_i))$
WCE	$-wy_i \log p_i - (1-y_i)\log(1-p_i), w = \frac{n-\sum_i p_i}{\sum_i p_i}$	—
Dice Loss	$1 - \frac{2\sum_i p_i y_i}{\sum_i(p_i^2+y_i^2)}$	$1 - \frac{2\sum_i \mathbf{w_i} p_i y_i}{\sum_i \mathbf{w_i}(p_i^2+y_i^2)}$
ASL$_\beta$	$1 - \frac{(1+\beta^2)\sum_i p_i y_i}{\sum_i(\beta^2 y_i + p_i)}$	$1 - \frac{(1+\beta^2)\sum_i \mathbf{w_i} p_i y_i}{\sum_i \mathbf{w_i}(\beta^2 y_i + p_i)}$
GDL	$1 - \frac{2\sum_{c=1}^2 w_c^2 \sum_i p_i y_i}{\sum_{c=1}^2 w_c^2 \sum_i(p_i^2+y_i^2)}, w_c = \frac{1}{\sum_i y_i}$	—

LUNA16 includes 816 (we have excluded 72 cases with nodules located outside of lung masks) annotated chest scans from LIDC/IDRI database [1]. For every image, we clip intensities between -1000 and 300 Hounsfield units (HU), and then set the voxels outside the given binary lung masks to -1000. Ground truth mask was formed by averaging 4 given annotations.

Metastases (private dataset) includes 1952 unique patients with the T1-weighted MRI of the head. We apply no preprocessing steps to these images.

LiTS includes 131 annotated CT abdomen scans. For every image, we clip intensities between -300 and 300 HU and then apply a given binary mask of liver the same way we did it with LUNA16 data.

Before passing through the network, we scale images to have voxel's intensities between 0 and 1.

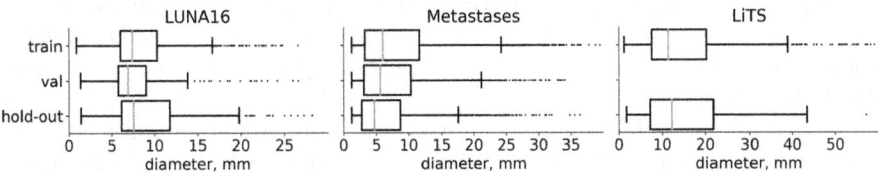

Fig. 2. Lesion diameters distribution. Metastases under 5 mm, lung nodules under 10 mm and liver tumors under 12 mm are considered *small*, according to the clinical recommendations [3, 12]

We use *train-validation* setup to compare different architectures and hyperparameters for loss functions. Then the merged combination of *training* and *validation* data is used to train the chosen methods and we report final results on previously unseen *hold-out* set. LUNA16 is presented as 10, approximately equal, subsets [10] thus we use the first 6 for *training* (534 images), next 2 for *validation* (178 images) and the last pair as *hold-out* (174 images). We divide Metastases into *training* (1250 images), *validation* (402 images) and *hold-out* (300 images). LiTS is also presented as 2 subsets, so we use the first for *training* (104 images) and the second as *hold-out* (27 images). We do not shrink the validation part of the LiTS, since this dataset is used only once for the final results reporting.

4.2   Architecture and Training

For all our experiments we consistently use a single CNN model – slightly modified 3D U-Net [6]. Implemented architecture within PyTorch framework is available in our repository along with a schematic image. Following the suggestion of [9], we do not focus our attention on fine-tuning the CNN model.

In all scenarios we train the model for 100 epochs, starting with learning rate of 10^{-2}, and reducing it to 10^{-3} at the epoch 80. Each epoch consists of 100 iterations of stochastic gradient descent with Nesterov momentum (0.9). At every iteration we sample patches of size $128 \times 128 \times 128$ and batch size of two. With the probability of 0.5 we sample the patch so that it contains at least one voxel with lesion, otherwise we sample it uniformly. The training takes about 26 hours on a 24 GB NVIDIA Tesla M40 GPU.

Note, that only two of the considered loss functions have hyperparameters: ASL (β) and Focal Loss (γ, α). We use ASL with $\beta = 1.5$ originally recommended in [8]. For Focal Loss we also use $\gamma = 2$ originally recommended in [13], but change α to be 0.75 chosen on validation.

4.3   Metric

Dice Score has a particular drawback measuring the delineation quality in the tasks with multiple lesions per image: big lesion overshadows small ones. We use **object Dice Score** – the average Dice Score over *unique found lesions*. Therefore it does not shift towards larger lesions. Note that we exclude missed lesions from this analysis, hence the delineation quality is independent from detection quality.

To measure the detection quality we suggest using a Free-response Receiver Operating Characteristic (FROC) curve analysis. It is extremely efficient operating with multiple targets and False Positive (FP) responses per case [7]. A FROC curve measures the sensitivity to detected objects instead of voxel-wise sensitivity, therefore does not have the same drawback of overshadowed lesions. A FROC curve summarizes the model's efficiency with the trade-off between the fraction of lesions detected (Recall) and the average number of FPs per image. But it gives us only visual representation of experimental results. To compare the performance of different methods we extract a single value from the curves. Authors of [20] suggested using the **average object-wise Recall** over the predefined FP values (1/8, 1/4, 1/2, 1, 2, 4, 8) which is also the main metric of

LUNA16 challenge [10]. This metric gives us the average fraction of detected lesions per case which is highly interpretable in terms of detection quality.

To calculate the confidence intervals for FROC curves and for average Recall we use bootstrapping. We sample 80% of test patients and build a curve on every of the 100 iterations. Average recall is calculated for every bootstrapped curve and we report the mean value along with the standard deviation.

4.4   Results and Discussion

We visualize our main contribution with the considerable improvement of the average object-wise Recall for all four chosen loss functions on all three datasets (Fig. 3). We also report our metrics separately for three groups of lesion sizes and show a solid contribution into the small lesion detection quality which satisfies our method's motivation. However, a comparison with WCE is worth a more detailed discussion.

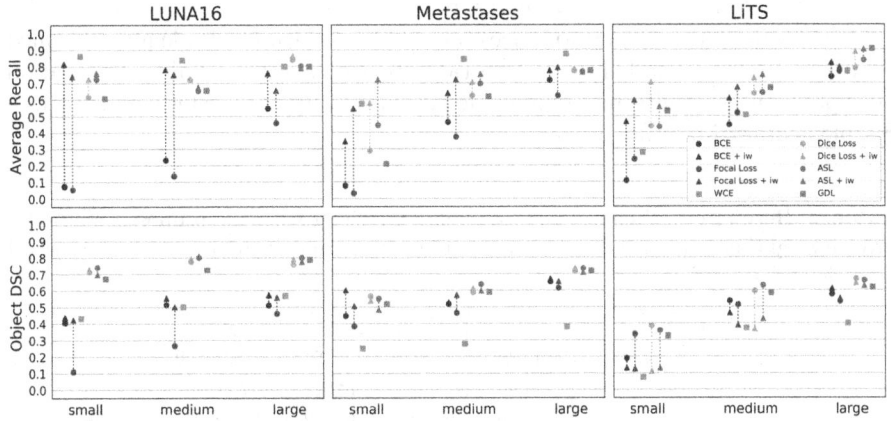

Fig. 3. The impact of inversely weighted loss functions in terms of average Recall and object-wise Dice Score. We show performance on three approximately equal subsets (1/3 each) of lesions divided by their size. Small and medium groups correspond to the clinical recommendations of small lesions (see Fig. 2).

Images from LUNA16 contain 1.3 nodules per scan on average, while Metastases and LiTS have 4.8 and 6.9 tumors per scan respectively. The latter means that LUNA16 is hardly an appropriate dataset to benefit from our method, since the majority of training patches contain only one lesion. One lesion per patch is clearly the *class imbalance* problem, and WCE outperforms the other methods in terms of average Recall. But nevertheless we show inverse weighting solving also the class imbalance task on the competitive level solidly improving BCE and Focal Loss performance. Finally, even the slight improvement in the detection quality of WCE comes with the dramatic delineation quality loss on the other two datasets, which is crucial for clinical tasks.

GDL failed to surpass inversely weighted loss function almost in all scenarios. But overall we find ASL and Dice Loss along with GDL and their inversely weighted modifications to be highly stable during the training. Respectively, Dice-like loss function sufficiently outperform BCE-like losses both in terms of the detection and the delineation qualities. We believe such a behaviour comes from two properties of Dice Loss. Firstly, it is designed to optimize the Dice Score metric, and one could clearly see the dominance of Dice-like losses in terms of object Dice Score (Fig. 3 and Table 2). Secondly, it partially solves the class imbalance problem, but only in the cases with exactly one object per patch. The latter is again perfectly demonstrated on LUNA16, as we put this dataset to be more about class imbalance problem in the previous paragraph. One could see the already high object Dice Scores and average Recall values of ASL and Dice Loss on LUNA16 along with minor changes of their reweighting.

However, modified with inverse weighting loss functions have a noticeable decrease in delineation quality on LiTS data. We consider this to be a side effect of highly increased object-wise Recall: *modified losses find more difficult cases, hence joint object Dice Score could decrease.*

Besides the separate performance on lesion sizes we also include more detailed results for all lesions in hold-out sets (Table 2). We give the visual representation of experimental results in terms of detection quality via FROC analysis (see Supplementary Materials).

Table 2. Results for all considered loss functions along with the proposed method – inverse weighting ("+" with iw, "−" without iw). The numbers in brackets are standard deviation.

	iw	LUNA16		Metastases		LiTS	
		avg Recall	obj DSC	avg Recall	obj DSC	avg Recall	obj DSC
BCE	−	.42 (.02)	.57 (.28)	.47 (.01)	.67 (.25)	.47 (.03)	.61 (.29)
	+	.67 (.01)	.56 (.20)	.52 (.01)	.66 (.23)	.59 (.03)	.53 (.27)
Focal Loss	−	.35 (.02)	.51 (.28)	.40 (.01)	.64 (.25)	.50 (.03)	.58 (.27)
	+	.55 (.01)	.54 (.20)	.52 (.01)	.63 (.21)	.62 (.03)	.48 (.27)
WCE	−	.74 (.01)	.50 (.17)	.54 (.01)	.39 (.22)	.52 (.04)	.41 (.29)
Dice Loss	−	.71 (.02)	.76 (.20)	.55 (.01)	.69 (.23)	.62 (.03)	.63 (.25)
	+	.73 (.02)	.77 (.16)	.57 (.01)	.68 (.21)	.72 (.03)	.49 (.30)
ASL	−	.68 (.02)	.77 (.16)	.55 (.01)	.71 (.20)	.66 (.03)	.63 (.24)
	+	.70 (.02)	.76 (.18)	.59 (.02)	.66 (.20)	.73 (.03)	.53 (.28)
GDL	−	.69 (.02)	.73 (.20)	.53 (.01)	.70 (.22)	.69 (.03)	.60 (.27)

5   Conclusion

We propose a universal approach to loss functions reweighting. It could be used with almost any state-of-the-art loss function. Our experiment demonstrates an improvement of network's ability to detect lesions for Cross-Entropy, Focal Loss, Dice Loss and Asymmetric Similarity Loss on three medical tasks with multiple targets per case. Moreover, we believe the method can also improve quality with other complex multi-stage pipelines or with any other CNN architecture which is the goal for our future research.

Acknowledgements. The results of the paper are based on the scientific research supported by the Russian Science Foundation under grant 17-11-01390. The authors also acknowledge the National Cancer Institute and the Foundation for the National Institutes of Health, and their critical role in the creation of the free publicly available LIDC/IDRI Database used in this study.

References

1. Armato III, S.G., et al.: The lung image database consortium (LIDC) and image database resource initiative (IDRI): a completed reference database of lung nodules on CT scans. Med. Phys. **38**(2), 915–931 (2011)
2. Bakas, S., et al.: Identifying the best machine learning algorithms for brain tumor segmentation, progression assessment, and overall survival prediction in the brats challenge. arXiv preprint arXiv:1811.02629 (2018)
3. Bankier, A.A., MacMahon, H., Goo, J.M., Rubin, G.D., Schaefer-Prokop, C.M., Naidich, D.P.: Recommendations for measuring pulmonary nodules at CT: a statement from the fleischner society. Radiology **285**(2), 584–600 (2017)
4. Bilic, P., et al.: The liver tumor segmentation benchmark (LiTS). arXiv preprint arXiv:1901.04056 (2019)
5. Brosch, T., Yoo, Y., Tang, L.Y.W., Li, D.K.B., Traboulsee, A., Tam, R.: Deep convolutional encoder networks for multiple sclerosis lesion segmentation. In: Navab, N., Hornegger, J., Wells, W.M., Frangi, A.F. (eds.) MICCAI 2015. LNCS, vol. 9351, pp. 3–11. Springer, Cham (2015). https://doi.org/10.1007/978-3-319-24574-4_1
6. Çiçek, Ö., Abdulkadir, A., Lienkamp, S.S., Brox, T., Ronneberger, O.: 3D U-net: learning dense volumetric segmentation from sparse annotation. In: Ourselin, S., Joskowicz, L., Sabuncu, M.R., Unal, G., Wells, W. (eds.) MICCAI 2016. LNCS, vol. 9901, pp. 424–432. Springer, Cham (2016). https://doi.org/10.1007/978-3-319-46723-8_49
7. DeLuca, P., Wambersie, A., Whitmore, G.: Extensions to conventional ROC methodology: LROC, FROC, and AFROC. J ICRU **8**(1), 31–5 (2008)
8. Hashemi, S.R., Salehi, S.S.M., Erdogmus, D., Prabhu, S.P., Warfield, S.K., Gholipour, A.: Asymmetric loss functions and deep densely-connected networks for highly-imbalanced medical image segmentation: application to multiple sclerosis lesion detection. IEEE Access **7**, 1721–1735 (2018)
9. Isensee, F., Kickingereder, P., Wick, W., Bendszus, M., Maier-Hein, K.H.: No new-net. In: Crimi, A., Bakas, S., Kuijf, H., Keyvan, F., Reyes, M., van Walsum, T. (eds.) BrainLes 2018. LNCS, vol. 11384, pp. 234–244. Springer, Cham (2019). https://doi.org/10.1007/978-3-030-11726-9_21
10. Jacobs, C., Setio, A.A.A., Traverso, A., van Ginneken, B.: Lung nodule analysis 2016 (2016). https://luna16.grand-challenge.org
11. Li, Z., Kamnitsas, K., Glocker, B.: Overfitting of neural nets under class imbalance: analysis and improvements for segmentation. In: Shen, D., et al. (eds.) MICCAI 2019. LNCS, vol. 11766, pp. 402–410. Springer, Cham (2019). https://doi.org/10.1007/978-3-030-32248-9_45

12. Lin, N.U., et al.: Response assessment criteria for brain metastases: proposal from the rano group. Lancet Oncol. **16**(6), e270–e278 (2015)
13. Lin, T.Y., Goyal, P., Girshick, R., He, K., Dollár, P.: Focal loss for dense object detection. In: Proceedings of the IEEE International Conference on Computer Vision, pp. 2980–2988 (2017)
14. Litjens, G., et al.: A survey on deep learning in medical image analysis. Med. Image Anal. **42**, 60–88 (2017)
15. Maier, O., et al.: Isles 2015-a public evaluation benchmark for ischemic stroke lesion segmentation from multispectral MRID. Med. Image Anal. **35**, 250–269 (2017)
16. Menze, B.H., et al.: The multimodal brain tumor image segmentation benchmark (BRATS). IEEE Trans. Med. Imaging **34**(10), 1993–2024 (2014)
17. Milletari, F., Navab, N., Ahmadi, S.A.: V-net: Fully convolutional neural networks for volumetric medical image segmentation. In: 2016 Fourth International Conference on 3D vision (3DV), pp. 565–571. IEEE (2016)
18. Ronneberger, O., Fischer, P., Brox, T.: U-net: convolutional networks for biomedical image segmentation. In: Navab, N., Hornegger, J., Wells, W.M., Frangi, A.F. (eds.) MICCAI 2015. LNCS, vol. 9351, pp. 234–241. Springer, Cham (2015). https://doi.org/10.1007/978-3-319-24574-4_28
19. Sudre, C.H., Li, W., Vercauteren, T., Ourselin, S., Jorge Cardoso, M.: Generalised dice overlap as a deep learning loss function for highly unbalanced segmentations. In: Cardoso, M.J., et al. (eds.) DLMIA/ML-CDS -2017. LNCS, vol. 10553, pp. 240–248. Springer, Cham (2017). https://doi.org/10.1007/978-3-319-67558-9_28
20. Van Ginneken, B., et al.: Comparing and combining algorithms for computer-aided detection of pulmonary nodules in computed tomography scans: the ANODE09 study. Med. Image Anal. **14**(6), 707–722 (2010)
21. Wong, K.C.L., Moradi, M., Tang, H., Syeda-Mahmood, T.: 3D segmentation with exponential logarithmic loss for highly unbalanced object sizes. In: Frangi, A.F., Schnabel, J.A., Davatzikos, C., Alberola-López, C., Fichtinger, G. (eds.) MICCAI 2018. LNCS, vol. 11072, pp. 612–619. Springer, Cham (2018). https://doi.org/10.1007/978-3-030-00931-1_70

Brain Tumor Segmentation with Missing Modalities via Latent Multi-source Correlation Representation

Tongxue Zhou[1], Stéphane Canu[1], Pierre Vera[2], and Su Ruan[1(✉)]

[1] Normandie Univ, INSA Rouen, UNIROUEN, UNIHAVRE, LITIS, Rouen, France
`tongxue.zhou@insa-rouen.fr, su.ruan@univ-rouen.fr`
[2] Department of Nuclear Medicine, Henri Becquerel Cancer Center,
Rouen 76038, France

Abstract. Multimodal MR images can provide complementary information for accurate brain tumor segmentation. However, it's common to have missing imaging modalities in clinical practice. Since there exists a strong correlation between multi modalities, a novel correlation representation block is proposed to specially discover the latent multi-source correlation. Thanks to the obtained correlation representation, the segmentation becomes more robust in the case of missing modalities. The model parameter estimation module first maps the individual representation produced by each encoder to obtain independent parameters, then, under these parameters, the correlation expression module transforms all the individual representations to form a latent multi-source correlation representation. Finally, the correlation representations across modalities are fused via the attention mechanism into a shared representation to emphasize the most important features for segmentation. We evaluate our model on BraTS 2018 datasets, it outperforms the current state-of-the-art method and produces robust results when one or more modalities are missing.

Keywords: Brain tumor segmentation · Multi-modal · Missing modalities · Fusion · Latent correlation representation · Deep learning

1 Introduction

Brain tumor is one of the most aggressive and fatal cancers in the world, early diagnosis of brain tumors plays an important role in clinical assessment and treatment planning of brain tumors. Magnetic Resonance Imaging (MRI) is commonly used in radiology to diagnose brain tumors since it can provide complementary information due to its dependence on variable acquisition parameters, such as T1-weighted (T1), contrast-enhanced T1-weighted (T1c), T2-weighted (T2) and Fluid Attenuation Inversion Recovery (FLAIR) images. Different sequences can provide complementary information to analyze different

© Springer Nature Switzerland AG 2020
A. L. Martel et al. (Eds.): MICCAI 2020, LNCS 12264, pp. 533–541, 2020.
https://doi.org/10.1007/978-3-030-59719-1_52

subregions of gliomas. T2 and FLAIR are suitable to detect the tumor with peritumoral edema, while T1 and T1c are suitable to detect the tumor core without peritumoral edema [16]. Therefore, applying multi-modal images can reduce the information uncertainty and improve clinical diagnosis and segmentation accuracy.

Segmentation of brain tumor by experts is expensive and time-consuming, recently, there have been many studies on automatic brain tumor segmentation [5,6,9,14,15], which always requires the complete set of the modalities. However, the imaging modalities are often incomplete or missing in clinical practice. Currently, there are a number of methods proposed to deal with the missing modalities in medical image segmentation, which can be broadly grouped into three categories: (1) training a model on all possible subset of the modalities, which is complicated and time-consuming. (2) synthesizing missing modalities and then use the complete imaging modalities to do the segmentation, while it requires an additional network for synthesis and the quality of the synthesis can directly affect the segmentation performance. (3) fusing the available modalities in a latent space to learn a shared feature representation, then project it to the segmentation space. This approach is more efficient than the first two methods, because it doesn't need to learn a number of possible subsets of the multi-modalities and will not be affected by the quality of the synthesized modality. Recently, there are a lot of segmentation methods based on exploiting latent feature representation for missing modalities. The current state-of-the-art network architecture is from Havaei, the proposed HeMIS [7] learns the feature representation of each modality separately, and then the first and second moments are computed across individual modalities for estimating the final segmentation. However, computing mean and variance over individual representations can't learn the shared latent representation. Lau et al. [11] introduced a unified representation network that maps a variable number of input modalities into a unified representation by using mean function for segmentation, while averaging the latent representations could averaging the latent representations could lose some important information. Chen et al. [4] used feature disentanglement to decompose the input modalities into content code and appearance code, and then the content code are fused via a gating strategy into a shared representation for segmentation. While the approach is more complex and time-consuming, because it requires two encoders for each modalities, and their proposed fusion method only re-weight the content code from spatial-wise without considering the channel-wise. Shen et al. [13] used adversarial loss to form a domain adaptation model to adapt feature maps from missing modalities to the one from full modalities, which can only cope with the one-missing modality situation.

The challenge of segmentation on missing modalities is to learn a shared latent representation, which can take any subset of the image modalities and produce robust segmentation. To effectively learn the latent representation of individual representations, in this paper, we propose a novel brain tumor segmentation network to deal with the absence of imaging modalities. The main contributions of our method are three-fold: 1) A correlation representation block is introduced to discover the latent multi-source correlation representation. 2) A fusion strategy based on attention mechanism with obtained correlation representation is proposed to learn the weight maps along channel-wise and spatial-wise for different modalities. 3) The first multi-modal segmentation network which is capable of describing the latent multi-source correlation representation and allows to help segmentation for missing data is proposed.

2 Method

Our network is inspired by the U-Net architecture [12]. To be robust to the absence of modalities, we adapt it to multi-encoder based framework. It first takes 3D available modalities as input in each encoder. The independent encoders can not only learn modality-specific feature representation, but also can avoid the false-adaptation between modalities. To take into account the strong correlation between multi modalities, we propose a block, named CR, to discover the correlation between modalities. Then the correlation representations across modalities are fused via attention mechanism, named Fusion, to emphasize the most discriminative representation for segmentation. Finally, the fused latent representation is decoded to form the final segmentation result. The network architecture scheme is depicted in Fig. 1.

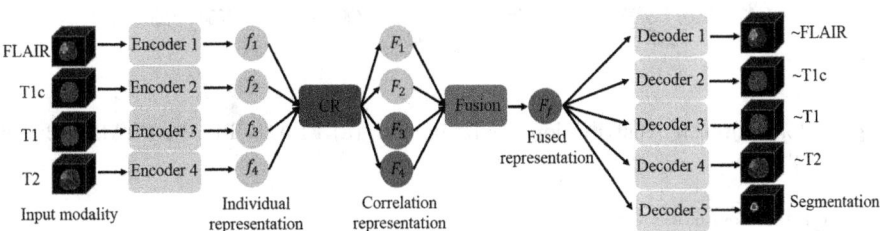

Fig. 1. A schematic overview of our network.

2.1 Modeling the Latent Multi-source Correlation

Inspired by a fact that, there is strong correlation between multi MR modalities, since the same scene (the same patient) is observed by different modalities [10]. From Fig. 2 presenting joint intensities of the MR images, we can observe a strong correlation in intensity distribution between each two modalities. To this end, it's reasonable to assume that a strong correlation also exists in latent representation between modalities. And we introduce a Correlation Representation (CR) block (see Fig. 3) to discover the latent correlation. The CR block consists of two modules: Model Parameter Estimation Module (MPE Module) and Linear Correlation Expression Module (LCE Module). The input modality $\{X_i, ..., X_n\}$, where $n = 4$, is first input to the independent encoder f_i (with learning parameters θ) to learn the modality-specific representation $f_i(X_i|\theta_i)$. Then, MPE Module, a network with two fully connected network with LeakyReLU, maps the modality-specific representation $f_i(X_i|\theta_i)$ to a set of independent parameters $\Gamma_i = \{\alpha_i, \beta_i, \gamma_i, \delta_i\}$, which is unique for each moddality. Finally the correlation representation $F_i(X_i|\theta_i)$ can be obtained via LCE Module (Eq. 1). Since we have four modalities, we learn four correlations from the complete modalities. For the test, if one modality is missing, its feature representation can be approximately recovered from the learned correlation expression with the available modalities. We replace the missing modality by the most similar one to always have four inputs for the trained model. In this way, we do not lose the information of the missing modality for segmentation.

$$F_i(X_i|\theta_i) = \alpha_i \odot f_j(X_j|\theta_j) + \beta_i \odot f_k(X_k|\theta_k) + \gamma_i \odot f_m(X_m|\theta_m) + \delta_i, (i \neq j \neq k \neq m) \tag{1}$$

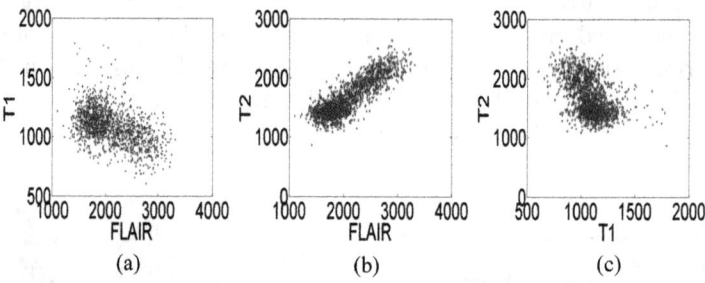

(a)　　　　　　　(b)　　　　　　　(c)

Fig. 2. Joint intensity distribution of MR images: (a) FLAIR-T1, (b) FLAIR-T2 and (c) T1-T2.

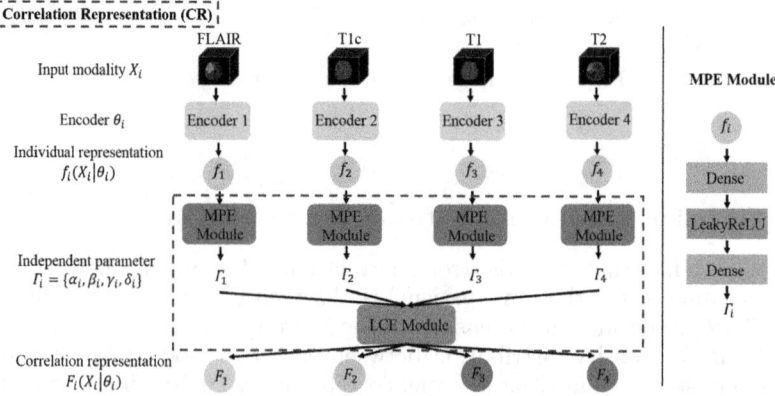

Fig. 3. Architecture of correlation representation block.

2.2   Fusion Strategy

The proposed fusion strategy is based on two blocks: a CR block which searches for latent correlations between the feature representations of the four modalities and a fusion block, described in Fig. 4, which seeks to weight the feature representations of the four modalities based on their contributions to the final segmentation. In our architecture, we use independently four encoders to obtain four feature representations corresponding to the four modalities. The CR block is then applied on the last layer of the encoders to learn the latent feature representation of each modality. Under our correlation hypothesis (Fig. 2), each feature representation is linearly correlated with the other three modalities. Thus, the CR block learns four new representations with latent correlation. To learn the contributions of the four feature representations for the segmentation, we propose a fusion block based on attention mechanism, which allows to selectively emphasize feature representations. The fusion block consists of channel (modality) attention module and spatial attention module. The first module takes four feature representations as input to obtain the channel-wise weights. While the second module focuses on spatial location to obtain the spatial-wise weights. These two weights are combined with the input representation F via multiplication to achieve the two attentional representations F_c and F_s, which are finally added to obtain the fused representation F_f. The greater the weight of a modality, the greater the final contribution to its segmentation. In this way, we can discover the most relevant characteristics thanks to the fusion block, and recover the missing features thanks to the CR block, making the segmentation more robust in the case of the missing modalities. The proposed fusion block can be directly adapted to any multi modal fusion problem, and it encourages the network to learn more meaningful representation along spatial-wise and channel-wise, which is superior than simple mean or max fusion method.

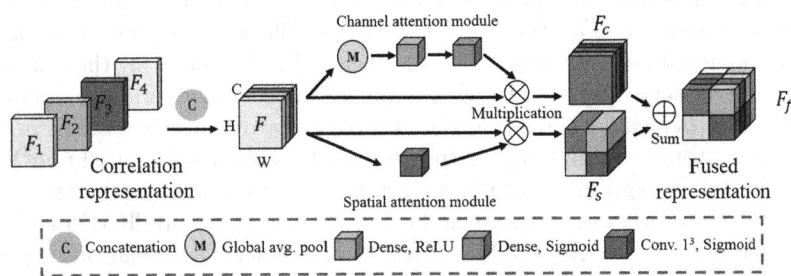

Fig. 4. The architecture of fusion block.

2.3   Network Architecture and Learning Process

The detailed network architecture framework is illustrated in Fig. 5. It's likely to require different receptive fields when segmenting different regions in an image, standard U-Net can't get enough semantic features due to the limited receptive field. Inspired by dilated convolution, we use residual block with dilated convolutions (rate = 2, 4) (res_dil block) on both encoder part and decoder part to obtain features at multiple scale. The encoder includes a convolutional block, a res_dil block followed by skip connection. All convolutions are $3 \times 3 \times 3$. Each decoder level begins with up-sampling layer followed by a convolution to reduce the number of features by a factor of 2. Then the upsampled features are combined with the features from the corresponding level of the encoder part using concatenation. After the concatenation, we use the res_dil block to increase the receptive field. In addition, we employ deep supervision [8] for the segmentation decoder by integrating segmentation layers from different levels to form the final network output. The network is trained by the overall loss function: $L_{total} = L_{dice} + L_1$, where L_1 is the mean absolute loss.

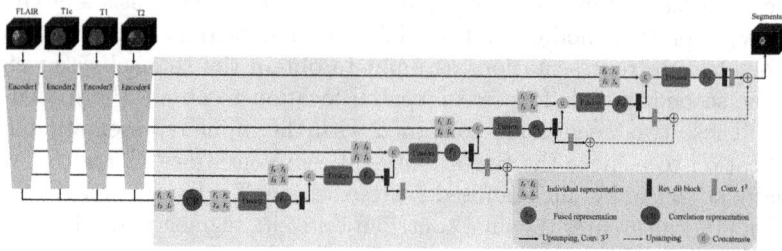

Fig. 5. Proposed segmentation network framework. Here only four encoders and the target segmentation decoder are shown.

3   Data and Implementation Details

Data and Pre-processing. The datasets used in the experiments come from BraTS 2018 dataset. The training set includes 285 patients, each patient has four image modalities including T1, T1c, T2 and FLAIR. Following the challenge, there are three segmentation classes: complete tumor, tumor core and enhancing tumor. The provided data have been pre-processed by organisers: co-registered to the same anatomical template, interpolated to the same resolution (1 mm^3) and skull-stripped. The ground truth have been manually labeled by experts. We did additional pre-processing with a standard procedure. The N4ITK [1] method is used to correct the distortion of MRI data, and intensity normalization is applied to normalize each modality of each patient. To exploit the spatial contextual information of the image, we use 3D image and resize it from $155 \times 240 \times 240$ to $128 \times 128 \times 128$.

Implementation Details. Our network is implemented in Keras. The model is optimized using the Adam optimizer (initial learning rate = 5e−4) with a decreasing learning rate factor 0.5 with patience of 10 epochs in 50 epochs. We randomly split the dataset into 80% training and 20% testing. All the results are obtained by online evaluation platform.

Table 1. Robust comparison of different methods (Dice %) on BraTS 2018 dataset, • denotes the present modality and ○ denotes the missing modality, ↑ denotes the improvement of CR block, bold results denotes the best score.

Modalities				Complete			Core			Enhancing		
F	T1	T1c	T2	HeMIS	Org	Our	HeMIS	Org	Our	HeMIS	Org	Our
○	○	○	●	**38.6**	31.4	**32.3**↑	**19.5**	14.9	15.7↑	0.0	6.2	**7.2**↑
○	○	●	○	2.6	29.7	**33.5**↑	6.5	49.3	**55.9**↑	11.1	50.0	**53.5**↑
○	●	○	○	0.0	3.3	**5.3**↑	0.0	4.3	**6.3**↑	0.0	4.5	**5.3**↑
●	○	○	○	55.2	71.4	**73.7**↑	16.2	46.2	**48.6**↑	6.6	5.0	**25.8**↑
○	○	●	●	48.2	45.1	**48.3**↑	45.8	48.1	**50.4**↑	**55.8**	52.0	52.4↑
○	●	●	○	15.4	11.4	**29.2**↑	30.4	22.6	**54.8**↑	42.6	24.8	**53.8**↑
●	●	○	○	71.1	75.9	**80.4**↑	11.9	47.4	**51.5**↑	1.2	7.7	**10.2**↑
○	●	○	●	**47.3**	31.6	35.5↑	**17.2**	12.9	14.3↑	0.6	2.5	**6.1**↑
●	○	○	●	74.8	80.4	**81.3**↑	17.7	20.7	**25.0**↑	0.8	9.3	**10.0**↑
●	○	●	○	68.4	80.3	**81.5**↑	41.4	65.7	**73.4**↑	53.8	62.7	**67.5**↑
●	●	●	○	70.2	81.1	**82.7**↑	48.8	71.7	**75.8**↑	60.9	65.7	**68.4**↑
●	●	○	●	75.2	83.5	**85.4**↑	18.7	41.3	**44.4**↑	1.0	11.1	**12.9**↑
●	○	●	●	75.6	87.5	**87.7**↑	54.9	74.2	**77.4**↑	60.5	65.4	**67.2**↑
○	●	●	●	44.2	46.9	**50.1**↑	46.6	51.2	**52.1**↑	**55.1**	54.3	54.8↑
●	●	●	●	73.8	87.9	**88.1**↑	55.3	76.2	**78.8**↑	61.1	68.1	**69.1**↑
Wins/15				2	0	13	2	0	13	2	0	13

4   Experiments Results

Quantitative Analysis. The main advantage of our method is using the correlation representation, which can discover the latent correlation representation between modalities to make the model robust at the absence of modalities. To prove the effectiveness of our model, we use Dice score as the metric, and compare two other approaches. (1) HeMIS [7], the current state-of-the-art method for segmentation with missing modalities. (2) Org, a specific case of our model without correlation representation block. From Table 1, for all the tumor regions, our method achieves the best results in most of all cases. Compared to HeMIS, the Dice score of our method just gradually drops when modalities are missing, while the performance drop is more severe in HeMIS. Compared to Org, the correlation representation block makes the model more robust in the case of missing modalities, which demonstrates the effectiveness of the proposed component and also proves our assumption. We can also find that, missing FLAIR modality leads to a sharp decreasing on dice score for all the regions, since FLAIR is the principle modality for showing whole tumor. Missing T1 and T2 modalities would contribute to a slight decreasing on dice score for all the regions. While missing T1c modality would contribute to a sever decreasing on dice score for both tumor core and enhancing tumor, since T1c is the principle modality for showing tumor core and enhancing tumor regions.

Qualitative Analysis. In order to evaluate the robustness of our model, we randomly select three examples on BraTS 2018 dataset and visualize the segmentation results in Fig. 6. We can observe that with the increasing number of missing modalities, the segmentation results produced by our robust model just slightly degrade, rather than a sudden sharp degrading. Even with FLAIR and T1c modalities, we can achieve a decent segmentation result.

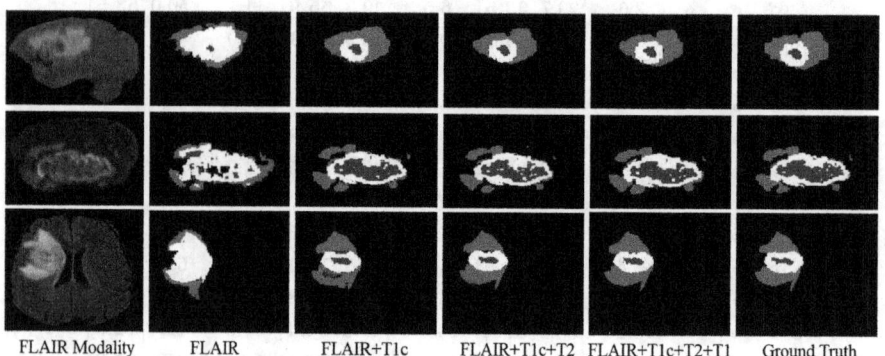

FLAIR Modality   FLAIR   FLAIR+T1c   FLAIR+T1c+T2 FLAIR+T1c+T2+T1   Ground Truth

Fig. 6. Examples of the segmentation results compared to ground truth. Red: necrotic and non-enhancing tumor core; Orange: edema; White: enhancing tumor. (Color figure online)

5   Conclusion

We propose a novel multimodal brain tumor segmentation network based on the latent multi-source correlation representation and fusion using attention mechanism for making the model robust to missing data. We demonstrate our method can yield competitive results on BraTS 2018 dataset under both full and missing modalities. The comparison results also show that the important roles of FLAIR and T1c on segmenting the complete tumor and tumor core, respectively. The proposed method can be generalized to other segmentation tasks with other modalities (e.g. MR and CT images). In the future we will test our method on other segmentation datasets and compare with other latent representation learning methods [2,3]. In addition, we will investigate more complex model to describe the multi-source correlation representation and adapt it to missing data issue.

References

1. Avants, B.B., Tustison, N., Song, G.: Advanced normalization tools (ANTS). Insight J **2**, 1–35 (2009)
2. Chartsias, A., Joyce, T., Giuffrida, M.V., Tsaftaris, S.A.: Multimodal MR synthesis via modality-invariant latent representation. IEEE Trans. Med. Imaging **37**(3), 803–814 (2017)

3. Chartsias, A., et al.: Multimodal cardiac segmentation using disentangled representation learning. In: Pop, M., et al. (eds.) STACOM 2019. LNCS, vol. 12009, pp. 128–137. Springer, Cham (2020). https://doi.org/10.1007/978-3-030-39074-7_14
4. Chen, C., Dou, Q., Jin, Y., Chen, H., Qin, J., Heng, P.-A.: Robust multimodal brain tumor segmentation via feature disentanglement and gated fusion. In: Shen, D., et al. (eds.) MICCAI 2019. LNCS, vol. 11766, pp. 447–456. Springer, Cham (2019). https://doi.org/10.1007/978-3-030-32248-9_50
5. Cui, S., Mao, L., Jiang, J., Liu, C., Xiong, S.: Automatic semantic segmentation of brain gliomas from MRI images using a deep cascaded neural network. J. Healthcare Eng. **2018** (2018). Article ID 4940593
6. Havaei, M., et al.: Brain tumor segmentation with deep neural networks. Med. Image Anal. **35**, 18–31 (2017)
7. Havaei, M., Guizard, N., Chapados, N., Bengio, Y.: HeMIS: hetero-modal image segmentation. In: Ourselin, S., Joskowicz, L., Sabuncu, M.R., Unal, G., Wells, W. (eds.) MICCAI 2016. LNCS, vol. 9901, pp. 469–477. Springer, Cham (2016). https://doi.org/10.1007/978-3-319-46723-8_54
8. Isensee, F., Kickingereder, P., Wick, W., Bendszus, M., Maier-Hein, K.H.: Brain tumor segmentation and radiomics survival prediction: contribution to the BRATS 2017 challenge. In: Crimi, A., Bakas, S., Kuijf, H., Menze, B., Reyes, M. (eds.) BrainLes 2017. LNCS, vol. 10670, pp. 287–297. Springer, Cham (2018). https://doi.org/10.1007/978-3-319-75238-9_25
9. Kamnitsas, K., et al.: Efficient multi-scale 3D cnn with fully connected CRF for accurate brain lesion segmentation. Med. Image Anal. **36**, 61–78 (2017)
10. Lapuyade-Lahorgue, J., Xue, J.H., Ruan, S.: Segmenting multi-source images using hidden Markov fields with copula-based multivariate statistical distributions. IEEE Trans. Image Process. **26**(7), 3187–3195 (2017)
11. Lau, K., Adler, J., Sjölund, J.: A unified representation network for segmentation with missing modalities. arXiv preprint arXiv:1908.06683 (2019)
12. Ronneberger, O., Fischer, P., Brox, T.: U-net: convolutional networks for biomedical image segmentation. In: Navab, N., Hornegger, J., Wells, W.M., Frangi, A.F. (eds.) MICCAI 2015. LNCS, vol. 9351, pp. 234–241. Springer, Cham (2015). https://doi.org/10.1007/978-3-319-24574-4_28
13. Shen, Y., Gao, M.: Brain tumor segmentation on MRI with missing modalities. In: Chung, A.C.S., Gee, J.C., Yushkevich, P.A., Bao, S. (eds.) IPMI 2019. LNCS, vol. 11492, pp. 417–428. Springer, Cham (2019). https://doi.org/10.1007/978-3-030-20351-1_32
14. Wang, G., Li, W., Ourselin, S., Vercauteren, T.: Automatic brain tumor segmentation using cascaded anisotropic convolutional neural networks. In: Crimi, A., Bakas, S., Kuijf, H., Menze, B., Reyes, M. (eds.) BrainLes 2017. LNCS, vol. 10670, pp. 178–190. Springer, Cham (2018). https://doi.org/10.1007/978-3-319-75238-9_16
15. Zhao, X., Wu, Y., Song, G., Li, Z., Zhang, Y., Fan, Y.: A deep learning model integrating fcnns and CRFs for brain tumor segmentation. Med. Image Anal. **43**, 98–111 (2018)
16. Zhou, T., Ruan, S., Canu, S.: A review: deep learning for medical image segmentation using multi-modality fusion. Array **3**, 100004 (2019)

Revisiting 3D Context Modeling with Supervised Pre-training for Universal Lesion Detection in CT Slices

Shu Zhang[1], Jincheng Xu[1], Yu-Chun Chen[2], Jiechao Ma[2], Zihao Li[2], Yizhou Wang[1,3,4], and Yizhou Yu[2,5(✉)]

[1] Department of Computer Science, Peking University, Beijing, China
[2] Deepwise AI Lab, Beijing, China
yizhouy@acm.org
[3] Advanced Institute of Information Technology, Peking University, Hangzhou, China
[4] Center on Frontiers of Computing Studies, Peking University, Beijing, China
[5] The University of Hong Kong, Pokfulam, Hong Kong

Abstract. Universal lesion detection from computed tomography (CT) slices is important for comprehensive disease screening. Since each lesion can locate in multiple adjacent slices, 3D context modeling is of great significance for developing automated lesion detection algorithms. In this work, we propose a *Modified Pseudo-3D Feature Pyramid Network* (MP3D FPN) that leverages depthwise separable convolutional filters and a group transform module (GTM) to efficiently extract 3D context enhanced 2D features for universal lesion detection in CT slices. To facilitate faster convergence, a novel 3D network pre-training method is derived using solely large-scale 2D object detection dataset in the natural image domain. We demonstrate that with the novel pre-training method, the proposed MP3D FPN achieves state-of-the-art detection performance on the DeepLesion dataset (**3.48%** absolute improvement in the sensitivity of FPs@0.5), significantly surpassing the baseline method by up to **6.06%** (in MAP@0.5) which adopts 2D convolution for 3D context modeling. Moreover, the proposed 3D pre-trained weights can potentially be used to boost the performance of other 3D medical image analysis tasks.

Keywords: Lesion detection · 3D context modeling · 3D network pre-training.

1 Introduction

With its high-resolution image and low cost, CT scan is critical in clinical decision and holds the key for making precise medical-care accessible to everyone around the world. Recently, deep learning methods have been introduced to detect lesions in CT slices [1–5]. Since it is difficult to distinguish lesions within

---

This work was done when Jincheng Xu was an intern at Deepwise AI Lab.

A. L. Martel et al. (Eds.): MICCAI 2020, LNCS 12264, pp. 542–551, 2020.
https://doi.org/10.1007/978-3-030-59719-1_53

a single axial slice, exploiting sufficient 3D context for accurate detection in volumetric CT data has emerged as a significant research focus.

Various architectures have been proposed for proper modeling of 3D context from neighboring CT slices. Yan *et al.* [1] adopts a late fusion strategy which stacked 2D features of neighboring slices to build 3D context enhanced features. Although the pseudo-3D contextual information has provided prominent performance gain [1–5], its late fusion strategy leads to notable losses of context information from early stages of the network. A direct way to address these issues is to employ 3D convolutions which introduce inter-slice connections hierarchically to learn 3D representations end to end. 3D convolutional filters can well preserve the 3D structure and texture information, but intensive memory and computation demands hinder its wide application in the universal lesion detection problem. What's worse, although 3D network pre-training has raised significant research attention [6–9], the lack of good pre-trained 3D models makes it even harder to achieve good performance with 3D based detectors.

In this paper, we focus on the problem of universal lesion detection in CT slices, where multiple adjacent CT slices are taken into consideration to localize 2D lesions for the target slice. We aim to develop a generic and efficient 3D backbone for 2D lesion detection with enhanced context modeling ability from multiple CT slices and devise a supervised pre-training method to boost its performance. Specifically, pseudo-3D convolutional filters [8] which use depthwise separable convolution are adopted to reduce the memory and computation overhead. The backbone in our method is a Modified Pseudo-3D ResNet (MP3D ResNet), which extracts context enhanced 3D features from multiple neighboring CT slices (9 in our case) and then converted the 3D features into 2D ones with a group transform module (GTM) for further 2D lesion detection in the target slice. Then, we feed backbone features extracted from MP3D ResNet into the neck of Feature Pyramid Network (FPN) to form the MP3D FPN for effective multi-scale detection. Finally, to facilitate efficient training of the MP3D FPN, we designed a novel supervised pre-training method, which exploits supervised signals from large-scale 2D natural image object detection dataset to pre-train the proposed MP3D detector. In summary, the main contributions of our paper are three folds:

1. We have proposed a generic framework to employ 3D network for 2D lesion detection in CT slices. The proposed MP3D FPN is computational and memory efficient, and it achieves state-of-the-art performance on the DeepLesion dataset.

2. We have derived a novel and effective way to adopt 2D natural images to pre-train 3D network with supervised labels, whose pre-trained weights can potentially benefit other 3D medical image analysis tasks (e.g. segmentation).

3. We have conducted comprehensive experiments to explore the effects of pre-trained weights for deep medical image analysis. The results suggest that pre-trained weights can not only lead to faster convergence in all sized datasets, but also help to achieve better results in smaller-scale ones.

2 Methodology

Figure 1 gives an overview of the proposed lesion detection framework. The proposed MP3D FPN comprises an MP3D ResNet as the backbone, a 2D FPN [12] as the neck and a 2D RPN/RCNN head. The MP3D ResNet takes multiple consecutive CT slices (e.g. 9) as input and generates 3D feature maps which bear the ability of 3D context modeling. Then a conversion block (GTM) further transforms the 3D feature maps into 2D ones for further 2D detection. Detailed architecture designs of the proposed MP3D backbone and the novel supervised pre-training scheme will be elaborated in the following sections.

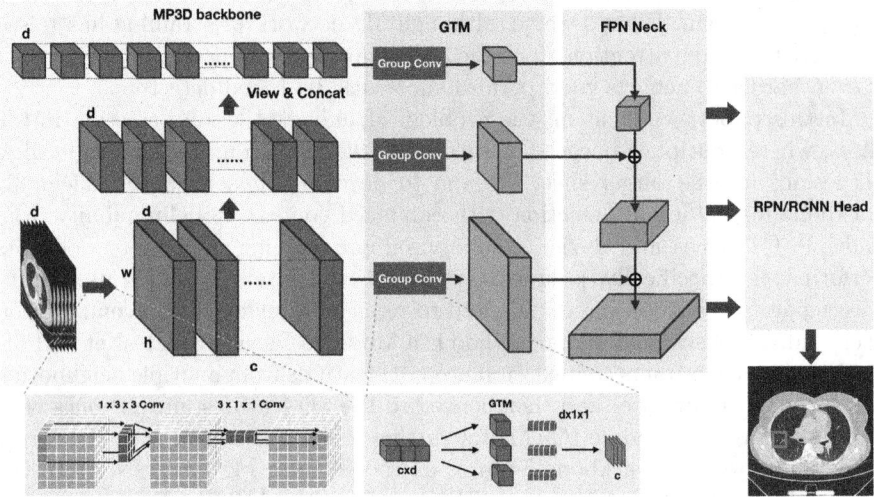

Fig. 1. Overview of the proposed MP3D FPN. MP3D ResNet extracts context enhanced 3D features and converts them to 2D ones with a group transform module (GTM). These context enhanced 2D features are then fed into the FPN neck and the RPN/RCNN head for further 2D lesion detection. The MP3D FPN is pre-trained on Microsoft COCO object detection dataset [15].

2.1 3D Context Modeling with an MP3D ResNet Backbone

In this work, we explore to employ 3D convolutions for effective 3D context modeling in the problem of lesion detection from consecutive CT slices (e.g. 9 slices). To advance the time and memory efficiency of normal 3D ResNet, we adopt the Pseudo-3D Residual Network (P3D ResNet) [8] as the prototype of our backbone network. The pseudo-3D convolution simulates $3 \times 3 \times 3$ convolution with $1 \times 3 \times 3$ filter on axial-view slices plus $3 \times 1 \times 1$ filter to build inter-slice connections on adjacent CT slices.

Lesion detection in CT slices aims to predict 2D bounding boxes in a certain slice, thus it requires 2D feature maps corresponding to the target slice for further prediction. Therefore, we need to convert the 3D feature maps to 2D ones for further prediction, meanwhile preserving the precise information of the target CT slice for accurate localization and classification. The designed Modified Pseudo-3D Residual Network (MP3D ResNet) highlights two aspects of modifications to fulfill such demands: 1) Instead of conducting isotropic pooling as in the original P3D ResNet, we neglect pooling operation in the inter-slice dimension. 2) A group transform module is introduced to generate the desired 2D feature maps from the context enhanced 3D features.

Neglecting pooling operation in the inter-slice dimension can help to preserve precise information of the target slice. In the meantime, since the number of input slices (e.g. 9) is rather small, we can get enough receptive field in the inter-slice dimension without downsampling. Regarding 2D feature map conversions, Fang et al. [13] proposed to extract C 2D feature maps ($1 \times 1 \times H \times W$) corresponding to the center slice and concatenate them to form the converted 2D feature map of size ($C \times H \times W$). However, this method can not fully exploit the 3D context information resided in other adjacent slices.

We, on the other hand, propose a group transform module (GTM) instead to includes all slice's features to compensate for the information loss. Specifically, we view 3D features ($C \times D \times H \times W$) into 2D ($CD \times H \times W$) and apply a group convolutional layer with the group size of C (every D channel is a group) to fuse all neighboring features to yield the final 2D feature maps ($C \times H \times W$).

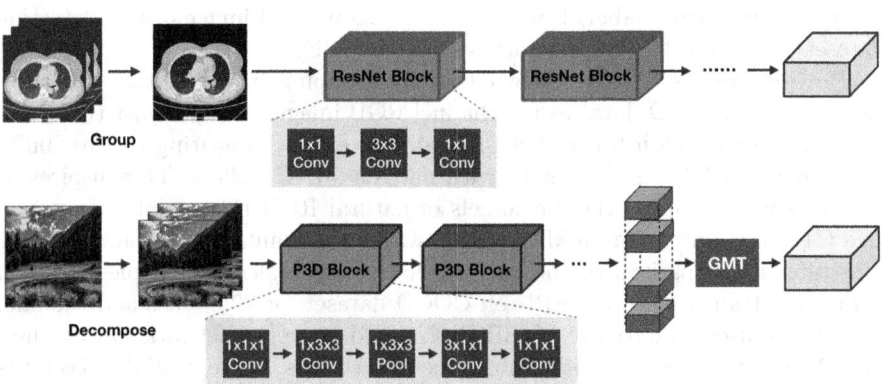

Fig. 2. Comparison between 1) using 2D Image-Net pre-trained weights for multi-slice medical image analysis and 2) decomposing 2D natural image to simulate multi-slice medical image for 3D network pre-training.

2.2 Supervised 3D Pre-training with COCO Dataset

Supervised pre-training from natural images has proven to be an effective way for 2D medical image transfer learning [1–5,10]. This indicates that using

Table 1. Sensitivities (%) at various FPs per image on the test set of DeepLesion. * indicates re-implementation of 3DCE using ResNet-50 FPN with the same configuration as our MP3D FPN.

Methods	0.5	1	2	4	$MAP@0.5$
3DCE, 27 slices [1]	52.86	64.80	74.84	84.38	–
MSB, 3 slices [2]	67.00	76.80	83.70	89.00	–
RetinaNet, 3 slices [3]	72.15	80.07	86.40	90.77	–
MVP-Net, 9 slices [4]	73.83	81.82	87.60	91.30	–
MULAN, 9 slices [5]	**76.12**	**83.69**	**88.76**	**92.30**	–
FPN+3DCE, 3 slices*	68.52	77.59	83.91	88.33	64.41
FPN+3DCE, 9 slices*	74.06	82.00	87.58	91.56	70.28
FPN+3DCE, 27 slices*	**74.67**	**82.89**	**88.17**	**91.62**	**70.82**
MR3D FPN, 9 slices	79.09	84.84	89.18	92.06	76.57
MP3D FPN, 9 slices	**79.60**	**85.29**	**89.61**	**92.45**	**76.87**
Imp over MULAN, 9 slices	↑**3.48**	↑1.60	↑0.85	↑0.15	–

supervised pre-training models from another domain can actually benefit the medical image analysis application. What's more, compared to self-supervised signals, we believe that supervised labels which carry the semantic information could enable the model to learn semantically invariant and discriminative features more effectively. Therefore, in this section, we aim to develop a method to exploit supervised labels from large-scale 2D natural image object detection dataset (e.g. coco [15]) to pre-train our MP3D FPN.

Previous works [1] have shown that by grouping 3 consecutive CT slices (which is natively 3D data) as a 3-channel RGB image, we can boost the detection performance with Image-Net pre-trained weights, indicating the feasibility of simulating RGB natural image with natively 3D CT slices. This inspires us to reversely decompose the 3 channels of natural RGB images into 3 consecutive CT slices, and train an MP3D FPN with such simulated 3D data. Figure 2 illustrates a comparison of the two correlative strategies. For implementation details, we train the MP3D FPN on COCO dataset for 72 epochs and the final weights are used to initialize MP3D ResNet. To drive the network to learn useful 3D contextual features from inter-slice connections, it is essential to keep the resolution in the inter-slice dimension unchanged for all stages of the backbone. The MP3D detector trained with a slice number of 3 can be used to initialize lesion detectors which takes variable number of slices as network input.

3   Experiments

3.1   Experimental Setup

Dataset and Metric: The NIH DeepLesion is a large-scale dataset for lesion detection, which contains 32,735 lesions on 32,120 axial CT slices captured from

4,427 patients. DeepLesion is splitted into training (70%), validation (15%), and test (15%) sets. We evaluate our MP3D FPN and all the compared methods on the test set by reporting the mean average precision (MAP@0.5) and average sensitivities at different false positives (FPs) per image.

Implementation Details: As in [3], the Hounsfield units (HU) are clipped into the range of $[-1024, 1050]$. We interpolate in the z-axis to normalize the intervals of all CT slices to 2.5 mm. Anchor scales are set to $\{16, 32, 64, 128, 256\}$ in FPN. Apart from horizontal and vertical flip, we resize the image to different scales of $\{448, 512, 576\}$ for data augmentation. MP3D-63 with group normalization [14] is used as the backbone in all our experiments, which has similar depth with the ResNet3D-50 model. The MP3D-63 model is derived from the conventional P3D-63 [8] model with the proposed modifications. Unless otherwise specified, the MP3D FPN takes 9 consecutive slices as input. We train all the models for 24 epochs at the base learning rate of 0.02, and reduce it by a factor of 10 after the 16-th and 22-th epoch (corresponding to the 2x learning schedule [11] on COCO dataset). We conduct experiments on the NVIDIA TITAN V GPU with 12 GB of memory, and mixed-precision training strategy is used in all our experiments to save memory.

3.2 Comparison with State-of-the-arts

Table 1 presents the comparisons with the previous state-of-the-art (SOTA) methods. Our model surpasses all the SOTA methods on sensitivities at different FPs and MAP@0.5, which includes 3DCE [1], MSB [2], RetinaNet [3], MVP-Net [4] and MULAN [5].

Without using any auxiliary supervision, MP3D FPN outperforms MULAN, the previous SOTA which additionally employs multi task learning and a deeper backbone (DenseNet-121) to improve the detection accuracy, by up to **3.48%** on the sensitivity of FPs@0.5. We re-implement 3DCE with ResNet-50 FPN using the same configuration as our MP3D FPN for fair comparison. Our proposed MP3D achieve a performance gain of **6.05%** on MAP@0.5 compared with this 2D convolution based context encoding method, demonstrating the superior 3D context modeling ability of our MP3D backbones. As shown in Table 1, MP3D FPN (248.93 GFLOPS, 45.16 M Params) and MR3D FPN (Modified ResNet 3D, 415.81 GFLOPS, 64.03 M Params) based detector achieve comparable results, but the MP3D based detector consumes much less time and memory. This strongly proves the efficacy and the thrift of our MP3D model.

3.3 Ablation Study

We perform a number of ablations to probe into our MP3D FPN. The results are shown as follows:

Input Slices: Table 2 shows the performance of the MP3D detector when applying 5,7,9 and 11 slices as input. The detector achieves higher detection accuracy

Table 2. Detection performance and computational cost with variable numbers of input slice. GFLOPS is used to characterize the computational cost.

Methods	0.5	1	2	4	$MAP@0.5$	$GFLOPS$
MP3D, 5 slices	76.86	83.44	88.13	91.54	75.01	156.84
MP3D, 7 slices	78.22	84.45	88.90	91.50	76.69	202.88
MP3D, 9 slices	79.60	85.29	**89.61**	92.45	76.87	248.93
MP3D, 11 slices	**80.05**	**85.77**	89.55	**92.45**	**77.64**	294.97

Table 3. Comparison of different conversion modules and different pooling strategies for pre-training.

Methods	0.5	1	2	4	$MAP@0.5$
MP3D w/ CTM	79.18	84.90	88.96	91.90	76.30
MP3D w/ GTM	**79.60**	**85.29**	**89.61**	**92.45**	**76.87**
MP3D w/ isotropic pooling	78.24	84.41	88.82	91.98	75.06
MP3D w/ proposed pooling	**79.60**	**85.29**	**89.61**	**92.45**	**76.87**

as more slices are used, meanwhile consuming more time and memory. MP3D with 7 slices as input get the best trade-off between effectiveness and efficiency.

Conversion Type: Table 3 demonstrates the comparisons of proposed GTM with the center-cropping transform module (CTM), which is proposed by Fang *et al.* [13]. The proposed GTM brings better results as it can efficiently aggregate information from all adjacent slices for further detection.

3.4   Effectiveness of the 3D Pre-trained Model

We conducted three groups of experiments to explore effectiveness of the pre-training method.

Comparison to Isotropic Pooling: In this work, to achieve 3D context modeling ability in the z-axis, we neglect pooling operation in the inter-slice dimension when pre-training the MP3D model on the Microsoft COCO dataset. We compared our proposed method to isotropic pooling for validation.

The pre-trained model takes three slices as input. When training with isotropic pooling, the z-axis degenerates to a single slice after the first two pooling layers, preventing further 3D convolution layers from learning useful 3D contextual information. As shown in Table 3, pre-trained weights learned from isotropic pooling gives worse results than the proposed method. This also proves that using decomposed natural image as input can actually helps the 3D model to gain context-encoding ability. Thus the learned weights can potentially be used to boost the performance of other 3D medical image analysis tasks.

Comparison to Training From Scratch: He *et al.* [11] demonstrated that with sufficient training data (around 35k from its experiment) and longer training

Table 4. Comparison of model performance with and without pre-training with different learning schedules. 1x, 2x and 6x indicates max training epochs of 12, 24 and 72 separately.

Methods	0.5	1	2	4	$MAP@0.5$
MP3D 1x w/o pretrain	70.12	78.00	83.95	88.23	67.60
MP3D 2x w/o pretrain	76.11	82.65	87.70	91.17	74.00
MP3D 6x w/o pretrain	**79.60**	85.29	89.26	92.19	76.75
MP3D 1x w/ pretrain	78.02	84.33	88.84	91.74	75.78
MP3D 2x w/ pretrain	79.58	**85.29**	**89.61**	**92.45**	**76.87**

Table 5. Training with variable dataset sizes (100% to 20%). For simplicity, we present the results of MAP@0.5.

Methods	100%	80%	60%	40%	20%
3DCE 9 slices 2x	70.28	69.22	67.08	63.61	57.02
3DCE 27 slices 2x	70.82	69.96	68.08	65.36	58.82
MP3D w/o pre-train 2x	74.00	71.58	68.79	63.40	50.67
MP3D w/o pre-train 6x	76.75	75.43	72.87	68.14	58.98
MP3D w/ pre-train 2x	**76.87**	**75.66**	**73.33**	**71.07**	**65.55**

schedule (6x), models trained from scratch could achieve comparable results to models training with pre-trained weights. Therefore, we examined the effectiveness of our proposed pre-training method by comparing MP3D with pre-training to model trained from scratch with longer schedule.

As shown in Table 4, when both trained for 1x learning schedule (12 epochs), MP3D with pre-trained weights significantly outperforms the one without pre-training, demonstrating faster convergence speed. And it turns out that with 2x learning schedule (24 epochs), model trained with the proposed pre-training weights can achieve comparable results with MP3D model trained from scratch with 6x learning schedule (72 epochs). These results validate the effectiveness of our proposed pre-training scheme.

Performance on Variable Dataset Sizes: In medical image analysis tasks, annotated data is often scarce. Therefore, it is appealing to gain a better understanding of the effects of pre-trained weights when dataset size is small. In this subsection, we compare the model performance of 2x, 6x training from scratch and 2x with pre-training on variable dataset sizes by randomly choosing 20%, 40%, 60% and 80% of the whole training data (Table 5). Pre-training based models achieve better performance with less training time on all the cases, and the smaller the size of the dataset, the larger the gap. A dramatic drop of performance starts when training with only 40% of the whole data. And when training with only 20% of the dataset, which is around 4,500 images, the model trained with our proposed pre-trained weights achieves an absolute performance gain of 6.57% on MAP@0.5, accounting for an 11% relative gain.

4   Conclusions

In this paper, we propose a generic model architecture to exploit 3D network for 2D lesion detection in CT slices. The proposed MP3D FPN can reduce computation and memory cost while providing enhanced 3D context modeling ability. A simple yet effective way for 3D network pre-training is also derived to facilitate efficient training. Without sophisticated structures and multi-supervision signals, it significantly improves the detection performance on the DeepLesion dataset, surpassing all the SOTAs. We have proved the benefits of pre-trained weights for variable dataset size, and we expect that the MP3D ResNet along with its pre-trained weights can serve as a benchmark backbone for 3D medical image analysis, making contributions towards accessible precise medication.

Acknowledgements. This work is funded by National Key Research and Development Program of China (No. 2019YFC0118101), MOST-2018AAA0102004 and NSFC-61625201. We would like to thank Yemin Shi for valuable discussions.

References

1. Yan, K., Bagheri, M., Summers, R.M.: 3D context enhanced region-based convolutional neural network for end-to-end lesion detection. In: Frangi, A.F., Schnabel, J.A., Davatzikos, C., Alberola-López, C., Fichtinger, G. (eds.) MICCAI 2018. LNCS, vol. 11070, pp. 511–519. Springer, Cham (2018). https://doi.org/10.1007/978-3-030-00928-1_58
2. Shao, Q., Gong, L., Ma, K., Liu, H., Zheng, Y.: Attentive CT lesion detection using deep pyramid inference with multi-scale booster. In: Shen, D., et al. (eds.) MICCAI 2019. LNCS, vol. 11769, pp. 301–309. Springer, Cham (2019). https://doi.org/10.1007/978-3-030-32226-7_34
3. Zlocha, M., Dou, Q., Glocker, B.: Improving RetinaNet for CT lesion detection with dense masks from weak RECIST labels. In: Shen, D., et al. (eds.) MICCAI 2019. LNCS, vol. 11769, pp. 402–410. Springer, Cham (2019). https://doi.org/10.1007/978-3-030-32226-7_45
4. Li, Z., Zhang, S., Zhang, J., Huang, K., Wang, Y., Yu, Y.: MVP-Net: multi-view FPN with position-aware attention for deep universal lesion detection. In: Shen, D., et al. (eds.) MICCAI 2019. LNCS, vol. 11769, pp. 13–21. Springer, Cham (2019). https://doi.org/10.1007/978-3-030-32226-7_2
5. Yan, K., et al.: MULAN: multitask universal lesion analysis network for joint lesion detection, tagging, and segmentation. In: Shen, D., et al. (eds.) MICCAI 2019. LNCS, vol. 11769, pp. 194–202. Springer, Cham (2019). https://doi.org/10.1007/978-3-030-32226-7_22
6. Zhou, Z., et al.: Models genesis: generic autodidactic models for 3D medical image analysis. In: Shen, D., et al. (eds.) MICCAI 2019. LNCS, vol. 11767, pp. 384–393. Springer, Cham (2019). https://doi.org/10.1007/978-3-030-32251-9_42

7. Chen, S., Ma, K., Zheng, Y.: Med3d: transfer learning for 3D medical image analysis. arXiv preprint arXiv:1904.00625 (2019)

8. Qiu, Z., Yao, T., Mei, T.: Learning spatio-temporal representation with pseudo-3D residual networks. In: proceedings of the IEEE International Conference on Computer Vision, pp. 5533–5541 (2017)

9. Yang, J., Huang, X., Ni, B., Xu, J., Yang, C., Xu, G.: Reinventing 2D convolutions for 3D medical images. arXiv preprint arXiv:1911.10477 (2019)

10. Lakhani, P., Sundaram, B.: Deep learning at chest radiography: automated classification of pulmonary tuberculosis by using convolutional neural networks. Radiology **284**(2), 574–582 (2017)

11. He, K., Girshick, R., Dollár, P.: Rethinking imagenet pre-training. In: Proceedings of the IEEE International Conference on Computer Vision, pp. 4918–4927 (2019)

12. Lin, T.Y., Dollár, P., Girshick, R., He, K., Hariharan, B., Belongie, S.: Feature pyramid networks for object detection. In: Proceedings of the IEEE Conference on Computer Vision and Pattern Recognition, pp. 2117–2125 (2017)

13. Fang, C., Li, G., Pan, C., Li, Y., Yu, Y.: Globally guided progressive fusion network for 3D pancreas segmentation. MICCAI 2019. LNCS, vol. 11765, pp. 210–218. Springer, Cham (2019). https://doi.org/10.1007/978-3-030-32245-8_24

14. Wu, Y., He, K.: Group normalization. In: Proceedings of the European Conference on Computer Vision (ECCV), pp. 3–19 (2018)

15. Lin, T.-Y., et al.: Microsoft COCO: common objects in context. In: Fleet, D., Pajdla, T., Schiele, B., Tuytelaars, T. (eds.) ECCV 2014. LNCS, vol. 8693, pp. 740–755. Springer, Cham (2014). https://doi.org/10.1007/978-3-319-10602-1_48

Scale-Space Autoencoders for Unsupervised Anomaly Segmentation in Brain MRI

Christoph Baur[1]([✉]), Benedikt Wiestler[4], Shadi Albarqouni[1,2],
and Nassir Navab[1,3]

[1] Computer Aided Medical Procedures (CAMP), TU Munich, Munich, Germany
c.baur@tum.de
[2] Computer Vision Laboratory, ETH Zurich, Zurich, Switzerland
[3] Whiting School of Engineering, Johns Hopkins University, Baltimore, USA
[4] Department of Diagnostic and Interventional Neuroradiology,
Klinikum rechts der Isar, TU Munich, Munich, Germany

Abstract. Brain pathologies can vary greatly in size and shape, ranging from few pixels (i.e. MS lesions) to large, space-occupying tumors. Recently proposed Autoencoder-based methods for unsupervised anomaly segmentation in brain MRI have shown promising performance, but face difficulties in modeling distributions with high fidelity, which is crucial for accurate delineation of particularly small lesions. Here, similar to these previous works, we model the distribution of healthy brain MRI to localize pathologies from erroneous reconstructions. However, to achieve improved reconstruction fidelity at higher resolutions, we learn to compress and reconstruct different frequency bands of healthy brain MRI using the laplacian pyramid. In a range of experiments comparing our method to different State-of-the-Art approaches on three different brain MR datasets with MS lesions and tumors, we show improved anomaly segmentation performance and the general capability to obtain much more crisp reconstructions of input data at native resolution. The modeling of the laplacian pyramid further enables the delineation and aggregation of lesions at multiple scales, which allows to effectively cope with different pathologies and lesion sizes using a single model.

Keywords: Anomaly segmentation · Anomaly detection · Unsupervised · Laplacian pyramid · Scale space · Autoencoders · Brain MRI

1 Introduction

Supervised Deep Learning has indisputably shown great performance in the segmentation of medical images, including pathologies in brain MRI. However, these

Electronic supplementary material The online version of this chapter (https://doi.org/10.1007/978-3-030-59719-1_54) contains supplementary material, which is available to authorized users.

© Springer Nature Switzerland AG 2020
A. L. Martel et al. (Eds.): MICCAI 2020, LNCS 12264, pp. 552–561, 2020.
https://doi.org/10.1007/978-3-030-59719-1_54

models make assumptions on the nature of pathologies they try to segment based on the labeled data they are trained from, in which rare cases might not be adequately covered and thus can potentially not be delineated properly. Generally, the unavailability of large quantities of labeled data poses a burden for the field. Recently, unsupervised representation learning and generative modeling based frameworks have emerged as promising tools to detect and segment arbitrary pathologies in MRI, without calling for pixel-precise expert annotations.

Methods based on GANs model the distribution of normal retinal OCT data and rely on the GANs' incapability to recover anomalous samples from the modeled distribution [10,11]. Similarly, in the context of brain imaging, Variational Autoencoders [7,13,14] (VAEs), Adversarial Autoencoders [2] (AAEs) and combinations of GANs and VAEs [1] have been proposed to model the distribution of healthy brain MRI. The feed-forward nature of these approaches allows to efficiently obtain reconstructions of input data. In those reconstructions anomalies likely have vanished as they are not part of the modeled distribution. The variational properties of these frameworks also allow to project input samples to a probabilistic latent space and to restore more likely, lesion-free counterparts by walking along the manifold [12]. Although promising results have been reported, some important aspects have not yet been adequately addressed: i) different pathologies appear at different sizes and might call for different image resolutions; ii) at high resolution, reconstruction fidelity is paramount to be able to delineate small lesions with precision, but frameworks like VAEs can only provide blurry, coarse reconstructions.

Here, we propose a framework for unsupervised anomaly segmentation based on the Laplacian Pyramid, tailored around the family of Autoencoders (AEs). Our approach allows to compress and reconstruct MR images of the brain with high fidelity while successfully suppressing anomalies. More precisely, inspired by [3], we model the distribution of the scale-space representation of healthy brain MRI rather than actual image pixels. Much like recently successful generative super-resolution methods [5,8], we split the modeling task into more easily solvable sub-problems. However, our method does not involve adversarial networks, such that optimization is more straightforward and computationally lightweight. A comparison to classic AEs and other AE-based State-of-the-Art methods on three different datasets with different pathologies shows both superior segmentation performance and higher reconstruction fidelity. The inherent multi-scale nature of the laplacian pyramid also allows us to segment anomalies at different resolutions and to aggregate the results, which further improves the performance and gives insights into which resolution is appropriate for diseases such as MS and Glioblastoma.

2 Methodology

Similar to previous work, we rely on modeling healthy anatomy with encoder-decoder networks and aim to localize anomalies from reconstruction residuals. However, we do not model the intensity distribution directly. Instead, we split

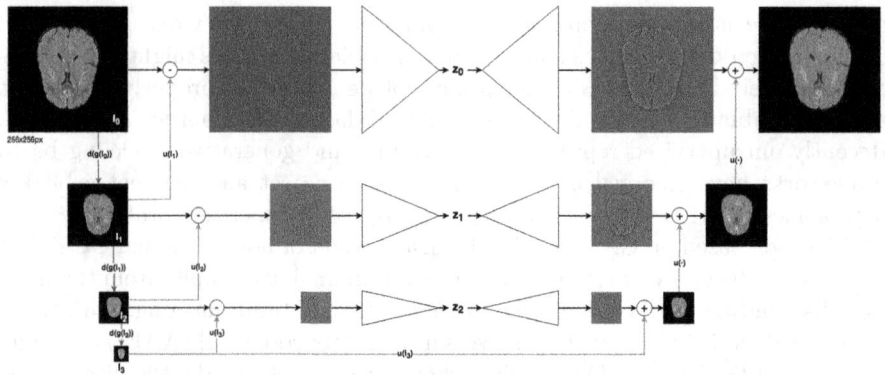

Fig. 1. An overview of the Scale-Space Autoencoder (SSAE) framework. A sample is decomposed into a 3-level laplacian pyramid, and every level uses a separate AE to compress and reconstruct the respective high frequency components.

the frequency band of the input data by learning to compress and reconstruct the laplacian pyramid of healthy brain MRI.

Given a gaussian kernel $g_\sigma(\cdot)$ with variance σ, a downsampling operator $d(\cdot)$ and an upsampling operator $u(\cdot)$, a laplacian pyramid with K levels can be obtained by repeatedly smoothing and downsampling an input image $\mathbf{x}$, i.e.

$$\mathbf{I}_0 = \mathbf{x}$$
$$\mathbf{I}_k = d(g_\sigma(\mathbf{I}_{k-1})) \qquad \forall 0 < k \leq K$$

and determining the high frequency residuals $\mathbf{H}_k$ at each level k:

$$\mathbf{H}_k = \mathbf{I}_k - u(\mathbf{I}_{k+1}) \qquad \forall 0 \leq k < K \tag{1}$$

An image $\mathbf{x}$ is completely represented by the low-resolution image $\mathbf{I}_K$ after K downsamplings and the high frequency residuals $\mathbf{H}_0, ... \mathbf{H}_{K-1}$. A reconstruction can be obtained recursively via

$$\hat{\mathbf{x}} = \sum_{k=0}^{K-1} u(\mathbf{I}_{K-k}) + \mathbf{H}_{K-1-k} \tag{2}$$

Let $\mathcal{X}_H$ be a set of healthy brain MR slices and $\mathbf{x}$ be a single sample $\in \mathcal{X}_H$. For every level k of the pyramid, we model the distribution of the respective healthy high frequency components $\mathbf{H}_k$ with an encoder-decoder network $\mathcal{M}_k(\cdot)$ by minimizing the discrepancy between $\mathbf{H}_k$ and its reconstruction $\hat{\mathbf{H}}_k = \mathcal{M}_k(\mathbf{H}_k)$ (see Fig. 1). To account for upsampling inaccuracies, we do not minimize the reconstruction error on the high frequency residuals directly. Instead, as a proxy, we minimize the difference between $\mathbf{I}_k$ and their reconstructed counterpart $\hat{\mathbf{I}}_k = u(\hat{\mathbf{I}}_{k+1}) + \hat{\mathbf{H}}_k$:

$$\mathcal{L}_k = \ell_2(\mathbf{I}_k, \hat{\mathbf{I}}_k) = \ell_2(\mathbf{I}_k, u(\hat{\mathbf{I}}_{k+1}) + \hat{\mathbf{H}}_k) \tag{3}$$

The overall loss is a weighted sum of losses at all scales:

$$\mathcal{L} = \sum_{k=0}^{K} \lambda_k \mathcal{L}_k \tag{4}$$

Since the laplacian pyramid of an image is often referred to as its *scale-space representation*, we refer to the resulting set of encoder-decoder networks as the Scale-Space Autoencoder (SSAE). The underlying encoder-decoder network $\mathcal{M}_k(\cdot)$ can be arbitrarily defined as a deterministic Autoencoder or as a VAE.

2.1 Anomaly Detection

Given a trained model and the scale-space representation of an image, it can be reconstructed at different resolutions from the recursive aggregation:

$$\hat{\mathbf{x}}_k = \hat{\mathbf{I}}_k = \sum_{i=k}^{K-1} u(\hat{\mathbf{I}}_{K-i}) + \mathcal{M}_k(\mathbf{H}_{K-1-i}) \tag{5}$$

Assuming that a model $\mathcal{M}_k$ is not capable to reliably reconstruct high frequency components of anomalies, an anomaly segmentation can be obtained from the residuals among $\mathbf{I}_k$ and $\hat{\mathbf{I}}_k$:

$$\mathbf{r}_k = \mathbf{I}_k - \hat{\mathbf{I}}_k$$

The recursive relation in Eq. 2 can also be applied on the residuals $\mathbf{r}_k$ to obtain an aggregated residual image $\mathbf{r}$ at full resolution, i.e. a multi-scale aggregation of lesion segmentations:

$$\mathbf{r}_* = \sum_{k=0}^{K-1} u(\mathbf{r}_{K-k}) + \mathbf{r}_{K-k-1} \tag{6}$$

3 Experiments and Results

In the following, we first introduce the datasets used in our experiments. In succession, we provide i) a comparison of our scale-space approach to a variety of State-of-the-Art methods, ii) a study on reconstruction fidelity and segmentation performance at multiple resolutions on different pathologies and iii) investigations of the proposed multi-scale aggregation.

3.1 Dataset

For evaluating our scale-space approach and the multi-scale aggregation, we employ four different datasets. To train our models, we use the FLAIR images from a dataset $\mathcal{D}_{healthy}$ of 100 healthy subjects from our clinical partners,

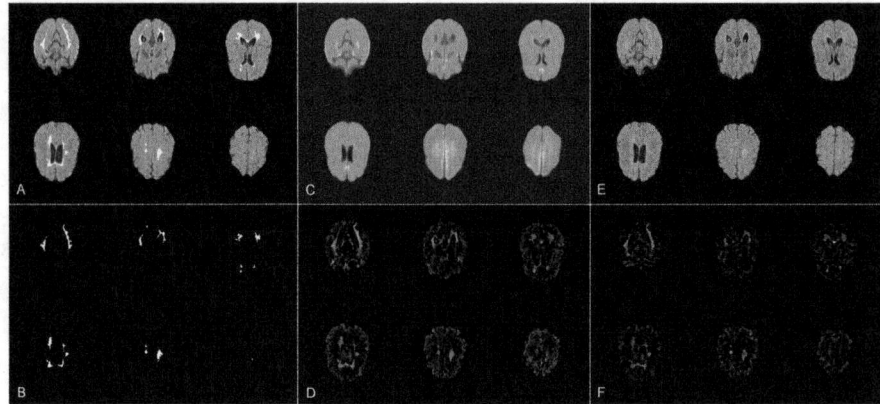

Fig. 2. Visual results. A: input; B: ground-truth segmentation; C: reconstruction from a normal AE; D: median-filtered residuals from C; E: reconstruction from our SSAE; F: median-filtered residuals from E. The high fidelity facilitated by our scale-space approach leads to fewer unwanted residuals.

acquired with a Philips Achieva 3T MR scanner. For testing, we use a dataset $\mathcal{D}_{MS}$ containing FLAIR scans of 49 subjects with MS, taken with the same scanner. Further, we rely on two datasets acquired with Siemens scanners: the nonpublic $\mathcal{D}_{GB}$, consisting of 26 subjects with Glioblastoma, and the publicly available MS dataset $\mathcal{D}_{MSLUB}$ from University Hospital of Lublijana [6]. All scans were skull-stripped using ROBEX [4], co-registered to the SRI24 ATLAS [9], and normalized by their 98th percentile into $[0; 1]$. In all our experiments, we use 2D axial slices which contain brain tissue.

3.2   Implementation

All our experiments were implemented in Python with TensorFlow and carried out on a commodity GPU. Each model was trained in batches of 8 until convergence using the ADAM optimizer with a learning rate of 0.001 and an automatic early-stopping heuristic. The lagrangian multipliers λ_k for each stage k in Eq. 4 were used in a one-hot fashion to train every stage of the pyramid separately, starting with the lowest level $k = 3$. For smoothing the images, we use a length 5 isotropic gaussian kernel with a σ such that $>99\%$ of the gaussian distribution are covered, and for the upsampling operator $u(\cdot)$ we adopt bilinear interpolation.

3.3   Comparison to State-of-the-Art

First, we compare three different variants of our scale-space approach, i.e. a dense, spatial and variational SSAE, against a variety of State-of-the-Art (SOTA) methods on all testing datasets. We measure the area under the

Precision-Recall curve (AUPRC) to reliably rate segmentation performance under heavy class imbalance. Further, we determine the optimally achievable DICE-score $\lceil DICE \rceil$ per dataset, which constitutes a theoretical upper-bound to a models segmentation performance and is determined via a greedy search for the threshold t which yields the highest DICE-score on a given test set. Modus operandi is 128×128px, as we were unable to obtain feasible results at higher resolution with all of the SOTA methods. Results are reported in Table 1. Among all reconstruction-based methods, our scale-space models always show noticeable improvements over their traditional counterpart, with the SSVAE being slightly inferior to the spatial and dense SSAE. However, on $\mathcal{D}_{MS}$ and $\mathcal{D}_{GB}$, the costly, iterative restoration-based approach from You et al. [12] shows the best overall performance.

Table 1. Variants of our scale-space approach compared to SOTA methods in terms of AUPRC and $\lceil DICE \rceil$ (higher is better). Methods marked with an * share the same model complexity. Top-2 methods in each column are bold-faced.

Approach	$\mathcal{D}_{MS}$		$\mathcal{D}_{GB}$		$\mathcal{D}_{MSLUB}$	
	AUPRC	$\lceil DICE \rceil$	AUPRC	$\lceil DICE \rceil$	AUPRC	$\lceil DICE \rceil$
AE (dense)* [1]	0.414	0.473	0.331	0.449	0.228	0.288
SSAE (dense)* **Ours**	**0.46**	**0.513**	**0.34**	0.422	0.217	0.285
AE (spatial)* [1]	0.213	0.317	0.27	0.337	0.122	0.198
SSAE (spatial)* **Ours**	0.435	0.485	**0.361**	**0.463**	0.222	**0.301**
VAE (dense)* [1]	0.283	0.372	0.267	0.389	0.156	0.217
SSVAE (dense)***Ours**	0.42	0.478	0.302	0.399	0.18	0.251
f-AnoGAN [10]	0.267	0.38	0.268	0.416	0.122	0.22
Context VAE [14]	0.434	0.487	0.26	0.39	**0.231**	**0.308**
GMVAE (You et al.) [12]	**0.495**	**0.522**	0.328	**0.474**	**0.236**	0.285

3.4 Reconstruction Fidelity

Next, we compare variants of AEs, i.e. dense AE, spatial AE and a VAE, against their scale-space counterparts in terms of their reconstruction capabilities. Again, all corresponding models share the same architecture and model complexity for a fair comparison. To measure fidelity, we collect the pixel-wise ℓ_1-errors among all healthy validation input slices and their reconstructions, normalized by the total number of pixels. Figure 3 shows the corresponding statistics on $r_0 = 256 \times 256$px, $r_1 = 128 \times 128$px and $r_2 = 64 \times 64$px. The upper limit of 256×256px was set by our training data $\mathcal{D}_{healthy}$. In comparison to their AE counterpart, all scale-space models show substantially lower reconstruction errors at all scales. As expected, reconstruction errors increase with image resolution, as the modeling task becomes more complex. The lowest error is achieved by a spatial SSAE, which reconstructs data almost perfectly due to the low level of compression in its bottleneck. Interestingly, a dense SSAE is on par with a

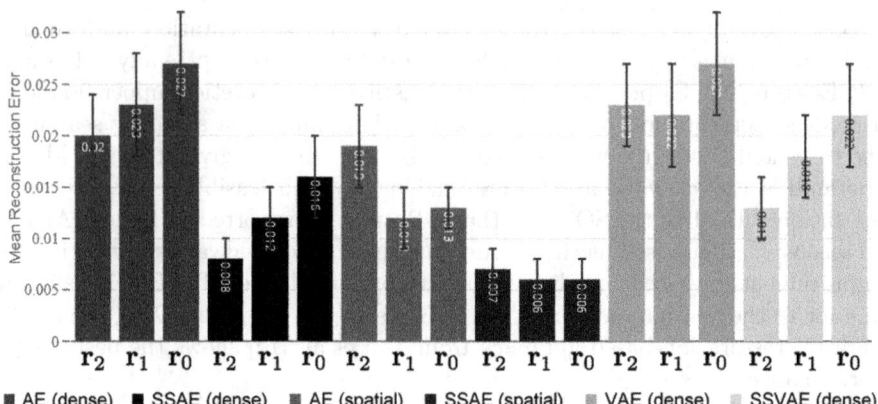

Fig. 3. Normalized reconstruction-errors at different resolutions using different AE and SSAE models on held-out healthy validation data (lower is better).

spatial AE, although it loses any spatial cues in its latent space. The achieved high fidelity can also be seen in our visual results (Fig. 2).

3.5   Investigating Resolution and Multi-scale Aggregation

Finally, we compare the different scale-space and traditional AE variants by their segmentation performance on the three datasets, again measured using the AUPRC & [DICE], at different resolutions and investigate the benefits of the proposed multi-scale aggregation of residuals (Eq. 6) at highest resolution (see Table 2). For MS lesions in $\mathcal{D}_{MS}$, which has been acquired with the same scanner as our healthy training data, best AUPRC is achieved by a dense SSAE at native resolution, yielding an absolute improvement of 19% over its corresponding dense AE. On $\mathcal{D}_{MSLUB}$, performance is significantly lower across the board due to lower contrast, but the dense SSAE still shows the best performance. On both datasets, additional 4% can be gained by aggregating residuals from multiple scales. In contrast to MS lesions, segmentation of tumors in $\mathcal{D}_{GB}$ works best at 128×128px with the majority of methods, and the proposed multi-scale aggregation shows no gains. The winning approach in this context is the spatial SSAE.

3.6   Discussion

The proposed scale-space formulation appears to be especially beneficial at native resolution, where it leads to considerably better reconstructions across all datasets. This is particularly useful for segmenting MS lesions, which can become very small. In this context, multi-scale aggregation also turns out to be beneficial, as these lesions can vary greatly in shape and size. For large, space-occupying lesions such as Glioblastoma ($\mathcal{D}_{GB}$), a resolution of 128×128px turns

Table 2. Segmentation comparing dense, spatial AEs and variational AEs/SSAEs at different resolution as well as our multi-scale aggregation.

Approach	Resolution	$\mathcal{D}_{MS}$		$\mathcal{D}_{GB}$		$\mathcal{D}_{MSLUB}$	
		AUPRC	⌈DICE⌉	AUPRC	⌈DICE⌉	AUPRC	⌈DICE⌉
AE (dense)	64 × 64	0.098	0.155	0.276	0.391	0.074	0.106
AE (dense)	128 × 128	0.414	0.473	0.331	0.449	0.228	0.288
AE (dense)	256 × 256	0.333	0.438	0.251	0.396	0.209	0.285
AE (dense)	*Aggr.*	0.358	0.459	0.258	0.38	0.236	0.317
SSAE (dense)	64 × 64	0.142	0.211	0.293	0.392	0.084	0.139
SSAE (dense)	128 × 128	0.46	0.513	0.34	0.422	0.217	0.285
SSAE (dense)	256 × 256	0.525	0.566	0.301	0.398	0.284	0.357
SSAE (dense)	*Aggr.*	0.564	0.59	0.303	0.389	0.325	0.39
AE (spatial)	64 × 64	0.131	0.203	0.309	0.422	0.099	0.144
AE (spatial)	128 × 128	0.213	0.317	0.27	0.337	0.122	0.198
AE (spatial)	256 × 256	0.029	0.064	0.235	0.405	0.034	0.083
AE (spatial)	*Aggr.*	0.517	0.546	0.342	0.446	0.342	0.422
SSAE (spatial)	64 × 64	0.139	0.209	0.297	0.391	0.09	0.142
SSAE (spatial)	128 × 128	0.435	0.485	0.361	0.463	0.222	0.301
SSAE (spatial)	256 × 256	0.371	0.435	0.357	0.463	0.207	0.296
SSAE (spatial)	*Aggr.*	0.494	0.53	0.324	0.418	0.322	0.388
VAE (dense)	64 × 64	0.067	0.134	0.21	0.307	0.049	0.083
VAE (dense)	128 × 128	0.283	0.372	0.267	0.389	0.156	0.217
VAE (dense)	256 × 256	0.242	0.356	0.143	0.255	0.124	0.195
VAE (dense)	*Aggr.*	0.269	0.383	0.145	0.253	0.156	0.23
SSVAE (dense)	64 × 64	0.139	0.203	0.281	0.385	0.073	0.125
SSVAE (dense)	128 × 128	0.42	0.478	0.302	0.399	0.18	0.251
SSVAE (dense)	256 × 256	0.472	0.526	0.272	0.388	0.227	0.307
SSVAE (dense)	*Aggr.*	0.516	0.558	0.277	0.377	0.262	0.341

out to be preferable. At native resolution, few additional False Positives lower the Precision. In this scenario, we find our scale-space approach not to provide much benefits, as it generates undesirably good reconstructions of large, homogenous lesions. Overall, the multi-scale aggregation leads to improvements in most of the cases, but generally is of greater value for normal AEs, whose anomaly detections appear to be more orthogonal among different resolutions and aggregate to a better consensus. Anomaly segmentations obtained from our scale-space models seem to correlate more across different resolutions.

4 Conclusion

In conclusion, we proposed to model normal brain anatomy in a laplacian pyramid representation to obtain high fidelity reconstructions and improved segmentation performance. We successfully demonstrate the use of this scale-space approach for unsupervised anomaly segmentation in brain MRI on different datasets with different pathologies. From the inherent multi-scale nature of our scale-space formulation, we derived a multi-scale residual aggregation technique for building an anomaly segmentation consensus among multiple resolutions, which i) turned out to be beneficial in most of the examined scenarios and ii) works for normal AEs as well. In future work, the design of a shared latent space between the different encoder-decoder networks could be investigated, and restoration approaches like [12] could be adapted for our framework. Recent generative super-resolution approaches [5,8] also offer great potential in high resolution anomaly detection & delineation, yet first require translation to the field. Using a scale-space representation of the MR data, we also see opportunities towards improved domain invariance in unsupervised anomaly segmentation methods.

Acknowledgements. S.A. is supported by the PRIME programme of the German Academic Exchange Service (DAAD) with funds from the German Federal Ministry of Education and Research (BMBF).

References

1. Baur, C., Wiestler, B., Albarqouni, S., Navab, N.: Deep autoencoding models for unsupervised anomaly segmentation in brain MR images. arXiv preprint arXiv:1804.04488 (2018)
2. Chen, X., Konukoglu, E.: Unsupervised detection of lesions in brain MRI using constrained adversarial auto-encoders. arXiv preprint arXiv:1806.04972 (2018)
3. Dorta, G., Vicente, S., Agapito, L., Campbell, N.D., Prince, S., Simpson, I.: Laplacian pyramid of conditional variational autoencoders. In: Proceedings of the 14th European Conference on Visual Media Production (CVMP 2017), p. 7. ACM (2017)
4. Iglesias, J.E., Liu, C.Y., Thompson, P.M., Tu, Z.: Robust brain extraction across datasets and comparison with publicly available methods. IEEE Trans. Med. Imaging **30**(9), 1617–1634 (2011)
5. Karras, T., Aila, T., Laine, S., Lehtinen, J.: Progressive growing of GANs for improved quality, stability, and variation. In: International Conference on Learning Representations (2018). https://openreview.net/forum?id=Hk99zCeAb
6. Lesjak, Ž., et al.: A novel public mr image dataset of multiple sclerosis patients with lesion segmentations based on multi-rater consensus. Neuroinformatics **16**(1), 51–63 (2018)
7. Pawlowski, N., et al.: Unsupervised lesion detection in brain CT using bayesian convolutional autoencoders (2018)
8. Pidhorskyi, S., Adjeroh, D.A., Doretto, G.: Adversarial latent autoencoders. In: Proceedings of the IEEE Computer Society Conference on Computer Vision and Pattern Recognition (CVPR) (2020, to appear)
9. Rohlfing, T., Zahr, N.M., Sullivan, E.V., Pfefferbaum, A.: The SRI24 multichannel atlas of normal adult human brain structure. Hum. Brain Mapp. **31**(5), 798–819 (2009)
10. Schlegl, T., Seeböck, P., Waldstein, S.M., Langs, G., Schmidt-Erfurth, U.: f-anogan: fast unsupervised anomaly detection with generative adversarial networks. Med. Image Anal. **54**, 30–44 (2019)

11. Schlegl, T., Seeböck, P., Waldstein, S.M., Schmidt-Erfurth, U., Langs, G.: Unsupervised anomaly detection with generative adversarial networks to guide marker discovery. In: Niethammer, M., et al. (eds.) IPMI 2017. LNCS, vol. 10265, pp. 146–157. Springer, Cham (2017). https://doi.org/10.1007/978-3-319-59050-9_12

12. You, S., Tezcan, K.C., Chen, X., Konukoglu, E.: Unsupervised lesion detection via image restoration with a normative prior. In: Cardoso, M.J., et al. (eds.) Proceedings of The 2nd International Conference on Medical Imaging with Deep Learning. Proceedings of Machine Learning Research, vol. 102, pp. 540–556. PMLR, London, 08–10 July 2019. http://proceedings.mlr.press/v102/you19a.html

13. Zimmerer, D., Isensee, F., Petersen, J., Kohl, S., Maier-Hein, K.: Unsupervised anomaly localization using variational auto-encoders. In: Shen, D., et al. (eds.) MICCAI 2019. LNCS, vol. 11767, pp. 289–297. Springer, Cham (2019). https://doi.org/10.1007/978-3-030-32251-9_32

14. Zimmerer, D., Kohl, S.A., Petersen, J., Isensee, F., Maier-Hein, K.H.: Context-encoding variational autoencoder for unsupervised anomaly detection. arXiv preprint arXiv:1812.05941 (2018)

AlignShift: Bridging the Gap of Imaging Thickness in 3D Anisotropic Volumes

Jiancheng Yang[1,2,3], Yi He[3], Xiaoyang Huang[1,2], Jingwei Xu[1,2], Xiaodan Ye[4], Guangyu Tao[4], and Bingbing Ni[1,2,5(✉)]

[1] Shanghai Jiao Tong University, Shanghai, China
nibingbing@sjtu.edu.cn
[2] MoE Key Lab of Artificial Intelligence, AI Institute, Shanghai Jiao Tong University, Shanghai, China
[3] Dianei Technology, Shanghai, China
[4] Shanghai Chest Hospital, Shanghai Jiao Tong University School of Medicine, Shanghai, China
[5] Huawei Hisilicon, Shanghai, China

Abstract. This paper addresses a fundamental challenge in 3D medical image processing: how to deal with imaging thickness. For anisotropic medical volumes, there is a significant performance gap between thin-slice (mostly 1 mm) and thick-slice (mostly 5 mm) volumes. Prior arts tend to use 3D approaches for the thin-slice and 2D approaches for the thick-slice, respectively. We aim at a unified approach for both thin- and thick-slice medical volumes. Inspired by recent advances in video analysis, we propose *AlignShift*, a novel parameter-free operator to convert theoretically any 2D pretrained network into thickness-aware 3D network. Remarkably, the converted networks behave like 3D for the thin-slice, nevertheless degenerate to 2D for the thick-slice adaptively. The unified thickness-aware representation learning is achieved by shifting and fusing aligned "virtual slices" as per the input imaging thickness. Extensive experiments on public large-scale DeepLesion benchmark, consisting of 32 K lesions for universal lesion detection, validate the effectiveness of our method, which outperforms previous *state of the art* by considerable margins without whistles and bells. More importantly, to our knowledge, this is the first method that bridges the performance gap between thin- and thick-slice volumes by a unified framework. To improve research reproducibility, our code in PyTorch is open source at https://github.com/M3DV/AlignShift.

Keywords: Imaging thickness · Anisotropy · DeepLesion.

1 Introduction

Deep learning has been dominating medical image analysis research in a wide range of tasks (*e.g.*, classification [6,33,34], segmentation [11,21], detection

---

J. Yang and Y. He—These authors have contributed equally.

© Springer Nature Switzerland AG 2020
A. L. Martel et al. (Eds.): MICCAI 2020, LNCS 12264, pp. 562–572, 2020.
https://doi.org/10.1007/978-3-030-59719-1_55

[22,29], registration [1,4]). However, deployment of the medical image AI systems is still challenging due to numerous difficulties, *e.g.*, open set scenarios [19], calibration and uncertainty quantification [7,10] in real-world distribution, label ambiguity in clinical annotations [12,30]. In this study, we focus on a fundamental issue in 3D medical image analysis: how to deal with the imaging thickness, which denotes the physical distance between axial slices. In practice, there exist both thin-slice (mostly 1 mm) and thick-slice (mostly 5 mm) for a same task, *e.g.*, lesion detection [28], organ and tumor segmentation [20]. Standard procedure treats this issue as pre-processing; spatial normalization is commonly applied to normalize the dataset into a same reference thickness (*e.g.*, 2 mm). However, the spatial normalization may amplify unwanted noises in medical images [5]. Figure 1 depict spatially normalized thin- and thick-slice computed tomography (CT) scans of a same subject. As illustrated, spatial normalization introduces significant artifacts to the thick-slice (note the sagittal and coronal views). If the spatially normalized thin- and thick-slice volumes are processed by a same CNN with standard convolutions, it will lead to domain shift. We conjecture that it is the reason why 3D approaches are preferred for thin-slice volumes, while 2D approaches tend to be superior for thick-slice/anisotropic volumes [11]. Spatial normalization for thick-slice data leads to larger information loss compared to that for thin-slice data. For this reason, we challenge the spatial normalization as a standard pre-processing procedure for 3D medical image processing.

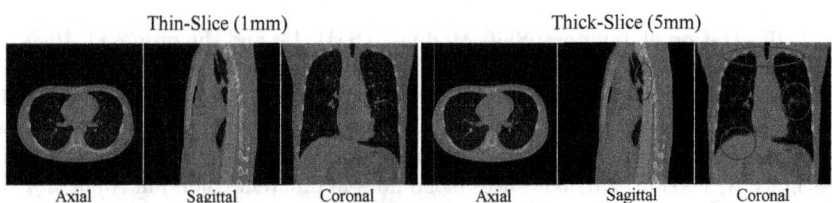

Fig. 1. Illustration of spatially normalized thin- and thick-slice computed tomography (CT) scans of a same subject. Data is from our custom dataset. Note that even though there is no significant difference between the axial slices, artifacts (the highlights on the plots) are not neglectable for the sagittal and coronal views in the thick-slice data, which results in domain shift for 3D approaches.

To address the thickness issue, we propose a novel parameter-free operator, *AlignShift*, to convert theoretically any 2D pretrained network into thickness-aware 3D network. The proposed *AlignShift* operator is inspired by Temporal Shift Module (TSM) in video analysis [14], which enables temporal (or 3D) information fusion by shifting adjacent slices (details in Sect. 2.1). Notably, TSM enables 2D-to-3D transfer learning, *i.e.*, pretrained 3D networks on 2D datasets, which is also highly related to previous studies [16,31]. Although superior to 2.5D approaches [13,27,35], TSM does not bridge the performance gap between thin- and thick-slice volumes (see Sect. 3.3). As a comparison, the *AlignShift* operator shifts and fuses aligned "virtual slices" as per the input imaging thickness, which results in unified thickness-aware representation learning (details in Sect. 2.2). Remarkably, the *AlignShift*-converted networks adaptively behave like 3D for the thin-slice, and like 2D for the thick-slice.

We validate the effectiveness of the proposed method on large-scale DeepLesion benchmark [28], a universal lesion detection dataset with 3D inputs and key-slice annotations of 32 K lesions. Without whistles and bells, the proposed methods outperform previous *state of the art* [13,27,35] by considerable margins. More importantly, our method closes the performance gap between thin- and thick-slice volumes compared to both 2.5D and TSM approaches; to our knowledge, we are the first to achieve this by a unified framework.

2   Methods

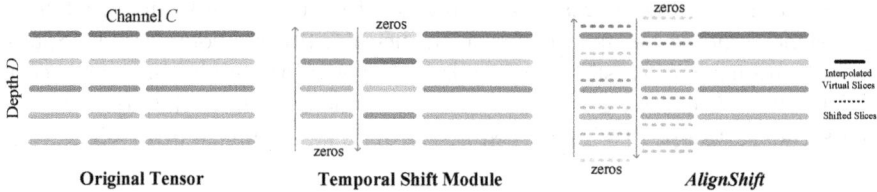

Fig. 2. Illustration of Temporal Shift Module (TSM) [14] and the proposed *AlignShift*. **Left:** A 3D tensor $(C \times D \times H \times W)$ with channel C, depth D, height H, width W, H and W are not depicted for simplicity. **Middle:** Temporal Shift Module (TSM). The channels are split into three parts for shifting up, shifting down and keeping original. Border slices are padded with zeros. **Right:** *AlignShift*. Instead of shifting physical slices in TSM, we shift "virtual" slices (solid lines in different colors) in *AlignShift*. The virtual slices are interpolated from shifted slices (dash lines) by a reference thickness r.

2.1   Preliminary: Temporal Shift Module (TSM)

Prior arts in 3D images processing utilize pure 2D network to leverage the 2D pretrained weights, while 3D randomly-initialized network is necessarily adopted to fuse the feature into 3D representations. 2.5D representation, *i.e.*, several slices as channels for 2D networks, is insufficient to capture 3D contexts. It is thus meaningful to directly convert a 2D pretrained network into a 3D counterpart. To this end, we introduce Temporal Shift Module [14] (TSM) from the field of video understanding, which enables 2D-to-3D network conversion. To our knowledge, this paper is the first to introduce TSM into medical images with proven effectiveness on DeepLesion [28] benchmark. TSM tries to leverage data shift operation [25] to capture 3D semantics under 2D CNN framework, in which data shift indicates shifting data along a dimension by a certain number of slices.

Algorithm 1: In-place *AlignShift* for 3D volumes (zero padding)

Input: input 3D feature $\boldsymbol{X} \in \mathbb{R}^{C \times D \times H \times W}$, input actual thickness $s \in \mathbb{R}^+$, shift channels $C^+, C^-, (C^+ + C^- < C)$, reference thickness $r \in \mathbb{R}^+$.
Output: $\boldsymbol{X} \in \mathbb{R}^{C \times D \times H \times W}$ (in-place assignment).

1 Compute align factor: $\alpha = r/s$;

2 Shift up: $\boldsymbol{X}^+ = [\boldsymbol{X}[: C^+], \boldsymbol{0}] \in \mathbb{R}^{C^+ \times (D+1) \times H \times W}$;

3 Obtain virtual slices: $\boldsymbol{X}[: C^+] = \alpha \cdot X^+[:, 1 :] + (1 - \alpha) \cdot X^+[:, : -1]$;

4 Shift down: $\boldsymbol{X}^- = [\boldsymbol{0}, \boldsymbol{X}[C^+ : (C^+ + C^-)]] \in \mathbb{R}^{C^- \times (D+1) \times H \times W}$;

5 Obtain virtual slices: $\boldsymbol{X}[C^+ : (C^+ + C^-)] = \alpha \cdot X^-[:, : -1] + (1 - \alpha) \cdot X^-[:, 1 :]$.

In practice, it is inserted as an operator before a $1 \times K \times K$ 3D convolution with kernel size K. Given a 3D tensor $(C \times D \times H \times W)$ with channel C, depth D, height H, width W, TSM shifts the slices in the depth dimension by $+1$ slice in one part of the channels, and by -1 slice in another part of the channels, while the rest part of channels remain static (see Fig. 2 Middle). Information between slices is fused by channel in this way. To some extent, TSM imitates 3D approaches by slices shifting. It is capable of processing 3D data in an efficient way. However, for medical images, TSM faces the issue of various imaging thickness, which is widespread in many medical image datasets such as DeepLesion [28]. TSM itself does not deal with this issue. Hence all the volumes are supposed to be normalized to the same thickness via interpolation before fed into a TSM model, no matter how large the volume imaging thickness is. To those volumes with thick-slice, the interpolation process could cause large distortion of information, as the highlighted artifacts showed in Fig. 1. According to the extensive experiments in Sect. 3, TSM has good performance over thin-slice volumes, while it declines enormously for thick-slice volumes.

2.2 *AlignShift*

We believe that spatial normalization by interpolation induces the performance gap between thin- and thick-slices volumes (see results in Table 3). Domain shift takes place when normalizing thick-slices volumes, which damages the performance. To address the thickness issue, we introduce virtual slices and propose *AlignShift* which enables adaptive data shift operation based on the given imaging thickness. *AlignShift* avoids spatial normalization to thick-slice volumes by treating thin- and thick-slice volumes separately. Without loss of generality, we define thick volumes as volumes that have a thickness larger than a reference thickness r, and vice versa. For thin-slice volumes, we normalize the thickness to the reference thickness r by interpolation as usual. For thick-slice volumes which could be easily skewed by interpolation, their original thicknesses s are kept. Given a 3D feature tensor $\boldsymbol{X}$ of shape $C \times D \times H \times W$ with channel C, depth D, height H, width W and physical thickness s on the depth dimension, *AlignShift* shifts part of channels up (denoted as C_+), and another part of channels down (denoted as C_-) along the depth dimension, while the rest channels remain static. In order to maintain a consistent "receptive field" in physical sense along the depth dimension, it shifts the data by a continuous step, whose step size (align factor) $\alpha = r/s$ depends on the reference thickness r and the volume's actual thickness s. As illustrated in Fig. 2, the shifted slice, called "virtual slice", is obtained by interpolation between the adjacent two slices. See Algorithm 1 for the mathematical formulation. Compared to our method, TSM discretely shifts the data by one full slice. The data shift strategy of TSM results in an inconsistent "receptive field" along the depth dimension in convolution, given the non-unified thickness. Thereby the data shift operation of TSM is so-called "unaligned" under this situation. Contrarily, our method aligns the 3D features of various thickness, allowing the network to learn thickness-aware representations with the same kernels. It is guaranteed by *AlignShift* that the physical distance between shifted and un-shifted channels is always consistent among volumes with different thickness. *AlignShift* bridges the performance gap between thin-slice and thick-slick CTs theoretically and empirically.

In practice, *AlignShift* is simple to use and implement. Similar to TSM, it is inserted as an operator before a $1 \times K \times K$ 3D convolution. No additional spatial normalization is needed. The original thickness is sent to the network to allow adaptive data shift operation. Compared to TSM, only modest modification is needed to gain a great performance boost. Note that *AlignShift* is able to capture 3D semantics like TSM, while it could degenerate to 2D for data with extremely large thickness, as a result of the align factor close to zero.

AlignShift serves as a parameter-free operator enabling to convert theoretically any 2D pretrained network into thickness-aware 3D network. The conversion process is straight-forward. Table 1 lists how main operators in 2D CNNs are converted to the counterpart in 3D CNNs.

Table 1. Convert a pretrained 2D backbone into 3D. We use DenseNet-121 [9]; *AlignShift* is only applied in the dense blocks. K denotes the kernel size.

2D Backbone	Conv2D $K \times K$	Pool2D $K \times K$	Norm2D
3D Backbone	$(AlignShift+)$Conv3D $1 \times K \times K$	Pool3D $1 \times K \times K$	Norm3D

2.3   3D Network for Universal Lesion Detection on Key Slices

We experiment with the proposed method on DeepLesion benchmark [28], which is a large-scale dataset on universal lesion detection. The inputs are 3D slices whereas only 2D key-slice annotations are available. We develop a 3D network with 2D detection heads, based on Mask RCNN [8]. As illustrated in Fig. 3, the 3D backbone is converted from the truncated DenseNet-121 [9] with *AlignShift*, serving as a 3D feature encoder. All the $K \times K$ 2D convolutions in the dense blocks are converted to *AlignShift*$+1 \times K \times K$ 3D convolutions. The encoder takes a grey-scale 3D tensor of $1 \times D \times 512 \times 512$ as input, where D is the length of

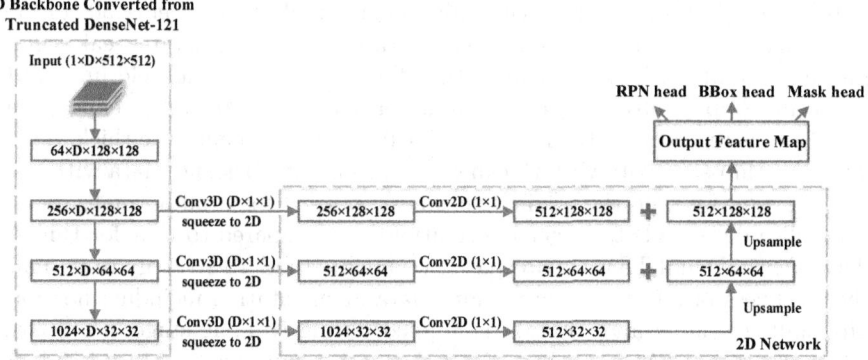

Fig. 3. The 3D network for universal lesion detection on DeepLesion [28]. The 3D backbone converted by a truncated DenseNet-121 [9,27] processes a grey-scale 3D input of $D \times 512 \times 512$, where D is the length of slices ($D = 3, 7$ in this study). 2D features of key slices are extracted, and then upsampled in a feature pyramid [15]. Detection is based on instance segmentation by Mask-RCNN [8]. Weak segmentation "ground truth" are generated from weak RECIST labels [35].

key slices ($D = 3, 7$ in this study), and extracts 3D features through three dense blocks. Each dense block increases the feature channels, downsamples the feature in the height and width dimension while maintaining the scale in the depth dimension. The feature output of each dense blocks is processed by a $D \times 1 \times 1$ 3D convolution and then squeezed into a 2D shape. A 2D decoder combines these features under different resolutions and upsamples the features step by step. The final feature map is fed into RPN head, BBox head and Mask head for detection and instance segmentation supervised by weak RECIST labels.

We implement the Mask-RCNN with PyTorch [17] and MMDetection [3]. As counterparts of the proposed *AlignShift*, we also implement 1) 2.5D Mask-RCNN, which stacks the slices as input channels for standard 2D networks, and 2) TSM-converted Mask-RCNN, which uses TSM instead of *AlignShift*. Note that the model sizes of the TSM models are strictly the same as the *AlignShift* models, and the 2.5 models are slightly smaller because of the Conv3D ($D \times 1 \times 1$) layer.

3   Experiments

3.1   Dataset and Experiment Setting

DeepLesion dataset [28] consists of 32,120 axial CT slices from 10,594 studies of unique patients. the thickness of the dataset is almost 1 mm (48.66%) and 5 mm (50.26%), which is appropriate to develop and evaluate the proposed method. There are 1 to 3 lesions in each slice, with totally 32,735 lesions from several organs, whose sizes vary from 0.21 to 342.5 mm. RECIST diameter (critical for tumor staging and prognosis assessment [32]) coordinates and bounding boxes were labeled on the key slices, with adjacent slices (above and below 30 mm) provided as contextual information. We use GrabCut [18] to generate weak segmentation "ground truth" from weak RECIST labels [2,35]. Hounsfield units of the input are clipped into $[-1024, 2050]$ and normalized. In *AlignShift* experiments, $r = 2$ mm is regarded as the reference thickness; we normalize the thickness into 2 mm for thin-slice data with thickness $<=2$ mm; for thick-slice data with thickness >2 mm, we keep the original thickness, since the spatial normalization for thick-slice data leads to larger information loss compared to that for thin-slice data. For 2.5D and TSM counterparts, we adapt standard strategy to normalize the thickness of all images into 2 mm. Data augmentation including horizontal flip, shift, rescaling and rotation is applied during training stage, no test-time augmentation (TTA) is applied. We resize each input slice to 512×512 before feeding into the networks. We use official data split (training/validation/test: 70%/15%/15%); following prior studies [13,27,35], sensitivity at various false positives levels (*i.e.*, FROC analysis) is evaluated on the test set.

Table 2. Sensitivity (%) at various false positives (FPs) per image of previous *state-of-the-art* and the proposed methods, on the large-scale DeepLesion benchmark [28]. Note that MULAN [27] uses extra tag supervision and an addition Score Refinement Layer (SRL) with tag inputs; We report the performance of MULAN under 171-tag supervision as well as that without SRL.

Methods	Slices	0.5	1	2	4	8	16	Avg. [0.5, 1, 2, 4]
3DCE [26] MICCAI'18	×27	62.48	73.37	80.70	85.65	89.09	91.06	75.55
ULDor [23] ISBI'19	×1	52.86	64.8	74.84	84.38	87.17	91.8	69.22
V.Attn [24] MICCAI'19	×3	69.10	77.90	83.80	–	–	–	–
Retina. [35] MICCAI'19	×3	72.15	80.07	86.40	90.77	94.09	96.32	82.35
MVP [13] MICCAI'19	×3	70.01	78.77	84.71	89.03	–	–	80.63
MVP [13] MICCAI'19	×9	73.83	81.82	87.60	91.30	–	–	83.64
MULAN [27] MICCAI'19	×9	76.12	83.69	88.76	92.30	94.71	95.64	85.22
w/o SRL [27] MICCAI'19	×9	–	–	–	–	–	–	84.22
Ours 2.5D	×3	71.27	79.82	86.30	90.61	93.75	95.70	82.00
Ours 2.5D	×7	72.66	81.45	87.07	90.98	93.40	95.30	83.04
Ours TSM	×3	70.24	79.52	86.28	90.90	94.06	96.09	81.73
Ours TSM	×7	75.98	83.65	88.44	92.14	94.89	96.50	85.05
Ours *AlignShift*	×3	72.90	80.74	87.15	91.92	94.85	96.48	83.18
Ours *AlignShift*	×7	**79.40**	**85.50**	**90.09**	**93.26**	**95.24**	**96.66**	**87.06**

3.2   Performance Compared with *State of the Art*

In Table 2, we depict sensitivity at various false positives per image (FPs), which shows that our proposed methods significantly outperform the previous *state-of-the-art* MULAN [27]. Notably, it is achieved without additional information beyond the CT images such as tags from medical reports and demographic information. The performance of our 2.5D counterparts is comparable to Improved RetinaNet [35] and MVP-Net [13]. The proposed TSM-converted networks outperform these studies [13,35], and even MULAN without tag supervision, which validates the superiority of pretrained 3D backbones over 2.5D. *AlignShift* further boosts performance and surpasses our TSM and previous *state-of-the-art* MULAN [27]. Due to memory constraints, we report the performance of maximum 7 slices, whereas more slices are expected with better performance.

Table 3. Detection performance analysis of our methods on all, thin-slice (mostly 1 mm) and thick-slice (mostly 5 mm) data. "diff." denotes the average sensitivity (Avg. [0.5, 1, 2, 4]) difference between thin/thick-slice data and that of all data.

Methods	Thinkness	0.5	1	2	4	8	16	Avg. [0.5, 1, 2, 4]	diff
2.5D ×3	All	71.27	79.82	86.30	90.61	93.75	95.70	82.00	–
	Thin	72.78	80.65	87.21	90.94	93.97	95.86	82.89	+0.89
	Thick	69.88	79.16	85.51	90.48	93.65	95.65	81.26	−0.74
2.5D ×7	All	72.66	81.45	87.07	90.98	93.40	95.30	83.04	–
	Thin	75.77	83.93	88.85	92.37	94.26	95.78	85.23	+2.19
	Thick	69.76	78.96	85.75	90.03	92.67	94.99	81.13	−1.91
TSM ×3	All	70.24	79.52	86.28	90.90	94.06	96.09	81.73	–
	Thin	73.74	81.84	87.54	92.21	94.92	96.72	83.83	+2.10
	Thick	67.03	77.37	84.98	89.95	93.16	95.44	79.83	−1.90
TSM ×7	All	75.98	83.65	88.44	92.14	94.89	96.50	85.05	–
	Thin	78.76	85.53	89.67	93.48	95.61	96.68	86.86	+1.81
	Thick	73.26	81.97	87.10	90.96	94.14	96.42	83.32	−1.73
AlignShift ×3	All	72.90	80.74	87.15	91.92	94.85	96.48	83.18	–
	Thin	73.51	81.59	87.62	92.37	94.87	96.51	83.77	+0.61
	Thick	72.85	80.18	87.10	91.94	94.91	96.54	83.02	−0.16
AlignShift ×7	All	79.40	85.50	90.09	93.26	95.24	96.66	87.06	–
	Thin	80.73	86.43	91.02	93.97	95.78	96.97	88.04	+0.98
	Thick	78.27	84.74	88.89	92.47	94.67	96.38	86.09	−0.97

3.3 Performance Analysis on Thin-Slice and Thick-Slice Data

To demonstrate the benefits of *AlignShift* on bridging the performance gap of thin- and thick-slice data, we conducted a performance analysis of our 2.5D, TSM and *AlignShift* models on the thin- and thick-slice data separately. As there is no open trained models available for prior *state of the art* [13,27,35], we believe our 2.5D models represent the performance of these studies, considering these studies follow 2.5D fashion. As illustrated in Table 3, there is a significant performance gap between thin- and thick-slice CTs for 2.5D and TSM approaches, which validates our argument (Sect. 1) that there is a significant domain shift if the thin- and thick-slice data are processed by a same CNN with standard convolutions. Note that the gap becomes larger when more slices are used, since the 3D information is less valuable for thick-slice data than the thin-slice. In comparison, by learning unified thickness-aware representation, the proposed *AlignShift* reduces the performance gap to neglectable for 3-slice setting; even for the 7-slice setting, the gap is closed compared to 2.5D and TSM approaches.

4   Conclusion

In this study, we challenge spatial normalization as a standard pre-processing approach to solve thickness issue in 3D medical images. Our experiment results indicate that both 2.5D and 3D (*i.e.*, TSM in this study) approaches do not fundamentally address the domain shift issue introduced by spatial normalization, which results in a significant performance gap between thin- and thick-slice data. In this regard, we propose a novel parameter-free operator *Align-Shift*, which enables us to convert theoretically any 2D pretrained network into thickness-aware 3D network. Extensive experiments on DeepLesion benchmark empirically validate that our methods bridge the gap between thin- and thick-slice data. Without whistles and bells, we establish a new *state of the art* on DeepLesion, which surpasses prior arts by considerable margins.

Acknowledgment. This work was supported by National Science Foundation of China (61976137, U1611461). This work was also supported by Interdisciplinary Program of Shanghai Jiao Tong University (YG2017QN661). Authors appreciate the Student Innovation Center of SJTU for providing GPUs.

References

1. Balakrishnan, G., Zhao, A., Sabuncu, M.R., Guttag, J., Dalca, A.V.: VoxelMorph: a learning framework for deformable medical image registration. IEEE Trans. Med. Imaging **38**, 1788–1800 (2019)
2. Cai, J., et al.: Accurate weakly-supervised deep lesion segmentation using large-scale clinical annotations: slice-propagated 3D mask generation from 2D RECIST. In: Frangi, A.F., Schnabel, J.A., Davatzikos, C., Alberola-López, C., Fichtinger, G. (eds.) MICCAI 2018. LNCS, vol. 11073, pp. 396–404. Springer, Cham (2018). https://doi.org/10.1007/978-3-030-00937-3_46
3. Chen, K., Wang, J., Pang, J., Cao, Y., et al.: MMDetection: open MMLab detection toolbox and benchmark. arXiv preprint arXiv:1906.07155 (2019)
4. Dalca, A.V., Balakrishnan, G., Guttag, J., Sabuncu, M.R.: Unsupervised learning for fast probabilistic diffeomorphic registration. In: Frangi, A., Schnabel, J., Davatzikos, C., Alberola-López, C., Fichtinger, G. (eds.) MICCAI 2018. LNCS, vol. 11070, pp. 729–738. Springer, Heidelberg (2018). https://doi.org/10.1007/978-3-030-00928-1_82
5. Glocker, B., Robinson, R., de Castro, D.C., Dou, Q., Konukoglu, E.: Machine learning with multi-site imaging data: an empirical study on the impact of scanner effects. In: Medical Imaging meets NeurIPS Workshop (2019)
6. Gulshan, V., et al.: Development and validation of a deep learning algorithm for detection of diabetic retinopathy in retinal fundus photographs. JAMA **316**(22), 2402–2410 (2016)
7. Guo, C., Pleiss, G., Sun, Y., Weinberger, K.Q.: On calibration of modern neural networks. In: ICML (2017)
8. He, K., Gkioxari, G., Dollár, P., Girshick, R.B.: Mask R-CNN. In: ICCV, pp. 2980–2988 (2017)
9. Huang, G., Liu, Z., Van Der Maaten, L., Weinberger, K.Q.: Densely connected convolutional networks. In: CVPR, vol. 1, p. 3 (2017)

10. Huang, X., Yang, J., et al.: Evaluating and boosting uncertainty quantification in classification. arXiv preprint arXiv:1909.06030 (2019)
11. Isensee, F., et al.: NNU-net: self-adapting framework for U-net-based medical image segmentation. arXiv preprint arXiv:1809.10486 (2018)
12. Kohl, S., et al.: A probabilistic u-net for segmentation of ambiguous images. In: NIPS, pp. 6965–6975 (2018)
13. Li, Z., Zhang, S., Zhang, J., Huang, K., Wang, Y., Yu, Y.: Mvp-net: Multi-view fpn with position-aware attention for deep universal lesion detection. In: Shen, D., et al. (eds.) MICCAI 2019. LNCS, vol. 11769, pp. 13–21. Springer, Heidelberg (2019). https://doi.org/10.1007/978-3-030-32226-7_2
14. Lin, J., Gan, C., Han, S.: TSM: temporal shift module for efficient video understanding. In: ICCV, pp. 7082–7092 (2019)
15. Lin, T.Y., Dollár, P., Girshick, R.B., He, K., Hariharan, B., Belongie, S.J.: Feature pyramid networks for object detection. In: CVPR, pp. 936–944 (2016)
16. Liu, S., et al.: 3D anisotropic hybrid network: transferring convolutional features from 2D images to 3D anisotropic volumeSs. In: Frangi, A.F., Schnabel, J.A., Davatzikos, C., Alberola-López, C., Fichtinger, G. (eds.) MICCAI 2018. LNCS, vol. 11071, pp. 851–858. Springer, Cham (2018). https://doi.org/10.1007/978-3-030-00934-2_94
17. Paszke, A., Gross, S., Chintala, S., Chanan, G., Yang, E., et al.: Automatic differentiation in pytorch (2017)
18. Rother, C., Kolmogorov, V., Blake, A.: "grabcut" interactive foreground extraction using iterated graph cuts. ACM TOG **23**(3), 309–314 (2004)
19. Scheirer, W.J., Rocha, A., Sapkota, A., Boult, T.E.: Toward open set recognition. IEEE T-PAMI **35**, 1757–1772 (2013)
20. Simpson, A.L., et al.: A large annotated medical image dataset for the development and evaluation of segmentation algorithms. arXiv preprint arXiv:1902.09063 (2019)
21. Tang, H., et al.: Clinically applicable deep learning framework for organs at risk delineation in CT images. Nat. Mach. Intell. 1–12 (2019)
22. Tang, H., Zhang, C., Xie, X.: Nodulenet: Decoupled false positive reduction for pulmonary nodule detection and segmentation. In: Shen, D., et al. (eds.) MICCAI 2019. LNCS, vol. 11769, pp. 266–274. Springer, Cham (2019). https://doi.org/10.1007/978-3-030-32226-7_30
23. Tang, Y.B., Yan, K., Tang, Y.X., Liu, J., Xiao, J., Summers, R.M.: ULDor: a universal lesion detector for CT scans with pseudo masks and hard negative example mining. In: ISBI, pp. 833–836. IEEE (2019)
24. Wang, X., Han, S., Chen, Y., Gao, D., Vasconcelos, N.: Volumetric attention for 3D medical image segmentation and detection. In: Shen, D., et al. (eds.) MICCAI 2019. LNCS, vol. 11769, pp. 175–184. Springer, Cham (2019). https://doi.org/10.1007/978-3-030-32226-7_20
25. Wu, B., et al.: SHIFT: a zero flop, zero parameter alternative to spatial convolutions. In: CVPR, pp. 9127–9135 (2017)
26. Yan, K., Bagheri, M., Summers, R.M.: 3D context enhanced region-based convolutional neural network for end-to-end lesion detection. In: Frangi, A.F., Schnabel, J.A., Davatzikos, C., Alberola-López, C., Fichtinger, G. (eds.) MICCAI 2018. LNCS, vol. 11070, pp. 511–519. Springer, Cham (2018). https://doi.org/10.1007/978-3-030-00928-1_58
27. Yan, K., et al.: Mulan: Multitask universal lesion analysis network for joint lesion detection, tagging, and segmentation. In: Shen, D., et al. (eds.) MICCAI 2019. LNCS, vol. 11769, pp. 194–202. Springer, Heidelberg (2019). https://doi.org/10.1007/978-3-030-32226-7_22

28. Yan, K., et al.: Deep lesion graphs in the wild: relationship learning and organization of significant radiology image findings in a diverse large-scale lesion database. In: CVPR, pp. 9261–9270 (2018)

29. Yang, J., Deng, H., Huang, X., Ni, B., Xu, Y.: Relational learning between multiple pulmonary nodules via deep set attention transformers. In: ISBI (2020)

30. Yang, J., Fang, R., Ni, B., et al.: Probabilistic radiomics: ambiguous diagnosis with controllable shape analysis. In: Shen, D., et al. (eds.) MICCAI 2019. LNCS, vol. 11769, pp. 658–666. Springer, Cham (2019). https://doi.org/10.1007/978-3-030-32226-7_73

31. Yang, J., Huang, X., Ni, B., Xu, J., Yang, C., Xu, G.: Reinventing 2D convolutions for 3D medical images. arXiv preprint arXiv:1911.10477 (2019)

32. Yang, Y., Yang, J., Ye, Y., Xia, T., Lu, S.: Development and validation of a deep learning model to assess tumor progression to immunotherapy. In: ASCO, vol. 37, pp. e20601–e20601 (2019)

33. Zhao, W., et al.: Toward automatic prediction of EGFR mutation status in pulmonary adenocarcinoma with 3D deep learning. Cancer Med. **8**, 3532–3543 (2019)

34. Zhao, W., et al.: 3D deep learning from CT scans predicts tumor invasiveness of subcentimeter pulmonary adenocarcinomas. Cancer Res. **78**(24), 6881–6889 (2018)

35. Zlocha, M., Dou, Q., Glocker, B.: Improving retinanet for CT lesion detection with dense masks from weak recist labels. In: Shen, D., et al. (eds.) MICCAI 2019. LNCS, vol. 11769, pp. 402–410. Springer, Cham (2019). https://doi.org/10.1007/978-3-030-32226-7_45

One Click Lesion RECIST Measurement and Segmentation on CT Scans

Youbao Tang[1](✉), Ke Yan[1], Jing Xiao[2], and Ronald M. Summers[1]

[1] Imaging Biomarkers and Computer-Aided Diagnosis Laboratory,
Radiology and Imaging Sciences, National Institutes of Health Clinical Center,
Bethesda, MD 20892-1182, USA
{youbao.tang,rms}@nih.gov
[2] Ping An Insurance Company of China, Shenzhen 510852, China

Abstract. In clinical trials, one of the radiologists' routine work is to measure tumor sizes on medical images using the RECIST criteria (Response Evaluation Criteria In Solid Tumors). However, manual measurement is tedious and subject to inter-observer variability. We propose a unified framework named SEENet for semi-automatic lesion *SE*gmentation and RECIST *E*stimation on a variety of lesions over the entire human body. The user is only required to provide simple guidance by clicking once near the lesion. SEENet consists of two main parts. The first one extracts the lesion of interest with the one-click guidance, roughly segments the lesion, and estimates its RECIST measurement. Based on the results of the first network, the second one refines the lesion segmentation and RECIST estimation. SEENet achieves state-of-the-art performance in lesion segmentation and RECIST estimation on the large-scale public DeepLesion dataset. It offers a practical tool for radiologists to generate reliable lesion measurements (*i.e.* segmentation mask and RECIST) with minimal human effort and greatly reduced time.

Keywords: Lesion RECIST estimation · Lesion segmentation · One-click human guidance · CT scans

1 Introduction

Lesion segmentation and measurement from computed tomography (CT) scans are important tasks in oncology image analysis. They are useful in quantitative assessment of the disease progression and therapy response. Generally, radiologists scan through the CT image to find lesions, and then measure their sizes using the RECIST (Response Evaluation Criteria In Solid Tumors) criteria [5]. They usually do not segment lesions, even though segmentations might prove helpful, due to time constraints. With these measurements, follow-up and quantitative analysis of tumor extents could be performed to provide valuable information for treatment planning and tracking. Such manual annotation processes are highly tedious and time-consuming, so it motivates many researchers to develop techniques to automate these processes.

A. L. Martel et al. (Eds.): MICCAI 2020, LNCS 12264, pp. 573–583, 2020.
https://doi.org/10.1007/978-3-030-59719-1_56

With the advent of deep learning, applications of medical image analysis [1,2,9–11,14,15,17–23,25,26,29] using deep learning have dramatically increased in the last few years. Many previous work focus on a single lesion type over a specific body part, e.g., lung nodule segmentation [22], lymph node segmentation [14] and liver tumor segmentation [10]. However, radiologists in their daily work need to find and measure all kinds of lesions, so single-type detection and segmentation algorithms are not scalable in practice. Recently, a large-scale DeepLesion dataset [27] covering different types of lesions over the entire body was released, which inspired techniques on universal lesion analysis. While universal lesion detection has received much attention [11,15,21,25,26,29], segmentation and RECIST estimation were not sufficiently studied. To accurately locate the lesion to segment or measure, existing work [1,2,16,17] require strong human guidance information, e.g., drawing a bounding box to cover the lesion region that should not be too tight or too large. This constraint is not user-friendly and increases time cost.

To overcome these problems, we propose a unified framework, SEENet, for joint lesion segmentation and RECIST estimation over the whole human body with only one click guidance. Unlike previous work [1,2,16,17] that ask radiologists to draw a bounding box to indicate the lesion of interest (LOI), this work only requires a single click, which is more convenient and efficient, without the need to carefully control the box size when drawing. More importantly, SEENet achieved better accuracy and robustness than [1,2,16,17]. SEENet consists of two main components. The first component (named MR-CNN) is responsible for simultaneous LOI extraction, initial lesion segmentation and RECIST estimation. We improved the Mask R-CNN [6] by adding a new branch for predicting the endpoints' heatmaps of RECIST. One-click guidance provided by users is required as the input of MR-CNN. For the second component, a model (named ARU-Net) is built by combining the advantages of U-Net [12], ResNet [7] and atrous spatial pyramid pooling module (ASPP) [3] for lesion segmentation and RECIST estimation refinement. ARU-Net is able to learn highly discriminative features that consider multiscale contextual information from image patches obtained according to the outputs of MR-CNN for full-size pixel-wise prediction.

The proposed SEENet is trained and evaluated on the large-scale DeepLesion dataset [27]. The coordinates of RECIST measurements provided in DeepLesion are use as supervisory information to learn the lesion segmentation task in a weakly-supervised way, so manual mask annotation for training is not needed. Extensive experimental results demonstrate that the proposed SEENet achieves the state-of-the-art performance in both universal lesion segmentation and RECIST estimation tasks, and MR-CNN without using the click information also achieves the competitive performance of fully automatic lesion detection. Overall, this work tries to solve a clinically important problem. It allows clinicians to easily control which lesion to segment and measure by one click and the rest is done accurately and automatically.

The main contributions of this work can be summarized as follows: 1) This work provides a solution to an important clinical task of lesion measurement annotation and segmentation. 2) A network based on Mask RCNN is built to extract lesion of interest, estimate RECIST measurement and segment lesion simultaneously. 3) A network that can learn multi-scale contextual information of lesions and perform full-size prediction is built to refine lesion segmentation and RECIST estimation results.

2   Methodology

Given a CT scan with lesions, we propose a unified framework to segment the lesion region and estimate the RECIST measurement accurately and simultaneously with one-click guidance from human. Figure 1 shows an overview of the proposed SEENet. It consists of two main components. The first one is designed based on an improved Mask R-CNN [6] for initial lesion segmentation and RECIST estimation. The second one is a U-Net [12] like architecture for lesion segmentation and RECIST estimation refinement. The motivation and detail of their design will be described in this section.

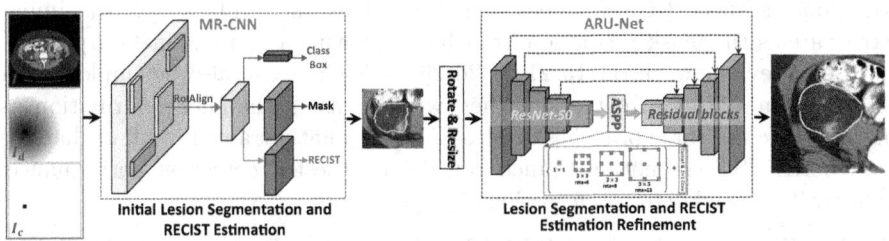

Fig. 1. Overview of the proposed SEENet. Yellow curves indicate the boundaries of the segmented lesions. Red and green spots indicate the endpoints of the long and short axes of the estimated RECIST measurement, respectively. (Color figure online)

Initial Lesion Segmentation and RECIST Estimation. Mask R-CNN [6] is able to detect and segment objects at the same time, and it has been successfully applied for lesion detection in [15]. With these inspirations, we propose a model (named MR-CNN) based on Mask R-CNN for simultaneous lesion segmentation and RECIST estimation. To achieve this goal, we need to first locate the lesion of interest (LOI), then predict lesion segmentation and RECIST estimation for the LOI.

Although previous works [11,15,21,25,26,29] contribute many efforts to improve the detection performance, there still exist many false positives in their lesion detection results. Our goal is to let radiologists segment and measure the lesion of their interest and not to distract them with false positive lesion detection results, so we need some manual input to indicate the LOI. Existing approaches [1,2,16,17] require radiologists to manually draw bounding boxes to obtain LOIs for their tasks. Compared with [1,2,16,17], a faster and easier way adopted in this work is to click around or inside the lesion region once. To effectively inject the one-click guide information into the model, a click image I_c and a distance transform image I_d are generated and truncated at 255 from the click point $\mathbf{p}$, where I_d is defined as $I_d(\mathbf{q}) = \|\mathbf{q} - \mathbf{p}\|_2$. Therefore, a three-channel image can be constructed as the input by concatenating the original 2D CT slice I, I_c and I_d, as shown in Fig. 1.

The original Mask R-CNN has two branches, one for detection and the other for segmentation. We hope the network to also predict the RECIST measurement, which consists of two lines: one measuring the longest axis of the lesion and the second measuring its longest perpendicular axis in the axial plane, see Fig. 2 for examples. Extending Mask R-CNN, the proposed MR-CNN outputs a RECIST estimation result in parallel by adding a new branch for predicting the heatmaps of four keypoints (*i.e.* the four endpoints of the RECIST axes), as shown in Fig. 1. Therefore, MR-CNN contains a backbone and three head branches for LOI extraction (classification and regression), mask prediction, and RECIST estimation over each LOI. Following the framework of [26], we remove the last dense block and transition layer of DenseNet-121 [8] and use it as the backbone in this work. The box recognition and mask prediction branches are the same as Mask R-CNN. The added RECIST estimation branch has a similar structure as the mask prediction branch except with a four-channel output.

Like previous work [11,15,21,25,26,29], MR-CNN can also be employed for fully automatic lesion detection when without using the click information as input. Since the three branches of MR-CNN are jointly trained, we find that the added RECIST estimation branch can enhance lesion detection performance. This will be validated in the section of experiments.

Lesion Segmentation and RECIST Estimation Refinement. The initial mask and RECIST prediction is not sufficiently accurate and fine-grained, since the output size of mask and RECIST branches is 28×28, which is too small to get accurate pixel-wise prediction. Therefore, we design a refinement model according to the following three principles: 1) performing full-size prediction, 2) using a strong backbone for feature extraction, and 3) considering rich contextual information at multiple scales due to the size variation of lesions. After investigating previous pixel-wise prediction approaches, we find that 1) the U-Net [12] is well designed for full-size prediction and has been successfully used in many medical image segmentation tasks, 2) ResNet-Pose [24] achieves good human pose estimation performance due to its powerful backbone (*i.e.* ResNet [7]), and 3) the atrous spatial pyramid pooling module (ASPP) [3] is able to learn multiscale feature representations with rich contextual information. Inspired by these works, we propose ARU-Net with a U-Net like architecture, using ResNet in the encoder and decoder, and ASPP as the junction between them for lesion segmentation and RECIST estimation refinement, as shown in Fig. 1.

Specifically, the first five blocks of ResNet-50 are used as the encoder of U-Net and the stride of the first convolutional layer is set as 1 instead of 2 to keep more spatial information in the output feature maps. Then, an ASPP module with 256 output channels and four different dilation rates (*i.e.* 1, 4, 8 and 12) follows the encoder, and their outputs are concatenated to form the multiscale contextual feature maps as an input of the decoder, as shown in Fig. 1. The decoder of U-Net consists of four upsampling blocks and one output block. Each upsampling block has a linear upsampling layer and two residual blocks. The output channel sizes of upsampling blocks are 512, 256, 128 and 64, respectively. The output block has two branches in parallel, one for mask prediction and the other for RECIST estimation.

Based on the results produced by the trained MR-CNN model (including a detected box, a predicted mask and an estimated RECIST), an adjusted LOI can be obtained as the input of ARU-Net with the following steps: 1) rotating the CT scan according to the center and the long axis' slope of the estimated RECIST; 2) cropping a square sub-image whose center is the predicted mask and whose width is two times the extent of the detected box's long side, so that sufficient visual context is preserved for ARU-Net training; 3) resizing the cropped image to 256 × 256.

Model Optimization. As done by the Mask R-CNN [6], a multi-task loss on each sampled RoI is defined as $L^1 = L^1_{cls} + L^1_{box} + L^1_{mask} + L^1_{recist}$ for MR-CNN training. The first three terms have the same definitions as the ones in [6]. L^1_{recist} is the mean squared error (MSE) loss. Another multi-task loss is defined as $L^2 = L^2_{mask} + L^2_{recist}$ for ARU-Net training, where both L^2_{mask} and L^2_{recist} are the MSE loss. For L^1_{mask} update, the pseudo masks of lesions are constructed based on GrabCut [13] from RECIST annotations following [17]. For L^2_{mask} update, we use the prediction of MR-CNN to refine the potentially noisy ground-truth. Specifically, the intersections of the segmentation results produced by MR-CNN and the pseudo masks are labeled as lesion and their differences are labeled as uncertain regions that will be ignored during training. For $L^1_{recist}(L^2_{recist})$ update, ground-truth keypoint heatmaps consist of four 2D Gaussian maps (with a standard deviation of 1(3) pixel(s)) centered on the endpoints of RECIST annotations. Both MR-CNN and ARU-Net are implemented in PyTorch. To mimic the radiologists' click behavior during training, we randomly sample the points from the dilated pseudo masks with five pixels for generating clicks. The ImageNet pre-trained models are used for weight initialization. MR-CNN and ARU-Net are separately trained. We first train MR-CNN using SGD with an initial learning rate of 0.004 for 8 epochs and decay it by 0.1 after 4 and 6 epochs, and then train ARU-Net using SGD with an initial learning rate of 0.01 for 150 epochs and decay it by 0.1 after every 50 epochs. Regular image transformations including scaling, rotation, and translation were used for data augmentation.

3   Experiments

Dataset. The DeepLesion dataset [27] is composed of 32,735 CT lesion images annotated with RECIST measurements from 10,594 studies of 4,459 patients. It contains a variety of lesions throughout the body such as lung nodules, liver lesions, and enlarged lymph nodes. Following the previous work [2], 1, 000 lesion images are randomly selected from 500 patients and manually segmented as a test set for quantitative evaluation. The remaining patients' images serve as a training set (90%) and a validation set (10%).

Evaluation Criteria. For lesion segmentation, the pixel-wise precision, recall, and dice similarity coefficient (Dice) are used for performance evaluation. For RECIST estimation, to quantify how our approach measures against the radiologists' annotations, we compare the RECIST annotations and those of our method by computing the mean and standard deviation of differences between their diameter lengths. As introduced in Sect. 2, MR-CNN can be used for fully automatic lesion detection. Therefore, we also evaluate the lesion detection performance using the free-response receiver operating characteristic (FROC), following previous works [11,15,21,25,26,29]. A detection result is considered as correct when the IoU between the predicted bounding box and the real bounding box is larger than 0.5.

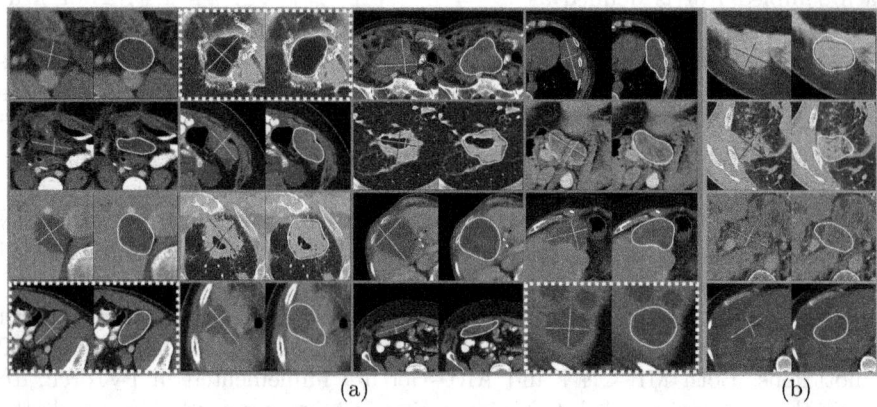

Fig. 2. Visual examples of results produced by SEENet. For clear visualization, the lesion segmentation and RECIST estimation results are shown separately. Therefore, each example includes two images. The left one presents the estimated RECIST (the green cross) and the RECIST annotation labeled by radiologists (the red cross). The right one presents the lesion segmentation result (the yellow curve) and the real lesion mask (the pink curve). The yellow dashed boxes indicate some cases where the manual RECISTs are imperfect, but SEENet can fix them (see text). (a) Sixteen good quality examples, (b) two over-estimated (top) and two under-estimated examples (bottom). All images in this figure are cropped from original CT scans according to the results produced by MR-CNN. Best viewed in color. (Color figure online)

Qualitative Results. Figure 2 shows several visual examples of the results produced by SEENet. From Fig. 2, all lesion regions are well cropped, suggesting that SEENet can successfully extract accurate lesion of interests (LOIs) with less human effort (*i.e.* one manual click) instead of manually drawing bounding boxes to include the lesion regions as done by previous work [1,2,16,17]. Some good quality examples are given in Fig. 2(a), where the automatic lesion segmentation results (the yellow curves) are very close to the manual segmentations (the pink curves) and the estimated RECISTs can well provide the information of lesions' long and short diameters. As demonstrated by [17], there is a large variation between RECIST annotations from different radiologists. Therefore, it's easy to understand that the endpoints of the estimated RECISTs are different from the ones of manual annotations. We also find that our estimation results are close to each other even the clicks are given at different positions. Sometimes, although the manual annotations cannot well touch the boundaries of the lesion regions, our estimated results can fix them (seeing the examples indicated with yellow dashed boxes). Two over(under)-estimated results are given in the top (bottom) of Fig. 2(b). In these cases, the boundaries of lesions are highly blurred, which makes SEENet fail to extract highly discriminative features from them to distinguish the lesions from their surrounding regions, especially for lesion segmentation, since only weak pixel-wise labels are used for training. These qualitative results intuitively demonstrate that the proposed framework SEENet can well perform the lesion segmentation and RECIST estimation simultaneously with one-click guide information during inference.

Table 1. Results of lesion segmentation and RECIST estimation. For lesion segmentation, the mean and standard deviation of pixel-wise recall, precision and Dice score are reported. For RECIST estimation, the mean and standard deviation of the differences of diameter lengths (mm) between radiologist RECIST annotations and those obtained by different methods are reported.

Method	Lesion segmentation			RECIST estimation	
	Precision	Recall	Dice	Long axis	Short axis
Cai *et al.* [2]	0.893 ± 0.111	0.933 ± 0.095	0.906 ± 0.089	–	–
Tang *et al.* [17]	–	–	–	1.893 ± 2.185	1.614 ± 1.874
MR-CNN	0.850 ± 0.115	0.820 ± 0.108	0.827 ± 0.092	2.361 ± 2.878	1.983 ± 2.293
MR-CNN+PSPNet [28]	0.893 ± 0.057	0.906 ± 0.121	0.887 ± 0.078	2.057 ± 2.215	1.730 ± 2.029
MR-CNN+DeepLabv3+ [4]	$\mathbf{0.909 \pm 0.051}$	0.896 ± 0.127	0.891 ± 0.067	2.023 ± 2.243	1.715 ± 2.007
MR-CNN+U-Net [12]	0.877 ± 0.076	0.881 ± 0.143	0.867 ± 0.084	2.153 ± 2.537	1.848 ± 2.153
MR-CNN+ResNet [24]	0.907 ± 0.047	0.875 ± 0.132	0.883 ± 0.077	2.076 ± 2.311	1.742 ± 2.041
MR-CNN+RU-Net	0.891 ± 0.053	0.913 ± 0.113	0.901 ± 0.063	1.913 ± 2.163	1.631 ± 1.911
MR-CNN+ARU-Net*	0.879 ± 0.061	0.935 ± 0.084	0.907 ± 0.051	1.908 ± 2.089	1.608 ± 1.902
MR-CNN+ARU-Net	0.883 ± 0.057	$\mathbf{0.947 \pm 0.074}$	$\mathbf{0.912 \pm 0.039}$	$\mathbf{1.747 \pm 1.983}$	$\mathbf{1.555 \pm 1.808}$

Note: - denotes the result is not reported. ⋆ denotes ARU-Net uses the LOI directly extracted by MR-CNN as input rather than the adjusted one.

Quantitative Lesion Segmentation & RECIST Estimation Results. To investigate the benefits of our designs, we evaluate the following experimental configurations: 1) only using the first component (MR-CNN); 2) using U-Net [12] as the second component (MR-CNN+U-Net); 3) using a good human pose estimation approach (*i.e.* ResNet-Pose [24]) as the second component (MR-CNN+ResNet); 4) using the designed second component without the ASPP module (MR-CNN+RU-Net); 5) directly using the output of MR-CNN as the input of ARU-Net (MR-CNN+ARU-Net*); 6) the fully proposed SEENet framework (MR-CNN+ARU-Net). For experimental comparisons, two state-of-the-art image segmentation methods (*i.e.* PSPNet [28] and DeepLabv3+ [4]) are used as the second component. Also, the best existing weakly-supervised universal lesion segmentation approach [2] and semi-supervised RECIST estimation approach [17] are compared.

Table 1 lists the quantitative results of lesion segmentation and RECIST estimation produced by different methods. From Table 1, we can see that 1) when using the second component for refinement, the performance of both lesion segmentation and RECIST estimation is improved significantly, demonstrating that the importance and effectiveness of the refinement step in the proposed framework. 2) Compared with U-Net and ResNet, RU-Net achieves better results, suggesting that RU-Net combining U-Net and ResNet is able to learn more representative features for performance improvement. 3) ARU-Net outperforms RU-Net, suggesting that the introduced ASPP module can extract multiscale contextual and discriminative features to strengthen the model's capability for lesion segmentation and RECIST estimation. 4) ARU-Net gets better results than ARU-Net*, especially for RECIST estimation. It demonstrates that the simple adjustment step can reduce the arbitrariness of lesion poses, which makes the model learn more discriminative features for our tasks. 5) Compared with the best approaches [1,2,16,17] customized for each specific task and requiring radiologists to draw bounding boxes to extract lesion of interests (LOIs), the proposed unified framework SEENet (*i.e.* MR-CNN+ARU-Net) still gets better performance on both tasks with less human effort (*i.e.* one click), demonstrating the effectiveness of the proposed method for simultaneous lesion segmentation and RECIST estimation. 6) Compared with the state-of-the-art image segmentation methods (*i.e.* PSPNet [28] and DeepLabv3+ [4]), the proposed ARU-Net achieves better results, meaning that the well-designed ARU-Net is more powerful and suitable for our tasks.

Quantitative Lesion Detection Results. Table 2 lists the quantitative results of lesion detection using different approaches. As mentioned, when without using the click information, MR-CNN can be used for fully automatic lesion detection, denoted by MR-CNN w/o click. It achieves competitive performance compared with the state-of-the-art lesion detection approaches [11,21,25,26,29]. If the RECIST estimation branch is removed (denoted by MR-CNN w/o click & RECIST), the detection performance drops about 3% of sensitivity at 1 false positive per image. It demonstrates the usefulness of the added RECIST estimation branch for lesion detection. When using the click information, MR-CNN achieves a sensitivity of 97.24% at 0.5 false positives per image, suggesting that the LOIs can be well extracted. We find that some errors happen when there are multiple lesions near the click position.

Table 2. Given an IoU of 0.5, sensitivity (%) at several specific average false positives per image on FROC curve. We average the results of MR-CNN with randomly clicking ten times.

Method	0.5	1	2	4	8	16
3DCE [25]	62.48	73.37	80.70	85.65	89.09	91.06
3DCE_CS_Att [21]	71.4	78.5	84.0	87.6	90.2	91.4
Zlocha et al. [29]	72.15	80.07	86.40	90.77	94.09	96.32
MVP-Net [11]	73.83	81.82	87.60	89.57	91.30	–
MULAN [26]	**76.12**	83.69	**88.76**	**92.30**	94.71	**95.64**
MR-CNN w/o click & RECIST	72.81	80.72	86.87	91.15	94.18	95.24
MR-CNN w/o click	75.92	**83.74**	88.13	92.11	**94.82**	95.63
MR-CNN	97.24	98.37	99.31	99.47	99.47	99.47

4   Conclusions and Future Work

We propose SEENet for automatic lesion segmentation and RECIST estimation on a variety of lesion types and require very simple human guide information, *i.e.* just one click. To obtain reliable lesion of interests, an improved Mask R-CNN model is designed by adding an extra two-channel input and a new branch for RECIST estimation. To further boost the performance of lesion segmentation and RECIST estimation, ARU-Net is designed to learn discriminative features with multiscale contextual information. Experimental results demonstrate the proposed method can work well on behalf of "click in and lesion measurements out" for clinicians. As such, it shows highly potential clinical values. Future work includes extending SEENet to 3D and making it end-to-end trainable.

Acknowledgments. This research was supported by the Intramural Research Program of the National Institutes of Health Clinical Center and by the Ping An Insurance Company through a Cooperative Research and Development Agreement. We thank Nvidia for GPU card donation.

References

1. Agarwal, V., Tang, Y., Xiao, J., Summers, R.M.: Weakly supervised lesion co-segmentation on CT scans. In: ISBI, pp. 203–206 (2020)
2. Cai, J., et al.: Accurate weakly-supervised deep lesion segmentation using large-scale clinical annotations: slice-propagated 3D mask generation from 2D RECIST. In: Frangi, A.F., Schnabel, J.A., Davatzikos, C., Alberola-López, C., Fichtinger, G. (eds.) MICCAI 2018. LNCS, vol. 11073, pp. 396–404. Springer, Cham (2018). https://doi.org/10.1007/978-3-030-00937-3_46
3. Chen, L.C., Papandreou, G., Kokkinos, I., Murphy, K., Yuille, A.L.: DeepLab: semantic image segmentation with deep convolutional nets, atrous convolution, and fully connected CRFs. IEEE Trans. Pattern Anal. Mach. Intell. **40**(4), 834–848 (2018)

4. Chen, L.C., Zhu, Y., Papandreou, G., Schroff, F., Adam, H.: Encoder-decoder with atrous separable convolution for semantic image segmentation. In: ECCV, pp. 801–818 (2018)
5. Eisenhauer, E.A., et al.: New response evaluation criteria in solid tumours: revised RECIST guideline (version 1.1). Eur. J. Cancer **45**(2), 228–247 (2009)
6. He, K., Gkioxari, G., Dollár, P., Girshick, R.: Mask R-CNN, In: ICCV. pp. 2961–2969 (2017)
7. He, K., Zhang, X., Ren, S., Sun, J.: Deep residual learning for image recognition. In: CVPR, pp. 770–778 (2016)
8. Huang, G., Liu, Z., Van Der Maaten, L., Weinberger, K.Q.: Densely connected convolutional networks. In: CVPR, pp. 4700–4708 (2017)
9. Jin, D., Xu, Z., Tang, Y., Harrison, A.P., Mollura, D.J.: CT-realistic lung nodule simulation from 3D conditional generative adversarial networks for robust lung segmentation. In: Frangi, A.F., Schnabel, J.A., Davatzikos, C., Alberola-López, C., Fichtinger, G. (eds.) MICCAI 2018. LNCS, vol. 11071, pp. 732–740. Springer, Cham (2018). https://doi.org/10.1007/978-3-030-00934-2_81
10. Li, X., Chen, H., Qi, X., Dou, Q., Fu, C.W., Heng, P.A.: H-DenseuNet: hybrid densely connected UNet for liver and tumor segmentation from CT volumes. IEEE Trans. Med. Imaging **37**(12), 2663–2674 (2018)
11. Li, Z., Zhang, S., Zhang, J., Huang, K., Wang, Y., Yu, Y.: MVP-Net: multi-view FPN with position-aware attention for deep universal lesion detection. In: Shen, D., et al. (eds.) MICCAI 2019. LNCS, vol. 11769, pp. 13–21. Springer, Cham (2019). https://doi.org/10.1007/978-3-030-32226-7_2
12. Ronneberger, O., Fischer, P., Brox, T.: U-Net: convolutional networks for biomedical image segmentation. In: Navab, N., Hornegger, J., Wells, W.M., Frangi, A.F. (eds.) MICCAI 2015. LNCS, vol. 9351, pp. 234–241. Springer, Cham (2015). https://doi.org/10.1007/978-3-319-24574-4_28
13. Rother, C., Kolmogorov, V., Blake, A.: "GrabCut": interactive foreground extraction using iterated graph cuts. ACM Trans. Graph. **23**(3), 309–314 (2004)
14. Tang, Y.B., Oh, S., Tang, Y.X., Xiao, J., Summers, R.M.: CT-realistic data augmentation using generative adversarial network for robust lymph node segmentation. In: SPIE Medical Imaging, vol. 10950, p. 109503V (2019)
15. Tang, Y.B., Yan, K., Tang, Y.X., Liu, J., Xiao, J., Summers, R.M.: ULDor: a universal lesion detector for CT scans with pseudo masks and hard negative example mining. In: ISBI, pp. 833–836 (2019)
16. Tang, Y., et al.: CT image enhancement using stacked generative adversarial networks and transfer learning for lesion segmentation improvement. In: Shi, Y., Suk, H.-I., Liu, M. (eds.) MLMI 2018. LNCS, vol. 11046, pp. 46–54. Springer, Cham (2018). https://doi.org/10.1007/978-3-030-00919-9_6
17. Tang, Y., Harrison, A.P., Bagheri, M., Xiao, J., Summers, R.M.: Semi-automatic RECIST labeling on CT scans with cascaded convolutional neural networks. In: Frangi, A.F., Schnabel, J.A., Davatzikos, C., Alberola-López, C., Fichtinger, G. (eds.) MICCAI 2018. LNCS, vol. 11073, pp. 405–413. Springer, Cham (2018). https://doi.org/10.1007/978-3-030-00937-3_47
18. Tang, Y., Tang, Y., Xiao, J., Summers, R.M.: XLSor: a robust and accurate lung segmentor on chest X-rays using criss-cross attention and customized radiorealistic abnormalities generation. In: MIDL, pp. 457–467 (2019)
19. Tang, Y.X., et al.: Automated abnormality classification of chest radiographs using deep convolutional neural networks. NPJ Digit. Med. **3**(1), 1–8 (2020)

20. Tang, Y., Tang, Y., Sandfort, V., Xiao, J., Summers, R.M.: TUNA-Net: task-oriented unsupervised adversarial network for disease recognition in cross-domain chest X-rays. In: Shen, D., et al. (eds.) MICCAI 2019. LNCS, vol. 11769, pp. 431–440. Springer, Cham (2019). https://doi.org/10.1007/978-3-030-32226-7_48

21. Tao, Q., Ge, Z., Cai, J., Yin, J., See, S.: Improving deep lesion detection using 3D contextual and spatial attention. In: Shen, D., et al. (eds.) MICCAI 2019. LNCS, vol. 11769, pp. 185–193. Springer, Cham (2019). https://doi.org/10.1007/978-3-030-32226-7_21

22. Wang, S., et al.: Central focused convolutional neural networks: developing a data-driven model for lung nodule segmentation. Med. Image Anal. **40**, 172–183 (2017)

23. Wang, Y., et al.: Weakly supervised universal fracture detection in pelvic X-Rays. In: Shen, D., et al. (eds.) MICCAI 2019. LNCS, vol. 11769, pp. 459–467. Springer, Cham (2019). https://doi.org/10.1007/978-3-030-32226-7_51

24. Xiao, B., Wu, H., Wei, Y.: Simple baselines for human pose estimation and tracking. In: ECCV, pp. 466–481 (2018)

25. Yan, K., Bagheri, M., Summers, R.M.: 3D context enhanced region-based convolutional neural network for end-to-end lesion detection. In: Frangi, A.F., Schnabel, J.A., Davatzikos, C., Alberola-López, C., Fichtinger, G. (eds.) MICCAI 2018. LNCS, vol. 11070, pp. 511–519. Springer, Cham (2018). https://doi.org/10.1007/978-3-030-00928-1_58

26. Yan, K., et al.: MULAN: multitask universal lesion analysis network for joint lesion detection, tagging, and segmentation. In: Shen, D., et al. (eds.) MICCAI 2019. LNCS, vol. 11769, pp. 194–202. Springer, Cham (2019). https://doi.org/10.1007/978-3-030-32226-7_22

27. Yan, K., Wang, X., Lu, L., Summers, R.M.: DeepLesion: automated mining of large-scale lesion annotations and universal lesion detection with deep learning. J. Med. Imaging **5**(3), 036501 (2018)

28. Zhao, H., Shi, J., Qi, X., Wang, X., Jia, J.: Pyramid scene parsing network. In: CVPR, pp. 2881–2890 (2017)

29. Zlocha, M., Dou, Q., Glocker, B.: Improving RetinaNet for CT lesion detection with dense masks from weak RECIST labels. In: Shen, D., et al. (eds.) MICCAI 2019. LNCS, vol. 11769, pp. 402–410. Springer, Cham (2019). https://doi.org/10.1007/978-3-030-32226-7_45

Automated Detection of Cortical Lesions in Multiple Sclerosis Patients with 7T MRI

Francesco La Rosa[1,2,3,4(✉)], Erin S. Beck[4], Ahmed Abdulkadir[5,6],
Jean-Philippe Thiran[1,3], Daniel S. Reich[4], Pascal Sati[4,7],
and Meritxell Bach Cuadra[1,2,3]

[1] LTS5, Ecole Polytechnique Fédérale de Lausanne, Lausanne, Switzerland
francesco.larosa@epfl.ch
[2] Medical Image Analysis Laboratory, CIBM, University of Lausanne,
Lausanne, Switzerland
[3] Radiology Department, Lausanne University Hospital, Lausanne, Switzerland
[4] Translational Neuroradiology Section,
National Institute of Neurological Disorders and Stroke,
National Institutes of Health, Bethesda, MD, USA
[5] University Hospital of Old Age Psychiatry and Psychotherapy, University of Bern,
Bern, Switzerland
[6] Center for Biomedical Image Computing and Analytics, Department of Radiology,
Perelman School of Medicine, University of Pennsylvania, Philadelphia, PA, USA
[7] Department of Neurology, Cedars-Sinai Medical Center, Los Angeles, CA, USA

Abstract. The automated detection of cortical lesions (CLs) in patients with multiple sclerosis (MS) is a challenging task that, despite its clinical relevance, has received very little attention. Accurate detection of the small and scarce lesions requires specialized sequences and high or ultra-high field MRI. For supervised training based on multimodal structural MRI at 7T, two experts generated ground truth segmentation masks of 60 patients with 2014 CLs. We implemented a simplified 3D U-Net with three resolution levels (3D U-Net⁻). By increasing the complexity of the task (adding brain tissue segmentation), while randomly dropping input channels during training, we improved the performance compared to the baseline. Considering a minimum lesion size of 0.75 µL, we achieved a lesion-wise cortical lesion detection rate of 67% and a false positive rate of 42%. However, 393 (24%) of the lesions reported as false positives were *post-hoc* confirmed as potential or definite lesions by an expert. This indicates the potential of the proposed method to support experts in the tedious process of CL manual segmentation.

Keywords: MRI · Ultra-high field · Multiple sclerosis · Cortical lesions · Segmentation · CNN

© Springer Nature Switzerland AG 2020
A. L. Martel et al. (Eds.): MICCAI 2020, LNCS 12264, pp. 584–593, 2020.
https://doi.org/10.1007/978-3-030-59719-1_57

1   Introduction

Multiple sclerosis (MS) is the most common demyelinating disease affecting the central nervous system. Demyelination results in focal lesions that appear in both the white matter (WM) and gray matter (GM) of the brain and of the spinal cord. Magnetic resonance imaging (MRI) is the conventional imaging tool used for the diagnosis and evaluation of disease progression and therapy response, with a focus on WM lesions (WMLs) dissemination in space and time. While WMLs remain a hallmark of MS, in 2017 cortical lesions (CLs) were added to the diagnostic criteria of MS [22]. CLs are associated with worse disability and with progressive forms of MS, and these associations appear to be at least partially independent of WML burden [3,23]. CLs can be divided into three subtypes: leukocortical (type I, involving the cortex and WM), intracortical (type II, entirely within the cortex but not touching the pial surface), and subpial (type III and IV, touching the pial surface of the cortex). There is increasing evidence that subpial lesions form due to inflammation in the overlying meninges, in a somewhat distinct mechanism from that of WM and leukocortical lesion formation [17]. Thus, it is important to understand the clinical implication of subpial lesions and their response to existing and novel MS treatments in order to optimize MS diagnostic and prognostic accuracy and maximize treatment efficacy.

CLs, however, are only visible with specialized advanced MRI sequences at high (3T) and ultra-high magnetic field (7T) [13,14]. Specifically, 7T MRI has become the reference *in vivo* technique for CL identification due to its increased signal-to-noise ratio (SNR) and often higher imaging resolution [13]. Moreover, 7T MRI is significantly more sensitive to intracortical and subpial lesions compared to 3T [18]. Magnetization-prepared 2 rapid acquisition with gradient echo (MP2RAGE) [14,19], in particular, has emerged as a promising sequence for detecting CLs at 7T [2], but different T2*-weighted (T2*w) contrasts have been suggested as well [18,20]. Overall, the combination of MP2RAGE and one (or more) T2*w sequence gives the highest sensitivity [2].

A wide range of machine learning algorithms have been proposed in order to automatically segment WMLs in MRI [10]. Recently, deep learning algorithms have achieved the best performance in terms of WML detection and segmentation [4]. However, the automated detection of CLs in MRI has been barely explored. CLs are smaller and show a lower intensity contrast compared to WMLs. Moreover, CLs locations (within the cortex and at its interface with WM) make their detection more challenging than lesions entirely within the WM. Finally, the need for advanced MRI sequences limits the dataset availability and thus the availability of training samples. Nevertheless, at 3T, four methods have been tested to automatically segment both WMLs and CLs [7,8,15,16]. All methods were applied in a multimodal setting, including advanced sequences such as MP2RAGE, 3D fluid-attenuated inversion recovery (FLAIR) and 3D double-inversion recovery (DIR) [7,8], or only MP2RAGE and 3D FLAIR [15,16].

At 7T, however, the problem of automatically detecting CLs differs from 3 T for three main reasons. Firstly, a significantly higher number of CLs is visible, including subpial ones which are almost not seen at lower magnetic fields. Secondly, the increased inhomogeneity in the radiofrequency (B1) field and local variations of the static magnetic field (B0) create artefacts and spatial distortions. Thirdly, the T2w 3D FLAIR sequence, commonly used at 1.5 and 3T, presents artefacts and alternative advanced sequences are acquired instead. Beyond these challenges and in the recent approval of the first 7T MRI scanner for clinical use, the development of automated tools for MS lesion segmentation at ultra-high field is needed to help physicians in better analysing those images. Pioneering work of Fartaria et al. [9] proposed an automated segmentation of MS lesions at 7T, based on the concatenation of skull stripping, tissue segmentation, and morphological operations. Their approach, based on a single MP2RAGE scan, segments both WMLs and CLs (mostly leukocortical), reporting an accuracy for CLs of 58% with 40% of false positives.

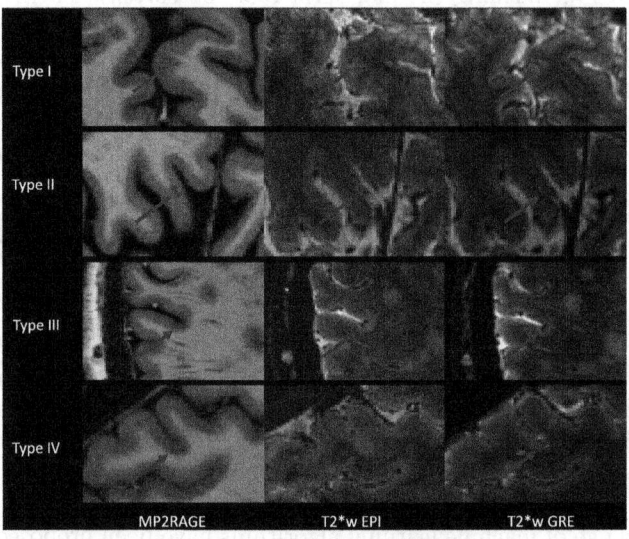

Fig. 1. Examples of the four types of CLs seen in the three different contrasts at 7T MRI.

In our work, we present a deep learning 7 T multimodal approach for CL detection only, considering MP2RAGE, T2*w echo planar imaging (EPI) [20, 21], and T2*w gradient recalled echo (GRE) sequences. This is the first attempt to detect CLs and classify them in two different types: leukocortical and subpial/intracortical. We implemented a 3D U-Net [5] with fewer resolution levels resulting in substantially fewer parameters. Considering this architecture as baseline, we increased the complexity of the prediction task by simultaneously predicting main tissue types and randomly dropping input channels during training. Another important contribution of this work is the validation framework. Compared to the only previous work in literature, we increase the number of patients and CLs used for validation: from 25 and 364 in [9] to 60 and 2014. Furthermore, we target small CLs with a minimum volume of 0.75 µL instead of 6 µL considered in [9].

2   Methodology

2.1   Dataset

MRI acquisitions were done on 60 patients (38/22 female/male, 49 ± 11 years old, age range [29–77] years) with Expanded Disability Status Scale (EDSS) scores ranging from 0 to 7.5 (median 2.0 ± 2.0), 17 were progressive and 43 relapsing remitting MS. Imaging was performed on a 7 T whole-body research system (Siemens Healthcare, Erlangen, Germany) using a 32-channel head coil. The MRI protocol included: (i) 3D MP2RAGE [14] (TR/TI1/TI2/TE = 6000/800/2700/5 ms, voxel size = $0.5 \times 0.5 \times 0.5\,mm^3$), (ii) 3D-Segmented T2*w EPI [20,21] (TR/TE = 52/23 ms, voxel size = $0.5 \times 0.5 \times 0.5\,mm^3$) acquired in two partially overlapping volumes, (iii) T2*w multi-echo GRE (TR/TE1/TE2/TE3/TE4/TE5 = 4095/11/23/34/45/56 ms, voxel size = $0.5 \times 0.5 \times 0.5\,mm^3$) acquired in three volumes.

The study was approved by the Institutional Review Board of our institution, and all patients gave written informed consent prior to participation.

Manual CL Detection and Tissue Segmentation. 2014 CLs were manually detected and classified by consensus by one neurologist and one neuroradiologist, both with several years of experience identifying CLs. They analyzed multiple planes and considered, if needed, all three MRI contrasts. Additional lesions which did not fully convince the experts, due to their poor intensity contrast, small size, or appearance on a single contrast, were marked as "possible CLs". The brain tissue was segmented in white and gray matter with the automatic software ANTs [1] for the training tissue labels.

Types of MS CLs. Our experts classified the CLs according to [3]. See Fig. 1 for an example of each type. Within our dataset, 38% of the CLs identified belong to type I, 7% to type II, 44% to type III, and 11% to type IV.

Pre-processing. The images of each subject were linearly registered to the same space (MP2RAGE), and intensity non-uniformities were corrected using a variant of the nonparametric nonuniform intensity normalization algorithm [24].

2.2   Network's Details

The chosen network architecture (Fig. 2) is inspired by the 3D U-Net [5], which has proved successful for several biomedical imaging segmentation tasks, including MS lesion segmentation [12]. Given the limited amount of data, to avoid overfitting we reduced the complexity of the network by removing one resolution layer, and thus the term U-Net⁻. We were interested in a voxel-wise segmentation of CLs with three levels (leukocortical lesions, subpial/intracortical lesions, and background), distinguishing CLs between these primarily in the GM (type II, III, and IV) and these affecting the interface between GM and WM (type I). We chose to work with patches of 68 × 68 × 68 as input yielding an output of 28 × 28 × 28 voxels. We propose an additional output layer (denoting this network as multi-task U-Net⁻) in order to guide the learning procedure. This additional task consisted of brain tissue segmentation in WM, GM, and background. A joint tissue and lesion segmentation has proven already to be promising in [6] regarding WM hyperintensities segmentation. Even though tissue segmentation is not the goal of this work, this architecture allows the network to be aware of the tissue location of the CLs and improved the detection metrics (see Sect. 3). Each lesion was sampled with the same probability, regardless of its size and was balanced with samples from the rest of the brain. The networks were trained with voxel-wise weighted cross-entropy in order to balance the two output maps. In the CLs output map weights of 15, 1, and 0 were assigned to CLs voxels, background, and WMLs respectively in order not to penalize the network if these are segmented (as some leukocortical lesions appear very similar to juxtacortical WMLs). In the tissue map, all the lesions had weight 0 to simplify the tissue segmentation in these regions, whereas other voxels had weight 1. The initial learning rate was set to 1e−4, and Adam was used as optimizer.

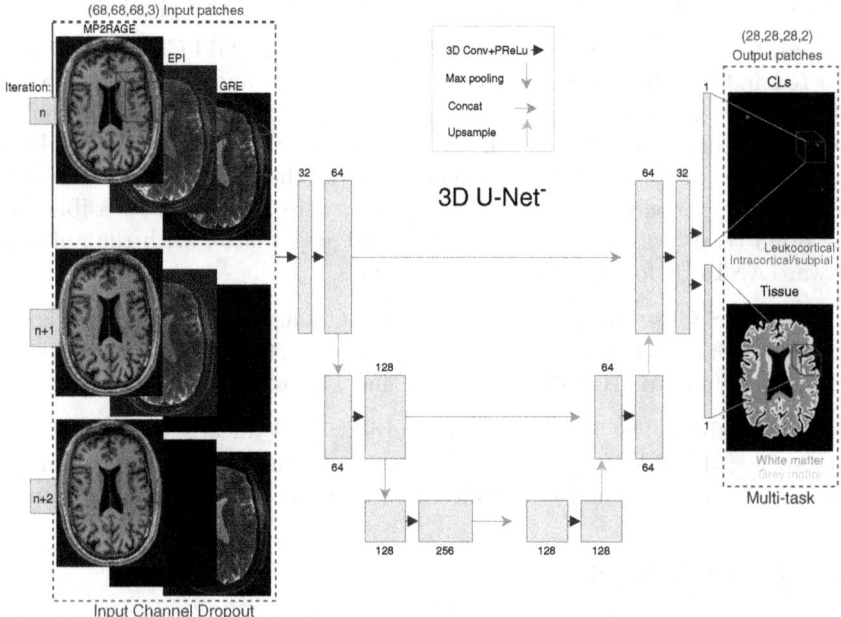

Fig. 2. Scheme of the 3D U-Net⁻ implemented. In input, the three MRI contrasts, with input channel dropout, in output a CLs mask and a tissue segmentation.

Data Augmentation. We applied extensive data augmentation to tackle the risk of overfitting. Random rotations of up to 180 degrees in all three planes and flipping of the axes were applied. Input-channel dropout (ICD) for the two T2*w contrasts was also evaluated. This consists in randomly dropping (eg. multiplying it by zero) one of the two T2*w contrasts at each training iteration. The main motivation is that small portions of the brain were occasionally missing on data from the T2*w GRE sequence, whereas the T2*w EPI shows several artefacts (see Fig. 3). We hypothesized this augmentation technique would improve the network robustness to these images' artefacts (see Sect. 3).

Training was performed on a NVIDIA TITAN X GPU for 50000 iterations and took approximately 22 hours per each fold. The code has been implemented in NiftyNet [11] running on top of Tensorflow. The code and models can be obtained from our research website[1].

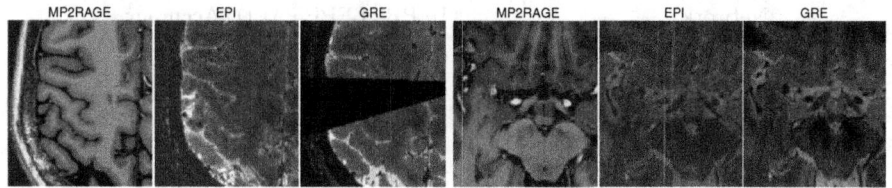

Fig. 3. On the left, a zoomed-in example where part of the brain is missing in the GRE sequence. On the right, artefacts affect the EPI.

2.3   Evaluation

We evaluated U-Net⁻, multi-task U-Net⁻ (adding the tissue segmentation output layer), and multi-task U-Net⁻ with ICD in a 6-folds cross-validation over the 60 cases available. We considered a minimum lesion size of 6 voxels (0.75 µL), much lower than the one previously considered by any method performing automatic MS lesion segmentation. As proposed in [4], we compute the following metrics: absolute volume difference (AVD), CLs lesion-wise true and false positives rates (LTPR and LFPR, respectively), CLs patient-wise true and false positives rates (TPR and FPR, respectively) and CL classification accuracy (Accuracy). Wilcoxon signed-rank test is performed to compare the TPR and FPR patient-wise of the different architectures. Differences are considered significant for p-value < 0.05.

3   Results

Lesion-Wise Analysis. Evaluation metrics of U-Net⁻, Multi-task U-Net⁻, and Multi-task U-Net⁻ + ICD are reported in Table 1. The latter outperforms the

---

[1] https://github.com/Medical-Image-Analysis-Laboratory.

others in all four metrics. This network achieves a CLs LTPR of 67%, LFPR of 42%, AVD of 36%, and CLs classification accuracy of 86%. We analyse the Multi-task U-Net⁻ + ICD LTPR depending on the minimum lesion size and per lesion type (see Fig. 5). As can be observed, CLs Type II are the most challenging ones, with a detection rate of 34% considering 0.75 µL as minimum lesion volume. Increasing the minimum lesion volume to 6µL (as in [9]), the network reaches an overall CL detection rate of 75%, with consistent improvements especially for type II and type III CLs. A qualitative example of the segmentation outputs is shown in Fig. 4 in comparison with the experts' ground truth.

Table 1. Lesion-wise TPR and FPR, patient-wise AVD, and CL classification accuracy reported for the different networks. Statistical differences are found for the AVD between all three methods (p-values < 0.01).

Network	LTPR	LFPR	AVD	Accuracy
3D U-Net⁻	0.63	0.53	1.22	0.82
Multi-task 3D U-Net⁻	0.66	0.44	0.55	0.85
Multi-task 3D U-Net⁻ + ICD	**0.67**	**0.42**	**0.36**	**0.86**

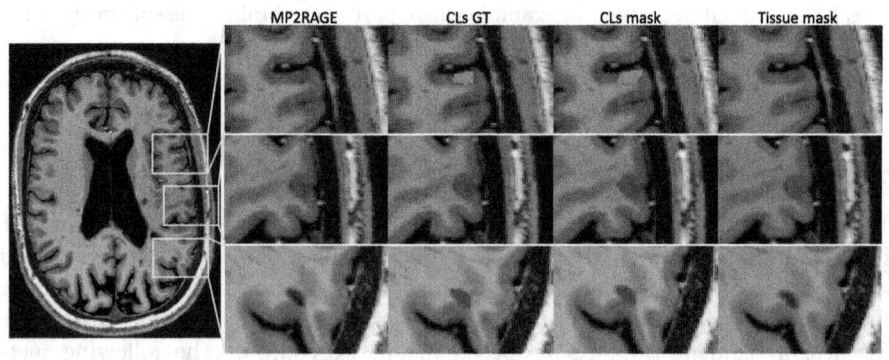

Fig. 4. Examples of CLs (leukocortical in red and subpial/intracortical in green) in the experts' ground truth compared to the output masks of Multi-task 3D U-Net⁻ + ICD. The tissue classes are color coded as red (WM) and green (GM). (Color figure online)

False Positives Analysis. Given the difficulty of the CL detection task, even for experts, we further analyzed the false positive lesions given by our best network architecture. Retrospectively, one of the experts re-evaluated each of the FP and assigned 24% of those (385 lesions) to actual CLs or "possible CLs". This is on one side clear evidence of the difficulty of the task, as two experts missed them, and on the other side, a sign of the practical value of the automatic method proposed, for instance to present candidate lesions to support and speed up the experts' routine MRI analysis.

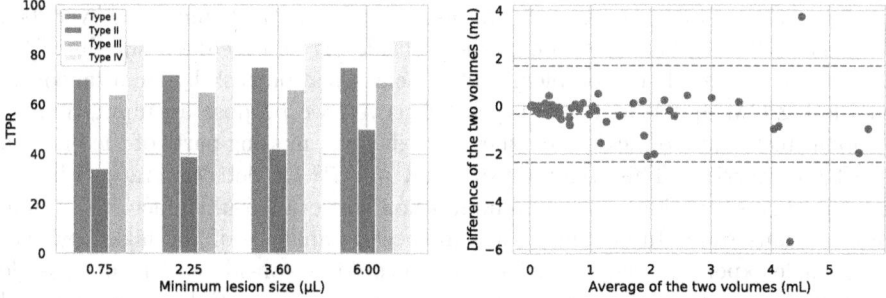

Fig. 5. On the left, the CL LTPR depending on the minimum lesion size considered, per lesion type. On the right, Bland-Altman plot (reference - prediction) of the manually and automatically segmented CL volumes.

Patient-Wise Analysis. The final architecture outperformed the two comparison networks also patient-wise (Fig. 6). Adding the output tissue segmentation map helped reduce false positives in the WM, and therefore the overall FPR. Statistical differences were found between multi-task 3D U-Net⁻ + ICD and the baseline 3D U-Net⁻ for both LTPR and LFPR. Bland-Altman plot of the manually and automatically CLs volume segmented per patient is presented in Fig. 5 right. Aside from two outliers, all differences are within mean ± 1.96 SD, and we do not observe any systematic error estimation bias as a function of the total lesion volume size.

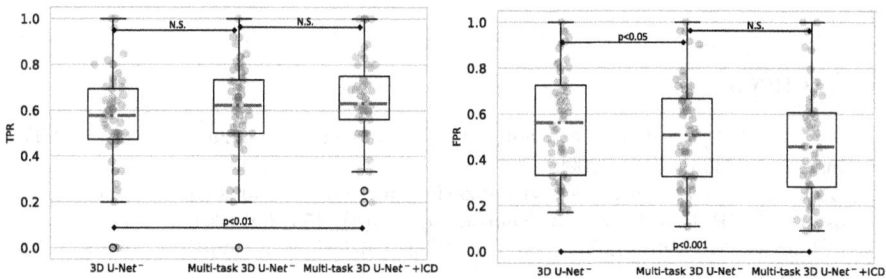

Fig. 6. TPR and FPR patient-wise for the three networks. N.S.: not significant.

4   Conclusion

In this work, we explore the capability of deep learning-based techniques for the automated detection of MS cortical lesions in advanced MRI sequences (MP2RAGE, T2*w EPI, and T2*w GRE) at 7T. To the best of our knowledge, this is the first automated method specifically proposed for MS CL detection at ultra-high field MRI. Furthermore, it differentiates them into two classes: leukocortical and intracortical/subpial.

Our work is evaluated on a large dataset of 60 MS patients including over 2000 CLs manually labelled by two experts. Considering as baseline a simplified 3D U-Net, we increased the complexity of the classification task by simultaneously predicting GM and WM tissue types. Moreover, we propose an input channel dropout technique to tackle the issues of artifacts or missing parts of the brain in the T2*w contrasts. This architecture achieves a 67% CL detection rate with 42% false positives, considering a minimum lesion size of 0.75 μL, much lower than any previous work. Interestingly, a retrospective analysis of the false positives by a single expert showed that 24% of them could be considered CLs or possible CLs missed in the initial labelling. This proves the potential of the proposed method for supporting experts in the tedious process of CL labelling, possibly presenting them with candidate lesions.

Future work will include exploring the T1 quantitative map of the MP2RAGE sequence, and experimenting during training a soft ground truth, which could help coping with the experts' definition of "possible cortical lesion".

Acknowledgments. This project is supported by the European Union's Horizon 2020 research and innovation program under the Marie Sklodowska-Curie project TRA-BIT (agreement No 765148), the Centre d'Imagerie BioMédicale of the University of Lausanne, the Swiss Federal Institute of Technology Lausanne, the University of Geneva, the Centre Hospitalier Universitaire Vaudois, and the Hôpitaux Universitaires de Genève. Erin S Beck is supported by a Career Transition Fellowship from the National Multiple Sclerosis Society. Pascal Sati, Erin S Beck, and Daniel S Reich are supported by the Intramural Research Program of the National Institute of Neurological Disorders and Stroke, National Institutes of Health, Bethesda, Maryland, USA. Ahmed Abdulkadir is supported by the Swiss National Science Foundation grant SNSF 173880.

References

1. Avants, B.B., Tustison, N., Song, G.: Advanced normalization tools (ANTS). Insight J **2**(365), 1–35 (2009)
2. Beck, E.S., et al.: Improved visualization of cortical lesions in multiple sclerosis using 7T MP2RAGE. Am. J. Neuroradiol. **39**(3), 459–466 (2018)
3. Calabrese, M., Filippi, M., Gallo, P.: Cortical lesions in multiple sclerosis. Nat. Rev. Neurol. **6**(8), 438 (2010)
4. Carass, A., et al.: Longitudinal multiple sclerosis lesion segmentation: resource and challenge. NeuroImage **148**, 77–102 (2017)
5. Çiçek, Ö., Abdulkadir, A., Lienkamp, S.S., Brox, T., Ronneberger, O.: 3D U-net: learning dense volumetric segmentation from sparse annotation. In: Ourselin, S., Joskowicz, L., Sabuncu, M.R., Unal, G., Wells, W. (eds.) MICCAI 2016. LNCS, vol. 9901, pp. 424–432. Springer, Cham (2016). https://doi.org/10.1007/978-3-319-46723-8_49
6. Dorent, R., Li, W., Ekanayake, J., Ourselin, S., Vercauteren, T.: Learning joint lesion and tissue segmentation from task-specific hetero-modal datasets. arXiv preprint arXiv:1907.03327 (2019)
7. Fartaria, M.J., et al.: Automated detection of white matter and cortical lesions in early stages of multiple sclerosis. J. Magn. Reson. Imaging **43**(6), 1445–1454 (2016)

8. Fartaria, M.J., Roche, A., Meuli, R., Granziera, C., Kober, T., Bach Cuadra, M.: Segmentation of cortical and subcortical multiple sclerosis lesions based on constrained partial volume modeling. In: Descoteaux, M., Maier-Hein, L., Franz, A., Jannin, P., Collins, D.L., Duchesne, S. (eds.) MICCAI 2017. LNCS, vol. 10435, pp. 142–149. Springer, Cham (2017). https://doi.org/10.1007/978-3-319-66179-7_17

9. Fartaria, M.J., et al.: Automated detection and segmentation of multiple sclerosis lesions using ultra-high-field MP2RAGE. Invest. Radiol. 54(6), 356–364 (2019)

10. García-Lorenzo, D., Francis, S., Narayanan, S., Arnold, D.L., Collins, D.L.: Review of automatic segmentation methods of multiple sclerosis white matter lesions on conventional magnetic resonance imaging. Med. Image Anal. 17(1), 1–18 (2013)

11. Gibson, E., et al.: Niftynet: a deep-learning platform for medical imaging. Comput. Methods Programs Biomed. 158, 113–122 (2018)

12. Kaur, A., Kaur, L., Singh, A.: State-of-the-art segmentation techniques and future directions for multiple sclerosis brain lesions. Arch. Comput. Methods Eng. 1–27 (2020)

13. Kilsdonk, I.D., et al.: Increased cortical grey matter lesion detection in multiple sclerosis with 7 T MRI: a post-mortem verification study. Brain 139(5), 1472–1481 (2016)

14. Kober, T., et al.: MP2RAGE multiple sclerosis magnetic resonance imaging at 3 T. Invest. Radiol. 47(6), 346–352 (2012)

15. La Rosa, F., et al.: Multiple sclerosis cortical and WM lesion segmentation at 3T MRI: a deep learning method based on FLAIR and MP2RAGE. NeuroImage: Clin. 102335 (2020). https://doi.org/10.1016/j.nicl.2020.102335. https://linkinghub.elsevier.com/retrieve/pii/S2213158220301728

16. La Rosa, F., et al.: Deep learning-based detection of cortical lesions in multiple sclerosis patients with FLAIR, DIR, and MP2RAGE MRI sequences. Multiple Sclerosis J. 25(CONF), 131–356 (2019)

17. Magliozzi, R., et al.: A gradient of neuronal loss and meningeal inflammation in multiple sclerosis. Ann. Neurol. 68(4), 477–493 (2010)

18. Maranzano, J., et al.: Comparison of multiple sclerosis cortical lesion types detected by multicontrast 3T and 7T MRI. Am. J. Neuroradiol. 40(7), 1162–1169 (2019)

19. Marques, J.P., Kober, T., Krueger, G., van der Zwaag, W., Van de Moortele, P.F., Gruetter, R.: MP2RAGE, a self bias-field corrected sequence for improved segmentation and T1-mapping at high field. Neuroimage 49(2), 1271–1281 (2010)

20. Sati, P., et al.: Rapid, high-resolution, whole-brain, susceptibility-based MRI of multiple sclerosis. Multiple Sclerosis J. 20(11), 1464–1470 (2014)

21. Sati, P., et al.: Rapid MR susceptibility imaging of the brain using segmented 3D echo-planar imaging (3D EPI) and its clinical applications. Magn. FLASH 68, 26–32 (2017)

22. Thompson, A.J., et al.: Diagnosis of multiple sclerosis: 2017 revisions of the McDonald criteria. Lancet Neurol. 17(2), 162–173 (2018)

23. Treaba, C.A., et al.: Longitudinal characterization of cortical lesion development and evolution in multiple sclerosis with 7.0-T MRI. Radiology 291(3), 740–749 (2019)

24. Tustison, N.J., et al.: N4ITK: improved N3 bias correction. IEEE Trans. Med. Imaging 29(6), 1310–1320 (2010)

Deep Attentive Panoptic Model for Prostate Cancer Detection Using Biparametric MRI Scans

Xin Yu[1], Bin Lou[1], Donghao Zhang[1], David Winkel[1,2], Nacim Arrahmane[1], Mamadou Diallo[1], Tongbai Meng[1], Heinrich von Busch[3], Robert Grimm[3], Berthold Kiefer[3], Dorin Comaniciu[1], and Ali Kamen[1(✉)]

[1] Digital Technology and Innovation, Siemens Healthineers, Princeton, NJ, USA
ali.kamen@siemens-healthineers.com
[2] Universitätsspital Basel, Basel, Switzerland
[3] Diagnostic Imaging, Siemens Healthcare, Erlangen, Germany

Abstract. Multi-parametric MRI (mp-MRI) has recently been established in major guidelines as a first-line diagnostic test for men suspected of having prostate cancer (PCa) primarily to detect and classify clinically significant lesions. However, widespread utilization is still challenged by 1) the difficulty of interpretation specifically for radiologists less experienced in reading mp-MRI scans, and 2) decreased productivity associated with increased time spent per case for reading these complex scans. Deep learning based lesion detection and segmentation methods have been proposed for radiologists to perform their tasks more accurately and efficiently. In this work, we present a novel panoptic lesion detection and segmentation method with both semantic and instance branches as well as an attention module to optimally incorporate both local and global image features. In a free-response receiver operating characteristics (FROC) analysis for lesion sensitivity on an independent dataset with 243 patients, our method has achieved 89% sensitivity and 85% with 0.94 and 0.62 false positives per patient, respectively. Using the proposed method, we have achieved an unprecedented area under ROC curve (AUC) of 0.897 in identifying clinically significant cases.

Keywords: Prostate cancer detection · Panoptic segmentation · Biparametric MRI

1 Introduction

Prostate Cancer (PCa) ranks as the second most frequent cancer and fifth leading cause of death in men worldwide [1]. Early PCa detection plays a crucial role in cancer treatment. Multi-parametric MRI (mp-MRI) and biparametric MRI (bp-MRI) based PCa diagnosis have been shown to be effective and lead to a superior

---

ProstateAI Clinical Collaborators–A list of members and affiliations appears at the end of the paper.

© Springer Nature Switzerland AG 2020
A. L. Martel et al. (Eds.): MICCAI 2020, LNCS 12264, pp. 594–604, 2020.
https://doi.org/10.1007/978-3-030-59719-1_58

biopsy yield rate as compared to standard systematic biopsy based on ultrasound guidance [7,14,15,23]. Computer-aided diagnosis (CAD) of PCa using mp-MRI or bp-MRI scans have become an active research area and many methods have recently been proposed [19,24]. However, there are still some major challenges for PCa detection. For example, there is a relatively high feature similarity between benign prostatic hyperplasia (BPH) and high grade PCa, specifically in the central/transition zone. Furthermore, for some clinically significant cases, there are only subtle differences between lesion features and those from normal prostate parenchyma. These together with varying shapes and sizes of lesions, and alignment errors across various imaging contrasts, make it very hard for a lesion detection system to capture all possible lesions (high sensitivity) with low false positive rate (high specificity).

Many attempts have been made to use convolutional neural networks (CNNs) for lesion detection (for example [3,17,19]). Currently, most of the methods for PCa detection are based on the semantic segmentation of lesions, where the problem is formulated as a combined detection and segmentation on the entire MRI images [2,20]. Contrastingly, region proposal based detection and instance segmentation have also been extensively explored [3,17] and applied in many other imaging tasks, but not particularly in PCa detection. While region based approaches utilizing local features have been pursued for the PCa lesion classification [19], to the best of our knowledge, it has not been used so far in the context of lesion detection. This could be due to the fact that region proposal based methods tend to pay more attention to local features whereas PCa lesion detection task is believed to work better when more global context is utilized. Recently, a new panoptic segmentation approach has been proposed [9], which aims to solve the semantic and instance segmentation in a single network, providing a novel way to utilize both local and global image features. Zhang et al. [25] first applied panoptic segmentation approach for medical image analysis. They improved the nuclei segmentation by combining semantic segmentation and instance segmentation and optimized the sum of loss functions coming from both branches. Liu et al. [13] further improved this work and proposed a feature fusion mechanism in the instance segmentation branch.

While observing radiologists reading prostate MR scans, we noticed that the task appears to be clearly demarcated into two steps of identifying suspicious areas as potential lesions based on a global context and then probing candidates carefully in the local context to separate them into clinically significant and non-significant classes. The overall scheme lends itself nicely to the semantic and instance segmentation methodology. Inspired by this and the related work mentioned above, and with the goal of learning both global and local features to detect and segment lesions in a unified framework, we propose a deep attentive panoptive model. In this model, we specifically devise to have branches of both semantic segmentation and instance segmentation. The semantic segmentation is focusing primarily on the difference between the general features of lesions and those from prostate parenchyma, while ignoring as much as possible variabilities of lesions-specific features. On the other hand, in the instance segmentation,

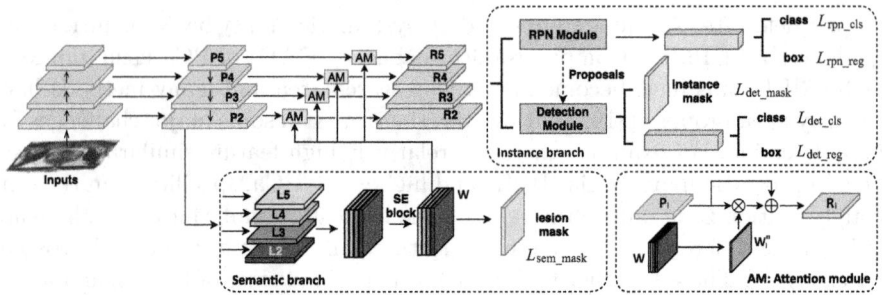

Fig. 1. Illustration of the overall architecture. Convolutional blocks are omitted for simplicity. L_{sem_mask}: semantic segmentation loss, L_{rpn_cls}: RPN classification loss, L_{rpn_reg}: RPN regression loss, L_{det_reg}: detection module regression loss, L_{det_cls}: detection module classification loss and L_{det_mask}: instance segmentation loss.

the focus is more on local features representing also the variabilities of individual lesions. Furthermore, we devised an attention module to perform more accurate detection by bringing in relevant information (at global feature level) from the semantic segmentation branch to the instance branch. We evaluated our proposed method on an independent test dataset with 243 patients based on three criteria of lesion-level free-response receiver operating characteristics (FROC), Dice coefficient for the detected lesions' contours, and patient-level detection of clinically significant cases using area under the ROC curve (AUC).

2 Methods

2.1 Architecture

The overall architecture of our proposed prototype system is depicted in Fig. 1. The network consists of a feature extraction backbone, a semantic segmentation branch, an instance segmentation branch, and an attention module. The details of our design are explained in the following subsections.

Feature Extraction Backbone. We adopted the deep residual network [4] with 50 layers (ResNet50) and a feature pyramid network (FPN) [11] as our backbone feature extraction network. To make it more suitable for our problem, we modified the starting filter size to 48 with the filter size increasing in a similar pattern as in ResNet50. The output of each stage of the ResNet50 all passed through 1×1 conv. layers separately resulting in a unified channel dimension of 192 and merged with corresponding top-down up-sampled features by element-wise addition [11].

Semantic Segmentation Branch. The features at different resolutions generated by the backbone (P_2, P_3, P_4, P_5) were inputs to the semantic segmentation branch. The input feature map sizes were $\frac{1}{4}$, $\frac{1}{8}$, $\frac{1}{16}$, and $\frac{1}{32}$ of the original image size, respectively. To generate a semantic feature map that fully exploited all features from different levels, we first used up-sampling blocks consisting of a 3×3 conv. layer, a group norm [22] layer, and bilinear up-sampling layers on P_3, P_4 and P_5 to match the size of feature P_2. The up-sampled features were named L_3, L_4 and L_5. A 3×3 convolutional block and a group norm were also used to calculate feature L_2 from P_2. All L_2 to L_5 features have a unified channel dimension of 96. We concatenated L_2-L_5 and used a Squeeze-and-Excitation (SE) block [5] with a dimension reduction ratio of 8 to re-weight each channel. This design explicitly adjusted contributions of different feature levels to the lesion semantic segmentation. The output of the SE block further went through a convolutional block consisting of 3 conv. layers with kernel size 1, 3, and 3 respectively, to reduce the channel dimension to 96, resulting in the feature map W. The re-weighted feature map W went through another 1×1 conv. layer and 4× up-sampling to achieve the original image size for final semantic segmentation. We believe that adding a lesion semantic segmentation branch facilitated the model to discriminate the lesion feature from a global prospective and also provided supplementary information to distinguish lesions from parenchyma.

Instance Segmentation Branch. The instance segmentation branch in our model is an extension of the Mask R-CNN [3] design with one major difference in the input features. In the original Mask R-CNN design, A Region Proposal Network (RPN) directly utilized features extracted by the backbone network (P_2-P_5) to generate region proposals. Proposals with smaller and larger sizes were assigned to feature levels with higher and lower resolutions, respectively. We believe that this feature assignment is not optimal and does not fully exploit the information from different feature levels. The higher resolution features contain richer instance information whereas lower resolution features have more semantic information, so these types of information should be considered as complementary to one another. Therefore, instead of using the feature extracted by the backbone (P_2-P_5) directly, we applied an attention module to refine the features P_2-P_5 and used those refined features (R_2-R_5) as inputs to the instance branch to generate region proposals. This can also be viewed as a multiscale strategy, which has been proven to be efficient in our previous work [24]. Moreover, in our design the RPN module can be viewed as localizing proposed candidate lesions. Candidates generated by the RPN may not be accurate enough because anchor sizes are predefined. The proposed regions were further analyzed in the detection module, where a binary classification is applied to distinguish lesions and non-lesion candidates. We observed this lesion qualification step significantly improved detection performance by filtering out false positives.

Attention Module. We designed an attention module to better integrate the global and local features from the aforementioned two branches. The input to the attention module was the feature map W coming from the semantic branch. The feature map W integrated multi-level features coming from the backbone network, which were then further re-weighted by the SE block to have higher emphasis on important features. Since the feature map W was derived from the semantic branch, it can provide complementary spatial information once shared with the instance segmentation branch. To incorporate feature W into the instance branch, feature $W \in \mathbb{R}^{C \times W \times H}$ first went through a 1×1 conv. layer to get compressed into a feature map with only one channel, $W' \in \mathbb{R}^{1 \times W \times H}$, and got activated by a rectified linear unit (ReLU). W' further went through a 1×1 conv. layer and got activated by a sigmoid function to achieve the weight map denoted by W''. After that, W'' was down-sampled to the size of P_2-P_5 to compute refined features R_2-R_5. For each feature map P_i, the operation can be formulated as:

$$R_i = P_i \otimes DS_i(W'') \oplus P_i \qquad (1)$$

where DS_i means down-sampling to the size of P_i. Moreover, $\otimes$ and $\oplus$ represent element-wise multiplication and addition, respectively. In general, the attention module can help to suppress features located outside lesions' regions of interest (ROIs) and enhance features within lesions' ROIs.

2.2   Loss Function

The final loss function is denoted as follows:

$$L_{total} = L_{sem\_mask} + L_{rpn\_reg} + L_{rpn\_cls} + L_{det\_reg} + L_{det\_cls} + L_{det\_mask}$$
$$(2)$$

where L_{sem_mask} is the binary cross entropy loss for the lesion segmentation in the semantic branch. L_{rpn_cls} and L_{rpn_reg} are the losses coming from the RPN module of the instance branch, representing the cross entropy classification loss and smoothed L1 bounding box regression loss, respectively. L_{det_reg}, L_{det_cls} and L_{det_mask} are coming from the detection module of the instance branch. L_{det_cls} is the cross entropy classification loss aiming at filtering out non-lesion proposals. L_{det_reg} is another smoothed L1 loss for bounding box regression. L_{det_mask} is the binary cross entropy loss for the lesion segmentation. All loss functions are displayed next to the corresponding network output in Fig. 1.

3   Experiments and Results

3.1   Datasets and Implementations

Training and validation were performed on a large dataset of 1502 cases acquired from 4 different institutions under either approved or exempted Institutional Review Board (IRB) protocols. The ground truth labels were built based on the Prostate Imaging Reporting and Data System (PI-RADS) scores noted in radiology reports and carefully reviewed/re-annotated in 3D by an expert radiologist with 4 years of experience. PIRADS ≥ 3 lesions were considered as clinically significant. The counts of PIRADS 3, 4, and 5 lesions in the training set were 239, 373, and 342, respectively. There were 769 clinically significant (positive) cases and 733 negative cases. The evaluations were performed on independent collection of 243 cases from the ProstateX challenge public dataset [12], which included 108 positive and 135 negative cases. The breakdown of PIRADS 3, 4, and 5 within the testing set was 29, 54, and 37, respectively. The system input included bi-parametric MR contrasts of T2-Weighted (T2W) and Diffusion-Weighted Images (DWI). For DWI, we used both the Apparent Diffusion Coefficient (ADC), which is a semi-quantitative parametric map derived from multiple sequences of DWI with various b-values and DWI b-2000 images. DWI ADC and DWI b-2000 images were registered to the corresponding T2W series and were all re-sampled to the size of 240×240×30 with a voxel spacing of 0.5 mm×0.5 mm×3 mm. All images were normalized to [0,1] to facilitate training: T2W images were linearly normalized based on 0.05 and 99.5 percentiles of pixels' intensity; DWI ADC images were normalized by a constant value; DWI b-2000 images were normalized by the median intensity of the corresponding DWI b-50 images within the prostate gland region. All images were concatenated and used as the input to the network.

The proposed method was implemented using Pytorch. The total loss of the network was optimized by Adam, which is a method for stochastic optimization, using the learning rate of 10^{-4} and trained for 100 epochs. Common data augmentations, including shift, rotation and vertical flip were adopted during training. Additionally, each slice was randomly cropped to 128×128 while assuring lesions were not being cropped. During inference, all slices were center cropped to 128×128. All networks were trained in 2D, whereas evaluations were all performed in 3D. During the evaluation, box predictions from different slices were mapped to the same plane and merged according to their Intersection over Union (IoU). Boxes belonging to neighboring slices were merged to form a 3D cube in order to be evaluated in 3D. In this process, we also used a non-maximum suppression (NMS) as described in [6].

3.2 Experimental Results

Model Comparison. We considered a U-Net [18] with residual blocks [4], a Mask R-CNN [3] and a Panoptic FPN [8] for comparison to our proposed method. We used the FROC analysis, which characterizes the relationship between detection sensitivity and false positive rate per case, for comparing performances of the methods. A true positive was identified if the IoU between detection and ground truth bounding box was greater than 0.4. For scenarios in which the network output did not include bounding boxes, we identified probability map extrema locations and used 10 mm distance to ground truth masks as the threshold [12]. In order to assess the importance of the attention module and its integration into the semantic branch, we included in our ablation experiments, an Panoptice FPN and our proposed method in two versions with and without the attention module. The FROC curves of all models are displayed in Fig. 2(A).

As shown in Table 1, Panoptic FPN is the best performing reference model at the sensitivity of 89%. The attention module further improves Panoptic FPN by lowering the false positive rate from an average of 1.75 to 1.21 per patient. The

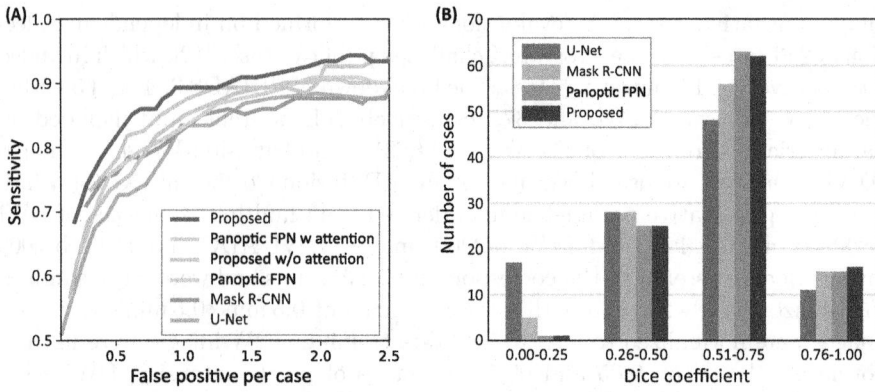

Fig. 2. Comparison of model performance on (A) FROC analysis and (B) the Dice coefficients distribution at the sensitivity of 86.7%.

best performing model is the proposed one, which included the attention module and has an average false positive rate of 0.94 per patient. Furthermore, our proposed model always achieved the highest sensitivity for a given false positive rate as shown in the first two right columns of Table 1. Figure 3 demonstrates two examples of detected lesions based on four different approaches.

Dice Analysis. One very important drawback of applying a U-Net-like semantic segmentation model for PCa lesion detection and its corresponding evaluation method as performed in [2,12] is that high overlap level between a true detection and the ground truth cannot always be guaranteed. An extreme example is shown in Fig. 3 (red arrow in the top left image). Although the detection based on the probability map maximum falls correctly within the ground truth mask, the lesion boundary is hugely under-estimated. In order to properly investigate this, we have analyzed the distribution of Dice coefficients between detected lesions and the corresponding ground truth masks. This evaluation was done only on true positive lesions, and our objective was to assess how well an approach

Table 1. Sensitivity (TPR) and false positive per patient (FP) comparison among different models and ablation experiments.

Models	FP@TPR = 89%	FP@TPR = 85%	TPR@FP = 1.0	TPR@FP = 0.75
UNet	3.02	1.32	83.2%	74.9%
Mask R-CNN	2.51	1.14	82.7%	79.3%
Panoptic FPN	1.75	1.14	82.9%	80.2%
Proposed w/o AM	1.58	1.02	84.9%	81.0%
Panoptic FPN w AM	1.21	0.85	87.3%	83.7%
Proposed	**0.94**	**0.62**	**89.3%**	**85.8%**

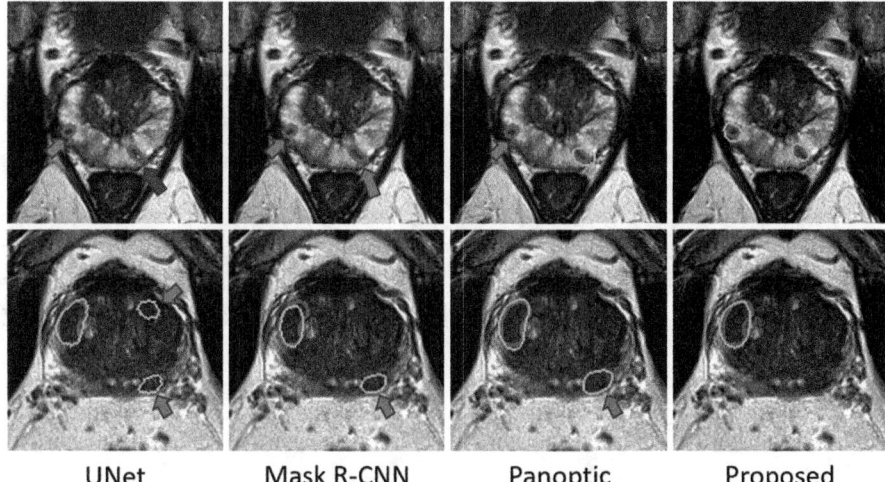

UNet   Mask R-CNN   Panoptic   Proposed

Fig. 3. Visualization of detection results on two sample cases (rows) using different approaches (columns). The blue and yellow contours represent ground truth and model detection, respectively. An orange arrow indicates a false negative detection and a green arrow indicates a false positive one. (Color figure online)

can estimate lesion size. In this analysis, false positives (FP) or false negatives (FN) did not have any influence. Furthermore, we chose an appropriate model-dependant operating point to have the identical sensitivity of 86.7% for all the models.

According to the result in Fig. 2(B), U-Net has many detected lesions with a Dice score less than 0.5, especially in the range [0, 0.25], while the other methods have comparable numbers of true positives in each range. Mask R-CNN has a slightly worse Dice distribution as compared to Panoptic FPN and the proposed method, which could be related to utilizing the semantic branch in these two approaches.

Case Level Study. Case level suspicion score reflects whether a patient has at least one clinical significant lesion, indicating the necessity for that patient to undergo a biopsy procedure. In this analysis, we defined the maximum value in the U-Net heatmap output or maximum value of the network output box score as the suspicion score of the case. For all these cases, we also had the ground truth from a radiologist in form of the Prostate Imaging Reporting and Data System (PI-RADS) score [16]. According to PI-RADS guideline, PI-RADS scores larger or equal to 3 and PI-RADS scores larger or equal to 4, can be considered at least equivocally clinically significant or likely clinically significant cancer cases, respectively.

We compared the AUC between PI-RADS score larger or equal to 3 and PI-RADS score larger or equal to 4 based on varying thresholds on the computed

Table 2. Case level AUC comparison.

PI-RADS	UNet	Mask R-CNN	Panoptic FPN	Proposed
PI-RADS $\geq$ 3	0.815	0.875	0.872	**0.897**
PI-RADS $\geq$ 4	0.841	0.914	0.908	**0.924**

suspicious scores from various models. The results are shown in Table 2. Our proposed method achieved the highest case level AUC as compared to other models, which means our method has a better discriminating power in detecting clinically significant cases.

4   Conclusions

In this paper, we presented a novel panoptic model for prostate cancer lesion detection and segmentation using bp-MRI scans. We designed a semantic branch and trained it jointly with an instance branch to capture both global and local image features. Furthermore, we adopted an attention module to combine features from these two steps and reduce FPs in a cooperative manner. Our experiments on an independent test dataset demonstrated that the proposed approach improves the performance of detecting clinically significant PCa cases. This result is consistent with previous studies on the attention mechanism, although employed in different forms ([10,21]). We believe this model has the advantage, which stems from facilitating the integration of complementary information from different sources. Although the proposed model was originally designed for PCa lesion detection, the strategy presented in this work has the potential to be extended to other medical imaging applications or even general computer vision tasks. Future work can be focused on the effect of integrating different semantic branches in the instance segmentation, and the generalizability of the proposed approach to other detection problems.

Disclaimer. The concepts and information presented in this paper are based on research results that are not commercially available.

ProstateAI Clinical Collaborators. *Henkjan Huisman[4], Angela Tong[5], Tobias Penzkofer[6], Ivan Shabunin[7], Moon Hyung Choi[8], Qingsong Yang[9], Dieter Szolar[10]*
[4]Radboud University Medical Center, Nijmegen, NL. [5]New York University, New York City, NY, USA. [6]Charité, Universitätsmedizin Berlin, Berlin, Germany. [7]Patero Clinic, Moscow, Russia. [8]Eunpyeong St. Mary's Hospital, Catholic University of Korea, Seoul, Republic of Korea. [9]Radiology Department, Changhai Hospital of Shanghai, China. [10]Diagnostikum Graz Süd-West, Graz, Austria.

References

1. Bray, F., Ferlay, J., Soerjomataram, I., Siegel, R.L., Torre, L.A., Jemal, A.: Global cancer statistics 2018: GLOBOCAN estimates of incidence and mortality worldwide for 36 cancers in 185 countries. CA: Cancer J. Clin. **68**(6), 394–424 (2018)
2. Cao, R., et al.: Joint prostate cancer detection and gleason score prediction in MP-MRI via FocalNet. IEEE TMI **38**(11), 2496–2506 (2019)
3. He, K., Gkioxari, G., Dollár, P., Girshick, R.: Mask R-CNN. In: Proceedings of ICCV, pp. 2961–2969 (2017)
4. He, K., Zhang, X., Ren, S., Sun, J.: Deep residual learning for image recognition. In: Proceedings of CVPR, pp. 770–778 (2016)
5. Hu, J., Shen, L., Sun, G.: Squeeze-and-excitation networks. In: Proceedings of CVPR, pp. 7132–7141 (2018)
6. Jaeger, P.F., et al.: Retina U-net: Embarrassingly simple exploitation of segmentation supervision for medical object detection. In: Machine Learning for Health Workshop, pp. 171–183 (2020)
7. Kasivisvanathan, V., et al.: MRI-targeted or standard biopsy for prostate-cancer diagnosis. NEJM **378**(19), 1767–1777 (2018)
8. Kirillov, A., Girshick, R., He, K., Dollár, P.: Panoptic feature pyramid networks. In: Proceedings of CVPR, pp. 6399–6408 (2019)
9. Kirillov, A., He, K., Girshick, R., Rother, C., Dollár, P.: Panoptic segmentation. In: Proceedings of CVPR, pp. 9404–9413 (2019)
10. Li, Y., et al.: Attention-guided unified network for panoptic segmentation. In: Proceedings of CVPR, pp. 7026–7035 (2019)
11. Lin, T.Y., Dollár, P., Girshick, R., He, K., Hariharan, B., Belongie, S.: Feature pyramid networks for object detection. In: Proceedings of CVPR, pp. 2117–2125 (2017)
12. Litjens, G., Debats, O., Barentsz, J., Karssemeijer, N., Huisman, H.: Computer-aided detection of prostate cancer in MRI. IEEE TMI **33**(5), 1083–1092 (2014)
13. Liu, D., Zhang, D., Song, Y., Zhang, C., Zhang, F., O'Donnell, L., Cai, W.: Nuclei segmentation via a deep panoptic model with semantic feature fusion. In: Proceedings of the International Joint Conference on Artificial Intelligence, pp. 861–868. AAAI Press (2019)
14. Loffroy, R., et al.: Current role of multiparametric magnetic resonance imaging for prostate cancer. Quant. Imaging Med. Surg. **5**(5), 754 (2015)
15. Pinto, F., et al.: Imaging in prostate cancer diagnosis: present role and future perspectives. Urol. Int. **86**(4), 373–382 (2011)
16. Purysko, A.S., Rosenkrantz, A.B., Barentsz, J.O., Weinreb, J.C., Macura, K.J.: PI-RADS version 2: a pictorial update. Radiographics **36**(5), 1354–1372 (2016)
17. Ren, S., He, K., Girshick, R., Sun, J.: Faster R-CNN: towards real-time object detection with region proposal networks. In: Advances in Neural Information Processing Systems, pp. 91–99 (2015)
18. Ronneberger, O., Fischer, P., Brox, T.: U-Net: convolutional networks for biomedical image segmentation. In: Navab, N., Hornegger, J., Wells, W.M., Frangi, A.F. (eds.) MICCAI 2015. LNCS, vol. 9351, pp. 234–241. Springer, Cham (2015). https://doi.org/10.1007/978-3-319-24574-4_28
19. Song, Y., et al.: Computer-aided diagnosis of prostate cancer using a deep convolutional neural network from multiparametric MRI. J. Magn. Reson. Imaging **48**(6), 1570–1577 (2018)

20. Tsehay, Y.K., et al.: Convolutional neural network based deep-learning architecture for prostate cancer detection on multiparametric magnetic resonance images. In: Medical Imaging 2017: Computer-Aided Diagnosis, vol. 10134, p. 1013405. International Society for Optics and Photonics (2017)
21. Wang, Y., et al.: Deep attentive features for prostate segmentation in 3D transrectal ultrasound. IEEE TMI **38**(12), 2768–2778 (2019)
22. Wu, Y., He, K.: Group normalization. In: Proceedings of ECCV), pp. 3–19 (2018)
23. Yacoub, J.H., Verma, S., Moulton, J.S., Eggener, S., Oto, A.: Imaging-guided prostate biopsy: conventional and emerging techniques. Radiographics **32**(3), 819–837 (2012)
24. Yu, X., et al.: False positive reduction using multiscale contextual features for prostate cancer detection in multi-parametric MRI scans. In: Proceedings of ISBI, pp. 1355–1359. IEEE (2020)
25. Zhang, D., et al.: Panoptic segmentation with an end-to-end cell R-CNN for pathology image analysis. In: Frangi, A.F., Schnabel, J.A., Davatzikos, C., Alberola-López, C., Fichtinger, G. (eds.) MICCAI 2018. LNCS, vol. 11071, pp. 237–244. Springer, Cham (2018). https://doi.org/10.1007/978-3-030-00934-2_27

Shape Models and Landmark Detection

Graph Reasoning and Shape Constraints for Cardiac Segmentation in Congenital Heart Defect

Tao Liu, Yun Tian$^{(\boxtimes)}$, Shifeng Zhao, and Xiaoying Huang

Beijing Normal University, Beijing 100875, China
tianyun@bnu.edu.cn

Abstract. Congenital heart defects (CHD) are the most common type of birth defect. The structures of the heart or great vessels of CHD patients have significant variations, which limit the application scope of existing whole heart segmentation methods. To solve this limitation, we propose a CHD segmentation method based on graph reasoning and shape constraints in the study. Graph reasoning is used to capture global relations, through projecting a set of features into the interaction space and then makes relational reasoning. After reasoning, relation-aware features are mapped back to the original feature map. The shape constraints are used to calculate the shape information of each substructure of the heart, this prior knowledge on shape constraints can improve the prediction accuracy. Our method is validated with 68 3D CT datasets with congenital heart defect. The evaluation results show that our method can increase the mean Dice score by 2.1% compared with the state-of-the-art methods. Code: https://github.com/liut969/CHD-Seg.

Keywords: Congenital heart defect · Segmentation · Shape constraint · Graph reasoning

1 Introduction

A congenital heart defect (CHD) is a defect in the structure of the heart or great vessels that is present from birth [9]. The structure of the heart and great vessel connections have been widely concerned due to its importance of the diagnosis and adjuvant treatment of heart diseases. However, in CHD patients, the cardiac structure varies greatly and the connection of great vessels is disordered. Therefore, the fully automated segmentation heart of CHD patients still remains a challenge.

The current methods of heart substructure segmentation mainly include two-stage segmentation and multi-view segmentation. The two-stage segmentation method first extracts region of interest (ROI), which is then fed into a CNN for subsequent classification [3,17], whereas the multi-view method trains multi-planar CNNs (axial, sagittal, and coronal views) to segment different views [8,13]. However, the structure of the heart or great vessels of CHD patients have

© Springer Nature Switzerland AG 2020
A. L. Martel et al. (Eds.): MICCAI 2020, LNCS 12264, pp. 607–616, 2020.
https://doi.org/10.1007/978-3-030-59719-1_59

significant variations, which limit the application scope of existing whole heart segmentation methods. For CHD, some semi-automated [10] and full-automated [14,16] whole heart segmentation methods have been proposed, but they have two limitations. First, they do not make use of global information since an individual layer can only capture local information. Second, prior knowledge about the shapes of the heart can improve the prediction accuracy, but they do not fully use shape information.

In this work, a CHD segmentation method based on graph reasoning and shape constraints is proposed. Inspired by the graph-based global reasoning networks [1], global reasoning is used to directly perform global relation reasoning. In this way, relation reasoning can be performed in early stages of a CNN model. Similar to the previous report [15], prior knowledge is added to the loss function to make the network focus on shape information during the training process. Our contributions are summarized as follows:

- A U-Net like network with graph-based global reasoning are designed. Graph reasoning is used in relation reasoning, through projecting a set of features into the interaction space for relation reasoning. After that, relation-aware features are mapped back to the original feature map;
- The shape constraints are employed to calculate the shape information. We add prior knowledge to the loss function to improve the prediction accuracy;
- Our method is validated with 68 3D CT datasets with CHD [14]. The evaluation results show that our method can increase the mean Dice score by 2.1% compared with the state-of-the-art methods.

2   Methods

2.1   Network Architecture

With U-Net [12] as a submodule of our framework, the contracting path and the expanding path in U-Net are retained, and all the standard square-kernel convolutional layers are replaced by Asymmetric Convolution Block [2] to enhance the skeletons at every layer. Moreover, a graph-based global reasoning unit [1] is added to the bottom of our framework to improve the global information. Therefore, a U-Net shaped network with graph-based global reasoning is designed in this study. The entire architecture of the network is illustrated in Fig. 1.

Asymmetric convolution blocks (Fig. 1(a)) are introduced to the contracting path and the expanding path in order to enhance the skeletons at every layer. Asymmetric convolution block (ACB) is an innovative structure as a building block to replace the standard convolutional layers without introducing any hyper-parameter. As for the repsquare-kernel $d \times d$ layer, the constructed ACB consists of three parallel layers with $d \times d$, $1 \times d$, and $d \times 1$ kernels, and the outputs are summed up to enrich the feature space. It should be noted that batch normalization (BN) is respectively applied on the three parallel layers, and then a rectified linear units (ReLU) is applied in the three BN-fused branches.

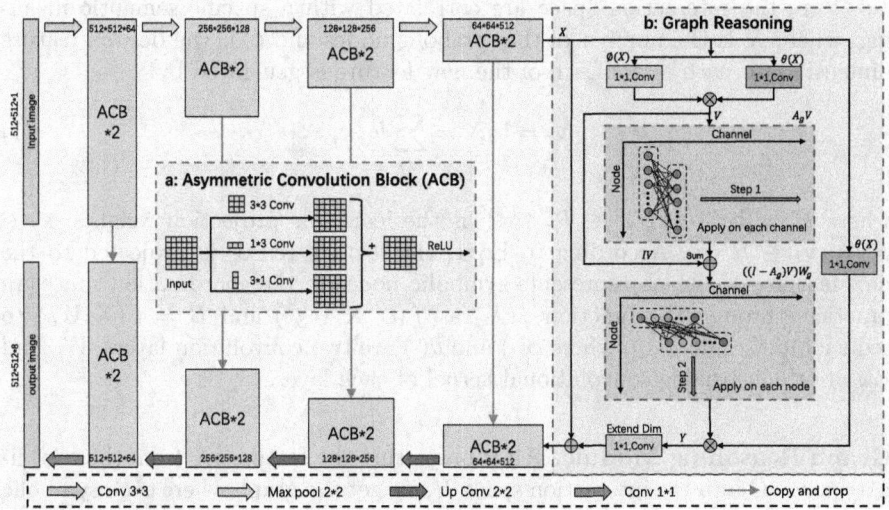

Fig. 1. Architecture of the proposed framework. (a): Asymmetric convolution block (ACB). For example, every 3×3 layer is replaced with an ACB comprising three layers with 3×3, 1×3 and 3×1 kernels, respectively, and their outputs are summed up. (b): Graph Reasoning. The architecture of the graph-based global reasoning unit, the input features X and output Y have the same size. More details are provided below.

2.2   Graph Reasoning

Commonsense knowledge graph is often used to describe different correlations among entities, and this correlation can be expressed in any form [7]. A knowledge graph $G = (\mathcal{V}, \mathcal{E}, A)$ is typically defined by its nodes $\mathcal{V}$, edges $\mathcal{E}$ and adjacent matrix A describing the edge weights. Based on this general formula, graph reasoning is usually operated on the feature maps $X \in \mathcal{R}^{H \times W \times C}$, where H and W are the height and weight of feature maps and C is the channel number.

The core of graph reasoning consists of three modules. First, the features X are projected from the coordinate space Ω to the features $\mathcal{V}$ in a latent interaction space $\mathcal{H}$, where each symbol node stores the new feature as its state. After that, a new fully-connected graph A_g is constructed in the interaction space $\mathcal{H}$, and a general graph convolution is applied on each node feature of the graph A_g to model and reason the context relationship between each pair of nodes. Finally, a reverse projection is performed to map the relation-aware features back to the original coordinate space, providing complementary features for the following layers to join forces of global reasoning. Each module of the graph reasoning used in this work are introduced below (Fig. 1(b)).

Local-to-Semantic Module. For a set of input feature tensors $X \in \mathcal{R}^{H \times W \times C}$ from convolution layers, our target is to project original features to the interaction space $\mathcal{H}$ by the projection function $f(\cdot)$. The new features $V = f(X) \in$

$R^{N \times C}$ in the interaction space are correlated with a specific semantic meaning, where N is the number of the symbolic nodes and C is the desired feature dimension for each node. Each of the new feature is generated by

$$\mathbf{v}_i = \mathbf{b}_i X = \sum_{\forall j} b_{ij} \mathbf{x}_j, \qquad (1)$$

where $B = [\mathbf{b}_1, \cdots, \mathbf{b}_N] \in R^{N \times HW}$ is the learnable projection weights, $\mathbf{x}_j \in R^{1 \times C}, \mathbf{v}_i \in R^{1 \times C}$. According to Eq. 1, the feature tensor is projected to the new features V, which represents symbolic nodes in the coordination space. In practice, through the function $f(X)$ as $f(\phi(\mathbf{X}; W_\phi))$ and $B = \theta(\mathbf{X}; W_\theta)$ to reduce input dimension, where $\phi(\cdot)$ and $\theta(\cdot)$ are two convolution layers, W_ϕ and W_θ are the learnable convolutional kernel of each layer.

Graph Reasoning Module. After projecting the features X from the coordinate space Ω into the interaction space $\mathcal{H}$, we get the graph where each symbolic node stores the new feature as its state. In the interaction space, with features as symbol nodes of fully connected graphs, symbolic nodes are combined with structured knowledge (i.e. node edges) to perform graph reasoning. Based on the symbol nodes, a single-layer graph convolution [5,6] is formulated as

$$\mathbf{Z} = GVW_g = ((I - A_g)V)W_g. \qquad (2)$$

where W_g denotes the state update function, G and A_g denote the $N \times N$ node adjacency matrix, $Z \in R^{N \times C}$ is the node after global reasoning. The adjacency matrix A_g is randomly initialized and learned during the training process. A_g reflects the relationship between the potential global semantic information of each node. After that, each node receives all necessary semantic information and stores the updated feature. In particular, two-direction 1D convolutions are used for graph convolution. One 1D convolution is applied on each channel and the other is applied on each node. This two step process is conceptually visualized in the middle of Fig. 1(b).

Semantic-to-Local Module. Finally, the evolved global representations of symbolic nodes $Z \in R^{N \times C}$ need to be projected back to the original coordinate space. In order to make them compatible with the current CNN architecture, the mapped modules Y need to be in the same size as the original input feature tensors $X \in \mathcal{R}^{H \times W \times C}$. The reverse projection aims to learn a mapping function $g(\cdot)$ that maps symbolic nodes to the original space. Each feature in the mapped modules $Y = g(Z)$ is generated by

$$\mathbf{y}_i = \mathbf{d}_i Z = \sum_{\forall j} d_{ij} \mathbf{z}_j \qquad (3)$$

with learnable reverse projection weights $D = [\mathbf{d}_1, \cdots, \mathbf{d}_{HW}] \in R^{HW \times N}$, $\mathbf{z}_j \in R^{N \times 1}, \mathbf{y}_i \in R^{1 \times C}$. The graph-based global reasoning unit can be easily incorporated into existing architectures to utilized global information. In practice, the graph reasoning unit is add to the bottom of our framework to reason global information. The connection of the graph reasoning unit and the backbone of our framework are illustrated in Fig. 1.

2.3   Shape Constraints

Traditional CHD segmentation methods are highly dependent on prior information and shape information of each substructure of the heart can significantly improve the prediction accuracy. However, the way using the shape information in the network to guide CHD segmentation is still a problem to be solved. In this work, in order to solve this problem, a novel shape-constraint loss function is proposed below:

$$L_{seg}(y, \hat{y}) = \frac{1}{n} \sum_{i=0}^{n} SC(P(y_i), P(\hat{y_i})) \times \left(1 - \frac{\sum_j y_{j,i} \hat{y}_{j,i}}{\sum_j y_{j,i} + \sum_j \hat{y}_{j,i}} \right) \qquad (4)$$

where y and $\hat{y}$ are respectively the ground truth and the predicted label. n represents the number of predicted classes, in this work $n = 7$ (background and seven substructures of the heart); $P(y_i)$ represents the i-th substructure of the heart in the ground truth, and $P(\hat{y_i})$ is the i-th substructure of heart with the predicted label $\hat{y}$; $y_{j,i}$ and $\hat{y}_{j,i}$ are the ground truth and the prediction probability of the j-th pixel of the i-th class; The shape constraint (SC) is a metric to measure the substructure shape similarity between $P(y_i)$ and $P(\hat{y_i})$. In this work, SC is defined as:

$$SC\left(P(y_i), P(\hat{y_i})\right) = \sum_{j=1...7} \left| \frac{1}{m_j^{P(y_i)}} - \frac{1}{m_j^{P(\hat{y_i})}} \right| \qquad (5)$$

where

$$m_j^{P(y_i)} = sign\left(h_j^{P(y_i)} \right) \cdot \log h_j^{P(y_i)}, \qquad (6)$$

$$m_j^{P(\hat{y_i})} = sign\left(h_j^{P(\hat{y_i})} \right) \cdot \log h_j^{P(\hat{y_i})}, \qquad (7)$$

and $h_i^{P(y_i)}$, $h_i^{P(\hat{y_i})}$ are respectively the Hu moments [4] of $P(y_i)$ and $P(\hat{y_i})$. SC measures the distance from the automatically predicted contour to the corresponding ground truth contour, averaged over all contours of cardiac substructures. A high SC value means that the two contours do not match with each other. When the automatically predicted contour is not similar to the ground truth contour, a larger penalty coefficient makes the value of the loss function larger and the network parameters are adjusted accordingly. In this way, shape information is used in the network to guide the CHD segmentation.

3   Experiment and Results

3.1   Datasets

In this study, we validate our method with 68 3D CT images captured by a Simens biograph 64 machine. This dataset containing 14 types of CHD is available[1]. The size of a set of the data is $512 \times 512 \times (130 - 340)$, and the typical voxel size is $0.25 \times 0.25 \times 0.5 \, mm^3$. The labeling was performed by experienced radiologists and the cardiac was marked with seven substructures: (1) LV: the left ventricle blood cavity; (2) Myo: the myocardium of the left ventricle; (3) RV: the right ventricle blood cavity; (4) LA: the left atrium blood cavity; (5) RA: the right atrium blood cavity; (6) Ao: the ascending aorta; (7) PA: the pulmonary artery. Figure 2 shows 3D views of some examples in our dataset with significant structure variations. PA is marked in red, Fig. 2(a) shows a normal heart structure, PA is connected to RV. Figure 2(b) and Fig. 2(c) have CHD, and PA and RV are partially or mistakenly connected.

(a)	(b)	(c)

Fig. 2. Comparison between the normal heart and the pulmonary artery in our CHD dataset. (a): normal heart, in which the PA marked in red is connected to the RV (as shown by the arrow.); (b): heart with CHD, in which the PA is small and there are few parts connected to the RV; (c): heart with CHD, in which PA and RV are mistakenly connected. (Color figure online)

3.2   Implementation Details

The proposed model is implemented in PyTorch and trained on NVIDIA GTX 2080Ti GPU. We employ a poly learning rate policy, in which the initial learning rate is multiplied by $\left(1 - \frac{iter}{total-iter}\right)^{0.9}$ after each iteration, and the base learning rate is set to $1e - 3$. Batch size are set to 2. Data augmentation, including rotation, translation, scale, and crop, is randomly performed to improve the

---

[1] https://github.com/XiaoweiXu/Whole-heart-and-great-vessel-segmentation-of-chd_segmentation/tree/master.

generalization ability of the network. We firstly train 20 epochs with a poly learning rate policy, and then fine-tune 10 epochs with shape constraints. The fine-tuned learning rate is $1e-6$. Similar to the previous report [14], the four-fold cross validation is performed.

3.3 Results

In order to verify the effectiveness of different modules, we conduct experiments on the connection of different modules. The modules involve in the ablation experiment include: ACB (introduced in Sect. 2.1), graph reasoning (introduced in Sect. 2.2) and shape constraints (introduced in Sect. 2.3). ACB aims to enhance the skeletons at every layer. Graph reasoning is used to capture global relations, and shape constraints are used to calculate shape information of each substructure of the heart. Table 1 lists the mean Dice score of different module connection methods. Different modules show some performance improvements. After introducing shape constraints into the loss function, our final CHD segmentation Dice score reach 80.4%.

Table 1. Ablation study of key components in our method.

ACB	Graph reasoning	Shape constraints	Dice scores
×	×	×	78.3
✓	×	×	78.9
✓	✓	×	80.1
✓	✓	✓	**80.4**

Table 2 shows the mean Dice score of the state-of-the-art methods and our method for seven substructures of cardiac. Compare with CHD segmentation method of Xu et al. [14], our method yield 0.8–6.7% higher mean Dice score across the heart substructures except Ao. The highest improvement is achieved in Myo since the structure of the myocardium of the left ventricle is relatively simple. Ao show the poor segmentation result due to the huge deformation of the ascending aorta caused by CHD.

Table 2. Mean of Dice score of the state-of-the-art methods and our method.

Methods	LV	RV	LA	RA	Myo	Ao	PA	Mean
Seg-CNN [11]	67.3	65.0	70.2	76.0	71.5	63.0	52.3	66.5
Xu et al [14]	82.4	77.6	78.6	82.7	77.3	**82.2**	67.1	78.3
Our method	**84.8**	**79.7**	**82.6**	**84.1**	**84.0**	79.6	**67.9**	**80.4**

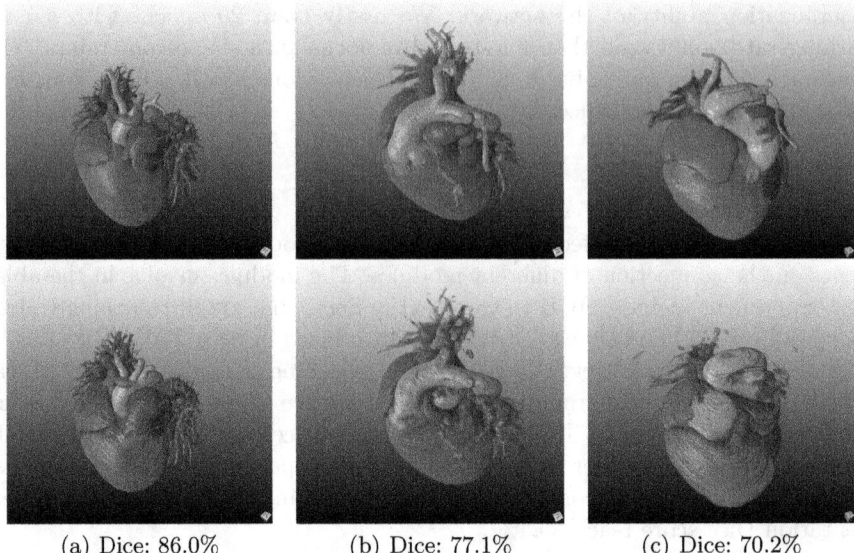

(a) Dice: 86.0%   (b) Dice: 77.1%   (c) Dice: 70.2%

Fig. 3. Visualization of our segmentation results and the ground truth. The first line is the ground truth, whereas the second line is the predicted segmentation result. (Color figure online)

Finally, the segmentation results obtained by our method achieved good, median, and poor Dice scores in test sets, and the visualization results are shown in Fig. 3. The bottom line in Fig. 3 represents the predicted segmentation results, and the top line is the corresponding ground truth. The segmentation result in Fig. 3(a) shows the higher accuracy, and most heart structures are segmented correctly compared with the ground truth. Figure 3(b) has some segmentation errors. Especially the segmentation of PA (highlighted in red) has many errors, and some blood vessels are lost. Figure 3(c) shows the boundary extraction errors between LA (highlighted in brown) and Ao (highlighted in cyan) and some small other tissue parts are incorrectly divided into heart tissue, thus leading to the poor Dice score. As shown in Fig. 3, a large quantity of pixel classification errors generally lead to a lower Dice score. In future work, we will solve the above problems.

4   Conclusion

This work proposes a CHD segmentation method based on graph reasoning and shape constraints. Graph reasoning is employed to capture global relations. Firstly, the features contained in the coordinate space are projected into nodes, and then the relation reasoning is performed via graph convolution. Shape constraint are used to calculate shape information, we adding this prior knowledge to the loss function to improve the prediction accuracy. Evaluation results obtained with 68 3D CT datasets with congenital heart defect indicated that our proposed network achieved more accurate segmentation results and outperformed the state-of-the-art methods in Dice measure.

Acknowledgments. This work is supported by National Natural Science Foundation of China (Grant Nos. 61472042 and 61802020), and by Beijing Natural Science Foundation (Grant No. 4174094), and by the Fundamental Research Funds for the Central Universities (Grant No. 2015KJJCB25).

References

1. Chen, Y., Rohrbach, M., Yan, Z., Shuicheng, Y., Feng, J., Kalantidis, Y.: Graph-based global reasoning networks. In: Proceedings of the IEEE Conference on Computer Vision and Pattern Recognition, pp. 433–442 (2019)
2. Ding, X., Guo, Y., Ding, G., Han, J.: Acnet: Strengthening the kernel skeletons for powerful CNN via asymmetric convolution blocks. In: Proceedings of the IEEE International Conference on Computer Vision, pp. 1911–1920 (2019)
3. Dormer, J.D., Ma, L., Halicek, M., Reilly, C.M., Schreibmann, E., Fei, B.: Heart chamber segmentation from CT using convolutional neural networks. In: Medical Imaging 2018: Biomedical Applications in Molecular, Structural, and Functional Imaging, vol. 10578, p. 105782S. International Society for Optics and Photonics (2018)
4. Flusser, J.: On the independence of rotation moment invariants. Pattern Recogn. **33**(9), 1405–1410 (2000)
5. Kipf, T.N., Welling, M.: Semi-supervised classification with graph convolutional networks. arXiv preprint arXiv:1609.02907 (2016)
6. Li, Q., Han, Z., Wu, X.M.: Deeper insights into graph convolutional networks for semi-supervised learning. In: Thirty-Second AAAI Conference on Artificial Intelligence (2018)
7. Liang, X., Hu, Z., Zhang, H., Lin, L., Xing, E.P.: Symbolic graph reasoning meets convolutions. In: Advances in Neural Information Processing Systems, pp. 1853–1863 (2018)
8. Mortazi, A., Burt, J., Bagci, U.: Multi-planar deep segmentation networks for cardiac substructures from MRI and CT. In: Pop, M., et al. (eds.) STACOM 2017. LNCS, vol. 10663, pp. 199–206. Springer, Cham (2018). https://doi.org/10.1007/978-3-319-75541-0_21
9. National Heart, L., Institute, B., et al.: What are congenital heart defects. Technical report, Accessed 3/12 (2015)
10. Pace, D.F., et al.: Iterative segmentation from limited training data: applications to congenital heart disease. In: Stoyanov, D., et al. (eds.) DLMIA/ML-CDS -2018. LNCS, vol. 11045, pp. 334–342. Springer, Cham (2018). https://doi.org/10.1007/978-3-030-00889-5_38
11. Payer, C., Štern, D., Bischof, H., Urschler, M.: Multi-label whole heart segmentation using CNNs and anatomical label configurations. In: Pop, M., et al. (eds.) STACOM 2017. LNCS, vol. 10663, pp. 190–198. Springer, Cham (2018). https://doi.org/10.1007/978-3-319-75541-0_20
12. Ronneberger, O., Fischer, P., Brox, T.: U-Net: convolutional networks for biomedical image segmentation. In: Navab, N., Hornegger, J., Wells, W.M., Frangi, A.F. (eds.) MICCAI 2015. LNCS, vol. 9351, pp. 234–241. Springer, Cham (2015). https://doi.org/10.1007/978-3-319-24574-4_28

13. Wang, C., Smedby, Ö.: Automatic whole heart segmentation using deep learning and shape context. In: Pop, M., et al. (eds.) STACOM 2017. LNCS, vol. 10663, pp. 242–249. Springer, Cham (2017). https://doi.org/10.1007/978-3-319-75541-0_26

14. Xu, X., et al.: Whole heart and great vessel segmentation in congenital heart disease using deep neural networks and graph matching. In: Shen, D., et al. (eds.) MICCAI 2019. LNCS, vol. 11765, pp. 477–485. Springer, Cham (2019). https://doi.org/10.1007/978-3-030-32245-8_53

15. Yang, H., Liu, Z., Yang, X.: Right ventricle segmentation in short-axis MRI using a shape constrained dense connected U-Net. In: Shen, D., et al. (eds.) MICCAI 2019. LNCS, vol. 11765, pp. 532–540. Springer, Cham (2019). https://doi.org/10.1007/978-3-030-32245-8_59

16. Yu, L., Yang, X., Qin, J., Heng, P.-A.: 3D FractalNet: dense volumetric segmentation for cardiovascular MRI volumes. In: Zuluaga, M.A., Bhatia, K., Kainz, B., Moghari, M.H., Pace, D.F. (eds.) RAMBO/HVSMR -2016. LNCS, vol. 10129, pp. 103–110. Springer, Cham (2017). https://doi.org/10.1007/978-3-319-52280-7_10

17. Zreik, M., Leiner, T., De Vos, B.D., van Hamersvelt, R.W., Viergever, M.A., Išgum, I.: Automatic segmentation of the left ventricle in cardiac CT angiography using convolutional neural networks. In: 2016 IEEE 13th International Symposium on Biomedical Imaging (ISBI), pp. 40–43. IEEE (2016)

Nonlinear Regression on Manifolds for Shape Analysis using Intrinsic Bézier Splines

Martin Hanik[1]([⊠])(ID), Hans-Christian Hege[1](ID), Anja Hennemuth[2](ID), and Christoph von Tycowicz[1](ID)

[1] Zuse Institute Berlin, Berlin, Germany
{hanik,hege,vontycowicz}@zib.de
[2] Charité – Universitätsmedizin Berlin, Berlin, Germany
anja.hennemuth@charite.de

Abstract. Intrinsic and parametric regression models are of high interest for the statistical analysis of manifold-valued data such as images and shapes. The standard linear ansatz has been generalized to geodesic regression on manifolds making it possible to analyze dependencies of random variables that spread along generalized straight lines. Nevertheless, in some scenarios, the evolution of the data cannot be modeled adequately by a geodesic. We present a framework for nonlinear regression on manifolds by considering Riemannian splines, whose segments are Bézier curves, as trajectories. Unlike variational formulations that require time-discretization, we take a constructive approach that provides efficient and exact evaluation by virtue of the generalized de Casteljau algorithm. We validate our method in experiments on the reconstruction of periodic motion of the mitral valve as well as the analysis of femoral shape changes during the course of osteoarthritis, endorsing Bézier spline regression as an effective and flexible tool for manifold-valued regression.

Keywords: Shape trajectory · Manifold-valued Bézier curves · Spline regression · Riemannian geometry

1 Introduction

Manifold-valued data arises in many medical applications, for example as image data or in the form of 2D/3D shapes, and sophisticated tools for its analysis have become increasingly important. Regression methods are central to modern statistics and research for their applicability to nonlinear spaces is fuelled by an ever-growing number of large longitudinal studies [11]. Consequently, geodesic regression [9,20] was introduced as a generalization of linear regression. It allows to test whether given instances in a Riemannian manifold can be well approximated by a generalized straight line. Nevertheless, there are processes that cannot be accurately described by a geodesic, e.g., periodic motion or processes with saturation which slow down after some time. In order to handle these

© Springer Nature Switzerland AG 2020
A. L. Martel et al. (Eds.): MICCAI 2020, LNCS 12264, pp. 617–626, 2020.
https://doi.org/10.1007/978-3-030-59719-1_60

cases, both non-parametric [8,17,23] and parametric models have been studied. In the latter category, Riemannian polynomials [14] and splines [22] have been considered for nonlinear regression. They are defined, for example by employing variational principles, as solutions to differential equations involving curvature terms. Therefore, evaluation and optimization is complicated and numerically expensive since there are no closed-form solutions available in general.

As an alternative, we propose to use manifold-valued Bézier curves [18,21]. They coincide with polynomial curves in Euclidean space, are intrinsic to the manifold (i.e., independent of a choice of coordinates) and more flexible than geodesics. In contrast to Riemannian polynomials, Bézier curves allow for explicit formulas, which enables us to evaluate them directly without time-discretization. This can improve computational speed without suffering a loss of accuracy. Furthermore, we can combine two such curves to a differentiable spline independently of the degrees of the Bézier segments. This is again an advantage over polynomial curves. While variational spline models allow for piecewise composition, there is no clear way to define them for even degrees [14]. Therefore, the introduction of flexible, intrinsic splines is a key contribution of this work. Our model features closed-form, numerically stable and efficient expressions for the gradient of the regression objective in terms of concatenated adjoint Jacobi fields [6]. In particular, we derive an algorithm that only requires basic Riemannian operations: the exponential and logarithmic map as well as certain Jacobi fields. Notably, closed-form expressions for these operations are available for many manifolds; in particular, they are known for Kendall's shape space [19] and shape models based on differential [25] and fundamental [3] coordinates.

While the method can be generally applied to data on any manifold, we provide two specific examples from shape analysis. First, we regress the data of 100 highly resolved femur geometries with different severeness of osteoarthritis against their grade in the Kellgren Lawrence grading system. Second, we reconstruct the full motion cycle of a mitral valve from 3D geometries that were derived from ultrasound images. To the best of our knowledge, we are the first to present intrinsic regression results of such a periodic process.

2   Spline Regression

Tools from Riemannian Geometry. Before we introduce Bézier curves on manifolds we recall some important facts from Riemannian geometry; for more information see for example [7]. As is often done, we use "smooth" synonymously with "infinitely often differentiable".

A Riemannian manifold is a differentiable manifold M together with a Riemannian metric $\langle \cdot, \cdot \rangle_p$ that assigns to each tangent space T_pM a smoothly varying scalar product. As a result, a distance function d is induced on M. Every Riemannian manifold comes with a unique connection ∇ called Levi-Civita connection. Given two vector fields X, Y on M it yields a natural way to differentiate Y along X; we denote the resulting vector field by $\nabla_X Y$.

A geodesic γ is a generalized straight line and its defining property is vanishing of acceleration, i.e., $\nabla_{\gamma'} \gamma' = 0$, where $\gamma' := \frac{\mathrm{d}}{\mathrm{d}t} \gamma$. An important fact is that every point in M has a so-called convex neighbourhood U. Each pair $p, q \in U$ can be joined by a unique length-minimizing geodesic $[0,1] \ni t \mapsto \gamma(t; p, q)$ that lies completely in U. In the following, we always assume to work in a convex neighbourhood. Then, γ is also differentiable with respect to its starting and end point. Explicit formula of these differentials involve the Riemannian curvature tensor R (which intuitively measures local deviation from flat space; see [7, Ch. 4]). It determines Jacobi fields J along γ as solutions to the linear second order differential equation $\nabla_{\gamma'} \nabla_{\gamma'} J + R(J, \gamma')\gamma' = 0$. Considering the boundary value problem $J(0) = X$, $J(1) = 0$, we denote its solution by J_X. Then, the derivative of γ w.r.t. its starting point p in direction $X \in T_p M$ is given by J_X, i.e., $d_p \gamma(t; \cdot, q)(X) = J_X(t)$ for all $t \in [0,1]$. Furthermore, since $\gamma(t; p, q) = \gamma(1 - t; q, p)$, endpoint variations are given analogously [6, Sect. 3.1].

Another important map is the Riemannian exponential. Let $X \in T_p M$ such that there is a geodesic $[0,1] \ni t \mapsto \gamma(t; p, q)$ in U with $X = \gamma'(0; p, q)$. The exponential map at p is then defined by $\exp_p(X) := q$. Its inverse is the Riemannian logarithm $\log_p$. In particular, we have $\log_p(q) = \gamma'(0; p, q)$.

The adjoint A^* of a linear operator $A : T_p M \to T_q M$ is given, as usual, by the linear operator from $T_q M$ to $T_p M$ that conserves the scalar product, i.e., $\langle AX, Y \rangle_q = \langle X, A^* Y \rangle_p$ for all $X \in T_p M$, $Y \in T_q M$.

Later, we want to calculate the gradient of a composition of functions. If $f : M \to M$ and $g : M \to \mathbb{R}$ are smooth, then the chain rule for gradients reads $\text{grad}_p(g \circ f) = d_p f^*(\text{grad}_{f(p)} g)$, i.e., the gradient of g at $f(p)$ is "transported" to the tangent space at p by the adjoint differential of f.

Bézier Curves. In the following we restrict the domain of definition to $[0,1]$ for clarity. This does not influence generality as reparametrizations are always possible. In particular, geodesics γ can be defined on arbitrary intervals by changing the speed of travel, i.e., the length of the velocity vector.

A set of $k + 1$ control points $p_0, \ldots, p_k \in U$ defines a *Bézier curve* $\beta : [0,1] \to M$ of order k according to the *generalized de Casteljau algorithm*

$$\beta_i^0(t) := p_i,$$
$$\beta_i^l(t) := \gamma(t; \beta_i^{l-1}(t), \beta_{i+1}^{l-1}(t)), \quad l = 1, \ldots, k, \quad i = 0, \ldots, k - l, \quad (1)$$

by $\beta(t) := \beta_0^k(t)$.

Note that $\beta(0) = p_0$ and $\beta(1) = p_k$. Furthermore, the velocities of β at these points are

$$\beta'(0) = k \log_{p_0}(p_1) \text{ and } \beta'(1) = -k \log_{p_k}(p_{k-1}); \quad (2)$$

see [21, Thm. 1]. The algorithm is visualized on the left of Fig. 1. Whenever of interest, we will make the dependence of β on its control points explicit by writing $\beta(t; p_0, \ldots, p_k)$. Note that if there are only 2 control points p_0, p_1, then β is just the geodesic from p_0 to p_1. In Euclidean space, the above algorithm is the ordinary de Casteljau algorithm (because there geodesics are straight lines) and it is a well known fact that then β is a curve with polynomials of order at most k as entries.

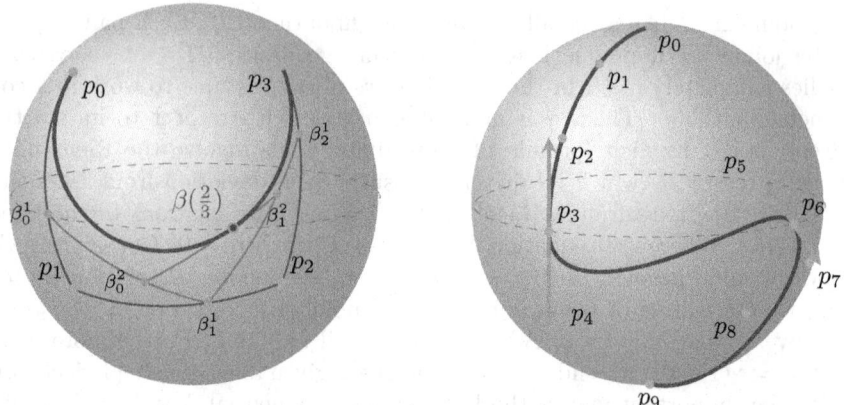

Fig. 1. Left: A cubic Bézier curve β on the sphere $\mathcal{S}^2$ and the construction of $\beta(2/3)$ by the de Casteljau algorithm. Right: A Bézier spline with 3 cubic segments on $\mathcal{S}^2$.

Property (2) allows us to fit Bézier curves of possibly different orders together to a differentiable spline. For $i = 0, \ldots, L-1$ let $p_0^{(i)}, \ldots, p_{k_i}^{(i)}$ be the control points of L Bézier curves such that

$$p_{k_i}^{(i)} = p_0^{(i+1)} \quad \text{and} \quad \gamma\left(\frac{k_i}{k_i + k_{i+1}}; p_{k_i-1}^{(i)}, p_1^{(i+1)}\right) = p_0^{(i+1)} \tag{3}$$

for all $i = 1, \ldots, L - 2$. Then, we define the *Bézier spline* B by

$$B(t) := \begin{cases} \beta(t; p_0^{(0)}, \ldots, p_{k_0}^{(0)}), & t \in [0, 1], \\ \beta(t - i; p_0^{(i)}, \ldots, p_{k_i}^{(i)}), & t \in (i, i+1], \quad i = 1, \ldots, L-1. \end{cases} \tag{4}$$

From (2) it follows that B is C^1, i.e., we can make B differentiable by aligning the three control points at the connections thereby removing one degree of freedom. For more details see [13, Sect. 2.3]. Note that we could add further restrictions to ensure that B is C^2 [21, p. 119].

If $L > 1$ and the first and last segment of B are at least cubic, we can consider closed Bézier splines. Then, B is C^1 and closed if and only if (3) extends cyclically, that is, we also have

$$p_{k_{L-1}}^{(L-1)} = p_0^{(0)} \quad \text{and} \quad \gamma\left(\frac{k_{L-1}}{k_{L-1} + k_0}; p_{k_{L-1}-1}^{(L-1)}, p_1^{(0)}\right) = p_0^{(0)}.$$

In the following, we set

$$K := \begin{cases} k_0 + k_1 + \cdots + k_{L-2} + k_{L-1}, & B \text{ non-closed}, \\ k_0 + k_1 + \cdots + k_{L-2} + k_{L-1} - 1, & B \text{ closed}, \end{cases}$$

and denote the set of $K + 1$ *distinct* control points of B by $p_0, \ldots, p_K$. In the non-closed case this means

$$(p_0, \ldots, p_K) := \left(p_0^{(0)}, \ldots, p_{k_0}^{(0)}, p_1^{(1)}, \ldots, p_{k_1}^{(1)}, \ldots, p_1^{(L-1)}, \ldots, p_{k_{L-1}}^{(L-1)}\right) \in M^{K+1},$$

while $p_0^{(0)}$ is left out for closed B. An example of a C^1 spline with three cubic segments and 10 distinct control points is shown on the right of Fig. 1.

The Model. Let N data points $q_i \in U$ with corresponding scalar parameter values t_i (for example points in time) be given. We suppose that the data points q_i are realizations of an M-valued random variable Q that depends on the deterministic variable $t \in \mathbb{R}$ according to the model

$$Q(t) = \exp_{B(t;p_0,\ldots,p_K)}(\epsilon).$$

Here, ϵ is a random variable that takes values in the tangent space $T_{B(t)}M$. The control points $p_0,\ldots,p_K$ are the unknown parameters. In Euclidean space it reduces to polynomial spline regression since Bézier curves and polynomials coincide. Note that our model is a generalization of geodesic regression [9], which it reduces to when B consists of a single segment with 2 control points.

Least Squares Estimation. Given N realizations $(t_j, q_j) \in \mathbb{R} \times U$, the *sum-of-squared error* is defined by

$$\mathcal{E}(p_0,\ldots,p_K) := \frac{1}{2}\sum_{j=1}^{N} d\Big(B(t_j;p_0,\ldots,p_K), q_j\Big)^2. \tag{5}$$

Then, we can formulate a least squares estimator of the Bézier spline model as the minimizer of this error, which under certain conditions agrees with the maximum likelihood estimation [9]. We would like to emphasize that none of the control points agrees with the data points as is the case in spline interpolation.

In general, minimizers of (5) are not known analytically, which makes iterative schemes necessary. Therefore, we apply Riemannian gradient descent. (For optimization on manifolds see [1].) The gradient of $\mathcal{E}$ can be computed w.r.t. each control point individually. We write $B_t(p_i)$ for the map $p_i \mapsto B_t(p_i) := B(t;p_0,\ldots,p_i,\ldots,p_k)$ and define the functions $p \mapsto \tau_j(p) := d(p,q_j)^2$. It is known that $\mathrm{grad}_p\tau_j = -2\log_p(q_j)$ for each $p \in U$. When we consider the j-th summand on the right-hand side of (5), the chain rule implies that its gradient w.r.t. the i-th control point is given by

$$\mathrm{grad}_{p_i}(\tau_j \circ B_{t_j}) = d_{p_i}B_{t_j}^*\Big(\mathrm{grad}_{B_{t_j}(p_i)}\tau_j\Big) = -2\,d_{p_i}B_{t_j}^*\Big(\log_{B_{t_j}(p_i)}(q_j)\Big).$$

Using (5) then gives the gradient of $\mathcal{E}$. The operator $d_{p_i}B_t^*$ "mirrors" the construction of the segment of B to which p_i belongs by transporting the vector $\log_{B_{t_i}(p_i)}(q_j)$ backwards along the "tree of geodesics" defined by the de Casteljau algorithm (1). More precisely, the result is a sum of vectors in $T_{p_i}M$ that are values of concatenated adjoint differentials of geodesics w.r.t. starting and end point. In symmetric spaces, for example, they are known in closed form. For a detailed inspection of $d_{p_i}B_t^*$ we refer to [6, Sect. 4].

As initial guess for the gradient descent, we choose $(p_0,\ldots,p_K)$ along the geodesic polygon whose corners interpolate the data points that are closest to knot points w.r.t. time.

3 Experiments

Although physical objects themselves are embedded in Euclidean space, their *shape features* are best described by more general manifolds requiring Riemannian geometric tools for statistical analysis thereon; see for example [4, 16, 25]. To test our regression method for shape analysis, we apply it to two types of 3D data: (i) distal femora and (ii) mitral valves given as triangulated surfaces. We perform the analysis in the shape space of *differential coordinates* [25]. That is, for homogeneous objects given as triangular meshes in correspondence, we choose their intrinsic mean [10] as reference template and view all objects as deformations thereof. (We assume that the meshes are rigidly aligned, e.g., by generalized Procrustes alignment [12].) On each face of a mesh, the corresponding deformation gradient is constant and, therefore, can be encoded as a pair of a rotation and a stretch, i.e., as an element of the Lie group of 3 by 3 rotation and symmetric positive definite matrices $SO(3) \times Sym^+(3)$. Denoting the Frobenius norm by $\| \cdot \|_F$, metrics are chosen such that the distance functions become $d_{SO}(R_1, R_2) := \| \log(R_1^T R_2)\|_F$ and $d_{Sym^+}(S_1, S_2) := \| \log(S_2) - \log(S_1)\|_F$, respectively. Suppose the number of triangles per object is m, then the full shape space is the product space $(SO(3) \times Sym^+(3))^m$. Using the product metric, statistical analysis thereon can be done face-wise and separately for rotations and stretches. We implemented a prototype of our method in MATLAB using the MVIRT toolbox [5].

Distal Femora. Osteoarthritis (OA) is a degenerative disease of the joints that is, i.a., characterized by changes of the bone shape. To evaluate our model, we regress the 3D shape of distal femora against OA severity as determined by the Kellgren-Lawrence (KL) grade [15]—an ordinal scale from 0 to 4 based on radiographic features. Our data set comprises 100 shapes (20 per grade) of randomly selected subjects from the OsteoArthritis Initiative (a longitudinal, prospective study of knee OA) for which segmentations of the respective magnetic resonance images are publicly available (https://doi.org/10.12752/4.ATEZ.1.0) [2]. In a supervised post-process, the quality of segmentations as well as the correspondence of the extracted triangle meshes (8,988 vertices/17,829 faces) were ensured.

Table 1. The computed R_{rel}^2 and R^2 statistics of the regressed (w.r.t. KL grade) geodesic, quadratic and cubic Bézier curve for data of distal femora

Order of Bézier curve	R^2	R_{rel}^2
1	0.05	0.57
2	0.07	0.78
3	0.08	0.90

For $i = 0, \ldots, 4$, the shapes with grade i are associated with the value $t_i = i/4$. We use our method to compute the best-fitting geodesic, quadratic and cubic Bézier curve. In order to compare their explanatory power, we calculate for each the corresponding manifold-valued R^2 statistic that, for $r_1, \ldots, r_N \in M$ and *total variance* $\mathrm{var}\{r_1, \ldots, r_N\} := 1/N \min_{q \in M} \sum_{j=1}^{N} d(q, r_j)^2$, is defined by [10, p. 56]

$$R^2 = 1 - \frac{\text{unexplained variance}}{\text{total variance}} := 1 - \frac{2/N \mathcal{E}(\beta)}{\mathrm{var}\{r_1, \ldots, r_N\}} \in [0, 1].$$

The statistic measures how much of the data's total variance is explained by β.

For $j = 1, \ldots, 20$ and $l = 0, \ldots, 4$, let $q_j^{(l)}$ be the j-th femur shape with KL grade l. Note that, for the described setup, the unexplained variance is bounded from below by the sum of the per-grade variances, i.e., $\sum_{l=0}^{4} \mathrm{var}\{q_1^{(l)}, \ldots, q_{20}^{(l)}\}$. In particular, for our femur data this yields an upper bound for the R^2 statistic of $R_{opt}^2 \approx 0.0962$. Hence, we also provide relative values $R_{rel}^2 := R^2/R_{opt}^2$ for comparison. The results are shown in Table 1.

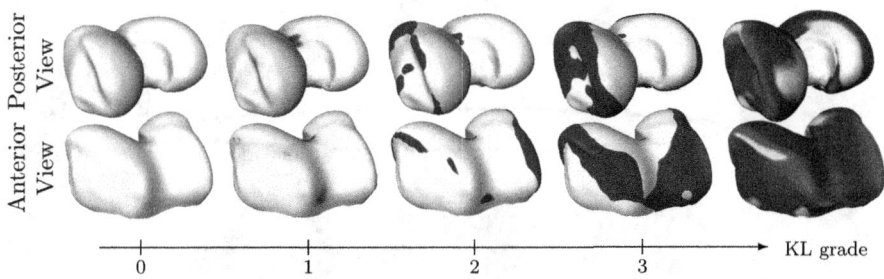

Fig. 2. Cubic regression of distal femora. Healthy regressed shape (KL = 0) together with subsequent grades overlaid wherever the distance is larger than 0.5 mm, colored accordingly (0.5 ▮▮▮▮▮▮ 3.0).

The computed cubic Bézier curve is displayed in Fig. 2. The obtained shape changes consistently describe OA related malformations of the femur, viz., widening of the condyles and osteophytic growth. Furthermore, we observe only minute bone remodeling for the first half of the trajectory, while accelerated progression is clearly visible for the second half. The substantial increase in R_{rel}^2 suggests that there are nontrivial higher order phenomena involved which are captured poorly by the geodesic model. Moreover, as time-warped geodesics are contained in the search space we can inspect time dependency. Indeed, for the cubic femoral curve the control points do not belong to a single geodesic, confirming higher order effects beyond reparametrization.

Mitral Valve. Diseases of the mitral valve such as mitral valve insufficiency (MI) are often characterized by a specific motion pattern and the resulting shape anomalies can be observed (at least) at some point of the cardiac cycle. In patients with MI, the valve's leaflets do not close fully or prolapse into the left atrium during systole. Blood then flows back lowering the heart's efficiency.

We compute regression with Bézier splines for the longitudinal data of a diseased patient's mitral valve. Sampling the first half of the cycle (closed to fully open) at equidistant time steps, 5 meshes (1,331 vertices/2,510 faces) were extracted from a 3D+t transesophageal echocardiography (TEE) sequence as described in [24]. Let $q_1, \ldots, q_5$ be the corresponding shapes in the space of differential coordinates. In order to approximate the full motion cycle we use the same 5 shapes in reversed order as data for the second half of the curve. Because of the periodic behaviour, we choose a closed spline with two cubic segments as model and assume an equidistant distribution of the data points along the spline, i.e., we employ $\{(0, q_1), (1/4, q_2), (1/2, q_3), (3/4, q_4), (1, q_5), (5/4, q_4), (3/2, q_3), (7/4, q_2)\}$ as the full set.

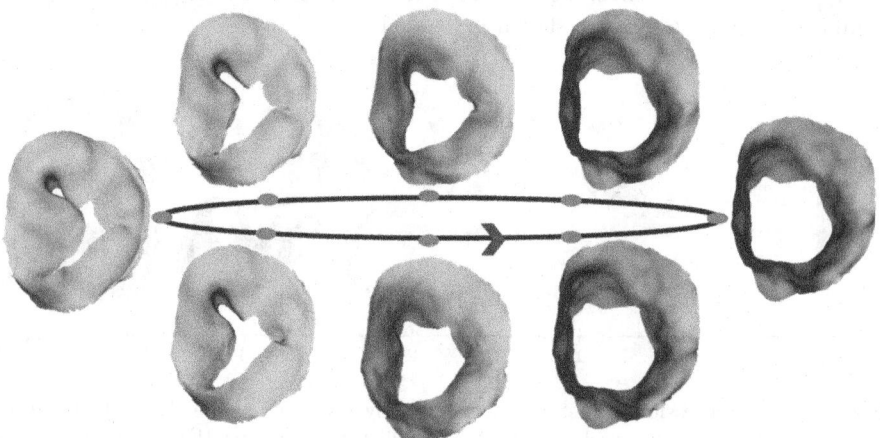

Fig. 3. Reconstructed meshes from regression of longitudinal mitral valve data covering a full cardiac cycle. The spline consists of two cubic segments.

The regressed cardiac trajectory is shown in Fig. 3. Our method successfully estimates the valve's cyclic motion capturing the prolapsing posterior leaflet. It shows the potential for improved reconstruction of mitral valve motion in presence of image artifacts like TEE shadowing and signal dropout. This, in turn, facilitates quantification of geometric indices of valve function such as orifice area or tenting height.

4   Conclusion

We presented a parametric regression model that combines high flexibility with efficient and exact evaluation. In practice, it can be used for many types of manifold-valued data as it relies only on three basic differential geometric tools that can be computed explicitly in many important spaces. In particular, we have presented two applications to shape data where we could model higher order effects and cyclic motion. A remaining question is, which Bézier spline (number of segments and their order) to choose for the analysis of a particular data set. This problem of model selection poses an interesting avenue for future work. Moreover, we plan to extend the proposed framework to a hierarchical statistical model for the analysis of longitudinal shape data, where subject-specific trends are viewed as perturbations of a population-average trajectory represented as Bézier spline.

Acknowledgments. M. Hanik is funded by the Deutsche Forschungsgemeinschaft (DFG, German Research Foundation) under Germany's Excellence Strategy – The Berlin Mathematics Research Center MATH+ (EXC-2046/1, project ID: 390685689). Furthermore we are grateful for the open-access dataset OAI (The Osteoarthritis Initiative is a public-private partnership comprised of five contracts (N01-AR-2-2258; N01-AR-2-2259; N01-AR-2-2260; N01-AR-2-2261; N01-AR-2-2262) funded by the National Institutes of Health, a branch of the Department of Health and Human Services, and conducted by the OAI Study Investigators. Private funding partners include Merck Research Laboratories; Novartis Pharmaceuticals Corporation, GlaxoSmithKline; and Pfizer, Inc. Private sector funding for the OAI is managed by the Foundation for the National Institutes of Health. This manuscript was prepared using an OAI public use data set and does not necessarily reflect the opinions or views of the OAI investigators, the NIH, or the private funding partners.) and the open-source software MVIRT [5].

References

1. Absil, P.A., Mahony, R., Sepulchre, R.: Optimization Algorithms on Matrix Manifolds. Princeton University Press, USA (2007). https://doi.org/10.1515/9781400830244
2. Ambellan, F., Tack, A., Ehlke, M., Zachow, S.: Automated segmentation of knee bone and cartilage combining statistical shape knowledge and convolutional neural networks: data from the osteoarthritis initiative. Med. Image Anal. **52**, 109–118 (2019). https://doi.org/10.1016/j.media.2018.11.009
3. Ambellan, F., Zachow, S., von Tycowicz, C.: A Surface-theoretic approach for statistical shape modeling. In: Shen, D., et al. (eds.) MICCAI 2019. LNCS, vol. 11767, pp. 21–29. Springer, Cham (2019). https://doi.org/10.1007/978-3-030-32251-9_3
4. Bauer, M., Bruveris, M., Michor, P.W.: Overview of the geometries of shape spaces and diffeomorphism groups. J. Math. Imaging Vis. **50**(1–2), 60–97 (2014). https://doi.org/10.1007/s10851-013-0490-z
5. Bergmann, R.: MVIRT, a toolbox for manifold-valued image restoration. In: IEEE International Conference on Image Processing, IEEE ICIP 2017, Beijing, China, 17–20 September 2017 (2017). https://doi.org/10.1109/ICIP.2017.8296271
6. Bergmann, R., Gousenbourger, P.Y.: A variational model for data fitting on manifolds by minimizing the acceleration of a Bézier curve. Front. Appl. Math. Stat. **4**, 1–16 (2018). https://doi.org/10.3389/fams.2018.00059
7. do Carmo, M.P.: Riemannian Geometry. Mathematics: Theory and Applications, 2nd edn. Birkhäuser, Boston (1992)
8. Davis, B.C., Fletcher, P.T., Bullitt, E., Joshi, S.: Population shape regression from random design data. In: 2007 IEEE 11th International Conference on Computer Vision, pp. 1–7 (2007). https://doi.org/10.1109/ICCV.2007.4408977

9. Fletcher, P.T.: Geodesic regression and the theory of least squares on Riemannian manifolds. Int. J. Comput. Vis. **105**(2), 171–185 (2013). https://doi.org/10.1007/s11263-012-0591-y
10. Fletcher, T.: 2 - Statistics on manifolds. In: Pennec, X., Sommer, S., Fletcher, T. (eds.) Riemannian Geometric Statistics in Medical Image Analysis, pp. 39–74. Academic Press (2020). https://doi.org/10.1016/B978-0-12-814725-2.00009-1
11. Gerig, G., Fishbaugh, J., Sadeghi, N.: Longitudinal modeling of appearance and shape and its potential for clinical use. Med. Image Anal. **33**, 114–121 (2016). https://doi.org/10.1016/j.media.2016.06.014
12. Goodall, C.: Procrustes methods in the statistical analysis of shape. J. Roy. Stat. Soc.: Ser. B (Methodol.) **53**(2), 285–321 (1991). https://doi.org/10.1111/j.2517-6161.1991.tb01825.x
13. Gousenbourger, P.Y., Massart, E., Absil, P.A.: Data fitting on manifolds with composite Bézier-like curves and blended cubic splines. J. Math. Imaging Vis. **61**(5), 645–671 (2019). https://doi.org/10.1007/s10851-018-0865-2
14. Hinkle, J., Fletcher, P.T., Joshi, S.: Intrinsic polynomials for regression on Riemannian manifolds. J. Math. Imaging Vis. **50**(1), 32–52 (2014). https://doi.org/10.1007/s10851-013-0489-5
15. Kellgren, J.H., Lawrence, J.S.: Radiological assessment of osteo-arthrosis. Ann. Rheum. Dis. **16**(4), 494–502 (1957). https://doi.org/10.1136/ard.16.4.494
16. Kendall, D., Barden, D., Carne, T., Le, H.: Shape and Shape Theory. Wiley Series in Probability and Statistics. Wiley, Hoboken (2009). https://doi.org/10.1002/9780470317006
17. Mallasto, A., Feragen, A.: Wrapped Gaussian process regression on Riemannian manifolds. In: 2018 IEEE/CVF Conference on Computer Vision and Pattern Recognition (CVPR), pp. 5580–5588. IEEE Computer Society, Los Alamitos (2018). https://doi.org/10.1109/CVPR.2018.00585
18. Nava-Yazdani, E., Polthier, K.: De Casteljau's algorithm on manifolds. Comput. Aided Geom. Des. **30**(7), 722–732 (2013). https://doi.org/10.1016/j.cagd.2013.06.002
19. Nava-Yazdani, E., Hege, H.C., Sullivan, T., von Tycowicz, C.: Geodesic analysis in Kendall's shape space with epidemiological applications. J. Math. Imaging Vis. **62**, 549–559 (2020). https://doi.org/10.1007/s10851-020-00945-w
20. Niethammer, M., Huang, Y., Vialard, F.-X.: Geodesic regression for image time-series. In: Fichtinger, G., Martel, A., Peters, T. (eds.) MICCAI 2011. LNCS, vol. 6892, pp. 655–662. Springer, Heidelberg (2011). https://doi.org/10.1007/978-3-642-23629-7_80
21. Popiel, T., Noakes, L.: Bézier curves and C2 interpolation in Riemannian manifolds. J. Approx. Theory **148**(2), 111–127 (2007). https://doi.org/10.1016/j.jat.2007.03.002
22. Singh, N., Vialard, F.X., Niethammer, M.: Splines for diffeomorphisms. Med. Image Anal. **25**(1), 56–71 (2015). https://doi.org/10.1016/j.media.2015.04.012
23. Su, J., Dryden, I., Klassen, E., Le, H., Srivastava, A.: Fitting smoothingsplines to time-indexed, noisy points on nonlinear manifolds. Image Vis. Comput. - IVC **30**, 428–442 (2012). https://doi.org/10.1016/j.imavis.2011.09.006
24. Tautz, L., et al.: Combining position-based dynamics and gradient vector flow for 4D mitral valve segmentation in TEE sequences. Int. J. Comput. Assist. Radiol. Surg. **15**(1), 119–128 (2019). https://doi.org/10.1007/s11548-019-02071-4
25. von Tycowicz, C., Ambellan, F., Mukhopadhyay, A., Zachow, S.: An efficient Riemannian statistical shape model using differential coordinates. Med. Image Anal. **43**, 1–9 (2018). https://doi.org/10.1016/j.media.2017.09.004

Self-supervised Discovery of Anatomical Shape Landmarks

Riddhish Bhalodia[1,2(✉)], Ladislav Kavan[2], and Ross T. Whitaker[1,2]

[1] Scientific Computing and Imaging Institute, University of Utah, Utah, USA
[2] School of Computing, University of Utah, Utah, USA
`riddhishb@gmail.com`

Abstract. Statistical shape analysis is a very useful tool in a wide range of medical and biological applications. However, it typically relies on the ability to produce a relatively small number of features that can capture the relevant variability in a population. State-of-the-art methods for obtaining such anatomical features rely on either extensive preprocessing or segmentation and/or significant tuning and post-processing. These shortcomings limit the widespread use of shape statistics. We propose that effective shape representations should provide sufficient information to align/register images. Using this assumption we propose a self-supervised, neural network approach for automatically positioning and detecting landmarks in images that can be used for subsequent analysis. The network discovers the landmarks corresponding to anatomical shape features that promote good image registration in the context of a particular class of transformations. In addition, we also propose a regularization for the proposed network which allows for a uniform distribution of these discovered landmarks. In this paper, we present a complete framework, which only takes a set of input images and produces landmarks that are immediately usable for statistical shape analysis. We evaluate the performance on a phantom dataset as well as 2D and 3D images.

Keywords: Self-supervised learning · Shape analysis · Landmark localization

1 Introduction

Statistical shape modeling (SSM)/morphological analysis [28] is an important resource for medical and biological applications. SSM broadly involves two distinct parts, (i) shape representation which involves describing the anatomy/shape of interest by giving an implicit or explicit representation of the shape, and (ii) using the shape representation to perform the subsequent

Electronic supplementary material The online version of this chapter (https://doi.org/10.1007/978-3-030-59719-1_61) contains supplementary material, which is available to authorized users.

analysis on shape population. Classical approaches relied on representing the shape via landmark points, often corresponding to distinct anatomical features. There have been many automated approaches for dense correspondence discovery which captures the underlying shape statistics [10, 26]. An alternate approach to shape representation is to leverage coordinate transformations between images or geometries, typically members of a population or to a common atlas [19]. Such a set of transformations implicitly capture the population shape statistics for the objects/anatomies contained in those images.

Automated shape representation via dense correspondences has its drawbacks; most such methods rely on heavily preprocessed data. Such preprocessing steps might include segmentation, smoothing, alignment, and cropping. These tasks typically require manual parameter settings and quality control thereby making this preprocessing heavy on human resources. In several cases, especially for segmentation a degree of specific anatomical, clinical, or biological expertise is also required, introducing even higher barriers to engaging in shape analysis. Additionally, automated landmark placement or registration rely on computationally expensive optimization methods, and often require additional parameter tuning and quality control. This heavy preprocessing and complex optimization often make statistical shape analysis difficult for nonexperts, especially when the data under study consists of primarily of images/volumes.

Systems that produce transformations and/or dense correspondences will typically produce high-dimensional shape descriptors, whereas many users prefer lower-dimensional descriptors to perform subsequent statistical analyses such as clustering, regression, or hypothesis testing. Therefore, there is typically an additional set of processes (e.g. PCA in various forms) that require further expertise (and research) to interpret these complex, high-dimensional outputs and distill them down to usable quantities.

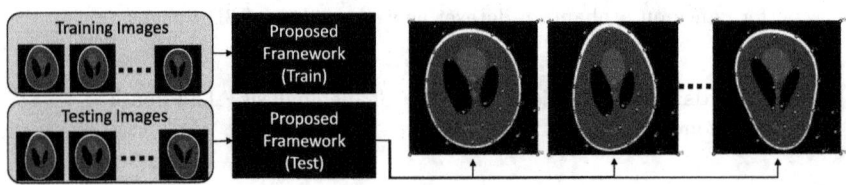

Fig. 1. Proposed method's advantage of being an end to end image to landmarks black-box(Color figure online)

These challenges point a need for an end-to-end system that takes in images and automatically extracts its shape landmarks, for direct statistical shape analysis. In this paper, we propose a system that takes collections of images as input and produces a set of landmarks that leads to accurate registration. Using image registration as the proxy task, we propose a self-supervised learning method using neural networks that discovers anatomical shape landmarks from a given image set. This method circumvents the intensive preprocessing and optimization required for previous correspondence based methods, while maintaining the simplicity of spatial landmarks of user specified dimension and complexity. Figure 1 showcases the usefulness of the proposed system, i.e. a black-box framework which trains on roughly aligned 2D or 3D images and learns to identify anatomical shape landmarks on new testing images from the same distribution.

2 Related Work

Statistical shape models have been extensively used in medical imaging (e.g. orthopedics [17], neuroscience [15] and cardiology [14]), however, they usually require some form of surface parameterization (e.g. segmentation or meshes) and cannot be applied directly on images. Explicit correspondences between surfaces have been done using geometric parameterizations [12,25] as well as functional maps [22]. Particle distribution models (PDMs) [16] rely on a dense set of particles on surfaces whose positions are optimized to reduce the statistical complexity of the resulting model [10,11]. These sets of particles are then projected to a low-dimensional shape representation using PCA to facilitate subsequent analysis [27]. Some recent works leverage convolution neural networks (CNNs) to perform regression from images to a shape description of these dense correspondences [5,7]. These methods are supervised and require an existing shape model or manual landmarks for their training.

Deformable registration is also widely used as a tool for modeling shape variation/statistics [3], as well as atlas building [19]. Recent works rely on neural networks to perform unsupervised registration to atlases [2] or random pairs [6], and the deformation fields produced by these methods can be used as a shape representation for individuals. Statistical deformation models [20,24] are applied which learns the probability model for the manifold of deformation fields and reduce the dimension to use it for shape analysis. However, in our experience users across a wide range of applications in medicine and biology prefer the simplicity and interpretability of landmarks. Many of these same users also balk at the complexity of the dimensionality reduction methods that are needed to make these deformation fields useful for statistical analysis.

Another relevant work is from computer vision literature, of using an image deformation loss to learn dense features/feature maps [13,23]. Other works use convolution neural networks to learn shape features on surfaces to discover correspondences [8], or to be used for subsequent correspondence optimizations [1]. In this work, we learn landmark points, rather than features/feature maps, in a purely unsupervised setting.

3   Methods

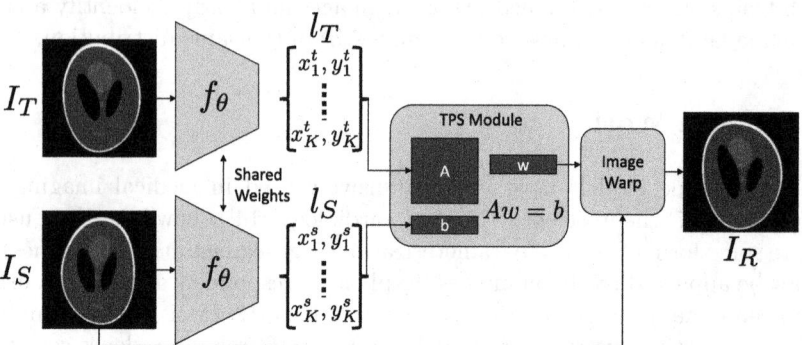

Fig. 2. Architecture for discovering anatomical shape landmarks in a self-supervised manner.

3.1   Model Description

The proposed self-supervised approach is that a NN should produce landmarks that best align the objects of interest in pairs of images, using as input many randomly chosen pairs from a set of images. The architecture contains a landmark regressor (NN) which discovers a vector of landmark positions on an image. The architecture includes a spatial transformer stage that takes as input the NN-generated landmarks and compares the resulting aligned images. For deformation we use a landmark-guided, radial basis function, *thin plate spline* (TPS) image registration, as in Fig. 2. For detecting landmarks, we need the system to be invariant pairing, i.e. always produce the same landmarks on an image. Therefore we use Siamese CNN networks [9] to extract the landmarks from source (I_S) and the target (I_T) images, and we denote these points l_S and l_T respectively. A single instance/sibling of the fully trained Siamese pair is the *detector*, which can be applied to training data or unseen data to produce landmarks. The output of a network (from the Siamese pair) is a $K \times d$ matrix, where K is the number of landmark points and d is the dimensionality of the image, typically either 2D or 3D. These features are treated as correspondences that go into the TPS solve module. The TPS registration entails the following steps: (i) create the kernel matrix A from l_T and the output position vector b using l_S, (ii) solve the linear system of equations ($Aw = b$) to get the TPS transformation parameters w, and (iii) using w the source image, warp the entire source grid into the registered image (I_R).

The loss for the entire network comprises of two terms:

$$\mathcal{L} = \mathcal{L}_{match}(I_T, I_R) + \lambda \mathcal{L}_{reg}(A) \tag{1}$$

The first term is the image matching term, any image registration loss which allows for backpropagation can be employed, in this work we work with L-2. However, more complex losses such as normalized cross-correlation [2] can also be used. The second term is the regularization term applied on the TPS transformation matrix kernel A, so that it does not become ill-conditioned, which can happen from the random initialization of the network or during optimization. To regularize A we use the condition number of the matrix using Frobenius Norm $(||A||_F = \sqrt{\sum_{i=1}^{M} \sum_{j=1}^{N} a_{ij}^2})$, defined as follows:

$$\mathcal{L}_{reg}(A) = \kappa_F(A) = ||A||_F ||A^{-1}||_F \tag{2}$$

A useful side effect of this regularization is as follows. The TPS kernel matrix becomes singular/ill-conditioned when two landmark positions are very close together, and therefore this regularization term, while preventing the matrix from being singular also encourages the resulting shape landmarks to be distributed in the image domain. This regularization loss is weighted by a scalar hyperparameter λ, which can be discovered via cross-validation for each dataset.

3.2 Training Methodology

The network is trained on a set of 2D/3D images in a pair-wise fashion. For smaller data sets, it is feasible to present the network with all pairs of images, as we have in the examples here. For larger image datasets, the n^2 training size may be too large and/or redundant, and random pairs could be used. For robust training, we train the Siamese network on images with a small added i.i.d Gaussian noise on the input, while using the original images for the loss computation on the transformed image. Finally, we whiten the image data (with zero mean and unit variance) before feeding it into the networks. We do not perform any data augmentation in the present results, however, to induce different invariances (e.g. intensity, rotation, etc.) one can employ sutible data augmentation in the training.

Landmarks Removal : As it can be seen in Fig. 1, when we discover landmarks there may be some which are *redundant*, i.e. they do not align with any significant anatomical features important for image registration. For this we propose a post-training method to weed out the redundant landmarks. After training the network, we re-register pairs of images by removing one landmark at a time, and we compute the difference in the registration loss computed using all the landmarks and by leaving one of them out. Averaging over all image pairs gives us an indicator of the importance of each landmark, and we can threshold and remove the ones with low importance. We apply this technique to the phantom data for testing. Figure 3 shows images/landmarks with and without the redundancy removal, demonstrating that landmarks in non-informative regions are removed. There are many alternative methods for culling landmarks, such as L1 regularized weights that the network might learn. We consider the study of alternative methods for landmark culling as beyond the scope of this paper.

4   Results

In this section we describe the performance of the proposed method on three datasets, (i) a Shepp-Logan (S-L) phantom (sythnthetic) dataset, (ii) a diatoms dataset with 2D images of diatoms of four morphological classes, (iii) a dataset of 3D cranial CT scans of infants for detection of craniosynostosis (a morphological disorder). We split each dataset into training, validation and testing images with 80%, 10%, 10% division, and the image pairs are taken from their respective set. For each dataset, the hyperparameter λ is discovered via 3-fold cross validation on the registration loss. In our experiments, we consider the registration loss as $\mathbb{L} - 2$ difference between the registered image and the target image. Detailed architecture for each dataset is presented in the supplementary material.

4.1   Phantom Dataset

We create a synthetic dataset using S-L phantom and creating randomly perturbed TPS warps using 6 control points, 2 on each ellipse endpoints, the boundary ellipse, and 2 black ellipses inside the phantom. We train our network on this dataset with 30 landmarks, with 4 constant landmarks placed on the corners of each image. We train the proposed network on this dataset for 20 epochs with a regularization coefficient of 0.0001, this gives an average test registration loss to reach 0.01%. Figure 3 showcases the results on this dataset, Fig. 3(a) and (b) are the source and target images overlayed with predicted features respectively, Fig. 3(c) represents the registered output. We also remove the redundant points

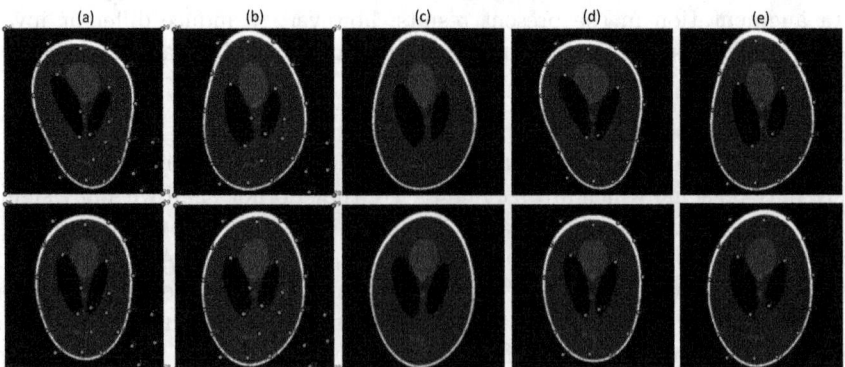

Fig. 3. Results on S-L phantom dataset, (a) and (b) an example of source-target image pair with learned landmarks overlayed, (c) the registered image (source image warped to target) and, (d) and (e) the same source and target pair with landmarks after the redundant points removal.

as described in Sect. 3.2, the retained points are shown in Fig. 3(d, e). Encouragingly, the redundancy metric shows high importance for points that are near the location of the control points from which the data was generated.

4.2 Diatoms Dataset

Diatoms are single-cell algae which are classified into different categories based on their shape and texture, which have biological applications [18]. The dataset consists of 2D diatom images with four different classes *Eunotia* (68 samples), *Fragilariforma* (100 samples), *Gomphonema* (100 samples) and *Stauroneis* (72 samples). We train the proposed network on a joint dataset of images from all four classes (all together, unlabeled/unsupervised), allowing the network to establish correspondences between different classes via discovered landmark positions. The goal is to see how well the discovered landmark positions describe the shape variation and distinguish the classes in the unsupervised setting. We whiten(zero mean, unit variance) the images before passing it through the network, use the regularization parameter set to 1e−5, and train the network to discover 26 landmarks. We train this dataset for 20 epochs which achieves the testing registration accuracy of 0.1%. Like with phantom data we compute the redundancy metric and remove landmarks below a threshold. Figure 4 (middle column) shows the images with only the retained landmarks and we see that the landmarks which did not lie on shape surfaces (left column) were removed for lack of impact on the losss function (point numbers 4, 6, 8, 14). We want to evaluate how well these landmarks used as shape descriptors perform on clustering these diatoms. For this, we use Spectral clustering [21] on the learned landmarks. We cluster landmarks coming from the training images and then predict the clusters for the validation as well as testing images (using the landmarks). The results are shown in the right column, which shows 2D PCA embedding of landmarks (shape features) labeled with ground truth clusters labels and the

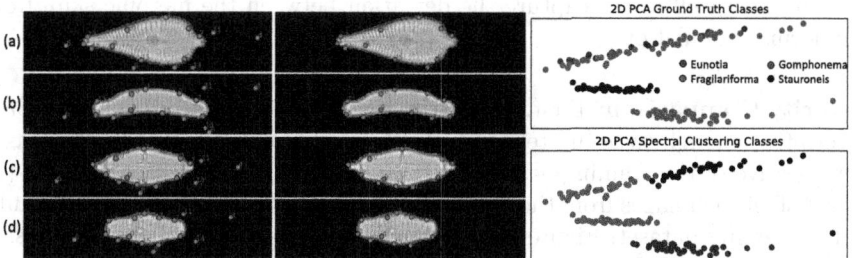

Fig. 4. The left image rows((a) Gomphonema, (b) Eunotia, (c) Stauroneis, (d) Fragilariforma) showcase 4 different images from test set corresponding to four different classes of diatoms and their predicted landmarks shown in cyan. The middle column shows the same images with redundant landmarks removed. The left column shows spectral clustering (in 2D PCA embedding space) evaluated on a test set and compared to ground truth labels.

predicted cluster label. The mismatch between *Eunotia* and *Fragilariforma* classes is due to the fact they both have a very similar shapes/sizes are typically also distinguished by intensity patterns, which are not part of this research.

4.3   Metopic Craniosynostosis

Metopic craniosynostosis is a morphological disorder of cranium in infants, caused by premature fusion of the metopic suture. The severity of metopic craniosynostosis is hypothesized to be dependent on the deviation of a skull's morphology from the shape statistics of the normal skull. There have been studies on diagnosing this condition [29] as well as characterizing the severity of the pathology [4] by various shape representation and modeling techniques. For this example we use 120 CT scans of the cranium with 93 normal phenotypical skulls with no deformity and 27 samples of metopic craniosynostosis (pathological scans for such conditions are generally less abundant). Each CT scan is a $101 \times 118 \times 142$ volume with an isotropic voxel resolution of $2\,mm$. We whiten (zero mean, unit variance) the data for training the network and train for 10 epochs with regularization weight of 0.00001 and 80 3D landmarks. The network saw both classes of scans but with no labels/supervision. After the redundancy removal we are only left with 49 landmarks. The registration performance of the system is shown in Fig. 5 (orange box) at the mid-axial slice of two source-target pairs. CT scans do not present with apparent information inside the skulls, however, with a very specific contrast setting (used in the figures) we can see grainy outlies of brain anatomy inside the skulls. An interesting thing to note is certain landmarks adhere to these low-contrast features, and are consistent across shapes. In row two of the figure, we show a normal skull as the source image and the target is a metopic skull, and trigonocephaly (triangular frontal head shape) which is a key characteristic in metopic craniosynostosis is captured by the three (in plane) landmarks, one on the frontal rim and two near the ears. Capturing this morphological symptom is essential in distinguishing the normal skulls from the metopic. Using these 49 landmarks as the shape descriptors we evaluate how well it can capture the deviation between the metopic skull from the normal population.

Severity Comparison: First, we want to study if the discovered landmarks are descriptive enough to accurately identify the pathology. We use all 120 images (irrespective of the training/testing set), we compute Mahalanobis distance (Z-score) of all the images from the base distribution formed using the normal skulls in the training dataset. Figure 5(green box) is the histogram of the Z-scores, it showcases that the Z-score of metopic skulls is larger on average than the normal skulls which support our hypothesis that the discovered low-dimensional landmark-based shape descriptor is enough to capture abnormal morphology. We also want to compare against a shape-of-the-art, correspondence-based shape model. We use *ShapeWorks* [10] as our PDM which involved segmenting the skulls, preprocessing (smoothing, anti-aliasing, etc.) and nonlinear optimizations, to place 2048 particles on each skull. *ShapeWorks* has been used in other

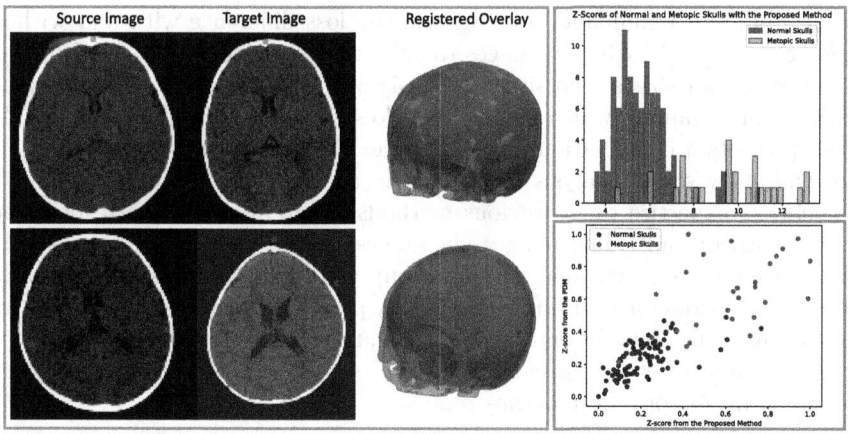

Fig. 5. (Orange Box) represents two instances of source and target 3D volumes, the first two images also show a specific contrast enhanced axial slice with discovered landmarks, and the third figure shows overlay of target segmentation and the registration segmentation. (Blue Box) Correlation between Z-scores from state-of-the-art PDM and Z-scores of landmark shape descriptors from the proposed method. (Green Box) Showcases the Z-scores from the landmark shape descriptor which is able to distinguish normal versus metopic skulls.(Color figure online)

metopic craniosynostosis severity analyses such as in [4]. We perform PCA to reduce the dense correspondences to 15 dimensions (95% of variability) and compute Z-scores (the base data to be the same scans as with the proposed method). We normalize Z-scores from both methods (PDM and the proposed one) and plot their scatter plot in Fig. 5 (blue box). We see that the correlation between the two methods is significant (correlation coefficient of 0.81), and hence, can predict/quantify the severity of metopic craniosynostosis equally well. This demonstrates that the landmarks discovered by our method are a good substitute for the state-of-the-art PDM model with very low amounts of pre- and postprocessing overhead. Also, it is much faster to get shape descriptors for new images as compared with conventional PDM methods.

5 Conclusions

In this paper, we present an end-to-end methodology for processing sets of roughly aligned 2D/3D images to discover landmarks on the images, which then can be used for subsequent shape analysis. Under the assumption that good landmarks can produce a better image to image registration, we propose a self-supervised neural network architecture that optimizes the TPS registration loss between pairs of images with an intermediate landmark discovery that feeds into the TPS registration module. Additionally, we also propose a regularizer that ensures TPS solvability and encourage more uniform landmark distribution.

We also apply a redundancy removal via the loss difference with and without a particular particle, which manages to cull uninformative landmarks. However, for future work there is a possibility of assigning importance to individual landmarks during training which can be used for removing redundant points. This paper presents a combination of technologies that result in a turn-key system, that will allow shape analysis to be used in a wide range of applications with a much less expertise than previous methods. In addition, the correspondence are provided on individual images via siamese network, which opens possibilities for using these correspondences for group-wise shape analysis as well as atlas building. We showcase that our methodology places landmarks qualitatively corresponding to distinct anatomical features and that these landmarks can work as shape descriptors for downstream tasks such as clustering for diatoms or severity prediction for metopic craniosynostosis.

Acknowledgements. This work was supported by NIH grants: R21 EB026061 and R01- HL135568, as well as supported by National Institute of General Medical Sciences of the National Institutes of Health under grant number P41 GM103545-18 'Center for Integrative Biomedical Computing'.

References

1. Agrawal, P., Whitaker, R.T., Elhabian, S.Y.: Learning deep features for automated placement of correspondence points on ensembles of complex shapes. In: Descoteaux, M., Maier-Hein, L., Franz, A., Jannin, P., Collins, D.L., Duchesne, S. (eds.) MICCAI 2017. LNCS, vol. 10433, pp. 185–193. Springer, Cham (2017). https://doi.org/10.1007/978-3-319-66182-7_22
2. Balakrishnan, G., Zhao, A., Sabuncu, M., Guttag, J., Dalca, A.V.: Voxelmorph: a learning framework for deformable medical image registration. IEEE TMI: Trans. Med. Imaging **38**, 1788–1800 (2019)
3. Beg, M.F., Miller, M.I., Trouvé, A., Younes, L.: Computing large deformation metric mappings via geodesic flows of diffeomorphisms. Int. J. Comput. Vis. **61**(2), 139–157 (2005)
4. Bhalodia, R., Dvoracek, L.A., Ayyash, A.M., Kavan, L., Whitaker, R., Goldstein, J.A.: Quantifying the severity of metopic craniosynostosis: a pilot study application of machine learning in craniofacial surgery. J. Craniofac. Surg. **31**(3), 697–701 (2020)
5. Bhalodia, R., Elhabian, S.Y., Kavan, L., Whitaker, R.T.: DeepSSM: a deep learning framework for statistical shape modeling from raw images. In: Reuter, M., Wachinger, C., Lombaert, H., Paniagua, B., Lüthi, M., Egger, B. (eds.) ShapeMI 2018. LNCS, vol. 11167, pp. 244–257. Springer, Cham (2018). https://doi.org/10.1007/978-3-030-04747-4_23
6. Bhalodia, R., Elhabian, S.Y., Kavan, L., Whitaker, R.T.: A cooperative autoencoder for population-based regularization of CNN image registration. In: Shen, D., et al. (eds.) MICCAI 2019. LNCS, vol. 11765, pp. 391–400. Springer, Cham (2019). https://doi.org/10.1007/978-3-030-32245-8_44
7. Bhalodia, R., et al.: Deep learning for end-to-end atrial fibrillation recurrence estimation. In: Computing in Cardiology, CinC, pp. 1–4. www.cinc.org (2018)

8. Boscaini, D., Masci, J., Rodoià, E., Bronstein, M.: Learning shape correspondence with anisotropic convolutional neural networks. In: Proceedings of the 30th International Conference on Neural Information Processing Systems, pp. 3197–3205. NIPS 2016, Curran Associates Inc. (2016)
9. Bromley, J., Guyon, I., LeCun, Y., Säckinger, E., Shah, R.: Signature verification using a "siamese" time delay neural network. In: Advances in Neural Information Processing Systems, pp. 737–744 (1994)
10. Cates, J., Fletcher, P.T., Styner, M., Shenton, M., Whitaker, R.: Shape modeling and analysis with entropy-based particle systems. In: Karssemeijer, N., Lelieveldt, B. (eds.) IPMI 2007. LNCS, vol. 4584, pp. 333–345. Springer, Heidelberg (2007). https://doi.org/10.1007/978-3-540-73273-0_28
11. Davies, R.H., Twining, C.J., Cootes, T.F., Waterton, J.C., Taylor, C.J.: A minimum description length approach to statistical shape modeling. IEEE Trans. Med. Imaging **21**(5), 525–537 (2002). https://doi.org/10.1109/TMI.2002.1009388
12. Davies, R.H., Twining, C.J., Cootes, T.F., Waterton, J.C., Taylor, C.J.: 3D statistical shape models using direct optimisation of description length. In: Heyden, A., Sparr, G., Nielsen, M., Johansen, P. (eds.) ECCV 2002. LNCS, vol. 2352, pp. 3–20. Springer, Heidelberg (2002). https://doi.org/10.1007/3-540-47977-5_1
13. DeTone, D., Malisiewicz, T., Rabinovich, A.: Superpoint: self-supervised interest point detection and description. In: CVPR Deep Learning for Visual SLAM Workshop (2018). http://arxiv.org/abs/1712.07629
14. Gardner, G., Morris, A., Higuchi, K., MacLeod, R., Cates, J.: A point-correspondence approach to describing the distribution of image features on anatomical surfaces, with application to atrial fibrillation. In: 2013 IEEE 10th International Symposium on Biomedical Imaging, pp. 226–229 (April 2013). https://doi.org/10.1109/ISBI.2013.6556453
15. Gerig, G., Styner, M., Jones, D., Weinberger, D., Lieberman, J.: Shape analysis of brain ventricles using spharm. In: Proceedings IEEE Workshop on Mathematical Methods in Biomedical Image Analysis (MMBIA 2001), pp. 171–178 (2001). https://doi.org/10.1109/MMBIA.2001.991731
16. Grenander, U., Chow, Y., Keenan, D.M.: Hands: A Pattern Theoretic Study of Biological Shapes. Springer, New York (1991)
17. Harris, M.D., Datar, M., Whitaker, R.T., Jurrus, E.R., Peters, C.L., Anderson, A.E.: Statistical shape modeling of cam femoroacetabular impingement. J. Orthop. Res. **31**(10), 1620–1626 (2013). https://doi.org/10.1002/jor.22389
18. Hicks, Y.A., Marshall, D., Rosin, P., Martin, R.R., Mann, D.G., Droop, S.J.M.: A model for diatom shape and texture for analysis, synthesis and identification. Mach. Vis. Appl. **17**(5), 297–307 (2006)
19. Joshi, S., Davis, B., Jomier, M., Gerig, G.: Unbiased diffeomorphic atlas construction for computational anatomy. NeuroImage **23**(Supplement1), S151–S160 (2004). Supplement issue on Mathematics in Brain Imaging
20. Joshi, S.C., Miller, M.I., Grenander, U.: On the geometry and shape of brain submanifolds. Int. J. Pattern Recog. Artif. Intell. **11**(08), 1317–1343 (1997)
21. Luxburg, U.V.: A tutorial on spectral clustering. Stat. Comput. **17**(4), 395–416 (2007)
22. Ovsjanikov, M., Ben-Chen, M., Solomon, J., Butscher, A., Guibas, L.: Functional maps: a flexible representation of maps between shapes. ACM Trans. Graph. (TOG) **31**(4), 30 (2012)
23. Rocco, I., Arandjelović, R., Sivic, J.: Convolutional neural network architecture for geometric matching. In: Proceedings of the IEEE Conference on Computer Vision and Pattern Recognition, pp. 6148–6157 (2017)

24. Rueckert, D., Frangi, A.F., Schnabel, J.A.: Automatic construction of 3-D statistical deformation models of the brain using nonrigid registration. IEEE Trans. Med. Imaging **22**(8), 1014–1025 (2003)
25. Styner, M., Brechbuhler, C., Szekely, G., Gerig, G.: Parametric estimate of intensity inhomogeneities applied to MRI. IEEE Trans. Med. Imaging **19**(3), 153–165 (2000)
26. Styner, M., Oguz, I., Xu, S., Brechbuehler, C., Pantazis, D., Levitt, J., Shenton, M., Gerig, G.: Framework for the statistical shape analysis of brain structures using spharm-pdm (07 2006)
27. Bieging, E.T., et al.: Left atrial shape predicts recurrence after atrial fibrillation catheter ablation. J. Cardiovasc. Electrophysiol. **29**(7), 966–972 (2018). https://doi.org/10.1111/jce.13641
28. Thompson, D.W., et al.: On growth and form. On growth and form. (1942)
29. Wood, B.C., Mendoza, C.S., Oh, A.K., Myers, E., Safdar, N., Linguraru, M.G., Rogers, G.F.: What's in a name? accurately diagnosing metopic craniosynostosis using a computational approach. Plastic and Reconstructive Surgery **137**(1), 205–213 (2016)

Shape Mask Generator: Learning to Refine Shape Priors for Segmenting Overlapping Cervical Cytoplasms

Youyi Song[1]([✉]), Lei Zhu[2], Baiying Lei[3], Bin Sheng[4], Qi Dou[5], Jing Qin[1], and Kup-Sze Choi[1]

[1] Center for Smart Health, School of Nursing, The Hong Kong Polytechnic University, Hong Kong, China
youyisong.song@connect.polyu.hk
[2] College of Intelligence and Computing, Tianjin University, Tianjin, China
[3] School of Biomedical Engineering, Shenzhen University, Shenzhen, China
[4] School of Mechanical Engineering, Shanghai Jiao Tong University, Shanghai, China
[5] Department of Computer Science and Engineering,
The Chinese University of Hong Kong, Hong Kong, China

Abstract. Segmenting overlapping cytoplasm of cervical cells plays a crucial role in cervical cancer screening. This task, however, is rather challenging, mainly because intensity (or color) information in the overlapping region is deficient for recognizing occluded boundary parts. Existing methods attempt to compensate intensity deficiency by exploiting shape priors, but shape priors modeled by them have a weak representation ability, and hence their segmentation results are often visually implausible in shape. In this paper, we propose a conceptually simple and effective technique, called shape mask generator, for segmenting overlapping cytoplasms. The key idea is to progressively refine shape priors by learning so that they can accurately represent most cytoplasms' shape. Specifically, we model shape priors from shape templates and feed them to the shape mask generator that generates a shape mask for the cytoplasm as the segmentation result. Shape priors are refined by minimizing the 'generating residual' in the training dataset, which is designed to have a smaller value when the shape mask generator producing shape masks that are more consistent with the image information. The introduced method is assessed on two datasets, and the empirical evidence shows that it is effective, outperforming existing methods.

Keywords: Shape mask generator · Refining shape priors · Overlapping cytoplasms segmentation · Cervical cancer screening

Electronic supplementary material The online version of this chapter (https://doi.org/10.1007/978-3-030-59719-1_62) contains supplementary material, which is available to authorized users.

© Springer Nature Switzerland AG 2020
A. L. Martel et al. (Eds.): MICCAI 2020, LNCS 12264, pp. 639–649, 2020.
https://doi.org/10.1007/978-3-030-59719-1_62

1   Introduction

Segmenting overlapping cytoplasm of cervical cells enables us to extract cell-level information of cervical cells, e.g. cytoplasm size, shape, etc. This level of information is required in the clinical practice for screening cervical cancer [1–3] which has been proven to be able to significantly reduce the incidence and mortality of cervical cancer [4,5]—the fourth most common cause of cancer and the fourth most common cause of death from cancer in women all over the world [6].

It is, however, a very challenging task, mainly due to the deficiency of intensity (or color) information in the overlapping region, as shown in Fig. (1) (a). In addition, it is rather difficult to leverage other successful segmentation algorithms, e.g. deep networks like U-Net [7], because this task is more general and complex; these successful algorithms just handle the special and simple case where one pixel just need to be segmented to one object and the objects' number is fixed and known, while in our task pixels in the overlapping region should be segmented to at least two objects and the objects' number is unknown and not fixed.

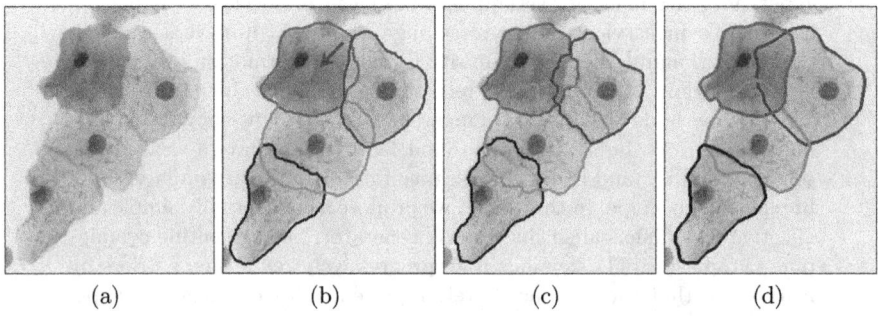

(a)	(b)	(c)	(d)

Fig. 1. Illustration of the challenge and problems of existing methods; (a) the challenge: intensity information in the overlapping region is deficient, (b) and (c) the problems: intensity-based method [13] is sensitive to image quality (b) while shape priors-based method [26] produces a visually implausible result (c), and (d) the ground truth.

There are two major streams of methods to deal with this challenging: (1) intensity- [8–16] and (2) shape priors-based [17–26]. Intensity-based methods attempt to exploit intensity and spatial information together, commonly by extending classic segmentation algorithms, e.g. thresholding [8–10], watershed [11–13], graph-cut [14], and morphological filtering [15,16]. They are sensitive to image quality, often failing when intensity information is seriously deficient; see Fig. (1) (b). Shape priors-based methods attempt to exploit shape priors for compensating intensity deficiency; they produce segmentation results by using modeled shape priors in shape-aware segmentation frameworks, e.g. level set model [27–29]. But they model shape priors by either a simple shape assumption (e.g. cytoplasm has a star shape [17] or an elliptical shape [18–20]) or a shape template matched from the collected set [21–26], resulting in a weak representation ability of the modeled priors, which often makes their segmentation results visually implausible in shape; see Fig. 1(c).

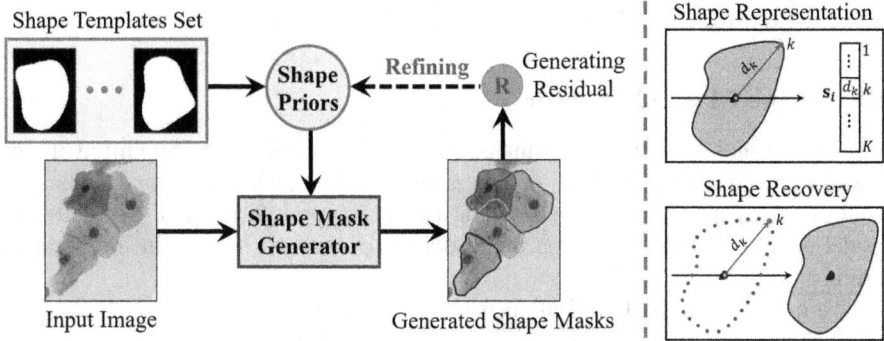

Fig. 2. The pipeline of the shape priors refinement procedure. Shape representation: we sample K boundary points with the same angle interval, and store the distance d_k (the boundary point k to nucleus' centroid) at the k-th entry of $\mathbf{s}_i$. Shape recovery: we first locate the corresponding K boundary points in the image, and then fill in the region outlined by these K points.

In this paper, we introduce a conceptually simple and effective technique, called shape mask generator, for segmenting overlapping cervical cytoplasms, with the key idea to progressively enhance shape priors' representation ability. Shape mask generator directly generates a shape mask for the cytoplasm as the segmentation, under the guidance of shape priors that are modeled from shape templates, allowing pixels to be segmented to several objects. Shape priors' representation ability is enhanced by learning to refine them, via minimizing the 'generating residual' in the training dataset. The generating residual is designed to have a smaller value when the generator producing shape masks that are more consistent with the image information. We assess the introduced method on two datasets, and the empirical results show that it (1) can enhance shape priors' representation ability and (2) works better than existing methods.

2   Methodology

Figure (2) shows the pipeline of how we learn to refine shape priors for guiding the shape mask generator to generate shape masks for segmenting overlapping cytoplasms. We start by modeling shape priors: $\boldsymbol{\mu}$ and $\mathbf{M}$, from shape templates, where $\boldsymbol{\mu}$ is the mean of collected templates and $\mathbf{M}$ consists of eigenvectors of collected templates' covariance matrix. Here note that shape is represented by a vector storing K boundary points' information, as shown in Fig. (2). We then refine $\boldsymbol{\mu}$ and $\mathbf{M}$ by solving for the following problem

$$\{\boldsymbol{\mu}^*, \mathbf{M}^*\} = \underset{\boldsymbol{\mu}, \mathbf{M}}{\operatorname{argmin}} \, \mathbb{E}_{\mathcal{D}} \big[\mathrm{R}\big(\mathbf{I}, \mathrm{G}(\mathbf{I}; \boldsymbol{\mu}, \mathbf{M})\big) \big], \tag{1}$$

where $\mathbb{E}_{\mathcal{D}}$ means the expectation on the training dataset $\mathcal{D}$, and R is a function to measure the generating residual between the generated shape masks $\mathrm{G}(\mathbf{I}; \boldsymbol{\mu}, \mathbf{M})$ and the training example $\mathbf{I}$, for evaluating shape masks' quality. Technical details are presented below.

2.1   Shape Mask Generator

We now present how the shape mask generator to work. Given the input image $\mathbf{I}$, and shape priors: $\boldsymbol{\mu}$ and $\mathbf{M}$, it generates a shape mask $\mathbf{s}_i$ for the cytoplasm i by finding an appropriate $\mathbf{x}_i$ according to the image information. Specially, we model $\mathbf{s}_i = \boldsymbol{\mu} + \mathbf{M}\mathbf{x}_i$. Below are the details of how to find $\mathbf{x}_i$ in an iterative manner.

We initialize $\mathbf{x}_i$ as $\mathbf{0}$, and align it to the image by

$$\operatorname{argmax}(B_i \cap B_c), \text{ s.t. } B_i \subset B_c, \tag{2}$$

where B_i is the aligned binary mask of cytoplasm i by rotating and scaling the binary mask of $\mathbf{s}_i$, and B_c is the binary mask of the clump area. Here note that for the alignment, we employ a multi-scale convolutional neural network (CNN) [30] to segment the clump area and nuclei, and how to transform $\mathbf{s}_i$ to its binary mask is illustrated in Fig. 2 (Shape Recovery).

We then check the quality of generated shape masks by

$$\mathbb{E}(B_c, \mathbf{x}) = \sum_{(x,y) \in \Omega_B} \big(B_u(x, y) - B_c(x, y) \big)^2, \tag{3}$$

where $\mathbf{x}$ collectively denotes all $\mathbf{x}_i$ for the clump, and $B_u = \bigcup B_i$ is the binary union. We can see that this function has the minimal value of 0 when the generated B_u is same as B_c, and is a monotone increasing function with the increase of the difference between B_u and B_c. We hence find a better value of $\mathbf{x}_i$ by decreasing this function, and once we have got a better value of $\mathbf{x}_i$, we repeat the above procedure (align and re-find) until this function cannot be decreased. The terminated $\mathbf{x}_i^*$ then is aligned to the image to produce the segmentation result of cytoplasm i, and the generating residual $\mathrm{R}\big(\mathbf{I}, \mathrm{G}(\mathbf{I}; \boldsymbol{\mu}\mathbf{M})\big)$ is set to $\mathbb{E}(B_c, \mathbf{x}^*)$.

We now go into how to decrease $\mathbb{E}(B_c, \mathbf{x})$. Our goal is to find a $\mathbf{p}$ such that $\mathbb{E}(B_c\mathbf{x} + \mathbf{p}) < \mathbb{E}(B_c\mathbf{x})$. To do so, we approximate $\mathbb{E}(B_c\mathbf{x} + \mathbf{p})$ as

$$\mathbb{E}(B_c\mathbf{x} + \mathbf{p}) \approx \mathbb{E}(B_c\mathbf{x}) + \nabla\mathbb{E}(B_c\mathbf{x})^T \mathbf{p} + \frac{1}{2}\mathbf{p}^T \nabla^2 \mathbb{E}(B_c\mathbf{x})\mathbf{p}, \tag{4}$$

where ∇ and ∇^2 are the gradient and the Hessian. This approximation is especially accurate when $\|\mathbf{p}\|_2$ is small; the approximation error is $O(\|\mathbf{p}\|_2^3)$. We then get the optimal value of $\mathbf{p}$ by

$$\mathbf{p}^* = \underset{\mathbf{p} \in \Omega_{\mathbf{p}}}{\operatorname{argmin}} \, \mathbb{E}(B_c\mathbf{x} + \mathbf{p}), \text{ s.t. } \|\mathbf{p}\|_2 \leq \triangle, \tag{5}$$

where $\triangle > 0$ is the radius that specifies the region in which we search $\mathbf{p}^*$. We solve the above equation (Eq. 5) by employing the trust-region algorithm [31] that automatically chooses the value of $\triangle$.

2.2 Refining Shape Priors

We now look at how we solve Eq. 1 for refining $\boldsymbol{\mu}$ and $\mathbf{M}$, given the training dataset $\mathcal{D} = \{(\mathbf{I}^j, B_c^j, \{\mathbf{s}_i^j\}_{i=1}^{N_j})\}_{j=1}^N$, where B_c^j is the binary mask of the clump area of the training example $\mathbf{I}^j$, and $\mathbf{s}_i^j$ is the shape template of cytoplasm i in $\mathbf{I}^j$ that has N_j cytoplasms. We first take out all shape templates $\{\mathbf{s}_i^j\}$ from $\mathcal{D}$, and compute $\boldsymbol{\mu}$ and the covariance matrix as

$$\boldsymbol{\mu} = \frac{1}{W} \sum_{j=1}^N \sum_{i=1}^{N_j} w_i^j \mathbf{s}_i^j \text{ and } \mathbf{M}_c = \frac{1}{N_c} \sum_{j=1}^N \sum_{i=1}^{N_j} (\mathbf{s}_i^j - \boldsymbol{\mu})(\mathbf{s}_i^j - \boldsymbol{\mu})^T, \qquad (6)$$

where W is the sum of templates' importance $\{w_i^j\}$ which are initialized as 1, and N_c is the number of all cytoplasms in $\mathcal{D}$. $\mathbf{M}$ is comprised of the first t eigenvectors of $\mathbf{M}_c$, in a column order with the decreasing eigenvalue; t's value is analyzed in the next section (Sec. 3).

We refine $\boldsymbol{\mu}$ and $\mathbf{M}$ by learning an appropriate value of $\{w_i^j\}$. We start by randomly taking an training example $(\mathbf{I}^j, B_c^j, \{\mathbf{s}_i^j\}_{i=1}^{N_j})$, and update $\{w_i^j\}_{i=1}^{N_j}$ one by one at each step. At each step, we continue to increase w_i^j by ℓ if the corresponding generating residual $\mathrm{R}(\mathbf{I}^j, \mathrm{G}(\mathbf{I}^j; \boldsymbol{\mu}\mathbf{M}))$ decreases; note that we define $\mathrm{R}(\mathbf{I}^j, \mathrm{G}(\mathbf{I}^j; \boldsymbol{\mu}\mathbf{M})) = \mathbb{E}(B_c^j, \mathbf{x}^*)$, as mentioned before. Once all $\{w_i^j\}_{i=1}^{N_j}$ have been updated, we update another new example. Once all examples have been updated, the updating procedure cycles again through all examples, until the generating residual cannot be decreased for all examples.

The refining algorithm is guaranteed to arrive at the right importance, and it holds regardless of which example and which shape template in the example we choose at each updating step. The formal proof is provided in the material. We here just give an intuitive explanation. The updating rule can be simply viewed as a random walk [32], moving towards $\mathbf{w}^*$ at some steps while also being away from $\mathbf{w}^*$ at other steps, where $\mathbf{w}^*$ denotes the right importance, meaning by which the generating residual is minimal for all training examples. This random walk is biased. $\mathbf{w}^T(t)\mathbf{w}^*$ grows linearly with t and $\mathbf{w}(t)$ is biased away from $\mathbf{w}(t-1)$ which makes $\|\mathbf{w}(t)\|$ grow at most as $\sqrt{t}$; $\mathbf{w}(t)$ denotes the learned importance at step t. So, if t was infinitely large, then $\frac{\mathbf{w}^T(t)\mathbf{w}^*}{\|\mathbf{w}(t)\|\|\mathbf{w}^*\|} \propto \frac{t}{\sqrt{t}} = \sqrt{t} = +\infty$. But $\frac{\mathbf{w}^T(t)\mathbf{w}^*}{\|\mathbf{w}(t)\|\|\mathbf{w}^*\|}$ cannot be greater than 1. This contradiction implies that t is finite, meaning that after finite t steps, $\mathbf{w}(t)$ makes the generating residual be minimal for all examples, which implies that $\mathbf{w}(t) = \mathbf{w}^*$.

3   Experimental Evaluation

3.1   Datasets

We assess our method on two datasets with different staining manners: Papanicolaou (Pap) stain and Hematoxylin and Eosin (H&E) stain. Pap stain dataset is obtained from [34]. It has 60 clumps with 316 cytoplasms; there are 5 cytoplasms on average in a clump. H&E stain dataset is obtained from [21]. It has 160 clumps with 962 cytoplasms; there are 6 cytoplasms on average in a clump.

3.2   Evaluation Metrics

We employed two metrics: (1) DSC, Dice Similarity Coefficient and (2) SSC, Shape Similarity Coefficient. DSC aims at measuring the matching extent of the segmentation result and ground truth by normalizing pixels' number in their intersection over the average of pixels' number in them. SSC aims at measuring the visually implausible extent of the segmentation result against ground truth; it is suggested by recent studies [25, 26]. They both have a value in $[0, 1]$, and a larger value of them indicates a better segmentation algorithm.

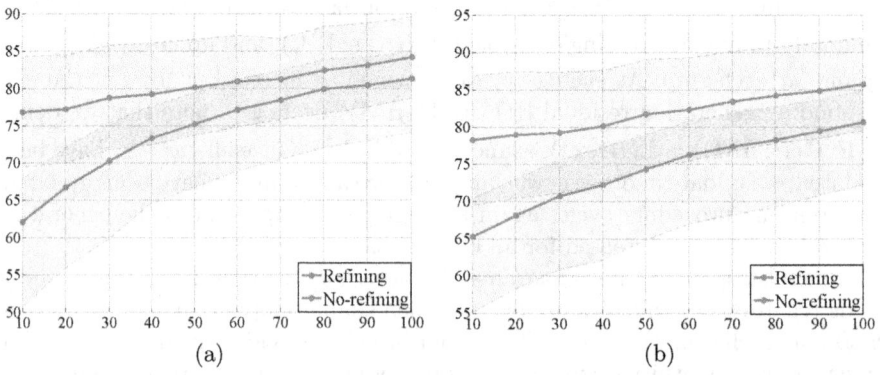

Fig. 3. Segmentation accuracy, (a) for DSC and (b) for SSC (both in a percentage manner), with and without refining the modeled shape priors, under different amounts of shape templates (from 10% to 100% of cytoplasms we have).

3.3   Parameters Selection

Our method has two parameters: (1) the number of boundary points (K) for representing cytoplasm's shape, and (2) the number of eigenvectors for getting the shape priors **M**. We set K to 360, such that each boundary point represents the shape at each integer angle of the shape. It also can be set to 180 or 720 (or even 90 or 1080) without any considerable performance varying, while a larger value of it consumes more computational cost. As for eigenvectors' number, a larger value of it, more local shape details are captured, and then the representative ability increases. But at the same time the dimension of $\mathbf{x}_i$ also increases, then consuming more computational resources. We finally set it to 20, as suggested in [35].

3.4   Experimental Results

Representative Ability Improvement : We first evaluate how much extent the representative ability of the modeled shape priors can be improved by refining them. To do so, we compared the segmentation accuracy of the proposed method with its variant that is without refining the modeled shape priors. We also considered the effect of shape templates' number; intuitively, more templates used, more shape information is available, and hence a stronger representative ability is likely to be obtained. We hence examined the segmentation accuracy on different amounts of shape templates, from 10% to 100% of cytoplasms we have (with an interval of 10%). In each examination, we randomly sampled shape templates, and tested algorithms on the whole dataset instead of the remaining examples in order to reduce the sampling bias. For further reducing the sampling bias, for each amount we examined 5 times, and reported their mean with the standard deviation.

Table 1. Segmentation results by DSC (%) under four different overlapping extents.

	Pap stain dataset				H&E stain dataset			
	$(0, \frac{1}{4})$	$[\frac{1}{4}, \frac{2}{4})$	$[\frac{2}{4}, \frac{3}{4})$	$[\frac{3}{4}, 1)$	$(0, \frac{1}{4})$	$[\frac{1}{4}, \frac{2}{4})$	$[\frac{2}{4}, \frac{3}{4})$	$[\frac{3}{4}, 1)$
LSF [19]	81.1 ± 7.4	77.4 ± 6.1	74.3 ± 7.1	71.9 ± 10.7	80.7 ± 8.0	75.2 ± 7.6	72.8 ± 8.4	69.4 ± 11.2
MCL [21]	80.1 ± 5.2	79.7 ± 6.4	77.3 ± 7.4	72.7 ± 8.7	81.3 ± 6.4	76.7 ± 8.2	72.2 ± 8.2	70.7 ± 9.3
MPW [13]	82.2 ± 6.4	80.4 ± 7.6	77.6 ± 7.0	73.2 ± 9.4	81.3 ± 7.2	79.1 ± 9.2	74.1 ± 8.3	71.6 ± 10.4
CF [26]	84.1 ± 8.2	82.1 ± 5.1	79.6 ± 6.7	77.2 ± 7.6	83.2 ± 7.1	81.3 ± 8.3	79.7 ± 8.4	75.2 ± 9.4
Ours	**85.4 ± 4.9**	**83.9 ± 4.7**	**82.3 ± 6.4**	**81.0 ± 6.3**	**84.6 ± 5.4**	**83.4 ± 5.2**	**82.1 ± 6.4**	**80.7 ± 7.2**

Table 2. Segmentation results by SSC (%) under four different overlapping extents.

	Pap stain dataset				H&E stain dataset			
	$(0, \frac{1}{4})$	$[\frac{1}{4}, \frac{2}{4})$	$[\frac{2}{4}, \frac{3}{4})$	$[\frac{3}{4}, 1)$	$(0, \frac{1}{4})$	$[\frac{1}{4}, \frac{2}{4})$	$[\frac{2}{4}, \frac{3}{4})$	$[\frac{3}{4}, 1)$
LSF [19]	77.8 ± 8.2	77.1 ± 8.4	75.6 ± 8.1	73.2 ± 8.4	78.1 ± 8.2	80.0 ± 8.7	75.6 ± 9.8	71.4 ± 10.1
MCL [21]	81.1 ± 7.5	79.6 ± 7.9	75.2 ± 8.9	74.1 ± 10.3	83.4 ± 8.7	81.2 ± 9.0	76.1 ± 10.7	72.1 ± 11.2
MPW [13]	82.4 ± 7.1	80.1 ± 7.3	77.2 ± 8.5	74.7 ± 9.2	84.3 ± 9.7	82.1 ± 10.4	77.4 ± 10.7	74.8 ± 10.4
CF [26]	86.3 ± 5.9	84.1 ± 6.7	79.7 ± 7.4	75.2 ± 8.7	86.7 ± 7.1	84.2 ± 7.7	80.1 ± 8.4	76.7 ± 8.2
Ours	**87.8 ± 5.4**	**86.1 ± 5.7**	**83.8 ± 6.3**	**81.7 ± 6.8**	**88.4 ± 7.2**	**86.4 ± 7.4**	**83.2 ± 7.6**	**81.3 ± 7.4**

Results are presented in Fig. (3) where DSC and SSC are both reported in a percentage manner. We can see that the segmentation accuracy is improved in all cases by refining shape priors, demonstrating that the proposed refining

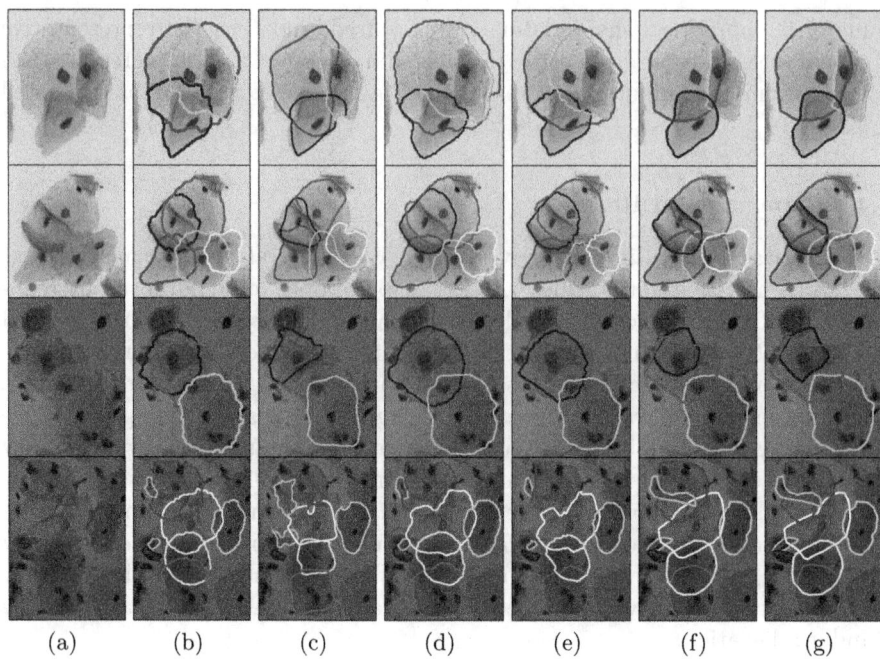

(a)   (b)   (c)   (d)   (e)   (f)   (g)

Fig. 4. Visual comparison of the proposed method against LSF [19], MCL [21], MPW [13], and CF [26] on four examples: (a) input images, (b)–(f) segmentation results of LSF, MCL, MPW, CF, and the proposed method, respectively, and (g) the ground truth. Note that examples' size has been scaled for better viewing, and that the first two examples come from the Pap stain dataset while the last two examples from the H&E stain dataset.

algorithm can improve shape priors' representative ability. We also can see that the segmentation accuracy is improved less with more shape templates used. It is mainly because in the specified dataset the improvement room is narrowing with more shape templates used. For example, when using 100% templates, theoretically the modeled shape priors should be able to represent all cytoplasms' shape, because all shapes have been seen, so their representative ability cannot be improved so much as that with fewer templates used.

Segmentation Accuracy Improvement : We now look at how much extent the segmentation accuracy can be improved by our method. We hence compare our method with LSF [19], MCL [21], MPW [13], and CF [26]. Among them, MPW is an intensity-based method by developing the watershed algorithm, while LSF, MCL, and CF belong to shape priors-based methods (LSF models shape priors by assuming cytoplasm has an elliptical shape, while MCL and CF by matching shape template). We produced their segmentation results by either re-running the implementation codes provided by the authors or using the implementation provided by the authors with the recommend parameter setting.

We acquired results based on a 5-fold cross-validation, and reported them in Table 1 for *DSC* and Table 2 for *SSC* (in a percentage manner), under four different overlapping extents for further evaluating how much overlapping extent the methods can deal with. The overlapping extent is defined as the length ratio of the occluded boundary part(s) against the whole boundary of that cytoplasm. It is observed from Table 1 and Table 2 that our method produced the most accurate segmentation result under all overlapping extents.

We now look at four visual examples shown in Fig. (4), for further visually evaluating the segmentation accuracy improvement. In all four examples, the intensity deficiency issue arises; in each example there is at least one cytoplasm whose occluded boundary part(s) is nearly visually invisible. We can see from Fig. (4) that the proposed method produced the most accurate results, and implausible results are substantially reduced compared with LSF [19], MCL [21], MPW [13], and CF [26]. Furthermore, some of our results are even comparable with the ground truth. These four examples demonstrate again that the proposed method works better than existing methods: LSF, MCL, MPW, and CF.

4   Conclusion

In order to screen cervical cancer, cell-level information is required in the clinical practice, which motivates us to segment overlapping cervical cytoplasms. The research problem is that intensity information is often deficient for recognizing the occluded boundary parts. Our idea is to refine shape priors such that it can represent most cytoplasms' shape. Our research assumption hence is that intensity deficiency can be substantially compensated by the representative shape priors. We concrete our idea by first (1) modeling shape priors from shape templates, then (2) using modeled shape priors to generate a shape mask for the cytoplasm as the segmentation result, and finally (3) refining modeled shape priors by minimizing the generating residual that encourages the generated shape masks to be consistent with image information. The refining algorithm is well designed such that it is strictly guaranteed to produce the most representative shape priors. The proposed method is assessed on two datasets with different staining manners, and the experimental evidence shows that (1) shape priors' representative ability can be effectively enhanced, (2) the segmentation accuracy can be effectively improved (especially, visually implausible results are substantially reduced compared with existing methods).

Acknowledgement. The work described in this paper is supported by a grant from the Hong Kong Research Grants Council (Project No. 15205919), a grant from the Hong Kong Polytechnic University (Project No. PolyU 152009/18E), a grant from the National Natural Science Foundation of China (Grant No. 61902275), a grant from the Innovative Technology Fund (Grant No. MRP/015/18), and a grant from the General Research Fund (Grant No. PolyU 152006/19E).

References

1. Davey, E., Barratt, A., Irwig, L., et al.: Effect of study design and quality on unsatisfactory rates, cytology classifications, and accuracy in liquid-based versus conventional cervical cytology: a systematic review. Lancet **367**(9505), 122–132 (2006)
2. Kitchener, H., Blanks, R., Dunn, G., et al.: Automation-assisted versus manual reading of cervical cytology (MAVARIC): a randomised controlled trial. Lancet Oncol. **12**(1), 56–64 (2011)
3. Guven, M., Cengizler, C.: Data cluster analysis-based classification of overlapping nuclei in Pap smear samples. Biomed. Eng. Online **13**(1), 159 (2014)
4. Schiffman, M., Castle, P.E., Jeronimo, J., Rodriguez, A.C., Wacholder, S.: Human papillomavirus and cervical cancer. Lancet **370**(9590), 890–907 (2007)
5. Saslow, D., et al.: American cancer society, American society for colposcopy and cervical pathology, and American society for clinical pathology screening guidelines for the prevention and early detection of cervical cancer. CA. Cancer J. Clin. **62**(3), 147–172 (2012)
6. WHO.: World cancer report, chapter 5.12 (2014). ISBN 9283204298
7. Ronneberger, O., Fischer, P., Brox, T.: U-Net: convolutional networks for biomedical image segmentation. In: Navab, N., Hornegger, J., Wells, W.M., Frangi, A.F. (eds.) MICCAI 2015. LNCS, vol. 9351, pp. 234–241. Springer, Cham (2015). https://doi.org/10.1007/978-3-319-24574-4_28
8. Harandi, N., Sadri, S., Moghaddam, N.A., Amirfattahi, R.: An automated method for segmentation of epithelial cervical cells in images of ThinPrep. J. Med. Syst. **34**(6), 1043–1058 (2010). https://doi.org/10.1007/s10916-009-9323-4
9. Plissiti, M., Vrigkas, M. and Nikou, C.: Segmentation of cell clusters in Pap smear images using intensity variation between superpixels. In: IEEE International Conference on Systems, Signals and Image Processing, pp. 184–187 (2015)
10. Kumar, P., Happy, S., Chatterjee, S., Sheet, D., Routray, A.: An unsupervised approach for overlapping cervical cell cytoplasm segmentation. In: IEEE International Conference on Biomedical Engineering and Sciences, pp. 106–109 (2016)
11. Sulaiman, S., Isa, N., Yusoff, I., Yusoff, I.A., Othman, N.H .: Overlapping cells separation method for cervical cell images. In: IEEE International Conference on Intelligent Systems Design and Applications, pp. 1218–1222 (2010)
12. Béliz-Osorio, N., Crespo, J., García-Rojo, M., Muñoz, A., Azpiazu, J.: Cytology imaging segmentation using the locally constrained watershed transform. In: Soille, P., Pesaresi, M., Ouzounis, G.K. (eds.) ISMM 2011. LNCS, vol. 6671, pp. 429–438. Springer, Heidelberg (2011). https://doi.org/10.1007/978-3-642-21569-8_37
13. Tareef, A., Song, Y., Huang, H., Feng, D., Chen, M., Wang, Y., Cai, W.: Multipass fast watershed for accurate segmentation of overlapping cervical cells. IEEE Trans. Med. Imaging **37**(9), 2044–2059 (2018)
14. Lee, H., Kim, J.: Segmentation of overlapping cervical cells in microscopic images with superpixel partitioning and cell-wise contour refinement. In: IEEE International Conference on Computer Vision and Pattern Recognition Workshops, pp. 63–69 (2016)
15. Guan, T., Zhou, D., Liu, Y.: Accurate segmentation of partially overlapping cervical cells based on dynamic sparse contour searching and GVF snake model. IEEE J. Biomed. Health Inf. **19**(4), 1494–1504 (2014)
16. Kaur, S., Sahambi, J.: Curvelet initialized level set cell segmentation for touching cells in low contrast images. Comput. Med. Imaging Graph. **49**, 46–57 (2016)

17. Nosrati, M. and Hamarneh, G.: Segmentation of overlapping cervical cells: a variational method with star-shape prior. In IEEE International Symposium on Biomedical Imaging, pp. 186–189 (2015)
18. Nosrati, M. and Hamarneh, G.: A variational approach for overlapping cell segmentation. In: IEEE International Symposium on Biomedical Imaging Overlapping Cervical Cytology Image Segmentation Challenge, pp. 1–2 (2014)
19. Lu, Z., Carneiro, G., Bradley, A.: An improved joint optimization of multiple level set functions for the segmentation of overlapping cervical cells. IEEE Trans. Image Process. **24**(4), 1261–1272 (2015)
20. Islam, Z. and Haque, M.: Multi-step level set method for segmentation of overlapping cervical cells. In: IEEE International Conference on Telecommunications and Photonics, pp. 1–5 (2015)
21. Song, Y., Tan, E., Jiang, X., et al.: Accurate cervical cell segmentation from overlapping clumps in Pap smear images. IEEE Trans. Med. Imaging **36**(1), 288–300 (2017)
22. Tareef, A., Song, Y., Cai, W., et al.: Automatic segmentation of overlapping cervical smear cells based on local distinctive features and guided shape deformation. Neurocomputing **221**, 94–107 (2017)
23. Song, Y., Cheng, J., Ni, D., Chen, S., Lei, B., Wang, T.: Segmenting overlapping cervical cell in Pap smear images. In: IEEE International Symposium on Biomedical Imaging, pp. 1159–1162 (2016)
24. Tareef, A., Song, Y., Huang, H., et al.: Optimizing the cervix cytological examination based on deep learning and dynamic shape modeling. Neurocomputing **248**, 28–40 (2017)
25. Song, Y., Qin, J., Lei, L., Choi, K.S.: Automated segmentation of overlapping cytoplasm in cervical smear images via contour fragments. In: AAAI Conference on Artificial Intelligence, pp. 168–175 (2018)
26. Song, Y., Zhu, L., Qin, J., Lei, B., Sheng, B., Choi, K.S.: Segmentation of overlapping cytoplasm in cervical smear images via adaptive shape priors extracted from contour fragments. IEEE Trans. Med. Imaging **38**(12), 2849–2862 (2019)
27. Kass, M., Witkin, A., Terzopoulos, D.: Snakes: active contour models. Int. J. Comput. Vis. **1**(4), 321–331 (1988)
28. Chan, T.F., Vese, L.A.: Active contours without edges. IEEE Trans. Image Process. **10**(2), 266–277 (2001)
29. Li, C., Xu, C., Gui, C., et al.: Distance regularized level set evolution and its application to image segmentation. IEEE Trans. Image Process. **19**(12), 32–43 (2010)
30. Song, Y., Zhang, L., Chen, S., et al.: Accurate segmentation of cervical cytoplasm and nuclei based on multiscale convolutional network and graph partitioning. IEEE Trans. Biomed. Eng. **62**(10), 2421–2433 (2015)
31. Nocedal, J., Wright, S.: Numerical Optimization. Springer, Berlin (2016)
32. Spitzer, F.: Principles of random walk. Springer Science & Business Media (2013)
33. Rosenblatt, M.: A central limit theorem and a strong mixing condition. Proceedings of the National Academy of Sciences of the United States of America **42**(1), 43 (1956)
34. Lu, Z., Carneiro, G., Bradley, A., et al.: Evaluation of three algorithms for the segmentation of overlapping cervical cells. IEEE Journal of Biomedical and Health Informatics **21**(2), 441–450 (2017)
35. Cootes, T.F., Taylor, C.J., Cooper, D.H., et al.: Active shape models-their training and application. Computer Vision and Image Understanding **61**(1), 38–59 (1995)

Prostate Motion Modelling Using Biomechanically-Trained Deep Neural Networks on Unstructured Nodes

Shaheer U. Saeed[1]([✉]), Zeike A. Taylor[2], Mark A. Pinnock[1], Mark Emberton[3], Dean C. Barratt[1], and Yipeng Hu[1]

[1] Centre for Medical Image Computing and Wellcome/EPSRC Centre for Interventional and Surgical Sciences, University College London, London, UK
zcemsus@ucl.ac.uk
[2] CISTIB Centre for Computational Imaging and Simulation Technologies in Biomedicine, Institute of Medical and Biological Engineering, University of Leeds, Leeds, UK
[3] Department of Urology, University College London Hospitals NHS Foundation Trust, London, UK

Abstract. In this paper, we propose to train deep neural networks with biomechanical simulations, to predict the prostate motion encountered during ultrasound-guided interventions. In this application, unstructured points are sampled from segmented pre-operative MR images to represent the anatomical regions of interest. The point sets are then assigned with point-specific material properties and displacement loads, forming the un-ordered input feature vectors. An adapted PointNet can be trained to predict the nodal displacements, using finite element (FE) simulations as ground-truth data. Furthermore, a versatile bootstrap aggregating mechanism is validated to accommodate the variable number of feature vectors due to different patient geometries, comprised of a training-time bootstrap sampling and a model averaging inference. This results in a fast and accurate approximation to the FE solutions without requiring subject-specific solid meshing. Based on 160,000 nonlinear FE simulations on clinical imaging data from 320 patients, we demonstrate that the trained networks generalise to unstructured point sets sampled directly from holdout patient segmentation, yielding a near real-time inference and an expected error of 0.017 mm in predicted nodal displacement.

Keywords: Deep learning · Biomechanical modelling · PointNet

1 Introduction and Related Work

Computational biomechanical modelling has applications in the areas of computer aided intervention, surgical simulation and other medical image computing tasks [8,9,11,12]. In particular, numerical approaches based on finite element

© Springer Nature Switzerland AG 2020
A. L. Martel et al. (Eds.): MICCAI 2020, LNCS 12264, pp. 650–659, 2020.
https://doi.org/10.1007/978-3-030-59719-1_63

(FE) analysis have been applied in a wide range of clinical tasks, such as modelling soft tissue deformation in augmented reality [9] and medical image registration [4,11]. For example, during transrectal ultrasound (TRUS) guided prostate biopsy and focal therapy, FE-based biomechanical simulations have been proposed to predict physically plausible motion estimations for constraining the multimodal image registration [11,12,24].

Due to the highly nonlinear behaviour of soft tissues, complex anatomical geometry and boundary condition estimates, FE simulations often rely on iterative algorithms that are computationally demanding. Many developments have made the modern FE solver highly efficient, such as using parallel computing algorithms with graphics processing units (GPUs) [22], simplifying the mechanical formulation [6,16], or learning reduced-order solutions [23]. However, a real-time solution remains challenging. In one of the approaches for the prostate imaging application, an average meshing-excluded computation time of 16s per simulation, on a GPU, was reported [11]. To meet the surgical requirement in efficiency, many turned to statistical learning approaches that summarise the FE simulations with a lower dimensional approximation [13,15,21,24].

Largely motivated by the representation capability and the fast inference, deep neural networks have been used to reduce computation time for biomechanical modelling problems. Meister et al have proposed to use neural networks to approximate the time integration, which allowed much larger time steps to accelerate the iterative optimisation [18]. Mendizbal et al presented a methodology for estimating the deformations from FE simulations using a U-Net variant, to efficiently predict a deformation field on regularly sampled grid nodes [19]. U-Mesh was able to make approximations for deformations in the human liver under an applied force and a mean absolute error of 0.22 mm with a prediction time of 3 ms was reported [19]. The model requires, as input, point clouds derived from tetrahedral meshes mapped to a sparse hexahedral grid. It also assumed that the deformable region has uniform material properties throughout. Liang et al used deep learning to estimate stress distributions by learning a mapping from a geometry encoding to stress distribution [17]. The model was trained on FE simulation data and was able to predict stress distributions in the aortic wall given an aorta geometry [17]. The constitutive properties were also assumed invariant throughout the entire geometry [17].

In this work, we adapt a PointNet [20] with a bootstrap aggregating sampling strategy, to model the biomechanics on a set of input feature vectors that represent patient-specific anatomy with node-wise boundary conditions and material properties. The use of unstructured data to represent the geometry potentially alleviates the need for meshing or shape encoding via principal component analysis. The incorporation of material properties within the proposed input feature vectors allows accommodation of more realistic inhomogeneous biological materials. We integrated these changes into the proposed PointNet based neural network training for deformation prediction tasks. The PointNet has been applied for a wide range of learning tasks with un-ordered point clouds as input, such as classification and segmentation.

We summarise the contributions in this work: 1) The proposed network provides a permutation-invariant deep network architecture over the unstructured input feature vectors, additionally allowing flexible point set sampling schemes without requiring pre-defined number of points or spatially regular nodal locations; 2) Out-of-nodal-sample generalisation ability is also investigated, based on the input feature vectors directly sampled from segmentation on holdout patient data; 3) The efficiency and accuracy of the proposed method is validated using a large holdout patient data set (30,000 simulations from 60 patients) in a real clinical application for predicting TRUS probe induced deformations in the prostate gland and the surrounding regions.

2   Methods

In Sects. 2.1-2.3, a deep neural network and its training strategy are described to learn a high-dimensional nonlinear mapping between a set of input feature vectors representing the geometry, applied loads and material properties, and a set of displacements on the input nodal locations.

2.1   Unstructured Input Feature Vectors

Without loss of generality, let $\{\mathbf{x}_n\}$ be a set of N un-ordered feature vectors $\mathbf{x}_n = [\mathbf{p}_n^T, \mathbf{b}_n^T, \mathbf{k}_n^T]^T$, where $n = 1, 2, ..., N$. $\{\mathbf{p}_n\}$ are the point coordinates; $\{\mathbf{b}_n\}$ represent the externally applied loads with known boundary conditions; and $\{\mathbf{k}_n\}$ specify the parameter values of the material property models.

For the prostate motion modelling application, $\mathbf{p}_n = [x_n, y_n, z_n]^T$ contain 3D Euclidean coordinates of the sampled points. $\mathbf{k}_n = [G_n, K_n]^T$ contain the shear and bulk moduli in an isotropic, elastic neo-Hookean material model [25]. The nodes with available displacement loads are assigned with vectors $\mathbf{b}_n = [1, b_n^x, b_n^y, b_n^z]^T$ where 1 indicates the availability of the assigned displacement for the node, while those without are assigned $\mathbf{b}_n = [0, 0, 0, 0]^T$. This representation can be readily generalised to dimension-specific loads by adding more 'switches', i.e. the first elements of the current vectors, and to other types of boundary conditions such as force.

2.2   Permutation-Invariant Nodal Displacement Prediction

The PointNet is adapted to predict displacement vectors $\{\hat{\mathbf{y}}_n\}$ from input features $\{\mathbf{x}_n\}$, as illustrated in Fig. 1. The adapted PointNet architecture is illustrated in Fig. 2, generalising the first transformation net T1-net to 9D space instead of the original 3D space. The readers are referred to [20] for other architectural details.

In this work, ground-truth displacements $\{\mathbf{y}_n\}$ are computed from finite element simulations (see Sects. 3.1 and 3.2). Mean squared error is minimised as the loss function to optimise the network weights: $\mathcal{L}(y, \hat{y}) = \Sigma_{n=1}^{N}(\mathbf{y}_n - \hat{\mathbf{y}}_n)^2/N$.

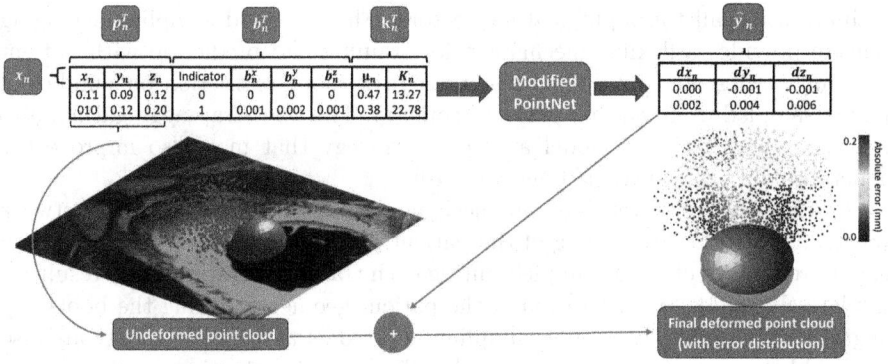

Fig. 1. Point cloud of prostate (red) with data flow (blue arrows) and error distribution of deformation prediction due to simulated TRUS probe (green sphere) movement. (Color figure online)

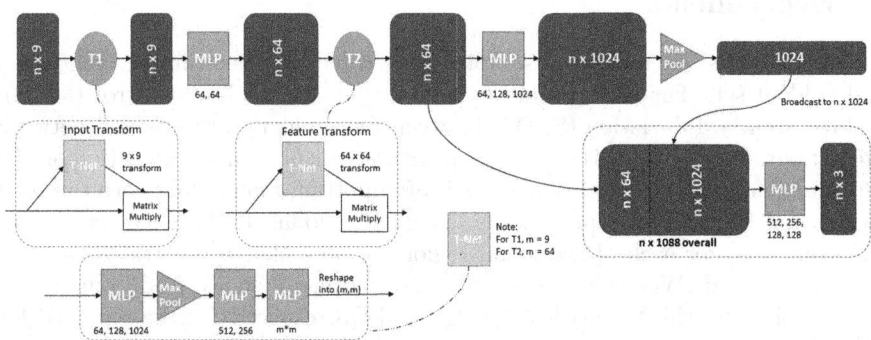

Fig. 2. Adapted PointNet architecture used for the displacement prediction task. Solid lines show data flow, blue boxes show data size and dashed lines show expanded views. (Color figure online)

2.3 Training-Time Bootstrap Aggregating

Although the adapted PointNet in theory accepts variable numbers of feature vectors as input during training and inference, an implementation with a fixed number of input vectors is much more efficient [20] with modern GPU parallel computing support. Reliably and efficiently mapping the often irregularly-shaped input to regular space, such as a cubic grid or a fixed number of points, remains an interesting challenge.

We propose an alternative bootstrap aggregating training strategy to randomly sample, with replacement, the input feature vectors, in each optimisation iteration. During inference, the final prediction is computed by averaging the predictions from a number of forward-passes of the trained network, which cover all the input feature vectors. We note that the expected back-propagated gradient remains the same using the proposed sampling and averaging scheme, as when training using all the input feature vectors. The proposed sampling-averaging scheme provides a flexible mechanism for training and prediction with patient anatomy represented by different point sets, without restriction on number of points sampled from varying patient geometry. The bootstrap aggregating, also known as bagging, is a model averaging strategy that may also improve the generalisability of the trained network [10].

In this work, the tetrahedron mesh nodes are used to train the network (Sect. 3.2), after solid meshing of the patient geometry. All mesh nodes have an equal probability of being sampled during each training iteration. This results in a relatively sparse representation of the patient geometry, during the bootstrap aggregating training. The same sampling and model averaging strategy are also applicable to input feature vectors with different and, potentially, simpler point sampling schemes other than finite element mesh nodes. One such example is validated in this study and described in Sect. 3.4.

3   Experiments

All the patients are randomly sampled into three groups, training, validation and holdout sets. For all experiments, we compute mean absolute error (MAE), and the standard deviation (St.D.), between FE simulation results and network predictions. Specific for this application, accurate displacement prediction on the prostate gland and its zonal structures is of importance in guiding both targeted biopsy and focal therapy procedures. Therefore, nodal displacement errors are also computed for each of the gland regions, represented by central zone (CZ) and whole gland (WG) with transition- and peripheral zones. Additionally, the first, second and third quartiles (Q1, Q2 and Q3 respectively) are reported for all nodes. Paired T-test results are reported for holdout set experiments.

3.1   Data Acquisition and Finite Element Simulations

T2-weighted MR images were acquired from 320 prostate cancer patients who underwent TRUS-guided transperineal targeted biopsy or focal therapy. Tetrahedron meshes of approximately $0.2 \times 0.2 \times 0.2 \, \text{m}^3$ volume of the patient abdominal region were generated, after the prostate glands and surrounding structures were manually segmented. In each simulation, two types of boundary conditions were applied: zero displacement on pelvic bones and sampled nodal displacements on the simulated TRUS probe. Sampled material properties were assigned to elements in different anatomical regions and zonal structures. For each patient, 500 finite element (FE) simulations were performed using NiftySim [14], resulting in 160,000 simulated motion data. Each predicts one plausible prostate motion due to change of ultrasound probe movement, acoustic balloon dilation, bony constraints and varying material properties. Averaged over all simulations, the maximum displacement value in the ground truth data is 5.21 mm, and the mean displacement over the entire point cloud is 0.83 mm. Further details of the finite element modelling can be found in [11,12]. Similar FE simulation strategies have been widely used and validated in the same applications [1,2,4,7,24].

3.2 Network Training and Hyperparameter Tuning

The point cloud node locations, boundary conditions and material properties used in the FE simulations were assembled into the input feature vectors $\{\mathbf{x}_n\}$, as the PointNet input. Batch normalization was used at each hidden layer, with additional dropout regularisation at a drop rate of 0.25, on the final fully connected layer. The Adam optimiser was used to minimize the mean squared error loss function, with an initial learning rate of 0.001 and a minibatch size of 32. The number of input feature vectors used for training was 14500. Based on preliminary results on the validation set, varying these hyperparameters produced limited impact on the network performance. Conversely, the global feature vector (GFV) size may impact performance significantly [20], as it linearly correlates with the number of trainable parameters, and affected model training and inference time in our validation experiments. Therefore, we report the network performance results with different GFV sizes, on the validation set. All the other hyperparameters were configured empirically and remained fixed throughout the validation and holdout experiments presented in this paper.

The networks were trained using 100,000 FE simulations from 200 patients, while validation and holdout sets each comprised data from 60 patients (30,000 simulations). Each network took approximately 32 h to train on two Nvidia Tesla V100 GPUs.

3.3 Sensitivity Analysis on Material Properties

Several previous studies have trained deep neural networks to predict finite element solutions with uniform material properties in the regions of interest [5,17,19]. This in principle is unrealistic for human anatomy; e.g. the prostate peripheral, transitional, and central zones are generally accepted to have differing material properties. The importance of material heterogeneity depends on the application, though Hu et al.'s results suggest it is significant for prostate motion predictions [11]. The proposed network readily includes material properties in the input feature vectors. We therefore investigated the difference between networks trained with and without region-specific material properties by treating region-specificity as a hyperparameter. Networks with homogeneous materials were correspondingly trained with reduced input feature vectors, which excluded material parameters: $\mathbf{x}_n = [\mathbf{p}_n^T, \mathbf{b}_n^T]^T$.

3.4 Generalisation to Points Sampled Directly from Segmentation

To demonstrate the generalisability of the network to alternative point sampling methods, we re-sampled all the point locations in the holdout set using a well-established region-wise cuboid tessellation approach. Each of the a anatomical regions was represented by c cuboid tessellations computed from segmentation surface points, without using the solid tetrahedral mesh. From each tessellation, f points were then randomly generated, this resulted in cf points per region and acf points in total. For training and validation purposes, material properties were assigned based on which tessellation the node belongs to, while BCs were interpolated using an inverse Euclidean-distance transform based on five nearest neighbouring nodes. It is noteworthy that, in general, $acf \neq n$ and the bootstrap aggregating, described in Sect. 2.3, still applies to the new input feature vectors.

4   Results

Global Feature Vector Size and Material Properties. Summarised in Table 1, results on the validation set suggest that increasing GFV size, up to a maximum of 1024, reduced error rates. However, further increasing GFV size from 1024 to 2048, the mean error increased from 0.010 ± 0.011 to 0.013 ± 0.015. This small yet significant increase (p-value $< 1e{-}3$) may suggest overfitting due to larger network size. Therefore, a GFV size of 1024 was subsequently used in holdout experiments. Also shown in Table 1, excluding material properties from the network inputs significantly increased nodal displacement errors, from 0.01 ± 0.011 to 0.027 ± 0.029 (p-value $< 1e{-}3$). Material parameters were therefore retained in the input feature vectors in the reported results based on the holdout set.

Network Performance on Holdout Set. As summarised in Table 1, the overall MAEs, on the holdout set, were 0.010 ± 0.012 mm and 0.017 ± 0.015 mm, for the FE tetrahedral mesh nodes and the points from the tessellation-sampling, respectively, with a significant difference (p-value $< 1e{-}3$). However, when these network-predicted displacements were compared with the nodal displacements produced with FE simulations, there was no significance found with p-values of 0.093 and 0.081, respectively. The error distributions were skewed towards zero, as can be observed based on the median, 25th and 75th percentile values reported in Table 1. Computed over all the cases in the holdout set, the average MAEs were 0.34 mm and 0.48 mm, for the points sampled from FE mesh nodes and points sampled using tessellation, respectively. We also report an inference time of 520 ms, when predicting displacements for approximately 14,500 nodes, using one single Nvidia GeForce 1050Ti GPU.

5   Discussion

Based on statistical test results on the holdout set, reported in Sect. 4, we conclude that the models presented in this study can predict highly accurate nodal displacements for new patients in our application. This provides an efficient alternative to FE simulations in time critical tasks, where additional computation can be offloaded to the model training phase, such as surgical simulation [3] and surgical augmented reality [9] where computation times need to be curtailed during deformation prediction. For the MR-to-TRUS registration application described in Sect. 1, rather than replacing the FE simulations for constructing a patient-specific motion model for intervention planning, we conjecture a possibility to

Table 1. Results from different experiments. All results presented in mm.

	All points/nodes				CZ	WG
	MAE ± St.D.	Q1	Q2	Q3	MAE ± St.D.	MAE ± St.D.
GFV Sizes	Results on validation set					
256	0.113 ± 0.091	0.043	0.094	0.165	0.107 ± 0.080	0.110 ± 0.094
512	0.065 ± 0.047	0.002	0.031	0.086	0.058 ± 0.052	0.063 ± 0.049
1024	0.010 ± 0.011	0.000	0.005	0.013	0.008 ± 0.013	0.009 ± 0.012
2048	0.013 ± 0.015	0.000	0.006	0.016	0.009 ± 0.011	0.009 ± 0.016
Input Feat. Vectors	Results on validation set					
$\mathbf{x}_n = [\mathbf{p}_n^T, \mathbf{b}_n^T, \mathbf{k}_n^T]^T$	0.010 ± 0.011	0.000	0.005	0.013	0.008 ± 0.013	0.009 ± 0.012
$\mathbf{x}_n = [\mathbf{p}_n^T, \mathbf{b}_n^T]^T$	0.027 ± 0.029	0.000	0.009	0.031	0.023± 0.021	0.029 ± 0.020
Sampling Strategy	Results on holdout set					
Tetrahedral Mesh	0.010 ± 0.012	0.000	0.007	0.018	0.009 ± 0.013	0.010 ± 0.012
Tessellation	0.017 ± 0.015	0.000	0.009	0.019	0.014 ± 0.020	0.017 ± 0.021

optimise the deformation prediction directly during the procedure, enabled by the highly efficient inference with non-iterative forward network evaluation.

An important contribution in this work is to provide evidence that, the proposed network can generalise to input feature vectors sampled from alternative methods other than the FE mesh, a simple and versatile tessellation method in this case. This is an important avenue for further investigation of the proposed method, especially for point spatial locations integrated with features like other types of BCs, material parameters and even other physiological measurements of clinical application interests.

The computational cost of data generation and model training is significant and this can be a hindrance in the deployment of deep learning models in practice. Augmentation can serve to alleviate a part of the problem by presenting augmented examples to the network for training. Re-sampling, like regional tessellation is a viable candidate, although this has yet to be investigated. More interestingly, the model generalisability to cases other than probe induced deformation prediction has not been investigated and this presents an opportunity for further research to investigate training strategies such as transfer learning and domain adaptation, which may substantially reduce the computational cost.

6 Conclusions

We have presented a PointNet based deep neural network learning biomechanical modelling from FE simulations, for the case of TRUS probe induced deformation of the prostate gland and surrounding regions. The PointNet architecture used for this task allows for randomly sampled unstructured point cloud data, representing varying FE loads, patient anatomy and point-specific material properties. The presented approach can approximate FE simulation with a mean absolute error of 0.017 mm with a sub-second inference. The method can be generalised to new patients and to randomly sampled 3D point clouds without requiring quality solid meshing. The proposed methodology is applicable for a wide range of time critical tasks, and we have demonstrated its accuracy and efficiency with clinical data for a well-established prostate intervention application.

Acknowledgments. This work is supported by the Wellcome/EPSRC Centre for Interventional and Surgical Sciences (203145Z/16/Z). ZAT acknowledges funding from CRUK RadNet Leeds Centre of Excellence (C19942/A28832).

References

1. du Bois d'Aische, A., et al.: Improved non-rigid registration of prostate MRI. In: Barillot, C., Haynor, D.R., Hellier, P. (eds.) MICCAI 2004. LNCS, vol. 3216, pp. 845–852. Springer, Heidelberg (2004). https://doi.org/10.1007/978-3-540-30135-6_103

2. Alterovitz, R., et al.: Registration of mr prostate images with biomechanical modeling and nonlinear parameter estimation. Med. Phys. **33**(2), 446–454 (2006)

3. Berkley, J., Turkiyyah, G., Berg, D., Ganter, M., Weghorst, S.: Real-time finite element modeling for surgery simulation: an application to virtual suturing. IEEE Trans. Vis. Comput. Graph. **10**(3), 314–325 (2004)

4. Hata, N., et al.: Evaluation of three-dimensional finite element-based deformable registration of pre- and intraoperative prostate imaging. Med. Phy. **28**(12), 2551–2560 (2001)

5. Brunet, J.-N., Mendizabal, A., Petit, A., Golse, N., Vibert, E., Cotin, S.: Physics-based deep neural network for augmented reality during liver surgery. In: Shen, D., et al. (eds.) MICCAI 2019. LNCS, vol. 11768, pp. 137–145. Springer, Cham (2019). https://doi.org/10.1007/978-3-030-32254-0_16

6. Cotin, S., Delingette, H., Ayache, N.: Real-time elastic deformations of soft tissues for surgery simulation. IEEE Trans. Vis. Comput. Graph. **5**(1), 62–73 (1999)

7. Crouch, J., Pizer, S., Chaney, E., Hu, Y., Mageras, G., Zaider, M.: Automated finite-element analysis for deformable registration of prostate images. IEEE Trans. Med. Imaging **26**(10), 1379–1390 (2007)

8. Erhart, P., et al.: Finite element analysis in asymptomatic, symptomatic, and ruptured abdominal aortic aneurysms: in search of new rupture risk predictors. Euro. J. Vasc. Endovasc. Surg. **49**(3), 239–245 (2014). https://doi.org/10.1016/j.ejvs.2014.11.010

9. Haouchine, N., Dequidt, J., Berger, M., Cotin, S.: Deformation-based augmented reality for hepatic surgery. Stud. Health Technol. Inf. **184**, 182–188 (2013)

10. Hastie, T., Tibshirani, R., Friedman, J.: The Elements of Statistical Learning, 12th edn. Springer Series in Statistics, Springer-Verlag, New York (2001)

11. Hu, Y., et al.: Mr to ultrasound registration for image-guided prostate interventions. Med. Image Anal. **16**(3), 687–703 (2012)

12. Hu, Y., et al.: Modelling prostate motion for data fusion during image-guided interventions. IEEE Trans. Med. Imaging **30**(11), 1887–1900 (2011)

13. Hu, Y., et al.: A statistical motion model based on biomechanical simulations for data fusion during image-guided prostate interventions. In: Metaxas, Dimitris, Axel, Leon, Fichtinger, Gabor, Székely, Gábor (eds.) MICCAI 2008. LNCS, vol. 5241, pp. 737–744. Springer, Heidelberg (2008). https://doi.org/10.1007/978-3-540-85988-8_88

14. Johnsen, S., et al.: Niftysim: a GPU-based nonlinear finite element package for simulation of soft tissue biomechanics. Int. J. Comput. Assist. Radiol. Surg. **10**(7), 1077–1095 (2015)
15. Khallaghi, S., et al.: Statistical biomechanical surface registration: application to MR-TRUS fusion for prostate interventions. IEEE Transac. Med. Imaging **34**(12), 2535–2549 (2015)
16. Lee, B., Popescu, D., Joshi, B., Ourselin, S.: Efficient topology modification and deformation for finite element models using condensation. Stud. Health Technol. Inf. **119**, 299–304 (2006)
17. Liang, L., Liu, M., Martin, C., Sun, W.: A deep learning approach to estimate stress distribution: a fast and accurate surrogate of finite-element analysis. J. Roy. Soc. Interface (2018). https://doi.org/10.1098/rsif.2017.0844
18. Meister, F., Passerini, T., Mihalef, V., Tuysuzoglu, A., Maier, A., Mansi, T.: Deep learning acceleration of total lagrangian explicit dynamics for soft tissue mechanics. Comput. Meth. Appl. Mech. Eng. **358**, 112628 (2020)
19. Mendizabal, A., Márquez-Neila, P., Cotin, S.: Simulation of hyperelastic materials in real-time using deep learning. Med. Image Anal. **59**, 101569 (2020). https://doi. org/10.1016/j.media.2019.10156, hal-02097119v3
20. Qi, C., Su, H., Mo, K., Guibas, L.: Pointnet: Deep learning on point sets for 3D classification and segmentation (2016). arXiv:1612.00593v2
21. Saito, A., Nakada, M., Oost, E., Shimizu, A., Watanabe, H., Nawano, S.: A statistical shape model for multiple organs based on synthesized-based learning. In: Yoshida, H., Warfield, S., Vannier, M.W. (eds.) ABD-MICCAI 2013. LNCS, vol. 8198, pp. 280–289. Springer, Heidelberg (2013). https://doi.org/10.1007/978-3-642-41083-3_31
22. Taylor, Z., Cheng, M., Ourselin, S.: High-speed nonlinear finite element analysis for surgical simulation using graphics processing units. IEEE Trans. Med. imaging **27**(5), 650–663 (2008)
23. Taylor, Z., Crozier, S., Ourselin, S.: A reduced order explicit dynamic finite element algorithm for surgical simulation. IEEE Trans. Med. imaging **30**(9), 1713–1721 (2011)
24. Wang, Y., et al.: Towards personalized statistical deformable model and hybrid point matching for robust MR-TRUS registration. IEEE Trans. Med Imaging **35**(2), 589–684 (2015)
25. Zienkiewicz, O., Taylor, R.: The Finite Element Method. Butterworth-Heinemann, The Netherlands, Oxford (2000)

Deep Learning Assisted Automatic Intra-operative 3D Aortic Deformation Reconstruction

Yanhao Zhang[1], Raphael Falque[1], Liang Zhao[1($\boxtimes$)], Shoudong Huang[1], and Boni Hu[1,2]

[1] Centre for Autonomous Systems, University of Technology Sydney, Sydney, Australia
liang.zhao@uts.edu.un
[2] School of Aeronautics, Northwestern Polytechnical University, Xi'an, China

Abstract. Endovascular interventions rely on 2D X-ray fluoroscopy for 3D catheter manipulation. The dynamic nature of aorta prevents the pre-operative CT/MRI data to be used directly as the live 3D guidance since the vessel deforms during the surgery. This paper provides a framework that reconstructs the live 3D aortic shape by fusing a 3D static pre-operative model and the 2D intra-operative fluoroscopic images. The proposed framework recovers aortic 3D shape automatically and computationally efficient. A deep learning approach is adopted as the front-end for extracting features from fluoroscopic images. A signed distance field based correspondence method is employed for avoiding the repeated feature-vertex matching while maintaining the correspondence accuracy. The warp field of 3D deformation is estimated by solving a nonlinear least squares problem based on the embedded deformation graph. Detailed phantom experiments are conducted, and the results demonstrate the accuracy of the proposed framework as well as the potential clinical value of the technique.

Keywords: 3D Aortic deformation reconstruction · Deep learning · Endovascular interventions

1 Introduction

Endovascular interventions provide a lower risk alternative to open surgery for cardiovascular diseases. The minimal incision benefits patients and broadens the

This work was supported by the Australian Research Council (ARC) Discovery project "Visual Simultaneous Localisation and Mapping in Deformable Environments" (DP200100982).

Electronic supplementary material The online version of this chapter (https://doi.org/10.1007/978-3-030-59719-1_64) contains supplementary material, which is available to authorized users.

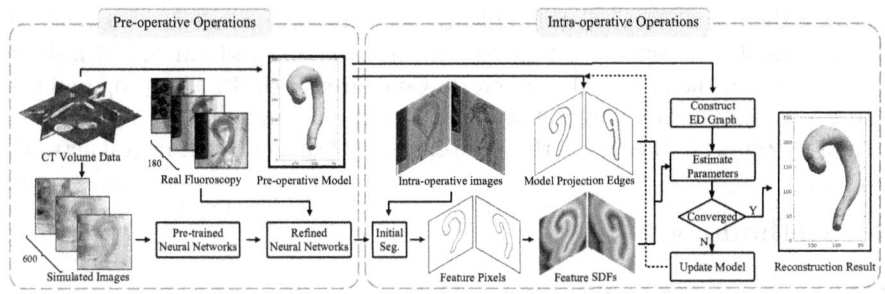

Fig. 1. Main processes of the proposed aortic deformation reconstruction framework.

options for age groups to receive the interventional treatment [7]. However, this therapy is challenging due to the requirement of a precise catheter manipulation in a highly dynamic surgical environment while limited visualisation is available [4]. Hence, the intra-operative recovery of vascular structure is needed for providing a 3D guidance on catheter surroundings and assisting catheter navigation.

The clinical approaches mainly rely on X-ray fluoroscopy for endovascular procedures. Recently, the new technology of angiography systems, e.g., biplane angiography systems, expands the viewing directions, but it only provides multiple 2D guidances for 3D operations. On the other hand, a 3D vessel structure is available pre-operatively by computed tomography (CT) scans. However, because of the dynamic nature of vasculature, the pre-operative data cannot be used directly to perfectly reflect aortic current shape, and therefore, the deformation should be updated intra-operatively [13].

In this paper, we propose a framework for 3D aortic deformation reconstruction. Pixels of vessel wall contours from each X-ray image are used as the observed features. The feature extraction is performed automatically based on a deep-learning image segmentation technique [8]. Using the extracted features, a signed distance field (SDF) based correspondence method is employed to provide observation constraints for the deformation reconstruction algorithm. The warp field for deformation reconstruction is formulated using embedded deformation (ED) graph [9], whose deformation parameters are estimated by solving a non-linear least squares problem. Currently, there are some works on the aortic deformation recovery using 3D pre-operative data and 2D intra-operative fluoroscopy. In [10], the distortion of overlaying per-operative data on fluoroscopic images is corrected, but the position of the inserted catheter is needed. Although distance field has been used for 2D/3D vessel registration, many works focus on aligning vessel's centerline [1,5]. By contrast, our work aims to recover aortic 3D shape which is more challenging. We need to deal with the stronger effect of overlaying structures from the image, and to reconstruct the vessel's deformation using a more complex deformation graph.

The proposed framework is based on our previous work [12]. Different from [12], in this paper, the features are extracted automatically based on a U-Net architecture [8]. In addition, by employing SDFs built from the extracted features, the iterative calculation of feature-vertex correspondences are avoided. Detailed validation using phantom experiments has been performed, which shows the accuracy of the proposed framework. Compared with [12], the proposed system is fully automatic, computationally more efficient, and achieves higher reconstruction accuracy, when using the same extracted features by the neural network.

2   Methodology

A flow chart describing the proposed framework is shown in Fig. 1. The preoperative operations are static model segmentation and neural network training. The intra-operative operations are feature extraction, SDF based correspondences calculation, and the 3D aortic deformation reconstruction.

2.1   Neural Network Based Feature Extraction

To deal with the view of partially occluded overlaying structures on fluoroscopic images, pixels presenting the vessel wall contours are used as the observed features. A U-Net architecture [8] is applied for the feature extraction. More formally, from a grayscale X-ray image input, the semantic segmentation problem that separates the background from the aorta is first solved. The boundary of the segmentation is then calculated as the features.

Compared with traditional edge detection methods, the neural network architecture is more suitable for handling less clear fluoroscopic images with occlusions or background artifacts. The lower layers are known to behave similarly to a Gabor filter [11] and therefore would have similar performance compared to traditional edge detectors. The upper layers can learn the semantic meaning of an aortic shape from data, thus provide a robust and automated method for contour detection from images with occlusions and outlier edges.

The network architecture can be decomposed in two parts: the input is first passed through a series of successive convolution block (which consists of max pooling, 2D convolutions, batch normalization (BN), rectified linear units (ReLU), 2D conv, BN, and ReLU) and is then upsampled through a series of deconvolution (which consists of upsampling, 2D conv, BN, ReLU, 2D conv, BN, and ReLU). A sketch of the architecture is shown in Fig. 2.

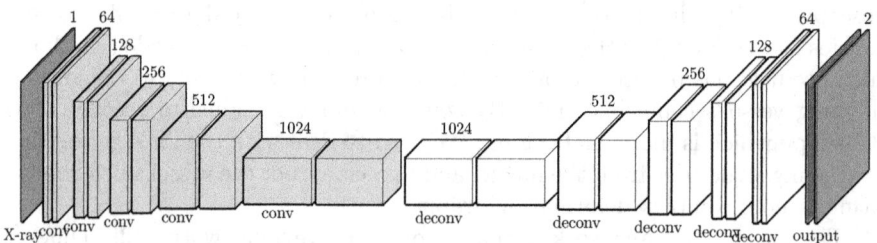

Fig. 2. U-NET architecture [8] used for the semantic segmentation of the grayscale X-ray images.

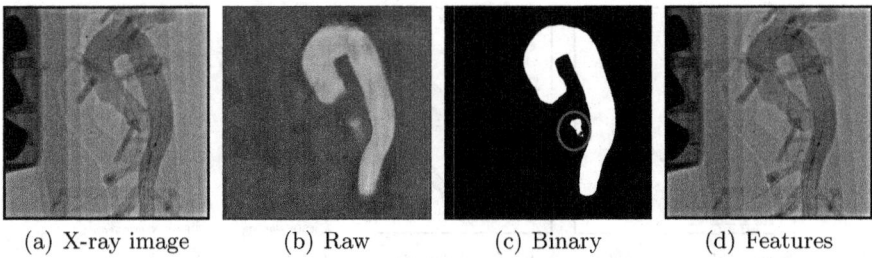

| (a) X-ray image | (b) Raw | (c) Binary | (d) Features |

Fig. 3. An example illustrating the feature extraction. The four figures are: X-ray image, raw segmentation from neural network, binarized raw segmentation, and the final extracted features after Moore-Neighbor tracing algorithm. The extraction is robust w.r.t. the redundant segmentation (red part in (b)) from U-Net. (Color figure online)

The training of the network is performed by loading weights trained on the SceneNet dataset [6] for RGB images. To adapt this network to our specific problem, the first and last layer of the network are resized to fit our segmentation problem (i.e., an input of $1 \times 512 \times 512$ which is the size of the grayscale X-ray image, and an output of $2 \times 512 \times 512$ where 2 is the number of classes for the segmentation and 512×512 is the size of the original image). The network weights optimization is performed using stochastic gradient descent (SGD), with a pixel-wise cross-entropy loss function.

Two refinement steps are then used for the fine tuning of the network weights. First, a training set of 600 simulated fluoroscopic images generated from different viewing directions by CT data are used to pre-train the network. Then a second training set of 180 real hand-labelled X-ray images is used for the final training. These are shown in the left part of Fig. 1. Throughout the fine tuning, different data augmentations (e.g., random flipping, changing of brightness and contrast, etc.) are employed to avoid overfitting and increase the generalization of the network.

The raw segmentation from the neural network is first binarized and the boundary of the binarized segmentation is then extracted using the Moore-Neighbor tracing algorithm [3]. One of the benefits of using aortic edge pixels as the observed features is the tolerance of wrong segmentation from the network. Figure 3 shows an example of the feature (boundary) extraction process. The redundant part segmented from the neural network can be easily removed after calculating the boundary.

2.2 SDF Based Correspondence Method

In this paper, the correspondence between extracted features and model vertices are calculated using a SDF based correspondence method. The orthographic projection of X-ray fluoroscopy is formulated as:

$$q(\mathbf{p}) = s\mathbf{U}\mathbf{R}(\mathbf{p} + \mathbf{t}), \qquad (1)$$

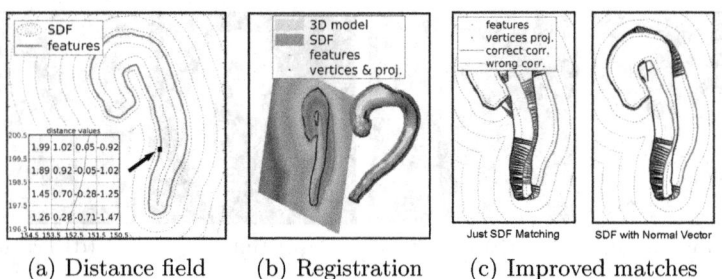

(a) Distance field   (b) Registration   (c) Improved matches

Fig. 4. An illustration of the SDF based correspondence method. During the optimization, model vertices are projected onto the SDF and the edge points of model projection (blue dots in (b)) are used to calculate the correspondence. (c) shows that the wrong matches introduced by pure SDF are avoided. It is noted that only SDFs are used when solving deformation parameters. (Color Figure online)

where $\mathbf{p} \in \mathbb{R}^3$ denote a model vertex, $\{\mathbf{R} \in SO(3), \mathbf{t} \in \mathbb{R}^3, s \in \mathbb{R}\}$ denote the relative transformation and the scale factor (reciprocal of pixel space) between model and image coordinates, $\mathbf{U}$ gets the two upper rows from $\mathbf{R}$.

Let $\mathcal{Q} = \{\mathbf{g}_{11}, \cdots, \mathbf{g}_{N^g N^g}\}$ denote the coordinate of $N^g \times N^g$ grids pixelated from the image space, $\mathcal{F} = \{\mathbf{f}_1, \cdots, \mathbf{f}_{N^o}\}$ denote N^o extracted features on this image. For each $\mathbf{g}_{ij}$, the closest corresponding feature $\tilde{\mathbf{f}} \in \mathcal{F}$ is calculated based on Euclidean distance. Both distance space $\mathcal{D}$ and normal vector of $\tilde{\mathbf{f}}$ are stored:

$$\mathcal{D}(\mathbf{g}_{ij}) = \text{sign}(\mathbf{g}_{ij}) \|\text{dist}(\mathbf{g}_{ij}, \mathcal{F})\|, \quad N(\mathbf{g}_{ij}) = n(\tilde{\mathbf{f}}), \qquad (2)$$

where $\text{dist}(\mathbf{g}_{ij}, \mathcal{F}) = n(\tilde{\mathbf{f}})^\top (\mathbf{g}_{ij} - \tilde{\mathbf{f}})$ is the point to line distance, $n(\cdot)$ is the 2D normal vector, and the $\text{sign}(\mathbf{g}_{ij})$ is equal to -1, 0, or 1 if $\mathbf{g}_{ij}$ is inside, on, or outside the aortic boundary. It is also easy to calculate the gradient $\nabla \mathcal{D}$ of the distance space $\mathcal{D}$.

Using the edge of model projection on each SDF, the observation constraints are provided to the reconstruction algorithm (observation term in Sect. 2.3). The model projection is performed using (1). The edge of the projected point cloud is calculated using the alpha-shape approach [2]. The normal vector $N(\cdot)$ is employed for avoiding the wrong matches, shown in Fig. 4c. To be specific, if the angle between $n \circ q(\mathbf{p})$ and $N \circ q(\mathbf{p})$ is larger than a threshold, this matching is discarded, where $\circ$ denotes function composition.

For each point from the edge of projected model, the corresponding distance, normal vector and the gradient of the distance space can be obtained directly, which means we do not need to recalculate the correspondence when the model is updated. Hence, the repeated calculation of correspondences in [12] are avoided when solving deformation parameters.

2.3   Deformation Reconstruction

The warp field for 3D deformation is built based on ED graph [9], which approximates the deformation using the weighted average of affine transformations around each ED nodes. Let $\{\mathbf{A}_j \in \mathbb{R}^{3\times3}, \mathbf{t}_j \in \mathbb{R}^3, \mathbf{g}_j \in \mathbb{R}^3\}$ denote the transformation and position of each ED node. For a model vertex $\mathbf{p}_i$, the new position is calculated using its K neighbouring nodes:

$$g(\mathbf{p}_i) = \sum_{j=1}^{K} w_{ij} \left[\mathbf{A}_j \left(\mathbf{p}_i - \mathbf{g}_j \right) + \mathbf{g}_j + \mathbf{t}_j \right], \quad w_{ij} = \left(1 - \|\mathbf{p}_i - \mathbf{g}_j\|/d_j \right) / n_j, \quad (3)$$

where d_j is the distance between $\mathbf{p}_i$ and the $K+1$ nearest node, n_j is a normalization factor. The warp field is solved by estimating $\{\mathbf{A}_j, \mathbf{t}_j\}$ using:

$$\underset{\mathbf{A}_j, \mathbf{t}_j}{\arg\min} \, w_{\mathrm{rot}} E_{\mathrm{rot}} + w_{\mathrm{reg}} E_{\mathrm{reg}} + w_{\mathrm{obs}} E_{\mathrm{obs}}. \qquad (4)$$

The rotation term E_{rot} aims to make the affine transformation close to a rigid transformation. The regularization term E_{reg} aims to prevent divergence of the neighbouring nodes. More details of E_{rot} and E_{reg} can be found in [9]. The observation term E_{obs} penalizes the misalignment between the back-projection of model deformation and the observation:

$$E_{\mathrm{obs}} = \sum_{l=1}^{L} \sum_{i \in \mathbb{N}(l)} \|\mathcal{D}_l \circ q_l \circ g(\mathbf{p}_i)\|^2, \quad \mathcal{J}_{\mathrm{obs}} = \nabla\mathcal{D}_l \cdot \frac{\partial q_l}{\partial g} \cdot \frac{\partial g}{\partial \mathbf{x}}, \qquad (5)$$

where $\mathcal{D}_l$, q_l, and $\nabla\mathcal{D}_l$ denote the distance space, projection formulation, and the gradient of distance space of the l-th image. $\mathbb{N}(l)$ is the index set of edge vertices with correspondence in this image, L is the total number of intra-operative images. $\mathcal{J}_{\mathrm{obs}}$ is the Jacobian of each observation residual $f_{\mathrm{obs}} := \mathcal{D}_l \circ q_l \circ g(\mathbf{p}_i)$ based on the chain rule. $\mathbf{x}$ is a concatenation vector of all deformation parameters. Both observation term and its Jacobian are computationally more efficient comparing with [12] as the SDF is employed.

Levenberg-Marquardt algorithm is applied to solve the non-linear least squares problem (4).

3 Experiments

Detailed real phantom experiments are performed to validated the reconstruction ability of the proposed framework.

3.1 Evaluation Metrics

The absolute point to plane distance is used to evaluate the accuracy of reconstruction result:

$$e = \|\tilde{n}(\mathbf{p}^{\mathrm{gt}})^\top (\hat{\mathbf{p}} - \mathbf{p}^{\mathrm{gt}})\|, \qquad (6)$$

where $\hat{\mathbf{p}} \in \mathbb{R}^3$ is the reconstructed position of a vertex, $\mathbf{p}^{\mathrm{gt}} \in \mathbb{R}^3$ is the corresponding vertex (nearest vertex from $\hat{\mathbf{p}}$) from ground truth, $\tilde{n}(\cdot)$ is the 3D normal vector.

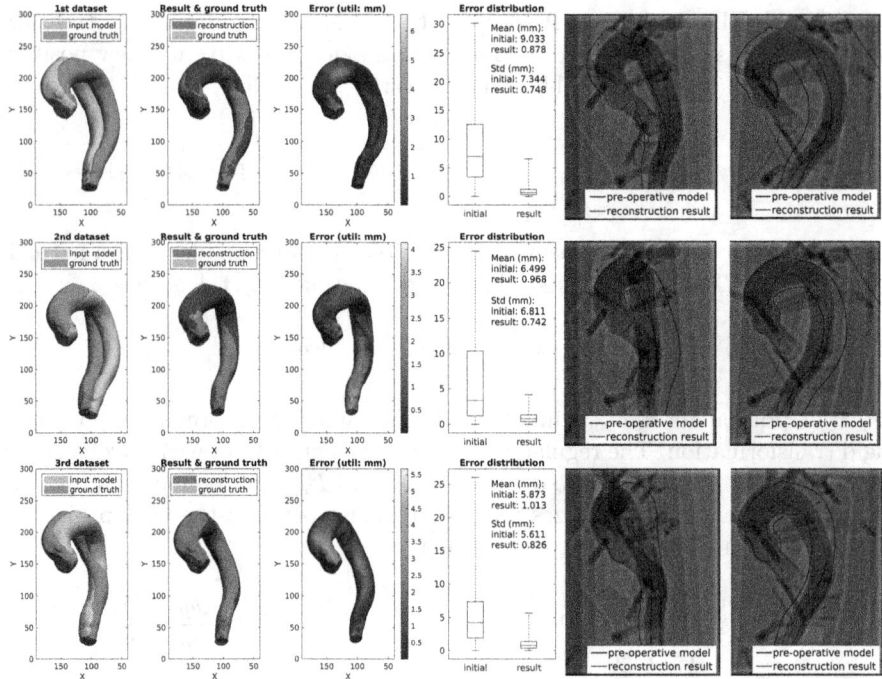

Fig. 5. Reconstruction result of phantom experiments. The 1st and 2nd column present the static model and the result. The 3rd and 4th column present the reconstruction error. The last two columns present the initial projection of pre-operative model (blue) and the reprejection of reconstruction result (red). After deformation reconstruction, the model reprojections are almost the same as the observations from the fluoroscopy. (Color figure online)

3.2   Phantom Experiments

A Silicon aortic phantom was used and different deformations were performed. For each deformation, the phantom was first scanned by CT. The X-ray images from four different viewing directions[1] were then collected as the intra-operative fluoroscopy. We used a GE C-arm system to collected the data of both CT and X-ray fluoroscopy. For each dataset, a triangular mesh of the aortic exterior surface was segmented from CT data, and used as the ground truth.

Here we present the reconstruction results of three different deformations, with six different experiments for each deformation. The simulated and real X-ray fluoroscopy of one deformation is used to train the neural network for feature

---

[1] The Positioner Primary Angles are close to $\{-15°, 0°, 15°, 30°\}$, and the Positioner Secondary Angles are close to $0°$. This paper uses LAO, RAO, and AP to denote +, −, and $0°$ of Positioner Primary Angle.

Table 1. Reconstruction accuracy comparison using same features

Data	3D init.	Method in [12]			Proposed framework		
		3D err.	3D imp.	2D err.	3D err	3D imp	2D err
1st	9.033	1.048	88.4%	0.420	0.878	90.3%	0.390
2nd	6.499	1.249	80.8%	0.358	0.968	85.1%	0.321
3rd	5.873	1.701	71.0%	0.389	1.013	82.8%	0.317

3D init.: initial difference (mm) between pre-operative model and ground truth.

3D err.: absolute error (mm) of 3D reconstruction.

2D err.: absolute error (mm) of reconstruction reprojection w.r.t. input features.

3D imp.: the 3D accuracy improvement by $\frac{\text{initial error} - \text{result error}}{\text{initial error}}$.

extraction described in Sect. 2.1. The F_1-score[2] of the other two deformation is 0.98 on average. Each deformation is reconstructed using different pre-operative models and the results are validated using the ground truth (first column in Fig. 5). In order to show the effect of occluded structures from fluoroscopy on the reconstruction accuracy, we choose the viewing directions with no, little, and medium occlusions from the X-ray images of each dataset. The results are shown in Fig. 5, where we can see that the mean error and the standard deviation of the 3D reconstruction are around 0.8 mm−1.0 mm and 0.7 mm−0.8 mm, respectively. Using the same features segmented from the neural network, a comparison of the reconstruction accuracy with our previous method in [12] is shown in Table 1. The 3D error was reduced by 28.5 % and 2D error by 11.9 % on average.

To show the effect of relative position of different viewing directions, we present the results of all 18 experiments in Fig. 6[3]. For real endovascular interventions, the high reconstruction accuracy can be achieved by choosing appropriate views of the aorta, e.g., from both sides (LAO-RAO) with fewer occlusions on the intra-operative images. This figure also presents a comparison with the the method in [12] using the same features, and overall, the proposed framework achieves higher accuracy.

---

[2] $F_1 = \frac{2}{\text{recall}^{-1} + \text{precision}^{-1}}$ can be used to show the segmentation accuracy, where recall and precision are calculated based on the hypothesis testing result.

[3] The viewing directions are LAO30-LAO15, LAO30-AP, LAO30-RAO15, LAO15-AP, LAO15-RAO15, and AP-RAO15.

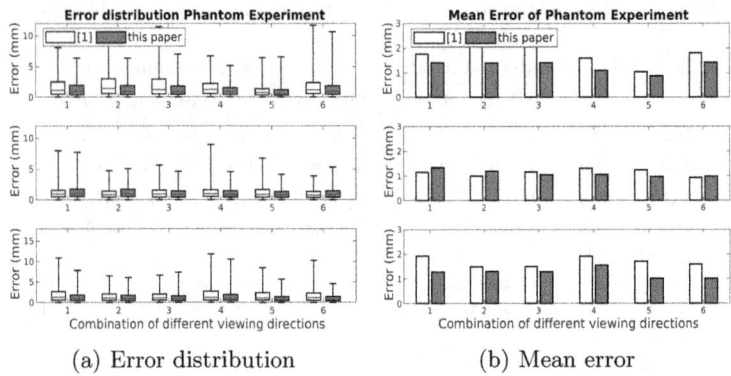

(a) Error distribution   (b) Mean error

Fig. 6. Distribution and mean reconstruction error of different relative viewing angles. Overall, the proposed framework outperforms the method in [12].

4   Conclusion

This paper presents a 3D aortic deformation reconstruction framework using a 3D pre-operative model and two intra-operative fluoroscopic images. Assisted by a deep-learning based image segmentation technique, the proposed framework recovers aortic 3D shape automatically. Using a SDF correspondence method, the redundant calculation of feature-vertex correspondence is avoided. The deformation field is formulated based on the deformation graph method. Phantom experiments are performed and the results demonstrate the ability of the proposed framework to recover the aortic deformation with low estimate error. Since our experiments used the phantom model with much larger deformation than clinical cases, we believe our proposed approach should generalize to clinical datasets, which will likely only require some fine tuning of the neural network. The proposed framework shows the potential clinical value to be used for endovascular interventions. In the future, we plan to include the image intensity information for finding feature-vertex correspondence. We also plan to improve the quality of correspondence by using the vessel's centerline.

References

1. Duong, L., Liao, R., Sundar, H., Tailhades, B., Meyer, A., Xu, C.: Curve-based 2D–3D registration of coronary vessels for image guided procedure. In: Medical Imaging 2009: Visualization, Image-Guided Procedures, and Modeling, vol. 7261, p. 72610S. International Society for Optics and Photonics (2009)
2. Edelsbrunner, H., Kirkpatrick, D., Seidel, R.: On the shape of a set of points in the plane. IEEE Trans. Inf. Theory **29**(4), 551–559 (1983)
3. Gonzalez, R.C., Woods, R.E., Eddins, S.L.: Digital Image Processing Using MATLAB. Pearson Education India, London (2004)
4. Kono, T., Kitahara, H., Sakaguchi, M., Amano, J.: Cardiac rupture after catheter ablation procedure. Ann. Thorac. Surg. **80**(1), 326–327 (2005)

5. Liao, R., Tan, Y., Sundar, H., Pfister, M., Kamen, A.: An efficient graph-based deformable 2D/3D registration algorithm with applications for abdominal aortic aneurysm interventions. In: Liao, H., Edwards, P.J.E., Pan, X., Fan, Y., Yang, G.-Z. (eds.) MIAR 2010. LNCS, vol. 6326, pp. 561–570. Springer, Heidelberg (2010). https://doi.org/10.1007/978-3-642-15699-1_59
6. McCormac, J., Handa, A., Leutenegger, S., Davison, A.J.: SceneNet RGB-D: Can 5M synthetic images beat generic imagenet pre-training on indoor segmentation?. In: 2017 IEEE International Conference on Computer Vision, pp. 2697–2706. IEEE (2017)
7. Mirabel, M., et al.: What are the characteristics of patients with severe, symptomatic, mitral regurgitation who are denied surgery? Europ. Heart J. **28**(11), 1358–1365 (2007)
8. Ronneberger, O., Fischer, P., Brox, T.: U-Net: convolutional networks for biomedical image segmentation. In: Navab, N., Hornegger, J., Wells, W.M., Frangi, A.F. (eds.) MICCAI 2015. LNCS, vol. 9351, pp. 234–241. Springer, Cham (2015). https://doi.org/10.1007/978-3-319-24574-4_28
9. Sumner, R.W., Schmid, J., Pauly, M.: Embedded deformation for shape manipulation. ACM Trans. Graph. **26**(3), 80 (2007)
10. Toth, D., Pfister, M., Maier, A., Kowarschik, M., Hornegger, J.: Adaption of 3D models to 2D x-ray images during endovascular abdominal aneurysm repair. In: Navab, N., Hornegger, J., Wells, W.M., Frangi, A.F. (eds.) MICCAI 2015. LNCS, vol. 9349, pp. 339–346. Springer, Cham (2015). https://doi.org/10.1007/978-3-319-24553-9_42
11. Zeiler, M.D., Fergus, R.: Visualizing and understanding convolutional networks. In: Fleet, D., Pajdla, T., Schiele, B., Tuytelaars, T. (eds.) ECCV 2014. LNCS, vol. 8689, pp. 818–833. Springer, Cham (2014). https://doi.org/10.1007/978-3-319-10590-1_53
12. Zhang, Y., Zhao, L., Huang, S.: Aortic 3D deformation reconstruction using 2D x-ray fluoroscopy and 3D pre-operative data for endovascular interventions. In: 2020 IEEE International Conference on Robotics and Automation, pp. 2393–2399. IEEE (2020)
13. Zhao, L., Giannarou, S., Lee, S.-L., Yang, G.-Z.: Registration-free simultaneous catheter and environment modelling. In: Ourselin, S., Joskowicz, L., Sabuncu, M.R., Unal, G., Wells, W. (eds.) MICCAI 2016. LNCS, vol. 9900, pp. 525–533. Springer, Cham (2016). https://doi.org/10.1007/978-3-319-46720-7_61

Landmarks Detection with Anatomical Constraints for Total Hip Arthroplasty Preoperative Measurements

Wei Liu, Yu Wang, Tao Jiang, Ying Chi$^{(\boxtimes)}$, Lei Zhang, and Xian-Sheng Hua

DAMO Academy, Alibaba Group, Hangzhou, China
xinyi.cy@alibaba-inc.com

Abstract. Total hip arthroplasty (THA) is a valid and reliable treatment for degenerative hip disease, and an elaborate preoperative planning is vital for such surgery. The key step of planning is to localize several anatomical landmarks in X-ray images for preoperative measurements. Conventionally, this work is almost conducted by surgeons manually that is labor-intensive and time-consuming. In this paper, we propose an automatic measurement method by detecting anatomical landmarks with the latest deep learning approaches. However, locating these landmarks automatically with high precision in X-ray images is challenging since image features of a certain landmark are subject to the variations of imaging postures and hip appearances. To this end, we impose the relative position constraints on each landmark by defining edges among landmarks according to the clinical significance. With multi-task learning, our method predicts the landmarks and edges simultaneously. Thus the correlations among these landmarks are exploited to correct the detection deviations implicitly in the network training. Extensive experiment results on two datasets have indicated the superiority of the anatomical constrained method and its potential for clinical applications.

Keywords: Landmarks detection · Anatomical constraint · Total hip arthroplasty · Preoperative planning

1 Introduction

Total hip arthroplasty is regarded as one of the most successful orthopedic operations, which improves quality of life in patients with hip pains. It is reported that more than 400,000 cases are implemented in China in 2018 [1] and there will be more cases in the future since the increasing number of aging population. An accurate and elaborate preoperative planning is vital for a successful surgery. Conventionally, surgeons need to take measurements such as neck-shaft angle, center-edge (CE) angle and femoral shaft axis on the anteroposterior and lateral X-ray images, which is time-consuming, labor-intensive and lacks of accuracy. A key step of these measurements is to localize the anatomical points on the femoral and the acetabulum, which could be achieved by identifying a set of

© Springer Nature Switzerland AG 2020
A. L. Martel et al. (Eds.): MICCAI 2020, LNCS 12264, pp. 670–679, 2020.
https://doi.org/10.1007/978-3-030-59719-1_65

landmarks on X-ray images. In this paper, we propose an automatic measurement method for THA preoperative planning by detecting accurate anatomical landmarks. Specifically, we train a deep convolutional neural network (CNN) to perform landmarks detection. By imposing anatomical constraints on the landmarks correlation, we achieve competitive results on both an in-house dataset and a public dataset as shown in experiments.

Anatomical landmarks detection in medical images is a prerequisite for many clinical applications, such as image registration, segmentation and computer-aided diagnosis (CAD). Due to the variations among patients and differences in image acquisition, it is difficult to detect the anatomical landmarks precisely. Traditional machine learning method mainly focused on predefined statistics priors, like classification of pixels [11,12] and regression with forest [5,6]. Recently, deep learning methods have demonstrated superior performances in medical image analysis to traditional methods. As for landmark detection, Zhang et al. [22] exploited two deep CNN to detect multiple landmarks on brain MR images, one learning associations between local image patches and target anatomical landmarks, and another predicting the coordinates of these landmarks. Yang et al. [21] utilized CNN to detect the geometric landmarks, and then segment femur surface with graph-cut optimization based on the identified landmarks. Bier et al. [2] detected the anatomical landmarks in pelvis X-ray images by a two-stage sequential CNN framework which is able to work in arbitrary viewing direction. Li et al. [8] presented a CNN model to learn spatial relationship between image patches and anatomical landmarks, and refining the positions by iterative optimization, which is effective for 3D ultrasound volumes. Noothout et al. [14] proposed a fully convolutional neural network (FCN) combined with regression and classification, in which they regressed the displacement vector from the identified image patch to the target landmark rather than its coordinates in cardiac CTA scans. Xu et al. [20] investigated the multi-task learning (MTL) method to perform view classification and landmark detection simultaneously by a single network on abdominal ultrasound images, and found that multi-task training outperforms the approaches that address each task individually. However, these methods hypothesized that the landmarks are independent, thus only using local information, without considering the relations between each other. To address such issue, Payer et al. [15] implicitly modeled the relationships by a spatial configurations block. Motivated by the intuition that anatomical landmarks generally lie on the boundaries of interested regions, Tuysuzoglu et al. [18] brought global context to landmarks detection by predicting their contours, and Zhang et al. [23] associated this task with bone segmentation. They have demonstrated the effectiveness of this idea, but the annotations of contours and segmentations are laborious especially for large datasets in practice.

Different from previous method, we propose an accurate anatomical landmarks detection model for THA preoperative planning in this paper, which adds an extra relation loss to model the relationships among the anatomical landmarks. The contributions of this work are summarized as follows. First, an automatic and accurate framework is proposed for anatomical landmark detection

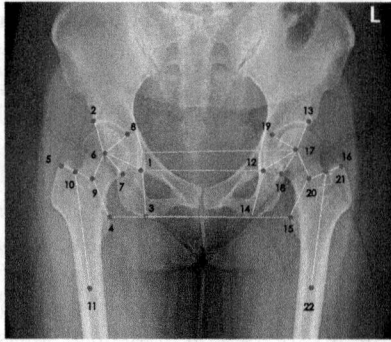

22 Landmarks			24 Edges		
Name	Right	Left	Right	Left	Cross
Teardrop	1	12	1-3	12-14	1-12
Upper Acetabulum Rim	2	13	6-1	17-12	3-14
Ischial Tuberosity	3	14	6-2	17-13	4-15
Lesser Trochanter	4	15	6-7	17-18	6-17
Greater Trochanter	5	16	6-8	17-19	
Femoral Head Center	6	17	6-9	17-20	
Lower Acetabulum Rim	7	18	9-4	20-15	
Top Acetabulum	8	19	9-10	20-21	
Femoral Neck Center	9	20	10-5	21-16	
Upper Femoral Shaft Axis	10	21	10-11	21-22	
Lower Femoral Shaft Axis	11	22			

Fig. 1. Illustration of the defined 22 landmarks and 24 clinical relevant edges on a anteroposterior hip X-ray image. The notations of each landmarks and edges are listed on the right. 10 edges on each side are illustrated as yellow lines, and 4 interaction edges across two sides are connected by green lines. (Color figure online)

with emphasis on THA preoperative planning. Second, the connections among landmarks are modeled to learn their relationships thus improving the detection precision. Third, extensive experiments on two datasets demonstrate that with our relation loss several state-of-the-art landmarks detection networks can be easily improved.

2   Method

To achieve the automatic measurement for THA preoperative planning, it is crucial to detect the anatomical landmark precisely. Rather than the conventional methods which only regress the coordinates or heatmaps of the landmarks, we further exploit the correlations of landmarks. As shown in Fig. 1, 11 landmarks (denoted as set V) on both left and right hip are selected on a anteroposterior X-ray image with the advice of orthopedics experts. Besides, the connection edges (denoted as set E) among these landmarks according to the clinical significance are introduced to model their relationships. Specifically, there are 10 edges on each side denoted as yellow lines, and 4 interaction edges across two sides are connected by green lines, totally 24 edges. These clinically relevant landmarks and edges are significant to the later measurements. Take the right hip as an example, the angle between the longitudinal axis of the femoral shaft (landmark 6 to landmark 9) and the central axis of the femoral neck (landmark 10 to landmark 11) is the neck-shaft angle, which is used to evaluate the force transmission of femur and normally lies in 125° to 140° [9]. The parallel lines of teardrops (landmark 1 to landmark 12) and lesser trochanter (landmark 4 to landmark 15) are utilized to assess the difference of two legs' length [9]. Taking such anatomical constraint into consideration, i.e., the edges, the deviation of a landmark could be corrected by others, thus improving the location accuracy.

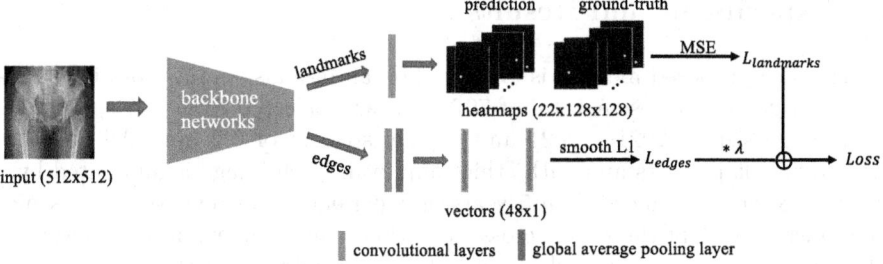

Fig. 2. The framework of proposed method.

In order to predict the landmarks as well as the edges simultaneously, we adopt the MTL strategy. The framework is shown in Fig. 2, which outputs two branches: (1) landmarks detection branch, and (2) edges prediction branch. A 2D X-ray image with size of 512×512 is firstly input into the backbone network to extract high-level features for the following two branches. For landmarks detection, each landmark is converted into a heatmap with a 2D Gaussian distribution centered at its coordinates. The distribution is normalized to the range of 0 to 1 and the Standard Deviation (Std) σ decides the shape of distribution. Several convolutional layers are utilized to regress these heatmaps from the high-level features, and output 22 channel feature maps with size of 128×128 where each channel represents a heatmap of a corresponding landmark. For edges prediction, each edge connecting two landmarks is denoted as a vector, as follows

$$e(v_i, v_j) = (x_{v_j} - x_{v_i}, y_{v_j} - y_{v_i}), \forall e \in E \tag{1}$$

where v_i and v_j are the connected landmarks, x_{v_i} and y_{v_i} is the coordinates of v_i on x and y directions respectively. The high-level features are firstly fed into convolutional layers to reduce dimensions and extract more relevant features, and then a global average pooling layer is followed to predict the vectors. In addition, the edge vector is normalized during experiment for faster convergence.

The loss of landmarks detection denoted as $L_{landmark}$ is formulated by Mean Square Error (MSE) that is consistent with previous literature [13,17], while the edges prediction error L_{edge} is evaluated by smooth L1 loss which is inspired by object detection tasks. And the final objective function L is combined with $L_{landmark}$ and L_{edge}:

$$L = L_{landmarks} + \lambda * L_{edges} \tag{2}$$

where λ is a balance factor. Added with the edges prediction loss that models the landmarks relations, the proposed method could correct the detection deviations implicitly during training.

3   Experiment and Results

Data. The proposed method is evaluated on an in-house dataset of 2D antero-posterior X-ray images. A total of 707 cases are collected from a hospital with an average size of 2021 × 2021 and a pixel spacing of 0.2 mm. All data are from different patients and with ethics approval. Each image is annotated by a clinical expert with more than 5 years of experience, and reviewed by a senior specialist. We adopt the simple cross-validation strategy in experiment and 80%, 10%, 20% of the data are randomly selected for training, validation, and testing. During preprocessing, all images are resized to 512 × 512 pixels with isotropic spacing of 0.79 mm. Besides, a supplementary experiment was conducted on a public dataset from the Grand Challenge [19] to further verify the effectiveness of our idea. The dataset contains 400 dental X-ray cephalometric images with 19 landmarks annotations from 2 experienced doctors, and the mean position of the two annotations is adopted as the ground truth. The resolution of an image is 1935 by 2400 pixels, and each pixel is about 0.1 mm. The data is divided into 3 subsets, 150 images for training data, 150 images for Test 1 data and 100 images for Test 2 data. As shown in Fig. 3, we also define 18 edges among the 19 landmarks according to the 8 measurement methods for detecting anomalies in the challenge. Likewise, all the images are firstly cropped to squares (1935 × 1935 pixels) and then resampled into the size of 512 × 512 with isotropic resolution of 0.38 mm during training.

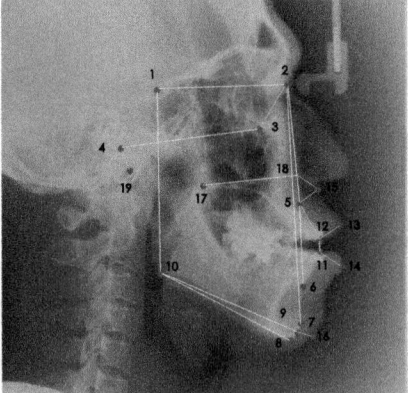

19 Landmarks		18 Edges	
Name	No.	Relevant	Auxiliary
Sella	1	1-2	2-3
Nasion	2	1-10	4-19
Orbitale	3	2-5	5-12
Porion	4	2-7	5-15
Subspinale	5	3-4	9-16
Supramentale	6	5-6	11-14
Pogonion	7	8-10	12-13
Menton	8	9-10	15-18
Gnathion	9	11-12	
Gonion	10	17-18	
Lower Incisal Incision	11		
Upper Incisal Incision	12		
Upper Lip	13		
Lower Lip	14		
Subnasale	15		
Soft Tissue Pogonion	16		
Posterior Nasal Spine	17		
Anterior Nasal Spine	18		
Articulate	19		

Fig. 3. Illustration of 19 landmarks and 18 edges on a X-ray cephalometric images. The measurement relevant landmarks are connected with yellow lines, and the others are linked with green lines followed the nearest neighbor principle for auxiliary.

Backbone Networks. The backbone network is utilized to extract high-level features from images for the following two branches of specific tasks. To eliminate the influence from backbone, we test 3 prevalent backbone networks in our experiment. The first is U-Net [16], a symmetrical downsample-upsample FCN framework with features concatenation, which is firstly applied to cell segmentation. The second is Hourglass [13], named for its hourglass like shape, in which features are processed across all scales to capture the various spatial relationships of human pose. Specifically, we used the stacked Hourglass network consisting of two Hourglass blocks. And the last is newly HRNet [17], which connects high-to-low resolution sub-networks in parallel and outputs reliable high-resolution representations with repeated multi-scale fusions. The small network HRNet-W32 from [17] is evaluated in our experiments.

Experiment Setup. The proposed model is implemented using Pytorch framework and running on a machine with 4 Nvidia P100 GPUs. Due to the limited data, the parameters of the network are initialized with the pre-trained model from the large public dataset ImageNet [4]. In addition, training datasets are augmented by flipping (with possibility of 0.5), random rotation (up to 45°) and random scaling (up to 50% difference). The network is optimized by Adam [7] with an initial learning rate (LR) of 1e-3, and is decreased to 1e-4 and 1e-5 at the 120th and 170th epochs. Optimization is carried out for 200 epochs with a batch size N of 32. The hyperparameter σ of Gaussian heatmaps is chosen to 2, and the balance factor λ is set to 1e-3 empirically.

Results. We compared landmarks detection performance of three backbone networks with the proposed edge constraints against their original ones without edges prediction branch on testing dataset. The quantitative comparison is measured by mean radial error (MRE), defined as

$$MRE = \frac{1}{n} \sum_{i=1}^{n} R_i \tag{3}$$

where n denotes the number of detected landmarks and R_i is the Euclidean distance between the predicted landmarks coordinates obtained by extracting the maxima on heatmaps and the ground-truth. The comparison results are reported in Table 1, and four randomly selected examples of predictions are given by each method as illustrated in Fig. 4. In Table 1, MREs of each individual landmark and the mean results are listed. It is obvious that the three backbone networks with the proposed edges prediction branch outperform their original ones, which validates our hypothesis that the relationships among anatomical landmarks are helpful for improving the locating precision. With the constraints of the landmarks connections, the mean MRE improvement percentiles of each backbone are: 2.3% (U-Net), 11.7% (Hourglass) and 5.1% (HRNet), which overpass the original state-of-the-art methods by a considerable margin. Among the three backbone networks, the HRNet model and Hourglass model work better than U-Net model since they have more sophisticated network structures. Furthermore, by using the intermediate supervision, Hourglass model with edge predictions get the best performance with mean MRE of 2.10 mm, which meets the clinical acceptable error 3 mm suggested by our orthopedics experts.

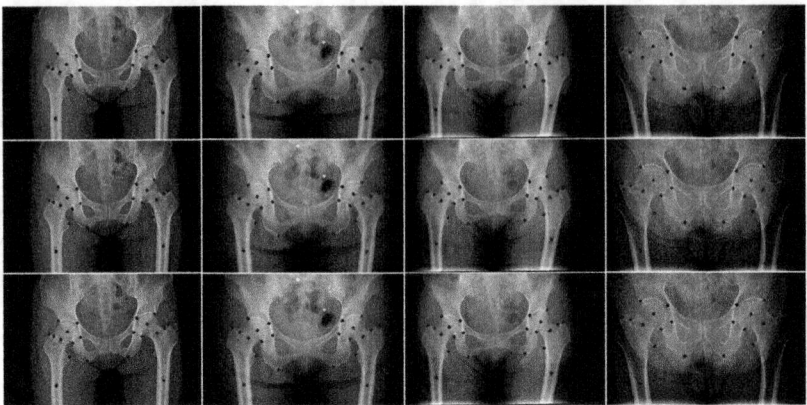

Fig. 4. Qualitative results of four randomly selected examples by each method: U-Net (top), Hourglass (middle) and HRNet (bottom). The predictions of original methods are shown in yellow circles, while the results of the methods with edge branches are shown in green circles. And the dots in red are ground truth.

Table 1. Quantitative comparison on an in-house hip dataset with MRE (mm).

Method	1	2	3	4	5	6	7	8	9	10	11	Mean
U-Net [16]	3.09	2.13	4.26	3.30	2.77	1.86	1.41	3.00	3.70	0.98	3.71	2.65
U-Net+edge	2.63	2.38	4.53	3.19	2.68	1.69	1.42	2.92	3.13	1.03	3.61	2.59
Hourglass [13]	2.15	2.38	4.07	3.17	2.24	1.52	1.25	2.99	2.88	0.69	3.62	2.38
Hourglass+edge	**1.72**	**1.73**	3.73	**2.49**	**2.00**	**1.35**	**1.08**	2.86	**2.69**	**0.64**	3.34	**2.10**
HRNet [17]	1.74	2.34	3.32	3.22	2.49	1.54	1.20	2.64	3.28	1.07	3.60	2.35
HRNet+edge	1.91	2.06	**3.23**	2.63	2.32	1.69	1.24	**2.42**	3.15	0.97	**3.21**	2.23

Having the accurate method for anatomical landmarks detection, we develop a simple demo for automatic THA preoperative measurement. Given an antero-posterior X-ray image, the demo can output the angles and lengths in 0.3 seconds, which is much faster than specialists. As shown in Fig. 5, the neck-shaft angle, the lateral CE angle and abduction angle are 131.76°, 36.83° and 55.93° on the right side, and 127.79°, 39.64° and 44.64° on the left side, respectively. The femoral offsets (FO) on each side are 39.94 and 42.80 mm, and the leg length difference is 9.12 mm.

To verify our idea, we further applied our method to the supplementary cephalometric dateset as described before. The results are show in Table 2 where successful detection rate (SDR) are adopted as the evaluation metric. The SDR shows the percentage of landmarks successfully localized within the radius of 2.0 mm, 2.5 mm, 3.0 mm, 4 mm. We use the Hourglass as the backbone network in this testing, and maximum iterations is reduced to 100 epochs to avoid overfitting due to the limited training data. Besides, three method are used for comparison. The first method from Lindner *et al.* [10] won the first place of the challenge, which explored the Random Forest regression-voting to detect

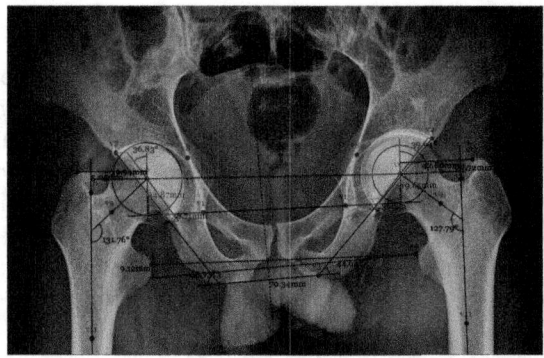

Fig. 5. A demo of automatics measurements for THA preoperative planning with the proposed method. The angles and lengths shown on the figure are automatically computed with the detected landmarks.

Table 2. Quantitative comparison on a public cephalometric dataset with SDR (%).

Test Dataset	Method	2.0 mm	2.5 mm	3.0 mm	4.0 mm
Test 1	Lindner *et al.* [10]	74.95	80.28	84.56	89.68
	Zhong *et al.* [24]	86.91	91.82	94.88	97.90
	Chen *et al.* [3]	86.67	92.67	**95.54**	**98.53**
	Hourglass	87.36	92.68	95.21	98.43
	Hourglass+edge	**89.05**	**93.93**	95.47	98.46
Test 2	Lindner *et al.* [10]	66.11	72.00	77.63	87.42
	Zhong *et al.* [24]	76.00	82.90	88.74	94.32
	Chen *et al.* [3]	75.05	82.84	88.53	**95.05**
	Hourglass	79.34	87.10	89.13	93.53
	Hourglass+edge	**80.42**	**87.84**	**89.68**	94.63

cephalometric landmarks, and the other two methods are based on deep learning approach. The former [24] regressed the heatmaps of landmarks from coarse to fine by a two-stages U-Net embeded with attention mechanism, and applied expansive exploration strategy to improve robustness during inferring. The later [3] achieved higher accuracy than existing deep learning-based methods with the help of a attentive feature pyramid fusion module. In terms of results, our method has achieved comparable performance with the others, especially in the case of higher location requirement, i.e., 2 mm and 2.5 mm. Meanwhile, it also indicates that our idea could generalized to wider clinical applications related to anatomical landmarks detection.

4   Discussion

In this paper, we propose an accurate anatomical landmarks detection method for THA preoperative planning, in which the connections among the landmarks are defined as the edges according to the clinical significance to model their relationships. By imposing such anatomical constraints, the deviation position of a landmark could be corrected by others implicitly, thus improving the detection accuracy. The extensive experiment results on two datasets have shown the superiority of the proposed method as well as the potential for clinical applications. In the future, we will extend this idea to more general landmark detection tasks.

References

1. How many total hip arthroplasty surgeries have been performed in china in 2018? https://www.sohu.com/a/299015396_100281680
2. Bier, B., et al.: X-ray-transform invariant anatomical landmark detection for pelvic trauma surgery. In: Frangi, A.F., Schnabel, J.A., Davatzikos, C., Alberola-López, C., Fichtinger, G. (eds.) MICCAI 2018. LNCS, vol. 11073, pp. 55–63. Springer, Cham (2018). https://doi.org/10.1007/978-3-030-00937-3_7
3. Chen, R., Ma, Y., Chen, N., Lee, D., Wang, W.: Cephalometric landmark detection by attentive feature pyramid fusion and regression-voting. In: Shen, D., et al. (eds.) MICCAI 2019. LNCS, vol. 11766, pp. 873–881. Springer, Cham (2019). https://doi.org/10.1007/978-3-030-32248-9_97
4. Deng, J., Dong, W., Socher, R., Li, L.J., Li, K., Fei-Fei, L.: Imagenet: A large-scale hierarchical image database. In: CVPR 2009, pp. 248–255. IEEE (2009)
5. Gao, Y., Shen, D.: Collaborative regression-based anatomical landmark detection. Phys. Med. Biol. **60**(24), 9377 (2015)
6. Han, D., Gao, Y., Wu, G., Yap, P.-T., Shen, D.: Robust anatomical landmark detection for MR brain image registration. In: Golland, P., Hata, N., Barillot, C., Hornegger, J., Howe, R. (eds.) MICCAI 2014. LNCS, vol. 8673, pp. 186–193. Springer, Cham (2014). https://doi.org/10.1007/978-3-319-10404-1_24
7. Kingma, D.P., Ba, J.: Adam: A method for stochastic optimization (2014). arXiv preprint arXiv:1412.6980
8. Li, Y., et al.: Fast multiple landmark localisation using a patch-based iterative network. In: Frangi, A.F., Schnabel, J.A., Davatzikos, C., Alberola-López, C., Fichtinger, G. (eds.) MICCAI 2018. LNCS, vol. 11070, pp. 563–571. Springer, Cham (2018). https://doi.org/10.1007/978-3-030-00928-1_64
9. Lim, S.J., Park, Y.S.: Plain radiography of the hip: a review of radiographic techniques and image features. Hip Pelvis **27**(3), 125–134 (2015)
10. Lindner, C., Cootes, T.F.: Fully automatic cephalometric evaluation using random forest regression-voting. In: ISBI 2015. Citeseer (2015)
11. Lu, X., Jolly, M.-P.: Discriminative context modeling using auxiliary markers for LV landmark detection from a single MR image. In: Camara, O., Mansi, T., Pop, M., Rhode, K., Sermesant, M., Young, A. (eds.) STACOM 2012. LNCS, vol. 7746, pp. 105–114. Springer, Heidelberg (2013). https://doi.org/10.1007/978-3-642-36961-2_13
12. Mahapatra, D.: Landmark detection in cardiac MRI using learned local image statistics. In: Camara, O., Mansi, T., Pop, M., Rhode, K., Sermesant, M., Young, A. (eds.) STACOM 2012. LNCS, vol. 7746, pp. 115–124. Springer, Heidelberg (2013). https://doi.org/10.1007/978-3-642-36961-2_14

13. Newell, A., Yang, K., Deng, J.: Stacked hourglass networks for human pose estimation. In: Leibe, B., Matas, J., Sebe, N., Welling, M. (eds.) ECCV 2016. LNCS, vol. 9912, pp. 483–499. Springer, Cham (2016). https://doi.org/10.1007/978-3-319-46484-8_29

14. Noothout, J.M., de Vos, B.D., Wolterink, J.M., Leiner, T., Išgum, I.: CNN-based landmark detection in cardiac CTA scans (2018). arXiv preprint arXiv:1804.04963

15. Payer, C., Štern, D., Bischof, H., Urschler, M.: Regressing heatmaps for multiple landmark localization using CNNs. In: Ourselin, S., Joskowicz, L., Sabuncu, M.R., Unal, G., Wells, W. (eds.) MICCAI 2016. LNCS, vol. 9901, pp. 230–238. Springer, Cham (2016). https://doi.org/10.1007/978-3-319-46723-8_27

16. Ronneberger, O., Fischer, P., Brox, T.: U-Net: Convolutional networks for biomedical image segmentation. In: Navab, N., Hornegger, J., Wells, W.M., Frangi, A.F. (eds.) MICCAI 2015. LNCS, vol. 9351, pp. 234–241. Springer, Cham (2015). https://doi.org/10.1007/978-3-319-24574-4_28

17. Sun, K., Xiao, B., Liu, D., Wang, J.: Deep high-resolution representation learning for human pose estimation. CVPR **2019**, 5693–5703 (2019)

18. Tuysuzoglu, A., Tan, J., Eissa, K., Kiraly, A.P., Diallo, M., Kamen, A.: Deep adversarial context-aware landmark detection for ultrasound imaging. In: Frangi, A.F., Schnabel, J.A., Davatzikos, C., Alberola-López, C., Fichtinger, G. (eds.) MICCAI 2018. LNCS, vol. 11073, pp. 151–158. Springer, Cham (2018). https://doi.org/10.1007/978-3-030-00937-3_18

19. Wang, C.W., et al.: Evaluation and comparison of anatomical landmark detection methods for cephalometric x-ray images: a grand challenge. IEEE Trans. Med. Imaging **34**(9), 1890–1900 (2015)

20. Xu, Z., et al.: Less is More: Simultaneous view classification and landmark detection for abdominal ultrasound images. In: Frangi, A.F., Schnabel, J.A., Davatzikos, C., Alberola-López, C., Fichtinger, G. (eds.) MICCAI 2018. LNCS, vol. 11071, pp. 711–719. Springer, Cham (2018). https://doi.org/10.1007/978-3-030-00934-2_79

21. Yang, D., Zhang, S., Yan, Z., Tan, C., Li, K., Metaxas, D.: Automated anatomical landmark detection ondistal femur surface using convolutional neural network. In: ISBI 2015, pp. 17–21. IEEE (2015)

22. Zhang, J., Liu, M., Shen, D.: Detecting anatomical landmarks from limited medical imaging data using two-stage task-oriented deep neural networks. IEEE Trans. Image Process. **26**(10), 4753–4764 (2017)

23. Zhang, J., et al.: Context-guided fully convolutional networks for joint craniomaxillofacial bone segmentation and landmark digitization. Med. Image Anal. **60**, 101621 (2020)

24. Zhong, Z., Li, J., Zhang, Z., Jiao, Z., Gao, X.: An attention-guided deep regression model for landmark detection in Cephalograms. In: Shen, D., et al. (eds.) MICCAI 2019. LNCS, vol. 11769, pp. 540–548. Springer, Cham (2019). https://doi.org/10.1007/978-3-030-32226-7_60

Instantiation-Net: 3D Mesh Reconstruction from Single 2D Image for Right Ventricle

Zhao-Yang Wang[1]([✉]), Xiao-Yun Zhou[1], Peichao Li[1], Celia Theodoreli-Riga[3,4], and Guang-Zhong Yang[1,2]

[1] The Hamlyn Centre for Robotic Surgery, Imperial College London, London, UK
zhaoyang.wang18@imperial.ac.uk
[2] Institute of Medical Robotics, Shanghai Jiao Tong University, Shanghai, China
[3] Regional Vascular Unit, St Marys Hospital, London, UK
[4] The Academic Division of Surgery, Imperial College London, London, UK

Abstract. 3D shape instantiation for reconstructing the 3D shape of a target from limited 2D images or projections is an emerging technique for surgical navigation. It bridges the gap between the current 2D intra-operative image acquisition and 3D intra-operative navigation requirement in Minimally Invasive Surgery (MIS). Previously, a general and registration-free framework was proposed for 3D shape instantiation based on Kernel Partial Least Square Regression (KPLSR), requiring manually segmented anatomical structures as the pre-requisite. Two hyper-parameters including the Gaussian width and component number also need to be carefully adjusted. Deep Convolutional Neural Network (DCNN) based framework has also been proposed to reconstruct a 3D point cloud from single 2D image, with end-to-end and fully automatic learning. In this paper, an Instantiation-Net is proposed to reconstruct the 3D mesh of a target from its single 2D image, by using DCNN to extract features from the 2D image and Graph Convolutional Network (GCN) to reconstruct the 3D mesh, and using Fully Connected (FC) layers as the connection. Detailed validation on the Right Ventricle (RV), with a mean 3D distance error of $2.21mm$ on 27 patients, demonstrates the practical strength of the method and its potential clinical use.

Keywords: 3D shape instantiation · Intra-operative 3D navigation · Right Ventricle · Graph Convolutional Neural Network

1 Introduction

Recent advances in Minimally Invasive Surgery (MIS) bring many advantages to patients including reduced access trauma, less bleeding and shorter hospitalization. However, they also impose challenges to intra-operative navigation,

---

Z.-Y. Wang and X.-Y. Zhou contribute equally to this paper. This work was supported by EPSRC project grant EP/L020688/1.

A. L. Martel et al. (Eds.): MICCAI 2020, LNCS 12264, pp. 680–691, 2020.
https://doi.org/10.1007/978-3-030-59719-1_66

where acquisition of 3D data in real-time is challenging and in most clinical practices, 2D projections or images from fluoroscopy, cross sectional Magnetic Resonance Imaging (MRI) and ultrasound are used. It is difficult to use these 2D images to resolve complex 3D geometries and therefore there is a pressing need to develop real-time techniques to reconstruct 3D structures from limited or even a single 2D projection or image in real-time intra-operatively.

For example, pre-operative 3D context from MRI or Computed Tomography (CT) was registered to intra-operative 2D ultrasound images with both spatial and temporal alignment, which facilitates intra-operative navigation for cardiac MIS [9]. Pre-operative 3D meshes from CT were adapted to intra-operative 2D X-ray images with as-rigid-as-possible method, which acts as an arterial road map for Endovascular Aneurysm Repair [14]. The 3D shape of a stent-graft at three different status: fully-compressed [17], partially-deployed [16] and fully-deployed [18] was instantiated from single 2D fluoroscopic projection with stent-graft modelling, graft gap interpolation, the Robust Perspective-n-Point method, Graph Convolutional Network (GCN), and mesh manipulation, which improves the navigation in Fenestrated Endovascular Aneurysm Repair. A review of bony structures reconstruction from multi-view X-ray images could be found in [7].

Recently, a general and registration-free framework for 3D shape instantiation was proposed [20] with three steps: 1) 3D volumes were pre-operatively scanned for the target at different time frames during the deformation cycle. 3D meshes were segmented and expressed into 3D Statistical Shape Models (SSMs). Sparse Principal Component Analysis (SPCA) was used to analyze the 3D SSMs to determine the most informative and important scan plane; 2) 2D images were scanned synchronously at the determined optimal scan plane. 2D contours were segmented and expressed into 2D SSMs. Kernel Partial Least Square Regression (KPLSR) was applied to learn the relationship between the 2D and 3D SSMs; 3) the KPLSR-learned relationship was applied to the intra-operative 2D SSMs to reconstruct the instantaneous 3D SSMs for navigation. Two deficiencies exist: 1) manual segmentation is essential; 2) two hyper-parameters including the Gaussian width and component number require to be carefully and manually adjusted. To avoid these drawbacks, a one-stage and fully automatic Deep Convolutional Neural Network (DCNN) was proposed to reconstruct the 3D point cloud of a target from its single 2D projection with PointOutNet and Chamfer loss [19]. However, 3D mesh with more details of the surface is more helpful and vital than point cloud.

In this paper, we propose an Instantiation-Net to reconstruct the 3D mesh of a target from its single 2D projection. DenseNet-121 is used to extract abundant features from the 2D image input. Graph Convolutional Network (GCN) is used to reconstruct the 3D mesh. Fully Connected (FC) layers are used as the connection. Figure 1 illustrates the framework for 3D shape instantiation is evolving from two-stage KPLSR-based framework [20], the PointOutNet [19], to the Instantiation-Net proposed in this paper. 27 Right Ventricles (RVs), indicating 609 experiments, were used for validation. An average 3D distance error around $2mm$ was achieved, which is comparable to the performance in [20] but with end-to-end and fully automatic training.

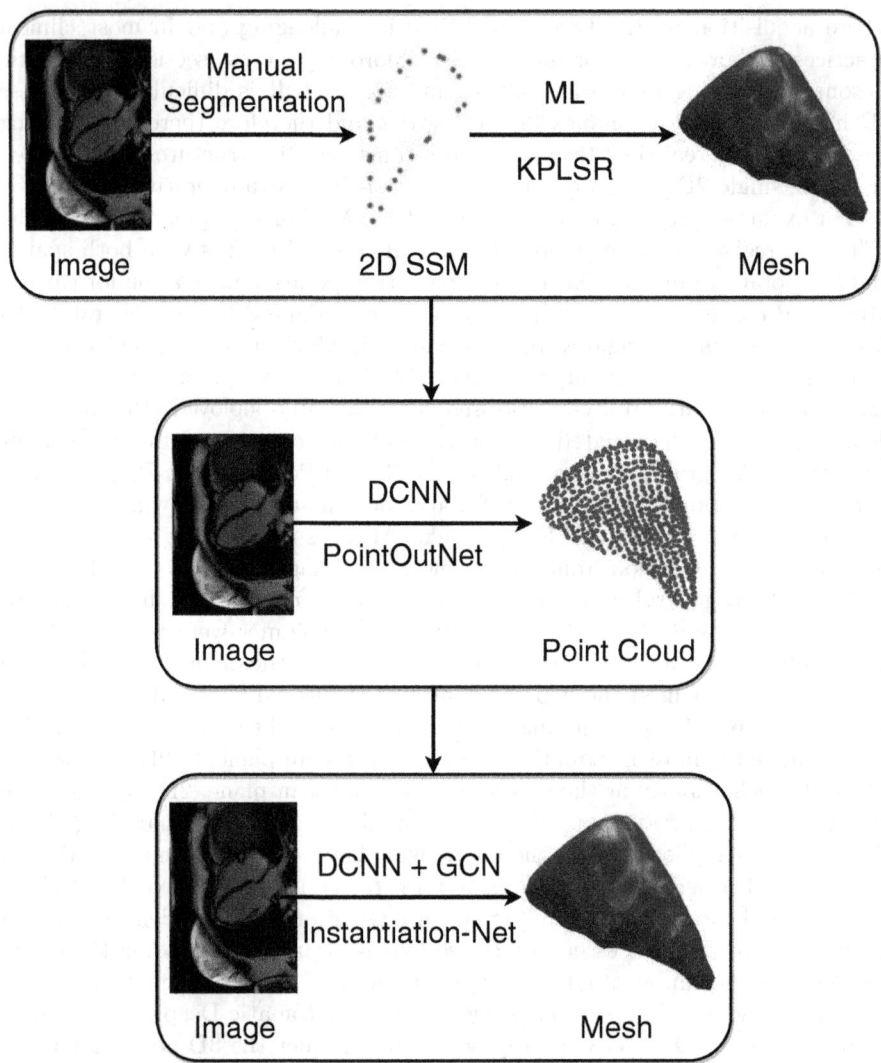

Fig. 1. An illustration of the evolution of 3D shape instantiation from two-stage approach based on KPLSR [20], PointOutNet based on deep learning [19] to the Instantiation-Net that could reconstruct 3D mesh from 2D image in end-to-end fashion.

2   Methodology

The input of Instantiation-Net is a single 2D image I with a size of 192×256 while the output is a 3D mesh $\mathscr{F}$ with vertex V and the connectivity A. Three parts including DCNN, FC and GCN consist of the proposed Instantiation-Net.

2.1 DCNN

For an image input $I_{N \times H \times W \times C}$, where N is the batch size and is fixed at 1 in this paper, H is the image height, W is the image width, C is the image channel and is 1 for medical images, multiple convolutional layers, batch normalization layers, average-pooling layers and ReLU layers[1] consist of the first part of Instantiation-Net - DenseNet-121 [8] for extracting abundant features from the single 2D image input. Detailed layer configurations are shown in Fig. 2.

DCNN		FC + GCN	
Layers	**Configuration**	**Layers**	**Configuration**
Convolution	7 × 7 conv, stride 2	Fully Connected	$[1,6,8,1024] \to 8 \to (M/4^4) \times 64$
Pooling	3 × 3 max pool, stride 2	Up-Sampling	$(M/4^4) \times 64 \to (M/4^3) \times 64$
Dense Block (1)	$\begin{bmatrix} 1 \times 1 \text{ conv} \\ 3 \times 3 \text{ conv} \end{bmatrix} \times 6$, stride 1	Convolution	$(M/4^3) \times 64 \to (M/4^3) \times 64$
Transition Layer (1)	1 × 1 conv 2 × 2 average pool, stride 2	Up-Sampling	$(M/4^3) \times 64 \to (M/4^2) \times 64$
Dense Block (2)	$\begin{bmatrix} 1 \times 1 \text{ conv} \\ 3 \times 3 \text{ conv} \end{bmatrix} \times 12$, stride 1	Convolution	$(M/4^2) \times 64 \to (M/4^2) \times 64$
Transition Layer (2)	1 × 1 conv 2 × 2 average pool, stride 2	Up-Sampling	$(M/4^2) \times 64 \to (M/4) \times 64$
Dense Block (3)	$\begin{bmatrix} 1 \times 1 \text{ conv} \\ 3 \times 3 \text{ conv} \end{bmatrix} \times 24$, stride 1	Convolution	$(M/4) \times 64 \to (M/4) \times 64$
Transition Layer (3)	1 × 1 conv 2 × 2 average pool, stride 2	Up-Sampling	$(M/4) \times 64 \to M \times 64$
Dense Block (4)	$\begin{bmatrix} 1 \times 1 \text{ conv} \\ 3 \times 3 \text{ conv} \end{bmatrix} \times 16$, stride 1	Convolution	$M \times 64 \to M \times 3$

Fig. 2. Detailed layer configurations of the proposed Instantiation-Net.

2.2 GCN

For a 3D mesh $\mathscr{F}$ with vertex of $\mathbf{V}_{M \times 3}$ and connectivity of $\mathbf{A}_{M \times M}$, where M is the number of vertex in the mesh, $\mathbf{A}_{M \times M}$ is the adjacency matrix with, $\mathbf{A}_{ij} = 1$ if the ith and jth vertex are connected by an edge, otherwise $\mathbf{A}_{ij} = 0$. The non-normalized graph Laplacian matrix is calculated $\mathbf{L} = \mathbf{D} - \mathbf{A}$, where $\mathbf{D}_{ii} = \sum_{j=1}^{M} \mathbf{A}_{ij}$, $\mathbf{D}_{ij} = 0$, if $i \neq j$, is the vertex degree matrix. For achieving Fourier transform on the mesh vertex, L is decomposed into Fourier basis as $\mathbf{L} = \mathbf{U}\Lambda\mathbf{U}^T$, where $\mathbf{U}$ is the matrix of eigen-vectors and Λ is the matrix of eigen-values. The Fourier transform on the vertex v is then formulated as $v_w = U^T v$, while the inverse Fourier transform is formulated as $v = \mathbf{U}^T v_w$. The convolution in spatial domain of the vertex v and the kernel s can be inversely transformed from the spectral domain as $v * s = \mathbf{U}((\mathbf{U}^T v) \odot (\mathbf{U}^T s))$, where s is the convolutional filter.

---

[1] For more details of these layers, please refer to [10, 12].

However, this computation is very expensive as it involves matrix multiplication. Hence Chebyshev polynomial is used to reformulate the computation with a kernel g_θ:

$$g_\theta(\mathbf{L}) = \sum_{k=0}^{K-1} \theta_k T_k(\tilde{\mathbf{L}}) \tag{1}$$

where $\tilde{\mathbf{L}} = 2\mathbf{L}/\Lambda_{max} - \mathbf{I}_n$ is the scaled Laplacian, θ is the Chebyshev coefficient. T_k is the Chebyshev polynomial and is recursively calculated as [2]:

$$\mathbf{T}_k(\tilde{\mathbf{L}}) = 2\tilde{\mathbf{L}}\mathbf{T}_{k-1}(\tilde{\mathbf{L}}) - \mathbf{T}_{k-2}(\tilde{\mathbf{L}}) \tag{2}$$

where $\mathbf{T}_0 = 1$, $\mathbf{T}_1 = \tilde{\mathbf{L}}$. The spectral convolution is then defined as:

$$y_j = v * s = \sum_{i=1}^{F_{in}} g_{\theta i,j}(\mathbf{L})v \tag{3}$$

where F_{in} is the feature channel number of the input V, $j \in (1, F_{out})$, F_{out} is the feature channel number of the output Y. Each convolutional layer has $F_{in} \times F_{out} \times K$ trainable parameters.

Except graph convolutional layers, up-sampling layers are also applied to learn the hierarchy mesh structures. First, the mesh $\mathscr{F}$ is down-sampled or simplified to a simplified mesh with M//S vertices, where S is the stride, and is set as 4 or 3 in this paper. Several mesh simplification algorithms can be used in this stage, such as Quadric Error Metrics [13], and weighted Quadric Error Metrics Simplification (QEMS) [5], The connectivity of the simplified meshes is recorded and used to calculate $\mathbf{L}$ for the graph convolution at different resolutions. The discarded vertexes during the mesh simplification are projected back to the nearest triangle, with the projected position computed with the barycentric coordinates. More details regarding the down-sampling, up-sampling and graph convolutional layers can be found in [13].

2.3   Instantiation-Net

For the DCNN part, DenseNet-121 from [8] is imported from Keras, with parameters pre-trained on ImageNet [3]. For the FC part, two FC layers with an output feature dimension of 8 are used. For the GCN part, four up-sampling and graph convolutional layers are adopted [13]. Detailed configurations of each layer are shown in Fig. 2. An intuitive illustration of the example Instantiation-Net with compacting multiple layers into blocks is shown in Fig. 3. The input is generated by tiling the 2D MRI image three times along the channel dimension. A 3D mesh can be reconstructed directly from the single 2D image input by the proposed Instantiation-Net in a fully automatic and end-to-end learning fashion.

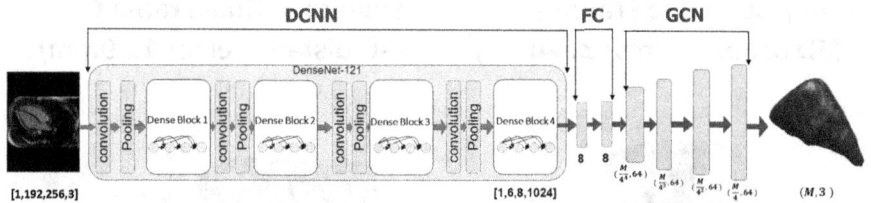

Fig. 3. An intuitive illustration of the proposed Instantiation-Net with compacting multiple layers into blocks.

2.4   Experimental Setup

The data used are the same as [19,20]. Following [19,20], Instantiation-Net was trained patient-specifically with leave-one-frame-out cross-validation: one time frame in the patient was used in the test set, while all other time frames were used as the training set. Stochastic Gradient Descent (SGD) was used as the optimizer with a momentum of 0.9, while each experiment was trained up to 1200 epochs. The initial learning rate was $5e^{-3}$ and decayed with 0.97 every $5 \times M$ iterations, where M is the number of time frame for each patient. The kernel size of GCN was 3. For most experiments, the feature channel and stride size of GCN were 64 and 4 respectively, except that some experiments used 16 and 3 instead. The proposed framework was implemented on Tensorflow and Keras functions. L1 loss was used as the loss function, because L2 loss experienced convergence difficulty in our experiments. The average value of the 3D distance errors of all the vertices is used as the evaluation metric.

3   Results

To prove the stability and robustness of the proposed Instantiation-Net to each vertex inside a mesh and to each time frame inside a patient, the 3D distance error for each vertex of four meshes and 3D distance error for each time frame of 12 patients are shown in Sect. 3.1 and Sect. 3.2 respectively. To validate the performance of the proposed Instantiation-Net, the PLSR-based and KPLSR-based 3D shape instantiation in [20] are adopted as the baseline in Sect. 3.3.

3.1   3D Distance Error for a Mesh

Four reconstructed meshes were selected randomly, showing the 3D distance error of each vertex in colors in Fig. 4. It can be observed that the error is distributed equally on each vertex and does not concentrate or cluster on one specific area. High errors appear at the top of the RV, which is normal, as the vertex number at the RV mesh top is less in the ground-truth than other areas.

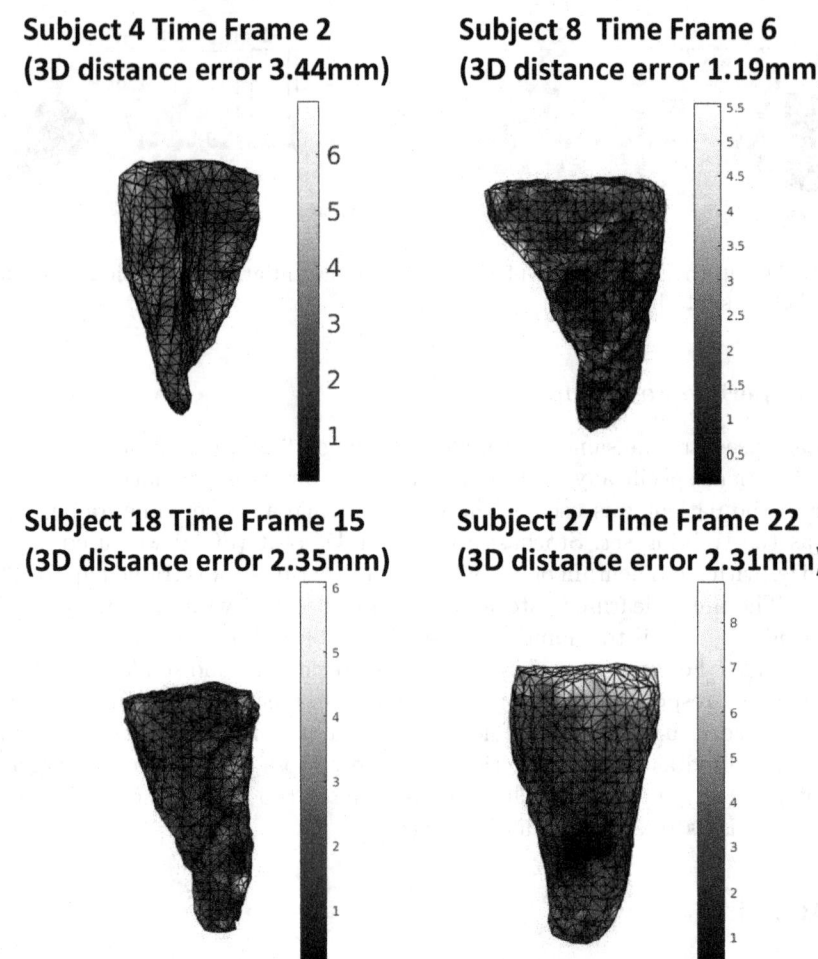

Fig. 4. The 3D distance error of each vertex of four randomly-selected meshes. The color bar is in a unit of mm.

3.2 3D Distance Error for a Patient

Figure 5 illustrates the 3D distance errors of each time frame of 12 subjects selected randomly. We can see that, for most time frames, the 3D distance errors are around $2mm$. High errors appear at some time frames, i.e. the time frame 1 and 25 of subject 7, the time frame 11 of subject 9, the time frame 9 of subject 5, the time frame 18 and 20 of subject 15, the time frame 13 of subject 26. This phenomenon was also observed in [19, 20], which is the boundary effect. At systole or diastole of the cardiac cycle, the shape of cardiac reaches its smallest or largest size, resulting in extreme cases of 3D mesh compared with other time frames. In the cross validation, if these extreme time frames are not seen in the training data, but are tested, the accuracy of the prediction will be lower.

3.3   Comparison to Other Methods

Figure. 6 shows the comparison of the reconstruction performance among the proposed Instantiation-Net, PLSR- and KPLSR-based 3D shape instantiation methods on the 27 subjects. These were evaluated by the mean of 3D distance errors across all time frames. We can see that the proposed Instantiation-Net out-performs PLSR-based 3D shape instantiation while under-performs KPLSR-based 3D shape instantiation slightly for most patients. The overall mean 3D distance error of the mesh generated by Instantiation-Net, PLSR-based and KPLSR-based 3D shape instantiation are $2.21mm$, $2.38mm$ and $2.01mm$ respectively. In addition, the performance of the proposed Instantiation-Net is robust across patients, no obvious outliers are observed.

All experiments were performed with a CPU of Intel Xeon® E5-1650 v4 and a GPU of Nvidia Titan Xp. The GPU memory consuming was around 11G which is larger than the 4G consumed by PointOutNet in [19], while PLSR-based and KPLSR-based method in [20] were trained on a CPU. The training time was around 1 h for one time frame which is longer than the $30mins$ of the PointOutNet in [19], while PLSR-based and KPLSR-based method in [20] took a few minutes. However, the inference of the end-to-end Instantiation-Net only took 0.5 seconds to generate a 3D mesh automatically, while KPLSR-based 3D shape instantiation needs manual segmentation.

4   Discussion

Due to limited coverage of the MRI images at the atrioventricular ring, less vertexes and sparse connectivity exist at the top of the 3D RV mesh, resulting in a higher error in this area, as shown in the right example in Fig. 4. In practical applications, the training data will cover all time frames pre-operatively, which can eliminate the boundary effect shown in Sect. 3.1.

DCNN has a powerful ability for feature extraction from images while GCN has a powerful ability for mesh deformation with both vertex deformation and connectivity maintenance. This paper integrates these two strong networks to achieve 3D mesh reconstruction from single 2D image, which crosses modalities. Based on the author's knowledge, this is one of the few pioneering works that achieve direct 3D mesh reconstruction from 2D images with end-to-end training. In medical computer vision, this is the first work that achieves 3D mesh reconstruction from single 2D image in an end-to-end and fully automatic training.

Apart from the baselines in this paper, there are also other works working on similar tasks, i.e. [1,4,6,11,15,19]. However, 3D occupancy grid is reconstructed in [1], point cloud is reconstructed in [4,11,19] and 3D volume is reconstructed in [6,15]. 3D occupancy grid, point cloud and 3D volume are different 3D data modalities compared to the 3D mesh reconstructed in this paper, hence it is difficult to conduct a fair comparison with them. In addition, two orthogonal X-rays are needed for a 3D volume reconstruction in [15] which can not work on a single image input in this paper.

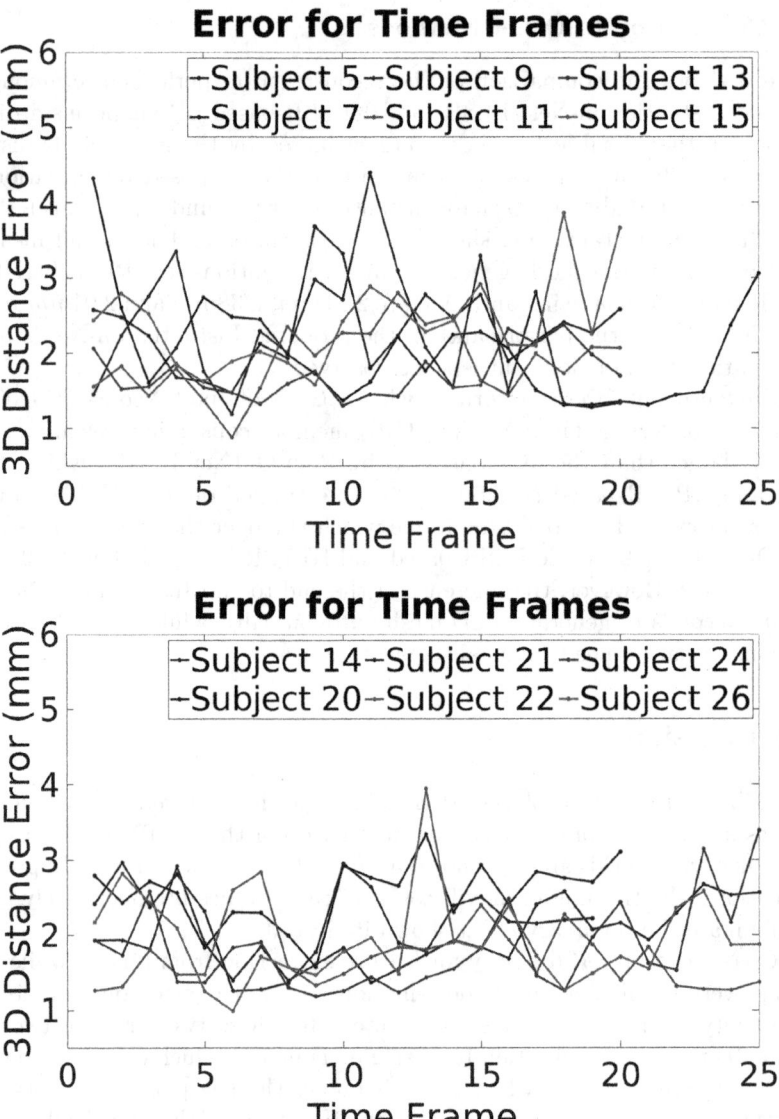

Fig. 5. The mean 3D distance errors of each time frame of 12 randomly selected patients.

One potential drawback of the proposed Instantiation-Net is that it requires both the larger consumption in GPU memory and the longer training time than that of the PointOutNet in [20] and the PLSR-based and KPLSR-based 3D shape instantiation in [19], but, the inference is quick and fully automatic.

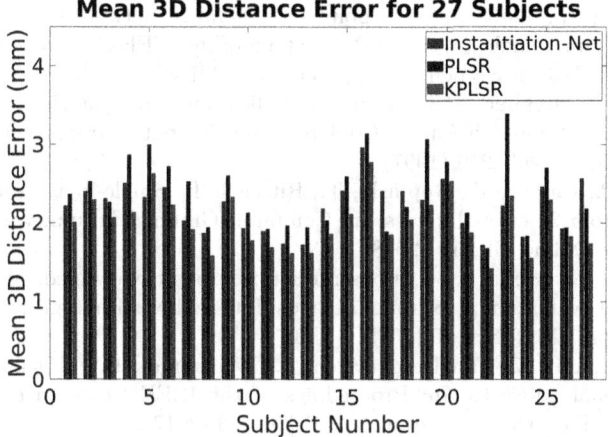

Fig. 6. The mean 3D distance errors of the mesh of 27 subjects generated by the proposed Instantiation-Net, PLSR- and KPLSR-based 3D shape instantiation.

5   Conclusion

In this paper, an end-to-end framework, called Instantiation-Net, was proposed to instantiate the 3D mesh of RV from its single 2D MRI image. DCNN is used to extract the feature map from 2D image, which is connected with 3D mesh reconstruction part based on GCN via FC layers. The results on 609 experiments showed that the proposed network could achieve higher/slightly lower accuracy in 3D mesh than PLSR-based/KPLSR-based 3D shape instantiation in [20]. According to the result, one-stage shape instantiation directly from 2D image to 3D mesh can be achieved by the proposed Instantiation-Net, obtaining comparable performance with the two baseline methods.

We believe that the combination of DCNN and GCN will be very useful in the medical area, as it bridges the gap between the image and mesh modality. In the future, we will work on extending the proposed Instantiation-Net to broader applications, i.e., reconstructing 3D meshes directly from 3D volumes.

References

1. Choy, C.B., Xu, D., Gwak, J.Y., Chen, K., Savarese, S.: 3D-R2N2: A unified approach for single and multi-view 3D object reconstruction. In: Leibe, B., Matas, J., Sebe, N., Welling, M. (eds.) ECCV 2016. LNCS, vol. 9912, pp. 628–644. Springer, Cham (2016). https://doi.org/10.1007/978-3-319-46484-8_38
2. Defferrard, M., Bresson, X., Vandergheynst, P.: Convolutional neural networks on graphs with fast localized spectral filtering. In: Advances in Neural Information Processing Systems, pp. 3844–3852 (2016)
3. Deng, J., Dong, W., Socher, R., Li, L.J., Li, K., Fei-Fei, L.: Imagenet: A large-scale hierarchical image database. In: 2009 IEEE Conference on Computer Vision and Pattern Recognition, pp. 248–255. IEEE (2009)

4. Fan, H., Su, H., Guibas, L.J.: A point set generation network for 3d object reconstruction from a single image. In: Proceedings of the IEEE Conference on Computer Vision and Pattern Recognition, pp. 605–613 (2017)
5. Garland, M., Heckbert, P.S.: Surface simplification using quadric error metrics. In: Proceedings of the 24th Annual Conference on Computer Graphics and Interactive Techniques, pp. 209–216 (1997)
6. Henzler, P., Rasche, V., Ropinski, T., Ritschel, T.: Single-image tomography: 3d volumes from 2d cranial x-rays. In: Computer Graphics Forum, vol. 37, pp. 377–388. Wiley Online Library (2018)
7. Hosseinian, S., Arefi, H.: 3d reconstruction from multi-view medical x-ray images-review and evaluation of existing methods. Int. Archives Photogrammetry Remote Sensing Spatial Inf. Sci. 40 (2015)
8. Huang, G., Liu, Z., Van Der Maaten, L., Weinberger, K.Q.: Densely connected convolutional networks. In: Proceedings of the IEEE Conference on Computer Vision and Pattern Recognition, pp. 4700–4708 (2017)
9. Huang, X., Moore, J., Guiraudon, G., Jones, D.L., Bainbridge, D., Ren, J., Peters, T.M.: Dynamic 2d ultrasound and 3d ct image registration of the beating heart. IEEE Trans. Med. Imaging $28(8)$, 1179–1189 (2009)
10. Ioffe, S., Szegedy, C.: Batch normalization: accelerating deep network training by reducing internal covariate shift. In: ICML, pp. 448–456 (2015). http://proceedings.mlr.press/v37/ioffe15.html
11. Jiang, L., Shi, S., Qi, X., Jia, J.: Gal: Geometric adversarial loss for single-view 3d-object reconstruction. In: Proceedings of the European Conference on Computer Vision (ECCV), pp. 802–816 (2018)
12. Krizhevsky, A., Sutskever, I., Hinton, G.E.: Imagenet classification with deep convolutional neural networks. In: Advances in Neural Information Processing Systems, pp. 1097–1105 (2012)
13. Ranjan, A., Bolkart, T., Sanyal, S., Black, M.J.: Generating 3d faces using convolutional mesh autoencoders. In: Proceedings of the European Conference on Computer Vision (ECCV), pp. 704–720 (2018)
14. Toth, D., Pfister, M., Maier, A., Kowarschik, M., Hornegger, J.: Adaption of 3D models to 2D X-ray images during endovascular abdominal aneurysm repair. In: Navab, N., Hornegger, J., Wells, W.M., Frangi, A.F. (eds.) MICCAI 2015. LNCS, vol. 9349, pp. 339–346. Springer, Cham (2015). https://doi.org/10.1007/978-3-319-24553-9_42
15. Ying, X., Guo, H., Ma, K., Wu, J., Weng, Z., Zheng, Y.: X2CT-GAN: reconstructing CT from biplanar x-rays with generative adversarial networks. In: Proceedings of the IEEE Conference on Computer Vision and Pattern Recognition, pp. 10619–10628 (2019)
16. Zheng, J.Q., Zhou, X.Y., Riga, C., Yang, G.Z.: Real-time 3D shape instantiation for partially deployed stent segments from a single 2-d fluoroscopic image in fenestrated endovascular aortic repair. IEEE Robot. Autom. Lett. $4(4)$, 3703–3710 (2019)
17. Zhou, X., Yang, G., Riga, C., Lee, S.: Stent graft shape instantiation for fenestrated endovascular aortic repair. In: Proceedings of the The Hamlyn Symposium on Medical Robotics. The Hamlyn Symposium on Medical Robotics (2016)
18. Zhou, X.Y., Lin, J., Riga, C., Yang, G.Z., Lee, S.L.: Real-time 3D shape instantiation from single fluoroscopy projection for fenestrated stent graft deployment. IEEE Robot. Autom. Lett. $3(2)$, 1314–1321 (2018)

19. Zhou, X.-Y., Wang, Z.-Y., Li, P., Zheng, J.-Q., Yang, G.-Z.: One-stage shape instantiation from a single 2D Image to 3D point cloud. In: Shen, D., et al. (eds.) MICCAI 2019. LNCS, vol. 11767, pp. 30–38. Springer, Cham (2019). https://doi.org/10.1007/978-3-030-32251-9_4

20. Zhou, X.Y., Yang, G.Z., Lee, S.L.: A real-time and registration-free framework for dynamic shape instantiation. Med. Image Anal. **44**, 86–97 (2018)

Miss the Point: Targeted Adversarial Attack on Multiple Landmark Detection

Qingsong Yao[1,3], Zecheng He[2], Hu Han[1,3], and S. Kevin Zhou[1,3(✉)]

[1] Medical Imaging, Robotics, Analytic Computing Laboratory/Engineering (MIRACLE), Key Lab of Intelligent Information Processing of Chinese Academy of Sciences (CAS), Institute of Computing Technology, CAS, Beijing 100190, China
yaoqingsong19@mails.ucas.edu.cn, {hanhu,zhoushaohua}@ict.ac.cn
[2] Princeton University, Newark, USA
zechengh@princeton.edu
[3] Peng Cheng Laboratory, Shenzhen, China

Abstract. Recent methods in multiple landmark detection based on deep convolutional neural networks (CNNs) reach high accuracy and improve traditional clinical workflow. However, the vulnerability of CNNs to adversarial-example attacks can be easily exploited to break classification and segmentation tasks. This paper is the first to study how fragile a CNN-based model on multiple landmark detection to adversarial perturbations. Specifically, we propose a novel Adaptive Targeted Iterative FGSM (ATI-FGSM) attack against the state-of-the-art models in multiple landmark detection. The attacker can use ATI-FGSM to precisely control the model predictions of arbitrarily selected landmarks, while keeping other stationary landmarks still, by adding imperceptible perturbations to the original image. A comprehensive evaluation on a public dataset for cephalometric landmark detection demonstrates that the adversarial examples generated by ATI-FGSM break the CNN-based network more effectively and efficiently, compared with the original Iterative FGSM attack. Our work reveals serious threats to patients' health. Furthermore, we discuss the limitations of our method and provide potential defense directions, by investigating the coupling effect of nearby landmarks, i.e., a major source of divergence in our experiments. Our source code is available at https://github.com/qsyao/attack_landmark_detection.

Keywords: Landmark detection · Adversarial examples.

1 Introduction

Multiple landmark detection is an important pre-processing step in therapy planning and intervention, thus it has attracted great interest from academia and industry [13,22,26,27]. It has been successfully applied to many practical medical clinical scenarios such as knee joint surgery [23], orthognathic and maxillofacial

This work is supported in part by the Youth Innovation Promotion Association CAS (grant 2018135) and Alibaba Group through Alibaba Innovative Research Program.

ⓒ Springer Nature Switzerland AG 2020
A. L. Martel et al. (Eds.): MICCAI 2020, LNCS 12264, pp. 692–702, 2020.
https://doi.org/10.1007/978-3-030-59719-1_67

surgeries [3], carotid artery bifurcation [24], pelvic trauma surgery [2], bone age estimation [5]. Also, it is an important step in medical imaging analysis [10,12,16], e.g., registration or initialization of segmentation algorithms.

Recently, CNN-based methods has rapidly become a methodology of choice for analyzing medical images. Compared with expert manual annotation, CNN achieves high accuracy and efficiency at a low-cost [3], showing great potential in multiple landmark detection. Chen et al. [3] use cascade U-Net to launch a two-stage heatmap regression [16], which is widely used in medical landmark detection. Zhong et al. [25] accomplish the task by regressing the heatmap and coordinate offset maps at the same time.

However, the vulnerability of CNNs to adversarial attacks can not be overlooked [19]. The attacks are legitimate examples with human-imperceptible perturbations, which attempt to fool a trained model to make incorrect predictions [7]. Goodfellow et al. [6] develop a fast gradient sign method (FGSM) to generate perturbations by back-propagating the adversarial gradient induced by an intended incorrect prediction. Kurakin et al. [9] extend it to Targeted Iterative FGSM by generating the perturbations iteratively to hack the network to predict the attacker desired target class. Adversarial attacks against CNN models become a real threat not only in classification tasks but also in segmentation and localization [21]. The dense adversary generation (DAG) algorithm proposed in [21] by Xie et al. aims to force the CNN based network to predict all pixels to target classes without L_∞ norm limitation. Other works that apply the adversarial attack to classification and segmentation [7,14,15] hack the network in both targeted and non-targeted manners with a high success rate.

A targeted attack on landmark detection is stealthy and disastrous as the detection precision is tightly related to a patient's health during surgical intervention, clinical diagnosis or measurement, etc. To study the vulnerability of landmark detection systems, we propose an approach for targeted attack against CNN-based models in this paper. Our main contributions are:

1. A simple yet representative multi-task U-Net to detect multiple landmarks with high precision and high speed.
2. The first targeted adversarial attack against multiple landmark detection, to the best of our knowledge, which exposes the great vulnerability of medical images against adversarial attack.
3. An Adaptive Targeted Iterative FGSM (ATI-FGSM) algorithm that makes the attack more effective and efficient than the standard I-FGSM.
4. A comprehensive evaluation of the proposed algorithm to attack the landmark detection and understanding its limitations.

2 Multi-task U-Net for Multiple Landmark Detection

Existing approaches for multiple landmark detection use a heatmap [16,25] and/or coordinate offset maps [3] to represent a landmark and then a U-Net-like network [17] is learned to predict the above map(s), which are post-processed

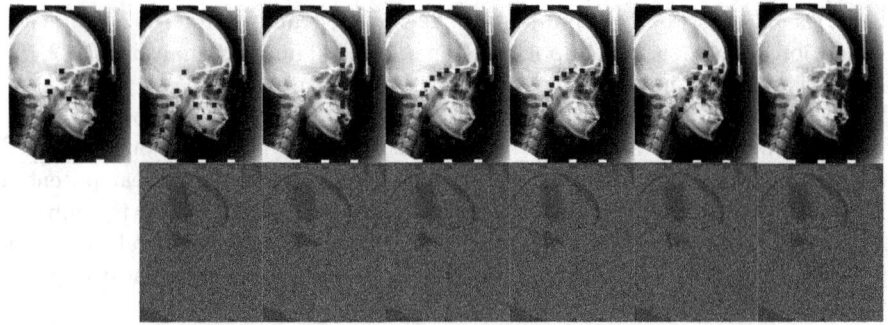

Fig. 1. An example of targeted adversarial attack against multiple landmark detection in a cephalometric radiograph. By adding imperceptible perturbations to the original image (left most), we arbitrarily position 19 landmarks to form the letters 'MICCAI'. The perturbation is magnified by a factor of 8 for visualization.

to derive the final landmark location. Here we implement a multi-task U-Net to predict both heatmap and offset maps simultaneously and treat this network as our target model to attack.

For the ith landmark located at (x_i, y_i) in an image X, its heatmap Y_i^h is computed as a Gaussian function $Y_i^h(x, y) = exp[-\frac{1}{2\sigma^2}((x-x_i)^2+(y-y_i)^2)]$ and its x-offset map $Y_i^{o_x}$ predicts the relative offset vector $Y_i^{o_x} = (x - x_i)/\sigma$ from x to the corresponding landmark x_i. Similarly, its y-offset map $Y_i^{o_y}$ is defined. Different from [25], we truncate the map functions to zero for the pixels whose $Y_i^h(x, y) \geq 0.6$. We use a binary cross-entropy loss L^h to punish the divergence of predicted and ground-truth heatmaps, and an L_1 loss L^o to punish the difference in coordinate offset maps. Here is the loss function L_i for the ith landmark:

$$L_i(Y_i, g_i(X, \theta)) = \alpha L_i^h(Y_i^h, g_i^h(X, \theta)) + sign(Y_i^h) \sum_{o \in \{o_x, o_y\}} L_i^o(Y_i^o, g_i^o(X, \theta)) \quad (1)$$

where $g_i^h(X, \theta)$ and $g_i^o(X, \theta)$ are the networks that predict heatmaps and coordinate offset maps, respectively; θ is the network parameters; α is a balancing coefficient, and $sign(\cdot)$ is a sign function which is used to ensure that only the area highlighted by heatmap is included for calculation.

To deal with the limited data problem, we fine-tune the encoder of U-Net initialized by the VGG19 network [18] pretrained on ImageNet [4]. In the test phase, a majority-vote for candidate landmarks is conducted among all pixels with heatmap value $g_i^h(X, \theta) \geq 0.6$, according to their coordinate offset maps in $g_i^o(X, \theta)$. The winning position in the ith channel is the final predicted i^{th} landmark [3]. The whole framework is illustrated in Fig. 2.

3   Adversarial Attack on Multiple Landmark Detection

A General Formulation. Given an original image X_0, the attacker attempts to generate a small perturbation P, such that (i) P is not perceptible to human beings and (ii) for the perturbed image, i.e., $X = X_0 + P$, its model prediction

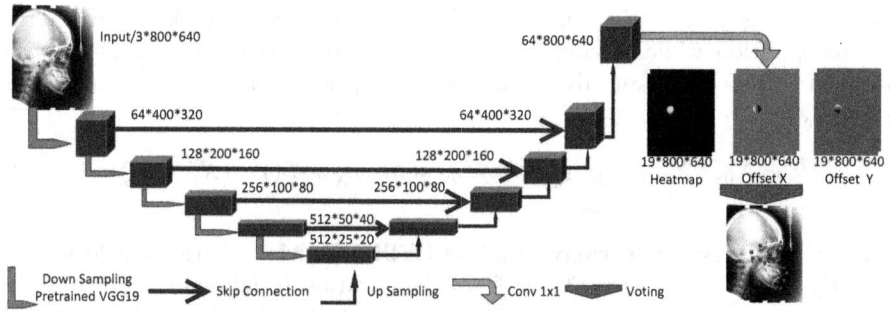

Fig. 2. Overview of our Multi-Task U-Net. For coordinate offset maps, we only focus on the areas with heatmap value ≥ 0.6. We set the value of the other areas to 0.

$g(X)$ is entirely controlled by the adversary. Follow the convention, we model the non-perceptive property of the perturbation as a constraint that the L_∞ norm of $P = X - X_0$ is less than ϵ. In the context of targeted adversarial attack on multiple landmark detection, taking full control of the model prediction means that, for an image with K landmarks, the attacker is able to move N arbitrary target landmarks to desired locations while leaving the remaining $(K - N)$ landmarks stationary.

We denote that the index set of all landmarks is given by $\Omega = \{1, 2, \dots, K\}$ and is split into two complementary subsets: $\mathcal{T} = \{t_1, t_2, \dots, t_N\}$ for the indices of target landmarks and $\mathcal{S} = \{s_1, s_2, \dots, s_{K-N}\}$ for the indices of stationary landmarks. We model the adversarial attack against the model prediction as minimizing the Euclidean distance between any target landmark $g_t(X, \theta)$ w.r.t. its corresponding adversarial target location (x_t, y_t), while keeping any stationary landmark $g_s(X, \theta)$ close to its original location (x_s, y_s):

$$\min_X \sum_{t \in \mathcal{T}} ||g_t(X, \theta) - (x_t, y_t)||_2 + \sum_{s \in \mathcal{S}} ||g_s(X, \theta) - (x_s, y_s)||_2 \tag{2}$$
$$s.t. \quad ||P||_\infty = ||X - X_0||_\infty \leq \epsilon, X \in [0, 256]^{C \times H \times M}$$

To accommodate the map-based landmark representation, the attacker sets an adversarial heatmap Y_t^h and coordinate offset maps Y_t^o based on the desired position. We then replace the corresponding Y_i^h and Y_i^o with Y_t^h and Y_t^o in Eq. (1). For a stationary landmark, we use heatmap $g^h(X, \theta)$ and coordinate offset maps $g^o(X, \theta)$ predicted by the original network as ground truth Y_s.

$$\min_X L(Y, g(X, \theta)) = \sum_{t \in \mathcal{T}} L_t(Y_t, g_t(X, \theta)) + \sum_{s \in \mathcal{S}} L_s(Y_s, g_s(X, \theta)). \tag{3}$$

Targeted iterative FGSM [9]. Targeted iterative FGSM is an enhanced version of Targeted FGSM [9], increasing the attack effectiveness by iteratively tuning an adversarial example. We adapt Targeted iterative FGSM from the classification task to multiple landmark detection task by revising its loss function L in Eq. (3). As L decreases, the predicted heatmaps and coordinate offset maps converge to the adversarial ones. This moves the targeted landmark to the desired position while leaving the stationary landmarks at their original positions. The process of an adversarial example generation, i.e., decreasing L, is given by:

$$X_0^{adv} = X_0, \quad X_{i+1}^{adv} = clip[X_i^{adv} - \eta \cdot sign(\triangledown_{X_i^{adv}} L(Y, g(X_i^{adv}, \theta))), \epsilon] \quad (4)$$

Adaptive Targeted Iterative FGSM (ATI-FGSM). There is a defect when directly adapting iterative FGSM from classification to landmark detection. In classification, each image is assigned a single label. However, for landmark detection, an input image contains multiple landmarks at various locations. The difficulty of moving each landmark varies significantly. Furthermore, the landmarks are not independent, thus moving one landmark may affect another. For example, moving a cohort of close landmarks (say around the jaw) to different locations at the same time is hard. To deal with this problem, we follow our intuition, that is, the relative vulnerability of each landmark to adversarial attack can be dynamically estimated based on the corresponding loss. A large loss term L_j at iteration i indicates that the landmark j is hard to converge to the desired position at round i and vice versa. Thus, we adaptively assign a weight for each landmark's loss term *in each iteration*, e.g., a hard-to-converge landmark is associated with a large loss, resulting in faster and better convergence during network back-propagation. Formally, in each iteration, we have:

$$L^{ada}(Y, g(X, \theta)) = \sum_{t \in \mathcal{T}} \alpha_t \cdot L_t(Y_t, g_t(X, \theta)) + \sum_{s \in \mathcal{S}} \alpha_s \cdot L_s(Y_s, g_s(X, \theta))$$
$$\alpha_j = L_j / mean(L(Y, g(X, \theta))) \quad j \in [1, K] \quad (5)$$

where $L(Y, g(X, \theta))$ is calculated by Eq. (3). The new $L^{ada}(Y, g(X, \theta))$, rather than the original $L(Y, g(X, \theta))$, is differentiated to generate gradient map in each iteration of our proposed ATI-FGSM attack.

4   Experiments

Dataset and Implementation Details. We use a public dataset for cephalometric landmark detection, provided in IEEE ISBI 2015 Challenge [20], which contains 400 cephalometric radiographs. Each radiograph has 19 manually labeled landmarks of clinical anatomical significance by the two expert doctors. We take the average annotations by two doctors as the ground truth landmarks. The image size is 1935 × 2400, while the pixel spacing is 0.1 mm. The radiographs are split to 3 sets (Train, Test1, Test2) according to the official website, whose numbers of images are 150, 150, 100 respectively. We use mean radial error (MRE) to measure the Euclidean distance between two landmarks and successful detection rate (SDR) in four radii (2 mm, 2.5 mm, 3 mm, 4 mm), which are designated by the official challenge, to measure the performance for both adversarial attack and multi-task U-Net. As MRE can be affected by extreme values,

Table 1. Comparison of five state-of-the-art methods and our proposed multi-task U-Net on the IEEE ISBI 2015 Challenge [20] datasets. We use the proposed multi-task U-Net as the target model to hack.

Model	Test Dataset 1					Test Dataset 2				
	MRE	2 mm	2.5 mm	3 mm	4 mm	MRE	2 mm	2.5 mm	3 mm	4 mm
Ibragimov et al. [8]	1.87	71.70	77.40	81.90	88.00	-	62.74	70.47	76.53	85.11
Lindner et al. [11]	1.67	74.95	80.28	84.56	89.68	-	66.11	72.00	77.63	87.42
Arik et al. [1]	-	75.37	80.91	84.32	88.25	-	67.68	74.16	79.11	84.63
Zhong et al. [25]	1.14	86.74	92.00	94.71	97.82	-	-	-	-	-
Chen et al. [3]	1.17	86.67	92.67	95.54	98.53	1.48	75.05	82.84	88.53	95.05
Proposed	1.24	84.84	90.52	93.75	97.40	1.61	71.89	80.63	86.36	93.68

we report median radial error (MedRE) for adversarial attacks additionally. Our multi-task U-Net is trained on a Quadro RTX 8000 GPU and optimized by the Adam optimizer with default settings. We set $\sigma = 40$. The learning rate is set to 1e-3 and decayed by 0.1 every 100 epochs. After multiple trials, we select $\alpha = 1.0$ for heatmaps in Eq. (1). We resize the input image to 800×640 and normalize the values to [-1, 1]. Finally, we train our multi-task U-Net for 230 epochs with a batch size of 8. In the adversarial attack phase, we set η=0.05 in Eq. (4) for the iterative increment of perturbations in our experiments.

Detection Performance of Multi-task U-Net. We report the performance of our multi-task U-Net and compare it with five state-of-the-art methods [1,3,8, 11,25] in Table 1. Our proposed approach predicts the positions of the landmarks only by regressing heatmaps and coordinate offset maps, which are widely used in the landmark detection task [3,16,25]. In terms of performance, our approach is close to the state-of-the-art methods [3,25] and significantly ahead of the IEEE ISBI 2015 Challenge championship [11].

4.1 Performance of ATI-FSGM

We evaluate the performance of the ATI-FGSM attack against the multi-task U-Net. To simulate the hardest scenario, our evaluation is established in a completely random setting. For each raw image in the two test datasets (250 images in total), we repeat twice the following: First randomly select a number of landmarks as targeted landmarks, leaving the rest as stationary landmarks. Then the target coordinates are randomly generated for the selected landmarks, from a huge rectangle ($x \in [100, 600], y \in [250, 750]$). So we have 500 attack attempts in total. This high level of randomness introduces significantly difficult cases for the adversarial attack. We generate adversarial examples by iterating 300 times (unless otherwise specified), under the constraint that $\epsilon = 8$. As in Fig. 3, the adversarial example moves the targeted landmarks (red) to the target positions (green) by fooling the network to generate incorrect heatmaps and coordinate offset maps. The small perturbation between the adversarial example and raw

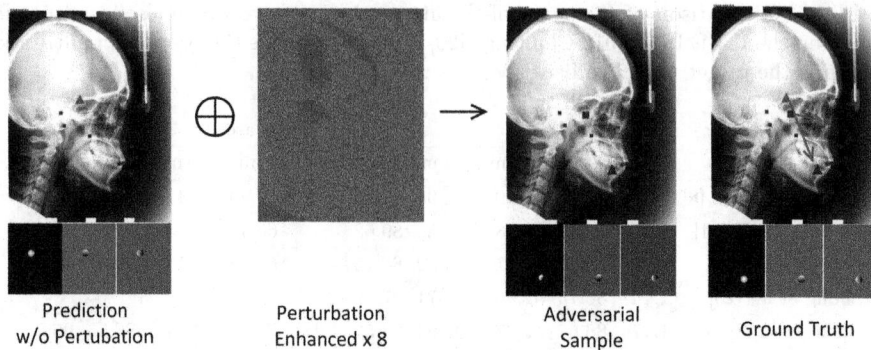

| Prediction w/o Pertubation | Perturbation Enhanced x 8 | Adversarial Sample | Ground Truth |

Fig. 3. An example of a targeted two-landmarks adversarial attack using our proposed Adaptive Targeted Iterative FGSM (ATI-FGSM). Red points highlight the predicted landmarks by the model on the original image, which are very close to the ground truth landmarks. After adding imperceptible perturbation to the input image, the model predicts the green points as the corresponding landmark positions. The green points are far away from their original positions (red), and can be controlled by the adversary. On the other hand, all other stationary points (blue) remain close to their original positions. (Color figure online)

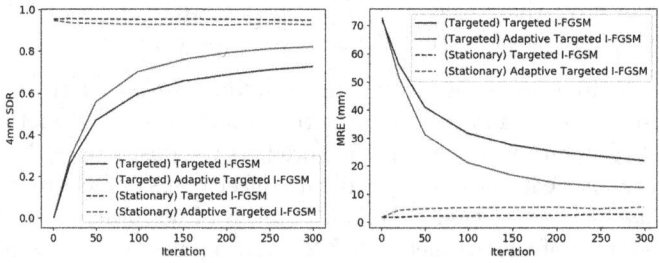

Fig. 4. Comparison between TI-FGSM and our ATI-FGSM. Our ATI-FGSM can arbitrarily move targeted landmarks away more efficiently and keep most of stationary landmarks in their original positions.

radiograph is hard to percept by humans. As in Table 2, the goals of our adversarial attack are quickly achieved in 300 iterations, and continuously optimized for the remaining 700 iterations. Evidently, the widely used method like heatmap regression [16] for landmark detection is very vulnerable to our attack.

Attack Performance vs Perturbation Strength. We evaluate our method under different constraints of perturbation intensity. Table 2 shows that the adversarial examples generated by our method can achieve low MedRE and high 4mm SDR by attacking randomly targeted landmarks successfully, while keeping most of the stationary landmarks at their original positions. Moreover, as the L_∞ norm constraint relaxes, MRE drops rapidly with more difficult landmarks hacked, but a few stationary landmarks are moved away.

Table 2. Attack performance at different iterations and L_∞ constraints.

# of iterations ($\epsilon = 8$)	1	20	50	100	150	200	250	300	400	600	750	1000
Targeted MRE (mm)	71.6	51.7	33.0	22.2	18.0	15.5	14.1	12.3	11.5	10.7	9.9	9.1
Stationary MRE (mm)	1.49	4.43	6.23	5.21	5.49	5.07	5.00	5.31	5.63	5.43	5.38	5.06
Targeted MedRE (mm)	69.2	49.6	1.32	0.67	0.55	0.42	0.42	0.42	0.42	0.42	0.36	0.33
Stationary MedRE (mm)	1.08	1.21	1.17	1.09	1.09	1.08	1.08	1.08	1.08	1.09	1.09	1.09
Targeted 4mm SDR (%)	0.7	31.1	55.2	68.2	73.8	77.5	79.6	82.2	83.4	84.9	86.2	87.3
Stationary 4mm SDR (%)	95.9	94.4	92.9	93.5	93.3	93.3	93.9	92.8	93.2	93.3	94.1	93.8
ϵ-value (# of iterations=300)	-	-	-	0.5	1	2	4	8	16	32	-	-
Targeted MRE (mm)	-	-	-	71.1	65.0	43.3	22.7	12.3	9.0	7.9	-	-
Stationary MRE (mm)	-	-	-	1.72	1.86	3.10	6.86	5.31	5.73	5.72	-	-
Targeted MedRE (mm)	-	-	-	72.2	65.1	34.1	0.5	0.42	0.42	0.42	-	-
Stationary MedRE (mm)	-	-	-	1.05	1.08	1.08	1.09	1.08	1.09	1.08	-	-
Targeted 4mm SDR (%)	-	-	-	1.17	9.69	38.3	68.5	82.2	87.3	88.2	-	-
Stationary 4mm SDR (%)	-	-	-	95.4	95.1	94.3	93.1	92.8	92.9	92.1	-	-

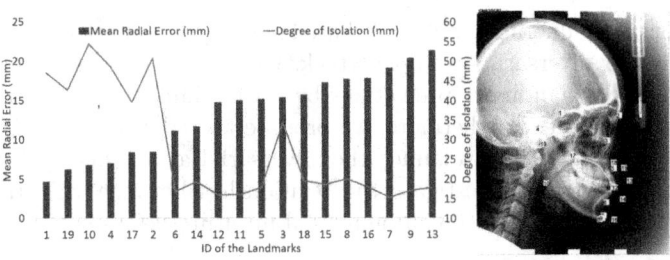

Fig. 5. Relationship between attack performance (measured by MRE) of each of 19 landmarks and its degree of isolation.

The effect of adaptiveness in ATI-FGSM. We compare the evaluation metrics and convergence speed of our method (green line) against Targeted I-FGSM (blue line) by generating 500 random adversarial examples with $\epsilon = 8$. The MRE and 4mm SDR (at 300 iterations) of our method are 12.28 mm and 82% while Targeted I-FGSM convergences to 21.84 mm and 72%, respectively. Besides, our method compromises the network more quickly, results in a shorter attack time. The results in Fig. 4 show the advantages of our method lie in not only the attack effectiveness but also efficiency. Note that the attacker can not keep all of the stationary landmarks still, a few stationary landmarks are moved away by our method.

Attack performance vs degree of isolation. As some landmarks are closely related, such as landmarks on the chin or nose, which are adjacent in all images, we set up an experiment to investigate the relationship between MRE and the degree of isolation. We define the degree of isolation of a landmark as the average distance between its five nearest neighbors. As shown in Fig. 5, we observe that MRE and degree of isolation are negatively correlated. Therefore, moving a couple of adjacent landmarks to random positions is more difficult than moving isolated ones. This is the major source of target deviation in our experiment, which may lead to potential defense.

A fancy attack. We draw 'MICCAI' on the same radiograph by attacking all of the 19 landmarks to the targeted position with $\epsilon = 8$ and 3000 iterations, which take 600s (per image) to compute on the GPU. As in Fig. 1, most landmarks are hacked successfully, which justifies that the CNN-based landmark detection is vulnerable to adversarial attacks.

5   Conclusion

We demonstrate vulnerability of CNN-based multiple landmark detection models when facing the adversarial-example attack. We show that the attacker can arbitrarily manipulate landmark predictions by adding imperceptible perturbations to the original image. Furthermore, we propose the adaptive targeted iterative FGSM, a novel algorithm to launch the adversarial attack more efficiently and effectively. At last, we investigate the relationship between vulnerability and coupling of landmarks, which can be helpful in future defense.

References

1. Arik, S.Ö., Ibragimov, B., Xing, L.: Fully automated quantitative cephalometry using convolutional neural networks. J. Med. Imaging **4**(1), 014501 (2017)
2. Bier, B., et al.: X-ray-transform invariant anatomical landmark detection for pelvic trauma surgery. In: Frangi, A.F., Schnabel, J.A., Davatzikos, C., Alberola-López, C., Fichtinger, G. (eds.) MICCAI 2018. LNCS, vol. 11073, pp. 55–63. Springer, Cham (2018). https://doi.org/10.1007/978-3-030-00937-3_7
3. Chen, R., Ma, Y., Chen, N., Lee, D., Wang, W.: Cephalometric landmark detection by attentive feature pyramid fusion and regression-voting. In: Shen, D., et al. (eds.) MICCAI 2019. LNCS, vol. 11766, pp. 873–881. Springer, Cham (2019). https://doi.org/10.1007/978-3-030-32248-9_97
4. Deng, J., Dong, W., Socher, R., Li, L.J., Li, K., Fei-Fei, L.: Imagenet: a large-scale hierarchical image database. In: CVPR, pp. 248–255 (2009)
5. Gertych, A., Zhang, A., Sayre, J., Pospiech-Kurkowska, S., Huang, H.: Bone age assessment of children using a digital hand atlas. Comput. Med. Imaging Graph. **31**(4–5), 322–331 (2007)
6. Goodfellow, I., Shlens, J., Szegedy, C.: Explaining and harnessing adversarial examples. In: ICLR (2015)
7. He, X., Yang, S., Li, G., Li, H., Chang, H., Yu, Y.: Non-local context encoder: robust biomedical image segmentation against adversarial attacks. AAAI **33**, 8417–8424 (2019)

8. Ibragimov, B., Likar, B., Pernus, F., Vrtovec, T.: Computerized cephalometry by game theory with shape-and appearance-based landmark refinement (2015)

9. Kurakin, A., Goodfellow, I., Bengio, S.: Adversarial machine learning at scale. In: ICLR (2017)

10. Li, H., Han, H., Li, Z., Wang, L., Wu, Z., Lu, J., Zhou, S.K.: High-resolution chest x-ray bone suppression using unpaired CT structural priors. IEEE Trans. Med. Imaging (2020)

11. Lindner, C., Cootes, T.F.: Fully automatic cephalometric evaluation using random forest regression-voting. Sci. Rep. **6**, 33581 (2016)

12. Litjens, G., et al.: A survey on deep learning in medical image analysis. Med. Image Anal. **42**, 60–88 (2017)

13. Liu, D., Zhou, S.K., Bernhardt, D., Comaniciu, D.: Search strategies for multiple landmark detection by submodular maximization. In: CVPR, pp. 2831–2838 (2010)

14. Ozbulak, U., Van Messem, A., De Neve, W.: Impact of adversarial examples on deep learning models for biomedical image segmentation. In: Shen, D., et al. (eds.) MICCAI 2019. LNCS, vol. 11765, pp. 300–308. Springer, Cham (2019). https://doi.org/10.1007/978-3-030-32245-8_34

15. Paschali, M., Conjeti, S., Navarro, F., Navab, N.: Generalizability vs. robustness: investigating medical imaging networks using adversarial examples. In: Frangi, A.F., Schnabel, J.A., Davatzikos, C., Alberola-López, C., Fichtinger, G. (eds.) MICCAI 2018. LNCS, vol. 11070, pp. 493–501. Springer, Cham (2018). https://doi.org/10.1007/978-3-030-00928-1_56

16. Payer, C., Štern, D., Bischof, H., Urschler, M.: Regressing heatmaps for multiple landmark localization using CNNs. In: Ourselin, S., Joskowicz, L., Sabuncu, M.R., Unal, G., Wells, W. (eds.) MICCAI 2016. LNCS, vol. 9901, pp. 230–238. Springer, Cham (2016). https://doi.org/10.1007/978-3-319-46723-8_27

17. Ronneberger, O., Fischer, P., Brox, T.: U-Net: Convolutional networks for biomedical image segmentation. In: Navab, N., Hornegger, J., Wells, W.M., Frangi, A.F. (eds.) MICCAI 2015. LNCS, vol. 9351, pp. 234–241. Springer, Cham (2015). https://doi.org/10.1007/978-3-319-24574-4_28

18. Simonyan, K., Zisserman, A.: Very deep convolutional networks for large-scale image recognition. In: ICLR (2015)

19. Szegedy, C., et al.: Fergus, R.: Intriguing properties of neural networks. In: ICLR (2014)

20. Wang, C.W., et al.: A benchmark for comparison of dental radiography analysis algorithms. Med. Image Anal. **31**, 63–76 (2016)

21. Xie, C., Wang, J., Zhang, Z., Zhou, Y., Xie, L., Yuille, A.: Adversarial examples for semantic segmentation and object detection. In: CVPR, pp. 1369–1378 (2017)

22. Yang, D., et al.: Automatic vertebra labeling in large-scale 3d ct using deep image-to-image network with message passing and sparsity regularization. In: IPMI, pp. 633–644 (2017)

23. Yang, D., Zhang, S., Yan, Z., Tan, C., Li, K., Metaxas, D.: Automated anatomical landmark detection ondistal femur surface using convolutional neural network. In: ISBI, pp. 17–21 (2015)

24. Zheng, Y., Liu, D., Georgescu, B., Nguyen, H., Comaniciu, D.: 3D Deep learning for efficient and robust landmark detection in volumetric data. In: Navab, N., Hornegger, J., Wells, W.M., Frangi, A.F. (eds.) MICCAI 2015. LNCS, vol. 9349, pp. 565–572. Springer, Cham (2015). https://doi.org/10.1007/978-3-319-24553-9_69

25. Zhong, Z., Li, J., Zhang, Z., Jiao, Z., Gao, X.: An attention-guided deep regression model for landmark detection in cephalograms. In: Shen, D., et al. (eds.) MICCAI 2019. LNCS, vol. 11769, pp. 540–548. Springer, Cham (2019). https://doi.org/10.1007/978-3-030-32226-7_60
26. Zhou, S.K. (ed.): Medical Image Recognition, Segmentation and Parsing: Machine Learning and Multiple Object Approaches. Academic Press, New York (2015)
27. Zhou, S.K., Greenspan, H., Shen, D. (eds.): Deep Learning for Medical Image Analysis. Academic Press, New York (2017)

Automatic Tooth Segmentation and Dense Correspondence of 3D Dental Model

Diya Sun[1], Yuru Pei[1(✉)], Peixin Li[1], Guangying Song[2], Yuke Guo[3],
Hongbin Zha[1], and Tianmin Xu[2]

[1] Key Laboratory of Machine Perception (MOE), Department of Machine
Intelligence, Peking University, Beijing, China
peiyuru@cis.pku.edu.cn
[2] School of Stomatology, Peking University, Beijing, China
[3] Luoyang Institute of Science and Technology, Luoyang, China

Abstract. In this paper, we propose an end-to-end coupled 3D tooth segmentation and dense correspondence network (c-SCN) for annotation of individual teeth and gingiva of clinically-obtained 3D dental models. The proposed model can be stacked on an existing graph convolutional network (GCN) for feature extraction from dental meshes. We devise a branch network for the instance-aware geodesic maps with respect to virtual tooth crown centroids for feature enhancement. The geodesic map encodes the spatial relationship of an individual tooth with the remaining dental model, and is concatenated with the GCN-based vertex-wise feature fields for simultaneous tooth segmentation and labeling. Furthermore, the label probability matrix from the multi-category classifier, indicating individual tooth regions and boundaries, is used to enhance the inference of dense correspondence. By utilizing the smooth semantic correspondence with the preservation of geometric topology, our approach addresses the attribute transfer-based landmark location. The qualitative and quantitative evaluations on the clinically-obtained dental models of orthodontic patients demonstrate that our approach achieves effective tooth annotation and dense correspondence, outperforming the compared state-of-the-art.

Keywords: Tooth annotation · Dense correspondence · Instance-aware geodesic map

1 Introduction

Digital dental models obtained by 3D scanning are widely used in clinical orthodontics, providing patient-specific 3D dentition configurations with geometric details, aiding clinical diagnose, virtual treatment planning, and quantitative treatment evaluations. Tooth segmentation and landmark location are essential to the computer-aided digital orthodontic applications, such as the virtual tooth rearrangement. Nevertheless, while the advances of tooth segmentation and correspondence made by the massive influx of research work are dramatic, the

© Springer Nature Switzerland AG 2020
A. L. Martel et al. (Eds.): MICCAI 2020, LNCS 12264, pp. 703–712, 2020.
https://doi.org/10.1007/978-3-030-59719-1_68

effective processing of orthodontic dental models is still a challenging issue due to dental abnormalities. The patient-specific tooth crowing and the impaction cause the tooth misarrangement with the order disruption along dental arcs. The point-wise dense correspondence allows attribute transfer from the labeled atlas. However, the tooth abnormalities make it hard to get semantic correspondences without prior interactively defined landmarks.

Traditional geometry-based methods utilize the curvature thresholding [9,22], the watershed-based region growing [11], and a morphologic skeleton [19] for teeth segmentation and rearrangement [21]. The geometric active contour method extracts the teeth-gingiva boundaries [8] with an initial snake around the tooth cusp. However, the geometry-based method is limited to handle the lingual-side teeth-gingiva boundaries without apparent curvature extremes. The recent deep learning-based methods, stacked on the existing bases, such as PointNet [25], the hierarchical Octree-based 3D CNN [14], and the Mask R-CNN [24], utilize the task-specific point-wise feature learning for segmentation of the individual tooth and the gingiva. However, the feature learning of discrete points or triangles does not address the labeling consistency of surrounding patches with arbitrary connections. The additional graph-cut and fuzzy clustering [2,20] are required for refinements in the postprocessing. Without the semantic priors of individual teeth, the hierarchical neural networks with separate teeth-gingiva segmentation and the teeth-teeth segmentation [6,20] are needed to handle the imbalanced multi-category classification. Moreover, the separate tooth detection module is required to locate the individual tooth [24,25]. Dense correspondence enables the attribute transfer from the annotated atlas. Recent deep neural network-based models allow the learning of the free-form deformation [7,10] and compute volumetric displacement fields [18] or vertex displacement vectors [5,23]. These recent works do produce vertex-wise correspondence while not explicitly address structure priors, such as boundary and regions, for the semantic correspondence of local structures, which limits the flexibility in dental meshes with abnormal tooth arrangements.

In this paper, we describe the c-SCN, a coupled 3D tooth segmentation and dense correspondence network that assigns vertex-wise labels to individual teeth and gingiva of the dental model. Moreover, the network produces a dense correspondence, facilitating the landmark location on teeth crowns. Unlike the previous work which does not consider vertex-wise labeling consistency in surrounding patches with arbitrary connections, we present an instance-aware geodesic map to encode the spatial relationship with the remaining dental model to enhance the GCN-based features in tooth segmentation and dense correspondence.

Our network can be stacked on an existing base GCN, such as the FeaSt-Net [16]. First, the network extracts the feature fields of the input dental model, which is bifurcated to the three passes: the decoder of the instance-aware geodesic maps, the multi-label classier, and the decoder of the dense displacements fields. Given the annotated training dataset with ground-truth vertex-wise labels, we use the geodesic maps with respect to the pseudo crown centroid of individual teeth to optimize the decoder of the geodesic map in a supervised manner. The geodesic map encodes the spatial relationship of an individual tooth with the remaining dental model, which is employed to enhance the feature fields for simultaneous tooth segmentation and labeling, as well as the dense correspondence. The acquirements of the ground-truth correspondence between dental models are challenging. We devise a semi-supervised scheme to learn the decoder of the dense displacements fields by penalizing the gap between the corresponding teeth. A difficulty in dense correspondence of 3D dental models is the labeling bleeding at the teeth boundaries. The dense correspondence decoder takes advantage of the combinational feature enhancement using the instance-aware geodesic maps and the probability matrix from the multi-category classifier with clues of tooth regions and boundaries for semantic correspondence. We evaluate our approach on real 3D dental models obtained in clinical orthodontics. Qualitative and quantitative comparisons demonstrate that our method outperforms the compared learning-based models. In conclusion, the contributions of this work are as follows:

- We present an end-to-end GCN-based model for tooth segmentation and dense correspondence of 3D clinically-obtained dental models.
- We introduce the instance-aware feature enhancement scheme by utilizing the geodesic map and the probability matrix from the multi-category classifier, which allows our model to be resilient to tooth misarrangement for segmentation and semantic correspondence.

2   Method

Our goal is to assign the vertex-wise labels of the incisor, the canine, the premolar, the molar, and the gingiva when given a 3D dental model. Moreover, our model produces dense correspondence, enabling vertex-to-vertex attribute transfer. We introduce an end-to-end coupled tooth segmentation and correspondence network (c-SCN) to predict the per-vertex labels and dense correspondence. The proposed framework is stacked on existing base GCN, the FeaStNet [16]. First, we extract the feature fields $F_0 \in \mathbb{R}^{N \times k_0}$ of the input dental model $X \in \mathbb{R}^{3N}$ using xyz coordinate, the normal vector, the curvature [4], the signature of histogram of orientation [15], and the shape diameter function. The feature field is sent to the FeaStNet, which dynamically updates the relationship between the convolutional filter weights and the local patch. The output feature fields $F_g \in \mathbb{R}^{N \times k_g}$ of the concatenated spatial graph convolution layers are bifurcated to three passes. The decoder of the geodesic maps takes F_g as input and outputs the instance-aware geodesic maps $M \in \mathbb{R}^{N \times k_m}$ with respect to k_m teeth centroids. Then, the geodesic maps are concatenated with the feature field F_g for the multi-label classification and dense correspondence. The vertex-wise classifier outputs the label probability matrix $P \in \mathbb{R}^{N \times k_c}$ with respect to k_c classes, indicating individual tooth regions and boundaries, is used to enhance the inference of dense correspondence. The decoder the displacement field produces the dense correspondence, enabling attribute transfer and landmark location.

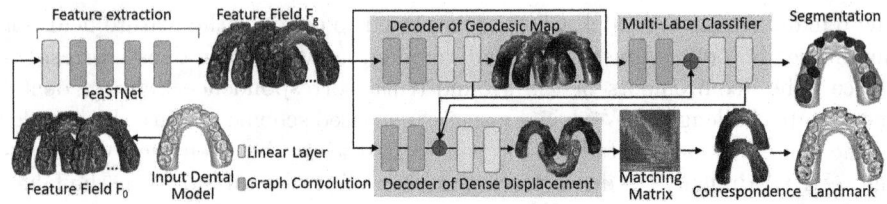

Fig. 1. Tooth segmentation and dense correspondence by the proposed c-SCN. The framework is stacked on an existing graph convolutional network, the FeaStNet, for feature extraction. The decoder of the geodesic maps take the GCN-based feature field as the input and output the instance-aware geodesic maps, which are used to reinforce the GCN-based feature fields for the multi-label classification and dense correspondence. The multi-label probability matrix with tooth region and boundary clues is used for dense correspondence, enabling attribute transfer and landmark location.

2.1   Instance-Aware Geodesic Maps

We present the instance-aware geodesic maps for feature enhancement. For each tooth, we define a pseudo landmark as the centroid of crown vertices projected to the crown surface in z direction. The geodesic distance map $M \in \mathbb{R}^{N \times k_m}$ encodes the spatial relationship of individual teeth with the remaining dental model, with entry $M_{i,l} = \frac{1}{\kappa} d_{geo}(x_i, x_l)$. Function $d_{geo}(x_i, x_l)$ returns the geodesic distance between the landmark l and vertex i. The constant κ is set to $\max d_{geo}(x_l, x_i)$ for normalization. As shown in Fig. 1, we build the decoder of geodesic maps using two graph convolution layers and two linear (with a kernel of 1×1) layers, which takes the feature volume F_g as the input and output the geodesic distance map M. The loss of the geodesic map decoder is defined as

$$L_{geo} = \|M - M'\|_F^2. \tag{1}$$

Here we use the Frobenius norm $\| \cdot \|_F$ to measure the difference between the predicted geodesic map M and the ground truth M'. Consider the centroid-based pseudo landmarks, the geodesic map accounts for the continuous spatial relationship of the individual tooth with the remaining dental model, facilitating the tooth instance location and vertex-wise annotation.

2.2   Multi-Label Classification

Given feature field F_g from the backbone network and the instance-aware geodesic maps, we employ the multi-label classifier to infer the probability distribution P of multiple teeth and the gingiva. Similar to the decoder of the geodesic maps, we utilize duplicated linear layers to predict the labeling probability. Since the geodesic map of the pseudo landmark indicates the spatial relationship of an individual tooth to the remaining dental model, we require the vertices labeled as the i-th tooth to have small values in the i-th column of the geodesic map $\lfloor M \rfloor_i$. The cross-entropy-based segmentation loss

$$L_{seg} = -\sum_{i=1}^{N} p_i \log p_i' + \alpha \sum_{i=1}^{K-1} \sum_{l(x_j)=i} |\lfloor M \rfloor_i(j)|, \tag{2}$$

where p_i and p_i' denote the predicted and the ground-truth labeling probability. The second term is used to ensure the vertex labeling consistent with the instance-aware geodesic maps. The vertex label $l(x_j)$ comes from the multi-label classifier. α is set to 0.5 empirically in our experiments. Note that the classification probability matrix P indicates the regions and boundaries of individual teeth. In the proposed framework (Fig. 1), the probability matrix P, combined with the geodesic map M, is used to augment features to infer the dense correspondence.

2.3   Dense Correspondence

The decoder of displacement field predicts the per-vertex displacement field $O \in \mathbb{R}^{3N_t}$ of the template $T \in \mathbb{R}^{3N_t}$, where the deformed template $T' = T + O$ closely fit the target 3D dental model. Inspired by [3], we define the chamfer distance-based loss function as follows:

$$L_{cd} = \sum_{i=1}^{K} \left\{ \sum_{x^t \in T'} \min_{x \in X, l(x) = l(x^t) = i} \|x^t - x\|_2^2 + \sum_{x \in X} \min_{x^t \in T', l(x^t) = l(x) = i} \|x - x^t\|_2^2 \right\} +$$
$$\left\{ \sum_{x^t \in \mathcal{B}(T')} \min_{x \in \mathcal{B}(X)} \|x^t - x\|_2^2 + \sum_{x \in \mathcal{B}(X)} \min_{x^t \in \mathcal{B}(T)} \|x - x^t\|_2^2 \right\}. \tag{3}$$

The chamfer distance-based loss function measures the distance between point clouds with the same tooth label l. Moreover, we measure the distance between the boundary point clouds $B(T')$ and $B(X)$ of the deformed template and the target model. In order to ensure the mesh smoothness and topology preservation, the Laplacian coordinates $Z(T')$ of the deformed template are required to be same as the original template mesh T, and $L_{smo} = \|Z(T) - Z(T')\|_2^2$.

Given the displacement field, we compute the matching matrix $Q \in \mathbb{R}^{N_t \times N}$ using the nearest neighbor searching scheme, where entry $q_{ij} = \exp(-\|x_i^t - x_j\|^2)$. Here we use the distance of Euclidean coordinates of $x_i^t \in T'$ and vertex $x_j \in X$ to define the matching probability, which is set to 1 when x_i and x_j' have the same coordinates. We perform the attribute transfer for landmark location, where the target landmark probability $G_l = G_l^T Q$. $G_l^T \in \mathbb{R}^{n_l \times N_t}$ denote the landmark map with entry set to 1 for n_l landmarks on the template. The target landmark coordinate of landmark l_i is computed as $x_{l_i} = \sum_{j=1}^{N} x_j G_{l_i,j}$.

The final loss function is defined as follows:

$$L = \gamma_{geo} L_{geo} + \gamma_{seg} L_{seg} + \gamma_{cd} L_{cd} + \gamma_{smo} L_{smo}. \tag{4}$$

The constant weights γ_{geo}, γ_{seg}, γ_{cd}, and γ_{smo} are used to balance the geodesic maps, the classier, the chamfer distance and the smoothness regularization, and set to 1, 1, 1, 0.5 in our experiments.

3   Experiments

Dataset and Evaluation. Experiments on the c-SCN have been conducted on 3D digital dental models obtained from orthodontic patients to show the performances on tooth and gingiva categories. The upper and lower dentition are segmented separately. We consider two sets of target categories with respect to the upper and the lower dentition. Each includes 15 classes of the symmetric incisor, the canine, the premolar, the molar, and the gingiva. The task is to segment teeth crowns and classify them. The dataset has 100 3D dental models, which is split randomly with 80 for training and remaining for testing. The 3D dental model has approx. $170k$ vertices, which is simplified to $15k$ using the quadric edge collapse-based algorithm in the preprocessing. The manually labeled tooth crown and the teeth landmarks are viewed as the ground-truth annotations, which are used for network training and evaluation. We utilize the nonrigid mesh deformation algorithm [13] to augment the dataset, where we assign 100 random deformation fields to each mesh, and obtain $8k$ synthetic dataset for training.

We evaluate the tooth segmentation using the Dice similarity coefficient (DSC), the average Hausdorff distance (AHD), and the label accuracy $e_a = \frac{n_p}{n}$, where n and n_p denote the number of testing vertices and those correctly labeled. The correspondence-based landmark location is evaluated using Euclidean metric $e_l = \frac{1}{k_l} \sum_{i=1}^{k_l} \|x_{li} - x'_{li}\|_2$, where x_{li} and x'_{li} denote the predicted and ground-truth landmark coordinates.

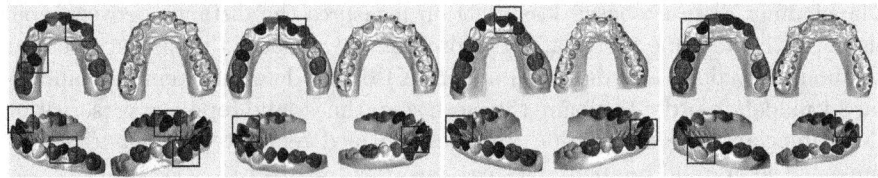

Fig. 2. Tooth segmentation (visualized in three views) and landmark location on clinically-obtained dental models.

Implementation detail. Our framework is stacked on the FeaStNet [16]. We incrementally train the model. First, we train the geodesic network using loss L_{geo}. Then, we train the label classifier using L_{seg} with the geodesic map decoder fixed. The dense correspondence network is pre-trained using $L_{cd} + L_{smo}$ with the backbone network fixed. Finally, we use the overall loss (Eq. 4) to fine-tune the network parameters. We consider symmetric 14 teeth, including 4 molars, 4 premolars, 2 canines, and 4 incisors, on the dental model. The category number k_c is set to 15 accordingly. The pseudo landmark number k_m is 14. The FeaStNet-based feature channel number $k_g = 128$. The framework is implemented using TensorFlow with the ADAM optimization algorithm on a PC with two NVIDIA 1080ti GPUs. The learning rates is set to 0.001. The training takes 24 hours with $60k$ iterations, and the online testing takes 1.59 seconds.

3.1   Qualitative Assessment

The proposed c-SCN realizes the tooth segmentation and landmark location by coupling the label classifier and correspondence-based attribute transfer as shown in Fig. 2. Note that our method is feasible to annotate the abnormal dentition with crowding and impacted teeth (red blocked). We think the reason is that the geodesic map-based feature enhancement helps to locate individual tooth by encoding instance-aware spatial relationship. Moreover, the dense correspondence enables consistent landmark location by exploiting the topology-preserving displacement fields.

Comparison with state-of-the-art. We compare tooth segmentation accuracies with the existing deep learning-based methods as shown in Fig. 3 (a). Instead of building neural networks on regular volume images [17], the point clouds [12,25], and triangle list [14], our GCN-based method utilizes arbitrary connections in the local patch for vertex feature learning and further tasks of labeling and dense correspondence. Our approach performs the segmentation of teeth and gingiva simultaneously, utilizing the geodesic map-based instance-aware spatial features enhancements for semantic labeling with an average accuracy of 0.987. As to the landmark location, we compare with the nonrigid ICP [1] and the deep learning-based 3D-Coded [26] as shown in Table 2. The proposed method outperforms the compared registration methods on both upper and lower dentitions by integrating the landmark-related continuous geodesic map, as well as the tooth regions and boundary clues, with the landmark errors of 0.96 mm vs. 0.99 mm of the NICP [1] and 1.44 mm of the 3D-Coded [26] methods.

Table 1. Segmentation accuracies with and without geodesic map (GM)-based feature enhancements on the upper and lower dentitions.

		DSC				AHD (mm)			
		Molar	Premolar	Canine	Incisor	Molar	Premolar	Canine	Incisor
Upper	w/o GM	0.89	0.90	0.92	0.92	0.23	0.25	0.19	0.13
	with GM	**0.98**	**0.98**	**0.98**	**0.97**	**0.06**	**0.08**	**0.08**	**0.05**
Lower	w/o GM	0.86	0.78	0.74	0.67	0.41	0.47	0.73	0.59
	with GM	**0.95**	**0.96**	**0.95**	**0.92**	**0.13**	**0.11**	**0.10**	**0.17**

Ablation study. We perform the ablation experiments on the geodesic map and labeling probability matrix-based feature enhancement for tooth segmentation and landmark location as shown in Fig. 3, Table 1, and Table 2. We report the tooth segmentation and landmark location accuracies of four kinds of teeth, including the incisor, the canine, the premolar, and the molar, with respect to the upper and lower dentition. The model with the GM-based feature enhancements produces performance improvements in both tooth segmentation and correspondence-based landmark location. We think the reason is that the geodesic maps with respect to the pseudo landmarks encode the instance-aware spatial relationships and facilitate the tooth location and semantic correspondence. Furthermore, an additional labeling probability matrix helps for the dense correspondence-based landmark location by providing clues of teeth boundaries and regions. For instance, the landmark error reduces from 2.03 *mm* to 0.96 *mm* with combinational feature enhancements concerning upper molars.

Table 2. Landmark location errors (mm) without feature enhancement (w/o FE), with the geodesic map (GM) and labeling probability matrix (PM)-based enhancements of the proposed method compared with the NICP (using 14 tooth-centroid landmarks)[1] and the 3D-Coded [26].

	Upper					Lower				
	w/o FE	GM	GM∘PM	NICP	3D-Coded	w/o FE	GM	GM∘PM	NICP	3D-Coded
Molar	2.03	1.27	**0.96**	0.99	1.44	2.06	1.38	**1.24**	1.30	2.35
Premolar	1.89	0.94	**0.86**	1.28	1.30	1.75	1.49	**1.23**	1.33	1.99
Canine	1.49	0.93	**0.71**	1.33	1.22	1.38	1.14	**0.99**	1.29	1.49
Incisor	1.47	0.83	**0.65**	0.93	1.36	1.13	0.75	**0.63**	0.78	1.71

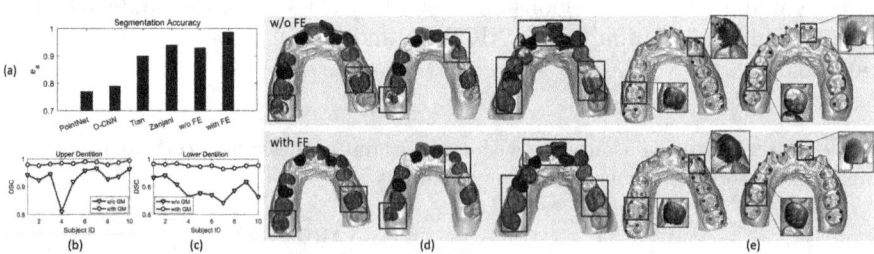

Fig. 3. Tooth segmentation accuracy of compared methods, including the PointNet [12], the O-CNN [17], Tian's [14], Zanjani's [25], and the proposed method with and without feature enhancements (FE). (b) and (c) are the DSCs of ten sampled dental models with and without GM-based feature enhancements. (d) Tooth segmentation and (e) correspondence-based landmark location with and without feature enhancement (FE). Dense correspondences of sampled individual teeth are visualized.

4 Discussion and Conclusion

In this paper, we propose a GCN-based framework for tooth segmentation and dense correspondence. We present an instance-aware geodesic map-based feature enhancement that enables robust vertex-wise classifier and the dense correspondence of dental models. We also employ the labeling probability matrix as the high-level categorical features to infer the vertex-to-vertex mapping. The solid and consistent vertex-wise labeling improvements suggest that the geodesic map and the category-based spatial relationship facilitate tooth segmentation and dense correspondence-based landmark location of 3D dental models with abnormal tooth arrangements in clinical orthodontics.

Acknowledgments. This work was supported by NKTRDP China 2017YFB1002601, NSFC 61876008, 81371192.

References

1. Amberg, B., Romdhani, S., Vetter, T.: Optimal step nonrigid icp algorithms for surface registration. In: 2007 IEEE Conference on Computer Vision and Pattern Recognition, pp. 1–8. IEEE (2007)
2. Boykov, Y., Veksler, O., Zabih, R.: Fast approximate energy minimization via graph cuts. In: Proceedings of the Seventh IEEE International Conference on Computer Vision, vol. 1, pp. 377–384. IEEE (1999)
3. Fan, H., Su, H., Guibas, L.J.: A point set generation network for 3d object reconstruction from a single image. In: Proceedings of the IEEE Conference on Computer Vision and Pattern Recognition, pp. 605–613 (2017)
4. Gal, R., Cohen-Or, D.: Salient geometric features for partial shape matching and similarity. ACM Trans. Graph. (TOG) **25**(1), 130–150 (2006)
5. Groueix, T., Fisher, M., Kim, V.G., Russell, B.C., Aubry, M.: 3d-coded: 3d correspondences by deep deformation. In: Proceedings of the European Conference on Computer Vision (ECCV), pp. 230–246 (2018)
6. Guo, K., Zou, D., Chen, X.: 3d mesh labeling via deep convolutional neural networks. ACM Trans. Graph. (TOG) **35**(1), 3 (2015)
7. Jack, D., et al.: Learning free-form deformations for 3D object reconstruction. In: Jawahar, C.V., Li, H., Mori, G., Schindler, K. (eds.) ACCV 2018. LNCS, vol. 11362, pp. 317–333. Springer, Cham (2019). https://doi.org/10.1007/978-3-030-20890-5_21
8. Kronfeld, T., Brunner, D., Brunnett, G.: Snake-based segmentation of teeth from virtual dental casts. Comput.-Aided Des. Appl. **7**(2), 221–233 (2010)
9. Kumar, Y., Janardan, R., Larson, B., Moon, J.: Improved segmentation of teeth in dental models. Comput.-Aided Des. Appl. **8**(2), 211–224 (2011)
10. Kurenkov, A., et al.: Deformnet: Free-form deformation network for 3d shape reconstruction from a single image. In: 2018 IEEE Winter Conference on Applications of Computer Vision (WACV), pp. 858–866. IEEE (2018)
11. Li, Z., Ning, X., Wang, Z.: A fast segmentation method for stl teeth model. In: 2007 IEEE/ICME International Conference on Complex Medical Engineering, pp. 163–166. IEEE (2007)

12. Qi, C.R., Su, H., Mo, K., Guibas, L.J.: Pointnet: Deep learning on point sets for 3d classification and segmentation. In: Proceedings of the IEEE Conference on Computer Vision and Pattern Recognition, pp. 652–660 (2017)
13. Sorkine, O.: Laplacian mesh processing. In: Eurographics (STARs), pp. 53–70 (2005)
14. Tian, S., Dai, N., Zhang, B., Yuan, F., Yu, Q., Cheng, X.: Automatic classification and segmentation of teeth on 3d dental model using hierarchical deep learning networks. IEEE Access **7**, 84817–84828 (2019)
15. Tombari, F., Salti, S., Di Stefano, L.: Unique signatures of histograms for local surface description. In: Daniilidis, K., Maragos, P., Paragios, N. (eds.) ECCV 2010. LNCS, vol. 6313, pp. 356–369. Springer, Heidelberg (2010). https://doi.org/10.1007/978-3-642-15558-1_26
16. Verma, N., Boyer, E., Verbeek, J.: Feastnet: Feature-steered graph convolutions for 3d shape analysis. In: Proceedings of the IEEE Conference on Computer Vision and Pattern Recognition, pp. 2598–2606 (2018)
17. Wang, P.S., Liu, Y., Guo, Y.X., Sun, C.Y., Tong, X.: O-cnn: Octree-based convolutional neural networks for 3d shape analysis. ACM Trans. Graph. (TOG) **36**(4), 72 (2017)
18. Wang, W., Ceylan, D., Mech, R., Neumann, U.: 3dn: 3d deformation network. In: Proceedings of the IEEE Conference on Computer Vision and Pattern Recognition, pp. 1038–1046 (2019)
19. Wu, K., Chen, L., Li, J., Zhou, Y.: Tooth segmentation on dental meshes using morphologic skeleton. Comput. Graph. **38**, 199–211 (2014)
20. Xu, X., Liu, C., Zheng, Y.: 3d tooth segmentation and labeling using deep convolutional neural networks. IEEE Trans. Vis. Comput. Graph. **25**(7), 2336–2348 (2018)
21. Yaqi, M., Zhongke, L.: Computer aided orthodontics treatment by virtual segmentation and adjustment. In: 2010 International Conference on Image Analysis and Signal Processing, pp. 336–339. IEEE (2010)
22. Yuan, T., Liao, W., Dai, N., Cheng, X., Yu, Q.: Single-tooth modeling for 3d dental model. J. Biomed. Imaging **2010**, 9 (2010)
23. Yumer, M.E., Mitra, N.J.: Learning semantic deformation flows with 3D convolutional networks. In: Leibe, B., Matas, J., Sebe, N., Welling, M. (eds.) ECCV 2016. LNCS, vol. 9910, pp. 294–311. Springer, Cham (2016). https://doi.org/10.1007/978-3-319-46466-4_18
24. Zanjani, F.G., et al.: Mask-MCNet: Instance segmentation in 3D point cloud of intra-oral scans. In: Shen, D., et al. (eds.) MICCAI 2019. LNCS, vol. 11768, pp. 128–136. Springer, Cham (2019). https://doi.org/10.1007/978-3-030-32254-0_15
25. Zanjani, F.G., Moin, D.A., Verheij, B., Claessen, F., Cherici, T., Tan, T., et al.: Deep learning approach to semantic segmentation in 3d point cloud intra-oral scans of teeth. In: International Conference on Medical Imaging with Deep Learning (2019)
26. Zhu, X., Liu, X., Lei, Z., Li, S.Z.: Face alignment in full pose range: a 3d total solution. IEEE Trans. Pattern Anal. Mach. Intell. **41**(1), 78–92 (2017)

Move Over There: One-Click Deformation Correction for Image Fusion During Endovascular Aortic Repair

Katharina Breininger[1(✉)], Marcus Pfister[2], Markus Kowarschik[2], and Andreas Maier[1]

[1] Pattern Recognition Lab, Friedrich-Alexander-Universität Erlangen-Nürnberg (FAU), Erlangen, Germany
katharina.breininger@fau.de
[2] Siemens Healthcare GmbH, Forchheim, Germany

Abstract. Fusing intraoperative X-ray with information from preoperative computed tomography for endovascular aortic repair has been shown to reduce radiation exposure, need for contrast agent, and procedure time. However, due to the instruments inserted during the intervention, the vasculature deforms and the fusion loses accuracy. In this paper, we propose an approach to use minimal user input obtained from a single 2D image for deformation correction in 3D. We integrate the 2D positional information as a projective constraint in an as-rigid-as-possible deformation model that allows for intraoperative correction of the deformation. Our method achieves clinically relevant accuracies while keeping user inputs to a minimum. We are able to recover the deformation at the right and left internal iliac bifurcation up to a 3D error of 1.9 mm, with an error of 0.5 mm orthogonal to the viewing direction, and an error of 1.7 mm in depth, while keeping the mean computation time below 6 s.

Keywords: Deformation modeling · Endovascular aortic repair · EVAR · Image fusion · Fluoroscopy

1 Introduction

Endovascular aortic repair (EVAR) has become the prevalent treatment strategy for elective repair of aortic aneurysms in the US [9]. During the procedure, stent grafts are inserted into the vessels under X-ray guidance to reduce pressure on the aneurysm wall and to prevent rupture. To facilitate navigation and correct placement of stent grafts without covering branching vessels, iodinated

Electronic supplementary material The online version of this chapter (https://doi.org/10.1007/978-3-030-59719-1_69) contains supplementary material, which is available to authorized users.

A. L. Martel et al. (Eds.): MICCAI 2020, LNCS 12264, pp. 713–723, 2020.
https://doi.org/10.1007/978-3-030-59719-1_69

contrast agent is applied to visualize the vasculature in the fluoroscopic images. Image fusion of intraoperative fluoroscopy with preoperative computed tomography angiography (CTA) [11,24] or magnetic resonance angiography (MRA) [23] has been proposed to aid navigation and to reduce procedure time, radiation exposure and the need for nephrotoxic contrast agent. However, due to the stiff tools inserted into the arteries during the procedure, the vasculature is deformed [14,15,17]. This renders the overlay inaccurate and reduces its value, which is an issue especially at vessel bifurcations, as accuracy at these landmarks is important to avoid accidental vessel occlusion.

Generally, approaches to model the intraoperative deformation can be divided into preoperative simulations and intraoperative corrections that aim to provide near real-time deformation during the procedure. Gindre et al. [10,18] simulated the insertion of stiff guide wires and the resulting vessel deformation for 28 patients. They reported a mean modified Hausdorff distance (mHD) of 3.8 ± 1.9 mm between intraoperative 3D information and the simulated wire. Accuracy at vessel bifurcations was not assessed. Mohammadi et al. [18] simulated the insertion of the stiff guide wires and the delivery system for four patients. The mean mHD between simulated and intraoperative instruments in the intraoperative 2D images was 2.99 ± 1.78 mm and 4.59 ± 3.25 mm on the ipsilateral and contralateral side, respectively. For the internal iliac ostium, they obtained an error of 2.99 ± 2.48 mm. In both approaches, the mean runtime for the simulation exceeded two hours. In [25], a deformation model using an as-rigid-as-possible (ARAP) deformation energy [22] is proposed, which allows for an intraoperative computation of the deformation. Given the course of the wire in one iliac artery, control points on the vessel surface are identified and pulled onto a specific position along the wire. For the internal iliac ostium in the modeled artery, they obtained a 2D projection error of 4.56 ± 2.81 mm. A similar approach presented in [6] allows for multiple instruments and more flexible modeling of the correspondences between the instruments and the vessel, such as slipping along the wire and uncertainty in the estimation of control points.

Commercial solutions offer for example the integration of pre-computed stiff wire simulations [2]. Other vendors support a manual correction where the user can adapt the shape manually using a set of "grab handles" to fit the overlay to a contrast injection using multiple rotation and translation steps [1], which allows for a very flexible adaptation but may also be time consuming intraoperatively. Similarly, Guyot et al. [12] proposed to integrate manual annotations as uncertainty ellipses in a non-rigid registration, but require multiple landmarks and two (contrasted) X-ray images.

Penney et al. [19] proposed a target accuracy of 3 mm based on half the diameter of the branching artery. All mentioned fully automatic approaches have reported errors above this threshold for a subset of patients and failure cases can be expected in practice. This can be either due to model simplification or, especially for preoperative approaches, because of differences between modeled devices and intraoperative decisions. User input can help to improve the accuracy, however, should require minimal interaction to avoid distractions in the clinical workflow.

As such we propose a "one-click" solution (for each landmark) to minimize user input while maintaining clinically acceptable accuracies. Based on a small contrast injection, inserted devices or calcifications, the user may identify a landmark, e.g., a vessel bifurcation, in a single intraoperative 2D X-ray image. Based on this information and the course of the wires [8,13,16], we deform the vascular anatomy using an extended as-rigid-as-possible formulation [6] that yields an accurate deformation in 3D and that is therefore still useful when the C-arm angulation is changed. At the same time, it allows for a computation time compatible with intraoperative use.

2 Methods

We assume a preoperative CT with a segmented vessel lumen and centerlines, a rigid registration of this data to the C-arm system, and known projection geometry for the acquired images. For the proposed correction, we additionally require the 3D centerline of one or more devices present in the current image. In the fluoroscopic image, they may be segmented using for example methods proposed in [3,8,16,28]. Then, the 3D course can be obtained by triangulation from two uncontrasted views [4,5,13], or reconstructed from a single view [7,20, 26]. Lasty, we require at least one "click" which identifies a 2D position in the current fluoroscopic image that corresponds to a 3D landmark in the preoperative vessel anatomy. In the following, we will first describe the model to integrate the guidewire information [6], and then continue with the integration of user input as a projective constraint in Sect. 2.2.

2.1 As-rigid-as-possible Deformation

To be able to deform the vasculature, we require a segmentation of the aorta and the left and right (common and external) iliac arteries. The vessel surface is represented by a triangle mesh $\mathcal{M}$ defined by a set of vertices $\mathcal{V} = \{\mathbf{v}_1, \mathbf{v}_2, \ldots, \mathbf{v}_{n_\mathcal{V}}\}, \mathbf{v}_i \in \mathbb{R}^3$, and a set of edges $\mathcal{E} = \{\mathbf{e}_1, \ldots, \mathbf{e}_{n_\mathcal{E}}\}, \mathbf{e}_i \in \mathcal{V} \times \mathcal{V}$.

The centerlines $\mathcal{C}^{\text{aorta}}, \mathcal{C}^{\text{liliac}}, \mathcal{C}^{\text{riliac}}$ of the vessels are represented as a sequence of equidistantly sampled points, i.e., $\mathcal{C}^a = (\mathbf{c}_1^a, \mathbf{c}_2^a, \ldots, \mathbf{c}_{n_a}^a)$, $\mathbf{c}_i^a \in \mathbb{R}^3$ for $a \in \{\text{aorta}, \text{riliac}, \text{liliac}\}$. $\mathcal{C}$ represents the union of all centerlines with $|\mathcal{C}| = |\mathcal{C}^{\text{aorta}}| + |\mathcal{C}^{\text{liliac}}| + |\mathcal{C}^{\text{riliac}}|$. Additionally, each centerline point $\mathbf{c}_i$ is connected to a set of mesh vertices, $\mathbf{skel}_i = (\mathbf{v}_{i1}, \ldots, \mathbf{v}_{i6})$, creating a skeleton fan. We define the combination of surface mesh, centerlines and skeleton as "skeleton mesh" $\mathcal{S}$.

Based on this, we can formulate an ARAP energy [22,27] for a given deformed skeleton mesh $\hat{\mathcal{S}}$ as follows:

$$
\begin{aligned}
E_{\text{arap}}(\mathcal{S}, \hat{\mathcal{S}}) = &\sum_{i \in |\mathcal{V}|} \sum_{\mathbf{v}_j \in \mathcal{N}_i} w_{ij} \|\mathbf{R}_{\mathbf{v}_i}(\mathbf{v}_i - \mathbf{v}_j) - (\hat{\mathbf{v}}_i - \hat{\mathbf{v}}_j)\|_2^2 \\
&+ \sum_{i \in |\mathcal{C}|} \sum_{\mathbf{v}_j \in \mathbf{skel}_i} w_{c_ij} \|\mathbf{R}_{\mathbf{c}_i}(\mathbf{c}_i - \mathbf{v}_j) - (\hat{\mathbf{c}}_i - \hat{\mathbf{v}}_j)\|_2^2 ,
\end{aligned}
\tag{1}
$$

where $\mathcal{N}_i$ represents the one-ring neighborhood of vertex $\mathbf{v}_i$, and the weights w_{ij} and $w_{c_{ij}}$ represent edge weights that account for a non-uniform tesselation. The rotation matrices $\mathbf{R}_{\mathbf{v}_i}$, $\mathbf{R}_{\mathbf{c}_i}$ are estimated such that the cost function is minimal for a given $\hat{\mathcal{S}}$, see [22].

We then aim to find deformed vertex and centerline positions $(\mathcal{S}^*)$ that adhere to a set of constraints for vertices and centerline points:

$$\mathcal{S}^* = \operatorname*{argmin}_{\hat{\mathcal{S}}} E_{\mathrm{arap}}(\mathcal{S}, \hat{\mathcal{S}}) \tag{2}$$

$$\text{subject to } \hat{\mathbf{v}}_h = \mathbf{v}_h^*, \quad \forall \mathbf{v}_h \in \mathcal{V}_h \tag{3}$$

where $\mathcal{V}_h \subset \mathcal{V} \cup \mathcal{C}$ is the set of handle points for which the deformation is known.

In the proposed application, the goal is to compensate for the deformation caused by stiff wires or the delivery system. Without additional information, only the position of the device relative to the preoperative vessel anatomy is known, and assigning a fixed mapping between a subset of undeformed vertices and targets as in [25] may be error-prone. In [6], constraints are formulated in a more flexible manner that allows the vessel to slip along the local direction of the instrument as described in the following. This idea is used as the basic deformation model and is extended by the projective constraints in Sect. 2.2.

Similar to [25], for each device, i.e., $\mathcal{G}^{\mathrm{r}}$ inserted via the right femoral artery and $\mathcal{G}^{\mathrm{l}}$ inserted via the left femoral artery, correspondences to the respective centerlines are established. For each centerline point proximal to the location of femoral access and distal to the proximal end of the respective device, a mapping $f(\mathbf{c}_i) = \mathbf{g}_i$ is obtained by equidistant sampling. Based on this mapping, translations $\mathbf{t}_i$ for each $\mathbf{c}_i$ are obtained as follows: If the line segment between $\mathbf{c}_i$ and $\mathbf{g}_i$ intersects with the surface at position $\mathbf{o}_i$, then

$$\mathbf{t}_i = \mathbf{g}_i - \mathbf{o}_i + g_{\mathrm{width}} \frac{\mathbf{g}_i - \mathbf{o}_i}{\|\mathbf{g}_i - \mathbf{o}_i\|} \,, \tag{4}$$

where g_{width} is the radius of the device. If no intersection occurs, the translation vector is interpolated in a linear fashion. Post-processing assures that the interpolation does not overcompensate for the deformation.

"Slipping" of the vessel along the device is permitted by penalizing the distance of the deformed point to the tangent g_i of the device at that position,

$$E_{\mathrm{dev}}(\hat{\mathbf{c}}_i, \mathbf{g}_i) = d(\hat{\mathbf{c}}_i, g_i)^2 \tag{5}$$

$$= \|\left(\mathbb{1} - \mathbf{n}_i \mathbf{n}_i^T\right)(\mathbf{t}_i - \hat{\mathbf{c}}_i)\|_2^2 \,, \tag{6}$$

where $\mathbb{1}$ is the identity matrix and $\mathbf{n}_i$ is the direction of the tangent.

Note that this assumes instruments that can be locally approximated by a line; this is generally the case for stiff wires and delivery devices, which are responsible for the bulk of deformation seen during EVAR.

Additionally, all points below the femoral access location in the groin and 25 cm proximal to the aortic bifurcation are integrated as immovable handle points in Eq. (3) [6], similar to the zero-displacement constraints in [10, 18].

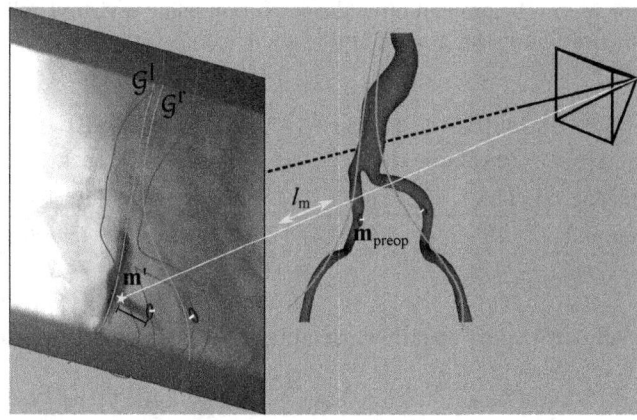

Fig. 1. Visualization of interaction and projective constraint: In the projection image, a 2D position $\mathbf{m}'$ is annotated that corresponds to a landmark $\mathbf{m}_{\mathrm{preop}}$ in the 3D volume.

2.2 Projective Constraints

For a given camera geometry, the transformation from 3D to 2D can be described by a projection matrix $\mathbf{P} \in \mathbb{R}^{3\times 4}$ with extrinsic camera parameters $\mathbf{R}, \mathbf{t}$ and intrinsic parameters $\mathbf{K}$:

$$\mathbf{x}'_{(h)} = \mathbf{P}\mathbf{x}_{(h)} = \mathbf{K}\begin{pmatrix}\mathbf{R} & \mathbf{t} \\ 0 & 1\end{pmatrix}\mathbf{x}_{(h)} \ , \tag{7}$$

where $\mathbf{x} \in \mathbb{R}^3$ is an arbitrary point in 3D, $\mathbf{x}' \in \mathbb{R}^2$ represents the projected point, and $\mathbf{x}_{(h)}, \mathbf{x}'_{(h)}$ represent the points in homogeneous coordinates.

From the 2D annotation ("click"), we obtain 2D coordinates $\mathbf{m}'$ in an image with projection geometry $\mathbf{P}$. These coordinates correspond to a landmark $\mathbf{m}_{\mathrm{preop}}$ in 3D located on or near a vertex $\mathbf{v}_m$ of the surface mesh. The goal is to recover the correct intraoperative position of this landmark $\mathbf{m}_{\mathrm{intraop}}$. Then, the position of the landmark in 2D can be backprojected to a line $l_m(\alpha) = \mathbf{c} + \alpha\mathbf{d}$ in 3D defined by the camera origin $\mathbf{c} = -\mathbf{R}^T\mathbf{t}$ and direction $\mathbf{d} = \tilde{\mathbf{d}}/\|\tilde{\mathbf{d}}\|$, where $\tilde{\mathbf{d}}_{(h)} = \mathbf{P}^+\mathbf{m}'_{(h)} - \mathbf{c}_{(h)}$. Here, $\mathbf{P}^+$ is the pseudo-inverse of $\mathbf{P}$. This idea is visualized in Fig. 1.

Based on this, we can integrate a landmark-matching cost into the energy function that penalizes the distance of the associated vertex $\mathbf{v}_m$ to the line:

$$E_{\mathrm{lm}}(\hat{\mathcal{S}}, \mathcal{L}) = \sum_{m\in|\mathcal{L}|} d(\hat{\mathbf{v}}_m, l_m)^2 \tag{8}$$

for all landmarks $\mathcal{L}$ that have information available both in 2D and 3D.

Table 1. Error in mm before and after the correction using a virtual "click" based on the forward projection of the ground truth landmark position from 30° LAO for RB and 30° RAO for LB.

	TRE_{3D} (median)	TRE_{3D} (mean ± std)	TRE_{orth} (mean ± std)	$\text{TRE}_{\text{depth}}$ (mean ± std)
Undeformed	11.6	11.6 ± 5.7	7.8 ± 4.4	7.9 ± 5.2
Proposed	1.3	1.9 ± 1.5	0.5 ± 0.4	1.7 ± 1.6

Bringing all constraints together, we aim to find the deformed skeleton mesh

$$\mathcal{S}^* = \underset{\hat{\mathcal{S}}}{\arg\min}\, E_{\text{arap}}(\mathcal{S}, \hat{\mathcal{S}}) + \lambda_{\text{dev}} \sum_{i \in |\mathcal{C}|} E_{\text{dev}}(\hat{\mathbf{c}}_i, \mathbf{g}_i) + \lambda_{\text{lm}} E_{\text{lm}}(\hat{\mathcal{S}}) \tag{9}$$

$$\text{subject to } \hat{\mathbf{v}}_h = \mathbf{v}_h, \quad \forall\, \mathbf{v}_h \in \mathcal{V}_h \ .$$

The cost function can be efficiently optimized in an iterative fashion by alternating between computing the rotation matrices $\mathbf{R}_{\mathbf{v}_i}$ and $\mathbf{R}_{\mathbf{v}_j}$ for the current estimate of $\hat{\mathcal{S}}$, and finding the least-squares solution for $\hat{\mathcal{S}}$ for given rotation matrices [6, 22].

3   Experiments and Results

3.1   Data

We validate the proposed approach on a data set of 13 patients (26 iliacs) treated with elective EVAR. A preoperative CTA was acquired and segmented semi-automatically using in-house prototype software to obtain the vessel surface mesh and 3D centerlines of the aorta, the common and external iliac arteries, and the femoral arteries. During the intervention, after deployment of the main stent graft trunk and before deployment of the iliac stent segments, a contrast-enhanced cone-beam computed tomography (CBCT) was acquired (Artis zeego, Siemens Healthcare GmbH, Forchheim, Germany). A trained radiologist identified the position of the left and right internal iliac bifurcation (LB, RB), and the aortic bifurcation (AB) in the preoperative segmentation and the CBCT, with the latter providing 3D ground truth (GT) landmark positions for the intraoperative deformation. Both volumes were registered using a semi-automatic, rigid 3D-3D registration with a focus on the lower lumbar vertebrae. In the intraoperative CBCT, the 3D course of the inserted wire was segmented and then extrapolated to the access point in the femoral artery using cubic splines. The 3D distances (target registration error - TRE_{3D}) between the predicted and the GT positions of the landmarks RB and LB, which are relevant for stent placement in the iliac arteries, are used as the main evaluation metric in this work. We further report the error orthogonal to the backprojection ray l_m (TRE_{orth}), which is comparable to the "in-plane" error reported in [19], and the error parallel to l_m ($\text{TRE}_{\text{depth}}$), which corresponds to the error in depth.

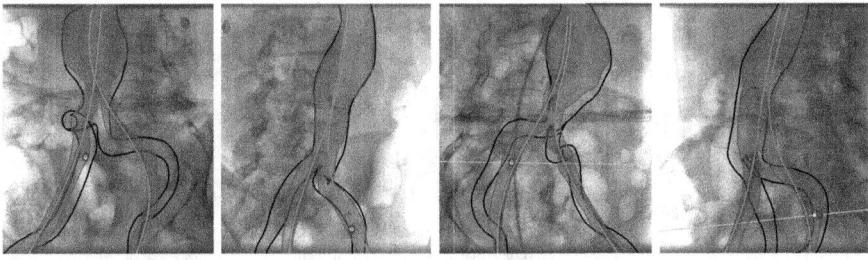

(a) Result in working projection.   (b) Result in orthogonal projection.

Fig. 2. Examples of corrected fusion images: The yellow point marks the ground truth position, the predicted position is represented in blue. The outline of the deformed vessel lumen is represented in red, with the undeformed surface mesh in black. In (b), the line constraint $l_m(\alpha)$ is visualized in yellow. Images courtesy of Sahlgrenska University Hospital, Gothenburg, Sweden. (Color figure online)

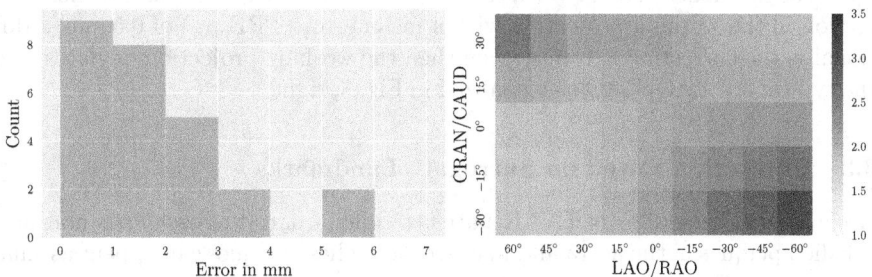

Fig. 3. Left: Histogram of 3D errors after correction for a working angulation of 30° LAO for RB and 30° RAO for LB. **Right:** Heat map of mean 3D error for RB and LB for annotations from different C-arm angulations. LAO/RAO angulation for LB is mirrored to yield comparable angular information.

3.2 Correction Based on Ostium Position

For the first set of experiments, we assume a C-arm angulation of 30° right anterior oblique (RAO) and 30° left anterior oblique (LAO). We obtain a virtual "click" in the image by forward projecting the 3D ground truth location of either LB (for 30° RAO) or RB (for 30° LAO) based on the respective projection geometry. In this experiment and all following experiments, we used $\lambda_{\mathrm{lm}} = 2.0$ for the projective constraint, and $\lambda_{\mathrm{dev}} = 0.8$ for the device. For all cases, the deformation improves the error considerably compared to the undeformed fusion with a 3D mean error of 1.9 mm (Table 1). Examples for deformation corrected fusion images are shown in Fig. 2. In all but four cases, the 3D error is below 3 mm (see Fig. 3, left). The two patients with the highest error additionally suffer from an iliac artery aneurysm for which the deformation is more challenging to model. Note that the error visible to the clinician is this severe only if the C-arm is rotated by 90°. In a typical clinical application, the change in C-arm angulation

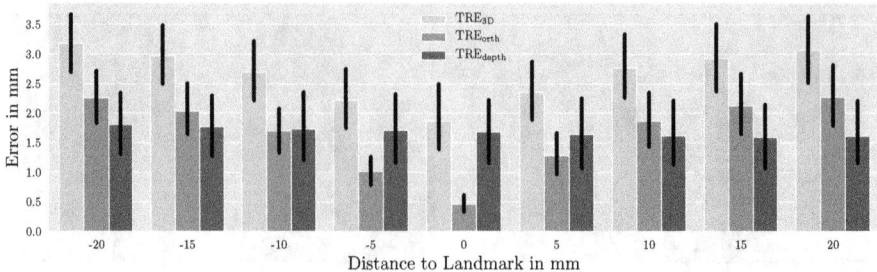

Fig. 4. Mean error and standard deviation when simulating a calcification landmark at different distances (negative: proximal, positive: distal) to the respective ostium for a working angulation of 30° LAO for RB and 30° RAO for LB.

while deploying a stent in one iliac will be considerably lower; accordingly, the utility of the fusion is retained. With the proposed approach, we see an excellent correction in the working projection with a mean error (TRE_{orth}) of 0.5 mm. Additionally, the correction is robust even then the working projection deviates from the typical 30° LAO/RAO as visualized in Fig. 3, right.

3.3 Correction Based on Surrogate Landmarks

A considerable number of EVAR patients suffer from atherosclerosis and have calcified plaques in the aorta and iliac arteries. These plaques can appear as small dark spots on X-ray images and, if located close to an anatomical landmark, may be used as a surrogate for the deformation.

To evaluate the potential of these surrogate landmarks, we insert a virtual calcification in the mesh at a predefined distance between 5 mm − 20 mm to the actual bifurcation and deform the model based on all available 3D ground truth landmarks. The projected position of this virtual calcification in the projection and the corresponding position in the undeformed model is then again used as described previously for a second deformation. The results for the error at the vessel bifurcation are presented in Fig. 4, evaluated on the same data set used in the previous experiments. As expected, the error increases with the distance of the surrogate landmark to the target bifurcation, mainly due to an increase in TRE_{orth}, however, it remains below 3.5 mm even for a distance of 20 mm.

4   Discussion and Conclusion

Any application used in an intra-operative environment should be easy-to-use with a high degree of automation and require minimal user interaction. We presented a method that allows for a simple and fast, yet accurate deformation correction of preoperative data to match the intraoperative vessel deformation seen during EVAR. With a single "click" in a 2D image, we are able to correct the fusion in 3D, retaining a corrected fusion when the C-arm angulation is changed.

For vessel ostia, the association between the click and the corresponding preoperative landmark may be easily obtained by selecting the landmark closest to the ray. A correction based on calcifications may be slightly more time consuming, as it additionally requires to identify the landmark in the preoperative CTA. This may, however, be simplified by (automatically) extracting potential candidates in the preoperative image, and then allowing for a selection via a drop-down list.

The average runtime for the correction was 5.6 s on a commodity computer, which allows for intraoperative use of this technique. Additional optimization and improvements like multi-resolution approaches potentially allow for a real-time correction that updates the overlay for each X-ray frame.

It should be noted that the proposed approach is limited by the care of the clinician when placing the preoperative landmarks as well as when marking the landmark in the 2D projection. Additionally, we assume an accurate rigid registration between the preoperative and the intraoperative images. The latter, however, is true for any fusion approach and since a bone registration is sufficient, no additional contrast agent is required. While a 3D-3D registration was employed in this work, a 2D-2D-3D registration and/or a 2D-3D re-registration can be used alternatively. In future work, automatic detection of relevant landmarks in contrasted and uncontrasted images may help to automatize the correction further.

Acknowledgment. We thank Dr. Giasemi Koutouzi and Dr. Mårten Falkenberg from Sahlgrenska University Hospital, Gothenburg, Sweden, for providing the data, annotations and registrations of intraoperative and preoperative scans.
Disclaimer. The methods and information presented in this work are based on research and are not commercially available.

References

1. Cydar, E.V.: Dynamic Morphology Correction. https://www.cydarmedical.com/product. Accessed 2 March 2020
2. Endonaut®, https://www.therenva.com/endonaut. Accessed 2 March 2020
3. Ambrosini, P., Ruijters, D., Niessen, W.J., Moelker, A., van Walsum, T.: Fully automatic and real-time catheter segmentation in X-Ray fluoroscopy. In: Descoteaux, M. (ed.) MICCAI 2017. LNCS, vol. 10434, pp. 577–585. Springer, Cham (2017). https://doi.org/10.1007/978-3-319-66185-8_65
4. Baert, S.A.M., van de Kraats, E.B., van Walsum, T., Viergever, M.A., Niessen, W.J.: Three-dimensional guide-wire reconstruction from biplane image sequences for integrated display in 3-D vasculature. IEEE Trans. Med. Imaging **22**(10), 1252–1258 (2003)
5. Bender, H.J., Männer, R., Poliwoda, C., Roth, S., Walz, M.: Reconstruction of 3D catheter paths from 2D X-ray projections. In: Taylor, C., Colchester, A. (eds.) Medical Image Computing and Computer-Assisted Intervention - MICCAI'99, pp. 981–989. Springer, Berlin Heidelberg, Berlin, Heidelberg (1999)
6. Breininger, K.: Machine Learning and Deformation Modeling for Workflow Compliant Image Fusion during Endovascular Aortic Repair. Ph.D. thesis (2020, in preparation)

7. Breininger, K., et al.: Simultaneous reconstruction of multiple stiff wires from a single x-ray projection for endovascular aortic repair. Int. J. Comput. Assist. Radiol. Surg. **14**(11), 1891–1899 (2019)

8. Breininger, K., et al.: Multiple device segmentation for fluoroscopic imaging using multi-task learning. In: Stoyanov, D., et al. (eds.) LABELS/CVII/STENT -2018. LNCS, vol. 11043, pp. 19–27. Springer, Cham (2018). https://doi.org/10.1007/978-3-030-01364-6_3

9. Dua, A., Kuy, S., Lee, C.J., Upchurch, G.R., Desai, S.S.: Epidemiology of aortic aneurysm repair in the United States from 2000 to 2010. J. Vasc. Surg. **59**(6), 1512–1517 (2014)

10. Gindre, J., et al.: Patient-specific finite-element simulation of the insertion of guidewire during an EVAR procedure: guidewire position prediction validation on 28 cases. IEEE Trans. Biomed. Eng. **64**(5), 1057–1066 (2017)

11. Goudeketting, S.R., et al.: Pros and cons of 3D image fusion in endovascular aortic repair: a systematic review and meta-analysis. J. Endovasc. Ther. **24**(4), 595–603 (2017)

12. Guyot, A., Varnavas, A., Carrell, T., Penney, G.: Non-rigid 2d–3d registration using anisotropic error ellipsoids to account for projection uncertainties during aortic surgery. In: Mori, K., Sakuma, I., Sato, Y., Barillot, C., Navab, N. (eds.) Medical Image Computing and Computer-Assisted Intervention - MICCAI 2013, pp. 179–186. Springer, Berlin Heidelberg, Berlin, Heidelberg (2013)

13. Hoffmann, M., et al.: Semi-automatic catheter reconstruction from two views. In: Proceedings of the 15th International Conference on Medical Image Computing and Computer-Assisted Intervention - Part II. pp. 584–591 (2012)

14. Koutouzi, G., Pfister, M., Breininger, K., Hellström, M., Roos, H., Falkenberg, M.: Iliac artery deformation during EVAR. Vascular **5**(27), 511–517 (2019)

15. Lalys, F., et al.: Identification of parameters influencing the vascular structure displacement in fusion imaging during endovascular aneurysm repair. J. Vasc. Interv. Radiol. **30**(9), 1386–1392 (2019)

16. Lessard, S., et al.: Automatic detection of selective arterial devices for advanced visualization during abdominal aortic aneurysm endovascular repair. Med. Eng. Phys. **37**(10), 979–986 (2015)

17. Maurel, B., et al.: Evaluation of visceral artery displacement by endograft delivery system insertion. J. Endovasc. Ther. **21**(2), 339–347 (2014)

18. Mohammadi, H., Lessard, S., Therasse, E., Mongrain, R., Soulez, G.: A numerical preoperative planning model to predict arterial deformations in endovascular aortic aneurysm repair. Ann. Biomed. Eng. **46**(12), 2148–2161 (2018)

19. Penney, G., Varnavas, A., Dastur, N., Carrell, T.: An image-guided surgery system to aid endovascular treatment of complex aortic aneurysms: description and initial clinical experience. In: Taylor, R.H., Yang, G.Z. (eds.) Information Processing in Computer-Assisted Interventions, pp. 13–24. Springer, Berlin, Heidelberg (2011)

20. Petković, T., Homan, R., Lončarić, S.: Real-time 3D position reconstruction of guidewire for monoplane X-ray. Comput. Med. Imaging Graph. **38**(3), 211–223 (2014)

21. Schulz, C.J., Schmitt, M., Böckler, D., Geisbüsch, P.: Fusion imaging to support endovascular aneurysm repair using 3D–3D registration. J. Endovasc. Ther. **23**(5), 791–799 (2016)

22. Sorkine, O., Alexa, M.: As-rigid-as-possible surface modeling. In: Proceedings of the Fifth Eurographics Symposium on Geometry Processing. pp. 109–116. SGP 2007, Eurographics Association, Aire-la-Ville, Switzerland (2007)

23. Tacher, V., et al.: Feasibility of three-dimensional MR angiography image fusion guidance for endovascular abdominal aortic aneurysm repair. J. Vasc. Interv. Radiol. **27**(2), 188–193 (2016)

24. Tacher, V., et al.: Image guidance for endovascular repair of complex aortic aneurysms: comparison of two-dimensional and three-dimensional angiography and image fusion. J. Vasc. Interv. Radiol. **24**(11), 1698–1706 (2013)

25. Toth, D., Pfister, M., Maier, A., Kowarschik, M., Hornegger, J.: Adaption of 3D models to 2D X-Ray images during endovascular abdominal aneurysm repair. In: Navab, N., Hornegger, J., Wells, W.M., Frangi, A.F. (eds.) MICCAI 2015. LNCS, vol. 9349, pp. 339–346. Springer, Cham (2015). https://doi.org/10.1007/978-3-319-24553-9_42

26. Trivisonne, R., Kerrien, E., Cotin, S.: Constrained stochastic state estimation of deformable 1D objects: application to single-view 3D reconstruction of catheters with radio-opaque markers. Comput. Med. Imaging Graph. **81**, 101702 (2020)

27. Zhang, S., Nealen, A., Metaxas, D.: Skeleton based as-rigid-as-possible volume modeling. In: Lensch, H.P.A., Seipel, S. (eds.) Eurographics 2010 - Short Papers. The Eurographics Association (2010)

28. Zhou, Y.-J., et al.: Real-time guidewire segmentation and tracking in endovascular aneurysm repair. In: Gedeon, T., Wong, K.W., Lee, M. (eds.) ICONIP 2019. LNCS, vol. 11953, pp. 491–500. Springer, Cham (2019). https://doi.org/10.1007/978-3-030-36708-4_40

Non-Rigid Volume to Surface Registration Using a Data-Driven Biomechanical Model

Micha Pfeiffer[1]([✉]), Carina Riediger[2], Stefan Leger[1], Jens-Peter Kühn[3],
Danilo Seppelt[3], Ralf-Thorsten Hoffmann[3], Jürgen Weitz[2,4],
and Stefanie Speidel[1,4]

[1] Translational Surgical Oncology, National Center for Tumor Diseases,
Dresden, Germany
micha.pfeiffer@nct-dresden.de
[2] Department for Visceral, Thoracic and Vascular Surgery,
University Hospital Carl-Gustav-Carus, Dresden, TU, Germany
[3] Institute and Policlinic for Diagnostic and Interventional Radiology,
University Hospital Carl-Gustav-Carus, Dresden, TU, Germany
[4] Centre for Tactile Internet with Human-in-the-Loop (CeTI),
Dresden, TU, Germany

Abstract. Non-rigid registration is a key component in soft-tissue navigation. We focus on laparoscopic liver surgery, where we register the organ model obtained from a preoperative CT scan to the intraoperative partial organ surface, reconstructed from the laparoscopic video. This is a challenging task due to sparse and noisy intraoperative data, real-time requirements and many unknowns - such as tissue properties and boundary conditions. Furthermore, establishing correspondences between pre- and intraoperative data can be extremely difficult since the liver usually lacks distinct surface features and the used imaging modalities suffer from very different types of noise. In this work, we train a convolutional neural network to perform both the search for surface correspondences as well as the non-rigid registration in one step. The network is trained on physically accurate biomechanical simulations of randomly generated, deforming organ-like structures. This enables the network to immediately generalize to a new patient organ without the need to re-train. We add various amounts of noise to the intraoperative surfaces during training, making the network robust to noisy intraoperative data. During inference, the network outputs the displacement field which matches the preoperative volume to the partial intraoperative surface. In multiple experiments, we show that the network translates well to real data while maintaining a high inference speed. Our code is made available online.

Keywords: Liver registration · Soft-tissue · Surgical navigation · CNN

Electronic supplementary material The online version of this chapter (https://doi.org/10.1007/978-3-030-59719-1_70) contains supplementary material, which is available to authorized users.

© Springer Nature Switzerland AG 2020
A. L. Martel et al. (Eds.): MICCAI 2020, LNCS 12264, pp. 724–734, 2020.
https://doi.org/10.1007/978-3-030-59719-1_70

1   Introduction

In navigated surgical interventions, the aim is to aid surgeons in finding structures of interest - such as tumors, vessels or planned resection lines. Often, a detailed, accurate and highly informative preoperative computer tomography (CT) scan is available and the challenge is to align this model with the intraoperative scene. Whenever deforming soft-tissue is involved, this requires a non-rigid registration. However, usually, only limited, sparse and noisy data can be acquired during the intervention. Furthermore, it is usually very difficult to find one-to-one correspondences between the pre- and intraoperative data, since they are subject to different types of noise and can look substantially different. Together with the large deformation (multiple centimeters), only partially visible surface (often less than 30%) and many unknown parameters (such as the organ's elastic properties, acting forces and boundary conditions) this makes the soft-tissue registration a challenging problem.

This work explores a deep-learning based approach to performing a non-rigid organ registration. We focus on laparoscopic liver surgery and register a given preoperative liver volume mesh to an intraoperative, partial surface of the same organ (obtained from a laparoscopic stereo video stream). We use a fully convolutional neural network (CNN), which analyses the two meshes and outputs a displacement field to register the preoperative organ volume to the intraoperative surface (see Fig. 1). To reach this aim, the network must learn to find a plausible solution for the surface correspondence problem, while at the same time learning about biomechanical deformation in order to constrain itself to physically realistic solutions. For training, a deformed intraoperative state of each preoperative mesh is simulated, using the Finite Element Method (FEM). We use synthetically generated, random organ-like meshes, which allows the trained network to generalize to new patients without the need to re-train

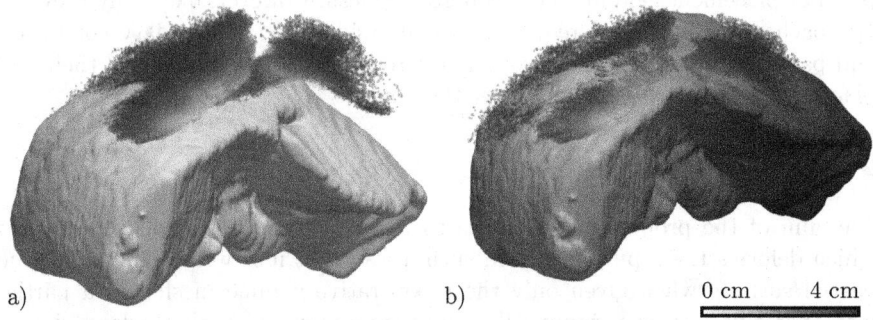

a)   b)   0 cm   4 cm

Fig. 1. Non-rigid registration using our CNN. Given the intraoperative point cloud of a partial liver surface and the preoperative liver mesh (a), our network estimates a displacement field, which deforms the preoperative volume to match the intraoperative surface (b). Displacement magnitude is encoded in shades of blue. (Color figure online)

for every liver. We call the approach *Volume-To-Surface Registration Network* (V2S-Net) and publish the code as well as the pretrained network online[1].

Related Work. State-of-the-art approaches in laparoscopic liver registration often rely on the FEM to model organ deformation [6,7,13,17,20]. These methods differ substantially in the intraoperative data which they use, either requiring dense surface data [17,20], sparse (annotated) surface data [6] or shading and contour cues [7,13]. While these methods can achieve high accuracies, they are usually computationally expensive and tend to either require manual assignment or careful engineering of boundary conditions.

Recently, the application of deep learning to simulate organ deformation has received a lot of attention, mainly due to the very low inference times [10,11,14, 16]. It has been shown that these data-driven models can achieve accuracies close to that of the FEM [10,14], can deal with partial surface information [2,16] and can even learn to deform real organs after training on synthetic data only [16]. However, all of the mentioned methods require the use of boundary conditions similar to the FEM. These are very difficult to obtain in a real surgical setting, since, for example, forces are extremely difficult to measure and estimating the surface displacement would require known surface correspondences.

On the other hand, the machine learning community has developed a large number of data-driven feature descriptors to efficiently describe and register 3D structures [5,18,21]. While this shows the ability of neural networks to interpret 3D data, in the case of organs, the lack of distinct features and large organ deformations require the incorporation of soft-tissue mechanics in order to find correct correspondences.

In design, our method is similar to the work of Suwelack et al. [20], who propose to morph the preoperative volume mesh into the intraoperative partial surface by simulating electric charge on the surfaces and solving the problem using the FEM. Similar to our work, they use the two meshes as input and output a displacement field for the preoperative mesh. However, like many previous approaches, their method requires manual assignment of boundary conditions and parameters, can become unstable if wrong values are chosen and their displacement estimation is much slower than ours.

2   Methods

The aim of the proposed V2S-Net is to learn to recover a displacement field which deforms the input volume in such a way that it is well aligned with the partial surface, when given only the preoperative volume mesh and a partial intraoperative surface as input. We train the network on synthetic data, since a real data set consisting of volume meshes as well as known displacement fields is not available. In addition to simulating deformations, we also generate the preoperative 3D meshes randomly, to ensure that the network will translate directly to new, unseen liver meshes.

---

[1] https://gitlab.com/nct_tso_public/Volume2SurfaceCNN.

2.1   Data Generation

Simulation. A random 3D surface mesh is generated by first creating an ico-sphere and then applying a set of extrusion, boolean, remeshing and smoothing operators. We use *Gmsh* [4] to fill the surface mesh with tetrahedral elements. The resulting volume mesh is considered to be our preoperative volume organ mesh V_P (Fig. 2, a). Next, up to three random forces (max. magnitude 1.5 N, over an area with random radius between 1 and 15 cm) and a zero-displacement boundary condition are assigned to random areas of the surface of the mesh. The steady-state deformation is calculated by the *Elmer* [9] finite element solver, using a neo-Hookean hyperelastic material model with a random Young's Modulus (2 kPa to 5 kPa) and Poisson's ratio of 0.35. The resulting deformed volume acts as the intraoperative state of the organ V_I (Fig. 2 b). For every vertex in V_P, we now know the displacement vector that needs to be applied in order to reach the intraoperative state V_I, resulting in the displacement field u.

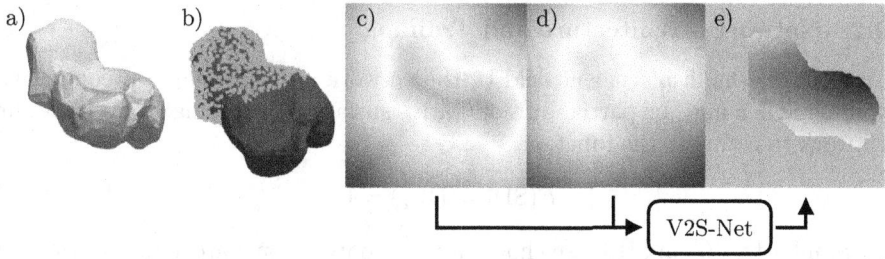

Fig. 2. a) Random preoperative volume mesh V_P, b) simulated intraoperative state V_I (green) and partial surface S_I (orange), c) signed distance field of preoperative volume SDF_P, d) distance field of partial surface DF_I, e) known displacement U (magnitude), which the V2S-Net learns to predict from the two distance fields. Afterwards, this displacement field can be used to infer the position of internal structures, such as vessels and tumors.

We extract a random surface patch of this deformed volume mesh. To simulate intraoperative noise and difference in imaging modalities, we resample this patch, delete random vertices and add uniform random displacements to the position of every vertex. The maximum of this noise is chosen randomly (in the range from 0 to 1 cm) for every mesh. Furthermore, random parts of the patch are deleted to simulate areas where surrounding tissues (like the falciform ligament) occlude the surface from the perspective of the laparoscope. The result is our intraoperative partial surface mesh S_I.

The use of random values sometimes leads to the generation of meshes for which the creation of tetrahedral elements fails or simulations for which the finite element solver does not find a solution. These samples are discarded. We also discard samples where the maximum displacement is larger than 20 cm or the amount of visible surface is less than 10%, since we assume these cases to be unrealistic.

Voxelization. To pass the meshes to the network, we represent them in the form of distance fields on a regular grid. For this, we define a grid of 64^3 points. At each point, we calculate the distance to the nearest surface point of the preoperative volume V_P as well as the intraoperative surface S_I. For the preoperative mesh, we flip the sign of all grid points that lie within the organ volume, resulting in a signed distance field SDF_P for the preoperative and a distance field DF_I for the intraoperative mesh (see Fig. 2 c and d).

Additionally, we interpolate the target displacement field u into the same grid with a gaussian kernel, resulting in an interpolated vector field U. For points outside the preoperative volume, U is set to $(0, 0, 0)^T$. In this way, we discretize a space of $(30\,\text{cm})^3$, which results in a voxel side length of roughly $4.7\,\text{mm}$.

We use the outlined process to generate 80 000 samples, which are split into training data (90%) and validation data (10%). By flipping each training sample along each combination of X-, Y- and Z-axes, we further increase the amount of training data by a factor of eight, resulting in roughly 460 000 samples.

2.2   Network Architecture and Training

To estimate the displacement field U, the network is given the full preoperative volume SDF_P and the partial intraoperative surface DF_I. Formally, we want our network to estimate the function:

$$F(\text{SDF}_P, \text{DF}_I) = \text{U}. \tag{1}$$

Similar to [10] and [16], we choose a fully convolutional architecture with 3D convolutions, an encoder-decoder structure and skip connections to allow for an abstract low-resolution representation while preserving high-resolution details. The precise architecture is shown in the supplementary material. Following [16], we let the network output the displacement field $\text{U}_{r,est}$ at multiple resolutions $r \in (64, 32, 16, 8)$. These are compared to the (downsampled) target displacement fields U_r using the mean absolute error L_r. We find that this process speeds up loss convergence during training. The final loss L is a weighted sum of these errors:

$$L_r = \frac{1}{r^3} \sum_{i=1}^{r^3} |\text{U}_r(i) - \text{U}_{r,est}(i)| \tag{2}$$

$$L = 10\,L_{64} + L_{32} + L_{16} + L_8.$$

We train the network with a *one cycle learning rate scheduler* [19] and the *AdamW* optimizer [8] for 100 epochs, after which the mean registration error on the validation data has converged to roughly $6\,\text{mm}$.

3   Experiments and Results

Since our network is trained on randomly generated meshes, it is vital to test on real patient data. However, reference data for real laparoscopic interventions is very difficult to obtain, since interventional CT scans during laparoscopy are very limited. To nevertheless capture all necessary aspects of the registration process, we conduct three experiments: one experiment with simulated liver deformations, one with real human liver deformations under breathing motion and one qualitative experiment on data from a laparoscopic setting. In all experiments, the used preoperative liver meshes were extracted from patient CT scans automatically using a segmentation CNN [1]. The process of estimating the displacement field (including upload to the NVidia GTX 1080 GPU) takes roughly 130 ms.

3.1 Liver Deformations (In Silico)

We generate a synthetic dataset as described in Sect. 2.1. However, instead of generating random meshes we use the mesh of a patient's liver and simulate 1725 deformations and partial intraoperative surfaces. This new dataset is not used for training and thus allows us to test how our method translates to a real liver mesh: We apply the network to all samples and calculate the displacement error for every point in the estimated displacement fields $U_{64,est}$ (results in Fig. 3). When the visible surfaces are large enough, registration errors tend to be small, even when the target deformations become large. Smaller visible areas lead to more interesting results, for example when the network cannot infer which part of the volume should be matched to the partial surface (see Fig. 4).

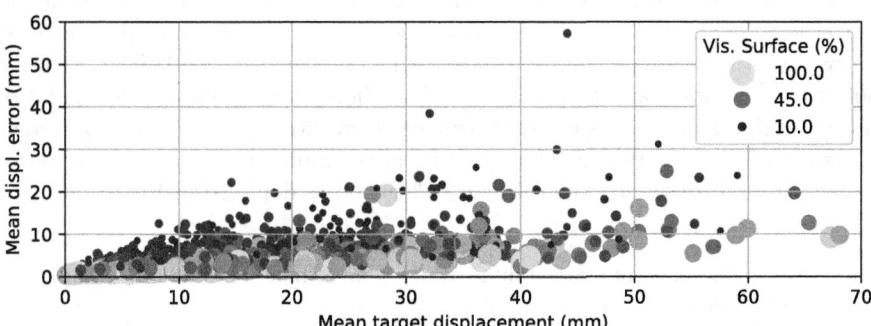

Fig. 3. Displacement error of each test sample, plotted over the target displacement. Both displacement error and target displacement are computed as the average over all grid points which lie inside the preoperative volume in the given test sample. Thus, the displacement error can be interpreted as a (mean) target registration error. As expected, this error tends to increase with larger target displacement and decrease with larger visible surfaces. With few exceptions, samples with a displacement error larger than 1 cm are those with very little visible surface.

3.2 Liver with Breathing Deformation (In Vivo)

During breathing motion, the human liver moves and deforms considerably. To assess whether our network translates to real human liver deformation, we evaluate on human breathing data. We extract liver meshes from two CT scans

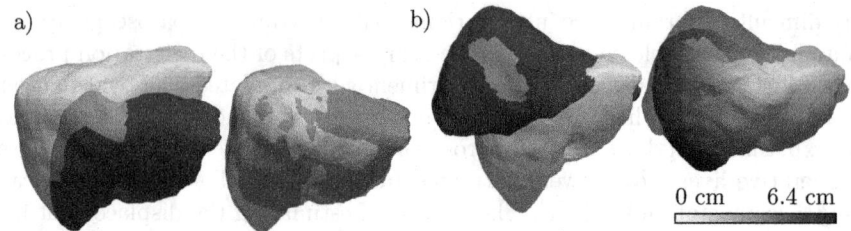

Fig. 4. From a real preoperative liver mesh (grey), a deformed intraoperative liver state (purple) is simulated. Given the preoperative mesh and a partial intraoperative surface (yellow), the V2S-Net estimates the deformed state (images 2 and 4). The magnitude of the error (red) indicates a successful registration for case a) (max. error 1.5 cm) and an unsuccessful registration for case b) (max. error 6.4 cm). When the randomly picked visible surface contains no distinct features (as is the case in b), or captures no areas of significant deformation, the network may estimate an incorrect but plausible deformation, resulting in the outliers in Fig. 3. This suggests that it is more important which areas of the liver are visible than the size of the visible surface.(Color figure online)

(one showing an inhaled and one an exhaled state) and let these represent the preoperative volume V_P and intraoperative surface S_I. We search for clearly visible vessel bifurcations and mark their positions in both scans. Given the distance fields of the two meshes, the network then estimates the displacement of every voxel in the inhaled state. The resulting displacement field $U_{64,est}$ is interpolated to the positions of the marked bifurcation points (gaussian interpolation kernel, radius 1 cm) and is used to displace them. We carry out this experiment for two patients. Average displacements and remaining errors after registration are shown in Table 1 and the result for Patient 1 is depicted in Fig. 5.

Table 1. Displacement of marked bifurcations (due to inhaling) and remaining errors after registration.

	Displacement (mm)		Error (mm)	
	Avg ± Std	Max	Avg ± Std	Max
Patient 1	21.4 ± 9.4	31.1	5.7 ± 2.8	9.8
Patient 2	28.3 ± 4.1	32.7	4.8 ± 0.7	5.4

3.3   Laparoscopic Liver Registration (In Vivo)

To validate whether our method works for our target task of navigated laparoscopy, we perform a qualitative evaluation on human in-vivo data acquired from a da Vinci (Intuitive Surgical) stereo laparoscope. We first reconstruct the intraoperative surface S_I from the video stream. For this, a 10 s camera-sweep

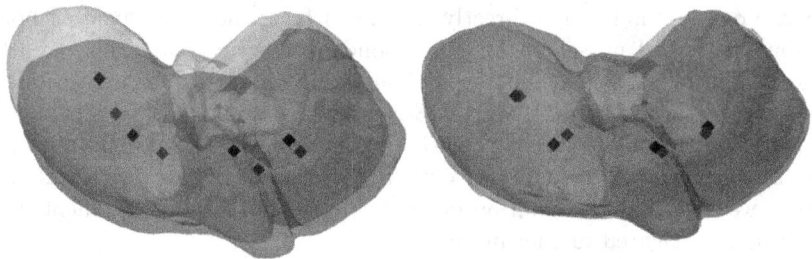

Fig. 5. Registration for Patient 1. The liver is deformed by breathing motion (inhaled and exhaled states, left). Four vessel bifurcations are marked in the first CT scan (black) and in the second CT scan (red). The network uses the surfaces to calculate a displacement field which registers the two liver states to each other (right). Applying this displacement field to the markers indicates a good approximation of the internal deformation. Results for Patient 2 can be found in the supplementary material. (Color figure online)

of the liver is performed at the beginning of the surgery. Since we lack positional information of the laparoscope, the OrbSLAM2 [12] algorithm is used to estimate the camera pose for each frame. Furthermore, the disparity between each pair of stereo frames is estimated (using a disparity CNN [22]) and a semantic segmentation is performed on each left camera frame to identify pixels which show the liver (using a segmentation CNN [15]). We reproject the pixel information into the scene using the disparity, camera calibration parameters and estimated camera pose, obtaining a 3D point cloud with color and segmentation information. While the camera moves, points which are close together and are similar in hue are merged together. After the sweep, we discard points if they have not been merged multiple times (i.e. points which were not seen from multiple view points) or if they were not segmented as *liver* in at least 70% of the frames in which they were seen. Additionally, we use a moving least squares filter (radius 0.5 cm) to smoothen the surface. After a manual rigid alignment which moves and rotates V_P so that it is roughly aligned with S_I, the distance fields for the pre- and intraoperative data are calculated and our network is used to estimate a displacement of the liver volume. Qualitative results are shown in Fig. 1 and in the supplementary material.

4   Conclusion

In this work, we have shown that a CNN can learn to register a full liver surface to a deformed partial surface of the same liver. The network was never trained on a real organ or real deformation during the training process, and yet it learned to solve the surface correspondence problem as well as the underlying biomechanical constraints.

Since our method works directly on the surfaces, no assignment of boundary conditions and no search for correspondences is necessary. The breathing motion experiment shows that, even though the segmentation process creates some artifacts in the surfaces, the V2S-Net finds a valid solution. The network was able to find the displacement without the need for a prior rigid alignment, likely because the full intraoperative surface was used. In cases with less visible surface, we find that the solution depends on the prior rigid alignment, which should be investigated further in future work.

Despite the relatively coarse computational grid, the method achieves registration accuracies which could be precise enough for surgical navigation. It is possible that these accuracies could be improved further with a finer discretization, but RAM and long training times are currently limiting factors. In the future, different data representations could be explored to overcome these limitations.

In our method, we outsource the complex and time consuming simulation of soft-tissue behavior to the data generation stage. This could be further exploited by adding additional information to the simulations, such as inhomogeneous material properties, surrounding and connecting tissues and more complex boundary conditions. Where these properties are measurable for a patient, they could be passed to the network as additional input channels. Furthermore, the training data could be extended with samples which include complex changes in mesh structure, such as surgical cuts. Since our method can directly adapt to new mesh topologies without needing to retrain, this could lead to a network which can deal with the dynamic mesh changes during surgery.

Our results show that there may be cases where the solution is ambiguous, for example when too little information is given and the network must guess how the hidden side of the liver is deformed. This issue is likely inherent to the ill-posed laparoscopic registration problem itself and not confined to our method. Since neural networks can estimate how confident they are of a solution [3], this probabilistic output could be used to assess how a solution should be interpreted and could give additional information to the surgeon.

References

1. Bilic, P., Christ, P.F., Vorontsov, E., Chlebus, G., Chen, H., Dou, Q., et al.: The liver tumor segmentation benchmark (LiTS). ArXiv abs/1901.04056 (2019)
2. Brunet, J.-N., Mendizabal, A., Petit, A., Golse, N., Vibert, E., Cotin, S.: Physics-based deep neural network for augmented reality during liver surgery. In: Shen, D., et al. (eds.) MICCAI 2019. LNCS, vol. 11768, pp. 137–145. Springer, Cham (2019). https://doi.org/10.1007/978-3-030-32254-0_16
3. Gal, Y., Ghahramani, Z.: Dropout as a bayesian approximation: representing model uncertainty in deep learning. In: Proceedings of the 33rd International Conference on International Conference on Machine Learning. vol. 48 (2016)
4. Geuzaine, C., Remacle, J.F.: Gmsh: A 3-d finite element mesh generator with built-in pre- and post-processing facilities. Int. J. Numer. Meth. Eng. **79**(11), 1309–1331 (2009)

5. Griffiths, D., Boehm, J.: A review on deep learning techniques for 3d sensed data classification. Remote Sensing **11**(12), 1499 (2019)
6. Heiselman, J., Clements, L., Collins, J., Weis, J., Simpson, A., Geevarghese, S.: Characterization and correction of intraoperative soft tissue deformation in image-guided laparoscopic liver surgery. J. Med. Imaging **5**(2), 021203 (2017)
7. Koo, B., Özgür, E., Le Roy, B., Buc, E., Bartoli, A.: Deformable registration of a preoperative 3d liver volume to a laparoscopy image using contour and shading cues. In: Descoteaux, M., Maier-Hein, L., Franz, A., Jannin, P., Collins, D.L., Duchesne, S. (eds.) MICCAI 2017. LNCS, vol. 10433, pp. 326–334. Springer, Cham (2017). https://doi.org/10.1007/978-3-319-66182-7_38
8. Loshchilov, I., Hutter, F.: Decoupled weight decay regularization. In: International Conference on Learning Representations (ICLR) (2017)
9. Malinen, M., Råback, P.: Elmer Finite Element Solver for Multiphysics and Multiscale Problems. Multiscale Modelling Methods for Applications in Materials Science, Forschungszentrum Jülich (2013)
10. Mendizabal, A., Márquez-Neila, P., Cotin, S.: Simulation of hyperelastic materials in real-time using deep learning. Med. Image Anal. **59**, 101569 (2019)
11. Mendizabal, A., Tagliabue, E., Brunet, J.N., Dallálba, D., Fiorini, P., Cotin, S.: Physics-based deep neural network for real-time lesion tracking in ultrasound-guided breast biopsy. In: Computational Biomechanics for Medicine XIV. Shenzhen, China (2019)
12. Mur-Artal, R., Tardós, J.D.: ORB-SLAM2: an open-source SLAM system for monocular, stereo and RGB-D cameras. IEEE Trans. Robot. **33**(5), 1255–1262 (2017)
13. Özgür, E., Koo, B., Le Roy, B., Buc, E., Bartoli, A.: Preoperative liver registration for augmented monocular laparoscopy using backward-forward biomechanical simulation. Int. J. Comput. Assist. Radiol. Surg. **13**, 1629–1640 (2018)
14. Pellicer-Valero, O.J., Rupérez, M.J., Martínez-Sanchis, S., Martín-Guerrero, J.D.: Real-time biomechanical modeling of the liver using machine learning models trained on finite element method simulations. Expert Syst. Appl. **143**, 113083 (2020)
15. Pfeiffer, M., et al.: Generating large labeled data sets for laparoscopic image processing tasks using unpaired image-to-image translation. In: Shen, D., et al. (eds.) MICCAI 2019. LNCS, vol. 11768, pp. 119–127. Springer, Cham (2019). https://doi.org/10.1007/978-3-030-32254-0_14
16. Pfeiffer, M., Riediger, C., Weitz, J., Speidel, S.: Learning soft tissue behavior of organs for surgical navigation with convolutional neural networks. Int. J. Comput. Assist. Radiol. Surg. **14**(7), 1147–1155 (2019). https://doi.org/10.1007/s11548-019-01965-7
17. Plantefeve, R., Peterlik, I., Haouchine, N., Cotin, S.: Patient-specific biomechanical modeling for guidance during minimally-invasive hepatic surgery. Ann. Biomed. Eng. **143**, 113083 (2015)
18. Qi, C.R., Su, H., Mo, K., Guibas, L.J.: Pointnet: deep learning on point sets for 3d classification and segmentation. In: 2017 IEEE Conference on Computer Vision and Pattern Recognition (CVPR) (2017)
19. Smith, L.N., Topin, N.: Super-convergence: very fast training of residual networks using large learning rates. CoRR abs/1708.07120 (2017)
20. Suwelack, S., et al.: Physics-based shape matching for intraoperative image guidance. Med. phys. **41**, (2014)

21. Wang, H., Guo, J., Yan, D.-M., Quan, W., Zhang, X.: Learning 3D Keypoint descriptors for non-rigid shape matching. In: Ferrari, V., Hebert, M., Sminchisescu, C., Weiss, Y. (eds.) ECCV 2018. LNCS, vol. 11212, pp. 3–20. Springer, Cham (2018). https://doi.org/10.1007/978-3-030-01237-3_1
22. Yang, G., Manela, J., Happold, M., Ramanan, D.: Hierarchical deep stereo matching on high-resolution images. In: The IEEE Conference on Computer Vision and Pattern Recognition (CVPR) (2019)

Deformation Aware Augmented Reality for Craniotomy Using 3D/2D Non-rigid Registration of Cortical Vessels

Nazim Haouchine[1]([✉]), Parikshit Juvekar[1], William M. Wells III[1,2], Stephane Cotin[3], Alexandra Golby[1], and Sarah Frisken[1]

[1] Harvard Medical School, Brigham and Women's Hospital, Boston, MA, USA
nhaouchine@bwh.harvard.edu
[2] Massachusetts Institute of Technology, Cambdridge, MA, USA
[3] Inria, Strasbourg, France

Abstract. Intra-operative brain shift is a well-known phenomenon that describes non-rigid deformation of brain tissues due to gravity and loss of cerebrospinal fluid among other phenomena. This has a negative influence on surgical outcome that is often based on pre-operative planning where the brain shift is not considered. We present a novel brain-shift aware Augmented Reality method to align pre-operative 3D data onto the deformed brain surface viewed through a surgical microscope. We formulate our non-rigid registration as a Shape-from-Template problem. A pre-operative 3D wire-like deformable model is registered onto a single 2D image of the cortical vessels, which is automatically segmented. This 3D/2D registration drives the underlying brain structures, such as tumors, and compensates for the brain shift in sub-cortical regions. We evaluated our approach on simulated and real data composed of 6 patients. It achieved good quantitative and qualitative results making it suitable for neurosurgical guidance.

Keywords: 3D/2D non-rigid registration · Physics-based modelling · Augmented Reality · Image-guided neurosurgery · Shape-from-Template

1 Introduction

Brain shift is a well-known intra-operative phenomenon that occurs during neurosurgical procedures. This phenomenon consists of deformation of the brain that changes the location of structures of interest from their locations in preoperative imaging [2,17]. Neurosurgical procedures are often based on pre-operative planning. Therefore, estimating intra-operative brain shift is important since it may considerably impact the surgical outcome. Many approaches have been investigated to compensate for brain shift, either using additional intra-operative imaging data [11,14,20,21] or advanced brain models to predict intra-operative outcome pre-operatively [3,7,8] The latter approach has the advantage of being hardware-independent and does not involve additional imaging in the operating room. However, even sophisticated brain models have difficulty modeling events

© Springer Nature Switzerland AG 2020
A. L. Martel et al. (Eds.): MICCAI 2020, LNCS 12264, pp. 735–744, 2020.
https://doi.org/10.1007/978-3-030-59719-1_71

that occur during the procedure. Additional data acquisition is then necessary to obtain a precise brain shift estimation. Various types of imaging techniques have been proposed to acquire intra-operative information such as ultra-sound [11,20,21], Cone-Beam Computed Tomography [19] or intra-operative MRI [14].

During a craniotomy, the cortical brain surface is revealed and can be used as an additional source of information. Filipe et al. [16] used 3 Near-Infrared cameras to capture brain surface displacement which is then registered to MRI scans using the coherent point drift method by considering vessel centerlines as strong matching features. A new deformed MRI volume is generated using a thin plate spline model. The approach presented by Luo et al. [15] uses an optically tracked stylus to identify cortical surface vessel features; a model-based workflow is then used to estimate brain shift correction from these features after a dural opening. Jiang et al. [12] use phase-shifted 3D measurement to capture 3D brain surface deformations. This method highlights the importance of using cortical vessels and sulci to obtain robust results. The presence of a stereo-miscroscope in the operating room makes it very convenient to deploy such methods clinically. Sun et al. [23] proposed to pre-compute brain deformations to build an atlas from a sparse set if image-points extracted from the cortical brain surface. These image-points are extracted using an optically tracked portable laser range scanner. Haouchine et al. [9] proposed to use a finite element model of the brain shift to propagate cortical deformation captured from the stereoscope to sub-structures. In a similar way Mohammadi et al. [18] proposed a projection-based stereovision process to map brain surface with a pre-operative finite element model. A pre-defined pattern is used to recover the 3D brain surface. In order to build a dense brain surface and gather more precise positions, Ji et al. [10] proposed a stereo-based optical flow shape reconstruction. The 3D shapes are recovered at different surgical stages to obtain undeformed and deformed surfaces. These surfaces can be registered to determine the deformation of the exposed brain surface during surgery.

Contribution: We propose a novel method to register pre-operative scans onto intra-operative images of the brain surface during the craniotomy. As shown in the pipeline of Fig. 1, our method uses images from a surgical microscope (or possibly a ceiling mounted camera), rather than intra-operative ultrasound or MRI which requires significant cost and time. Unlike previous methods, we rely solely on a single image to avoid tedious calibration of the stereo camera, laser range finder or optical stylus. Our method considers cortical vessels centerlines as strong features to drive the non-rigid registration. The intra-operative center-lines are automatically extracted from the image using convolutional deep neural networks, while the pre-operative centerlines are modelled as a network of linked beams capable of handling non-linear deformations. Our approach is formulated as a force-based shape-from-template problem to register the undeformed pre-operative 3D centerlines onto the deformed intra-operative 2D centerlines. This problem is solved by satisfying a combination of physical and projective constraints. We present our results through the microscope occulars using Augmented Reality view by overlaying the tumor model in the miscropcic view after accounting for the estimated brain shift deformation.

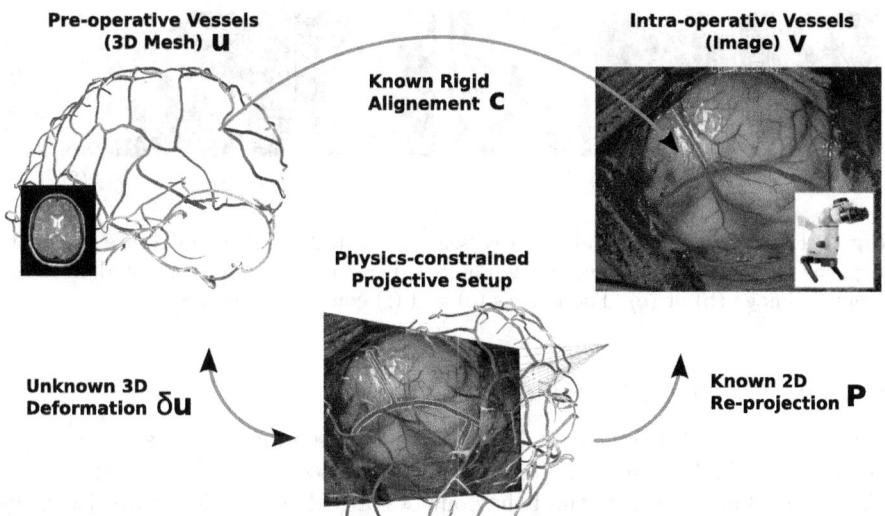

Fig. 1. Problem formulation: we aim at recovering the deformed 3D vessels shape δu from its known reprojection in the image $\mathbf{v}$, the known pre-operative 3D vessels at rest $\mathbf{u}$ and known rigid alignment $\mathbf{c}$, satisfying physical and reprojective constraints $\mathbf{P}$.

2   Method

2.1   Extracting 2D Cortical Brain Vessels

To extract the vessels from microscopic images we rely on a deep convolutional network following a typical U-Net architecture [22]. The input is a single RGB image of size $256 \times 256 \times 3$ and the final layer is a pixel-wise Softmax classifier that predicts a class label $\{0,1\}$ for each pixel. The output image is represented as a binary image of size 256×256 as illustrated in Fig. 2. the segmentation can suffer from class imbalance because microsopic images of the cortical surface are composed of veins, arteries and parenchyma of different sizes. We thus rely on a weighted cross-entropy loss L to account for imbalanced depths [6], formulated as follows:

$$L = -\frac{1}{n}\sum_i w_{c_i}\cdot c_i^*\cdot log(c_i) \quad with \quad c_i = \frac{e^{z_i}}{\sum_c e^{z_i,c_i}} \quad and \quad w_{c_i} = \frac{med(f_{c_i}|c_i \in C)}{f_{c_i}} \quad (1)$$

where n is the number of pixels, C is the set of classes, c_i^* is the ground truth label of pixel i, c_i is the probability of classifying pixel i with class c_i. (z_i, c_i) is the output of the response map and w_{c_i} is the class-balanced weight for class c_i, with f_{c_i} being the frequencies of class c_i and $med(\cdot)$ the median. Once segmented, the vessel centerlines are extracted from the binary image by skeletonization. We denote $\mathbf{v}$, the vector of 2D points corresponding to the intra-operative centerlines.

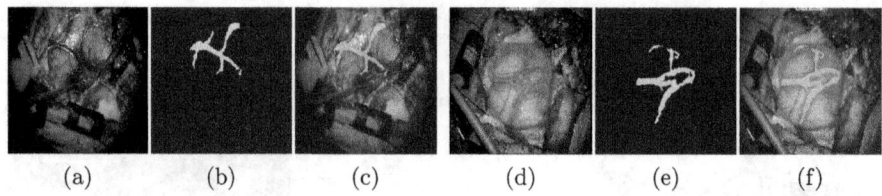

(a)   (b)   (c)   (d)   (e)   (f)

Fig. 2. Extracting 2D cortical brain vessels: A classical U-Net architecture is used to segment the microscopic images. The input images (a) or (d) are segmented to obtain a binary image (b) or (e). The images (c) and (f) consist of overlays.

2.2   3D Vascular Network Modelling

Let us denote $\mathbf{u}$ the vector of 3D vertices representing the vessel centerlines derived from MRI scans. This set of vertices is used to build a non-rigid wire-like model that represents the behaviour of cortical vessels. More precisely, the vessels are modeled with serially linked beam elements that can handle geometric non-linearities while maintaining real-time computation. This model has previously been used to simulate guide wires and catheters [4]. Each beam element is delimited by two nodes each having 3 spatial and angular degrees of freedom. These node positions relate to the forces applied to them thanks to a stiffness matrix $\mathbf{K}_e$ and account for rotational degrees of freedom through a rotational matrix $\mathbf{R}_e$. At each node i, the internal forces $\mathbf{f_i}$ generated by the deformation of the structures is formulated as:

$$\mathbf{f_i} = \sum_{e=i-1}^{i} \mathbf{R}_e(\mathbf{u})\mathbf{K}_e(\mathbf{R}_e(\mathbf{u})^T(\mathbf{u} - \mathbf{u}_e) - \mathbf{u}^{rest}) \qquad (2)$$

where e is the index of the two beams connected to this i^{th} node. $\mathbf{u}_{i-1}$, $\mathbf{u}_i$ and $\mathbf{u}_{i+1}$ are the degrees of freedom vectors of the three nodes (respectively $i-1$, i, $i+1$) and belong to the two beams in the global frame. $\mathbf{u}_{ej}$ denotes the middle frame of the jth beam that is computed as an intermediate between the two nodes of the beam, where $\mathbf{u}^{rest}$ corresponds to the degrees of freedom at rest in the local frame. The global force $\mathbf{f}$ emanating from the 3D vessels can be computed as $\mathbf{f} = \sum_j^{n_u} \mathbf{f}_j$, with n_u being the number of nodes of the vascular tree.

2.3   Force-Based Shape-from-Template

A shape-from-template problem is defined as finding a 3D deformed shape from a single projected view knowing the 3D shape in rest configuration [1]. In our case, the 3D shape at rest consists of the pre-operative 3D centerlines $\mathbf{u}$. The single projected view consists of the 2D intra-operative centerlines $\mathbf{v}$. The unknown 3D deformed shape $\delta\mathbf{u}$ is the displacement field induced by a potential brain shift. As in most registration methods, an initial set of n_c correspondences $\mathbf{c}$ between the image points and the model points has to be established. We thus initialise our non-rigid registration with a rough manual rigid alignment. Once aligned, a vector **c** is built so that if a 2D point $\mathbf{v}_i$ corresponds to a 3D point $\mathbf{u}_j$ then $c_i = j$ for each point of the two sets. Assuming that the camera projection matrix **P** is known and remains constant, registering the 3D vessels to their corresponding 2D projections amounts to minimize the re-projection error $\|\mathbf{Pu}_{c_i} - \mathbf{v}_i\|$ for $i \in n_c$. However, minimizing this error does not necessarily produces a correct 3D representation since many 3D shapes may have identical 2D projections. To overcome this issue, we add to the re-projection constraints the vessels' physical priors following the beams model introduced in Eq. 2. This will force the shape of the vascular tree to remain consistent in 3D while minimizing the reprojection error in 2D. This leads to the following force minimization expression:

$$\underset{\delta \mathbf{u}}{\operatorname{argmin}} \sum_i^{n_c} \left(\mathbf{f}_{c_i} - \kappa \|\mathbf{Pu}_{c_i} - \mathbf{v}_i\| \right)^2 \tag{3}$$

where κ is the stiffness coefficient that permits the image re-projection error to be translated to an image bending force. Note the subscript c_i that denotes the correspondence indices between the two point sets. This minimization can be seen as enforcing 3D vessel centerlines to fit sightlines from the camera position to 2D vessels centerlines while maintaining a coherent 3D shape.

2.4 Mapping Tumors with Cortical Vessels Deformation

In order to propagate the surface deformation to tumors and other sub-cortical structures, we use a linear geometrical barycentric mapping function. We restrict the impact of the cortical vessel deformations to the immediate underlying structures (see Fig. 6).

Formally speaking, if we denote the vector of vertices representing a 3D tumor by **t**, we can express each vertex $\mathbf{t}_i$ using barycentric coordinates of facet vertices **u**, such that $\mathbf{t}_i = \sum_{j=1}^{3} \phi_j(x_i, y_i, z_i)\mathbf{u}_j$, where $\phi(x, y, z) = a + bx + cy$ with (a, b, c) being the barycentric coordinates of the triangle composed of nodal points $\mathbf{u}_j$, with $1 \le j \le 3$. This mapping is computed at rest and remains valid during the deformation.

3   Results

We tested our method on simulated data of a 3D synthetic human brain. The 3D vessel centerlines were extracted from the vessels mesh surface using a mean curvature skeletonization technique. The number of centerline nodes to build the wire-like model is set in a range between 12 and 30 nodes (only a subset of the vascular network has been considered). The stiffness matrix of the vessels is built with a Young's modulus set to 0.6 MPa and Poisson's ratio to 0.45 to simulate a quasi-elastic and incomprehensible behaviour where vessels thickness is set to 0.5 mm [5]. We used the Sofa framework (www.sofa-framework.org) to build the 3D beam-elements model.

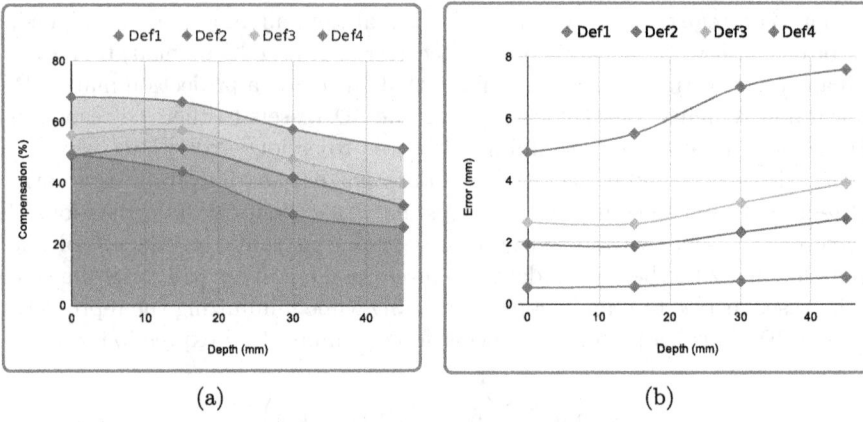

Fig. 3. Quantitative evaluation on simulated data: Charts (a) and (b) show the percentage of compensation and target registration error respectively w.r.t to depth and brain shift amplitude. The depth axis correspond to the position of the target in the brain where 0mm represent the cortical surface and 45mm the deep brain.

We quantitatively evaluated our method by measuring the target registration error (TRE) on different locations. We considered four in-depth locations from 0 mm to 45 mm, 0 mm being the cortical surface. We simulated a brain shift to mimic a protrusion deformation that can occur due to brain swelling after the craniotomy. The deformations were of increasing amplitudes: Def1 = 1.7 mm, Def2 = 4 mm, Def3 = 6 mm and Def4 = 10 mm. We extracted 2D centerlines of each deformation by projecting the deformed 3D centerlines w.r.t a known virtual camera. We added Gaussian noise with a standard deviation of 5 mm and a 5 clustering decimation on the set of 2D points composing the centerlines. The results reported in Fig. 3 suggest that using our method achieves small TRE ranging from 0.53 mm to 1.93 mm, on the cortical surface and the immediate sub-cortical structures ($\leq$ 15 mm). Since the TRE depends on the amount of brain shift, we also quantify the brain-shift compensation by measuring the difference between the initial and the corrected error (normalized by the initial error). Brain shift compensation of up to 68.2 % is achieved, and at least a 24.6 % compensation is reported for the worst configuration. We can also observe that errors and compensation at the cortical surface are very close to the immediate sub-cortical location ($\leq$ 15 mm). They increase when the targets are located deeper in the brain ($\geq$ 30 mm) or the amount of deformation increases ($\geq$ 6 mm).

Our craniotomy dataset was composed of 1630 microscopic images with labels obtained through manual segmentation. The model is trained on mini-batches of size 32 for 200 epochs using Adam optimizer [13] with a learning rate of 0.001 that is decreased by a factor of 10 each 100 epochs. We used the Tensorflow framework (www.tensorflow.org) on an NVidia GeForce GTX 1070.

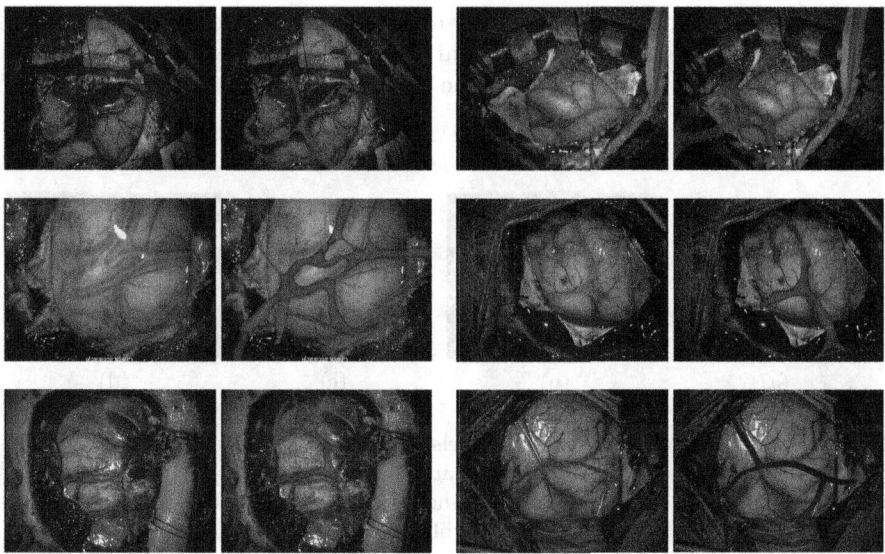

Fig. 4. Augmented Reality views after applying our method on 6 patient data sets retrospectively. The non-rigid registration provided a good estimation of deformation of the cortical surface, as viewed by overlays of the deformed 3D vessels on their 2D projections seen through the surgical microscope.

We tested our method on 6 patient data sets retrospectively. The cortical vessels, brain parenchyma, skull and tumors were segmented using 3D Slicer (www. sliced.org). The miscroscopic images were acquired with a Carl Zeiss surgical microscope. We only used the left image of the sterescopic camera.

The pre-operative vessels are first aligned manually on the image to obtain the rigid transform, then the 3D/2D non-rigid registration was performed, and used to drive deformation of the underlying tumors. Figure 4 shows the resulting Augmented Reality rendering and exhibits good mesh-to-image overlay. Figure 5 shows the measured deformation amplitude on each vessel after non-rigid registration. The deformations range from 0 to 3 mm and are non-uniformly distributed on the vascular trees which suggest a non-rigid deformation.

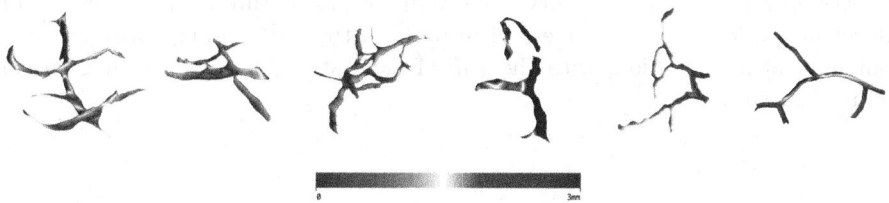

Fig. 5. Color-coded estimated deformation on the vessels.

Finally, we show in Fig. 6 the ability of our method to rectify tumor positions through their mapping with the cortical vessels. We can clearly see that tumor positions are corrected according to the brain shift estimated from the cortical vessels registration.

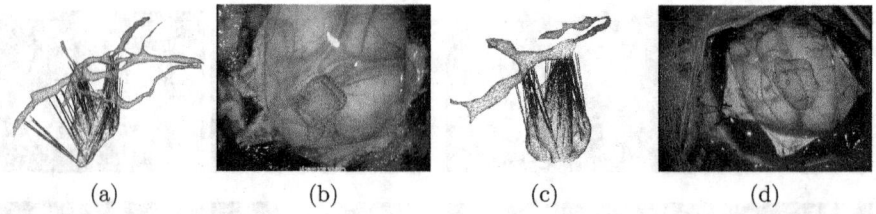

    (a)   (b)   (c)   (d)

Fig. 6. Mapping tumors with cortical vessels: In (a) and (c), a visualization of the mapping mechanism. Blue lines represent the attachments. In (b) and (d), an Augmented Reality visualization of the tumors with the estimate displacement induced from the mapping w.r.t to initial positions (dotted blue lines). (Color figure online)

4   Conclusion and Discussion

We proposed here a brain-shift aware Augmented Reality method for craniotomy guidance. Our method follows a 3D/2D non-rigid process between pre-operative and intra-operative cortical vessel centerlines using a single image instead of a stereo pair. Restricting our method to a single image makes it more acceptable in operating rooms but turns the registration process into an ill-posed problem. To tackle this issue we proposed a force-based shape-from-template formulation that adds physical constraints to the classical reprojection minimization. In addition, our pipeline takes advantage of recent advances in deep learning to automatically extract vessels from microscopic images. Our results show that low TRE can be obtained at cortical and sub-cortical levels and compensation for brain shift with up to 68% can be achieved. Our method is however sensitive to the outcome of the cortical vessels segmentation. A fragmented segmentation may lead to discontinuous centerlines and thus produce aberrant vascular trees that can affect the whole pipeline. One solution could be the use of the complete vessels segmentation in addition to centerlines to make advantage of the use of more featured such as radii, curves and bifurcations. Future work will consist of developing a learning-based method to perform the non-rigid registration without manual initialisation, with the aim of facilitating its usage by surgeons in clinical routines.

References

1. Bartoli, A., Gérard, Y., Chadebecq, F., Collins, T., Pizarro, D.: Shape-from-template. IEEE Trans. Pattern Anal. Mach. Intell. **37**(10), 2099–2118 (2015)
2. Bayer, S., Maier, A., Ostermeier, M., Fahrig, R.: Intraoperative imaging modalities and compensation for brain shift in tumor resection surgery. Int. J. Biomed. Imaging 2017, 1–18 (2017)
3. Bilger, A., Dequidt, J., Duriez, C., Cotin, S.: Biomechanical simulation of electrode migration for deep brain stimulation. In: Fichtinger, G., Martel, A., Peters, T. (eds.) MICCAI 2011. LNCS, vol. 6891, pp. 339–346. Springer, Heidelberg (2011). https://doi.org/10.1007/978-3-642-23623-5_43
4. Cotin, S., Duriez, C., Lenoir, J., Neumann, P., Dawson, S.: New approaches to catheter navigation for interventional radiology simulation. In: Duncan, J.S., Gerig, G. (eds.) MICCAI 2005. LNCS, vol. 3750, pp. 534–542. Springer, Heidelberg (2005). https://doi.org/10.1007/11566489_66
5. Ebrahimi, A.: Mechanical properties of normal and diseased cerebrovascular system. J. Vasc. Interv. Radiol. **2**(2), 155–162 (2009)
6. Eigen, D., Fergus, R.: Predicting depth, surface normals and semantic labels with a common multi-scale convolutional architecture. In: Proceedings of the 2015 IEEE International Conference on Computer Vision (ICCV). p. 2650–2658. ICCV 2015, IEEE Computer Society, USA (2015)
7. Essert, C., Haegelen, C., Lalys, F., Abadie, A., Jannin, P.: Automatic computation of electrode trajectories for deep brain stimulation: a hybrid symbolic and numerical approach. Int. J. Comput. Assist. Radiol. Surg. **7**, 517–532 (2011)
8. Hamzé, N., Bilger, A., Duriez, C., Cotin, S., Essert, C.: Anticipation of brain shift in deep brain stimulation automatic planning. In: 2015 37th Annual International Conference of the IEEE Engineering in Medicine and Biology Society (EMBC). pp. 3635–3638 (2015)
9. Haouchine, N., Juvekar, P., Golby, S., Wells, W., Cotin, S., Frisken, S.: Alignment of cortical vessels viewed through the surgical microscope with preoperative imaging to compensate for brain shift. SPIE Image-Guided Procedures, Robotic Inter. Model. **60**(10), 11315–11360 (2020)
10. Ji, S., Fan, X., Roberts, D.W., Hartov, A., Paulsen, K.D.: Cortical surface shift estimation using stereovision and optical flow motion tracking via projection image registration. Med. Image Anal. **18**(7), 1169–1183 (2014)
11. Ji, S., Wu, Z., Hartov, A., Roberts, D.W., Paulsen, K.D.: Mutual-information-based image to patient re-registration using intraoperative ultrasound in image-guided neurosurgery. Med. Phys. **35**(10), 4612–4624 (2008)
12. Jiang, J., et al.: Marker-less tracking of brain surface deformations by non-rigid registration integrating surface and vessel/sulci features. Int. J. Comput. Assist. Radiol. Surg. **11**(9), 1687–1701 (2016). https://doi.org/10.1007/s11548-016-1358-7
13. Kingma, D.P., Ba, J.: Adam: A method for stochastic optimization (2014), http://arxiv.org/abs/1412.6980, Published as a conference paper at the 3rd International Conference for Learning Representations, San Diego (2015)
14. Kuhnt, D., Bauer, M.H.A., Nimsky, C.: Brain shift compensation and neurosurgical image fusion using intraoperative mri: current status and future challenges. Crit. Rev. Biomed. Eng. **40**(3), 175–185 (2012)

15. Luo, M., Frisken, S.F., Narasimhan, S., Clements, L.W., Thompson, R.C., Golby, A.J., Miga, M.I.: A comprehensive model-assisted brain shift correction approach in image-guided neurosurgery: a case study in brain swelling and subsequent sag after craniotomy. In: Fei, B., Linte, C.A. (eds.) Medical Imaging 2019: Image-Guided Procedures, Robotic Interventions, and Modeling, vol. 10951, pp. 15–24. International Society for Optics and Photonics, SPIE (2019)

16. Marreiros, F.M.M., Rossitti, S., Wang, C., Smedby, Ö.: Non-rigid deformation pipeline for compensation of superficial brain shift. In: Mori, K., Sakuma, I., Sato, Y., Barillot, C., Navab, N. (eds.) MICCAI 2013. LNCS, vol. 8150, pp. 141–148. Springer, Heidelberg (2013). https://doi.org/10.1007/978-3-642-40763-5_18

17. Miga, M.I., et al.: Clinical evaluation of a model-updated image-guidance approach to brain shift compensation: experience in 16 cases. Int. J. Comput. Assist. Radiol. Surg. 11(8), 1467–1474 (2015). https://doi.org/10.1007/s11548-015-1295-x

18. Mohammadi, A., Ahmadian, A., Azar, A.D., Sheykh, A.D., Amiri, F., Alirezaie, J.: Estimation of intraoperative brain shift by combination of stereovision and doppler ultrasound: phantom and animal model study. Int. J. Comput. Assist. Radiol. Surg. 10(11), 1753–1764 (2015). https://doi.org/10.1007/s11548-015-1216-z

19. Pereira, V.M., et al.: Volumetric measurements of brain shift using intraoperative cone-beam computed tomography: preliminary study. Oper. Neurosurg. 12(1), 4–13 (2015)

20. Reinertsen, I., Lindseth, F., Askeland, C., Iversen, D.H., Unsgård, G.: Intraoperative correction of brain-shift. Acta Neurochir. (Wien) 156(7), 1301–1310 (2014). https://doi.org/10.1007/s00701-014-2052-6

21. Rivaz, H., Collins, D.L.: Deformable registration of preoperative mr, pre-resection ultrasound, and post-resection ultrasound images of neurosurgery. Int. J. Comput. Assist. Radiol. Surg. 10(7), 1017–1028 (2015)

22. Ronneberger, O., Fischer, P., Brox, T.: U-Net: convolutional networks for biomedical image segmentation. In: Navab, N., Hornegger, J., Wells, W.M., Frangi, A.F. (eds.) MICCAI 2015. LNCS, vol. 9351, pp. 234–241. Springer, Cham (2015). https://doi.org/10.1007/978-3-319-24574-4_28

23. Sun, K., Pheiffer, T., Simpson, A., Weis, J., Thompson, R., Miga, M.: Near real-time computer assisted surgery for brain shift correction using biomechanical models. IEEE J. Transl. Eng. Health Med. 2, 1–13 (2014)

Skip-StyleGAN: Skip-Connected Generative Adversarial Networks for Generating 3D Rendered Image of Hand Bone Complex

Jaesin Ahn[1], Hyun-Joo Lee[2], Inchul Choi[1], and Minho Lee[1(✉)]

[1] School of Electronics Engineering, Kyungpook National University,
Daegu, South Korea
amoeba04@gmail.com, sharpic77@gmail.com, mholee@gmail.com
[2] Department of Orthopedic Surgery, Kyungpook National University Hospital,
Daegu, South Korea
lidmania@daum.net

Abstract. Computed tomography (CT) is commonly used for fracture diagnosis because it provides accurate visualization of shape with 3-dimensional(3D) structure. However, CT has some disadvantages such as the high dose of radiation involved in scanning, and relatively high expense compared to X-ray. Also, it is difficult to scan CT in the operation room despite it is necessary to check 3D structure during operation. On the other hand, X-ray is often used in operating rooms because it is relatively simple to scan. However, since X-ray only provides overlapped 2D images, surgeons should rely on 2D images to imagine 3D structure of a target shape. If we can create a 3D structure from a single 2D X-ray image, then it will be clinically valuable. Therefore, we propose Skip-StyleGAN that can efficiently generate rotated images of a given 2D image from 3D rendered shape. Based on the StyleGAN, we arrange training sequence and add skip-connection from the discriminator to the generator. Important discriminative information is transferred through this skip-connection, and it allows the generator to easily produce an appropriately rotated image by making a little variation during the training process. With the effect of skip-connection, Skip-StyleGAN can efficiently generate high-quality 3D rendered images even with small-sized data. Our experiments show that the proposed model successfully generates 3D rendered images of the hand bone complex.

Keywords: Generative adversarial networks · CT · X-ray · 3D rendering · Hand bone complex · Skip-connection · Skip-StyleGAN.

Electronic supplementary material The online version of this chapter (https:// doi.org/10.1007/978-3-030-59719-1_72) contains supplementary material, which is available to authorized users.

© Springer Nature Switzerland AG 2020
A. L. Martel et al. (Eds.): MICCAI 2020, LNCS 12264, pp. 745–754, 2020.
https://doi.org/10.1007/978-3-030-59719-1_72

1   Introduction

In the clinical situation, visualizing 3-dimensional (3D) shape of human internal structures, such as organs or bones, is the essential part for the accurate diagnosis of disease. Currently, computed tomography (CT) is commonly adopted for the visualization of 3D internal structures of human because it can easily provide rendered 3D model from the stack of tomography scans. These 3D models are especially useful when doctors have to estimate complex fractures from several 2D tomography images of bone.

However, CT increases the risk of excessive radiation exposure during scanning process, therefore it is not recommended for frequent use. Furthermore, it requires relatively large expense for both scanning equipment and scanning itself. Therefore, surgeons usually rely on only 2D X-ray images to estimate 3D structure when they are on the operation. This could degrade the reliability of diagnosis and inevitably increase the patient's risk. If multiple views of 3D internal structures can be easily estimated from a few 2D X-ray images, it can greatly enhance the accuracy of diagnosis in the medical field, especially during the operation. For this reason, several researches attempted to reconstruct 3D model or interpolate the unseen view of 3D shape from a few 2D tomography images. In the medical imaging field, Femur [16] reconstructed a simple bone structure from 2D images based on traditional methods, such as intensity-based registration or similarity-based registration. However, such pre-processing methods bring high computational overhead and involve manual process for obstruction removal and boundary extraction. Therefore it is hard to be applied for other complex 3D bone structures. Recently, there is a research which adopts a deep learning based method for the same purpose. It uses Variational AutoEncoder [11] to generate a 3D structure from the 2D images of coronal, sagittal, axial [1]. However, it needs at least 3 images to reconstruct 3D shape of the target structure. In the non-medical field, there are similar researches with respect to the human face. They generate the multiple views of 3D face based on a given view of the face image. For multi-view image generation, those researches either focused on a 3D model reconstruction [2,17,18] or generative adversarial network(GAN) [4] based inference. The 3D reconstruction oriented models usually need additional information, such as landmarks or contour from 2D images [12]. GAN based models produce the low quality or distorted images as the view rotation angle increases. Moreover, their main purpose is the face recognition which does not require high quality images [7,14,15]. Therefore, those models are not appropriate for medical purpose.

In this paper, we propose a novel generative model, Skip-StyleGAN to address those problems. The main contributions of our model are following: (1) Adopting skip-connection to transfer discriminative information, training difficulty is reduced and high-quality multi-view images are generated. It also reduces the information that the model needs to generate, so that Skip-StyleGAN can be trained with small-sized data. (2) Unlike other generative models, we don't use a separate encoder network, instead we use a discriminator as an encoder network for a generator. (3) To improve the quality of image generated by a large view angle rotation, we utilize a neighboring image with smaller view angle rotation while training the model. With those modifications, our Skip-StyleGAN produces high quality multi-view images of a target 3D model rotated from the original view of a given image, even for 180 degree. To the best of our knowledge, our model is the first attempt in the medical field to generate multi-views of 3D CT rendering structure based on a single 2D X-ray image. In experiments, we show that proposed model generates high quality multi-view images even compared to the state-of-the art GAN based multi-view generation models. We illustrate the details of our model in the following section.

2 Proposed Method

Our model aims to generate high quality multi-view images of 3D structure based on a single 2D image of a target. For this purpose, we propose a novel GAN architecture for generating only neighboring view of current input image. Based on this model, we can sequentially generate multi-view images of a target structure. Following sections illustrate overall architecture and its main components with corresponding loss functions.

2.1 Skip-StyleGAN

Skip-StyleGAN is a neighboring view generation model based on the StyleGAN but utilizes skip-connections to transfer multi-scale feature information of discriminator to the generator for training efficiency.

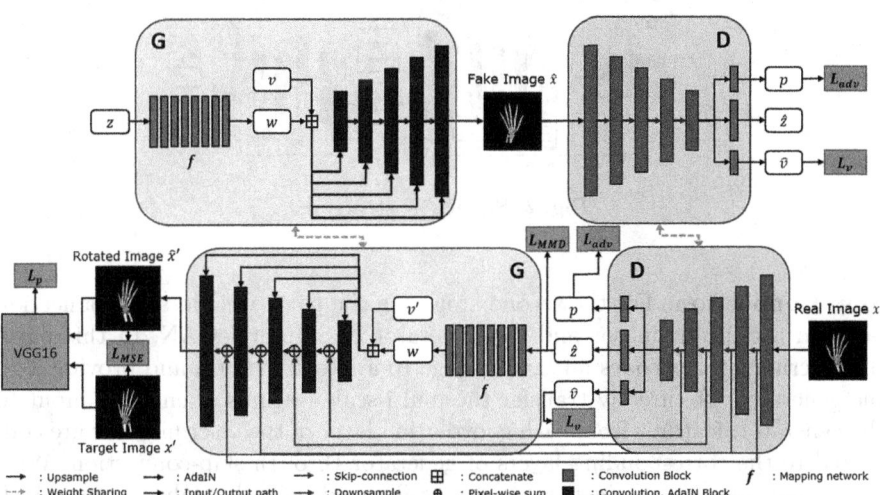

Fig. 1. The overall structure of Skip-StyleGAN with skip-connection. We adopt Style-GAN to our neighboring view generation model and add skip-connection between discriminator and generator.

Overview. As shown in Fig. 1, Skip-StyleGAN has cyclic paths, from the discriminator(D) to the generator(G), to generate a neighboring view. The whole cyclic path can be divided into two steps. In the first step, as shown in the first row of Fig. 1, the network is trained as conventional generative adversarial networks. In the second step, the second row of Fig. 1, the discriminator and the generator, with the trained weights in the first step, are connected with the encoded vector $\hat{z}$, similar to the auto-encoder, to generate rotated images. The entire architecture consists of only one generator and discriminator, and it is represented as weight sharing in Fig. 1. In this architecture, the discriminator produces three vectors, encoded input image $\hat{z}$, predicted view code $\hat{v}$, and the probability of real or fake p from the given input images. From these outputs, the generator produces an image for original view or a neighboring view according to the view code v.

StyleGAN. StyleGAN [10] is designed to generate high-resolution images with multi-scale training. Since the StyleGAN is sequentially trained for each resolution, it learns the feature representation for each scale. As shown in Fig. 2, the mapping network f converts input latent vector z to the intermediate latent vector w which enables scale specific control over image synthesis. The adaptive instance normalization(AdaIN) layer integrates this latent vector with features from each scale, and provides control over the strength of image features at different scales.

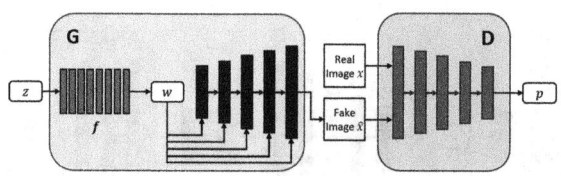

Fig. 2. StyleGAN structure.

Skip-Connection. For the second step of cyclic path, we add skip-connection between the discriminator and the generator of Skip-StyleGAN. In this path, the discriminator encodes an input image to a latent vector z and provide it to the generator. To directly transfer the multi-scale features of encoded input to the generator, features from each convolution layer of the discriminator are connected to the corresponding layers of generator through skip-connection. With this skip-connection, the generator can easily produce high quality image which is more close to the real data. It also contributes to reducing the computational complexity of training and enable our model to generate high quality multi-view images without relying on additional information, such as contour, landmarks.

Neighboring View Generation Model. Skip-StyleGAN adopts additional label for generator input to learn the latent space for rotating a view of input image. However, instead of learning the whole space of rotation, our model only focuses on the relation between the input view and neighboring view in the latent space. The generator is trained with two input vectors, random vector z and view code v for controlling the view. By providing only two types of the view code, original view or a neighboring view, the generator learns to reflect the semantics of the input view code for generating neighboring view image. Furthermore, the discriminator is used as an autoencoding network to provide better latent representation $\hat{z}$ to the generator in the cyclic path of training.

The discriminator of our model also classifies whether the given input image corresponds to an original view or a neighboring view, and outputs the result $\hat{v}$. This latent view code $\hat{v}$ is used for minimizing binary cross-entropy loss, view classification loss(L_v), as following:

$$L_v = -vlog\hat{v} - (1-v)log(1-\hat{v}) \tag{1}$$

This loss enforce the model to generate images according to view code v.

In addition to the classification of view, the discriminator encodes the input image to a latent vector $\hat{z}$. From this output, we minimize Maximum Mean Discrepancy (MMD) loss [3,5] between encoded $\hat{z}$ and random vector z to reduce the difference between the data distribution and the latent space z. With this MMD loss, generator learned from random normal distribution can be used to generate images from the encoded vector $\hat{z}$ which represents the real data distribution. MMD loss is computed as below:

$$\begin{aligned} L_{MMD} = &\frac{1}{n^2}\sum_{i=1}^{n}\sum_{j=1}^{n}k(z_i, z_j) - \frac{2}{nm}\sum_{i=1}^{n}\sum_{j=1}^{m}k(z_i, D(x_j)) \\ &+ \frac{1}{m^2}\sum_{i=1}^{m}\sum_{j=1}^{m}k(D(x_i), D(x_j)) \end{aligned} \tag{2}$$

For the stable training of GAN structure, we also adopt WGAN-GP [6] loss for the training our model. WGAN-GP loss is computed as following:

$$L_{adv} = E_{\hat{x}\sim P_g}[D(\hat{x})] - E_{x\sim P_r}[D(x)] + \lambda E_{\tilde{x}\sim P_{\tilde{x}}}[(\|\nabla_{\tilde{x}}D(\tilde{x})\|_2 - 1)^2] \tag{3}$$

where x is a real image and $\hat{x}$ is a fake image created by $\tilde{x} = \alpha x - (1-\alpha)\hat{x}$.

When the generator is producing a neighboring view of input image based on the encoded $\hat{z}$, we always apply a view code v' which is fixed to represent the neighboring view. In this way, our model learns to generate the neighboring view of input image which is rotated to one direction.

To generate enhanced quality image, we adopt Mean Squared Error(MSE) loss and Perceptual loss [9] for model training.

$$L_{MSE} = \frac{1}{n}\sum_{i=1}^{n}(x' - G(D(x), v))^2 \tag{4}$$

$$L_p = \frac{1}{n} \sum_{i=1}^{n} \sum_{j=1}^{m} (\phi_i(x) - \phi_i(\tilde{x}))^2 \tag{5}$$

where x' represents rotated version of a real image x and $\phi_i(x)$ means features extracted from the pre-trained model VGG16 [13].

The total loss L_{total} is the sum of all the above loss functions.

$$L_{total} = L_{adv} + L_v + L_{MMD} + L_{MSE} + L_p \tag{6}$$

2.2 Training Algorithm

Skip-StyleGAN is trained with two steps. At the first step, based on a random latent vector z and view label v, generator produces fake image and discriminator tries to distinguish it from real one. As shown in Algorithm 1, the first step consists of 1~4. At the second step, given a real image x, discriminator outputs p, $\hat{z}$, $\hat{v}$, and generator tries to produce rotated image $\hat{x}'$ based on $\hat{z}$ and view label v'. In Algorithm 1, the second step consists of 5~8.

Algorithm 1: Skip-StyleGAN

Input : Sets of view labeled image X, max iteration T, batch size B
Output: Trained network G and D
for $t = 1$ **to** T **do**
    for $i = 1$ **to** B **do**
        1. Sample $z_i \sim P_z$ with v_i and $x_j \sim P_x$ with v_j;
        2. $\hat{x}_i \leftarrow G(v_i, z_i)$;
        3. $(p_i, \hat{z}_i, \hat{v}_i) \leftarrow D(\hat{x}_i)$;
        4. Update D by L_v and G by L_v;
        5. $(p_j, \hat{z}_j, \hat{v}_j) \leftarrow D(x_j)$;
        6. Update D by L_v, L_{MMD}, and L_{adv}, and G by L_v;
        7. $\hat{x}'_j \leftarrow G(v', \hat{z}_j)$;
        8. Update D, G by L_{MSE} and L_p;
    end
end

---

3 Experiments

3.1 Dataset and Evaluation

For the training of Skip-StyleGAN, we collected hand bone complex dataset from 121 patients' CT and X-ray DICOM images at university hospital. Among 121 patients, 191 hands are collected when we separate the left and right hands. Before training, we make 2D view images from 3D rendered hand bone shapes in 10° intervals using open software, 3D Slicer. Unusual data that may disturb training are excluded during this process. Therefore, we use 157 hands for training, and 10 hands for testing. Skip-StyleGAN needs multi-resolution data for the original and neighbor views, so, 1570 multi-resolution images, which has sizes of 8 × 8, 16 × 16, 32 × 32, 64 × 64, 128 × 128, are used to train one Skip-StyleGAN. For example, the first Skip-StyleGAN that generates 10° view rotated images requires 157 of 0° images and 157 of 10° images for every 5 resolutions. Skip-StyleGAN is implemented by PyTorch, and executed on NVIDIA Titan RTX GPU.

For the evaluation, we sequentially combine the output of Skip-StyleGAN for 0° to 90° rotation with the result from the 180° to 90°rotation. We train Skip-StyleGAN with left direction for 0° to 90° rotation and the right direction for 180° to 90° rotation. For the initial input of Skip-StyleGAN, we convert front view X-ray images to rendered bone image by using MUNIT [8] which has trained with 109 X-ray images and 157 rendered images.

3.2 Multi-view Image Generation

We compare the multi-view generation performance of our model with CRGAN [14] which is a state-of-the-art multi-view generation model. As shown in Fig. 3, Skip-StyleGAN generated rotated views of bone structure which are very close to the ground truth images. The structural accuracy of Skip-StyleGAN generated images is even better than CRGAN model and the comparison for the fine details are shown in Fig. 4. From Fig. 4, we can clearly see that Skip-StyleGAN generates more accurate multi-view images in its shapes comparing to CRGAN. For the quantitative evaluation, see supplementary material.

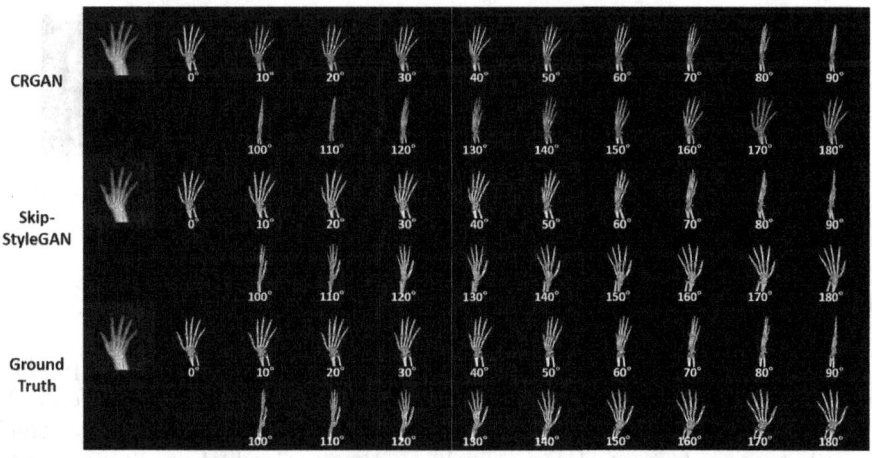

Fig. 3. Comparison of multi-view generation performance.

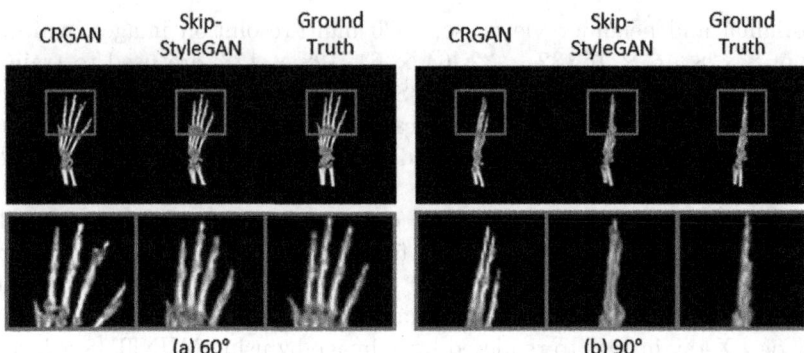

Fig. 4. Comparison of multi-view generation performance. (a) 60° result, (b) 90° result.

3.3 Skip-Connection

We evaluate the effect of skip-connection on Skip-StyleGAN with an ablation study. Figure 5 shows the multi-view image comparison between Skip-StyleGAN with and without skip-connection models. As shown in the result, for the without case, the shape of bone structure in the rotated view is severely distorted as the rotation angle increases. In contrast, the skip-connection added model successfully generates multi-view images while correctly maintaining the hand bone shape.

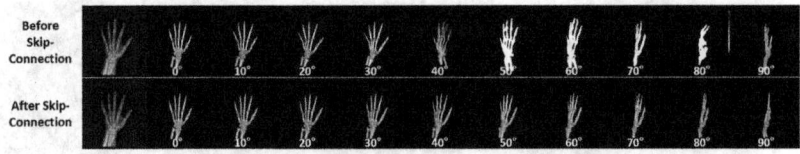

Fig. 5. Comparison of before and after skip-connection.

4   Discussion and Conclusion

In this paper, we propose a novel GAN architecture, Skip-StyleGAN, to produce high-quality multi-view images of 3D CT rendering images from a single 2D X-ray image of front view. Skip-StyleGAN consists of (1) skip-connection which contributes to reducing training difficulty and generating high-quality images by transferring more details of feature; (2) discriminator that is used for both view classification and input encoding to generate multi-view images; (3) neighboring view generation model which learns the latent space between two consecutive view angle rotated images. In experiments, we show that Skip-StyleGAN generates superior quality of multi-view images compared to other state-of-the art models. To the best of our knowledge, it is the first work to generate multi-view images of 3D CT rendered shape from a single 2D X-ray image. Considering the superior performance of our work, we are expecting that Skip-StyleGAN contributes significantly to the efficiency and reliability of diagnosis in the medical field.

Acknowledgement. This work was partly supported by Institute of Information & Communications Technology Planning & Evaluation(IITP) grant funded by the Korea government(MSIT) (2016-0-00564, Development of Intelligent Interaction Technology Based on Context Awareness and Human Intention Understanding) and Institute for Information & communications Technology Promotion(IITP) grant funded by the Korea government(MSIT) (2018-0-00861, Intelligent SW Technology Development for Medical Data Analysis).

References

1. Cerrolaza, J.J., et al.: 3D fetal skull reconstruction from 2dus via deep conditional generative networks. In: Frangi, A.F., Schnabel, J.A., Davatzikos, C., Alberola-López, C., Fichtinger, G. (eds.) MICCAI 2018. LNCS, vol. 11070, pp. 383–391. Springer, Cham (2018). https://doi.org/10.1007/978-3-030-00928-1_44

2. Cui, J., Li, S., Xia, Q., Hao, A., Qin, H.: Learning multi-view manifold for single image based modeling. Comput. Graph. **82**, 275–285 (2019)

3. Dziugaite, G.K., Roy, D.M., Ghahramani, Z.: Training generative neural networks via maximum mean discrepancy optimization. arXiv preprint arXiv:1505.03906 (2015)

4. Goodfellow, I., et al.: Generative adversarial nets. In: Advances in Neural Information Processing Systems. pp. 2672–2680 (2014)

5. Gretton, A., Borgwardt, K., Rasch, M., Schölkopf, B., Smola, A.J.: A kernel method for the two-sample-problem. In: Advances in Neural Information Processing Systems. pp. 513–520 (2007)

6. Gulrajani, I., Ahmed, F., Arjovsky, M., Dumoulin, V., Courville, A.C.: Improved training of wasserstein gans. In: Advances in Neural Information Processing Systems. pp. 5767–5777 (2017)

7. Huang, R., Zhang, S., Li, T., He, R.: Beyond face rotation: global and local perception gan for photorealistic and identity preserving frontal view synthesis. In: Proceedings of the IEEE International Conference on Computer Vision. pp. 2439–2448 (2017)

8. Huang, X., Liu, M.Y., Belongie, S., Kautz, J.: Multimodal unsupervised image-to-image translation. In: Proceedings of the European Conference on Computer Vision (ECCV). pp. 172–189 (2018)

9. Johnson, J., Alahi, A., Fei-Fei, L.: Perceptual losses for real-time style transfer and super-resolution. In: European Conference on Computer Vision. pp. 694–711. Springer (2016)

10. Karras, T., Laine, S., Aila, T.: A style-based generator architecture for generative adversarial networks. In: Proceedings of the IEEE Conference on Computer Vision and Pattern Recognition. pp. 4401–4410 (2019)

11. Kingma, D.P., Welling, M.: Auto-encoding variational bayes. arXiv preprint arXiv:1312.6114 (2013)

12. Moniz, J.R.A., Beckham, C., Rajotte, S., Honari, S., Pal, C.: Unsupervised depth estimation, 3d face rotation and replacement. In: Advances in Neural Information Processing Systems. pp. 9736–9746 (2018)

13. Simonyan, K., Zisserman, A.: Very deep convolutional networks for large-scale image recognition. arXiv preprint arXiv:1409.1556 (2014)
14. Tian, Y., Peng, X., Zhao, L., Zhang, S., Metaxas, D.N.: Cr-gan: learning complete representations for multi-view generation. arXiv preprint arXiv:1806.11191 (2018)
15. Tran, L., Yin, X., Liu, X.: Disentangled representation learning gan for pose-invariant face recognition. In: Proceedings of the IEEE Conference on Computer Vision and Pattern Recognition. pp. 1415–1424 (2017)
16. Whitmarsh, T., Humbert, L., De Craene, M., Barquero, L.M.D.R., Frangi, A.F.: Reconstructing the 3d shape and bone mineral density distribution of the proximal femur from dual-energy x-ray absorptiometry. IEEE Trans. Med. Imaging **30**(12), 2101–2114 (2011)
17. Yin, X., Yu, X., Sohn, K., Liu, X., Chandraker, M.: Towards large-pose face frontalization in the wild. In: Proceedings of the IEEE International Conference on Computer Vision. pp. 3990–3999 (2017)
18. Zhu, X., Lei, Z., Liu, X., Shi, H., Li, S.Z.: Face alignment across large poses: a 3d solution. In: Proceedings of the IEEE Conference on Computer Vision and Pattern Recognition. pp. 146–155 (2016)

Dynamic Multi-object Gaussian Process Models

Jean-Rassaire Fouefack[1,2,3](✉) ⓘ, Bhushan Borotikar[3,4,5] ⓘ,
Tania S. Douglas[1] ⓘ, Valérie Burdin[2,3] ⓘ, and Tinashe E. M. Mutsvangwa[1,3] ⓘ

[1] Division of Biomedical Engineering, University of Cape Town,
7935 Cape Town, South Africa
ffcjea001@myuct.ac.za, {tania.douglas,tinashe.mutsvangwa}@uct.ac.za
[2] Department Image and Information Processing, IMT-Atlantique, Brest, France
valerie.burdin@imt-atlantique.fr
[3] LaTIM INSERM U1101, Brest, France
bhushan.borotikar@gmail.com
[4] CHRU de Brest, Brest, France
[5] University of Brittany Occidental, Brest, France

Abstract. Statistical shape models (SSMs) are state-of-the-art medical image analysis tools for extracting and explaining shape across a set of biological structures. A combined analysis of shape and pose variation would provide additional utility in medical image analysis tasks such as automated multi-organ segmentation and completion of partial data. However, a principled and robust way to combine shape and pose features has been illusive due to three main issues: 1) non-homogeneity of the data (data with linear and non-linear natural variation across features), 2) non-optimal representation of the $3D$ Euclidean motion (rigid transformation representations that are not proportional to the kinetic energy that moves an object from one position to the other), and 3) artificial discretization of the models. Here, we propose a new dynamic multi-object statistical modelling framework for the analysis of human joints in a continuous domain. Specifically, we propose to normalise shape and dynamic spatial features in the same linearized statistical space, permitting the use of linear statistics; and we adopt an optimal 3D Euclidean motion representation for more accurate rigid transformation comparisons. The method affords an efficient generative dynamic multi-object modelling platform for biological joints. We validate the method using controlled synthetic data. The shape-pose prediction results suggest that the novel concept may have utility for a range of medical image analysis applications including management of human joint disorders.

Keywords: Combined 3D shape and pose analysis · Generative models · Statistical Euclidean motion representation · Gaussian process

This work is based on research supported by the National Research Foundation (NRF) of South Africa (grant no's 105950 and 114393); the South African Research Chairs Initiative of the NRF and the Department of Science and Technology (grant no 98788); the South African Medical Research Council and the French Ministry of Higher Education, Research and Innovation (MESRI), Brest Métrople, France (grant no 17-178).

© Springer Nature Switzerland AG 2020
A. L. Martel et al. (Eds.): MICCAI 2020, LNCS 12264, pp. 755–764, 2020.
https://doi.org/10.1007/978-3-030-59719-1_73

1   Introduction

A well established and understood formalism for analysing 3D geometric variation in a linearized statistical space exists in the form of statistical shape modelling (SSM). SSMs (also known as point distribution models (PDMs)) typically
model the data in Euclidean vector space using principal component analysis
(PCA), treating feature variation changes as a linear combination of local translations only [2,4,8,10]. While limited in capturing the non-linearity in shape
space, the validity of this linearization for rigid shapes has been codified in the
literature for single anatomical structures [2,4,8]. Efforts for faithfully representing the non-linearity of shape space have been reported but have not become
mainstream due to computational inefficiency and a lack of robustness [12].
Recently, *Luthi et al.* [8] introduced a generalisation of SSMs, referred to as Gaussian process morphable models (GPMMs). In this framework, the parametric
low-dimensional model was represented as a Gaussian process over deformation
fields obtained from training examples. In contrast to discrete models that are
dependent on artificial discretization, GPMMs are inherently continuous, that
is, permitting of the arbitrary discretization of the domain on which the model is
defined. However, GPMMs do not embed inter-object shape correlation, nor the
anatomo-physiological relationship between articulating objects. Thus, current
SSMs and GPMMs are unable to represent, in a statistically robust and intuitive
way, an articulating anatomical complex composed of several rigid substructures
which can move relative to each other.

Various efforts have been reported in the literature to model shape and pose
features together. *Fletcher and colleagues* [5] proposed the analysis of pose variation through principal geodesic analysis (PGA); a non-linear extension of PCA.
Bossa and Olmos [3] proposed parametric low-dimensional models of several
structures of brain in different poses. Shape and pose features of these brain
structures were concatenated in a long vector and standard multivariate statistics were extracted [3]. Both the above shape and pose PGA based models
used a standard representation (Rodrigues, quaternion and Euler representation) for modelling the rigid transformations describing the pose. *Moreau et al.*
[9] reported that the standard representation is limited in its ability to model
rigid transformations of non-compact objects (with respect to a shape compactness measure). They instead proposed a new norm for statistical analysis
of rigid transformations that is robust for analysing non-compact objects. However, they demonstrated this new norm only for SPMs without considering shape
and pose variability analysis. A non-linear shape modelling approach based on
differential coordinates (thus avoiding global rigid transformation through local
rotation and stretching) has been reported [1,12]. While this approach captures
the inherent non-linearity in shape variation, it still suffers from artificial discretization which prevents marginalization of the resultant probabilistic model.
Additionally, it does not allow for modelling multi-object structures.

We propose a novel method that incorporates 1) morphology and pose normalisation to obtain an homogeneous analysis space; 2) an optimal representation of 3D Euclidean motion allowing for an efficient associated norm for

comparison of rigid transformations; and 3) a continuous domain for our modelling space. Our method permits the modelling of shape and pose variation of complex articulated objects composed of multiple rigid objects. We refer to the proposed modelling framework as Dynamic Multi-object-Gaussian Process Modelling (DMO-GPM).

2   Dynamic Multi-object Gaussian Process Models

Before describing our DMO-GPM framework, we summarise the main concepts behind GPMMs on which we will capitalise to synthesize the dynamic multi-object concept. In GPMMs [8], shape correspondence, established across n examples, leads to deformation fields $u_i, i = 1 \ldots n$ defined from the reference shape Γ_S to i^{th} examples in the training data. These deformations are then modelled as Gaussian Processes (GP) on the reference shape domain Ω_S ($\mathbb{R}^3 \supset \Omega_S \supset \Gamma_S$) thus making them independent of discretization. The GPMMs are formulated as $\{\Gamma_R + u(\Gamma_R)\}$ with $u \sim GP(\mu, k)$ and μ is the mean and k the covariance (kernel function).

2.1   Optimal Representation of $3D$ Euclidean Motion

The literature on shape and pose models (SPMs) usually emphasizes the common shape-pose space required in medical image processing. The standard representation (SR) of rigid transformations may not always encapsulate the kinetic energy necessary to move points on an object from one position to another, particularly for non-compact shapes. This reduces the efficiency of this parameterization for statistical analysis of rigid transformations [9]. Thus, we propose to extend the kinetic energy based representation by *Moreau et al.* [9] in a continuous space and use it to encode a rigid transformation in DMO-GPM. We refer to this new transformation representation as the energy displacement representation (EDR).

Lets start by representing a multi-object complex as a set of N objects; each object defined by its shape and its spatial position parameters. A multi-object may then be represented as a concatenated vector space and denoted as $X = [X_S, X_K]^T$ where $X_S = [S^1, \ldots, S^N]^T$ and $X_K = [K^1, \ldots, K^N]^T$ with S^j and K^j representing the point domain of the shape and the spatial orientation features for the jth object of the joint ($j = 1, \ldots, N$), respectively.

Now let us assume there are n multi-object examples in the training dataset. Furthermore, let us explicitly define the rigid transformation representation which is the displacement field representation that extends [9] in a continuous domain and will be used to define joint feature representations. We can now define the EDR of the ith example of the object j on its reference spatial position domain $\Omega_K^j \subset \mathbb{R}^3$ with their respective reference shape Γ_S^j and reference pose points Γ_K^j. The EDR δ_i^j and its associated metric d are defined as:

$$\delta_i^j(x) = h_i^j(x) - Id(x), x \in \Omega_K^j, i = 1 \ldots n$$

$$h_i^j = \arg\min_{h \in SE(3)} \|\overrightarrow{h(S_i^j)} - \overrightarrow{\Gamma_S^j}\|^2 \text{ and } d^2(h_i^j, Id) = \overrightarrow{\delta_i^j(\Gamma_K^j)}^T \overrightarrow{\delta_i^j(\Gamma_K^j)}, \tag{1}$$

$SE(3)$ being a lie group of rigid transformations.

2.2   Normalising Dynamic Multi-object Features for Homogeneous Representation

As mentioned, SPMs in the literature are embedded in a non-homogeneous analysis space due to the non-optimal representation of the poses. We define a unified representation of shape and relative spatial dynamics comprising joint deformation fields over which a GP may be defined (Sect. 2.3). A reference multi-object joint, $\Gamma = \cup_{j=1}^{N}(\Gamma_S^j \cup \Gamma_K^j) \subset \mathbb{R}^3$ is chosen from the training examples. A joint deformation field of the ith example in the training data-set is then a pair of deformation fields (u_S^i, u_K^i), where u_S^i maps a point x of the reference shape objects $\cup_{j=1}^{N}\Gamma_S^j$ to the point $u_S^i(x)$ of its corresponding shape example; and u_K^i maps a point x of the reference pose objects $\cup_{j=1}^{N}\Gamma_K^j$ to the point $u_K^i(x)$ of its corresponding pose example. We define the ith joint deformation field as:

$$\begin{cases} u_S^i(x) \text{ if } x \in \Omega_S = \cup_{j=1}^{N}\Omega_S^j \\ u_K^i(x) \text{ if } x \in \Omega_K = \cup_{j=1}^{N}\Omega_K^j. \end{cases} \text{ where } \begin{cases} u_S^i(x) = u_i^j(x), \text{ if } x \in \Omega_S^j \\ u_K^i(x) = h_i^j(x), \text{ if } x \in \Omega_K^j. \end{cases} \quad (2)$$

Before obtaining residual features (around the mean) that will represent normalised features, the joint function of the mean shape and spatial transformations needs to be defined. We can estimate this mean function, μ_{MO}, using the mean pose deformation fields as:

$$\frac{1}{n}\sum_{i=1}^{n}u_i^j(x), \text{ if } x \in \Omega_S^j \text{ and } \mu_K^j(x) \approx \bar{h}^j(x), \text{ if } x \in \Omega_K^j. \quad (3)$$

with $\bar{h}^j = \underset{h \in SE(3)}{\arg min}\left\|\overrightarrow{h\left[\frac{1}{n}\sum_{i=1}^{n}\delta_i^j(\Gamma_K^j)\right]} - \Gamma_K^j\right\|^2.$

Thanks to the EDR, $\bar{h}$ is directly computed from the vector field mean, which is the Fréchet mean approximation.

Thus far, pose representations across the training data-set belong to a manifold which is a non-linear space. To linearise rigid transformations we can project onto a linearized space to the manifold at the mean rigid transformation (tangent space) using the EDR (Eq. 1), in order to obtain the unified space of shape and pose features. The relative spatial transformations are then linearized through a exp / log bijective mapping presented below.

Let us define the exp / log functions associated to the EDR between two rigid transformations $h_{i_1}^j, h_{i_2}^j$:

$$\begin{cases} \log[h_i^j] = \delta_i^j, j = 1\ldots N, i = 1\ldots n \\ \log_{h_{i_1}^j}[h_{i_2}^j] = \log[(h_{i_2}^j)^{-1} \circ h_{i_1}^j]. \end{cases} \text{ and } \begin{cases} \exp[\delta_i^j] = \underset{h \in SE(3)}{\arg min}\|h[\delta_i^j(\Gamma_K^j)] - \Gamma_K^j\|^2 \\ \exp_{h_{i_1}^j}[\delta_{i_2}^j] = h_{i_1}^j \circ \exp[\delta_{i_2}^j]. \end{cases} \quad (4)$$

The linearized deformation fields, over which the GP will be defined, are denoted by $\{u_i^{MO}\}_{i=1}^n$ with

$$u_i^{MO}(x) = u_S^i(x) - \mu_{MO}(x), x \in \Omega_S \quad \text{and} \quad u_i^{MO}(x) = \log_{\mu_{MO}}[u_K^i](x), x \in \Omega_K. \tag{5}$$

2.3 Dynamic Multi-object Modelling in a Continuous Domain

From a training dataset of n examples with N objects each, the deformation fields $\{u_i^{MO}\}_{i=1}^n$ defined on the continuous domain, $\Omega = \cup_{j=1}^N(\Omega_S^j \cup \Omega_K^j)$, can be modelled by a GP defined by $u \sim GP(\mu_{MO}, k_{MO})$, where k_{MO} is the kernel function:

$$k_{MO}(x,y) = \frac{1}{n}\sum_{i=1}^n u_i^{MO}(x)u_i^{MO}(y)^T, x,y \in \Omega \tag{6}$$

The multi-object deformation fields u^{MO} can then be represented by an orthogonal set of basis functions denoted by $\{\phi_m^{MO}\}_{m=1}^M$, $M \leq n$ and defined as:

$$\phi_m^{MO}(x) = \phi_m^S(x) \text{ if } x \in \Omega_S, \text{ and } \phi_m^{MO}(x) = \phi_m^K(x) \text{ if } x \in \Omega_K. \tag{7}$$

where ϕ_m^S and ϕ_m^K represents the shape and the energy displacement component of the mth basis function.

In this continuous domain we can model the jth object as a combination of the shape deformation field and a rigid transformation (obtained using exponential mapping) as defined below:

$$
\begin{cases}
\mu_{MO}(x) + \sum_{m=1}^M \alpha_m \sqrt{\lambda_m^{MO}}\phi_m^{S_j}(x), \text{ if } x \in \Omega_S^j, \\
h^j : \exp_{\mu_{MO}}\left(\sum_{m=1}^n \alpha_m \sqrt{\lambda_i^{MO}}\phi_m^{K_j}(x)\right), \text{ if } x \in \Omega_K^j.
\end{cases}
\tag{8}
$$

where $\alpha \sim \mathcal{N}(0,1)$ and the pair $(\lambda_m^{MO}, \phi_m^{MO})_{m=1...M}$ represent the mth eigenvalue and eigenfunction couple. These couples are obtained using Karhunen-Loève expansion and Nyström approximation as in [8]. The mth eigenfunction ϕ_m^{MO} is a continuous multi-object deformation field defined on Ω, in the tangent space to $SE(3)$. A shape instance of the jth object and its associated spatial position can be generated from our probabilistic model for $\alpha = (\alpha_m)_m \sim \mathcal{N}(0,1)$ as:

$$\text{shape\&pose}^j = h^j(\text{shape}^j) \text{ with shape}^j = \sum_{m=1}^M \alpha_m \sqrt{\lambda_m^{MO}}\phi_m^{S_j}(\Gamma_S^j) \tag{9}$$

where $\Gamma_S^j \subset \Omega_S^j$ is the reference shape of the jth object.

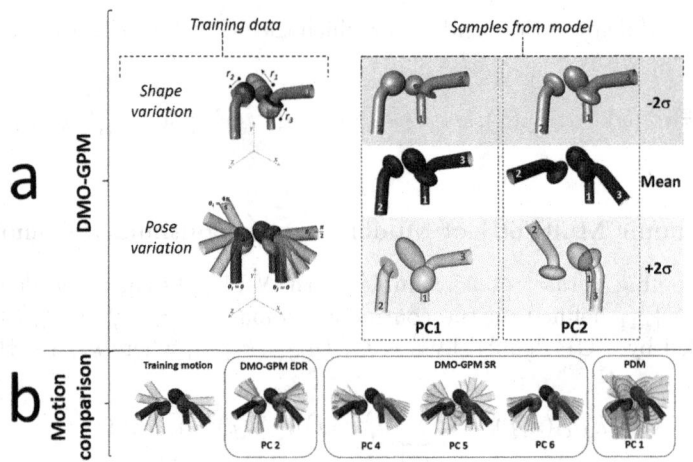

Fig. 1. Model training data and sampling. a: Shape and pose training data (left) and samples extracted from the DMO-GPM (right). b: Model pose sampling comparison: DMO-GPM with EDR (pose marginalized), SR (pose marginalized), and PDM.

3   Experiment and Results

3.1   Data

To validate the DMO-GPM framework, we created a synthetic data set with precisely defined modes of shape and pose variation consisting of surface mesh data of three "lollipops" as defined in [7]. Each lollipop has a shaft, a neck and head. We prescribed shape differences for each shape by varying the length of the major axis defining the ellipsoid of the head of each lollipop. We created artificial joints using three lollipops per scenario. Each joint was composed of three lollipops with major axes for corresponding pairs of lollipops of r_1, r_2 and r_3, for object 1, object 2 and object 3, respectively. The span of the data-set of joints was created by varying r_1 and r_2 as $\{(r_1, r_2, r_3) = (r, 31 - r, 17 - r), i = 1, \ldots, 15\}$ creating a shape correlation between them. For joint motion, for each joint generated above, we rotated the second lollipop (object 2) relative to the first one (object 1) and the third relatively to object 2 using the Euler's angle convention for describing rigid transformations (φ, θ, ψ). The second lollipop was moved in the yz-plane by four angles $(\theta = \frac{1}{5}\pi, \frac{2}{5}\pi, \frac{3}{5}\pi, \frac{4}{5}\pi)$. The third object was moved in the yz-plane by four angles $(\theta = \frac{1}{2}\pi, \frac{1}{3}\pi, \frac{2}{9}\pi, \frac{1}{9}\pi)$ defining a Euclidean motion correlation with that of the second object. Finally, we applied our method to real shoulder data as described in [6].

3.2   Validation

Shape-Pose Capturing Performance: We evaluated the performance of our model in providing a statistical analysis space for shape and its spatial orientations. As expected, the first two principal components (PC) explained almost the

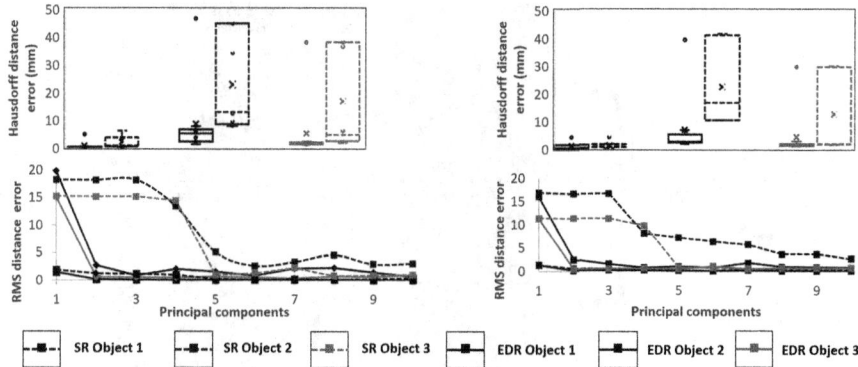

Fig. 2. Quantitative comparison of the DMO-GPM with EDR (our model) and DMO-GPM with SR. Left: Specificity performance (Hausdorff distance and RMS errors) using DMO-GPM with EDR and SR. Right: Generalisation performance (Hausdorff distance and RMS) using DMO-GPM with EDR and SR.

total variation (99%) across the lollipop training data. The first PC explained shape variation preserving shape correlation between different objects (Fig. 1a). The second accounted for their relative positions as well as the pose correlation between the second and the third object, as observed in Fig.1a. PC1 with samples from −2 to +2 standard deviations shown in Fig. 1a, explains the same shape variation as in the training data (Fig. 1.a: Top left) and PC2 explains the same pose dynamic as in the training data (Fig. 1.a: Bottom left). We also compare the performance of the EDR (our model) in explaining the transforms describing the degrees of freedom (DOF), to that of SR and point distribution model (PDM). Figure 1b, from the left to the right, shows the DOF of the training data, the pose marginalized DMO-GPM with EDR, the pose marginalized DMO-GPM with SR and the PDM. Our model captures the training motion with one PC while the one with SR needs up to 3 PCs to explain the motion that is in one plane in the training data. As expected PDM led to unrealistic shape variations.

Specificity and Generality: We quantitatively compared our model using EDR to the standard representation (SR). We first measured the specificity; measuring the capacity of the model in explaining variation within the training data, in terms of number of PCs used. We fitted the DMO-GPM to 10 training examples, which included shape and pose variation. The fitting was performed using the Markov Chain Monte Carlo (MCMC) method as in [11]. Figure 2 shows the box plot of the Hausdorff and the average root mean square (RMS) surface-to-surface distance errors (left column) in terms of the number of PCs for the first, the second and the third objects. Our model (DMO-GPM with EDR) outperforms the one with SR for specificity. Secondly, we measured the generalisation ability; measuring the capacity of the model in explaining

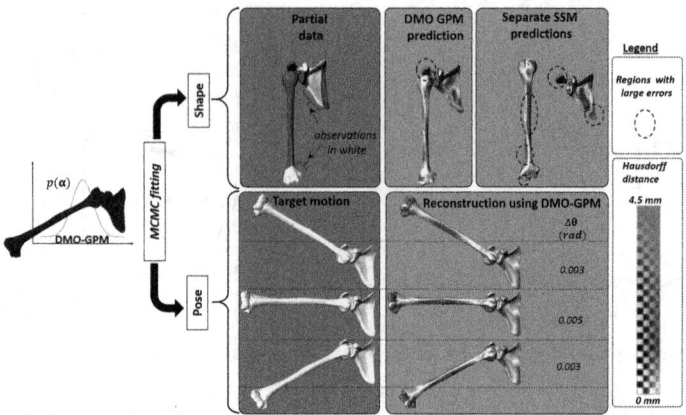

Fig. 3. Reconstruction of target shoulders. Left: our probabilistic model (DMO-GPM) Top-row: DMO-GPM marginalized shape prediction (middle) and PDM based shape prediction (right). Bottom-row: The DMO-GPM marginalized pose prediction at multiple poses.

examples outside the training data. Again our model outperforms the one with SR as shown in Fig. 2 (right column). This illustrates the robustness of the proposed method in representing $3D$ Euclidean motion as well as in explaining associated shape variations.

Shoulder Joint Prediction: To evaluate the performance of the DMO-GPM in predicting real joint data, we predicted the simulated abduction motion in [6]. The scapula and the humerus were predicted with the humerus at different poses relative to the scapula. Five poses were generated within the motion range $(0, \frac{3}{10}\pi, \frac{1}{2}\pi, \frac{7}{10}\pi, \frac{4}{5}\pi)$; these test poses simulated the abduction motion in the training data-set. Moreover, distal humeral and scapula blade fractures were simulated, and both DMO-GPM and individual bone PDMs were used to reconstruct fractured bones. Again the prediction was done using DMO-GPM and MCMC with a comparator method using PDM. The reconstructed shoulder with humerus and scapula at different relative poses using the DMO-GPM are shown in Fig. 3 (bottom-left). They predicted well at each relative position. The poses were predicted with the average of 0.003 rad and the average Hausdorff distance shape error was 3.1 ± 0.4 mm. The reconstructed shoulder fracture is also shown in Fig. 3 (top) for both DMO-GPM and individual PDMs. The DMO-GPM not only preserves the relative orientation of the bone but also shows better prediction of shape.

4   Conclusion

In the context of multi-shape prediction under 3D Euclidean motion invariance, we proposed a data driven model that is robust in providing a statistical analysis space of multi-shapes and their spatial dynamics. Our method shows significant improvement in finding a latent space that explains multi shape (compact and non-compact) variation with the associated 3D Euclidean motion compared with state-of-the-art [3,5]. Our method creates a new paradigm in modelling multi-object shapes; modelling them as deformation fields in a continuous domain. The continuous property of our model domain allows marginalization to a region of interest that has so far only been possible with single shape modelling [8]. Moreover, the framework can be used to model single non-linear shapes as in [1] by rigidly subdividing them and applying our method. We have demonstrated that our method yields highly predictive motion descriptors in experiments on the shoulder joints. In future work, we will investigate how to embed intensity in the pipeline for $3D$ image segmentation and data augmentation.

References

1. Ambellan, F., Zachow, S., von Tycowicz, C.: A surface-theoretic approach for statistical shape modeling. In: Shen, D., et al. (eds.) MICCAI 2019. LNCS, vol. 11767, pp. 21–29. Springer, Cham (2019). https://doi.org/10.1007/978-3-030-32251-9_3
2. Blanc, R., Székely, G.: Confidence regions for statistical model based shape prediction from sparse observations. IEEE Trans. Med. Imaging **31**(6), 1300–1310 (2012)
3. Bossa, M.N., Olmos, S.: Multi-object statistical pose+ shape models. In: 2007 4th IEEE International Symposium on Biomedical Imaging: From Nano to Macro, pp. 1204–1207. IEEE (2007)
4. Cootes, T.F., Taylor, C.J., Cooper, D.H., Graham, J.: Training models of shape from sets of examples. In: Hogg, D., Boyle, R. (eds.) BMVC92, pp. 9–18. Springer, London (1992). https://doi.org/10.1007/978-1-4471-3201-1_2
5. Fletcher, P.T., Lu, C., Pizer, S.M., Joshi, S.: Principal geodesic analysis for the study of nonlinear statistics of shape. IEEE Trans. Med. Imaging **23**(8), 995–1005 (2004)
6. Fouefack, J.R., Alemneh, T., Borotikar, B., Burdin, V., Douglas, T.S., Mutsvangwa, T.: Statistical shape-kinematics models of the skeletal joints: application to the shoulder complex. In: 2019 41st Annual International Conference of the IEEE Engineering in Medicine and Biology Society (EMBC), pp. 4815–4818. IEEE (2019)
7. Gee, A.H., Treece, G.M.: Systematic misregistration and the statistical analysis of surface data. Med. Image Anal. **18**(2), 385–393 (2014)
8. Lüthi, M., Gerig, T., Jud, C., Vetter, T.: Gaussian process morphable models. IEEE Trans. Pattern Anal. Mach. Intell. **40**(8), 1860–1873 (2017)
9. Moreau, B., Gilles, B., Jolivet, E., Petit, P., Subsol, G.: A new metric for statistical analysis of rigid transformations: application to the rib cage. In: Cardoso, M.J., et al. (eds.) GRAIL/MFCA/MICGen -2017. LNCS, vol. 10551, pp. 114–124. Springer, Cham (2017). https://doi.org/10.1007/978-3-319-67675-3_11

10. Mutsvangwa, T., Burdin, V., Schwartz, C., Roux, C.: An automated statistical shape model developmental pipeline: application to the human scapula and humerus. IEEE Trans. Biomed. Eng. **62**(4), 1098–1107 (2015)
11. Schönborn, S., Egger, B., Morel-Forster, A., Vetter, T.: Markov chain monte carlo for automated face image analysis. Int. J. Comput. Vision **123**(2), 160–183 (2017)
12. von Tycowicz, C., Ambellan, F., Mukhopadhyay, A., Zachow, S.: An efficient riemannian statistical shape model using differential coordinates: with application to the classification of data from the osteoarthritis initiative. Med. Image Anal. **43**, 1–9 (2018)

A Kernelized Multi-level Localization Method for Flexible Shape Modeling with Few Training Data

Matthias Wilms[1,2,3]($\boxtimes$), Jan Ehrhardt[4], and Nils D. Forkert[1,2,3]

[1] Department of Radiology, University of Calgary, Calgary, Canada
matthias.wilms@ucalgary.ca
[2] Hotchkiss Brain Institute, University of Calgary, Calgary, Canada
[3] Alberta Children's Hospital Research Institute, University of Calgary,
Calgary, Canada
[4] Institute of Medical Informatics, University of Lübeck, Lübeck, Germany

Abstract. Statistical shape models (SSMs) are a standard generative shape modeling technique and they are still successfully employed in modern deep learning-based solutions for data augmentation purposes or as shape priors. However, with few training samples they often fail to represent local shape variations. Recently, a new state-of-the-art method has been proposed to alleviate this problem via a multi-level model localization scheme using distance-based covariance manipulations and Grassmannian-based level fusion during model training. This method significantly improves a SSMs performance, but heavily relies on costly eigendecompositions of large covariance matrices. In this paper, we derive a novel computationally-efficient formulation of the original method using ideas from kernel theory and randomized eigendecomposition. The proposed extension leads to a multi-level localization method for large-scale shape modeling problems that preserves the key characteristics of the original method while also improving its performance. Furthermore, our extensive evaluation on two publicly available data sets reveals the benefits of Grassmannian-based level fusion in contrast to a method derived from the popular Gaussian Process Morphable Models framework.

Keywords: Statistical shape models · Kernels · Few training data

1 Introduction

Statistical shape models (SSMs)[3] are a classical generative modeling technique that has been used intensively over the past 25 years to integrate learned prior information about plausible shape variations into medical image segmentation

Electronic supplementary material The online version of this chapter (https:// doi.org/10.1007/978-3-030-59719-1_74) contains supplementary material, which is available to authorized users.

© Springer Nature Switzerland AG 2020
A. L. Martel et al. (Eds.): MICCAI 2020, LNCS 12264, pp. 765–775, 2020.
https://doi.org/10.1007/978-3-030-59719-1_74

or registration methods [10,11,26]. Even in an era where state-of-the-art results are mostly obtained via deep learning-based solutions, SSMs are still highly useful: (1) They are frequently used for model-based data augmentation purposes when training neural networks [12–14,19,20] and (2) several deep learning architectures make use of or directly integrate SSMs as priors [16,27,28].

SSMs estimate a low-dimensional affine subspace of plausible shape configurations based on the variability seen in a training dataset. New shapes can then be sampled from the model in data augmentation scenarios and existing shapes can be projected onto the subspace for regularization purposes. Their linear nature imposes a strong prior on the learned representation and results in simple closed-form solutions to transport data between subspace and embedding space, which still makes them an attractive choice. However, their generalization ability strongly depends on the amount and variability of the training samples used.

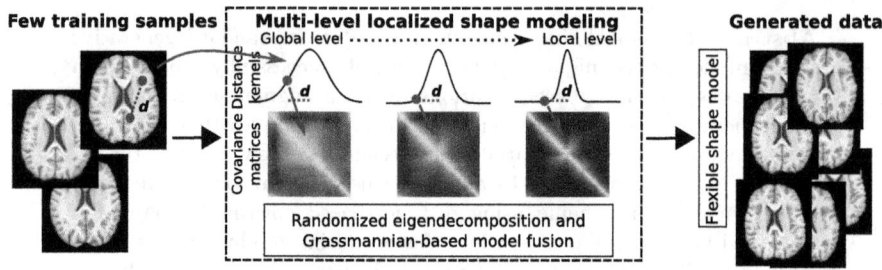

Fig. 1. Graphical overview of the proposed multi-level localization method using kernels for large-scale, distance-based covariance matrix manipulation and eigendecomposition. The approach can be employed to build flexible shape models from few training samples that are, for example, useful in deep learning data augmentation scenarios.

With few training data, SSMs frequently fail to represent local variability [25]. This problem can be alleviated by integrating local prior information into the training process, which usually consists of an eigendecomposition of the training samples' covariance matrix. A popular option is to apply the principle of locality by assuming that the shape variability at a specific point is mainly influenced by its immediate surrounding [4,15,22,25], which can be implemented via distance-based covariance matrix manipulations to reduce covariances of distant points.

In [25], this idea was generalized to a hierarchical multi-level training scheme that results in a significantly improved accuracy in limited data scenarios. One of its key components is a Grassmannian manifold-based fusion technique, which allows to incorporate information from different locality levels into a single SSM. The approach has, for example, been successfully employed for 2D data augmentation [20] but its applicability is currently limited to smaller problems due to its high computational complexity (e.g., explicit representation of the covariance matrix is required). This prevents its use in modern large-scale scenarios like 3D data augmentation [29] where multiple objects and their relations are encoded via dense displacement fields with potentially millions of elements.

In this paper, we propose a novel extension of [25] that enables its use for large-scale problems in limited training data scenarios while preserving its main characteristics (e.g., Grassmannian-based fusion). This is achieved by deriving a kernelized formulation of the original method that is computationally highly efficient because of the use of a randomized low-rank eigendecomposition approach (see Fig. 1 for an overview). We evaluate our extension on two publicly available data sets and also compare the Grassmannian-based level fusion technique to the popular Gaussian Process Morphable Models framework [15].

2   Background

In this Section, we will first briefly introduce our mathematical notation for describing SSMs and summarize the original localization method from [25].

2.1   Classical Statistical Shape Models and Affine Subspaces

For SSM training, we assume a training population of $(\mathbf{s}_s)_{s=1}^{n_s}$ vectorized shape representations $\mathbf{s}_s \in \mathbb{R}^{n_p n_d}$ to be given. Each vector $\mathbf{s}_s$ is formed by vertically stacking the n_d sub-coordinates of a shape's n_p points. Points need to be in correspondence across the population and can either be sparsely sampled from an object's surface (contours or meshes) or densely distributed across its volume when derived from images or registration-based displacement fields.

Following [3], a SSM is then generated via eigendecomposition of the population's positive semi definite (p.s.d.) covariance matrix $\mathbf{C} \in \mathbb{R}^{m \times m}$ ($m = n_p n_d$):

$$\mathbf{C} = \frac{1}{n_s} \sum_{s=1}^{n_s} (\mathbf{s}_s - \bar{\mathbf{s}})(\mathbf{s}_s - \bar{\mathbf{s}})^T = \frac{1}{n_s} \mathbf{S}\mathbf{S}^T = \mathbf{P}\mathbf{\Lambda}\mathbf{P}^T \text{ with } \bar{\mathbf{s}} = \frac{1}{n_s} \sum_{s=1}^{n_s} \mathbf{s}_s. \quad (1)$$

Here, $\bar{\mathbf{s}}$ denotes the mean shape, columns of $\mathbf{P} \in \mathbb{R}^{m \times m}$ are the orthornomal eigenvectors of $\mathbf{C}$, and the diagonal matrix $\mathbf{\Lambda} \in \mathbb{R}^{m \times m}$ holds the corresponding eigenvalues. Usually, only the eigenvectors $\mathbf{P}_q \in \mathbb{R}^{m \times q}$ with the $q \ll m$ largest positive eigenvalues $\mathbf{\Lambda}_q \in \mathbb{R}^{q \times q}$ are used to form a SSM $(\mathcal{A}, \mathbf{\Lambda}_q)$. $\mathcal{A} = \{\bar{\mathbf{s}} + \mathbf{w} | \mathbf{w} \in \text{span}(\mathbf{P}_q)\}$ is a q-dimensional affine subspace of maximum shape variation in $\mathbb{R}^m$ with eigenvalues $\mathbf{\Lambda}_q$. Transport between $\mathbb{R}^m$ and $\mathcal{A}$ is possible via $\mathbf{s} = \bar{\mathbf{s}} + \mathbf{P}_q \mathbf{z}$ and $\mathbf{z} = \mathbf{P}_q^T(\mathbf{s} - \bar{\mathbf{s}})$. New shapes $\mathbf{s}$ similar to the training data can conveniently be generated by sampling parameters $\mathbf{z} \in \mathbb{R}^q$ from a normal distribution $\mathcal{N}(\mathbf{0}, \mathbf{\Lambda}_q)$.

When $n_s \ll m$ (few training samples), the expressiveness and flexibility of the SSM is limited as q cannot exceed the rank of $\mathbf{C}$: $q \leq \text{rank}(\mathbf{C}) \leq (n_s - 1)$. As a result, a low dimensional subspace will usually predominantly cover global shape variability and frequently fail to represent local variations. Furthermore, this low-rank structure allows to avoid costly explicit estimation of large $\mathbf{C}$ by computing $\mathbf{P}_q$ from $n_s \times n_s$ inner-product $\mathbf{S}^T\mathbf{S}$ instead [3].

2.2   Multi-level Localized Shape Models

In [25], additional flexibility is introduced into the training procedure by removing the covariances estimated from the training data between distant points (principle of locality). This artificially increases the rank of $\mathbf{C}$ beyond n_s and potentially results in more flexible, localized shape models. To do so, a symmetric distance function (e.g. Euclidean or geodesic) $d : \mathbb{R}^{n_d} \times \mathbb{R}^{n_d} \to \mathbb{R}_{\geq 0}$ between points $\mathbf{x}_i, \mathbf{x}_j \in \mathbb{R}^{n_d}$ on the mean shape and an accompanying distance threshold $\tau \in \mathbb{R}_{\geq 0}$ are defined. A thresholded matrix $\mathbf{C}_\tau \in \mathbb{R}^{m \times m}$ is then generated from the n_p^2 submatrices $\mathbf{C}_{ij} \in \mathbb{R}^{n_d \times n_d}$ of $\mathbf{C}$ by setting elements for which $d(\mathbf{x}_i, \mathbf{x}_j) > \tau$ to zero while data for closer points is preserved:

$$(\mathbf{C}_\tau)_{ij} = \begin{cases} \mathbf{C}_{ij} & , \text{ if } d(\mathbf{x}_i, \mathbf{x}_j) \leq \tau \\ \mathbf{0}_{n_d \times n_d} & , \text{ otherwise} \end{cases} . \tag{2}$$

$\mathbf{C}_\tau$ is then used instead of $\mathbf{C}$ to estimate the SSM. The idea is then to model the shape variability at n_l different levels of localization (from global to local) by manipulating $\mathbf{C}$ with a series of increasing thresholds $\tau_1 > \ldots > \tau_{n_l}$ resulting in a hierarchy of localized SSMs/affine subspaces $(\mathcal{A}_l)_{l=1}^{n_l}$ with dimensions $q_1 \leq \ldots \leq q_{n_l}$. They are then successively fused/combined into a single subspace $\mathcal{A}_{n_l}^*$ with dimension q_{n_l}, which preserves properties of more global levels and adds complementary more local information introduced at each additional level. The main idea underlying this scheme is that more global information can usually be estimated more robustly from limited real data and such information should therefore be given priority over more local variability.

Starting with $\mathcal{A}_1^* = \mathcal{A}_1$ (optimal most global model) and $\mathcal{A}_2$ (more local), this idea can be efficiently implemented via iteratively solving $n_l - 1$ optimization problems on the Grassmannian manifold of q_l-dimensional subspaces (see [25]):

$$\mathcal{A}_l^* = \underset{\mathcal{A} \in Gr(q_l, m)}{\arg\min} \ d_{Gr}(\mathcal{A}, \mathcal{A}_l) \quad \text{s.t.} \quad \mathcal{A}_{l-1}^* \subseteq \mathcal{A} . \tag{3}$$

Here, $\mathcal{A}_l^*$ is the optimal, fused model at level l that preserves the more global information from $\mathcal{A}_{l-1}^*$ (previous lvl.) while being as close as possible to the more local subspace $\mathcal{A}_l$ (current lvl.). This is quantified via the geodesic distance $d_{Gr}(\cdot, \cdot)$ on the Grassmannian $Gr(q_l, m)$ of q_l-dimensional subspaces of $\mathbb{R}^m$.

Computational requirements preventing its use for large m: Implementing this scheme as suggested in [25] has two major shortcomings: (1) Generating $m \times m$ matrix $\mathbf{C}_\tau$ in Eq. (2) and its eigendecomposition leads to a time and space complexity[1] of $\mathcal{O}(m^3)$ and $\mathcal{O}(m^2)$, respectively, for the entire pipeline. (2) Matrix $\mathbf{C}_\tau$ is frequently non-p.s.d. with negative eigenvalues [25]. In [25], this problem is tackled by converting $\mathbf{C}_\tau$ into the closest p.s.d. covariance matrix, which again requires several eigendecompositions. Both of these aspects prevent its use when m is large (= many points n_p) even on modern hardware.

---

[1] Naive implementation of the eigendecomposition algorithm is assumed here.

3 Kernelized Multi-level Localization Method

Our goal is to extend the multi-level localization method from Sect. 2.2 in a way that allows its use with large m while preserving its main characteristics (distance-based thresholding, hierarchy of subspaces, level fusion on Grassmannian). To achieve this, we propose to replace the costly eigendecomposition of full $\mathbf{C}_\tau$ with a recent efficient and accurate approximative decomposition approach for large p.s.d. matrices [21] that only uses few random samples from $\mathbf{C}_\tau$.

3.1 Randomized Low-Rank Eigendecomposition

The basic idea is to compute $\mathbf{P}_q \in \mathbb{R}^{m \times q}$ from a low-rank approximation $\mathbf{C}_\tau \approx \mathbf{RWR}^\mathbf{T}$ with $q \le r \ll m$, $\mathbf{R} \in \mathbb{R}^{m \times r}$, and $\mathbf{W} \in \mathbb{R}^{r \times r}$. Here, $\mathbf{R}$ is composed of randomly sampled entries of $\mathbf{C}_\tau$ and $\mathbf{W}$ is computed from a random sketch of $\mathbf{C}_\tau$ as well, with r being an user-specified sampling factor related to the desired rank and accuracy. In total and with our configuration ($r \approx 10q$), the algorithm from [21] only needs to see (roughly) $mr + (10r)^2 \ll m^2$ entries of $\mathbf{C}_\tau$. This results in an eigendecomposition time and space complexity (slightly simplified here) of $\mathcal{O}(mr^3 + mr^2)$ and $\mathcal{O}(mr + r^2)$, respectively, both linear in m.

3.2 Kernel-Based Covariance Thresholding

Using the randomized decomposition method requires (1) an efficient way to compute entries of $\mathbf{C}_\tau$ for random sampling and (2) $\mathbf{C}_\tau$ to be p.s.d.. The second aspect in particular requires a modification to the pipeline described in Sec. 2.2 to prevent $\mathbf{C}_\tau$ from becoming non-p.s.d. through thresholding. We will jointly address both requirements by deriving a kernel-based formulation here.

Let a scalar-valued kernel $k : \mathcal{X} \times \mathcal{X} \to \mathbb{R}$ be a symmetric, positive definite (p.d.) function over domain $\mathcal{X}$ [24]. Moreover, a matrix-valued kernel is a symmetric function $K : \mathcal{X} \times \mathcal{X} \to \mathbb{R}^{n_d \times n_d}$ generating symmetric p.s.d. matrices [1]. Multiplication preserves kernel properties [24] allowing us to combine Eqs. (1–2):

$$(\mathbf{C}_\tau)_{ij} = K_{cov}(\mathbf{x}_i, \mathbf{x}_j) k_{mod}(\mathbf{x}_i, \mathbf{x}_j; \tau) \text{ with}$$

$$K_{cov}(\mathbf{x}_i, \mathbf{x}_j) = \frac{1}{n_s} \sum_{s=1}^{n_s} (\mathbf{s}_s[\mathbf{x}_i] - \bar{\mathbf{s}}[\mathbf{x}_i])(\mathbf{s}_s[\mathbf{x}_j] - \bar{\mathbf{s}}[\mathbf{x}_j])^T = \mathbf{C}_{ij} . \tag{4}$$

Here, K_{cov} is a kernel computing the $n_d \times n_d$ block of covariances between points $\mathbf{x}_i$ and $\mathbf{x}_j$ and k_{mod} is the scalar-valued thresholding kernel used to manipulate covariances based on the distance between $\mathbf{x}_i$ and $\mathbf{x}_j$ with threshold τ.

Constructing $\mathbf{C}_\tau$ with valid kernels K_{cov} and k_{mod} guarantees the matrix to be p.s.d. and also provides an easy way to compute blocks or single elements for the randomized sampling. As K_{cov} is a kernel by construction, $\mathbf{C}_\tau$ not always being p.s.d. in [25] means that hard thresholding following Eq. (2) does not lead to a valid kernel k_{mod} (see suppl. material for an interpretation of a kernel k_{mod} arising from Eq. (2) as a Heaviside function that cannot be guaranteed to be p.d.). Hence, we need to use a valid distance-based kernel for k_{mod}.

The positive definiteness of a distance-based kernel function is heavily influenced by the actual distance $d(\cdot,\cdot)$ used. Therefore, kernel and distance always need to be chosen as pairs. Research on this issue is scarce and proofs only exist for standard choices (see [8]). In this work, we will only use exponential kernels

$$k_{mod}(\mathbf{x}_i,\mathbf{x}_j;\tau) = \exp\left(-\gamma d(\mathbf{x}_i,\mathbf{x}_j)^p\right) \text{ with } \gamma,p \in \mathbb{R}_{>0}, \tag{5}$$

for which, for example, p.d. proofs exist for $p = 2$ (Gaussian kernel) when $d(\cdot,\cdot)$ is an Euclidean distance. Note that a Gaussian kernel cannot generally be used with geodesic distances [8]. Depending on its exact parameterization (here: $\gamma = 1/(2\tau^2)$ and $p = 2$), k_{mod} now mimics the thresholding from Eq. (2) in a p.d. way. After kernel-based manipulation/eigendecomposition, the Grassmannian-based fusion approach from Eq. (3) can be applied to fuse a sequence of subspaces.

Relation to Gaussian Process Morphable Models: Our method shares similarities with the Gaussian Process Morphable Models framework [11,15] that also allows for kernel-based covariance manipulation for shape model localization in a Gaussian Process (GP)-like [24] environment. In contrast to our work, this approach does not directly aim for multi-level localization and uses Nyström-based eigendecomposition. However, in [15], a standard technique from GPs (linear combinations of kernels are kernels [24]) is employed to do multi-scale shape analysis. We adopt this idea to directly derive a single manipulated covariance matrix $\mathbf{C}^*_{n_l}$ that contains localization information from all n_l levels leading to a combined subspace $\mathcal{A}^*_{n_l}$:

$$(\mathbf{C}^*_{n_l})_{ij} = K_{cov}(\mathbf{x}_i,\mathbf{x}_j) \sum_{l=1}^{n_l} w_l k_{mod}(\mathbf{x}_i,\mathbf{x}_j;\tau_l). \tag{6}$$

Here, $w_l \in \mathbb{R}$ is a level-specific weight to emphasize specific levels. Equation (6) will be used as an alternative fusion method in our experiments.

4   Experiments and Results

Our evaluation's three main goals are: (1) Comparison of the proposed kernelized multi-level localization method with its original formulation when used with few training samples. (2) Effectiveness of its performance for large-scale modeling. (3) Comparison of Grassmannian- and kernel-based multi-level model fusion.

Data: Two publicly available data sets are used. (1) The JSRT/SCR chest radiograph database [9,18] includes manually defined, point-based 2D shapes for 5 different structures (right & left lung, heart, right & left clavicle; in total represented by $n_p = 166$ points; Fig. 2) from 247 patients. This data was also used in [25] and we follow their scheme and divide the 247 cases into training/test sets of 123/124 shapes. (2) The 581 T1 brain MRI images from the IXI database[2]

---

[2] https://brain-development.org/ixi-dataset/.

for which no manually defined shape data is available. Hence, we start by non-linearly registering all images to a IXI-specific brain template ([2]; $256 \times 256 \times 150$ voxel; spacing $\approx 1\,mm$; Fig. 2) using ITK's *VariationalRegistration* [7,23]. The resulting dense displacement fields encode multi-object shape differences between the template's anatomy and all patients. Masked versions of the displacement fields (template's brain mask with 1159091 voxels) are used as inputs for shape modeling. 19 cases with mis-registrations had to be excluded. All remaining 562 displacement fields are randomly split into a training/test set of 250/312 cases.

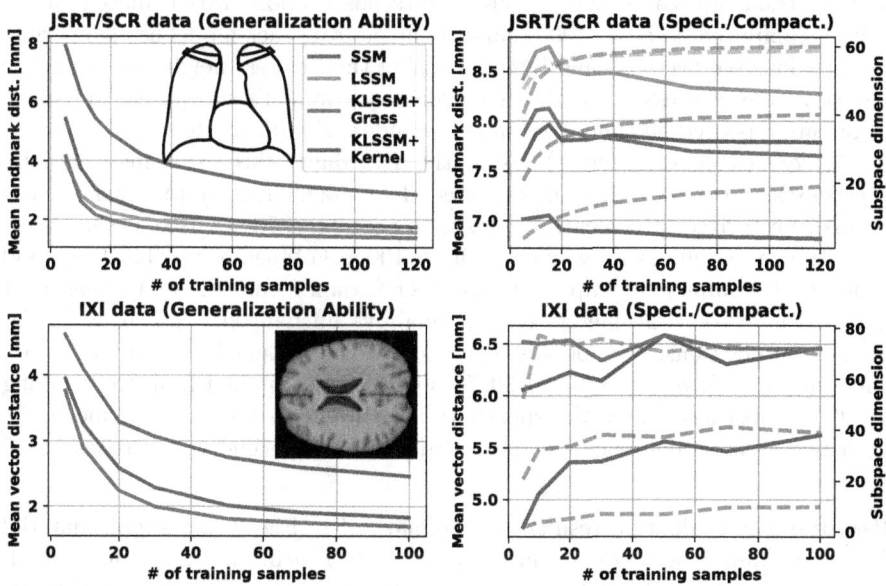

Fig. 2. Visualization of the results for both experiments averaged over all repetitions (JSRT/SCR: top; IXI: bottom). Right: solid lines indicate specificity (lower = better); dashed lines correspond to compactness. See suppl. material for table version. Furthermore, the JSRT/SCR mean shape and the IXI brain template are visualized.

Experimental Design: We conduct two different experiments: (1, *small-scale experiment*) This experiment uses the JSRT/SCR data and aims at confirming that the new kernelized version is as effective in few training data scenarios as the original approach. 2D point data of all five structures are fused into one shape vector per case to handle multiple objects with $m = 332$ ($n_p = 166$; $n_d = 2$). From the training set, subsets of $n_s \in \{5, 10, 15, 20, 30, 40, 70, 120\}$ shapes are randomly sampled to simulate training scenarios of varying sizes. Then, four different modeling approaches are trained on the sampled sets: Standard PCA model (Sect. 2.1, *SSM*); Non-kernelized localized model (Sec. 2.2, *LSSM*); Kernelized localized model with Grassmannian fusion (Sec. 3 & Eq. (3), *KLSSM+Grass*); *KLSSM* with kernel-based fusion (Eq. (6), *KLSSM+Kernel*;

equivalent to a GP Morphable Model). Code and parameters for *SSM* and *LSSM* (e.g., $n_l = 5$) are taken from [25]. Our code is available on github[3]. For both *KLSSM* variants, we use the heuristically chosen Gaussian kernel from Sec. 3.2, $r = 332$ for eigendecompositions, and $d(\cdot, \cdot)$ is the Euclidean distance in $\mathbb{R}^2$. The combined Euclidean/geodesic distance from [25] is not compatible with the Gaussian kernel. For all models/levels subspace size q is chosen to cover 95% of the variability according to a model's eigenvalues and for *KLSSM+Kernel*, $w_l = \frac{1}{n_l}$ for all levels. Models are analyzed via generalization ability, specificity, and compactness [5]. For generalization ability, mean landmark distances between test shapes and their model-based reconstructions are calculated. Specificity is computed based on 1000 shapes sampled from each model using a normal distribution (see Sec. 2.1) and by determining their closest neighbours from the test set. Compactness is the dimensionality of a model's subspace. All experiments are repeated 50 times to minimize random sampling effects.

(2, *large-scale experiment*) Using the IXI data, this experiment mimics a large-scale scenario (e.g., model-based data augmentation to generate new brains). Vectorized displacement fields with $m = 3477273$ are used as shape vectors. Here, a $m \times m$ matrix would require ≈ 100 TB of memory (64bit float), and hence *LSSM* cannot be employed. All other variants from the first experiment are used here too. Parameters remain (mainly) unchanged (e.g., $n_l = 5$). For eigendecompositions, $r = 700$ is selected, $d(\cdot, \cdot)$ is the Euclidean distance in $\mathbb{R}^3$, and subsets with $n_s \in \{5, 10, 20, 30, 70, 50, 100\}$ are sampled from the training set. Generalization ability and specificity measurements are based on mean displacement vector differences to the test data. All experiments are repeated 10 times.

Results: The evaluation results are summarized in Fig. 2 (see suppl. material for tables) and generally confirm the advantage of using localized shape models as they consistently and significantly outperform the *SSM* models in terms of generalization ability for all n_s (paired t-tests with $p < 0.05$). Results for the JSRT/SCR data also illustrate that *KLSSM+Grass* (new method) is as effective as *LSSM*. Only for $n_s = 5$, *LSSM* reaches a slightly superior generalization ability than *KLSSM+Grass* (3.96 ± 0.44 vs. 4.15 ± 0.37). For all other n_s, *KLSSM+Grass* even significantly outperforms *LSSM* with equally compact models but better specificity scores. This could indicate that levels generated via kernelization are globally more consistent than those from the p.d. correction step used with *LSSM* leading to more plausible samples. From the results for the IXI data, we see that *KLSSM+Grass* is able to handle massive data. It consistently and significantly outperforms *SSM* for all n_s (see also suppl. material Fig. 1) and models can be trained in ≈ 30 min on 4 cores of an Intel Xeon 6148 CPU @ 2.40 GHz with 64 GB RAM. This confirms the effectiveness of the proposed kernelized formulation.

Comparing *KLSSM+Grass* and *KLSSM+Kernel* reveals that Grassmannian-based level fusion leads to models with better generalization abilities than the

---

[3] https://github.com/wilmsm/localizedssm.

kernel-based fusion derived from the GP Morphable Models framework (diffs. significant for all experiments). *KLSSM+Grass* models tend to be larger with a slightly reduced specificity for very small sample sizes. However, analyzing their generalization abilities at the same specificity level (see suppl. material Fig. 2) shows that *KLSSM+Grass* still significantly outperforms *KLSSM+Kernel*. We, therefore, conclude that *KLSSM+Grass*'s additional dimensions are informative.

5   Conclusion

In this paper, we presented a novel, kernel-based extension of a recent state-of-the-art multi-level localization approach for building flexible shape models from few training samples [25]. While the original method can only handle small shapes, our extension allows its use on large-scale shape modeling problems. We, therefore, see many new applications for this method in previously unreachable scenarios like 3D data augmentation for deep learning [20] or other large-scale scenarios where shape models are used to guide segmentation, image registration, or classification approaches.

The results of our extensive evaluation on two publicly available data sets do not only illustrate the effectiveness of the proposed extension but also show that kernelization improves the method's general performance for shape modeling with few training data. Furthermore, our results indicate a superior performance of the Grassmannian-based model fusion technique, a key element of the proposed method, in comparison to multi-level localization within the popular Gaussian Process Morphable Models framework [15]. Further research could, therefore, explore its use in other applications where models need to be combined (e.g., [17]). In terms of kernel-based localization, we are currently working on ways to directly employ (multi-object) geodesic-like distances naturally arising in shape modeling scenarios. We also plan to analyze the effects different kernels/parameterizations as well as other eigendecomposition strategies [6] have on the localization results.

Acknowledgements. This work was supported by the University of Calgary's Eyes High postdoctoral scholarship program and the River Fund at Calgary Foundation.

References

1. Alvarez, M.A., Rosasco, L., Lawrence, N.D., et al.: Kernels for vector-valued functions: a review. Found. Trends Mach. Learn. **4**(3), 195–266 (2012)
2. Avants, B., Tustison, N.: ANTs/ANTsR brain templates (2014). https://doi.org/10.6084/m9.figshare.915436.v2
3. Cootes, T., Taylor, C., Cooper, D., Graham, J.: Active shape models-their training and application. CVIU **61**(1), 38–59 (1995)
4. Cootes, T.F., Taylor, C.J.: Data driven refinement of active shape model search. In: British Machine Vision Conference - BMVC, 1996, pp. 1–10 (1996)

5. Davies, R., Twining, C., Cootes, T., Waterton, J., Taylor, C.: A minimum description length approach to statistical shape modeling. IEEE Trans. Med. Imaging **21**(5), 525–537 (2002)

6. Dölz, J., Gerig, T., Lüthi, M., Harbrecht, H., Vetter, T.: Error-controlled model approximation for gaussian process morphable models. J. Math. Imaging Vision **61**(4), 443–457 (2019)

7. Ehrhardt, J., Schmidt-Richberg, A., Werner, R., Handels, H.: Variational registration - a flexible open-source itk toolbox for nonrigid image registration. Bildverarbeitung für die Medizin **2015**, 209–214 (2015)

8. Feragen, A., Lauze, F., Hauberg, S.: Geodesic exponential kernels: when curvature and linearity conflict. In: Proceedings of the IEEE Conference on Computer Vision and Pattern Recognition, pp. 3032–3042 (2015)

9. van Ginneken, B., Stegmann, M.B., Loog, M.: Segmentation of anatomical structures in chest radiographs using supervised methods: a comparative study on a public database. Med. Image Anal. **10**(1), 19–40 (2006)

10. Heimann, T., Meinzer, H.P.: Statistical shape models for 3d medical image segmentation: a review. Med. Image Anal. **13**(4), 543–563 (2009)

11. Jud, C., Giger, A., Sandkühler, R., Cattin, P.C.: A localized statistical motion model as a reproducing kernel for non-rigid image registration. In: Descoteaux, M., Maier-Hein, L., Franz, A., Jannin, P., Collins, D.L., Duchesne, S. (eds.) MICCAI 2017. LNCS, vol. 10434, pp. 261–269. Springer, Cham (2017). https://doi.org/10.1007/978-3-319-66185-8_30

12. Karimi, D., Samei, G., Kesch, C., Nir, G., Salcudean, S.E.: Prostate segmentation in MRI using a convolutional neural network architecture and training strategy based on statistical shape models. Int. J. Comput. Assist. Radiol. Surg. **13**(8), 1211–1219 (2018)

13. Kollias, D., Cheng, S., Ververas, E., Kotsia, I., Zafeiriou, S.: Deep neural network augmentation: generating faces for affect analysis. Int. J. Comput. Vision **128**(5), 1455–1484 (2020). https://doi.org/10.1007/s11263-020-01304-3

14. Lin, A., Wu, J., Yang, X.: A data augmentation approach to train fully convolutional networks for left ventricle segmentation. Magn. Reson. Imaging **66**, 152–164 (2019)

15. Lüthi, M., Gerig, T., Jud, C., Vetter, T.: Gaussian process morphable models. IEEE Trans. Pattern Anal. Mach. Intell. **40**(8), 1860–1873 (2018)

16. Milletari, F., Rothberg, A., Jia, J., Sofka, M.: Integrating statistical prior knowledge into convolutional neural networks. In: Descoteaux, M., Maier-Hein, L., Franz, A., Jannin, P., Collins, D.L., Duchesne, S. (eds.) MICCAI 2017. LNCS, vol. 10433, pp. 161–168. Springer, Cham (2017). https://doi.org/10.1007/978-3-319-66182-7_19

17. Ploumpis, S., Wang, H., Pears, N., Smith, W.A., Zafeiriou, S.: Combining 3d morphable models: A large scale face-and-head model. In: CVPR, pp. 10934–10943 (2019)

18. Shiraishi, J., et al.: Development of a digital image database for chest radiographs with and without a lung nodule: receiver operating characteristic analysis of radiologists' detection of pulmonary nodules. Am. J. Roentgenol. **174**(1), 71–74 (2000)

19. Tang, Z., Chen, K., Pan, M., Wang, M., Song, Z.: An augmentation strategy for medical image processing based on statistical shape model and 3D thin plate spline for deep learning. IEEE Access **7**, 133111–133121 (2019)

20. Uzunova, H., Wilms, M., Handels, H., Ehrhardt, J.: Training CNNS for image registration from few samples with model-based data augmentation. In: Descoteaux, M., Maier-Hein, L., Franz, A., Jannin, P., Collins, D.L., Duchesne, S. (eds.) Med Image Comput Comput Assist Interv - MICCAI 2017. LNCS, vol. 10433, pp. 223–231. Springer, Cham (2017)
21. Wang, S., Zhang, Z., Zhang, T.: Towards more efficient SPSD matrix approximation and CUR matrix decomposition. J. Mach. Learn. Res. **17**(210), 1–49 (2016)
22. Wang, Y., Staib, L.H.: Boundary finding with prior shape and smoothness models. IEEE Trans. Pattern Anal. Mach. Intell. **22**(7), 738–743 (2000)
23. Werner, R., Schmidt-Richberg, A., Handels, H., Ehrhardt, J.: Estimation of lung motion fields in 4D CT data by variational non-linear intensity-based registration: a comparison and evaluation study. Phys. Med. Biol. **59**(15), 4247–4260 (2014)
24. Williams, C.K., Rasmussen, C.E.: Gaussian processes for machine learning, vol. 2. MIT press, Cambridge (2006)
25. Wilms, M., Handels, H., Ehrhardt, J.: Multi-resolution multi-object statistical shape models based on the locality assumption. Med. Image Anal. **38**(5), 17–29 (2017)
26. Wilms, M., Handels, H., Ehrhardt, J.: Representative patch-based active appearance models generated from small training populations. In: Descoteaux, M., Maier-Hein, L., Franz, A., Jannin, P., Collins, D.L., Duchesne, S. (eds.) MICCAI 2017. LNCS, vol. 10433, pp. 152–160. Springer, Cham (2017). https://doi.org/10.1007/978-3-319-66182-7_18
27. Yu, X., Zhou, F., Chandraker, M.: Deep deformation network for object landmark localization. In: Leibe, B., Matas, J., Sebe, N., Welling, M. (eds.) ECCV 2016. LNCS, vol. 9909, pp. 52–70. Springer, Cham (2016). https://doi.org/10.1007/978-3-319-46454-1_4
28. Zhang, H., Li, Q., Sun, Z., Liu, Y.: Combining data-driven and model-driven methods for robust facial landmark detection. IEEE Trans. Inf. Forensics Secur. **13**(10), 2409–2422 (2018)
29. Zhao, A., Balakrishnan, G., Durand, F., Guttag, J.V., Dalca, A.V.: Data augmentation using learned transformations for one-shot medical image segmentation. In: CVPR 2019, pp. 8543–8553 (2019)

Unsupervised Learning and Statistical Shape Modeling of the Morphometry and Hemodynamics of Coarctation of the Aorta

Bente Thamsen[1] (iD), Pavlo Yevtushenko[1], Lina Gundelwein[2], Hans Lamecker[2], Titus Kühne[1,3] (iD), and Leonid Goubergrits[1,4(✉)] (iD)

[1] Institute for Imaging Science and Computational Modelling in Cardiovascular Medicine, Charité - Universitaetsmedizin Berlin, Berlin, Germany
leonid.goubergrits@charite.de
[2] 1000shapes GmbH, Berlin, Germany
[3] DZHK (German Centre for Cardiovascular Research), Partner Site Berlin, Berlin, Germany
[4] Einstein Center Digital Future, Berlin, Germany

Abstract. Image-based patient-specific modeling of blood flow is a current state of the art approach in cardiovascular research proposed to support diagnosis and treatment decision. However, the approach is time-consuming, and the absence of large data sets limits the applicability of Machine Learning (ML) technology. This study employs Statistical Shape Models (SSM) and unsupervised ML to interconnect the morphometry and hemodynamics for the congenital heart disease coarctation of the aorta (CoA). Based on magnetic resonance imaging (MRI) data of 154 subjects, an SSM of the stenosed aorta was developed using principal component analysis, and three clusters were identified using agglomerative hierarchical clustering. An additional statistical model describing inlet boundary velocity fields was developed based on 4D-flow MRI measurements. A synthetic database with shape and flow parameters based on statistic characteristics of the patient population was generated and pressure gradients (dP), wall shear stress (WSS), kinetic energy (KE) and secondary flow degree (SFD) were simulated using Computational Fluid Dynamics (STAR CCM +). The synthetic population with 2652 cases had similar shape and hemodynamic properties compared to a real patient cohort. Using Kruskal Wallis test we found significant differences between clusters in real and synthetic data for morphologic measures (H/W-ratio and stenosis degree) and for hemodynamic parameters of mean WSS, dP, KE sum and mean SFD. Synthetic data for anatomy and hemodynamics based on statistical shape analysis is a powerful methodology in cardiovascular research allowing to close a gap of data availability for ML.

Keywords: Cardiovascular modelling · Computational Fluid Dynamics · Coarctation of the aorta · Machine Learning · Cluster analysis · Statistical Shape Model

© Springer Nature Switzerland AG 2020
A. L. Martel et al. (Eds.): MICCAI 2020, LNCS 12264, pp. 776–785, 2020.
https://doi.org/10.1007/978-3-030-59719-1_75

1 Introduction

Congenital heart diseases (CHD) such as coarctation of the aorta (CoA), which manifests in a constriction of the aortic arch, are associated with abnormal hemodynamic conditions [1, 2]. Survival rates after surgical repair of the obstruction have improved significantly over the last decades. Nevertheless, long-term complications such as high blood pressure are frequently observed [3] with an unknown causality.

Computational modeling of the cardiovascular system in combination with advanced medical imaging is a promising tool to improve clinical diagnostics and support treatment decisions [4]. Especially patient-specific Computational Fluid Dynamics (CFD) simulations facilitate a detailed evaluation of hemodynamics and subsequent tailoring of individual treatment options [5, 6]. Such simulations still have a high demand of computational power and require trained specialists, which makes their integration into clinical routine nearly impossible.

Machine Learning (ML) methods on the other hand allow for quick and low-cost computations. ML enhances the understanding of complex biophysical systems, enables the discovery of patterns in large datasets and is already used in the cardiovascular field [7, 8]. Unsupervised hierarchical clustering of the three-dimensional aortic shape has previously been used to identify clinically meaningful subgroups of CHD patients [9]. Combining such analysis with descriptive statistics may reveal new insights into a disease and identify unknown relations between the symptoms and the anatomical shape of the diseased organ. However, ML algorithms usually need a large database in order to achieve adequate and meaningful results.

In this work, we aim to connect numerical simulation and ML to identify and quantify intra- and inter-correlation of the morphometry and the hemodynamics of the CoA. The final objective of this work is to generate novel knowledge that could support the diagnosis and treatment of CoA.

2 Methods

2.1 Patient Population and Data Acquisition

A large synthetic database of realistic CoA cases was generated based on a relatively small patient cohort of 154 subjects. A Statistical Shape Model (SSM), which captures the shape variability of the aortic arch was used. Magnetic resonance imaging (MRI) data acquired from patients with different indications (CoA, aortic or mitral valve disease) and healthy volunteers at the German Heart Institute Berlin served as training data. The study met the requirements of the Helsinki Declaration and was approved by the institutional ethics committee. Written informed consent was obtained from all study participants and/or their legal guardians. The study was registered with ClinicalTrials.gov (NCT02591940).

A 1.5T Philips Achieva (Philips Medical Systems, Best, The Netherlands) was used with balanced 3D steady-state free-precession (SSFP) imaging for the assessment of aorta anatomy attaining an acquired voxel size of $1.5 \times 1.5 \times 3.2$ mm^3 and a reconstructed voxel size of $0.66 \times 0.66 \times 1.6$ mm^3, with a repetition time of 4 ms, an echo time of 2 ms, a flip angle of 90° and 3 signal averages (navigator gated and ECG triggered).

In 53 CoA patients and 14 healthy subjects, 4D flow measurements were simultaneously performed. The respective acquired voxel size was $2.55 \times 2.55 \times 2.5$ mm^3, reconstructed voxel size $1.72 \times 1.72 \times 2.5$ mm^3, repetition time 3.5 ms, echo time 2.2 ms, flip angle $5°$ and the number of signal averages 1. The velocity encoding adapted to optimize velocity resolution was around 4 m/s.

Demographic data and key shape and flow parameters are summarized in Table 1. We conducted a Kolmogorov-Smirnov test using Matlab (The MathWorks, Inc., Natick, MA, USA) to test for normal distributions, in which case, mean and standard deviation are reported instead of median and interquartile range (IQR).

Table 1. Patient demographics (A) and shape with flow parameters (B) of training data set.

A:	n=154	
Sex F/M (count, percentage)	48, 31 / 106, 69	
Age (median, IQR)	25 [15-54]	
Weight (kg) (mean ± std)	62.2 ± 22.2	
Height (cm) (median, IQR)	168 [152-177]	
BSA (median, IQR)	1.79 [1.42-1.94]	
Disease (CoA/ CoA+AVD/ AVD/ MVD/ Control) (count, percentage)	75/3/24/8/44, 48.7/2.0/15.6/5.2/28.6	
Bicuspid Aortic Valve (count, percentage)	47, 30.5	

B:	Definition	
Aortic Length (mm) (mean ± std)		237.4 ± 50.1
Inlet Diameter (mm) (mean ± std)		27.1 ± 8.1
Height/Width (H/W) ratio (-) (mean ± std)		0.64 ± 0.14
Stenosis degree (%) (median, IQR) Stenosis diameter D_{sten}, nominal descendens diameter D_{nom}	$SD = \left(1 - \dfrac{D_{sten}}{D_{nom}}\right) \cdot 100$	33.4 [17.1-65.5]
Ascendens Flow rate (mL/s) (mean ± std)		386.5 ± 113.4
Descendens Flow rate (mL/s) (mean ± std)		189.7 ± 84.9
Secondary Flow degree (-) (mean ± std) Mean in-plane velocities $v_i^{in-plane}$ and mean normal-to-plane velocities v_i^{normal}	$SFD = \dfrac{v_i^{in-plane}}{v_i^{normal}}$	0.51 ± 0.35

2.2   Pre-processing of Image and Flow Data

Aortic arch geometries were segmented from MRI images with the software package ZIB Amira (v. 2015.28, Zuse Institute Berlin, Germany) by combining a threshold-based filling algorithm and manual adjustments described in detail earlier [10]. Consistent aortic arch models were generated via cutting the aorta ascendens at the sinotubular junction, the three supra-aortic branches at approx. 15 mm length, and the aorta descendens at the height of the left ventricle apex. Further, the centerlines were extracted from the segmented geometries and the local radii were mapped onto the lines reflecting the thickness distribution of the vessel and its branches at 390 points. To generate a surface mesh describing the computational domain for the CFD, hull of circles of the respective local radii at each centerline point are connected and the result is processed with a smoothing algorithm.

From the 4D-flow MRI measurements, peak systolic flow rates in ascending and descending aorta as well as inlet vector fields at the sinotubular junction are obtained using the software MEVIS Flow v10.3 (Fraunhofer MEVIS, Bremen, Germany).

2.3 Statistical Models for Aortic Shapes and Inlet Vector Fields

Statistical shape models are an important tool, employed to enhance medical image data segmentation and anatomy reconstruction and widely used for statistical analysis of morphometric data in general [11]. Previously, SSM methodology was employed to study the aortic morphology and was shown to provide valuable insights about the link between aortic anatomy and clinical outcome [9, 12–15]. As a prerequisite for an SSM the training data must be aligned into a common coordinate system.

For the shape model of the aorta, the centerlines with radii were used as corresponding representations. Subsequently, a mean shape was identified, and all shapes were rigidly aligned by minimizing the sum of squared distances between corresponding points. No scaling was performed in order to maintain the size information.

Next, a Principal Component Analysis (PCA) was performed on the centerline coordinates and radii. PCA is a standard method to reduce the dimensionality of large datasets and to enhance interpretability, described in detail in literature [16]. To compensate for the different dimensions in the centerline model consisting of coordinates and radii, PCA was computed using the correlation matrix instead of the covariance matrix. The modes of variations (eigenvalues) resulting from the PCA together with the mean shape determine the SSM (see Fig. 1-B).

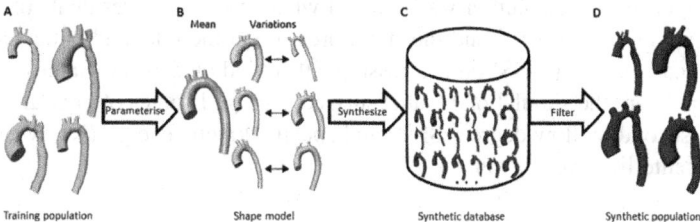

Fig. 1. The patient data (A) provide training data for the SSM (B) generation, which enables to synthesize new aortic shapes of a synthetic database (C) used to create custom populations (D).

Additionally, to provide a realistic velocity inlet profile for each shape, an SSM for the inlet velocity vector field was created. A representation of the training data is found by sampling the measured inlet velocity vector fields on a circular plane with a fixed mesh of 1028 points and 1956 faces. Second, the plane and vector fields are aligned to achieve a consistent spatial orientation of inlet boundaries. Third, the modes of variation are attained through a PCA.

2.4 Computational Fluid Dynamics Simulation

Hemodynamics of real and synthetic cases were computed with CFD simulations using the commercial software package Star CCM+ (Siemens, Munich, Germany). Unsteady Reynolds Averaged Navier-Stokes (URANS) equations were numerically solved with second order discretization for stationary boundary conditions at peak systole with a time step of 1 ms. Further, we assumed a rigid vessel wall and blood as an incompressible

Non-Newtonian fluid with shear-thinning characteristics implemented with the Carreau-Yasuda model [17]. Since Reynolds numbers are expected to be well above the transition value of 2300 for a pipe flow at the inlet, turbulence was considered with the k-ω Shear Stress Transport (SST) RANS turbulence model. A velocity inlet profile was prescribed using either the 4D-flow MRI vector field for the real cases if available or the statistical vector field model for the synthetic cases and real cases without 4D-flow MRI data. Turbulence intensity was assumed with 5% at the inlet boundary. At the outlet boundaries a flow split outlet was set defining the outflow rate relative to the inlet flow rate. The branching vessel flows F_i were specified according to Murray's law using the ascendens and descendens flow rates F_{asc} and F_{desc} and the branch vessel diameters D_i:

$$F_i = (F_{asc} - F_{desc}) \cdot \frac{D_i^3}{\sum_j^{N_B} D_j^3} \tag{1}$$

A polyhedral mesh with four inflation layers on the walls to resolve near wall flow was generated using StarCCM+ . Cell refinement at the walls ensured wall y+ values of below or close to one. A mesh independence study revealed a base cell size of 1.2 mm to be the best compromise between accuracy and computational effort. This base size results in average cell and vertex counts of around 600 k and 3 M, respectively, depending on the volume of the specific case.

Convergence of the solution was reached when normalized residuals of mass and momentum were below $1e^{-5}$ and the static pressure at the inlet and outlets as well as the wall shear stresses (WSS) on the vessel wall settled on constant values within a $\pm$ 5% margin. From the simulation results, surface-averaged values of pressure and WSS as well as secondary flow degree (SFD) and specific kinetic energy (KE) were derived along the centerline every 2 mm.

2.5 Synthetic Cohort

The SSM and the statistical vector field model now enabled new CoA cases to be synthesized by altering the weights of the principal modes of variation. By randomization a large database of >10000 synthetic shapes and inlet velocity vector fields were generated. Then, a stepwise filtering approach was applied to extract a synthetic population with characteristics simulating a realistic patient cohort. As shown in Fig. 1.

As a first step, the distribution properties of the training population were used to restrict the shape space for the synthetic population. Next, the simulated hemodynamics served to further eliminate non-physiological cases by neglecting all cases with pressure values lower than 0 mmHg or WSS larger than 100 Pa. Finally, we established a synthetic population that contained only diseased cases, thus, disregarding shapes with a stenosis degree lower than 20%. This way, a synthetic population of 2652 aortic morphologies and corresponding inlet velocity profiles was obtained.

2.6 Cluster Analysis

Descriptive statistics and clustering techniques were used to analyze, characterize and compare the real and synthetic CoA population. To identify clusters in the patient data, we used an agglomerative hierarchical clustering technique, which is an inherently unsupervised ML method since no prior information about the population is needed. The analysis was carried out on the shape vectors of the patient data consisting of the weights for each PCA mode. Further, we disregarded the first mode as it includes the size variance, which is mainly age related. Clustering settings were the average linkage method and the correlation distance metric, adapted to achieve clusters with similar sizes and large distances. Cluster assignments were transferred to the synthetic population by 1-nearest-neighbor classification using the correlation metric.

3   Results

Figure 2 illustrates the resulting SSM for the aortic shape including mean shape and shapes according to minimum and maximum weights for the first three PCA modes and the same for three clusters. The analysis found that 9 modes explain 90% of the cumulative shape variance, the first 3 modes already capture 70%.

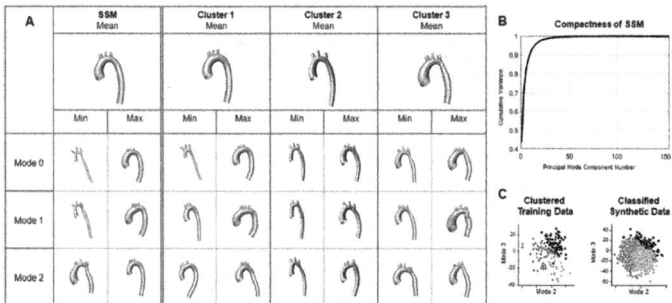

Fig. 2. A: Mean shapes with minimum and maximum weights of modes. B: Compactness of the SSM described by cumulative variance. C: Results of the clustering and classification procedure for the real training and synthetic data with regard to PCA modes 2 and 3.

3.1   Comparison of Real and Synthetic Population

The synthetic population is very similar to the training data distribution (see Fig. 3).

No significant differences were found according to Mann-Whitney U-test except for the inlet SFD ($p \leq 0.05$). Still, the median SFD values are close (0.4 and 0.51 for the real and synthetic population, respectively) and the range is very similar with only 3.7% of data points being outliers beyond 1.5 times the IQR.

3.2   Cluster Analysis

Three clusters, which included respectively 35, 25, and 22 cases, were identified. Respective clusters of synthetic data included 631, 1276, and 745 cases. Figures 4 and 5 show differences between clusters. Kruskal-Wallis test and a follow-up multiple comparison

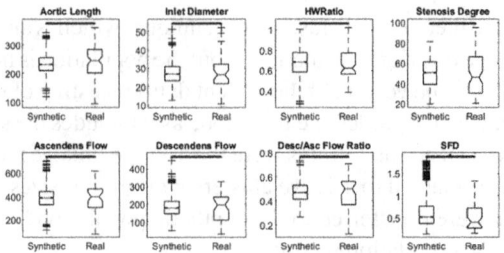

Fig. 3. Comparison of synthetic and patient populations for major morphometric and hemodynamic boundary conditions.

test found in the cluster 1 significantly lowest H/W ratios in comparison to cluster 2 (p = 0.005), lowest stenosis degrees were significant only when compared to cluster 3 (p < 0.001). WSS (p = 0.011), sum of KE (p < 0.001) and mean SFD (p = 0.003) were significantly lower in cluster 1 in comparison to cluster 2. Pressure gradients were significantly lower in cluster 1 vs. clusters 2 and 3 (p = 0.002).

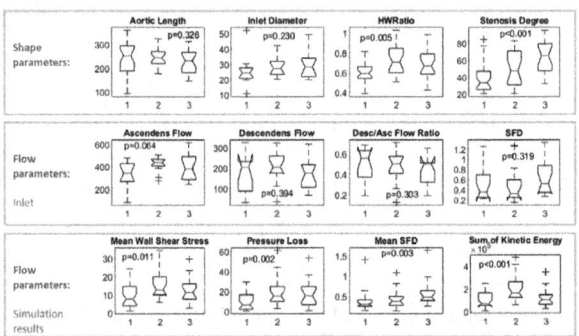

Fig. 4. Shape and flow parameters of the three clusters within the training data. Included p-values of Kruskal Wallis test indicate significant differences between the clusters.

The multiple comparison test for the synthetic data revealed for cluster 1 having significantly lower stenosis degrees, largest descendens flow rate, lowest mean WSS and lowest pressure loss. Cluster 2 had significantly lower aortic lengths and inlet diameters, lowest ascendens flow rates and largest mean WSS, pressure losses and sum of KE. In cluster 3, we found largest inlet diameters with largest inlet SFDs and largest simulated mean SFDs. However, the identified clusters show no direct correlation (see Fig. 6) with clinically introduced types of the aortic shape such as gothic, crenel, normal or S-kinked shapes [3].

4 Discussion and Conclusion

A large synthetic database using an SSM approach based on a relatively small number of 154 real cases including 44 healthy subjects was created to study shape and flow

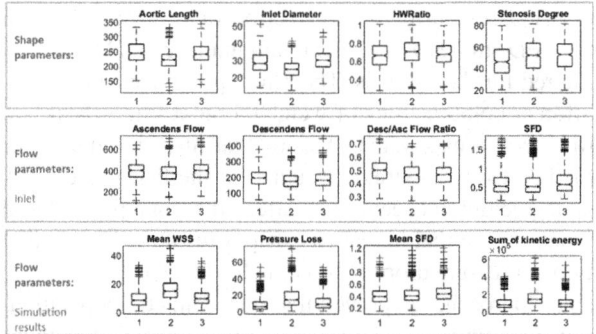

Fig. 5. Comparison of shape and flow parameters between three clusters within the synthetic population, Kruskal Wallis test found significant differences for all parameters with p < 0.001.

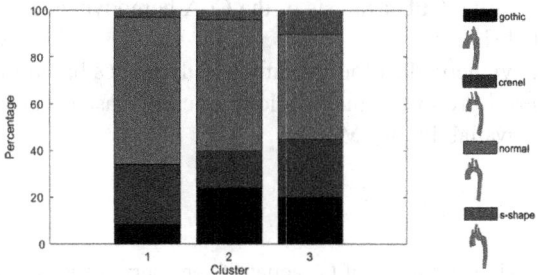

Fig. 6. Distribution of different anatomical shapes of the aorta in clusters.

characteristics of CoA. Similarly, Bruse et al. presented an SSM of the stenosed aorta but without side branches based on 60 cases including 20 healthy subjects and 40 CoA cases [9]. Thea found that the first 19 PCA modes explained 90% of the shape variability. Casciaro et al. explained 80% with the first three modes interpreted as size, arch unfolding and symmetry [15]. To identify shape clusters, we employed unsupervised hierarchical clustering and further analyzed differences in CFD derived hemodynamic parameters associated with abnormal hemodynamics [18]. Bruse et al. used hierarchical clustering to distinguish between shapes related to predefined clinically meaningful groups [9]. In our study we used the same approach as an unsupervised learning aiming to find new shape biomarkers. Such meaningful clustering may reveal new insights into CoA pathology and ultimately stimulate novel diagnosis and treatment strategies. It will be part of future work to relate the identified clusters to clinical diagnosis. Cluster analysis was done without the first mode. The first shape mode describes the scaling of the aorta, which correlates strongly with the patient age. Considering it during clustering, would result in clusters of the age groups represented in the training set. As scale is furthermore often not considered to be a parameter of shape, the clustering was done on the remaining modes.

To derive hemodynamics for the synthetic database we performed advanced semi-automized CFD simulations permitting a simulation of 82 untreated real and more than

2500 synthetic CoA cases during a short period of one year. This approach clearly outnumbers other CFD studies with a maximum number of 115 simulations [19].

Data were filtered for the analysis. The filtering removes unrealistic shapes, which can occur by different combinations of weighted modes, mostly if several modes are weighted towards the min/max value. We saw that filtering with regard to aortic size mostly disregarded cases with extreme weights for the first mode, while cases filtered by their stenosis degree did not seem to be effected by one particular mode but by the combination of many. Note that unrealistic shapes result in unrealistic hemodynamics such as, for example, pressure drops >100 mmHg.

To validate our approach, we proved that our synthetic population was similar in anatomic shape and hemodynamic characteristics to a real patient population. Therefore, the synthetic cohort is an adequate means to overcome the shortage of patient data. Employing SSM in combination with CFD was also reported by Khalafvand et al. to study hemodynamics in the left ventricle [20]. The current study does not include a clinical validation for the CFD analysis of the CoA hemodynamics since it was a part of our earlier study [5].

In conclusion, synthetic data for anatomy and dynamics based on statistical shape analysis is a powerful promising methodology in cardiovascular research allowing to close a gap of data availability for ML.

References

1. Brown, M.L., et al.: Coarctation of the aorta: lifelong surveillance is mandatory following surgical repair. J. Am. Coll. Cardiol. **62**, 1020–1025 (2013)
2. Kenny, D., Hijazi, Z.M.: Coarctation of the aorta: from fetal life to adult- hood. Cardiol J. **18**, 487–495 (2011)
3. Ou, P., et al.: Late systemic hypertension and aortic arch geometry after successful repair of coarctation of the aorta. Eur. Heart J. **25**, 1853–1859 (2004)
4. Kelm, M., et al.: Model-Based therapy planning allows prediction of haemodynamic outcome after aortic valve replacement. Sci. Rep. **7**(1), 9897 (2017)
5. Goubergrits, L., et al.: MRI-based computational fluid dynamics for diagnosis and treatment prediction: clinical validation study in patients with coarctation of aorta. J. Magn. Reson. Imaging **41**(4), 909–916 (2015)
6. Goubergrits, L., et al.: Is MRI-based CFD able to improve clinical treatment of coarctations of aorta? Ann. Biomed. Eng. **43**(1), 168–176 (2015)
7. Yu, K.-H., Beam, A.L., Kohane, I.S.: Artificial intelligence in healthcare. Nat. Biomed. Eng. **2**(10), 719–731 (2018)
8. Retson, T.A., Besser, A.H., Sall, S., Golden, D., Hsiao, A.: Machine learning and deep neural networks in thoracic and cardiovascular imaging. J. Thorac. Imaging **34**(3), 192–201 (2019)
9. Bruse, J.L., et al.: Detecting clinically meaningful shape clusters in medical image data: metrics analysis for hierarchical clustering applied to healthy and pathological aortic arches. IEEE Trans. Biomed. Eng. **64**(10), 2373–2383 (2017)
10. Goubergrits, L., et al.: The impact of MRI-based inflow for the hemodynamic evaluation of aortic coarctation. Ann. Biomed. Eng. **41**(12), 2575–2587 (2013)
11. Lamecker, H., Zachow, S.: Statistical shape modeling of musculoskeletal structures and its applications. In: Zheng, G., Li, S. (eds.) Computational Radiology for Orthopaedic Interventions. LNCVB, vol. 23, pp. 1–23. Springer, Cham (2016). https://doi.org/10.1007/978-3-319-23482-3_1

12. Bosmans, B., et al.: Statistical shape modeling and population analysis of the aortic root of TAVI patients. J. Med. Devices **7**(4), 040925-1–040925-2 (2013)

13. Bruse, Jan L., et al.: A non-parametric statistical shape model for assessment of the surgically repaired aortic arch in coarctation of the aorta: how normal is abnormal? In: Camara, O., Mansi, T., Pop, M., Rhode, K., Sermesant, M., Young, A. (eds.) STACOM 2015. LNCS, vol. 9534, pp. 21–29. Springer, Cham (2016). https://doi.org/10.1007/978-3-319-28712-6_3

14. Bruse, J.L., et al.: Looks do matter! Aortic arch shape after hypoplastic left heart syndrome palliation correlates with cavopulmonary outcomes. Ann. of Thorac. Surg. **103**(2), 645–654 (2017)

15. Casciaro, M.E., Craiem, D., Chironi, G., Graf, S., Macron, L., Mousseaux, E., Simon, A., Armentano, R.L.: Identifying the principal modes of variation in human thoracic aorta morphology. J. of Thorac. Imag. **29**(4), 224–232 (2014)

16. Jolliffe, I.T., Cadima, J.: Principal component analysis: a review and recent developments. Phil. Trans. R. Soc. A **374**, 20150202 (2016)

17. Arora, D: Computational Hemodynamics: Hemolysis and Viscoelasticity. PhD thesis, Department of Mechanical Engineering and Materials Science, Rice University, Houston, TX (2005)

18. Yevtushenko, P., et al.: Surgical aortic valve replacement: are we able to improve hemodynamic outcome? Biophys. J. **117**(12), 2324–2336 (2019)

19. Ong, C.W., et al.: Computational fluid dynamics modelling of hemodynamic parameters in the human diseased aorta: a systematic review. Ann. Vasc. Surg. **6**, 336–381 (2020)

20. Khalafvand, S.S., et al.: Assessment of human left ventricle flow using statistical shape modelling and computational fluid dynamics. J. Biomech. **74**, 116–125 (2018)

Convolutional Bayesian Models for Anatomical Landmarking on Multi-dimensional Shapes

Yonghui Fan[(⊠)] and Yalin Wang

School of Computing, Informatics, and Decision Systems Engineering,
Arizona State University, Tempe, AZ, USA
yfan61@asu.edu

Abstract. The anatomical landmarking on statistical shape models is widely used in structural and morphometric analyses. The current study focuses on leveraging geometric features to realize an automatic and reliable landmarking. The existing implementations usually rely on classical geometric features and data-driven learning methods. However, such designs often have limitations to specific shape types. Additionally, calculating the features as a standalone step increases the computational cost. In this paper, we propose a convolutional Bayesian model for anatomical landmarking on multi-dimensional shapes. The main idea is to embed the convolutional filtering in a stationary kernel so that the geometric features are efficiently captured and implicitly encoded into the prior knowledge of a Gaussian process. In this way, the posterior inference is geometrically meaningful without entangling with extra features. By using a Gaussian process regression framework and the active learning strategy, our method is flexible and efficient in extracting arbitrary numbers of landmarks. We demonstrate extensive applications on various publicly available datasets, including one brain imaging cohort and three skeletal anatomy datasets. Both the visual and numerical evaluations verify the effectiveness of our method in extracting significant landmarks.

Keywords: Anatomical landmarking · Gaussian process kernels

1 Introduction

Statistical shape models are widely used to describe anatomical structures and morphological differences in medical image analysis [4]. The anatomical landmarking (or called saliency detection in some literature) is often implemented as the first step in anatomical shape analyses such as registration [21], segmentation [30,31] and reconstruction [33]. Hence, inferring reasonable landmarks from shape models is a prerequisite to the success of these applications [23,32].

The most reliable landmarking is manual labeling by experts. But obviously, this is impossible to be widely implemented. An observation is that a point has a higher likelihood to be a qualified landmark if its geometric features are more

© Springer Nature Switzerland AG 2020
A. L. Martel et al. (Eds.): MICCAI 2020, LNCS 12264, pp. 786–796, 2020.
https://doi.org/10.1007/978-3-030-59719-1_76

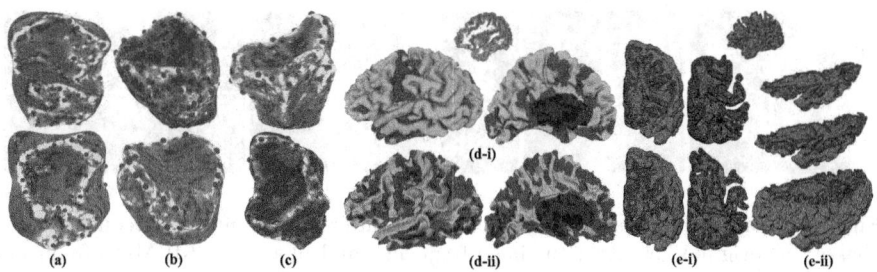

Fig. 1. shape models used in this paper: (a) Molars; (b) Metatarsals; (c) Distal radii; (a)-(c) are rendered by the normalized Gaussian curvatures. Yellow regions stand for high curvature areas. Landmarks are marked by red spheres. (d) The pial (d-i) and white (d-ii) surfaces of the grey matter. 1500 landmarks and their 50 neighboring vertices are marked in red. (d) A grey matter tetrahedral mesh on (d-i) coronal cutting planes and (d-ii) horizontal cutting planes. The landmarks are colored in green. (Color figure online)

significant [5,7]. For example, as shown in Fig. 1(a)-(c), points on ridges of the teeth and the epiphysis of the bones are more likely to be landmarks than points on flat regions. This insight inspires a thought of acquiring reasonable anatomical landmarks by using quantified geometric features [10]. Most, if not all, of existing methods use existing geometric feature descriptors and take the feature computation as a standalone step before the landmarking. However, this design often shows a feasibility restriction to different dimensional shapes because the classical geometric features are usually limited to certain types of shapes. For example, a weighted Gaussian process landmarking method (W-GP) proposed in [10] uses two curvatures to direct the landmark inference. It works well on surface shapes, but it is ineffective on tetrahedral models because both curvatures have no definitions on interior structures. Another example is the morphometric Gaussian process landmarking method proposed in [8]. This method solves the landmarking on tetrahedral meshes, but is not applicable to surface meshes because of the missing support from interior structures. Furthermore, the calculation of the geometric features increase the computational cost, which impedes applications on large-scale data.

In this paper, we introduce a convolutional Bayesian model to address these problems. The inspiration comes from the success of convolutional neural networks (CNN) and the strong reasoning ability of the Gaussian process (GP). The convolutional operation helps to capture significant structural features from different types of vision inputs. The GP is capable of making continuous reasonable inferences from the prior knowledge. This motivates us to integrate them together towards a universal and robust landmarking technique. Our contributions are summarized into two-folds:

- We propose a GP model with a multi-frequency multi-phase periodic diffusion kernel (mmPDK) to solve the problems of anatomical landmarking on multi-dimensional shape models. The multi-frequency multi-phase setting is

Fig. 2. Illustrations of periodic diffusion kernels after adding multiple frequencies and phases. (a) original kernels with single frequency and phase. (b)-(d) Multi-frequency and multi-phase Kernels after adding two, three and four sets of frequencies and phases. This is analogous to the results of different convolutional operations.

analogous to convolutional layers with different hyperparameters. Hence, the mmPDK mimics the accumulated results of convolutional operations with different patterns. The utilization of mmPDK guarantees that the high-quality geometric features are encoded into the prior knowledge of a GP, so the posterior inference is geometrically reasonable. Each landmark is determined based on the maximized uncertainty of GP posterior inferences. By using a GP regression framework with an active learning strategy, our method is flexible with demands on arbitrary numbers of landmarks.

- We apply anatomical landmarking to various shape models. We demonstrate extensive applications and experimental results including visualizations of uncertainty maps and landmarks, registrations between surfaces, and classifications with simplified feature space. The results verify the effectiveness of our method. Figure 1 shows two types of shape models from four datasets used in our work. A reasonable theoretical insight is that our method is feasible to more types of medical image data, such as closed surface meshes and images.

2   Methods

Notations: Given a shape model $\mathcal{G} = \{\mathcal{V}, \mathcal{E}, \mathcal{F}, \mathcal{T}\}$ in $\mathbb{R}^3$, where $\mathcal{V}$ is the indexed vertex set of the size $|\mathcal{V}|$. $\mathcal{E}, \mathcal{F}$ and $\mathcal{T}$ are indexed edge set, face set and tetrahedron set, respectively. $\mathcal{E}, \mathcal{F}$ and $\mathcal{T}$ can be empty in some data types. v_n is the nth vertex. $\tilde{v}^n$ is the nth landmark. t denotes for a temporal variable. Define a zero-mean GP as $\mathcal{GP}(0, K)$, where K is the kernel. Here, we interchangeably use kernel and covariance function to represent any positive semi-definite matrix. $\|\cdot\|$ denotes the distance lag, it can be L1 norm, L2 norm or some other spatial metrics. Some other notations are defined near to the places they are referred.

2.1   Multi-frequency Multi-phase Periodic Diffusion Kernel

The inference ability of a zero-mean GP is uniquely determined by its kernel function. So we start by investigating an effective kernel. In a convolutional neural network, the spatial features of an image is well captured by the patch-wise convolutional operations. This inspires us to construct similar computational

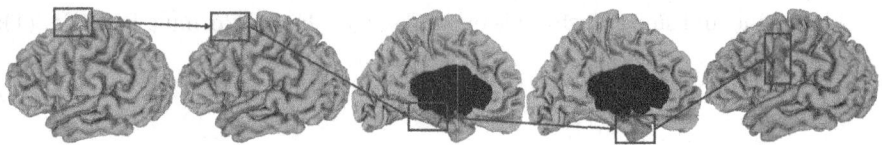

Fig. 3. A sequential landmarking process. We render the selected vertex and its 100 neighboring vertices in green as the current salient area. (Color figure online)

structures in a kernel construction. The bridge linking two concepts together is the diffusion process. A diffusion process is a solution to a stochastic differential equation [19]. When the scenario is the heat diffusion problem, the diffusion process stands for a heat distribution at a certain time. The diffusion process of the heat diffusion equation is essentially the result of a convolutional filtering [6]: $f(x,t) = \int_{\chi} f_0(x')h_t(x,x')dx' = (f_0 * h_t)(x)$. This theorem has been applied for extracting features on manifold-valued medical shapes [13]. Let $T(x,t)$ denote the heat at position x at time t in region D in $\mathbb{R}^d$. Given proper initial boundary conditions, a diffusion process solves this parabolic partial differential equation (PDE) for T: $\frac{\partial T}{\partial t} = \alpha \Delta T + F$ $(t \geq 0)$, where Δ is the Laplace operator; F is a spatial-temporal potential function describing the properties of heat sources, which is also written as the multiplication of a Dirac delta function and a temporal function $h(t)$: $F = h(t)\delta(x - x')$, where constant α is 1. Denoting Green's function of Δ under the Dirichlet boundary condition as G, a fundamental solution to the above PDE is: $T(x,x',t) = \int_0^t G(x,x',t-s)h(s)ds$. Green's function in $\mathcal{R}^d$ diffusion problems has the standard form: $G = \frac{e^{-x^2/4t}}{(4\pi t)^{d/2}}$. A periodic potential gives $h(t) = cos(\omega t)$. Then the diffusion process with the standard Green's function and the periodic potential is: $T = \int_0^t cos\omega(t-s)\frac{e^{-x^2/4s}}{(4\pi t)^{d/2}}ds$.

The Green's function of Δ in 3D diffusion problem is a specific realization from the family of functions $f(t) = t^{d-1}e^{-\frac{1}{4}at}$ in $\mathbb{R}^d, d = 3$. The integral Laplace transform of this family of functions is available in Eq. (1). An interesting observation is that the solution of the integral is structurally similar to the popular Matérn kernel:$C(\tau) = \frac{\sigma^2}{\Gamma(d)2^{d-1}}(2\sqrt{d}\tau\kappa)^d\mathcal{K}_d(2\sqrt{d}\tau\kappa)$. Both of them have terms such as the modified Bessel function of the second kind $\mathcal{K}_d$ and functions of the same dimension order d. This indicates a solid kernel from Eq. (1).

$$\int_0^\infty t^{d-1}e^{-\frac{1}{4}at}e^{-st}dt = 2\left[(\frac{1}{4}a)^{\frac{1}{2}}s^{-\frac{1}{2}}\right]^d \mathcal{K}_d(a^{\frac{1}{2}}s^{\frac{1}{2}}) \qquad (1)$$

However, a practical explicit solution to such an integral is not directly derivable [22]. So we estimate the integral to be the summation of a cosine Fourier transform$\hat{f}_c(\omega)$ and a sine Fourier transform$\hat{f}_s(\omega)$ if $t \to \infty$:

$$T = cos(\omega t)\int_0^t cos(\omega s)G(s)ds + sin(\omega t)\int_0^t sin(\omega s)G(s)ds$$
$$\approx cos(\omega t)\hat{f}_c(\omega) + sin(\omega t)\hat{f}_s(\omega) \qquad (2)$$

The cosine and sine transform is expanded with Euler's formula from Eq. (1):

$$\hat{f}_c(\omega) = 2^{-1-d/2}\pi^{-d/2}\left[(\sqrt{-i\omega})^{d-2}\Sigma_1 + (\sqrt{i\omega})^{d-2}\Sigma_2\right] \tag{3}$$

$$\hat{f}_s(\omega) = -i2^{-1-d/2}\pi^{-d/2}\left[(\sqrt{-i\omega})^{d-2}\Sigma_1 - (\sqrt{i\omega})^{d-2}\Sigma_2\right] \tag{4}$$

$$\Sigma_1 = (\|x\|\sqrt{-i\omega})^{1-d/2}\mathcal{K}_{1-d/2}(\|x\|\sqrt{-i\omega}) \tag{5}$$

$$\Sigma_2 = (\|x\|\sqrt{i\omega})^{1-d/2}\mathcal{K}_{1-d/2}(\|x\|\sqrt{i\omega}) \tag{6}$$

Substituting Eq. (3)-(6) into Eq. (2):

$$\begin{aligned}
T = {} & 2^{-1-d/2}\pi^{-d/2}\left[(\sqrt{-i\omega})^{d-2}\Sigma_1 + (\sqrt{i\omega})^{d-2}\Sigma_2\right]cos(\omega t) \\
& - i2^{-1-d/2}\pi^{-d/2}\left[(\sqrt{-i\omega})^{d-2}\Sigma_1 - (\sqrt{i\omega})^{d-2}\Sigma_2\right]sin(\omega t)
\end{aligned} \tag{7}$$

When the data is in $\mathbb{R}^3, d = 3$, we get an initial kernel expression from Eq. (7):

$$T(\|x\|,\omega,t) = \frac{1}{4\pi}e^{-\|x\|\sqrt{\frac{1}{2}\omega}}cos(\|x\|\sqrt{\frac{1}{2}\omega} + \omega t) \tag{8}$$

For simplicity, we define a frequency term $\lambda = \sqrt{\frac{1}{2}\omega}$ and a phase term $\phi = \omega t$. Then the initial kernel expression is simplified to be:

$$T(\|x\|,\lambda,\phi) = \frac{1}{4\pi}e^{-\lambda\|x\|}cos(\lambda\|x\| + \phi) \tag{9}$$

We define the final version of mmPDK as a weighted squared form: $K = TWT$, where the T and weight matrix W are defined in Eq. (10). The weight matrix W is a diagonal matrix with the absolute sum of each row as the diagonal entry. This design is inspired by the kernel principal component analysis (KPCA) which uses a weighted multiplication of the covariance matrix. We define N frequencies with $\lambda = \sqrt{0.2\pi n}, n = [1, ..., N]$. We assign ϕ with the values by dividing $[0, \frac{\pi}{2}]$ into N equal line-spaces. T equals to the summation of N different convolutional filterings.

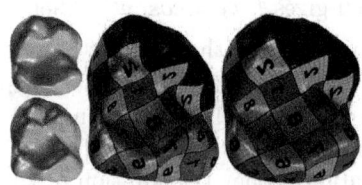

Fig. 4. An illustration of the surface registration. The source and target meshes are on the left column. The two textured meshes show the registration result.

$$T(\|x\|,N) = \frac{1}{4\pi N}\sum_{n=1}^{N}e^{-\lambda_n\|x\|}cos(\lambda_n\|x\| + \phi_n), \quad W(x) = \sum|T(x,\cdot)| \tag{10}$$

The heat kernel (HK) has a similar theoretical background [3]. But HK considers a zero potential while mmPDK is in a dynamic scenario that has more variations. Figure 2(a) shows five kernels with single frequency and phase, which is analogous to the HK. Figure 2(b)-(d) show the two to four summations of multi-frequencies and multi-phases kernels. More filtering patterns are observed.

2.2   Anatomical Landmarking via GP Uncertainty Estimation

The main algorithm for anatomical landmarking is a GP regression process with an active learning strategy. We assume a multivariate Gaussian distribution with mmPDK as the kernel: $\mathcal{GP}_\mathcal{G}(0, K)$. Supposing $\mathcal{S} \leq |\mathcal{V}|$ landmarks are needed. For each vertex, we choose $N_\mathcal{G}$ neighboring vertices and use their pairwise distance lags to build the kernel. For surface models, we use the fast marching algorithm to calculate the geodesic distance and choose the nearest $N_\mathcal{G}$ neighboring vertices. For high dimensional models, we use K-Nearest Neighbor (KNN) algorithm with the Euclidean distance as the spatial metric. The kernel is a sparse matrix. Define the uncertainty map of $\mathcal{G}$ during selecting the sth landmark as:

$$\Sigma_\mathcal{G}(v) = diag(K)_v - K_{v,\tilde{v}^{s-1}}^T K_{\tilde{v}^{s-1},\tilde{v}^{s-1}}^{-1} K_{v,\tilde{v}^{s-1}}, s \leq \mathcal{S} \tag{11}$$

$$K_{v,\tilde{v}^{s-1}} = \begin{pmatrix} K(v,\tilde{v}^1) \\ \vdots \\ K(v,\tilde{v}^{s-1}) \end{pmatrix}, \quad K_{\tilde{v}^{s-1},\tilde{v}^{s-1}} = \begin{pmatrix} K(\tilde{v}^1,\tilde{v}^1) & \cdots & K(\tilde{v}^1,\tilde{v}^{s-1}) \\ \vdots & & \vdots \\ K(\tilde{v}^{s-1},\tilde{v}^1) & \cdots & K(\tilde{v}^{s-1},\tilde{v}^{s-1}) \end{pmatrix} \tag{12}$$

The uncertainty map is initialized as $diag(K)$. The landmark is the vertex with the largest uncertainty score on the map: $argmax(\Sigma_\mathcal{G})$. From Eq. (11) we can see that the whole process follows an active learning strategy. The uncertainty map is updated by adding the covariance information of the newly-selected landmark to the prior knowledge after each selection. This update keeps happening until $\mathcal{S}$ landmarks are selected. This framework has been successfully implemented in other work [8,10]. Figure 3 shows the process of selecting the

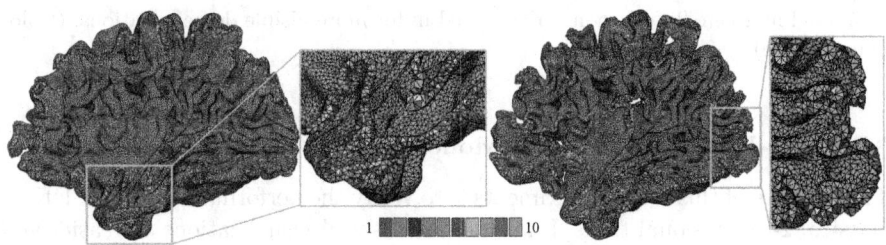

Fig. 5. Illustrations of uncertainty maps on a grey matter tetrahedral mesh. All the vertices are divided into ten classes. 1 and 10 denote the highest and lowest uncertainty classes, respectively. Two zoom-in regions are provided for more visible demonstrations.

first five landmarks on a pial surface. We render the landmark and its 50 neighboring faces to highlight the region where the landmark comes from. Figure 1(a) shows the landmarks on skeletal surfaces. The mesh is rendered by normalized Gaussian curvatures. Figure 1(a) shows 1500 landmarks and their 50 neighbors on pial and white surfaces. Some landmarks in sulci are invisible.

3   Experiments

Common Settings: Wave Kernel Signature (WKS) [2] is used as the vertex-wise feature descriptor in registration and classification experiments. Surface-based WKS is computed by regular cotangent form. Tetrahedron-based WKS is computed by using the discretized eigenproblem method in [9]. Python-based GPyTorch [11] and Matlab-based GPML [28] are used as development tools. The tetrahedral mesh is formatted and visualized in the way of TetView [24].

Comparison Methods: (1) Heat kernel GP (HK) ; (2) Spectral mixture kernel GP (SMK) [29]; (3) Periodic kernel GP (PK) [27]; (4) Mesh saliency (MS) [16]. This is a highly cited classical method in saliency detection on meshes; and (5) The W-GP in [10]. The diffusion kernel also has the same theoretic background with mmPDK and HK [15]. But we skip it in this paper because of similar performances with HK. We also test the Matérn kernel family [25] but we neither demonstrate the results because the performances are not comparable. The mesh saliency method and W-GP are not applied to three-dimensional models.

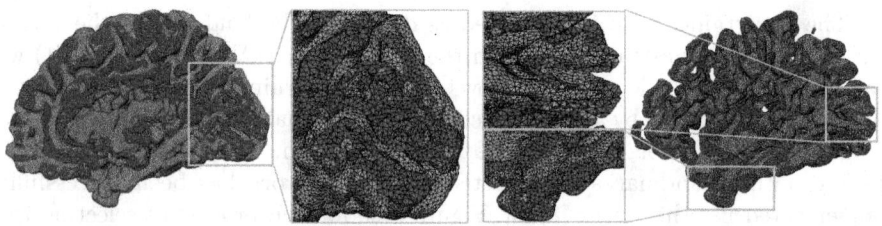

Fig. 6. Demonstration of landmarks in a grey matter tetrahedral mesh. The landmark is marked in green. Two regions are zoomed in for more visible demonstrations. (Color figure online)

3.1   Two-Dimensional Shape Models

The purpose of this set of experiments is to verify the performance of mmPDK on classical 2-dimensional tasks. Implementations and visualizations are easier and more visible on 2-dimensional models. Three datasets released in [5] are used: (i) "Mandibular molars", or "molar", contains 116 teeth triangle meshes; (ii) "First metatarsals", or "metatarsal", contains 57 models; (iii) Distal radii contains 45 models. One prime reason for employing these datasets is the availability of ground-truth landmarks from experts.

The regions of interest in these models are the marginal ridges, teeth crowns and outline contours where distinguishable geometric features are rich in [5,12]. If taking the normalized Gaussian curvature as the measurement of geometric features, the above regions have high curvatures. Figure 1(a)-(c) show the landmarking results with mmPDK. The meshes are rendered by the normalized Gaussian curvatures and the landmarks are marked by red spheres. Visually, we can see that the selected vertices are clustered in bright yellow regions which stand for high curvature regions. This demonstration visually proves that mmPDK is capable of capturing significant spatial information and yielding reasonable inferences. Figure 1(d-i) and (d-ii) demonstrate the landmarking results on pial and white surfaces, which indicate potential in surface-based cortical structure analysis.

Next, we apply the landmarks to a surface registration application for numerically evaluating the significance of the selection. We randomly select 10 pairs of models within each dataset and use the Bounded distortion Gaussian process landmark matching algorithm to do the registration [10,17]. The continuous Procrustes distance is used to numerically measure the performance of correspondence [1]. Figure 4 shows a textured mapping of two registrated meshes by using mmPDK as an example. The average Procrustes distances of different methods are: HK 0.14, SMK 0.127, PK 0.142, MS 0.118, W-GP 0.086 and mmPDK 0.084. The Procrustes distance of ground-truth landmarks is 0.081. We see that the result of mmPDK is closer to the ground-truth result.

3.2 Three-Dimensional Shape Models

In this set of experiments, we verify the performance of mmPDK on 3-dimensional models by applying landmarking to the morphological study of Alzheimer's disease (AD). Structurally, AD causes abnormal atrophy of the cerebral cortex, which results in a gradually thinner grey matter, i.e. thinner cortical thickness, than the normal aged people [20,26]. We use 275 structural 3D magnetic resonance imaging (MRI) data of left cerebral hemispheres (88 AD patients and 187 Cognitively Unimpaired (CU) visitors) from the baseline collection of Alzheimer's Disease Neuroimaging Initiative phase 2 (ADNI2) [14,18]. We follow the pipeline in [9] to generate the grey matter tetrahedral meshes and solve the discretization eigenproblem. Each mesh contains about 160,000 vertices.

Initially, we demonstrate two visualization results. We randomly choose one mesh and visualize one of its uncertainty maps in Fig. 5. The uncertainty of the mesh is divided into ten classes in the descending order. Then, we compute 5,000 landmarks with mmPDK and visualize them in Fig. 6. For better visual effects, we render the faces that the landmarks belonging to and provide several zoom-in views. In morphological studies, these landmarks stand for positions that are most sensitive to structural changes. The visualization results show that points mainly centralize in ROIs such as the temporal pole and temporal gyrus etc. Previous studies show that these regions may be closely related to AD judged by their functionalities, clinical diagnosis and morphometry changes [20].

Table 1. Grey matter atrophy classifications with 1000, 2000 and 3000 landmarks. The global feature is taken as the reference. mmPDK shows a leading performance.

		HK	PK	SMK	mmPDK	Global
1000	ACC	0.950	0.900	0.964	**0.971**	0.973
	SEN	0.954	0.903	0.947	**0.961**	0.957
	SPE	0.946	0.897	0.984	**0.984**	0.993
2000	ACC	0.942	0.900	0.950	**0.978**	0.973
	SEN	0.955	0.864	0.929	**0.970**	0.957
	SPE	0.925	0.944	0.977	**0.987**	0.993
3000	ACC	0.941	0.913	0.950	**0.980**	0.973
	SEN	0.953	0.930	0.930	**0.974**	0.957
	SPE	0.928	0.892	0.973	**0.988**	0.993

Next, we use anatomical landmarking as a manifold learning technique. The general idea is using the WKS features of landmarks to form a simplified feature expression of one subject. The significance of different landmarking methods is numerically reflected by the classification results. The SVM and 10-folds cross-validation are used in classifications. The performance is measured by accuracy (ACC), sensitivity (SEN) and specificity (SPE). 275 left cerebral hemisphere structural MRIs including 88 AD patients and 187 Cognitively Unimpaired (CU) visitors are used. We select 1000, 2000 and 3000 landmarks on each subject and concatenate their WKS together to a feature matrix. Considering the landmarks of different subsects are not registered, we compute the principal component of the feature matrix and reshape it to a vector. We take this vector as the final subject-wise expression of features. Table. 1 lists the classification results. It shows that a well-selected set of landmarks may be more discriminative than using global features regarding accuracy. One explanation is that such a massive mesh usually contains redundancies and a representative subset is able to decrease the side effects of redundant information. In general, we decrease the feature dimension from a hundred thousand to thousand and this simplified feature space is statistically representative of the original massive data.

Overall, the experiments verify the effectiveness of mmPDK. Our work brings insights on the potential of convolutional Bayesian techniques, or more general advanced Bayesian learning techniques, for effective medical image analysis.

Acknowledgements. This work is supported in part by NIH (RF1AG051710 and R01EB025032) and Arizona Alzheimer Consortium.

References

1. Al-Aifari, R., Daubechies, I., Lipman, Y.: Continuous procrustes distance between two surfaces. Commun. Pure Appl. Math. **66**(6), 934–964 (2013)
2. Aubry, M., Schlickewei, U., Cremers, D.: The wave kernel signature: a quantum mechanical approach to shape analysis. In: 2011 IEEE International Conference on Computer Vision Workshops (ICCV Workshops), pp. 1626–1633. IEEE (2011)
3. Berline, N., Getzler, E., Vergne, M.: Heat Kernels and Dirac Operators. Springer, Heidelberg (2003)
4. Bonaretti, S., Seiler, C., Boichon, C., Reyes, M., Büchler, P.: Image-based vs. mesh-based statistical appearance models of the human femur: implications for finite element simulations. Medical Eng. Phys. **36**(12), 1626–1635 (2014)
5. Boyer, D.M., Lipman, Y., Clair, E.S., Puente, J., Patel, B.A., Funkhouser, T., Jernvall, J., Daubechies, I.: Algorithms to automatically quantify the geometric similarity of anatomical surfaces. Proc. Natl. Acad. Sci. **108**(45), 18221–18226 (2011)
6. Bronstein, M.M., Bruna, J., LeCun, Y., Szlam, A., Vandergheynst, P.: Geometric deep learning: going beyond euclidean data. IEEE Signal Process. Mag. **34**(4), 18–42 (2017)
7. Couette, S., White, J.: 3D geometric morphometrics and missing-data. can extant taxa give clues for the analysis of fossil primates? C.R. Palevol **9**(6–7), 423–433 (2010)
8. Fan, Y., Lepore, N., Wang, Y.: Morphometric gaussian process for landmarking on grey matter tetrahedral models. In: 15th International Symposium on Medical Information Processing and Analysis, vol. 11330, p. 113300H. International Society for Optics and Photonics (2020)
9. Fan, Y., Wang, G., Leporé, N., Wang, Y.: A tetrahedron-based heat flux signature for cortical thickness morphometry analysis. Med. Image Comput. Comput. Assist. Interv. **11072**, 420–428 (2018)
10. Gao, T., Kovalsky, S.Z., Boyer, D.M., Daubechies, I.: Gaussian process landmarking for three-dimensional geometric morphometrics. SIAM J. Math. Data Sci. **1**(1), 237–267 (2019)
11. Gardner, J., Pleiss, G., Weinberger, K.Q., Bindel, D., Wilson, A.G.: Gpytorch: blackbox matrix-matrix gaussian process inference with GPU acceleration. In: Advances in Neural Information Processing Systems, pp. 7576–7586 (2018)
12. Guennebaud, G., Germann, M., Gross, M.: Dynamic sampling and rendering of algebraic point set surfaces. In: Computer Graphics Forum, vol. 27, pp. 653–662. Wiley Online Library (2008)
13. Huang, S.G., Lyu, I., Qiu, A., Chung, M.K.: Fast polynomial approximation of heat kernel convolution on manifolds and its application to brain sulcal and gyral graph pattern analysis. IEEE Trans. Med. Imaging **39**(6), 2201–2212 (2020)
14. Jack Jr., C.R., et al.: The alzheimer's disease neuroimaging initiative (ADNI): MRI methods. J. Mag. Resonance Imaging Off. J. Int. Soc. Magnet. Resonance Med. **27**(4), 685–691 (2008)
15. Kondor, R.I., Lafferty, J.: Diffusion kernels on graphs and other discrete structures. In: Proceedings of the 19th International Conference on Machine Learning, vol. 2002, pp. 315–322 (2002)
16. Lee, C.H., Varshney, A., Jacobs, D.W.: Mesh saliency. ACM Trans. graphics (TOG) **24**(3), 659–666 (2005)

17. Lipman, Y.: Bounded distortion mapping spaces for triangular meshes. ACM Trans. Graphics (TOG) **31**(4), 1–13 (2012)
18. Mueller, S.G., et al.: The alzheimer's disease neuroimaging initiative. Neuroimaging Clin. **15**(4), 869–877 (2005)
19. Øksendal, B.: Stochastic Differential Equations. U. Springer, Heidelberg (2003). https://doi.org/10.1007/978-3-642-14394-6
20. Pini, L., et al.: Brain atrophy in alzheimer's disease and aging. Ageing Res. Rev. **30**, 25–48 (2016)
21. Salhi, A., Burdin, V., Brochard, S., Mutsvangwa, T.E., Borotikar, B.: Clinical relevance of augmented statistical shape model of the scapula in the glenoid region. Med. Eng. Phys. **76**, 88–94 (2020)
22. Särkkä, S.: Linear operators and stochastic partial differential equations in gaussian process regression. In: Honkela, T., Duch, W., Girolami, M., Kaski, S. (eds.) ICANN 2011. LNCS, vol. 6792, pp. 151–158. Springer, Heidelberg (2011). https://doi.org/10.1007/978-3-642-21738-8_20
23. Seim, H., Kainmueller, D., Heller, M., Zachow, S., Hege, H.C.: Automatic extraction of anatomical landmarks from medical image data: an evaluation of different methods. In: 2009 IEEE International Symposium on Biomedical Imaging: From Nano to Macro, pp. 538–541. IEEE (2009)
24. Si, H.: Tetgen, a delaunay-based quality tetrahedral mesh generator. ACM Trans. Math. Softw. (TOMS) **41**(2), 1–36 (2015)
25. Stein, M.L.: A kernel approximation to the kriging predictor of a spatial process. Ann. Inst. Stat. Math. **43**(1), 61–75 (1991)
26. Wang, G., Wang, Y., Initiative, A.D.N., et al.: Towards a holistic cortical thickness descriptor: heat kernel-based grey matter morphology signatures. Neuroimage **147**, 360–380 (2017)
27. Williams, C.K., Rasmussen, C.E.: Gaussian Processes for Machine Learning, vol. 2. MIT press, Cambridge (2006)
28. Wilson, A., Adams, R.: Gaussian process kernels for pattern discovery and extrapolation. In: International Conference on Machine Learning, pp. 1067–1075 (2013)
29. Wilson, A.G.: Covariance kernels for fast automatic pattern discovery and extrapolation with Gaussian processes. Ph.D. thesis, University of Cambridge (2014)
30. Wu, Z., et al.: Intrinsic patch-based cortical anatomical parcellation using graph convolutional neural network on surface manifold. Med Image Comput Comput Assist Interv **11766**, 492–500 (2019)
31. Xie, W., et al.: Statistical model-based segmentation of the proximal femur in digital antero-posterior (AP) pelvic radiographs. Int. J. Comput. Assist. Radiol. Surg. **9**(2), 165–176 (2014)
32. Zhang, J., Liu, M., Shen, D.: Detecting anatomical landmarks from limited medical imaging data using two-stage task-oriented deep neural networks. IEEE Trans. Image Process. **26**(10), 4753–4764 (2017)
33. Zheng, G., Gollmer, S., Schumann, S., Dong, X., Feilkas, T., Gonzülez Ballester, M.A.: A 2D/3D correspondence building method for reconstruction of a patient-specific 3D bone surface model using point distribution models and calibrated X-ray images. Med. Image Anal. **13**(6), 883–899 (2009)

SAUNet: Shape Attentive U-Net for Interpretable Medical Image Segmentation

Jesse Sun[1,4], Fatemeh Darbehani[1,2,3], Mark Zaidi[2], and Bo Wang[1,2,3(✉)]

[1] Peter Munk Cardiac Center, Toronto, Canada
[2] University of Toronto, Toronto, Canada
{fatemeh.darbehani,mark.zaidi}@mail.utoronto.ca
[3] Vector Institute, Toronto, Canada
bowang@vectorinstitute.ai
[4] University of Waterloo, Waterloo, Canada
j294sun@uwaterloo.ca

Abstract. Medical image segmentation is a difficult but important task for many clinical operations such as cardiac bi-ventricular volume estimation. More recently, there has been a shift to utilizing deep learning and fully convolutional neural networks (CNNs) to perform image segmentation that has yielded state-of-the-art results in many public benchmark datasets. Despite the progress of deep learning in medical image segmentation, standard CNNs are still not fully adopted in clinical settings as they lack robustness and interpretability. Shapes are generally more meaningful features than solely textures of images, which are features regular CNNs learn, causing a lack of robustness. Likewise, previous works surrounding model interpretability have been focused on post hoc gradient-based saliency methods. However, gradient-based saliency methods typically require additional computations post hoc and have been shown to be unreliable for interpretability. Thus, we present a new architecture called Shape Attentive U-Net (SAUNet) which focuses on model interpretability and robustness. The proposed architecture attempts to address these limitations by the use of a secondary shape stream that captures rich shape-dependent information in parallel with the regular texture stream. Furthermore, we suggest multi-resolution saliency maps can be learned using our dual-attention decoder module which allows for multi-level interpretability and mitigates the need for additional computations post hoc. Our method also achieves state-of-the-art results on the two large public cardiac MRI image segmentation datasets of SUN09 and AC17.

Keywords: Semantic segmentation · Medical imaging · Interpretability

Electronic supplementary material The online version of this chapter (https://doi.org/10.1007/978-3-030-59719-1_77) contains supplementary material, which is available to authorized users.

A. L. Martel et al. (Eds.): MICCAI 2020, LNCS 12264, pp. 797–806, 2020.
https://doi.org/10.1007/978-3-030-59719-1_77

1   Introduction

Cardiovascular magnetic resonance imaging (CMR) is currently used as the gold standard for the non-invasive assessment of various cardiovascular functions. Moreover, CMR plays a crucial role in the diagnosis of diseases such as cardiomyopathies, myocarditis, and congenital heart diseases in which measurements of the left and right ventricular volumes, along with heart rate, can be used to quantify cardiac output. For example, an increase in cardiac output at resting state is associated with the development of cardiovascular disease caused by atherosclerosis. One of the greatest challenges in bi-ventricular volume estimation is the segmentation of the left and right ventricular endocardium at end-systolic and diastolic timepoints. In a clinical setting, there is a high reliance on manual annotations for ventricular volume estimation. CMR accredited operators will typically annotate short-axis slices by drawing a polygon around the left ventricle (LV) on slices that contain it. The inclusion criteria for which slices to annotate the LV on is ambiguous and can range from slices containing at least 50 to 75% of the cavity being surrounded in the myocardium. Furthermore, if a slice contains both ventricle and atrial myocardium, the operator may choose to trace through the junction in a straight line. Since detailed contouring is very time consuming, one method to annotate the LV includes drawing a circle around the endocardium and performing binary thresholding to create a mask of all pixels with an intensity comparable to that of blood. In either case, there is a heavy reliance on a human operator to calculate LV volume. Geometrical models have been developed in an attempt to decrease the time spent performing annotations, however both manual annotations and geometric modeling suffer from poor intra-observer and inter-observer variability [13]. Recent advances in imaging and computing have led to a drastic rise in the use of machine learning for medical imaging [16]. The advent of deep learning allows for much higher levels of abstraction for feature selection and discretization. Convolutional neural networks (CNNs) have been shown to learn abstractions obtained from multidimensional medical images, learning features hard to define by humans. This is one of the reasons why CNNs excel at object recognition and segmentation.

A disadvantage shared by many neural networks including U-Net is a lack of interpretability. Neural networks interface with many convolutional layers simultaneously making it challenging to visualize what features it is learning on. This effectively renders the neural net a "black box", which poses a challenge when attempting to find the root cause of a misclassification, and gives an advantage to potential adversarial attacks. Furthermore, CNNs are highly influenced by dense pixel values which are not robust features compared to shapes of objects [7]. Thus, shapes of objects should be learned to allow generalizability and robustness of the model which goes hand-in-hand with transparency. A lack of model transparency and robustness will hinder its translation into a clinical setting. By affording a higher accuracy in segmentation and verifying that an algorithm is not perpetuating biases, a valuable tool can be created to help solve the challenges numerous clinicians face in medical image analysis.

To the best of our knowledge, past attempts in incorporating shape information in medical imaging segmentation involve forming a new loss function [1,2,5]. Furthermore, limited works on model interpretability for medical imaging have been published. As such, the contributions of this work are:

- The addition of a secondary stream that processes shape features of the image in parallel with the U-Net. Rather than constructing a new loss function, we suggest learning shape features can be built into a model. Further, the output of the shape stream is a shape attention map that can be used for interpretability.
- The usage of spatial and channel-wise attention paths in the decoder block for interpretability of features the model learns at every resolution of the U-Net.

We evaluate our model on large public MRI ventricular volume estimation and segmentation datasets SUN09 [18] and AC17 [4] and demonstrate our method yields state-of-the-art results. We then provide an analysis of the spatial and shape attention maps to interpret the features our model learned. Consequently, our method not only yields strong performance, it is also interpretable at multiple resolutions.

2   Method

We propose a new interpretable image segmentation architecture called Shape Attentive U-Net (SAUNet). A SAUNet is composed of two streams - the texture stream and the gated shape stream. The texture stream is the same structure as a U-Net [20], however the encoder is replaced with dense blocks from DenseNet-121 due to the strong gradient flow and improved performance shown by [9] and the decoder block used is our proposed dual attention decoder block. Dense pixel information and features are learned through the texture stream but not shape features. Takikawa et al. [23] proposed Gated-SCNN, in which the authors first introduced the idea of a gated shape stream to help remove noise and produce finer segmentation on the Cityscape dataset. We propose and show that on top of producing finer segmentations, the gated shape stream gets the model to learn object shapes (see Fig. 2 and *supplementary materials*) and this is consequently interpretable. Hence, we propose the usage of a secondary stream on-top of our U-Net variant that processes shape and boundary information, the gated shape stream, explained in detail in Sect. 2.1.

2.1   Gated Shape Stream

The gated shape stream processes and refines relevant boundary and shape information using features processed by the encoder from the texture stream. The fusion of shape information from the shape stream flow with texture information is done by the gated convolutional layer.

Shape Stream

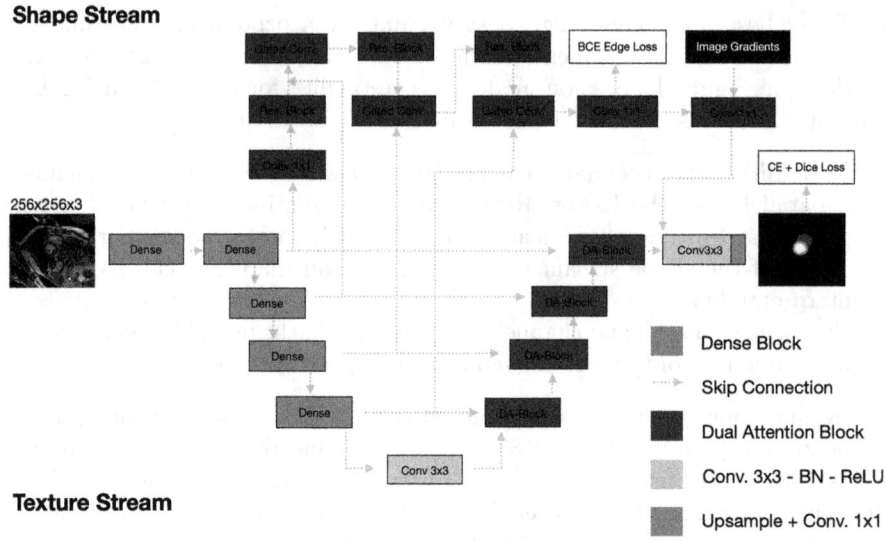

Texture Stream

Fig. 1. Our proposed Shape Attentive U-Net. The proposed model is composed of two main streams - the shape stream that processes boundary information and the texture stream. The shape stream is composed of gated convolutional layers and residual layers. The gated convolutional layers are used to fuse texture and shape information while the residual layers are used to fine-tune the shape features.

Gated Convolutional Layer. Let $C_{1\times1}(x)$ denote the normalized 1×1 convolution function applied on feature map x, and let $R(x)$ denote the residual block function applied on feature map x. The residual block used is composed of two normalized 3×3 convolutions with a skip connection. The function $C_{1\times1}(x)$ returns a feature map of the same spatial dimensions as x but shrinks the number of channels down to one. The gated convolutional layer computes an attention map, α_l, of boundaries by using information from the shape stream flow and the texture stream. Formally, denote the shape stream feature maps as S_l and the texture stream feature maps as T_t where l denotes the layer number in our shape stream and t indexes the encoder block the texture stream feature maps are outputted from. Bilinear interpolation is applied to T_t if needed to match the dimensions of S_l. Since we want precise boundaries of the shape, no pooling layers should be used in the shape stream. We define each residual block as a layer for the shape stream. Then, α_l is computed as,

$$\alpha_l = \sigma(C_{1\times1}(S_l||C_{1\times1}(T_t)))\tag{1}$$

where σ is the sigmoid function and $||$ denotes the channel-wise concatenation of feature maps. α_l is stacked channel-wise to match the dimensions of S_l. Then, the output of the gated convolutional layer, $\hat{S}_l$, is the inputted shape stream feature map S_l element-wise multiplied with α_l,

$$\hat{S}_l = S_l \otimes \alpha_l \tag{2}$$

where $\otimes$ is the Hadamard product. The feature map of the next layer of the shape stream is computed as,

$$S_{l+1} = R(\hat{S}_l) \tag{3}$$

and the same procedure to refine S_{l+1} is applied (equations 1–2 but now T_{t+1} is used).

Output of Gated Shape Stream. The predicted class boundaries from the shape stream are deeply supervised to produce L_{edge}. L_{edge} is the binary cross entropy loss between the ground truth class boundaries and the predicted class boundaries by the shape stream. Now, an objective of the model is to learn the shapes of the classes correctly. Since the entire gated shape stream is differentiable, the gradients propagate back to even the texture stream encoders. Intuitively, the texture stream encoders will learn some relevant shape information as well. The output of the gated shape stream is the predicted shape feature maps of the classes of interest concatenated channel-wise with the Canny edges from the original image. The output is then concatenated with the texture stream feature maps before the last normalized 3×3 convolution layer of the texture stream.

2.2 Dual Attention Decoder Block

The decoder module fuses feature maps outputted by the encoder from the skip connection along with the feature maps of lower resolution decoder blocks that capture more contextual and spatial information. Naturally, we would like to understand what features the model is detecting in these blocks to make the model less black-box. We propose the dual attention decoder block that is comprised of two new components after the standard normalized 3×3 convolution on the concatenated feature maps. The two new components are the spatial attention path for interpretability and a channel-wise attention path for improved performance as demonstrated by Hu et al. [8].

Spatial Attention Path. Let d denote the number of channels coming into the spatial attention path. Then, the spatial attention path is composed of a normalized 1×1 convolution followed by another 1×1 convolution. The first convolution reduces the number of channels to $\frac{d}{2}$ and the second convolution reduces the number of channels to 1. A sigmoid is applied to map the pixel values in the single channel into the range of $[0, 1]$ to obtain F'_s. F'_s is then stacked channel-wise d times to obtain F_s. This is done to match the dimensions of the spatial attention path output, F_s, with the output from the channel-wise attention path, F_c, in order to perform element-wise multiplication.

Channel Attention Path. The channel-wise attention path is comprised of a squeeze and excitation module that produces a scale coefficient in $[0,1]$ for each channel from the skip connection. Each channel from the skip connection feature map is then scaled by their respective coefficient to obtain F_c.

Channel and Spatial Attention. The output, F, of our proposed dual-attention decoder block is a fusion of channel and spatial attentions,

$$F = (F_s + 1) \otimes F_c \tag{4}$$

Operator $\otimes$ denotes the Hadamard product. The $+1$ is included so that the spatial attention originally in the range of $[0,1]$ can only amplify features rather than zeroing out features that may be valuable in later convolutions.

2.3   Dual-Task Loss Function for Learning Shapes

We propose the loss function used to be composed of the segmentation loss and the shape stream boundary loss. Let L_{CE} and L_{Dice} denote the cross entropy loss and Dice loss of the predicted segmentation, respectively. Let L_{Edge} denote the binary cross entropy loss of the predicted shape boundaries. Then, our total loss, L_{total}, is defined as,

$$L_{total} = \lambda_1 L_{CE} + \lambda_2 L_{Dice} + \lambda_3 L_{Edge} \tag{5}$$

where λ_1, λ_2, and λ_3 are hyper-parameters to weigh each measure. In our experiments, we found setting $\lambda_1 = \lambda_2 = \lambda_3 = 1$ works well. We observed a drop in segmentation performance occurs when $\lambda_3 \gg \lambda_1 + \lambda_2$ as segmentation quality measured by L_{CE} and L_{Dice} are marginally considered relative to the entire loss term, L_{total}. Moreover, we found that using L_{CE} without L_{Dice} and vice versa results in the model not learning well and quickly. Hence, both L_{CE} and L_{Dice} are used. Intuitively, the model learns to predict individual pixel values correctly through L_{CE} and also learns to consider overlap through L_{Dice}.

3   Experiments

To evaluate our proposed model, we conduct our experiments on the SUN09 [18] and AC17 [4] left and bi-ventricular segmentation datasets, respectively. We present our results in the following sections. The Dice Coefficient metric is used for evaluation consistent with other benchmarks and works. The experiments were completed on one NVIDIA Quadro RTX 5000 GPU with 16GB of memory. For each experiment, each image slice was z-score normalized. The following data augmentations were performed during runtime: rotations in $[-\pi, \pi]$, horizontal and vertical flips with 50% chance, elastic deformations, and gamma shifts with a factor sampled from $[0.5, 2.0]$ uniformly distributed. All the code used is publicly available on our GitHub: https://bit.ly/38Xrluf.

3.1 SUN09

For SUN09, training our proposed model for 120 epochs took 1.5 hours for each class' dataset. No hyper-parameter tuning was done for our model trained with the shape stream. Our scores along with the previous top five scores are reported in Table 1.

Table 1. Test set Dice scores for SUN09. Only the previous top five works with the highest reported accuracies (Dice scores) are listed. No hyper-parameter tuning was required for our SAUNet model.

Model	Endocardium	Epicardium
Tran [24]	0.92	0.96
Curiale et al. [6]	0.90	0.90
Yang et al. [26]	0.93	0.93
Romaguera et al. [19]	0.90	–
Avendi et al. [3]	0.94	–
SAUNet (Ours)	**0.952**	**0.962**

3.2 AC17 Segmentation

For AC17, training our proposed model for 180 epochs took 3.5 hours. The Dice scores for the left ventricle, right ventricle, and myocardium segmentation structures are presented in Table 2 along with the scores from previous published works on AC17. The results presented are for the model trained with RAdam and a learning rate of 5E-4.

Table 2. AC17 test set results. Our proposed method yields state-of-the-art results for end-to-end models in all classes in terms of Dice score. Notably, our performance in the right ventricle class is significantly better than previous works, and this is perhaps due to the help of the shape stream learning the irregular shape of the right ventricle.

	LV	RV	MYO
Wolterink et al. [25]	0.930	0.880	0.870
Patravali et al. [17]	0.925	0.845	0.870
Khened et al. [13]	0.920	0.870	0.860
Ilias et al. [10]	0.905	0.760	0.785
Jang et al. [11]	0.938	0.890	0.879
SAUNet (Ours)	**0.938**	**0.914**	**0.887**

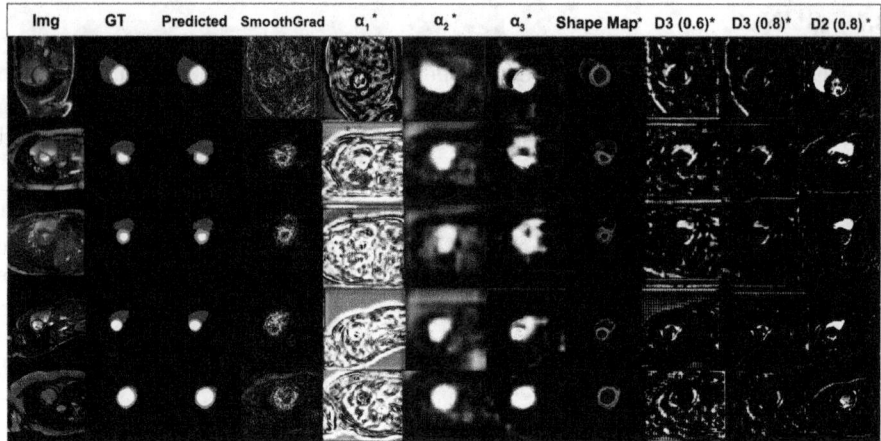

Fig. 2. Our models predictions and attentions on AC17's validation set. * denotes proposed method. α_l is l^{th} shape attention map, $DX(Y)$ is X^{th} decoder block threshold of Y.

4   Interpretability

The learned shape and spatial attention maps are extractable from our model. The spatial attention maps can be used to interpret the regions of high activation for each decoder block while the learned shape maps can be used to deduce that the model has learned the correct shape of the classes of interest. Figure 2 contains the spatial attention map of the last two dual-attention decoder blocks, intermediate shape stream attentions α_l, the final shape attention map, and saliency maps generated using SmoothGrad [22].

Higher-resolution decoder blocks learned the feature of the right ventricle primarily according to column 11, $D2(0.8)$, where the maps are thresholded by 0.8. In the last row, the right ventricle in the image is not visible so high attention was placed on the left ventricle. The right ventricle seems to have the highest attention and priority as its shape is unique and hence serves as a robust feature for localization. The attention maps from decoder block 3 are at a lower resolution level compared to decoder block 2 and according to column 10, $D3(0.8)$, where the spatial attention maps are thresholded by 0.8, fewer areas of high activation are present compared to decoder block 2. Lower resolution blocks process more global information, so similar attention is placed among many regions of the image. To support this claim, column 9, $D3(0.6)$, presents the same attention maps but thresholded by 0.6. Not only traces of attention around the right ventricle are apparent, many other regions like the brim of the structure are also in focus. Furthermore, the shape stream narrows down on the shape of the structures of interest evident in columns 5–8.

5   Conclusion

In this work, we present a new inherently interpretable medical image segmentation model called Shape Attentive U-Net. Our proposed method is able to learn
robust shape features of objects via the gated shape stream while also being
more interpretable than previous works via built-in saliency maps using attention. Furthermore, our method yields state-of-the-art results on the large public
bi-ventriciular segmentation datasets of SUN09 and AC17. Through this work,
we hope to take a step in making deep learning methods clinically adoptable
and hopefully inspire more work on interpretability to be done in the future.

References

1. Al Arif, S.M.M.R., Knapp, K., Slabaugh, G.: Shape-aware deep convolutional neural network for vertebrae segmentation. In: Glocker, B., Yao, J., Vrtovec, T., Frangi,
   A., Zheng, G. (eds.) MSKI 2017. LNCS, vol. 10734, pp. 12–24. Springer, Cham
   (2018). https://doi.org/10.1007/978-3-319-74113-0_2
2. Al Arif, S.M.M.R., Knapp, K., Slabaugh, G.: SPNet: shape prediction using a
   fully convolutional neural network. In: Frangi, A.F., Schnabel, J.A., Davatzikos,
   C., Alberola-López, C., Fichtinger, G. (eds.) MICCAI 2018. LNCS, vol. 11070, pp.
   430–439. Springer, Cham (2018). https://doi.org/10.1007/978-3-030-00928-1_49
3. Avendi, M.R., Kheradvar, A., Jafarkhani, H.: A combined deep-learning and
   deformable-model approach to fully automatic segmentation of the left ventricle in
   cardiac MRI (2015)
4. Bernard, O., et al.: Deep learning techniques for automatic MRI cardiac multi-
   structures segmentation and diagnosis: is the problem solved? IEEE Trans. Med.
   Imaging 37(11), 2514–2525 (2018)
5. Chen, X., Williams, B.M., Vallabhaneni, S.R., Czanner, G., Williams, R., Zheng,
   Y.: Learning active contour models for medical image segmentation. In: The IEEE
   Conference on Computer Vision and Pattern Recognition (CVPR), June 2019
6. Curiale, A.H., Colavecchia, F.D., Kaluza, P., Isoardi, R.A., Mato, G.: Automatic
   myocardial segmentation by using a deep learning network in cardiac MRI (2017)
7. Geirhos, R., Rubisch, P., Michaelis, C., Bethge, M., Wichmann, F.A., Brendel, W.:
   Imagenet-trained CNNs are biased towards texture; increasing shape bias improves
   accuracy and robustness. In: ICLR (2019)
8. Hu, J., Shen, L., Albanie, S., Sun, G., Wu, E.: Squeeze-and-excitation networks.
   In: The IEEE Conference on Computer Vision and Pattern Recognition (CVPR),
   pp. 7132–7141 (2018)
9. Huang, G., Liu, Z., Weinberger, K.Q., van der Maaten., L.: Densely connected convolutional networks. In: 2017 IEEE Conference on Computer Vision and Pattern
   Recognition (CVPR), pp. 2261–2269 (2016)
10. Ilias, G., Tziritas, G.: Fast fully-automatic cardiac segmentation in MRI using
    MRF model optimization, substructures tracking and B-spline smoothing, pp. 91–
    100, Jan 2018
11. Jang, Y., Hong, Y., Ha, S., Kim, S., Chang, H.-J.: Automatic segmentation of LV
    and RV in cardiac MRI. In: Pop, M., et al. (eds.) STACOM 2017. LNCS, vol.
    10663, pp. 161–169. Springer, Cham (2018). https://doi.org/10.1007/978-3-319-
    75541-0_17

12. Jetley, S., Lord, N.A., Lee, N., Torr. P.: Learn to pay attention. In: ICLR (2018)
13. Khened, M., Alex, V., Krishnamurthi, G.: Densely connected fully convolutional network for short-axis cardiac cine MR image segmentation and heart diagnosis using random forest. In: Pop, M., et al. (eds.) STACOM 2017. LNCS, vol. 10663, pp. 140–151. Springer, Cham (2018). https://doi.org/10.1007/978-3-319-75541-0_15
14. La Gerche, A., et al.: Cardiac MRI: a new gold standard for ventricular volume quantification during high-intensity exercise. Circulation. Cardiovascular Imaging 6(2), 329–338 (2013)
15. Liu, L., et al.: On the variance of the adaptive learning rate and beyond (2019)
16. Martin, T.N., et al.: St-segment deviation analysis of the admission 12-lead electrocardiogram as an aid to early diagnosis of acute myocardial infarction with a cardiac magnetic resonance imaging gold standard. J. Am. Coll. Cardiol. 50(11), 1021–1028 (2007)
17. Patravali, J., Jain, S., Chilamkurthy, S.: 2D-3D fully convolutional neural networks for cardiac MR segmentation. In: Pop, M., et al. (eds.) STACOM 2017. LNCS, vol. 10663, pp. 130–139. Springer, Cham (2018). https://doi.org/10.1007/978-3-319-75541-0_14
18. Radau, P., Lu, Y., Connelly, K., Paul, G., Dick, A., Wright, G.: Evaluation framework for algorithms segmenting short axis cardiac MRI, July 2009
19. Romaguera, L.V., Costa, M.G.F., Romero, F.P., Filho, C.F.F.C.: Left ventricle segmentation in cardiac MRI images using fully convolutional neural networks. In: Armato III, S.G., Petrick, N.A. (eds.) Medical Imaging 2017: Computer-Aided Diagnosis. volume 10134, pp. 760–770. International Society for Optics and Photonics, SPIE (2017)
20. Ronneberger, O., Fischer, P., Brox, T.: U-Net: Convolutional Networks for Biomedical Image Segmentation. In: Navab, N., Hornegger, J., Wells, W.M., Frangi, A.F. (eds.) MICCAI 2015. LNCS, vol. 9351, pp. 234–241. Springer, Cham (2015). https://doi.org/10.1007/978-3-319-24574-4_28
21. Selvaraju, R.R., Cogswell, M., Abhishek, D., Vedantam, R., Parikh, D., Batra, D.: Grad-CAM: visual explanations from deep networks via gradient-based localization. The IEEE International Conference on Computer Vision (ICCV), Venice, 2017, pp. 618–626. https://doi.org/10.1109/ICCV.2017.74
22. Smilkov, D., Thorat, N., Kim, B., Viégas, F.B., Wattenberg, M.: SmoothGrad: removing noise by adding noise. ArXiv, abs/1706.03825 (2017)
23. Takikawa, T., Acuna, D., Jampani, V., Fidler, S.: The IEEE International Conference on Computer Vision (ICCV), pp. 5229-5238 (2019)
24. Tran, P.V.: A fully convolutional neural network for cardiac segmentation in short-axis MRI (2016)
25. Wolterink, J.M., Leiner, T., Viergever, M.A., Išgum, I.: Automatic segmentation and disease classification using cardiac cine MR images. In: Pop, M., et al. (eds.) STACOM 2017. LNCS, vol. 10663, pp. 101–110. Springer, Cham (2018). https://doi.org/10.1007/978-3-319-75541-0_11
26. Yang, X., Zeng, Z., Yi, S.: Deep convolutional neural networks for automatic segmentation of left ventricle cavity from cardiac magnetic resonance images. IET Comput. Vision 11(8), 643–649 (2017)

Multi-task Dynamic Transformer Network for Concurrent Bone Segmentation and Large-Scale Landmark Localization with Dental CBCT

Chunfeng Lian[1], Fan Wang[1], Hannah H. Deng[2], Li Wang[1], Deqiang Xiao[1],
Tianshu Kuang[2], Hung-Ying Lin[2], Jaime Gateno[2,3], Steve G. F. Shen[4,5],
Pew-Thian Yap[1], James J. Xia[2,3(✉)], and Dinggang Shen[1(✉)]

[1] Department of Radiology and BRIC, University of North Carolina at Chapel Hill,
Chapel Hill, NC, USA
dinggang.shen@gmail.com
[2] Department of Oral and Maxillofacial Surgery, Houston Methodist Hospital,
Houston, TX, USA
jxia@houstonmethodist.org
[3] Department of Surgery (Oral and Maxillofacial Surgery), Weill Medical College,
Cornell University, New York, NY, USA
[4] Department of Oral and Craniomaxillofacial Surgery,
Shanghai Jiao Tong University, Shanghai, China
[5] Shanghai University of Medicine and Health Science, Shanghai, China

Abstract. Accurate bone segmentation and anatomical landmark localization are essential tasks in computer-aided surgical simulation for patients with craniomaxillofacial (CMF) deformities. To leverage the complementarity between the two tasks, we propose an efficient end-to-end deep network, i.e., multi-task dynamic transformer network (DTNet), to concurrently segment CMF bones and localize large-scale landmarks in one-pass from large volumes of cone-beam computed tomography (CBCT) data. Our DTNet was evaluated quantitatively using CBCTs of patients with CMF deformities. The results demonstrated that our method outperforms the other state-of-the-art methods in both tasks of the bony segmentation and the landmark digitization. Our DTNet features three main technical contributions. *First*, a collaborative two-branch architecture is designed to efficiently capture both fine-grained image details and complete global context for high-resolution volume-to-volume prediction. *Second*, leveraging anatomical dependencies between landmarks, regionalized dynamic learners (RDLs) are designed in the concept of "learns to learn" to jointly regress large-scale 3D heatmaps of all landmarks under limited computational costs. *Third*, adaptive transformer modules (ATMs) are designed for the flexible learning of task-specific feature embedding from common feature bases.

Keywords: Craniomaxillofacial (CMF) · Multi-task learning · Segmentation · Landmark localization

A. L. Martel et al. (Eds.): MICCAI 2020, LNCS 12264, pp. 807–816, 2020.
https://doi.org/10.1007/978-3-030-59719-1_78

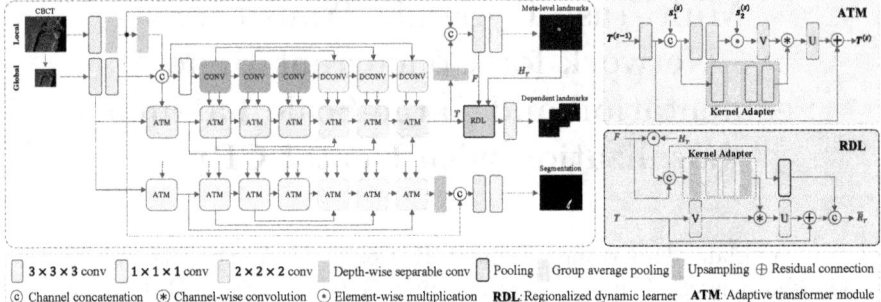

Fig. 1. End-to-end DTNet for concurrent jaw segmentation and large-scale landmark localization. For illustration simplicity, here we only show the landmarks from one anatomical region and the common part of all ATMs (i.e., pooling and up-sampling for the encoding and decoding path are ignored).

1   Introduction

Cone-beam computed tomography (CBCT) scans are routinely used in quantifying deformity and planning orthognathic surgery for patients with jaw deformity. The planning pipeline starts from accurately segmenting the bones from the background and digitizing (localizing) anatomical landmarks onto three-dimensionally (3D) reconstructed models [18]. In current clinical practice, surgeons have to manually segment the bones and soft tissues, and digitize the landmarks. This task is very time-consuming and highly depends on surgeons' experience. Thus there is an urgent need, from surgeons, to develop reliable and fully automatic method for segmentation and landmark digitization.

Automated CMF bone segmentation and landmark localization are practically challenging. This is mainly because that CBCT scans typically have severe image artifacts (e.g., caused by amalgam dental fillings, and orthodontic braces), significant appearance variations, and a large volume (typically around $600 \times 600 \times 500$ voxels, 0.4 mm^3 isotropically per voxel). Most of the traditional methods, including atlas- [15], model- [3], and learning-based methods [17], formulate the segmentation and the localization as two independent tasks, despite of the fact that the bony landmarks are the anatomically meaningful points located on the skeletal surface—both tasks are naturally associated [20]. Recently, deep learning methods leveraging fully convolutional neural networks (FCNs) [7,8,10,14] have been proposed to perform CMF bone segmentation and landmark localization in a unified framework. Torosdagli et al. [16] applied a dense variant of the U-Net [14] to segment mandible, based on which they designed another U-Net to regress the geodesic maps revealing landmark locations. Zhang et al. [21] designed a different cascade of two 3D U-Nets, where the first U-Net provides contextual guidance (i.e., voxel-wise displacements to landmarks) to assist the training of the second U-Net with two parallel outputs for the concurrent segmentation of bony structures and regression of landmark heatmaps.

To a degree, these methods did achieve the performance in both segmentation and localization. However, they still have a number of technical limitations that hampered them to be used in real clinical settings. *First*, they are typically implemented using small image patches (e.g., $96 \times 96 \times 96$) sampled from a large CBCT volume to compensate the bottleneck of the memory size of graphic processing unit (GPU). It can significantly sacrifice the global view of the whole bony structure, which is important for both semantic segmentation [2] and discrimination between different landmarks [22]. *Second*, while the efficacy of heatmap regression has been verified in other landmark detection tasks [12,19], these methods can only jointly localize a limited number of CMF landmarks (e.g., 15 landmarks in [21]), due to the heavy memory consumption for the respective 3D heatmaps. That problem greatly limits its capability of efficiently addressing the realistic demand of large-scale landmarks (e.g., more than 60 on the mandible) for orthognathic surgical planning. *Third*, both [16] and [21] consist of multiple steps (or networks) implemented in an isolated fashion, while potential heterogeneity between different steps may lead to suboptimal results.

In this paper, we propose an *end-to-end* deep learning method, called multi-task dynamic transformer network (DTNet), for concurrent bone segmentation and landmark localization from CBCT images. Once a large clinical CBCT volume is directly input into DTNet, it can efficiently output the segmentation result and large-scale heatmaps for the landmarks *in one-pass* (Fig. 1).

The main technical contributions of our work are: *First*, our DTNet contains two collaborative branches, i.e., a light-weight branch to capture the local image details from the high-resolution input, and another deep branch to learn the global context from the down-sampled input. *Second*, we design a regionalized dynamic learner (RDL) in the "learning-to-learn" framework to leverage the stable dependency between spatially neighboring landmarks. The RDL first localizes a meta-level landmark in each predefined anatomical region by regressing the high-resolution heatmap. Based on that, it further predicts region-specific dynamic convolutional kernels to efficiently localize other neighboring landmarks in the down-sampled image space. *Third*, as an end-to-end network, our DTNet extends the state-of-the-art multi-task architecture (i.e., MTAN [9]) by introducing adaptive transformer modules (ATMs) to jointly learn task-oriented feature embedding from common feature pools.

2 Multi-task Dynamic Transformer Network

Our DTNet contains three important components, i.e., collaborative local and global branches, adaptive transformer modules, and regionalized dynamic learners besides the fundamental convolutional (Conv), deconvolutional (DConv), pooling, and upsampling operations. The schematic diagram is shown in Fig. 1.

Collaborative Local and Global Branches: Inspired by recent advances in real-time high-resolution segmentation [2,13], our DTNet designs a two-branch architecture to efficiently learn the local details and global context for high-resolution volume-to-volume predictions from a large 3D input (size: $L \times W \times H$). A light-weight local branch works on the original input to capture local details, while a deep global branch works on a significantly down-sampled input (size: $\frac{L}{5} \times \frac{W}{5} \times \frac{H}{5}$) to learn both shared and task-specific contextual representations.

Specifically, the local branch consists of only two general $3 \times 3 \times 3$ Conv layers (both with unit stride and zero-padding) and a $5 \times 5 \times 5$ depth-wise separable Conv layer [5] (5 strides without padding) to control the number of learnable parameters. The second Conv layer outputs feature maps describing fine-grained image details, which are transferred by a long-range skip connection to the top of DTNet for high-resolution inference. The third Conv layer transfer these local features into the global branch to assist the learning of deep contextual feature representations from the down-sampled input.

The global-branch network adopts FCNs as the backbone to develop a multi-task architecture for concurrent bone segmentation and landmark localization. Inspired by [9], it consists of a single 3D U-Net to learn common feature representations shared between two tasks, based on which two light-weight subnetworks are further designed to learn adaptive feature embedding for each specific task. To begin with, the backbone applies two Conv layers to learn from the down-sampled input the local features, which are further merged with the corresponding features from the local branch, forming multi-scale representations of image details to assist the construction of the subsequent Conv and DeConv blocks with residual connections [4]. Each Conv block in the encoding path contains two convolutional layers, where the first two of them are followed by pooling. Symmetrically, each DeConv block in the decoding path starts with bilinear up-sampling, followed by two Conv layers. Built upon the shared U-Net, task-specific subnetworks apply a series of adaptive transformer modules (ATMs) to learn from each Conv/DConv block the respective feature embedding.

Adaptive Transformer Modules: We assume that the feature maps produced by each block of U-Net form *a common feature pool* shared across complementary tasks, upon which ATM learns *task-oriented feature embedding* in a "learning-to-learn" fashion [1]. According to the diagram shown in Fig. 1, ATM in the encoding path combines task-specific features $\mathbf{T}^{(s-1)}$ from the preceding scale and initial common features $\mathbf{S}_1^{(s)}$ at current scale (e.g., from the 1st Conv layer of a Conv block) to predict a task adapter, which further applies on the following common features $\mathbf{S}_2^{(s)}$ (e.g., from the 2nd Conv layer of a Conv block), yielding task-specific feature representations $\mathbf{T}^{(s)}$ at current scale. The task adapter performs joint feature selection and transformation from $\mathbf{S}_2^{(s)}$, using online predicted spatial attentions and *dynamic* Conv [1]. Specifically, $\mathbf{T}^{(s-1)}$ is first processed by a general $3 \times 3 \times 3$ Conv to obtain $\widehat{\mathbf{T}}^{(s)}$, which is merged with $\mathbf{S}_1^{(s)}$ via channel-wise concatenation, such as $[\widehat{\mathbf{T}}^{(s)}; \mathbf{S}_1^{(s)}]$. The attention map $\mathbf{A}^{(s)}$

in terms of the merged features is then defined as

$$\mathbf{A}_{\mathrm{T}}^{(s)} = \mathbf{W}_{\mathrm{sigmoid}}^{(s)} * \mathbf{W}_{\mathrm{relu}}^{(s)} * \left([\widehat{\mathbf{T}}^{(s)}; \mathbf{S}_1^{(s)}]\right), \tag{1}$$

where $\mathbf{W}_{\mathrm{sigmoid}}^{(s)}$ and $\mathbf{W}_{\mathrm{relu}}^{(s)}$ are the kernel weights of two $1 \times 1 \times 1$ Convs followed by sigmoid and ReLU activations, respectively, and $*$ denotes the Conv operator. Since $\mathbf{A}_{\mathrm{T}}^{(s)}$ and $\mathbf{S}_2^{(s)}$ have the same size, the task-relevant features are selected via element-wise multiplication, i.e., $\mathbf{A}_{\mathrm{T}}^{(s)} \odot \mathbf{S}_2^{(s)}$. Regarding $\mathbf{A}_{\mathrm{T}}^{(s)} \odot \mathbf{S}_2^{(s)}$ (with m_{i} channels) as a set of bases, a dynamic $1 \times 1 \times 1$ Conv is further learned for task-oriented transformation of the selected common features. Considering that predicting all learnable parameters $\mathbf{W}^{(s)}$ is computationally infeasible even for $1 \times 1 \times 1$ kernels, the dynamic Conv is factorized in an analog of SVD [11]. Therefore, the output $\mathbf{T}^{(s)}$ (with m_{o} channels) is defined as

$$\mathbf{T}^{(s)} = \mathbf{W}^{(s)} * (\mathbf{A}_{\mathrm{T}}^{(s)} \odot \mathbf{S}_2^{(s)}) \oplus \widehat{\mathbf{T}}^{(s)} \approx \mathbf{U}^{(s)} * \widetilde{\mathbf{W}}^{(s)} *_c \mathbf{V}^{(s)} * (\mathbf{A}_{\mathrm{T}}^{(s)} \odot \mathbf{S}_2^{(s)}) \oplus \widehat{\mathbf{T}}^{(s)}, \tag{2}$$

where $*$ and $*_c$ denote general and *channel-wise* Convs, respectively; $\oplus$ denotes the residual connection; $\mathbf{U}^{(s)}$ and $\mathbf{V}^{(s)}$ are the parameter matrices of two $1 \times 1 \times 1$ Convs with m_{o} and m_{i} output channels, respectively; and $\widetilde{\mathbf{W}}^{(s)}$ is a diagonal matrix with only m_i learnable parameters, which are one-shot determined by a light-weight kernel predictor in terms of $[\widehat{\mathbf{T}}^{(s)}; \mathbf{S}_1^{(s)}]$. The kernel predictor has an architecture similar to squeeze-and-excitation [6], but learns the output coefficients from distinct input sources. It starts with a $1 \times 1 \times 1$ Conv, followed by global average pooling (GAP) and another two $1 \times 1 \times 1$ Convs to predict $\widetilde{\mathbf{W}}^{(s)}$.

Notably, the encoding and decoding ATMs have similar structures, except that the former contains pooling while the latter contains bilinear up-sampling. In each of them, we set $m_{\mathrm{o}} < m_{\mathrm{i}}$, which effectively controls the number of learnable parameters and realizes task-oriented low-dimensional feature embedding.

Regionalized Dynamic Learners: Since jointly regressing large-scale 3D heatmaps in high-resolution image space is memory infeasible, our DTNet integrates an efficient localization module by explicitly modeling the dependencies between spatially neighboring landmarks. To this end, we separate the 3D model of the jaw as several predefined anatomical regions, with each of them grouping a set of landmarks that have stable intra-region displacements. For each region, a meta-level landmark is first localized by regressing its high-resolution heatmap. Leveraging the strong guidance provided by this meta-level landmark, an RDL is further constructed to learn dynamically region-aware representations for the localization of other dependent landmarks under very limited memory costs.

Specifically, let $\mathbf{F}$ be a high-resolution representation, produced by fusing the localization-related global-branch representation (i.e., $\mathbf{T}$ from the last ATM) and the local-branch image details. As shown in Fig. 1, a $1 \times 1 \times 1$ Conv layer with sigmoid activations works on $\mathbf{F}$ to predict meta-level heatmaps $\{\mathbf{H}_r\}_{r=1}^R$, corresponding to R different anatomical regions. To detect other dependent landmarks located within each (e.g., the r-th) region, the respective RDL combines $\mathbf{H}_r$ and

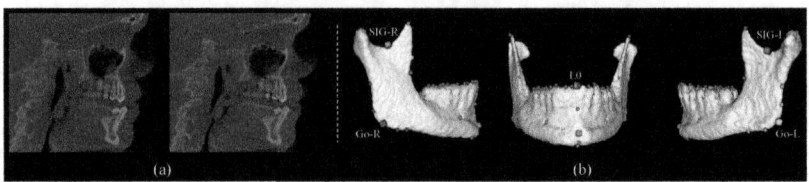

Fig. 2. An representative subject in our dataset, where (a) shows the slice-view of the ground-truth mandible segmentation, and (b) shows the 6 anatomical regions with different colors. The dilated points denote the meta-level landmarks for each region.

$\mathbf{F}$ to learn a region-aware dynamic Conv layer, which applies on $\mathbf{T}$ to regressing the heatmaps of these dependent landmarks in significantly down-sampled image space. In more detail, a set of $3 \times 3 \times 3$ channel-wise Conv kernels is first predicted as $\widetilde{\mathbf{W}}_r = f_r([\mathbf{H}_r \odot \mathbf{F}; \mathbf{F}])$, where $\mathbf{H}_r$ provides high-resolution *regional attention*, and $f_r(\cdot)$ is a light-weight kernel adapter consisting of depth-wise separable Convs and general $2 \times 2 \times 2$ Convs with double strides. The *region-aware representation* $\widetilde{\mathbf{R}}_r$ for down-sampled heatmaps regression is finally defined as

$$\widetilde{\mathbf{R}}_r = [\mathbf{U}_r * \widetilde{\mathbf{W}}_r *_c \mathbf{V}_r * \mathbf{T} \oplus \mathbf{T}; \overline{\mathbf{H}}_r \odot \overline{\mathbf{F}}; \overline{\mathbf{F}}] \tag{3}$$

where $\mathbf{U}_r * \widetilde{\mathbf{W}}_r *_c \mathbf{V}_r * \mathbf{T} \oplus \mathbf{T}$ denotes residual SVD-factorized Conv [11] of $\mathbf{T}$, and $\overline{\mathbf{H}}_r \odot \overline{\mathbf{F}}$ and $\overline{\mathbf{F}}$ are meta-level feature representations after average pooling.

Implementation: Following [16], we attempt to segment the mandible and localize the associated landmarks, as it is the most frequently deformed bony structure that needs orthognathic surgical correction. The respective DTNet was implemented with PyTorch on a general GPU (i.e., NVIDIA TITAN Xp, 12 GBytes). It takes as input a big CBCT volume (size: $160 \times 160 \times 160$), concurrently output in one-pass the segmentation map of the mandible and 64 heatmaps of all landmarks located on the mandible, costing less than 40 seconds (including loading data and saving results). Using the Adam optimizer, the network was trained by minimizing the combination of three Dice losses for jaw segmentation, high-resolution heatmap regression, and down-sampled heatmap regression, respectively. Dropout and group normalization were used in the network to accelerate training and improve generalization capacity. Training samples were mirror flipped for data augmentation.

3   Experiments

Dataset and Experimental Setup: Our method was evaluated quantitatively using 77 sets of CBCT images of patients with non-syndromic CMF deformities, and 63 sets of CT images of normal subjects taken for the reason other than CMF deformities. All personal informations were de-identified.

Table 1. The segmentation and localization results (mean ± standard deviation) obtained by our DTNet and other three competing methods. The localization results were quantified in terms of RMSE for the 6 meta-level and all 64 landmarks, respectively. Notably, all competing methods leveraged our two-branch architecture and RDLs to deal with large input CBCT volume and large-scale landmarks.

Method	Mandible segmentation (%)			Landmark localization (mm)	
	DSC	SEN	PPV	Meta-level	All
U-Net	92.49 ± 2.13	92.47 ± 5.13	93.32 ± 4.43	2.18 ± 0.54	2.99 ± 0.33
MTU-Net	92.34 ± 2.06	93.59 ± 4.42	91.53 ± 5.10	2.01 ± 0.55	2.85 ± 0.40
MTAN	92.66 ± 2.23	94.17 ± 4.16	91.43 ± 4.84	2.02 ± 0.51	2.91 ± 0.45
DTNet	**93.95 ± 1.30**	**94.24 ± 1.37**	**93.68 ± 1.78**	**1.95 ± 0.43**	**2.52 ± 0.31**

The study was approved by Institutional Review Board. The ground-truth of the segmented bones and digitalized landmarks were manually established by two experienced CMF surgeons. The 64 landmarks on the mandible were divided to 6 groups based on anatomical regions, including Ramus Upper Right (RUR), Ramus Low Right (RLR), Ramus Upper Left (RUL), Ramus Low Left (RLL), Distal Mandible (DMand) and Lower Teeth (LT). For each anatomical region, one landmark was preselected as the meta-level landmark based on a surgeon's experience, including SIG-R, Go-R, SIG-L, Go-L, Pg, and L0 (Fig. 2). All images were spatially normalized to the same resolution of $0.8 \times 0.8 \times 0.8 \,\text{mm}^3$, and the gray-scale values were also normalized using histogram matching to reach similar gray-scale distributions. The 3D heatmap of each landmark was generated using a Gaussian filter with the standard deviation of 3 mm. We randomly split 20 CBCT images for performance evaluation, and used the remaining 57 patients' CBCT and 63 normal CT images for network training.

Using the same settings in loss function and optimizer, our **DTNet** was compared to the other state-of-the-art methods, including **MTAN** [9], multi-task U-Net (**MTU-Net**) [21], and the original mono-task **U-Net** [14]. All competing networks were adjusted to a comparable number of learnable parameters. Specifically, we first replaced the global-branch subnetwork of our DTNet with MTAN, MTU-Net and U-Net to evaluate the efficacy of the proposed ATMs and RDLs for adaptive multi-task learning and large-scale landmark localization, respectively. In addition, we compared DTNet to the U-Net implemented with smaller patches (size: $96 \times 96 \times 96$), denoted as **SU-Net**, to evaluate the efficacy of the proposed collaborative two-branch architecture in capturing local details and global context for high-resolution inference. Finally, the segmented results of the mandible were quantitatively compared to the ground truth in dice similarity coefficient (DSC), sensitivity (SEN) and positive prediction value (PPV). The landmark localization results were also quantitatively evaluated by calculating the root mean squared error (RMSE, in mm) between algorithm-detected and ground-truth landmark coordinates.

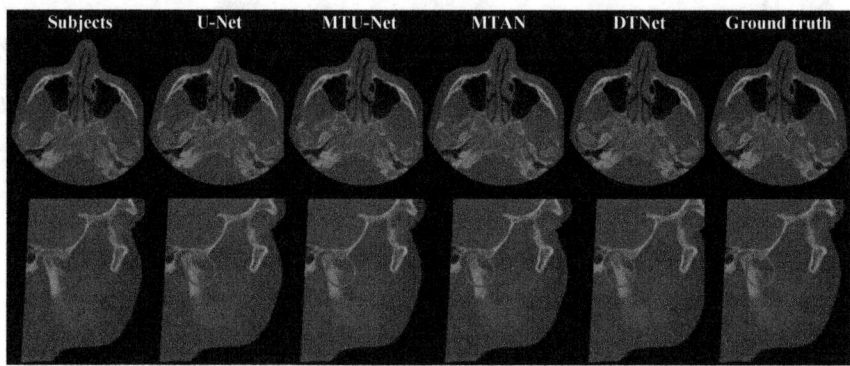

Fig. 3. Representative results obtained by our DTNet and other competing methods for the segmentation of mandible. The marks in red indicate the challenging bony structures with low-contrast boundary. (Color figure online)

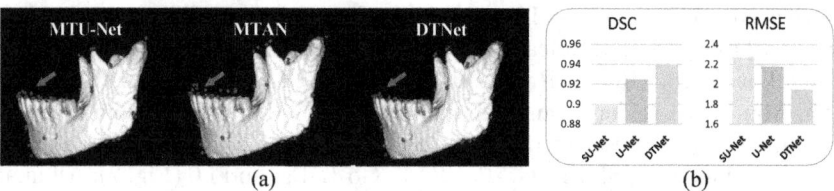

Fig. 4. (a) Representative localization results obtained by different multi-task networks, where blue and red points denote the detected and ground-truth landmarks, respectively. (b) A comparison between small-patch U-Net (i.e., SU-Net) and two-branch networks (i.e., U-Net and our DTNet).

Results: Table 1 presents the quantitative results obtained by different automated methods for both mandible segmentation and landmark localization. From Table 1, we can have the following observations. *First*, compared with the mono-task U-Net, the three multi-task networks (i.e., MTU-Net, MTAN, and our DTNet) led to better segmentation and localization results in most cases. It suggests that the two tasks are correlated and can provide each other auxiliary information for performance enhancement. *Second*, compared with the state-of-the-art multi-task architectures (i.e., MTU-Net and MTAN), our DTNet has superior performance with respect to all metrics, which implies that the proposed ATM modules are effective, and more powerful than simple task-specific attention, in extracting task-specific representations from shared feature bases for adaptive multi-task learning. *Third*, by performing intra-method comparisons between the localization results of the meta-level landmarks and all landmarks, we can observe that there is no big differences in terms of RMSE. It indicates that the proposed RDL can generally work with different architectures for the efficient localization of large-scale landmarks. In addition to the quantitative comparisons, the representative examples of mandible segmentation and landmark localization are shown in Fig. 3 and Fig. 4 (a), respectively. These qualitative comparisons between our DTNet and other multi-task methods further justify the efficacy of our DTNet, especially in segmenting low-contract structures and localizing landmarks in challenging anatomical regions (e.g., on the lower teeth).

To evaluate the efficacy of the collaborative two-branch design in capturing both local details and global context from large CBCT images, our DTNet and the above two-branch U-Net were further compared with SU-Net, which was implemented with smaller image patches. The corresponding results of the mandible segmentation and meta-level landmark localization are summarized in Fig. 4 (b), from which we can see that both U-Net and our DTNet largely outperformed SU-Net. It implies that the integration of local image details and global context is important for high-resolution volume-to-volume inference, which also verifies the effectiveness of our collaborative two-branch design to this end.

4   Conclusion

In this paper, we have proposed a multi-task deep neural network, DTNet, for concurrent mandible segmentation and large-scale landmark localization in one-pass for large-volume CBCT images. Our DTNet uses a collaborative two-branch architecture to efficiently capture both local image details and global context for high-resolution volume-to-volume inference. Adaptive transformer modules are designed in the "learning-to-learn" framework to learn dynamically task-specific feature embeddings from a common feature pool. Regional dynamic learners are also proposed to leverage the local dependencies among the neighboring landmarks for efficient large-scale localization. The experimental results confirm the performance of our DTNet on real-patient CBCT data.

Acknowledgements. This work was supported in part by NIH grants (R01 DE022676, R01 DE027251 and R01 DE021863).

References

1. Bertinetto, L., et al.: Learning feed-forward one-shot learners. In: NeurIPS, pp. 523–531 (2016)
2. Chen, W., et al.: Collaborative global-local networks for memory-efficient segmentation of ultra-high resolution images. In: CVPR, pp. 8924–8933 (2019)
3. Gupta, A., et al.: A knowledge-based algorithm for automatic detection of cephalometric landmarks on CBCT images. Int. J. Comput. Assist. Radiol. Surg. **10**(11), 1737–1752 (2015)
4. He, K., et al.: Deep residual learning for image recognition. In: CVPR, pp. 770–778 (2016)
5. Howard, A.G., et al.: MobileNets: efficient convolutional neural networks for mobile vision applications. arXiv preprint arXiv:1704.04861 (2017)
6. Hu, J., et al.: Squeeze-and-excitation networks. In: CVPR, pp. 7132–7141 (2018)

7. Lian, C., et al.: Multi-channel multi-scale fully convolutional network for 3D perivascular spaces segmentation in 7T MR images. Med. Image Anal. **46**, 106–117 (2018)

8. Lian, C., et al.: Hierarchical fully convolutional network for joint atrophy localization and Alzheimer's disease diagnosis using structural MRI. IEEE Trans. Pattern Anal. Mach. Intell. **42**(4), 880–893 (2020)

9. Liu, S., et al.: End-to-end multi-task learning with attention. In: CVPR, pp. 1871–1880 (2019)

10. Long, J., et al.: Fully convolutional networks for semantic segmentation. In: CVPR, pp. 3431–3440 (2015)

11. Nie, X., et al.: Human pose estimation with parsing induced learner. In: CVPR, pp. 2100–2108 (2018)

12. Payer, C., Štern, D., Bischof, H., Urschler, M.: Regressing heatmaps for multiple landmark localization using CNNs. In: Ourselin, S., Joskowicz, L., Sabuncu, M.R., Unal, G., Wells, W. (eds.) MICCAI 2016. LNCS, vol. 9901, pp. 230–238. Springer, Cham (2016). https://doi.org/10.1007/978-3-319-46723-8_27

13. Poudel, R.P., et al.: ContextNet: exploring context and detail for semantic segmentation in real-time. In: BMVC (2018)

14. Ronneberger, O., Fischer, P., Brox, T.: U-Net: convolutional networks for biomedical image segmentation. In: Navab, N., Hornegger, J., Wells, W.M., Frangi, A.F. (eds.) MICCAI 2015. LNCS, vol. 9351, pp. 234–241. Springer, Cham (2015). https://doi.org/10.1007/978-3-319-24574-4_28

15. Shahidi, S., et al.: The accuracy of a designed software for automated localization of craniofacial landmarks on CBCT images. BMC Med. Imaging **14**(1), 32 (2014)

16. Torosdagli, N., et al.: Deep geodesic learning for segmentation and anatomical landmarking. IEEE Trans. Med. Imaging **38**(4), 919–931 (2018)

17. Wang, L., et al.: Automated segmentation of dental CBCT image with prior-guided sequential random forests. Med. Phys. **43**(1), 336–346 (2016)

18. Xia, J.J., et al.: New clinical protocol to evaluate craniomaxillofacial deformity and plan surgical correction. J. Oral Maxillofac. Surg. **67**(10), 2093–2106 (2009)

19. Yang, D., et al.: Automatic vertebra labeling in large-scale 3D CT using deep image-to-image network with message passing and sparsity regularization. In: Niethammer, M., et al. (eds.) IPMI 2017. LNCS, vol. 10265, pp. 633–644. Springer, Cham (2017). https://doi.org/10.1007/978-3-319-59050-9_50

20. Zhang, J., et al.: Automatic craniomaxillofacial landmark digitization via segmentation-guided partially-joint regression forest model and multiscale statistical features. IEEE Trans. Biomed. Eng. **63**(9), 1820–1829 (2015)

21. Zhang, J., et al.: Context-guided fully convolutional networks for joint craniomaxillofacial bone segmentation and landmark digitization. Med. Image Anal. **60**, 101621 (2020)

22. Zhong, Z., Li, J., Zhang, Z., Jiao, Z., Gao, X.: An attention-guided deep regression model for landmark detection in cephalograms. In: Shen, D., et al. (eds.) MICCAI 2019. LNCS, vol. 11769, pp. 540–548. Springer, Cham (2019). https://doi.org/10.1007/978-3-030-32226-7_60

Automatic Localization of Landmarks in Craniomaxillofacial CBCT Images Using a Local Attention-Based Graph Convolution Network

Yankun Lang[1], Chunfeng Lian[1], Deqiang Xiao[1], Hannah Deng[2], Peng Yuan[2], Jaime Gateno[2,3], Steve G. F. Shen[4], David M. Alfi[2,3], Pew-Thian Yap[1], James J. Xia[2,3(✉)], and Dinggang Shen[1(✉)]

[1] Department of Radiology and BRIC, University of North Carolina at Chapel Hill, Chapel Hill, NC, USA
dinggang.shen@gmail.com
[2] Department of Oral and Maxillofacial Surgery, Houston Methodist Hospital, Houston, TX, USA
jxia@houstonmethodist.org
[3] Department of Surgery (Oral and Maxillofacial Surgery), Weill Medical College, Cornell University, Ithaca, NY, USA
[4] Department of Oral and Craniofacial Surgery, Shanghai 9th Hospital, Shanghai Jiaotong University College of Medicine, Shanghai, China

Abstract. Landmark localization is an important step in quantifying craniomaxillofacial (CMF) deformities and designing treatment plans of reconstructive surgery. However, due to the severity of deformities and defects (partially missing anatomy), it is difficult to automatically and accurately localize a large set of landmarks simultaneously. In this work, we propose two cascaded networks for digitizing 60 anatomical CMF landmarks in cone-beam computed tomography (CBCT) images. The first network is a U-Net that outputs heatmaps for landmark locations and landmark features extracted with a local attention mechanism. The second network is a graph convolution network that takes the features extracted by the first network as input and determines whether each landmark exists via binary classification. We evaluated our approach on 50 sets of CBCT scans of patients with CMF deformities and compared them with state-of-the-art methods. The results indicate that our approach can achieve an average detection error of 1.47 mm with a false positive rate of 19%, outperforming related methods.

Keywords: Craniomaxillofacial (CMF) surgery · Landmark localization · GCN · Deep learning

1 Introduction

Craniomaxillofacial (CMF) surgeries aim to correct congenital or acquired deformities of the head and face [10]. Due to the complexity of CMF anatomy, detailed

© Springer Nature Switzerland AG 2020
A. L. Martel et al. (Eds.): MICCAI 2020, LNCS 12264, pp. 817–826, 2020.
https://doi.org/10.1007/978-3-030-59719-1_79

surgical planning is often carried out with the help of cone-beam computed tomography (CBCT) images. CMF landmark localization, also called "landmark digitization", is an important step to quantify deformities for surgical planning. An automated landmark digitization method is highly valuable for effective and efficient surgical planning.

Deep learning-based methods, such as convolutional neural networks have been proposed to learn task-specific features for anatomical landmark localization in medical images. For example, Payer et al. [6] applied fully convolutional network (FCN) [4,5,7] to predict a non-linear mapping from input image patches to the respective heatmap patches. Zhang et al. [13] employed a cascade of two FCNs to detect multiple anatomical landmarks simultaneously, where the 3D displacements generated by the first FCN are used in combination with the image patches in the second FCN to regress the respective landmark heatmaps. Wang et al. [8] developed a multi-task network for segmentation and landmark localization in prenatal ultrasound volumes.

Although yielding promising prediction results in landmark localization, the above methods suffer from a number of limitations. First, for patients with facial trauma or post-ablative surgery, some anatomical landmarks might be missing due to deformities. Failure to consider this will lead to false-positive detections, affect deformity quantification, and mislead surgical planning. Second, these methods localize each landmark independently without considering the inter-dependency between landmarks. Most CMF landmarks are located on bony boundaries and are related via a relatively fixed geometrical structure. Explicitly modeling this kind of inter-dependency can reduce misdetections.

In this paper, we focus on localizing CMF landmarks and at the same time determine their existence. We propose a coarse-to-fine two-stage approach to gradually detect CMF landmarks in CBCT images. In the first stage, a cascade of two networks is employed for coarse but reliable landmark localization. The first network is derived from U-Net, which takes a down-sampled 3D image as input, and outputs a set of attention maps. To model the dependence between landmarks, we first group all landmarks according to 7 pre-defined anatomical regions and encode their spatial relationships in an adjacency matrix. We then employ a second network based on a graph convolution network (GCN) with the adjacency matrix and features extracted from the attention maps as inputs to determine the existence of each landmark. In the second stage, image patches with a higher resolution are sampled in the vicinity of the landmark locations estimated in the first stage. These patches are used to train a high-accuracy network [3] to further refine landmark localization.

The contribution of our paper is two-fold. First, we introduce a new attention feature extraction mechanism for feature learning. Second, we encode the dependency of all landmarks in the form of a graph to be adopted in a GCN to predict the existence of each landmark. The accuracy of this method will be demonstrated via quantitative evaluation.

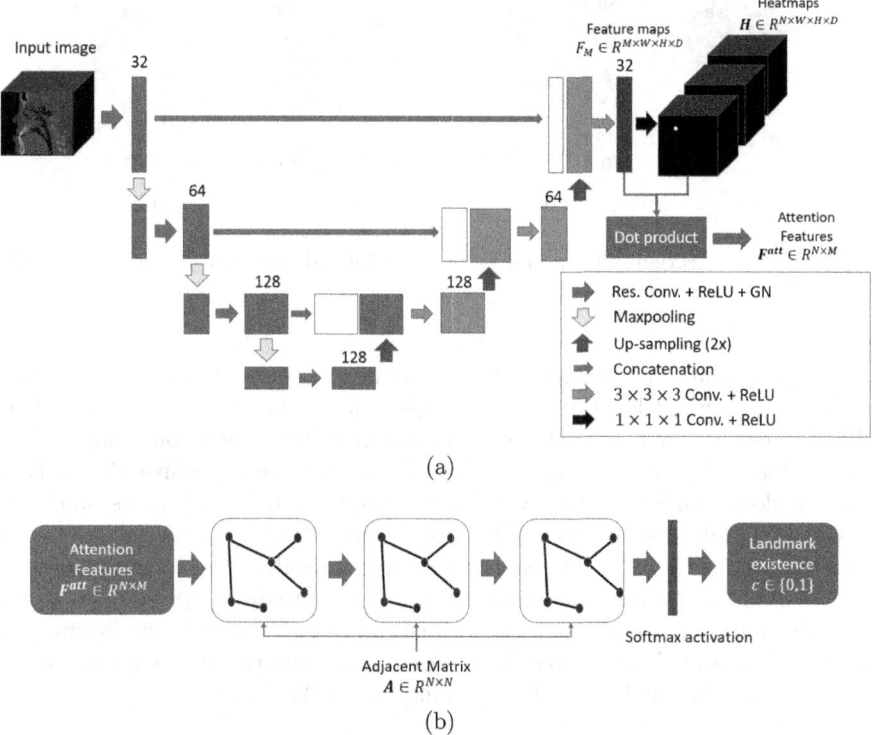

Fig. 1. The proposed network for CMF landmarks detection. (a) Attention feature extraction network for localizing landmarks and generating attention features. (b) GCN for determining landmark existence (0 for negative and 1 for positive).

2   Method

To improve the accuracy of CMF landmark localization on CBCT images, we use a coarse-to-fine framework that adopts a proposed network to gradually and jointly refine the predicted locations of all landmarks. Specifically, we adopt GCN to solve the problem of landmark existence determination. The proposed network is shown in Fig. 1 (a), (b). Different from other GCN networks in [2], we use a feature extraction network to automatically learn the features used as inputs for GCN. Moreover, we design an adjacent matrix to model the dependencies of landmarks in the same anatomic region. Details of our proposed network is introduced in the following sections.

2.1   Attention Feature Extraction Network

The purpose of Attention Feature Extraction Network (AFEN) is to generate N numbers of feature vectors for the subsequent GCN, and to predict landmark

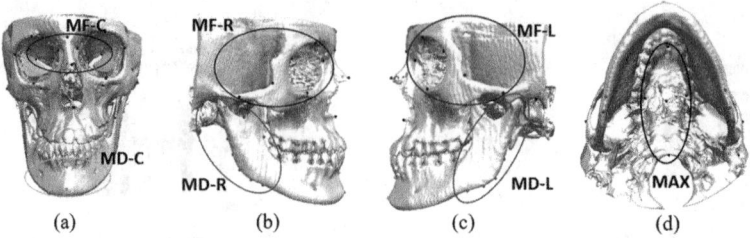

Fig. 2. The illustrations of landmarks in 7 predefined anatomical regions shown in (a)–(d).

locations by heatmap regression. Each landmark is represented by a heatmap, where the landmark location has the highest intensity. As shown in Fig. 1(a), AFEN is constructed as a U-Net, with a contraction path consisting of four residual blocks [1], and an expansion consisting of three expansive blocks. Each residual block consists of two $3 \times 3 \times 3$ convolutional (conv) layers, and each conv layer is followed by Rectified Linear Units (ReLU) activation and Group Normalization (GN) [9]. Between two subsequent residual blocks, a max pooling layer is used to down-sample feature maps and increase receptive field. In the expansive path, each expansive block consists of two $3 \times 3 \times 3$ conv layers, each followed by a ReLU activation. N numbers of heatmaps are generated after a $1 \times 1 \times 1$ convolutional layer. The training loss of AFEN is:

$$L_{AFEN}(H_i, \hat{H}_i) = \frac{1}{N} \sum_{i=1}^{N} (H_i - \hat{H}_i)^2 \tag{1}$$

where H_i is the regressed heatmap for landmark i, and $\hat{H}_i$ is the corresponding ground-truth heatmap. N is the number of landmarks.

The generated heatmap should be a probability distribution map with large probability value around the location of each landmark. Meanwhile, probability values are close to zero at other locations far away from the landmark. Therefore, in this work, we use the regressed heatmap as attention map rather than activating the features maps by Softmax or Sigmoid functions as introduced in the conventional attention mechanisms [14,15]. Each element of the attention feature F_i^{att} for the i-th landmark is calculated by:

$$F_{i_j}^{att} = H_i * F_{M_j} \tag{2}$$

where $*$ is the dot product. F_{M_j} is the j-th feature map in the last layer of U-Net as shown in Fig. 1(a). H_i is the i-th regressed heatmap. F_i^{att} gathers all the information from each feature map near the landmark locations.

2.2 Graph Convolution Network

Due to the fact that the locations of CMF landmarks follow a stable structure, a graph is formed by all landmarks, where each node represents one landmark.

The edge between each pair of landmarks is determined by whether the two landmarks are in the same anatomical regions. All 60 landmarks are pre-defined to be located in 7 non-overlapped regions: Midface-left (MF-L), Midface-Central (MF-C), Midface-Right (MF-R), Maxilla (MAX), Mandible-Left (MD-L), Mandible-Right (MD-R), and Mandible-Central (MD-C), as shown in Fig. 2(a)–(d) using different colors. The landmark dependency is represented by an adjacent matrix defined as:

$$A = \begin{bmatrix} a_{11} & \cdots & a_{1N} \\ \vdots & a_{ij} & \vdots \\ a_{N1} & \cdots & a_{NN} \end{bmatrix} \tag{3}$$

where a_{ij} is the value of the edge between landmark i and j defined as:

$$a_{ij} = \begin{cases} 1, & \text{if } i = j, \text{ or } i, j \in R_k \\ 0, & \text{otherwise} \end{cases} \tag{4}$$

where R_k is the k-th anatomical region.

Our GCN consists of three graph convolutional layers as shown in Fig. 1(b). Each layer takes feature $F_i \in R^{N \times M_i}$ and the adjacent matrix A as input, and outputs a high level feature $F_i^{'} \in R^{N \times M_i^{'}}$, where M_i and $M_i^{'}$ is the numbers of input and output feature channels, respectively. The output of each layer $F_i^{'}$ is calculated by the definition in [2]. Specially, the number of output feature channels $M_i^{'}$ is set to be 32, 16 and 2 for each layer. The first layer takes $F_1 = F^{att} \in R^{N \times M}$ and A as input, and the output of the last layer is $F_3^{'} = F^o \in R^{N \times 2}$, followed by a softmax activation layer. The training loss of GCN is defined as:

$$L_{GCN} = -\sum_{i=1}^{N} \hat{c}_i log(\sigma(F_i^o)) + (1 - \hat{c}_i)log(1 - \sigma(F_i^o)) \tag{5}$$

where $\hat{c}_i \in \{0, 1\}$ is the ground truth of the existence of the i-th landmark, σ is the softmax activation. The total training loss of our network is:

$$L = \lambda_A L_{AFEN} + \lambda_G L_{GCN} \tag{6}$$

where λ_A and λ_G are the training weights.

2.3   Implementation and Inference Procedure

At each stage, our detection network was trained by back-propagation and stochastic gradient descend (SGD) in an end-to-end manner. The initial learning rate was set to 0.001, decaying by 20% after every 5 epochs. The total number of training epochs was 20, and each epoch contained 12,000 iterations. For the first stage, to simplify the training, at the first 5 epochs, a large weight ($\lambda_A = 1.0, \lambda_G = 0.3$) was assigned for heatmap regression losses (i.e., (1)) to produce reliable attention maps. After that, we reduced the heatmap regression weights and increased the landmark existence classification weights, such as

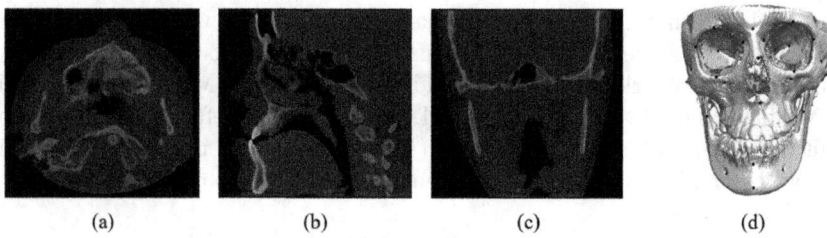

      (a)   (b)   (c)   (d)

Fig. 3. The illustrations of (a)–(c) the original image and (d) 60 landmarks on bony structure from a random subject in our dataset.

$\lambda_A = 0.3, \lambda_G = 1.0$. We first pre-trained our models using randomly selected 50 sets of normal spiral CT images (scanning matrix: 0.488×0.488 mm^2; and slice thickness: 1.25 mm) provided by clinic. After the pre-training, we subsequently trained our network using CBCT images of patient subjects. For training the network in the second stage, the training parameters were set exactly same as described in [3] with the size of input image patch as $64 \times 64 \times 64$.

During the inference procedure, all landmarks on a testing CBCT image were jointly detected using the trained two-stage coarse-to-fine framework. From the second stage, we only sampled image patches centered at the algorithm-localized landmark positions from the previous stage (with the size of $64 \times 64 \times 64$), that is, totally 60 image patches for each testing image, which can significantly reduce the time for testing. The trained model only takes around 1–3 min to process a CBCT volume (size: $536 \times 536 \times 440$) for the joint prediction of 60 landmarks.

3   Experiments

3.1   Experimental Data and Methods

Our method was evaluated quantitatively using randomly selected 50 sets of CBCT images (resolution: 0.3 or 0.4 mm^3 isotropically) from patients with non-syndromic jaw deformities from our digital archive of Oral and Maxillofacial Surgery Department at Houston Methodist Hospital. IRB approval was obtained prior to the study (Pro00013802). Each volume was larger than $536 \times 536 \times 440$. Figure 3 shows an example. For each dataset, the midface and the mandible were manually segmented and 60 landmarks, with 33 on the midface and 27 on the mandible, were digitized and verified by two experienced CMF surgeons using the AnatomicAligner system [11]. 40% of our CBCT dataset are patients with defect due to imcompleted scaning or trauma. Using 5-fold cross-validation, we orderly selected 35 sets of data for training, 5 for validation, and the remaining 10 for testing. Prior to the training, the resolution of each dataset was resampled to 0.4 mm^3 isotropically, and the intensity was normalized to the same distribution by histogram matching and Gaussian normalization constant (GNC). For training in the first stage, each image was down-sampled to a resolution of 1.6 mm^3 and then padded to the size of $128 \times 128 \times 128$. Resolution and size of image patch in the second stage is 0.4 mm^3 and $64 \times 64 \times 64$, respectively. Data augmentation (e.g. rotation, flipping) was also used to increase the training set and the robustness of our models. The landmark localization was completed under an environment of Intel Core i7-8700K CPU with a 12 GB GeForce GTX 1080Ti graphics processing unit (GPU).

We quantitatively compared our method to three baseline deep-learning methods: 1) a basic U-Net proposed in [7]; 2) an extended Mask R-CNN proposed in [3]; and 3) a joint bone segmentation and landmark digitization (JSD) network proposed in [13]. The details of each method are described below.

1) U-Net: We used the same two-stage training strategy to train this network. The networks in the first and the second stages were trained with $128 \times 128 \times 128$ images (resolution: 1.6 mm^3 isotropically) and $96 \times 96 \times 96$ image patches (resolution: 0.4 mm^3 isotropically), respectively. Each landmark position was decided by the coordinates of the highest-value voxel in the predicted heatmap. All 60 landmarks were compared.
2) Extended Mask R-CNN: We used the same parameters and the three-stage coarse-to-fine training strategy introduced in [3] to train this network. The size of image (or image patches) in the three stages is $128 \times 128 \times 128$ (resolution: 1.6 mm^3 isotropically), $64 \times 64 \times 64$ (resolution: 0.8 mm^3 isotropically) and $64 \times 64 \times 64$ (resolution: 0.4 mm^3 isotropically), respectively. We also used the same predefined anatomical regions to model landmark dependencies. All 60 landmarks were compared.
3) JSD. We trained the network for landmark localization by using $96 \times 96 \times 96$ image patches (resolution: 0.4 mm^3 isotropically) as inputs. Network architecture and training parameters were set as those described in [13]. However, JSD method required a large amount of GPU memories for restoring displacement maps, which made it infeasible for detecting all 60 landmarks. Therefore, in JSD comparison, we only detected and compared 15 most clinically relevant landmarks, which were evenly located in 7 regions.

Root mean squared errors (RMSEs) and 95% of confidence intervals (95% Cis) were calculated. The false positive rate was also calculated by $FP/(FP + TN)$, where FP and TN is the numbers of false positives and true negatives, respectively.

3.2   Results

Table 1 shows the comparison of the RMSEs and their 95% CIs between the algorithm-localized and ground-truth landmarks, where negative landmarks (the landmarks not existing) were also taken part into calculation (the ground truth of missing landmark location is set to be $[0.0, 0.0, 0.0]$). RMSE of using our proposed method was 1.47 mm, which was well within the clinical tolerance of 2 mm [12]. It also had the lowest FP rate of 19%, which showed the effectiveness of the proposed mechanism in determining the existence of negative landmarks by using GCN with the explicit modeling of local dependencies between landmarks and the attention features extraction.

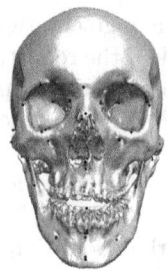 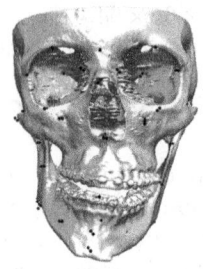 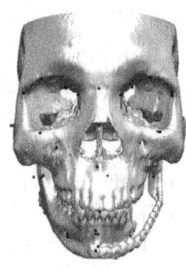

Fig. 4. The results of landmark localization using our method. Condition severity of patients ranged from mild deformity, severe deformity, to discontinuity defect (partially missing anatomy). The detected landmarks are shown as red points, with the ground-truth landmarks shown as green points. (Color figure online)

In contrast, the results achieved with the U-Net had the largest RMSE of 2.67 mm, and reached the highest FP rate of 100% since this network was not capable of determining the landmark existence. The extended Mask R-CNN had a better accuracy than U-Net. However, the false positive rate was still very high (95%). For both methods, RMSEs in MF-L, MF-R, MD-L and MD-R were relatively higher than those in other regions due to the high FP. The results achieved with JSD method reached the accuracy of 1.69mm, and in some regions (MAX, MD-C) the accuracy is higher than those obtained by our approach. However, FP in MD-L and MD-R is still high (100%). Meanwhile, the high GPU memory cost made it difficult to be used for large-scale landmark detection. Nonetheless, this network was also not able to determine the missing landmarks.

Our approach took 1–3 min to jointly localize 60 landmarks from a large CBCT volume with the size of $536 \times 536 \times 440$, while U-Net took 1–2 min, and the extended Mask R-CNN took 2–6 min. It took less than 1 min for JSD to detect 15 landmarks.

Figure 4 illustrates the results of three different subjects whose condition severity ranged from slight deformity, severe deformity, to discontinuity defects (partial anatomy was missing) using our method. No missing landmark was miss-detected.

Table 1. Root mean squared error (mm) of landmark detection (on top) and the corresponding confidence intervals (on bottom) in the predefined 7 regions.

	MF-L	MF-C	MF-R	MAX	MD-L	MD-R	MD-C	Overall
U-Net in [7]	2.05	1.54	3.83	1.42	3.85	3.91	2.04	2.67
	[1.66, 2.44]	[1.16,1.92]	[3.42, 4.24]	[1.08, 1.76]	[3.48, 3.92]	[3.53, 4.22]	[1.67, 2.41]	[2.33, 3.01]
M R-CNN in [3]	1.86	1.58	1.61	1.57	2.05	2.41	1.67	1.82
	[1.73, 1.99]	[1.31, 1.85]	[1.45, 1.77]	[1.34, 1.79]	[1.74, 2.36]	[2.11, 2.71]	[1.34, 1.99]	[1.57, 2.17]
JSD in [13]	**1.42**	1.38	1.61	**1.32**	2.43	2.37	**1.31**	1.69
	[1.32, 1.52]	[1.20, 1.56]	[1.50, 1.72]	**[1.17, 1.47]**	[2.15, 2.71]	[2.16, 2.58]	**[1.23, 1.39]**	[1.46, 1.92]
Our approach	1.63	**1.36**	**1.58**	1.37	**1.41**	**1.37**	1.35	**1.47**
	[1.51, 1.74]	**[1.16, 1.56]**	**[1.49, 1.67]**	[1.19, 1.56]	**[1.30, 1.52]**	**[1.24, 1.50]**	[1.28, 1.42]	**[1.26, 1.68]**

4 Discussion and Conclusion

In this work, we have proposed a two-cascade-network for digitizing 60 anatomical craniomaxillofacial landmarks on CBCT images. Specially, the first network, the U-Net, outputs the regressed heatmaps for localizing the landmark locations, as well as attention features extracted by a proposed extraction mechanism. The second network, Graph Convolution Network, takes the attention features with a designed adjacent matrix as input and outputs the existence of each landmark as a binary classification. The results of quantitative evaluation have proven the location accuracy and also the reduced false positive rate when our method was used. The proposed network can be trained in an end-to-end manner and output large-scale landmarks simultaneously.

Acknowledgment. This work was supported in part by NIH grants (R01 DE022676, R01 DE027251 and R01 DE021863).

References

1. He, K., Zhang, X., Ren, S., Sun, J.: Deep residual learning for image recognition. In: Proceedings of the IEEE Conference on Computer Vision and Pattern Recognition, pp. 770–778 (2016)
2. Kipf, T.N., Welling, M.: Semi-supervised classification with graph convolutional networks. arXiv preprint arXiv:1609.02907 (2016)
3. Lang, Y., et al.: Automatic detection of craniomaxillofacial anatomical landmarks on CBCT images using 3D mask R-CNN. In: Zhang, D., Zhou, L., Jie, B., Liu, M. (eds.) GLMI 2019. LNCS, vol. 11849, pp. 130–137. Springer, Cham (2019). https://doi.org/10.1007/978-3-030-35817-4_16
4. Lian, C., Liu, M., Zhang, J., Shen, D.: Hierarchical fully convolutional network for joint atrophy localization and Alzheimer's disease diagnosis using structural MRI. IEEE Trans. Pattern Anal. Mach. Intell. (2018)
5. Lian, C., Zhang, J., Liu, M., Zong, X., Hung, S.C., Lin, W., Shen, D.: Multi-channel multi-scale fully convolutional network for 3D perivascular spaces segmentation in 7t MR images. Med. Image Anal. **46**, 106–117 (2018)
6. Payer, C., Štern, D., Bischof, H., Urschler, M.: Regressing heatmaps for multiple landmark localization using CNNs. In: Ourselin, S., Joskowicz, L., Sabuncu, M.R., Unal, G., Wells, W. (eds.) MICCAI 2016. LNCS, vol. 9901, pp. 230–238. Springer, Cham (2016). https://doi.org/10.1007/978-3-319-46723-8_27
7. Ronneberger, O., Fischer, P., Brox, T.: U-Net: convolutional networks for biomedical image segmentation. In: Navab, N., Hornegger, J., Wells, W.M., Frangi, A.F. (eds.) MICCAI 2015. LNCS, vol. 9351, pp. 234–241. Springer, Cham (2015). https://doi.org/10.1007/978-3-319-24574-4_28
8. Wang, X., Yang, X., Dou, H., Li, S., Heng, P.A., Ni, D.: Joint segmentation and landmark localization of fetal femur in ultrasound volumes. In: 2019 IEEE EMBS International Conference on Biomedical & Health Informatics (BHI), pp. 1–5. IEEE (2019)
9. Wu, Y., He, K.: Group normalization. In: Proceedings of The European Conference on Computer Vision (ECCV), pp. 3–19 (2018)

10. Xia, J.J., Gateno, J., Teichgraeber, J.F.: New clinical protocol to evaluate craniomaxillofacial deformity and plan surgical correction. J. Oral Maxillofac. Surg. **67**(10), 2093–2106 (2009)

11. Yuan, P., et al.: Design, development and clinical validation of computer-aided surgical simulation system for streamlined orthognathic surgical planning. Int. J. Comput. Assist. Radiol. Surg. **12**(12), 2129–2143 (2017). https://doi.org/10.1007/s11548-017-1585-6

12. Zhang, D., Wang, J., Noble, J.H., Dawant, B.M.: Headlocnet: deep convolutional neural networks for accurate classification and multi-landmark localization of head CTS. Med. Image Anal. **61**, 101659 (2020)

13. Zhang, J., et al.: Joint craniomaxillofacial bone segmentation and landmark digitization by context-guided fully convolutional networks. In: Descoteaux, M., Maier-Hein, L., Franz, A., Jannin, P., Collins, D.L., Duchesne, S. (eds.) MICCAI 2017. LNCS, vol. 10434, pp. 720–728. Springer, Cham (2017). https://doi.org/10.1007/978-3-319-66185-8_81

14. Zhang, L., Singh, V., Qi, G.J., Chen, T.: Cascade attention machine for occluded landmark detection in 2D X-Ray angiography. In: 2019 IEEE Winter Conference on Applications of Computer Vision (WACV), pp. 91–100. IEEE (2019)

15. Zhu, M., Shi, D., Zheng, M., Sadiq, M.: Robust facial landmark detection via occlusion-adaptive deep networks. In: Proceedings of the IEEE Conference on Computer Vision and Pattern Recognition, pp. 3486–3496 (2019)

Author Index

Printed in the United States
By Bookmasters